ROOSEVELT:
THE LION AND THE FOX

JAMES MacGREGOR BURNS

Roosevelt:

THE LION AND
THE FOX

A Harvest Book
Harcourt Brace & Company
San Diego   New York   London

Library of Congress Catalog Card Number: 56-7920

ISBN 0-15-678870-5 (Harvest: pbk.)

Printed in the United States of America

FF EE DD CC

FOR Jan
David
Timothy
Deborah
Antonia

A prince, wrote Machiavelli, must imitate the fox and the lion, for the lion cannot protect himself from traps, and the fox cannot defend himself from wolves. One must therefore be a fox to recognize traps, and a lion to frighten wolves. Those that wish to be only lions do not understand this. Therefore, a prudent ruler ought not to keep faith when by so doing it would be against his interest, and when the reasons which made him bind himself no longer exist. If men were all good, this precept would not be a good one; but as they are bad, and would not observe their faith with you, so you are not bound to keep faith with them.

PREFACE

THIS BOOK is, first of all, a political biography of Franklin D. Roosevelt. It treats much of his personal as well as his public life, because a great politician's career remorselessly sucks everything into its vortex—including his family and even his dog. How did Roosevelt become what he was? Why was he so effective in winning power? How strong a leader was he in the long run? Where did he fail, and why? What meaning does his life hold for Americans and for American statecraft today?

This book is also a study in political leadership in the American democracy. It focuses chiefly on the man, but it treats also the political context in which he acted, for my approach is based on the central findings of social scientists that leadership is not a matter of universal traits but is rooted in a specific culture. We can understand Roosevelt as a politician only in terms of his political, social, and ideological environment, the way he shaped his society and in turn was shaped by it.

Roosevelt was one of the master politicians of his time, certainly the most successful vote getter. His political artistry grew out of long experience with the stuff of American politics: men's ambitions, fears, and loyalties operating through conventions, primaries, elections, offices, constitutions, opinion agencies. Hence this book is concerned with political methods in the United States.

But methods are not enough. What are the ends to which the methods are geared? This is a central question in regard to Roosevelt. Politics is, among other things, the art of compromise; but should the democratic politician compromise with questionable forces to attain a high good? The democratic politician must win elections; but what if he makes concessions in seeking votes that gravely imperil his chance of putting through his program? In this era of Machiavellians, must the democratic politician act as the fox? To what extent can he take the posture of the lion?

ix

Roosevelt won brilliant victories—yet during his second term he became ensnarled in forces he could not control and thwarted by men he could not master. That term is, I think, by far the most significant phase of his career. It not only throws light on Roosevelt's personality, on his improvising and the implications of that improvising, but it raises the more fundamental question of whether the American political system can meet the crises imposed on it by this exacting century. So this book, finally, is an effort to probe the inner workings of personality and politics in order to throw some light on current problems of political leadership.

Any biographer undertaking at this time to treat Roosevelt's whole life faces a dilemma. The war years represented the culmination for both Roosevelt and his country of so much that went before that they deserve full attention; unhappily, scholars as yet do not have the records, memoirs, and other data necessary for a full account and analysis. I have tried to meet this dilemma by treating the war years synoptically and by presenting in the Epilogue and elsewhere an estimate of Roosevelt's character that may help explain his handling of certain war problems as well as the nature of his earlier leadership. The full account of the war years must wait.

A note on footnotes: there are none in the text itself; references are in the Bibliographies at the back of the book. The reason simply is that to list every reference to the thousands of letters and other documents consulted at the Franklin D. Roosevelt Library and elsewhere would have meant a book half again as long. But the reader may wish to know sources of some of the main conclusions, the general nature and scope of the material used, the author's evaluation of it, and his methods of analysis. I hope that the Bibliographies will serve this purpose.

I have so many debts for help received that these, too, must be acknowledged in the back of the book. But two persons deserve special mention. One is my fellow political scientist at Williams, William H. Brubeck, who undertook a great deal of research with me at Hyde Park, helped shape many of the ideas in this volume, and gave the various drafts searching criticism. The other is my wife, Janet Thompson Burns, who did all these things, and who also managed to perform clerical and stenographic chores and, with the help of the children, to create at home those conditions in which hard and sustained work was possible. To my colleague and to my wife I am profoundly grateful.

J. M. B.

CONTENTS

xi

ILLUSTRATIONS

following page 46

PART 1   *The Education of a Politician*

ONE *A Beautiful Frame*

Abound HALFWAY from Albany to New
York the Hudson River flows into a narrow channel, crooks slightly
leftward, and then resumes its promenade toward the Atlantic.
East of this bend lie a railroad and a siding; from the siding a dirt
road climbs steep slopes, through dense woods, to a gently rolling
plateau. On a knoll of this plateau, commanding the sweep of the
river south, stands today a spacious mansion topped by a widow's
walk and breasted by a long porch and balustrade.

In 1882 the middle part of this mansion stood alone, without its
present wings—a roomy, clapboarded house with shutters and a
narrow veranda. January 30 of that year dawned cold and windy,
with a hint of snow in the air. Inside the house all was tenseness and
anxiety: servants bustled to and fro; kettles of water steamed in the
kitchen. Attention centered on the mistress of the house lying in a
small room upstairs. In this room late in the day, after hours of
agony and heavy doses of chloroform, Sara Delano Roosevelt gave
birth to a child. That night in her diary her husband James wrote:
"At quarter to nine my Sallie had a splendid large baby boy. He
weighs 10 lbs., without clothes."

Crowing and chortling in his large carved bassinet, Franklin
Delano Roosevelt seemed a happy child from the outset. Life in the
sunny upstairs room went on at a tranquil pace. Sara breast-fed her
baby for almost a year; she recalled later—with a shade of satisfaction—that "Nurse and I used our own discretion about his feed-
ings," and that no formula was used. To the baby, the moving blur
above him slowly changed into his mother's face—serene, harmonious features, dark hair combed back into a bun, heavy eyebrows,
deep chin. Often in the room was his father, a man slender in face
and body, of medium height, with side whiskers, strong hands, gentle
touch and voice.

Franklin was an only child. His mother did not "pamper" him—
indeed, James thought she nagged him—but the household seemed
to revolve around the little boy. There were no brothers or sisters
to compete for attention, to wrest toys from him, or to bring the life

of school or playground to him outside his parents' ken. The servants doted on him. Family quarrels, jarring words, harsh discipline he never knew. Sara and James agreed exactly on what they wanted to do with their son: to shape him gently but firmly in the mold of a Hyde Park gentleman. A governess said, "He was brought up in a beautiful frame."

Parents and child formed the focal point of a large establishment. House and grounds were peopled with nurse, maids, cook, gardener, coachman, stable boys, farm hands. The estate spread over several hundred acres, embracing fields and forests, gardens, greenhouse, grapery, icehouses, barns, and stables. Timidly Franklin explored the world of Hyde Park. At first he was excessively shy with people outside his family, but he liked to accompany his father as the squire, booted and spurred, bowler on his head and riding crop in hand, made his inspections.

Slowly, reluctantly, Sara let Franklin go on his own. Until he was five he wore dresses and long blond curls; he left skirts only for kilts and Lord Fauntleroy suits; and he was almost eight and a half when he wrote his father: "Mama left this morning and I am going to take my bath alone." But soon he was making the estate his kingdom. He coasted on the slopes below the house; roamed the woods with bow and arrow; watched while huge cakes of ice were hauled up from the river; snowshoed across the fields (most memorably after the blizzard of '88); skated and iceboated on the river; built a crow's-nest in a hemlock near the house; rode his pony Debby and cared for his red setter Marksman; swam in the Hudson, bobbing in the wake of the heavy river traffic; shot birds for his collection. In the house he played steeplechase, deployed his toy soldiers, started a stamp collection.

Often Sara and James shared these activities with him. He had the companionship of his father to a much greater extent than the average American child. The boy's affection for his parents is reflected in his letters. Thus, on May 18, 1888, at the age of six he wrote:

My dear mamma
    I went fishing yesterday after noon with papa   we caught a dozen of minnows   we left them on the bank   papa told me it would frighten the fish to put them in the pond   how is dear grandpapa   I hope he is better dear mamma   I send you a kiss   your loving son
                                                                                    Franklin

Of course Franklin played frequently with the children of other prominent Hyde Park families. But he was with adults much more than with other children. And virtually all his associates, young and old, were joined tight in the Delano or Roosevelt clans or came from a handful of Hudson River families.

The strongest loyalty was to the family, and this loyalty fused with a pervasive sense of community. Parents and child often took trips—to Fairhaven, Massachusetts, to Campobello in the Bay of Fundy, to England and the Continent—yet travel simply meant new places but the same kind of people. When the Roosevelts went by rail, they traveled in a private car. On the ship, as Sara said, there were always "people one knows." Places they visited swarmed with cousins and aunts. Franklin saw the world through the eyes of his family—and they presented the world to him as they saw it. And always, at the beginning and the end, was Hyde Park, the little imperium under his parents' scepter.

It was a secure world. The nation was at peace; by the 1880's it had largely bound up the deep gash of civil war. The real capital of the United States was seventy-five miles down the Hudson in New York. Here the capitalists thought big and acted big; they were building America as generals fight wars, recruiting immigrant Swedes, Germans, Bohemians at the docks, throwing masses of men into action at strategic points, establishing railroads, mines, factories, whole cities. These men, it has been aptly observed, spoke little and did much; in Washington were politicians who did little and spoke all too much. On Capitol Hill the congressmen bickered over patronage, tariffs, reform, states' rights, while the big decisions were made on Wall Street. Parties alternated in power—in 1889 the stout, dependable Cleveland was succeeded by the stout, respectable Harrison—but the party battle seemed often a sham battle.

Across the sea, Victoria, a tiny figure on a huge throne, ruled majestically in the fifth decade of her seemingly endless reign. The Queen's navy policed the oceans of the world. Europe, too, was at peace; the "Concert of Europe" may have given forth few notes of harmony, but the powers felt safe enough to fight little wars at home and to build big empires abroad. Weekly, the *Illustrated London News* brought to Hyde Park a picture of this Europe—of Hohenzollerns and Hapsburgs secure on their thrones, of parades and palaces, of international society moving from Paris to London to Vienna, to spa to fox hunt to fancy ball.

Hyde Park knew little of the hates and conflicts simmering just under the surface of affairs—of Mary Lease telling farmers to "raise less corn and more hell," of strikers and finks locked in murderous little battles, of immigrants packed in grimy tenements, bewildered by this strange new world. Certainly Hyde Park knew nothing of some of the men these forces would help thrust above the surface of twentieth-century affairs. Alfred E. Smith, born in a Manhattan tenement, the son of a teamster who died when Al was thirteen, spent the 1880's as an altar boy, newsboy, fishmonger. In the hills of Pennsylvania, Tom Lewis, blacklisted for leading a strike, wandered from pit to pit, holding a job until the dreaded list caught up with him, trying to feed his family; his son, a pugnacious boy named John, would soon leave school for the mines. In West Branch, Iowa, Herbert Hoover was swimming under the willows down by the railroad bridge, catching sunfish on a butcher-string line, picking potato bugs for a penny a hundred.

In Romagna in central Italy—a classic land of political turbulence—Benito Mussolini slept on a sack of corn leaves; born a year after Franklin, the son of a socialist blacksmith, he was sent away to school, ate at third-class tables, and was expelled at the age of eleven. Toward the end of the decade, in a small town on the Bavarian border, a man in his fifties, who had the square face of a Hindenburg but who was only a petty civil servant, fathered a child whose strange dreams and artistic bent he could not understand; at fifteen Adolf Hitler was orphaned and soon cast loose to become a vagrant. In the 1880's, in Georgia, Josef Djugashvili, later Joseph Stalin, was a swarthy, pock-marked boy three years older than Franklin; the son of a peasant cobbler, he lived in a leaky adobe hut and grew up in a land seared by national and racial hatreds.

THE SEED AND THE SOIL

Someday, in some political arena, Roosevelt would come to grips with all these men, and he would overcome, in some way, all but the last of them. Here lies the first paradox of his paradoxical life. There are reasons why an Adolf Hitler or a John L. Lewis should acquire a lust to dominate. Anxious, insecure, adrift in their early years, they made of life an insatiable quest for power.

But what about Roosevelt? He was no product of a broken home or of a ruined land. He knew nothing of family strife, physical want, contemptuous glances. His father "never laughed at him," Sara once remarked. He adored his parents, and as an only child he never suffered even the common experience of dethronement by younger children taking over the center of the family circle. His environment laid no stress on competitive achievement in business or politics. He was to be a Hyde Park gentleman.

Was the pursuit of power in Franklin's genes? His mother always set great store by heredity, and she thought that she saw much of the "Delano influence" in him. On the Roosevelt side there is the striking fact that, after six generations of unremarkable men, "in the seventh generation, this dynasty of the mediocre suddenly blazed up with not one but two, of the most remarkable men in American history." Is there some clue to Franklin D. Roosevelt the politician in the Roosevelts who went before?

The common progenitor of both Franklin and Theodore Roosevelt was Nicholas Roosevelt, whose father had sailed to New Amsterdam from Holland in the 1640's. Nicholas had two sons, Johannes (1689-?) and Jacobus (1692-1776). From the first of these issued the line that was to produce Theodore, from the second, Franklin.

Only one of Franklin's forebears was a politician of any importance. This was Jacobus' son Isaac (1726-1794), a prosperous sugar merchant with no love for the British trade laws that discriminated against his business. Siding with the patriots, he helped draft New York's first constitution after the outbreak of the Revolutionary War and won membership to its first senate. As a Federalist member of the state convention he voted under Alexander Hamilton's brilliant leadership to ratify the new federal Constitution in opposition to the great landowners along the Hudson.

Then the line veered steadily away from politics. Isaac's son James (1760-1847) went to Princeton, became a sugar refiner and banker, was a Federalist member of the New York State Assembly for one term, bred horses, and bought land along the Hudson near Poughkeepsie. His son Isaac (1790-1863) had no interest in politics: he was a Princeton man, a student of medicine and botany, a breeder of cattle and horses, and became a Dutchess County squire. Meanwhile, as the generations passed, the Dutch blood blended with English, German, and other strains. Isaac's son James (1828-1900)—Franklin's father—was of mainly Anglo-Saxon inheritance.

"My son Franklin is a Delano, not a Roosevelt at all," Sara used to say. If so, any clue to Roosevelt's political development is still missing. To be sure, the Delano family liked to trace its ancestry to William the Conqueror, and a Delano held a cabinet seat under Grant. But most of the Delanos passed politics by; they were shipowners, merchants, speculators, philanthropists, industrialists, and country gentlemen. They were proud of their derivation from Philippe De La Noye, who arrived in Plymouth in 1621. Sara's father, Warren Delano, as a young man won a fortune in the China trade, lost much of it in the depression of 1857, returned to Hong Kong to recoup his losses, and retired to an estate on the west bank of the Hudson with his wife and eleven children. Warren was a lifetime Republican who liked to say—perhaps not wholly in jest—"I will not say that all Democrats are horse thieves, but it would seem that all horse thieves are Democrats." He carefully kept his children insulated from his business cares and from people outside his class.

"The Delanos," it has been said, "carried their way of life around them like a transparent but impenetrable envelope wherever they went."

The riddle remains. One looks in vain for any foretoken of Franklin D. Roosevelt the politician in these Delano and Roosevelt lines. Political skills cannot, of course, be inherited as such; genes cannot transmit specific traits and attitudes. But biological inheritance cannot be ignored. It supplies the stuff from which personality is shaped; it sets limits within which variation is constrained. Basic traits, such as motor skills and reaction speed, are certainly influenced by heredity, while temperamental traits, such as stability of mood and emotionality, may be as well. And heredity might have particular importance in a family as prone to intermarriage as the Roosevelts.

Roosevelt at birth was simply a cluster of possibilities. In his forebears the seeds of personality, such as they were, had issued in seafaring, money-making, gaining social prestige. In another generation they were to emerge in vote-getting and power-holding. The seed was there, but what about the soil? The first of Franklin's environments was that created by James and Sara Roosevelt, themselves influenced by the environments of Roosevelts and Delanos who went before. Was it in this soil that Roosevelt's political personality and drive began to grow?

Graduating from Union College in 1847 and from Harvard Law School four years later, James Roosevelt had moved steadily into the life of squire and businessman—except for one remarkable occasion in his youth when he and a mendicant priest, on a walking tour in Italy, joined Garibaldi's army, wore red shirts for a month or two, and then resumed their walking trip. Through his mother's family James became involved in coal and transportation. Eventually he became vice-president of the Delaware and Hudson Canal Company, president of some smaller transportation enterprises, and a director in a number of other companies. Most of the earnings of the Delaware and Hudson came from its heavy investments in anthracite coal. These activities gave James Roosevelt a secure base on which to maintain his expensive but unostentatious home in Hyde Park.

Yet James wanted to be more than a railroad executive. Three times he gambled for high stakes in money and power—and each time he lost. He helped build a huge bituminous coal combination, but the company took heavy losses in the 1873 panic, and the stockholders voted Roosevelt and his friends out of control. He and other capitalists tried to set up a holding company to gain control of an extensive railroad network in the South, but this venture failed too. He helped form a company to dig a canal across Nicaragua, won an act of incorporation from Congress and President

Cleveland, raised six million dollars, started construction—and then the depression of 1893 dried up the sources of funds.

James's unlucky plunges, it has been said, forever turned his son against successful businessmen and speculators. This is unlikely. For most of his life Roosevelt displayed no animus against money-makers. He seemed to regard his forebears' mishaps as joking matters. Moreover, James would not have allowed his setbacks to disturb the family home. He had a striking capacity to compartmentalize his life, moving easily from the quiet of his Hyde Park estate to the rough and tumble of the business world, and back. In later years his son would look longingly toward home at the very time he was launched on daring political ventures.

Although they were sixth cousins, James and Sara did not meet until 1880, at the New York City home of the Theodore Roosevelts. James was fifty-two years old. His first wife had died four years earlier; their only son, James Roosevelt Roosevelt, was now twenty-six years old—the same age as Sara—and had married an Astor, a good beginning for the life he would lead as sportsman, trustee, philanthropist, and minor diplomat.

Tall, gracious, beautiful, Sara was the product of an upper class of international scope. As a girl she had sailed to Hong Kong on a square-rigger; she had been educated abroad; she had moved in society in New York, Boston, London, and Paris. Sara was irresistibly attracted by the widower's courtly ways, hearty good humor, and tenderness. She overcame the objections of her father, who knew and liked James as an old business associate but deemed him too old for his daughter. James Roosevelt and Sara Delano were married in October 1880. After a long tour abroad, they retired to James's Hyde Park estate.

The family, it has been said, is "the psychological broker of society"—the chief agent in molding people's life habits and life attitudes. Did James and Sara Roosevelt, by design or by chance, fashion a world for their son that would encourage an interest in politics? One looks in vain for any such evidence. It was not a world of envy, ambition, or power. It was a world of benevolent authority, with class lines separating the close little family of three at the top from the nurses and governesses, and these in turn from the maids and cooks indoors, and these in turn from the stableboys and farm hands outside. It was a world with the sound and smack of the sea, carried in Sara's rendering of the sea chanteys she had learned on the long voyage to China. It was a world of broad horizons, where Paris and London and Nauheim were familiar places one visited almost every year. Socially it was an insulated world, which looked with equal distaste on the squabbling Irish politicians in Poughkeepsie, the closefisted tradesmen in Hyde Park, the vulgar millionaires at the new resorts. It was a world with deep roots in the American past, asking nothing for the future except a gracious life and a secure estate on the banks of the Hudson.

GROTON: EDUCATION FOR WHAT?

Sara kept her son in this insulated world as long as she could Under her watchful eye Franklin's formal education began in the family; in a sense it never passed outside it. James took an active interest in the Hyde Park public school, but it probably never occurred to Sara to send Franklin there. The boy's only taste of public school came one summer in a German *Volksschule*. His mother thought this "very amusing," but doubted that he learned much. Franklin seemed to enjoy going to school with "a lot of little mickies," as he called them.

Sara herself gave the boy his first schooling. At six he went to a kind of kindergarten under a German governess at the house of some family friends nearby. Then began a succession of governesses and tutors at home. One of these, Mlle. Jeanne Sandoz, had a sense of social justice that probably influenced the boy to an extent. But her main job was to drill Franklin in Latin, French, German, penmanship, and arithmetic; a little European history was thrown in. Sara remained in active charge of her son's education, and a governess either deferred to her wishes or left.

But Franklin could not be schooled at home forever, and Sara had long before laid plans against the time when he would leave. The year after their son's birth she and James had visited friends in Groton, Massachusetts, a small town forty miles northwest of Boston. These friends had given land nearby to a young clergyman, Endicott Peabody, to found a school for boys. Peabody's idea attracted Sara. Resolving to keep his school small, he saw it as simply a large family, with himself as paterfamilias. The headmaster and the trustees—including Phillips Brooks, William Lawrence, and J. Pierpont Morgan—came from eminently respectable families.

Sara clung to her son until he was fourteen. Although Peabody was reluctant to admit boys except for the whole six-year period, Franklin began school as a third former. His Hyde Park neighbor Edmund Rogers entered with him, and his nephew Taddy Roosevelt—grandson of James and his first wife—was a class ahead. When in September 1896 the Roosevelts deposited their son at Groton, Sara wrote plaintively in her diary: "It is hard to leave our darling boy. James and I feel this parting very much."

Here were the makings of a real trial—if not a crisis—for the fourteen-year-old boy. He was out, very late, from under his mother's sheltering wing. He had been the center of attention, even adoration, at Hyde Park; now he was but one of 110 boys. He had had many comforts; now he lived in a cubicle, almost monastic, with a cloth curtain across the doorway, and he washed with a tin basin in soapstone sinks. At home his tempo had been his own; now he had to conform to a rigidly laid out day, from chapel in the morning to study period in the evening, and punctuality was enforced.

Every new boy at Groton faced such problems, but Franklin had others. Joining his form in the third year, he had to break through the icy crust that his classmates put up against "new boys." He spoke with the trace of an English accent. Having a nephew older than he was a source of embarrassment; soon he was dubbed "Uncle Frank." Moreover, Taddy was a "queer sort of boy"—a reputation that could easily spread to a relative. Franklin, in short, was a trifle unorthodox, and unorthodoxy at Groton could encounter harsh penalties at the hands of the older boys. One of these penalties was the "bootbox"—being shoved forcibly, doubled up, into a small locker, and being left there. Another, also permitted by the faculty, was "pumping"—sixth formers would call out the name of an offender in study period, drag him quailing and shaking to a nearby lavatory, bend him face upward over a trough, and pour basins of water over his face and down his throat until he went through the sensations of drowning.

But Franklin Roosevelt was never bootboxed, never pumped— and he won the Punctuality Prize his second year. He got few black marks from his masters; indeed, he was almost relieved when he did, "as I was thought to have no school-spirit before." If the boys called him Uncle Frank, "I would sooner be Uncle Frank, than Nephew Rosy as they have been calling Taddy!" Franklin quickly sided with the dominant majority, not the rebellious few. He was a bit contemptuous of the "new kids" who arrived at school. "The Biddle [Moncure] boy is quite crazy, fresh and stupid, he has been boot-boxed once and threatened to be pumped several times," he reported with relish.

If stresses and strains were concealed behind this easy adaptability, they found no reflection in Franklin's chatty letters to his parents. "I am getting on finely both mentally and physically," he wrote in his first letter home. He conformed fully with Groton mores—he played intramural football on a fourth-string eleven, happily endured numerous scrapes, bruises, and lacerations, cheered himself hoarse at varsity football games, sang in the choir, got into little mischief, criticized the food, and begged for goodies from home. "He strikes me as an intelligent & faithful scholar, & a good boy," Peabody reported to the parents.

How explain this smooth passage from home to school? The reason in part was that Franklin found himself among boys of the same social-economic class that he had known in Hyde Park. His shift was geographical, not social. Of the other boys in his form, nine were from New York City, seven from Boston, two from Philadelphia. Blagden, Chadwick, Greenough, Peabody, Ramsford, Thayer—the names in his form, including his own, were those of wealthy, socially established families from a few centers on or near the eastern seaboard. A random sampling of Groton classes during the early years, according to one authority, showed that over 90 per cent of the boys were from families listed in social registers.

Another reason was the Rector. Doubtless Peabody came to serve as something of a substitute for Franklin's own father, who was entering his seventies and ailing. This remarkable headmaster seems to have put the stamp of his personality on every Grotonian, and not least on young Roosevelt.

A large, vigorous, uncomplicated man with blond hair and an athletic frame, Peabody was thirty-nine when Franklin arrived at Groton. He was a dull teacher, a stuffy preacher, and he had little interest in intellectualism, religious or otherwise. An autocrat, he had a withering "look" that could quell the most bumptious boy. "You know," Averell Harriman once said to his father, "he would be an awful bully if he weren't such a terrible Christian." When a defiant boy told the headmaster in front of the school that he had been unfair, Peabody gave him six black marks and told him that "obedience comes before all else." Peabody believed in religion, character, athletics, and scholarship, seemingly in that order. "Instinctively he trusted a football-player more than a non-football-player, just as the boys did," according to his biographer. He was as puritanical as his forefathers, forbidding the boys to skate on Sunday, chiding Groton alumni for their moral lapses long after they had left the fold.

But Peabody had big virtues that dwarfed his failings. His sense of dedication and warmth of personality enveloped the whole school. He knew precisely what he wanted—to cultivate "manly Christian character, having regard to [the] moral and physical as well as intellectual development" of his charges, and he was the living embodiment of these purposes. Striding solidly through classrooms, in his blue suit, starched collar, and white bow tie, or taking part energetically in the boys' games, he dominated the campus and personified the lusty Christianity in which he believed. The boys loved and feared him; they could not ignore him. One alumnus, otherwise critical of the Rector, said that from Peabody the boys learned determination and to be unafraid.

Roosevelt needed this kind of example. Despite the easy transition from Hyde Park, at times he felt insecure and uncertain of himself at Groton. Often he feared that he would not pass examinations. He submitted a story to the school magazine; "there is precious little chance of its being accepted," he wrote home. Actually, Franklin's occasional feelings of inadequacy were not without cause: he had much to feel inadequate about. Despite his excellent tutoring at home as a child and his oral facility, his grades in his first years at Groton averaged about C (D was failing), and in the later years he brought them up barely to the B level. Despite his enthusiastic participation in football, baseball, hockey, golf, tennis—Peabody required group sports for all boys and merely tolerated individual sports—he was distinguished in nothing but the "high kick." In this he set a school record—significant only because his successful kicks of over seven feet meant landing painfully on his left side and arm, and suggested an intense drive on Franklin's part to excel in some arena.

Franklin's life at Groton followed an inexorable routine: chapel and classes took up the morning, sports the afternoon, and chapel and study hall the evening, until the boys, all in Eton collars, blue suits, and pumps, filed past the Peabodys, shook hands, and said good night. Autumns were filled with football excitement; then came the Christmas season, with the unforgettable reading of Dickens's *Christmas Carol* by the Rector's father. In winter the short afternoons were taken up with coasting, tobogganing, and skiing. With spring came boating, swimming, golf, and drilling for the Memorial Day parade. Absorbed in this routine, Groton had little interest in the outside world. The dramatic events of 1898, however, broke through with a thunderous roar. Franklin was immensely excited by the war with Spain. Indeed, he and two boys planned to decamp from Groton in a pieman's cart and enlist, but at the crucial moment he came down ingloriously with scarlet fever.

At vacation time, a Grotonian later recalled, the boys reacted to the close, monastic life of the school like sailors taking shore leave. But not Franklin. If he got into escapades, or even mischief, there is no hint of it. During short vacations he joyously threw himself back into the life of Hyde Park. Summers he spent usually at Campobello, where his greatest pleasure was in sailing his twenty-one-foot sailboat, *New Moon*, which his father had given him. He still showed little interest in girls. While he duly observed the social amenities, he spent a good deal of time evading certain girls whom he called "pills" or "elephantine."

As the four years at Groton came to an end, Roosevelt was showing more maturity and assurance. He had gained more independence from his mother, who had frequently visited him at school. His schoolwork improved, he became a dormitory prefect and manager of the baseball nine Some of his schoolmates considered him self-assertive and quarrelsome. Others liked him strongly; one remembered him as "gray-eyed, cool, self-possessed, intelligent," with the "warmest, most friendly and understanding smile." But there is evidence that Roosevelt did not consider himself a success at Groton. He did not win the prized position of senior prefect, and he felt bitter toward the Rector for his "favoritism" in choosing others. In his senior year he still patronized the "new kids," but he himself was a tall, gangling youth with pince-nez and with braces on his teeth.

"He was a quiet, satisfactory boy," the Rector summed him up many years later, "of more than ordinary intelligence, taking a good position in his Form but not brilliant. Athletically he was rather too slight for success. We all liked him."

What influence did Groton have on Roosevelt as a future politician? The question takes on special interest because Peabody made much of his eagerness to educate his boys for political leadership. Himself a graduate of Cheltenham and Cambridge, he was impressed by the fact that the English public (*i.e.*, private) schools had been recruiting stations for British leadership; Eton had supplied half a dozen prime ministers in the nineteenth century, and some cabinet meetings seemed like reunions of old Harrovians. Could Groton serve the same high purpose in America? "If some Groton boys do not enter political life and do something for our land," he said, "it won't be because they have not been urged." And he exhorted them.

Exhortation—but little else. Certainly Groton did not equip her youths with any kind of political expertness. In a democracy the indispensable political skill is facility in dealing with all sorts of people. Grotonians, one of them remarked, could "gaze fixedly two inches over the head of a slight acquaintance while they carried on a conversation." Ten years after Groton, during his early political life, Roosevelt was still throwing his head up and looking down his nose at people. The only political skill Franklin seems to have learned at Groton was an effective debating style, but this kind of argumentation was of little use in his later political battles.

Nor was the Groton curriculum likely to quicken a boy's interest in the politics of his own country. Languages—especially the dead languages of Greece and Rome—made up much of the program. History was European history. No course dealt directly with the United States. The Rector and most of his masters taught by rule and by rote; the students were drilled rather than educated. "I studied Sacred Studies for six years at Groton," said one of Franklin's schoolmates. "I never heard of Renan or of Tom Paine; and I was never told that the Old and the New Testament are full of the most potent contradictions." Franklin's hundreds of letters during his four years give hardly a hint of any intellectual excitement. Classes were obstacle courses to be run.

It has been said that Roosevelt's concern for the underprivileged was born at Groton. This is true only in a special sense. Peabody was something of a Christian Socialist. He worried about the needy, and Groton maintained a summer camp for poor boys, where Franklin sometimes helped out. But the Rector's socialism somewhat resembled that of his Cambridge teacher Charles Kingsley, who ended up more interested in better sanitation than in economic or social reform. The Rector's humanitarianism never went much beyond a concern for the cleanliness and morals of the masses. Franklin's main interest in the poor was to give charity to them. As for specific public issues, Roosevelt in his debates argued for a larger navy, against the annexation of Hawaii and for the independence of the Philippines, against guaranteeing the integrity of China—taking sides that were probably assigned rather than chosen —but he displayed no interest in the developing economic and social problems of a rising industrialism at home.

In one way, at least, Groton failed the future politician completely. Politics to Peabody was a kind of crusade in which Grotonian knight-errants, presumably dressed in Eton collars, would charge eagerly into the political arena and clash noisily with the forces of evil. Politics must be "purified," he told Franklin and his schoolmates. But his exhortations ignored the cruel questions facing the American politician bent on success. Never lie, the Rector said—without taking up the further question whether in politics lies are sometimes necessary to reach "good" ends. Never compromise with evil, the Rector said—without arguing whether politicians must work with corrupt forces to carry out popular mandates. Peabody's goals were good ones for a humanitarian politician, but his artless homilies were simply irrelevant to the harsh lesson of American politics, the lesson Lincoln Steffens finally learned, that "honesty is not enough," that effective politics in a democracy requires knowledge, courage, will power, humor, leadership.

To be sure, Peabody was struggling with an old and formidable problem. For at least two millenniums societies have struggled with the problem of discovering and educating political talent. In Greece, in the spirit of Paideia, young men were tested to see who possessed the essential qualities of leadership—common sense, intellectual capacity, devotion to the public welfare. For centuries printing presses flooded Europe with books on how princes should be educated and how rulers should behave—Machiavelli's *Prince* is the best-known example. The English public schools educated generation after generation for political leadership. Groton and other

American private schools borrowed Etonian and Harrovian forms, just as they aped the athleticism of Greece and the monasticism of the middle ages. But they borrowed only forms—and the forms were meaningless in a different culture, in the unique democratic politics of America.

"I count it among the blessings of my life that it was given to me in formative years to have the privilege of your guiding hand," Roosevelt wrote to Peabody forty years after he graduated from Groton. The Rector came to stand as a unique personal compound of Christian ideals. Groton, too, became a bundle of precious memories—memories of walking to town for cider and apples, of youthful voices floating across the soft May evenings, of the sun streaming through the chapel windows, of the Rector stabbing the air with taut fingers as he strove to drive home his simple precepts. Peabody and the school helped shape Roosevelt's basic attitudes toward social problems, but they throw little light on the emergence of Roosevelt as a politician. None of his political battles was won on the playing fields of Groton.

HARVARD: THE GOLD COAST

"My dearest Mama and Papa," Franklin Roosevelt wrote home in September 1900, "Here I am, in Cambridge and in twelve hours I shall be a full registered member of the Class of 1904." His room looked as if it had been "struck by sheet Lightning," his sitting room lacked curtains and carpets, the bed looked "inhabitable"— but he was happy. He was about to become a Harvard man.

The transition from Groton was an easy one. Many of his old classmates were entering Harvard with him. He immediately began eating at a Groton table rather than in one of the large common dining halls. Some evenings he went to Sanborn's billiard parlor where he could see most of the "Groton, St. Marks, St. Pauls and Pomfret fellows." His roommate, Lathrop Brown, was a Grotonian. Together they shared a suite of rooms in Westmorly Court, amidst Harvard's "Gold Coast" of high-priced dormitories and select clubs.

Unlike Groton, Harvard was not isolated from the world. Across the Charles River lay Boston, basking in its golden afternoon. The "Hub of the Universe," the "Athens of America" boasted of its Brahmin families, of its Bulfinch State House, of the Athenaeum, its outstanding private library, and—now that it was getting used to her—of beer-drinking, Buddha-worshiping Mrs. Jack Gardner, whose fabled art palace was opened in young Roosevelt's junior year. For this Boston, Harvard was a kind of genteel brain trust. The relation between city and gown was a close but not always happy one. Boston, said a Harvard historian, was a "social leech" on the college; Beacon Hill hostesses—"Boston mammas," he called them—wanted to entertain Harvard's "appetizing young men" and balked all efforts to make a "social democracy" of the college. Roosevelt was immediately engaged on the Boston-Cambridge social circuit. With Proper Bostonians he got along very well; their families, while socially far grander, were much like those he had known at Hyde Park: rich, wellborn, and inbred. Hardly a week went by during his four years at Harvard that he did not conduct a round of social calls, duly handing his card to formidable butlers. "My dress-suit looked like a dream and was much admired," he reported home. His height, his almost-handsome head—hair parted in the middle, close-in, deep-set eyes, long, lean nose and chin, sensitive lips—his ready smile, no longer showing braces, his easy ways, stood him in good stead.

But on the athletic field his physique failed him. As at Groton he wanted desperately to make good in a big sport. He weighed only 146 pounds, however, and he was not athletically skillful. Trying out for end on the freshman football team, he lasted only two weeks. There was consolation in winning the captaincy of one of the scrub teams after the first day of practice. He also worked hard for crew —but here again he could rise no higher than stroke on intramural teams.

Roosevelt made up for his athletic frustrations by plunging into extracurricular activities. He was pleased at being elected secretary of the Freshman Glee Club. Most important was the *Crimson*. The day he reported home that he had "left" the freshman team he added that he was trying out for the undergraduate daily, "& if I work hard for two years I may be made an editor." Work he did —often several hours a day—and in his junior year he won the top post of editor in chief. Luck, or connections, played a part; upon calling Cousin Theodore Roosevelt in Boston to ask to see him, Franklin discovered that the vice-president was to lecture in a Harvard course and thereby he won a scoop for his paper. But his success was due mainly to doggedness.

Obviously Roosevelt wanted to make good at Harvard. What was the source of this ambition? Doubtless it lay largely in his anxiety to gain the respect of his classmates in general, and of the social elite in particular. Throughout his college career Roosevelt was a joiner. But some organizations one did not join—one was asked. The club system that Roosevelt encountered at Harvard was one of the most harshly exclusive in the country. Sophomores were first sifted out by the "Hasty Pudding," which gave special social prominence to the first group chosen. Then came the real test—election to one of the "final" clubs. At one time affiliated with national fraternities, the chapters at Harvard had not enjoyed brotherhood with provincials in Ohio and points west and had gladly given up their charters. They had become a direct link between Harvard and Boston society. Behind their elegantly dowdy exteriors few activities of any importance went on; the important thing was to belong to them, not to be active in them.

Delightedly Franklin entered the social lists. "I am about to be slaughtered, but quite happy, nevertheless," he wrote home after hearing that he had been picked for a sophomore club. As a Roosevelt and as a Grotonian, he was almost sure of membership in a final club. But which one? At the top of the hierarchy stood Porcellian, which years before had tapped Cousin Theodore. Franklin made a high-ranking club, the Fly, but was passed over by Porcellian. This blow gave him something of an inferiority complex, according to Eleanor Roosevelt; it was the bitterest moment of his life, according to another relative. Evidence is conflicting on this point, but one thing is certain: social acceptance was of crucial importance to the young Roosevelt.

There was time for classes too. Roosevelt took the liberal arts course; his program included English and French literature, Latin, geology, paleontology, fine arts, and public speaking; but he concentrated on the social sciences, enrolling in a dozen history courses and in several courses each in government and economics. These were European history, English history, American history, American government, constitutional government, tendencies of American legislation, international law, currency legislation, economics of transportation, of banking, and of corporations. As at Groton he was only a fair student, attaining a "gentleman C" average. He had anticipated several courses at Groton, however, and hence was able to meet his requirements for a bachelor's degree in three years. He stayed a fourth year at Harvard in order to edit the *Crimson*, registering in the graduate school, but he did not take his courses too seriously and was not granted a master of arts degree.

During much of the college year he saw his mother frequently. James Roosevelt died at the age of seventy-two, during his son's freshman year, after a long struggle with heart disease. "I wonder how I lived when he left me," Sara said afterward. She managed to endure one lonely winter at Hyde Park; after that she took an apartment in Boston only a few miles from her son. Franklin's relation with her was close but relaxed. He dealt with her tactfully and affectionately and made a brave effort to shoulder some of the responsibilities of Hyde Park and Campobello. He saw a good deal of his mother during the summers, which took the old easy pattern. Following his freshman and junior years he made trips to Europe, touring the Norwegian coast, Germany, Switzerland, France, and

England. But these trips left time for golf, tennis, and sailing Campobello.

Roosevelt's activities at Harvard spilled over into many fields. At the suggestion of a Boston bookseller he began a collection, starting with Americana in general, narrowing this down to "ships" and finally to United States warships. He became head librarian of the Fly Club, but his duties were light. He continued his charitable activities, teaching occasionally at a club for poor boys in Boston. He even led the cheers at a football game, though he "felt like a D... F... waiving my arms & legs before several thousand amused spectators!" But much of his college career is summed up in a line written to his mother: ". . . am doing a little studying, a little riding & a few party calls."

Half a century before Roosevelt finished Harvard, Henry Adams, descendant of two presidents, had entered there. The Harvard of his day, Adams said later, was a mild and liberal school which sent young men into the world as respectable citizens. But "leaders of men it never tried to make. . . . It taught little, and that little ill, but it left the mind open, free from bias, ignorant of facts, but docile." Much had happened to the college since Adams's years there, especially during Charles W. Eliot's presidency, but the remark aptly states Harvard's effect on Franklin Roosevelt.

His courses seemed admirably suited for educating a future statesman, but they lacked meaningful content. Roosevelt's government courses, for example, stressed constitutional formalities and legal abstractions rather than political realities. His program, Roosevelt himself complained, was "like an electric lamp that hasn't any wire." He wanted a "practical idea of the workings of a political system—of the machinery of primary, caucus, election and legislature." His first course in government was taught by one of the dullest lecturers in Harvard's history.

The fault was not merely that of the college. Roosevelt was largely indifferent to his studies—and might have been indifferent even if the courses had been far more exciting. Not one of his letters home reflects interest in the intellectual side of Harvard beyond meeting course requirements and cramming for examinations. When a myopic lecturer bored him he had no compunction, along with most of the rest of the class, in escaping from the hall by a rear window and stealing down the fire escape.

Certainly the doctrines taught Roosevelt at Harvard had little relation to the views of the politician of the 1930's. The man who as president would dominate Congress and try to "pack" the Supreme Court learned in college about the eternal verity of a nice and fixed balance among the branches of government. The man who as president would try "crazy" economic experiments and currency schemes received a solid grounding in classical economics ("I took economics courses in college for four years, and everything I was taught was wrong," he said later). The man who would be called the "master political psychologist of his time" took no psychology and quit his only philosophy course after three weeks. He might have learned a good deal about the role of the West in American history and politics from Frederick Jackson Turner, but he missed the first six weeks of Turner's lectures.

His professors ranged from extreme right wing to moderately liberal. He became close friends with only one of them, a handsome socialite economics teacher named Abram Piatt Andrew, who later went into politics and won appointment as assistant secretary of the treasury under Taft. Abbott Lawrence Lowell might have taught him something about practical politics—Lowell had won office as member of the Boston School Committee though neither party would nominate him for a second term—but Roosevelt seems to have had only occasional contact with him. Lowell and at least two others of Roosevelt's teachers who were still alive during his presidency would later hotly oppose most of the New Deal.

What was Roosevelt's own social outlook during his college days? To the extent that he had one, it was a mixture of political conservatism, economic orthodoxy, and anti-imperialism, steeped in a fuzzy altruism and wide ignorance. "Yes, Harvard has sought to uplift the Negro," he wrote in his junior year, "if you like, has sought to make a man out of a semi-beast." After Theodore Roosevelt helped settle the great coal strike of 1902 Franklin criticized his cousin for interfering in the affair and for his "tendency to make the executive power stronger than the Houses of Congress." Although he had heard the great historian Edward Channing debunk hero worship and historical humbug, Roosevelt as a senior wrote a most adulatory and inaccurate essay on Alexander Hamilton. On the other hand, he helped establish a "Boer Relief Fund," and in a thesis on the Roosevelt family before the Revolution he lauded his forebears for their "very democratic spirit" and their sense of responsibility.

Perhaps the best measure of Roosevelt's views at Harvard lies in his *Crimson* editorials. In the fall, obsessed by football problems, he wrote indignant editorials about weak cheering at the games, smoking in the grandstand, lack of enthusiasm by the spectators, poor spirit in the team. When winter came he moved right on to problems of winter sports. Interspersed were editorials on matters that have occupied student editors for decades: inadequate fire protection in the dormitories, the need for board walks, overly congested college calendars, and the like. He went to some pains to draw attention to political speakers at the university. He showed absolutely no interest in matters outside Harvard.

Roosevelt met little success in campus politics. When in his freshman year some of the "outlanders" in the class broke the Groton grip on the class presidency, Roosevelt was on the sidelines. Senior year he was nominated for the prized office of class marshal but lost out at the hands of an organized slate. He did win office, however, as permanent chairman of the class committee, thanks largely to his prominence as editor of the *Crimson*. But he showed none of the political craft at Harvard that Herbert Hoover had displayed ten years earlier at Stanford in leading the "barbarians" in a triumphant attack on fraternity control of the campus.

About the time Roosevelt was at Harvard a Tammany district boss named George Washington Plunkitt, seated on his favorite bootblack stand, was explaining how to get ahead in politics. You must study human nature, he said, not books—they were just a hindrance. "If you have been to college, so much the worse for you. You'll have to unlearn all you learned." The secret? "You have to go among the people, see them and be seen." Roosevelt's early education violated all Plunkitt's time-tested precepts. Yet the young man from Hyde Park would vanquish the Plunkitts in the years to come. How he stuck to boyhood ideals nurtured at Hyde Park, Groton, and Harvard, and tried to realize these ideals by plunging into the rough and tumble of American politics was to be the theme of the life ahead.

TWO *Albany: The Young Lion*

I T IS A STRIKING fact that some of the great
popular leaders of our time have risen to power from outside the national "heartland." Lloyd George came not from England but from
Wales, Hitler not from Prussia but from Austria, Stalin not from
Mother Russia but from Georgia, MacDonald not from England
but from northern Scotland, just as Napoleon earlier was not a
Frenchman but a Corsican. In a geographical sense Roosevelt was
no outlander, but in a cultural sense he was. His shift from Hyde
Park, Groton, and Harvard to New York City was a journey between two worlds—from the class-bound gentility of home and
school to the bustling, bawling urban America of the 1900's.

This urban America was in economic and political ferment. Between the time young Franklin Roosevelt first looked out at side-
wheelers straining against the Hudson current and the time on that
June day in 1904 when he sat in cap and gown on the commence-
ment platform, important changes had taken place. In that year an
economist found that two mammoth groups—the Morgan and the
Rockefeller combinations—had come to "constitute the heart of the
business and commercial life of the nation." In the four years that
Roosevelt studied classical economics at Harvard, over 150 trusts
had been formed. Ten of these combinations were capitalized at
one hundred million dollars or more; trusts were pyramiding into
supertrusts. Despite depressions, despite the Sherman Anti-Trust
Act of 1890, despite populist and socialist attacks, the capitalists
bore their power with bland assurance.

The system had not gone unchallenged. In 1896 young William
Jennings Bryan, his face impassioned under the prairie sun, his
voice in turn imploring, commanding, lashing out, had aroused
the West against Wall Street and the forces of gold. But the challenge had come to naught. Outwardly unruffled, William McKinley
had sat the campaign out on his front porch. The Boy Orator lost
every electoral vote in the East, every county in New England.
Four years later he did even worse. To many Easterners Bryanism
seemed a far-off western trouble, supported in the East only by the

flotsam and jetsam of the larger cities. To Franklin Roosevelt, starting at Groton in the middle of Bryan's first campaign and at Harvard during his second, it meant nothing: the cries of the Bryanites were muffled by the academic walls around him. But in the early 1900's things were different. Suddenly—overnight, it seemed later—the intoxicating aroma of reform was everywhere. A host of pushing, sharp-eyed journalists began reporting on the ills of twentieth-century America. These ills had little to do with the stale complaints of horny-handed farmers or grubby socialists. These evils were hurting respectable people too. Patent medicines, it was revealed, were often poisonous—and they could kill anyone. Life insurance companies gambled with other people's money—including that of the middle class. Canned goods on sale just around the corner at the grocery store might be filthy or even poisonous. Courts were crooked; the Senate was corrupt. And in many a city the black trail of wrongdoing, the muckrakers reported, ran straight from fat madams and grafting policemen through politicians and mayors to churchgoing traction magnates and utility executives.

These revelations were not buried in obscure Marxist journals or in populist weeklies. Mass-circulation magazines—*Collier's, McClure's, American, Cosmopolitan*—screamed them forth. Time was when a magazine "was very ca'ming to the mind," said Mr. Dooley, the Archey Road philosopher-bartender. "But now whin I pick me fav-rite magazine off th' flure, what do I find? Ivirything has gone wrong." Reformism stirred not only bartenders but barbers, housewives, ministers, professors, young people.

Muckraking was well under way when Roosevelt graduated from Harvard in 1904. During the next six years the revolt of the American conscience, as Frederick Lewis Allen called it, came into full tide. These years Roosevelt spent in New York, first as a student at Columbia Law School, then as a young lawyer. He could not have been in a more strategic place to absorb the atmosphere of reform. For the New York of the 1900's embodied both the portent and promise of the time: it was the city of a million immigrants, of the unspeakable Hell's Kitchen, of Tammany and Boss Murphy, of corruption on a colossal scale, but it was also headquarters for most of the muckraking magazines, the seat of numerous reform movements, the place where Cousin Theodore had been a swaggering police commissioner and unsuccessful candidate for mayor.

How much effect did this environment have on Roosevelt? The direct and immediate impact was not profound; as in the past, Roosevelt tended to be sensitive to people rather than doctrines. But the ultimate, indirect impact was important. In the long run Roosevelt could no more escape the pervasive atmosphere of reformism than he could shut out the air around him. And there were two people who served as vital links between the new America and himself. Significantly they were both members of his social class, and both members of his family.

UNCLE TED AND COUSIN ELEANOR

On one occasion when he was five years old Franklin Roosevelt cavorted around his nursery floor with Eleanor Roosevelt on his back; she was then two years old and a member of the Oyster Bay Roosevelts. But they met only occasionally during following years. The first member of the Oyster Bay branch to make an impression on Franklin was his fifth cousin Theodore.

Twenty-four years older than Franklin, Theodore was always just far enough ahead of him to assume heroic proportions in the boy's eyes. During Franklin's childhood "Cousin Theodore" or "Uncle Ted" was out West capturing desperadoes. While Franklin was at Groton, Theodore was successively in New York bossing the police, in Washington helping run the navy, a hero in the war with Spain, and then governor of New York. The Rough Rider loved to impart his energetic fervor to youth. "For a man merely to be good is not enough," he told his admiring cousin and a dazzled audience of Grotonians, his teeth and spectacles gleaming, "he must be shrewd and he must be courageous."

Theodore met the Groton ideal perfectly: he was a bold crusader for "clean government," against corruption, graft, and obvious types of political sin. As governor of New York he attacked the bosses, and they were delighted to help ease him out of the state and into the vice-presidency. Who could anticipate a crazed anarchist's bullet? Another boss—the head of the Republican party—was aghast. "I told William McKinley it was a mistake to nominate that wild man at Philadelphia," Mark Hanna exclaimed. "Now, look, that damned cowboy is President of the United States!" And to T.R. he wrote, "Go slow."

"I shall go slow," the President had answered. But physically and temperamentally he seemed unable to go slow. Seven months after taking office he demanded dissolution of the Northern Securities Company in the face of J. P. Morgan's suave reply that if the company had done anything wrong "send your man [the attorney general] to my man and they can fix it up." In the following years the President advocated workmen's compensation and child-labor laws, pure food and drug laws, stronger national regulation of railroads, income and inheritance taxes, sweeping conservation measures. To be sure, he was not a consistent or thoroughgoing reformer. As a student of reform has said, "He could be brutally militaristic, evasive about trusts, compromising on social legislation, purblind to the merits of reformers who did not equate reform with Theodore Roosevelt." But he dramatized reform, and even gave it an air of respectability.

Franklin Roosevelt could not escape this "condition of excitement and irritation in the public mind," as Uncle Ted once described it. The man who had won the boy's admiration as a Rough Rider kept it as a reformer. Franklin saw the President at the White House on a number of occasions both before and after his marriage to the President's niece. He must have speculated on the parallels between his career and his cousin's early one: Theodore had gone to Harvard, had failed there to win election as class marshal, had gone on to Columbia Law School—and then into politics. Franklin could hardly miss the potential parallel. One day in 1907 he told his fellow law clerks that he had his career well in mind: first a seat in the state assembly, then assistant secretary of the navy, then governor of New York—and then the presidency. His friends did not laugh at him; he seemed in earnest, and had not Cousin Theodore had just such a career?

But one great parallel was missing. Theodore had always been a Republican, but Franklin—what was Franklin? His father, believing that the national government should be honest, frugal, and limited in scope, had been a Cleveland Democrat, and so was the son. But these were difficult times for a Roosevelt who was a Cleveland Democrat. In 1896 James, an eastern capitalist, certainly could not have supported Bryan; he probably voted for McKinley. In 1898 James campaigned for Theodore for governor of New York, and Franklin wrote from Groton that "we were all wild with delight when we heard of Teddy's election." In 1900 Franklin joined the Harvard Republican Club and marched miles through Boston in a torchlight procession for the McKinley-Roosevelt ticket. In 1904 he cast his first ballot for Theodore. Again family ties were strongest.

Was Franklin a Democrat during his early years? By inheritance yes, but when it came down to specific cases he supported Republicans. Actually his party leanings were as amorphous as his ideological ones. Why did he not enter politics as a Republican? He then could have put himself directly in line for Theodore's political inheritance. The most likely explanation seems to be that Theodore's power in the Republican party, thanks partly to his flat statement in 1904 that he would not run for another term, was waning when Franklin finished law school, and so was progressivism in the Republican party. In 1910 Franklin, probably by chance more than by design, was in a position to run for office on either major party ticket. It was less by conviction that he became a Democrat than by virtue of the fact that the Democratic party needed him and went to him.

Eleanor Roosevelt was the daughter of Theodore Roosevelt's younger brother, Elliott, and of Anna R. Hall. Franklin was her fifth cousin once removed. It was by no means unimportant to Franklin that she was the niece of Uncle Ted, with all the glamour that went with membership in the presidential family. But this was the least of it. Growing up she had been a gawky, pensive girl, with a brace and the prominent Rooseveltian teeth. Suddenly, during his later college years, Franklin saw a tall willowy girl with a sweet, expressive face under a great mass of hair. He fell in love, and late in 1903 proposed to her. She accepted. Franklin was only twenty-two years old and Eleanor only nineteen, but, she said later, "it seemed an entirely natural thing and I never even thought that we were both rather young and inexperienced."

But Sara did. She was stunned by her son's sudden announcement. Having lost her husband only three years before, she had looked forward to companionship with her son, who, she hoped, would settle down at Hyde Park. They were far too young to get married, she told Franklin. But her son was firm—and diplomatic. "I know my mind . . ." he wrote her. "And for you, dear Mummy, you know that nothing can ever change what we have always been & always will be to each other—only now you have two children to love & to love you. . . ." And from Eleanor came a plaintive note that was also a truce offer: ". . . I do so want you to learn to love me a little. You must know that I will always try to do what you wish for I have grown to love you very dearly during the past summer."

Sara tried to delay things by taking Franklin on a Caribbean cruise early in 1904 to think things over. When he returned he was as determined as ever to marry Eleanor. Sara gave in. She did not object to Eleanor as a person. Indeed, she was pleased at Franklin's choice, if he had to choose so early. The engaged couple, carefully chaperoned, spent a few weeks together at Campobello getting to know each other better.

Franklin and Eleanor were married March 17, 1905. Endicott Peabody officiated, and Uncle Ted, just inaugurated president in his own right, came up from Washington to give his niece away. Inevitably T.R. stole the show; guests clustered around the genial chief executive, leaving the newlyweds standing quite alone. "When he goes to a wedding he wants to be the bride, and when he goes to a funeral he wants to be the corpse," remarked a relative sourly as he watched the proceedings. Franklin and Eleanor had a European honeymoon in the grand tradition: Brown's hotel in London, art galleries in Paris, moonlight gondola rides in Venice, a leisurely trip north through the Alps, visits with family friends on estates in England and Scotland.

The woman Franklin married had had as unstable and unhappy a childhood as his had been sunny and secure. Her early life in gloomy brownstone houses in New York City was of the stuff of an Edith Wharton novel. Her mother, a somber unsympathetic person racked by violent headaches, died when Eleanor was eight. A brother died a few weeks later. She adored her father, a radiant, warmhearted man who called her "Little Nell" and became the object of her dreams. But he was an alcoholic who spent long periods in sanitariums, and he died in Eleanor's tenth year. "My aunts told me, but I simply refused to believe it," she remembered, "and while I wept long and went to bed still weeping, I finally went to sleep and began the next day living in my dream world as usual." She was reared by her mother's family, who made no effort to build up the child's self-confidence. Her mother, annoyed by Eleanor's solemn face and graceless ways, had called her "granny" to her face; an aunt said that she was an old maid who could never hope to marry. To make matters worse, another aunt had a series of desperately unhappy love affairs, an uncle drank heavily, and the whole Hall family carried on a dizzy social life that was far beyond their means.

In her mid-teens Eleanor had three years of schooling in England, and she came back to New York a far more secure and poised person. But her early years had given her a sympathetic interest in fellow sufferers that she was never to lose. She was haunted for months by the face of a wretched-looking man who had tried to snatch a purse from a woman sitting near her. She was interested in the ragged little newsboys to whom she had helped her father serve Thanksgiving dinner. By the age of nineteen she was teaching in a settlement house and investigating working conditions of women for the Consumers' League. Inevitably her qualities of compassion and sensitivity added a new dimension to Franklin's social outlook.

But this was a long-term process, and the couple were concerned with more immediate things when they returned from their honeymoon in the fall of 1905. They moved into a house on East 36th Street, which had been rented and furnished by Sara, and they lived here for two years until Sara had finished building two adjoining houses on 65th Street, one for herself and one for her son and daughter-in-law. Their first child, Anna, was born in May 1906. Five more children would be born during the next ten years, including one who died in infancy from the flu. These were hard years for Eleanor. She was not ready for many domestic responsibilities. She reproached herself bitterly over the baby who died, although she was not at fault. Her mother-in-law tried to plan her life for her, and often succeeded.

Wanting desperately to share in her husband's activities, Eleanor tried to learn to drive Franklin's little Ford car and to ride Franklin's horse Bobby. But she ran the car into a gatepost, and she could not control Bobby. She practiced golf by herself for days and then ventured on the green with her husband, who, after watching her cut at the ball for a few minutes, said that she might just as well give it up. She did.

Franklin seemed insensitive to his young wife's feelings of inadequacy, her restlessness under Sara's maternal domination, her wish to share more of his life. When he found Eleanor once weeping at her dressing table at their—or Sara's—house on 65th Street, he reacted more with bewildered dismay than with anxious compassion. "What on earth is the matter with you?" he demanded. Though he gave his wife and family warm affection and plunged into family picnics and yacht trips with zest and vigor, he could spend many a Saturday afternoon playing poker at the University Club in New York City. Like his father, he seemed able to compartmentalize his life with ease.

Roosevelt had begun Columbia Law School in the fall of 1904 and he entered his second year soon after returning from his honeymoon. Here he repeated the pattern of Harvard, minus the extracurricular activities. Although the Columbia faculty included a distinguished group of law professors, the courses failed to interest Franklin. His grades once again averaged C. He failed two courses —one of them Pleading and Practice I—and had to take make-up examinations. After passing the New York bar examinations before the end of his third year he promptly dropped his courses, thus failing to win his LL.B. degree. Clearly the study of the law did not challenge young Roosevelt.

Law practice was something else. Through his connections he got a clerkship at the old Wall Street law firm of Carter, Ledyard, and Milburn. It was an unpaid job the first year and his work was rather routine. But cases came his way—many of them from his rather litigious family—and he enjoyed the practical higgle and haggle of legal negotiation. He was surprised and depressed at the gap between legal education and legal practice. He saw little connection between legal "grand principles" and the problems of a relative's trunk destroyed on a Le Havre dock, the interpretation of a will, or a deed of transfer of land.

Roosevelt was not excited by the broader points of law. If he had been, his future at Carter, Ledyard, and Milburn—and his whole career—might have been much different. The firm defended such clients as Standard Oil of New Jersey and the American Tobacco

Company against the government's attacks on the trusts; it was saturated with the spirit of sober, responsible defense of corporate interests in the face of progressivism. As it turned out, Roosevelt was influenced far more by his everyday contacts with clients, lawyers, claimants, and the politicians and would-be politicians around the courts than he was by office ideology.

After a time, however, he was bored by the law. Something inside him was pushing him to wider fields of action.

The six years after Harvard were outwardly uneventful ones for Roosevelt, aside from family affairs. They were years of intellectual latency. But beneath the surface was a flux and flow, stirred by the nature of the times, by his wife and associates, and by the demands of his work. The year 1910 brought this period to a close and found Roosevelt ready for any opportunity that lay ahead.

THE RACE FOR THE SENATE

The average American politician follows a well-trod path to elective office. He strikes deep roots in a likely community. He joins countless organizations where he can make useful contacts: Masons, Grange, Elks, veterans' groups, and the like. He is active in his church, in charities, in civic affairs. Carefully skirting controversies that divide people, he quickly puts himself at the head of any movement that commands wide community backing. Above all he makes a point of being a good "mixer" with all classes of people.

Roosevelt did virtually none of these things. He may have dreamed of running for office, but certainly he made little preparation for it. In 1910 he had not lived the year round in Hyde Park since leaving for Groton fourteen years before. He stayed at his mother's house many week ends and summers, but he saw little of the townspeople. He became vice-commodore of the Hudson River Ice Yacht Club and vestryman of the St. James Episcopal Church—activities hardly calculated to bring him in touch with a cross section of the people. To be sure, he joined Hyde Park's Eagle Engine Company No. 1 and Rescue Hook and Ladder Company No. 1—but only *after* he was elected senator.

Roosevelt did not create his first great opportunity. That opportunity came to him.

It first came to him early in 1910 in New York City when John E. Mack, district attorney of Dutchess County and a leading Poughkeepsie Democrat, visited Roosevelt on a legal errand. It seemed possible, Mack said, that Lewis Stuyvesant Chanler, a prominent socialite politician, might quit his current post of state assemblyman. Would Roosevelt be interested in running? Roosevelt was highly responsive. At party functions later in the year Dutchess

County Democrats looked over the young man. They had mixed feelings about him. His patrician and somewhat supercilious bearing and speech, his slight acquaintance with the district, his youth and inexperience, above all his unpredictability were a source of worry. On the other hand, he bore the magic name of Roosevelt. And he had money—money for his own campaign and perhaps enough left over for the party treasury.

Roosevelt had few qualms. He wanted to try his hand at politics. He was eager to return to Hyde Park to live. Most important, he had a good chance to win. Poughkeepsie with its Irish and other Democratic forces made up much of Chanler's district. To be sure, his mother was dubious about the idea, and so were a number of friends and relatives. It struck them a bit like an English gentleman's going "into trade." But Uncle Ted was pleased, even though Franklin was entering politics on the Democratic side. As for Eleanor, now pregnant for the fourth time, she merely acquiesced; it never occurred to her that she had any part to play. By early summer Roosevelt was intent on running.

Then came a blow. Chanler, it seemed, had no intention of giving up his assembly post. Elected lieutenant governor in 1906, and unsuccessful Democratic candidate for governor in 1908, he was not ready to quit the political arena. In vain Roosevelt took Chanler out to dinner and urged him to run for state senator. Embracing several agricultural counties, the senatorial district was traditionally Republican. Only once since 1856 had the Democrats won the district, and that occasion had been a three-cornered contest. Chanler would not take the risk.

What was Roosevelt to do? His alternatives were to try for state senator himself or to back out altogether. He hesitated to take on what seemed a hopeless contest. On the other hand, his enthusiasm was now pushing him on. Even an unsuccessful campaign would be good political experience, and it might put him in line for the assembly seat whenever Chanler gave it up. The district, moreover, was not hopelessly Republican; Senator John F. Schlosser, the incumbent, had won in 1908 only by 18,366 to 16,294. The party leaders pressed him; they "told me it was my duty to accept," Roosevelt said shortly afterward, "and thinking it over for twenty-four hours, I felt inclined to agree with them in as much as there was such a dearth of material."

Once Roosevelt had made up his mind, the party leaders managed things easily. They gave him formal standing in the party by appointing him a delegate to the senatorial district convention that was to nominate him. They steered his nomination through without difficulty. Roosevelt benefited from the ease with which the leadership could control the convention; if the state senatorial nominee had been chosen in party primaries in those days as he is today, some zealous young attorney looking for publicity or law business might have run against Roosevelt and damaged his chances in the election. But no one did.

"As you know," said Roosevelt in his acceptance speech, "I accept this nomination with absolute independence. I am pledged to no man; I am influenced by no special interests, and so I shall remain." He pledged himself to the cause of good government and asked the aid of "independent thinking voters."

Then he struck a T.R. note. "We are going to have a very strenuous month," he said.

A strenuous month it was. More important, it was a highly successful one. By design or by chance Roosevelt fashioned precisely the correct strategy for his district in the light of the national and state situations.

By late 1910 deep fissures were cleaving the Republican party. The stewing and simmering of the past decade, brought to a boil by muckrakers and rabble rousers, had aroused passions too strong for the easygoing man in the White House to subdue or divert. President Taft had signed a high tariff bill, had allowed most of Theodore Roosevelt's cabinet to resign and had appointed more conservative men, and had generally lined up with the Republican Old Guard in Congress. Lost from sight was Taft's progressive side, his sober trust busting, his conservation program. The people wanted a man who looked like a reformer. "There is no use trying to be William Howard Taft with Roosevelt's ways . . ." the President said wistfully. T.R. was back from Africa, not yet fifty-two, and jobless. Republican insurgents in Congress had disarmed Speaker Joseph G. Cannon and were training their guns on the portly figure in the White House.

The national situation was reflected in New York State. Farmers and dairymen were disturbed by the tariff, which seemed to raise the cost of overalls, gingham, and hardware but not the price they got for milk. The Old Guard in the state was led by a group of bosses whose reputation was little better than Tammany's. In an open onslaught against the conservatives in his party, Theodore Roosevelt, still powerful in the state, picked Henry L. Stimson as the Republican candidate for governor; the issue, said T.R., was "bossism," control of the party by Old Guard leaders. This situation played directly into Franklin Roosevelt's hands. Ordinarily, an upstate Democratic candidate had to answer charges of Tammany control of his party. Now Roosevelt could point to bossism in the opposition party, and cite his Republican cousin to prove his case. Even better, young Roosevelt had a convenient target in his own district—a local Republican boss who had been called by the noted Republican leader Elihu Root "a stench in the nostrils of the people" of New York.

Otherwise the district presented formidable difficulties. The farmers—dairymen, poultrymen, and fruit and vegetable raisers— were unhappy over bossism and corruption but at the same time they were orthodox Republicans. Most of the press was stoutly Republican. Senator Schlosser, a candidate for re-election, was a man of substance and reputation. Born in Poughkeepsie and a graduate of Union, he had opened a law office in Fishkill Landing and steadily climbed the political ladder. His extensive activity in local volunteer firemen's associations had given him strategic contacts in every locality. But he had one crucial weak point. In his two terms in the senate he had generally lined up with the Old Guard.

Faced with this situation, Roosevelt decided to make bossism versus clean government the issue. It was easy for him to do this; he was equipped to do little else. At Groton and Harvard, politics had been pictured for him as a battleground of good men against bad. Clean government rather than progressive government had been the battle cry of his father and other Cleveland Democrats. What could be more natural than to pitch his campaign on this note? To be sure, Roosevelt exploited the Republican cleavage between standpatters and progressives. But even though this was 1910, progressivism was not the issue on which the young politician based his campaign.

Quite the contrary. Roosevelt's essential strategy was to blur over the progressive-conservative split and to direct his appeals as much to Republicans and independents as to Democrats. This nonpartisan strategy took these forms:

He denounced Democratic and Republican bosses with equal fervor.

He talked in generalities, avoiding specifics that might leave him in a partisan posture.

He virtually ignored the state Democratic ticket and party record.

He played up his relationship with Uncle Ted. "I'm not Teddy," he started off at one meeting. "A little shaver said to me the other day that he knew I wasn't Teddy—I asked him 'why' and he replied: 'Because you don't show your teeth.' "

He shunned national issues that might split the voters along party lines. "I have personally never been able to see that the National politics of a candidate for a State or local office makes very much difference," he wrote later to a Republican.

He allied himself with "good" Republicans. After Roosevelt had denounced Schlosser for blocking the reform measures of Charles Evans Hughes, Republican governor of New York at this time, Roosevelt was asked if he favored Hughes's policies. "You bet I do," he shot back.

This strategy was pointless, however, unless Roosevelt solved the basic problem facing all campaigners—getting through to the people, establishing contact with them. He began with the handicap of not being well known even in his home town of Hyde Park. To cover his huge, 25,000-square-mile district by horse and buggy would be hopeless. He met the problem head on in Rooseveltian fashion. There was only one automobile in the area—a big red Maxwell, with shining brass lamps but lacking windshield or top. This Roosevelt hired and decorated with flags and bunting. Cars at the time were unpredictable and they scared farmers' horses, but the Maxwell covered much of the area at twenty-five miles an hour and attracted a good deal of attention. So successful was this method that a charge by Representative Hamilton Fish (father of Roosevelt's New Deal opponent) that Roosevelt was not even a bona fide resident of the district fell rather flat.

Roosevelt was not yet an orator. "He spoke slowly," his wife remembered later, "and every now and then there would be a long pause, and I would be worried for fear he would never go on." But he quickly picked up political gimmicks. He remembered to speak a good word for the particular town he was in. He learned quickly to adapt his arguments to his audience. Like a good salesman he brought up his own candidacy only after establishing a bond between his audience and himself on other matters. Already he was using the phrase "my friends." Sometimes there were traces of the oratorical techniques to come, such as his use of the repetitive phrase when he said that he did not know whether Schlosser (Roosevelt had not yet learned the importance of ignoring his opponent's name) represented the local boss or represented only Schlosser, but "I do know that he hasn't represented me and I do know that he hasn't represented you." In general, however, his speeches were earnest and plain spoken rather than eloquent.

Actually, not platform oratory but talking with people face to face was the main job in a local campaign. Talk Roosevelt did— to teamsters passing on the road, to men idling in stores, to farmers picking apples and husking corn. Roosevelt was on the road long hours every day. "I think I worked harder with him than I ever have in my life," said a companion many years later. As he campaigned the quick smile and handshake became automatic. "Call me Franklin—I'm going to call you Tom," he said to an astonished house painter. Touring with experienced Democratic politicians who knew voters by name in every locality helped Roosevelt considerably; despite his nonpartisanship he leaned heavily on his Democratic fellow candidates, who knew hundreds of voters in the district. It was no one-man campaign.

The opposition at the beginning made the fatal mistake of discounting the twenty-eight-year-old candidate's chances. A Republican newspaper doubted that Schlosser would be "greatly disturbed." Too late the Republicans sensed the drift of affairs. At the last minute an opposition newspaper played up Roosevelt's connection with a New York firm of lawyers "for some of the great trusts which are being prosecuted by President Taft's administration. . . ." This was a clumsy move, for it simply strengthened Roosevelt's position with Republicans as a Democrat not tainted with Bryanism.

Roosevelt gave his final talk in Hyde Park. After paying tribute to his home town, he expressed his wish to follow in his father's footsteps by keeping in close touch with Hyde Park affairs. He denounced Schlosser once more for being "a member of that little ring of Republican politicians who have done so much to prevent progress and good government." The issues remained the same— honesty and economy in the state government.

Election Day in November 1910 was cold and wet. The returns came in slowly, but the trend soon became clear. Roosevelt defeated Schlosser 15,708 to 14,568, a plurality of 1,140. He won Hyde Park by 406 to 258, Dutchess County by a margin of 850, Columbia County by 469, and lost Putnam County by 179. His victory was part of a national trend. Democrats won almost three-fifths of the seats in the national House of Representatives, the governorship and both houses of the legislature in New York. Woodrow Wilson won in New Jersey. Tally sheets across the nation showed the results of a decade of protest: a tidal wave against Taft, a trend toward the Democrats.

Was Roosevelt merely a chip on this wave? Certainly to some extent. But his victory cannot be explained simply in terms of a lucky year. He ran in his district nearly 700 votes ahead of John A. Dix, the Democratic candidate for governor. To be sure, Dix's opponent, Henry L. Stimson, was more formidable than Schlosser, but Roosevelt also ran generally ahead of the Democratic candidates for assembly in his district. An important reason for this margin was his nonpartisan strategy, which had clearly paid off. It seems likely that Roosevelt would have won by a thin majority in any "average" year.

But the senator-elect probably spent little time on such speculation. It was enough that he had won. He rented a large, expensive house in Albany, conveniently near the capitol. At the end of the year 1910 he moved there with his wife and family. For a young man not yet twenty-nine, he had a large establishment. Following his first child, Anna, two sons had been born: James in December 1907 and Elliott in September 1910. There was the usual retinue of nurses and servants. Eleanor was still weighted down with family worries: James had a heart murmur and had to be carried up steps; she had a wet nurse for the infant Elliott, and she went through agonies of fear that the wet nurse's own baby would suffer when the mother went with the Roosevelts to Albany. Her husband was sympathetic toward her difficulties, but he was mainly absorbed in the job that lay ahead. On the threshold of his political career, the state senator-elect looked forward to his new role with high hopes and excitement.

THE COLLEGE KID AND THE TAMMANY BEAST

There is a story, perhaps true, that Big Tim Sullivan, lounging in an Albany hotel with another Tammany boss early in January 1911, watched a tall young man stride across the lobby. To some at this time Roosevelt, with his spare figure and lean face, gold bowed

First published sketch of Roosevelt, Jan. 19, 1911, J. Norman Lynd, New York *Herald,* © New York *Sun,* Inc.

spectacles and frock coat, looked like a student of divinity. Others noted his well-modeled features, lithe figure, and slightly curling hair—enough to "set the matinee girl's heart throbbing with subtle and happy emotion," one reporter said. But to Big Tim that day he looked like a cocky, bumptious "college kid," still wet behind the ears.

So that was Roosevelt? "You know these Roosevelts," Big Tim growled. "This fellow is still young. Wouldn't it be safer to drown him before he grows up?"

Within a few weeks Big Tim must have wished that he had followed his own advice. The young politician who had assailed boss-ism in his campaign was to seize a superb opportunity to lead a pitched fight against Tammany before he hardly had time to warm his senatorial chair.

At this time United States senators from New York were chosen not directly by the voters but by the state assembly and senate meeting in joint session. The Democrats had won control of both houses in the 1910 election; if they stuck together they could name the next senator. When Roosevelt first arrived in Albany the field seemed open and a number of candidates were lining up support in the legislature. Suddenly the whole situation changed. Charles F. Murphy, boss of Tammany, passed the word down that the Democrats' man would be William F. Sheehan. "Blue-eyed Billy," as he was called, did not represent the worst of Tammany, but not the best either. Originally a Buffalo politician, he had savagely fought the rising Grover Cleveland. Later he had won riches and influence in New York City as a traction and utilities magnate. Now he yearned for a place in the Senate—the "most exclusive club in the world"—to bring his career to a grand finale.

Everything about the case—Sheehan's early opposition to Cleveland, his later record, Boss Murphy's easy assumption that the Democrats would fall in line, Tammany's influence in general—was calculated to goad the young senator into action. Besides, an excellent "honest government" candidate was available in Edward M. Shepard of Brooklyn, counsel for the Pennsylvania Railroad and a civic leader. "Shepard is without question the most competent to fill the position," Roosevelt wrote in his diary on January 1, "but the Tammany crowd seems unable to forgive him his occasional independence and Sheehan looks like their choice at this stage of the game. May the result prove that I am wrong! There is no question in my mind that the Democratic party is on trial, and having been given control of the government chiefly through up-State votes, cannot afford to surrender its control to the organization in New York City."

Tammany showed its power at the first Democratic caucus that Roosevelt attended. Senator Tom Grady, leader of the Democrats in the senate, was occasionally given to independence and to alcohol. In the caucus Murphy easily deposed him. Roosevelt was pleased with the development. Grady's ability was unquestioned, he noted loftily in his diary, but "not so his habits or his character." Indeed, if Tammany had not ditched Grady, Roosevelt might have bolted the party then and there. Robert F. Wagner, a steady young senator from Manhattan's upper East Side, took Grady's place. Alfred E. Smith, another young Tammanyite, who in seven terms of office had shown himself a dexterous, trigger-swift legislator, became majority leader in the assembly. The method of party control was simple. The Democrats commanded a majority in each chamber. Tammany commanded a majority of the Democrats. Thus, if all went according to party custom, a minority of Tammanyites could control the whole legislature, including the election of a United States senator.

During early January rumblings of opposition to Sheehan reached Murphy's ears. His response was in character: no patronage or committee appointments would be given out until the Democrats toed the line. This was too much for a small group of assemblymen led by Edmund R. Terry of Brooklyn. They decided to boycott the caucus in order not to be bound by the caucus decision; by joining with the Republicans they could deny Tammany the necessary votes for Sheehan's election.

Roosevelt got wind of this development and immediately joined the rebel group. On the night of January 16, while most of the Democrats went to their caucus to choose Sheehan, Roosevelt and Terry met in their headquarters. Both were nervous. Murphy was bringing pressure on the rebels, and Governor Dix was standing by the Tammany boss. Slowly the rest of the Insurgents, as they were called, arrived, and it became clear that the Democratic caucus could not command enough votes to put Sheehan over. Hopefully the rebels waited for a truce offer from Tammany, but none came. Murphy had only begun to fight.

Schooled in the politics of the Gas House district of New York City, Murphy had fought his way up through the Tammany hierarchy with his fists and wits. A big, glum, taciturn man who liked to receive his satraps at Delmonico's, he was used to rebellions and he knew how to handle them. His moves against the Insurgents were ingenious and ruthless. From Boss William Barnes, who was delighted at the rupture in Democratic ranks, he got a promise that the Republicans would stand firm for their own man, incumbent Senator Chauncey M. Depew, until Murphy could overcome the rebels. He lined up state committeemen in the Insurgents' districts to exert pressure on their most vulnerable flank: the next election. Insurgents' appointees in government jobs were fired, their law firms boycotted, and other reprisals were threatened. Finally—and most harassing of all—Tammany whispered that the attack on Sheehan was simply an attack on Catholics and Irishmen. "Every conceivable form of pressure" had been brought to bear on the group, Roosevelt told the press with some exaggeration.

Although not the initiator of the revolt, Roosevelt gradually became its leader. He was informally chosen chairman at an early meeting and he usually spoke for the group. Acting essentially as a presiding officer rather than a dominant chieftain, he conducted diplomatic negotiations with the Tammany forces. His leadership was partly due to the proximity of his home, and to the fact that he was a senator and the others virtually all assemblymen. It was also due to his resoluteness, good humor, and resourcefulness.

As the struggle deepened the Insurgents won nationwide attention. The fight against bossism struck a popular note. Progressives had long denounced the United States Senate as a "millionaires' club" packed with hirelings of the trusts. The national Senate was under a drumfire of criticism for holding up a proposed constitutional amendment to require direct election of senators. Woodrow Wilson, just installed in the governor's mansion in Trenton, was battling a move in the New Jersey legislature to send a noted boss to the Senate, and Theodore Roosevelt, who had come out in 1910 for direct primaries, seemed to favor popular election of senators. These changes, along with the initiative and referendum, were key parts of the Progressives' apparatus of reform.

Newspapers throughout the country featured the fight that this new Roosevelt was making against bossism. Even more gratifying to the young senator were the hundreds of letters he received from his constituents. "Stand firm," most of them urged. A few letters were hostile. "You know what they done to your Uncle Teddy," he was warned. But his mail from the district ran heavily in favor of the Insurgents.

Early in the fight Sheehan warned Roosevelt to his face that he would go into the Insurgents' constituencies and "show up their characters." The Tammany politician carried out his threat, but his invasion of Dutchess County was a conspicuous failure. Regular Democratic leaders in Poughkeepsie, seeking to keep on friendly relations with the powerful Tammany elements in the party, gave a dinner for Sheehan and collected 265 names on a petition demanding that Roosevelt go along with the caucus decision. The petition did not worry Roosevelt. The more opposition from regular Democrats, the more popularity he gained with independents and Republicans.

On January 30 Murphy himself sought out Roosevelt. Was there any chance the Insurgents would change their minds? "No, Mr. Murphy," Roosevelt answered. The Insurgents held strategic ground. They would not give in.

To hand out statements to the press, to deal with Murphy on equal terms, to assume heroic proportions in the eyes of voters back home —all this was heady stuff for the twenty-nine-year-old Roosevelt. But before the end his appetite for the fight palled.

For one thing, the struggle became unduly protracted. Week

after week went by with no break in the deadlock. Staying in session these extra weeks was expensive and inconvenient for the legislators, who received only $1,500 a year and ordinarily were in Albany only one or two days a week during the first three or four months of the year. They tended to blame the Insurgents. Pressures on the small group steadily built up, and Roosevelt and Terry had trouble holding their cohorts in line. Moreover, the struggle became increasingly complex as time passed. As Sheehan's chances dwindled, more and more candidates—at least a score of them—entered the lists. Every new candidate changed the pattern of pressures and loyalties amid which the Insurgents were operating.

Even more important, at least for Roosevelt, was the change in the moral climate of the struggle. It was easy to soar on a high ethical plane, to be on the side of righteousness against wickedness. But was the issue this simple? Tammany was not a monolithic evil. Roosevelt could not but respect the honesty and integrity of men like Wagner and Smith. The machine, he discovered, was not really a machine, but a collection of men with crisscrossing loyalties and motivations. Revolts against Murphy flared in the strongest Tammany districts. Even more surprising, Murphy himself was not a dead-ender for Sheehan; as the deadlock continued and Sheehan's chances faded, Murphy quietly began to line up support for Dan Cahalan, his lieutenant and son-in-law. Boss Barnes and his Republican minions played a crafty game, negotiating at one point with Tammany, at the next with the Insurgents. Instead of a grand rally between clean-cut opposing forces, the struggle began to look like Tolstoi's picture of war as a confused scramble of men and groups.

Strange maneuverings took place on the Insurgent side too. Unable to make headway with Barnes, Roosevelt tried to arrange a bipartisan deal with influential Republicans through a group of eminent and conservative Cleveland Democrats, most notably Francis Lynde Stetson, attorney for J. P. Morgan. Roosevelt hoped to win over Republican support for a conservative, clean-government Democrat for senator. But some of the Stetson group apparently wanted a *quid pro quo*—an understanding that the anti-Tammany Democrats would continue as an anti-Progressive group pledged to oppose bills such as the then pending income-tax amendment. When Samuel Untermeyer looked like a possible compromise candidate, this same group, remembering Untermeyer's antitrust and anti-Morgan activities, helped destroy his chances. Murphy did not miss his opportunity. He charged that the Insurgents were but a front for the reactionary Stetson group.

By late March the struggle had become a bitter war of nerves. Roosevelt and Terry were losing control of their small group; "we came near going on the rocks several times," Roosevelt said later. Tammany was still uneasy about a possible deal between Republicans and Insurgents. At this point Murphy staged an elaborate maneuver. He suggested a compromise candidate in Justice Victor J. Dowling. Knowing that the Insurgent tail could not wag the Democratic dog, Roosevelt and his group agreed. But a day later, as the Insurgents met just before going to the caucus they had boycotted so long, word came that Dowling had refused the nomination and Murphy had substituted the name of Justice James A. O'Gorman, formerly Grand Sachem of Tammany Hall.

Could the Insurgents swallow O'Gorman? Could they afford not to? O'Gorman, despite his Tammany connections, had shown independence from the machine. Moreover, he was ex-president of the Friendly Sons of St. Patrick and beloved by the Irish. Some of the Insurgents had previously said they would accept O'Gorman. Two of the group left immediately to enter the caucus and vote for O'Gorman. The rest, badly divided, debated the matter for hours during that afternoon. Finally a majority, with Roosevelt and a few others still opposed, decided to go along with O'Gorman, after Smith and Wagner promised that there would be no reprisals. Roosevelt's little band was deserting him.

The end was inglorious. Hoots, groans, and hisses greeted the Insurgents as they filed into the chamber for the final vote. They had done their duty as they saw it, Roosevelt said lamely. "We are Democrats—not irregulars, but regulars." The press felt that the Insurgents had been outgeneraled. Roosevelt maintained that the Insurgents had won, but a defensive note crept into his letters to his constituents. And he was wary about future Insurgent strategy. "I believe it will be a mistake for us to try to get all of the former Insurgents together again," he wrote to a friend, "but there are ten or twelve of us who can form a pretty good nucleus to work."

Roosevelt could mark up some gains from the struggle. He had won national attention, he had strengthened his position in his district, and Progressives probably remembered his lengthy fight against Tammany long after they forgot the anticlimactic ending. Perhaps more important in the long run, the young politician had been given a telling education in the tactics of pressure and intrigue.

But he had suffered losses too. Midway in the struggle Sumner Gerard had urged him toward moderation. "If you go too far, needlessly, you run the danger of impairing your future political effectiveness." Roosevelt knew what Gerard meant by his "future political effectiveness." An aroused Tammany would spike any statewide ambitions the senator might have. But Roosevelt was in no mood to compromise. When a constituent warned him of the Tiger's long memory, Roosevelt said, "No, right is right, no matter who it hurts."

He was not willing to let the issue die. Months after the Sheehan fight he told a Buffalo audience that Murphy "and his kind" must be destroyed, that the "beasts of prey have begun to fall." Tammany lashed back. The "silly conceits of a political prig," said a Murphy lieutenant. The party should not tolerate these fops and cads, these political accidents who "come as near being political leaders as a green pea does a circus tent." The Tammany man compared Roosevelt's education and background with his own leadership, which, he said, depended on "human sympathy, human interest, and human ties among those with whom I was born and bred. . . ."

The struggle between the high-minded patrician and the earthy, human bosses was to go on a long time. But perhaps the last words in the Sheehan struggle were uttered by Roosevelt to Frances Perkins many years later when he was President: "You know," he said, "I was an awfully mean cuss when I first went into politics."

FARMER-LABOR REPRESENTATIVE

The fight against Sheehan over, the senate settled down to the business of legislating. Senator Roosevelt threw himself into the work. Years later Frances Perkins remembered him on the floor of the senate: ". . . very active and alert, moving around the floor, going in and out of committee rooms, rarely talking with the members, who more or less avoided him, not particularly charming (that came later), artificially serious of face, rarely smiling, with an unfortunate habit—so natural that he was unaware of it—of throwing his head up." During his two years in the senate Roosevelt seemed to be looking down his nose at people, but he was learning the craft of parliamentary politics with remarkable speed.

Roosevelt's early legislative activities were not all of one pattern. Much of the time he was fighting a running battle with Tammany; on occasion he would go along with a dubious project of the bosses. He noisily held aloft the banner of clean government, yet he filled many minor positions with patronage appointments carefully cleared with Democratic leaders in his district; making appointments in this way, he said privately, was "vitally necessary if there is to be any organization in the party." He paid special attention to the interests of his constituents, yet on one occasion he moved to strike out of an appropriation bill a bridge-repair item for his district. He hewed close to the local farm interests, yet in October 1912 the New York State Federation of Labor said that Roosevelt's record on their bills was "excellent." Roosevelt's record as state senator was compounded in parts of insurgency, orthodoxy, and trial and error.

When "moral" issues arose he could still vault onto his white charger and attack the enemy with vim, to the delight of his constituents. Although occasionally he himself gambled in a small way, Roosevelt opposed legalizing race-track gambling. He criticized prize fighting and Sunday baseball. He drew laudatory letters from clergy in his district by working hard for the "one day of rest in seven" bill. He hedged on Prohibition through the time-honored device of the state politician: coming out for "local option," which would allow voters to decide the issue for their own local areas. He favored a national uniform divorce law, and won unanimous support from the legislature—and from the National Christian League for Promotion of Purity.

In his early months Senator Roosevelt's progressivism was political in content rather than economic or social. He introduced a well-received resolution urging New York State congressmen to work for direct election of senators, he supported municipal home rule, and, after some vacillation, he came out for woman suffrage. The direct primary for party nominations was the kind of reform that enlisted his full energies. Considered but not adopted by previous legislatures, endorsed by both parties in 1910, direct primaries for party nominations came before the legislature not long after the "Sheehan business" and touched off another angry brawl. Roosevelt, so uncompromising in the Sheehan fight, was more willing to negotiate with the bosses in this matter, although some of his Insurgent colleagues were not. After holding out strenuously for a strong primary bill in July 1911, two months later he voted for a weak primary bill, riddled with concessions to Tammany; the following year, after helping to arouse the voters, he worked with a bipartisan group of Progressives to bring about changes that would cut down the party organization's influence in the primaries, but he made little progress against the regulars.

Labor legislation—the dull and grimy side of progressivism—was something else. When Roosevelt first came to Albany his views on labor, to the extent he had any, were benevolently paternalistic. He favored help for foreign seamen coming into New York City; he wanted purer milk for needy children. He flatly opposed legislation to legalize boycotts by unions, and took an evasive stand on workmen's compensation and on measures to forbid working boys of sixteen to twenty-one more than fifty-four hours per week. But in the next two years his attitude changed sharply. He not only backed the fifty-four-hour bill but during the debate on this bill held the senate floor with a talk on birds until none other than Big Tim Sullivan himself could be routed out of bed to supply a vitally needed vote. He came out for workmen's compensation legislation despite opposition from some constituents. By February 1913 he was willing to speak at a legislative hearing in favor of the whole batch of thirty-two bills drawn up by the Factory Investigating Commission.

How account for this change? The cause did not lie in a shift in Roosevelt's basic social outlook, for he had not developed a philosophy of government. Partly, no doubt, Roosevelt was influenced by his cousin Theodore, who by mid-1912 was vociferously supporting workmen's compensation, limited injunction in labor disputes, and social welfare legislation for women and children. Partly it was the climate of the times: America was moving toward a climax of progressive debate and action in the election of 1912. Partly it was the realization that his Tammany colleagues, whatever their failings, had a concern for social justice that rivaled his own. Most important, the investigations, reports, and debates in the senate gave him a vivid, harsh lesson in how the "other half" lived.

Indeed, the whole senate experience was a political education for Roosevelt. He learned quickly from old Albany hands like Smith and Wagner, from newspapermen, lobbyists, and state officials. He mastered knacks of the political trade: how to avoid taking a stand on issues and becoming involved in destructive local squabbles, how to deal with local party leaders, how to handle patronage without making an undue number of enemies, how to attract publicity, how to answer importunate letters. Above all, he learned the lesson that democratic politicians must learn: that the political battle is not a simple, two-sided contest between opposing parties, or between right and wrong, or between regulars and irregulars, but, as in the Sheehan episode, a many-sided struggle that moved over broad sectors and touched many interests. A simple farm bill, for example, involved not merely individual farmers but county agricultural societies, canneries, university professors, merchants, railroads, and government officials, and divisions over policy might occur not merely between such groups but within them.

Sometimes education came at painful cost. Tammany could still outmaneuver the young senator when it had a mind to. Backed by reformers, Roosevelt late in 1911 attacked a charter for New York City that was sponsored by Tammany. Senate lines were closely drawn and Roosevelt was in a position to kill the charter, but Tammany closed in on him from the rear: it threatened to reshuffle congressional districts and put Dutchess County into a hopelessly Republican area. Under pressure Roosevelt faltered. He came out for the charter, then, after progressive outcries, again took a stand against it. This was not the only time that Roosevelt vacillated as he tried to balance the perversely conflicting factors of his own political ambitions, his various principles about the right thing to do, the complex relationships of state leaders in both parties, the welfare of his constituents, and the multifarious strands of public opinion in district, state, and nation.

Climbing the political ladder to the presidency, according to one theory, is essentially a matter of luck; the winner has simply won an incredible run at throws of the dice. This theory can easily be applied to Roosevelt; his wealth, name, family connections, appearance were bestowed upon him, and he had the good luck to run for office during two Democratic years. Yet he had bad luck too. In 1912, in the middle of his campaign for re-election to the state senate, he was stricken by typhoid and put out of action for the rest of the contest.

In this emergency he called in Louis McHenry Howe to run his campaign. Albany correspondent for the New York *Herald* and a kind of minor political operator around the capitol, Howe, with his dwarfish body, ferret-like features, and untidy clothes, looked like a troll out of a Catskill cave. He was out of a job in 1912 and glad to work for a man who, he felt, seemed likely to have a shining political future. To the little man Eleanor Roosevelt took an immediate dislike that lasted many years, but her husband saw his many uses. While Roosevelt lay in bed, on occasion despairing of the outcome, Howe managed the fight with verve, imagination, and guile. Armed with substantial funds, he sent thousands of "personal" letters from Roosevelt to farmers throughout the district. He published large advertisements in the newspapers. He played up specific measures that Roosevelt had proposed—or would propose—for his constituents, including lower license fees for shad fishermen along the Hudson and legislation for standard-size barrels for apple growers. He dealt with complaints from regular Democrats about Roosevelt's handling of patronage and his attitude toward Tammany.

Howe had some twists of his own, such as his denunciation of Roosevelt's opponent, a banker and utility president named Jacob Southard, for not visiting Columbia County during the campaign; his rather free distribution of five-dollar checks to scores of campaign workers; and his crafty ways of arousing discord within the Republican ranks. But his strategy was essentially that of his chief two years before: to proclaim Roosevelt's agrarian progressivism, his bipartisanship, his antibossism, and his concern for the specific needs of his constituents.

Once again the strategy worked. Roosevelt got 15,590 votes to 13,889 for Southard and 2,628 for George Vossler, the Bull Moose candidate. He ran in his district 800 votes ahead of the Democratic candidates for president and for governor. Vossler received 1,400 fewer votes in the district than Theodore Roosevelt. To be sure, the young senator won about a thousand fewer votes than his opponents combined, but it seems likely that at least half of Vossler's vote would have gone to Franklin Roosevelt in a straight party fight. A close observer estimated that, on the average, eight Democrats in every election district deserted Roosevelt but thirty Republicans swung over to him.

To Fruit Growers!

I am convinced after careful investigation that the present law making a 17 1-8 inch barrel the legal standard for fruit is unjust and oppressive to fruit growers.

I pledge myself to introduce and fight for the passage of an amendment to the law making a Standard Fruit Barrel of 16 1-2 Inches.

This barrel to be the legal standard for fruit and to be marked, "Standard Fruit Barrel."

The justice of this seems so plain that I feel assured of the passage of the amendment.

I wish to acknowledge my indebtedness to Mr. Alexander Hoover, the Democratic candidate for Assembly, from Columbia County, who is himself a practical fruit grower, for the clear and convincing presentation of the facts in this matter which led me to the conviction that this law must be changed.

With Mr. Hoover's practical knowledge and the experience in overcoming the parliamentary obstacles that the commission men's lobby will use to obstruct the passage of the bill that I have acquired through two years' service in the Legislature, I feel certain that this wrong can be righted.

Franklin D. Roosevelt,

Candidate For State Senator.

When Franklin Roosevelt says he will fight for a thing, it means he won't quit until he wins—you know that.

Political poster issued by Roosevelt in 1912 campaign for re-election to the New York State Senate

In the new senate, convening in January 1913, Roosevelt moved with his usual vigor. In their 1912 sweep the Democrats had won majorities in both chambers as well as the governorship, and Roosevelt was now chairman of the Committee on Agriculture. One of his first moves was to redeem a promise made during the election: that he would do something about the wide margin between what the New York City commission merchants paid the farmers for produce, and what the merchants sold it for. Roosevelt promptly introduced a measure providing for the regulation of commission merchants through licensing, inspection, and publicity. While Howe, now employed as a lobbyist, built fires under the state Grange in behalf of the bill, Roosevelt held hearings at the capitol. He received a vivid lesson in interest-group politics: 250 commission merchants showed up in Albany, but practically no farmers. While Roosevelt took a firm stand for his bill, he was willing to make a number of concessions to the merchants.

Roosevelt introduced several other agricultural bills that he had drafted in collaboration with the Grange and with agricultural experts. These bills would give backing by the state government to farmers' co-operative associations, both marketing and purchasing; would allow agricultural credit banks to lend money for farm improvements; would provide state aid to county farm bureaus. On conservation matters, too, the senator took advanced positions. He sided with Hughes and other Republican progressives on state development of water power, and he vainly fought to extend state control of forestation, in the face of intense opposition from lumber interests.

The sweep of Senator Roosevelt's farm and conservation bills was impressive. Considered with his position on labor legislation, these bills sharply raise the question whether Roosevelt moved essentially to a "New Deal" position on farm and labor matters twenty years before the New Deal was to be inaugurated. In major respects he did. But this shift came not in response to a new philosophy of government but to specific problems that seemed to him to call for specific action. "He probably could not have formulated his political philosophy very well at this time," Eleanor Roosevelt said later. He was interested less in the philosophy than in the "science of government," as he called it—how to understand people, how to influence them.

By the time the farm bills came up for a vote, Roosevelt was no longer in the state senate. A wider field of action had beckoned him.

'The mold of a Hyde Park gentleman'

Mother and son, 1893

Franklin D. Roosevelt and his father, 1883

Young Franklin (center, dark sailor suit) with his grandparents, aunts, uncles, and cousins, Newburgh, N. Y., July 13, 1890 (*photo by R. E. Atkinson*)

Three-year-old Franklin and his dog preparing for a ride at Hyde Park

Fourth-string football player at Groton (lower left, white sweater), 1899

A young lawyer and his cousins

Cousin Eleanor (fifth cousin once removed) in 1906, one year after their marriage

Cousin Jean Delano, sailing at Campobello, around 1910

Franklin Roosevelt with his wife, his mother, and his daughter, Anna, on Daisy, the pony, 1911

Family affairs

The family in Washington, 1916—Elliott, at left; James, center, behind Franklin Jr.; John on his mother's lap, Anna Eleanor, at right

(photo by Harold L. Ritch)

A Roosevelt on the job

His first political post, in the New York Senate, 1911

Assistant Secretary of the Navy in the
Navy Yard, New York, 1913 (*International News Photo*)

Roosevelt with Charles F. Murphy, his old Tammany adversary, and John
A. Voorhis at Tammany Hall, July 4, 1917 (*New York* Daily News *photo*)

The rising politician campaigning for Vice-President on the 1920 Democratic ticket—at Dayton, Ohio (*photo by F. W. Emmert*)

'Something of a lion, something of a fox'

On crutches in 1924, with John W. Davis, who won the presidential nomination, and Al Smith (at right), who lost it, after Roosevelt's "happy warrior" speech (*photo by F.P.G.*)

'A New Deal for the American people'

The Democratic nominee for President arriving by plane in Chicago with his family, July 2, 1932, to address the convention (*United Press photo*)

At the Democratic convention, July 4, 1932, with Louis McHenry
Howe (left) and his campaign manager, James A. Farley (*Wide World
photo*)

'Nothing to fear but fear itself'

The President and his First Lady after arrival in Washington, D. C.,
March, 1933, before his first inauguration (*Wide World Photo*)

'A man of many roles'

F.D.R. joking with Vice-President Garner at a dinner for James A. Farley (right), Feb. 15, 1937; behind Garner, Henry A. Wallace; behind Roosevelt, Cordell Hull; behind Farley, Henry A. Morgenthau

A dismal fishing cruise off Miami during the recession, with Robert H. Jackson (standing, center), Harry Hopkins (right of Jackson), and Harold Ickes (seated, right), Nov. 29, 1937 (*United Press photo*)

After hot dogs and a picnic at Hyde Park, President and Mrs. Roosevelt wave farewell to the King and Queen of England at the railroad station, June 11, 1939

The President and his secretaries: (left to right) Marguerite Le Hand, Marvin H. McIntyre, and Grace Tully, Hyde Park, Nov. 4, 1938

'The inner circle'

The President and his cabinet: (clockwise) Henry Morgenthau, Secretary of the Treasury; Homer S. Cummings, Attorney General; Claude Swanson, Secretary of the Navy; Henry A. Wallace, Secretary of Agriculture; Frances Perkins, Secretary of Labor; Harry H. Woodring, Secretary of War; Cordell Hull, Secretary of State, Sept. 27, 1938 (*United Press photo*)

The campaign (1932—*International News photo*)

The press (aboard campaign train, Sept. 13, 1932—*Wide World photo*)

The crowds (at Newburgh, N. Y., Nov. 4, 1940—*United Press photo*)

The polling booth (with his wife and mother at Hyde Park's Town Hall, Nov. 8, 1938—*United Press photo*)

The inauguration (Chief Justice Charles Evans Hughes administering the oath of office, Jan. 20, 1937—*International News photo*)

A drought year—but when Roosevelt spoke, it rained —Charlotte, N. C., Sept. 10, 1936

The Roosevelt smile

Roosevelt laughing at his crippled legs to put others at ease, Hollywood Bowl, Sept. 24, 1932 (*Wide World photo*)

'Never . . . a man who was loved as he is'

At Warm Springs, Ga., Dec. 1, 1933 (*United Press photo*)

Commander in chief

The President reviewing the fleet from the *U.S.S. Houston* at San Francisco, July 14, 1938 (*Wide World photo*)

THREE *Washington:*
  The Politician as Bureaucrat

POLITICAL affairs swept along pell-mell on the
national scene during State Senator Roosevelt's years in Albany.
Early in 1912 Theodore Roosevelt, steadily swinging to the left,
began a strenuous campaign for the Republican presidential nomination. "I don't want to fight," said Taft, but "even a rat in a corner will fight." Although T.R. won most of the presidential primaries, Taft's power over office-holding delegates and the party
machinery brought him the Republican nomination late in June
1912. The Rough Rider promptly bolted, and the presidential
chances of a Democrat soared.

Who was this Democrat to be? Franklin D. Roosevelt had already made his choice. During 1911 he had watched admiringly
as Woodrow Wilson, the new governor of New Jersey, split with
the political machine that had ushered him into politics, shouldered Boss Jim Smith out of a United States senatorship, and commanded the progressive forces of the state in a successful fight for
public-utilities regulation, workmen's compensation, a corrupt-
practices act, primary and elections legislation, municipal reform.
Wilson was Roosevelt's kind of Democrat—clean, cultivated, and
progressive but not too progressive. Late in 1911 Roosevelt visited
the governor in New Jersey to tender him his support.

Wilson's spare frame, lean, bespectacled face, and grave bearing gave him a scholarly, almost austere look, but his attitude was
not academic. After some friendly conversation he went straight to
the point. How many New York delegates to the Democratic national convention would be for him? About thirty out of the delegation of ninety, Roosevelt replied, but Murphy would control
most of the delegates, and under the unit rule (by which the whole
delegation vote is cast for the candidate who has the majority vote
of the delegation) the whole ninety would be anti-Wilson.

Despite the odds, Roosevelt was so enthusiastic for the New Jersey progressive that he went home ready to work with other pro-
Wilson Democrats in the state. He hoped to arouse enough Wilson
sentiment in New York to weaken Murphy's hold on the delegation

47

to the convention. Once again Roosevelt ran head on into massed Tammany power. Of a score or more upstate Democrats he invited to a Wilson dinner, only three accepted. At the Democratic state convention Murphy easily put through his slate of ninety delegates. Roosevelt was not even able to become an alternate delegate. He and his friends set up the New York State Wilson Conference, organized some Wilson clubs, and hired Howe to spread propaganda, but it was hardly more than a gesture. Murphy sat tight with his batch of convention votes.

Late in June 1912 Democrats swarmed into Baltimore to nominate "the next President." The air was electric, battle lines were fluid and confused. Roosevelt made up in energy for what he lacked in office and influence. With others he opened a Wilson conference headquarters near the convention hall, bombarded the delegates with arguments, and, after the nominating speech for Wilson, set off a demonstration of upstate Wilson men while Murphy's delegates sat stonily in their places. But he was far from the centers of power—the smoke-filled rooms where Champ Clark's men and Wilson's men battled each other desperately for votes. When Murphy, to Roosevelt's despair, suddenly threw New York's votes to Clark, William Jennings Bryan redressed the balance by switching to Wilson. Day after day the interminable ballots continued. Slowly Wilson picked up strength; on the forty-sixth ballot he won.

WILSON NOMINATED THIS AFTERNOON ALL MY PLANS VAGUE SPLENDID TRIUMPH, Roosevelt wired his wife in Campobello. His plans were not vague for long. His own position was suddenly changed; now he was an "original Wilson man" in a state whose delegation had stuck to Clark until the end. He had no doubt that Wilson would win New York over the split opposition. Tammany was boxed in; its leaders might not give Wilson enthusiastic support, but they would not dare knife him. To Roosevelt the time seemed ripe for a jolting blow against Tammany's influence in the state. He and his friends quickly organized the "Empire State Democracy" made up of pro-Wilson progressives and constituting virtually a party within the Democratic party.

The strategy was impressive, at least on paper. "This is the year to go ahead and strike," Roosevelt told two hundred Democrats at an organization meeting late in July, "and we've got the club. We hope we won't have to use it. . . ." What was this club? It was the threat to introduce a whole separate state ticket and thereby upset Murphy's plans to win the governorship easily with a mediocre Tammany slate over the T.R. and Taft candidates. To be sure, this was a dog-in-the-manger approach; the slate of the Empire State Democracy would not win either. But the threat would be enough, it was calculated, to force Murphy to accept a "good" Democrat.

Bad luck, poor management, and Murphy's astuteness sent the plans awry. The anti-Murphy movement was racked by warring splinter groups, the Empire State Democracy ran out of funds at the crucial moment, and Roosevelt came face to face with the need to win renomination and re-election for state senator in his own district. In September he bolted the sinking Empire State Democracy. To Roosevelt's delight Wilson asked Murphy for an unbossed state convention; to Roosevelt's dismay the Tammany leader was perfectly agreeable. Certainly the convention would be unbossed, he said—and promptly demonstrated his point by dropping his choice for the nomination, lackluster Governor Dix, and leaving the nomination wide open. Amazed and delighted, the anti-Murphy forces let their guard down—and Murphy helped switch the convention to a man with whom he felt he could do business, William ("Plain Bill") Sulzer of Tammany Hall. The insurgents had no choice but to endorse Sulzer.

By now Roosevelt was fighting his own battle for re-election to the senate. While he lay sick in bed and Howe scurried round the district, the national campaign roared to a tumultuous climax. "I am fighting," proclaimed Woodrow Wilson, "not for the man who has made good, but for the man who is going to make good—the man who is knocking and fighting at the closed doors of opportunity." "We are for liberty," shouted Theodore Roosevelt, "but we are for the liberty of the oppressed. . . ." When an anti-third-term fanatic shot him in the breast as he was leaving for a speech, he treated the country to old-time Teddy Roosevelt heroics; "I will make this speech or die," he said, and he made the speech. Taft and Eugene Debs, the Socialist candidate, scouted for votes to the right and to the left of the main stars. On Tuesday November 5 the voters gave the verdict: Wilson 6,293,019; Roosevelt 4,119,507; Taft 3,484,956; Debs 901,873.

The Wilson administration had every reason to make a place for Senator Roosevelt. In January he got an appointment with the President to discuss patronage matters, and at this time Roosevelt may have expressed an interest in going to Washington. Shortly before Wilson's inauguration, William Gibbs McAdoo, the prospective Secretary of the Treasury, had sounded out the young state senator on a place in his department. But Roosevelt had his eye on something else. On the morning of Inauguration Day he ran into Josephus Daniels, the new Secretary of the Navy. The North Carolina editor-politician liked the stamp of Roosevelt's progressivism, his reputation as a Tammany-baiter, his bubbling enthusiasm, and the fact that he came from a different part of the country from

Daniels and thus would lend geographical balance to the navy office. Roosevelt congratulated him on his appointment as Secretary of the Navy. "How would you like to come to Washington as Assistant Secretary of the Navy?" Daniels asked.

Roosevelt beamed. "How would I like it? I'd like it bully well. It would please me better than anything in the world." An old hand at congressional protocol, Daniels cleared the appointment with Senator O'Gorman. The Senator consented, but without enthusiasm. As a courtesy Daniels also consulted Elihu Root, Republican Senator from New York.

A queer look came over Root's face. "You know the Roosevelts, don't you?" he asked. "Whenever a Roosevelt rides, he wishes to ride in front."

A ROOSEVELT ON THE JOB

From the start, the new Assistant Secretary did try to ride in front. Two days after his installation, when Secretary Daniels was out of town, he told reporters half-jokingly, "There's a Roosevelt on the job today. You remember what happened the last time a Roosevelt occupied a similar position?"—a gratuitous reminder of T.R.'s belligerent orders to Dewey two months before the Spanish-American War. Often during the next seven and one-half years Franklin Roosevelt differed with his chief, and made little effort to conceal his feelings. The surprising thing was Daniels' willingness to put up with the brash young man. Even more surprising was Roosevelt's quick mastery of the political dimensions of his job.

Traditionally the Assistant Secretary's job was a management job. Even in 1913 it was a big one. Most federal agencies of the time were small and somewhat sleepy operations; less than two decades previously, a Vanderbilt was spending more money on farming and forestry than was the United States Government. The United States Navy, however, had heavy and far-flung responsibilities; it employed civilians in scores of yards and installations and maintained a sizable fleet of battleships. Roosevelt, the only Assistant Secretary in the department, had charge of civilian personnel, handled awkward relations between military and civilian officials, helped prepare the navy's budgets. But his interests were far-ranging. "I get my fingers into everything," he used to say, "and there's no law against it."

A bureaucracy, it has been said, is no testing field for heroes. It can smother a man in a blanket of rules, customs, formalities, in endless ribbons of influence and deference. It might have smothered Roosevelt, who had had no experience in a large organization. But it did not. He never gained from his job the dramatic effects

that his Uncle Ted had, but from the start—with one exception—
he showed a capacity for political administration that was to serve
him well in later years.

The exception involved his chief. Josephus Daniels was a man
the young Dutchess County patrician took many years to understand. Born in North Carolina during the Civil War, Daniels had
grown up among farmers and politicians who were struggling
against tobacco and railroad interests. Editor of a small-town newspaper most of his life, he was a Bryanite, a pacifist, a prohibitionist, an agrarian radical. His black string tie, homespun face, and
rustic courtliness were the perfect cover for a full grasp of the art
of politics and the arts of politicians.

Daniels was the only administrative superior Roosevelt ever had
in his political career. The young man chafed at the older man's
ways: he thought Daniels "the funniest looking hillbilly" he had ever
seen, he mimicked the Secretary before society friends, and he wrote
him amazingly tactless memorandums. Only Daniels' large-mind-
edness and his love for Roosevelt—"love at first sight," the older
man said—saved the Assistant Secretary. It was Daniels, moreover,
who handled the main job that faces any department head—the job
of getting along with Congress. Roosevelt dealt with Senators and
Representatives on a host of secondary matters, but Daniels did the
slow, stubborn work of negotiating with the powerful men on
Capitol Hill who appropriated money for the navy.

The admirals, of course, liked Roosevelt, just as they disdained
the puritanical Methodist whom Wilson, by some grim joke, they
felt, had made their chief. The young Assistant Secretary loved
ships, he spoke nautical lingo, he dealt with them as social equals,
and his wife was nice to their wives. They may have chuckled a
bit at young Roosevelt's enjoyment of the seventeen-gun salutes
fired in his honor, and at his designing an Assistant Secretary's
flag to fly when he was aboard ship. But they respected, too, his
ability to pilot a high-speed destroyer through the narrow strait
between Campobello Island and the mainland.

The chief link between Roosevelt and the admirals, however,
rose above personalities. He was from the start a "big navy" man.
"I hope when you 'put this uniform on' you will not, like the Right
Honorable Winston Churchill, First Lord of the Admiralty, be
carried away by the zeal for a big navy which has eaten up so many
Secretaries," a friend wrote him shortly after he took office. But
Roosevelt came out immediately for a "large and efficient navy."
Daniels himself favored naval expansion, but Roosevelt's enthusi-
asm outran his chief's.

The heaviest organized pressure for a big navy came from the
Navy League of the United States, which was run largely by steel,

shipping, and financial magnates. Roosevelt gave a "big navy" speech to the League's convention before he had been in office a month. "This is not a question of war or peace," he said. "I take it that there are as many advocates of arbitration and international peace in the navy as in any other profession. But we are confronted with a condition—the fact that our nation has decided in the past to have a fleet, and that war is still a possibility." The speech fell within the bounds of Wilsonian ideology. But behind the scenes Roosevelt showed a cordiality toward the League that was in marked contrast with the pacifism of Secretary of State Bryan and even of Daniels himself. For example, a general meeting to discuss plans for the League's convention was held in Roosevelt's office, and the League asked him to preside.

The largest and potentially most difficult group Roosevelt had to deal with was organized labor. Relations with the thousands of civilian workers in the yards and depots offered plenty of snarls and pitfalls. Many of the men were organized in craft unions of the American Federation of Labor, an organization of importance to the Wilson administration and to any political ambitions Roosevelt might have. At the same time the voters wanted naval economy, the admirals wanted a disciplined labor force, departmental engineers wanted more efficiency in the yards, and congressmen wanted special favors for constituents employed by the navy.

Roosevelt skirted these formidable shoals in impressive fashion. Typical was his handling of problems involved in "scientific management." The Taylor "stop-watch" system of timing, standardizing, and routing jobs had been hailed by management as the road to productive efficiency; the unions, however, saw the system as scientific exploitation leading to wage cuts and layoffs. Eager to establish a record for efficiency, Roosevelt became highly interested in the possibilities of the Taylor system. But he was quick to see the objections of the workers. In the end he did not push the system; while there must be authority and discipline, he said, he was impressed with the findings of a congressional investigating committee that "neither the Taylor system nor any other should be imposed from above on an unwilling working force."

Some of Roosevelt's administrative decisions represented compromises that, from a narrow management viewpoint, were defective. But the great lesson he learned during these years was that bureaucrats, workers, and sailors were human beings with human problems and failings. He saw that people wanted recognition as well as promotions or better wages; he tried, for example, to have labor representatives appointed to wage boards. "I want you all to feel," he told a group of machinists, "that you can come to me at any time in my office and we can talk matters over." His labor policies worked. After his years as Assistant Secretary Roosevelt was able to boast, with only slight exaggeration, that the navy had not had a single strike during the previous seven and one-half years.

In Washington, Roosevelt entered a world of far broader perspectives than he had known at Hyde Park, Harvard, or Albany. He came to know Oliver Wendell Holmes, Louis D. Brandeis, Felix Frankfurter; important foreigners like the British ambassador, Sir Cecil Spring-Rice, the French Ambassador, Jean Jules Jusserand; and, of course, the leaders in the Wilson administration, including Secretary of the Interior Franklin K. Lane and First Assistant Postmaster General Daniel C. Roper. He saw much of the younger diplomatic set. When Joseph E. Davies organized a small Common Counsel Club to promote principles of "progressive Democracy" Roosevelt became one of the members.

It was by *people*—all sorts of people—that he continued to be educated in the tough, knotty ways of government. "Young Roosevelt is very promising, but I should think he'd wear himself out in the promiscuous and extended contacts he maintains with people," Secretary Newton Baker said to Frances Perkins. "But as I have observed him, he seems to clarify his ideas and teach himself as he goes along by that very conversational method." Roosevelt at times seemed like a sponge soaking up information and ideas indiscriminately. But some reactive organism was at work; he was more than a sponge. One night in June 1913, for example, after dining with Colonel George Harvey, the eminent editor and amateur politico, Roosevelt wrote in his diary: "Col. Harvey is brilliant—too much so to argue—he changes the battle front or else closes debate with a final statement. I want to see more of him, but have a feeling we shall clash."

Absorbed in the navy, Roosevelt was only on the fringe of the main action of the Wilson administration. "No one can mistake," the new President said in his inaugural address, "the purpose for which the Nation now seeks to use the Democratic Party." He soon was demonstrating that purpose. In the next nine months he steered through Congress the Federal Reserve Act, which reshaped the national banking and currency system, and a tariff act that dropped duties to the lowest point since the Civil War. Attached to the latter was a graduated federal tax on incomes, potentially the most radical measure of all. Other important legislation ground through Congress during following years: acts to prevent unfair competition, to improve the lot of seamen, to develop vocational education, to require the eight-hour day on railroads.

The atmosphere of Washington was the atmosphere of Wilsonian reform. Roosevelt supported the President's proposals; indeed, they represented on a national level the kind of thing he had fought for in Albany. Not that he had yet developed, however, a rounded philosophy of government, although he did try to have one. Once, for example, while state senator, he had bravely advanced the thought at a People's Forum in Troy, New York, that the new idea in politics must be "cooperation," which began "where competition leaves off." Co-operation was the "struggle for liberty of the community rather than liberty of the individual . . . and by liberty, we mean happiness and prosperity. . . ." On the surface, his argument fell somewhere between T.R.'s New Nationalism and Wilson's New Freedom; analyzed closely it was pretentious nonsense. The only merit his argument had was in the realm of semantics: co-operation, he assured his audience, was a more acceptable term politically than "community interest" (too socialistic), "brotherhood of man" (too idealistic), or "regulation" (would alarm "old fogies"). He evidently felt he ought to think out a philosophy of government, but his heart was not in it.

But a philosophy of government, after all, was not necessary to run the navy. As it turned out, Roosevelt's pragmatic, undoctrinaire approach to governmental matters often brought him to a "progressive" policy in Washington just as it had in Albany. A case in point was the Navy Department's handling of monopoly. Roosevelt and Daniels had to tussle with steel manufacturers who handed in identical bids on armor plate, with mine owners who had a monopoly of high-grade coal, with high-cost middlemen and block bidders. Daniels saw the problem from the point of view of an agrarian foe of the trusts, Roosevelt from that of a bureaucrat trying to stretch his funds to buy as many ships as possible. Different motives brought the two men to a common posture of opposing trusts.

With Wilson himself Roosevelt had only sporadic contacts, but the relationship was cordial. The Assistant Secretary was able to view at close hand Wilson's masterly handling of Congress. And he remembered years later how the President said to him on one occasion: "It is only once in a generation that a people can be lifted above material things. That is why conservative government is in the saddle two-thirds of the time."

TAMMANY WINS AGAIN

"You can rest assured," Roosevelt wrote to a former constituent soon after arriving in Washington, "that I am not through with politics or public affairs in the State of New York." His navy job gave him excellent political leverage in more than one direction. The navy itself hired thousands of civilian workers in New York

State alone. His Poughkeepsie friend John Mack said later that Roosevelt "took care" of every job seeker Mack wrote him about during the navy years; the Brooklyn Navy Yard was well sprinkled with political appointees of the assistant secretary. In Washington, Roosevelt also could keep in touch with Postmaster General Albert S. Burleson and Secretary of the Treasury McAdoo, and other administration chiefs who controlled hundreds more federal positions in the state.

Roosevelt's political administration of naval affairs, moreover, gave him valuable publicity and contacts in key places in the nation. He conducted numerous inspections of navy yards, and he made a point of talking about expanding the facilities; bettering conditions for navy personnel, including enlisted, commissioned, and civilian; improving housing; stabilizing employment; and the like. His inspections were well staged: guns boomed salutes, Marines stood at attention, brass bands blared out marches. Reporters played up his appeals to local interests and civic pride. Years later Louisiana politicians were remembering that he had got the New Orleans navy yard reopened.

Doggedly helping Roosevelt in all these political activities was Louis Howe. Officially, as Roosevelt's assistant, Howe worked on procurement, contracts, construction, labor relations, and he spent a good deal of time on such matters. Actually he was assistant in charge of politics—a congenial job for a man who had made his chief's advancement his own life aim. Day after day Howe coached Roosevelt on the fine points of political thrust and parry. A typical bit of advice involved a letter from one Frank Cooper, an office seeker, which Roosevelt had marked to be answered. Don't answer it, counseled Howe. "Clute [a rival to Cooper] has now been confirmed by the Senate and if you should write Cooper expressing your regrets he would be the first to show the letter to Clute some fine day when he wanted something of Clute or in case you did not do something he wanted you to do for him." Howe was instinctively hostile toward any politician who might stand in Roosevelt's way— a trait that was often vindicated by events but one that gained Howe a good many enemies.

Howe's chief service to Roosevelt was curbing his young chief's impetuosity when conditions called for a policy of watchful waiting. Unhappily, Howe was not around to advise him when Roosevelt made the decision to run for United States Senator—a decision that led to the only real election defeat of his career and to a resounding victory for Tammany. Informing Howe of his decision, Roosevelt was almost apologetic. "My senses have not yet left me," he said.

Perhaps Roosevelt's political sense had left him. The story of his try for the Democratic nomination for United States Senator in

1914 is a story of improvisation, faulty intelligence work, and bad luck.

The political situation in New York in 1913 had taken a dramatic turn. The new governor, "Plain Bill" Sulzer—the instrument of Murphy's defeat of Roosevelt and the Empire State Democracy in 1912—had turned on Tammany even before taking office. From the executive mansion—renamed by Plain Bill the "People's House"—issued a torrent of denunciation of the bosses. Murphy hit back hard. Tammany started impeachment proceedings against Sulzer on the grounds of misusing campaign funds; in October 1913 Sulzer was convicted and removed from office. Lieutenant Governor Martin H. Glynn, an Albany politician close to Murphy, took his place. The divided Democrats lost heavily in the assembly elections the following month.

To Roosevelt this seemed the golden opportunity to strike a demolishing blow against Murphy. In the election, Tammany had lost control of New York City and much of its patronage; the national administration regarded it with distaste; if the Tiger's grip on the state government was severed it might starve to death. Roosevelt himself was under much pressure, especially from the old Empire State Democracy group, to run for governor the next year.

Everything depended on President Wilson. Armed with administration backing and patronage, Roosevelt could take a commanding position in state affairs. Without Wilson's permission the assistant secretary, as a member of the administration, could take no decisive action at all. Months went by, but Wilson did not give him the signal. On the contrary, the President continued to dole out patronage to Tammanyites and independent Democrats alike. When in March 1914 Roosevelt asked Wilson for "five minutes" to see how far he might go in speaking out on New York politics, Wilson wrote in reply: "My judgment is that it would be best if members of the administration should use as much influence as possible but say as little as possible in the politics of their several states"; particularly in this case, the President added, for in New York "the plot is not yet clear."

Roosevelt wanted to make the plot clear. Barred from open action, he flirted briefly with the New York Progressive party. He evidently hoped to gain the Progressive as well as the Democratic nomination for governor, unless, of course, the Progressives nominated Cousin Theodore; "I will not run against him," said Franklin. "You know blood is thicker than water." But Cousin Theodore neither ran himself nor helped turn Progressive support to Franklin. The latter then redoubled his efforts to strengthen the anti-Tammany Democrats through patronage. He was assisted in this by McAdoo, who had long-term interests of his own in building up the independent Democracy. Together they managed to get some appointments for anti-Tammany men and rumors spread that soon there would be more.

Stung on its most tender flank, Tammany was quick to retaliate. The chairman of the important Committee of Appropriations of the House of Representatives warned Wilson that he and the other Democratic congressmen from New York City would not stand being slandered by persons professing to be authorized spokesmen for the President. The Democratic state chairman of New York said that the party upstate had become so demoralized as a result of the patronage situation that he doubted if the Democrats could elect a single congressman.

Wilson saw the danger signals. He put out a conciliatory statement toward Tammany. And Roosevelt, who had been making formal disavowals of his candidacy, issued an announcement on July 23 that sounded as though he really meant it.

Wilson's strategy was as careful as Roosevelt's was clumsy. The President liked the young assistant secretary, but he knew that more important matters were at stake than Rooseveltian efforts to purify New York State. To put his program through Congress he needed a united party. Several Tammany representatives held key chairmanships as a result of their seniority. Patronage was important; only after Wilson appointed an acceptable person to the prized New York City customs collectorship did Senator O'Gorman vote for the Federal Reserve bill. The President, moreover, had to keep in mind his own prospects for re-election in 1916. His chances in the key state of New York would be forlorn if the party should be divided.

Roosevelt had been rebuffed. Three weeks after he gave up hope for the governorship, however, he suddenly announced that he was a candidate for Senator. Why?

Despite Roosevelt's coyness he was eager throughout the latter part of 1913 and the early part of 1914 to make a statewide run for an important office in New York. Partly it was the example of Uncle Ted, who had entered the executive mansion in Albany two years after becoming assistant secretary of the navy. Partly it was Franklin Roosevelt's feeling that he must strike out in state politics while memories of his anti-Sheehan fight were still warm, or while the Republicans and the Bull Moosers were still divided. Perhaps, too, it was a fear that rising men in New York Democratic politics would take the center of the stage if he stayed too long in the wings. It is certain that even while he was giving up his gubernatorial ideas he was thinking of the senatorship; "I *might* declare myself a candidate for U.S. Senator in the Democratic and Progressive Primaries," he wrote on July 19 to his wife, who was waiting the arrival of a child. "The Governorship is, thank God, out of the question. . . . I really would like to be in the Senate just so as to get a summer really with my family once in every three or four years!"

Roosevelt did not clear his candidacy with Wilson. His tactic was to get into the race fast since "this would necessarily place any other candidate who may be put forward by Charles F. Murphy in the position of opposing me," as he wrote to a friend. "I want to throw the burden of proof on the other attorney." Also, if he was the first man in the race, he could ask prominent New York leaders for support without embarrassing them. After a series of conferences he teamed up with John A. Hennessy, who would be the anti-Tammany candidate for the gubernatorial nomination.

For a while it seemed that Roosevelt might have no opponent, or that if he did it would be William Randolph Hearst. Either prospect delighted Roosevelt; he felt he could beat the notorious publisher "in spite of his wad and his papers." But Roosevelt made no effort to keep a Murphy man out of the race; on the contrary, his denunciations of the Tammany boss were so sharp, as Howe himself admitted, that it would "almost force them to put someone in the field against him."

Once again Roosevelt underestimated Murphy's resourcefulness. Reports soon were spreading that Tammany would back James Gerard, ambassador to Germany, for the nomination. An upright, well-liked member of Tammany, Gerard was a Wilson man who at the moment was enjoying a good deal of notice for helping Americans stranded by the outbreak of the European war. For days Roosevelt refused to believe that Gerard would accept the tempting bait Murphy held out for him. Howe had confidential information that there was not the "slightest chance" Gerard would run. Neither Roosevelt nor Howe knew that Gerard cabled Bryan and Wilson to clear his acceptance and the President made no objection.

Gerard threw his hat in the ring—but from a distance. He said that his duties would not permit his return to campaign. He knew he could afford to leave his affairs in Murphy's hands. Roosevelt demanded of Gerard whether he would be controlled by Murphy if elected senator; the ambassador did not reply. The assistant secretary said that a man who would leave his military post of duty was not fit to be a senator; he said nothing about his own absence from his navy post while the conflagration was blazing up in Europe.

Despite this blow, and despite his pessimism as to the outcome, Roosevelt conducted a strenuous campaign. Ranging through upstate New York, he repeatedly attacked Murphy and demanded that Gerard stay at his post. Securing labor endorsements from his union friends in Washington he had tens of thousands of copies of the endorsement—some uphappily lacking the union label—handed out at plant gates. Under Howe's guidance he wrote friendly letters to dozens of newspaper editors, at the same time arranging for advertising. But he rarely could find mass audiences; the primary, which took place late in September 1914, during the first great battles of the war, did not attract much attention.

"He is quiet and unassuming," one editor wrote, "has the demeanor and poise of the student, and with his youthful scholarly face and soft accent, he gives no indication of the stubborn attitude that his friends claim he can assume on occasion. . . . Some of his utterances were planned with the skill of an old campaigner. . . ." But the editor—a Republican—was not overly impressed. Roosevelt had not made his position on the "great questions of the day" at all clear in his speech, he said, and compared to retiring Senator Elihu Root he cut a sorry figure as a great statesman.

Back in headquarters Howe was fighting the patronage battle. By a last-minute manipulation of jobs he hoped to hold friends firm and win over recalcitrants among the small bands of Democrats who would bother to vote. When Roosevelt asked one of his appointees, John B. Judson, for support and Judson replied candidly but pleasantly that he could not back him, Howe was ruthless. He could not "too strongly urge the importance of sudden and swift reprisal in this case." Wherever possible Judson's friends must lose their appointments and his "bitterest enemies" be given jobs. An influential Democrat might be induced to break with Judson if given control of some patronage, and anti-Judson newspapers must be used. Roosevelt agreed that the deserter should be punished.

All in vain. On primary day the absentee Gerard beat Roosevelt 210,765 to 76,888, with 23,977 votes going to a third candidate. Murphy's candidate, Glynn, defeated Hennessy by a somewhat heavier vote. Roosevelt had the consolation of winning over a third of the state's sixty-one counties, including Dutchess County by a sweeping vote, but Democrats were sparse in most of these counties. Tammany had shown its strength even upstate, where Gerard ran better than two to one. All in all, it was a bad beating for the young politician.

Roosevelt promptly cabled Gerard his congratulations, adding that he would campaign for him if the ambassador would declare his unalterable opposition to Murphy's leadership. Gerard smoothly replied that of course he would represent the whole party and people and no faction or individual if elected, and Roosevelt made some speeches for him. In the November elections, however, both Gerard and Glynn lost to their Republican rivals. "I am sorry . . ." said Roosevelt, "but not entirely surprised."

Roosevelt could not have been surprised at his own defeat in the primaries. As a state senator he had argued with keen insight that direct nominations in primaries would not destroy party organizations. Differing with ardent supporters of the primary who viewed it as the cure for democracy's ills, he predicted that few would vote and that the organization would get its own people to the polls. He favored direct nominations, however, for at least they would arouse greater interest in candidates. His own experience in 1914 amply justified his reasoning.

His drubbing hurt Roosevelt keenly for a time, but defeat is a stringent educational process. He discovered that it took more than federal patronage to beat a strong state machine; he experienced the problems of a state-wide campaign, husbanding voice and energy; and he learned how to take defeat.

More important, the young politician got another harsh lesson in the power of Tammany. He could win a rural upstate district against the organization, but not the whole state. And a general election in November could rarely be won unless the Democracy was united. Much as they hated each other, the machine and the independents needed each other. The moral issue, moreover, was still a fuzzy gray rather than black and white. Tammany was headed by Murphy, but it was also made up of honest men like Gerard and rising young progressives like Al Smith.

Roosevelt learned his lesson. Never again did he take on Tammany in a knightly onslaught.

The Assistant Secretary's political setback was quickly swallowed in epochal events on the international stage. The assassination of an archduke in far-off Bosnia had been almost forgotten by Americans when suddenly the European powder keg exploded. On August 1, 1914, Germany declared war on Russia. Roosevelt got the news while he was on the way to Reading, Pennsylvania, to dedicate an anchor of the battleship *Maine* as a memorial. "A complete smash up is inevitable," he wrote his wife on the train. "It will be the greatest war in the world's history."

Roosevelt had long been psychologically prepared for the smash up. He had, indeed, been through one or two dress rehearsals. During a Japanese-American war scare in 1913 he had drawn up a hypothetical war plan and had put the submarine torpedo flotilla at Newport through an emergency mobilization. When American forces occupied Vera Cruz, Mexico, early in 1914, Roosevelt had said, "I do not want war," but he had thought the United States must "go down there and clean up the Mexican political mess . . . right now." During his months in office he had ridden far ahead of Daniels in his efforts at naval preparedness.

Now war had come and his impatience spilled over. On arriving in Washington, Roosevelt went straight to the department, "where as I expected I found everything asleep and apparently oblivious to the fact that the most terrible drama in history was about to be enacted." He was doing the real work, he wrote his wife again a few days later; Daniels was "bewildered by it all, very sweet but very sad." Daniels and Bryan, he said, had as much conception of what a general European war means as four-year-old Elliott "has of higher mathematics."

These remarks foreshadowed Roosevelt's role during the months of "neutrality" that lay ahead. He sided with the admirals in pressing for stepped-up expansion of the navy, urged Wilson to set up a Council of National Defense, came out for universal military training. His zeal led him onto dubious ground: he maintained contacts with Theodore Roosevelt, Henry Cabot Lodge, and other critics of Wilson's policies, and even passed on naval intelligence information to Republicans who used it in attacking Daniels for naval unpreparedness.

If Roosevelt was zealous to the point of insubordination, his attitude stemmed in part from a realistic grasp of the difficulties ahead. At the outbreak of the war he realized it would probably be a long one. In contrast to some of his banker friends, he saw that lack of money would not shorten the war for any determined nation. He had a sure sense of the implications of world war for naval strategy; he held a long correspondence with Admiral Alfred Thayer Mahan, who warned him against splitting the fleet between the Atlantic and the Pacific. He understood the need for great reserve strength in men and matériel if war should come. Week after week he toiled with the tough, irksome details of rearmament.

"We've got to get into this war," Roosevelt was telling his chief by the fall of 1916. Daniels did not need to ask on whose side. Roosevelt had been pro-Ally from the start. "Rather than long drawn-out struggle I hope England will join in and with France and Russia force peace *at Berlin!*" he had written on hearing that Germany had invaded France. He was elated by the Belgians' "glorious resistance." Wilson had asked Americans to be neutral in thought as well as action, but early in 1915 Roosevelt lamented to his wife, "I just *know* I shall do some awful unneutral thing before I get through!"

Roosevelt's aggressive stand for preparedness might have left him in an exposed position, but events came to the rescue. Following the sinking of the *Lusitania* in May 1915 Secretary Bryan resigned his office rather than go along with Wilson's protests against German submarine policy—protests he feared might have to be made good by war. A year later preparedness was in full swing; the Naval

Appropriation Act of that year would have made the United States Navy in time the largest in the world. In the 1916 election the administration closed ranks. Whatever his private doubts of the past, Roosevelt hotly defended Wilson and Daniels against the Republican accusation of unpreparedness. "Misquotations and misrepresentations—yea, lies—have been used by the President's opponents," he declared in a speech in Providence. "I say lies because this is a good 'Roosevelt' word to use."

Furious at Wilson's "tame" policy toward Germany, Theodore Roosevelt ditched the Progressives in June 1916 and came out for the Republican nominee, Charles Evans Hughes. Their ranks reunited, the Republicans seemed sure to win the presidency as Election Day neared. The first returns bore out such predictions, and Franklin Roosevelt, like Wilson, went to bed sure that Hughes had won. But the next day the returns from the West told a different story: it was the "most extraordinary day of my life," Roosevelt wrote his wife excitedly. Final returns gave Wilson 9,129,-606 popular votes over Hughes's 8,538,221, making a difference in the electoral college of 277 to 254.

"It is rumored," joked the happy and relieved Assistant Secretary of the Navy a few days later, "that a certain distinguished cousin of mine is now engaged in revising an edition of his most noted historical work, *The Winning of the West*."

WAR LEADER

On January 9, 1917, the Kaiser presided nervously over a fateful crown council at his headquarters in a Silesian castle. During the previous year the war had gone badly for Germany and her allies: the Allied lines had sagged under the massive blow at Verdun, but held; after Jutland the German navy did not dare to risk another heavy encounter with the British; the Allied blockade was sapping Germany's economic strength. There was only one way out, the military chiefs argued: unrestricted submarine warfare. For over two years the diplomats had fought successfully against this drastic policy on the ground that it would drive the United States into the war. At this meeting the military won. Shortly, orders were flashed to U-boat commanders to start unrestricted warfare February 1.

Roosevelt was in Santo Domingo early in February 1917 when the radio reported Germany's announcement. Daniels called him home immediately. Anxious weeks followed as the country moved indecisively toward war. Roosevelt pressed for action. Early in March he asked Wilson's permission to have the fleet fitted out for war. "No," said the President, as Roosevelt remembered it later,

". . . I do not want the United States to do anything in a military way, by way of war preparations, that would allow the definitive historian in later days . . . to say that the United States had committed an unfriendly act against the central powers." But soon reports were coming in of American ships torpedoed, and a united cabinet advised Wilson to ask Congress to declare war.

On a rainy April night Franklin and Eleanor Roosevelt listened to Wilson's eloquently solemn war message. Eleanor went home "still half dazed by the sense of impending change." The address, said her husband to the press, "will be an inspiration to every true citizen no matter what his political faith, no matter what his creed, no matter what the country of his origin."

The die cast, Roosevelt plunged into war administration with vigor and aplomb. Much had to be done—vast extension of procurement and recruitment, stepped-up naval construction, quick defense measures, the fashioning of a naval plan of action, coordination with the merchant marine, careful arrangements with the British and French on deployment of ships, and a host of other matters. Handling big jobs in a big way inspirited him. He liked to act quickly, even if it meant not always acting wisely. Emory S. Land's comments about his suggestions on ship design—"He was a great trial and error guy, but he did have some good ideas"—characterized his activities in general.

War mobilization did not end the need for Roosevelt's political approach to administration. Seeking to gain a discount on copper from Daniel Guggenheim late in 1916, Roosevelt won his goal by warning Guggenheim that a price cut would show the public that businessmen were not interested in preparedness simply for selfish reasons. When wage disputes arose during the war he talked face to face with union chiefs. Contracts were awarded efficiently but not always on a strictly nonpolitical basis.

One of Roosevelt's attempted political maneuvers would have rendered unnecessary a historic episode during the breathless weeks before Wilson's call for war. Wishing to provide navy guns for merchantmen crossing submarine-infested waters, Roosevelt discovered that he could not sell guns to private owners, but he decided that under an old law he could *lease* them. He so informed Wilson through Daniels, but the President would not exploit the loophole. Instead he asked Congress for the necessary authority—only to have the bill killed by a filibuster on the part of a "little group of willful men," as Wilson called them. Roosevelt must have watched with wry satisfaction when the President later ordered guns on merchantmen without congressional authority—and he could hardly have forgotten the incident in preparing his Lend Lease step in 1940.

Roosevelt needed all the political craft he could muster to put through some of his proposals. One of these was to lay a mine barrage between Scotland and Norway to keep U-boats out of the Atlantic. The cost was so staggering and technical difficulties so formidable that Roosevelt ran into opposition from both the British Admiralty and Admiral William S. Sims in London. However, the invention of an electric antenna firing device, the dispatch of a high-ranking admiral to pilot the project through naval channels in London, and Roosevelt's continual pressure finally broke the log jam. The project finally proved wholly practical, although it was started too late to have more than a minor role in antisubmarine warfare.

In the months before the war Roosevelt's impatience with Daniels' deliberate ways reached a new height. "J. D. is too damned slow for words," he wrote to his wife in November 1916. The Assistant Secretary did not, however, lend any support to an organized campaign spearheaded by the Navy League to make Roosevelt Secretary during Wilson's second term. He had no use, he said, for a subordinate who was constantly thinking up ways of stepping into his boss's shoes; he knew, too, that Daniels was personally and politically close to Wilson. After hostilities started, conflict tended to revolve more around methods than objectives, but in private Roosevelt still was sharply critical of his chief. At one point he helped the American novelist Winston Churchill draft a series of criticisms of naval administration which Churchill presented personally to Wilson. Roosevelt's idea of getting a job done was to grab scissors and slash away at red tape; he did not fully realize that much of the red tape was simply the complicated line of clearance and consultation that Daniels, dealing with a multitude of decision-makers, had to wind up before effective action could be taken.

"I am trying to forget that there is such a thing as politics," Roosevelt said early in 1918. But he could not. Friends kept urging him to run for governor. More important, Tammany was making overtures.

This surprising development was largely a result of a change in Roosevelt's own approach to Tammany. He had not forgotten the lessons of 1914 and the years before. Quietly he had adopted a policy of live and let live. In 1915 he did patronage favors for some of the very Tammany congressmen who had attacked him so bitterly the previous year. In 1916, taking his cue from Wilson, he followed a party harmony policy in both the state and national election. He showed the utmost cordiality toward Smith, Wagner, and other progressive-minded Tammany men. Peace was consummated on the Fourth of July, 1917, when Roosevelt, at Tammany's invitation, gave the main talk in the Wigwam and was photographed with his old adversary Murphy. By the spring of 1918 he had received reports that at least a dozen New York City leaders were for him, perhaps even Murphy himself. Actually, Tammany had no sudden love for Roosevelt, but saw him as a man who could win upstate votes.

Roosevelt quite likely could have had the nomination—and the election. But in June 1918 he indicated decisively that he did not want to run.

His heart lay somewhere else. He was keenly aware that one vital element was missing in his political career. At a time when hundreds of thousands of men were in uniform, he was not. He was not even overseas. Uncle Ted, desperately eager himself to fight in France, had urged him to get into the war, but Daniels would not let him go. The next best thing was to get near the fighting, if only as a civilian. He finally induced the Secretary to send him on an official mission to inspect navy bases and confer with Allied leaders. Eager for adventure, Roosevelt departed early in July 1918 on a destroyer bound for Europe.

It was an exciting and satisfying trip. Zigzagging across the Atlantic Roosevelt's destroyer experienced nothing more than a few false alarms, but even these furnished the basis for future yarns. In England he met and talked with Lloyd George ("What impressed me most was his tremendous vitality," he said later), Lord Balfour, Winston Churchill (neither made much impression on the other at the time), Clemenceau, Orlando, and a host of famous admirals and generals. It was no mere junket. He spent a good deal of time going into humdrum details of contracts, supplies, and personnel. He tried, none too successfully, to straighten out a ticklish diplomatic and military tangle over the operations—or lack of them—of the Italian navy.

And finally he saw war. This was his main goal in the trip; it is significant that the only time he lost his poise was when a naval attaché tried to detour him around the fighting areas; Roosevelt persecuted the poor man for months afterward. He toured the sector where Marines had fought, describing the war-torn area with a vivid eye for detail. He saw fighting at a distance. Most exciting of all, he came under sporadic artillery fire.

It was exciting—but he still was not in uniform. He left for home in September determined to ask Daniels for a commission. Exhausted by his trip, however, he fell ill with influenza and pneumonia, and had to be taken ashore on a stretcher. He took weeks to recover, and time was running out. Around the end of October he went to Wilson with Daniels' permission to request a commission. It was too late, the President told him—he had received the first overtures for an armistice, and he hoped the war would be over soon.

Roosevelt was keenly disappointed but he tried to make the best of it. "Though I did not wear a uniform," he wrote later to a Grotonian who was preparing a World War tablet at the school, "I believe that my name should go in the first division of those who were 'in the service,' especially as I saw service on the other side, was missed by torpedoes and shells. . . ."

He was not nearly as disappointed as a young Austrian soldier who on November 11, 1918, lay weeping on a hospital bed in Prussia—weeping for the first time, he said later, since the death of his mother. He wept not because he had missed the war (he had fought bravely for four years, had been gassed and wounded) but because Germany was defeated and prostrate. At this time, Adolf Hitler wrote in *Mein Kampf*, "I resolved I would take up political work "

FOUR

Crusade for the League

THE WAR YEARS had a maturing effect on Roosevelt. Long hours, tough decisions, endless conferences, exhausting trips, hard bargaining with powerful officials in Washington and abroad turned him into a seasoned politician-administrator. Much of the time he was aggressively pushing forward, spurring his superiors and subordinates to action. This was easy for him—the hard part was patiently following the circuitous path that led to action. Much of the work was painstaking and inglorious.

Physically the years showed their marks. Faint lines appeared on his forehead; the smooth, almost soft face of the Albany years was a bit leaner and more furrowed. His hair was thinning above the temples. Dark shadows—a family characteristic—showed under his blue eyes. Yet he kept his essentially youthful appearance. Still lean and supple, he could play fifty-four holes of golf on a hot summer day; he could vault over a row of chairs with ease. "A beautifully built man, with the long muscles of the athlete," said Walter Camp, the celebrated Yale coach whom Roosevelt brought to Washington to set up a physical fitness program for the navy.

His family responsibilities had increased too. His children now numbered five. Franklin D. Roosevelt, Jr., had been born in August 1914 and John Roosevelt in March 1916. The family lived in Washington most of the year, with the invariable sojourns in Campobello during the summer and frequent visits to Hyde Park in between. A flock of servants—sometimes as many as ten—attended the family. Roosevelt's salary and investments together brought him about $27,000 a year, but life was expensive, and occasionally his mother helped him out.

Public life also exacted another toll. He was away from the family much of the time—away when children came down with semiserious illnesses, away when one of them was burned in a picnic fire. His anxiety only increased at a distance; during a polio epidemic he badgered Daniels unmercifully until the secretary allowed him to dispatch a destroyer to Campobello to take his children home by sea. His personal life, like that of other public figures, was fair game for rumor-mongers. A story went the rounds that he had fallen in love with another woman and that Eleanor had offered him his freedom. At best the long separations were the source of difficulty. "You were a goosy girl," he wrote his wife from Washington, "to think or even pretend to think that I don't want you here *all* the summer, because you know I do! But honestly *you* ought to have six weeks straight at Campo, just as *I* ought to, only you can and I can't. . . ."

The image Roosevelt presented to the world during the immediate postwar period was that of the brisk young executive. His job now called for a multitude of immediate "practical" duties rather than the glamorous actions of war, and much of the supervision of this work fell to the assistant secretary. He now became highly interested in improving the organization and administration of the federal government. Showing a keen grasp of the political context of public administration, he repeatedly urged that the President be given more control of budget-making, that Congress put its own houses in order by consolidating its appropriations activities in one general committee, that promotion be based on efficiency rather than length of service, that existing agencies be reorganized and functions redistributed, and that heads of executive departments be given more authority.

Toward politics he was cautious. "Quite frankly," he wrote a supporter in February 1920, "I do not personally intend to make an early Christian martyr of myself this fall if it is going to be a strongly Republican year." Yet this was precisely what he was to do.

CHALLENGE AND RESPONSE

Roosevelt spent the first few weeks of 1919 on navy business in Europe. While he helped tidy up the debris of war, Woodrow Wilson in Paris tried to lay the foundations of peace. The President was at the peak of his career; his tour of Europe had been that of an uncrowned monarch. "No one has ever had such cheers," an observer said. "I saw Foch pass, Clemenceau pass, Lloyd George, generals, returning troops, banners, but Wilson heard from his carriage something different, inhuman—or superhuman."

On a wintry day in mid-February Wilson left France for home. He carried with him triumphantly a draft of the Covenant of the proposed League of Nations. On the same ship was the Assistant Secretary of the Navy, returning to Washington with his wife. One day the Roosevelts lunched with the Wilsons and their party. The talk was mostly an exchange of stories, but at one point the President spoke of the League of Nations. "The United States must go in," he said, "or it will break the heart of the world, for she is the only nation that all feel is disinterested and all trust."

After their ship docked in Boston, the Roosevelts rode in the triumphal parade that escorted the President to his hotel. An estimated 200,000 Bostonians roared a welcome to the President, and even Governor Calvin Coolidge was moved to "feeling sure the people would back the President." Watching the crowds cheer the President wildly at every station on the way to Washington, Eleanor Roosevelt felt sure that they had "grasped his ideals."

Perhaps they had. But the Covenant was part of a treaty that had to win the votes of two-thirds of the Senate of the United States. And the Senate numbered men as proud and stiff-necked as Wilson himself, men jealous of senatorial prerogative in foreign relations, sensitive to large national-origin groups at home, keenly aware of the presidential election that lay ahead. The Senate, moreover, was under Republican management; despite Wilson's plea to the people in 1918 for Democratic control of Congress for the sake of "unified leadership," the voters had put the opposition party in control of both houses by slim margins.

Roosevelt watched with dismay as the President's foes in the Senate outmaneuvered the administration in skirmish after skirmish. In February 1919 the Republicans, still a minority, filibustered vital appropriations bills to death in the last weeks of the Democratic-controlled Congress, thereby forcing Wilson to summon, months ahead of the normal session, an extraordinary session of Congress which the Republicans would control. Just before the short session ended, Senator Henry Cabot Lodge by a parliamentary stratagem presented the Senate with the "Round Robin"—a pronunciamento that the Covenant was unacceptable "in the form now proposed" to thirty-nine Republican senators or senators-elect. In July, after weeks of hard negotiating with Lloyd George and Clemenceau in Paris, Wilson laid the treaty before the Senate. In August the President expressed willingness to accept mild Senate reservations to the treaty stated in a separate resolution, but the Senate Foreign Relations Committee proceeded to rip the treaty. In September Wilson went to the country, gave forty passionate speeches, suffered a breakdown, and returned spent and stricken. In November the President urged Democratic Senators to vote against the Lodge reservations to the treaty, and these were defeated, but unconditional ratification failed by a vote of 38 for to 53 against.

What had happened? Early in 1919 Wilson's fight for a League had been applauded by American and European alike; at the end of the year his hopes were in ruins. Many explanations were put forward. Italo-Americans were aroused by the refusal to let Italy have Fiume, Irish-Americans by England's control of "six seats" in the Assembly, German-Americans by Allied treatment of the old country. Other Americans were simply tired of Europe and its troubles; they were distracted by labor troubles, high prices, the Red Scare. The League question was caught in a bitter battle between parties. Above all, Wilson continued to talk about idealism after the cynical men at Versailles had produced a treaty of *real-politik;* he continued to insist on the Covenant as he framed it long after concessions were in order.

Whatever the truth, it is notable that Roosevelt's approach to the matter was somewhat different from the President's. The Assistant Secretary was, of course, pro-League, but his speeches lacked Wilson's fine moral fervor. While Wilson talked about following "the vision," about "destiny," about "lifted eyes," about America's duty, about Americans' dreams, Roosevelt was more pragmatic, more experimental. "It is important not to dissect the document," Roosevelt said in March 1919. "The important thing is first to approve the general plan." Unless the United States came in, he warned, the League would become simply a new Holy Alliance. "The League may not end wars, but the nations demand the experiment."

He was more willing to compromise than Wilson seemed to be. As early as March 29, 1919, he favored an amendment recognizing the Monroe Doctrine, but he thought the League should be tried even if desired amendments were not forthcoming. Other reservations to the League Covenant would be necessary, he warned at the end of the year. He had little hope that the League, even with United States membership, would prevent all future wars; several months after the war he still wanted compulsory military training.

"I have read the draft of the League three times," he said in July, "and always find something to object to in it, and that is the way with everybody. . . . Personally I am willing to make a try on the present instrument." Only once during this period did Roosevelt talk grandiloquently in Wilsonian terms. This was in a speech to a meeting sponsored by the League to Enforce Peace, when he put the League of Nations on a plane with the Magna Charta and the Constitution. He knew what his audience wanted.

Unlike Wilson, who became more and more obsessed with the treaty and League alone, Roosevelt during the postwar period seemed concerned with a variety of issues, great and small. During 1919 and early 1920 he gave a remarkable number of speeches on a remarkable variety of subjects. He delivered over a score of talks describing and defending the navy's record in World War I. He repeatedly advocated peacetime universal military training as the fairest way of maintaining an army. He called for administrative and legislative reorganization. He even had time to take a politician's straddle on a minor but touchy subject: vivisection was necessary for scientific research, he told a meeting of humane societies, but the medical profession should stop abuses of it.

Some of his ideas were simply fatuous. He expressed the hope on one occasion that state and national governmental affairs would be as "free from politics" after the war as during the war. Some of his talks were of the spread-eagle type, filled with references to "good Americanism," "clean living," "straight thinking." But certain threads ran through many of his speeches: nationalism ("Americanism") rather than localism or sectionalism, internationalism rather than nationalism, the use of government to solve problems, the improvement in governmental machinery to handle heavier burdens.

He was still a Wilson man. "The progressive movement within the Republican Party has been dying ever since 1916—yesterday it died," he said late in May in a speech before the Democratic National Committee in Chicago the day after conservative Republicans had won a victory in the Senate. The Republican party was still the party of "conservatism and reaction," of "little Americanism and jingo bluff." He predicted a party realignment with Republican liberals joining the Democrats while the Tories in his own party shifted to the opposition. He lambasted the new Republican Congress, just convened, for its concern over restoring the "old form of preferential tariff for pet groups of manufacturers," for truckling to the returned soldiers but doing very little for them, for revising the income tax to benefit millionaires, for mudslinging and slander.

It was a rousing speech—a "humdinger," said a local editor. He was simply trying, Roosevelt commented afterward, "to go back to certain fundamentals as old as the country itself."

1920—THE SOLEMN REFERENDUM

With the advent of election year, Roosevelt's friends as usual pressed him to run for governor or Senator. And as usual he was evasive. Much would depend, he told his supporters during the early months of 1920, on the type of candidate nominated at the Democratic national convention in July.

The Democrats were in an awkward position. Their party chief was an invalid in the White House. The Republicans, no longer riven by Progressive secession, were turning Congress into an anti-administration sounding board, and were exploiting the crop of domestic and foreign problems that followed the war. Opposition to the League seemed to be increasing not only among conservatives but also among progressive elements on whose support the Wilsonian Democracy had come to rely.

Many Democratic leaders wanted to discard the League as a major campaign issue. City bosses of the North, at odds with the President over patronage matters, wanted to shake off Wilson as party leader and symbol. But it could not be done. As tightly as he could, Wilson had tied his party to his League. Convinced that the people were with him, he told his party publicly that the election must be a "great and solemn referendum" on the settlement of the war and the shape of the peace. Sick at heart over the prospects of the League in the Senate, thousands of Democrats looked to the election as a means of breaking the deadlock.

One of these Democrats was Roosevelt. In sharp contrast to his status in 1912 he enjoyed a good deal of influence in the 1920 Democratic convention in San Francisco. He was both an important member of the administration and a full-fledged delegate, elected by fellow Democrats in his congressional district. His one vote, moreover, would count. He tried unsuccessfully to induce the New York Democrats to drop the unit rule, under which a majority of the New York delegates (under Murphy) could control the votes of the whole delegation, as they had in 1912. The rules committee of the convention, however, came to his rescue by holding, over the protests of Tammany, that the unit rule did not apply to delegations selected by primary elections.

Roosevelt grasped a chance to dramatize his support of Wilson on the opening day of the convention. The unveiling of a huge oil portrait of the stricken President touched off a noisy demonstration. Delegation after delegation poured into the aisles and waved their placards. But not the New York delegates—they sat conspicuously in their seats. "Get up, New York!" the paraders shouted, but in vain. This was too much for Roosevelt. He ran over to a bulky Tammany leader who was tightly grasping the state standard, grabbed with such force as to pull the indignant Tammanyite to his feet, wrestled with him for a moment, and then bore the standard triumphantly down the aisle.

For several days and two-score ballots the convention was deadlocked in a seesaw race among Governor James M. Cox of Ohio, Attorney General A. Mitchell Palmer, and William G. McAdoo, former secretary of the treasury and now a son-in-law of the President. Roosevelt seconded the nomination of Governor Alfred E. Smith of New York, but after Smith and other favorite sons had dropped out, he and most of the other upstate New Yorkers voted several times for McAdoo. McAdoo, however, was not an avowed candidate and he was scornfully labeled the "Crown Prince" by those who feared Wilson's influence over the convention. Wilson himself was silent.

Cox won on the forty-fourth ballot. It was as logical for the Democrats to nominate him as it had been earlier for the Republicans to choose another Ohio editor-politician, Warren G. Harding, after a conference of party leaders. Cox was a compromise candidate. Sufficiently pro-Wilson not to have alienated the administration, he still did not suffer the handicap of being a "Wilson man." He had made a progressive and efficient record in the gubernatorial office—a place where he could sidestep some of the more ticklish national issues. On liquor he was wet, but not excessively so.

As usual, choosing the vice-presidential candidate was a convention afterthought. By long tradition he must balance the ticket. Geographically he must come from a different part of the country from the presidential candidate. Politically he must represent different interests in the party. In contrast to Cox, Roosevelt was identified with the Wilson administration, he was a moderate dry, and he was considered an independent in the party. Moreover, he had a good record in government, and his name might bring over some progressives from the Republican camp, T.R. having died the previous year.

The nomination was accomplished easily. Presented with a list of available candidates, Cox expressed a preference for Roosevelt, but as an experienced politician he wanted to clear the matter with Tammany, which had gone down the line for him in the convention. When Cox's manager, Edmund H. Moore, called Murphy out of bed, the Tammany chief was blunt.

"I don't like Roosevelt," he said. "He is not well known in the country, but, Ed, this is the first time a Democratic nominee for the Presidency has shown me courtesy. That's why I would vote for the devil himself if Cox wanted me to. Tell him we will nominate Roosevelt on the first ballot as soon as we assemble."

Murphy as usual was as good as his word. Several other candidates were put in nomination, but word traveled quickly through the hall that Cox and Murphy wanted Roosevelt. When Al Smith seconded the nomination of the assistant secretary, Tammany's position was made clear. The other nominations were withdrawn, and Roosevelt was nominated by acclamation. He had had no part in his selection.

Viewed in retrospect, Roosevelt's nomination seemed wholly natural if not inevitable. But it was not. Other candidates met the eligibility requirements. Roosevelt had no organized machine working in his behalf, although some of his friends had started a small boom for him. He had been a McAdoo man, and Cox had never met him. Roosevelt himself was caught somewhat by surprise at the outcome. If his nomination was due in part to fortuitous circumstances, such as his name and place of residence, it was due also to his improved relations with Tammany, a political reputation that *had* spread outside New York, and to his record in the navy.

Roosevelt and Cox at the outset faced a critical question of strategy. To what extent should they base their campaign on the League issue? Obviously they could not be rid of it, but they could soft-pedal it and play up a number of domestic matters—tried and tested issues such as the tariff or "Republican reaction." This was precisely what many Democratic leaders urged them to do. It was pointed out—quite accurately, as it turned out—that the Republicans, not being committed to the Covenant, could hold both supporters and opponents of the League in line for Harding, while large elements of the Democratic party—especially the Irish and Italians—would desert.

The decision of Cox and Roosevelt, however, was to make the League the central issue of their campaign. Together they visited the President to symbolize this intention. Wilson sat on the White House portico, gray and gaunt, a shawl covering his paralyzed left arm. Cox said, as Roosevelt later remembered it, "Mr. President, we are going to be a million per cent with you, and your Administration, and that means the League of Nations." The President seemed to come to life. "I am very grateful" was all he could manage to say.

The Democratic candidates also decided on an aggressive campaign, despite advice that, as the representatives of the party in power, they should allow the Republicans to carry the election to them. Harding, on the other hand, elected to conduct a front-porch campaign in McKinley fashion. Roosevelt was itching to take to the road. Between mid-August and Election Day he traveled almost ceaselessly, usually in a car attached to regular trains, sometimes by auto, and once by airplane. He took a wide swing through the Northwest in August, then into New England and New York in September, then swung west again by a more southerly route as far as Colorado, and campaigned intensively in his home state again during the last days of the campaign, winding up in Madison Square Garden at the end of October. He probably made more than a thousand speeches.

Ahead of him ranged a Democratic party publicity agent, named Stephen Early; with the candidate was a general assistant, Marvin McIntyre; Howe helped out in Washington and New York and later on the campaign train. Early's staccato reports gave the candidate the political lay of the land. "Washington state is DRY," he telegraphed to McIntyre from Spokane. "Interest centers on reclamation of lands and destruction of Non-Partisan League. The Boss will be asked to express himself on Non-Partisan League and their kind of radicals. This section of country vitally interested. . . . Advise strongly that you do not hit the NPL directly. Lumber is the big industry. Wheat is the big crop. Agricultural development is the aim of all. . . ."

There was little interest in the League of Nations, Early concluded. Wilson had failed to arouse interest in it on his tour. As Roosevelt moved on, the reports on League sentiment were even more discouraging. Almost everywhere, it seemed, the situation varied between apathy and downright opposition. "New Hampshire is hopeless," Early reported, "the Irish are rampant." In Minneapolis, McIntyre found a lack of interest in the League—people were thinking of their "breadbaskets and not of their war allies."

But Roosevelt stuck to the League issue. Desperately he tried to put the opposition on the defensive with a direct question to the Republican candidate. "If the United States can enter the existing League of Nations in such a way that the will of the League cannot be imposed on us against our will, and if it is made clear that our Constitutional and Congressional rights regarding war are in every way preserved, would you then, Senator Harding, favor our going in?" Roosevelt knew that he would get no answer, that Harding would remain silent for fear of alienating either the anti-League Republicans headed by Senator Hiram Johnson or the pro-League Republicans led by ex-President Taft. In his maddening way Harding continued to utter banalities on his porch.

Roosevelt did not spend all his ammunition on the League issue, however. He touched on a variety of subjects—the tariff, Harding's reported espousal of dollar wheat for the farmers, excessive campaign spending by the Republicans, control of Harding by a small gang of men. He advanced a program that in a rough way antedated later ones: better marketing facilities and living conditions for farmers, a billion-dollar conservation and development program, higher labor standards, improved relations with Latin America, and closer economic relations with all nations. He endorsed the legislation passed under the Wilson administration.

Most of the time Roosevelt waged a skillful, aggressive campaign which drew attention without stealing the show from the star, Governor Cox. He also committed mistakes, the worst of which occurred at Butte. Stung by Republican charges that Britain would control six votes in the League Assembly, Roosevelt said that the United States would control a dozen—namely those of her little brothers to the South. Indeed, he went on, he and Daniels really controlled two of these votes, for they "had something to do with the running of a couple of little republics." He added with a smile that while in the navy he had written Haiti's constitution himself.

It was a dreadful boner. Republicans pointed with alarm, Latin Americans felt insulted, and the State Department was upset. Roosevelt took the politician's way out—he claimed he was misquoted and "clarified" his remarks.

The Roosevelt name continued to exert its spell. Pressing up to the candidate people would say, "I voted for your father" and "You're just like the Old Man." To offset this annoying misapprehension the Republicans sent young Colonel Theodore Roosevelt, Jr., on his cousin's trail. "He is a maverick," the colonel said of his distant cousin; "he does not have the brand of our family." More important, Harding finally left his porch and delivered some stump speeches.

Although he knew that a candidate tends to be carried away by his cheering audiences and well-wishers, Roosevelt was in high hopes the day before the election. His hopes were soon dashed. The Republicans won the presidency by over seven million votes, 16,-152,220 to 9,147,553, one of the most sweeping victories in presidential history. Republicans would control the House 300 to 132, the Senate 59 to 37. Harding polled more than twice as many votes as Cox in Roosevelt's own state.

Wilson was bitter. "We had a chance to gain the leadership of the world," he said. "We have lost it, and soon we shall be witnessing the tragedy of it all." Cox accepted defeat with the grace of a veteran. So did Roosevelt, but he looked forward. The moment of defeat, he said to a friend, was the best time to lay plans for Democratic victories in the future.

THE RISING POLITICIAN

One Sunday evening late in 1917 Sara Delano Roosevelt sat, book in hand, in the living room that she had recently added in the new south wing of her Hyde Park home. She enjoyed this gracious, comfortable room, with the Gilbert Stuart portrait of James's great-grandfather, large windows, marble fireplaces. high bookshelves. But this evening her heart was heavy. Franklin and Eleanor had been up for the week end and there had been a long talk that ended in something unusual at Hyde Park—a family argument. In part it was a disagreement that had at its core a devoted mother's attempt to keep her son at home in the safe arms of his family estate, an attempt that was doomed to failure. But more than that it was based on her inability to understand why a man born to aristocracy should wish to identify himself with the crowd and with the crudities and compromises of political life. The young couple had just left, and she thought of them as they neared their home in New York. At length she closed her book, walked to her Snuggery next to the living room, and sat down at her writing desk to pour her thoughts out to her son and daughter-in-law.

". . . Perhaps dear Franklin," she wrote, "you may on second thoughts or *third* thoughts see that I am not so far wrong. . . . One can be democratic as one likes, but if we love our own, and if we love our neighbor, we owe a great example." She deplored the trend to shirt sleeves, she said, to the giving up of the old-fashioned virtues of family life, of tradition and dignity, to the tendency of some to be "all things to all men." "I cannot believe that my precious Franklin really feels as he expressed himself." For Sara Delano Roosevelt, it was ⁺he duty of the aristocrat to be better than others, to serve as an example for the less fortunate to follow. To her—and to many others like her—welfare was more personal than public and the past was more precious than the future. But her son, though understanding and affectionate, had moved beyond the perimeter of Hyde Park.

The letter was a mother's despairing effort to keep a hold on her son; it was, even more, a forlorn cry from the Hyde Park of old to the rising political man who had to be "all things to all men." In hardly a dozen years Roosevelt had moved from the narrowly circumscribed life of Hyde Park, Groton, and Harvard into the varied and strenuous roles of politician, legislator, bureaucrat, and war leader. The descendant of country squires, of Hudson Valley aristocrats, was dealing on equal terms with the shirt-sleeved men of labor, with the derby-hatted men of Tammany. No wonder the mother wondered why her son had journeyed so far from Hyde Park. But the journey had begun many years ago.

The family has been well called a miniature political realm in which habits relating to later political life are ingrained. In childhood, the most striking trait apparent in young Franklin's personality was his responsive receptivity to his family and, after a time of shyness, to servants. He was usually willing to come to terms easily with the dominant forces in his environment. It was not merely the ability to adjust but to find ways of getting along with a variety of dissonant groups and personalities at the same time without upsetting the delicate equilibrium that made him into the man he was. At Groton he had so little trouble with the masters that he had to redress the balance by deliberately incurring a penalty at the hands of "Old Nutty" to keep in favor with his mates. At Harvard, he managed to keep one foot in the exclusive clubs with the other in class political affairs. At Albany he won and kept the backing of farm groups even while establishing close relations with labor and other groups important to his political future. In the navy, he was on good terms simultaneously with admirals, labor leaders, "big navy" men, local politicians, and leaders of the Wilson administration, as well as some groups hostile to Daniels and the President.

The breadth and ease of Roosevelt's associations apply in a class sense as well. Born a patrician, he never gave up his class associations and activities. Even in the busiest days of the war he took time and pains to sponsor friends' admissions to exclusive New York clubs, to maintain relations with leading Dutchess County families, to participate in Washington social life. His friendships reached across party lines; he kept on friendly terms with Henry Cabot Lodge, Augustus P. Gardner, and other Republicans even when they vigorously attacked Wilson and Daniels. His class contacts were of enormous help to him: they provided entree to a remarkable variety of important people. Indeed, his class, cutting across political parties, had something of the power and influence of a city machine, except that it was bound together by personal ties of family and social rank rather than by patronage and food baskets.

Sara Roosevelt was probably troubled more than she needed to be that Sunday night at Hyde Park. For, in the supreme sense, Roosevelt never left home. Somehow he traversed almost a cross section of American life, moving ever into new groups and activities, without tearing his roots from Hyde Park. The general precepts and values he had learned from his parents and from Peabody were always very much part of him. His mother sometimes could not see in him the hard deposit of Hyde Park simply because Roosevelt could move out into other worlds with such outward assurance.

Outward assurance—but with a good deal of inward assurance too. The latter was another product of his formative years. Roosevelt was born with security, position, status. He had a powerful sense of belonging; he "knew who he was." He had no reason to feel loss of identity or a cutting of roots when he launched into new fields. He could shift roles with ease because he never doubted where he had come from and where some day he would return. There was ever continuity in change. So too, Roosevelt had no need of an elaborate social philosophy; unlike the intellectual, who constructs an ideology and then throws himself into it for the security it offers, he had a home of his own. He was content with its simple moralities, duties, and benevolence.

Roosevelt's later career was so dazzling that it has tended to obscure his earlier political attainments. Actually his rise before November 1920 was a spectacular one. He had made a notable record and drawn considerable attention both in Albany and Washington. He had won the vice-presidential nomination of a major party at the age of thirty-eight; even T.R. had been four years older when the Republicans nominated him for vice-president in 1900.

It is easy to explain all this away. Only a chain of fortuitous circumstances, it can be argued, could be responsible for the early career. *If* the Dutchess County Democrats had not needed a candidate in 1910, *if* 1910 and 1912 had not been good years for upstate New York Democrats, *if* the Sheehan incident had not occurred, Roosevelt would have remained a respectable New York corporation lawyer. One trouble with this "if" approach is that it can be completely turned around. If Roosevelt had played his cards differently in the Sheehan fight—if, for example, he had acted as intermediary between Tammany and the rebels instead of leader of the latter—he would have been a likely compromise choice for statewide office in 1912 or 1914 or 1916. If he had won such office he probably would have entered the cabinet or gone into uniform during the war; and in either case he would have been a leading contender for the Democratic presidential nomination in 1920.

Such an "if" approach is a fruitless one. On the contrary, Roosevelt's early career can be understood only as the dynamic interaction of an emerging political personality and a responsive environment. Despite his outward coyness during the decade between 1910 and 1920, Roosevelt almost constantly had his eye out for the main chance. If on occasion the situation was hostile to his ambitions, as in 1914, most of the time it was favorable. The political environment was not merely passively receptive to his ambitions; it was not simply a static backdrop; it had a life and momentum of its own. Both in 1910 and 1920, for example, the Democracy turned to Roosevelt, just as he had turned to the party in 1914. Time and place, prevailing ideology, and political configuration all played their part. Maturing in a time of social flux and flow, living in a strategic place in a strategic state, exploiting prevailing hostility to bossism and corruption, attaching himself to a party that enjoyed a decade of success after a half-century of repeated defeat, Roosevelt was in a favorable position from the start.

Roosevelt's success, however, was not simply a matter of sheer luck. Luck there was, of course—in his name, in his family and class connections, in his comfortable income, and in the assurance that he gained from all these. But these elements of good fortune would not have been enough without two other qualities of his: keen ambition and a capacity to learn.

Compared to his Uncle Ted's fierce drive to excel as boxer, cowboy, soldier, politician, and big-game hunter, the younger Roosevelt's ambition might have looked puny indeed. But it was there, and the more he became involved in competitive relationships the more it seemed to grow. The fact that Roosevelt could try for United States Senator from the most populous state in the union only four years after entering politics and at the age of thirty-two was a measure of that ambition.

To some extent Roosevelt's drives fed on his inadequacies. He could adjust quickly to new situations, he could act with assurance —but he could not always excel. At Groton he was neither an admired athlete nor a notable scholar. At Harvard he failed to make Porcellian. In New York City he made no special mark as a lawyer. When he aspired too high in state politics he came down with a bad jolt. In the navy he was not top dog; more important, he was not in uniform at a time when his country and his class expected its able-bodied young men to go to war.

Roosevelt's request, following the war, that Groton put him on the first division of the school's war tablet was ludicrous, yet highly revealing too. Clearly he wanted the kind of recognition that Uncle Ted had tasted so fully after his exploits as a Rough Rider. Following the war Franklin Roosevelt applied for membership in the American Legion. As the years passed his stories of his military experiences and risks overseas became more and more expansive—to the point where he was claiming that he had probably seen more of the war than anyone else.

But directing Roosevelt's ambition was a capacity to learn quickly from experience. In two major instances in his early political career he did not come quickly to terms with his environment, and in both cases his failure furthered his political education. The first of these was his attack on Tammany: it brought happy immediate returns in publicity and applause but only at the cost of endangering his hopes for state-wide political office. His response was to bury the hatchet with Tammany, although doing so discreetly enough not to antagonize much of his good-government support. The campaign on the League of Nations issue in 1920 was another example of defying political realities without avail. Cox and Roosevelt knew that the League was a dangerous issue, but by a combination of circumstances they campaigned largely on this plank. It was a gallant gesture and it failed. Indeed, the result was worse than failure: actually the election had been lost for many other reasons besides the League, but the Republicans could interpret the result as an endorsement of isolationism.

Roosevelt never forgot these lessons. He was to show keen appreciation throughout his later career of the principle that politics is the art of the possible. He profited from Uncle Ted's warning at Groton that being good was not enough—a man must be shrewd and he must be courageous. He had learned at first hand the wisdom of Machiavelli's advice to princes that they must act at times with great valor and at times with great prudence—that they must be something of a lion and something of a fox.

PART 2 *The Rise to Power*

FIVE

Interlude:
The Politician as Businessman

O N A W A R M autumn afternoon in the 1920's,
at the height of what Charles and Mary Beard later called the
summer solstice of Normalcy, the head of Burns Bros., coal dealers, embarked on the *Berengaria* for a vacation in Europe. Halfway
up the gangway he turned and looked down at a group of his
clerks assembled on the pier to see him off. With a cry, "Here's
luck, boys!", he pulled from his pocket a handful of silver and gold
coins and sent them clattering on the cobblestones. He watched for
a moment with relish as his clerks grabbed for the coins, and then
turned and disappeared into the ship.

Reading about the incident in the next day's *Herald Tribune,*
Louis Howe was shaken out of his usual hard-boiled attitude toward his fellow man. Grown-up men scrambling like so many starving children in the dirt—this, he exploded in a letter to Roosevelt,
was a perfect example of the business attitude of the day. More, it
was an illustration of the Republicans' economic philosophy of
money trickling down from rich to poor. He urged his boss to use
the story in future speeches.

If this was normalcy to Howe, others looking back on the 1920's
had their own memories of something that seemed to symbolize the
decade. Perhaps it was the monkey trial in Tennessee, or mah-
jongg, or bathtub gin, or Teapot Dome, or the Lone Eagle, or Al
Capone, or the expulsion of five socialists from the New York State
Assembly as "traitors," or the frenetic chattering of stock market
tickers late on an October day in 1929. Historians looking back
noted more basic facts—the low level and instability of farm income, the slow decline of labor unionization during the decade,
the spread of crime. Business boomed: automobiles, radios, refrig-
erators, cosmetics, telephones. Stocks climbed erratically upward;
profits soared. Advertising became a big industry. It was a decade
given over to Business, without muckrakers.

As for Roosevelt, he adjusted to the business decade with ease.
He became a businessman. Shortly after his defeat in the fall of
1920 he took a job as vice-president of a large surety bonding firm,

the Fidelity and Deposit Company of Maryland, in charge of its New York office at $25,000 a year (five times his navy salary), and he returned to the practice of law. During the next eight years he took part in a variety of business ventures. The most important of these involved foreign investments. Roosevelt backed a Canadian corporation that was buying up devalued German marks to purchase stock in various German corporations, and which later liquidated with high profits. He bought shares in another company that invested in German securities, and he was an incorporator of the Federal International Investment Trust, designed to help American investors take securities guaranteed by foreign banks in payment of credit balances due for American exports. Of these speculations, only the Canadian venture brought Roosevelt any profit.

These investments were conservative compared with some of Roosevelt's other speculations, however. He bought two thousand shares of stock in a company that unsuccessfully wildcatted for oil in Wyoming. He lost over $25,000 in a scheme to buy lobsters and hold them off the market until prices rose; lobster prices failed to rise. With Owen D. Young and others he started an enterprise to run dirigibles between New York and Chicago, but this soon proved to be, technologically, a misguided enthusiasm. A chain of resort hotels, the harnessing by General Electric of tidal power at Passamaquoddy Bay, vending machines, commercial forestry, selling advertising space in taxicabs—these and other schemes Roosevelt conceived with the enthusiasm and imagination of an old-time investment plunger.

A plunger Roosevelt was. To some at the time, this behavior seemed entirely out of character, yet it showed a side of the man that came into view many times in his career. As war administrator, as businessman, as President, he liked to try new things, to take a dare, to bring something off with a flourish. Taking a plunge, moreover, was easy for him. He had the security—his and Eleanor's inherited income and the availability of Sara's help in case of need—that allowed it. There was an interesting parallel between his business and his intellectual ventures. He could speculate with money because he had a financial heritage; he could speculate with ideas because he had a vague but deep-rooted ideological heritage to fall back on.

Even so, many of his business activities had more of a political than a commercial tinge. If he exhibited the daring of the speculator, he displayed, too, the cautiousness of a politician who refuses to gamble all on one election. Roosevelt in the end neither lost nor gained heavily because he seldom invested very much at a time. The political atmosphere was thickest at Roosevelt's Fidelity and Deposit Company office. The bonding business was a key part of the company's activities, and city and state politicians controlled a good deal of bonding. Roosevelt not only boasted of how he got business through his political connections in Albany and Washington but criticized associates for failing to cultivate the "big men" who had contracts to give out. He could later contend quite rightly that he had made a success of this business.

The most curious of Roosevelt's business activities was a post he took early in the '20's as a "czar" of the building industry. During the war and postwar years builders had lost the confidence of the public as a result of profiteering, shoddy work, and high prices. Their aim in setting up the American Construction Council was to form an organization embracing 250 national organizations, including architects and engineers as well as contractors and building trades laborers, and capable of policing itself. The builders wanted, also, to head off further demands for forthright prosecution of building trades associations under the antitrust laws. Roosevelt served as a respectable figurehead; more than that, he took a keen interest in gathering data and in long-range planning to iron out sharp seasonal fluctuations in the industry.

To some extent Roosevelt absorbed the political attitudes of the businessmen and promoters who surrounded him in the 1920's. Just before taking his building industry post he struck out at government regulation: it was too unwieldy and expensive, he said. Education, rather than protective legislation, he asserted on another occasion, was the only way to stop investors from losing money on securities. When he denounced governmental subsidies to the merchant marine as being too costly, he was probably reflecting the antagonism that other small shippers like himself had toward the big shippers who were getting most of the favors from Washington.

On the other hand, Roosevelt did not adopt all the root postulates that governed the business approach. He never accepted the idea that the businessman should make the essential decisions in society, or that government should pursue a strictly hands-off policy toward business, or that popular government was dangerous. Even as a businessman he was still something of a Wilsonian. He did accept, especially in his building-industry job, the doctrines of a basic harmony of interests among economic groups and of a measure of self-regulation by business. These ideas would crop up again after he became President.

One reason that Roosevelt spurned business doctrine was his aversion to any kind of sweeping theory; he thought and acted in terms of immediate problems, not of eternal absolutes. Another reason was his distaste for the cardinal goal of most of his business friends: money-making. He was more absorbed in the game of speculation itself than the financial outcome. Above all, even as a businessman he was keeping his eye on the main chance, which to him was politics.

And well he might, for no one fades from the limelight faster than a defeated vice-presidential candidate. Roosevelt's situation could have been especially vexing, since now another Roosevelt—Theodore, Jr.—was Assistant Secretary of the Navy, was inspecting navy yards and receiving salutes. But Franklin had no intention of fading away. He became president of the Navy Club, chairman of the New York organization of Boy Scouts, and a trustee of Vassar; he raised money for the American Legion and for the (Episcopal) Cathedral of St. John the Divine; he remained active in Harvard affairs, and he took a leading part in organizing the Woodrow Wilson Foundation, to help commemorate his old chief's ideals.

This period was to be but an interlude in his political career. He would lie low for a while until "this bunch in Washington show either that they can make good or that they are hopeless failures," he wrote to a friend. He told Stephen Early that he looked to him for many things in the days to come—"Thank the Lord we are both comparatively youthful!" But his prospects were suddenly changed.

ORDEAL

The summer of 1921 was an unpleasant one for Roosevelt. In line with American political tradition, Republicans were raking through the ashes of the preceding administration in a search for political ammunition. They felt they had a good case in a situation at Newport, Rhode Island, where after the war immoral practices involving liquor, drugs, and homosexuality had sprung up. Roosevelt had looked into the situation and appointed an investigating squad to get evidence. The investigators themselves, however, had used improper and revolting methods; when he discovered this Roosevelt had ordered them to stop. Republican members of a Senate investigating committee accused him of direct responsibility for the improper methods, which he denied. Roosevelt went to Washington in July 1921 to present his case, only to find that the committee majority was publishing its report unchanged before he could present his testimony. He was galled by what he felt was a breach of faith. He looked tired when he finally left New York for this vacation at Campobello.

Then on a sunny day in mid-August Roosevelt slipped and fell overboard while cruising off Campobello. He suffered a slight chill, but the next day resumed his usual vigorous vacation life. That day, spying a forest fire from their small boat, he and his family landed and spent several hours beating out the flames. Then in rapid succession Roosevelt went for a swim in a nearby lake, dogtrotted a mile and a half, took a dip in the piercingly cold waters of the Bay of Fundy, and sat in a wet bathing suit for half an hour reading some mail.

Suddenly feeling chill, he went to bed. The next day he had severe pain in his back and legs and a high fever. Mrs. Roosevelt sent for a doctor, who diagnosed simply a cold. One more day and Roosevelt could not walk or move his legs. Another doctor—an "expert diagnostician" who happened to be in the vicinity—thought it was a blood clot that had settled in the lower spinal cord, and then changed his mind and decided it was a lesion in the spinal cord. Only after two weeks of illness did another specialist make a correct diagnosis—poliomyelitis.

During much of the time Roosevelt was in agony. His bladder and the rectal sphincter were paralyzed and he had to be catheterized. At one time his arms and back were paralyzed. His temperature varied from very high to subnormal. He suffered also from acute mental depression, heightened by the indecision of the doctors and his failure to improve. All this time—and for weeks afterward —he was flat on his back.

Sleeping on a couch in her husband's room, Mrs. Roosevelt nursed him night and day during the first month of illness. "The jagged alternations between hope and despair; the necessity of giving blind trust to a physician even when the physician, cruelly pressed, could scarcely trust himself; the fearsome responsibility involved; above all the unpredictable oscillations of mood in the patient himself, which had to be ministered to with the utmost firmness, subtlety, and tenderness" were part of the ordeal she went through, as described by John Gunther. Sara Roosevelt had been in Europe and arrived home at the end of August to get a carefully written letter from Eleanor: "Franklin has been quite ill and so can't go down to meet you on Tuesday to his great regret. . . ."

Howe had gone to Campobello earlier in the summer and was fortunately still there when Roosevelt was stricken. His first instinct was to keep the public from knowing the extent of the attack. He issued vague announcements to the press, and he and Eleanor told the less immediate members of the family that Roosevelt was ill from the effects of a chill and was recovering. Howe finally let out the dread word poliomyelitis only when he could quote doctors as saying that there definitely would be no permanent effect. When Roosevelt was finally able to be taken to New York in mid-September, Howe managed to get him moved in his stretcher from a launch onto a luggage dray and then into a private railway car while the hopeful onlookers, by a ruse, were gathered elsewhere.

Roosevelt spent six weeks in Presbyterian Hospital in New York. After the first week there his specialist, Dr. George Draper, reported that he was "much concerned at the very slow recovery both as regards the disappearance of *pain*, which is very generally present, and as to the recovery of even slight power to twitch the muscles." The lower extremities, he found, presented a depressing picture. There was a little motion in the toes of each foot, but the patient could not extend his feet. Roosevelt could not sit up; only by pulling himself up by a strap over his head could he even turn in bed. When he was discharged from the hospital at the end of October the medical record reported, "Not improving."

Dr. Draper was most concerned about Roosevelt's psychological condition. "He has such courage, such ambition, and yet at the same time such an extraordinarily sensitive emotional mechanism," he reported, "that it will take all the skill which we can muster to lead him successfully to a recognition of what he really faces without crushing him." Partly because of careful handling by Eleanor and the doctors, partly because of some inner strength and stability, he became cheerful once the initial period of nervous collapse was over.

It took Roosevelt years to realize that he would never walk again. He was eternally hopeful. In the hospital he was convinced that he would leave in two or three weeks on crutches. Soon he was stating in cheery letters that he would completely recover. Repeatedly during the following years he told friends that he would soon walk independently on crutches, and eventually with nothing more than canes. Almost six years after his attack he wrote to one of his doctors: "My own legs continue to improve," but "I cannot get rid of the brace on that left leg yet. It is still a mystery as to why that left knee declines to lock. . . ."

Roosevelt spent seven years searching for a cure. He found a doctor in Marion, Massachusetts, who taught him some exercises. He spent parts of four winters on a houseboat off Florida; sometimes he swam and crawled around lonely beaches for hours. His great discovery was Warm Springs, Georgia, where warm waters heavy with mineral salts allowed extended exercise without overtiring or enervating the patients. He went there winter after winter and from a rather seedy resort developed it into a leading hydrotherapeutic center.

So much for the medical story. What effect did polio have on Roosevelt the politician?

A vast legend has grown up on this subject—namely, that his illness converted Roosevelt from a rather supercilious young socialite and amateur politico into a political leader of ambition and power and democratic convictions. The reason for this legend is clear. Roosevelt's battle with polio has all the drama and plot of a modern folk saga. The young man who had strode down convention aisles "looking like a Greek God" now had to be carried around like a baby, or pushed in a wheel chair. The man of only forty who had struck everyone with his animation and vitality spent hours crawling on the floor as he tried to learn to walk again. People jumped from the fact of physical change to the fiction of personality transformation.

The evidence is that Roosevelt's illness did not alter but strengthened already existent or latent tendencies in his personality.

Polio, for example, did not teach him patience. He had already shown this trait to a marked degree in his lengthy maneuverings in state politics, in his dealings with local politicians, in his handling of the endless trivia of patronage and position. Nor did his illness give him a sudden new confidence in himself. His confidence in his capacity to win battles, political or otherwise—"cockiness," his political rivals called it—had steadily expanded as his public activities broadened.

There was no basic change in his political ideas. Those who see a new humanitarian rising from the sickbed ignore Roosevelt's decade of immersion in Wilsonian progressivism. Actually, he showed himself after his illness, just as he did before it, as a shrewd politician who kept his eye on the main chance and who was willing to bend his own views in adjusting to political realities. His position on the political spectrum remained the same—a little left of center. While insisting that he was a good liberal or progressive—he used the terms interchangeably—he insisted, too, that his position was one of "constructive progress" between conservative Republicanism and the "radicalism" of La Follette and the Progressives. On matters like the League of Nations and prohibition, too, he took a politician's straddling position.

Doubtless his illness gave him opportunity for thinking out some of his ideas, but he took little advantage of this opportunity. He started two rather ambitious intellectual and creative projects— a history of the United States and an analysis of the practical workings of American government. In each case he wrote a dozen or so pages and then dropped the project. Neither fragment reflects any new or original ideas, although the few pages of the history reveal a marked socio-economic interpretation, as against the "great man" theory of history. He did a good deal of reading during his long convalescence—some biography and history, practically no econom ics, poetry, or philosophy, but both before and after his illness he liked books of travel and adventure best.

He was a man of many thoughts, not a man of trenchant ideas. A talk he gave at Milton Academy—a talk he considered of some importance and which was published in 1926 as a book with the pretentious title *Whither Bound?*—shows a wide-ranging mind in action but only a grab bag of thoughts. He skipped along, touching dexterously on the revolution of science, the need to accept change, the importance of equality of opportunity, the tendency of the majority to be progressive in outlook but divided over means. Utterly lacking was a central idea or unifying thread. Columns he wrote later for newspapers in Georgia and New York show the same tendencies.

Was there ever a time during this period when Roosevelt's future as a politician trembled in the balance? Clearly a conflict rose between Eleanor and Sara Roosevelt as to whether Franklin should carry on an active political career, as his wife hoped, or retire to the ease of Hyde Park, as his mother wanted. However intense the struggle between wife and mother, it was of little long-run significance. There was never the slightest chance of Roosevelt's retiring from politics. If anything, his illness made him want to be more active, more involved. "You are built a bit like me," he wrote to a close friend within a year of the attack, "you need something physically more active, with constant contact with all kinds of people in many kinds of places." In 1924 he left the law firm of Emmet, Marvin and Roosevelt, which he had helped form in 1920, mainly because estates and wills and the like "bored him to death," for a new firm of Roosevelt and O'Connor, where he would be working with "live people" directly involved in more active ventures.

All this does not mean that polio had no major consequences for Roosevelt and his political career. Physically he went through a transformation; as if compensating for his crippled legs, he developed heavy, muscular shoulders and chest which, he exclaimed delightedly, "would make Jack Dempsey envious." His disablement meant that he could move about only in a wheel chair or on people's arms—Howe ruled that he must never be carried in public—but his attendants became adept in these arrangements. His legs became, actually, something of a political asset. They won him sympathy—something he might never have had otherwise. Millions of Americans were electrified in later years by Roosevelt's public appearances—the tense, painfully awkward approach to the center of the stage, the bustle of aides and politicians around him, climaxed with Roosevelt's radiant smiles and vigorous gestures.

His handicap was also a convenience. Since he was perfectly natural about the state of his legs, he was able again and again to use his disability as an excuse for not taking part in political activities he wished to avoid. It was an excuse no one could contradict, until Al Smith did so successfully in pressuring him to run for governor in 1928. His illness also had the highly advantageous effect of bringing Eleanor Roosevelt more actively into politics than might otherwise have been the case. She joined the Women's Trade Union League and became a leader in Democratic women's organizations in the state. She often brought her Democratic and trade-union "girls" to see her husband. Howe, too, who had planned to go into business in 1921, stayed on with his chief during and after the crisis.

The chief political importance of Roosevelt's illness was simply in the realm of time. While it interrupted his vast political contacts and correspondence for only a few weeks, it postponed for years the day when he might run for office; he did not want to seek office until he had made as full a recovery as possible. This was something of a blessing, since the mid-1920's were not auspicious years for many Democrats. As it turned out, his return to politics was delayed until he was much closer to the years of the flood tide of Democratic strength.

DEAR AL AND DEAR FRANK

Right after the November 1921 election victorious Democrats in the state assembly races got letters of congratulation from Roosevelt. This was the signal that he was not through with politics. A few months more, and he was deeply involved in the maneuvers that preceded Al Smith's attempt to recapture the governorship in 1922.

Events of the 1920's were to throw Roosevelt and Smith into a tight political embrace. When their careers first intertwined, during the Sheehan shenanigans, they were ranged on opposite sides: Smith was a regular and Roosevelt a rebel; their alliance was to fall to pieces years later with Roosevelt in power and Smith in rebellion. But beginning in 1920, when each seconded the other's nomination at the Democratic national convention, until 1928, when Smith drafted Roosevelt for party duty, they worked in unison, with Smith as the senior partner.

The reason for the alliance was simple: each needed the other. Together they spanned, geographically, religiously, and socially, the breadth of the Democratic party; to win elections each needed the support that the other could command. Personally they were friendly and respected each other's political talents. Reporters could draw elaborate contrasts between the patrician and the plebeian, between the upstater and the New Yorker, between the Episcopalian and the Catholic, but both men were too big-minded, too worldly wise, to be concerned with such matters. On the surface during this period their relations were impeccable. Underneath they both had a seasoned tough-minded understanding of the complex mechanics and dynamics of intraparty politics; doubtless they both knew that theirs was essentially a political friendship.

Al's candor had impressed Roosevelt in the Sheehan fight: Smith as majority leader in the assembly had told the rebels frankly that if they attended the caucus they would have to vote for the caucus candidate. Roosevelt had been something less than candid with Smith in respect to the gubernatorial campaign in 1918; the assistant secretary later proclaimed that he had backed Al for the Democratic nomination, while actually he and Howe had been exceedingly cagey on the matter. He probably expected Smith to lose in 1918 and thus leave the way clear for himself in 1920, but Al won. In 1920 Smith lost his bid for re-election but he won over a million more votes in New York than did Cox and Roosevelt.

Even in defeat Smith remained the leading Democrat in New York. Roosevelt could no longer oppose or evade him, so he had to "join" him. Events of early 1922 gave Roosevelt his opportunity. William Randolph Hearst wanted the Democratic nomination for governor, and Murphy was letting him line up delegates. Smith did not want to leave his profitable trucking business, but he could never forget that the publisher had accused him during his first administration of allowing poisoned milk to be distributed to children in New York City. At the last minute Smith agreed to a draft and Roosevelt was chosen to issue the call. A cordial exchange of "Dear Al" and "Dear Frank" letters followed.

Murphy now wanted Hearst to run for the Senate. Despite tremendous pressure Smith steadily refused to accept the publisher as his running mate, and Hearst pulled out of the race. Roosevelt could probably have had the senatorial nomination, but he did not yet feel ready. Finally, Murphy and Smith compromised on Dr. Royal S. Copeland, a Hearst protégé, for senator. Roosevelt worked for the ticket and served as honorary head of Copeland's campaign. Smith defeated incumbent Governor Nathan L. Miller, and swept Copeland in with him.

Smith's victory marked him as a leading candidate for the presidency in 1924. Although Roosevelt carefully maintained good relations with Bryan and other national leaders of the Democracy, he had no alternative but to support his fellow New Yorker. He was keenly concerned, however, that Smith might command insufficient national appeal. Several times he urged Smith to speak out on national questions. But the governor wanted to stick to his New York problems.

Most of all Roosevelt feared that Smith would become irretrievably branded as a "wet" and lose all hope of gaining votes from the dry forces in the party. When the governor was faced with the awkward choice of signing or vetoing a liquor bill, Roosevelt wrote him, "I am mighty sorry for the extremely difficult position in which you have been placed over this darned old liquor question," and proceeded to outline an elaborate stratagem whereby Smith could veto the bill without alienating either side, and then call the legislature into special session to pass new legislation. Smith rejected the advice. He took a more direct and honest line of action, but one that left him more vulnerable to attacks from the drys.

"If I did not still have these crutches I should throw my own hat in the ring," Roosevelt wrote a friend in the late summer of 1923. Within a few months, indeed, Howe was lining up complimentary first-ballot votes for his chief among several delegations to the national convention. But this was not a serious gesture. At the end of April 1924 the governor announced that Roosevelt would head the New York Smith-for-President committee. There was talk that the Smith forces wanted Roosevelt for the sake of his name only, but immediately he plunged into the job of winning delegate votes for the governor.

This was no easy task. Democrats everywhere agreed that Smith had been an honest, efficient, progressive governor. But Democratic candidate for president? Impossible. At this time the Ku Klux Klan was not merely a band of nightshirters, it was a powerful subterranean influence that reached into governors' mansions and state assemblies. Even those Democrats who feared no "popish" control of the White House if Al won were reluctant to gamble on victory with a Catholic and a wet. Nevertheless, Roosevelt set to work. Through a massive correspondence and an elaborate intelligence system he acquired information on the personalities and politics of state delegations. For the first time in his life he saw in detail and on a national scale the confused currents and crosscurrents, the rival personalities and factions, the electoral law and machinery, that lay behind the pushing and hauling in the convention. He won few delegates for Smith but he added a course in his own political education.

Smith, after trying out several other speakers, asked Roosevelt to make his nominating speech. It was Roosevelt's first important address since 1920, and he rose above the occasion. He won the attention of the delegates with a speech free from claptrap and stentorian phrases, and when he called Smith the "happy warrior of the political battlefield" the phrase was so apt that it galvanized Smith's rooters and the last few sentences of the speech were drowned out. Mark Sullivan termed the speech a "noble utterance." Walter Lippmann called it "moving and distinguished." Ironically, when the "happy warrior" phrase was first suggested to Roosevelt, he was afraid it was too poetic, and, as it turned out, he used it prematurely, instead of waiting for the climactic final sentence. Nevertheless, the speech won him the spotlight and Democrats remembered it for years. Possibly Roosevelt was really drawing a picture of himself in the phrase happy warrior; certainly it was another case of his furthering his own career in the process of aiding Al.

But no speech could affect that convention. Ballot after ballot dragged on in the smoky heat of Madison Square Garden until it became clear that neither the forces centered in the East supporting Smith nor the forces centered in the South and West behind McAdoo could muster the vital two-thirds. Roosevelt took part in the conferences that, on the 103rd ballot, gave John W. Davis the nomination. Davis was a saddlemaker's grandson who had become ambassador to Great Britain and had been called "one of the most perfect gentlemen I have ever met" by the King himself. The kind of conservative who believed in civil liberties, Davis was a lifelong Democrat and a distinguished lawyer. But he was a lackluster compromise, without Al's color or McAdoo's Wilsonian background. As a weary, cynical gesture to progressivism the delegates chose the Peerless Leader's brother, Charles W. Bryan, for the vice-presidency, and departed.

The convention was a disaster for the Democratic party and a setback for Smith, but it was a personal victory for Roosevelt. His eloquent, moderate speeches, his gay, gallant air that made people forget his crutches, his loyalty to Al combined with his friendliness toward other factions, all left a deep imprint on the rank and file of the Democracy. Lippmann congratulated him on his service to New York, and Tom Pendergast, Democratic boss of Kansas City, told a mutual friend that Roosevelt had the most magnetic personality he had ever encountered. Praise from two men near the opposite poles of political life was a tribute to Roosevelt's broad appeal.

But his triumph was short lived. In accordance with political tradition, Davis men quickly moved in after the convention to take over the machinery of the national Democratic party. Roosevelt was left on the sidelines. Smith ran again for governor, but Roosevelt played little part in the state campaign. Indeed, the whole month before the election he spent in Warm Springs. His pessimism about the Democrats' chances was amply justified. Coolidge beat Davis by over seven million votes, and the Republicans won decisive majorities in both House and Senate. But Smith in New York breasted the Republican tide. His victory over Theodore Roosevelt, Jr., marked the end of the latter's political career and laid the ground for the reappearance of Franklin Roosevelt four years later.

The dreary convention fight and the dismal election results of 1924 left the Democrats divided and leaderless. "Something must be done, and done now," Roosevelt wrote in December 1924, to restore the voters' confidence in the party. But what? His almost singlehanded effort to rejuvenate the party in 1925 gave him a harsh lesson in the internal power arrangements of the Democratic party.

He had long worried over the condition of the party. His campaign in 1920 had confirmed his suspicions that the party's machinery was archaic and outgrown, as he wrote to Cordell Hull, national chairman of the party, late in 1921. Hull agreed but could do nothing. Three years later the picture seemed blacker. There was room, Roosevelt said, for but two parties. The Republican party was conservative; "the Democratic Party is *the* Progressive Party of the country," he insisted. The progressives had been badly divided in 1924. But there must be no overtures to the La Follette party; all progressives must get together in the Democratic party.

So much was clear to him. But could the Democratic party be made into an instrument for winning elections and governing the country? Not unless it was reformed, he felt. He was appalled by the lack of national organization—the national headquarters consisted of "two ladies occupying one room in a Washington office building," he said impatiently. The man Davis had bequeathed as national chairman, Clem Shaver, was out visiting millionaires asking them to endorse notes for the party. "Could anything be more of a farce?" Roosevelt demanded. "We have no money, no publicity, no nothing!" He wanted the party to unite more closely, to get rid of its "factionalism" and "localism," to do a better publicity job, to get on a firmer financial basis.

Roosevelt laid his plans artfully. He feared that the national committee would stymie any reform effort because the committee, consisting largely of old party work horses from each state, was the seedy fruit of the existing arrangements. He decided to bypass the national leaders and appeal directly to local party leaders, including delegates to the recent national convention. To 3,000 of these leaders he wrote a letter that asked for their advice on improving the party but consisted mainly of a statement of Roosevelt's views on what should be done. "I take it that we are all agreed on certain fundamental truths," he said casually, and he proceeded to name them: the national party organization should be more active and work more closely with state organizations; publicity should be improved; party leaders should meet more often to plan for united action.

His letters aroused all the ancient vexations among the rank and file: Southerners complained about the party's liberalism, Westerners about the city bosses, Easterners about Bryanism and the anti-Catholic and antiliquor forces. But most of the several hundred respondents, doubtless taking their cue from Roosevelt's letter, called for drastic party reform. They wanted more unity, better organization, more leadership, more discipline, less factionalism and localism. "The Democrats are just a mob," an Iowan said disgustedly. Most, but not all, wanted the party to become or remain a liberal organization.

Fortified by these opinions, Roosevelt proposed a small national conference of the party to discuss issues and organization. At first, prospects for the plan seemed bright. Well-known Democrats including Davis, Cox, Hull, and Daniels backed it, and there was much favorable publicity. Since some elements in the party suspected that the project was a bid by Roosevelt for party leadership on Smith's behalf or his own, it seemed imperative to Roosevelt and Howe that Shaver as national chairman issue the call for the conference. But this Shaver would not do. The party's first job, he said, was to cut its organization to the bone and pay off its debt. The harder Roosevelt tried to force Shaver's hand the clearer it became that the national chairman was following party leaders who opposed reform.

Who were these leaders? Roosevelt had little trouble finding out. They were the Democratic chieftains in Congress, who were far more concerned about keeping their seats from their own states and districts than in re-forming ranks for a presidential victory in 1928. Many of the Democratic leaders were Southerners who had piled up committee seniority as representatives of one-party areas that monotonously returned them to office in election after election. Although these congressmen maintained a congressional campaign committee, they had little unity or organization. Their real fear was that a concerted national effort by the party might jeopardize the position of some congressmen who could survive politically only by deserting the party platform and taking a position congenial to local interests. They would do nothing positive, Howe observed, unless driven to it by a purely local situation—but their districts were usually not of the type to reflect national trends or conflicts. The Democratic congressmen could hardly have been pleased, either, by Roosevelt's admitted plan of inviting only half a dozen Democratic members from each House.

"We have practically no leaders in a National sense at all," Roosevelt concluded; it was an "unspeakable groping about in the darkness." Howe undoubtedly reflected Roosevelt's feelings when he remarked that the selection of the donkey as the Democratic emblem was prophetic.

Roosevelt was also unsuccessful in reforming methods of party finance. He was indignant that Jesse Jones was raising money from big contributors. When Jones heard of this he wrote Roosevelt a surprised letter—he was paying off the party's debt, said the Texan, wasn't this enough? Roosevelt replied that the party should be financed from small contributions. He had estimated that if every election district of one thousand people contributed only five dollars per district, the Democrats could raise half a million dollars. Nothing came of this proposal either.

Nationally the Democratic party remained a divided, leaderless aggregation of state factions and sectional groupings. It followed precisely the policy Roosevelt feared most—a policy of opportunism, or as he described it, a posture of waiting with hands folded for the Republicans to make mistakes. The weaknesses of the party were to affect his plans for re-entering politics; years later they would plague the Democrats as the party in power and Roosevelt as president and party leader.

SUMMONS TO ACTION

Seemingly Roosevelt's political influence sank to its nadir during the mid-1920's. Then, in the space of six weeks, he vaulted into the governorship of the nation's largest state and became automatically a leading presidential possibility. The remarkable thing was not the feat itself but the way it came about. The sudden change in Roosevelt's political fortunes was initially less an act on Roosevelt's part than a summons by his party.

The collapse of his party reform efforts in 1925 left him as impotent politically as the party itself. He had no position in the party—he was now only the defeated vice-presidential candidate once removed—and some anti-Smith Democrats felt that the whole reform enterprise had been an artifice to promote the Happy Warrior's candidacy in 1928. Actually, if the project was intended to promote the interest of any one Democrat, it was that of Roosevelt himself.

His position in the state was ambiguous. For a time after the 1924 election he professed to be neutral toward Democratic candidates. "A plague on all individuals who would like to be President!" he wrote. Smith's capture of a fourth gubernatorial term in 1926, however, confirmed the governor's power both in New York and in the Democratic presidential race. During the pre-1928-convention period Roosevelt campaigned for Smith, even to the extent of spending two weeks in the Midwest trying to round up delegates.

He was politically close to Smith but not one of the inner circle who confabbed endlessly with their chief in the famous "Tiger Room" in the penthouse of a wealthy Manhattan contractor. During this period—indeed, during all the period between 1913 and 1928— Roosevelt had no office in the state aside from an unpaid position as chairman of the Taconic State Park Commission.

The American politician clings to power by keeping a foothold in one level of party or government even when he is dislodged from some other level. Ironically, Roosevelt's influence dwindled in his local Dutchess County party during the 1920's. One reason was his long absences from Hyde Park. He tried to break the grip of the old "courthouse gang" on the party, but with no success. He had about given up on the Dutchess County Democracy by 1928. There were "too many local leading Democrats," he complained, "tied up for financial reasons with the Republicans."

In view of all this, what is the explanation of Roosevelt's continued political standing—a standing so great that the Democratic leaders of New York hoped he would take the nomination for United States Senator in 1926 and drafted him for governor two years later?

Part of the answer is that Roosevelt continued to work hard at politics during this period. He wrote thousands of letters—letters of congratulation to winning Democrats, of commiseration to losers, of inquiry and advice to friends throughout the state and nation dating from his senatorial and navy days. Passing through Washington he made a point of meeting Democratic congressmen. Even in the South he managed to cultivate political friendships: he invited AFL officials to his houseboat in Florida, visited Bryan in Miami (before the latter's death in 1925), conferred with Southern political leaders at Warm Springs.

His position on party issues helped him politically. He was moderately liberal in a moderately liberal party. He believed the party should stand for "progressivism with a brake on," not "conservatism with a move on." He followed closely and commented knowledgeably on a variety of international and national issues, such as war debts, banking, conservation, the one-party press, and Mississippi River flood control. On touchy matters like prohibition he took a position midway between the party extremes. He managed in a state convention keynote speech for Smith to tread the liquor tightrope so adroitly as to win from Daniels, a dry, the encomium: "I think you took only a light bath and came out in fine shape. From that speech nobody would call you an immersionist like Al Smith; they would rather think you took yours by sprinkling or pouring. . . ."

It was easy for Roosevelt to turn down the senatorial nomination in 1926. He had just begun his Warm Springs cure and he hoped for rapid progress in the next years. Moreover, he did not feel cut out to be a Senator. Most important were considerations of his career. If he ran for senator and lost, he would have accumulated a string of three consecutive defeats. If he ran and won, he must, perforce, take positions in the Senate that would antagonize some wing of the divided Democratic party.

But the situation in 1928 was different. In that year Smith went to the Democratic convention with a commanding lead. Roosevelt again nominated the governor, in a speech notable chiefly for the fact that it was written with the radio audience specifically in mind; Roosevelt already had sensed the future political importance of this new medium, and he made effective use of it at Houston. "A model of its kind," the New York *Times* commented, "—limpid and unaffected in style and without a single trace of fustian." He also served as Smith's floor manager, but the show was largely in the hands of Smith's immediate associates. The affair—for a Democratic convention—was rather tranquil. Smith easily won the nomination on the first roll call.

Knowing of Roosevelt's business contacts, Smith asked him to organize business and professional men for the campaign, while Eleanor Roosevelt, who had become increasingly active in state Democratic affairs, helped run the Bureau of Women's Activities. Roosevelt did not participate too actively in the campaign; Howe usually represented him at headquarters. Roosevelt, in fact, was not happy over the way the campaign was managed. He objected to Smith's choice of John J. Raskob for national chairman, for Raskob was a wet, a Catholic, and a wealthy General Motors executive—factors, Roosevelt feared, that would only intensify the already strong anti-Smith feeling in the Protestant South and the Progressive West.

"Smith has burned his bridges behind him," he wrote his close friend Van Lear Black late in July. "My own particular role will be that of the elder statesman who will not be one of the 'yes men' at headquarters." He felt that Smith's lieutenants were excluding him from the top campaign councils. He was unhappy about the publicity program, which was being handled by a Smith underling with the help of the General Motors advertising experts. "In other words, it is a situation in which you and I can find little room for very active work, but we shall be in a more advantageous position in the long run. . . ."

What did Roosevelt mean by "in the long run"? Perhaps these words give some clue to his motives in the confused situation that shortly developed.

In mid-September Roosevelt went to Warm Springs. He knew

before leaving New York that party leaders wanted him to run for governor; Smith had already approached him. Why was Roosevelt so unwilling? First of all, there was his health. In one brief exhilarating moment at Warm Springs he had taken a few steps without canes. Two more years of Warm Springs, he felt, and he might discard them entirely (but not, of course, his braces, which he must have accepted by then as permanent). He was also concerned about the success of Warm Springs, in which he had invested a large sum of money.

But his main motives were those of a politician. He had long been pessimistic about the Democrats' chances in 1928 and his hopes had not risen after the convention. The country was prosperous; Hoover was a strong candidate for the Republicans; and Smith's vulnerability as a Catholic and a wet became increasingly evident as the campaign progressed. To run in 1928 might mean going down with the ship; but if Smith lost, all sorts of possibilities would open up for the future.

Late in September the state Democratic convention met in Rochester. Smith and his lieutenants anxiously canvassed the gubernatorial prospects. How much Smith himself wanted Roosevelt to run is uncertain. Most of the pressure came from state leaders who feared that the Republicans, with Al out of the way, would regain control in Albany. Howe, who was dead set against his chief's running in 1928, wired Roosevelt that only the jobholders really wanted him. He warned: "Beware of Greeks bearing gifts."

Whatever his own feelings, Smith took the lead in pressuring Roosevelt. Roosevelt made himself inaccessible during the first day of the convention, but Smith finally got him on the telephone. One by one the governor pushed Roosevelt's objections aside. Raskob would help finance Warm Springs. The governor's duties were not arduous enough to interfere with his program of recovery. Above all, the party needed him; it wanted to draft him.

Undoubtedly it was this last argument that moved Roosevelt. His long-term political hopes clearly limited his personal choice in the matter. Smith and the other leaders pressed their demands to the point where further refusal would appear as an act of disloyalty, an act that in itself might cause a bitterness in the party toward Roosevelt that would jeopardize his future prospects.

Smith seemed to sense the weakness. Would Roosevelt decline to run if the convention nominated him?

Roosevelt hesitated. This was a situation that he could not control. Smith saw his advantage and hung up. On October 2, 1928, the Rochester convention nominated Roosevelt for governor of New York. Thus it happened that Roosevelt, against his own intentions and the advice of Howe and with his wife unsure of her own mind, took the first direct step to the presidency. It was significant that his return to politics, like his original entrance eighteen years before, came about chiefly at the behest of his party.

When news of Roosevelt's nomination by acclamation reached Warm Springs the little cottage had an air more of gloom than of triumph. From Howe came a sour wire: BY WAY OF CONGRATULATIONS DIG UP TELEGRAM I SENT YOU WHEN YOU RAN IN SENATORIAL PRIMARIES—a reminder of Howe's opposition to his chief's ill-fated effort against Gerard in 1914. Soon Roosevelt's cheerful voice rang out: "Well, if I've got to run for governor, there's no use in all of us getting sick about it!"

The Republicans promptly took the line that the crippled Roosevelt was a sacrificial offering to Smith's presidential ambitions. The drafting was pitiless and pathetic, one newspaper said. Smith met the attack head on. "We don't elect a Governor for his ability to do a double back flip or a handspring," he said. "The work of the Governorship is brainwork." Roosevelt's answer was a bit more calculated. He had not been dragooned into running, he asserted. Smith had been willing to abide by his reluctance to run. "I was drafted because all of the party leaders when they assembled insisted that my often-expressed belief in the policies of Governor Smith made my nomination the best assurance to the voters that these policies would be continued." But the best answer, Roosevelt felt, would be a vigorous campaign around the state.

Both party tickets mirrored the New York melting pot. Roosevelt's Republican opponent was Albert Ottinger, a prominent Jew and an experienced politician who had won the state attorney generalship despite Smith's hold on the governorship. Running with Roosevelt for lieutenant governor was Herbert Lehman, also a Jew, head of a lucrative private banking firm and a heavy contributor to Smith's campaigns. Senator Copeland was up for a second term.

Roosevelt already had the nucleus of the staff that would go on with him to the White House. Recognizing his limited knowledge of current state problems, he asked Maurice Bloch, his campaign manager and the Democratic leader in the assembly, to find someone to help him. Bloch recommended Samuel I. Rosenman, a young former state legislator who had served on the legislative bill drafting commission for the past three years. In charge of the Roosevelt headquarters in New York City was James A. Farley, a contractor and state boxing commissioner who had recently been appointed secretary of the state Democratic committee. Edward J. Flynn, boss of the turbulent Democracy in the Bronx, worked for Roosevelt in New York. Howe, quickly overcoming his pique, had his hand in everything; one of his main jobs was setting up a number of "independent" committees for Roosevelt that catered to special groups such as businessmen and professional men.

Lugging suitcases filled with red Manila envelopes neatly marked "Labor," "Taxes," and other state issues, Rosenman met Roosevelt on the Hoboken ferry as the campaign party left for the 1,300-mile campaign around New York. It was mid-October, with three weeks to election. Rosenman had heard stories that Roosevelt was something of a playboy, that he was weak and ineffective. "But the broad jaw and upthrust chin, the piercing, flashing eyes, the firm hands"—these, Rosenman said later, did not fit the picture.

For three days Roosevelt ignored Rosenman. The campaign seemed to be a curiously unplanned affair. At first Roosevelt concentrated on national issues to such an extent that Bloch wired Rosenman: TELL THE CANDIDATE THAT HE IS NOT RUNNING FOR PRESIDENT BUT FOR GOVERNOR. . . . Roosevelt, however, enjoyed little freedom of action. He had to run on Smith's record as governor—an excellent record, but one that did not enable Roosevelt to proclaim bold new plans. And he had to run in the midst of the anti-Catholic, anti-Irish prejudice that was strong in New York State as well as the rest of the country.

This bigotry Roosevelt denounced in his first major talk, and he did so in a city—Binghamton—that had been a Ku Klux Klan stronghold earlier in the century. He told of the printed handbills he had seen in Georgia stating that if Smith became president Protestant marriages would be void and children made illegitimate. "Yes, you may laugh," he said, but it was a serious problem. "I believe that the day will come in this country when education—and, incidentally, we have never had a Governor in the State of New York who has done more for the cause of education than Alfred E. Smith—when education in our own State and in every other State, in the cities and the hamlets and the farms, in the back alleys and up on the mountains, will be so widespread, so clean, so American, that this vile thing that is hanging over our heads in this Presidential election will not be able to survive."

For two days the campaign train chugged through the tier of agricultural counties above the Pennsylvania line. In Jamestown, Roosevelt endorsed the state platform's pledge to name a commission to study the problem of farm taxes and distribution, but he openly went beyond the platform to say that he wanted to see "the farmer and his family receive at the end of each year as much for their labor as if they had been working . . . as skilled workers under the best conditions in any one of our great industries." In 1928 this was an extreme version of "parity"—more extreme than Roosevelt probably realized.

By the time he reached Buffalo he was using Rosenman's meaty envelopes of facts on state legislation. He showed Rosenman the art of converting a dull sheaf of facts into a political speech—how to make a speech sparkle with wit and irony, how to turn statistics into a broadside without seeming to use statistics, how to gird details around a central dramatic theme. Not that Roosevelt himself had become the accomplished speaker he was later to be. Many of his speeches had the air of improvisation, lacking any central theme. He made the mistake of repeatedly mentioning Ottinger's name. On the other hand, he knew and used such devices as attacking the Republican leadership—especially the leaders in the state legislature—rather than the Republicans as a whole. Generally his speeches ran the register nicely from cheery good will to indignation at the promises and "misrepresentations" of the enemy.

Because he wanted close contact with the voters, the candidate switched to an automobile for the campaign in the western counties and for the long trip through the Mohawk Valley in central New York to the Albany area, and then down to New York City. Behind lurched two buses, one for newsmen and the other for stenographers, mimeographers, and their equipment. Traveling by car enabled Roosevelt to shake hands at the crossroads. Speaking in halls was difficult; sometimes the candidate had to be carried up fire escapes and back stairs. Watching one of these entrances, Frances Perkins realized that this man had accepted the ultimate humility that comes from being helped physically, and accepted it smiling. "He came up over that perilous, uncomfortable, and humiliating 'entrance,' and his manner was pleasant, courteous, enthusiastic. He got up on his own braces, adjusted them, straightened himself, smoothed his hair, linked his arm in his son Jim's, and walked out on the platform as if this were nothing unusual."

Roosevelt delighted in telling his audiences of his strenuous campaign—of the seven speeches in one day, the side trips, being "kidnapped" to make extra appearances. "Too bad about this unfortunate sick man, isn't it?"

Batavia, Rochester, Canandaigua, Syracuse—slowly the caravan wound its way through country brilliant with fall colors. In Rochester the candidate advocated a broader state health program, a better old-age pension law, and repeal of the state's archaic poor law. In Syracuse, one hundred miles south of the outlet of the St. Lawrence into Lake Ontario, he declared that the people wanted "their" power sites—like the Long Saulte Rapids on that river—developed by a state power authority and not by a private corporation. In Utica, a center of dry feeling, he came out flatly against a "baby Volstead act" that would establish state enforcement of prohibition side by side with national—a position that made him almost as wet as Smith himself. Back in Manhattan he promised that the Democrats would enact a "real 48-hour law." In the Bronx he outlined an ambitious program of judicial reform. In Yonkers he mentioned scornfully that a leading magazine had featured an article under the title, "Is Hoover Human?" No one in his wildest dreams, he proclaimed, could ask the same question about Al Smith.

Did his campaign win votes for Roosevelt? Undoubtedly—but it was probably no more important an element than others hidden far below the surface of events. Ottinger was badly knifed in Erie County by a Republican faction there. In New York City some whispered that he was not a "good Jew"—and the candidate had to state publicly that he was "bar mitzvah [confirmed] in the Central Synagogue." But it was Smith who suffered real desertions. Thousands of New Yorkers who had given him their votes for governor failed to support him for the presidency. His Bowery mien, his harsh resonance over what he called the "raddio," his natty dress with the bright pocket handkerchief—all these clashed with their idea of the man who should occupy the White House.

On election eve Smith and Roosevelt glumly listened to the election returns in a New York armory. By midnight it was clear that Smith had lost both New York and the nation. "Well," Al is reported to have said, "the time just hasn't come yet when a man can say his beads in the White House." The race for governor was close, and returns came in slowly. Knowing the reputation of some Republican election officials upstate for holding back returns until they could estimate their party's needs, Roosevelt and Flynn telephoned warnings to upstate sheriffs that a "staff of 100 lawyers" would leave the next morning to hunt for election frauds. This was partly bluff, but it may have helped. Roosevelt went to bed. Flynn told him in the morning that he had won. Final returns were 2,130,193 for Roosevelt to 2,104,629 for Ottinger—a margin of 25,564 votes.

It was a hairbreadth victory for Roosevelt and an ironic defeat for Smith in his own state. The former ran about 73,000 votes ahead of the latter upstate, but only 33,000 behind him in New York City. Thus Roosevelt's tactic of nursing his upstate strength while at the same time keeping friendly with Tammany seemed to pay off. On the whole he emerged relatively unscathed from the maelstrom of factional desertions and party shifts. Even so, Roosevelt's showing was not impressive. He ran behind Lehman and Copeland; the latter had had the backing of Hearst, who openly opposed Roosevelt.

The Republicans won the presidency on the prosperity as well as the religious issue. The day after the election a "victory boom" in Wall Street roared the stock exchange to the second biggest day up to that time.

Amid POMP and circumstance and the booming of guns Roosevelt took the oath as governor of the state of New York on the first day of 1929. An audience of notables watched the ceremony in the brightly draped assembly chamber in Albany. Making his farewell speech, Al Smith described the progress of the state in the quarter-century since he had first come to Albany. Then he turned and looked up at the man standing next to him.

"Frank, I congratulate you," Smith said earnestly. "I hope you will be able to devote that intelligent mind of yours to the problems of this state."

Roosevelt responded in kind. The day was significant, he said in beginning his inaugural address, less for the inauguration of a new governor than for the departure of the old. He spoke of Smith's "wise, efficient, and honorable" administration of the state's affairs. The new governor handled skillfully the problem of giving Smith credit for past achievements while showing at the same time that great tasks lay ahead. "To secure more of life's pleasures for the farmer; to guard the toilers in the factories and to insure them a fair wage and protection from the dangers of their trades; to compensate them by adequate insurance for injuries received while working for us; to open the doors of knowledge to their children more widely; to aid those who are crippled and ill; to pursue with strict justice, all evil persons who prey upon their fellow men; and at the same time, by intelligent and helpful sympathy, to lead wrongdoers into right paths—all of these great aims of life are more fully realized here than in any other State in the Union. We have but started on the road, and we have far to go; but during the last six years in particular, the people of this State have shown their impatience of those who seek to make such things a football of politics or by blind, unintelligent obstruction, attempt to bar the road to Progress. . . ."

The ceremony symbolized a turning point in the closely entwined careers of the two politicians. Until the fateful election of 1928 their relation had an ordered pattern: Smith was the senior partner, Roosevelt the junior, and each gained political strength in the strengthening of the other. Roosevelt was eight years younger than Smith; if the latter had gone to the White House in 1928, Roosevelt, as governor or perhaps as cabinet member, would have been the likely Democratic nominee eight years later—in 1936, the year Howe had long slated for the capture of the White House.

As it happened, the political bond between the two men was snapped by the tiny percentage in New York State who voted for Roosevelt but against Smith in 1928. Roosevelt became the kingpin of New York politics, Smith the titular head of the national Democracy but, like all defeated presidential nominees, actually lacking office, authority, and title.

The new situation bristled with potentialities for misunderstanding. Smith had talked Roosevelt into running and could justifiably feel that Roosevelt owed much to him; Roosevelt could contend, with equal justification, that he had discharged the debt by working hard for the Happy Warrior in the campaign upstate. It was a bitter fact for Smith that many New Yorkers had voted for Roosevelt and against him; but it was a fact, too, that the new governor had jeopardized such support by identifying himself closely with Smith's cause. Finally, Smith not only wanted to remain active in state governmental affairs but thought that Roosevelt needed—indeed, wanted—his help. He did not realize that Roosevelt felt fully capable of taking over the reins and was eager to strike out on his own.

Sharpening the situation were the groups around the two men. Smith hoped his department heads would be kept in office by Roosevelt, and the new governor did retain many of them. But the immediate staff was another matter. Belle Moskowitz had served Smith with masterful talent and zeal, but Roosevelt did not keep her on. Nor did he retain Robert Moses, another official close to Smith, as secretary of state; in his place he installed Flynn of the Bronx. Farley took command of the state party; Rosenman became counsel to the governor; Howe looked after his chief's interests in New York City. One inner circle, intensely devoted, loyal, ambitious for its chief, took the place of another.

There was no open break between Smith and Roosevelt, only a growing strain and conflict that would come to a head when greater matters were at stake.

Any doubts about Roosevelt's ability to bear the burden of the governorship on his own shoulders quickly disappeared. For one thing, the burden was not unduly heavy. Smith had left a well-functioning state government; he had bequeathed no pressing problems calling for dramatic action or all-night conferences. Roosevelt, moreover, was able to handle the job without changing the pattern of his life significantly. Three or four winter months in Albany, April and May in Warm Springs, summer in Albany punctuated by long week ends at Hyde Park and travels inside and outside the state, several more weeks in Warm Springs in the late fall, Christmas at Hyde Park, and then back to Albany—this was the rhythm of the gubernatorial years.

In all these places Roosevelt lived amid a pleasant whirl of affairs in which political activities seemed to merge gracefully with domestic. His four sons and their friends, back from school or college, filled the air with endless chatter and clatter, whether at the ugly old executive mansion or in Hyde Park. Eleanor Roosevelt, still active in Democratic party and educational affairs, brought a variety of friends and associates to the family meals. Secretaries hurried in and out. Visitors to Hyde Park were struck by the picture—like a Currier and Ives print, Frances Perkins said—of the family sitting on the terrace: Sara Roosevelt reading in her wicker chair, Eleanor knitting, Roosevelt, an unopened book in his lap, looking at the Hudson where it came to view toward the south. Even Sara was drawn into the political orbit, entertaining his political allies and reminding him of the wedding anniversaries and birthdays of old friends.

Roosevelt moved amiably and deftly among the concentric worlds of politics, family, and statecraft. Ernest K. Lindley, a young reporter close to the official family in Albany, could not forget a scene at the executive mansion:

"The tea things are taken away. . . . One of Roosevelt's secretaries arrives from the Capitol with two brief cases filled with letters dictated earlier in the day. Roosevelt reads and signs the letters, occasionally altering one and putting it aside for retyping. As he does so he answers questions at length. It is St. Valentine's Day. In the adjoining dining-room, behind drawn curtains, one gathers that the table is being prepared for a dinner for the Governor's office staff. Louis Howe, the diabolic impresario of such occasions, has been busy all afternoon with cardboard and scissors and paints making a fancifully humorous centerpiece and valentines peculiarly appropriate to each guest. Occasionally a shriek of laughter comes through the curtain. One overhears a voice in the hall reporting that Howe's masterpiece is an excruciatingly funny valentine for the Governor. Roosevelt looks up for an instant, smiles knowingly, and returns to the dual business of editing his letters and answering questions. Mrs. Roosevelt slips in, hands him a piece of paper with a head pasted on it and whispers that he will have to draw the valentine for Howe. He puts aside his correspondence for a second, swiftly sketches an absurd picture of a man in a long nightgown, holding a candle, and puts on a nightcap for a finishing touch. He puts some caption beneath it which makes them both burst into laughter. Mrs. Roosevelt exits and he returns to his work again. He is finished in a few minutes and ready to go up-stairs to dress for dinner. Just then another visitor arrives, a department head of sober demeanor.

" 'Come along and talk to me up-stairs,' says the Governor. They start down the hall, conversing very seriously. At the entrance to the dining-room, Roosevelt turns aways for an instant, draws back the curtains, shouts triumphantly, 'I've seen it.' Shrieks and moans from within are his reply. He turns back to his visitor and, continuing their conversation, they enter the elevator."

THE POLITICS OF THE EMPIRE STATE

The state over which Roosevelt was to preside for four years is a proving ground for national leadership. Six presidents have graduated from its strenuous political life: Van Buren, Fillmore, Arthur, Cleveland, and the two Roosevelts. Other New Yorkers have been presidential candidates of distinction: Greeley, Tilden, Hughes, Smith, Dewey. Still others—men like Root, Stimson, Wagner, Lehman, Harriman, Dulles—have gained national leadership in cabinet and Congress.

The reasons for this prominence are severalfold. For one thing, New York is a big state—big in population, big in industry, finance, commerce, and agriculture, and, for the East, big in area. The Empire State has something of the might and majesty of the nation itself. New York City is the financial, commercial, artistic, and intellectual hub of the country and of much of the world. Its polyglot citizenry resembles less a melting pot, one politician has said, than a boiling pot. Stretching to the north alongside three New England states, New York embraces mountain chains, magnificent farm land, and the long valleys dropping down to the St. Lawrence River. The "peninsula" of the state that juts west is a little subculture of its own, with important industrial and transport centers like Buffalo and Rochester, a half-dozen colleges and universities, and strong political traditions.

To win statewide office in New York, a politician must court a medley of groups that are almost as multifarious as those throughout the nation. Not only does New York City have "more Irish than Dublin, more Italians than Rome, more Greeks than Athens," as its mayors like to boast, but an upstate city like Buffalo has dozens of groups of different national origin. The large Jewish and Catholic minorities are well organized; so are the main economic groups of farmers, workers, and businessmen.

The struggle for political power in this rich, variegated land has produced a robust two-party system, and the sharp competition between the two parties has prepared local politicians for national leadership. In this century no other state has surpassed New York in thoroughness of party organization or vigor of party leadership. Each party is virtually statewide in scope, based on county committeemen in the great majority of the state's nine thousand districts. Formally, each party constitutes a pyramid, every layer of which is a cluster of party committees organized for the conquest of elective offices, running from the precinct, ward, and city committees at the base, up through assembly districts to the state party committee at the top. Actually, each party has been led by small but shifting coalitions of state officials and city and rural bosses.

The party struggle in New York is often pictured in terms of New York City Democrats versus upstate Republicans, but this is an oversimplification. Republicans have run up slim majorities in Queens and Richmond in the city, and heavy majorities in the growing suburbs outside. The Democrats are strong in the industrial belt that cuts across the middle of the state from Troy to Buffalo. To be sure, the political issue of "who gets what, when, and how" sometimes does break down to a clean-cut tug of war between New York City and the rest of the state. With well over half the state's population, New York City has usually paid about three-quarters of the state's taxes each year, and has got back little more than half in the form of state aid. The state, moreover, holds sovereign power over the city, which legally is merely its instrument. "New York City," proclaimed Boss George Washington Plunkitt mournfully, "is pie for the hayseeds."

New York City, despite its voting majority, is unable to control the state government because the system of legislative representation in the historic American pattern gives representation to rural areas at the expense of urban. Long ago each of the state's sixty-two counties (except for two sparsely populated counties) was guaranteed at least one member of the assembly, and the membership of this lower house was fixed "forever" at 150, leaving New York City with a minority. Representation in the Senate was also rigged against the city. Thus the stage was set in New York for the classic tug of war between governor and lawmakers. The New York legislature has been called "Republican by constitutional law"; the Democrats have carried both houses only twice in this century, while they have won the governorship twelve times. A Democratic governor elected by an urban-based majority must deal with a senate and assembly responsive to pressures from rural areas and small towns.

All these factors were present in 1929 when Roosevelt took office. Elected mainly by city voters, he confronted a Republican legislature. Pledged to face up to some of the looming problems of industrialism and urbanism, he had to deal with men representing areas far removed from the tensions of modern life. Given Roosevelt's temperament and the power and pride of the legislators, it was doubtless inevitable that the two forces would soon collide.

He hoped, Roosevelt had said in his inaugural address, that his administration would mark an "Era of Good Feeling." He pledged that he would not let state business become involved in partisan politics and that he would not claim undue credit for accomplishing things on which he and the legislators agreed. This pledge was only a gesture. Roosevelt had written to Mrs. William Jennings Bryan less than two weeks before: "Eleanor and I are getting ready for a strenuous two years. I expect to be the target of practically all of the Republican artillery, but, as you know, I am a little like my dear friend, Mr. Bryan, in liking a good fight." Government business is inseparable from politics, and politicians win votes by taking credit for the things voters like and disclaiming responsibility for things they do not like. Smith had made great political capital by appealing over the heads of balky Republican legislators to the voters.

Given the conditions dividing Roosevelt and lawmakers, the era of good feeling could not last long, and it did not. It collapsed suddenly in April 1929 in a sharp quarrel over the power of governor and legislature to control the budget.

The exact issue was complex. After years of agitation the people of New York through a constitutional amendment had adopted the so-called "executive budget," intended to center immediate decision-making on the details of spending in the governor while keeping general control in the senate and assembly. The legislature could uphold or strike out the governor's items, but it could not add new items without his approval. Both Roosevelt and the Republican leaders flouted the new procedure. The governor's budget was not clearly itemized, and when the legislators brought the revised budget out of committee, it did not show just what items had been changed. Moreover—and this was especially galling to Roosevelt—the legislators ruled that itemization of certain lump sums had to be approved by the chairmen—Republicans, of course—of the two house committees as well as by the governor.

Behind the cloak of legal technicalities was the scuffle of politicians. The executive budget aimed to free the legislature of budgetary detail—but it was precisely in the details that politicians were interested. Legislators had debts to those who helped them gain office, debts that could be paid off in the currency of state contracts, jobs, purchases, and the like. Every legislator had a par-

ticular stake in state spending in his own district. Budget-making
in the legislature inevitably became a game of logrolling, umpired
by the two finance chairmen who, through their power to itemize,
bolstered their legislative leadership by judicious awarding and
withholding of budgetary favors to the rank and file of Republican
legislators.

Each side assumed a lofty posture of constitutional righteousness.
"I raise the broad question," Roosevelt said, "affecting the division
of governmental duties between the executive, the legislative, and
the judicial branches of the government." The legislators retorted
that "the rights of the people must be preserved from the arrogance
and presumption of an overzealous executive." Roosevelt seemed to
enjoy the fight. "I am in one continuous glorious fight with the
Republican legislative leaders," he wrote a friend happily.

When the legislature handed him the amended budget the governor pondered for two weeks and then vetoed the whole $56,000,-
000 bill. He admitted that this was drastic action, but, he said,
"Either the State must carry out the principles of the Executive
Budget, which embody fifteen years of effort to place the affairs of
the State on a modern efficient business basis, or we shall drift into
a hopeless situation of divided responsibility for administration of
executive functions." Roosevelt resubmitted the bill in the same
form as his first budget. The Republicans made the same changes
and promptly adjourned. They were fortified in their position by
a legal opinion from the attorney general, a Republican who by
an election quirk had won office in 1928 and who now, of course,
was siding with his fellow partisans in the legislature.

What could Roosevelt do now? His advisers were divided. Some
felt that he had demanded a too rigid construction of the executive budget amendment, that he should now retire gracefully by
signing the law, or call the legislature into what all knew would be
a futile special session. Others held that he had a sound legal position and that he should submit the question to the courts. Roosevelt decided on the latter step. The Republicans chose as counsel
none other than former Governor Nathan L. Miller, a Republican
who had never been troubled by having to share power with the
two finance chairmen, since, as Roosevelt commented privately, "the
group of three constituted a little family tea party which Miller
was able to dominate." In June 1929 a decision of the Appellate
Division of the New York Supreme Court sustained the legislature's
position, but several months later the Court of Appeals upheld the
governor's case on the major points.

Roosevelt had won the fight, but in a curiously un-Rooseveltian
way. He had appealed to the courts rather than to the people, perhaps out of a conviction that the issues were too technical for popu-

lar understanding or arousal. The position he had taken both in public and private—that he was fighting for "Constitutional Government, carrying out the original American theory of separation of powers between the executive, legislative, and judicial branches" —was a remarkable stand for a politician who in Albany and later in Washington would try to bypass some of the ancient barriers between the three branches of government.

In any event, the budget fight was only a skirmish in a larger political battle that Roosevelt was not to win.

THE ANATOMY OF STALEMATE

The trouble was that Roosevelt could find no way to overcome the stubborn fact that the legislature shared governmental power with him but mirrored a different pattern of political power. He tried the formula of nonpartisanship, but pious gestures could not wave away the realities of politicians' conflicting loyalties and ambitions. He tried appealing to the people over the heads of the Republican leaders, but the latter gave enough ground to take the sting out of public resentment and then took up another obstructive position. He knew that he could carry his case to the voters in the 1930 election, but the Republicans would probably still retain their grip on the legislature. And always he labored under the difficulty that even the Empire State was not strong enough to cope with problems that were national or international in character. The fight over St. Lawrence power—an issue closer to Roosevelt's heart than any other during his governorship—illustrated the intractable nature of the political stalemate.

After piling up in the Great Lakes water flows into the St. Lawrence River and then races down through a narrow gorge to the Gulf of St. Lawrence and the Atlantic. "In the brief time that I have been speaking to you," Roosevelt said midway through his inaugural address, "there has run to waste on their paths toward the sea, enough power from our rivers to have turned the wheels of a thousand factories, to have lit a million farmers' homes. . . ." Much of this unused power was spilling through the St. Lawrence. Roosevelt knew the background of the situation—how the legislature years before had given and then rescinded a free grant to a private company to develop the power of the Long Saulte Rapids, how Smith had conducted a long running battle over water power with the Republican leadership, how strongly represented the utility interests had always been in the Republican legislature. By 1929 the private power interests seemed as potent in New York Republican circles as before; H. Edmund Machold, the former speaker of the assembly and soon to be chairman of the Republican state committee, was a partner of Floyd L. Carlisle, the "power baron" of northeastern New York, as his enemies called him.

Campaigning in central New York State, Candidate Roosevelt had solemnly preached "Thou shalt not steal" and proceeded to belabor the Republican leaders as schemers and thieves. Now Governor Roosevelt told the legislature that it was intolerable that the use of the "stupendous heritage" of water power should be longer delayed by "petty squabbles and partisan dispute." The Republicans were not impressed. The next day, in his message to the legislature, the governor reiterated that the people's control of their water power could not be alienated by long-term leases; then he looked up at his audience and added with a smile, "This is one of those questions on which I hope we can reach agreement."

Skeptical laughter rippled through the assembly chamber. It was clear that agreement was impossible. But at least Roosevelt was able to define the central issue: How much should be done by the state in both developing and distributing electricity from the people's water power, and how much by private enterprise?

What was Roosevelt's answer to the question? He had no detailed program when he came to office, but he learned quickly. He learned mainly from experts in the field. Leland Olds, a student of utility regulation, was one of those invited to the executive mansion. He arrived on a late afternoon in February and got a warm welcome from the governor. Olds watched Roosevelt and Rosenman splash in a heated pool built in an old hothouse behind the mansion, sat wonderingly during dinner while every subject except the business at hand was batted briskly around the table. After dinner Roosevelt reminisced about Hyde Park history and the farmers in Dutchess County who could not get electricity. Then came questions to Olds until after midnight—long, searching questions about accounting methods, the valuation theory, court decisions, a people's counsel for rate cases. Watching these proceedings, Rosenman felt that the governor had exhausted both Olds and the subject.

By March 1929 Roosevelt was ready with a plan for the St. Lawrence. The power should be developed by the state, he said, but transmitted and distributed by private enterprise. The rub lay in the rates charged by the companies. Rate regulation by the state Public Service Commission, Roosevelt told the legislature, had become ineffective, largely because the courts had allowed high profits based on inflated valuations. Frankly proposing the theory of contract rather than the theory of regulation, he urged that the state be authorized to make contracts with transmitting and distributing companies, "under which a fair price to the consumer will be guaranteed, this price to make allowances only for a fair return to the companies on the actual capital invested in the transmitting and distributing of this particular power energy." This proposal was a departure from Smith's reliance on rate regulation by the Public Service Commission.

Roosevelt's only specific request of the legislature was for the creation of a body to submit a specific plan for St. Lawrence development to the lawmakers. To give the bills a bipartisan character the governor asked the Republican leaders to introduce them, but they refused to do this or even to let the Democrats bring the bills on the floor. The 1929 session ended with the measures quietly stifled in committee.

The next session saw a different outcome, largely because 1930 was an election year. Roosevelt had asked Howe to get comparative bills for New Yorkers using private power and Canadians using publicly developed electricity, and he was ready to use the findings in his fight with the utilities. The opposition was divided; W. Kingsland Macy, a rising young Republican leader in Suffolk County, demanded the resignation of the new head of the state Republican committee, an associate of former chairman Machold, on the ground that it was issues like water power that the "party is licked on." In January 1930 the water power bill was introduced in the legislature along the lines Roosevelt had asked. "A complete triumph," Walter Lippmann wrote the governor.

But this was only a first step. During late 1930 the St. Lawrence Power Development Commission appointed by the governor made a study of the situation, and Roosevelt kept the issue alive in his re-election campaign. The report of the commission in January 1931 was highly favorable to the project from both the engineering and financial standpoints. The commission majority followed Roosevelt's previous stand on state development of the power and private distribution through the contract method. Two months later a bill was introduced embodying these recommendations.

Then another altercation flared up—and once again it was over the power of the governor and legislature. Senator John Knight, Republican leader of the senate, introduced an amendment canceling the right of the governor to appoint the members of the power authority, and specifying five individuals by name. Roosevelt was indignant. He had warned the Republican leaders in a conference that he would not accept such a provision; he was forced to the conclusion, he announced, that the Republicans were trying to insure a veto. Power development, he said, fell under the governor's powers—"Executive responsibility must be armed with Executive authority." Both sides knew that the right to name the new authority meant control over the actual use of the vast power of the St. Lawrence.

Roosevelt's tactic was a direct appeal to the people. He dramatized the Republican move as a play by the utilities to balk the people's development of their own power. He announced his plan to go on the air a few days later, but just before the scheduled talk Knight and his followers surrendered. The governor used his radio time to sermonize that the influence of "Mr. and Mrs. Average Voter" was stronger than that of private corporations and a handful of political leaders.

Perhaps it was. Yet even with the bill finally passed and a Roosevelt-minded power authority appointed, the whole project was to fail. For now it ran into a configuration of stubborn facts—the fact that only the national government could make a treaty with Canada involving the St. Lawrence, the fact that President Hoover was sensitive to the opposition of private power and railroad interests, the fact that by late 1931 Roosevelt was already emerging as Hoover's likely opponent the following year. A week after Roosevelt accepted the Democratic nomination in July 1932 he asked for a conference with Hoover to discuss, prior to completion of negotiations with Canada, New York's share of the cost of development. In a sullen reply Hoover said that it would not "be necessary for you to interrupt your cruise by a visit to Washington."

As it turned out, more than a quarter-century was to pass before the swift-running waters of the St. Lawrence would light the homes and run the separators for the farmers of northern New York.

The flaccid hand of stalemate lay over all Roosevelt's major programs during his governorship. The legislature's response to his proposals wavered near a point of unstable equilibrium between the dislike of the rural-based legislators for Roosevelt's progressive recommendations and their fear of writing a record of negation and obstruction on which the next Republican statewide ticket would ride to defeat. Since for the most part they had little fear for their own seats and their concern for the ticket was not profound, the point of equilibrium was much nearer do-nothingism than action. And if Roosevelt somehow spurred the legislature to legislate, he confronted the bleak fact that even the Empire State was still but one of forty-eight, and its legal and material powers were sharply circumscribed.

Do-nothing government had become a far more critical problem during Roosevelt's second year of office than ever before, for in that year the Depression began to bite deep into the flesh and bone of the state's economy. Production dwindled, prices shrank, wages declined, farm income fell off sharply. New York City's Bank of the United States collapsed in the largest bank failure in American history. Thousands of jobless were soon walking the streets. As income from taxes diminished, the state's responsibility to prevent suffering increased. So did the need for drastic action—but the need ran head on into the stalemate in Albany.

Farm policy was a case in point. Roosevelt knew the plight of the farmers, who had suffered eight years of high industrial prices and somewhat depressed agricultural markets even before the advent of the Great Depression. He knew, too, that the difficulties were deep-reaching, involving factors of supply and demand, middlemen's costs and profits, tariffs, farm abandonments, urbanization, and others. "The ultimate goal," he said in his annual message to the legislature in 1929, "is that the farmer and his family shall be put on the same level of earning capacity as his fellow American who lives in the city." He understood specific aspects of agricultural economics—transportation costs, the national interrelationships of farming, the tendency of milksheds to cut across state lines, land misuse, the haphazard planlessness of much farm production and marketing.

His speeches impressed farmers and farm politicians outside New York State as well as inside. "We thought you were acquainted only with Wall Street magnates," wrote a Wisconsin official after Roosevelt had described vividly the gap between the prices farmers got and the prices consumers paid.

But the actual legislation passed was almost trifling compared with the immensity of the problem. More state aid for highway construction, for snow removal, for grade crossing elimination, and for agricultural research met some of the farmers' specific complaints but hardly changed the economic dimensions of their lives. As the Depression deepened in 1930 and 1931 more basic measures were adopted, such as a bill providing more credit facilities for crop production. The obstacle to more drastic action did not lie mainly with the legislature, which was fairly responsive to farm needs and anxious to stop the governor from capturing farm leadership. It lay in the iron fact that a single state could not cope with a national situation.

In the case of labor legislation Roosevelt faced both a hostile legislature and a nationwide problem. During his first term he won from the legislature measures providing a half-holiday a week for women working in factories and stores, changes in the use of labor injunctions, and a slight expansion of workmen's compensation. Only in 1931 did the legislature pass a bill limiting women and children to a six-day, forty-eight-hour week. More sweeping proposals, such as minimum-wage measures, met the inevitable—and often in some cases unanswerable—argument that the resulting higher costs might force industry to leave the state.

Thus the limited nature of the state program was a gauge of hard political circumstances, not of Roosevelt's own philosophy.

Operating even then a "little left of center," to use his later term, he anticipated many of the New Deal programs in his continuous search for specific ways to meet specific problems. As the severity of the problems broadened during the Depression, so did the scope of his solutions. In his thinking he was ranging somewhat ahead of most politicians in the Northeast. "Is there any possible device to be worked out along volunteer lines," Roosevelt wrote a Nebraska bank president early in 1930, "by which the total wheat acreage of the nation could gradually be exhausted to the point of bringing it in line with the actual national consumption figure?" Long before TVA he was talking about the need of public competition with private utilities, "at least as a yardstick."

The outlook of his major appointees was further testament to Roosevelt's general liberalism. His industrial commissioner was Frances Perkins, the slim, pretty, serious-minded woman who had been a social worker when she first met Roosevelt in his senate years, and who for ten years had served as a member, and then chairman, of Smith's Industrial Board. In making her commissioner, Roosevelt put her in an administrative post with supervision over many men—at the time a move that caused some lifting of eyebrows—and he left her free rein in running the agency. His advisers on water power and utilities included men who were later to become prominent in the New Deal: Morris L. Cooke, Leland Olds, James C. Bonbright, and, unofficially, Felix Frankfurter, a professor at Harvard Law School. Other future New Dealers advised him on farm policy, social security problems, and relief.

On the whole, Roosevelt made an impressive record as governor. Considering that brilliant achievements were impossible in the wake of Smith's eight productive years in the office, considering, too, that the legislature stood ready to spike any ambitious effort at reform, Roosevelt made the most of what opportunities he had. He won no single striking victory, but he operated with telling results in a wide range of state activities, including social welfare, government efficiency, prison reform, and utility regulation, as well as in the face of more serious problems stemming from the crisis in field and factory. And as the Depression deepened and state problems multiplied, Roosevelt showed growing power and vigor in meeting them.

Above all, the governor possessed the indispensable quality of accepting the need for change, for new departures, for experiments. He recognized that government was not a bogy but an instrument for meeting the problems of change. And he had the capacity to learn. It was these things that made his governorship truly an apprenticeship in politics and statecraft.

THE POWER OF PARTY

Early in his first term Roosevelt discovered that the state had a small boat for inspecting canals. Why not take it over for his own inspection trips? This was just the kind of innovation he liked. It was a comical sight—the large figure of the governor and his ample family and crew perched on the small craft as it poked slowly from lock to lock, with the official car and chauffeur and a horde of state police tagging along on the nearest highway. But it was also, politically, a shrewd move, dramatizing Roosevelt's interest in upstate affairs.

These excursions were genuine inspection trips for the governor, even though Mrs. Roosevelt had to serve as his eyes and ears. Carried from the barge to a car, he could do little more than drive around the grounds of hospitals, asylums, and other state institutions, but she quickly learned to find out the things her husband wanted to know: Did the inmates actually get what the menus listed? Were beds too close together, or folded up during the day, indicating congestion? How did the patients seem to feel and act toward the staff? "We have got to de-institutionalize the institutions," Roosevelt wrote to Howe in the summer of 1929.

Roosevelt also began his famous "fireside chats" during his first term. Direct and pleasing in tone, these radio talks were aimed especially at upstate New Yorkers, who got most of their information through the Republican press. Radio still faced a host of technical difficulties, and Farley had to send questionnaires throughout the state asking local Democrats how good the reception was from various stations. Roosevelt, of course, began the first of his talks with the claim that they would be nonpartisan reports. Actually, most of them were highly partisan thrusts at the Republican legislators.

Indeed, Roosevelt played politics expertly and tirelessly throughout his gubernatorial days. While he occasionally donned the cloak of nonpartisanship, he was essentially a party politician. The American governor is usually the leader of his state party, operating through lieutenants of his choice. Such was Roosevelt. But in leading the New York State Democracy he ran into the same weaknesses that he had found—and vainly tried to solve—in the national party in previous years.

An investigation by Farley confirmed Roosevelt's worst suspicions. "There is no such thing as a Democratic organization upstate," Farley reported bluntly. The few militant local organizations to be found were interested only in local elections; in some cases they traded votes with the enemy, backing Republicans for state and national office in exchange for local offices. Farley found much apathy and discouragement; there was little sense of "being part of a triumphant state organization." The state committee was moribund. Its lists of upstate workers were almost useless; its chairman, William Bray, installed by Smith, was an aged politico, lacking energy and imagination.

Together, Roosevelt and Farley worked out a scheme to bypass Bray and the committee and to strengthen the Democracy's roots upstate. The scheme bore the earmarks of Roosevelt's earlier thinking. A new organization—the Union of Democratic Clubs—would be constituted, not out of committeemen, but directly out of rank-and-file Democrats with energy and enthusiasm. With the help of the Union, stagnant local leadership would be weeded out and aggressive young Democrats put in command.

Crucial in the plan was the election of Farley as secretary of the Union; since he was already secretary of the Democratic state committee he could co-ordinate all party activities. This role Farley performed brilliantly. In endless trips about the state he patched up local factional quarrels, invigorated dead committees, hunted out political talent. Local leaders got used to receiving almost daily his urgently written letters, signed in green ink, imploring their ceaseless attention to the vital minutiae of political campaigns: registration, absentee ballots, first voters, election inspectors, literacy tests, endless lists of names. In 1930 Roosevelt eased Bray out of the chairmanship and Farley took his place.

Roosevelt tackled another problem he had long worried about—the Republican-dominated rural press. "I am not concerned about prejudice, personal stupidity or wrong thinking," he wrote to his friend Henry Morgenthau, Jr., after looking over a survey of opinion in rural areas, "so much as by the sheer, utter and complete ignorance displayed by such a large number of farmers." On Morgenthau's suggestion a press bureau was set up in Albany mainly to feed Democratic material to upstate rural newspapers.

Frequent tours of the state, radio talks, press handouts, and, above all, stepped-up party activity—this kind of intensive activity lay behind what was to be, statistically at least, Roosevelt's greatest election triumph.

"You and I have the same kind of sense of obligation about going through with a task once undertaken," Roosevelt wrote to Lehman in May 1930. The thought of not running probably never occurred to him. A confident state convention at Syracuse heard Smith laud the governor's "clear brain" and "big heart"; it unanimously renominated him. His doctrine, the governor said in accepting the renomination, was the same as two years before: "that progressive Government, by its very terms, must be a living and a growing thing, that the battle for it is never ending and that if we let up for one single moment or one single year, not merely do we stand still but we fall back in the march of civilization."

The Democrats had good reason for confidence. The deepening Depression was tying the Republicans into a political noose of their own making: having claimed credit in 1928 for past prosperity, now they had to take the blame for current hard times. Roosevelt had used Republican obstructionism skillfully to dramatize his program, and he was far better known than anyone the Republicans could nominate. Despite his protestations of nonpartisanship, his governorship had been a continuous campaign for re-election.

Two possible danger areas loomed for the Democrats. One of these was prohibition. Roosevelt had long hedged on this issue; he had expressed the fervent hope that it would disappear from politics. It did not, but it changed in a direction favorable to the Democrats. By the end of the 1920's—a decade of speakeasies, raids by Treasury men, gang wars, and intemperance—New York Republicans were finding prohibition to be a political liability. Roosevelt had no intention of running as a wet. But when he heard that the probable Republican nominee was about to come out for repeal, the governor moved fast to outflank him on the wet side. In a letter to Senator Wagner in September 1930 he favored outright repeal and the restoring of liquor control to the states.

It was a potent move. The Republicans failed to pick up much wet support, yet they outraged the drys upstate. The outcome was nomination of a prohibitionist candidate, which threatened to split off a sizable segment of the Republican vote.

The other problem was not so easily managed. The corruption issue, which had been seething for over a year, erupted a month before the election, after evidence had come to light of traffic in judicial offices. Roosevelt turned the case over to the state's attorney general, a Republican, and designated a Republican Supreme Court justice to convene an extraordinary grand jury. He also asked the Appellate Division of the Supreme Court to make a general investigation of the magistrates' courts. Roosevelt was directly involved in the situation because he had made a routine short-term appointment of a Tammany man to a General Sessions judgeship, and the judge was alleged to have bought his place from Tammany for thirty thousand dollars.

The Republicans saw a grand opportunity to force Roosevelt into a political trap: if he cracked down on Tammany, they figured, he might lose election support from the organization, and if he failed to act he could be dubbed a Tammany pawn. Staking most of their hopes on this move, they nominated for governor the United States attorney for the southern district of New York, a pugnacious redhead named Charles H. Tuttle, who had nosed along the labyrinthine trail between Tammany and the judges and had won some well-publicized indictments.

Roosevelt evaded the net by the tactic of compromise. He took formal steps to enable the Republicans to investigate Tammany, but he never allowed a situation to arise where he was arrayed directly in an investigatory attack on Tammany. This awkward posture took considerable explaining, especially to friends who wondered why a man who had a reputation for acting quickly and firmly in some fields should stand on legal niceties in this one. The situation, Roosevelt wrote to an anxious Harvard classmate and rector in New York City, was not one between Tammany and himself; "it is one between constitutional government and a political campaign. More than that, it is one between the retention of constitutional government and a breaking down of the safeguards of liberty in the same way that they have been broken down both in the Italy of Mussolini and in the Russia of Lenin." He went on to describe the limitations on the power of the governor to investigate.

"In thinking this over, for the love of Mike," Roosevelt ended his letter, "remember that I am just as anxious as you are to root out this rottenness, but that on January 1st, 1929, I took a certain oath of office." Undoubtedly Roosevelt's stand lost him the support of some independent Democrats in New York City. While the Democratic New York *Times* and the independent Republican *Sun* backed him, the *World,* which was strongly pro-Smith, withheld its support and the *News* came out for Tuttle.

The campaign revolved around Tuttle's ceaseless hammering at Roosevelt on the corruption issue and the governor's insistent attempt to focus the debate on water power, agriculture, labor, public works, utility regulation, and other general state matters. Was his opponent running for governor or district attorney? Roosevelt asked caustically. Following his usual procedure, he devoted each campaign speech to a defense of a major state program. In Buffalo he read a strong letter of endorsement by President Green of the AFL. In Rochester he talked about prisons, hospitals, public works. In Syracuse he described the high cost of electricity to the housewife in terms so vivid and concrete that people around there long after were talking about the "waffle iron campaign."

But people were interested in another issue, too: jobs. Democratic candidates throughout the country were taunting the Republicans for failing to cope with depression after all the talk about the "full dinner pail" in 1928. Secure in the White House for at least another two years, President Hoover was already beginning to play the historic role he was to hold for more than a generation: the scapegoat for hard times. In his speech in Buffalo—an especially hard-hit city—Roosevelt quoted some of the Republican claims of 1928. He looked out at his audience. "Those extracts read strangely tonight." He cited them, he added, not to gain partisan advantage but to show that no party had any monopoly on prosperity.

The Republicans counterattacked Roosevelt later in the campaign by bringing up reserves from Washington in the form of cabinet members, most notably the Secretary of State, Henry L. Stimson. By this time Tuttle needed help; his one-issue campaign was losing public interest, partly because, busy electioneering, he was running low on new revelations. In a radio speech from Washington, Stimson said that Roosevelt had "shown his unfitness to deal with the great crisis now confronting New York State."

Roosevelt's reply—given in New York City on the eve of the election—carefully played on state pride and resentment against the national administration. "I say to these gentlemen: We shall be grateful if you will return to your posts in Washington, and bend your efforts and spend your time solving the problems which the whole Nation is bearing under your Administration. Rest assured that we of the Empire State can and will take care of ourselves and our problems."

Roosevelt defeated Tuttle by 1,770,342 to 1,045,341, a margin of 725,001 votes. More remarkable, he won forty-one out of the fifty-seven counties outside New York City, carrying upstate New York by 167,784, an unprecedented feat for a Democrat. Most of this margin was due to the splitting tactics of the prohibitionist candidate; but even without this helpful intervention, Roosevelt would have run close to Tuttle upstate. His half-million plurality in New York City vindicated his straddling policy on the corruption issue.

It was a strikingly personal victory. All the other statewide Democratic candidates won by smaller majorities than Roosevelt; more important, the Republicans still held majorities in the state senate and assembly, and the Democrats failed to capture a single one of the twenty Republican congressional seats upstate. Despite all Farley's work, it was an executive, not a legislative—and thus not a party—victory.

But it was no time for cavil. A Republican-controlled legislature had its uses for Roosevelt. And bigger things lay ahead. Three weeks after the election he wrote Farley about the latter's work: "It is not merely a fine record, but a great opportunity for us to consolidate the gains.

"When I think of the difficulties of former State Chairmen with former Governors and vice versa (!), I have an idea that you and I make a combination which has not existed since Cleveland and Lamont—and that is so long ago that neither you nor I know anything about it except from history books."

SEVEN *Nomination by a Hairbreadth*

THE DAY AFTER his re-election Farley and Howe threw Roosevelt's hat into the presidential ring. "I do not see how Mr. Roosevelt can escape becoming the next presidential nominee of his party," Farley proclaimed in a victory statement, "even if no one should raise a finger to bring it about." When Farley notified the governor of this move, Roosevelt laughed. "Whatever you said, Jim, is all right with me."

Never before this occasion, according to Farley, had he discussed Roosevelt's candidacy with his chief. This is not surprising. Even with his associates Roosevelt had maintained the fiction of concentrating solely on New York affairs. He had a politician's superstition against planning campaigns too far ahead; moreover, he knew that a victory in 1930 was the decisive step to victory in 1932. The effect of his re-election was to fix the timetable; 1932 was to be the year.

"Eddie," the governor said to Flynn a week or two after his election, ". . . I believe I can be nominated for the Presidency in 1932 on the Democratic ticket."

He might have added, "and elected." With every new slump in economic conditions in 1930, Democratic hopes for 1932 went soaring. Rarely has a party been caught so neatly in a cul-de-sac of its own making as the Republicans during the Depression. Prosperity was safe under the G.O.P., their orators had chanted in 1928; they had made it the chief issue of the campaign. HOOVER AND HAPPINESS OR SMITH AND SOUP HOUSES? WHICH SHALL IT BE? G.O.P. signs had demanded. The position was as intellectually dishonest as it was politically dangerous for the Republicans, following in general a laissez-faire ideology, shrank from any real commitment to national governmental action to prevent depression. But the strategy had worked.

And now breadlines were stretching block after block, soup kitchens were handing out thin porridge and coffee, and "Hoovervilles"—little settlements of shacks, discarded cars, and packing boxes—were springing up near the dumps and mud flats of big

123

cities. Yet the Depression was a remarkably passive affair. There were few riots or even strikes. The American people seemed benumbed. Or perhaps they were simply waiting—waiting for the upturn that had always come in past depressions, perhaps waiting for their leaders to act. Hoover acted: he organized private relief activities, ordered federal departments to economize, asked businessmen to maintain wage standards, created the Reconstruction Finance Corporation to lend funds to banks and other institutions, reluctantly supported federal aid to states for relief. But nothing he did seemed to help.

Roosevelt's first reaction to the stock market crash in 1929 was more that of a Republican businessman than a Democratic politician. While the market was tumbling on October 24 a newspaper asked for his outlook. He did not know detailed conditions, Roosevelt wired back, but he firmly believed fundamental industrial conditions to be sound. Shortly afterward, in a Poughkeepsie speech, he assailed speculation. Five weeks later, after stock prices had reached their 1929 low point, he told Howe, "It is just possible that the recent little Flurry down town will make the prices comparatively low," and asked him to check on the condition of certain stocks.

Curiously, it took Roosevelt some time to realize that finally there had come the hard times he had long prognosticated would break the Republicans' grip on the White House. By the fall of 1930, however, he was exploiting the situation in his campaign speeches. In December of that year came a warning to his office from William Allen White in Kansas.

"These are great days for you Democrats but don't be too cagey," wrote the editor of the Emporia *Gazette*. "If the old brig rights herself within the next year, whether by reason of good seamanship or by the chance of wind or wave, the people will forget that she ever listed. But what I fear is that if she does not right herself soon the crew will come running out of the Fo'c's'le, and throw the whole brass colored quarter deck crowd into the sea, Democrats, Republicans, and all."

But the old brig did not right herself. As the "black depression" came to grip the urban sections of his state, Roosevelt took increasingly drastic action. His first major step had been to set up in March 1930 an emergency unemployment committee, headed by a banker, to consider long-range proposals for stabilizing unemployment, and later in the year steps were taken for immediate relief of distress and for expanded public works. At a time when the American Federation of Labor was still opposed to compulsory unemployment insurance as a "dole or handout," Roosevelt favored such a plan, and eventually he proposed a state program. In August 1931 he got the legislature to create the Temporary Emergency

Relief Administration. Twenty millions were appropriated to tide desperate New Yorkers over the melancholy winter of 1931-32, and a sallow, sharp-faced young social worker named Harry Hopkins came in to run the agency.

During most of the early Depression years Roosevelt did not differ fundamentally from Hoover over domestic relief and recovery policies. Both opposed direct relief spending by the federal government; both favored putting main reliance on state and private agencies; both believed that government should cut its regular expenses to the bone. Yet each presented a different image to the public—Roosevelt, that of a man in motion, Hoover, a man stuck fast. Roosevelt, of course, made the most of his position. Early in 1931 he called and presided over a well-publicized regional conference in Albany of governors of industrial states. And he skillfully used opposition in the legislature as a foil.

"I am glad that you believe with me," Roosevelt wrote Bernard M. Baruch in December 1931, "that issues this coming year will be more economic than anything else." The nation demanded, he added, a more definite leadership.

THE POLITICAL USES OF CORRUPTION

The story of Roosevelt's presidential nomination is the story of how a battle almost won in the early stages was almost lost by mistake after mistake during the last critical months of the contest.

Roosevelt began the fight with tremendous advantages. The Democrats were hungry for a presidential winner; after the gubernatorial victory in 1930 he became a leading choice for 1932. His rural appeal impressed a party whose strength in the East was grounded in urban areas. His good record as governor, his name, his standing in the most populous state, his Wilsonian background, his radio voice, and his appearance all gave him a long head start. How could he lose?

The dangers were threefold. Scenting Democratic victory, a host of Democratic candidates, including favorite sons, was entering the fray. Roosevelt's lead made him the object of concerted action by his rivals. And he had to win not a mere majority but two-thirds of the votes in the convention, for the Democrats still had their century-old rule requiring a candidate to poll this fraction of votes for the party nomination.

Partly to cloak his front-runner position, Roosevelt long kept up the pretense that he was not a candidate for President. "I am sitting tight, sawing wood, and keeping my mouth shut—at least for the present!" he said in March 1931. How anyone could want to be President in such a period he could not understand, he remarked even to friends. His tactic was in sharp contrast to that of Albert C. Ritchie, governor of Maryland, who was eying the nomination race. Asked by a newspaper if he would like to be President Ritchie said, "Of course I would. Who wouldn't?"

Roosevelt's method was to leave the actual management of the campaign to Howe and Farley in New York City and to his friends throughout the country, while making the key decisions himself. His two lieutenants formed a remarkable combination. Howe—more gnarled and hollow-eyed than ever—served as the governor's adviser, spur, and confidant. Implacably jealous of anyone who got too close to his "Franklin," darkly suspicious of anyone who was not 100 per cent for Roosevelt's cause, armed with a Machiavellian flair for hunting out the complex trails of influence, Howe tirelessly played the game of plot and counterplot, working off his frustrations in tirades against his rivals and enemies. Quite the opposite was Farley. He could get along with anybody, even with Howe, which was part of his effectiveness. He had a large limber body to insert between warring factions, and a smooth pink face that looked as if it were sanded and buffed by his intermediary's role. He was a joiner, a mixer, a glad-hander who could remember names—anybody's name.

Part of Roosevelt's strength stemmed from the pains he took not to alienate any major faction of the party. To be sure, he had come out for repeal of the Eighteenth Amendment in 1930, but he played down the subject in following years. He had fully retreated from his support in 1920 of American entry into the League of Nations—so much so as to bring scores of bitter letters from disappointed League supporters who remembered his stand in 1920. He favored U.S. adherence to the World Court, but refused to come out publicly for it. Even on the historic Democratic issue of the tariff Roosevelt straddled; he placated high-tariff groups in the West by suggesting to them that the tariff was really a local matter. On most economic and social matters, however, Roosevelt was ahead of the drift of opinion.

The upshot of this situation was that the South looked on Roosevelt as a wet but a reasonable wet, the West saw him as a progressive (largely because of his water-power policies), the East rated him as mildly wet and reasonably liberal.

Roosevelt's first real move for the nomination was well disguised. In July 1931 Farley set out for Seattle to attend a convention of the Benevolent and Protective Order of Elks, of which he was a high dignitary. Armed with a map, he and Roosevelt had laid out an elaborate trip through eighteen states, where Farley could stop off for chats with state chairmen ostensibly about party affairs but actually to sound out sentiment for the New York governor. For nineteen days Farley shook hands, carefully noted names, and warily discussed candidates. Where he found Roosevelt supporters he urged them to try to get their state delegations pledged to his chief as early as possible. "Have indicated that they must all get away from the 'favorite-son' idea," Farley reported to the governor, "on the theory that it is only used for the purpose of tying up blocks of delegates to be manipulated." He warned delegates not to expect that by plumping for their governors or senators they could trade off support for the vice-presidential nomination.

Farley's findings showed the extent of Roosevelt's strength even before his active candidacy. In California he found "no sentiment for any one else at the moment except for the Governor." He thought everything was "all right in Illinois." Roosevelt's friends in Indiana would have "absolute control of the delegation. . . ." In half a dozen more states the situation was at least satisfactory. Farley was bubbling over with optimism by the time he returned to New York.

Actually, Farley's reports were generally far too enthusiastic and in some cases misleading. A newcomer to national politics, he did not realize the extent of factionalism in some states; his one- or two-day trips did not give him time to explore the many centers of power. Party leaders who promised to deliver solid delegations simply were not able to come across. The attachments of delegates to presidential candidates were inextricably tied up with conflicting loyalties to a variety of candidates for state and local offices.

This miscalculation was important, for it led Farley to pin his hopes and strategy on an overwhelming show of strength at the convention and to make repeated predictions of victory on the first ballot. To be sure, these predictions helped bring some delegates off the fence, but they also helped concentrate the pack in opposition to the front runner. And they prompted the question: What if Roosevelt does not win on the first ballot?

All during 1931 trouble was piling up for Roosevelt in his own state. The great strength of a New York governor seeking the presidential nomination lies in the fat bloc of delegates he can take to the convention. By all the ordinary rules Roosevelt should have commanded such support in 1932. But he did not.

The trouble arose on his traditionally weak sector, Tammany. One of the incidental effects of the Depression was to put severe pressure on the Hall for jobs and favors. Boss Murphy had been succeeded by men unable to provide leadership or discipline. Most of the corruption was petty, but it reached up to the higher Tammany levels and erupted in dramatic incidents—the murder of a redheaded adventuress, the revelations of Sheriff Thomas Farley about graft and his "little tin cup"—that helped make news of corruption for months on end.

Once again Roosevelt had to walk the tightrope, but this time he leaned to the anti-Tammany side. He co-operated with the Republicans in establishing a well-armed legislative investigation committee, he appointed the redoubtable Samuel Seabury to look into charges against the office of the Tammany district attorney, and he gravely considered charges of laxness against Tammany's

June 1932, William Ireland
Columbus *Dispatch*

beloved jack-a-dandy, Mayor James J. Walker of New York City. Roosevelt also was most circumspect in his relations with Tammany leaders, often using Howe, Rosenman, or his law partner, Basil O'Connor, as intermediaries.

Mildly spanking Tammany was perfectly safe for Roosevelt as long as the Hall had no other candidate to support for the presidential nomination. There was Smith, of course, but for several years Smith's relations with the organization had been cool. But toward the end of 1931, as Tammany saw Roosevelt under mounting pressure from anti-Tammany forces and from Republicans eager to split the New York Democracy, the Hall looked around for a way out of its predicament. During this very period Smith was making up his mind to seek the nomination. A *rapprochement* between Smith and the Hall was in order.

Smith's entry into the race caught the Roosevelt forces off balance; for a long time they refused to believe that he was anything but a stalking-horse for some other candidate. Farley and Flynn had begun working for Roosevelt only on Smith's assurances that he would not run in 1932. Sickened by the wave of religious prejudice that had helped beat him in 1928, Smith doubtless meant this disavowal at the time. But two things changed his mind. One was the increasing indication during 1931 that the Democrats would win. The other was the steady deterioration of his relations with Roosevelt.

The smoldering conflict broke out into the open in the November election of 1931. Roosevelt was sponsoring a $20,000,000 reforestation amendment as Referendum No. 3, which Smith attacked in a blistering speech at a Tammany rally. "What a queer thing that was for Al to fight so bitterly on No. 3!" the governor wrote to a friend. "I cannot help remembering the fact that while he was Governor I agreed with almost all the policies he recommended but I was against one or two during those eight years. However, for the sake of party solidarity, I kept my mouth shut. . . ." Passage of the amendment was seen as proof of Roosevelt's influence in the state.

In December Roosevelt got definite word as to the extent of Smith's feeling in a letter from Clark Howell, publisher of the Atlanta *Constitution*, who had just visited Smith in his office in the Empire State Building. After some preliminaries, Howell had asked Smith whether there was any ground for personal hostility on his part against Roosevelt. Smith had answered that their personal relations were pleasant, but then he rose, stamped his foot, according to Howell, and demanded: "Do you know, by God, that he has never consulted me about a damn thing since he has been Governor? He has taken bad advice and from sources not friendly to me. He has ignored me!" Raising his voice and banging his fist on the table Smith went on to charge that Roosevelt had refused to tell Smith about his candidacy, that he was dodging on prohibition, and that his "damn fool friends" were arranging Roosevelt dinners and the like. A political friendship had collapsed for political reasons.

Tammany—like Boss Plunkitt—saw its opportunity and took it. Smith was the lesser of the two evils; moreover, he was still popular with the New York City Democracy's rank and file. The New York delegation was made up of delegates at large chosen by the state committee, and of district delegates elected locally. In open defiance of Roosevelt, Tammany forces on the state committee chose a delegate-at-large slate largely composed of their own men; the district delegates were split about equally between Roosevelt and Tammany. Shrewdly Tammany left the delegates at large uninstructed so that they could be used as a club against the governor in the corruption situation. The upshot was that Roosevelt found himself in control of less than half of his own state delegation.

BATTLE AT THE GRASS ROOTS

On January 23, 1932—a week before his fiftieth birthday—Roosevelt formally announced his candidacy for the Democratic nomination for President by authorizing the Democratic Central Committee of North Dakota to enter his name in the preferential primary of that state. Two weeks later Smith announced that he would accept the nomination if it should be offered to him, but that he would not conduct an active campaign—an announcement that politicians correctly interpreted as meaning his supporters would conduct an active campaign. Half a dozen other candidates were entering or eying the arena.

By now Roosevelt's campaign had become a major operation. Outside the immediate entourage of Howe and Farley and their assistants was a circle of old Roosevelt friends and supporters. Colonel Edward House, the indefatigable little Texan who had served and then left Wilson, was quietly pulling strings with his friends throughout the country. Such influential senators as Cordell Hull of Tennessee, Alben W. Barkley of Kentucky, and Thomas J. Walsh of Montana helped Roosevelt in Washington. No national organization could do the job, however; Farley and Howe relied mainly on state politicians. The campaign took money—almost $90,000 in the first three months—but money was not a serious problem. Large donations came from Lehman, Henry Morgenthau, Sr., William H. Woodin, Joseph P. Kennedy, Robert W. Bingham, and a score of other financiers, merchants, and industrialists. Central in the operation was Roosevelt himself, conducting a huge correspondence, entertaining prominent out-of-state politicos in Albany or Hyde Park, almost daily advising Farley and Howe on their activities. Roosevelt was at his best in entertaining visiting national politicians. Senator Clarence C. Dill of Washington remembered years later how the governor had got wind that he was in Albany and invited him to dinner. "I talked with him three hours and came away a devoted and enthusiastic booster. . . ."

Roosevelt's supporters were a remarkably varied lot—a strange assortment of old Harvard friends, city bosses, millionaires, Western radicals, Southern Bourbons, opportunistic Midwesterners who knew how to jump on the right bandwagon, Ku Kluxers, old Wilsonites, old Bryanites, professors, high-tariff men, low-tariff men. Directly or indirectly he was dealing with leaders who were then, or later, some of the most controversial personalities in American life: Hearst, Huey P. Long, Thomas J. Pendergast of Missouri, James

M. Curley of Boston. This diversity of support was a source of both strength and weakness—strength in that it gave him the appearance of nationwide appeal, weakness in that his supporters might lack unity and staying power at the convention.

Presidential nominations are usually won not by one great campaign through the nation but by a series of guerrilla battles, by tortuous, often undercover manipulations in each of the states and territories. Grand strategy must give way to petty strategy, and petty strategy to the mastery of detail. The network of detail surrounding a thousand potential convention delegates was Farley's forte.

Backed by a year's strenuous effort, the Roosevelt forces pulled far ahead in the early contests of 1932. Alaska, Washington, North Dakota, Georgia, Iowa, Maine, and Wisconsin fell to Roosevelt in an impressive demonstration of the wide compass of his support Yet Roosevelt never took a decisive lead. The difficulty was two-fold. Running ahead of even the combined opposition was not enough for the Roosevelt forces; they had to win the magic two-thirds. And sensing a possible stalemate ahead, several state delegations did the precise thing that Farley had been trying so desperately to avoid—they pledged to favorite sons as a means either of hoarding their votes for future bargaining purposes or of capturing the nomination in a stalemate. Oklahoma instructed its delegates to vote for their rustic governor, Alfalfa Bill Murray, whose political antics and dripping mustache had become a cartoonist's delight. Missouri pledged its thirty-six delegates to prickly Senator James Reed, the old anti-Wilson isolationist. Maryland plumped for Ritchie, who rivaled Roosevelt in bearing, background, and eloquence, and who had won the Maryland governorship four times by ever-increasing majorities. Illinois with its fifty-eight votes went to Senator J. Hamilton Lewis, the old Populist spellbinder, whose wig, pink whiskers, and gay attire had won him the name the "Aurora Borealis of Illinois."

Late in April 1932 the Roosevelt machine seemed to stall. Smith carried the Massachusetts primary by a popular vote of three to one; he would have the entire delegation with its thirty-six votes. Pennsylvania gave a majority of its votes to Roosevelt, but Smith showed unexpected strength, especially in the wet districts. Early in May came the worst blow of all. In a three-way contest for California's forty-four votes with Smith and Speaker John N. Garner of the House of Representatives, Roosevelt unexpectedly ran second after Garner, although ahead of Smith. Prospects of a first-ballot victory began to look slim. What had happened?

The Massachusetts situation was badly bungled. Early in the

game Mayor James M. Curley of Boston had suddenly jumped on the Roosevelt bandwagon. Long the bully boy of Boston politics, Curley had often been counted out, but he always bounced back, soothing the crowds with his honey-sweet voice, thwacking the old-line, respectable Democrats hip and thigh. Curley's motives were simple: he saw Roosevelt as a political comer whom he could use in advancing his own ambitions to win the governorship over the opposition of Senator David I. Walsh, Governor Joseph B. Ely, and the state organization. Curley had some luck, too. Roosevelt's oldest son, James, had gone into the insurance business in Boston and he was eager to dabble in politics. Curley established a solid alliance with him. The father in Albany was touched and pleased at his son's interest in politics. Like many another political leader in history, he may have allowed a family situation to spoil his good judgment.

Curley simply ran away with Roosevelt's campaign in Massachusetts. But aside from his own faction he made little headway. "No attention was paid to the country districts where our strength lay, nor was the slightest attempt made to get out the rural vote," Howe wrote later in an angry account of Curley's "wretched" management of the campaign. "Curley insisted on making it a city fight throughout the state with all the organization and voting officials under the control of Walsh and Ely. This is on a par with his early agreement with me to have the campaign run by a committee of six mayors with himself only responsible for Boston—a promise which he failed utterly to carry out and which left at least four [of] the mayors somewhat lukewarm to Roosevelt's cause. . . ." The main effect of Curley's campaign was to goad the opposition into a strenuous counteraction, and the availability of Smith, who was idolized by Massachusetts Democrats, fell in perfectly with their needs.

Sensing defeat, Roosevelt at the eleventh hour tried to compromise. A peace conference in Boston that excluded Curley made some progress until news came in that Curley had chosen that afternoon to lash out at Smith for deceiving the people and wrecking the party; the meeting broke up. Curley himself tried to work out a deal where Smith would have the whole delegation on early ballots if Roosevelt could have it intact later. But Walsh and Ely saw no need to compromise. The campaign ended in a typical "Curley-Burley" in which Roosevelt was lost in a storm of personal and factional invective.

Part of Roosevelt's difficulty in Massachusetts lay in some uncertainty whether Smith actually hoped to win for himself or planned to throw his strength at some point to someone else. In this sense, too, Roosevelt's early start was a disadvantage; his opponents knew that he was out for himself, but he could never know who would emerge as his real opponent out of the makeshift combinations that the "Stop Roosevelt" forces were piecing together. He encountered the same difficulty in California.

In the beginning the Roosevelt forces had been optimistic about this state, partly because they discounted both Garner's interest and availability. A small-town banker and realtor from western Texas—the "goat country," he liked to call it—Garner had risen to be the shrewd and militant leader of the Democratic forces in the House. Considered an extreme wet and hostile to Eastern business interests, he lacked national appeal, but two factors gave him strength in California: a huge "Texas California" association that loved any son of the mother state, and backing from Hearst. Garner ran far ahead in Los Angeles, as did Smith in San Francisco.

Seeking nationwide support in the party, Roosevelt was at a disadvantage facing candidates who could take a position that had local appeal. On many matters, such as liquor and Tammany, he treaded carefully, or remained silent. But failure to take a position also could be politically dangerous. "Do you wish to win for yourself the undesirable title of the 4-P's Candidate: Pusillanimously-Pussyfooting-Pious-Platitudinous Roosevelt," a fellow Harvard alumnus wrote him angrily. Oswald Garrison Villard, editor of the liberal *Nation,* in an open letter addressed to Roosevelt fourteen flat questions such as "Are you a protectionist or not? Yes or no?" "Are you for repeal of the Eighteenth Amendment? Yes or no?" The governor refused to answer; these were "Have-you-stopped-beating-your-wife?" questions, he wrote to Villard indignantly—and privately.

On general economic questions, however, Roosevelt took a militant stand. "These unhappy times," he said in a radio speech in April 1932, "call for the building of plans that rest upon the forgotten, the unorganized but the indispensable units of economic power, for plans . . . that build from the bottom up and not from the top down, that put their faith once more in the forgotten man at the bottom of the economic pyramid." The Forgotten Man became one of his most remembered phrases. "The country needs and, unless I mistake its temper, the country demands bold, persistent experimentation," he told a graduating class at Oglethorpe University. Almost a year before March 1933 he was proclaiming that America was facing an emergency at least equal to war itself.

Smith was waiting to outflank him on the right. "I will take off my coat and vest," he said shortly after Roosevelt's Forgotten Man speech, "and fight to the end any candidate who persists in any demagogic appeal to the masses of the working people of this country to destroy themselves by setting class against class and rich against poor."

While fighting Smith with his right hand, Roosevelt had to hold off other candidates with his left. Newton D. Baker was an especially worrisome threat. A reform mayor of Cleveland, secretary of war under Wilson, an eminent corporation lawyer, Baker had not been taken seriously as a possible candidate because of his repeated advocacy of United States entry into the League of Nations. In January 1932, however, he backslid, stating that he would not take the country into the League "unless an enlightened majority of the people favored the step." As the convention neared, Farley and Howe busily stoked backfires against Baker's possible candidacy, warning Westerners that Baker was pro-League and labor leaders that he was the candidate of the "financial crowd."

But all eyes came back to Smith. "I do hope that Al will not make a bitter or a mean fight," Roosevelt wrote to a friend in June. "It does nobody any good and, though he may block the convention and raise cain generally, it would be much better for the country if he would forget self and work primarily for the country itself. . . ."

THE MAGIC TWO-THIRDS

At Roosevelt headquarters in Chicago Farley posted a gaudy map —"Field Marshal Farley's map," it was soon dubbed—showing his chief's strength across the nation. The map also showed Roosevelt's weakness. For it was clear when the Democratic convention opened on June 27, 1932, that Roosevelt could not win the often predicted first-ballot victory unless a stampede was touched off at the end of the roll. Who would touch it off? Farley still did not know. He had met disappointment after disappointment in trying to win the extra one hundred votes that would mean victory.

The key, he felt, lay in a bloc of three Midwestern states: Ohio, Indiana, and Illinois. Earlier Ohio had looked hopeful, but now it was holding its delegates behind its favorite son, Governor George White, in order, according to reports, to lead a procession to Baker later. Indiana was a baffling disappointment; Farley offered a high convention post to Paul V. McNutt if he would help negotiate an instructed delegation for Roosevelt, but McNutt would not, or could not, come across. Illinois was the worst blow of all. Senator Lewis withdrew just before the convention and his votes were expected to go to the New York governor, but the withdrawal was timed too early. The Illinois delegation simply trotted out another favorite son, a Chicago banker, and stood pat.

Under mounting pressure, the Roosevelt forces at the eleventh hour embarked on a risky maneuver that almost lost them the fight. This was the repeal of the two-thirds rule. The idea was simple:

Each national convention at the outset adopted its own rules by straight majority vote; sure of commanding such a majority the Roosevelt men needed only to change the rules and then nominate their candidate by a straight majority.

The tactic might have worked if it had been properly timed. But it was not. The issue came up at an organization meeting of Roosevelt delegates called by Farley before the convention opened. Suddenly Senator Huey P. Long of Louisiana took the floor to offer a resolution setting forth that the governor's friends would fight for a straight majority rule. Coat open, arms pumping, the Kingfish raised his pudgy, pock-marked face in a bellowing call to action. Farley dared not restrain the man who held Louisiana's delegates' votes in his pocket, and who had told Flynn that he backed Roosevelt only because he had met the other contenders. The resolution went through.

The opposition blazed up in wrathful indignation. A nomination won in such a way, said Senator Carter Glass, would be "damaged goods obtained by a gambler's trick." Roosevelt's opponents, hitherto divided, now had a moral issue around which to unite. Even worse, pro-Roosevelt delegations in the South showed signs of deserting on the majority rule issue, for the two-thirds rule had become a venerable mechanism for protecting the power of the South in the party.

After conferring over the telephone with Roosevelt in Albany and with Howe in Chicago, Farley decided to surrender. He had been careful not to implicate his chief in the original decision. Actually, Roosevelt had been directly involved in the two-thirds maneuver just as he was in all major decisions in the nomination fight, but he and Farley had lost control of the timing through Long's precipitous action. The governor's withdrawal was as graceful as circumstances allowed. "I believe and always have believed," he said, "that the two thirds rule should no longer be adopted. It is undemocratic. Nevertheless, it is true that the issue was not raised until after the delegates to the convention had been selected, and I decline to permit either myself or my friends to be open to the accusation of poor sportsmanship or to the use of methods which could be called, even falsely, those of a steam-roller. . . ."

Repairing their fractured ranks, the Roosevelt men now faced the first battles over convention organization. In these tests of strength only a straight majority was needed to win, and the Roosevelt forces mobilized enough votes to seat friendly delegations from Louisiana and Minnesota and elect Senator Thomas Walsh of Montana as permanent chairman over Smith's candidate, Jouett Shouse. The permanent chairman contest aroused new charges of deceit against the Roosevelt men, who had indicated earlier in the year that they would back Shouse. The 626 to 528 vote on the chairman race suggested how close the nomination race might be. The Smith forces, however, gained heart from a smashing victory for a "dripping wet" repeal plank—a plank that drew far more attention than the party's declarations on economic recovery.

At last came the roll call on nomination. Farley was everywhere, pumping hands, claiming victory, exhorting delegations to get on the bandwagon while there was still room. In a hotel room Howe was conducting last-minute espionage operations and putting out feelers to key men in favorite-son delegations. In Albany, Roosevelt waited by the radio, frequently counseling with his lieutenants over a private telephone wire. Biting on a cigar, Smith sat amid Tammany delegates so hostile to Roosevelt that Farley had difficulty finding a seat in order to vote during roll calls. It was past four o'clock on the morning of July 1 when the nominating and seconding speeches finally came to an end. Exhausted by ten hours of turgid oratory, demonstrations, and blaring band music, the delegates slumped in their chairs.

The first roll call went according to expectations. Roosevelt moved far ahead near the outset and kept a long lead. His final tally on the first roll call of 666¼ dwarfed Smith's 201¾, Garner's 90¼, and White's 52, but it was about one hundred short of two-thirds. While tellers were making their check, Farley sat back on the platform, waiting for the bandwagon rush to start.

Nothing happened.

Farley sprinted down to the floor and pleaded with delegations to shift. He had the vice-presidential nomination to offer, but the delegations were stalling while they waited to see if the current went in another direction. Weary delegates were eager to adjourn but the Roosevelt forces wanted another roll call before their own delegations weakened. On the second roll call Roosevelt picked up 11½ votes, an increase so small that it dramatized the extent to which Farley had staked his hopes on the first ballot.

Still no delegation came over. Now it was the opposition forces that wanted another roll call. Roosevelt, they proclaimed, was stopped. On the third ballot Roosevelt crept up five more votes. His ranks at least were holding firm—but so were the enemy's. At 9 A.M., after the third roll call, the convention adjourned and the delegates tottered out into the sunshine.

The next few hours would be decisive. Farley had to win a sizable bloc of votes before his own ranks buckled. The breaking away of one delegation might start an avalanche toward Garner, who had picked up eleven votes on the third ballot. Already Mississippi's twenty votes were in jeopardy; this delegation was supporting Roosevelt under the unit rule by a 10½ to 9½ vote, and had been barely saved for the governor on the third roll call. Alabama, Arkansas, and Minnesota also had soft spots.

The only card Farley had left was a big one. For some time he had been in touch with a group of men close to Garner, including Representative Sam Rayburn of Texas. Garner was a serious candidate, but he did not want a deadlocked convention, and he personally opposed the two-thirds rule. Farley had also been in direct touch with Hearst, warning him that in a deadlock the prize might go to Baker, whose internationalist views the publisher hated. Hearst hated Smith even more. Farley had been putting every possible form of pressure on Garner's men at the convention. Now—while Roosevelt leaders were proffering the vice-presidency in a dozen different directions—Farley was able to make a definitive offer. The deal was quickly made. All during the day Smith was trying to reach Garner in Washington, but the Speaker would talk to no one but Rayburn. Late in the afternoon Rayburn got an official release from Garner. It was none too soon. Mississippi had cracked and gone over to the coalition.

Winning Garner's consent to release his delegates was one thing; winning his supporters' was something else. The big Texas delegation had come to Chicago to nominate Jack Garner. Farley, moreover, faced a special handicap. Early in the spring the Roosevelt forces had tried to capture the Texas delegation; they had failed badly, and the Garner forces kept all but a few Roosevelt men off the delegation. Now the Texans balked at going to the New York governor. Their caucus was tumultuous: last-ditch Garner leaders were pleading with the delegates to stand firm; women were crying hysterically; and delegates from other states had filtered into the room and were busy promising more votes for Garner on the next ballot. Ironically, a good many anti-Roosevelt delegates were absent trying to win votes for the Speaker in other delegations. In the confusion Rayburn barely managed to push the pro-Roosevelt stand through, fifty-four to fifty-one.

Now the Roosevelt avalanche began. The shift of Texas brought around California too. On the fourth roll call McAdoo, a victim of the two-thirds rule eight years before, came to the rostrum. The pro-Smith galleries drowned him out with groans and boos, but finally his voice came through. "California came here to nominate a President of the United States," he shouted. "She did not come to deadlock the Convention or to engage in another devastating contest like that of 1924. California casts 44 votes for Franklin D. Roosevelt."

The frenzied cheering echoed over the radio in Roosevelt's study. He leaned back and grinned broadly. "Good old McAdoo." **The** delegations swiftly fell in line—all but Smith's diehard supporters. who refused to make the nomination unanimous.

On a roof garden in Washington a little man sat smoking a cigar. A reporter recognized him. "You've gone to Roosevelt?" "That's right, son." The reporter expressed surprise. The cigar glowed. "I'm a little older than you are, son. And politics is funny." In Chicago the delegates were asking why Garner had shifted. Even as he was giving way, several states were breaking loose for him. To be sure, he was duly nominated for vice-president, but exchanging the certainty of the speakership for the uncertainty of the vice-presidency seemed a strange swap for the canny Texan. Was it really fear of a deadlock? Was it Hearst? His supporters were at a loss. "It's a kangaroo ticket," said a disappointed Texas politician. "Stronger in the hindquarter than in front."

The Roosevelt forces had won—yet they had lost too. They had gone for a running mate to a section of the country that was certain to vote Democratic in November. They had disappointed some of their Western supporters who had worked for Roosevelt long before Chicago. They had made some serious mistakes. Yet the nomination fight had shown the essential strength of their candidate—a strength that could weather his and his lieutenants' errors. The real test lay ahead.

EIGHT *The Curious Campaign*

ROOSEVELT began his election campaign with the kind of dramatic gesture he loved. While the convention waited, he flew from Albany to accept the nomination on the spot rather than follow tradition and acknowledge it weeks later. Buffeted by head winds, the flimsy trimotored plane was hours late, and convention chiefs, for once out of Democratic speeches, had to turn to bandleaders and songsters to keep the weary delegates in their seats. During the flight the governor serenely worked on his speech and then fell asleep, while Mrs. Roosevelt, Rosenman, and the others shivered, and son John was quietly sick in the tail of the plane.

The trip from the airport to the convention was a triumphant procession. His coming out to accept the nomination, Roosevelt told the convention, was a symbol of his intention to avoid hypocrisy and sham. "Let it also be symbolic that in so doing I broke traditions. Let it be from now on the task of our Party to break foolish traditions and leave it to the Republican leadership, far more skilled in that art, to break promises."

The speech was long and rambling—due in part to a fierce struggle that had been waged over its composition by Roosevelt's advisers and to Roosevelt's willingness—while he was bowing and waving to the crowds between airport and convention hall—to placate Howe by substituting the latter's opening paragraphs for his own. The speech was essentially an appeal for an experimental program of recovery that would steer between radicalism and reaction, that would benefit all the people without falling into an "improvised, hit-or-miss, irresponsible opportunism." The people that year wanted a real choice, he said. "Ours must be a party of liberal thought, of planned action, of enlightened international outlook, and of the greatest good to the greatest number of our citizens." Endorsing the party platform "100 per cent," he lambasted the Republican leaders for their failures and set out in hazy terms a program on taxes, agriculture, tariffs, and recovery.

"I pledge you, I pledge myself, to a new deal for the American people," Roosevelt wound up in his peroration. The two words nestling in the speech had meant little to Roosevelt and the other speech writers; soon they were to be more important than the sum of all the other words. Next day a cartoon by Rollin Kirby showed a new "man with a hoe" looking up puzzled but hopeful at an airplane labeled "New Deal."

THE FOX AND THE ELEPHANT

How to get the new program off the ground was the mission of Farley, who on Roosevelt's recommendation was elected the chairman of the Democratic National Committee. The new chairman inherited a superb publicity man in Charles Michelson, ghost writer of scores of speeches that had slashed and pummeled the Hoover

May 26, 1932, Elmer Messner, Rochester *Democrat and Chronicle*

HELPFUL FARM HINTS FROM HYDE PARK, Oct. 25, 1932, Ding Darling, © 1932, New York *Herald Tribune*, Inc.

administration. Roosevelt's personal organization was quickly converted into the campaign high command, with headquarters in New York. Soon six hundred people were working through a score of specialized divisions. Considerable attention was devoted to the women's division, which was headed by a group of imaginative and indefatigable women workers, including Eleanor Roosevelt.

On one thing Roosevelt and Farley were insistent: they must bypass the cumbersome pyramid of state and county committees and establish a direct personal link with 140,000 local party workers whose names had been collected during the preconvention campaign. Along with millions of buttons and leaflets these committeemen received personal letters from Roosevelt and Farley, the latter's signed in green ink. Farley saw the campaign as a party battle and sought to keep control under the top Democratic regulars. "We are going to have every kind of club function we can," he told a meeting of party leaders early in August, "but we don't want them running wild." Farley wanted to prevent crossed wires, but straight party control had its disadvantages too. Special groups did not get full attention; labor especially was handled in a slipshod fashion.

The softest spot in the Roosevelt forces, however, was Tammany. What would the Sachems do? Farley got an answer the day he returned from Chicago, when he had the temerity to invade the Hall during a patriotic ceremony. The gallery hissed; the Sachems on the platform sat in stony silence. But Tammany had little freedom of action; its course depended largely on two men, Smith and Walker.

Crushed and bitter, Smith had left Chicago before Roosevelt arrived. It was nip and tuck for a while whether he would openly attack the victor. He did not—but when Roosevelt emissaries urged him to support the ticket, he balked. "I think he wants to work it out in his own way and in his own time," Roosevelt wrote Frankfurter. Al did; in the final weeks before the election he campaigned vigorously for Roosevelt in Massachusetts and Connecticut.

Walker presented a different problem. Seabury's probe of corruption in New York City had come to a head—as it had been deliberately timed to do in order to embarrass him, Roosevelt suspected —in the weeks just before the convention with charges against the mayor. Walker, who had swaggeringly voted against Roosevelt in the convention, shortly afterward filed his answers. During late August, with the election campaign under way, Roosevelt presided over a series of hearings in Albany. The situation required all his political finesse. Some Tammany leaders were in an ugly mood and openly talked of bolting the ticket; even Father Charles Coughlin, the radio priest, wrote from Detroit asking that Walker be given his day in court. The Republicans blew the case into a national issue of Roosevelt and Tammanyism. Day after day the governor in judicial mien patiently questioned the mayor about his tangled affairs. Under mounting pressure, Walker suddenly resigned, accusing Roosevelt of "unfair, unAmerican" conduct of the hearing. The governor had walked the political tightrope expertly. He stripped the Republicans of a national issue without losing Tammany, which was divided on the matter and in any case did not dare to turn against Roosevelt openly.

With the Walker case disposed of, Roosevelt could begin his campaign in earnest. He had received a good deal of advice to the effect that (a) the election was already "in the bag," and (b) a campaign tour might jeopardize the Democratic lead. Roosevelt spurned both ideas. He was cautious—almost superstitious—about assuming victory. He believed that a campaign trip would carry the attack to Hoover; moreover, it would demonstrate his physical vigor and silence the whispering against his health. Besides—he simply wanted to go. "My Dutch is up," he told Farley.

Never, perhaps, has a candidate had as large and varied a group of advisers as Roosevelt collected for his campaign. They ranged from idealistic college professors to cynical party politicians, and they spoke for almost every political viewpoint of right, left, and center. One or two advisers tried to sort out the ideas in logical form for the candidate, but it was a trying task. Roosevelt loved to juggle ideas, he hated to antagonize people, he was looking for proposals that would appeal to a wide variety of groups, whatever the lack of internal consistency. While the candidate toured the streets and talked from the back platform of trains, fierce fights broke out in speech-drafting sessions between high-tariff and low-tariff men, among advocates of various farm policies, between the budget-balancers and public works advocates.

What did the candidate say? At this critical juncture of the nation's affairs, what program did he offer the American people?

As in past campaigns, Roosevelt devoted each major speech to a major topic. In Topeka he promised to reorganize the Department of Agriculture; he favored the "planned use of land," lower taxes for farmers through tax reform, federal credit for refinancing farm mortgages, and lower tariffs; and he came out for the barest shadow of a voluntary domestic allotment plan to handle farm surpluses. In Salt Lake City he outlined a comprehensive plan of federal regulation and aid for the floundering railroad industry. In Seattle he let loose a thundering attack on high tariffs. In Portland he demanded full publicity as to the financial activities of public utilities, regulation of holding companies by the Federal Power Commission, regulation of the issuing of stocks and bonds, and use of the prudent-investment principle in rate-making. In Detroit he called for removing the causes of poverty—but he refused to spell out the methods because it was Sunday and he would not talk politics!

One speech in particular excited observers on the left. At the Commonwealth Club in San Francisco Roosevelt talked eloquently about the need for an economic constitutional order, about the role of government as umpire, with federal regulation as a last resort. Although the implications of these ideas for a specific program were left vague, the speech was studded with phrases about economic oligarchy, the shaping of an economic bill of rights, the need for more purchasing power, and every man's right to life, which

Roosevelt defined as including the right to make a comfortable living. But these ideas seemed to fade away later in the campaign as the candidate turned to other notions, some of them more orthodox than those of Hoover himself.

It was all very confusing to the close observer. He was sure that Roosevelt was against prohibition, reporter Elmer Davis wrote, but for the rest—"You could not quarrel with a single one of his generalities; you seldom can. But what they mean (if anything) is known only to Franklin D. Roosevelt and his God."

Roosevelt found it easier to assail Hoover's policies than to spell out clear proposals of his own. The administration, he declared, had encouraged speculation and overproduction through its fake economic policies. It had tried to minimize the gravity of the Depression. It had wrongly blamed other nations for causing the crash. It had "refused to recognize and correct the evils at home which had brought it forth; it delayed relief; it forgot reform." And Roosevelt and a thousand orators painted President Hoover as sitting in the White House inert, unconcerned, withdrawn.

Hoover launched a vigorous counteroffensive. He concentrated his fire on what he called the radicalism and collectivism in Roosevelt's proposals. It was perhaps to meet this attack, perhaps for other reasons unknown, that Roosevelt toned down the sweep of his proposals midway in the campaign. He so modified his tariff-reduction stand that his position differed little from that of his adversary in the White House. He hoped that governmental interference to bring about business stabilization could be "kept at a minimum"—perhaps limited simply to publicity. He took a weak stand on unemployment, pledging that no one would starve under the New Deal, that the federal government would set an example on wages and hours, seeking to persuade industry to do likewise, and would set up employment exchanges, leaving unemployment insurance to the states. He promised co-operation with Congress—and with both parties in Congress. And in one of the most sweeping statements of his campaign he berated Hoover for spending and deficits, and he promised—with only the tiniest of escape clauses—to balance the budget.

Here was no call to action, no summons to a crusade. Roosevelt had no *program* to offer, only a collection of proposals, some well thought out, like the railroad plan, others vague to the point of meaninglessness. On the whole he was remarkably temperate; there was little passion or pugnacity. Some of his speeches, indeed, had the flavor of academic lectures, as Roosevelt led his audience through the Hoover policies and then described his own. For a nation caught in economic crisis, it was a curious campaign.

What was Roosevelt up to? He was trying to win an election, not lay out a coherent philosophy of government. He had no such philosophy; but he knew how to pick up votes, how to capture group support, how to change pace and policy. "Weave the two together," he said to an astonished Raymond Moley when the academic man presented Roosevelt with two utterly different drafts on tariff policy. "I think that you will agree," he wrote to Floyd Olson about his Topeka farm speech, "that it is sufficiently far to the left to prevent any further suggestion that I am leaning to the right."

"A chameleon on plaid," Hoover growled. With his orderly engineer's mind he could not come to grips with this antagonist who fenced all around him, now on the left, now on the right, now in attack, and now in sudden retreat. Nor could Norman Thomas, the Socialist candidate for President, with his elaborate, eloquent, detailed platform. It was not 1896, or 1912, or even 1928. In the gravest economic crisis of their history the American people, still benumbed and bewildered, seemed only to stir lethargically amid the tempests of the politicians.

On election eve Roosevelt gave a last talk to his neighbors in Poughkeepsie. He spoke of the "vivid flashes" of the campaign—the great crowd under the lights before the capitol in Jefferson City, the Kansans listening patiently under the hot sun in Topeka, the "strong, direct kindness" of the people in Wyoming who had come hundreds of miles to see him, the sunset in McCook, Nebraska, the children in wheel chairs at Warm Springs, the stirring trip north through New England.

"A man comes to wisdom in many years of public life. He knows well that when the light of favor shines upon him, it comes not, of necessity, that he himself is important. Favor comes because for a brief moment in the great space of human change and progress some general human purpose finds in him a satisfactory embodiment."

The light of favor shone brightly. Election night Roosevelt sat happily among his friends at campaign headquarters in New York City as the returns poured in. He won 22,815,539 votes to Hoover's 15,759,930, carrying 42 states and 472 electoral votes. It was almost a nationwide sweep; only Pennsylvania, Delaware, Connecticut, Vermont, New Hampshire, and Maine went Republican. It was, in part, a personal victory for the Democratic candidate: outside the South and New England Roosevelt's percentage topped that of the Democratic candidates for Representative in four-fifths of the states. But it was a party victory too. The new Senate would be Democratic by 59 to 37, the new House Democratic by 312 to 123.

During the night a telegram of congratulation arrived from

Hoover. The next morning, sitting in bed in the 65th Street house, Roosevelt scribbled a reply on the back of Hoover's wire:

"I appreciate your generous telegram. I want to assure you that subject to my necessary executive duties as Governor, I hold myself in readiness to cooperate with you in our—"

Roosevelt stopped and crossed out the last eight words.

"—ready to further in every way the common purpose to help our country."

THE STAGE IS SET

The place that a great man holds in history, it has been said, is largely determined by the manner in which he makes his exit from the stage. The same could be said for his entrance. "No cosmic dramatist," Robert Sherwood said, "could possibly devise a better entrance for a new President—or a new Dictator, or a new Messiah—than that accorded to Franklin Delano Roosevelt."

The President-elect enjoyed all the advantages, Sherwood noted, of having a good act to follow. Hoover was meeting the fate of defeated presidents—his popularity ebbed even more after the election. Roosevelt's cardinal object was to keep clear of the wrecked Hoover administration. The four months between election and inauguration saw a dogged, undercover duel between the two politicians as Hoover sought to salvage his reputation in the face of mounting economic crisis, while Roosevelt warily shied off from any involvement.

The issue was precipitated shortly after the election when the foreign debt situation suddenly came to a head. On November 12, 1932, Hoover had notified Roosevelt that Britain had asked for a suspension of payments due the United States and for a review of the whole debt situation. Would the President-elect meet with him on the matter? Roosevelt saw treacherous ground ahead. Hoover viewed the war debt problem in terms of his basic assumption that the Depression was foreign-made and could be met best by international action—an assumption his opponent had assailed during the campaign. Roosevelt, moreover, had no firsthand acquaintance with the problem. During the 1920's he had asked for a constructive over-all Democratic party position on the matter, and he had scoffed at Coolidge's remark, "Well, they hired the money, didn't they?" But he had gone little beyond this.

Whatever the pitfalls, Roosevelt knew that he had to respond to the popular demand that he co-operate with the outgoing Chief Executive for the sake of national unity. His tactic was to observe all the formalities of co-operation—to meet with Hoover, to exchange letters and telegrams with him—but to refuse to take joint action that would imply joint responsibility. His official position was that President Hoover had the power to act if action was needed, that it was not necessary for the President-elect to appoint interim representatives, that he would make no commitments before March 4. Unofficially, he told reporters that "it was not his baby." After a month of futile sparring Hoover released the whole correspondence to the press with the cold comment: "Governor Roosevelt considers that it is undesirable for him to assent to my suggestions for cooperative action on the foreign proposals outlined in my recent message to Congress. I will respect his wishes."

The state of the nation in January 1933 formed a fitting backdrop to these fruitless negotiations. Farm prices had slid badly since summer; factory production, retail trade, stocks and bonds were all down. Unemployment rose by one or two million to around fifteen million. Farmers were using shotguns to keep homes from being foreclosed. In the cities, unemployed white-collar people were suddenly on every corner, selling apples. Through financial circles trickled underground reports of serious trouble in leading Detroit banks.

Congress, meanwhile, fribbled and dawdled. Weighted down by 158 members who had been handed their walking papers by the voters in November, divided in party control, surly toward the President, unsure of the President-elect, the legislators could find no basis for action. Roosevelt made his views known on a few matters through Democratic leaders, but he did not emulate Wilson's example in 1912-13 of mobilizing his leaders and drafting legislation weeks before he took office. Where does the President-elect stand? asked a Republican representative. "He is here today and there tomorrow." Wearily congressmen squabbled over beer, deadlocked over relief, put off action on banking, farm mortgage relief, bank deposit legislation. Lacking presidential leadership they could not act.

Across the seas crisis glowed and flickered. On January 30, 1933—Roosevelt's fifty-first birthday—a befuddled President Hindenburg dismissed the chancellor and put in his place Adolf Hitler, who promptly dissolved the Reichstag, ordered an election, arrested opposition leaders, and terrorized the voters with a manufactured panic. Censured by the League of Nations for its aggression in Manchuria, Japan truculently withdrew its representatives from the Assembly. Mussolini's Italy, it was disclosed, was shipping arms into Austria to arm the fascists there. Latin-American countries were seething with discontent.

During these long weeks Roosevelt remained buoyant and imperturbable. He cleaned up his gubernatorial affairs, shuffled and reshuffled appointment lists, conferred on foreign affairs with Secretary of State Stimson and his own advisers, spent several weeks in Warm Springs and on Vincent Astor's yacht, kept in touch with congressional leaders, and found time to tour the Tennessee River area with Senator George W. Norris. But all his actions were in slow waltz time. Despite the pleadings of reporters, despite the strictures of editorial writers, he refused to issue statements on the sharpening economic crisis or to announce his plans. He merely waited.

If anything more was needed to heighten the tension of the pre-inauguration weeks, it was supplied in mid-February by a short, dark man who stood in a crowd around Roosevelt's car in Miami. Shouting that "too many people are starving to death," Zangara fired shot after shot at the President-elect; knocked upward by a woman's quick move, his gun missed Roosevelt but hit several bystanders and mortally wounded Mayor Cermak of Chicago. Moley, who was near the scene, was not surprised that Roosevelt's nerve held in front of the crowd. But he was amazed to see no letdown later on when the President-elect was among his friends. There was nothing, Moley said, "not so much as the twitching of a muscle, the mopping of a brow, or even the hint of a false gaiety" to indicate that anything unusual had happened.

By mid-February the banking situation was approaching crisis. On February 17, the day Roosevelt returned from his yacht trip, Hoover wrote him an anxious letter in longhand. Confidence was steadily degenerating, the President said. He urged Roosevelt to assure the country that there would be no "tampering or inflation of the currency," that the budget would be balanced even if it meant more taxes, that government credit would be maintained. The President-elect answered that mere statements would not avail. Doubtless Roosevelt suspected—as Hoover privately admitted—that by making such statements he would be approving the Hoover policies that he had attacked during the campaign. The President-elect kept silent; he had two weeks to wait.

At the end of February Hoover launched a last despairing effort. He wanted to issue an executive order controlling bank withdrawals, but he was not sure of his power to do so, and he feared that a Democratic Congress might repudiate such action. Would the President-elect approve such action? Roosevelt would not. The President, he said, had the authority to act on his own. Matters were now coming to a head. Frantic bankers, sitting late in their offices totaling withdrawals, wondered whether their banks would pull through. In the Treasury Department the night before the inaugural, officials were pleading with the governors of New York and Illinois to close the banks to prevent fatal runs on the banks the next morning.

Roosevelt did not foresee that the banking situation would reach a dramatic climax on Inauguration Day. No man could have. But he played his cards perfectly. Despite the pleadings of the administration and the fervent advice of his friends, he refused to tip his hand. No untimely action marred his entrance on the great stage.

Cabinet appointments, too, Roosevelt held off announcing until near the end of the interregnum. Their revelation only served to throw the figure of the new chief executive into sharper relief.

His selections comprised a mixed collection that gave little hint of Roosevelt's program. Cordell Hull, a spare, graying man of sixty-one, was an obvious choice for Secretary of State. Hull's downcast eyes, stooped shoulders, and soft voice masked a strength and tenacity that had marked his long career as a representative and later senator from Tennessee, and as chairman of the Democratic National Committee. A Cleveland Democrat and conservative in his economic viewpoints, Hull for years had led the fight for lower tariffs, clearing the legislative halls with his statistic-studded speeches on foreign trade. He would serve as a useful liaison between the President and conservative members of Congress.

Roosevelt's first choice for Secretary of the Treasury was Carter Glass, who had served in this post under Wilson. The peppery Virginian shied away, partly because of an ailing wife, partly because he feared that Roosevelt might try out unorthodox fiscal policies. Instead the President-elect picked William Woodin, an industrialist who had provided an invaluable combination of ideas and money in the presidential campaign. A little man with a heart-shaped face and an artless, almost elfin manner, Woodin was head of the American Car and Foundry Company. His economic views, while not hidebound, were as orthodox as those of Glass; clearly Roosevelt was not looking for radicals for the Treasury Department.

Roosevelt's candidate for Attorney General from the beginning had been Senator Thomas J. Walsh of Montana. The skillful and relentless exposer of the Teapot Dome scandals, Walsh had ably served the Roosevelt campaign as a prominent Rocky Mountain politician and as chairman of the 1932 Democratic convention. But shortly before the inauguration Walsh married a widow from Cuba, and he died suddenly en route to Washington from his honeymoon. In his place Roosevelt hurriedly chose Homer S. Cummings of Connecticut, who had been slated for Governor General of the Philippines. The replacement of Walsh by Cummings, a seasoned, middle-of-the-road Democratic politico, gave a more easterly cast to his cabinet than Roosevelt had originally planned.

The President-elect filled his two military posts in an almost cavalier fashion. He had come to like personally Governor George H. Dern of Utah, who had been a pillar of strength in the West, and he simply wanted Dern somewhere in his cabinet. Roosevelt's first place for Dern was Secretary of the Interior, but Dern had local antagonisms in Utah, and Secretary of War seemed to be a convenient slot. In the navy post Roosevelt installed Senator Claude Swanson, a benign old Virginian who wore high, wing collars and a frock coat. Swanson's appointment indicated that Roosevelt would be his own Secretary of the Navy; it had the advantage, too, of enabling Roosevelt's old friend, Harry F. Byrd, to be appointed Swanson's successor in the Senate.

A final concession to the Old Democracy came in the choice for Secretary of Commerce of Daniel C. Roper, a onetime political lieutenant of Wilson's who had later served as a leader in the McAdoo faction of the party. A bespectacled South Carolinian, Roper had views and associations that made him eminently acceptable to business. Symbol of the rising Democracy was Jim Farley, who knew of his designation as Postmaster General only when Roosevelt impishly commented on a story that "Jim's predecessor" had bought a new government limousine to allow more room for his silk hat.

In filling his labor, farm, and "Western" places Roosevelt moved left of center. He chose for Secretary of Labor his New York industrial commissioner, Frances Perkins, who had learned how to advance social-welfare legislation by getting along with the politicians, and who enabled Roosevelt to shatter another tradition in naming a woman to his cabinet. For Secretary of Agriculture he turned to Henry A. Wallace, a leader of the more militant farmers of the Corn Belt, son of a Republican Secretary of Agriculture, and a rustic, diffident man who had pioneered in developing new strains of corn and in breeding hogs and chickens. Roosevelt had offered Interior first to Hiram Johnson and then to Bronson Cutting, both of whom declined. After one meeting with Harold L. Ickes, Roosevelt tendered him the place; Ickes, a Chicagoan, had a reputation for independent Republicanism, honesty, and pugnacity. "I liked the cut of his jib," Roosevelt said.

Perhaps the historians of the future would find some underlying principle in Roosevelt's selections, Moley (who served as a go-between in the process) wrote later, but he could not. Time makes the task no easier. To some extent the cabinet met the classical American tradition: a collection of party war horses, sprinkled with a few independents, drawn from state and national politics, somewhat representative of the nation geographically. Like almost all previous cabinets it differed sharply with the British system of choosing party leaders who had long trod the political course in close harness; indeed, several members of the new cabinet had never met one another.

But even for America, Roosevelt's cabinet was a strange assortment. Ideologically, it embraced Democratic conservatives and Democratic progressives, a Republican conservative and two Republican progressives, inflationists and anti-inflationists, an ex-Bull Mooser along with old Wilson men, social-welfare New Dealers along with Cleveland Democrats, mild nationalists along with internationalists, Republicans of various hues along with partisan Democrats. Politically, it catered to almost every major group: business, industry, farmers, labor; Catholics and Protestants; North, South, Midwest, Far West. Yet even this was not an organizing principle. Roosevelt did not follow slavishly the wishes of group leaders. Wallace was not liked by some farm leaders; President William Green of the AFL announced angrily that labor would never be reconciled to Miss Perkins's appointment; and there was no Jew in the cabinet. Personally, it was an elderly group; the average age of fifty-eight suggested both experience and caution; and it was the first cabinet to include a woman.

The only principle in the cabinet's make-up was, in short, its lack of essential principle. Roosevelt had no rounded program; hence he could not recruit his official family along programmatic lines.

The real significance of the cabinet lay in Roosevelt's leadership role. He could count on loyalty from his associates: almost every one was "FRBC"—for Roosevelt before Chicago—and not a single one had been an important opponent in the 1932 convention. There was not a likely presidential possibility in the lot—no one who would try to push himself ahead of Roosevelt, at least during the first term. It was a cabinet the new President could easily dominate. By no means a "ministry of all the talents," it was a body that would gain life and meaning through the vigorous overarching leadership of Roosevelt himself.

The President-elect thus made no final commitment to any person, idea, or program in his cabinet. Nor did he do so in his immediate entourage. Howe, who was to be *the* secretary to the President, had a hand in many policy decisions, but he tended to reflect Roosevelt's own notions rather than to serve as a source of original thinking. Moreover, Howe's health was beginning to fail badly. Roosevelt chose as his assistant secretaries his old lieutenants of the 1920 campaign, Stephen Early and Marvin McIntyre, the former to handle press relations, and the latter appointments with the President. Both had a journalist's interest in personalities; both were shrewd political operators; but neither was especially concerned with policy or program. Clearly Roosevelt was not disposed to establish a powerful chief of staff or dominating idea man in the White House.

No one stole the show from the main actor. All eyes were on Roosevelt as Inauguration Day drew near.

ROOSEVELT ON THE EVE

The presidency, Roosevelt said shortly after his election, "is preeminently a place of moral leadership." From Washington, who personified the ideal of federal union, to T.R. and Wilson, who used the presidency as a pulpit, "all our great Presidents were leaders of thought at times when certain historic ideas in the life of the nation had to be clarified."

The presidential office is a "superb opportunity for reapplying, applying in new conditions, the simple rules of human conduct to which we always go back. Without leadership alert and sensitive to change, we are all bogged up or lose our way."

While Roosevelt was extolling the great leaders of the past, Americans were wondering what kind of leader he would be. There were some who saw him as little more than a Democratic Harding. The "corkscrew candidate of a convoluting convention," snorted Heywood Broun, the pugnacious liberal columnist. An "amiable man with many philanthropic impulses," but with neither a firm grasp on public affairs nor very strong convictions, Walter Lippmann said. Critic Edmund Wilson probed deeper. He could not find a particularly arresting personality—Roosevelt seemed essentially a boy scout with a spirit of cheerful service. There was a flatness, a hollowness, Wilson felt, in his ideas about American democracy. He was sensible, decent, diplomatic, efficient—but politically was there anything durable?

Others saw a different man. Beneath the charm and amiability they felt a tough center—shrewdness, courage, tenacity, and conviction. His old friends found impressive growth since the war years. They remembered him as attractive, eager, and able, but somewhat impressionable, immature, and certainly lacking in greatness. The man of 1932, they felt, had gained strikingly in force and power. If he had changed so much in a dozen years, would he not grow even more in the exacting presidential job?

The man at the center of this controversy was, in December 1932, approaching the end of his fifty-first year. He was tall, weighing about 180 pounds, a big man except for his thin, limp legs. His endless exercises had given him an exceptionally well-developed torso. His abdominal muscles had been entirely regenerated since the polio attack and his thigh muscles had come back to some extent.

He had not conquered the effects of polio on his legs—although even in 1932 he hoped he might restore them further—but he had compensated for some of the restrictions of his crippled state. He had a specially equipped Ford that he loved to drive around the Hyde Park estate. He swam a good deal and had developed a powerful backstroke; in the Warm Springs pool he liked to give his friends a head start and then, turning over on his back and dragging his legs after him, overtake them with a few tremendous strokes. He could even ride horseback, gripping the saddle with the upper part of his legs.

He was not a whit sensitive or embarrassed about his crippled condition. While scores of people around watched in covert embarrassment, he would be bodily lifted into or out of a car or train without losing his composure. His only worry about his legs was that some might fear he was not strong enough for a demanding job. During his second campaign for governor he ostentatiously took out over half a million dollars of life insurance through twenty-two companies and saw that the highly favorable medical report was well publicized. He instructed his staff not to send out letters that referred to his health or his crippled condition.

His composure under stress was remarkable. He had the quality of grace under pressure that Ernest Hemingway once called the highest form of courage. When tension arose he told a joke, or turned quickly to another subject, or launched into a long anecdote. This unruffled quality was evidently more than skin deep, for a medical examination following an especially strenuous week showed that his heart and blood pressure were normal. Even so, one thing could be counted on to upset Roosevelt's composure even in the years before the presidency: attacks by the press that he considered unfair.

The main reason for Roosevelt's composure was his serene and absolute assurance as to the value and importance of what he was doing. Another was his staff, which learned over the years how to operate smoothly with their chief. His secretary, Marguerite Le Hand, a handsome woman with prematurely graying hair, had a superb talent for managing his schedule, his callers, and his immediate office. Grace Tully, another secretary, took his dictation; together they could handle dozens of letters an hour as the President ordered replies written and sketched out their contents in a few short phrases. Louis Howe still acted for Roosevelt through the entire range of his affairs, fending off unwanted visitors, carrying out undercover political missions, arguing with "Franklin" to his face as few other people dared.

Eleanor Roosevelt managed to work closely with her husband and at the same time live some of her life separately. During the first part of the week she helped run a school for girls in New York City, then caught a train for Albany and resumed her place as official hostess. On the side she made speeches to women's organizations, saw that two or three houses were in running order, kept an eye on a furniture shop in Hyde Park, and found time to ride horseback. The children were rapidly leaving the family circle. Anna and James were both married, Franklin, Jr., was entering Harvard and John would follow. Elliott, not wanting to go to college, had deliberately failed some of his entrance examinations and was now earning his own living.

Outside his family and personal staff were a host of advisers, political associates, and correspondents. These men provided something of a measure of the President-elect's ideas and purposes.

Two things were remarkable about the men around Roosevelt in 1932: the variety of their backgrounds and ideas, and the fact that not one of them dominated the channels of access to Roosevelt's mind. It was a varied group because Roosevelt's test of a man was not his basic philosophy, or lack of one, but the sweep of his information, his ability to communicate, and his willingness to share ideas. Without any plan, a "brain trust," as reporters came to call it, grew up around him.

One of the chief brain trusters at this time was Raymond Moley, a Columbia University professor. Moley's high, domed forehead, shrewd, close-set eyes, and thin lips faithfully mirrored the complexities of the personality underneath: a cultured, widely read man of thought who had a passion for action, a subtle, sensitive man who liked to knock around with politicians high and low. His career had been wide-ranging: an Ohio boyhood, some time in local politics, then long periods of teaching and research, a decade of close study of the relation between politics and criminal justice, and a final climactic year with the Seabury investigation. Essentially a conservative despite his reputation as one of Roosevelt's radical professors, Moley believed in a kind of benevolent partnership between government and business that would leave capitalists with power and status while achieving efficiency through national planning, and ending the aimlessness and wastefulness of free competition and rugged individualism.

Others around Roosevelt leaned toward national planning, but with a less procapitalistic orientation. Rexford Tugwell, a curly-haired, good-looking Columbia professor of only forty-two, liked to shock friends and enemies with easy talk about "doing America over," but his studies of agricultural economics and a visit to Soviet Russia had left him with deep concern over the chaos of atomistic competition during the Depression. Another professor, Adolf A. Berle, Jr., was an authority on corporation law and coauthor of the classic study *The Modern Corporation and Private Property*. A child prodigy who, his enemies said, had continued to be a child long after he had ceased being a prodigy, Berle was still a brash young man of thirty-seven, who could overwhelm banker and bureaucrat alike with his biting tongue and his vast information on financial practices.

Newspapermen made much of the brain trust and its supposed hold on Roosevelt's mind. They still did not know their man. If the President was excited by the young men and their sparkling notions, he was receptive, too, to many others in the host of advisers around him, among them Professor George F. Warren and his monetary theories, James Bonbright, a utilities expert, Frank A. Pearson, another monetary theorist, and Schuyler Wallace, a student of public administration.

And professors were only part of Roosevelt's stable of advisers. He consulted a good deal with financiers like Bernard Baruch, wise old politicos like Cox and Colonel House, labor leaders like William Green of the American Federation of Labor, with businessmen, farm politicians, state officials, newspaper editors, old friends, party leaders. Especially important were a number of senators and representatives who had helped line up delegates for Roosevelt in their states. In their ideas these legislators stretched across the political spectrum, but Roosevelt was under special obligation to a group of Southerners, most notably the men of Texas: Garner, Rayburn, and Senator Tom Connally.

Roosevelt knew how to use these men for his own purposes; he resembled Hawthorne's picture of Andrew Jackson as one who compelled every man who came within his reach to be his tool, and the more cunning the man, the sharper the tool. But the process worked the other way, too. Through these men Roosevelt was supplementing his own ideas gained from the Square Deal and the New Freedom, from his state and navy years, with the ideas of men who had been immersed in one or another of the great range of American political traditions. He was sinking taproots into the whole American experience.

For in this group—sometimes in the same person—mingled and jostled ideas stretching back to a variety of thinkers and movements: back to Democratic heroes like Jefferson and Cleveland who preached against big government; back to the state laboratories of La Follette and Hughes and their testing out of social reforms; back to thinkers like Thorstein Veblen, with his sardonic examination of waste under capitalism, or like Herbert Croly and his ideas of a national concert of interests under a strong national government, or like John Dewey, with his zest for experimentation and practicality; back to the populist revolt against the Eastern money power; back to Samuel Gompers and his fight for labor's place in the sun; back to Louis Brandeis and his passion for hard facts and statistics; back to the economic internationalism of the South and the nationalism of the Midwest; back to the idea of governmental control and development of national resources—especially water and electric power—that had flowered notably in the Northwest; back to a host of men and movements hoping for salvation through tinkering with money and credit; back to the muckrakers and their campaigns for clean government and civic virtue; back to Theodore Roosevelt and his eagerness to use government to curb economic power and special privilege; back to Wilson's fight for the little man and for his right to compete effectively against the economic giants; back to the World War I experience of fighting a war by mobilizing and integrating the whole industrial weight of a nation; back to the idea of the American Construction Council and of many businessmen that business must curb excessive competition and draw together in larger, more harmonious units.

Many of these ideas were mutually contradictory, and some would be squeezed out in the press of crisis. In any event, Roosevelt did not swallow them all equally. He had an order of priority which amounted to something of a political creed. He believed—most of the time—that government could be used as a means to human betterment. He preached the need to make government efficient and honest. He wanted to help the underdog, although not necessarily at the expense of the top dog. He believed that private, special interests must be subordinated to the general interest. He sought to conserve both the natural resources and the moral values of America.

These made up a collection of general concepts rather than an operating program, and some of Roosevelt's associates were amazed and even frightened by his receptivity to any notion that might fit under the broad umbrella of his mind. Usually sparing in his use of time, he could spend hours in excited and happy talk with men who seemed little more than cranks. Voracious and prehensile in his quest for information, Roosevelt had a startling capacity to soak up notions and facts like a sponge, and to keep this material ready for instant use. He could overwhelm miners with a vast array of facts about the dismal coal situation; he could impress businessmen with a detailed description of the intricacies of their enterprises. He had, observed Tugwell, a flypaper mind.

Even with this receptivity, though, there was no final commitment. Roosevelt liked people and he liked their ideas, but just as he depended entirely on no one person, he had final trust in no single idea. Even his chief adviser, Moley, Roosevelt let it be known, was to be a clearinghouse for ideas, not a source of definite policy. His mind, Moley noticed, skipped and bounced through subject after subject, just as Roosevelt himself could run through a series of conferences with a variety of people and emerge fresh and relaxed. This lack of final commitment in the long run would have its dangerous aspects, but it had high merit in 1932, when the old dogmas had helped leave the economy prostrate.

Not only the needs of the day, not only Roosevelt's intellectual make-up, but the American political tradition itself resisted systematic doctrines and unified philosophies. There was a real philosophy neither of the left nor of the right to compel the New Dealers of 1932 to examine first principles and shape an integrated and consistent program. The Socialists had made heavy compromises with ideas of reform and melioration, and even so were not a threat politically. A coherent body of conservative thought hardly existed, except to the extent business philosophers had shaped absolutist ideas of laissez faire to advance the interests of private enterprise. As for the progressive and liberal traditions, both T.R. and Woodrow Wilson had altered their programs in the face of stubborn economic and political facts. Everything conspired in 1932 to make Roosevelt a pragmatist, an opportunist, an experimenter.

All in all, it was hardly surprising that observers in 1932 differed so much on Roosevelt's capacities. To some he seemed, quite rightly, lacking in persistence, conviction, and intellectual depth and maturity. Others had seen a different side of the man. To them he had a grasp on Jefferson's deeply humane ends and on Hamilton's creative means; he had Bryan's moral fervor without the Great Commoner's mental flabbiness; he had Wilson's idealism without his inflexibility; he had some of Bob La Follette's and Al Smith's hardheadedness without their hardness and bitterness; he had much of T.R.'s vigor and verve.

Perhaps no one sized up Roosevelt at this time as trenchantly and truly as a picturesque old man was to do. Early the following year, shortly after entering the presidency, Roosevelt paid a visit in Washington to retired Justice Oliver Wendell Holmes. Holmes, now ninety-two, remembered Roosevelt from the war years as a good fellow but with rather a soft edge. After the President had left his study the great jurist sat musing. A friend looked at him inquiringly.

"You know," Holmes said, "his Uncle Ted appointed me to the court."

"Yes, Mr. Justice?"

The old man looked at the door through which Roosevelt had just left.

"A second-class intellect." The words flashed. "But a first-class temperament!"

PART 3 *Rendezvous with Destiny*

NINE *A Leader in the White House*

THE EVENING of February 27, 1933, at Hyde Park was cloudy and cold. A stiff northwest wind swept across the dark waters of the Hudson and tossed the branches of the gaunt old trees around the Roosevelt home. Inside the warm living room a big, thick-shouldered man sat writing by the fire. From the ends of the room two of his ancestors looked down from their portraits: Isaac, who had revolted with his people against foreign rule during an earlier time of troubles, and James, merchant, squire, and gentleman of the old school.

Franklin D. Roosevelt's pencil glided across the pages of yellow legal cap paper. "I am certain that my fellow Americans expect that on my induction into the Presidency I will address them with a candor and a decision which the present situation of our Nation impels." The fire hissed and crackled; the large hand with its thick fingers moved rapidly across the paper. "The people of the United States want direct, vigorous action. They have made me the instrument, the temporary humble instrument"—he scratched out "humble"; it was no time for humility—"of their wishes."

Phrase after phrase followed in the President-elect's bold, pointed, slanting hand. Slowly the yellow sheets piled up. By 1:30 in the morning the inauguration speech was done.

But not quite done. During the next two days frightening reports continued to reach Hyde Park. Piece by piece, the nation's credit structure was becoming paralyzed. Crisis was in the air—but it was a strange, numbing crisis, striking suddenly in a Western city and then in the South a thousand miles away. It was worse than an invading army; it was everywhere and nowhere, for it was in the minds of men. It was fear. But at Hyde Park the next President was serene, even cheerful. Between conferences with worried advisers he worked over his inaugural, adding phrases, shortening sentences, stepping up the pace.

On March 1 the President-elect left Hyde Park for New York City, where he spent the night. The news in the morning was worse. Twelve more states had closed or constricted their banks.

161

The crisis now was nearing Wall Street, the last citadel. That day authorities announced that several thousand New York relief workers would be dropped because funds were running low. Newark defaulted on its payroll. Led by police cars with shrieking sirens, followed by a car filled with baggage, Roosevelt was driven to his train for the capital. While the train passed through Pennsylvania and Maryland where the banks were closed, he talked calmly with his advisers.

Washington was somber under a cold March rain. A crowd quietly waited while the train, glistening with its jewellike lights, backed into Union Station. Policemen in black raincoats bustled around the rear car; secret service men, hands in their overcoat pockets, searched through the faces in the crowd. Wearing a gray hat and dark overcoat, hardly visible in the gloom, Roosevelt walked slowly out on the back platform, his wife at his side. His sons James and John helped move him swiftly to a car. He sat back confidently, with a smile. Photographers closed in and aimed their cameras; the flaming flash bulbs blanketed the big figure and his smile in a blaze of light; they faded, and the car pulled away.

Tension in Washington was mounting. The Federal Reserve Board reported that a quarter billion dollars' worth of gold had poured out of the system in a week. It seemed likely that the New York banks would have to be closed. Word came to Roosevelt's suite in the Mayflower from an exhausted, heartsick President: Would the President-elect join him in an emergency proclamation? After anxious conferences Roosevelt's answer went back: The President was still free to act on his own.

In his hotel room, Roosevelt worked over his speech. Nearby was a copy of Thoreau, with the words "Nothing is so much to be feared as fear."

Only one formality remained before the inauguration—the President-elect's traditional call on the outgoing Chief Executive. When Roosevelt arrived at the White House on March 3 he found that Hoover planned to use the meeting for a final plea for joint action to stop the bank panic. Sitting stiffly in their carefully spaced chairs, the two politicians sparred with each other. Roosevelt still refused to act. As he rose to go, the President-elect murmured that since the President was so busy, he—Roosevelt—would understand if the President did not return the call. Hoover looked him hard in the face: "Mr. Roosevelt, when you have been in Washington as long as I have been, you will learn that the President of the United States calls on nobody."

"A DAY OF CONSECRATION"

Saturday, March 4, dawned cloudy and cheerless. Almost all the nation's banks were closed. "We are at the end of our string," Hoover cried. Roosevelt went to church, where old Endicott Peabody of Groton assisted with the services. President and President-elect motored to the Capitol, Roosevelt trying to make conversation, Hoover dully acknowledging the cheers of the crowds. As he waited impatiently in the Capitol Roosevelt scribbled an opening sentence for his speech: "This is a day of consecration." Out before the Capitol rotunda, a vast crowd waited silently. Slowly, slowly, Roosevelt, coatless and hatless, moved out on the high white platform, between Grecian columns strung with ivy and bedecked with flags.

Chin outthrust, face grave, Roosevelt repeated the oath of office after Chief Justice Hughes in a high, ringing voice. The cold wind riffled the pages of his speech as he turned to face the crowd. The words came clearly to the black acres of people in front of him and the millions at their radios throughout the nation:

"This is a day of national consecration. I am certain that my fellow Americans expect that on my induction into the Presidency I will address them with a candor and a decision which the present situation of our Nation impels. This is preeminently the time to speak the truth, the whole truth, frankly and boldly. Nor need we shrink from honestly facing conditions in our country today. This great Nation will endure as it has endured, will revive and will prosper."

The great crowd waited in almost dead silence.

"So, first of all, let me assert my firm belief that the only thing we have to fear is fear itself—nameless, unreasoning, unjustified terror which paralyzes needed efforts to convert retreat into advance. In every dark hour of our national life a leadership of frankness and vigor has met with that understanding and support of the people themselves which is essential to victory. I am convinced that you will again give that support to leadership in these critical days. . . ."

The trouble, he said, lay in material, not spiritual, things. "Plenty is at our doorstep, but a generous use of it languishes in the very sight of the supply." This was mainly because rulers of the exchange of mankind's goods had failed and abdicated. "The money changers have fled from their high seats in the temple of our civilization." The task now was to apply social values nobler than mere monetary profit. But restoration called not for changes in ethics alone. "This nation asks for action, and action now."

The undemonstrative crowd stirred somewhat to the words: "Our greatest primary task is to put people to work." This could be done by "direct recruiting by the Government itself." Resources must be better used, purchasing power raised, homes and farms protected from foreclosure, costs of all government reduced, relief activities unified, transportation and communication planned on a national basis. There must be "an end to speculation with other people's money," and provision for an adequate but sound currency.

In foreign relations he would dedicate the nation to the policy of the "good neighbor—the neighbor who resolutely respects himself and, because he does so, respects the rights of others. . . ." But international economic relations, though vastly important, "are in point of time and necessity secondary to the establishment of a sound national economy." First things must come first. He would work to restore world trade, but the emergency at home could not wait.

Roosevelt's face was stern and set. "If I read the temper of our people correctly, we now realize as we have never realized before our interdependence on each other; that we cannot merely take but we must give as well; that if we are to go forward, we must move as a trained and loyal army willing to sacrifice for the good of a common discipline. . . . We are, I know, ready and willing to submit our lives and our property to such discipline, because it makes possible a leadership which aims at a larger good. This I propose to offer. . . ."

Roosevelt's voice struck a lower, grimmer note. Leadership and discipline were possible under the Constitution, he said, and he hoped that the normal balance of executive and legislative power would be adequate to meet the task. But a temporary departure from normal might be necessary. He would "recommend the measures that a stricken Nation in the midst of a stricken world may require." He would try to get speedy action on his measures or such other measures as Congress proposed.

"But in the event that the Congress shall fail to take one of these two courses, and in the event that the national emergency is still critical, I shall not evade the clear course of duty that will then confront me. I shall ask the Congress for the one remaining instrument to meet the crisis—broad Executive power to wage a war against the emergency, as great as the power that would be given to me if we were in fact invaded by a foreign foe."

The people had asked for direct, vigorous action, for discipline and direction under leadership. "In the spirit of the gift I take it." He closed with a plea for divine guidance.

At the end Roosevelt waved to the crowd and suddenly smiled his great electrifying smile. Herbert Hoover shook hands and left.

Roosevelt rode alone before dense crowds back to an immediate round of conferences.

"It was very, very solemn, and a little terrifying," Eleanor Roosevelt said afterward as she talked with reporters in the White House. "The crowds were so tremendous, and you felt that they would do anything—if only someone would tell them what to do."

"ACTION, AND ACTION NOW"

It was like a war. While soldiers and sailors marched smartly in the long inaugural parade, while couples waltzed gaily in the inaugural balls, haggard men conferred hour after hour at their desks. In the huge marble buildings along Pennsylvania Avenue the lights burned late, dully illuminating the confetti and debris strewn along the street below. Democrats newly arrived in Washington and Republican holdovers sat side by side, telephoning anxious bankers, feeling the financial pulse of the nation, drawing up emergency orders. Early in the morning they would snatch a few hours' sleep, then rush back to their posts. Outside, the reporters waited hour after hour, breathlessly interviewing comers and goers for tidbits of news. Washington was electric with rumor and hope.

FINIS.

March 3, 1933, Jerry Doyle, Philadelphia *Record*

In the White House—now a command post to handle economic crisis—sat the new President, unruffled and smiling. His own account of his busy first day and its crucial decisions he set down in his diary (which he kept two days and then abandoned). After attending church with his whole family and lunching with family and friends, he plunged into a round of meetings. "Two-thirty P.M. meeting in Oval Room with all members of Cabinet, Vice-President and Speaker Rainey, outlining banking situation. Unanimous approval for Special Session of Congress Thursday, March ninth. Proclamation for this prepared and sent. This was followed by conferences with Senator Glass, Hiram Johnson, Joe Robinson and Congressmen Steagall and Byrnes and Minority Leader Snell—all in accord. Secretary Woodin reported bankers' representatives much at sea as to what to do. Concluded that forty-eight different methods of handling banking situation impossible. Attorney General Cummings reported favorably on power to act under 1917 law, giving President power to license, regulate, etc., export, hoarding, earmarking of gold or currency. Based on this opinion and on emergency decided on Proclamation declaring banking holiday. . . . Hurried supper before Franklin, Jr., and John returned to school. Talked with Professor Warren in evening. Talked with representatives of four Press Associations explaining bank holiday Proclamation. Five minute radio address for American Legion at 11.30 p.m. Visit from Secretary of State. Bed." Such was the breathless course of the President's first day as he recorded it.

The banking crisis dominated Roosevelt's whole first week. The President and his advisers sensed that the key problem was one of public psychology. The people wanted action. The President had promised it. The curious fact was that the important actions had already been taken by the states and by the banks themselves: the banks had closed. Roosevelt played his role of crisis leader with such extraordinary skill that his action in *keeping* the banks closed in itself struck the country with the bracing effect of a March wind. His action was essentially defensive, negative, and conservative—but he made of it a call to action. He even deceived the reporters; the President himself complained to them in a press conference that in reporting his extension of the bank holiday they played up the extension rather than the exceptions he was going to make.

Summoned by the new President, Congress convened in special session on Thursday, March 9. While freshman members were still looking for their seats, the two houses hastily organized and received a presidential message asking for legislation to control resumption of banking. The milling representatives could hardly wait to act. By unanimous consent Democratic leaders introduced an emergency banking act to confirm Roosevelt's proclamation and to grant him new powers over banking and currency. Completed by the President and his advisers at two o'clock that morning, the bill was still in rough form. But even during the meager forty minutes allotted to the debate, shouts of "Vote! Vote!" echoed from the floor. "The house is burning down," said Bertrand H. Snell, the Republican floor leader, "and the President of the United States says this is the way to put out the fire." The House promptly passed the bill without a record vote; the Senate approved it a few hours later; the President signed it by nine o'clock.

Swift and staccato action was needed, Woodin had said. The very next day—March 10—the President sent Congress a surprise message on economy. It was couched in crisis tones. The federal government was on the road to bankruptcy, Roosevelt said. The deficit for the next fiscal year would exceed a billion dollars unless immediate action was taken. "Too often in recent history liberal governments have been wrecked on rocks of loose fiscal policy." He asked Congress for wide power to effect governmental economies, to trust him to use that power "in a spirit of justice to all." The proposed bill bore the portentous title "To Maintain the Credit of the United States Government."

Caught by surprise, lobbyists of the American Legion and other veterans' organizations wired their state and local bodies that veterans' benefits were endangered. A deluge of telegrams hit Capitol Hill. Defying organized veterans was a stiff dose for Congress, which again and again during the past decade had passed veterans' legislation over presidential vetoes. Revolt erupted among the House rank and file, and for a time the Democratic leaders lost control of the situation. A caucus of Democratic representatives almost agreed to an emasculating provision, and adjourned after heated wrangling. On the floor the leaders helped restore discipline through free use of the President's name.

"When the *Congressional Record* goes to President Roosevelt's desk in the morning," one leader warned, "he will look over the roll call we are about to take, and I warn you new Democrats to be careful where your names are found." The barbed point touched off hisses and groans. Despite the parliamentary powers of the leaders, the bill passed the House only because sixty-nine Republicans crossed the aisle to back the President. Ninety Democrats, including seven party leaders, deserted their new chief in the White House on his second bill. More trouble was brewing in the Senate, as the telegrams from American Legion posts piled up.

But nothing could stem the President's momentum. On March 12, at the end of his first week, he established direct contact with the people in the first of his "fireside chats." The President's reading copy of his talk disappeared just before the talk, but he calmly took a newspaperman's mimeographed copy, mashed out a cigarette stub, turned to the microphone, and began simply, "I want to talk for a few minutes with the people of the United States about banking. . . ." For twenty minutes or so his warm, reassuring voice welled into millions of homes, explaining the banking situation in simple terms without giving the impression of talking down to his listeners. The speech was a brilliant success.

The President stayed on the offensive. The next day, when a divided Senate was to consider the economy bill, he shot a terse seventy-two-word message to Congress on a new subject: beer. He recommended immediate modification of the Volstead Act to legalize the manufacture and sale of beer and light wines; he asked also for substantial taxes on these beverages. The shattered ranks of Democratic congressmen quickly solidified behind this popular move, which had been promised in their national platform. Roosevelt skillfully timed his message for maximum effect. The Senate passed the economy bill on the fifteenth, the beer bill the next day.

A dozen days after the inauguration a move of adulation for Roosevelt was sweeping the country. Over ten thousand telegrams swamped the White House in a single week. Newspaper editorials were paeans of praise. The new President seemed human; he seemed brave; above all, he was acting. A flush of hope swept the nation. Gold was flowing back to financial institutions; banks were reopening without crowds of depositors clamoring for their money; employment and production seemed to be turning upward.

"I will do anything you ask," a congressman from Iowa wrote the President. "You are my leader."

But the President did not deceive himself. The efforts so far, he realized, had been essentially defensive. Even with the first three measures through, he told reporters, "we still shall have done nothing on the constructive side, unless you consider the beer bill partially constructive." Originally he had planned for Congress to adjourn after enacting the first set of bills, then to reassemble when permanent legislation was ready. But why not strike again and again while the mood of the country was so friendly? The leaders were willing to hold Congress in session; a host of presidential advisers were at work in a dozen agencies, in hotel rooms, anywhere they could find a desk, drawing up bills. The result was more of the fast and staccato action that would go down in history as the "Hundred Days."

March 16—The President asked for an agriculture bill to raise farmers' purchasing power, relieve the pressure of farm mortgages, and increase the value of farm loans made by banks. Hastily framed by Secretary Wallace and his aides, the measure was based partly

Ding Darling, © 1933, New York *Herald Tribune*, Inc.

on recommendations of a conference of farm leaders. It was the most dramatic and far-reaching farm bill ever proposed in peace-time, the President said later. The House passed the bill by a 315-98 vote on March 22 after five and a half hours of debate, the Senate by an equally lopsided vote five weeks later. In mid-May the President signed the Agricultural Adjustment Act into law.

March 21—The President asked for quick authorization of a civilian conservation corps for the purposes of both reforestation and humanitarianism. This bill interested Roosevelt himself as much as any single measure of the Hundred Days. It was designed to put a quarter of a million young men to work by early summer, building dams, draining marshlands, fighting forest fires, planting trees. Congress pushed the measure through in ten days by voice vote.

March 21—The President asked for federal grants to the states for direct unemployment relief. His move represented a break with the previous administration's policy; flatly opposed to giving money to the states for relief, Hoover in the end had grudgingly backed loans to states and cities. Proclaiming that the nation would see to it that no one starved, Roosevelt was prepared to launch the biggest relief program in history. Congress passed the Federal Emergency Relief Act by heavy majorities and authorized the Reconstruction Finance Corporation to make available five hundred millions through the Federal Emergency Relief Administration.

March 29—The President asked for federal supervision of traffic in investment securities in interstate commerce. To the old doctrine of *caveat emptor,* he said, must be added the further doctrine, "let the seller beware." The essential goal was full publicity for new securities to be sold in interstate commerce. In an effort to restore public confidence, heavy penalties would be levied for failure to lodge full and accurate information about securities with the government. The bill passed early in May. Another measure, the Banking bill of 1933, was intended to impose on banks a complete separation from their security affiliates. Early in May the two Houses passed the measure to help drive the money-changers out of the temple.

April 10—The President asked for legislation to create a Tennessee Valley Authority, charged with the duty of planning for the "proper use, conservation and development of the natural resources of the Tennessee River drainage basin and adjoining territory. . . ." Roosevelt's vision was broad: he saw the project as transcending mere power development and entering the wide fields of flood control, soil erosion, afforestation, retirement of marginal lands, industrial distribution and diversification—in short, "national planning for a complete river watershed. . . ." The measure had a dramatic background: for over a decade George W. Norris of Nebraska and other members of Congress had desperately fought efforts to sell the government-built Muscle Shoals dam and power plant to private interests. They had barely staved off such a sale. Now Roosevelt was urging that Muscle Shoals be but a small part of a vast program that would tie together and invigorate a huge, underdeveloped region. Involving extensive public ownership and control, the measure was almost pure socialism, but Congress passed it by decisive majorities. The President signed the bill May 18, with Senator Norris exultantly looking on.

April 13—The President asked for legislation to save small home mortgages from foreclosure. With foreclosures rising to a thousand a day, he wanted safeguards thrown around home ownership as a guarantee of social and economic stability. Machinery would be provided through which mortgage debts on small homes could be readjusted at lower interest rates and with provision for postponing interest and principal payments in cases of extreme need. Roosevelt had his legislation within a month.

May 4—The President proposed emergency railroad legislation under which a co-ordinator of transportation would be authorized to promote or compel action by carriers to avoid duplications of service, prevent waste, and encourage financial reorganizations. He recommended repeal of the recapture provisions of the Interstate Commerce Commission Act and the regulation of railroad holding companies by the ICC. Both Houses passed bills within a month of Roosevelt's request.

May 17—The President proposed machinery for "a great cooperative movement throughout all industry in order to obtain wide reemployment, to shorten the working week, to pay a decent wage for the shorter week and to prevent unfair competition and disastrous overproduction." He asked also for full power to start a large program of direct employment, and estimated that $3,300,000,000 could be invested in public construction to put the "largest possible" number of people to work. The National Industrial Recovery bill got a severe lambasting in the Senate, especially from the left, but it passed substantially intact, and the President signed it June 16.

"A LEADERSHIP OF FRANKNESS AND VIGOR"

The display of action was dazzling and heartwarming. But what did it all amount to? Where was the country headed? At a press conference late in March a reporter admitted to some confusion. The President's first actions, he noted, had been deflationary, but his later bills, like the farm bill, seemed to mean more government spending. Roosevelt's answer was cautious. Local machinery would be used and the budget for ordinary governmental running expenses would be balanced. But "you cannot let people starve," the President finished.

Roosevelt was following no master program—no "economic panaceas or fancy plans," as he later called them derisively. He not only admitted to, he boasted of, playing by ear. He was a football quarterback, he liked to tell reporters, calling a new play when he saw how the last one turned out. The situation had "moved so fast," he wrote Colonel House in mid-May, "that what is a problem one day is solved or superseded the next. As you will realize, snap judgments have had to be made."

But what lay back of the snap judgments? If Roosevelt's actions were frankly experimental, what shaped the experiments? The main influences working on Roosevelt were embodied in his party, his advisers, and in Congress.

Americans like to scoff at party platforms and campaign promises, but Roosevelt's action during the Hundred Days can be understood only against the party and election background. He had promised economy in government, and the economy bill was a determined effort to honor that promise. The party had promised beer, and his short message on beer quoted the party plank almost word for word. The farm bill had been generally forecast in the Democratic platform and in Roosevelt's acceptance and Topeka speeches. Virtually every other major action had been outlined in more or less detailed form in platform or addresses or both. Never before had a President converted so many promises into so much legislation so quickly.

One result, of course, was that the program of the Hundred Days reflected the inconsistencies of platform and election pledges. But nothing better illustrates Roosevelt's capacity to throw himself into a role than the fact that he really believed in the rightness of his major actions, however inconsistent with one another. Economy was an example. Amid tremendous projects for governmental spending Roosevelt prepared plans for parsimonies in government—for example, cutting a war veteran totally disabled in civil life from $40 to $20 a month. And when Daniels wrote him in concern because state legislatures were drastically reducing school appropriations, Roosevelt in reply complained that teachers' salaries were too high. In the White House, meanwhile, Eleanor Roosevelt was instituting nineteen-cent luncheons, which the President duly ate.

Partly by design, partly by chance, Roosevelt had gathered around him a group of advisers as diverse in philosophy as the New Deal itself. One of the most influential of these during 1933 was the President's budget director, Lewis W. Douglas. His plain, open face and lean frame gave Douglas the look of a cowboy rather than what he really was, scion of a copper-rich Arizona family, and an able politician who had served in the national House of Representatives. So well did he help the President economize that Roosevelt was calling him "in many ways the greatest 'find' of the administration" within a month of the inauguration. Keeping a tight hold on the purse strings, Douglas quickly won a reputation as a do-or-die budget-balancer.

He had numerous allies. Centered in the Treasury Department was a group of men pressing for government economy and orthodox fiscal policies. Woodin was ill much of the spring and summer of 1933, and Dean Acheson, a dapper young lawyer and old Grotonian, often took his place at the White House. Fussy, scholarly looking Henry Morgenthau, Jr., an old friend of the President's, advised him on farm credit and other agricultural matters; although fundamentally humanitarian in outlook, Morgenthau was cautious and conservative in his approach to many economic problems. Roosevelt installed his old friend Jesse Jones, Texas banker and Democrat, as head of the Reconstruction Finance Corporation.

Other enclaves of orthodox thinking were the Commerce Department and the Federal Reserve Board.

But fresh minds and new ideas also had full scope at the White House. Roosevelt installed Raymond Moley in the State Department as Assistant Secretary with the understanding that he would continue to work closely with the President. Harry Hopkins, appointed Federal Relief Administrator, had a voice in many relief and recovery decisions. Tugwell, now Assistant Secretary of Agriculture, did not confine his advice to farm matters. Berle helped draft several key bills of the Hundred Days. But these were only four of a host of zealous, indefatigable lawyers, economists, teachers, social workers, some of them amazingly young, who were flocking into key staff positions in the old departments and in the new emergency agencies that were springing up all around town.

Some of these idea men were more influential than they might have guessed, for Roosevelt did not let the weight of his office squeeze out fresh notions and projects. Interesting new ideas were often relayed to him by Wallace, Ickes, or Miss Perkins, and he pounced on them avidly. Sometimes he would winnow them from abstracts of the long reports that his secretaries piled on his desk. Much advice and information came by mail; the names of his correspondents already were beginning to look like a small "Who's Who of America."

Of incalculable influence was Eleanor Roosevelt. Varied and imposing though her new duties were, the First Lady was not content with presiding over the White House. She was so much a center of interest and activity that by the end of 1933 she had received over three hundred thousand pieces of mail. In that year she began the trips that would take her to an incredible number of places throughout the country, and eventually to many parts of the world. A *New Yorker* cartoon showing a miner at the bottom of a deep shaft looking up and exclaiming to his mate "Why, it's Mrs. Roosevelt!" nicely captured the popular reaction of surprise and delight at the First Lady's gadding about.

Roosevelt was still teaching his wife how to observe conditions and report back to him. "Watch the people's faces," he told her. "Look at the condition of their clothes on the wash line. You can tell a lot from that. Notice their cars." As soon as possible after her return the President would question her closely. When she got back from a trip to the Gaspé Peninsula, for example, he wanted to know everything about the lives of the fishermen—what they had to eat, how they lived, what the farms were like, how the houses were built, what kind of education was provided.

So eager was the President for intelligence, no matter how great the ensuing clutter and confusion, that he deliberately organized his office to cast as wide a net as possible. Not content with the varied advice available in the cabinet, he established in July 1933 an Executive Council that included all the cabinet members along with a dozen or so heads of recovery agencies. Still not content, he established later in the year the National Emergency Council with many of the same members. These agencies were clumsy affairs: they were too big to act effectively; petty difficulties were raised along with big problems; they often wasted the time of the busy men who attended. Moreover, they undercut the cabinet, which dwindled in importance, until eventually Ickes was quietly taking cat naps at cabinet meetings and hoping that the President did not see him.

But one great function the cabinet and the two councils did serve: week after week they gave Roosevelt a vivid picture of the vast array of problems, big and small, that were arising in the first headlong, exuberant, haphazard months of the New Deal. And more, they exposed the heads of thirty of forty agencies firsthand to Roosevelt's contagious drive and enthusiasm. Sitting confidently in the midst of his admiring lieutenants, telling stories, making jokes, knocking heads together, urging action, demanding quick reports and recommendations, Roosevelt almost singlehanded gave pace and direction to the New Deal battalions.

"After spending an hour with the President," an ordinarily rather sober agency chief exclaimed to a friend, "I could eat nails for lunch!"

Supposedly sharing co-ordinate power with the President, even during crises, were 96 senators and 435 representatives on Capitol Hill. What would be their relation to the new president? The question was partially answered in the House of Representatives as soon as Congress convened. As a result of a three-way trade among the Tammany, Tennessee, and Texas congressional delegations, Representative Henry T. Rainey of Illinois was elected Speaker, the first Northern Democrat so chosen in over half a century. Under the deal the floor leadership went to Joseph W. Byrns of Tennessee, and a Texan succeeded to the chairmanship of the Appropriations Committee. Two other leading party positions went to Northerners. In the Senate three friends of Roosevelt were dominant: Vice-President Garner, who was attending cabinet meetings, President Pro Tem Key Pittman of Nevada, and Floor Leader Joseph T. Robinson of Arkansas, a party stalwart.

Within the two Houses, however, powerful forces were working toward both the left and the right. Southerners, generally conservative in outlook, except for their hostility toward Wall Street, were chairmen or ranking members of most of the committees as a result of storing up seniority during the long years of Democratic defeats in the North. Along with the time-honored blocs—public works, reclamation, farmers, labor, and the like—were factional groups propelled by depression-sharpened discontent: silverites, inflationists, veterans. A wholly unpredictable factor lay in the scores of freshman representatives, some of them stridently offering panaceas, others silent and bewildered by the capital kaleidoscope. The Senate had responded more slowly to political trends, but it too embraced a multitude of ideological splits, bipartisan blocs, and party factions.

Left without direction the Democratic ranks in Congress would break up into guerrilla armies. Senate Democrats set up a steering committee and a policy committee, dominated by old hands friendly to the President. The new leadership of the House established a hierarchy of committees designed ostensibly to canvas members' opinions but actually aimed more at siphoning off protest and holding rebels in line. But no congressional strong man was put at the top. Who would direct the steering committee, the whips, the caucus? What program would be followed? The question was not long left in doubt. Casually identifying the Democratic party's program with the administration, Rainey said, "We will put over Mr. Roosevelt's program."

The Chief Executive was Chief Legislator. It was only at the level of the presidential office that party interests, the crisscrossing legislative *blocs,* and the bustling bureaucrats were given some measure of integration in meeting national problems. The fact that Roosevelt's leadership provided the unifying force did not mean, however, that Congress lacked effect on policy. The price of congressional support was that Roosevelt often yielded unduly to congressional pressures. And a striking feature of Congress in 1933 was the sentiment for more of a New Deal than Roosevelt was willing to give. Most of the congressmen wanted more inflation than Roosevelt, less economy in government, a more open hand with veterans and farmers, larger public works, tougher policies toward finance. Divided as it was, Congress had the effect of pushing Roosevelt a bit further toward the left.

If Roosevelt could ride the whirlwind, it was because he himself was always in motion. Throughout the Hundred Days he rarely lost the initiative. He had promised a leadership of vigor, and he was the living incarnation of the phrase. Gay, laughing, confident, he dominated the life of the White House. While still in bed in the morning, his large torso looming over the shrunken legs that hardly ribbed the sheets, he spouted ideas, questions, instructions to his aides. Wheeling rapidly through the White House corridors, he easily swung into his office chair for long hours of visitors, letters, telephone calls, emergency conferences. He did not spare himself. Where Coolidge had disposed of visitors by his formula "Don't talk back to 'em," Roosevelt outtalked his advisers, outtalked the cabinet, and even outtalked visiting senators.

A leadership of vigor—and a leadership of frankness too. Appealing features of the Rooseveltian personality were his candor and his humility. Such was the image projected to the people in his second fireside chat. "I do not deny that we may make mistakes of procedure," he said. "I have no expectation of making a hit every time I come to bat." He quoted Theodore Roosevelt's remark that he would be happy to be right 75 per cent of the time. Economic conditions looked a little better, but "we cannot ballyhoo ourselves back to prosperity." In his press conferences Roosevelt talked much the same way. "Oh, I am learning a lot about banking," he exclaimed early in March, amid laughter. The administration had made some ten-yard gains, he said late in April.

"But it is a long field."

AMERICA FIRST

Even the rush and roar of breath-taking events at home could not drown out offstage sounds of crisis abroad. The international situation had taken ominous turns. Once installed as chancellor, Hitler had, in a few weeks by terror and by decree, crushed all organized opposition, suppressed trade unions, outlawed other parties, and proceeded to erect a totalitarian regime. Japanese troops were swarming toward the Great Wall of China. So serious was the situation in the East that at the second cabinet meeting Roosevelt gravely discussed the ultimate possibility of war with Japan.

Foreign affairs did not seem serious enough to Roosevelt, however, to warrant any departure from old ways of choosing men to represent the United States abroad. Loyal Democrats were waiting for their reward, and the President did not disappoint them. To Mexico City was dispatched Josephus Daniels; to the Court of St. James's, Robert W. Bingham, editor of the Louisville *Courier-Journal* and a longtime friend of the President; to Paris, Jesse I. Straus, who had helped finance the campaign. Roosevelt offered Berlin to his old running mate of 1920, James Cox, who declined. In the State Department, however, was a group of career men including Under Secretary William Phillips, a close friend of the President since Wilson days, Herbert Feis, an economist, and Stanley K. Hornbeck, a Far Eastern expert. Urged by Hull to divide his diplomatic appointments about fifty-fifty between career men and politicos, the President kept some Republican appointees on in the lesser capitals.

European economic problems were pressing when the President entered office, and these he handled with a politician's wariness and a Rooseveltian bent for personal diplomacy. High on the agenda were the intertwined problems of war debts and monetary stabilization. These matters could not be held off long, for a World Economic Conference had long been scheduled for spring or summer 1933. During April and May 1933 Roosevelt discussed economic problems with a succession of visiting foreign leaders, including Prime Minister Ramsay MacDonald and Premier Edouard Herriot. Stressing the "exploratory" nature of their talks, the President and his visitors issued bland statements filled with pious nothings.

Roosevelt had good reason for his caution. On foreign policy the Democratic party platform was vague and platitudinous, and Roosevelt had almost ignored foreign affairs during the campaign. He had few foreign policy pegs on which to hang his hat. More important, he was shaping domestic policies in order to raise farm and industrial prices somewhat. Such a moderate inflation, he feared, might be washed out by an inundation of cheap goods from abroad. To prevent this the President got power from Congress to raise the tariff even higher than Smoot-Hawley levels. Clearly Roosevelt still believed, as he had said on March 4, that international trade relations, though important, were secondary to recovery at home.

But pressures from the opposite direction were strong too. Despite Roosevelt's own shift to a more nationalist policy in the 1920's, many leaders in his party still prized the internationalist tradition of Wilson. If the Democratic party had stood for any traditional policy, they pointed out, it was lower tariff walls. Nor could the President ignore the strong sentiment, especially along the Eastern seaboard, for a positive attack on the jumble and chaos of economic affairs among nations.

These conflicting pressures played on the President through his close associates. Hull was making no secret of his expectation that the secretaryship would crown his life work for expanded trade and economic co-operation among nations. Roper and Swanson in the cabinet were old Wilson men, as were some influential congressmen. On the other hand, Moley, Ickes, Hopkins, Tugwell, and others in the presidential entourage favored priority for the domestic front. Some business friends of the President took the same position, and Baruch wrote him early in July that "there can possibly be no ground for criticism either here or abroad upon the position you take that internal matters come first." Privately Roosevelt struck out at international financiers—"the fellows in Amsterdam and Antwerp, etc."—whose speculations, he felt, were undermining the dollar.

Given these crossed purposes and mixed councils, it was inevitable that matters would come to an unhappy climax. This they did, in the painfully public arena of the World Economic Conference in London. Despite early worries about the gathering, Roosevelt had thrown himself into the role of world leader in his reception of foreign representatives and his preparations for the conference. But his preparations were sadly amiss. He chose for the American delegation a group of men, headed by Hull, who had divergent economic ideas and varying expertness in the field. Made up of some of the most eminent political leaders and economists of the time, the conference had aroused high hopes that it could point the way toward better economic relations among nations. Much depended, it was generally agreed, on the attitude of the United States delegation. But in London the Americans wandered in a fog of confusion, and Moley's arrival with fresh instructions from the President only sharpened the tension within the delegation and aroused the foreign representatives' hopes.

Suddenly on July 3 came a sharp message from Roosevelt in effect rapping the conference for trifling with efforts for an artificial and temporary monetary stability "on the part of a few large countries only," and for ignoring fundamental economic ills. The message threw the conference into confusion. It went on twitching for a few days, as an observer remarked, before it rolled over and died, amid savage recriminations and general hopelessness.

Roosevelt had torpedoed the conference. Why? The answer lay largely in the turn of events at home while the conferees were debating in London. The measures of the Hundred Days seemed to be achieving more monetary stability in the United States, and Roosevelt, at the height of his popularity at home, was not ready to jeopardize this happy condition by trying prematurely to tie the dollar to foreign currencies. Economists divided over his position; some denounced his "nationalistic" path, while in Britain John Maynard Keynes, an advocate of managed currencies, wrote that Roosevelt was "magnificently right." Politically the President was caught in a cross-fire. Those who favored "putting our own house in order" applauded his action; but the internationalists were surprised and disappointed. Hull returned home indignant over his treatment and furious at Moley's intervention.

Equally abortive was America's participation in the disarmament conference that had been dragging along for over a year at Geneva. In mid-May 1933 Roosevelt sent an eloquent direct appeal to heads of states proposing a "solemn and definite pact of non-aggression" among all the nations of the world. But the conference could not break out of the deadlock of hate and fear, and Roosevelt, his hands tied by his repudiation of the League in 1932, was able to offer no more than passive co-operation in any program of collective security. The conference finally collapsed in the face of Hitler's withdrawal from both the conference and the League.

On war debts, another gnawing problem of the year, Roosevelt was equally cautious. He refused to treat them as part of a general international economic problem; he refused even to give the delegates in London authority to discuss debts. "That stays with Pop —right here," he said.

If, then, the war for economic recovery was to be waged mainly at home, what was the over-all strategy for the prosecution of that war? The President was a magnificent leader—but along what paths were Americans to be led? As the Hundred Days came to an end, people searched for a pattern in the rapid-fire actions of the preceding weeks.

That there were orderly continuities with the past could not be doubted. The President had grasped the standard of Wilsonian reform in his measures for federal supervision of securities, friendliness to labor, business regulation. He had trod Cousin Theodore's old path in conservation and in the elements of planning in the AAA. He had filched a plank from American socialism in the public ownership features of TVA. Most strangely, he had taken over— indeed sharpened—such precepts of the Hoover administration as budget-balancing and government economy. And his foreign policies were remarkably like the economic and political nationalism of the 1920's.

Continuities—but what of the present? Try as he might, the most resourceful political philosopher could not extract consistency from the jumble. The Square Deal, the New Freedom, the New Nationalism, the associational activities of the 1920's, all elbowed one another in uneasy intimacy. There was nothing but contradiction between the spending for public works and the economy act, between the humanitarianism of direct relief and the miserliness of veterans' cuts, between the tariff-raising provisions of the AAA and the new internationalism of the State Department, between Roosevelt's emphasis on the strengthening of government as a tool for social betterment and his reducing the cost of government, including the salaries of government workers.

But Roosevelt was now cast as the man of action, as the experimenter, as the quarterback, and consistency was a small virtue. "What are you going to say when they ask you the political philosophy behind TVA?" Senator Norris asked him shortly before the bill went to Congress. "I'll tell them it's neither fish nor fowl," the President answered gaily, "but, whatever it is, it will taste awfully good to the people of the Tennessee Valley."

Nothing better exemplified this pragmatism—both in the manner it was drawn up and in its major provisions—than the National Industrial Recovery Act, described by Roosevelt as probably the most important and far-reaching legislation ever enacted by the American Congress. As the mainspring of the early New Deal, this measure for two years embodied its hopes and its liabilities.

Faintly foreshadowed in Roosevelt's Commonwealth Club speech, the NRA had its immediate origin with a number of persons working separately in Washington during the interregnum. Several congressmen introduced bills to modify antitrust laws in order to prevent "unfair and excessive" competition. Business representatives in Washington wanted to bring some order out of anarchy by establishing stronger associations or councils in the main sectors of industry, trade, and finance, with some power of self-government. Others favored more stringent economic planning, with a governmental board in charge. Labor leaders were pressing for protection of collective bargaining and labor standards. Some persons favored huge governmental loans to industry; others wanted to step up public works and direct relief.

At first the President moved slowly. Aware of the ferment of radical thinking on over-all economic policy, he preferred to push through his crisis bills before turning to reconstruction measures. Moreover, he felt that recovery ideas had not crystallized enough. It was the Senate that forced the President's hand. On April 16 the upper chamber passed, 53-30, a bill introduced by Senator Hugo L. Black of Alabama that would forbid interstate commerce in commodities produced by persons working more than five days a week or six hours a day. This drastic, rigid thirty-hour bill worried the President, especially since it had the backing in Congress of liberal and prolabor groups. As the Black bill gained momentum on the Hill, Roosevelt began to pay more attention to the possibility of an industrial recovery program. He had commissioned several persons to explore such a program, doing this quietly so that he would not jeopardize his friendly relations with Black and his group. On May 10 he convened a White House meeting of the leaders of groups working on recovery programs.

For two hours the discussion ranged through a score of proposals. Finally the President remarked that the group seemed basically divided between a large public works program and government-industry codes. Why not do both? someone spoke up. "I think you're right," the President said quickly, and he designated several present to "lock themselves into a room" until they reached agreement.

The resulting bill did not have easy going in Congress. It was beset on all sides by groups asserting that antitrust laws must not be relaxed, or that the bill was a "sellout" to industry, or that it regimented industry too much, or that it failed to provide for currency inflation. Would Roosevelt's strategy of combining many disparate proposals, thereby gaining support from various elements in Congress, offset the voting strength of the opposition should the dissident groups combine against the bill? His strategy worked, but only because the great bulk of congressmen had an almost blind faith in him—one representative called him a "Moses" leading the people out of the wilderness—and because ticklish political issues were left to the President to decide by delegation of power. The Black bill was sidetracked.

The final act was a compromise among many groups and theories. Industrial councils could draw up codes of fair competition, but these had to be approved by the President. These codes were exempted from antitrust laws, but monopolistic practices were still barred. The essence of the measure was voluntary self-government by industry, but the government had a rigid licensing power to force businessmen in line. In Section 7a labor received a vague guarantee of the right to bargain collectively with employers through their own representatives, and equally vague provisions for wage and hour standards in the new codes. In an entirely different title of the bill, over three billion dollars were authorized for a huge spending effort through public works.

With this measure signed and Congress adjourned in mid-June, the President left for Groton, where he watched Franklin, Jr., graduate, then boarded an auxiliary schooner with son James and a small crew. He sailed contentedly along the New England coast to Maine, even sandwiching in political conferences at stops en route. The bright June skies above the little schooner seemed to be

March 10, 1933, H. M. Talburt, New York *World-Telegram*, Scripps-Howard Newspapers

smiling on the American people too. A production index had shot up from 56 in March to 93 in June. The nation was already feeling the effects of stepped-up relief spending, AAA and CCC checks, heightened business confidence. One leader, manning the tiller off the rocky New England coast, was still the center of public approbation.

"How do you account for him?" William Allen White wrote to Ickes that spring. "Was I just fooled in him before the election, or has he developed? As Governor of New York, I thought he was a good two-legged Governor of a type that used to flourish in the first decade of the century under the influence of La Follette and Roosevelt. We had a lot of them but they weren't presidential size. . . .

"I thought your President was one of those. Instead of which he developed magnitude and poise, more than all, power! I have been a voracious feeder in the course of a long and happy life and have eaten many things, but I have never had to eat my words before. I shall wait six months and . . . if they are still on the plate, down they go with a gusto. And I shall smack my lips as my Adams apple bobs."

TEN

President of All the People?

During the first half of his first term Roosevelt tried a Grand Experiment in government. He took the role of national father, of bipartisan leader, of President of all the people. Playing this role with consummate skill, he extracted from it the last morsel of political power and government action. Eventually his biparty leadership was to falter, and he would turn in new directions. But during these first two years, 1933 and 1934, he savored the heady feeling of rising above parties and groups and acting almost as a constitutional monarch armed with political power.

The New Deal, the President told a Wisconsin crowd in August 1934, "seeks to cement our society, rich and poor, manual worker and brain worker, into a voluntary brotherhood of freemen, standing together, striving together, for the common good of all." Such government would not hurt honest business, he said; in seeking social justice it would not rob Peter to pay Paul. Government, he told a convention of bankers two months later, was "essentially the outward expression of the unity and leadership of all groups." His own role as president? It was "to find among many discordant elements that unity of purpose that is best for the Nation as a whole." Throughout Roosevelt's speeches of 1934 ran this theme of government as conciliator, harmonizer, unifier of all major interests. He was the master broker among the many interests of a great and diverse people.

As president of all the people Roosevelt tried to stay above the political and ideological battles that raged all around him. Insisting that he did not want to be drawn into controversy, he asked his supporters to take over the burden of answering attacks on the New Deal from the extreme right or left. He was forever acting as umpire between warring administrators or congressmen. When his advisers differed over policy he time and again ordered: "Put them in a room together, and tell them no lunch until they agree!" When Tugwell and Senator Copeland were at swords' points over food and drug legislation, the President suggested that they battle it out together while he sat in and held the sponge. He told his agency chiefs that he was operating between the 15 per cent on the extreme left and the 15 per cent on the extreme right who were opposing him for political reasons or "from pure cussedness." He insisted that he was going neither right nor left—just down the middle.

The country enjoyed a brief era of good feelings, and presiding jauntily over the era was Roosevelt himself. While the New Deal came in for some sharp criticism, everybody, it seemed, loved the President. William Randolph Hearst was a guest at the White House. The Scripps-Howard newspapers lauded his New Deal. Pierre Du Pont and other businessmen wrote him friendly letters. Farm leaders rallied to the cause. "To us," wrote Ed O'Neal of the American Farm Bureau Federation, "you are the Andrew Jackson of the Twentieth Century, championing the rights of the people. . . ." Father Coughlin defended him. William Green and other leaders of labor had little but words of praise for the man in the White House. Across the seas a man who seemed to love nobody had a good word for him. "I have sympathy with President Roosevelt," remarked Adolf Hitler in mid-1933, "because he marches straight to his objective over Congress, over lobbies, over stubborn bureaucracies."

Some Democrats could not understand Roosevelt's nonpartisan line. When one of them naïvely suggested early in 1934 that the President come to a celebration for the Democratic party's patron saint, the President gently rebuked him. He would take no part in Jefferson Day celebrations that year: "Our strongest plea to the country in this particular year of grace," he said, "is that the recovery and reconstruction program is being accomplished by men and women of all parties—that I have repeatedly appealed to Republicans as much as to Democrats to do their part." Much as he loved Jefferson, it would be better if "nonpartisan Jefferson dinners" should be held, with as many Republicans as Democrats on the banquet committees. He made no objection to a nationwide tribute to himself on the occasion of his birthday, in the interest of crippled children.

Republican party leaders were perplexed too. During the first months they were content to mute their protests and to bask in the patriotic posture of "country before party." But slowly the party emerged from its torpor. Its task was formidable at best. Republican leadership had been decimated in two national elections. Living almost in oblivion, Hoover was a scapegoat even for his own party, and the Republican leaders in Congress seemed pedestrian and heavy-footed next to the lustrous, fast-moving figure in the White House. By early 1934 they were trying hard to act as a real opposition party.

A MASTER OF BOTH INSTRUMENTS, Nov. 18, 1934, Edwin Marcus, reprinted by permission of the New York *Times*

But what were they to oppose? A cardinal aspect of Roosevelt's nonpartisanship was his quarterbacking now on the right, now on the left, now down the center of the political field. As in the 1932 campaign, he did not leave an opening at either end of his line through which the Republicans could try to carry the ball. Indeed, the Grand Old Party itself tended to split into factions to the right and to the left of the President's erratic middle-of-the-road course. Despite their minority position in the party, the progressive Republicans like Norris and McNary had the advantage of White House smiles and favors.

A remarkable aspect of this situation was that Roosevelt continued in 1934 to take a more moderate and conservative stand on policy than did the majority of congressmen. On silver, on inflation, on mortgage refinancing, on labor, on spending, Congress was to the left of the President. In contrast with later periods, Roosevelt's main job in 1933 and 1934 was not to prod Congress into action, but to ride the congressional whirlwind by disarming the extremists, by seeking unity among the blocs, and by using every presidential weapon of persuasion and power.

AN ARTIST IN GOVERNMENT

The classic test of greatness in the White House has been the chief executive's capacity to lead Congress. Weak presidents have been those who had no program to offer, or whose proposals have been bled away in the endless twistings and windings of the legislative process. Strong presidents have been those who finessed or bulldozed their programs through Congress and wrote them into legislative history. By this classic test Roosevelt—during his first years in the White House—was a strong President who dominated Congress with a masterly show of leadership.

If Roosevelt had ever stopped during these turbulent days to list his methods of dealing with Congress, the result might have looked something like this:

1. Full use of constitutional powers, such as the veto
2. Good timing
3. Drafting of measures in the executive branch
4. Almost constant pressure, adroitly applied
5. Careful handling of patronage
6. Face-to-face persuasiveness with legislative leaders
7. Appeal to the people.

But it would have been out of character for the President to catalogue his methods in such systematic fashion. He cheerfully played the legislative game by ear, now trying this device and now that, as the situation dictated.

He experimented even with a policy of hands off for a short period. Late in March 1934 the President ostentatiously left Washington for two weeks of deep-sea fishing off the Bahamas. White House pressure was relaxed. Soon Congress was looking like a schoolroom of disorderly boys with the master gone. A wrangle broke out among Democrats over regulation of stock exchanges. Over one hundred representatives, breaking away from their leaders, lined up in favor of a mortgage refinancing bill so inflationary that Roosevelt sent word to Garner and Rayburn from his yacht to tell Congress "if this type of wild legislation passed the responsibility for wrecking recovery will be squarely on the Congress, and I will not hesitate to say so to the nation in plain language." Garner said that in thirty years he had never seen the House in such abject turmoil.

The hands-off experiment was a dismal failure. Welcomed by a group of congressmen on his return Roosevelt remarked pointedly that he had learned some lessons from the barracuda and sharks. He added with a smile, "I am a tough guy."

The presidential reins were tightened, but the President never got really tough. He depended mainly on conferences with congressional leaders to put across his program. He even denied that there was such a thing as "must legislation."

"The word 'must' is a terrible word," he told reporters. "I would not use 'must' to Congress. I never have, have I?" he finished amid laughter.

His formal constitutional powers in legislation Roosevelt exploited to the hilt. Reviving Wilson's practice, he delivered his reports on the state of the union to Congress in person. He outlined general proposals in well-timed messages, and he followed these up by detailed legislative proposals drafted in the executive departments and introduced by friendly congressmen. Individual legislators were drawn into the executive policy-making process not as representatives of Congress nor of their constituencies, but as members of the administration. The President met frequently with congressional leaders and committee chairmen, and occasionally with other members of Congress. In practice he fashioned a kind of "master-ministry" of bureaucrats and congressmen with Roosevelt at the top.

The President could say no, too. During his first two years he used his veto powers to a far greater extent than the average of all the previous presidents. Many of the vetoed bills involved special legislation, which Roosevelt had his assistants scrutinize carefully. More important than the veto was the President's threat to use it. Again and again he sent word through congressional leaders that he would turn down a pending bill unless it was changed. On one occasion in 1934, when Congress passed an immigration bill that seemed to Roosevelt filled with inequities, he simply proposed that the two Houses pass a concurrent resolution of recall—otherwise he would veto the bill. Only once did the Seventy-third Congress override Roosevelt; this occasion followed a legislative revolt against the President's economy program.

Roosevelt played the patronage game tirelessly and adroitly. Major appointments were allotted on the basis of lists the President drew up of "our friends" in various states; an opponent he carefully designated simply as "not with me." Routine jobs he turned over to Farley. Thousands of applicants besieged Farley in his office and hotel until the Postmaster General had to sneak back and forth to his office as if he were dodging a sheriff's writ. Farley flouted custom by openly accepting and systematizing patronage procedures. When his outer office became packed, he calmly went about the room followed by a stenographer taking the name of each person and the kind of job he wanted. Only because the new emergency agencies were hiring employees outside the classified civil service (about a hundred thousand such jobs by July 1934) was Farley able to take care of the host of deserving Democrats.

Congressmen wanted jobs too, and the President saw that they got them. When a delegation of Democratic representatives complained to him about the treatment they had got on patronage from departments, he promptly asked the cabinet to be as helpful as possible with congressmen on this matter. The President was shrewd enough, however, to postpone job distribution during the first session long enough to apply the test of administration support, with the result, it was said, that "his relations with Congress were to the end of the session tinged with a shade of expectancy which is the best part of young love."

Roosevelt was not above back-alley horse trades. In the spring of 1934 Senator "Cotton Ed" Smith of South Carolina pigeonholed the Chief Executive's nomination of Tugwell as Under Secretary of Agriculture. But Smith also badly wanted a United States marshalship for a henchman who had a good reputation except for a slight case of homicide. So Roosevelt made the deal, and greeted an astonished Tugwell with the cheery remark: "You will never know any more about it, I hope; but today I traded you for a couple of murderers!"

Roosevelt often fell back on his own charm and resourcefulness in dealing with congressmen. Ickes watched in admiration one day as the President handled a ticklish problem of patronage. Senate Majority Leader Robinson was insisting on the appointment as commissioner of Indian affairs of a man whom Ickes felt to be totally disqualified. When an ugly row seemed in the offing, the President had the two antagonists to tea. First he established a friendly atmosphere by discussing with Robinson a number of pending bills that the President and Senator both favored. Then he let Robinson and Ickes briefly make their cases about the appointment. Before an argument could develop, the President turned the subject back to general policies. When dinner was announced, Roosevelt said pleasantly to Robinson, "Well, Joe, you see what I am up against. . . ." Robinson replied that there was nothing further he could say, and left. Even so, the President waited a day or two, and then sent in the name of another man.

Roosevelt was a genius at placating his bickering lieutenants. Ickes was a chronic grumbler, staying after cabinet sessions to pour out his troubles. Sometimes harassed officials, feeling that their chief had forgotten them, used the threat of resigning as a means of getting their way—or, at the least, of getting attention from the White House. The President bore these pinpricks with marvelous good humor. But he knew how to teach a lesson too. Once when he heard that an important administrator was about to resign he telephoned him: "I have just had some bad news, Don. Secretary Hull is threatening to resign. He is very angry because I don't agree with him that we ought to remove the Ambassador to Kamchatka and make him third secretary to the Embassy at Svodia." Quickly catching on, the official agreed that his threat to resign was very foolish indeed.

Roosevelt's way with the press also showed his mastery of the art of government. He made so much news and maintained such a friendly attitude toward the newspapermen covering the White House that he quickly and easily won their sympathy. The newspapermen were especially pleased that the President had reinstituted the press conference, thus enabling them to question him directly. No one knew better than Roosevelt, however, that the press conference was a two-edged sword: he could use it to gain a better press, but the reporters could also use it to trip him. Much depended on knowing when *not* to answer a question.

One day, while instructing his agency chiefs on public relations, Roosevelt told them how he had handled an awkward query. A reporter had asked him to comment on a statement by Ambassador Bingham in London urging closer relations between the United States and Britain. If he had done the natural thing of backing up Bingham, the newspapers would have made headlines of the President's statement, with likely ill effect on naval conversations then under way with Japan. If he had said "no comment," he would have sounded critical of Bingham's statement. So he simply said he had not seen it—although in fact he had.

Roosevelt used his most tactical weapons for dealing with Congress. "The coming session will be comparatively easy to handle," Roosevelt wrote to Colonel House in December 1933, "though it may not be noiseless." The President did not make the near-perfect score in this session that he had the year before, but he got through most of his program and staved off bills he disliked. To Hull's infinite satisfaction Congress passed the Reciprocal Tariff Act as an emergency measure to stimulate foreign trade without disturbing any "sound" or "important" American interest, as the President put it. The Gold Reserve Act was passed in virtually the form Roosevelt had asked; he hailed it as a decisive step by which the government took firmly in its own hands control of the gold value of the dollar. Farm benefits were extended to growers of cotton, tobacco, and other commodities. The President's requests for stock exchange regulation and for two billions in bonds for refinancing farm mortgages were converted into legislation.

On other issues, however, the outcome was different. Roosevelt had to negotiate with the silver bloc for weeks before reaching a

IT LOOKS AS THOUGH AT LAST WE MIGHT HAVE A VAMP-PROOF PRESIDENT, June 6, 1933, John T. McCutcheon, Chicago *Tribune*

WASHING BEHIND THE EARS WON'T BE ENOUGH, March 26, 1933, Tom Carlisle, Washington *Star*

bargain under which the Treasury would purchase heavy amounts of silver and thus shore up the domestic silver market. On a clear-cut sectional issue, the St. Lawrence Waterway Treaty, the President met defeat, with Democratic senators from states supposedly hurt by the waterway voting against the treaty and killing it. And both chambers by sweeping majorities overrode a presidential veto of an appropriations bill that would have restored part of Roosevelt's pay cut for government employees.

When Congress could not interfere, Roosevelt acted with decision. Constitutionally the President had exclusive power to grant or withhold recognition of foreign governments. On November 17, 1933, Roosevelt announced the resumption of diplomatic relations between the United States and the Soviet Union. This action came after lengthy haggling over terms. Moscow promised to refrain from abetting revolutionary activity against the American political or social order, and to protect the right of free religious worship of Americans in Russia. Rosy plans were laid for expansion of trade between the two nations. Although some of the President's friends (and his mother) opposed recognition, the action seemed to be well received by most Americans, including many businessmen and Republicans.

Many measures passed by Congress granted sweeping powers to the President. By the close of the Seventy-third Congress he held unprecedented controls over a peacetime American economy. Yet Roosevelt did not seek all the power he got. In several instances Congress granted him wide discretion, simply because the factions on Capitol Hill split wide open on thorny political matters and could agree only on leaving final decision with the White House. This was true of farm relief, the NRA, and the tariff. Power, it is said, goes to the power-seeking, but in these cases it was also the temper of the times and the divisions in Congress that enlarged presidential power.

The Roosevelt technique with Congress dazzled the country; but there were misgivings. One of those who was not enchanted was a keen student of national politics at Harvard named E. Pendleton Herring. Analyzing the first two sessions of Roosevelt's Congress, Herring noted the extent to which presidential control had rested on unsteady bases such as patronage, government funds and favors, the co-operation of congressional leaders, and the crisis psychology of the people. Even so, Herring noted, the administration could do little more than "keep order in the bread-line that reached into the Treasury." The more powerfully organized groups got much of what they wanted; the weaker groups, such as labor and consumers, did not do so well. The President had shown himself as an astute politician rather than a crusader. Responsible executive leadership seemed weak in the face of organized minorities.

"Can the presidential system," asked Herring, "continue as a game of touch and go between the Chief Executive and congressional *blocs* played by procedural dodges and with bread and circuses for forfeits?"

It was a good question—but the American people in 1933 and 1934 were more concerned with "bread and circuses" than with academic anxieties.

THE BROKER STATE AT WORK

If the New Deal had circus-like qualities during the first years, the center ring was occupied by the National Recovery Administration, and the ringmaster presented a fresh new visage on the American scene. General Hugh S. Johnson looked like the old cavalry man that he was; he had a hard, leathery face, squint eyes, and a rough bark of a voice, but underneath, curious qualities crowded one another: he was a sentimentalist, an old hand with businessmen and business ways, a West Pointer, and as mercurial and picturesque as a sideshow barker. Although Johnson's long-time boss Bernard Baruch rated him as only a "good No. 2 man," the general impressed the President enough to win the job of running the biggest experiment in peacetime governmental control of the economy that America had ever seen.

Johnson's main task was to induce businessmen to draw up codes of fair competition, which on the President's approval had the full force of law. Administered under the general's supervision by a code authority in each industry, the codes were supposed to stop wasteful competition, to bring about more orderly pricing and selling policies, and to establish higher wages, shorter hours, and better working conditions for workers. Antitrust policies would be softened so that businessmen could co-operate in setting up the codes. Johnson had expected to administer the vast public works section of the bill too, but at the last minute Roosevelt put this under Ickes. So furious was the general that he threatened to quit the whole business then and there; the President asked Miss Perkins to "stick with Hugh and keep him sweet," which she did by driving him for hours around Washington until he mastered himself and promised to go on with his part of the job.

And a job it was. Within weeks the NRA burst on the American people like a national call to arms. The NRA eagle was suddenly in every shop window, on magazine covers, in the movies, on girls in chorus lines. Rushing from city to city in an army plane, issuing pronunciamentos at every stop, Johnson orated, politicked, wisecracked, coaxed businessmen into signing codes drawn up by industry representatives hurriedly collected in Washington. The general became the symbol of recovery; for hours he reviewed a climactic parade up Fifth Avenue, trying desperately to greet the endless river of humanity without appearing to give the despised Mussolini salute. Not since 1917 had the whole nation savored such a throbbing sense of unity, of marching together.

But marching where? Almost at the start the President had virtually lost control of the NRA. He told the cabinet one day how Johnson, coattails standing out behind, had rushed into his office, and handed the President three codes to sign. As Roosevelt was signing the last one, Johnson looked at his watch, said he had five minutes to catch his plane, and dashed out, the codes in his pocket. "He hasn't been seen since," Roosevelt added brightly. The President was hardly more than a front man in whose name an elaborate re-employment agreement was arranged and a thousand other actions taken. Johnson himself had to delegate huge policy-making powers to hastily summoned businessmen who might or might not be representative of the myriad interests in their industries. And in the first flush of enthusiasm the NRA coverage was extended so far that the machinery was nearly swamped. An extreme case was the St. Louis bootblack who signed the re-employment agreement, cut his hours to forty a week, and promptly asked the NRA to make up his pay.

The NRA was essentially an expression of the broker state—that is, of the government acting for, and mediating among, the major interest groups. The NRA was the institutional expression of

Roosevelt's plan for a partnership of all groups, achieved through friendly co-operation between the government and group leaders. But who were the leaders? It was not surprising that in the haste and confusion Johnson dealt with the business and labor leaders closest at hand, those who were most vocal, best organized, most experienced in dealing with politicians and bureaucrats. Who could speak for that amorphous group, the consumers? A Consumers' Advisory Board was set up but was eased to one side; a member quit indignantly within a few weeks of its establishment.

By the end of 1933 the NRA eagle was fluttering through heavy weather. "N.R.A. is the worst law ever passed," some disillusioned Cleveland grocers wired the President. "N.R.A. means National Run Around," read a labor placard hoisted by a Baltimore picket line. Protests rose in Congress. William Connery, chairman of the House Labor Committee, asked Roosevelt to tell Johnson to work with "true representatives" of labor. Roosevelt answered patiently that as one "a great deal older than you" he advised the Congressman not to overstate his case. "Most of us who consider ourselves liberals have the same ultimate objective in view. . . ." But the President could not ignore the protests. In March 1934 he appointed a review board under the old reformer and defense attorney Clarence Darrow, which soon was reporting that the codes had allowed the more powerful interests to seize control or extend their control of industries. Roosevelt trimmed NRA's powers, limited its jurisdiction, eased Johnson out, and put a more domesticated chief, Donald Richberg, in his place. But by the time the Supreme Court administered the *coup de grâce* shortly before NRA's second birthday, it was near administrative and political collapse.

If NRA was the mainspring of the New Deal in shop and factory, the Agricultural Adjustment Act was its counterpart on the farm. The object of the measure was to restore farm prices to parity—to the relationship, that is, they bore to nonagricultural prices in the years 1909 to 1914. To reach this goal, processing taxes were to be levied equal to the difference between the actual prices and parity. The money raised was to finance restriction of production either by renting land and keeping it out of production or by paying benefits to farmers in return for their agreement to reduce production—"to kill every third pig or plow every third row under," as the newspapers were soon putting it. But like the NRA, Triple-A was soon revealing the insuperable problems of Roosevelt's middle way.

The act bore telltale marks of its birth pangs. It was drawn up by spokesmen from the larger farm organizations and the farm journals, under the direction of Henry Wallace. The viewpoint of the larger commercial farmers, organized in the American Farm Bureau Federation and the National Grange, had the most weight in the early, vital policy-making process, while the Farmers Union, generally embracing the smaller farmers on more marginal land, and inheriting the old Populist tradition, was scarcely represented. Millions of farmers belonged to no organization at all; they could not afford the dues, they lacked the time, they could not travel fifty miles to meetings. And no real organization even existed for countless farm laborers on vast, Middle Western farms, southern sharecroppers, illiterate farm hands, and migratory workers following the crops in battered Model-T Fords. Dirt farmers, rough in speech and countenance, returned from Washington deriding the men in neckties and white shirts they had seen testifying for the AAA bill.

Growers of "basic" crops covered by the act, such as wheat, cotton, corn, and tobacco, got quick benefits from the federal checks handed out in return for crop limitation. On other farmers the only effect of the program was to raise their hopes and expectations. By fall Roosevelt admitted that the West was seething with unrest. A letter from a Minnesota farmer named Olson to Eleanor Roosevelt poignantly illustrated the agricultural situation.

Painfully scrawling on cheap scratch paper, Olson described his "tradgety." "I am trying to hold my farm and get food for my children but it is hard this year. Money is scarce and hard to get. . . ."

Eleanor Roosevelt showed her husband this letter. "I am glad you wrote . . ." the President replied to him. "You are absolutely right that many things which the farmers raise have not by any means reached a proper level. . . ." He mentioned his own cattle raising in Georgia, and expressed the hope that AAA coverage would be extended. "All I can ask you to do is to believe that we are honestly trying to do our best, and that we think we are slowly but surely improving conditions."

Roosevelt's reassurances were partly justified. AAA benefits were extended to new crops in 1934, and farm prices and prosperity advanced. But discontent remained. The "big boys"—the large commercial farmers, farming corporations, banks and insurance companies—seemed to be getting more than their share of the take. Even worse, it was charged, AAA checks enabled recipients to buy machinery; by "tractoring" hired hands off the land and "plowing every third row under" farm managers cut down the need for farm labor. Vainly the Farmers Union denounced "scarcity economics" and insisted that the trouble with agriculture was not overproduction but underconsumption.

"The government wouldn't let us plant," tenant farmers complained, "so we had to go on relief."

Roosevelt knew that the acid test of the New Deal was recovery. During 1933 and 1934 he watched the ups and downs of the nation's economic temperature like a doctor following the condition of a feverish patient.

He was delighted when employment rose sharply the first four months after he took office. He proudly showed reporters a chart from which farm prices had dropped clear off the bottom of the sheet—the line had now reappeared and was headed up. But in July came a stock market crash and, even worse, a drop in production. The President dismissed the crash as due to gamblers: "everybody got to speculating and things went too fast; that got a perfectly natural corrective," he told reporters. Anyway, he said, employment looked good. By fall of 1933 he was worried about employment too: "There aren't nearly enough people back at work," but he thought things were improving. He wrote Garner about this time that business was "not nearly as badly off as the New York crowd is howling about, but unemployment is still serious."

It was all so strange. Things seemed better—the NRA was going strong; the breath of recovery filled the air—yet the prosaic gauges of recovery—wages, prices, spending, employment—were moving up erratically and unpredictably where they were moving up at all. The situation looked so serious that in September 1933 the President instructed Secretary of War Dern to make ready army rolling kitchens for feeding the needy where local relief was inadequate. By the end of 1933 the alarmed and disconcerted President was looking for scapegoats. Prices had dropped, he said, because some people had not approved of NRA codes and because "some of our foreign friends" were deliberately trying to increase the exchange value of the dollar. Curiously, the President was almost embracing the idea of foreign causes of depression—an idea he had lambasted when Hoover used it in 1932.

Casting about for a solution, Roosevelt took up a notion that George F. Warren, a Cornell professor, had been pressing for some time. Drawn from the old quantity theory of money, the idea was that an increase in the value of gold would be the decisive factor in restoring higher prices. In October 1933 the President decided on this approach. In what has been called probably the "boldest attempt ever made to give the widest public a brief instruction in complicated economic doctrine and maneuver," Roosevelt told the people in a fireside chat about his plan to buy gold. "This is a policy and not an expedient," he said defensively. But while a government market for gold became a lasting policy, the Warren theory proved an abortive one; raising the price of gold did not boost commodity prices.

"Our troubles will not be over tomorrow, but we are on our way and we are headed in the right direction," the President said in his radio talk. During 1934 employment did improve somewhat. The cause lay largely in programs that Roosevelt viewed as essentially humanitarian rather than recovery-producing.

The first of these programs was run by Hopkins, more driving and sharp-tongued than ever. Told by Roosevelt to get help to the people fast, he had sat down at his desk while it was waiting in a hallway to be moved into his office, and in a few hours authorized millions of dollars of relief. Spurring and goading his subordinates, infuriating state politicians while playing his own brand of New Deal politics, ignoring bureaucratic protocol, Hopkins spent several hundred millions through the states during the early months of the New Deal and almost a billion on "quicky" projects through the Civil Works Administration in late 1933 and the first half of 1934.

Hopkins' main concern was to act fast. Told of a project that would work out in the long run, he answered bitingly that people "don't eat in the long run—they eat every day." Operating at a much slower pace was Ickes and his Public Works Administration. Suspicious, cantankerous, stubborn, "Honest Harold," as he was called to his discomfiture, authorized projects only after he had satisfied himself as to their legal propriety, economic value, and engineering practicality. But by 1934 money was moving out through PWA into the hands of contractors, manufacturers, engineers, laborers, truckers, carpenters, architects, and deep into the arteries of the economy.

Other agencies added to this outpouring of money. The Reconstruction Finance Corporation, continued from the Hoover days, was lending more money than ever. The TVA, beginning its vast development program in the Tennessee Valley, was converting an area that had been a drain on the economy into a source of economic stimulation. The AAA put into farmers' hands money that quickly found its way to Sears, Roebuck and the local hardware store, and thence to manufacturers, banks, workers.

Roosevelt used all these instruments; he put full reliance on no single one of them. As leader of all the people, as broker among major organized interests, he would take the middle way. He adopted spending policies, but only as a temporary measure until the budget was balanced. He favored tariff reduction, but not where it hurt major American interests. He wanted a "reflationary" price rise, but not an "inflationary" one. He was favorable to organized labor, but only to the point consistent with a partnership of industry, labor, and farmers with government.

Nowhere was the President's role as buffer among major interests, as conciliator of rival viewpoints, more sharply revealed than in a statement he made to a press conference in December 1933: "Douglas' job is to prevent the Government from spending just as hard as he possibly can. That is his job. Somewhere between his efforts to spend nothing . . . and the point of view of the people who want to spend ten billions additional on public works, we will get somewhere, and we are trying to work out a program."

THE POLITICS OF BROKER LEADERSHIP

Every politician tries to win elections by simple "followership"—that is, by gauging carefully group attitudes, opinion trends, party activities, and then taking that position that will reap the most votes on Election Day. A leader, by contrast, actively shapes his political context; he seeks to change the constellation of political forces about him in a direction closer to his own conception of the political good.

The genius of great party leaders lies in their power to forge a majority combination of voters around burning issues of government, and through their personal qualities of leadership to put this combination behind some philosophy of government and program of action. Jefferson, for example, built a national following out of Southern planters, Western grain growers, Northern laborers, frontiersmen, debtors, and other sectional and group elements, and this following, roughly organized in the Republican party, put him into the White House. Jackson, too, was a broker of sections and groups, as all national leaders must be, but he was also a majority leader equipped with definite notions about government and able to win popularity with the great mass of people. Jefferson and Jackson as presidents acted for great popular majorities, and they stand in history for a conception of government by a majority working through a broadly based political party.

Roosevelt during 1933-34 was no Jefferson, no Jackson. He did not conceive of himself as the leader of a majority on the left, as a party leader building a new alignment of political power. His job, as he saw it, was to patch up an ailing economic system, to rescue human lives, to bring about generally agreed-on reforms, and above all to promote economic recovery. These goals—especially the last—could be achieved by coaxing and conciliating leaders of major interests into a great national partnership.

Viewed as a matter of political leadership, Roosevelt's Grand Experiment took the form of what can be called broker leadership. During his first two years in office he seemed to conceive of his presidential role as one of dealing with and mediating among the leaders of organized groups, especially labor, farmers, and businessmen. If the economics of the broker state meant improvisation, a host of energetic and ill-assorted government programs, and economic betterment without real recovery, the politics of broker leadership brought short-term political gains at the expense, perhaps, of long-term strategic advance.

Roosevelt was no theorist. It is doubtful that he chose this course as a result of a well-defined political philosophy. It simply emerged, shaped only roughly by his underlying concept of the public good, from the day-to-day projects and improvisations of his regime. It probably never occurred to him that the NRA, with its functional representation of business and labor groups, and the AAA, dominated by the big farm groups, showed some likeness to the corporate state fashioned by Benito Mussolini, with its syndicates of workers and employers. But George Peek, AAA chief, saw that the power of special interest groups could not be separated from the state, even in a democracy. "The truth is," he said bluntly, "that no democratic government can be very different from the country it governs. If some groups are dominant in the country, they will be dominant in any plan the government undertakes."

Such an approach had profound implications for Roosevelt's political leadership. It meant that he took the more passive method of responding to major political and economic pressures, rather than the more positive one of deliberately building up some voting alignment on the left or right that would recast the basic pattern of political power. It meant that he ignored the possibilities for the future of a voting alignment of great strength—one composed of less privileged farm groups, masses of unorganized or ill-organized industrial workers, consumers, Negroes, and other minority groups. It is significant that the President allowed consumers short shrift in NRA and AAA, that he failed to put pressure behind the food and drug bill that Tugwell had drawn up for the protection of consumers, that he allowed postponement of unemployment and old-age pension measures, that he showed little interest at first in Wagner's efforts to strengthen labor's right to organize, that he was hazy and cool on the subject of a pending antilynching bill.

From the standpoint of immediate political gains, however, Roosevelt's way was most effective. The congressional elections of 1934 were coming up. In an "off" election year, with no presidential contest to give a national orientation to the thousands of state and local contests across the nation, American elections tend to break up into forty-eight different arenas, and each of these arenas in turn presents a jumble of guerrilla contests revolving around personalities, patronage, local issues, and hardy election perennials such as corruption and crime. Parties and programs tend to be lost in the dust of battle as candidates and their personal factions stuggle for votes.

Speaking for "all the people," unhampered by rigid party control or obligations to a set program, the President was able to adjust his tactics to the needs of each state. He was all the more effective because of his pretense that he was taking no part in state or local campaigns, even in state Democratic politics. Actually, he stuck a finger into a number of crucial contests. Nothing better illustrated his opportunism and flexibility than his handling of the Pennsylvania situation.

Pennsylvania in the early 1930's presented the materials for major political realignment. Governor of the state in 1934 was Gifford Pinchot, the onetime chief forester who had been ousted by Taft in a *cause célèbre,* and later a Bull Mooser with Theodore Roosevelt. Pinchot had long led the progressive elements in the Republican party against such regulars as the oldtime bosses Pew and Grundy. Coming up for re-election to the United States Senate in 1934 was David Reed, a Republican regular. The Pennsylvania Democrats, who had lost part of their liberal potential to the Republican progressives and had not won a Senate seat in sixty years, nominated two able, colorless, organization Democrats, Joseph F. Guffey for Senator and George Earle for governor.

Roosevelt and Pinchot were old friends. They had both fought the Old Guard in their parties, Pinchot far more bellicosely and openly than the other. Although a Republican, Pinchot was vigorously supporting Roosevelt in 1934, and some kind of political tie-in seemed desirable. Early in 1934 the President suggested to Pinchot that he run for the Senate and indicated that Democratic support might be forthcoming. It soon became clear, however, that the Pennsylvania Democrats would not nominate the governor, for they expected to win with a man of their own. So Pinchot had to run in the Republican primaries, denouncing Old Guard Republican Reed as a mouthpiece of the Mellons and praising Roosevelt. But Roosevelt kept hands off; he would not even allow Ickes to speak for Pinchot in the primary, and Reed won. The governor —and his wife, who was indefatigably ambitious for her husband— thereupon tried to work out a new Progressive Republican-Democratic ticket on which Pinchot would run for Senator and Earle for governor. The Pennsylvania Democracy was not interested, and Roosevelt would not help. In the end Pinchot came out for his arch-enemy, Reed.

It was a bitter Pinchot who wrote Roosevelt shortly before the election. He wanted to continue to support Roosevelt, Pinchot said, but he could not support Guffey and Earle. "The nomination by the Democrats of two utterly unfit men for the highest offices of this Commonwealth, and my opposition to them, will not make me your enemy unless you so elect. . . . The last word is yours."

Roosevelt's reply was a bit lofty—and revealing. He could not understand why Pinchot would support a reactionary like Reed.

"Also, my dear Gifford, I know you won't mind my telling you that I think you and I have always worked for principles in government above anything else—i.e., the purposes and objectives. You and I also know from long public experience that time and again we cannot get just the men we would select to help us attain these principles and objectives. I am not speaking of Pennsylvania but I do know in New York that I have had to work through many people whom I did not like or even trust—but I have worked with them and through them, in order to obtain the ultimate goal."

That being the case, he concluded, in Pinchot's place he would have kept his hands out of the fight. After this exchange, the breach between the two men was complete, and a Progressive Republican-Democratic coalition was never achieved.

In other states too, the President followed tactics of expediency. California posed a special problem. In that turbulent state Upton Sinclair, the old muckraker and long-time Socialist, had won the Democratic nomination for governor with the backing of hundreds of thousands of supporters of his End Poverty in California plan to enable California's jobless to produce for their needs in state-operated factories and farms. Sinclair's thumping primary victory over the old-time McAdoo-George Creel faction late in August 1934 put the White House in a dither. Should Farley issue the usual routine congratulations to Democratic primary winners? What position should the President take? When Sinclair forced the issue by asking to see the President, Roosevelt decided to deal with the situation personally.

Arriving in Hyde Park, Sinclair found Roosevelt at his most charming. The President told stories with gusto, listened sympathetically while Sinclair described his plan, and then intimated that he would himself come out for "production for use" in a few weeks. He even told the improbable story that his mother had read Sinclair's *The Jungle* to him at breakfast and spoiled his appetite. Striking a liberal posture, he told the Californian, "I cannot go any faster than the people will let me."

Roosevelt thoroughly charmed Sinclair, but if he thought he had weakened the old radical's determination to wage an all-out campaign for EPIC, he mistook his man. By October California was witnessing the most bitter campaign in its history, and regular Democrats like Creel were deserting Sinclair in droves. Faced with this thorny situation, Roosevelt kept hands off. The President's instructions on Sinclair's candidacy, Early told Eleanor Roosevelt, were "(1) Say nothing and (2) Do nothing."

Other administration officials did not follow this injunction. Comptroller of the Currency J. F. T. O'Connor returned to his native state to size up the situation and to try to induce Sinclair to withdraw in favor of the nominee of the Commonwealth and Progressive parties. Failing in this, O'Connor talked with Governor Frank F. Merriam, the Republican candidate for re-election. Whether or not an out-and-out deal was made, the upshot was that Merriam put out some pro-Roosevelt statements, the President never spoke out for either Sinclair or "production for use," and the Republican trounced the Democrat at the polls.

Wisconsin presented another ticklish situation. For some time Roosevelt had maintained close political relations with Senator Robert La Follette, Jr., and other Progressive Republicans. In spring 1934 the La Follette Progressives broke away from the Republican party and established the Progressive party. La Follette had supported Roosevelt measures in the Senate, and the President hoped that he would be re-elected. Wisconsin Democrats felt differently. They had plans of their own, and hoped to exploit the split between Progressives and regular Republicans. To complicate matters further, Progressives in 1932 had combined with Democrats to elect A. G. Schmedeman the first Democratic governor in half a century. But now, in 1934, the Progressives had a gubernatorial candidate of their own in Philip F. La Follette, and Schmedeman was running for re-election.

Worried Democrats in Wisconsin urged Roosevelt not to endorse Bob La Follette. Aroused Progressives demanded recognition for the "best New Dealer in the Senate." What would Roosevelt do? "My own personal hope is that they will find some way of sending Bob La Follette back here," Roosevelt told reporters off the record. "But I cannot compel the Democracy of Wisconsin to go ahead and nominate him." Lacking presidential direction, the Wisconsin Democracy put up a regular Democrat against Senator La Follette.

Faced with this predicament, Roosevelt decided to take a bipartisan stand. Speaking at Green Bay, Wisconsin, early in August, he patted both Senator La Follette and Governor Schmedeman on the back and praised them for their co-operation. Election time brought happy results for Roosevelt, but not for the Wisconsin Democrats. Both La Follette brothers won over their Democratic foes, and the local Democracy continued as a weak opposition party lacking New Deal support either in Washington or at home.

Minnesota combined still different hues in the splotchy pigmentation of state-by-state politics. Here, too, a New Dealish third party—

the Farmer Labor party—was involved, and here, too, the Democrats were shot through with factionalism and dominated by patronage bosslets; but in Minnesota, one Democratic faction had been virtually an adjunct of the Farmer-Laborites. Who wore the Roosevelt mantle in Minnesota? By 1934 regular Democrats suspected that Roosevelt would recognize the Farmer-Laborite governor, Floyd B. Olson, and the Farmer-Laborite Senator, Henrik Shipstead, both candidates for re-election against regular Democrats.

They suspected correctly. Roosevelt wrote in longhand to Farley: "In Minnesota *hands off*—don't encourage opposition to Shipstead or Oleson [sic]." Roosevelt himself was "in a quandary" about Minnesota, he told reporters. In the end both Farmer-Laborites won handsomely.

In New Mexico, a childhood friend of Roosevelt, Senator Bronson Cutting, was running for re-election as a progressive Republican. The President and Cutting had had a falling out over the bonus bill, and administration patronage had gone largely to the Democratic organization. Cutting and his Democratic opponent, Dennis Chavez, fought a close race that went into the Senate as a disputed contest; flying back to New Mexico for some election affidavits, Cutting was killed in a plane crash. Roosevelt said later that he had told Cutting that he was willing to give Chavez a job to drop the fight, but Cutting had turned down the offer. Roosevelt had taken no further action except to tell reporters that Cutting was a "very old boyfriend of mine" but Chavez was a pretty good congressman.

"I am trying to get across the idea that if we have the right kind of people," Roosevelt had said to his press conference, "the party label does not mean so very much." Of course, he added amid a burst of laughter, that had to be kept off the record.

RUPTURE ON THE RIGHT

The President's tactics paid off at the polls. One of the few permissible generalizations about American politics had been that a President's party loses some strength during nonpresidential or off-year elections. Such was not the case in 1934. Democratic strength rose from 313 to 322 in the House and—incredibly—from 59 to 69 in the Senate, and Democrats took over governorships in a number of states.

"Some of our friends think the majority top heavy," Garner wrote the President, "but if properly handled, the House and Senate will be all right and I am sure you can arrange that."

Certain results were especially satisfying to the President. Both Guffey and Earle won in Pennsylvania. Bob La Follette, Jr., swept

Wisconsin. Olson and Shipstead triumphed in Minnesota. Pittman won in Nevada, Wheeler in Montana, and a newcomer named Harry S. Truman in Missouri. Roosevelt was by no means disturbed by Sinclair's defeat in California.

The outcome was a tribute not merely to Roosevelt's tactics in 1934. It was a tribute much more to Roosevelt himself—and to the New Deal, which in all its excitement and ambiguities he symbolized. As no President had since Theodore Roosevelt, he towered over his administration and his age. At a time when Americans wanted a man of action in the White House, he provided action or at least the appearance of action. At a time when they wanted confidence, he talked bravely, reassuringly about the future; whatever the mistakes, we were "Looking Forward," we were "On Our Way," the titles of two books he put out in 1933 and 1934. At a time when Americans wanted good cheer, he filled the White House with laughter.

Some leaders have the power to inspire intense love and devotion in the circle of friends and subordinates immediately around them, while appearing frigid and aloof to the millions out beyond. Other leaders possess just the reverse qualities. To a remarkable degree Roosevelt appealed both to his immediate circle and to the great public as well. "I have been as close to Franklin Roosevelt as a valet," said Louis Howe, no sentimentalist, as he lay slowly dying in a Washington hospital, "and he is still a hero to me." Even crusty, churlish Harold Ickes melted under the Rooseveltian charm. "The President is a fine companion . . ." he noted in his diary after a trip with Roosevelt. "He is highly intelligent, quick-witted, and he can both receive and give a good thrust. He has a wide range of interests and is exceedingly human." Watching the patients at Warm Springs swarming around Roosevelt's car, singing to him, laughing with him, treating him like a big jolly brother, Ickes said, "I have never had contact with a man who was loved as he is."

But Roosevelt's ultimate strength was always his hold on the people. During his second year in office he maintained his popularity through timely action, unfailing cheerfulness in public and private, and a masterly grasp of public opinion. Millions sat by their radios to hear his warm, reassuring words; hundreds of thousands saw their radiant Chief Executive during his extensive trips throughout the country. These trips were tonic for the people; they were also tonic for Roosevelt. He believed that he could read people's feelings by their faces. Telling his Emergency Council after a Western trip the difference between the faces of 1932 and those of 1934, he said: "You could tell what the difference was by standing on the end of the car and looking at the crowd. They were a hopeful people. They had courage written all over their faces

They looked cheerful. They knew they were 'up against it,' but they were going to see the thing through. . . ."

It was not strange that a Chicago welder or an Atlanta housewife or a Waco filling station proprietor wrote the President letters of affection, told him of their hopes and worries and troubles. But it was notable that men who were themselves leaders turned to the President for direction and support. Late in 1934 McIntyre informed his chief that publisher Roy Howard, who had been "carrying the flag for the New Deal," had reached the point now where he would like to come in to get fresh information before he got off on the wrong tack through misunderstanding. Businessmen, labor chiefs, bankers, newspaper editors, farm leaders left the White House cheered, impressed, relieved.

He needed people, too, and he reached out for them. A visiting professor like Harold Laski, the British Socialist, or a prominent businessman with ideas, or a traveler with an interesting report on a foreign land, or an elder statesman like Colonel House, or an observant politician in from the West—any of these might expect an invitation to the White House. Mrs. Roosevelt continued to have "interesting" people in to tea, and Felix Frankfurter assiduously sent along men with fresh minds. Roosevelt exploited visitors as more introverted leaders might use books—as sources of information.

In projecting his charm out to the masses, the President made full

HIS GREATEST FIGHT LIES AHEAD.

Aug. 1, 1933, Jerry Doyle, Philadelphia *Record*

use of the two great media of communication, press and radio. He
continued to captivate the reporters in his press conferences with
his joshing and fun-making, his swift repartee, his sense of the dramatic, his use of first names and easy geniality. Again and again the
press conferences erupted in bursts of laughter.

But Roosevelt's most important link with the people was the
"fireside chat." Read in cold newspaper print the next day, these
talks seemed somewhat stilted and banal. Heard in the parlor, they
were fresh, intimate, direct, moving. The radio chats were effective
largely because Roosevelt threw himself into the role of a father
talking with his great family. He made a conscious effort to visualize
the people he was talking to. He forgot the microphone; as he
talked, "his head would nod and his hands would move in simple,
natural, comfortable gestures," Miss Perkins noted. "His face would
smile and light up as though he were actually sitting on the front
porch or in the parlor with them." And his listeners would nod
and smile and laugh with him.

In his first two years in office Roosevelt achieved to a remarkable
degree the exalted position of being President of all the people.
Could it last? Could he keep a virtually united people behind him?

He could not. Even during his first year there were subdued
rumblings of discontent. In 1934 opposition was taking organized
form, especially on the right.

The opposition on the right was a mixture of many elements. It
was compounded in part of a national reaction to certain elements
of the New Deal: the reaction of nineteenth-century individualists
to the collectivism of NRA and AAA; of believers in limited government to the leviathan that Roosevelt seemed to be erecting; of
champions of thrift to government spending; of opponents of labor
organization to politicians who admitted union leaders into high
places in the new partnership; of fanatic believers in the sanctity of
the gold standard. But there must have been a deeper, more pervasive explanation for the hatred of Roosevelt on the part of people
who in many cases had benefited from the New Deal. In the outcries
of the anti-Roosevelt sections of business and industry was a sharp,
querulous note betraying loss of status, class insecurity, lessened
self-esteem.

The President was remarkably sensitive to pinpricks from the
right, especially from people in his own class. Writing to a Boston
banker and Harvard classmate, he went out of his way to mention
remarks that he had heard his friend had made, and concluded
"because of what I felt to be a very old and real friendship these
remarks hurt." Roosevelt's ire rose at reports of conversations about
him in business circles. "I wish you could have heard the dinner-

party conversations in some of the best houses in Newport," he wrote to a business friend. He talked caustically to reporters about "prominent gentlemen" dining together in New York and criticizing him.

Ironically enough, Roosevelt made the same complaint against his critics that they directed against him. He said they were doctrinaire, impractical. When his friend James P. Warburg broke with the New Deal because of its monetary policies, Roosevelt wrote Warburg that he had read the latter's book with great interest. He then urged Warburg to get a secondhand car, put on his oldest clothes, and make a tour of the country. "When you have returned, rewrite 'The Money Muddle' and I will guarantee that it will run into many more editions!" The President made much of the fact that conservatives were criticizing the New Deal without offering constructive alternatives.

It was one thing to deal with malcontents off in New York—the "speculators," as Roosevelt called some of them disdainfully, or "that crowd." It was something else when opposition developed among his own advisers. His anger rose to white heat when Treasury Adviser O. W. M. Sprague, who he felt had offered no constructive advice toward recovery and who had evidently tried to call protest meetings against New Deal financial policies, resigned late in 1933. Scribbling on some scrap paper, the President wrote Sprague a scorching letter, in which he told him that he would have been dismissed from the government if he had not resigned, and that Sprague's actions had come close to the border line of disloyalty to the government. The letter was never sent, however. Other advisers resigned: Peek of the AAA, Douglas, Acheson.

Roosevelt seemed almost relieved when the conservative opposition coalesced and organized in the broad light of day. In August 1934 the American Liberty League was chartered, dedicated to "teach the necessity of respect for the rights of persons and property," the duty of government to protect initiative and enterprise, the right to earn and save and acquire property. Not only were there industrialists like the Du Ponts, automobile manufacturers like William S. Knudsen, oil men like J. Howard Pew, and mail-order house magnates like Sewell L. Avery among its members or spokesmen; there were also illustrious Democratic politicians such as Al Smith, Jouett Shouse, John W. Davis, and Bainbridge Colby. At a press conference the President said amiably that Shouse had been in and had pulled out of his pocket a couple of "Command ments"—the need to protect property and to safeguard profits. What about other commandments? Roosevelt asked. What about loving your neighbor? He quoted a gentleman "with a rather ribald sense

THE BEST THEY HAVE TO OFFER.

Aug. 11, 1934, Rollin Kirby, New York *World-Telegram*

of humor" as saying that the League believed in two things—love God and then forget your neighbor.

"There is no mention made here in these two things," the President went on, "about the concern of the community, in other words the government, to try to make it possible for people who are willing to work, to find work to do. For people who want to keep themselves from starvation, keep a roof over their heads, lead decent lives, have proper educational standards, those are the concerns of Government, besides these points, and another thing which isn't mentioned is the protection of the life and liberty of the individual against elements in the community which seek to enrich or advance themselves at the expense of their fellow citizens. They have just as much right to protection by government as anybody else. I don't believe any further comment is necessary after this, what would you call it—a homily?"

By the fall of 1934 Roosevelt's break with the Liberty League conservatives seemed irreparable. His own feelings were sharpening. He told Ickes that big business was bent on a deliberate policy of sabotaging the administration. When an ugly general strike broke out in San Francisco, he blamed "hotheaded" young labor leaders, but even more the conservatives who, he said, really wanted the strike. The President's thoughts must have been far from the grand concert of interests when, referring to his inaugural address, he told reporters, "I would now say that there is a greater thing that America needs to fear, and that is those who seek to instill fear into the American people." His hopes must have been far from a partnership of all the people when he wrote Garner, after a visit to the Hermitage in November 1934, "The more I learn about old Andy Jackson the more I love him."

Such was the beginning of the rupture on the right. Much more momentous were the forces of unrest gathering on the left.

THE SOWER, Jan. 4, 1934, Rollin Kirby, New York *World-Telegram*

ELEVEN *The Grapes of Wrath*

STUDENTS of history have long observed the tendency of social movements to overflow their channels. Moderate reformers seize power from tired regimes and alter the traditional way of things, and then extremists wrest power from the moderates; a Robespierre succeeds a Danton; a Lenin succeeds a Kerensky. Often it is not actual suffering but the taste of better things that excites people to revolt.

Such was the danger of the early years of the New Deal. The Hoover years had been a period of social statics; the Depression seemed to have frozen people into political as well as economic inertness. Then came the golden words of a new leader, the excitement of bread and circuses, the flush of returning prosperity. Better times led to higher expectations, and higher expectations in turn to discontent as recovery faltered. America had been in a political slack water; now the tide was running strong toward new and dimly seen shores.

Riding this swift-running tide were more radical leaders with new messages for America. They sensed that millions wanted not merely economic uplift but social salvation. They estimated correctly. In a time of vast change and ferment many Americans yearned for leaders who could bring order out of chaos, who could regulate a seemingly hostile world. The New Deal benefits had not reached all these people, nor had even Roosevelt himself. Sharecroppers, old people, hired hands, young jobless college graduates, steel puddlers working three months a year, migratory farm laborers—millions of these were hardly touched by NRA or AAA. Many of them, especially in rural areas, were beyond Roosevelt's reach; they had no radios to hear his voice, no newspapers to see his face; they belonged to no organized groups.

Politics, like nature, abhors a vacuum, and in the ferment of the early 1930's these new leaders were busy breeding and capturing discontent. Their main technique was to offer simple, concrete solutions to people bored and confused by the complexities of the New Deal, and to do so by a direct, dramatic pitch. Their appeal was personal rather than formal, mystical rather than rational. With their mass demonstrations, flags, slogans, and panaceas, they unconsciously followed Hitler's advice to "burn into the little man's soul the proud conviction that though a little worm he is nevertheless part of a great dragon."

The high point in these currents of the great tide came in 1935. It was in this year that Roosevelt came face to face with the men who were turning against the administration and who were hoping to build new citadels of power from the ashes of the New Deal.

THE LITTLE FOXES

On a hot June day early in Roosevelt's first term a young man with a snub nose, dimpled chin, and wavy hair, strode into the office of the President of the United States. He was Senator Huey P. Long of Louisiana, and he was in a huff. After a few pleasantries he went straight to the point. Huey P. Long, he proclaimed, had swung the nomination to Roosevelt at Chicago. And he had supported the administration's program. But what had Roosevelt done for him? Nothing. Patronage had gone to the Senator's enemies in Louisiana, and the President had kept on some of Huey's old enemies in the administration.

Perched on top of Long's red hair was a sailor straw hat with a bright-colored band, and there it stayed during the interview, except when the Senator whipped it off and tapped it against the President's knee to drive home his complaints. This open defiance of presidential amenities upset Farley, who was sitting by, and put McIntyre, who was lurking by the door, into a teeth-clenching rage. But Roosevelt, leaning back in his chair, did not seem to mind a bit. The big smile on his face never left. He answered Long's arguments pleasantly but firmly. He took no blame for the past, made no promises for the future.

After a few minutes the Senator admitted defeat. He took his hat off and kept it off; shortly afterward he made his departure. Outside the White House he said to Farley: "What the hell is the use of coming down to see this fellow? I can't win any decision over him." It was the last meeting between Roosevelt and Long. Within a few months the Louisianian had started total war against the administration.

Long had emerged from a background almost the antithesis of Roosevelt's. Winn Parish in northern Louisiana, where he had been born in a log cabin in 1893, was a land of scrawny cattle, harvests, and people, a spawning ground of political protest. Vocal and energetic from the start, Huey ran away at ten, tried his hand at auc-

June 24, 1934, C. K. Berryman,
Washington *Star*

THE PIED PIPER IS WILLING TO PASS OVER HIS PIPES.

tioneering, helping in a printer's office, peddling books, selling a cooking compound and medicines for "women's sickness," went through the three-year law course at Tulane in eight months, and got a special examination from a Louisiana court to enter the bar at twenty-one. He "came out of that courtroom running for office."

Run for office he did—and much more. Unlike most Louisiana politicians, Huey tried fresh techniques. He attacked the big corporations and seemed to mean it, he outfought the political old guard, and he came through on his promises of free schoolbooks, better roads and hospitals, more public works. He won the governorship in 1928 after a cyclonic campaign, stood off a move to impeach him, and crushed the opposition. His "theory of democracy" was simple. "A leader gets up a program and then he goes out and explains it, patiently and more patiently, until they get it," he said. And if he wins office, "he don't tolerate no opposition from the old-gang politicians, the legislatures, the courts, the corporations or anybody." Huey didn't, and in a few years he made Louisiana his fiefdom.

With his base increasingly secure, Huey roamed into wider fields. Elected Senator in 1930, he had found the perfect national forum. In the Senate, he thumped august senatorial backs, lambasted "Prince Franklin, Knight of the Nourmahal" [a yacht owned by Vincent Astor that Roosevelt occasionally used], "Lord Corn Wallace," "Chicago Chinch Bug" Ickes, accused Farley of profiteering, and turned the Senate Office Building into national headquarters for his Share-Our-Wealth movement. If the means were vague, the goals were definite and glowing: free homesteads and education, cheap food, veterans bonuses, a limitation of fortunes, a minimum annual income of two thousand dollars. Every man a king, and Huey the kingfish.

Bragging that he would go to the White House in 1936, or at the latest in 1940, Long cast about for allies, and other leaders loomed as possible auxiliaries of the Louisianian. One of these was Father Coughlin, of Royal Oak, a Detroit suburb. A burly young man with a smooth face and a smoother tongue, Coughlin had had the wit late in the 'twenties to turn to his natural instrument, the radio. He had met with phenomenal success. One of his denunciations of "Hoover prosperity" had brought a million letters; he averaged eighty thousand a week. When his 150 assistants opened the mail, money would tumble out—up to half a million dollars a year, it was said.

For a time Coughlin strongly supported Roosevelt. "The New Deal is Christ's Deal," he proclaimed, and the two men had exchanged friendly letters. When Coughlin solicited a naval appointment for a priest in September 1934, the President interceded with the Navy Department. But Coughlin's program went far beyond Roosevelt's. He wanted currency inflation, a "living annual wage," nationalization of banking, currency, and national resources. His relations with Roosevelt suddenly turned cold in 1934, perhaps because his leading backer was discovered by the administration to be a big operator in foreign exchange. The voice from the Shrine of the Little Flower, first low and solemn, then keening high and plaintive, was soon lumping Roosevelt with the "godless capitalists, the Jews, communists, international bankers, and plutocrats."

Meanwhile a third figure loomed on the western horizon—a lean, bespectacled oldster named Dr. Francis E. Townsend. A former city health officer, almost destitute himself, Townsend had absorbed some of the economic panaceas floating around California. He was brooding over the plight of himself and his generation when—so the story went—he looked out his bathroom window one morning and saw three old women rummaging in a garbage pail for scraps to eat. From that moment the old man's crusade was on. He came up with a plan that—to old people at least—was spine-tingling in its sweep and simplicity. Everyone sixty or over would get a monthly pension of two hundred dollars provided—and what a wonderful proviso it was—that he spent his money within thirty days. Financed by a "transactions tax" the vast forced spending would invigorate the whole economy.

The truth about Townsend soon blended inseparably with legend, but the context of the movement was clear. America's population was aging; the old rural family sheltering aunts and uncles and grandparents was declining; the self-sufficient community was disappearing. Etched deep on the faces of the old people who crowded around the doctor was the pitiless story of a generation: complicated machines that had thrown them out of factories, new routines that had eluded them, perhaps a long trek westward to the end of the line—and finally the Great Depression, casually breaking several million old people on the economic wheel.

The Townsend movement mushroomed with startling speed. In September 1933—seven months after Roosevelt's New Deal started —the doctor sent his plan to a local newspaper; within a year a thousand or more Townsend clubs were organized. Another thousand or so were set up in early 1935. As the New Deal honeymoon waned the cause seemed to be gaining momentum. Striking deep roots in the subsoil of discontent, it had the indispensable material for a protest movement: a leader who symbolized the cause; a strongly religious twist to the appeal; a concrete program directly related to old people's needs and indigenous to the "American way of life," scorning radical and "unChristian" methods.

Roosevelt's friends were alarmed by the burgeoning power of the agitators. Report after report came to the White House of huge mass meetings aroused by anti-Roosevelt speeches. There was talk, Colonel House warned the President, that Long could do to him what Theodore Roosevelt had done to Taft in 1912. Even Howe got worried after Dan Tobin of the teamsters union reported that members—"decent and honest fellows" too—were asking if they should form Share-Our-Wealth clubs. Stanley High, a White House assistant, returned from the West with gloomy reports in August 1935. The Townsend movement was vital and fast-moving, he warned the White House; it was his guess that the biggest mistake in 1936 would be made by those who thought Townsend could be laughed off.

Guesswork was one thing; factual reports something else. Alarmed by Long's activities, Farley asked the National Democratic Committee's statistician, Emil Hurja, to make a secret poll of Long's national strength. Hurja's findings were disquieting. The Kingfish had drawn from the President sizable sections of his 1932 vote. Long's strength was not restricted to Louisiana and a few nearby states; he had surprising support across the nation—enough, possibly, to tip the balance toward Republicans in 1936 elections. To make matters worse, he was openly threatening to "get" some of his foes in the Senate. This threat had a sharp edge to it. In 1932 Long had invaded Arkansas in a whirlwind, circus-like campaign to help Hattie Caraway succeed to her late husband's Senate seat—"one poor little widow woman against six big-bellied bullies," he said— and Hattie had won more votes than her six opponents combined.

How would Roosevelt respond to the little foxes? He followed closely the activities of Long & Co., but he was not unduly alarmed. He seemed more concerned that the Republicans—especially progressive Republicans like La Follette and Nye—might fish in troubled waters, resulting in both a progressive Republican ticket and a Long ticket in 1936. "There is no question that it is all a dangerous situation," the President wrote House, "but when it comes to Show-down these fellows cannot all lie in the same bed and will fight among themselves with almost absolute certainty."

Roosevelt quickly discerned a critical weakness of the protest movements: their timing. It was better, he wrote House, to have the "free side-show" in 1935 than the next year, when the main performance would start. When Ray Stannard Baker, Wilson's biographer, urged him in March 1935 to keep before the country a vision of high moral purpose, Roosevelt demurred. Public psychology, he said, "cannot, because of human weakness, be attuned for long periods of time to a constant repetition of the highest note in the scale." Wilson had stirred moral convictions, but he had lacked T.R.'s power to arouse people to enthusiasm over specific events.

"There is another thought which is involved in continuous leadership," the President went on. People "tire of seeing the same name day after day in the important headlines of the papers, and the same voice night after night over the radio. For example, if since last November I had tried to keep up the pace of 1933 and 1934, the inevitable histrionics of the new actors, Long and Coughlin and Johnson, would have turned the eyes of the audience away from the main drama itself!" But Roosevelt agreed that the time would come for a "new stimulation of united American action," and he would be ready.

But that time was not yet. Roosevelt's way of dealing with rival leaders meanwhile was not to try to steal their ideological thunder, but to outmaneuver them in some close and tricky infighting.

His attack against Long was of this order. Patronage was doled out to the enemies of the Kingfish in Louisiana, and his supporters holding non-civil service jobs were fired. Theodore Bilbo, a Mississippi politician who had been given a job by the administration, was assigned the task of warding off Long's forays against neighboring senators. In August 1935, after an administration friend had won a primary election in Mississippi, Bilbo wired Roosevelt that the first treatment had been administered "that madman Huey Long" and more would follow. "I am watching your smoke," Roosevelt answered enthusiastically. Federal agents roamed Louisiana checking the financial affairs of Long and his gang.

Coughlin, too, felt the stiletto rather than the rapier. The last thing Roosevelt wanted was a head-on encounter with the priest:

he was upset when cabinet members spoke up against Coughlin. The President preferred to work under cover against the priest through prominent Catholics such as Frank Murphy, ex-mayor of Detroit, and administration friends in the hierarchy and in Catholic laymen's organizations. An elaborate study was submitted to Roosevelt of Coughlin's broadcasting network, and Farley checked on postal receipts at the Royal Oak post office as a measure of the response to one of the priest's appeals for funds. The White House had a hopeful report from Cardinal O'Connell in Boston that the Father was to be called to Rome to head the American College there, but nothing came of this.

If much of this maneuvering was ineffective, Roosevelt did not seem to be concerned. He could wait. To many of the inner circle during the early months of 1935, however, the administration seemed to be drifting and the President losing ground politically.

LABOR: NEW MILLIONS AND NEW LEADERS

On the labor front, too, the New Deal unleashed surging and dynamic forces. Probably Roosevelt never fully understood these new forces or the new leaders they lifted to power. Certainly he had little conscious role in bringing about social and legislative changes that were to recast radically the structure of political power in the 1930's.

The Depression had sapped the morale and strength of organized labor. Union membership, which had slowly fallen off during the 1920's, sank deep after 1930 as workers lost jobs and as a huge reservoir of unemployed made the strike a feeble and often suicidal weapon. The more cautious union leaders tried to batten down the hatches as the industrial storms blew. Sporadic strikes of desperation swept bituminous coal and textile centers, but they were poorly organized and usually ebbed away amid shootings, arrests, terrorism, aimless destruction. By early March 1933 the relative strength of organized labor was about what it had been a quarter-century before.

Quite unwittingly the new President acted as midwife in the rebirth of labor action. The Rooseveltian militance and exuberance of the Hundred Days aroused workers just as they aroused the rest of the population. But even more decisive was a little provision in the NRA act, Section 7a, which provided that "employees shall have the right to organize and bargain collectively through representatives of their own choosing, and shall be free from the interference, restraint, or coercion of employers of labor, or their agents, in the designation of such representatives. . . ." Neither Roosevelt nor Miss Perkins had much to do with this provision.

Framed mainly by congressmen and labor leaders, it was simply part of a bargain under which labor joined the NRA's great "concert of interests." Moreover, the provision opened up a Pandora's box of complexity and ambiguity; lawyers argued endlessly over its interpretation.

But labor leaders made it simple enough. "To hell with the legal talk," they told their organizers. PRESIDENT ROOSEVELT WANTS YOU TO JOIN THE UNION, proclaimed posters that John L. Lewis plastered by the thousands throughout the mining area. Unionism, labor organizers shouted, was now good Americanism. As business improved during 1933, workers flocked into unions—into the United Mine Workers, into David Dubinsky's International Ladies Garment Workers Union, into Sidney Hillman's Amalgamated Clothing Workers, into the United Textile Workers Union, tens of thousands more into embryonic rubber, steel, auto, aluminum, cement, metal-mining unions.

There was a virtual uprising of workers for union membership, incredulous AFL leaders reported. Workers held mass meetings and sent word they wanted to be organized.

With growing unionism came a rash of strikes. Hackies in New York City, shipyard mechanics in New Jersey, aluminum workers in Pennsylvania, Milwaukee streetcar men, Butte copper miners, California fruit pickers, grocery clerks, newspapermen, furriers, teamsters, lumberjacks left their work. More workers struck in the summer of 1933 than in the whole period of 1930 and 1931. And the strike wave surged upward during 1934 and 1935. Symptomatic of the general unrest was the longshoremen's strike on the West Coast which spread to milk-wagon drivers, carpenters, and other workers. So alarmed were Secretaries Hull and Cummings by this situation—the President was on a cruise—that Miss Perkins found them gravely discussing whether or not this was a "general strike" as defined in an article in the Encyclopaedia Britannica.

When the strikes inundated the NRA mediation machinery, Roosevelt established a National Labor Board under his old friend Senator Robert Wagner of New York. Successful at first, the board collapsed in the face of employer intransigence in late 1933 and early 1934. Wagner now saw the need for a permanent law outside the NRA structure, establishing legal sanction for collective bargaining through unions of workers' own choosing. With no help from the President, who in 1934 was still keeping his chips on the NRA partnership method, the New York Senator, Secretary of Labor Perkins, and a group of administration labor experts hammered out a bill that would give Section 7a force and precision. This bill ran head on into opposition from employers and the press and vacillation in the White House. Finally, Roosevelt backed a compromise resolution that went through Congress with bipartisan support and under which the President set up a temporary National Labor Relations Board. The new law was fuzzy on major points. Roosevelt still had no collective bargaining policy; he was still floundering from crisis to crisis.

And more crises were building up. The events of 1933 and 1934 had released labor forces that were putting the old machinery of the labor movement under severe strain. Spunky young leaders were emerging in great industrial centers—men who had left assembly lines only a few months back to form unions, lead strikes, organize picket lines, cope with bosses, scabs, cops, judges. Eager to organize the new millions, the AFL was still dominated by leaders of craft-type unions who had an old and tested way of recruiting members—put them into "federal" unions, rigidly controlled by the AFL labor chiefs, and keep them in these recruiting stations until they could be parceled out, trade by trade and craft by craft, to the Blacksmiths, the Carpenters, the Electricians, the Pipe Fitters, the Sheet Metal Workers, and a score of other craft unions.

Confronting giant, nationwide, integrated industrial empires like General Motors, United States Steel, Goodyear, and Du Pont, the grass-roots leaders saw that this slicing-up process meant disunity and weakness. Ready to back them up was a minority group of AFL leaders: Lewis, Murray, Hillman, Dubinsky, and a dozen others. What part craft versus industrial unionism, labor statesmanship, personal ambition, and ancient grudges played in the ensuing infighting was obscured in the dust and clamor of battle, but the Federation was soon shaken to its foundations. In the fall of 1935 Lewis and his followers set up the Committee for Industrial Organization.

"Dear Sir and Brother," Lewis wrote Green on November 23, 1935, "Effective this date I resign as vice-president of the American Federation of Labor." A new dimension was being added to the shape of American power.

And where was Roosevelt in all this? His part was not much more than that of an onlooker. The fact was that internal politics of the unions did not interest him. The political implications of a vastly expanded labor movement solidly grounded in the millions of workers in the great mass-production industries seemed to escape him.

And yet vital questions and possibilities were hidden in the complexities of government policy toward collective bargaining and in the skirmishes of union chiefs. They were questions and possibilities of economic and political power. Section 7a put the weight of government behind unions. The question now was the *kind* of union. Much depended on governmental policy concerning questions like the nature of the bargaining unit, the method of election, craft versus industrial representation, the definition of company unions. When, for example, Roosevelt in March 1934 threw his influence behind a kind of proportional representation for auto workers, he weakened the solidarity and power of the workers against management. When labor officials backed company-wide unions and representation based on majority-rule elections, they were building up the power of mass industrial unions.

Humdrum matters, but important. John L. Lewis was shrewd enough to understand the implications for the future. "Isn't it right," he asked the 1935 convention of the AFL in his growling, thundering way, "that we should contribute something of our own strength, our own knowledge, our own influence toward those less fortunately situated? . . . If we help them and they grow strong, in turn we will be the beneficiaries of their changed status and their strength. . . . And whereas today the craft unions may be able to stand upon their own feet, and like mighty oaks before the gale, defy the lightning, the day may come when this changed scheme of things—and things are rapidly changing now—when these organizations will not be able to withstand the lightning and the gale." Lewis was calling for a deliberate policy of broadening the labor movement in order to deepen the economic strength of a labor coalition.

If Roosevelt failed to see the potentialities of an enlarged labor movement for the political coalition behind the New Deal, the reason lay in part in his attitude toward labor. He looked on labor from the viewpoint of a patron and benefactor, not as a political leader building up the labor flank of future political armies. He was concerned about their wages, hours, and conditions; he saw them as people with concrete troubles. It is significant that when he talked with reporters about a visit auto workers had paid him, he said nothing about the union situation in this vital industry but quoted line by line his conversation with the men about their problem of making ten dollars a day but working only sixty-five days a year.

The supreme test of Roosevelt's leadership in this area was his handling of the Wagner Act. This was the most radical legislation passed during the New Deal, in the sense that it altered fundamentally the nation's politics by vesting massive economic and political power in organized labor. Unlike much of Roosevelt's reform and relief program, the act cut through the heart of existing labor-management relations. It had an essential part in building powerful unions that in turn would furnish votes, money, and organization to future liberal coalitions.

Yet for months Roosevelt was cool to the Wagner bill; he threw his weight behind the measure only at the last moment, when it was due to pass anyway. He long showed a special indifference, even obtuseness, to the cardinal question of employee representation. In May 1934 he told reporters with some irritation that the workers could choose as representatives whomever they wished—including the Ahkoond of Swat, or the Royal Geographic Society, or a union, or the Crown Prince of Siam. He failed to see that the essence of the problem was whether or not workers could still be represented by company unions and by a variety of minority and craft spokesmen whose disunity would weaken the workers in dealing with employers and in forging a new political arm.

When Wagner went ahead and introduced his National Labor Relations bill into Congress in February 1935, he not only got no help or encouragement from the President, but it was all he could do to stop Roosevelt from lining up with Senators Robinson and Harrison in the latter's efforts to stall the bill to death. Questioned in press conferences, Roosevelt was invariably cool or evasive. Almost singlehanded Wagner shaped political strategy, won grudging acceptance of the bill from the AFL old guard, fought the bill through the Senate against a hostile press and indifferent leadership. The bill passed the Senate, 63-12, on May 16, 1935.

Eleven days later the Supreme Court invalidated the Recovery Act, including whatever legal support the act had given unionization. It might be logically supposed that it was this action, knocking the props from under the President's collective bargaining policy, that forced him into Wagner's camp. But no; on May 24, three days *before* the court decision, Roosevelt came out for the bill. Why? The explanation lies largely in his simple, pragmatic reaction to the immediate situation. The bill's top-heavy majority in the Senate made House passage seem certain. By coming out for the bill Roosevelt could influence some important provisions still open, and he could wangle his way out of what might be called an administration defeat. He may have been influenced, too, by the fact that Chamber of Commerce leaders, who had been generally sympathetic to his program, openly broke with him early in May. The Supreme Court decision simply reinforced a decision already made.

With typical Rooseveltian agility, he dropped his weight heavily on the scales, once he had decided to jump. By June the Wagner measure was a "must bill." Roosevelt helped push the bill over the hurdles in the House; he ignored the frantic entreaties of businessmen to stop the measure. After the bill passed the House without a roll call, the President congratulated Chairman Connery of the House Labor Committee, adding, "It is a tremendous step forward."

In this curious way Roosevelt and labor first became partners.

LEFT! RIGHT! LEFT!

Roosevelt's sudden reversal on the Wagner Act was symptomatic of his policy-making during 1935. The first session of the Seventy-fourth Congress stands as one of the strangest examples of presidential leadership and congressional followership in modern times. That session had passed several mild New Deal measures and was apparently coming to an end when it suddenly showed a burst of energy and enacted, during the hot summer of 1935, some of the most significant measures of Roosevelt's first term. But if the President's course seemed erratic, the explanation was clear. He was picking his way, step by step, among great pressures, now forced left and now right as he faced specific problems, always moving toward a goal that was fixed only generally in his mind.

The President's State of the Union speech to Congress in January 1935 had given little foretaste of the stormy days ahead. Despite references to the need for more social justice, it was moderate in tone and called for a rather limited program. "We can, if we will," said the President, "make 1935 a genuine period of good feeling, sustained by a sense of purposeful progress." He told the receptive legislators that he was ready to submit a broad security program, embracing natural resources, unemployment insurance, old-age insurance, and better homes. He promised an extensive new program of public works and work relief. He mentioned briefly other needed measures such as extending the NRA and improving taxation "forms and methods." The New Deal, evidently, was to be clarified, improved, and consolidated, rather than extensively broadened.

This attempt by the President to follow a wobbling way between the left and right threatened for months to mire his program in a legislative swamp. The *via media* still would not work.

The huge work relief bill sharply etched the difficulties of the middle way. "The Federal Government must and shall quit this business of relief," the President told Congress. He was not willing that the vitality of the people should be further sapped by handing out cash or market baskets or by giving a few hours' work cutting grass or raking leaves. The most exciting thing about the bill was Roosevelt's request for $4,880,000,000—a sensational sum for peacetime—but this sum was actually about halfway between the nine billions urged by progressives in the Senate and the small "dole" favored by some conservative legislators. Roosevelt also took the precaution of having the director of procurement, rather than the controversial figures Ickes and Hopkins (who would administer it), present the bill to the House Committee.

Steered firmly by the House leaders, the bill went through the lower chamber with relative ease. In the Senate the story was different. With unlimited debate at their disposal, groups on the right and left ripped into the bill. The goal of the conservatives was simple: to reduce the appropriation and turn the bill into poor relief. The labor bloc wished to expand the bill's coverage, but, above all, they hoped to write in a provision that labor would be given the prevailing wage paid by private employers in the area. This provision the President flatly opposed; he preferred a "security wage" of perhaps fifty dollars a month, partly to spread relief farther, partly to appease private employers' fears of wage competition. Lining up first with the left and then with the right were inflationists, Senators mainly concerned with converting the program into a pork barrel that they could open up back home, and adventurers like Long. Muddying the waters further were Ickes and Hopkins as they enlisted legislators to back their own favorite provisions.

Joining in a policy of opportunism, these disparate groups pushed a prevailing wage amendment through by one vote. Roosevelt's response was to have the resolution temporarily killed by being sent back to committee. The President was finding his course hard going. Ickes felt that he was dispirited, looking tired, and lacking his usual fighting vigor and buoyancy. In the Senate, Long was cock of the walk. While the White House tried to find a compromise on the prevailing wage, the Kingfish taunted: "I see by the newspapers that some votes are being switched on the prevailing wage amendment. I resent anyone calling on anybody for a trade without calling on me first. . . . I might cut the price a little bit." He rambled on. "I am a dyed-in-the-wool party man. I do not know just what party I am in right now, but I am for the party."

By compromising with the liberal-labor bloc the administration was finally able to stave off crippling amendments and push the bill through. Passage was due less to Roosevelt—who was cruising on the *Nourmahal* during the latter stages and complaining that the Senate was a "headache" and the whole situation "too childish for grownups"—than to administration leaders on the Hill and to the legislators' willingness to compromise on certain issues by leaving them to the President. Roosevelt had to accept some losses: most notably a provision requiring senatorial confirmation for employees under the measure who earned more than $5,000 a year.

By early April when the relief bill passed, Roosevelt had only this victory in three months. He had appealed to the Senate to ratify United States adherence to the World Court, but the effort had failed amid a deluge of hostile telegrams, many of them stirred up by Coughlin. His social security bill, which would commit the nation to a program of assisting the jobless and the poor through federal and state action, was floundering between the same forces that had almost ground the relief bill to death: the liberals were sorely disappointed by its limited coverage and by the reliance it put on state participation; the conservatives thought it went too far. A veterans' bonus bill had passed the House with more than enough votes to override the expected presidential veto.

Never had Roosevelt been so squeezed among opposing political forces as during the spring of 1935. Spokesmen of the United States Chamber of Commerce sharply attacked the administration. Meeting with the President in mid-May, progressive senators La Follette, Wheeler, Norris, and Johnson, backed up by Ickes and Wallace, urged him to assert the leadership that the country, they said, was demanding. Roosevelt's old adviser Felix Frankfurter reported that Justice Louis Brandeis had sent word that it was the eleventh hour. La Follette reminded the President that Theodore Roosevelt had taken open issue with members of his own party.

Roosevelt indicated to the progressives that he would take a firmer stand. But despite the pressure from left and right, and from the agitators of discontent, he was not yet ready to jettison the middle way. He was still pinning his hopes on an extension of NRA for two years. The NRA was not Little Orphan Annie, he told reporters, but "a very live young lady" and he expected the two-year extension to go through.

Then, late in May, came the unanimous decision of the Supreme Court invalidating the NRA, mainly on the grounds that Congress had exercised power beyond the scope of the interstate commerce clause and had delegated too much of this power outside its own reach. It was a jolting blow to the heart of Roosevelt's middle way.

For four days the President was silent, while the country waited expectantly. Then, on May 31, he gave his answer in a carefully staged performance. As the reporters trooped up to his desk, they saw an open copy of the high court's opinion on one side, and on the other a dozen or more telegrams. Eleanor Roosevelt was there, knitting on a blue sock. The President leaned back in his chair, lighted a cigarette, jestingly asked, as he so often did, whether the reporters had any news. Did he care to comment on the NRA? a reporter asked.

"Well, Steve, if you insist. That's an awful thing to put up to a fellow at this hour of the morning just out of bed." But the President was eager to talk. And talk he did, for almost an hour and a half.

His monologue was not that of a liberal outraged by a tory court.

It was a long dissenting opinion by a man who had been following a moderate course helping and mediating among businessmen, workers, and farmers alike, and now to his surprise finds the props knocked from under him. One by one he quoted from the pile of telegrams. These "pathetic appeals," as he called them, came not from unemployed workers or from desperate farmers but from businessmen—drugstore proprietors in Indiana, a candy seller in Massachusetts, a Georgia businessman, a large department store owner, a cigar store operator. Pushing the telegrams aside, the President paused dramatically. What were the implications of the decision? It simply made impossible national action, collective action, the great partnership. Clearly he was attacking the decision not because it was conservative or antilabor but because it thwarted action by the national government to help all groups, including business.

Again and again the President insisted it was not a partisan issue. Where to go next? "Don't call it right or left; that is just first-year high school language, just about. It is not right or left. . . ." Then he slashed at the Court again. A "horse-and-buggy definition of interstate commerce." And he let the reporters quote that phrase.

FDR—'HORSE-AND-BUGGY DECISION' shouted next day from front pages across the nation. Most people took this remark figuratively as a New Dealer's attack on conservative judges. Actually Roosevelt was speaking literally—he was dissenting with judges who thought that national problems could be solved by forty-eight separate states. Pressed by reporters as to how he would cope with the effect of the decision, the President said, "We haven't got to that yet."

Then began the second Hundred Days.

Congress, which had been idling for weeks and had come to a standstill after the court decision, was galvanized into action. Roosevelt threw himself into the legislative battle. No longer was he squeamish about putting the lash to congressional flanks. Now he was bluntly telling congressional leaders that certain bills *must* be passed. Administration contact men ranged amid the legislative rank and file, applying pressure. Late in the afternoon they would report back to the President. When they mentioned a balking congressman, the big hand would move instantly to the telephone; in a few moments the President would have the congressman on the wire, coaxing him, commanding him, negotiating with him. To scores of others Roosevelt dictated one- or two-sentence chits asking for action. He and his lieutenants, working late into the night, acting in close concert with friendly leaders on Capitol Hill, stayed one or two jumps ahead of the divided opposition. Congressmen complained, balked, dragged their heels, but in the end they acted.

The Wagner Labor Relations Act went through with a rush before the end of June, and the President signed it enthusiastically. The Social Security Act was passed, also by heavy majorities. Banking and Tennessee Valley legislation were strengthened. The AAA was modified in an attempt to protect it against judicial veto. The holding company bill, which was designed to curb the power of giant utility holding companies over their operating subsidiaries, and which Roosevelt had been urging since January, went through under intensified administration pressure. And a controversial tax bill became law despite intense opposition from business and grumbling among congressmen that the President was pushing them too hard.

Nothing better showed Roosevelt's sudden change of direction than the tax bill. He had said nothing about such a measure in his January message; his budget message had suggested that no new taxes would be needed. He had toyed with a "share-the-wealth" scheme of the Treasury's in February, but as late as May 22 he seemed to be sticking to his January position. Unexpectedly on June 19 the President asked Congress for an inheritance tax as well as the estate tax, gift taxes to balk evasion of the inheritance tax, stepped-up income taxes on "very great individual incomes," and a corporation income tax graduated according to the size of corporations, with a dividend tax to prevent evasion. Leaving Congress "tired, sick, and sore, and in confusion," as one Senator said, the President then departed for the Yale-Harvard boat races.

What had happened? Had the President turned left?

Viewed in retrospect, Roosevelt's course seemed to many a sudden and massive shift leftward, away from the *via media* of the first two years to a commanding position on the left. From such a view it was an easy step to the further assumption that Roosevelt had shifted left to meet the rising hurricanes among labor, farmers, Long, Coughlin, Townsend & Co. The trouble with this theory is that it does not fit the way Roosevelt actually behaved. His reaction to the hurricanes set off by agitators of discontent was to outmaneuver the leaders and to give way a bit to the blast, not to steal the ideological thunder of the left. He did not exploit the potentialities of encouraging and allying himself with the new millions of labor.

What did happen was the convergence of a number of trends and episodes at a crucial point—June 1935—that left Roosevelt in the posture of a radical. The Supreme Court demolished the main institutional apparatus of the middle way by invalidating NRA. In filling this void, Roosevelt salvaged 7a (in the form of the Wagner Act) and other NRA provisions that had been concessions to the left. The Court's decision made impossible the resurrection of the code features that had been the NRA's attraction for certain business and industrial groups. The result of this situation was that merely carrying on prolabor elements of the NRA meant a leftward shift.

This was one reason for Roosevelt's new posture; another was the practical effect of dealing with Congress. Following a middle way between the progressive and conservative factions had not been as easy in 1935 as it had been earlier. For one thing, Congress had shifted leftward in interest and ideology after the November 1934 election. In the early months of 1935 Roosevelt's program had been bombarded from right and left, and narrowly escaped destruction. The exigencies of congressional politics pulled him to a more liberal program, and it was significant that his new position, harmonizing more smoothly with the majority in Congress on the left, resulted in an even more important array of measures than those of the first Hundred Days.

But the main reason for the new posture was the cumulative impact of the attacks from the right. He had been following a mid-

APPLYING THE PRESSURE, May 1, 1935, C. H. Sykes, Philadelphia *Public Ledger*

dle way; "as he looked back on it all," recalled Moley, who was watching him closely during this period, "he was, like Clive, amazed at his own moderation." The undercover attacks of business, the criticism that filled most of the press, the open desertion of big businessmen as symbolized in the Liberty League and smaller businessmen as represented in the Chamber of Commerce, the drifting away of conservative advisers like Moley—all these played their part. The desertion of the right, especially in the NRA decision, automatically helped shift Roosevelt to the left.

The theory that Roosevelt executed a swing left for ideological reasons as a result only of the NRA decision runs hard up against other strands of Roosevelt's development. His program had always embraced liberal measures as well as orthodox ones. Social security had long been in the works—Roosevelt in 1930 had been the first leading politician to advocate unemployment insurance—and it was put off to 1935 mainly because of administrative and drafting difficulties. The President urged the holding company bill throughout the session. He lined up for the Wagner Act before the NRA decision was announced. The speech he planned to give if the Supreme Court ruled against the abrogation of the Gold Clause would, except for the Court's 5-4 majority for the government, have precipitated a grave constitutional crisis in February 1935.

Roosevelt, in short, made no consciously planned, grandly executed deployment to the left. He was like the general of a guerrilla army whose columns, fighting blindly in the mountains through dense ravines and thickets, suddenly converge, half by plan and half by coincidence, and debouch into the plain below.

That Roosevelt had made no final ideological commitment to the left was made clear in an exchange of letters between the President and newspaper publisher Roy Howard shortly after Congress adjourned. Certain elements of business, Howard warned, had been growing more hostile to the administration, and considered the tax bill an attempt at revenge on business. They hoped for a breathing spell for industry, a recess from further experimentation. In a cordial response Roosevelt defended the tax measure and spoke for a "wise balance" in the economy. But, he added, the administration's basic program had now reached substantial completion. The "breathing-spell" was here—"very decidedly so." The zig had been followed by another zag.

Possibly Roosevelt really meant what he wrote to Howard. But events have ways of committing leaders to new positions. The great legislative victories of 1935 had unloosed forces that were to carry Roosevelt further from the middle way toward partisanship and party leadership. The second Hundred Days pointed the way toward the triumph of 1936—and toward the defeats that lay beyond.

TWELVE *Thunder on the Right*

THE PRESIDENT himself seemed to take a breathing spell during the latter weeks of 1935. Exulting over the "grand and glorious" congressional session, he left Washington in September for a train trip across the country, with a stop for the politician's happy task of dedicating Boulder Dam. A "million eager people" had received him in Los Angeles, he wrote his mother. At San Diego he gave an address on the menacing clouds of "malice domestic and fierce foreign war," and again he sounded the theme of social co-operation and concord. Then, with Ickes and Hopkins in tow, he boarded the cruiser *Houston* for a leisurely cruise south through the Panama Canal, and north to Charleston.

Telling long anecdotes, playing poker until late at night, making fun of Hopkins and Ickes, jubilantly landing huge sailfish, the President was in high spirits. He had time after his return for trips to Hyde Park and Warm Springs, and for some of the horseplay that he loved to indulge in with subordinates. When told that his genial military aide, "Pa" Watson, and Admiral Grayson were arguing jocularly over their exploits in a turkey shoot, Commander in Chief Roosevelt solemnly compiled formal charges and ruled that after being tied to trees one hundred paces apart, "each be armed with a bow and arrow, that each be blindfolded, that each be required to emit turkey calls, and that thereafter firing shall begin. . . ."

It was a pleasant lull, but it could be no more than that. Events were marching on. In October 1935 Italy invaded Ethiopia, and in December Britain and France agreed to the dismemberment of Haile Selassie's beleaguered country. At home, lines were forming for the election year that lay ahead. Late in December Roosevelt told Moley he wanted a "fighting speech" for his annual message— a keynote speech for 1936. Once again the President set the stage carefully. Over Republican protests he insisted on a joint session in the evening, when he could reach the widest radio audience.

The atmosphere was heavy with partisan feeling on the night of January 3, 1936, when the President slowly made his way up the ramp to the House rostrum, carefully placed his pince-nez beside his manuscript, took a firm grip on the sides of the desk, and launched into his speech.

He recalled, as usual, the dire days at home of March 1933, when he took office. But the world picture of that day had been an image of substantial peace. This image had lasted in the Americas. In the rest of the world—"Ah, there is the rub." Were he to give an inaugural speech now, he could not limit his comments on world affairs to one paragraph. In Europe and Asia were growing ill will, aggressive tendencies, increasing armaments, shortening tempers. And what was the policy of the United States?

"As a consistent part of a clear policy, the United States is following a twofold neutrality toward any and all Nations which engage in wars that are not of immediate concern to the Americas. First, we decline to encourage the prosecution of war by permitting belligerents to obtain arms, ammunition or implements of war from the United States. Second, we seek to discourage the use by belligerent Nations of any and all American products calculated to facilitate the prosecution of a war in quantities over and above our normal exports of them in time of peace."

Suddenly Roosevelt's voice seemed to take on a more vibrant, sonorous tone. His bipartisan state paper completed, he was now giving a campaign speech. Within our own borders, as in the world at large, he said, popular opinion was at war with a power-seeking minority. "In these latter years we have witnessed the domination of government by financial and industrial groups, numerically small but politically dominant. . . ." These groups, happily, did not speak the true sentiments of the "less articulate but more important elements that constitute real American business." Since 1933 he and Congress had contended for and established a new relationship between government and people. They had appealed from "the clamor of many private and selfish interests, yes, an appeal from the clamor of partisan interest, to the ideal of the public interest." Control of the federal government had been returned to Washington.

Lowering his voice confidentially, rocking back and forth behind the rostrum, Roosevelt was now drawing blood. Cheers and rebel yells burst from the Democrats, while the little band of Republicans looked on sourly.

"We have earned the hatred of entrenched greed." After abdicating in 1933, these groups were seeking "the restoration of their selfish power." Inexorably Roosevelt went on. "They steal the livery of great national constitutional ideals to serve discredited special interests. As guardians and trustees for great groups of individual stockholders they wrongfully seek to carry the property and interests entrusted to them into the arena of partisan politics. They seek—this minority in business and industry—to control and often do control and use for their own purposes legitimate and highly honored business associations; they engage in vast propaganda to spread fear and discord among the people—they would 'gang up' against the people's liberties.

"The principle that they would instill into government if they succeed in seizing power is well shown by the principles which many of them have instilled into their own affairs: autocracy toward labor, toward stockholders, toward consumers, toward public sentiment. . . ."

Spiked with searing phrases, the speech was a far cry from the mellow, philosophical discourse of the year before. Partisan Democrats greeted it joyously as the kickoff for the presidential campaign. Republican congressmen, who had burst into derisive laughter when Roosevelt in closing referred to his speech as a message on the state of the union, called it a great stump speech but a dismal address for a chief of state. The Liberty League and other conservative groups feverishly prepared replies. Radicals had a mixed reaction. They liked the bristling words, but where was Roosevelt's program? The President had proposed no new legislation. With millions out of jobs, with farmers still desperate, was he going to coast on the New Deal record?

The answer came four days later.

THUNDERBOLTS FROM THE BENCH

For months now, a heavy judicial hand had been smothering vital parts of the New Deal. Federal district judges had issued over one thousand injunctions restraining the government from carrying out acts of Congress. Corporation lawyers went shopping for the most helpful courts, and often they were rewarded both with the requested injunction and with a stump speech from the bench. "Usurpation," one judge had snorted about the NRA. By the beginning of 1936 appeals were piled up, awaiting action by the Supreme Court.

Sitting loftily behind the immense mahogany bar in their magnificent red-draped chamber, the nine old men of the Supreme Court seemed far above the reach of partisan politics. Never in all its history had the Court so faithfully met the popular stereotype of majestic judges enunciating almost divinely inspired law. In the exact center sat Chief Justice Hughes, with his chiseled features, white goatee, and bushy eyebrows. Flanking him were eight other elderly, dignified men, whose tenure stretched back over the decades. One had been appointed by President Taft, two by Wilson, the rest by Harding, Coolidge, and Hoover, none by Franklin D. Roosevelt. Their average age in 1936 was seventy-one.

But if all was quiet in the High Court, it was, as Justice Holmes had once said, the quiet of a storm center. Behind the judicial masks there burned passionate convictions about politics and policy. Judges are human, and their decisions, in the words of a close student of the judiciary, are not brought by constitutional storks, but are born out of the travail of economic and social circumstances. Most of the justices had once been vote-seeking politicians; all of them had climbed to their judicial eminence through the push and jostle of the competitive world.

Like a legislature, the Court had its right, its left, and its center. Lined up as a solid phalanx on the right were the learned Willis Van Devanter, an Old Guard Republican who had helped McKinley beat Bryan in 1896; the churlish James Clark McReynolds, successively a Gold Democrat, Wilson's Attorney General, and now the most outspoken conservative on the Court; the bewhiskered George Sutherland, a Taft man in 1912, president of the American Bar Association in 1918, rewarded by Harding with a seat on the high bench in 1922 after he had failed of re-election to the Senate; and the tall, bulky Pierce Butler, an Irish Catholic railroad attorney and conservative Democrat appointed by Harding over the bitter protests of Senator Norris. The main tie binding these men was their common origin in or near the pioneer life of the frontier, their common belief in the ideology of *laissez faire,* individualism, and free competition.

"Steady the boat," Chief Justice Taft had admonished the four shortly before he retired, and they were still steadying the boat.

On the left was a remarkable trio. Most distinguished was the ascetic-looking Louis D. Brandeis, the famous "People's Advocate" whose appointment to the Court by Wilson had met the bitter opposition of Taft, Root, and five other ex-presidents of the American Bar Association. Harlan F. Stone, a granite-faced New Englander, had been dean of Columbia Law School and Coolidge's Attorney General before his fellow Amherst alumnus appointed him to the Court. White-thatched Cardozo had been a brilliant New York State judge and legal craftsman for many years before Hoover elevated him on Norris's and Borah's urgings.

In the middle were the "swing men": Roberts and Chief Justice Hughes. At sixty-four the youngest member of the Court, Roberts had been a law professor, corporation lawyer, and Coolidge's prosecutor of the oil cases, before Hoover chose him for the Court in 1930. First appointed to the Court by Taft, Hughes had resigned to campaign for President against Wilson in 1916; he served as Harding's and then Coolidge's Secretary of State and returned to the Court as Chief Justice in 1930. An old acquaintance of Roosevelt's, Hughes had a meticulous sense of constitutional checks and balances; although the President had written Cardozo that he hoped he could have at least in part the same type of "delightful" relations with the Supreme Court that he had had with the Court of Appeals in Albany, Hughes, aside from official functions, had carefully kept his judicial distance from the White House.

Teetering on these three- or four-way divisions, the Court had followed a mixed course in passing on the social and economic measures of the 1930's. It had upheld state moratorium laws on mortgage foreclosures, state price-fixing legislation and milk control laws. Five to four it had sustained the congressional resolution voiding gold payment requirements in private contracts, with Mc-Reynolds storming that the Constitution was "gone." Then in staccato blows in the spring of 1935 the Court had struck down the Railroad Retirement Act, the NRA, the Frazier-Lemke Farm Mortgage Act. Most ominous for the New Deal was the solidity of the conservative four and the unpredictability of the swing men. Was Roberts—perhaps even Hughes too—now enlisted on the right for the duration?

At precisely high noon on January 3, 1936, the Chief Justice parted the center curtains and he and his eight brethren suddenly appeared behind their chairs while the clerk intoned his "Oyez" and concluded, "May God save the United States." Slowly, precisely, hardly looking at the pages before him, Justice Roberts began the Court's opinion in *U.S.* v. *Butler*, involving the constitutionality of the Agricultural Adjustment Act. This case concerned no horny-handed farmer rebelling against bureaucratic controls from Washington, but the refusal of receivers of a bankrupt New England textile company to pay processing taxes under the act. Their coun-sel, conservative old ex-Senator George Wharton Pepper, attacking the constitutionality of the act, had concluded his argument with a plaintive plea that not in his time would "the land of the regimented" be accepted as a worthy substitute for "the land of the free."

While the packed audience waited anxiously for some clue, Roberts' dry voice went interminably on. First he reviewed the old story of Hamilton's broad view versus Madison's narrow view of the power of Congress to tax for and spend for the general welfare. When Roberts plumped for the Hamiltonian view, the audience stirred with the thought that the AAA was safe. But no —now Roberts was saying that the processing tax was not merely a tax but part of a plan. And what was the plan? By the AAA "the amount of the tax is appropriated to be expended only in payment under contracts whereby the parties bind themselves to regulation by the Federal Government." Congress was trying to buy a compliance it was powerless to command. The asserted power of choice was an illusion.

Then Roberts conjured up a parade of imaginary horribles—things that Congress might regulate, such as shoes and education, if the claimed national power was sustained. This brought him to the heart of his real, though veiled, position. Although Roberts early in the case had said that the Court could not consider the merits of laws but could merely lay the Constitution beside the statute to see if the latter "squares with" the former—this later came to be called the "slot machine" theory of judicial review—Roberts went on to violate his own theory by questioning the whole idea of legislative power. He simply had no confidence in the capacity of Congress to act with self-restraint, or ultimately in the wisdom of the people who elected it. He feared that Congress would become "a parliament of the whole people, subject to no restrictions save such as are self-imposed." And for this position Roberts had enlisted not only the "steady four" but Hughes as well.

"A tortured construction of the Constitution," Stone declared in an indignant dissent for himself, Brandeis, and Cardozo. "Courts are not the only agency of government that must be assumed to have capacity to govern. Congress and the courts both unhappily may falter or be mistaken in the performance of their constitutional duty. But interpretation of our great charter of government which proceeds on any assumption that the responsibility for the preservation of our institutions is the exclusive concern of any one of the three branches of government, or that it alone can save them from destruction is far more likely, in the long run, 'to obliterate the constituent members' of 'an indestructible union of indestructible states' than the frank recognition that language, even of a constitution, may mean what it says: that the power to tax and spend includes the power to relieve a nationwide economic maladjustment by conditional gifts of money."

Stone reminded the Court of Holmes's famous injunction: "It must be remembered that legislators are the ultimate guardians of the liberties and welfare of the people in quite as great a degree as the courts." Perhaps the subtle barb struck home, but the "steady four" remained impassive. They had the votes.

In the White House, Roosevelt was talking with Secretary of War Dern when a secretary came in with the bad news on a slip of paper and laid it before him. Eager reporters crowded around Dern afterward: How had the President reacted to the news? "He just held the sheet of paper in front of him," said Dern, "and smiled."

The smile was significant. To this decision Roosevelt would

enter no dissenting opinion, no "horse-and-buggy" remark. The situation had gone far beyond such talk. More than any other previous decision, Attorney General Robert H. Jackson later remembered, the *Butler* case had turned the thoughts of men in the administration toward the impending necessity of a challenge to the Court. Roosevelt's smile was that of a fighter ready for the struggle ahead, perhaps too of a tactician watching his opponent overextend himself.

"It is plain to see," wrote Ickes in his diary after a cabinet meeting later in the month, "from what the President said today and has said on other occasions, that he is not at all averse to the Supreme Court declaring one New Deal statute after another unconstitutional. I think he believes that the Court will find itself pretty far out on a limb before it is through with it and that a real issue will be joined on which we can go to the country. For my part, I hope so."

If such was Roosevelt's tactic, the Supreme Court walked straight into the trap. There was a lull when the TVA won validation of its right to sell power generated at Wilson Dam, with only McReynolds dissenting. But on May 18 the work of demolition was resumed. In *Carter* v. *Carter Coal Co.* Hughes sided with Roberts and the rightists in ruling invalid the labor provisions of the Bituminous Coal Conservation Act of 1936. A week later the Court in another 5-4 split voided the Municipal Bankruptcy Act on the ground that it infringed on the rights of states to deal with their municipalities.

The climax came on June 1, 1936. With the national conventions only a few weeks off, the Court took a step that was bound to plunge it into the political turbulence of the year. By another 5-4 decision it invalidated the New York minimum wage law—and in effect those of other states as well. Probably more than any other action, concluded a historian of the Court, this decision "revealed the grim and fantastic determination of the narrow Court majority to preclude legislative intervention in economic and social affairs." For all its fine words about the reserved powers of the states, the Court seemed to be as much against state New Deals as it was against the national one. In a ringing dissent Stone warned that a legislature must have necessary economic powers or government would be rendered impotent. Privately Hughes was deeply troubled by the excesses of the "steady four."

Roosevelt put his finger on the crucial consequence of the decision. The Court, he said, was creating a "no-man's-land" where neither state nor federal government could function.

"How can you meet that situation?" a reporter asked.

"I think that is about all there is to say on it," Roosevelt replied. The President would not tip his hand—yet.

Another result of the Court's actions was to make necessary a fuller legislative program than the President originally had planned. The Court's upset of the AAA left Congress floundering until Wallace and farm organization leaders worked out a method of crop control through an expansion of the Soil Conservation Act of 1935. After the AAA's derailing denied the government half a billion in processing taxes, the President, without consulting even the House Ways and Means Committee, sent specific instructions on a new tax program. Swallowing their pride, congressmen voted for those features most palatable in an election year—a graduated tax on undivided profits and on all corporate income, and a "windfall" tax aimed at those processors who had profited as a result of the *Butler* decision. A legislative item left over from the second Hundred Days and from the vacuum created by the NRA overthrow was the Walsh-Healey bill regulating labor standards of firms receiving government contracts.

On other matters the President held the presidential reins over Congress rather loosely. A conspicuous example was the veterans' bonus bill. The year before, Roosevelt had vetoed the bill in a brilliant message that he had delivered orally to Congress, and Congress had sustained him by a hair. This year the congressmen were scrambling for their cyclone cellars, fearful of veterans' wrath in November. Recognizing their plight, Roosevelt forsook his valiant role of yesteryear and sent Congress a feeble note indicating that he had not changed his mind. Congress passed the bill over presidential veto. What was good election politics for the President was evidently not good election politics for congressmen. By this method of playing both ends against the middle, both the President and his cohorts could live to fight another day.

A final consequence of the judicial demolition was further to confirm Roosevelt in his leftward direction. After years of wobbling back and forth along a middle way, the President was now committed to a militant if still somewhat ambiguous and limited progressivism. And this development raised the whole question of Roosevelt's relationship to the American right.

ROOSEVELT AS A CONSERVATIVE

For months a vast bitterness against the President had been welling up from what Ickes later would call the grass roots of every country club in America. This bitterness varied in tone from the august denunciations of the Liberty League and the big business associations to the stories that went the rounds of club and bar. Some of these, touching on the President's egoism and compulsion to dominate, were genuinely funny, and no one laughed louder at them than did Roosevelt. Others were mean and smutty, told behind cupped hands in Pullman cars. Still others were simply fantastic, such as the widely circulated stories about maniacal laughter someone had heard from the President's study in the White House, about doctors wheeling away a limp, gabbling figure.

Roosevelt could laugh at his right-wing foes. He roared at a story that George Earle brought him about four wealthy members of Philadelphia's exclusive Rittenhouse Club who were sitting in the library late in 1935 sipping drinks and damning the President and all his works. After a while one of them happened to turn on the mahogany-encased radio. Suddenly a well-known voice came out referring scornfully to criticisms of the New Deal by "gentlemen in well-warmed and well-stocked clubs." It was Roosevelt, making a speech in Atlanta.

"My God!" exclaimed one of the men, according to Earle's story, "do you suppose that blankety blank could have overheard us?"

But the President was also confused and hurt by the rancor from the right. He had not sought it. Had he not saved the capitalistic system? It was with political guile but also in real perplexity that later in the year he told his fable:

"In the summer of 1933, a nice old gentleman wearing a silk hat fell off the end of a pier. He was unable to swim. A friend ran down the pier, dived overboard and pulled him out; but the silk hat floated off with the tide. After the old gentleman had been revived, he was effusive in his thanks. He praised his friend for saving his life. Today, three years later, the old gentleman is berating his friend because the silk hat was lost."

What had happened? It has often been said that Roosevelt betrayed his class, historian Richard Hofstadter has noted, "but if by his class one means the whole policy-making, power-wielding stratum, it would be just as true to say that his class betrayed him." If so, how can this be explained?

The mystery deepens when Roosevelt is viewed less in his familiar posture as a liberal or progressive, and more as a conservative acting in the great British conservative tradition. That tradition has its cloudy and contradictory aspects, but certain of its elements have shown a tenacity and continuity down through the years. They are: the organic view of society, compelling a national and social responsibility that overrides immediate class or group interest; a belief in the unity of the past, the present, and the future, and hence in the responsibility of one generation to another; a sense of the unknowable, involving a respect for the limits of man's knowledge and for traditional forms of religious worship; a recog-

"MOTHER, WILFRED WROTE A BAD WORD!", Dorothy McKay, reprinted from
Esquire, November, 1938, copyright by *Esquire,* Inc., 1938

nition of the importance of personal property as forming a foundation for stable human relationships; personal qualities of gentility,
or gentlemanliness, that renounce vulgarity and conspicuous display
and demand sensitivity to other persons' needs and expectations;
and an understanding of the fact that while not all change is reform, stability is not immobility.

If such are some of the chief lineaments of an enduring conservatism, Roosevelt seems to have been a conservative by many tests.

During his first two years in office Roosevelt could hardly have
displayed more loyalty to the conservative belief in the need for
an abiding devotion to some national or general interest that transcended party, or group, or sectional concerns. He called for a national effort against economic crisis; he played down the role of
party and partisanship. He proclaimed the need for a true concert
of interests, and the NRA, as he visualized it, was simply the in-
stitutionalization of that idea. He was leader of all the people, and
he was perfectly willing to subordinate the interests of his class to
his idea of the national interest at the same time that all other interests found an equal place in the national plan.

A belief in the unity of past, present, and future? This central
concept of Edmund Burke was a root principle in Roosevelt. It
revealed itself in his absorbing concern for his ancestors, for Dutchess
County history, for local customs and traditions; in his lifelong
interest in tree farming; in his solicitous concern for the national
heritage, however vaguely he conceived it, that was passing through
one generation of Americans after another. Probably the most
persistent interest he had in public policy involved conservation
of natural and human resources.

Roosevelt was a religious man—"a very simple Christian," his
wife once called him. He was christened in St. James Episcopal
Church in Hyde Park, became a vestryman there in 1928, and later
the senior warden, as his father had been before him. He liked
the hymns and Psalms, the order and routine of the church. The
intensity of his religious feeling is not easy to gauge; certainly there
was a strong conventional element, and church attendance for him
was at least as much a politically and symbolically important ritual
as it was an opportunity for communion. He was unconcerned
about religion as a philosophy, although toward the end of his life
he became interested in Kierkegaard.

A belief in personal property? Roosevelt, like most other leaders
of property-hungry masses through American history, wanted not
the suppression of property but its broader distribution. He believed in the family-sized farm—the farm that a man and his wife
and his sons could live on. He believed in enabling workers to own
their houses; he experimented long and hard with resettlement

projects that gave people a chance to maintain their own houses and till their own plots. To Roosevelt there was a difference not in degree but in kind between this type of property owning and corporate ownership. A prudent householder himself, he handled his own property with affection and circumspection.

Roosevelt was a gentleman in all but the prissy sense of the term. "He was decent; he was civilized; he was kind," Gunther wrote. He disdained coarseness or vulgarity; he never used more than the milder, more conventional forms of profanity; he avoided excessive show of feeling and expected other people to; he expected people to have good manners; he hated the kind of ostentation that he had seen in fashionable centers. His consummate ability to identify his own feelings with other people's was, of course, an essential part of his political technique. He had a continuing sense of responsibility for the health and well-being of his staff and of other people around him.

Roosevelt's attitude toward change cannot be so simply set forth. He had a love for innovation and experimentation in government that clashed with the conservative's repugnance for unnecessary change; at the same time, he had a curious instinct for fixity in his personal affairs, such as the arrangements in his bedroom and office; and his tenderness for Hyde Park rested in part on his sense that here was a point of stability in a relentlessly changing world. To the extent that he thought about the implications of governmental change, moreover, Roosevelt defended change as essential to holding on to the values of lasting importance. For over a century conservatives in Britain had been demonstrating, through such reforms as factory acts and social welfare services, that minor changes in institutions and laws were necessary to conserve enduring ends. And in this sense, too, Roosevelt was a conservative.

The argument should not, of course, be overstated. Roosevelt was too much of an opportunist and pragmatist to be catalogued neatly under any doctrinal tradition, no matter how broad it might be. Moreover, he did not believe in such conservative ideas as the need for hierarchy in society, the natural inequality of man, and the pessimistic view of man and his potentialities. His mind, open to almost any idea and absolutely committed to almost none, welcomed liberal and radical notions as well as conservative. But if any balance could be drawn, he was far closer to the conservative tradition than any other. He could say—and did say—with the great conservatives: "Reform if you would preserve."

The question insistently asserts itself: Why—if Roosevelt was in the broader sense a conservative, at least in his first two years in office—did American "conservatives" forsake him? The answer is that the American right was not acting in a great conservative tradition, that it had little concern with enduring conservative values. True conservatism—that of Burke, and of John Adams and some of the other Federalists—was shouldered out of the way by moneyed groups that draped narrow interests in the finery of enduring principles. But the exclusive concern with temporary self-interest was there for all to see. The fact was that by the end of the 1920's business conservatism was showing little understanding of its "stewardship" or preserving function. It had no standards, no traditions, no coherence—only a grab bag of fetishes and stereotypes.

The right had muffed its big chance. At a critical point in his first term—the early months of 1935—Roosevelt still was balanced precariously between right and left. He was still sticking to his idea that he could represent overriding national interests, that he could be leader of all the people. New Deal reforms had been accepted by most elements in the business community; even the continuing unemployment and the rumblings from labor and Long & Co. were not enough to push him leftward. Then business seemed to declare war on the President; the Chamber of Commerce lambasted his program, the Supreme Court vetoed parts of it. In the second Hundred Days and in January 1936 business got its answer.

Why did business declare war? Partly because some New Deal measures were bothersome and expensive. Taxes did go up, restrictions did increase, labor did get "uppity," forms and questionnaires did multiply. Yet business profits also mounted sharply during 1933 and 1934; as Roosevelt said, the old gentleman's life was saved, even if not his top hat. Mounting business opposition to Roosevelt cannot be explained in terms of reasoned self-interest alone. The explanation lies also in two other areas, ideological and psychological.

The business community had become the prisoner of its own idea-system. The key concept in this system was the belief in *laissez faire,* in the idea that government should not interfere in man's social, and especially his economic, affairs. The generous liberalism of the nineteenth century was divested of its broader philosophical dimensions and squeezed into the cramped mold of a narrowed and restrictive economic orthodoxy. The individual, in reality a mysterious, many-sided figure, was distorted into the ungainly creature of Economic Man. Forgetting that actual man interacts with the world about him in a multitude of different ways, forgetting, too, that governmental restraint is only one of many restraints upon him and often the least important, forgetting that broadened governmental functions in the economic and social realm do not necessarily contract but may enlarge individual freedom, the rugged individualists preached that the way to free mankind was to remove the political controls from him. And they erected large signs around themselves, their workers, and their property, "Government, keep out."

Nowhere had this central idea been more augustly or authoritatively set forth than in the opinions of the Supreme Court of the United States. By an astonishing feat of legerdemain the justices had taken the Fourteenth Amendment, which had been adopted ostensibly to protect the newly freed Negroes against white retaliation, and converted it into a powerful means of protecting corporations against governmental regulation. Some judicial opinions were essays on economic individualism that might have been lifted out of Adam Smith or even Herbert Spencer. It was no coincidence that the business revolt against Roosevelt coincided with the judicial revolt. The "steady four" were merely reiterating on the bench the precepts that had guided their steps from the frontier through the struggles in business and politics to the legal pulpit that was the Court. And because much of American life, as Thorstein Veblen had shown, reflected the business philosophy so superbly enunciated by the judges, the business creed of economic individualism was also the creed of organized lawyers, organized doctors, newspaper and magazine publishers, and of large sections of religion and education.

Behind all this, however, were factors that lay far deeper in the human psyche than symbols and ideologies. The vehemence of the rightist revolt against Roosevelt can be explained only in terms of feelings of deprivation and insecurity on the part of the business community. Roosevelt had robbed them of something far more important than their clichés and their money—he had sapped their self-esteem. The men who had been the economic lords of creation found themselves in a world where political leaders were masters of headlines, of applause, and of deference. Men who felt that they had shouldered the great tasks of building the economy of the whole nation found themselves saddled with responsibility for the Depression. Men who had stood for Righteousness and Civic Virtue found themselves whipping boys for vote-cadging politicians. And government was ceaselessly becoming more and more dominant. "Business which bears the responsibility for the pay checks of private employment has little voice in government," complained the Liberty League.

Roosevelt had exploded one of the most popular myths in America, a perceptive Frenchman said to Joseph Kennedy. He had dissociated the concept of wealth from the concept of virtue.

Only wounds rubbed raw by this psychological deprivation can explain the tortured protests of the businessmen of 1934 and 1935. When Lewis Douglas wrote the President late in 1934 that he hoped "most fervently" that Roosevelt would really try to balance the budget, and that on this hung not only Roosevelt's place in history but "conceivably the immediate fate of western civilization," he was not merely converting a governmental income-outgo balance sheet into an Eternal Principle; he was revealing his own deep psychological commitment to a business way of doing things. When Herbert Bayard Swope wrote Farley early in 1935 of a sense of fear that was beginning at the top, growing downward, and spreading as it grew in the form of misgiving about the President, he was reporting on an essentially irrational hatred of Roosevelt that had begun long before the second Hundred Days had given the business community some kind of rational basis for that hatred.

And because the hatred on the right seemed so bitter and illogical, Roosevelt was tempted to respond in kind. The hardening opposition of the press especially aroused him. In August 1935 the President somehow got hold of a message from a Hearst executive to Hearst editors and to its news service: "The Chief instructs that the phrase Soak the Successful be used in all references to the Administration's tax program instead of the phrase Soak the Thrifty hitherto used, also he wants the words Raw Deal used instead of New Deal." Roosevelt was indignant. He even had a press release prepared—"The President believes that it is only fair to the American people to apprise them of certain information which has come to him. . . ." But more prudent counsels prevailed, and the release was not issued. The editorial lions roared louder and louder. Early in 1936 the Chicago *Tribune* was already running as its "platform" the slogan "Turn the rascals out," with the admonition "Only 201 [or 101, or 17] days in which to save your country. What are you doing to save it?"

Conservatism is betrayed when it becomes the private property of a narrow economic or social minority. And the failure of the American right to rise above its concern with property, myth, and status and to follow a conservative creed in the great British and early American tradition powerfully influenced both the character of Roosevelt's leadership and the attitude of the left toward the New Deal.

ROOSEVELT AND THE RADICALS

Violently waving his hands, twisting his mouth down into the familiar old near-snarl, Al Smith arraigned the New Deal before a cheering, guffawing crowd of Liberty Leaguers in Washington late in January 1936. Al's hair was silvered, his face was lined and hollowed, but the wisecracks were as biting as ever. The brain trusters, he shouted, had caught the Socialists in swimming and had run away with their clothes. The New Deal had fomented class warfare. It had carried out one Socialist plank after another. While a dozen Du Ponts, John W. Davis, Shouse, and Raskob applauded, Smith concluded on a dark note of Marxist threats to the American system.

Roosevelt, who had directly challenged the Liberty League in his message to Congress earlier in the month, was not disturbed by Smith's threat to "take a walk." He had already written Smith off, and he left it to his lieutenants to parry the attack. Jumping into the fray, Ickes the next evening quoted Smith's answer to a Hoover charge of socialism in 1928; this cry, Al had said then, was always raised by powerful interests eager to stop progressive legislation. Senator Joseph Robinson, Smith's running mate in 1928, lashed the "Unhappy Warrior" for deserting his party.

The most agonized reply came from no New Dealer but from a tall handsome Socialist leader with long patrician features and a vibrant voice. The New Deal was socialism? cried Norman Thomas over the radio a few days later. Emphatically not. Roosevelt had not carried out the Socialist platform—except on a stretcher. One by one Thomas ticked off the New Deal reforms. The banks? Roosevelt had put them on their feet and turned them back to the bankers. Holding company legislation? True Socialists would nationalize holding companies, not try to break them up. Social security? The Roosevelt act was a weak imitation of a real program. The NRA? It was an elaborate scheme for stabilizing capitalism through associations of industries that could regulate production in order to maintain profits. The AAA? Essentially a capitalist scheme to subsidize scarcity. TVA? State capitalism. CCC? Forced labor.

Roosevelt's slogan was not the Socialist cry, "Workers of the world, unite," Thomas proclaimed. Roosevelt's cry was "Workers and small stockholders unite, clean up Wall Street." And that cry was at least as old as Andrew Jackson.

As a political maneuver, Thomas's speech was transparent. He was desperately trying to keep the rank and file from falling under Roosevelt's spell. The unions, though, were too busy with their immediate problems to pay much heed. The Wagner Act was helping them organize. The WPA and PWA were putting men to work. Even Socialist leaders were deserting to take jobs in government.

But as ideological analysis, Thomas's answer was beyond dispute. If socialism had any coherent meaning, it meant the vesting of the ownership and control of capital, land, and industry in the whole community. With the exception of TVA, nothing important in the New Deal was of this description. The only plausible aspect to the Liberty League's equation of the New Deal and socialism was the Socialists' habit of advancing a host of immediate, "practical" reforms along with their basic program of socialization.

Roosevelt, like major party leaders before him, had no compunction about plucking popular planks from the Socialist party platform—planks such as unemployment compensation and public housing. But he spurned the central concept of socialization. Even more, his aversion had been tested in the crucible; in 1933 he probably could have won congressional assent to the socialization of both banking and railroads, but he never tried. He wanted to reform capitalism, not destroy it. And in this sense he was a conservative. It was precisely because the Socialists had a coherent economic and social doctrine rooted in a systematic philosophy that they recognized Roosevelt's true conservatism. It was precisely because the Liberty Leaguers lacked such a philosophy that they totally miscalculated Roosevelt's New Deal.

And the Communists? During Roosevelt's first two years they denounced his program as a capitalist ruse, as fascism disguised in milk-and-water liberalism. "The 'New Deal' of Roosevelt," proclaimed a party resolution in 1934, "is the aggressive effort of the bankers and trusts to find a way out of the crisis at the expense of the millions of toilers. Under cover of the most shameless demagogy, Roosevelt and the capitalists carry through drastic attacks upon the living standards of the masses, increased terrorism against the Negro masses, increased political aggression and systematic denial of existing civil rights. . . ."

Then came a flip-flop. Shaken by Hitler's looming power Moscow put aside revolutionary tactics and called for a popular front of Socialists and *bourgeoisie* against the Fascists. Obediently the American Communists wheeled around a 180-degree turn. Roosevelt now must be supported as a leader of anti-Fascist forces. The reversal was useful to the Communists, for popular-front tactics helped them to infiltrate the burgeoning trade unions and other progressive groups. But it was an acceptance of Roosevelt on opportunistic, not doctrinal, grounds.

The antagonism of the independent left to the New Deal was equally sharp. In the spring of 1935 Heywood Broun called Roosevelt labor's Public Enemy No. 1. The chubby, unkempt columnist poked fun at the labor leaders who invaded the White House, were charmed by Roosevelt into a happy trance, and woke up, Broun said, with something like the automobile code. The myth of Roosevelt as a crusading radical was as empty as the masterful politician myth, wrote the *Nation*'s Washington correspondent. Roosevelt was a nonintellectual—a man who lived and thought on the skin of things.

Even the more drastic legislation of the second Hundred Days seemed to make no difference to the left. The Social Security Act was weak, genuine public works had gone by the board, the Wagner Act had been forced on the President. Even Roosevelt's fighting speech of January 1936 left them cold; it was empty of concrete proposals. Perhaps the radicals were still bemused by the picture they had created of Roosevelt as the "gay reformer," lacking doctrine and direction; more likely they saw the rejuvenated New Deal of 1935 as merely a stepped-up program of moderate reform. If in the end many radicals voted for the President, it was not because they loved Roosevelt more but because they loved the Republicans less.

"Governor," said an old friend to Roosevelt during the second Hundred Days, "did you see this morning's *Times?* You don't have a thing to worry about. The Communist Party has decided to pat you on the head." The President roared. Nothing could have amused him more than this kind of leftist support.

When Roosevelt expressed amazement that people could call him a radical, he was mainly play acting. As a politician, he knew perfectly well that this cry was an old, if somewhat soiled, practice in American politics. Yet there was an element of genuine incredulity in his reaction. He knew he had been taking some kind of middle road; more important, the hostility he felt toward Marxist doctrines, whether socialist or communist, made the charges seem ridiculous to him. This hostility was not merely ideological. It was psychological in the sense that Roosevelt distrusted the kind of doctrinaire and systematic thinking that was implicit in intellectual radicalism.

Roosevelt, in fact, was an eminently "practical" man. He had no over-all plans to remake America but a host of projects to improve this or that situation. He was a creative thinker in a "gadget" sense: immediate steps to solve specific day-to-day problems. He had ideas such as the tree shelter belt in the drought areas; transcontinental through-highways with networks of feeder roads; huge dams and irrigation systems; resettlement projects for tenant farmers; civilian conservation work in the woods; a chain of small hospitals across the country; rural electrification; regional development; bridges and houses and parks. Not surprisingly, virtually all these ideas involved building tangible things. What excited Roosevelt was not grand economic or political theory but concrete achievements that people could touch and see and use.

But all this was little known to the American people in 1935 and 1936. By some incredible process of inversion, the popular press of the day painted a picture of Roosevelt as thinker that was utterly false. Cartoons showed him as a bemused dreamer, attired in cap and gown and attended by crackpot professors, following wild intellectual theories. Business magazines drubbed him for his "impractical" theories. It was incredible that in a country where newspapers and magazines devoted oceans of ink and forests of pulp to covering the White House, there emerged a totally reversed image of the presidential mentality.

Actually the shoe was on the other foot. It was not Roosevelt who was the impractical theorist but the businessmen themselves. In turning every question of statecraft into a question of Eternal Principle, they followed precisely the course that Roosevelt rejected.

Roosevelt saw this. He was no little exasperated with the tendency of his business friends to take refuge in abstractions. Again and again he chided them for their failure to address themselves to specific issues. When the dean of the Harvard Business School criticized the President in the New York *Sun*, Roosevelt wrote a friend sadly that he had talked with the dean for an hour once: "I put several problems up to him and he had not one single concrete answer to any of them." In a long correspondence with Fred Kent, an economist and banker, Roosevelt took a particular delight in ignoring Kent's generalizations and asking for specific suggestions on specific problems.

Nowhere was the contrast between the practical Roosevelt and the doctrinaire businessman better etched than in his friendly arguments with a big New York realtor. If the federal government did not provide five dollars a room for housing, Roosevelt asked this businessman, could private builders take care of families earning under a thousand dollars a year? "Housing is particularly and always has been a private matter and absolutely local," the realtor replied. "There is nothing whatever in the Constitution or our scheme of government authorizing or indicating any Federal interest in the housing question." He feared that the government was starting on a voyage which "I frankly must call communistic or socialistic."

"What are we going to do with them?" Roosevelt answered. "Are we going to compel them to live under slum conditions? . . . Has society as a whole no obligation to these people? Or is society as a whole going to say we are licked by this problem?"

He noted that the realtor had quoted Lincoln. Another President —Cleveland—had said, "We are faced with a condition and not a theory." Roosevelt ended: "I wish you would give me a solution."

The President struck the same note in a press conference with editors of trade papers early in 1936. Referring to industrial leaders, he said that he was waiting for them to come and give some kind of answer. But instead of doing that, they were going around the country saying "We have to have a balanced budget. We have to have a balanced budget."

The President plainly wanted to answer Douglas and all the other impractical men who were chanting this account-book liturgy.

"A balanced budget isn't putting people to work. I will balance the budget as soon as I take care of the unemployed. In other words, I am not being helped.

"Hell, I can stop relief tomorrow. What happens? Tell me that! You know. I don't mean, by that, the policy of the owner of your paper. You know, as human beings, what happens if I stop relief tomorrow. It isn't any joke."

A day or two after Al Smith's biting assault on the New Deal before the Liberty League, Roosevelt asked an aide to dig up a quotation from Lincoln that the President vaguely remembered. The passage was soon on his desk:

"I do the very best I know how—the very best I can; and I mean to keep on doing so until the end. If the end brings me out all right, what is said against me won't amount to anything. If the end brings me out wrong, 10,000 angels swearing I was right would make no difference."

THIRTEEN *Foreign Policy by Makeshift*

OOSEVELT'S practical, day-to-day approach to government was even more pronounced in foreign policy making than in domestic. It was not surprising. He had burned his fingers in the election campaign of 1920 in which he and Cox had fought for adherence to the League of Nations and to the principle of collective security. Candidate Roosevelt's ditching of the League in 1932 showed how far he would compromise with previous principles to realize immediate goals.

But even after Roosevelt was safely in office he cautiously skirted foreign policy shoals on which he feared his political popularity and his domestic program might be wrecked. His treatment of the London Economic Conference, his nationalist economic policies during 1933, his continuation of the Hoover policies on the League and on war debts seemed on their face a planned and consistent retreat from the internationalist tendencies of the Democratic party of Wilson and Cox. But they were not. For alongside these policies he fashioned measures of international co-operation that enabled him to veer back and forth between isolationism and internationalism as political conditions required.

The political climate and terrain in which the President acted did not make a foreign policy of principle any easier. To be sure, the framers of the Constitution a century and a half before had wisely given the chief executive a good deal of initiative and power in foreign policy making. But disapproval of treaties had been left in the hands of one-third plus one of the senators, and most international projects called for funds that could be denied by a majority of legislators in either House, or by a stubborn committee. Even in the executive branch he headed the President faced centrifugal forces: the cliquishness of Foreign Service officers; the narrow class loyalties of some of the "striped pants" set; the tangle of bureaucratic rivalries; and curious tie-ins between careerists in the ugly old building that housed the State Department and powerful congressmen on Capitol Hill. A host of politicians had their fingers in the foreign policy pie.

247

Outside Washington were the millions of voters who held the destinies of foreign policy makers in their hands. And here was the most unstable foundation of all on which to build a consistent program of foreign relations. Great numbers of these voters were colossally ignorant of affairs beyond the three-mile limit; as the old story went, they were more concerned about a dogfight in Main Street than a flare-up in distant Ruritania. Others were rigidly bound by loyalties absorbed in the countries of their national origin. Still others were prisoners of ancient fears and shibboleths: that wily foreign diplomats always played Uncle Sam for a sucker, that America had never lost a war and never won a peace conference, that salvation lay in keeping free of entangling alliances.

Yet all this was only one dimension in which Roosevelt had to shape foreign policies. For these policies by definition were influenced in turn by the political climate in foreign lands. The character of the Nazi ideology, the balance of power in the French Chamber of Deputies, the foreign policy attitudes of British labor, the silent struggle within the Kremlin, the fortunes of Chinese war lords, were all elements in the equation of world power. Reading long letters from his ambassadors, lunching with foreign envoys, quizzing his unofficial agents who had just seen MacDonald or Goering or Mussolini, leafing through lengthy studies by State Department economists, Roosevelt had to make judgments day after day on mighty imponderables imperfectly understood.

Even worse, all these forces were in ceaseless motion. An assassination in Japan, an election in France, a palace revolt in South America, a crucial cabinet session in Downing Street, the rising misery of Asiatic millions, the vast fermenting and steaming of distant ideologies—any of these could jar the unstable equilibrium of world politics. The United States was no exception. Not only was its politics plagued by the usual unpredictabilities, but the American people, lacking stable attitudes built on long experience in foreign policy making, swung fitfully from one foreign policy mood to another, from isolation to neutralism to participation in world politics.

No wonder that Roosevelt moved warily on the darkling plain of foreign policy. No wonder that he wrote a friend early in 1934, "In the present European situation I feel very much as if I were groping for a door in a blank wall. The situation may get better and enable us to give some leadership." But what if the situation grew worse, and leadership all the more imperative?

GOOD NEIGHBORS AND GOOD FENCES

Lacking a general principle by which to make foreign policy, Roosevelt improvised from one situation to another. The result was a jumble of separate and somewhat clashing policies. The President ranged back and forth from the old political internationalism of the Democratic party to the economic nationalism implicit in the New Deal, from the anti-imperialism of the Bryan Democrats to traditional power politics.

In veering from one policy to another Roosevelt was less concerned with fitting his policy into a larger framework than with overcoming immediate problems. In a sense he followed a middle way in foreign policy as he did in domestic. Yet again his middle way was no straight line between two ordered philosophies, but only a kind of geometric median across which Roosevelt tacked from one policy to another.

The gnawing problem of war debts hung on through the first term. Roosevelt departed little from the Hoover policies. Congress had forbidden the Executive to reduce or cancel the debts, and he made no attempt to alter this stand; but he knew too that full payment was impossible. In this impasse the President explored a variety of schemes, shifting figures around on scratch paper. All this came to naught, and Congress grew more and more testy as the nations sent token payments or no payments at all. The upshot was passage in 1934 of a bill of the belligerent old isolationist Hiram Johnson that forbade the floating of loans in this country by defaulting nations. Over objections from the State and Treasury departments Roosevelt, in a concession to congressional isolationists, signed the measure into law.

Disarmament was a sterner test of United States harmony with its old allies. The World Disarmament Conference at Geneva had been deadlocked for almost a year when Roosevelt took office, and Hitler's seizure of power made prospects seem even more dismal. In May 1933 the President sent a personal appeal to the heads of fifty-four nations asking that they enter a nonaggression pact, eliminate offensive weapons, and sharply curb arms and armies. A few days later Roosevelt and Hull authorized Norman Davis, chairman of the United States delegation at Geneva, to go much further. If arms could be reduced, he announced, Washington would be willing not only to consult with other nations but to refrain from any action tending to defeat a collective effort against a nation breaching the peace, if we agreed with the rightness of that effort.

If this bald announcement represented a trial balloon, it was quickly shot down by salvos from more than one quarter. Germany was already readying orders for aircraft, and its factories were pouring out chemicals, steel, and small arms. France, fearful as ever of German *revanche,* was holding out for special guarantees. And in the ornate old room on Capitol Hill where met the Senate Committee on Foreign Relations, potent senators opposed this gesture toward internationalism. The disarmament conference was soon deadlocked again.

In October Hitler announced Germany's withdrawal from both the conference and the League. The greatest arms race in history was on.

The collapse of the conference pushed Roosevelt and Hull back into a new emphasis on naval disarmament. Japan was demanding naval parity, and Roosevelt sought to join with the British in a common stand against the looming threat in the Orient. But the British, more concerned about German than Japanese rearmament, were not easy to work with. In November 1934 an angry Roosevelt told Davis that he must constantly impress Sir John Simon, British foreign secretary, "and a few other Tories" with the "simple fact that if Great Britain is even suspected of preferring to play with Japan to playing with us, we shall be compelled, in the interest of American security, to approach public sentiment in Canada, Australia, New Zealand, and South Africa in a definite effort to make these Dominions understand clearly that their future security is linked with us in the United States." He added that Davis would "best know how to inject this thought into the minds of Simon, Chamberlain, Baldwin, and MacDonald in the most diplomatic way."

Here was an astonishing move—a threat in effect to detach the sympathies of the dominions from the mother country, and to establish with them an anti-Japanese alignment with the United States as the center stone. The effort came to naught; a week later Hull was instructing Davis on the need for an early, open, and conclusive indication of American and British alignment on naval limitation. Roosevelt's threat was significant, however, in showing how the hard steel of power politics showed through the velvet of diplomatic relations even between two friendly nations.

As for American participation in international organizations, Roosevelt continued to play a most cautious game. Speaking to the Woodrow Wilson Foundation shortly after Christmas 1933, he paid tribute to the League as a common meeting place for international discussion, as a means of settling disputes, and as an aid in labor, health, and other matters. The United States was cooperating openly in using its machinery. But, he continued, "we are not members and we do not contemplate membership." At one time he thought of appointing an American ambassador to the

League, but he feared the reaction of the isolationists. And he was cautious even on technical co-operation. When Phillips told him that the Department of Agriculture wanted to have a representative on a committee of League experts on the international meat trade, Roosevelt replied: "What would be the effect of this? Is it perhaps going too far toward official membership in a direct official committee of the League itself?"

Of a milder political coloration than the League were two other world agencies: the International Labor Organization and the Permanent Court of International Justice. It was on Miss Perkins' initiative that the Senate and House passed by simple majority vote a joint resolution authorizing membership in the ILO. Roosevelt had said to her, "I may be President of the United States, I may be in favor of the ILO, but I can't do it alone." The result was that Miss Perkins did it alone. On Roosevelt's advice and with his blessing—but with no other help from him—she trudged from Pittman to Johnson to Borah explaining that the ILO had existed before the League, was not part of it, and no loss of sovereignty was involved. After thus patiently lining up virtually every member of the Foreign Relations Committee, she got the resolution through.

Joining the World Court also seemed politically feasible. Both party platforms in 1932 had called for adherence to the watered-down protocols that safeguarded United States sovereignty. Largely on Hull's initiative, Roosevelt decided to push ratification at the beginning of the 1935 session. Trouble loomed from the start. Roosevelt's cabinet was divided, and Chairman Key Pittman of the Senate Foreign Relations Committee was so lukewarm that he asked the President to get Robinson to lead the fight. For a while Roosevelt and Hull thought they had the needed two-thirds of the senators. But a lightning mobilization of isolationist opinion commanded by Hearst, Father Coughlin, Will Rogers, and others unloosed a flood of telegrams onto Capitol Hill, and enough senators wavered to defeat the measure.

Although Roosevelt had not thrown himself into the fight as had Hull, he was stung by the rebuff. Ickes at a cabinet meeting noticed a bitter tinge to his laughter, and a hint that he wanted to hurt the thirty-six dissenters. If the thirty-six ever got to heaven, Roosevelt wrote Robinson, "they will be doing a great deal of apologizing for a very long time—that is if God is against war—and I think He is." But Roosevelt's chief reaction was a feeling that he had to wait out public opinion. Adherence would come eventually, he wrote Elihu Root, "but today, quite frankly, the wind everywhere blows against us." And to Stimson he sent somber words:

"Thank you for that mighty nice note. It heartens me. You are right that we know the enemy In normal times the radio and other appeals by them would not have been effective. However, these are not normal times; people are jumpy and very ready to run after strange gods. This is so in every other country as well as our own.

"I fear common sense dictates no new method for the time being —but I have an unfortunately long memory and I am not forgetting either our enemies or our objectives."

Most internationalist of all the administration's foreign policies was the trade agreements program. Chiefly responsible for the program, however, was Hull, not Roosevelt, who remained perched between isolationists and internationalists in his own administration and party.

In his maiden speech to Congress at the age of thirty-six Hull had called for lower tariffs; he had fought for them ever since; and now, as Secretary of State, the tenacious old Tennessean saw his great opportunity. Roosevelt had given him the impression during the years before 1932 that he favored reciprocal tariff agreements between nations. But when Hull tried to push his ideas during the first Hundred Days, he ran straight into the nationalistic emphasis in AAA and NRA. His trade program was sidetracked. On one thing, though, Hull and Roosevelt were fully agreed. No substantial tariff reduction could be achieved unless power was delegated to the President. To run a low tariff bill through the congressional gantlet was to expose it to decimation by congressmen with special interests. Only the President could act for a more general interest.

But would Roosevelt act? Slowly he came round during 1933 to some kind of trade agreements program; when, however, he set up a committee to co-ordinate foreign trade relations, he picked as head a vigorous opponent of tariff reductions, George N. Peek. At the same time that the President was pushing ahead with a trade agreements bill he named Peek foreign trade adviser. Hull was stunned by this appointment. A few months after the bill became law, the President allowed Peek to negotiate a barter agreement with Germany. When Hull and Peek disagreed over the most-favored-nation clause, Roosevelt asked Hull to spend "a couple of hours some evening" with Peek talking things over. "In pure theory you and I think alike," Roosevelt wrote Hull, "but every once in a while we have to modify a principle to meet a hard and disagreeable fact!"

Such a tug of war could not last. Under heavy pressure from Hull, the President finally swung against Peek and his barter plans. Later Peek resigned with a bitter statement.

Hull also took the lead in applying the Good Neighbor doctrine to the rest of the Americas, but here he had full backing from the President. Torn by strife and discontent, resentful of the years of interference by its Big Brother of the North, Latin America was skeptical toward Democratic party promises of no more meddling in its internal affairs. The real test of the new line could come only in a concrete situation, and Cuba, long a ward of the United States, provided such a test. When palace revolt followed revolt in Havana during 1933, the ugly situation seemed to threaten American commercial interests in the island. Worried by the rioting and army mutinies, Ambassador Sumner Welles in Cuba proposed a "strictly limited intervention," but Hull and Roosevelt refused. Later they erased a festering sore by abrogating the Platt Amendment, which had restricted Cuba's sovereignty. As further proof of the Good Neighbor policy Roosevelt also withdrew marines from Haiti and eased relations with Panama. Capping the whole program was the patient nurturing of friendly relations by Hull at the seventh Pan-American Conference in Montevideo, the first such meeting that an American Secretary of State had attended as a delegate.

By 1936 Roosevelt could call the Good Neighbor policy "a fact, active, present, pertinent and effective." Yet it was notable that the foreign policy on which he took the most fixed and principled stand was essentially a negative policy—one of noninterference—whatever positive results might flow from it. To be sure, persistent noninterference was not easy, but it was far easier than a persistent policy of intervention or collective security.

In any event, Roosevelt did not put all his bets on treaties and noninterference as a basis for good neighborliness, at least outside the Americas. Good fences, too, made for good neighbors, and some of his fences bristled with spikes and spears. Within a week of Roosevelt's inauguration Swanson announced that the navy would be built up to treaty strength, and three months later the President allotted almost a quarter billion from NRA appropriations for this purpose. But the build-up of armed strength during the first term was slow and quiet. Roosevelt did not want to publicize defense unduly. When McIntyre told him early in 1934 that patriotic organizations were asking him to proclaim "National Defense Week," Roosevelt answered tersely, "Don't do it."

STORM CLOUDS AND STORM CELLARS

In the white marble caucus room of the Senate Office Building late in 1934 sat the stage managers of a carefully planned, elaborately staged drama. In the center behind the long table was the hero of the drama, a stern, hard-faced young senator named Gerald P. Nye; flanking him were other idols of American isolationism—Arthur H. Vandenberg, Bennett Champ Clark, Homer T. Bone. Of villains in this drama there were many: evil, bloodsucking "merchants of death," who paraded before the committee day after day to confess their sins. Of heroines there was only one: an ethereal being, always appealed to but never seen, a figure named Peace. Crowded behind the villains was the chorus, the spectators who craned their necks and muttered with indignation as the play unfolded.

Such was the Nye committee investigating the munitions industry. Like many other famous Senate investigations, the Nye probe was less a search for data than a dramatization of things already known or rightly suspected. But the charges were dramatic and shocking. Arms makers had bribed politicians, shared patents, divided up business, reaped incredible profits, evaded taxes—all in the sordid trade of death weapons. Even worse, munitions makers helped foment wars to boost their profits.

Rarely have Senate hearings fallen with such heavy impact on the stream of American opinion. Horrendous titles suddenly blazoned forth in book stores and magazine stands: "merchants of death" were deep in "iron, blood and profits"; it was "one hell of a business." The timing was flawless. The revelations coincided with and contributed to a deep revulsion against entanglement in European quarrels. Writers were busy showing that 1917 was not due to German submarines or a conception of neutral rights, but to a few greedy capitalists. Germany was not so guilty after all. The Americans had been saps and suckers.

With war clouds piling up again in Europe, millions of Americans vowed, "Never again." Women organized peace societies. College students formed the "Veterans of Future Wars" to collect their bonuses now, before they had to fight and die. Isolationism was strong everywhere, but especially in the Midwest, Northwest, and Rockies; in election after election these sections sent to Congress men like William E. Borah of Idaho, Key Pittman of Nevada, Burton Wheeler of Montana, young Bob La Follette of Wisconsin, and Nye of North Dakota, who championed the isolationist cause. This cause, charged with emotion and bitterness, had now become a force of awesome, almost primeval power.

Where was Roosevelt in all this? Certainly he had a deep stake in preventing a mobilization of public opinion that might in turn shackle him in making foreign policy. But the President's relation to the Nye investigation was a passive one. Largely by default, Nye, a Republican isolationist, was allowed to chair the committee. Gliding with the current of opinion favoring the probe, Roosevelt not only joined the chorus denouncing the arms trade but allowed Nye access to executive papers that were greatly to aid the Senator's efforts to dramatize the skulduggery of bankers and diplomats. Even more, he tolerated—and to some extent encouraged—the Nye committee in its ambition to use intensifying disgust with arms makers as an anvil on which to beat out a rigid policy of isolationism for the United States.

At this crucial juncture Roosevelt offered little leadership. It was not inevitable that popular hatred of arms makers and war profiteers should deepen popular feeling that America ought to isolate itself from foreign entanglements and thus from foreign wars. That hatred might as well have bolstered a public desire to work with other nations in order to stop war and hence end the grim accouterments of battle, including merchants of death. But such a channeling of opinion demanded an active program of education—in short, leadership. Roosevelt only drifted.

Given the powerful ground swell of isolationist feeling, the brilliance of the isolationists in marshaling their forces, the passivity of the administration, and the tension in Europe, only one outcome was possible—a national stampede for a storm cellar to sit out the tempests ahead. During the second Hundred Days, the isolationists on Capitol Hill were pressing for legislation requiring the President, in the event of war abroad, to embargo export of arms to all belligerents. Roosevelt and Hull favored such embargo authority, but they wanted to empower the President to discriminate between aggressor and victim by embargoing exports of arms only to the former. Such discretionary power, they reasoned, would help deter aggressors.

But the isolationists would have none of it. Such discretion, they shouted, would mean sure entanglement in alien quarrels. Pittman was hostile and surly. The President was riding for a fall, he warned the White House, if he insisted on "designating the aggressor in accordance with the wishes of the League of Nations." The senator said he was willing to introduce such a discretionary provision, but the President would get "licked."

The President did get licked. Mandatory arms embargo legislation passed both chambers by almost unanimous votes. Roosevelt dared not stand against the tide; he had urgent domestic bills to get through, and the isolationists were threatening to filibuster. The President signed the measure, but he warned that the inflexible provisions might drag us into war instead of keeping us out.

Why, then, did Roosevelt sign the bill? He acted mainly out of expediency. For one thing, the mandatory arms embargo section of the act was to expire in six months, and Roosevelt and Hull reasoned that they might gain discretionary power in the revision. For another, they both liked one feature of the bill—the setting up of regulation of arms traffic. Most important, Mussolini for months had been making plans for an attack on Ethiopia. A mandatory arms embargo against both nations would hurt Italy, with its need for modern arms and its possession of ships to transport them, far more than it would hurt Haile Selassie's flintlock-armed native troops. When Roosevelt told reporters dryly that the measure met the "needs of the existing situation," he was more than hinting at his almost Machiavellian expediency.

And so it was that Roosevelt, at the very moment that dictators girded for war in Europe and Asia, was stripped of power to throw his country's weight against aggressors.

As Roosevelt scrawled his name on the Neutrality Act at the end of August 1935, Italian troops, tanks, and airplanes were pouring through the Suez Canal toward Ethiopia. To military and diplomatic strategists in chancelleries of great nations, the Neutrality Act came as confirmation of America's refusal to throw its weight into the balance of world politics. Yet Roosevelt could not stay clear of the looming conflict.

For months he and Hull had been watching the approach of that conflict. So had politicians and diplomats in Europe: Prime Minister Baldwin and Foreign Secretary Sir Samuel Hoare of Britain, and Foreign Minister Pierre Laval of France. The precise nature of the division in Europe during 1935 was shrouded in the rhetoric of collective security and the murk of secret negotiations, but two things were clear. One was the reluctance of France and Britain to antagonize Mussolini irretrievably as long as they feared Hitler more and hoped to keep the two dictators apart. The other was Mussolini's determination to grab Ethiopia, preferably through an act of violence.

Roosevelt had had a measure of grudging admiration for Mussolini; and the dictator had responded with some friendly words for the President and his New Deal. Ambassador Breckinridge Long in Rome wrote enthusiastically in 1933 about the rejuvenation of Italy, including the punctuality of the trains. Even on the very eve of invasion, Long was drawing up elaborate plans for giving Italy large slices of Ethiopia as part of a general European settlement. Roosevelt's reaction to Mussolini's war preparations during 1934 was more equivocal. On the one hand, he believed that war would be a threat to peace everywhere, and thus America was involved; on the other hand, he shied away from any involvement in the situation by refusing to do more than urge Mussolini to settle the issue peacefully. When Mussolini said it was too late—Italy had mobilized a million men and spent two billion lire—Roosevelt still hoped Italy would take the "magnificent position" of settling the issue by arbitration. But more than moral support to Ethiopia or to the idea of collective security he would not offer. Hull made clear that the United States would not join the League of Nations in imposing sanctions.

"I am very much more worried about the world situation than about the domestic," Roosevelt wrote to Senator Josiah Bailey at the end of August 1935. "I hope that there will be no explosion before I take my trip on the boat"—a reference to a long cruise that the President planned to take on the U.S.S. *Houston*. But the explosion was imminent. On October 3, 1935, Mussolini's legions thrust into Ethiopia. What now?

News of the attack came to Roosevelt on the *Houston* as the cruiser plowed along serenely off the California coast. His attitude toward Italy hardened at once. "Good!" he exclaimed loudly when news reports favorable to Ethiopia were flashed to the ship. The sympathies of Hopkins, Ickes, and his other companions were with Ethiopia. The President had left a draft neutrality proclamation with Hull, and he waited impatiently while Hull tried to find out whether hostilities formally existed. "They are dropping bombs on Ethiopia—and that is war," Roosevelt exclaimed. "Why wait for Mussolini to say so?"

In Washington, Hull had problems of his own. Some of his advisers were urging him not to issue a neutrality proclamation because it might prejudice action by the League Council, which was preparing to name Italy as an aggressor nation. But Hull wanted to act before the League did. His reason stemmed directly from the decisive element in American foreign policy making—the isolationists' hostility toward American co-operation with Geneva. Roosevelt wired him to act immediately. They both recognized that much depended on staying clear of the League.

By an extraordinary conjuncture of two events—the passage of the Neutrality Act and the invasion of an agrarian country by a nation badly needing imports of the sinews of war—Roosevelt was in the happy situation where the more he sought to cut off exports to Italy in the name of neutrality, the more he was able to assist in the imposing of economic sanctions against the aggressor. This whole tactic depended, however, on keeping Geneva's actions separate from Washington's in the public eye. The President and Hull were equal to the task. When Hoare sounded them out on some kind of action under the Kellogg Pact, they coldly rejected the idea. And so worried were they that the League might ask them to co-operate formally in sanctions, thus inviting a refusal that might throw cold water on the League's efforts, that they warned Geneva not to issue such an invitation. The British and French agreed not to.

The Neutrality Act, however, embargoed only arms and munitions; it did not embargo raw materials that Italy could convert into weapons for her warriors. From the start Roosevelt and Hull recognized this massive shortcoming. The President asked the State

Department to study the possibility of adding copper and steel to the list, in case League sanctions should include these items, and he was even ready to limit sharply the transshipment of our exports by neutrals. Informed that the Neutrality Act could not be stretched this far, Roosevelt fell back on a "moral embargo" based on the "spirit" of the act. On October 30 he denounced profiteering in Italian trade that might help prolong the war.

Despite these appeals, exports of war materials to Italy mounted. On November 15, with League sanctions slated to take effect three days later, Hull warned stiffly against an increase in such exports as oil, copper, trucks, and scrap steel. His warning covered more materials than the League sanction list, which omitted the crucial item of oil. Menaced on its most vulnerable flank, Italy hotly protested Hull's action.

But that action was still only "moral." Would the administration put teeth into it? Britain especially was eager to know the answer to this question. Her "businessmen's government" feared that if the League imposed an oil embargo against Italy, American oilmen, scorning Hull's moralities, would grab the whole Italian oil market. Britain also had the problem of dealing with the slippery figure of Laval, who had long wanted to appease Mussolini by jettisoning Ethiopia and who had stalled off a League oil embargo.

So Britain's Ambassador put the question straight to Hull. Would the United States stop increased oil exports to Italy if the League embargoed oil? Hull hesitated. Only Congress could take such action, but to appeal to Congress to embargo oil in conjunction with the League was to establish the fearful link between American policy and League collective security that he and Roosevelt had fought so hard to avoid. "We have gone as far as we can," he replied. He could not speak for Congress.

Frustrated by the administration's fear of the isolationists, the resourceful diplomats of Downing Street turned to other expedients. Hoare and Laval in Paris agreed on a plan to end the war by dismembering Ethiopia and handing over large chunks to Mussolini. Publication of the agreement set off a storm of denunciation; Hoare was sacked, and the plan was killed. But the sordid proposal also killed the high hopes for effective sanctions. The League continued to equivocate. The war went on. Italian troops struck deeper into Ethiopia, burning, bombing, spraying poison gas from the clouds.

The Hoare-Laval plan caught Roosevelt and Hull by surprise. The President was outraged; "our British friends," he said, "have come a sad cropper." For months Haile Selassie's natives fought on. Forsaken by the League, the emperor made a last appeal before he fled his country. Did the people of the world realize that he had fought on to protect not only his people but also collective security? Were they blind to his fight for the whole of humanity? Where were his tardy allies?

"If they never come, then I say prophetically and without bitterness, 'The West will perish.' "

THE LAW OF THE JUNGLE

Ethiopia's betrayal left American internationalists in a sea of uncertainty and despondency. Isolationists jeered that once again Uncle Sam had been gulled by European diplomats. Most Americans were merely confused. As for Roosevelt, not since entering the White House had he been so perplexed and worried by developments abroad.

"The situation changes so fast from day to day that it is hard to do more than make wild guesses in regard to the European future," he wrote his minister in Bucharest late in January 1936. To Ambassador Straus in Paris he wrote in even more pessimistic vein. The whole European situation, the President said, was black.

"I have been increasingly concerned about the world picture ever since May, 1933. There are those who come from England and France and Germany who point to the fact that every crisis of the past three years has been muddled through with a hope that each succeeding crisis will be met peacefully in one way or another in the next few years. I hope that point of view is right but it goes against one's common sense."

To Congress the President addressed an urgent warning: "Not only have peace and good-will among men grown more remote in those areas of the earth during this period, but a point has been reached where the people of the Americas must take cognizance of growing ill-will, of marked trends toward aggression, of increasing armaments, of shortening tempers—a situation which has in it many of the elements that lead to the tragedy of general war." People in such nations might wish to change aggressive policies, but lacking freedom, they were following blindly and fervently those who sought autocratic power. Such nations had not shown patience in trying to solve their problems.

"They have therefore impatiently reverted to the old belief in the law of the sword, or to the fantastic conception that they, and they alone, are chosen to fulfill a mission and that all the others among the billion and a half of human beings in the world must and shall learn from and be subject to them."

Brave words—but they masked a central ambiguity in Roosevelt's approach to neutrality. Outwardly he took the isolationists' position that arms and trade embargoes would keep America out of war by keeping American merchants and others disentangled from war. Privately he took the internationalists' position that such embargoes—if they could be administered with discretion—could keep America out of war by discouraging aggressors from starting war. Between the two approaches a vast difference loomed. But the President made no effort to educate the people on this cardinal difference. He hoped that they would be educated by events. Unhappily for the President, events such as the Hoare-Laval agreement seemed to educate the people in the wrong direction.

And time was running out. In February of 1936 the Neutrality Act of the previous September was to expire. Roosevelt and Hull hoped to gain from Congress both legal standing for the "moral" embargo of war materials and—crucial to their whole strategy—presidential discretion in applying such an embargo. When Hull appealed to Congress for these two new provisions, he ran into a stone wall. Within a few weeks the battle was lost. Why?

The immediate reason was the power of the isolationists on Capitol Hill. Johnson and Borah lashed Hull's bill mercilessly. They were riding high on a massive wave of isolationist feeling whipped by the failure of collective security in Europe, and by new revelations of the indefatigable Nye at home. Led by Nye, Johnson & Co., the isolationists forced Roosevelt and Hull to accept an extension of the 1935 act, with some changes. Lacking guidelines from the administration, the internationalists stood by helplessly.

As Americans huddled in their storm cellars, dictators turned to the sword.

At dawn on March 7, 1936, advance units of the German army thrust into the Rhineland. In Berlin a few hours later Hitler addressed cheering members of the Reichstag, while foreign diplomats looked on in stony silence. His troops had moved, the Fuehrer announced, but Germany wanted peace. He proposed a twenty-five-year nonaggression pact with France; reciprocal demilitarization of the frontier (i.e., scrapping of France's famed Maginot Line); and bilateral nonaggression pacts with Germany's eastern neighbors (but not with Soviet Russia). For ninety minutes he shouted and beseeched; then, surrounded by hundreds of armed men, he strode out of the hall.

France hesitated, and was lost. Later it became known that some of Hitler's generals had opposed the move, and that Hitler's troops would have turned back had France resisted. But the Quai d'Orsay did not dare act alone, and Downing Street equivocated. Other nations only fumed and sputtered. The League declared Germany guilty of breaching the Versailles and Locarno treaties. Roosevelt and Hull privately took a grave view of the step. But no one acted.

Throughout Roosevelt's first term Japanese soldiers, merchants, and bureaucrats were consolidating positions on the Asiatic mainland. Like a great musty fruit lying in the sun, China was decomposing on its exposed edges. In 1933 Jehol was annexed to Manchukuo, in 1935 Japanese troops seized Chahar, in 1936 they penetrated Suiyuan. Having shaken off the old naval treaties, Tokyo was now building up its fleet. Ominous as these events seemed to Roosevelt and Hull, even more fateful was the merciless struggle in Japan of militarist extremists against the moderates.

Only a month after taking office Roosevelt had written House that he wondered if a Japanese diplomat's criticism of the President's decision to keep the fleet in the Pacific had stemmed from a desire to "ingratiate himself against assassination by the Junker crowd when he gets home." The remark was prophetic. On a night late in February 1936, Ambassador Joseph Grew in Tokyo was showing the film *Naughty Marietta* to former Premier Saito and Grand Chamberlain Suzuki; a few hours later Saito was shot dead and Suzuki wounded. The insurgents were rounded up and executed but Japanese politicians had a frightening glimpse of the explosive forces breaking through the surface.

Tension was mounting in Europe. In July 1936, an Italian bomber squadron was alerted for duty in Spain. A few days later General Francisco Franco took command of revolting Moors and Foreign Legionnaires in Spanish Morocco. People's militia put down army uprisings in Madrid and other centers, but the revolt gained momentum in the north and south. Iberia quickly became a European battleground, with Italy and Germany taking the initiative. Italian troops and airmen, Nazi agents and technicians poured into rebel territory by the thousands. Within a few weeks Rome and Berlin simultaneously recognized Franco as Spain's ruler.

"What an unfortunate and terrible catastrophe in Spain!" Roosevelt wrote Ambassador Claude Bowers. But United States neutrality, he added, would be "complete." Britain and France forbade their citizens to sell arms to the Spanish government; Hull put a moral embargo on American exports, although the Neutrality Act did not apply to civil war. Italy and Germany agreed not to intervene, and kept on intervening.

In the fall of 1936 Germany and Japan signed the Anti-Comintern Pact. The Axis could now forge strategic plans of united action. The democracies, divided and irresolute, were hamstrung by isolationists and appeasers in strategic positions. The West was still floundering.

THE POLITICIAN AS FOREIGN POLICY MAKER

The record is clear. As a foreign policy maker, Roosevelt during his first term was more pussyfooting politician than political leader. He seemed to float almost helplessly on the flood tide of isolationism, rather than to seek to change both the popular attitudes and the apathy that buttressed the isolationists' strength.

He hoped that people would be educated by events; the error of this policy was that the dire events in Europe and Asia confirmed the American suspicion and fear of foreign involvement rather than prodding them into awareness of the need for collective action by the democracies. In short, a decisive act of interpretation was required, but Roosevelt did not interpret. At a minimum he might have avoided the isolationist line about keeping clear of joint action with other nations. Yet at a crucial moment—when he approved the Neutrality Act shortly before Italy's attack on Ethiopia —he talked about co-operating with other nations "without entanglement."

The awful implications of this policy of drift would become clear later on when Roosevelt sought to regain control of foreign policy making at home as the forces of aggression mounted abroad. But the immediate question is: Why did Roosevelt allow himself to be virtually immobilized by isolationist feeling? Why did he not, through words or action, seek to change popular attitudes and thus rechannel the pressures working on him?

The enigma deepens when Roosevelt's private views are considered. In his private role he was an internationalist. He believed, that is, in the proposition that America's security lay essentially in removing the economic and social causes of war and, if war threatened, in uniting the democracies, America included, against aggressive nations. But in his public role he talked about keeping America disentangled from the political affairs of other nations; he often talked, in short, like an isolationist.

The mystery deepens still further when one considers that the President had emphatic, though perhaps ill-defined, ideas about the need for leadership in a democracy. He must have recognized the potential in leadership when, in addressing the Woodrow Wilson Foundation at the end of 1933, he asserted roundly that the "blame for the danger to world peace lies not in the world population but in the political leaders of the population." At the same time he was concerned about the perennially weak leadership that the politicians gave France. He was perhaps aware, too, that simply following a line of policy lying at the mean between two extremes would not necessarily lead to the wisest course. In the case of Ethiopia, for instance, the British and French through their indecisive maneuverings succeeded neither in keeping Mussolini out of Germany's orbit nor in vindicating the ideals of collective security. Washington's foreign policies were equally muddled.

The reasons for the sharp divergence between Roosevelt's private and public roles in foreign policy making were several. In the first place, the President's party was cleft through the middle on international issues. The internationalist wing centered in the southern and border states was balanced by isolationists rooted in the West and Midwest. To win the nomination Roosevelt had given hostages to both groups. Part of the price of success in 1932 had been categorical opposition to United States co-operation with the collective security efforts of the League, and a cautious policy of neutrality based on nonentanglement. In the second place, Roosevelt in his campaign had so ignored foreign policy, or fuzzed the issue over when he did touch on it, that he had failed to establish popular attitudes on foreign policy that he could later evoke in support of internationalism. Moreover, during his first term the President gave first priority to domestic policies; a strong line on foreign affairs might have alienated the large number of isolationist congressmen who were supporting the New Deal. Indeed, many isolationists seemed to believe that any marked interest in foreign affairs by the President was virtually a betrayal of progressivism.

In addition, the President had surrounded himself with men from both sides. Men like Hull and Howe and Morgenthau were generally on the international end of the spectrum, but others like Moley and Hopkins and Hugh Johnson and Ickes were at the opposite end. Ickes had been so pleased by the Senate action on the World Court that he had telephoned and congratulated Hiram Johnson, whom he found "as happy as a boy." The development of the New Deal's policies of economic nationalism, tinged with the rhetoric of international good will and economic co-operation, resulted from and reinforced this division.

But the main reason for Roosevelt's caution involved the future rather than the past. The election of 1936 was approaching, and at this point he was not willing to take needless risks. It was significant that after he and Mackenzie King had signed a trade agreement in Washington—and a rather moderate one at that—Roosevelt wrote to King in April 1936 that "in a sense, we both took our political lives in our hands. . . ." The immediate goal of re-election was the supreme goal; the tasks of leadership, he hoped, could be picked up later.

FOURTEEN *1936: The Grand Coalition*

S TUDYING the rulers of foreign lands, Anne O'Hare McCormick of the New York *Times* found that they had shriveled or aged during these tortured years. "On the faces of Mussolini, Hitler, Stanley Baldwin, even the rotating governors of France," she reported, "strain and worry have etched indelible lines. Caught off guard, when they are alone, they are tired and baffled men who have paid a heavy price for power."

Not so Roosevelt. Home again, Mrs. McCormick marveled that he was so little shaken by the seismic disturbances over which he presided. "On none of his predecessors has the office left so few marks as on Mr. Roosevelt. He is a little heavier, a shade grayer; otherwise he looks harder and in better health than on the day of his inauguration. His face is so tanned that his eyes appear lighter, a cool Wedgwood blue; after the four grilling years since the last campaign, they are as keen, curious, friendly, and impenetrable as ever."

If other leaders bent under the burdens of power, Roosevelt shouldered his with zest and gaiety. He loved being President; he almost always gave the impression of being on top of his job. Cheerfully, exuberantly, he swung through the varied presidential tasks: dictating to Miss Tully pithy, twinkling little notes for friends and subordinates; splashing in the White House pool for the delighted photographers; showing off the incredible gewgaws that littered his desk; greeting delegations of Indians, of Boy Scouts, of businessmen, of Moose, of 4-H Club leaders, of Democratic ladies; relating long anecdotes about his ancestors to luncheon guests; scratching his name on bills with a dozen pens and carefully awarding each to a congressional sponsor solemnly standing behind the President's big chair; conferring genially with congressional leaders, agency heads, party leaders, foreign emissaries; poking fun at reporters while deftly turning aside their questions.

The variegated facets of the presidential job called for a multitude of different roles, and Roosevelt moved from part to part with ease and confidence. He was a man of many faces. Presiding over meetings of chiefs of his emergency agencies, he was the brisk administrator investing the sprawling bureaucracy with pace and direction, and patiently educating his subordinates on the *Realpolitik* of administrative management. Entertaining visitors on a yacht, he was the quintessence of sociableness and charm. Addressing a party meeting, he was the militant political leader, trenchant, commanding, cocky, assertive. Motoring through the woods at Hyde Park, he was the country squire, relaxed, casual, rustic. Attending Harvard's tercentenary in top hat and morning coat, he was the chief of state, august, sedate, and solemn.

Watching the President perform at a press conference midway through the first term, John Gunther was struck by the incredible swiftness with which he struck a series of almost theatrical poses. In twenty minutes, Gunther noted, Roosevelt's features expressed amazement, curiosity, mock alarm, genuine interest, worry, rhetorical playing for suspense, sympathy, decision, playfulness, dignity, and surpassing charm. And when the reporters roared at Roosevelt's remarks, he was clearly pleased at this audience response; after one such burst of laughter, the President took a sort of bow with a tilt of his huge head.

In all these roles Roosevelt gave an impression of directness and simplicity, and winning qualities these were. Ushered into the presidential bedroom one morning, Ickes found him shaving in the adjoining bathroom. Roosevelt invited him to sit on the toilet seat while they talked; the President was then wheeled to his bed where he reclined, still talking, while being dressed. He had his braces put on to greet a delegation, then returned to his room to take his braces off and relax again. "I was struck all over again," Ickes exclaimed that night, "with the unaffected simplicity and charm of the man." But this apparent simplicity was most deceiving—as Ickes himself was to discover.

The staff, as the last year of the first term arrived, reflected some of the change in Roosevelt's political posture and in the alignment of forces amid which he operated. Howe had died in April, until the end toying with great schemes for Roosevelt's triumphant re-election. Douglas, Acheson, and most of the other conservatives had long since left. By 1936 only Moley remained from the right wing of the original brain trust—and the graying, anxious professor was not to stay long. For months he had watched with rising alarm as the New Deal veered left. In turn captivated by Roosevelt's charm and pained by his policies, Moley somehow stayed on until a night in June when the President in a small gathering began taunting him about his new conservatism. Moley replied with heat, an angry quarrel followed, and the old relationship was over.

New faces in the White House took the place of old. There was

Stanley High, a smooth-mannered, bespectacled young man whose religious background helped him supply the President with what his more irreverent White House aides called "inspirational messages." There was Tommy Corcoran, a brash, engaging lawyer, only thirty-six years old, whose role as White House court jester with his jokes, Irish ballads, and mimicry seemed to belie his growing reputation as a tough-minded puller of governmental wires and manipulator of politicians and bureaucrats. There was Corcoran's "Gold Dust twin," Ben Cohen, a dreamy intellectual who had shown brilliant powers in drafting New Deal bills and coping with legal technicalities. Others fluttered in and out of the White House limelight: Robert H. Jackson, William O. Douglas, Isador Lubin—militant legal and economic technicians of a changing social order.

The President steered his kitchen cabinet with an easy rein. Its members in fact made up his staff for legislative, propaganda, and election campaigns, but he never institutionalized it. He casually borrowed personnel from agencies as he needed them. Presidential business was carried on in a catch-as-catch-can turmoil of personal conferences, sudden telephone calls, handwritten chits circulated among key advisers. The most valuable member of the kitchen cabinet was still Eleanor Roosevelt, who not only reached millions of people with her endless trips and with a newspaper column on "My Day," but continued to bring a stream of new faces and new ideas into the White House.

Yet to single out even this half-dozen or so White House personalities is to risk underestimating the vital role that the others in the executive establishment would play in 1936. For, as convention and election time approached, it became clear that Roosevelt would campaign squarely on the basis of the new benefits and the new hope that the New Deal administrators and their alphabetical agencies had brought to America.

THE POLITICS OF THE DEED

Perhaps it was Roosevelt's grasp of the cardinal fact of New Deal benefits to the people that largely explains his optimism about reelection. "We will win easily next year," he told his cabinet in November 1935, "but we are going to make it a crusade." His steady optimism continued into the early months of 1936. And well it might. For the New Deal program, partly by design and partly by chance, was coming to a climax in the election year.

By almost any test the economic surge since 1932 had been remarkable. Unemployment had dropped by about four million since the low point early in 1933; at least six million jobs had been created. Pay rolls in manufacturing industries had doubled since

1932; stock prices had more than doubled. Commercial and industrial failures in 1936 were one-third what they had been four years before. Total cash income of farmers had fallen to four billion in 1932 and recovered to almost seven billion in 1935. Capital issues had shot up sixfold since 1933. The physical volume of industrial production had almost doubled.

When the President wrote to agency heads in 1936 asking them for detailed lists of their achievements that could be used in his campaign, the responses underlined the central part that the New Deal had played in this upsurge. In three years federal and other relief agencies had poured over five billion dollars into work projects and related relief activities. Another four billion had gone into public works: roads, dams, sewage systems, public buildings, and the like. The Agricultural Adjustment Administration was supplying a substantial chunk of farm income through its direct benefit and rental payments. The Reconstruction Finance Corporation, a major carry-over from the Hoover administration, had stepped up its huge lending operations.

Most important of all—in a long-run sense—was the social security program, which began operating in 1936. Its main provisions involved unemployment and old age, although there was a small appropriation for preventive public health. The program was financed through pay-roll taxes, which began at a low rate and were to rise in the years ahead. Social security in 1936 was only a modest beginning. Benefits were small, and would not be received for some time. There were grave administrative difficulties. Since money was being collected and not distributed, the effect of the program in 1936 was deflationary. But the towering fact was that at last the national government had acted to underpin the future security of Americans.

A remarkable aspect of the New Deal was the sweep and variety of the groups it helped. Not only the millions of farmers and industrial workers, but great numbers of people in other categories had benefited from New Deal largesse. The Home Owners Loan Corporation conducted a vast rescue job, making over a million loans to mortgage-ridden home owners. The WPA put to work not only blue-collar workers but artists, writers, actors, teachers—and in jobs that salvaged their self-respect. The National Youth Administration helped thousands of hard-pressed high-school and college students to continue their education. Old people were looking forward to their pensions. Bank depositors had a guarantee of the security of their savings. Businessmen gained from government contracts, broadened purchasing power, freer lending policies.

Behind the cold statistics was the picture of a nation again on the march. The impact of Roosevelt and his New Deal had been to arouse the energies and aspirations of a people chilled by the bleak hand of depression. To them the New Deal was not a list of figures. It was a group of farmers stringing up electric wires in the Missouri Ozarks. It was a towering dam in California, water sluicing through an irrigation ditch in Colorado, a hospital in Jersey City, cars streaming through a tunnel under the Hudson. It was men swarming back to work in Pittsburgh, a widow keeping her home in Ohio, Negroes watching a slum-clearance project in Chicago. It was grass cover holding soil onto a hill in Georgia, a farmer buying a new tractor in Iowa, a river in Tennessee running fast and clear where once the water had been brown with topsoil.

The New Deal had brought a new condition for man; more than this, it had brought a new condition in the relations among men. The old subserviency of worker to employer, of mortgagee to mortgage holder, of farmer to shipper and middleman, of tenant farmer to landlord, of small businessman to banker, may have remained in its essential form; but the laws and spirit of the New Deal had instilled in these relations some of the equality and dignity that marked the old American dream. "My friends," Roosevelt said to a crowd of young Democrats in April 1936, "the period of social pioneering is only at its beginning." And that pioneering in the readjustment of human relationships had been accomplished with zest and—on the whole—with good will, rather than in an atmosphere of bitterness and reprisal. "Once again," Roosevelt could say on the same occasion, "the very air of America is exhilarating."

There were, to be sure, grave deficiencies in the transformations wrought by the New Deal. For all the talk of re-employment, eight to nine million Americans still had no jobs in 1936. The spending of the New Deal had not markedly improved the lot of millions in areas that could not be easily reached by government. Pay rolls had gone up, but so had living costs. Conditions compared favorably with early 1933—but not so favorably with 1929. Some programs, especially housing, had hardly got off the ground. Over most of the New Deal emergency agencies hung an aura of improvisation, wasted effort, and inefficiency. And despite the expansionist philosophy of the New Deal, its basic program for farmers was restrictive.

But in 1936 such matters could be left for the Republicans to enunciate. Of his own role the President had no doubt. It was to herald the gains of the New Deal and to assert that even better days lay ahead. It was to proclaim—again and again and again—the contrast between the America he had found in March 1933 and the America of 1936. Nothing would be allowed to soften the vividness of that contrast. When the National Emergency Council early in 1936 submitted to Roosevelt some statistical tables and statements implying that recovery began in 1932, Early indicated that this would not do at all. Changes must be made in the report.

"The President is insistent," he wrote to the NEC, "that the low point in the depression be fixed as March, 1933, or early in the year 1933—this for obvious reasons."

A voice boomed out from the back of a crowd in Hyde Park as the President stood on the platform of his special train.

"Boss man! You're out in front now. Show 'em your heels!"

Roosevelt waggled his head jauntily.

"There's something in that," he shot back.

But how much was there in that? Was the President really out front? Was it enough to capitalize on the politics of the deed and to roll to re-election on the wave of rising prosperity? If so, he could assume a defensive posture and hoard his strength until Election Day. Or did the battle still have to be won? If so, a hard, militant campaign lay ahead.

Throughout the early months of 1936 Roosevelt wrestled with this cardinal tactical problem. And, characteristically, he ended up by shifting back and forth between two tactical lines and sometimes following them simultaneously.

Early in the year the President seemed decided on a defensive campaign. The White House passed word to Congress that its session should be a brief one, devoted to appropriating money and passing routine administrative bills. A bill regulating conditions of employment of firms receiving government contracts was passed as a final plugging of the gap left by the NRA's demise. The Supreme Court's AAA decision forced the passage of a new farm bill and indirectly led to a controversial proposal by the President for a corporate-surplus tax in order to make up for the lost revenue. But the President failed to make a vigorous fight either for the new tax bill or for an effective housing program. He seemed ready to rest on his record.

Politically this tactic involved soft-pedaling the party and also some fence-mending. Democrats were grumbling that Roosevelt hardly mentioned his party, even in a Jefferson Day dinner speech. In March the President tried to soothe businessmen by giving a long White House luncheon to members of Commerce Secretary Roper's Business Advisory Council; he talked anew about a cut in spending, and he laid plans for organizing businessmen in the campaign ahead. He asked Ickes to call in Norris, Johnson, and other Republicans to revamp the Progressive League.

Far more ambitious was a plan for tapping the enormous reservoirs of votes contained in the huge religious, economic, and civic organizations across the nation. American politics is largely group politics; and Roosevelt characteristically approached these groups through their leaders. He set up a new organization with the innocent title of the Good Neighbor League. Stanley High solicited the use of their names from religious leaders like Rabbi Lazarus, labor leaders like George Harrison of the Railway Brotherhoods, civic leaders like George Foster Peabody, women's leaders like Lillian Wald and Carrie Chapman Catt. This organization of the forces of piety, hope, and feminism, decked out in the demure garments of nonpartisanship, became a smooth vote-getting machine for Roosevelt, financed actually by the Democratic National Committee.

Late in April Roosevelt seemed still undecided between a "unity" crusade and a partisan campaign directed against the business groups that opposed him. Then in late spring came a tactical change in the other direction—toward a partisan campaign based on a promised expansion of the New Deal. By early May he was denouncing, in private conversation, the business and press opposition and asserting that he welcomed their hatred. He was telling Moley, in one of their last long conversations, that the country needed less talk and obstructionist criticism and more leadership.

The main reason for the shift lay in political developments. By May the Republicans were gathering their forces and heading toward their national convention in Cleveland. More important, one candidate had clearly emerged as a front runner in the quest for the Republican nomination. This was Alf M. Landon. Governor of Kansas, a successful businessman, attached irretrievably to neither the Republican Old Guard nor the liberal wing of the party, Landon had just the qualities of common sense, homely competence, cautious liberalism, and rocklike "soundness" that the Republican leaders hoped would appeal to a people tiring, it was thought, of the antics and heroics in the White House. Middle class by every test and in every dimension, he had the shrewd, guileless face, the rimless glasses, and the slightly graying hair that made him indistinguishable from a million other middle-aged Americans. At the Republican convention in Cleveland, Landon won overwhelmingly over Borah on the first ballot.

Later it would become fashionable to joke about Landon, but he was no joke to the Democrats in June of 1936. For one thing, Landon had made a powerful run for the nomination against strong candidates—Borah, Vandenberg, and several others. For another, the Republicans, eying the great prize of the presidency and the obvious appeal of New Deal prosperity and reform, enunciated a moderately liberal platform. Landon himself was no mossback reactionary; he had deserted the Old Guard for the Bull Moosers in 1912, and he impressed the country when he boldly stated his position on certain planks of the 1936 platform in such a way as to put him a few degrees left of the party. More imponderable than all, in the late spring of 1936, was the potential of Al Smith and of the Jeffersonian Democrats who were splitting away from the New Deal. There were rumors that the anti-New Deal Democrats might set up a third party.

Faced by this mobilization of the conservatives, Roosevelt found himself still harried elsewhere by the forces of Coughlin, Townsend, and Long. Huey Long had been shot to death in his state capitol in September 1935, but the Louisianian's nationwide following had not fallen apart with his assassination; one of Long's organizers, a handsome, slick-talking Louisiana minister named Gerald L. K. Smith, had sprung forward to grab the reins and the mailing lists. By June 1936 this ill-assorted trio was joining hands and preparing to set up the Union party. The only basis for their harmony was hatred of Roosevelt and the realization that his defeat would favor their own chances in later elections.

The attacks from left and right brought a sudden little drop in Roosevelt's popularity in June 1936, and his sensitive political ears doubtless caught this. The Supreme Court's extreme swing rightward in the New York minimum wage law case at the beginning of June also probably influenced the President. In any event, the force of the opposition made it clear that he would have to wage a strong campaign. But Roosevelt evaded for a time the question of whether or not he would promise an extension of the New Deal, and whether or not he would wage a party fight. His way of delaying a decision on these tactical matters was to play up the presidential personality.

"There's one issue in this campaign," he told Moley. "It's myself, and people must be either for me or against me."

"I ACCEPT THE COMMISSION"

Like all party conventions, the Democratic national assemblage in Philadelphia had its smoke-filled room—but it was the President's study 150 miles away in the White House. Roosevelt dominated the proceedings throughout. He drafted the platform, passed on the major speeches, made the main convention decisions, and brought the affair to a stunning climax with his acceptance speech.

The platform was, of course, a string of hosannas to the New Deal. One plank reflected a major decision on Roosevelt's part. The ticklish problem of the Supreme Court could be handled either by a plank boldly calling for a constitutional amendment broadening congressional power over the economy, or by silence on the matter —or by generalities, assuming, of course, that the President had not

yet formulated the plan he was to present to Congress seven months
later. Beset with conflicting advice, Roosevelt chose the method of
generality. After asserting that national problems demanded national action, the platform went on cautiously: "If these problems
cannot be effectively solved by legislation within the Constitution,
we shall seek such clarifying amendment" as would allow the state
and federal legislatures, within their respective spheres, to pass laws
adequate to regulate commerce, protect public health and safety,
and safeguard economic security. "Thus we propose to maintain
the letter and spirit of the Constitution."

Still, the platform was an unusually outspoken and eloquent
document. *"We hold this truth to be self-evident—*that government
in a modern civilization has certain inescapable obligations to its
citizens, among which are: (1) Protection of the family and the
home; (2) Establishment of a democracy of opportunity for all the
people; (3) Aid to those overtaken by disaster." While ambiguous
on foreign policy, the declaration was an emphatic pledge to continue and to expand the domestic New Deal. Most revealing, perhaps, of Roosevelt's militance of the moment was the inclusion in
the same sentence of a promise to "rid our land of kidnapers,
bandits, and malefactors of great wealth." After considerable wrangling in the resolutions committee, a period and a few words were
set between the criminals and the malefactors—but they stayed in
the same paragraph.

The fight over the period was symptomatic of convention proceedings. The delegates had little to decide. Farley kept the huge
assembly in session for five days, partly because he wanted to give
the Philadelphia businessmen, who had donated $200,000 to have
the convention in the City of Brotherly Love, their money's worth,
partly because he saw a chance to drench the air waves with Democratic propaganda day after day, and partly because Roosevelt
wanted to give his acceptance speech on a Saturday, as he had four
years before. Time was consumed by endless speeches and parliamentary formalities; the delegates were amused by songs, stunts,
and the ousting of a group of Al Smith Democrats who had the
temerity to call out their hero's name.

But the convention did make one decision of potential importance. The President was still determined on the abrogation of the
two-thirds requirement for nomination, and Bennett Champ Clark,
son of the victim of the rule in 1912, had the satisfaction of moving
the adoption of the majority rule. Mollified by a promise of increased convention representation for their section, the Southerners
put up only a token fight; but the governor of Texas wondered
out loud about the implications of the change for 1940.

By the time Roosevelt's neighbor John E. Mack placed the President's name in nomination, the convention had become a wild political jamboree. "With our decks cleared for battle," shouted Mack, "with justice and right and progress with us, we are ready for more action under the inspired leadership of that great American whose name I give you as your candidate for President, no longer a citizen merely of one State, but a son of all the 48 States, Franklin Delano Roos——" An hour-long political demonstration followed the climactic uttering of the magic name: delegates milled about, cheering hoarsely, waving banners, tooting horns, jabbering, whistling.

Hardly less enthusiastic was the candidate himself. To Mack he exclaimed over the telephone: "John, you were grand! You had the jury right in the hollow of your hand—perfectly grand. I hope they will find for your client. It's all right. You were in grand voice. It came over the air marvelously. It's great stuff. . . ."

While the seconding speeches—no less than fifty-six of them—droned on, Roosevelt was putting the last touches on his acceptance speech. This speech would set the tone for the campaign. Once again Roosevelt faced the problem of whether to give a "sweetness and light" address appealing to all groups or a partisan talk to a partisan throng; and once again he was for a time undecided. At first he turned to Moley for a draft stressing the theme of unity and co-operation; later he got from Rosenman and High a "militant, bare-fisted statement of the necessity for economic freedom," as Rosenman later described it. The night before he was nominated, with the embattled speeches of party militants in Philadelphia still echoing in his ears, the President hammered out a rough draft—"so rough that I didn't like it," he told reporters the next day, "being a peaceful man." Sweetness and light were still in it—and something else too.

A theatrical setting awaited the President in Philadelphia Saturday night. Masses of humanity—over one hundred thousand persons—sat in great banks in the Franklin Field stadium. Rain had been falling, but by the time Roosevelt's long black car slid up the ramp to a curtained-off area behind the platform, stars were showing through the splotchy clouds. Behind the curtain the smiling President started his slow, stiff-legged walk toward the stage. Suddenly he spotted in the crowd around him the benign, white-bearded face of Edwin Markham. Reaching out to seize the poet's outstretched hand, the President was thrown off balance, and down he went. Pulled back to his feet, white, shaken, and angry, he snapped, "Clean me up."

But only for an instant did he lose his composure. A moment later, when the curtain was parted, there stood the President—calm, erect, smiling. The crowd burst into frenzied, ecstatic cheering.

Roosevelt opened serenely on a note of national unity. "I come not only as a leader of a party, not only as a candidate for high office, but as one upon whom many critical hours have imposed and still impose a grave responsibility." He thanked members both of his own party and of other parties for their unselfish and nonpartisan effort to overcome depression.

"America will not forget these recent years, will not forget that the rescue was not a mere party task. It was the concern of all of us. In our strength we rose together, rallied our energies together, applied the old rules of common sense, and together survived. In those days we feared fear. . . . We have conquered fear."

The President's voice sounded clearly in the soft summer air. "But I cannot, with candor, tell you that all is well with the world. Clouds of suspicion, tides of ill-will and intolerance gather darkly in many places." Even in America, the rush of modern civilization had raised new problems that must be faced if Americans were to preserve the political and economic freedom for which Washington and Jefferson had fought. Political tyranny had been wiped out at Philadelphia on July 4, 1776. But economic tyranny had risen to threaten Americans.

A hundred spotlights set the President off brilliantly from the dark masses around him. "It was natural and perhaps human that the privileged princes of these new economic dynasties, thirsting for power, reached out for control over Government itself. They created a new despotism and wrapped it in the robes of legal sanction. In its service new mercenaries sought to regiment the people, their labor, and their property. And as a result the average man once more confronts the problem that faced the Minute Man. . . .

"The royalists of the economic order have conceded that political freedom was the business of the Government, but they have maintained that economic slavery was nobody's business. They granted that the Government could protect the citizen in his right to vote, but they denied that the Government could do anything to protect the citizen in his right to work and his right to live. Today we stand committed to the proposition that freedom is no half-and-half affair. If the average citizen is guaranteed equal opportunity in the polling place, he must have equal opportunity in the market place."

Roosevelt's voice was rising in crescendo after crescendo. "These economic royalists complain that we seek to overthrow the institutions of America. What they really complain of is that we seek to take away their power." The crowd roared its approval. "Our allegiance to American institutions requires the overthrow of this kind of power. In vain they seek to hide behind the Flag and the Constitution." Roosevelt's phrases cut through the cheering—"democracy, not tyranny . . . freedom, not subjection . . . dictatorship by mob rule and the overprivileged alike . . . the resolute enemy within our gates . . ."

Roosevelt lowered his voice. "Governments can err, Presidents do make mistakes, but the immortal Dante tells us that divine justice weighs the sins of the cold-blooded and the sins of the warm-hearted in different scales. Better the occasional faults of a Government that lives in a spirit of charity than the consistent omissions of a Government frozen in the ice of its own indifference.

"There is a mysterious cycle in human events. To some generations much is given. Of other generations much is expected. This generation of Americans has a rendezvous with destiny. . . ."

Roosevelt looked up at the crowd.

"I accept the commission you have tendered me. I join—"

A clamorous roar swept through the stadium, drowning out the last words "—with you. I am enlisted for the duration of the war." Like a prize fighter, Roosevelt held his clasped hands over his head, then seized John Garner's. Slowly the President made his way back to his car. As the ecstatic crowd cheered, he circled the field twice; then his car disappeared into the night.

From the center of the stage Roosevelt moved back into the wings. He gave two or three "nonpolitical" dedicatory speeches, and then he entered the fullest blackout a President can enjoy, by cruising for two weeks off the New England coast. The President's vacation was carefully timed. He was perfectly willing to let the Republicans take over the stage; his time would come later. "The Republican high command," he wrote Garner, "is doing altogether too much talking at this stage of the game."

Others were not so serene. Watching the Landon build-up in the press, Ickes grumbled that the Democratic campaign was drifting and the President was defeating himself. Eleanor Roosevelt warned that the Landon headquarters was moving quickly into action. Without Roosevelt's direct control things fell into disorder; even Early and High were disturbed. "The President smiles and sails and fishes," Ickes complained, "and the rest of us worry and fume."

Roosevelt could afford to smile and sail. In a broad sense he had been campaigning for re-election ever since taking office, and he had begun setting his campaign machine in action months before his nomination. He had asked many of his ambassadors abroad to come back for the campaign; he had assigned propaganda jobs, including the preparation of a "Life of Governor Landon" that would picture the Kansan as a pleader for federal relief; he had directed the setting up of special campaign groups like the Good Neighbor League, reviewed campaign tracts, helped draft Lehman for renomination as governor to strengthen the whole ticket in New York, in-

structed his campaign aides not to mention any Republican candidate. When Farley forgot this last precept and referred to the Republican candidate as the governor of a "typical prairie state," the President chided him none too gently. It would have been all right if
Farley had said "one of those splendid prairie states," the President
wrote him, but the word "typical" coming from a New Yorker was
meat for the opposition.

Within a few weeks after the Philadelphia convention Farley had
campaign headquarters actively functioning in New York. The national chairman wrote 2,500 local Democratic leaders for their ap-
praisal of the situation in their area. "I want the true picture,"
Farley warned, and it was on the basis of these and succeeding
estimates that he later made his remarkably accurate prediction of
the election results.

Farley set up the usual campaign divisions, including business,
veterans, foreign language, and the like. The Democrats paid special
attention to labor. Lewis and other CIO chiefs organized Labor's
Nonpartisan League, a wholly partisan agency for mobilizing Roosevelt votes in the industrial centers. Perhaps its most important contribution to the campaign was a gift of half a million dollars. In
the face of the widening labor schism between Lewis's CIO and the
American Federation of Labor, the Democrats were careful not to
jeopardize their good relations with the AFL. Administration officials lobbied among Federation chiefs to hold labor's ranks together
at least until November. Roosevelt kept in close touch with Green,
and the AFL chief publicly promised after a visit to Hyde Park that
90 per cent of labor's vote would go to the President.

While Farley framed a party campaign during midsummer, while
Landon and his hard-driving running mate, Frank Knox, stumped
the country, the President serenely kept his posture of nonpartisanship. Actually he was closely directing aspects of the campaign, even
to the extent of specifying the kind of paper and color process to
be used in pamphlets. Publicly, however, the President seemed occupied with his presidential duties. Of course, as President he could
continue to exploit the politics of the deed. He deflated Republican
criticism of the Democratic spoils system by putting postmasters
under civil service regulations. He anticipated a Landon pronouncement on farm problems by creating a crop insurance committee for
protection against farm surpluses.

As President, too, Roosevelt could make pronouncements of nonpartisan character but with wide popular appeal. Such an occasion
was his Chautauqua address. "I have seen war. I have seen war on
land and sea. I have seen blood running from the wounded. . . . I
hate war." Carefully skirting dangerous political shoals, the President fell back on his old formula of shunning political commit-

ments, such as those involved in the League, but warning that peaceful nations could be involved as long as war existed anywhere in the world. "I have passed unnumbered hours, I shall pass unnumbered hours, thinking and planning how war may be kept from this Nation. . . ."

Nature, too, aided the President's guise of nonpartisanship. By the summer of 1936 a belt of land running from Canada to Texas had been seared and baked by drought. With the sun remorselessly drying up streams and killing off crops, the President decided on one of his "look-sees." Any politics on the drought trip? reporters asked. "It is a great disservice to the proper administration of any government," the President said piously, "to link up human misery with partisan politics."

The trip was a political master stroke. The President made a score of back-platform speeches in nine states; he saw, and was seen by, tens of thousands of voters. Never did he mention the campaign, except in an offhand, humorous way, and never did he mention the Republican opposition. But he often pointed out the contrast between the conditions he had seen in 1932 and the conditions he saw now, even in the drought areas. As the politician joked and politicked with local officials, the inspection train took on the aura of a campaign train. Roosevelt himself seemed to take on magical qualities as his trips through the parched country time and again brought rain.

But the tour was a work trip, too, and the President had a chance to talk with scores of federal and local officials. The climax came in Des Moines when Roosevelt conferred with state governors—including the governor of Kansas. The meeting was called in part to put Landon "on the spot" in regard to farm relief, but the Kansan held his own. Roosevelt took care to be thoroughly briefed for the encounter. "You will not remember," Landon said at one point, "but the first talk with me when you invited me to Washington in 1933—"

Roosevelt cut in: "About the water?"

"I am amazed you remember," Landon said.

The President's main difficulties came at the hands not of Landon but of blunt-talking Governor Ernest Marland of Oklahoma, where drought conditions were at their harshest. At the end the Oklahoman demanded: "Mr. President, what are we going to tell the 100,000 hungry farmers in Oklahoma tomorrow when we go home?"

"You are going to tell them that the Federal agencies are getting busy on it just as fast as the Lord will let them. . . . You can accomplish something in one week, but you cannot accomplish the impossible."

"That is small consolation for a hungry farmer," the governor persisted.

"What more can you say to the hungry farmer, Governor? The machinery will be put in gear just as fast as the Lord will let you."

"WE HAVE ONLY JUST BEGUN TO FIGHT"

The grand strategy in this battle, Herbert Bayard Swope wrote Roosevelt in August, "is to be firm without being ferocious; to be kindly rather than cold; to be hopeful instead of pessimistic; to be human rather than to be economic; to be insistent upon every man having a chance, and above all, to make yourself appear to be the President of *all* the people. . . ."

"I agree with all you say," Roosevelt replied. And during September, while the people and the politicos waited for the old campaigner to open up, Roosevelt doggedly kept his nonpartisan pose. He spoke to the nation on conservation, to a world power conference on "human engineering," to the Conference on the Mobilization for Human Needs, to a national convention of philatelists, to the tercentenary celebration of Harvard, where he was booed by the undergraduates and where he brought smiles even to the faces of stiff-necked Republican alumni by saying: "At that time [one hundred years ago] many of the alumni of Harvard were sorely troubled by the state of the Nation. Andrew Jackson was President. On the 250th anniversary of the founding of Harvard College, alumni again were sorely troubled. Grover Cleveland was President." A pause. "Now, on the 300th anniversary, I am President."

But still the President took no notice of the campaign, of the Republicans and their charges. "Say, Steve," a reporter asked Early jocularly, "is this going to be a nonpolitical campaign?"

Farley could take no such lofty stand. As the rallier of party forces, he was fair game for Republican thrusts. Day after day he was charged with using relief jobs and public funds to bribe millions of voters, with operating a colossal spoils machine, with neglecting the post office. The Republicans hoped their shots would glance off Farley and demolish Roosevelt; more likely, their drumfire against the Postmaster General simply helped Roosevelt in his tactic of staying above the battle.

Farley's worst troubles came from Democrats rather than Republicans. Roosevelt's bipartisanship of 1934 had left Democrats disorganized and disgruntled in half a dozen states. The Wisconsin Democracy had warned Farley against any further administration flirting with the Progressives, and they had put up another candidate to fight Philip La Follette for the governorship. The EPIC groups, still in control of the Democratic party organization in California, had toyed with third party ideas but were now grudgingly supporting Roosevelt. Farmer-Laborites in Minnesota had been openly critical of the New Deal but were now lining up behind Roosevelt, to the discomfiture of the Democratic factions. And it was to Farley, the party leader, that the angry Democrats turned to demand help from the national administration.

The kind of problem Farley faced was typified by the situation in Idaho. Mutual friends of Senator Borah and Roosevelt had tried to induce Farley to withdraw administration support from Borah's Democratic foe in exchange for the Idaho senator's support for Roosevelt against Landon. The proposed deal was backed also by a Democratic faction in Idaho opposed to the Democratic nominee, and Borah was willing to play along with the idea. But Farley reported to the go-betweens that the Democratic candidate was in the fight to stay. Borah never took a stand between Roosevelt and Landon.

Another pro-Roosevelt but non-Democratic senator was Norris of Nebraska—and Norris was a man Roosevelt especially esteemed. Late in 1935 the President had urged Norris to run for re-election in 1936, but the old white-haired Nebraskan allowed the party primaries to go by without filing. He cut off his ties with organization Republicans by denouncing the 1936 platform, and he continued to attack organization Democrats, including Farley, for their spoils activities. But he came out for the President; "Roosevelt is the Democratic platform," the Senator announced. Nominated on petitions as an independent by thousands of his followers late in the summer of 1936, Norris confronted the regular nominees of the two parties. The Democratic nominee, Terry M. Carpenter, appealed for support to his national party leaders, but in vain. To make matters worse for Carpenter, key Democratic leaders in the state came out for Norris against their own party nominee. Carpenter could merely hope that Roosevelt would remain silent.

In planning his mid-October campaign, the President handled state situations such as these with his usual versatility. He kept entirely clear of California, Wisconsin, and Idaho, and thus avoided hostile factions in those states. He planned to go to Minnesota, but before he arrived the local Democrats had been induced to withdraw their state ticket in favor of the Farmer-Laborites, so that the President's main task in this state was to soothe the injured feelings of the ticketless Democratic leaders. As for Nebraska—here he intended to be as direct and outspoken as elsewhere he had been evasive.

Roosevelt opened his formal campaign with a speech at the end of September to the New York Democratic convention in Syracuse. He used the occasion to answer charges of Coughlin, Hearst, and others that the Communists were supporting the New Deal. The President had been urged to answer these charges by denouncing

Soviet violations of treaty agreements, but he believed that a flat statement would be enough. "I have not sought, I do not seek, I repudiate the support of any advocate of Communism or of any other alien 'ism' which would by fair means or foul change our American democracy," he asserted. The New Deal, he said, had saved the country from the threat of communism posed by the social and economic wreckage of 1932. Liberalism was the protection of the farsighted conservative. "Reform if you would preserve."

With biting sarcasm Roosevelt struck out at the "me-too" speeches of the Republicans. "Let me warn you and let me warn the Nation against the smooth evasion which says,"—and here Roosevelt arched his eyebrows and raised his voice to a near falsetto—"Of course we believe all these things; we believe in social security; we believe in work for the unemployed; we believe in saving homes. Cross our hearts and hope to die, we believe in all these things; but we do not like the way the present Administration is doing them. Just turn them over to us. We will do all of them—we will do more of them—we will do them better; and, most important of all, the doing of them will not cost anybody anything."

As Roosevelt's campaign train rolled slowly through the Midwest during October, the patterns of his attack became clear. Over and over again, in rear-platform talks and formal speeches, he stressed three simple themes: the contrast between conditions in March 1933 and conditions in October 1936; the role of the New Deal in getting the country out of depression; and the interdependence of the American people—of workers and businessmen, of farmers and consumers, of state governments and the national government. With homely examples he drove these points home.

Although the President said on one occasion, "We are here to proclaim the New Deal, not to defend it," to a surprising degree he devoted his talks to a point-by-point answer to Republican charges. Again and again he answered Landon's charges of waste and wild spending with the simple question, "If someone came to you and said, 'If you will borrow $800 and by borrowing that $800 increase your annual income by $2,200,' would you borrow it or not?" When some Republican orator accused him of bringing out a new farm program every year, like new automobile models, he accepted the simile and said the nation had passed beyond Model-T farming. "While his speeches did not resound with Webster's sonorous roll, or shimmer with the polished hardness of Woodrow Wilson's rhetoric," Charles and Mary Beard wrote not long afterward, "his prose, although sometimes dull and repetitious, often glowed with poetic warmth and was enlivened by the flight of speeding words."

It was notable, though, that Roosevelt talked little about the future during his Western swing. He was making the New Deal record, not the New Deal promises, the issue. He implied that the New Deal would be enlarged if he stayed in office. But it was no more than an implication; and his speeches were studded with conciliatory remarks for businessmen, doctors, beet sugar growers, and others. Foreign policy he almost completely ignored.

When he wished to take a forthright position the President did so with a flourish. Such was his endorsement of Norris. Speaking in Omaha, the President said that outside of his own state of New York he had consistently refrained from taking part in state elections. But to this rule "I have made—and so long as he lives I always will make—one magnificently justified exception. George Norris' candidacy transcends State and party lines." Roosevelt appealed directly to the cheering crowd to help Norris win re-election.

Always Roosevelt was the gay campaigner, easy in his way with crowds, quick on the trigger, homey, laughing, waving, obviously enjoying himself. In Emporia, Kansas, he looked through the crowd for Editor White, who was supporting Landon. "I wish he were here," the President said genially. "He is a very good friend of mine for three and a half out of every four years."

There was a rustle in the crowd and White appeared. "Shoot not this old gray head," he cried out in mock alarm as he went up to the rear platform of the train.

"Hello, Bill, glad to see you," Roosevelt said. Then turning to the crowd: "Now that I see him, I shall not say anything about the other six months." The crowd laughed and applauded as the two men shook hands, and the train pulled out.

By late October battle lines had stiffened between the two main parties. The Union party, denied a place on the ballot in a dozen states, riven by cleavages among the strange assortment of men who founded it, was visibly faltering. Coughlin had antagonized people by stripping off his black coat and Roman collar at the Union party convention and calling Roosevelt a betrayer and liar. Townsend in October was urging supporters to vote for Landon in states where they could not vote for the Union candidate, William Lemke. Greeted by deep, ominous booing and cold, dead silence in some cities, the Republican candidate was grimly plugging away at his anti-New Deal line. But his hopes ran high on the crest of support from the great majority of newspapers and of denunciations of the New Deal by Democrats Smith and Davis. Moreover, the *Literary Digest*, whose polls had been accurate in past elections, showed Landon holding a decisive edge over his opponent.

Roosevelt late in October set out on a ten-day tour of the urban Northeast. In an almost literal sense the tour was not a campaign trip but a triumphal procession. The President himself said that the trip brought out the "most amazing tidal wave of humanity" he had ever seen. There was something terrible about the crowds that lined the streets, Roosevelt remarked to Ickes—he could hear men and women crying out, "He saved my home," "He gave me a job." Roosevelt made the entire New England swing in an open car, and even hard-bitten reporters were incredulous over the wild enthusiasm of the crowds. For mile after mile people lined the roads, not only in the cities but in the outskirts as well. Boston Common was overrun by a seething mass of 150,000 people. In Connecticut cities the candidate's entourage—including Eleanor Roosevelt—could hardly get through the crowded streets. In New York City the Roosevelt car traveled more than thirty miles without passing a block whose sidewalks were not jammed.

As he waved and talked to such crowds Roosevelt seemed to catch their militancy. His speeches took on a sharper edge, struck a more positive note. In New York City he promised national legislation for better housing. In Wilkes-Barre he attacked scathingly the "propaganda-spreading employers" who were putting anti-social security law slips into pay envelopes. In Brooklyn he stated the task still to be done—to destroy "the glaring inequalities of opportunity and security which, in the recent past, have set group against group and region against region."

Before a wildly fervent, chanting crowd in Madison Square Garden, Roosevelt on the last day of October brought his campaign to a passionate climax.

". . . We have not come this far without a struggle and I assure you that we cannot go further without a struggle.

"For twelve years our Nation was afflicted with hear-nothing, see-nothing, do-nothing Government. The Nation looked to that Government but that Government looked away. Nine mocking years with the golden calf and three long years of the scourge! Nine crazy years at the ticker and three long years in the breadlines! Nine mad years of mirage and three long years of despair! And, my friends, powerful influences strive today to restore that kind of government with its doctrine that that Government is best which is most indifferent to mankind."

Explosive cheers were punctuating the President's sentences. He was deftly modifying the transitions in his prepared text as he caught the rhythm of the crowd. "For nearly four years now you have had an Administration which instead of twirling its thumbs has rolled up its sleeves. And I can assure you that we will keep our sleeves rolled up.

"We had to struggle with the old enemies of peace—business and financial monopoly, speculation, reckless banking, class antagonism, sectionalism, war profiteering. *They* had begun to consider the Government of the United States as a mere appendage to their own affairs. And we know now that Government by organized *money* is just as dangerous as Government by organized *mob*."

Roosevelt's voice had been in turn stern with indignation, sonorous with moral fervor, solemn, and even cheery. Now his tone hardened. "Never before in all our history have these forces been so united against one candidate as they stand today. They are unanimous in their *hate* for *me—and I welcome their hatred*."

A raucous, almost animal-like roar burst from the crowd, died away, and then rose again in wave after wave. Roosevelt began again, gently.

"I should like to have it said of my first Administration that in it the forces of selfishness and of lust for power met their *match*." The words came faster, rang with increasing militancy. "I should like to have it said—" Cheers, cowbells, horns, clackers drowned out the words.

"Wait a moment!" Roosevelt commanded. The old performer would not have his lines spoiled. The din subsided.

"I should like to have it said of my second Administration that *in it these forces met their master*." The roar from the crowd was like that at a prize fight—a massive sound through which the promptings of individuals could be faintly heard.

A few days before, Landon had stood where the President was now standing, and had demanded that Roosevelt indicate his future course if re-elected. The President picked up the challenge but did so in his own terms. Again and again hitting the refrain "For all these we have only just begun to fight," he said:

"This is our answer to those who, silent about their own plans, ask us to state our objectives.

"*Of course* we will continue to seek to improve working conditions for the workers of America. . . . *Of course* we will continue to work for cheaper electricity in the homes and on the farms of America. . . . *Of course* we will continue our efforts in behalf of the farmers of America. . . . *Of course* we will continue our efforts for young men and women . . . for the crippled, for the blind, for the mothers, our insurance for the unemployed, our security for the aged. *Of course* we will continue to protect the consumer . . . will continue our successful efforts to increase his purchasing power and to keep it constant.

"For these things, too, and for a multitude of things like them, we have only just begun to fight. . . ."

ROOSEVELT AS A POLITICAL TACTICIAN

Reporters groped for words. The election results were a tidal wave, an earthquake, a landslide, the blizzard of '36. Roosevelt carried every state but Maine and Vermont. He won over Landon by 27,752,309 to 16,682,524 votes, the biggest popular plurality in history; his 523 to 8 ratio of electoral votes—exactly as predicted by Farley—was the biggest since 1820. He helped enlarge the already top-heavy Democratic margins in Congress. The new House would have 334 Democrats and 89 Republicans, against 321-104 before; sitting in the Senate would be 75 Democrats and only 17 Republicans, as compared to the old 70-23 ratio. If there had been a coattails effect, Roosevelt had the longer tails; Lehman in New York and Frank Murphy in Michigan had been urged to run to help the President; Roosevelt ran far ahead of both of them.

Roosevelt's political reputation soared. Tumbling over one another, observers called him the master politician, the champion campaigner. What was the secret of his political sorcery? Some of his techniques were as old as politics itself; a few were new; all were invested with the deft Roosevelt touch. If categorized, they might go as follows.

Grasp of Public Opinion. Roosevelt showed such a sure sense of popular moods and attitudes that some believed he had intuition or a sixth sense in this field. Actually, his understanding was rooted in solid, day-to-day accumulation of facts on what people were thinking. Roosevelt read half a dozen newspapers a day. He kept up a vast correspondence. Tens of thousands of letters came to the White House every week reporting people's views and problems. He got some understanding from crowds—the way they looked, how they reacted to certain passages in his speeches. As President he enjoyed special advantages. Through favored journalists he could put up trial balloons and test public reaction. He had special voting polls conducted, and he often received advance information on other polls. Administrators in regional and state offices sent in a good deal of information, as did state and local party leaders. A huge division of press intelligence clipped hundreds of newspapers and compiled digests.

Timing Roosevelt's timing also seemed intuitive, but it too was largely calculated. Essential in his timing was the care he took not to confront his political opposition when it was mobilizing and moving hard and fast; he believed, for example, that presidents could expect to lose some popular support during congressional sessions, and that the President should wait until Congress adjourned before seizing the offensive again. Sometimes he moved fast, before the opposition could mobilize. "I am like a cat," Roosevelt said once. "I make a quick stroke and then I relax." More often, he waited for the crest of the opposition wave to subside, then he acted. In the 1936 campaign he was under intense pressure from his political advisers to attack Landon when the Republican tide was running strong in early summer, but he refused. When he told Rosenman that tides turned quickly in politics, he was recognizing a shiftiness and moodiness in certain sectors of public opinion that have since been tested and proved in opinion and voting studies.

Attention to Political Detail. Roosevelt showed infinite patience in dealing with the day-to-day routine of politics, involving in most cases the ambitions, hopes, and desire for recognition of countless politicians. The White House establishment was carefully organized for this purpose. A memo to Roosevelt during the campaign from one of his aides read:

1. Dan Tobin needs a little pat on the back. What do you think of taking him along on the New England trip? . . .
2. Jim [Farley] suggests the possibility of taking John J. O'Connor up through New England since he's an old Massachusetts man—nose a bit out of joint, etc.
3. Jim thinks the Connecticut trip should include Meriden. It is Frank Maloney's home town. . . .

Or take the case of David E. Fitzgerald, a Democratic leader in New Haven. In 1935 the White House sent him an autographed picture of the President. Fitzgerald traveled with Roosevelt's entourage during the New England tour in 1936; his note of congratulations brought a "Dear Dave" reply from the President. Each of three Fitzgerald letters in 1940 was answered by a warm little note from Roosevelt; a postelection wire of congratulations brought a presidential letter in which "Dear Mr. Fitzgerald" was crossed out and "Dear Dave" substituted. When Fitzgerald caught cold campaigning, the White House sent him flowers. In 1941, another "Dear Dave" letter; a year later Fitzgerald died, and a warm presidential letter went to his widow, who replied, in a widow's tremulous handwriting, "Mr. Fitzgerald was always an ardent admirer of yours. . . ."

Attention to Intragroup Factions. The White House checked carefully on the political situation within groups, in order both to keep on friendly terms with all the factions and to avoid being compromised by some faction of politically suspect leanings. Splits among Negroes, Jews, labor groups, bankers, veterans, and the like were followed with care. Through administration officials who had longtime connections with national associations, the White House got deeply involved in the internal politics of some groups, but always covertly. Pro-Roosevelt activities in the groups were often defensive, designed to offset opposing factions which might swing the formal association against the President during an election campaign.

Separating Opposition Leaders from Rank and File. Splitting enemy leaders from their followers is an old political tactic, but few politicians have used it as persistently or as meticulously as Roosevelt. Almost invariably he attacked "Republican leaders" or "Republican spokesmen," never the Republican party or Republicans generally. "There are thousands of people," Roosevelt had said to Rosenman as far back as 1930, "who think as you and I do about government. They are enrolled as Republicans because their families have been Republicans for generations—that's the only reason; some of them think it is *infra dig* to be called a Democrat; the Democrats in their village are not the socially 'nice' people the enrolled Republicans are. So never attack the Republicans or the Republican party—only the Republican *leaders*. Then any Republican voter who hears it will say to himself: 'Well, he doesn't mean me. . . .'"

Fighting on Your Own Battleground. Offensively this meant attacking the opposition at its weakest point in an effort to force it to accept the gage of battle on the worst ground for it. Defensively it meant answering the opposition's most extreme or absurd attacks. In 1930 Roosevelt ignored Republican charges against his handling of the New York City situation until almost the end of the campaign. In his Madison Square Garden speech in 1936 he skillfully converted Landon's effort to put him on the defensive into a superb defense of the New Deal on his own terms.

Personal Charm and Political Craft. No political technique is effective unless employed with skill in a given situation. Immensely strengthening all Roosevelt's tactics were the calculated flattery he could use in winning over critics and the sheer astuteness with which he outmaneuvered rival leaders. An example of the latter was his handling of John L. Lewis's campaign donation in 1936. The CIO chief came into Roosevelt's office one day with a check for $250,000 and with a photographer to record the ceremony. Roosevelt was all smiles, but he would not take the check.

"No, John," he said. "Just keep it, and I'll call on you if and when any small need arises."

Lewis left, grumbling that he had been outsmarted. He had been. During the next few weeks requests for money flowed in from Farley and from independent Roosevelt groups. In vain Lewis tried to stem the torrent by insisting on a written order from the President. Roosevelt backed up the requests with orders or with telephone calls. In the end Lewis's treasury was drained of almost half a million dollars—and without undue notice in the press.

Undeniably, the triumph was largely a personal victory for Roosevelt. "I am the issue," he had said to Moley; and Farley had built his campaign around the Roosevelt personality. So the post-election huzzas were justifiably for Roosevelt, rather than for his party or even for his cause.

Drowned out by the applause were some misgivings about certain aspects of the election results. Roosevelt himself, according to one report, was disturbed by the shriveled Republican strength in House and Senate. Without strong party opposition, he foresaw that splits might more easily develop within the huge Democratic majorities as shifting factions fought with one another. Ickes said bluntly that the President had pulled through to victory men whose defeat would have been better for the country. On the other hand, Roosevelt was pleased with his own sweep. If Landon had gained over Hoover he feared that the "reactionary element" would exploit that fact during the next Congress.

The personal nature of the sweep had other implications. For one thing, it left in some obscurity the nature of the mandate the voters had given him. He had run mainly on the New Deal record; what was the New Deal future to be—a continuation of the present program, an enlargement, a shift in new directions? To be sure, Roosevelt in the eleventh hour of the campaign had uttered his magnificent "we-have-only-just-begun-to-fight" statement. Was this a bit of campaign oratory, or a pledge to an expanded New Deal?

Roosevelt's victory, too, had been realized at some expense to the party that he headed. In several states the Democratic organization was left stranded, and in New York State the American Labor Party, composed largely of unionists suspicious of both major parties, boasted of the voters who had supported the President on its ticket. It was odd, and yet significant, that within a few days of the Democratic party nominee's great victory, observers were predicting a party realignment, and possibly even a national labor party, by 1940.

Another aspect of the personal nature of Roosevelt's victory was the ambiguity of the class groupings supporting him. In 1932 voters from all income classes had flocked to his standard out of their common deprivations during the Depression. Roosevelt's fuzzy position on many issues that year had made it possible for his vote to cut across class lines. What had happened in 1936? Polling results suggested that a class cleavage had begun to divide the voters at a point about midway through the first term, and had widened considerably by 1936. But later studies were to show that the cleavage in 1936 was not as sharp as some had supposed. This was due in part to the breadth of the President's appeal—he won votes not only from the great majority of the poor, but from a surprising percentage of the better off too.

There is a rule of economy in politics. "The perfect party victory," it has been said, "is to be won by accumulating a relatively narrow majority, the mark of the skillful conduct of politics." To win a great majority of votes may involve such commitments as to make victory politically embarrassing. From such a standpoint Roosevelt's landslide was political extravagance. Of course, he had not expected to win by such a sweep, and he did not have the benefit of hindsight. But much would depend on the decisions he made as he strove to govern with his top-heavy majority.

Such speculations as these, however, would have seemed academic indeed in November of 1936. Roosevelt was at the peak of his political form. When he sailed on the *Indianapolis* for a good-will tour to South America late that month, he left an America that was itself bursting with good will toward its leader. Rested by the trip and greeted by huge throngs in Rio de Janeiro and Buenos Aires, he was as captivating as ever.

He looked forward confidently and eagerly to his second term, which would start in January 1937 rather than March as a result of the passage of a constitutional amendment. All seemed well and calm at home—his only worry was the situation abroad. ". . . I still don't like the European outlook," he wrote Eleanor at the end of November.

PART 4 *The Lion at Bay*

FIFTEEN   *Court Packing:*
The Miscalculated Risk

Wwas it an omen? The famous Roosevelt
luck seemed to forsake the President on the January day in 1937
when he entered his second term. Bursts of cold rain soaked the
gay inaugural decorations, furled the sodden flags around their
staffs, and drenched dignitaries and spectators alike while they
gathered below the Capitol rotunda. The rain drummed on the
cellophane that covered Roosevelt's old family Bible, as he stood
with upraised hand facing Chief Justice Hughes.

They eyed each other, the old judge, his wet whiskers quivering
in the wind, the resolute President, jaw stuck out. Hughes read the
oath with slow and rising emphasis as he came to the words "promise to support the Constitution of the United States." Roosevelt
gave the words equal force as he repeated the oath. At this point,
he said later, he wanted to cry out, "Yes, but it's the Constitution
as *I* understand it, flexible enough to meet any new problem of democracy—not the kind of Constitution your Court has raised up as
a barrier to progress and democracy."

The President turned to the rain-spattered pages of his inaugural
address. "When four years ago we met to inaugurate a President, the
Republic, single-minded in anxiety, stood in spirit here. We dedicated ourselves to the fulfillment of a vision—to speed the time
when there would be for all the people that security and peace essential to the pursuit of happiness. We of the Republic pledged
ourselves to drive from the temple of our ancient faith those who
had profaned it; to end by action, tireless and unafraid, the stagnation and despair of that day. We did those first things first."

But the covenant "with ourselves" did not stop there. "Instinctively we recognized a deeper need—the need to find through government the instrument of our united purpose to solve for the individual the ever-rising problems of a complex civilization. Repeated attempts at their solution without the aid of government
had left us baffled and bewildered. For, without that aid, we had
been unable to create those moral controls over the services of science which are necessary to make science a useful servant instead

of a ruthless master of mankind. To do this we knew that we must find practical controls over blind economic forces and blindly selfish men."

The rain poured down, dripped off Roosevelt's bare head, dulled the cutting edge of some of his sentences. As the intricacies of human relationships increased, he said, so power to govern them also must increase—power to stop evil, power to do good. "The essential democracy of our Nation and the safety of our people depend not upon the absence of power, but upon lodging it with those whom the people can change or continue at stated intervals through an honest and free system of elections." Did the Chief Justice, sitting a few feet away on the President's right, catch the faint warning in the sentence?

The President was turning now to the future. "Shall we pause now and turn our back upon the road that lies ahead?" He looked at the crowd. "Many voices are heard as we face a great decision. Comfort says, 'Tarry a while.' Opportunism says, 'This is a good spot.' Timidity asks, 'How difficult is the road ahead?'" The nation had come far since the days of stagnation. But dulled conscience, irresponsibility, and ruthless self-interest already were reappearing. Here was the challenge to American democracy:

"In this nation I see tens of millions of its citizens—a substantial part of its whole population—who at this very moment are denied the greater part of what the very lowest standards of today call the necessities of life.

"I see millions of families trying to live on incomes so meager that the pall of family disaster hangs over them day by day.

"I see millions whose daily lives in city and on farm continue under conditions labeled indecent by a so-called polite society half a century ago.

"I see millions denied education, recreation, and the opportunity to better their lot and the lot of their children.

"I see millions lacking the means to buy the products of farm and factory and by their poverty denying work and productiveness to many other millions.

"I see one-third of a nation ill-housed, ill-clad, ill-nourished.

"It is not in despair that I paint you that picture. I paint it for you in hope—because the Nation, seeing and understanding the injustice in it, proposes to paint it out. . . .

"To maintain a democracy of effort requires a vast amount of patience in dealing with differing methods, a vast amount of humility. But out of the confusion of many voices rises an understanding of dominant public need. Then political leadership can voice common ideals, and aid in their realization.

"In taking again the oath of office as President of the United

States, I assume the solemn obligation of leading the American people forward along the road over which they have chosen to advance. . . ."

BOMBSHELL

Just two weeks later Roosevelt and Hughes faced each other once again—this time in the gracious, brilliantly lighted East Room of the White House. It was the President's annual dinner for the judiciary. At the center of the scene were the President, jauntily waving his cigarette holder to point up his stories, and the great jurist. Both were in a jovial mood; the talk ran fast and free. Around them were banked others of the nation's great—cabinet members, judges, senators, bankers, even the Gene Tunneys.

The jollity barely concealed a certain tension in the air. Key New Deal measures were crowding the Supreme Court's docket. Rumors were running through Washington that Roosevelt, armed with his huge popular endorsement, was aiming some kind of attack on the Court. Besides the President only a handful present knew the truth of the rumors. Watching Roosevelt and Hughes, Attorney General Cummings wished the secret were out. "I feel too much like a conspirator," he complained to Rosenman. Roosevelt, on the other hand, was probably savoring the irony of the moment. On the eve of a great battle the commander of one side was giving a banquet to his adversaries.

But the President was a bit nervous too. During the next two days he pored over his message to Congress, adding, erasing, shifting phrases and sentences. His main concern was to keep his plan secret; he had not told some of his closest aides. On February 4 he called an extraordinary meeting of cabinet members and congressional leaders for the following day. Amazed White House stenographers were told to report at 6:30 the next morning to mimeograph documents for this meeting and for a press conference.

Next morning the cabinet and congressmen waited wonderingly in the long, low-ceilinged cabinet room. The President was quickly wheeled in. He called out cheery greetings, then turned directly to the business at hand. Announcing his intention to meet the challenge posed by the Court, he read excerpts from his message that would go to Congress in an hour.

Amid dead silence, he outlined his plan. For every Supreme Court justice who failed to quit the bench within six months after reaching seventy, the President would be empowered to appoint a new justice up to a total of six. The message to Congress talked much of judicial efficiency, congestion in the courts, the need for new blood, the problem of injunctions; and the President's bill involved new appointments at the district and circuit court level too. But the crux of the proposal leaped out from the long legal phrases—the power Roosevelt was asking to flank Hughes and his brethren with six New Deal justices.

The meeting was a study in mixed emotions. Ickes was elated that the President had moved at last. Cummings, twiddling his pince-nez with a slightly self-important air, was pleased to have long been a part of the unfolding drama. But the congressional delegation sat as if stunned. Garner and Rayburn said not a word. Robinson, deep concern written on his face, gave a feeble indication of approval. Henry Ashurst, chairman of the Senate Judiciary Committee, must have thought of his heated denial during the campaign that Roosevelt would try to pack the Court, but he loyally spoke out in support of the bill. Speaker Bankhead bore a poker face throughout.

There was virtually no discussion; the President solicited no opinions from his party's leadership. At the end he wheeled off to meet a waiting group of newspapermen. Over this session Roosevelt presided like an impresario. Again and again bursts of laughter punctuated his reading of his message to Congress, as he interpolated telling little points; the President threw his head back and joined in the laughter. Once again he demanded absolute secrecy until the message was released.

Driving back to Capitol Hill from the White House, Garner and his colleagues were still silent. Suddenly Hatton Sumners of Texas, chairman of the House Judiciary Committee, turned to the others. "Boys," he said, "here's where I cash in." The group took the news to Congress with them. By the time the message was read, the cloakrooms were filled with little knots of legislators asking one another, "What do you think of it?" In the first hours it seemed as though the proposal cut through each House, down the middle. Two sons of Texas signalized the extremes. In the House, New Deal Representative Maury Maverick grabbed a mimeographed copy of the bill, scribbled his name on it, and threw it into the bill hopper almost before the reading clerk was finished. In the Senate lobby Garner held his nose with one hand and vigorously shook his turned-down thumb.

A messenger hurried across the plaza to the Supreme Court building. Inside, the justices were hearing an argument. Only Brandeis had heard the news; just before the justices entered the Court, Corcoran, with Roosevelt's consent, had "crashed the sacred robing room" to tell him, and Brandeis had instantly expressed his disapproval. Now a page slipped through the draperies behind the dais and handed a paper to each Justice. The attorney at bar, sensing the sudden tension on the bench, paused a moment. Hughes shifted restlessly in his chair, Van Devanter looked grim, Butler seemed to chuckle. But judicial mien quickly reappeared, and proceedings continued.

Blazing headlines carried the news to the people during the afternoon. Next morning, reading the newspapers in bed over his breakfast tray, the President was not surprised at the howls of anguish in the editorial columns. He had expected this; what he was banking on was the approval of the people. As it turned out, the proposal at the outset split the American people neatly in half. Could Roosevelt mobilize a popular majority behind his plan? Could he convert such a majority into congressional action?

The suddenness of Roosevelt's move, the obvious pleasure he found in presenting his handiwork, and the utter secrecy that surrounded its preparation all gave the impression of a proposal that had been hastily cooked up after the election. Actually Roosevelt had been considering judicial reform for over two years.

Even before the Court's all-out attack on the New Deal in 1935 Roosevelt was thinking of enlarging the Court to protect his legislation. That he would not brook judicial opposition on a crucial matter was apparent from the radio address to the nation he planned in the event that the Court found against him in the gold cases. Only the Court's slim vote in his favor turned him from defiance of the Court through presidential proclamation and an appeal to Congress. When the Court voided the NRA and other measures, the President's view that action must be taken steadily hardened.

But what to do? For a while Roosevelt had toyed with the idea of a constitutional amendment. Various types were possible: directly enlarging congressional authority in specific economic and social fields; granting Congress power to re-enact and thus "constitutionalize" a measure voided by the Court; requiring a six to three or even a seven to two vote in the Supreme Court to strike down an act of Congress; setting an age limit on judges or giving them terms instead of appointments for life. Eventually Roosevelt decided against the amendment method. At best it would take too long. More likely, an amendment, even if it won two-thirds majorities in House and Senate, would never hurdle the barriers carefully contrived by the framers of the Constitution—three-quarters of the state legislatures or of state conventions—especially since these assemblies tended to overrepresent conservative, small-town interests and attitudes.

"Give me ten million dollars," the President said later, "and I can prevent any amendment to the Constitution from being ratified by the necessary number of states."

Could an act of Congress do the trick? A measure that directly challenged the High Court by trying to curb its power would probably be voided by the Court itself. There was another method, however, that seemed certainly constitutional because it was sanctioned by precedent. This was to enlarge the Court's membership, as previous presidents had done, by inducing Congress to authorize new appointments. At first, packing the Court seemed distasteful to the President, perhaps because the objective would be so transparent. But he kept returning to the idea. He was fascinated by a historical precedent—Asquith's and Lloyd George's threat through the King to pack the House of Lords with new Peers if that chamber refused to bow to the supremacy of the House of Commons.

Clearly the President feared a direct assault on the Court. Perhaps he sensed—as polls indicated—that in late 1935 most of the people opposed restriction on the Court's veto power. The Democratic platform of 1936 had come out only for some "clarifying amendment." During the campaign Hoover and others demanded that the President confirm or deny that he planned to pack the Court. Roosevelt not only ignored the specific question—as a seasoned campaigner would—but he skirted the whole problem of the Supreme Court. Doubtless his silence helped him roll up his great majority—but it also meant that he gained no explicit mandate to act on the Court.

At the first cabinet meeting after the election Roosevelt raised the Court issue. He expected, he said with mock glumness, that McReynolds would still be on the bench at the age of one hundred and five. An appeal to the people might be necessary. The problem "must be faced," he wrote to Joseph Patterson of the New York *Daily News*. But how to face it? Before Roosevelt left on his cruise to South America, he set Cummings to work in Washington poring over a sheaf of plans for overcoming the nine old men—or at least five of them.

Mulling over various proposals one December morning, Cummings ran across a recommendation that Attorney General—now Justice—McReynolds had made in 1913 that when any federal judge, except Supreme Court justices, failed to retire at the age provided by law, the President should appoint another judge to preside over the Court and to hold precedence over the older one. Why not, thought Cummings, apply the idea to the Supreme Court?

"The answer to a maiden's prayer!" Roosevelt reportedly exclaimed when Cummings brought in his idea. And so it must have seemed. The plan was clearly constitutional. It was, compared with most of the other proposals, quite moderate in character, involving no change in the venerable system of checks and balances. Most important, the plan could be presented to the country as part of a broader program of reconstructing the whole federal judiciary in the name not of liberalism but of greater efficiency and expedition in the courts. And Roosevelt, with his penchant for personalizing the political opposition, must have delighted in the thought of hoisting McReynolds by his own petard.

All that remained was the matter of how to present the plan. Why did Roosevelt insist on almost conspiratorial secrecy? Why did he spring the plan suddenly on Robinson, who would have to manage the fight in the Senate; on Ashurst, who just before had hotly denied that Roosevelt had any plans for packing the Court, on his old progressive ally Norris, on Brandeis and Stone, on Rayburn and Garner, on Farley and Ickes, even on McIntyre and Early? Roosevelt explained to Farley that he feared premature disclosure by the press. This explanation is unconvincing. Roosevelt was too astute a politician to think that secrecy was worth the price of excluding key leaders from the decision-making conferences. Moreover, Roosevelt himself had leaked the essence of the plan to a *Collier's* writer a few weeks before the announcement.

The explanation lies deeper—deep in Roosevelt's personality. He had won what he considered to be a personal election victory over the Old Guard. Now the Old Guard remained entrenched in the ramparts of the judiciary. The stage was set for a Rooseveltian onslaught against the citadel as exhilarating and triumphant as his rout of the Republicans. He set the stage with his old flair for timing and suspense. His final presentation combined in a curious fashion two Rooseveltian traits—his instinct for the dramatic and his instinct for the adroit and circuitous stratagem rather than the frontal assault.

Both instincts failed him. "Too clever—too damned clever," said one pro-New Deal newspaper. The President's liberal friends were disturbed. Some of them had hoped that Roosevelt would make a direct attack on the Court's conservative veto. Others used his disingenuousness as an excuse to desert the cause. Still others disagreed with his particular plan. Years before, Roosevelt had lamented that reform came slowly because liberals had such difficulty in agreeing on means. His words would fly back to mock him in 1937.

GUERRILLA WARFARE

Battle lines formed quickly but not in a way that was to Roosevelt's liking. He was not surprised that Republicans and conservative Democrats flared up in opposition. This was to be expected. But alarming reports reached the White House from the Senate. Two noted progressives, Burt Wheeler and Hiram Johnson, were opposed. So were Democrats Joseph O'Mahoney of Wyoming, Tom

Connally of Texas, Bennett Clark of Missouri, Ed Burke of Nebraska, and a dozen others of the kind of men on whose loyalty the President had counted. And—worst blow of all—Norris. Although in the end he supported the bill, the old Nebraskan, within a few hours of Roosevelt's announcement, said quietly, "I am not in sympathy with the plan to enlarge the Supreme Court."

Something was happening to the Grand Coalition that had carried Roosevelt to his election triumph. Something was happening to the Republicans too. Knowing that their little band in Congress could not overcome the President in a straight party fight, they resolved to stay silent and let the Democrats fight one another. When Hoover, Landon, and other national leaders wanted to rush to the microphone and make the court plan a party issue, congressional Republicans McNary, Borah, and Vandenberg, acting quickly, headed them off. The Liberty League, moribund after November 1936, was silent. Roosevelt found himself aligned not against Republicans but against his own fellow partisans.

"What a grand fight it is going to be!" Roosevelt wrote Creel. "We need everything we have got to put in it!" To visitors he declared confidently that "the people are with me." Were they? Within a few days it was clear that the proposal had struck deep into the complex of American emotions. There was a crescendo of protest. The New York *Herald Tribune* gave seven of its eight front-page columns to the proposal. Patriotic groups moved quickly into action. New England town fathers called mass meetings. Bar associations met and denounced. Mail flooded congressional offices; some senators received over a thousand letters a day. What amazed congressmen was less the amount of opposition than the intensity of it. There was a pervasive element of fear—"fear of the unknown," columnist Raymond Clapper thought—and a deep reverence for the Supreme Court.

Many of the protestants cited their middle-class background, their little property holdings, their fear of labor and radical elements. Events helped sharpen these fears. During the early months of 1937 a rash of sit-down strikes broke out. The picture of grinning, insolent workers barricading factories against the owners was disturbing to people who wanted law and order, and a curious, emotional link was created in the conservative middle-class mind between the court plan and labor turbulence. For the first time, William Allen White wrote Norris, opposition to Roosevelt was coming "not from the plug hat section but from the grass roots."

The protest was not wholly spontaneous. Busily stoking the fires were Roosevelt's old friend Frank Gannett and other prominent conservatives. "Get busy fast!" Borah urged Gannett; the New York publisher put $49,000 into the campaign and raised almost $150,000 more from several thousand contributors. Full-page advertisements blossomed in the newspapers; fervent oratory filled the air waves; speeches were franked by the tens of thousands through congressional offices and out to the country. And still the hand of Republican leaders was hardly visible.

One early effect of this surge of protest was to strip Roosevelt's proposal of its "efficiency" façade and to show it plainly as an attempt to liberalize the Court. Abruptly shifting his tactics, the President decided to wage his campaign squarely on this basic issue. And he resolved on a direct appeal to the country. "The source of criticism is concentrated," he wrote a friend late in February, "and I feel that as we get the story to the general public the whole matter will be given wide support."

Significantly, his first appeal was to his party. Addressing a resplendent Democratic victory dinner at the Mayflower Hotel on March 4, the President summoned his partisans to defend his proposal. Roosevelt seemed in the best of humor, but his voice was stern and commanding. He warned his party that it would celebrate victories in the future only if it kept faith with the majority that had elected it. "We gave warning last November that we had only just begun to fight. Did some people really believe we did not mean it? Well—I meant it, and you meant it."

A new crisis was at hand, the President asserted—a crisis different from but even graver than four years before. It was the ever-accelerating speed of social forces now gathering headway. The President dwelt at length on the fate of remedial measures at the hands of the courts. Then he brought his speech to a stunning climax:

"It will take courage to let our minds be bold and find the ways to meet the needs of the Nation. But for our Party, now as always, the counsel of courage is the counsel of wisdom.

"If we do not have the courage to lead the American people where they want to go, someone else will.

"Here is one-third of a Nation ill-nourished, ill-clad, ill-housed—NOW!

"Here are thousands upon thousands of farmers wondering whether next year's prices will meet their mortgage interest—NOW!

"Here are thousands upon thousands of men and women laboring for long hours in factories for inadequate pay—NOW!

"Here are thousands upon thousands of children who should be at school, working in mines and mills—NOW!

"Here are strikes more far-reaching than we have ever known, costing millions of dollars—NOW!

"Here are Spring floods threatening to roll again down our river valleys—NOW!

"Here is the Dust Bowl beginning to blow again—NOW!

"If we would keep faith with those who had faith in us, if we would make democracy succeed, I say we must act—NOW!"

The President's fireside chat a few days later was more pallid and more defensive. Again he dwelt on the conditions of four years before, the "quiet crisis" that faced the country, the failure of the Supreme Court to pull together with the other horses in the "three-horse team" of the national government. The Constitution must be saved from the Court, and the Court from itself. He directly met the charge of packing the Court by denying that he had any intention of appointing "spineless puppets." He explained at length why he had not chosen the amendment alternative. He pointed to his own record of devotion to civil and religious liberty.

"You who know me will accept my solemn assurance that in a world in which democracy is under attack, I seek to make American democracy succeed. You and I will do our part."

The President was not depending on oratory alone. From the outset a special White House staff, under Roosevelt's close direction, managed an aggressive campaign. They dispatched speakers to the country, channeled ideas and arguments to friendly legislators, and put pressure on senators hostile or silent on the measure. The form of this pressure was a subject of open wrangling among Democrats. At the very least, Corcoran and the other administration agents put it up to senators in stiff terms to back up the President. Senators were tempted with new patronage arrangements and with federal projects for their states, and even with judicial appointments for themselves. Pressure was also brought to bear on a number of senators through Democratic organizations in their home states, including Chicago's Kelly-Nash machine and Pendergast's Kansas City organization. Some senators—certainly Robinson himself—could hardly forget that passage of the measure would mean that the President could allot six Supreme Court judgeships—the most highly prized appointive job in America.

Roosevelt's appeal to the people had some impact. Support for the plan reached its highest point in mid-March. But the actual deciding would be done on Capitol Hill, and here things were not going so well.

Roosevelt's aides were not operating on Capitol Hill with their usual efficiency. Part of the trouble was caused by James Roosevelt, whom his father had appointed as an assistant early in 1937. Eleanor Roosevelt, foreseeing the pressures amid which James would have to work, opposed the appointment, but her husband saw no reason why the fact that he was President should deprive him of his oldest son's help. Eleanor's doubts were vindicated. James made promises that seemed to have special authenticity but in fact did not;

the efforts of the other aides on the Hill were undermined; and congressional friction and bitterness increased.

The senatorial opposition, on the other hand, was functioning with extraordinary skill and smoothness. The Republicans were still relatively quiet. On the Democratic side Carter Glass supplied the moral indignation and Wheeler and O'Mahoney the liberal veneer, while middle-of-the-road Democrats like Royal S. Copeland of New York, Frederick Van Nuys of Indiana, and Connally furnished the anchor line of votes. Against them was aligned a solid core of New Dealers and a group of senators who went along with the bill largely out of personal loyalty to the President. A score of senators were—openly, at least—on the fence.

In mid-March the seat of battle shifted to the reverberant, multi-columned Senate caucus room, where the Judiciary Committee held hearings on the measure. Cummings led off for the administration with a statement that reflected the President's original plea for a more efficient judiciary. He was followed by Assistant Attorney General Robert H. Jackson, who tried valiantly to bring the subject back to the issue of liberalizing the Court. Both were subjected to a barrage of unfriendly questions. So effective was the cross-examination that a dozen experts from the American Bar Association were rumored to be in Washington furnishing ammunition. Other administration witnesses testified over the next ten days, including President Green of the AFL, political scientists Edward S. Corwin and Charles Grove Haines, Editor Irving Brant of the St. Louis *Star-Times*. Then it was the opposition's turn.

Shrewdly handled, the congressional hearing can be a powerful weapon against the executive. Although not himself a member of the Judiciary Committee, Wheeler was ready, through his friends on the committee, to use it to turn the administration's flank. A veteran of Montana's stormy politics, he was a man temperamentally at his best in opposition: tireless, vengeful, resourceful, and often choleric. Despite his protestations of love for the President, he had reason to feel disgruntled; an early and strenuous worker for Roosevelt's nomination, he had had little recognition, and he knew that he—who had been, after all, the Progressive party running mate of the great La Follette in 1924—had taken a more liberal position than the President on many relief and reform measures.

Wheeler opened the attack on the court bill before the committee. Suddenly he produced the opposition's bombshell—a letter from Chief Justice Hughes showing categorically that the Supreme Court was abreast of its work and arguing that a larger court would lower its efficiency. In the few minutes the letter took to read it made three things clear: that a coalition had been forged between the senatorial opposition and the politicians of the judiciary, who were quietly doing what they could against the plan; that this coalition was attacking Roosevelt on his weakest salient, his original charge of inefficiency; and that the political skill of Hughes himself had been thrown into the fight.

Outwardly Hughes had preserved his usual benignity in the face of the court plan. "If they want me to preside over a convention," he said, "I can do it." But the old politician's fighting instincts were aroused. He wished to speak out—but how could he in the face of the restraints that tradition imposed on the Court? Roosevelt's use of the inefficiency argument gave him the perfect opportunity to attack the plan in the guise of supplying data. The Chief Justice was ready even to appear personally before the committee, but Brandeis objected, so a letter had to do. Working feverishly over a week end to meet Wheeler's timetable, the Chief Justice turned the letter over to the Senator with a smile. "The baby is born."

Hughes's political leadership and shrewdness matched Roosevelt's. He had not been able, he informed the committee, to consult with every member of the Court, but he was confident that his letter was in accord with their views. Actually, at least one justice, Stone, resented Hughes's failure to consult him and disagreed with part of the letter. Perhaps the Chief Justice knew or suspected that Stone disparaged Hughes's reputation as a liberal Justice, that Stone, through Irving Brant of the St. Louis *Star-Times*, was letting his views be known to the White House. In any event, Hughes's strategy was perfectly executed.

Dismayed by Hughes's counterthrust, the administration had to sit by idly while the committee heard witness after witness. For days on end their arguments against the President's plan filled the press and radio. Roosevelt hoped that "things would move faster from now on," as he wrote a friend, but the opposition saw the advantages of delay. To make matters worse, the administration had no one on the committee with Borah's or Wheeler's or Connally's brilliance in cross-examination. Here, too, the President was paying a price for his secrecy; Senator Hugo Black, a tenacious and resourceful parliamentarian, had left the Judiciary Committee at the beginning of the year.

During the critical weeks of late March and early April popular support for the plan slowly, steadily ebbed away. The backing that Roosevelt aroused in his two speeches lacked stability and depth; it simply disintegrated as the long fight wore on. Much of the trouble lay in the deep fissures running through workers and farmers, the two great group interests that Roosevelt had counted on because of their unhappy experiences with the Court. The AFL was now locked in trench warfare with the CIO, and labor rallies organized by the administration fell apart in the face of this split, local Democratic party quarrels, and general apathy. The farm organizations were not acting as though there had ever been an AAA decision. Leaders of the powerful Farm Bureau Federation were silent; the Grange was against the plan; and—worst of all—the Farmers Union was divided. Evidently the farm leaders were responding less to a sense of calculated self-interest than to the currents of feeling sweeping middle-class America: respect for the "vestal virgins of the court"; fear of labor turbulence; concern for law and order and property rights.

In this extremity Roosevelt turned to the Democratic party. Farley industriously toured the party circuit, trying to build grass fires behind lagging Democratic congressmen and vaguely threatening punishment to deserters. All in vain—on this issue the party lacked vigor and militance. Moreover, prominent Democratic leaders outside the Senate were decamping on the court issue. In the cabinet itself Hull was quietly hostile. In Roosevelt's own state his old comrade in arms Governor Lehman came out against the bill, and even Boss Flynn of the Bronx, the most stolid of party war horses, was opposed.

At the beginning of April the President was still optimistic. Corcoran, Pittman, La Follette, and others had been reporting enthusiastically on the chances of victory. When Senator Black warned him of the opposition's determination and tactics of delay, Roosevelt replied: "We'll smoke 'em out. If delay helps them, we must press for an early vote."

BREACHES IN THE GRAND COALITION

Roosevelt was wrong. By April the chances for the court plan were almost nil. The President simply could not command the needed votes in either Senate or House. Then on April 12 came a clinching blow. In a tense, packed courtroom Hughes read the Supreme Court's judgment sustaining the Wagner Act.

If Roosevelt had been as acutely sensitive to political crosscurrents during this period as he usually was, the Court's shift would not have surprised him. A few weeks after the election, while Roosevelt and Cummings were leafing through court plans, Roberts had told the Chief Justice privately that he would vote to sustain a Washington minimum-wage law and overturn a contrary decision of a few months back. Hughes was so pleased he almost hugged him. Final decision was delayed, however, because Stone was ill for some time, and because Hughes saw the disadvantages of appearing to yield before the court-packing plan. By the end of March the time seemed ripe for the decision on this case and on three others favorable to the administration. Still, these were only straws in the wind, and they had little effect on Roosevelt's plans. The Wagner Act decision two weeks later, however, showed the decisive alignment of Hughes and Roberts with the three liberals.

Once again the Chief Justice had outfoxed the President. How much he changed his technical position to meet the tactical needs of the hour is a subject of some dispute among constitutional experts. Certainly Hughes's position on the companion cases to the main case of April 12 seemed a long jump from some of his earlier judgments; on the other hand, the Chief Justice, like most politician-judges, had been flexible enough in his positions to make the jump possible. His new position was more important politically than legalistically. He had consolidated a majority of the Court behind him; he had taken the heart out of the President's argument; he had upheld a measure dear to labor and thus reduced even further its concern over the Court—and he had done all this without undue sacrifice of the Court's dignity.

Outwardly Roosevelt's reaction to the Court's move was gleeful. "I have been chortling all morning," he told reporters. "I have been having a perfectly grand time." He compared the *Herald Tribune's* enthusiastic hailing of the decision with its approval two years before of the Liberty League lawyers' opinion against the constitutionality of the Wagner Act.

"Well, I have been having more fun!" Roosevelt went on amid repeated guffaws from the reporters. "And I haven't read the Washington Post, and I haven't got the Chicago Tribune yet. Or the Boston Herald. Today is a very, very happy day. . . ." He quoted with relish a remark a friend had made to him: the No Man's Land had been eliminated but "we are now in 'Roberts' Land.'"

Inwardly the President was more puzzled than pleased. Should he press on with the court fight? He must have sensed immediately that Hughes had given the plan's chances a punishing blow; he had hoped for a complete veto of New Deal legislation so that the issue would be sharpened for the people. He soon learned, moreover, that Robinson and others of his lieutenants were talking compromise. "This bill's raising hell in the Senate," Robinson reportedly told a White House representative. "Now it's going to be worse than ever, but if the President wants to compromise, I can get him a couple of extra justices tomorrow." On the other hand, Robinson himself posed a problem. It had long been understood that the doughty Arkansan would receive the first vacant justiceship and thus fulfill a life ambition. But the Senator's appointment would clearly be a recognition of service to Roosevelt rather than a recognition of legal distinction or ingrained liberalism; once on the Court, moreover, Robinson might swing right. To offset this appointment there must be others.

Roosevelt had further reasons to stand pat on his proposal. He was now in the fight to the hilt, and compromise would be interpreted as defeat for him and victory for Wheeler and the other rebels. He still hankered for six of his own appointees—liberal-minded judges with whom he could establish friendly personal relations such as he had enjoyed with the state judges when he was governor. Crucial New Deal measures were still to come before the Court, and the justices might swing right again if the pistol at their head was unloaded. Finally, the President still thought that he could win. Had he not saved many a measure during the first term, when prospects looked bleak, simply by sticking to his guns?

So the order was full speed ahead. "We must keep up—and strengthen—the fight," the President wrote Congressman David Lewis. As if to flaunt his confidence over the outcome he made plans to fish in the Gulf of Mexico at the end of April. Roosevelt's manner was still buoyant.

"I am delighted to have your rural rhapsody of April twelfth and to know that the French Government has spring fever," he wrote on April 21 to Ambassador William C. Bullitt in Paris. "Spring has come to Washington also and even the Senators, who were biting each other over the Supreme Court, are saying 'Alphonse' and 'Gaston' to each other. . . .

"I, too, am influenced by this beautiful spring day. I haven't a care in the world which is going some for a President who is said by the newspapers to be a remorseless dictator driving his government into hopeless bankruptcy."

The Supreme Court turnabout marked a decisive shift in the character of the court fight. No longer was the issue one of Roosevelt New Deal versus Old Guard Court. Now the fight lay between the President and Congress. When the Court upheld the Social Security Act a few weeks later, it served to take the Court as an institution even further out of the struggle. But not its members. In May and June, Hughes made speeches that were hardly veiled assaults on the court proposal.

Roosevelt returned from his fishing in mid-May. He was in a militant mood. After talking with precinct committeemen during the train trip back, he told the cabinet, he was as certain as ever that the people were still behind the bill. Democrats in Congress who opposed it, he added, might expect defeat at the polls. Roosevelt warned Garner privately that he, the President, had brought a lot of congressmen in on his coattails, and that he might openly oppose Democrats who were against the bill. He had Robinson and other leaders in, laughed off their fears, explained away the defections they gloomily reported, and sent them back to the battle.

That battle was still going badly. Shipstead came out against the bill, as did several other senators on whom Roosevelt was relying. Party leaders were warning of a deepening split among the Democrats. Even White House assistants were losing confidence and counseling compromise. Other New Deal measures were being pulled down with the court bill. Then, on May 18, the opposition played another card. Wheeler and Borah, knowing of Van Devanter's wish to retire, got word to the justice that a resignation timed to coincide with an expected vote by the Judiciary Committee against the court bill would help the plan's opponents. For Wheeler knew what that vote would be. A few minutes after Roosevelt read Van Devanter's notice of retirement on the morning of May 18 and had written in longhand a cool but polite note of acceptance, the Senate Judiciary Committee met in executive session. After brushing aside several compromise measures it voted 10-8 that the President's bill "do not pass." The committee line-up symbolized the split in the ranks of the Grand Coalition: six Democrats of diverse ideological hues deserted the President.

Face to face with this deepening split, Roosevelt executed one of the rapid tactical shifts that so often threw his opponents off guard. He turned to the possibility of compromise. But his freedom of maneuver here was unhappily narrowed by a conjunction of circumstances that stemmed partly from sheer bad luck and partly from the way in which he had handled matters. Van Devanter's retirement not only knocked one more prop from under the President's plea for new blood on the Court; it also precipitated in acute form the old problem of rewarding Robinson with a justiceship without alienating the "true" liberals and making a mockery of Roosevelt's arguments for the bill. Within a few hours of Van Devanter's retirement, almost as if by plan, both opposition senators and supporters of the bill were crowding around Robinson's front-row desk in the Senate chamber, pumping his hand, calling him "Mr. Justice." The Senate was in effect nominating Robinson to fill the vacancy.

In this extremity Roosevelt turned to the direct person-to-person persuasion for which he had such a flair. Against the advice of Corcoran and Jackson, who wanted him to let the bill go over to another session or even to accept defeat and take the issue to the country, the President decided on a shrewd but risky tactical move. Through Farley he let it be known to Robinson that the Senator could expect to take Van Devanter's place. Then the President called Robinson in and agreed to accept a compromise on the bill, but he added that if there was a bride there must be bridesmaids. He asked Robinson to take full leadership of the fight for a compromise bill. The President was now seeking to turn the senatorial support for Robinson's appointment to his own advantage. If the senators wanted to help their old colleague, they would have to provide some extra appointments as well. The danger in the plan was that everything depended on Robinson.

And the President did not fully trust the majority leader. He complained to Ickes that Robinson had lost his punch, that there was no leadership in Congress. Speaker Bankhead was not strong in the House, he said, and Rayburn was so anxious to succeed to the speakership that he feared to offend anyone. The President was especially upset about Garner. Exclaiming that "my ears are buzzing and ringing," the Vice-President had left on a long-planned vacation in Texas just as the fight in the Senate was coming to a head. But the President never expressed his feelings directly to Garner. Instead, after the Vice-President had been away several weeks Roosevelt urged his return in a letter that offered every bait that might lure the sulking Texan. Knowing of Garner's fears about government spending and labor violence, and his old populist distrust of bankers, the President predicted a balanced budget for the coming year and declared that the public was "pretty sick of the extremists which exist both in the C.I.O. and some of the A.F. of L. unions and also of the extremists like Girdler and some of his associates backed by the Guarantee [sic] Trust Co., etc." Roosevelt ended his appeal on a personal note.

"And finally, just to clinch the argument for your return, I want to tell you again how much I miss you because of you, yourself, and also because of the great help that you have given and continue to give to the working out *peacefully* of a mass of problems greater than the Nation has ever had before." But the Vice-President stayed in Texas.

Garner's own sit-down strike signalized the state of the Democratic party. It was not the court plan alone that was splitting apart the Grand Coalition. The attack on the plan served as a rallying cry for the conservatives who feared the rising tide of labor turbulence, for the "old" liberals who disliked the President's indirections and his personal handling of party matters, for New Deal liberals who prized orderly processes and constitutional traditions. Seeking to placate these elements Roosevelt, when asked about the deadlock between labor and management, said calculatedly, "A plague on both your houses." Lewis's howl of indignation and the icy silence of the party Old Guard indicated that in striving to veer between the various factions Roosevelt was keeping the warm support of none.

At the end of June Roosevelt tried another tack—and one that again illustrated his preference for direct personal handling of affairs. A grand political picnic was arranged at Jefferson Island in

Chesapeake Bay, to which Democratic congressmen were invited. The plan was to submerge intraparty bickering in three days of good fellowship. The President was at his best. Seated in an arm-chair under a big locust tree, he chatted congenially and drank beer with groups of shirt-sleeved legislators. He even allowed Martin Dies of Texas to induct him into the Demagogue's Club, involving a pledge to favor all spending bills and no tax bills, to do nothing to harm his chances for a third term, never to be consistent—and not to send controversial proposals to Congress.

In sharp contrast to this bucolic scene was the grim atmosphere of the Senate. There, day after day, Robinson was making the rounds of the Democrats, pleading with them to support his compromise plan. The new measure was mild enough, allowing the President to appoint only one coadjutor justice a year for any justice who had passed seventy-five and failed to retire. Even so, Robinson found it hard going, and often he had to resort to a personal plea to embarrassed senators for help in realizing his life ambition. When Robinson opened debate on the bill in the Senate he seemed to reporters, as he sawed the air with violent gestures and beat off his interrogators, like an aging bull tormented by the fast-moving picadors around him and stung by their *banderillas*. Day after day Robinson roared his arguments and threats at the opposition, meanwhile desperately counting and recounting the small majority he had lined up. But he had come to the end of his road. On the morning of July 14 he rose from his hotel bed, took one step, and fell dead, a copy of the *Congressional Record* in his hand.

The stroke that ruptured Robinson's heart ruptured as well the bonds of personal loyalty on which the majority leader had been depending for his compromise plan. There was a sudden rush away from the bill. Even as Robinson was buried in Little Rock the congressmen who had escorted the body out on the funeral train were busy sparring over the bill. On the train back to Washington, Garner, who had joined the delegation in Little Rock, went down the aisles systematically counting noses. On the morning of July 20 he reported to the President.

"How did you find the court situation, Jack?" Roosevelt asked.

"Do you want it with the bark on or off, Cap'n?"

"The rough way," Roosevelt said with a laugh.

"All right. You are beat. You haven't got the votes."

NOT WITH A BANG BUT A WHIMPER

The end of the court fight was anticlimactic. Roosevelt asked Garner to arrange the best compromise that he could. Whether the

Vice-President tried to salvage something out of the bill or simply surrendered is shrouded in the obscure maneuvering of the last days. By now Congress was outside anyone's control; "everything on the Hill seems to be at sixes and sevens," Ickes complained. Appropriately enough, the Judiciary Committee served as executioner by offering a motion to recommit the court bill. Only twenty senators voted against recommittal. A week later the Senate rushed through an emasculated bill, making minor reforms and improvements, which the President halfheartedly signed into law.

The last episodes of the court fight were entangled with a struggle over the Democratic leadership in the Senate. Pat Harrison of Mississippi and Alben W. Barkley of Kentucky were vying for Robinson's mantle in one of those contests that become all the more bitter because they cleave the membership of an intimate club. The court fight sharpened tempers of the opposing factions. Roosevelt was on good terms with both senators, but he had several reasons to prefer Barkley. The Kentuckian was a more reliable New Dealer and was personally more loyal to Roosevelt; he had, for example, given active support to the court bill while Harrison was passive. And if Harrison won the position, he would probably have to vacate the chairmanship of the Senate Finance Committee and this vital post would fall into the hands of a conservative Democrat.

Clearly Roosevelt had his preferences—but could he act upon them? Not if he was to follow the custom that forbids presidential interference in the Senate's internal affairs. Roosevelt's method of resolving this problem was characteristic. Openly he took a neutral position; to be sure, he addressed a letter to "My Dear Alben" urging a continued fight for the principles of the court bill, but Barkley's position as acting majority leader permitted this public show of friendship.

Privately the President was not neutral at all. A check showed that Senate Democrats were split almost evenly between the two candidates. Every vote would count. An obvious weak link in Harrison's ranks was Senator William H. Dieterich, who owed his Senate seat largely to Boss Ed Kelly of Chicago. Roosevelt asked Farley to telephone Kelly to use his influence with Dieterich. Farley refused on the grounds that he had promised the principals that he would keep hands off. The President thereupon turned to Hopkins and Corcoran, who threw White House pressure on Dieterich and others. The Harrison forces mobilized pressure too. Senator Harry Truman, who had pledged his vote to Barkley, had to ask the Kentuckian to be released of his promise. Among the shifters was Dieterich—from Harrison to Barkley. Barkley's victory by one vote

THE ILLEGAL ACT, June 3, 1935,
Ernest H. Shepard, *Punch*

PRESIDENT ROOSEVELT: "I'M SORRY,
BUT THE SUPREME COURT SAYS I MUST
CHUCK YOU BACK AGAIN."

was an important victory for the President, but one that sharpened
the ill temper of the Senate.

The court fight over, Roosevelt sought to regain direction of
his general legislative program. Congress, he told his cabinet, must
take responsibility for what was done and what was left undone.
The President was especially concerned about the farm situation.
If farm prices fell next year, he said, a good many Democrats would
be defeated in the next election. While Roosevelt talked, Ickes
scribbled on a piece of paper and passed it to Farley: "The President seems to be indulging in a curtain lecture for the benefit of
the Vice President."

Congress was still wallowing in confusion. Earlier in the session
it had passed, under Roosevelt's proddings, several important bills.
One of these was the Guffey-Vinson bituminous coal bill providing
for governmental and private co-operation in marketing, price control, and trade practices. Others were a revised Neutrality Act and
renewal of the Trade Agreements Act. Congress had also enacted
the Farm Tenancy bill, authorizing federal loans to farm tenants,
sharecroppers, and laborers to help them buy their own farms. This
was work done, but it seemed strikingly small in the light of the President's broad challenge, in his inaugural, of "one third of a nation
ill-housed, ill-clad, ill-nourished."

Could that challenge still be met? By the end of July five administration measures awaited action in Congress: wages and hours,
low-cost housing, executive reorganization, comprehensive farm

program, and creation of seven regional agencies patterned somewhat after the TVA. When Congress adjourned late in August, only
one of these measures had been made into law. This was the Wagner
Housing bill. It was significant that this lone administration victory
was due far more to Wagner and an indefatigable group of public-
housing enthusiasts and lobbyists than to the President. Roosevelt,
to be sure, did help persuade a key chairman in the House to report the bill out of committee, but only after weeks of backing and
filling in the White House.

Equally significant was the reason that the rest of Roosevelt's
program failed. In part that failure stemmed from Roosevelt's
original calculation that court reform would have a better chance
if other major bills were postponed in its behalf. Later he appeared
to swing to the opposite view that at least one of the measures—
wage-hour regulation—would be so popular that it would unify
Democratic ranks split over court reform. Both calculations proved
wrong.

But there was a more important reason for Roosevelt's legislative
difficulties—a reason that reflected the strategic weakness of his
political position. The trouble was that the ample coalition that
he had summoned to his personal support in November—and which
had responded to that summons—was already falling apart.

The blocking of the wage-hour bill showed how extensive were
the fractures in the coalition. When Senator Black introduced his
proposed Fair Labor Standards Act late in May, Roosevelt vigorously urged passage. "We have promised it," he said. "We cannot
stand still." Quickly the bill ran into snags. Southerners from low-
wage states, including Harrison, deserted the President on the issue.
Sharp differences developed among labor groups, not only between
AFL and CIO leaders but also within the two organizations. As if
all this was not enough, a fight broke out between low-tariff and
high-tariff Democrats over a protectionist clause in the bill. Pressure
against the bill was put on Farley and Roosevelt through Democratic
leaders in the South. After a struggle the bill passed the Senate,
and by calling in President Green of the AFL and acceding to his
major demands Roosevelt was able to ease the bill through the
House Labor Committee. Then the bill stalled in the face of a
coalition of Republicans and Southern Democrats on the Rules
Committee. In vain Democratic leaders summoned a caucus to put
force behind the bill; not enough Democrats showed up to make
it an official caucus.

By mid-August the President was ready to give up the fight for
the rest of his program. He decided to call Congress back in special
session during the fall. Let the congressmen get back to their dis-

tricts, he said, and they would return with a strengthened feeling for the New Deal.

But one task remained for the President before adjournment—and a most pleasant task. Van Devanter's seat on the Court was still open.

A pleasant task—but not an easy one. Roosevelt wanted a durable New Dealer, a relatively young man, either a Southerner or Westerner, and a competent lawyer, who at the same time would clear the Senate without difficulty. This last was the rub, for in the sweltering Washington heat the senators seemed to be more bitter and unpredictable than ever. For this reason the President leaned toward a New Deal Senator. He finally chose Black over other senatorial possibilities mainly because the Alabaman had gone down the line for Roosevelt's policies; the President felt drawn to Black also because he faced a hard battle for re-election and perhaps because Black had an only child suffering from deafness. While Roosevelt did not rate Black's legal talents very high, he was more concerned about seasoned liberalism than expertness. Despite some grumbling in the Senate, the usual clubby feeling prevailed, and after a brief debate Black was readily confirmed.

"So Hugo Black becomes a member of the Supreme Court of the United States while the economic royalists fume and squirm and the President rolls his tongue around in his cheek," Ickes crowed in his diary. The President was not to roll his tongue long. A week or so later, after Black had left for a vacation in Europe, a Pittsburgh newspaper produced categorical proof that the new Justice had been a member of the Ku Klux Klan. The rumors that Black had neither confirmed nor denied during the confirmation debate were true. The press exploded with shrill attacks on both Black and the President.

"I did not know that Black belonged to the Ku Klux Klan," Roosevelt said to a friend. "This is very serious." The President was deeply disturbed. He told reporters that nothing could be said until Black returned from Europe. Privately he did what he could. He asked Ickes to go to Borah and see if he would help out. Wheeler and others had been demanding that the President investigate Black, and Roosevelt particularly wanted Borah's backing for the proposition that the President had no right to make such an investigation. Borah fully agreed. By the time Black returned from Europe Roosevelt had left on a Western tour, and all eyes were on the justice.

Harried by reporters, Black turned to the radio and laid his case before perhaps fifty million people. He denounced intolerance, and pointed to his congressional record in defense of civil liberties. Then, in his soft, strained Southern voice he admitted that he had been a member of the Klan, but asserted that he had long ago disassociated himself from it. After referring again to his civil liberties record, he ended with a sad "good night."

And thus ended Roosevelt's battle against the Court.

Roosevelt's enemies could not help gloating. Surely the President had suffered a dizzy fall in the short span of six months. At the beginning of the year he had towered over the political scene, with his colossal vote of approval in November and with his huge majorities in Congress. Then he seemed invincible. Yet now he had been beaten.

Why had this political colossus stumbled and fallen? Roosevelt's critics were quick with an explanation: Pride goeth before a fall. Intoxicated with success, Roosevelt had recklessly attacked a venerable American institution. Overly sure of himself, he had made mistake after careless mistake. His potency had gone to his head. Learned pundits quoted Lord Acton: "Power tends to corrupt, and absolute power corrupts absolutely."

Was it really so simple? A closer look at the court fight showed that the real story was much more complex than this morality tale suggested.

Roosevelt did not go about the job of court reform recklessly. Quite the contrary—he struck at the Court only after a long period of waiting, and under what he considered to be the best possible conditions. His plan was not hastily conceived; he had searched through a variety of proposals to find one that would have a good chance of clearing Congress and at the same time achieve his purpose. Nor was his plan a radical one. Compared with some of the constitutional and legislative proposals of the day, it was mild indeed.

That Roosevelt's cocksureness led to mistake after mistake and thus defeated the plan was another explanation of the time—and one that was assiduously promoted by those who, like Hopkins and Ickes, had little to do with conducting the fight for the court bill. Such a view fails to explain, among other things, why the remarkably astute Roosevelt of 1936 became the bungler of 1937. The theory that Roosevelt did not direct the fight personally and the mistakes were made by subordinates is incorrect; he was in command throughout. Much was made of Roosevelt's stubbornness in clinging to the original plan; but this stubbornness was precisely the quality that had saved measures in previous terms—when it had been called firmness or resoluteness. Certainly Roosevelt made mistakes in the court fight, but so did his opponents.

All such explanations ignored the probability that the original court plan never had a chance of passing. This was the crucial point. For—if the plan was indeed doomed from the start—the Court's switch and Van Devanter's resignation and Robinson's death became mere stages in the death of the bill rather than causes of that death.

That the court bill probably never had a chance of passing seems now quite clear. Roosevelt's original proposal evidently never commanded a majority in the Senate. In the House it would have run up against the unyielding Sumners, and then against a conservative Rules Committee capable of blocking the bill for weeks. From the start Democratic leaders in the House were worried about the bill's prospects in that chamber. Robinson's compromise plan might have gone through the Senate if he had lived. More likely, though, it would have failed in the face of a dogged Senate filibuster, or later in the House.

Any kind of court reform would have had hard going. The popular reverence for the Constitution, the conception of the Supreme Court as its guardian, the ability of the judges—especially Hughes—to counterattack in their own way, the deep-seated legal tradition in a Congress composed of a large number of lawyers—all these were obstacles. Yet there was tremendous support in Congress and in the country for curbing the Court's excesses. Undoubtedly some kind of moderate court reform could have gone through.

The fatal weakness of Roosevelt's plan lay partly in its content and partly in the way it was proposed. The plan itself seemed an evasive, disingenuous way of meeting a clear-cut problem. It talked about judicial efficiency rather than ideology; it was aimed at immediate personalities on the Court rather than long-run problems posed by the Court. The manner of presentation—the surprise, Roosevelt's failure to pose the issue more concretely in the election, his obvious relish in the job, his unwillingness to ask his cabinet and his congressional leaders for advice—alienated some potential supporters. More important, this method of presentation prevented Roosevelt from building a broad coalition behind the bill and ironing out multifarious tactical details before springing the attack —behind-the-scenes activities in which Roosevelt was highly adept.

That this masterly politician should make such errors even before his bill was born is explained partly by Roosevelt's personality, partly by his view of the political circumstances at the end of 1936.

Clearly Roosevelt had come to love—perhaps he had always loved—the drama, the suspense, the theatrical touches, and his own commanding role in projects that astonished the country and riled the enemy. But it was more than this. Roosevelt had fought the campaign on a highly personal basis. And he had built a winning coalition around himself—not the Democratic party, not the Democratic platform, not the liberal ideology—but around himself. He had won a stunning victory in spite of the doubters, the rebels, and the perfectionists. The master strokes in the campaign were largely of his own devising.

Roosevelt's handling of the court fight was the logical extension of his presidential campaign. But now he met a new set of factors, and some of the old tricks did not work. Now he was trying to push a controversial bill through Congress, not win popular votes for himself as a beloved leader. He could not maneuver as he once had; victory depended on conciliating key congressmen and clearing labyrinthine channels. The Grand Coalition seemed to have shriveled away. With the President's blessing, Stanley High tried to activate the Good Neighbor League—it failed to respond. The mighty legions of farm and labor, so powerful in November, seemed to melt away in the spring. Roosevelt turned to the Democratic party; it was a scattered and disorganized army. He appealed for support on the basis of a "quiet crisis," but people saw no crisis. It was not March 1933.

The Black appointment repeated the whole problem in minor theme. Here again Roosevelt consulted only with two or three persons, and not with his congressional leaders. It was well known on Capitol Hill that the Alabaman had had Klan connections, and as Ickes said after the sensation broke, the leaders could have helped protect the President if Roosevelt had let them in on the decision beforehand. As it was, Roosevelt had to take personal responsibility for a personal appointment. Black went on to make a distinguished record as a justice, especially in the field of civil liberties—but this could not help Roosevelt at the time.

All in all, the court fight was a stunning defeat for the President. Whether or not it was a fatal or irretrievable one, however, depended on the events to follow. Two years later, with his eye on a string of pro-New Deal Court decisions, the President exulted that he had lost the battle but won the war. As matters turned out in Congress and party, it could better be said that he lost the battle, won the campaign, but lost the war.

ROOSEVELT tried to make the best of his court-packing defeats. He pointed to the Court's new position on New Deal measures. He felt that the country had been educated in the need for a broad interpretation of the Constitution. But he believed, too, that the battle was not over. "Judicial reform is coming just as sure as God made little apples," he wrote Senator Green. "Keep at it with me!"

But underneath he was deeply stung and shaken by his defeat. Farley found him outwardly as debonair as ever, but inwardly seething at the party rebels. In cabinet meetings he sent jocular but pointed barbs in Garner's direction, while the Vice-President kept a poker face under his shaggy white eyebrows. A few times during the last fretful weeks of the court fight Roosevelt lost his usual poise. The President roundly scolded Early for putting out a statement on the court fight that the newspapers had garbled. Roosevelt even lost his temper in front of the White House press corps; he was angry because Lindley and other reporters had interpreted a social visit of Boss Flynn's as proof of presidential intervention in the New York mayoralty fight. This was no sudden flare-up on Roosevelt's part; he deliberately turned a forty-minute press conference into a long beratement, again and again demanding that Lindley apologize.

Even more remarkable was Roosevelt's treatment of General Johnson, now a fiery anti-New Deal columnist. The President had been infuriated by Washington rumors that despite his promise he never intended to put Robinson on the Court; when Johnson in his column charged Roosevelt with intended treachery, the old NRA chief was summoned to the White House. Roosevelt went over the columns, making caustic comments. To Ickes next day the President related the ensuing dialogue:

"Hugh, do you know what fine, loyal old Joe Robinson would have said to you if you had written that while he was alive?"

"No."

"He would have said, Hugh, that you are a liar, a coward, and a cad."

As Johnson's face reddened, Roosevelt slowly repeated the line. Then, according to the President's story, Johnson cried.

Significantly, all Roosevelt's outbursts involved the press. "As you know," he wrote Ambassador Bowers in Spain, "all the fat-cat newspapers—85% of the whole—have been utterly opposed to everything the Administration is seeking, and the best way to describe the situation is that the campaign of the spring, summer and autumn of 1936 is continuing actively throughout the year 1937. However, the voters are with us today just as they were last fall." To detour around the reporters and their publishers, to feel again the bracing enthusiasm of the crowds, to take his program to the people before the special session, the President decided on a trip to the Northwest.

Late in September the long presidential special headed out of the Capital, rolled across the cornfields of the Midwest and through the long valleys of Wyoming, Idaho, Montana, Oregon, and Washington. It was like the election campaign all over again, as Roosevelt gave his chatty little homilies from the back platform, grasped the hands of local politicians, confabbed with governors and senators. The President told a Boise crowd that he felt like Antaeus—"I regain strength by just meeting the American people." But as the President dedicated dams and inspected reclamation systems, friendly reporters thought of him not as Antaeus but as a modern Paul Bunyan, talking about the big jobs ahead even as he exulted in the huge construction projects under way.

The President got in a few licks at party rebels too. In Nebraska he studiously avoided inviting Senator Ed Burke, who had fought the court bill, to join his party. In Montana he heaped praise on Murray while ignoring Wheeler. In Wyoming, O'Mahoney was not invited either, but when the senator boarded the presidential train as a member of a welcoming committee, Roosevelt, undaunted, greeted him cheerily; later, however, he told a Caspar audience that the people disliked politicians who gave lip service to objectives while doing nothing to attain them. And in Boise—was it a warning to rebellious Democrats throughout the nation?—Roosevelt had only smiles for Republican Senator Borah.

The President was buoyed up by the popular response to his trip. The crowds seemed to him even bigger than a year before. He sensed that the people had not grasped the court issue, but they still wanted his objectives. And it was objectives that he stressed in speeches on the trip back as he called for an expanded farm program and wages and hours legislation. Then in Chicago on October 5 he abruptly changed the subject and created a sensation.

Hundreds of thousands lined the President's route that day from the station to the PWA bridge he was to dedicate. He had deliberately chosen Chicago, Roosevelt told the crowd, to speak on a subject of "definite national importance." In a few moments he was talking about the world situation—and doing so in a fashion that no President had for sixteen years. Referring indirectly to the increasing hostilities in Spain and China, he said sternly that the very foundations of civilization were threatened by the current reign of terror and international lawlessness. If conditions got worse, America could not expect mercy; the Western Hemisphere could not avoid attack.

"The peace-loving nations must make a concerted effort in opposition to those violations of treaties and those ignorings of humane instincts which today are creating a state of international anarchy and instability from which there is no escape through mere isolation or neutrality." No nation could isolate itself from the spreading upheavals. "The peace, the freedom and the security of ninety per cent of the population of the world is being jeopardized by the remaining ten per cent who are threatening a breakdown of all international order and law." Then came a Rooseveltian climax.

"When an epidemic of physical disease starts to spread, the community approves and joins in a quarantine of the patients in order to protect the health of the community against the spread of the disease." He was determined, the President added quickly, to adopt every practicable measure to avoid involvement in war. His speech ended on a mixed note. "We are adopting such measures as will minimize our risk of involvement, but we cannot have complete protection in a world of disorder in which confidence and security have broken down."

The crowd shouted its approval. Back on his train the President asked Miss Tully, "How did it go, Grace?" When she expressed enthusiasm over the reception, he nodded and said, "Well, it's done now. It was something that needed saying."

But what did the President mean? What kind of collective action? What kind of quarantine? Back in Washington, Hull, surprised and shocked by Roosevelt's strong words, remained quiet. Other party leaders were silent. It was the opposition that spoke up. Pacifists charged the President with starting the people down the road to war. Isolationist congressmen threatened him with impeachment. The AFL resolved against involvement in foreign wars. A telegraphic poll of Congress showed a heavy majority against common action with the League in the Far East.

"It's a terrible thing," Roosevelt said later to Rosenman, "to look over your shoulder when you are trying to lead—and to find no one there." He was indignant at the silence of party leaders who should have spoken up. Cut off from his troops, he had to re-establish contact. The next day, as reporters strove to interpret the speech, Roosevelt was all caution. His speech, he said, was not a repudiation of neutrality—it might even be an expansion.

"You say there isn't any conflict between what you outline and the Neutrality Act," Lindley said. "They seem to be on opposite poles to me and your assertion does not enlighten me."

"Put your thinking-cap on, Ernest," the President said.

"I have been for some years. They seem to be at opposite poles. How can you be neutral if you are going to align yourself with one group of nations?"

"What do you mean, 'aligning'?" the President asked. "You mean a treaty?"

"Not necessarily," Lindley said. "I meant action on the part of peace-loving nations."

"There are a lot of methods in the world that have never been tried yet."

Lindley was persistent. "But, at any rate, that is not an indication of neutral attitude—'quarantine the aggressors' and 'other nations of the world.'"

"I can't give you any clue to it. You will have to invent one. . . ."

A few days later the President pulled in his horns further. He announced United States participation in a forthcoming conference of the parties to the Treaty of Washington over the Far Eastern situation—a clear indication, since Japan and China were signatories to the treaty, that sanctions against aggressor nations were out of the question, at least for the time.

But by now—October 1937—a storm was blowing up from a new quarter.

CLOUDBURST

Late in the summer stocks had slackened off. At first the drop seemed a normal one, and the usual explanations—readjustment, corrective realignment, and so on—were trotted out. But things rapidly got worse. Wave after wave of selling hit the market and spilled stocks to new lows. Suddenly it seemed like 1929 all over again. Selling orders poured in from all over the country, transactions went to seven million shares in a single day, the ticker tape fell far behind.

There was some disposition in the cabinet to see the drop as an artificial one; Miss Perkins reported in mid-September that her statisticians expected an early upturn in business. A week later the President was even cautiously hopeful in a press conference that the country had moved out of its long-term basic emergency, and early in October cabinet members were still speaking of a "corrective dip" in the market.

Roosevelt was in a paradoxical situation. He believed that economic conditions were fundamentally sound. "I have been around the country and know conditions are good," he said to the cabinet on October 8. "Farmers are getting good prices." He suspected that big business was trying to drive the market down as a move against the administration. "Everything will work out all right if we just sit tight and keep quiet."

Yet the President dared not show his optimism in public. Above all he feared the dread parallel with Hoover, whose hopeful declarations month after month in the early 1930's had become a grim joke. "Dan," Roosevelt said sharply to Roper, who had been trying to calm his business constituency, "I wish you would stop giving out so many Hooverish statements!"

Sitting tight worked no better for Roosevelt than it had for Hoover. Stocks kept on dropping; the whole economy was now showing a decline. The financial community was suffering a bad case of jitters, Morgenthau reported. Morgenthau's own jitters were severe. "We are headed right into another depression," he told Roosevelt. "The question is, Mr. President—what are we going to do about it?" Roosevelt knew his Secretary of the Treasury too well to be alarmed by him. Nor was he alarmed by the deluge of wires from businessmen offering warnings, advice, frantic pleas to do something—anything. He joked with reporters about the industrialist who insisted in a three-page telegram that he was talking not for the big or medium-sized speculators but for the small investors— the kind of investor who carried little brokerage accounts of ten to twenty thousand dollars.

But the harsh indices of economic decline could not be laughed off. At a cabinet meeting early in November Miss Perkins reported that employment was dropping at a time when it usually rose. A long discussion followed. When Morgenthau suggested that Roosevelt publicly compare current conditions with those of early 1933 to reassure business, the President betrayed his anxiety. "Oh, for God's sake, Henry, do you want me to read the record again?" he demanded. The discussion revealed a cabinet deeply split on the course to take. Morgenthau, Farley, and Roper wanted a conciliatory approach to business, while Ickes, Perkins, and Wallace sought an expansion of New Deal measures. Government economists were badly divided too.

Roosevelt was plainly at sea. Ickes had never seen him so worried over the drift of events, so eager for counsel from his cabinet. A former president, beset by conflicting advice, had once exclaimed,

"I can't make a damn thing out of this tax problem. I listen to one side and they seem right—and then—God!—I talk to the other side and they seem just as right. . . . God, what a job!" If Roosevelt was more urbane than Harding, he was no less perplexed. He told reporters about two letters he had received from two leading economic experts:

"One says the entire question is one of the velocity of capital turnover credit, so do not pay any attention to purchasing power. The other one says: forget all this algebraic formula about the velocity of capital turnover credit; the whole question is purchasing power on the part of one hundred and thirty million people.

"It is a fascinating study," the President wound up almost ruefully.

By mid-November, when Congress met in special session, the decline had become so severe that it could not be openly ignored. "Since your adjournment in August," the President declared to Congress, "there has been a marked recession in industrial production and industrial purchases following a fairly steady advance for more than four years." He quickly added that he had been aware of uncertainties in the economic picture before the recession began, and that the decline had not reached serious proportions. "But it has the effect of decreasing the national income, and that is a matter of definite concern." The job was both to check the recession and to lay the groundwork for a more permanent recovery.

But it was no crisis program that the President presented to Congress. The two items that might affect recovery—a permanent national farm act and wages and hours—were leftovers from the regular session. So were the other two recommendations—administrative reorganization and regional planning. That Roosevelt would serve this warmed-up assortment was a measure of his inability to decide on a basic economic program.

Perhaps it made no difference, for the special session was a shambles. The Senate at the start ran into a wrathful filibuster over Wagner's antilynching bill. In the House Roosevelt's leaders through a variety of trades squeezed out enough signatures on a petition to pry the wages and hours bill out of the Rules Committee; then the bill was dashed to pieces on the rocks of opposition from AFL factions and from Southern congressmen. The farm bill made faster progress but encountered a split between Secretary Wallace and President O'Neal of the Farm Bureau. The reorganization and regional planning bills simply made no progress at all. When Congress adjourned a few days before Christmas it had passed not one of Roosevelt's four proposals.

Roosevelt's political opponents were alert. They remembered some sentences from an extemporaneous talk the President had made in Charleston over two years before. "Yes, we are on our way back—not just by pure chance, my friends, not just by a turn of the wheel, of the cycle," Roosevelt had said on that occasion. "We are coming back more soundly than ever before because we are planning it that way. Don't let anybody tell you differently." And now Republican orators were mockingly throwing the words back in Roosevelt's face.

A reporter cautiously sounded Roosevelt out on the matter. The President was unruffled. That was perfectly true in Charleston in 1935, he said. "The things we had done, which at that time were largely a monetary and pump-priming policy for two years and a half, had brought the expected result, perfectly definitely." But, he added, there had been a great drop in pump priming, and NRA and AAA had been knocked into a cocked hat.

Roosevelt's answer was disingenuous. It was not the Court alone that had blocked New Deal planning. The President himself had shifted back and forth in his search for viable economic policies. To look on his policies as the result of a unified plan, as Moley acidly commented later, was to believe that the accumulation of stuffed snakes, baseball pictures, school flags, old tennis shoes, and the like in a boy's bedroom were the design of an interior decorator. Indeed, Roosevelt himself had boasted of his experimentation. In five years he had changed direction, reversed speed, and doubled back on his trail.

Economically the New Deal had been opportunistic in the grand manner. Roosevelt had tried rigid economy, then heavy spending, then restriction of spending again. He had shifted back and forth from spending on direct relief to spending on public works. He had tried controlled inflation and then policing of prices. He had tried economic nationalism, and then encouraged Hull's program of economic internationalism. His monetary policies had been jumbled—the abandonment of gold, the abortive experiment with the Warren price theory, a flirtation with inflationary silver economics, and later a monetary stabilization agreement with Britain and France.

Yet experimentation is a means to an end, not an end in itself. Roosevelt recognized this. He argued that his twists and turns were all aimed at a common goal—a more secure and prosperous economy, better living conditions for the mass of people, especially the one-third of the nation ill-housed, ill-clad, ill-nourished. Changing methods, he said, were simply a response to changes in the economic situation as he strove for the greater goal. This argument was convincing as long as business conditions were improving. In the fall of 1937 it seemed an empty apology.

On one economic matter, however, Roosevelt had shown a dogged tenacity and consistency. This was balancing the budget. Not, of course, that he had balanced the budget—but it remained a central objective of his fiscal policies. Again and again during the first term he had returned to the point until it had become a refrain. He had promised to balance the budget during the 1936 campaign, and early in 1937 he had looked forward hopefully to a balanced budget in a year or two. "I have said fifty times that the budget will be balanced for the fiscal year 1938," Roosevelt had exclaimed to Garner during the court fight. "If you want me to say it again, I will say it either once or fifty times more."

Curiously, the recession seemed only to harden the President's determination to get the budget in balance. He expected it to be "definitely balanced by the next fiscal year," he announced at Bonneville at the end of September. He made the same statement time after time in press conferences. He grew indignant over the disposition of Congress to spend money without raising taxes for it, and throughout the fall of 1937 he was busy searching for ways of cutting spending.

The high point in this effort came on the night of November 10, when Morgenthau, who had been pressing the President for an end of deficits, announced to the Academy of Political Science in New York that the administration positively intended to balance the budget. This was nothing new—but it amazed the New Deal economists around Roosevelt, for in a series of conferences with the President a day or so before the speech they had got the impression that he was contemplating a resumption of heavy spending. Was Morgenthau, they wondered hopefully, speaking out of turn? No, it developed that Roosevelt had gone over the secretary's address in advance.

Whatever his private doubts, Roosevelt was outwardly determined on government economy and a balanced budget. Probably he hoped that this reassurance would buoy up business confidence and check the deepening recession. But business did not pick up.

It was a dismal December. The President took Hopkins and Ickes on a fishing trip in the Gulf of Mexico, but he had to cut the cruise short because of an infected jaw. Ickes had never seen him so listless and despondent; he even talked of letting Congress have its head. In mid-December Japanese bombers sank the United States gunboat *Panay* and killed three Americans. A crisis seemed in the making until Japan met American demands just before Christmas. The President's Christmas greeting to the nation was, in substance, a sermon to "love thine enemy." One of his last official acts of 1937, however, was to indicate that he expected to expand the country's naval power. Love thine enemy—but carry a big stick.

PALACE STRUGGLE FOR A PROGRAM

The new year—1938—brought no turn in the economic situation. Business indices were still falling; a special census of unemployment confirmed the administration's worst fears. Between eight and eleven million people were jobless.

The President maintained an air of self-assurance. To Congress he delivered a long message that was in effect an earnest and persuasive restatement of the New Deal. He again called for a balanced budget, but not if it meant that Americans must starve or go on the dole. Resubmitting his program of 1937, Roosevelt vowed that he would not "let the people down." His Jackson Day dinner address early in January was a summons to the "overwhelming majority of our citizens" to join him in the spirit of Jefferson and Jackson and Lincoln to curb the power and privileges of small minorities. "We know that there will be a few—a mere handful of the total of businessmen and bankers and industrialists—who will fight to the last ditch to retain such autocratic control over the industry and finances of the country as they now possess. With this handful it is going to be a fight—a cheerful fight on my part, but a fight in which there will be no compromise with evil—no letup until the inevitable day of victory."

"Bert," said the President to House Republican leader Snell following his speech to Congress, "as they used to say on the East Side of New York, 'that wasn't esking them, that was telling them!' "

But telling them what? Actually Roosevelt was still a highly puzzled man. He did not conceal this fact from himself. There was something both pitiable and engaging in the way in which, five years after becoming President and in the midst of deepening economic crisis, he set about re-educating himself in the mysterious ways of the economic system. As in the past, he consulted men rather than books. To a New York banker who had warned him against consulting visionary and dangerous theorists the President wrote that he was seeing more businessmen than any other group. "If you could sit in my office beside me for a week it would be very helpful to you, for you would be gaining in education in every line as greatly as I am gaining as each day passes." Once again the President was talking with men late into the night, rummaging through their minds.

Unhappily, the more Roosevelt turned for advice to the men around him and to others he called in, the more he risked becoming entangled in the arguments over economic policy within his own staff, within his cabinet, within his whole circle of advisers. And the more he was plunged into the middle of the intellectual warfare among academic economists.

During the fall and early winter Roosevelt's conservative advisers seemed to have the upper hand. Morgenthau's budget-balancing speech, the President's continued assurances on the same subject, his well-publicized demands for government economy, his frequent distinction between the great number of businessmen and the tiny minority of wrongdoers—all these were designed to bolster business confidence, to embolden investors, to shore up the stock market. In his "budget seminar" with reporters shortly after the new year began Roosevelt said that the most important fact was the cut of over half a billion in estimated spending for the next fiscal year.

The President's caution did little to placate business. It served mainly to arouse the New Dealers around him. By the end of 1937 they were taking their case directly to the people. But this was a flanking effort—their main goal was to drive a salient into the economic mind of Roosevelt himself.

By this time the New Dealers had become a relatively stable and unified group. Their leaders in the cabinet were Ickes, Wallace, Perkins—and perhaps more influential with Roosevelt than any of these by 1938—Hopkins. Behind these notables was as remarkable and able a group of idea men as Washington had ever seen. The ebullient Corcoran was as active as ever, showing his uncanny capacity to move back and forth between exacting technical jobs and tough backstairs politicking. An official of increasing influence during this period was the chairman of the Board of Governors of the Federal Reserve System, a sharp-faced banker from Utah named Marriner Eccles. Two other rising stars were William O. Douglas, the sandy-haired ex-professor who now chaired the Securities Exchange Commission, and Robert H. Jackson, a New York lawyer who had won wide attention for his work in the Justice Department. Behind these men, backing them up with charts and memorandums and analyses, were a dozen barely known economists and lawyers—Isador Lubin in the Labor Department, Mordecai Ezekiel in Agriculture, Herman Oliphant in Treasury, Lauchlin Currie under Eccles, Leon Henderson and David K. Niles under Hopkins.

By the end of 1937 little knots of these and other New Dealers had been meeting secretly and holding feverish discussions on how to salvage the New Deal. They were at odds, however, over economic strategy. The out-and-out Keynesians wanted Roosevelt to start a bigger and better spending program. Others called for an old-fashioned, slam-bang attack on the trusts. The New Dealers were too unsure of Roosevelt's current political mood to let him in on their plans; besides, their tactic was to force his hand by building up pressure on the left.

As it turned out, though, Roosevelt unwittingly decided the issue between the spenders and the trust busters for a time. His private complaints during the fall that certain business interests were ganging up on him showed which way the presidential mind was leaning. Jackson, in the tradition of his namesake a century before the New Deal, opened up the counterattack on business by blaming monopolists and profiteers for the recession. Ickes followed with a denunciation of the "sixty families" that, he cried, controlled the American economy. The New Dealers were not content to deplore the economic power of the monopolists. They flayed them for seeking political power, for trying to defy the popular mandate of 1936, even for leading the country toward fascism. Ickes waited anxiously for the President to back up the onslaughts. Roosevelt did, after a fashion—but he took care to reiterate that only a small minority of businessmen were guilty of "poor citizenship."

So trust busting was the order of the day. Nothing could have been better calculated to inflame the war between New Deal and business or to sharpen the alternatives facing Roosevelt. For the essence of the businessmen's argument was that the recession stemmed directly from lack of confidence by investors in Roosevelt's policies and ultimate intentions. Lack of confidence meant lack of investment, and faltering investment meant a slowing of the wheels of industry. As the New Dealers thwacked them hip and thigh, businessmen turned to Roosevelt for a repudiation of his radical advisers.

But the President was silent. He was still groping. As long as he could not see his way clear he steered cautiously between the New Dealers and the conservatives and avoided alienating either wing. And he continued to go to school. During the early weeks of 1938 businessmen flocked to the White House on the President's invitation to tell him their ideas. The administration sponsored in Washington a conference of small businessmen that became so turbulent that the police had to be called. The Business Advisory Council met and its spokesman, Averell Harriman, asked the President to provide leadership around which they could rally, but the businessmen suspected that the President was still planless. Other meetings were more ominous. One hundred thousand workers turned out for a relief demonstration in Detroit; three thousand youth delegates convened in Washington to demand a "youth act" that would provide part-time jobs.

Pressed to act but not knowing what to do, Roosevelt turned from one scheme to another. For a time he toyed with ideas for a revival of some kind of public and private national planning, although not to the extent of the NRA. Soon he was taking a different tack; in conferring with utility magnates he spoke strongly against utility holding companies, themselves a form of private planning. He denounced various marketing practices of big business, but he also made clear that he was not leaning toward any form of socialism. In the fashion of Hoover several years back, the President warned against wage reductions; but he expressed concern also over high prices in some fields and low prices in others. Roosevelt insisted that all his policies were designed to promote full employment. He failed, however, to back up his policies with more than cajolery, and as business conditions worsened, the nation saw only a policy of improvisation and drift.

A number of economists urged Roosevelt to increase government spending and thus prime the economic pump so that business could step up its own activity. These appeals—many of which came from academic men—did not move Roosevelt, at least at that moment. Pump priming had been proper in 1933, he believed, but it was not desirable in 1938 when business indices were off by only about a third. Here Roosevelt was somewhat a victim of circumstances. The two men close to him who had both an intellectual and vocational interest in spending were inactive, for different reasons. Hopkins had recently had part of his stomach removed because of cancer, and was recuperating in the early weeks of 1938. And Ickes during these months was putting virtually all his political energies behind his obsessive efforts to wrest the Forest Service away from the Agriculture Department and affix it to his own domain.

Roosevelt was now more sorely pressed than ever. Once again, as in early 1935, he was being squeezed by forces beyond his control. His enemies in Congress taunted him for his failure to come to grips with the recession. His friends pleaded for a reassertion of his moral leadership. "Mr. President," wrote Wallace, "[you] must furnish that firm and confident leadership which made you such a joy to the nation in March of 1933." It was all Roosevelt could do to get enough money out of Congress to meet immediate and essential relief needs. He warned a congressional leader that if Congress cut relief he would post a big sign in front of the White House announcing WPA NEED NOT APPLY HERE—with a big arrow pointing to Capitol Hill.

It was a condition, not a theory, that finally moved the President. In March the stock market's halting decline turned suddenly into a panicky drop, and other indices slumped badly. Unemployment was still rising. In fact, the decline from the previous September was the sharpest the country had ever known. Even a number of business leaders were now calling guardedly for spending. When

Roosevelt left Washington for Warm Springs late in March he was worried and tense. He stopped off in Georgia to deliver one of the most bitter attacks of his life on minority selfishness, on feudalism that he described as virtual fascism. By now Hopkins was back in action, and, armed with memorandums from New Deal economists, he met Roosevelt at Warm Springs and urged on him a large-scale spending program.

Roosevelt knew that he must act. And he knew that he must act for the people—the people who loved him and who had sustained him. On the train back to Washington from Georgia he looked out of the window at the nondescript men and women who—five years after his inauguration—were still waiting for him along the track to wave and smile at him. He turned to an assistant. "*They* understand what we're trying to do."

Soon after arriving in Washington Roosevelt told Morgenthau that he had decided to scrap budget balancing and resume spending. When Morgenthau cried that he might resign, the President answered, "You just can't do this!" It would wreck the administration, and Morgenthau would go down in history as having quit under fire. Morgenthau stayed.

As usual, when the President shifted, there was little looking back. In mid-April he proposed to Congress a three-billion-dollar spending program, and in a long fireside chat took his new program to the people. Two weeks later he asked Congress to launch a thorough study of the concentration of economic power in American industry and the effect of that concentration upon the decline of competition. Congress responded enthusiastically to his proposals and passed the legislation by heavy majorities within a few weeks. Three billion was appropriated for spending and lending during the next fiscal year, and the Temporary National Economic Committee, consisting of senators, representatives, and government officials, and staffed by scores of experts, was established under the chairmanship of Senator Joseph C. O'Mahoney to conduct a full-scale investigation of the economy. Within a few months business indices were edging up again, but a large lump of unemployment continued to weigh down the economy.

ROOSEVELT AS AN ECONOMIST

One day late in Roosevelt's second term Marriner Eccles reported at the White House to raise some pressing economic questions with the President. He had been promised an hour-long luncheon engagement—a prize that an administrator might spend weeks conniving for. To his dismay, he found that Senator McAdoo was cutting into his time. When Eccles finally got into the President's study the burly old Californian was standing over Roosevelt and declaiming about the political situation back home.

"Bring up a chair, Marriner," the President said. To McAdoo he added: "Marriner and I are just about to have lunch."

McAdoo was too engrossed in his problems to take the hint. "Oh, that's all right," he said, "you two boys go right ahead—I'll talk while you eat."

Reaching to a warming oven next to his chair, Roosevelt pulled out a plate. It was burning hot. Juggling it awkwardly, he managed to place it before Eccles. While the President shook his scorched fingers and Eccles burned inside, McAdoo continued to talk. He finally wound up:

"Now, remember, Franklin. I want to leave one last thought with you. When it comes to appointing any of those federal judges in California, I wish you would take the matter up with me instead of with that son-of-a-bitch Downey. . . ."

McAdoo finally left. Marveling at Roosevelt's good humor through all this, Eccles leaned forward to talk. But as the waiter rolled away the tray there was a new diversion. Fala bounded in, Roosevelt took a ball out of his desk, and for several minutes the dog played retriever for his master, while Eccles feebly voiced words of praise.

"That's enough now," Roosevelt said to Fala. "I've got to get back to work." Eccles started talking, but after a few minutes he saw that he had lost his audience. Roosevelt was looking around the room for Fala. Suddenly the President burst out: "Well, I'll be God-damned! Marriner, do you see what I see?"

Eccles did. Over in a corner Fala was committing an indiscretion on the rug. Several more minutes elapsed while Roosevelt summoned a guard, had Fala's nose rubbed in the mess, and delivered a post mortem. By now Eccles' time was almost up. He left in a blind rage. To his associates awaiting him expectantly at the Federal Reserve Building he could report only on California politics and on the doings of Fala.

This sort of thing happened many times. People were amazed at Roosevelt's governmental habits—at his way of running through a series of wholly unrelated conferences like a child in a playroom turning from toy to toy, at his ability seemingly to put one matter out of his head when he turned to another, above all at his serenity and even gaiety under the pitiless pressures of men and events. The methods, of course, reflected the man. Roosevelt's mental agility and flexibility were well suited to the experimental phase of the New Deal. In 1938 Roosevelt was still the improviser, still the pragmatist.

Was practicality enough? Roosevelt's fumbling and indecisiveness during the recession showed his failings as an economist and thinker. His distrust of old and doctrinaire economic theories freed him from slavery to ideas that would have been risky in the 1930's. But at the same time, that distrust helped cut him off from the one economist and the one economic idea that might have provided a spectacular solution to Roosevelt's chief economic, political, and constitutional difficulties.

The man was the noted British economist John Maynard Keynes. An academician who was yet a leader in the bizarre Bloomsbury set, an economist who had won and lost fortunes as a speculator, a Cambridge don who also ran insurance companies, a prickly intellectual who was close to men of affairs throughout the world, a reformer who believed in liberal capitalism, Keynes for two decades had been provoking British opinion with his unorthodox views of economics, industry, and international affairs. In 1936 he had published the capstone of his economic thought, *The General Theory of Employment, Interest, and Money*. Bristling with critical references to cherished theories and honored names, filled with strange terms and equations, punctuated by lengthy appendixes, the *General Theory* had been read by few. But its impact on liberal economists in America was already making itself felt.

For, out of all the complexities and involutions of Keynes's writings, there emerged a central idea that was dazzling in its stark simplicity. Classical economics dictated that in bad times governments must permit if not encourage lower wages, lower prices, and rigorously balanced budgets. Purged and cleansed by this stringent process, the economy could then right itself and once again march up the long foothills to the mountain peaks of the business cycle. Keynes boldly assaulted this notion. The nub of his advice to government in time of depression was to unbalance the budget deliberately by heavy spending and low taxes. Only through heavy spending by consumers and investing by government or private capitalists could the economy right itself.

To call any single doctrine a "solution" is, of course, dangerous business. Keynesianism, moreover, is still a highly controversial topic among economists and policy makers; its usefulness is sharply limited depending on the nature of an economy, the people, the condition, and the time. Yet it seems clear that if ever the idea of deficit financing had urgent applicability, it was to the America of the 1930's, with its huge army of unemployed, its vast raw materials, and the state of its industrial arts.

In the first place, deficit spending was constitutional. When at a social gathering Justice Stone whispered to Miss Perkins, "My dear, the taxing power is sufficient for everything you want and need," he was in effect reminding the administration of its plenitude of power in the whole fiscal realm as compared with other avenues that could be blocked off by judicial action. Indeed, a great authority on the Constitution, Professor Edward S. Corwin of Princeton, had predicted the "twilight of the Supreme Court" because the Court, by making difficult a legal challenge to federal appropriations, had left to Congress power over spending and taxing.

Massive deficit spending was politically feasible too. Despite the ceaseless talk of economy on the Hill, Congress, at least during Roosevelt's first five years, was eager to spend. It is an old political bromide that congressmen want to vote for all spending bills and against all taxing bills—which happens to be just the right combination for deficit spending. The President often had to throw his weight *against* the congressional spenders, as in the case of the veterans' bonus. If Roosevelt had urged spending programs on Congress rather than the court plan and certain reform measures in 1937, he probably could have both met his commitments to the one-third ill-housed, ill-fed, and ill-clothed and achieved substantial re-employment.

Deficit spending was ideally suited to Roosevelt's ideology and program. He was no doctrinaire capitalist; twenty years before his presidency he was a New Deal state senator favoring a host of governmental controls and reforms, and he had stood for progressivism as a Wilson lieutenant and as governor. He was no doctrinaire socialist; he had never embraced the idea of central state ownership of the means of production. Rejecting both doctrinaire solutions, Keynesian economics was a true middle way—at a time when New Dealers were groping for a middle way that worked.

As a practical man, Roosevelt liked to apply the test, "Will it work?" Deficit spending *had* worked in 1935 and 1936 with the huge relief programs, veterans' bonus payments, and monetary expansion. Then had come a shift to the opposite policy: relief spending had been cut, reserve requirements for commercial banks raised, holdings of securities by banks reduced, and the growth of loans slowed. This shift from deficit spending had *not* worked. Both experiments had been fairly conclusive, each in its way; Roosevelt might have wanted the chance to experiment further, but a nation can hardly be expected to serve indefinitely as a laboratory.

Why did this most practical of men miss out on what probably would have been the ideal solution for his economic, political, and judicial problems?

Not because Keynes had failed to reach him. The Englishman had corresponded with the President, and he had talked with him in 1934. The two men liked each other, but the intellectual and the politician were cut from different cloth: Roosevelt was dubious about Keynes's "rigmarole of figures" and seemed surprised to find him a mathematician rather than a political economist; for his part

Keynes was disappointed that the President was not more literate in economics.

From England, Keynes had watched the sharp decline of late 1937 with mounting anxiety. On February 1, 1938, he had written the President a long and eloquent letter. "You received me so kindly when I visited you some three years ago that I make bold to send you some birds eye impressions. . . ." After a disclaimer of omniscience, Keynes delivered a polite but candid attack on the administration's recent economic policies. There had been an "error of optimism," he said, in 1936. Recovery was possible only through a large-scale recourse to public works and other investments. The administration had had an unexampled opportunity to organize increased investment in durable goods such as housing, public utilities, and transport.

Could the administration, asked Keynes, escape criticism for the failure of increased investment? "The handling of the housing problem has been really wicked," and housing could be the best aid to recovery. As for utilities, their litigation against the government was senseless. But as for the allegedly wicked holding companies, no one had suggested a way to unscramble the eggs. The President should either make peace with the utilities or be more drastic. Keynes leaned toward nationalizing them, but if public opinion was not yet ripe for that, what was the point of "chasing the utilities around the lot every other week"? As for railroads, either take them over or have pity on the overwhelming problems of the managers.

Keynes even tried to educate the President on the nature of businessmen. They had a different set of delusions from politicians, he warned, and thus required different handling. "They are, however, much milder than politicians, at the same time allured and terrified by the glare of publicity, easily persuaded to be 'patriots,' perplexed, bemused, indeed terrified, yet only too anxious to take a cheerful view, vain perhaps but very unsure of themselves, pathetically responsive to a kind word. You could do anything you liked with them, if you would treat them (even the big ones), not as wolves and tigers, but as domestic animals by nature, even though they have been badly brought up and not trained as you would wish."

It was a mistake, Keynes went on, to think that businessmen were more immoral than politicians. "If you work them into the surly, obstinate, terrified mood of which domestic animals, wrongly handled, are so capable, the nation's burden will not get carried to market; and in the end, public opinion will veer their way. . . ."

"Forgive the candour of these remarks," Keynes had concluded. He listed half a dozen administration policies he supported with enthusiasm. "But I am terrified lest progressive causes in all the democratic countries should suffer injury, because you have taken too lightly the risk to their prestige which would result from a failure measured in terms of immediate prosperity. There *need* be no failure. But the maintenance of prosperity in the modern world is extremely *difficult;* and it is so easy to lose precious time."

The eloquent appeal had not moved the President. He asked Morgenthau to write a reply to Keynes for him, and the President signed as written the banal little letter that Morgenthau produced. Two months later Roosevelt did resume spending, of course, but it was not the kind of massive spending that Keynes was calling for.

Part of the reason for Roosevelt's failure to exploit Keynes and his ideas lay in the web of political circumstances. Lacking a coherent economic philosophy in 1932, Roosevelt had opportunistically pummeled Hoover from both right and left, attacking him both for do-nothing government *and* for unbalancing the budget. Roosevelt had thus committed himself to a balanced budget, at least in the long run, and during his presidential years he mired himself further in this swamp. The more he unbalanced the budget, the more—literally scores of times—he insisted that eventually he would balance it. The more he promised, the more he gave hostages to the conservatives on the Hill and in his party. His personal stand became party policy in both the 1932 and 1936 platforms.

Another reason for the failure lay with Roosevelt's advisers. Some of them, of course, opposed any type of heavy spending; but even those who leaned toward a new economic program were committed to particular doctrines or policies and hence were unable to exploit the full potential of Keynes's idea. Some of them were mainly concerned about price rigidity—so concerned, indeed, that they wished to make this the main basis of a campaign against big business. Some were more worried about inflation than continuing unemployment. Some wanted to penalize business by raising taxes —good politics, perhaps, but a contradiction of the Keynesian idea of lowering taxes while increasing spending. Some, lacking faith in the long-term prospects of capitalism in America, believed in a theory of secular stagnation that did not admit that Keynesian economics was a basic solution. Some were believers only in pump priming; the government could pour heavy doses of purchasing power into the economy, as it had in 1935 and 1936, but after that business was supposed to man the pumps.

These splits even among his liberal advisers reflected to some extent the haphazard fashion in which Roosevelt had assembled his brain trust. Even so, there were few out-and-out Keynesians in the government, and most of these were in the lower echelons and lacked access to the President. And Keynesian theory was so new that certain statistical and analytical tools were lacking.

The main reason for Roosevelt's failure in the economic sphere, however, lay neither in the political situation nor in his divided advisers. With his immense political resourcefulness and volatility Roosevelt could always have broken out of the party and congressional web, at least in 1936 and early 1937. He could always have changed his advisers. His main trouble was intellectual. Roosevelt was simply unable as a thinker to seize the opportunity that Keynesian economics gave him. His failure as an economist was part of a broader intellectual failure.

What was the nature of this failure? Roosevelt's mind was an eminently operative one, quick, keen, fast, flexible. It showed in his intellectual habits. He disdained elaborate, fine-spun theories; he paid little attention to the long and abstract briefs that academic people were always sending him on ways of improving administration, on strengthening the cabinet as an institution, on dealing with Congress. He hated abstractions. His mind yearned for the detail, the particular, the specific. Invariably he answered general questions in terms of examples—in terms of an individual business, of a farmer in Kansas, of a problem in Hyde Park, of a situation during the Wilson administration. He had a passion for the concrete.

His working habits bespoke his mind. From the start of his day to the end, from his skimming through a half-dozen newspapers at breakfast through a schedule of quick conferences on a score of different subjects to his playing with his stamps before bedtime, his mind sped from topic to topic, picking them up, toying with them, and dropping them. His intellectual habits were not disorderly; they were staccato.

Roosevelt's mental way of life was nourished by its own successes. He liked to outwit the reporters in fast repartee. He liked to show off the incredible knowledge of a wide variety of specific matters that he carried in his head. Sometimes there was a touch of fakery in this, for the President could steer a conversation toward a subject on which he was newly briefed. But to an extraordinary extent he grasped an immediate, specific situation in all its particulars and complexity. He knew, for example, the tangled political situations and multitude of personalities in each of the states; he could talk for hours about the housing, roads, people, and history of Hyde Park; he could describe knowledgeably the activities and problems of a host of businesses and industries; he could pull out of his head hundreds of specific prices, rents, wages; he could identify countless varieties of fish, birds, trees; he could not be stumped on geography.

His self-esteem as a practical man must have been fed, too, by the ignorance of so many of his critics. Many men of affairs were slaves to the theories of defunct economists, and Roosevelt could puncture their pretensions with his knowledge of their own business and its relation to the rest of the world. His indignant complaints to his friends about the businessmen's failure to advance specific constructive suggestions was the lament of the practitioner against the theorist. Undoubtedly Roosevelt's emphasis on his own practicality had an element of overcompensation too. Cartoonists in 1938 were still picturing him as a fuzzy theorist surrounded by bemused brain trusters; and a friend who had romped with him as a child in the Hyde Park nursery, and who had evidently learned little since those days, rebuked him with the words: "You are not an essentially practical person."

And now, by a supreme irony, fate placed before this man of practicality an economic theory that seemed to embody only uncommon sense. The idea of boosting spending and holding down taxes and of doing this year after year as a deliberate policy, the idea of gaining prosperity by the deliberate creation of huge debts —this idea in its full dimensions seemed but another fanciful academic theory, and Roosevelt by 1938 had had a bellyful of such theories. Pump priming as a temporary emergency measure he could understand—but not deficit spending as the central, long-term approach to full-scale economic recovery.

Deficit spending posed a special intellectual problem for the President. If there had been consistency in his handling of economic affairs, it was his habit of trying to make economic decisions by combining opposites. "Lock yourselves in a room and don't come out until you agree," he would say blithely to people who differed hopelessly in their economic premises—to free traders and nationalists, to deflationists and inflationists, to trust busters and collectivists, to spenders and economizers. The trouble with deficit spending was that halfway application did not work. It had utility only through full and determined use; otherwise it served only to antagonize and worry business by increasing the public debt without sufficiently raising spending and investment.

A Keynesian solution, in short, involved an almost absolute commitment, and Roosevelt was not one to commit himself absolutely to any political or economic method. His mind was a barometric reflection of the personal and policy pressures around him. "We are at one of those uncommon junctures of human affairs," Keynes said in the 1930's, "when we can be saved by the solution of intellectual problems and in no other way." But Roosevelt's mind was attuned to the handling of a great variety of operational and tactical matters, not to the solving of intellectual problems.

Roosevelt's deficiencies as an economist were as striking as his triumphs as a politician. It was a major failure of American democracy that it was not able in the late 1930's to show that a great nation could provide jobs for its workers and food, clothes, and houses for its people. What Roosevelt could not achieve World War II would achieve as a by-product enabling Republicans to charge later that the New Deal could end depression only through war. It was a personal failure for Roosevelt too. Halfway through his second term the man who had ousted Hoover on the depression issue knew that eight or nine million people were walking the streets. He knew that millions were still living in shanties and tenements, and that some were not far from starvation. Would the great promise of January 1937 become a mockery?

SEVENTEEN

Deadlock on the Potomac

IN MOST SOCIETIES, people's love for their leaders is strongly mixed with hatred and fear. Certain tribes set off a time each year for the throwing of dung at their chiefs. In America, as Mr. Dooley once remarked, people build their triumphal arches out of brick so that they will have something handy to throw at the hero when he comes through. As economic conditions deteriorated during early 1938, so did Roosevelt's popularity. By the summer months of that year barely half the people questioned in a nationwide survey said that they would vote for Roosevelt if they were going to the polls at that time.

The rancor among sections of the rich was sharper and uglier than ever. The President seemed to be hated more bitterly in conservative quarters than any American progressive since Bryan. A corporation lawyer openly solicited pledges in Wall Street for a large fund to be presented to Roosevelt on condition he resign within five months.

Any trouble in the Roosevelt family was fair game for the Roosevelt haters. During his early presidential years his sons got into the usual scrapes at school—especially traffic offenses—and these were duly inflated in the press. A highly publicized article in the *Saturday Evening Post* accused James of exploiting his family connection in writing insurance. Several actual or impending divorces in the family got full attention, especially in the gossip columns. While the father did what he could to bring about reconciliations, he did not expect his children to subordinate their private lives to his public life. He said little about these problems except in the immediate family circle, but the attacks on his offspring—and through them on him—hurt. They must have hurt all the more because he knew that for the last ten years he had had little time to devote to family affairs and problems.

Roosevelt stories made their rounds of country club and dinner party; one of the more ingenious was about the philatelist who took some of his most prized stamps to the White House to show them to the President, how Roosevelt filched several of the choicest when his guest was not looking, how Mrs. Roosevelt summoned the collector to a New York hotel a week later and quietly paid him off. Fashionable men and women, fastidious about everything except their obsession with the man in the White House, talked on and on about his mind, his legs, his morals, and the morals of his family.

All this Roosevelt could write off—indeed, had long before written off. But the drop in his popularity among other classes was a different matter. With his acute sensitivity to shifts in attitudes, he could not ignore the fateful parallel between 1938 and the Hoover years. Roosevelt in 1938 was losing popular support not only among the prosperous but to an even greater extent among the middle- and lower-income groups. The Supreme Court fight and the Black appointment had turned people against the New Deal—but not nearly so much as had the Roosevelt recession.

But how far had this desertion gone? The decisive fact of 1938 was that most people *thought* Roosevelt had lost popular favor to a greater extent than he really had. His actual drop between early 1936 and late 1938 in the public polls was a matter of a few percentage points. Even at the lowest point of his popularity in 1938 he commanded the support of a bare majority of the people—and a majority that was probably a trifle larger than during certain periods of the first term. The difference was that during the first term Roosevelt always gave the *impression* of popularity, while in 1938 that impression no longer existed.

The popular attitude toward Roosevelt was marked by a deep ambivalence. On the one hand, almost everyone liked him as a person. Asked, "On the whole, do you like or dislike his personality?" eight out of ten Americans in the spring of 1938 answered "like" to only one who answered "dislike." Negroes, the poor generally, labor, the unemployed were enthusiastically for Roosevelt the person. The Southwest as a section delivered a resounding 98 per cent for him, and other sections were not far behind. Most remarkable of all, not a single occupation group—not executives, nor professional people, nor proprietors—"voted" for the presidential personality by less than three-quarters of that group.

Reports from journalists squared with the findings of the pollsters. "They love Roosevelt," reported liberal journalist Richard Neuberger from the Northwest after talking with Idaho ranchers, Seattle streetcar motormen, a lumberjack in Coeur d'Alene, a Union Pacific brakeman, a Portland electrician, and others. Whatever the objections to the New Deal, Neuberger found, people liked Roosevelt because they believed that he was doing things for *them*. Many referred to him as "our President," and as long as he remained "our President," concluded Neuberger, Roosevelt would continue to be the dominant influence in the nation's politics.

But Roosevelt's general economic objectives, his methods of achieving these objectives, his advisers, many of his policies—these were different matters. Fewer than half of those polled in the spring of 1938 favored Roosevelt's economic goals; more than half were opposed, doubtful, or uninformed. More people disliked his "methods" than liked them. Of five major economic groups—Negroes, poor, lower middle, upper middle, and prosperous—all but the first two registered majorities against the President's methods.

Running through this opposition was a streak of fear of Roosevelt's apparent political power. As an abstract matter a large section of the people believed that the President of the United States should have less authority. About half of those with opinions said that Roosevelt himself had too much power, and about one-quarter of those who approved his economic objectives shared this alarm. The worry over presidential power extended to all economic classes; although tending to parallel general class attitudes toward Roosevelt and his policies, it was somewhat marked among the lower middle class.

The state of public opinion in the spring of 1938 posed a dilemma for the President. His great strength lay in his own political personality, in the magic spell that he could still cast over the voters. His weakness lay in the anxiety of millions over his seemingly great political power—an anxiety like that of a wife who adores a gay and vibrant husband without wholly trusting his judgment or his self-control. Could he convert his personal popularity into political strength and leadership? Could he convert the majority popular support he still retained into congressional majorities necessary to consolidate and extend the New Deal? Could he maintain and even strengthen his own power without frightening further those who already feared the extent of presidential power?

By the spring of 1938 events on Capitol Hill were bringing these questions into sharp focus.

SQUALLS ON CAPITOL HILL

"For God's sake," a congressional spokesman telephoned the White House in April 1938, "don't send us any more controversial legislation!"

Here spoke the authentic voice of Congress. Now in the sixth year of the New Deal, senators and representatives were balking at Roosevelt's leadership as they never had before. They were tired of "must" bills, tired of crises, tired of charges of rubber-stamp Congress, tired of bustling, pushing young zealots from the White House.

Most congressmen were no less fond of Roosevelt as a person in 1938 than they had been four or five years before. But like the people as a whole, they were more jealous and distrustful of his ambitions and his powers.

Despite the personal ties between Roosevelt and many congressmen, there had always been a political and psychological breach between the New Deal President and Capitol Hill. Only during the crisis days of the early New Deal had President and legislators suspended their historic conflict—a conflict artfully contrived and institutionalized by the framers of the Constitution. So, too, Congress embraced a way of life that was alien to the brisk pace, the electric atmosphere of the White House. Things moved more sedately in the soft, casual life of cloakroom and committee chamber. Signing their mail and genially chatting with one another while forensic gales lashed the air, the senators in particular embodied old ways of politics amid the marble columns and statuary of their nineteenth-century chamber.

Presiding over this legislative way of life were men who felt supremely secure in their positions of power. Still holding seats in 1938 on Capitol Hill were two senators and two representatives who had entered Congress thirty years before, when Roosevelt was still a law clerk. These four men had seen six presidents come and five presidents go, and they doubtless expected to be in Congress after Roosevelt had gone too. Perhaps two hundred members of Congress had entered the Senate or House before Roosevelt's first inaugural. Men who had won election after election, decade after decade, had no undue fear of a president who was limited by tradition to two terms. Many congressional leaders had almost unshakeable grips on their states or districts. Perhaps they served city machines, or had ties with dominant economic interests, or had won the hearts of their constituents by indefatigable errand-running, or had built powerful political organizations of their own.

Buttressing the power of the congressional leaders were certain arrangements on the Hill. By far the most important was the seniority rule, which inexorably elevated to chairmen those in the majority party with the longest continuous service on committees. And chairmanships meant the right to call committee meetings or not to call them, the right to speed bills on their way or to pocket them, the right to a dominant voice over policy within the committee jurisdiction. These lord-proprietors, as Woodrow Wilson once called them, had built close ties with bureaucrats who catered to their constituents, and with agents for the great national organizations that maintained their headquarters in Washington. Steeped in the lore and mores of Capitol Hill, they were artistic parliamentarians who knew the shades and nuances of quorum calls, points of order, filibusters, and a score of other weapons in the arsenal of obstruction and delay.

Because of the one-party system and sluggish politics of the South it was inevitable that Southerners would accumulate senior-ity and hence capture important chairmanships during periods of Democratic rule. Chairing the two great fiscal committees of the Senate in 1938 were anti-New Deal Democrats: the pert, white-haired lord of Virginia politics, Carter Glass, of Appropriations, and Mississippi's droll, plump Pat Harrison, of Commerce. Chief of Agriculture and Forestry was crusty old Cotton Ed Smith of South Carolina who, when a Negro rose to preach in the 1936 conven-tion, had stalked out, muttering "the man is black—black as melted ink." Southerners ran many committees of the lower chamber too. Agriculture was chaired by a Texan, Banking and Currency by an Alabaman, Judiciary by a Texan, Public Lands by a Louisianian, Ways and Means by a North Carolinian.

Another reason for Southern influence in Congress lay perhaps in commitments Roosevelt seems to have made to gain his nomina-tion in 1932. Garner's willingness to accept the vice-presidential nomination was due in part to Roosevelt's willingness to recognize Southern, and especially Texan, power in Congress. The most im-portant understanding was that Rayburn would be in line for the majority leadership and later the speakership of the House. It was the President's recognition of Rayburn's claim that accounted in part for the desertion of the New Deal by a rival aspirant, Repre-sentative John O'Connor of New York. Roosevelt also had 1932 debts to pay to other Southerners.

To be sure, a number of key committees in both Houses were under the chairmanship of Northerners. Some of these chieftains, like Roosevelt's old friends Wagner of Banking and Currency in the Senate, and Mary T. Norton of Labor in the House, had con-sistently voted for New Deal measures. But happenstance, the prides and jealousies of office, and the factionalism and sectionalism of American party politics had brought to chairmanships a number of Northerners who had turned against much of the Roosevelt New Deal: in addition to O'Connor, that bellicose New Yorker who bossed the most powerful single committee on Capitol Hill, the House Rules Committee, there were Senator Royal S. Copeland of New York, whose relations with Roosevelt had been cool for many years, and Wheeler of Montana, who had clashed with Roosevelt over the Supreme Court and by now was off the reservation.

"Who does Roosevelt think he is?" Wheeler once demanded scornfully of a White House aide. "He used to be just one of the barons. I was baron of the Northwest. Huey Long was baron of the South." He mentioned other sectional leaders. But the President had turned against Long and now against the Senator from Montana. "He's like a king trying to reduce the barons."

This Congress of 1938 had little wish to repeal the New Deal. But neither did it wish to extend the New Deal in order to meet the Roosevelt challenge of the one-third ill-housed, ill-clad, ill-nourished.

Because the Soil Conservation and Domestic Allotment Act of 1936 had been a hurried measure to fill the gap left by the Supreme Court's voiding of the original AAA, Congress moved quickly in its 1938 session to pass a new Agricultural Adjustment Act. Embracing cotton, rice, and tobacco as well as wheat and corn, this measure assigned production quotas to producers of these crops and gave money to those who planted within certain acreage allotments and who followed prescribed soil conservation methods. The government could also make loans on various farm commodities both to prevent farm prices from collapsing in the face of huge surpluses and to establish an ever-normal granary. If two-thirds of the farmers approved, artificial market control of surplus crops could be established. Providing also for freight rate studies, research in new uses for farm products, purchase of surplus farm products for persons on relief, the act set the pattern for federal regulation of agriculture for years to come.

This much for the farmer. What about the worker? Passage of a weak wages and hours bill in mid-1938 seemed to drain the cup of congressional willingness to extend the New Deal. And when it came to giving Roosevelt power to control his own executive branch, the men on Capitol Hill broke into open revolt.

By early 1938 some New Dealers had given up hope that any wage-hour bill could pass through Congress. In the regular and special sessions of 1937 the original bill had been ground to pieces between the Southern Democrats and the labor bloc. But the President was determined to press for the bill. Angry though he was about Southern desertions from the measure, he reluctantly ceded a North-South wage differential in the bill to gain Southern votes. He sounded out the AFL on the price of its support. But Roosevelt would not go too far. When Representative Martin Dies asked for further concessions for the South, the President's patience was exhausted.

"Call up Martin Dies," he instructed McIntyre, "and tell him that any idea of having an individual State vary a national Wages and Hours bill is not only unsound, but would destroy the effectiveness of building up a purchasing power in those sections most needing it, and the President regards it as the weakest, most dangerous proposition he has ever heard. Tell him further that if we start to legislate for the oil industry, we'll be aiding and abetting those people who want to exempt the canners, the cheese factories, and the lumber mills, and that is completely unsound."

But could any bill pass without "unsound" concessions? For weeks the White House and Labor Department searched for a formula. No single approach satisfied all factions. By mid-April the House Labor Committee was facing a harsh choice between an AFL bill that lacked a North-South differential and a draft backed by Southerners that empowered a five-man board to grant such a differential. Whipsawed between two blocs, members of the Labor Committee tried to stall off a decision. Roosevelt would not let them. After the Labor Committee voted down the Southerners' draft, Chairman Mary Norton managed to hold the protesting committeemen in session until they reported out the AFL version.

Stripped of the North-South differential, the bill now ran into the hardened opposition of the Southerners dominating the Rules Committee. A discharge petition was necessary to pry the bill out of committee. But would enough congressmen sign the petition? One such effort had succeeded, but another one had failed. In this extremity the administration resorted to a crafty political maneuver.

Senator Claude Pepper, a staunch Roosevelt man, was engaged in a slam-bang race for renomination in Florida. To many observers Pepper's chances did not seem too good, but the White House had reliable information that Pepper would win. It was reasoned that if Pepper could be induced to speak vigorously for the wage-hour bill during the campaign, his later victory would be interpreted as a test of sentiment on the bill in the South. At least $10,000 was turned over to Pepper's campaign managers by Roosevelt's assistants, who had got the money from a radio corporation executive on the basis of another deal.

The stratagem worked. On May 3 Pepper won a decisive victory. Three days later the discharge petition was opened for signatures. So many representatives swarmed around the "honor roll" that House proceedings were drowned out, and in less than three hours the list of signatures reached the necessary 218. On May 24, after a tumultuous session lasting twelve hours, the House passed the bill by a heavy vote. Since the House version now differed radically from the Senate draft of the previous year, the bill was in danger until the end. Southerners talked about filibuster, and Green threatened to oppose the bill if differentials were reinserted. But a conference committee skillfully worked out a set of compromises, and the bill finally became law in June.

"That's that," said Roosevelt with a sigh of relief as he signed the measure. His sigh was one of disappointment too. The bill had been so watered down in its long journey through Congress that it could have little impact on the national economy. And perhaps it was a sigh of prophecy. The wage-hour bill was the last of Roosevelt's basic New Deal measures to pass Congress. During the final stages of its passage, the President had suffered a staggering defeat in Congress that was a gauge of his loss of legislative control.

The measure that occasioned this defeat was, on its face, one of the least controversial Roosevelt had ever proposed. Even more, it was designed to meet the insistent demands from business quarters that executive management be improved in the name of efficiency and economy. Previous chief executives, including Taft and Hoover, had proposed reorganization measures hardly less radical than Roosevelt's. Formulated by a group of political scientists and public administration experts headed by Louis Brownlow, the President's recommendations called for expanding the White House staff; strengthening his management agencies, including the substitution of a personnel director for the three-member Civil Service Commission; extending the merit system "upward, outward, and downward to cover practically all non-policy-determining posts"; setting up two new cabinet departments, Social Welfare and Public Works, and putting independent agencies under line departments; placing responsibility for accounts and transactions under the President while strengthening independent control of post-auditing under an auditor-general.

When Roosevelt first urged these changes in January 1937 they met apathy and quiet hostility in Congress. For months the proposals marked time while the Supreme Court bill held the center of the stage. Not until late in February 1938 did reorganization come before the Senate.

The times were not auspicious. Roosevelt was still floundering in the face of depression. The wage-hour bill was still splintering Congress into factions. Alarmed by the opposition's strength, Roosevelt and a dozen of his lieutenants—Ickes, Farley, Hopkins, Corcoran, Jesse Jones, and others—threw themselves into the fray. Urgent telephone calls went to state politicos asking them to put pressure on irresolute senators; enticing patronage plums were held out; favors were bargained off. Even so, the measure barely survived a series of test votes in the Senate.

By late March a hurricane of opposition was rising from the country. Reorganization was dubbed the "dictator bill." It was a question, proclaimed Senator Walsh of Massachusetts, "of plunging a dagger into the very heart of democracy." It was a fight against possible Hitlerism, a columnist declared. Committees to "uphold constitutional government" showered the country with letters and advertisements. Orators at New England town meetings thundered and protested. Over a hundred Paul Reveres, mounted on horses carrying banners reading NO ONE MAN RULE, converged on Washington and clattered along Pennsylvania Avenue. Father Coughlin fulminated over the radio. It was the Supreme Court fight all over again—but perhaps even more sharp and passionate.

One day during the fight the object of all this wrath and fear sat with his usual smile as the reporters trooped in. On the President's desk was a yataghan, a Turkish saber someone had presented him. "I can put it in the wall at thirty paces," Roosevelt said gleefully.

"How far down Pennsylvania Avenue can you throw it?" asked a reporter. The President laughed but did not answer. Even yataghans could not help now. When the measure finally emerged from the Senate and moved to the House, the hurricane roared to a climax. Hundreds of thousands of telegrams denouncing the plan poured in on the legislators. Because O'Connor and his Rules Committee opposed the plan, the leaders could not get a special rule governing debate. They lost control of the bill at the start, and soon it was caught in parliamentary tangles. Obstructionists delayed consideration by endless points of order, quorum calls, questions of personal privilege. As debate raged day after day, powerful interest groups pressed their claims for exempting their pet bureaus from reorganization.

Forced back on the defensive, Roosevelt took steps both to counteract the group pressures and to quiet the popular fear of presidential power that had been whipped up. Remembering the charges that he had lost the Supreme Court fight because he made compromises too little and too late, he began to negotiate concessions. The Office of Education was exempted in the face of a wave of fear among religious groups that its relocation in the bureaucratic structure would mean more federal control. So was the Veterans Bureau in the wake of protests by ex-servicemen's groups. Other key agencies got immunity. The most important concession involved a crucial question of presidential power. In the original bill Congress had had power to veto presidential reorganization proposals only by a two-thirds vote in both Houses; by a compromise, only a majority vote was required, with the effect that presidential reorganization plans would be far easier to defeat.

Roosevelt's move to calm popular fear was sudden and dramatic. Reporters at Warm Springs were summoned late at night to receive a presidential announcement. It read:

"A: I have no inclination to be a dictator.

"B: I have none of the qualifications which would make me a successful dictator.

"C: I have too much historical background and too much knowledge of existing dictatorships to make me desire any form of dictatorship for a democracy like the United States of America."

The President went on to denounce a "carefully manufactured partisan and political opposition." He promised that in almost every case he would go along with congressional opinion on specific reorganization. He mentioned examples of "silly nightmares conjured up at the instigation either of those who would restore the government to those who owned it between 1921 and 1933, or of those who for one reason or another seek deliberately to wreck the present administration." The harshness of Roosevelt's words betrayed the hurt and vexation he felt.

All to no avail. On April 8, by a razor-thin margin of 204 to 196, the House returned the measure to committee. As the vote was announced wild cheering broke out among representatives in the chamber. Congress was in open revolt. The White House was in a quandary. Farley and Early wanted the President to conciliate Congress. Ickes, heartsick over losing his chance to annex the Forest Service, implored Roosevelt to carry on the fight. It was up to the President, Corcoran declared, to show whether he was going out like Herbert Hoover or like Andrew Jackson. But Roosevelt would not press the fight. Already he was turning to another urgent matter: his spending program. He dispatched a letter to Majority Leader Rayburn. "Thanks for the good fight . . ." He added that there should be no personal recrimination.

No retaliation—yet.

THE BROKEN SPELL

"The old Roosevelt magic has lost its kick," Hugh Johnson crowed happily in the spring of 1938. "The diverse elements in his Falstaffian army can no longer be kept together and led by a melodious whinny and a winning smile." Pundits of press and radio across the nation sagely nodded agreement. The spell was broken. But why? On this there were a host of theories.

Some argued that the old politician was losing his touch, but the reporters who watched Roosevelt closely scoffed at the notion. The President's fireside chats were as warm and stirring as ever; he was perhaps even more charming and persuasive with visitors; he appeared to have lost none of his cocky self-assurance. His mental reflexes had, if anything, been sharpened during the presidential years. In the semiweekly jousting of the press conferences, the President usually came out on top. Asked one day what he thought of a Senator's proposal to make it a felony for a newspaper knowingly to publish a falsehood, he answered, quick as a flash, "I'm trying to pare expenses and I don't want any more prisons!" Trying to outsmart him, some reporters at a Press Club dinner wrote on the back of a menu, "I hereby nominate Herbert —— [a fellow reporter] as Ambassador to the North Pole," folded the words over to conceal them, and sent the menu to the guest of honor for his "autograph." When the nomination paper came back they discovered that Roosevelt had changed "North" to "South" and had innocently added "North Pole already occupied."

No, nothing had happened to Roosevelt's political skill or acuteness. Another theory was that Roosevelt's election triumph of 1936 had left him with a bad case of overconfidence, that this overconfidence had led to the bungling tactics of the court reform defeat, and this defeat had brought down Roosevelt's political house of cards. This interpretation made some sense as long as it could be argued that a better presentation of the court bill or greater willingness to accept a compromise might have saved the proposal. It was clearer in retrospect that no court reform bill of significance nor, indeed, any administrative reform bill of any significance could have won passage in the 1937-38 Congress. In short, the reasons for Roosevelt's defeats on Capitol Hill lay deeper than such simple explanations assumed.

Searching for these deeper reasons, students of politics noted the historical fact that even the stronger presidents—men like Jefferson and Wilson and Theodore Roosevelt—had met formidable difficulties in their second terms. With a president's power due to evaporate at a set date, the focus of power shifts from the White House to cabinet members and senators jockeying for the throne. Was not Roosevelt simply encountering the centrifugal forces inherent in this historic situation? To some extent he was. But as a resourceful politician, Roosevelt could also exploit a great countervailing force—namely, his control of the 1940 nomination. Roosevelt insisted to intimates—and the word got out fast enough—that the nomination would go to a Democrat who met the tests of a New Dealer by the President's standards. He planned, in short, to choose his successor. And there was always the possibility that Roosevelt himself would run—a possibility that Roosevelt had skillfully played up, even while ostensibly dismissing it, only six weeks after his second term began, when he spoke laughingly at the Democratic victory dinner of his plans for January 20, 1941.

Another explanation of Roosevelt's loss of leadership over Congress was quite simple. The President's popularity with the voters, it was pointed out, had slipped considerably during the Roosevelt recession, and congressmen were jumping off the presidential bandwagon as soon as they found this drop in their own constituencies. That explanation, too, had some merit; on the other hand, Roosevelt had lost the court fight before the recession and at a time when his personal popularity was still high. Moreover, his standing with the people had slipped badly during the first term—only to rise again in 1936. No congressman could dare count on continued unpopularity for the resilient politician in the White House.

What, then, could explain the revolt in Congress? It was not surprising that the real explanation eluded the observers of the day. Only as Roosevelt's first term fell into fuller perspective and as the precise nature of his relations with Congress during that period was revealed did the basic situation become clear. The essence of the situation was this: Roosevelt had led Congress during his first term by his adroit and highly personal handling of congressional leaders and by exploiting the sense of crisis; but, intent on immediate tactical gains on Capitol Hill, he had neglected to build up a position of strength with the rank and file of Congress.

With his usual pragmatism, Roosevelt at the outset had faced up to the hard facts of the distribution of power in Congress. Since committee chiefs had power, he would deal with committee chiefs. And he did so with such charm, such tact, such flexibility, such brilliant timing, such sensitivity to the leaders' own political problems that the President's personal generalship often meant the difference between passage and defeat of key bills. Time and time again he won the support of men like Glass and Harrison and Tydings and Sumners and Doughton not because they liked the New Deal in general or the measure in particular but because they liked and were willing to defer to the man who was President. Roosevelt's leadership talents lay in his ability to shift quickly and gracefully from persuasion to cajolery to flattery to intrigue to diplomacy to promises to horse-trading—or to concoct just that formula which his superb instincts for personal relations told him would bring around the most reluctant congressman.

"It is probably safe to say," said onetime presidential assistant Stanley High, "that during 1933, 1934, and 1935 a record-breaking number of men of some political eminence went to the President's office in a state of incipient revolt and left it to declare to the world their subscription to things that they did not subscribe to."

A good method while it worked—and it did work for four years. The supreme test of that method came in the second Hundred Days. To put through a restless and bewildered Congress the enduring legislation of the New Deal at the fag end of the 1935 session was the ultimate tribute to Roosevelt's capacity to prod and charm and reason balking legislators into acting.

But there was a price to pay. Boiling under the surface even while the great measures thrashed their way through Congress was a deep bitterness toward the White House. Men like Glass deserted the administration as the program of 1935 revealed the shape of things to come. Even loyalists like Byrnes complained that they had had to "swallow a lot" for the White House; they were close to the breaking point. As Roosevelt in his foxlike fashion crossed and recrossed his own trail in maneuvering his bills through Congress, congressmen had to reverse positions and cover up for the White House. They had to take the rap—and they were tired of taking the rap.

Bitterness was sharpest in the House. Administration supporters there complained to Roosevelt that party organization and discipline were nonexistent. The Democratic Steering Committee—the logical link between the President and his partisans in the House—was virtually ignored by the White House. When Hopkins held a peace conference with this committee in July 1935, member after member rose to excoriate the administration's flouting of rank-and-filers, to complain about appointments, even to threaten reprisal against the White House.

Roosevelt's breathing spell of late 1935, his limited legislative program for 1936, and the closing of ranks in the campaign staved off rebellion for a time. But the President's effort to carry out his program to help the needy one-third of the people precipitated the new and sterner battles of the second term.

Had the New Deal, then, really been dealt? Was it all over? What about the scores of young New Dealers washed into Congress by the Roosevelt tidal wave of 1936? Were not they the makings of congressional majorities for an expanded New Deal?

They might have served this purpose—but they never had the chance. For another price that Roosevelt had to pay for his dependence on the old ranking Democrats was the consolidation of the powers of these leaders in Congress. He had confirmed their political status, their high-priority claims on administration favors, their near monopoly of access to the White House. He had failed to encourage rank-and-file organization in Congress behind a New Deal program.

When Pittsburgh Democratic boss David Lawrence wanted to bring in three new Democratic congressmen to meet the President early in 1937, Roosevelt put him off, finally allotted three minutes, and then postponed even this appointment. "There is a group of aggressive progressive Democrats who have stuck by you through thick and thin, about seventy-five in number, as well as a number of other progressives not classed as Democrats," Representative Kent Keller wrote the President in April 1938, "and I do not believe that you have ever called in a single one of this group in consultation as to administration policies." Roosevelt, he said, was dealing only with a small group of congressional leaders. Characteristically the President told McIntyre, "Have him come in to see me." But things went on as before; the rank and file remained adrift. When a year later another friendly congressman urged him to establish contact with the rank and file by inviting them to the White House in small groups, the President replied that he would like to do this but his day was simply too crowded.

The President hoped that the Democratic legislators would remain responsible to the party platform of 1936. The congressmen, however, had had little part in drawing up the platform. They felt responsible to the majorities that had elected them in their districts; in any event, it was the voters in their districts who would determine whether or not they would stay in Congress. And not only this; something of tremendous importance was happening throughout the mid-1930's within the American electorate.

It is often said that a coalition of labor and farm groups created the New Deal. But this can be reversed. It is just as true—and of greater significance—that the New Deal helped create a new labor movement and a new farm movement in America, along with a dozen other immensely strengthened groups. And it was this massive swelling in the size and number and strength of politically oriented groups that changed decisively the pattern of power in counties and townships and wards and precincts, where congressmen were elected and defeated.

Labor was the most striking case in point. Sapped and crippled by depression, the unions had recruited millions of new members with the help of Section 7a and the Wagner Act. By 1937 the Committee for Industrial Organization had broken completely with the AFL and was gathering in millions of workers in steel, autos, rubber, electrical goods, and other mass-production industries. As fiery young leaders debouched from the ranks, unions took on a new militance and a new exhilaration. Contributing its funds and ordering its organizers into the precincts, the CIO had given Roosevelt's re-election campaign a mighty boost. Then, for month after month, the country had seen turbulent labor erupting in mass demonstrations, sit-down strikes, quickie stoppages, parades, police violence.

Striding across the front pages of the nation's newspapers was the new army's glowering, blustering commander, John L. Lewis. "The Huey Long of labor," Huey himself had called him, and no one could have better personalized Roosevelt's political predicament in his second term than the burly, pug-faced CIO chief. By 1938 Lewis was seething over Roosevelt's "ingratitude." For all his denunciations of businessmen, Lewis had a commercial approach to politics. The President, he felt, should pay off for favors granted. But what had Roosevelt done? He had taken a neutral stand during the period of sit-down strikes with his famous statement, "A plague on both your houses." He had publicly rebuked Lewis for demanding White House recognition of its 1936 friends. The President, Lewis growled, was even stealing his lieutenants—especially Sidney Hillman—away from him by giving them government jobs and drawing them into the charmed White House circle. Roosevelt and Hopkins, he complained, were balking CIO efforts to organize WPA workers. Where, demanded Lewis, was the pay-off?

Conflict between the two men was inevitable even if they both had not been prima donnas. To speak and act for his followers, Lewis had to move toward leftist politics and direct action. Roosevelt, with a different constituency and needing support in Congress, had to continue his delicate balancing act among power blocs. Lewis derided Roosevelt's public role as a great humanitarian and forthright fighter for the underdog; Roosevelt, he said, was weak, tricky, and lacking in conviction. Distrusting the mine leader, and fearing that he would disrupt the coalition, Roosevelt struck out at him at critical moments. And Lewis, fighting for his organization's life during the crucial organizing drives, recoiled from what he called Roosevelt's "catlike scratches."

If farmers lacked such a spectacular leader to dramatize their claims, they presented an even better case than labor of the New Deal's impact on groups. Indeed, rarely has an organization owed its power more directly to governmental action than the strongest farm group, the American Farm Bureau Federation. For the thousands of county farm bureaus that made up the Federation had originally been established as semigovernmental units, and their extension agents took on much of the practical administration of the New Deal farm programs at the same time that they served as unofficial recruiting officers for the Federation. As the farm programs expanded, so did the Federation's membership, which more than doubled between 1933 and 1938.

The Federation's relation to the New Deal was curious: administratively it was geared in with programs, while politically it could operate as an independent force, putting pressure on Roosevelt and Wallace. Other farm groups were active too. The commodity associations burgeoned as the New Deal poured benefits into the hands of woolgrowers, beet sugar raisers, pork producers, cattle raisers, peanut growers, and a host of other groups. And the bigger the association, the more pressure it could turn on Washington.

The situation was duplicated in other sectors of American life. The WPA brought into being the Workers Alliance, whose leaders —some of them members of the Communist party—were agitating noisily for more and bigger work projects. The National Youth Administration was a focus of interest for youth groups. Lending and housing programs stimulated a host of associations linked to these activities. Government lawyers had a large part in forming the National Lawyers' Guild, as a rival group to the conservative American Bar Association.

"You know," Roosevelt said to *Nation* editor Max Lerner in 1938, "this is really a great country. The framework of democracy is so strong and so elastic that it can get along and absorb a Huey Long and a John L. Lewis." A perceptive remark—but an incomplete one. While powerful new forces were straining within the Grand Coalition, while these forces were acting like a centrifuge that spun locally elected congressmen into their separate orbits, forcible leadership was all the more necessary in the White House as a focus for the national interest, as a rallying point for the liberal majority, and as a unifying force for government action. This was the supreme crisis of leadership that Roosevelt faced in the spring of 1938.

TOO LITTLE, TOO LATE

"There is no question," Roosevelt wrote Ambassador Biddle in Warsaw late in 1937, "that the German-Italian-Japanese combination is being amazingly successful—bluff, power, accomplishment or whatever it may be." The President could not say the same about his own foreign policy making. Stalled on the domestic front, he faced formidable congressional opposition in his efforts to awaken the country to the rising dangers abroad. Indeed, Roosevelt's handling of foreign policy making was especially ineffective because there his program and strategy were even more opportunistic than at home.

The President of course had definite opinions about certain aspects of the international situation. The aggressions of Italy, Japan, and Germany were to him simply "armed banditry," and he was not reluctant to say so in private. He wished—again privately—for "more spine" in the British Foreign Office. Squarely opposing the idea of peace at any price, he wanted co-operation among the democratic nations to save the peace. But on crucial operating questions concerning the kind of international co-operation, the extent of German-Italian-Japanese participation in peace programs, and above all the commitments to be undertaken by the United States, he was uncertain. In late 1937 and 1938 he was still searching for a peace formula, with his eye always cocked on the barons of isolationism on Capitol Hill.

Following the disappointing reaction to his "quarantine" speech in October 1937, Roosevelt tried again to take the initiative, although in a different direction. He had long toyed with the idea of sponsoring a dramatic meeting at sea of chiefs of state. Late in October he decided the time was ripe for a somewhat less spectacular move—an Armistice Day meeting of all diplomatic representatives in the White House, to hear a message from the President. Based on suggestions from Under Secretary Sumner Welles, who had been working closely with the President and somewhat independently of Hull, the message would propose a new effort to reach agreement on basic principles of peaceful international relations, on ways of giving all peoples access on equal terms to the world's raw materials, on methods of changing international agreements peacefully, and on the rights and obligations of neutrals in the unhappy event of war. Surely a moderate program—except for the suggestion of treaty revision to remove certain inequities of Versailles.

The plan died a-borning. Hull was utterly opposed to it. He feared that a short day or two of open deliberations would arouse false hopes, unduly provoke the dictators, and produce little practical good. The very features that appealed to the President—a colorful White House assemblage suddenly convened as a world forum for a dramatic Rooseveltian pronouncement—troubled this most undramatic of men. Yet actually, since he believed strongly in the basic principles the President would espouse, the reasons for Hull's opposition lay deeper than this. Part of the trouble was Welles's key role in the project. More important, Hull feared that forthright presidential action would arouse Congress. An old hand at wheedling and appeasing the lawmakers, he was alarmed lest his efforts to bring Congress around to internationalism would be set back. Reluctantly Roosevelt dropped the plan for the time being.

While democratic leaders diddled, dictators acted. In November 1937 they formally established the Rome-Berlin-Tokyo Axis. Japanese troops drove even deeper into China. The Brussels Conference failed utterly to alleviate the crisis in the Far East. Everywhere the arms rush was intensifying. And on November 5 Hitler summoned his generals to the Reichstag, told them of his plans for the conquest of eastern Europe, and ordered them to prepare for inevitable war. The generals knew that Austria was first on their Fuehrer's list.

Shortly after New Year's Day 1938, Roosevelt again turned to his plans for an international conference. This time, however, he followed Hull's suggestion of sounding out Britain first. Prime Minister Chamberlain's reply was like a douche of ice water. The President's plan, he wrote, would cut across his own efforts at "a measure of appeasement" of Italy and Germany. He had been working for months toward this end, he protested, and the stage had been carefully set. Would the President hold up action for a time?

The President would and did. But he was anxious over certain revelations in Chamberlain's letter: the prime minister had indicated that to appease Mussolini he was prepared to recognize Italy's conquest of Ethiopia. Roosevelt promptly urged Chamberlain not to take this step—for it would seriously affect American public opinion. Hull told the British Ambassador bluntly that recognition would be a corrupt bargain that would rouse a feeling of disgust in America.

Chamberlain's rebuff of Roosevelt and the ensuing rift shocked a keen student of world affairs watching from the wings. The rejection of the President's proffered hand, Churchill wrote ten years later, was the loss of the last frail chance to save the world from tyranny otherwise than by war. Yet Chamberlain, unlike Roosevelt, was pursuing a calculated course of action, designed at best to turn the Axis away from attacking the democracies and at least to spar for time to rearm. And a key element in his calculations was that, owing to isolationist feeling in America, Roosevelt could not be relied on to back up his principles with action. "It is always best and safest," Chamberlain said acidly, "to count on nothing from the Americans but words."

As it turned out, Chamberlain later sent a second, more cordial letter to Roosevelt welcoming the President's proposal. The prime minister's hand was forced by his young foreign secretary, Anthony Eden, who had returned to London from a vacation trip to hint at his resignation unless Chamberlain altered his policies. But it was now too late. Hitler was already moving resolutely ahead.

Early in February the Fuehrer consolidated his military position at home by ousting the generals who had spoken out against his war program and appointing himself commander in chief. At once Hitler turned his eye to the south where lay the glittering prize of Austria, portal to Czechoslovakia and the lands beyond. Summoning Austrian Chancellor von Schuschnigg to his retreat just over the border in Berchtesgaden, Hitler scolded and bullied him for hours. "Perhaps I shall be suddenly overnight in Vienna, like a spring storm," he ranted. "Do you want to turn Austria into another Spain?" Schuschnigg gave in to Hitler's demands, but he tried to strengthen his hand by holding a plebiscite on the issue of Austrian independence. This Hitler would not brook. With Mussolini acquiescent and Britain passive, he knew that he could afford to strike. On March 12 German tanks and troops swept across the border, and within a few hours Austria was his.

The news brought a quick flare-up of public opinion in America. Newspaper editorials were indignant. Roosevelt was silent, but a few days later he wrote "Grand!" on a speech of Hull's that served as a kind of official statement. The secretary's statement, however, was the same old litany—a bold stand against "international lawlessness," a warning against isolationism, and a shying away from American commitments.

Roosevelt was silent—but not passive. "I am in the midst of a long process of education—and the process seems to be working slowly but surely," he wrote a friend. But how slow would education be? Always his thoughts returned to the isolationists and their leaders on Capitol Hill. He was amused to read a letter from an Englishman, sent on to him by a Boston schoolmaster.

"That is a delightful letter," he wrote back. "Is it not a funny thing that no European has the foggiest notion of our system of government or of our public thought in regard to European politics? His suggestion that the President should present 500 aeroplanes to Great Britain is particularly joyous. Almost it makes me feel like a dictator! Can you see the expression on the face of the Congress or on the face of the Editors of the Boston Transcript and the Boston Herald if I were to ask for such authority from Congress? I am not even considering what the Boston Irish or the Kansas New Englanders would do. . . ."

Editors and congressmen, Irishmen and Kansans—could they be educated in time by Roosevelt, or would they be educated too late by events?

Events were hurrying on at an ever dizzier pace. By 1938 Spain had become a cockpit of international combat. Tens of thousands of Italian "volunteers," thousands of German officers and technicians, quantities of Axis tanks, artillery, and aircraft braced Franco's attacks. The government, with the help of its International Brigade and later of Soviet arms, had twice staved off heavy attacks on Madrid. But the Loyalists' Aragon offensive failed in the summer of 1937; Italian forces captured Bilbao; Santander and Gijou fell. The League Assembly announced that "veritable foreign army corps" were operating in Spain. By 1938 Loyalist chances looked dim.

Roosevelt from the start had favored the Loyalist cause. He understood the international character of the war; he looked on the Madrid government as the constitutional authority, under the control of a popular-front coalition that included the Communists. Publicly, however, the President was adamantly neutral. His first decisive step—taken significantly during the 1936 campaign—was to put a moral embargo on the export of arms to both sides. When several American exporters readied shiploads of war material, the President asked Congress to extend the arms embargo of the Neutrality Act to Spain. In all Congress only one person—a Farmer-

Laborite—voted against the measure. One load of planes cleared the three-mile limit just in time, only to fall later into Franco's hands.

As the months passed Roosevelt felt increasingly distressed over the course of events in Spain. Noninterference became in effect "non-noninterference," for Franco benefited from the policy. A savage bombing of the Basque shrine city of Guernica by German and Italian planes aroused American opinion. From Spain Ambassador Bowers warned the administration that the embargo was playing into the hands of Franco and Mussolini and Hitler. Ickes was outspokenly indignant about what he called America's shameful role in Spain. In the State Department, Welles was gravely troubled; he saw that a Franco victory would mean a decisive strategic advance for Italy in the Mediterranean. Even some ardent nonInterventionists—men like Norman Thomas and Senator Borah —opposed Roosevelt's policy as unjust and, indeed, unneutral.

There were arguments and forces on the other side. Great Britain, France, and a score of other nations were following a policy ostensibly of strict nonintervention, designed to localize the conflict in Spain. Roosevelt feared to undertake action that cut across these efforts. Any inclination he had to shift policy ran into the stubborn opposition of Hull, backed by a group of career officials who were eager to follow the British lead on the question. Roosevelt's hands were tied also by the sweeping endorsement that administration and Congress had given to neutrality at almost any cost.

Beset by these pressures, Roosevelt wavered. At one point in the spring of 1938 he considered raising the embargo on arms to Madrid. Senator Nye himself had introduced a resolution to raise the embargo, and the New York *Times* reported that Roosevelt was on the verge of acting.

But nothing happened. "A black page in American history," Ickes told the President. Roosevelt argued that lifting the ban would be pointless, for munitions could not go across the Spanish frontier. When Ickes showed how these difficulties could be overcome, the President shifted his ground. He had discussed the matter with congressional leaders that morning, he told Ickes. To raise the embargo would mean the loss of every Catholic vote in the coming fall election, Roosevelt said, and Democratic congressmen opposed it.

So the cat was out of the bag—the "mangiest, scabbiest cat ever," Ickes barked into his diary a few days later. "This proves up to the hilt," Ickes went on, "what so many people have been saying, namely, that the Catholic minorities in Great Britain and America have been dictating the international policy with respect to Spain."

Ickes was only partly right. Not merely the caution of congressmen but Roosevelt's own indecision was involved in policy toward Spain. Indeed, the President wavered again later in 1938 as the rebel forces pressed on to Madrid, and once again Hull had to dissuade his chief from acting. Still, Ickes had put his finger on the heart of the problem. The men on Capitol Hill and the minority groups behind them had their grip on levers of action or obstruction that touched directly the balance of power and the flow of events far outside the country's borders. Unredeemed by decisiveness in the White House, the congressional deadlock on the Potomac cast its shadow across the world.

EIGHTEEN *Fissures in the Party*

T HE SCENE was the livestock pavilion of the University of Wisconsin. The time was late April 1938. Under a huge banner emblazoned with a circle around a cross, a slim, gray-haired man with a boyish face was orating before a rapt audience of several thousand. Football players sporting huge W's patrolled the aisles. The speaker was Governor Philip La Follette of Wisconsin, scion of the great Fighting Bob, brother of young Senator Bob. The occasion was the launching of a new party, National Progressives of America.

By the time La Follette finished, hair tousled and coat awry, reporters were sure that history had been made—perhaps even to the degree it had been at Ripon, Wisconsin, eighty-four years before, when the Republican party was founded. The young Progressive, they said to one another, had hit Roosevelt where it hurt. He had scored New Deal economics and New Deal politics at their weakest points. For ten years, according to La Follette, "the Republicans and the Democrats have been fumbling the ball." The people had had enough of relief and spoon feeding and scarcity economics. They wanted jobs and security. The new party would be no popular front, "no conglomeration of conflicting, opposing forces huddled together for temporary expediency." It was an obvious fling at Roosevelt and his personal coalition. How would the New Deal's chief respond?

The President, it seemed, was inclined to scoff. While the crowd was carried away with the enthusiasm of the moment, he wrote Ambassador William Phillips in Rome, most people seemed to think La Follette's new emblem was just a feeble imitation of the swastika. "All that remains is for some major party to adopt a new form of arm salute. I have suggested the raising of both arms above the head, followed by a bow from the waist. At least this will be good for people's figures!"

Actually Roosevelt had mixed feelings toward the new party. He knew that La Follette had planned his move carefully, with assiduous cultivation of farm and labor leaders. The movement could not be dismissed. Roosevelt hoped, though, that it might serve as a useful warning to conservative Democrats that their party was in danger of losing liberal support. Everything depended on Phil and Bob not going too far To keep them from going too far, Roosevelt told Ickes, he would invite Bob on a Potomac cruise; he would suggest to the Senator that after 1940 he could have the secretaryship of state, and Phil could take his place in the Senate.

It was a typical Rooseveltian stratagem, but it seemed too late for stratagems. Phil went serenely ahead, courting progressive groups and third-party leaders throughout the northern Central states. Nor did his efforts have any discernible influence as a warning to conservative Democrats. In Congress, which adjourned in mid-June, they kept on jabbing and thundering against the New Deal. Aside from the spending bill, the chief accomplishments of the Seventy-fifth Congress had been the revived agricultural program for farmers and the weak wage-hour bill for workers. A new housing program had been authorized, but one that would hardly touch the mass of the "ill-housed." The New Deal, as a program for the general welfare, had been little advanced—certainly not when compared with the glowing promises of January 1937.

Slowly Roosevelt came to his decision—the time had come for a party showdown.

The idea of purging the party of conservative congressmen was not a new one. For months at the White House there had been talk of a purge, especially on the part of Corcoran, Ickes, and Hopkins. But the fact that Roosevelt could embrace this ultimate weapon was a measure of his true feelings in the spring of 1938. Not only was a purge directly contrary to the President's general first-term policy of noninterference in local elections, but even more, it forced him into the posture he hated most—the posture of direct, open hostilities against men who were in his party and some of whom were his friends, of almost complete commitment to a specific method and a definite conception of party.

Only resentment and exasperation of the greatest intensity could have moved Roosevelt to such action, and that was his state of mind in the spring of 1938. Despite his usual surface geniality, for months he had simmered and stewed over the obstructionists who were gutting his program. Again and again in the presence of intimates and even of visitors he struck out at his foes—at the lobbyists who tried to exempt special interests from regulation, at the "yes but fellows" who piously agreed with the need for reform but never agreed with Roosevelt's way of doing it, at the millionaires who found legal devices to avoid taxes, at the columnists and commentators who told lies to scare the people, at the "fat cat" newspaper publishers who ganged up on the administration, and, above all, at the congressmen who had ridden into power on his coattails and now were sabotaging his program.

In a free society, only the last of these were within reach of presidential retaliation. As La Follette fished in troubled political waters and threatened to split the Grand Coalition in June 1938, Roosevelt decided to act.

THE DONKEY AND THE STICK

On a hot night late in June the President fired the opening salvo. In a fireside chat he stated that the Seventy-fifth Congress, elected on a "platform uncompromisingly liberal," had left many things undone. On the other hand, he said, it had done more for the country than any Congress during the 1920's, and he listed a number of its achievements. People had urged him to coast along, enjoy an easy presidency for four years, and not take the party platform too seriously.

"Never in our lifetime has such a concerted campaign of defeatism been thrown at the heads of the President and Senators and Congressmen" as in the case of this Congress. "Never before have we had so many Copperheads" who, as in the War between the States, wanted peace at any price. The President dwelt for a moment on the economic situation. Leaders of business, of labor, and of government had all made mistakes, he asserted. Government's mistake, however, was in failing to pass the farm and wage-hour bills earlier, and in assuming that labor and capital would not make mistakes.

Then Roosevelt got down to the business at hand. The issue in the congressional primaries and elections, he said, was between liberals who saw that new conditions called for new remedies, including government action, and conservatives, who believed that individual initiative and private philanthropy would solve the country's problems and who wanted to return to the kind of government America had had in the 1920's.

"As President of the United States, I am not asking the voters of the country to vote for Democrats next November as opposed to Republicans or members of any other party. Nor am I, as President, taking part in Democratic primaries.

"As the head of the Democratic Party, however, charged with the responsibility of the definitely liberal declaration of principles set forth in the 1936 Democratic platform, I feel that I have every right to speak in those few instances where there may be a clear issue between candidates for a Democratic nomination involving these principles, or involving a clear misuse of my own name.

"Do not misunderstand me. I certainly would not indicate a

preference in a State primary merely because a candidate, otherwise liberal in outlook, had conscientiously differed with me on any single issue. I should be far more concerned with the general attitude of a candidate toward present day problems and his own inward desire to get practical needs attended to in a practical way." And again the President struck out at "yes but fellows."

ROOSEVELT DECLARES WAR ON PARTY REBELS, read the next day's headlines. Yet the declaration of war was an ambiguous one. Politicians anxiously questioned one another. What was the President's test of a conservative? Was it only a vote against the court plan? Would Roosevelt limit himself to speaking out? And what did he mean by his statement that he was acting as party leader rather than as President?

Confusion deepened after Roosevelt left Washington in his air-cooled, ten-car train that would take him on a zigzag route across the nation. Roosevelt seemed to have a different tactic in each state. In Ohio he gave a mild nod of approval to a mild New Dealer, Senator Robert J. Bulkley, who had a primary fight on his hands. In Kentucky the President pulled no punches. Alben Barkley, his stalwart Senate leader, was hard pressed by Governor "Happy" Chandler, who had a big grin, a rousing platform manner, and a firm grip on his political machine. Roosevelt was so eager for Barkley to win and so worried that a defeat would mean Senator Pat Harrison's capture of the Senate leadership that he had even welcomed John L. Lewis's proffer of aid in the race.

Greeting Roosevelt's train, Happy deftly slid into a place next to the President in the parade car and took more than his share of the bows, while Barkley smoldered and Roosevelt showed his usual *sang-froid*. Happy soon got his comeuppance. In a speech showering Barkley with praise the President dismissed Chandler as a young man who would take many years to achieve the experience and knowledge of Alben Barkley. "Any time the President can't knock you out, you're all right," said the irrepressible Happy, who was determined to keep at least a thumb hooked into the President's coattails. But a few hours later Roosevelt shook even the thumb loose by hinting that Chandler had proposed to the White House a deal in judicial appointments in order to get to the Senate.

Having spoken like a lion, the President moved as stealthily as a fox during his next stops. In Oklahoma he mentioned his "old friend" Senator Elmer Thomas but he did not snub Thomas' primary opponent. In Texas he smiled on several liberal congressmen, including Lyndon Johnson and Maury Maverick, and he threw Senator Connally, a foe of the court bill, into an icy rage by announcing from the back platform the appointment to a federal judgeship of a Texan whom Connally had not recommended. In Colorado another court bill opponent, Senator Alva Adams, shifted uneasily from foot to foot while the President elaborately ignored him. But Adams' opponent, who had seemingly launched his campaign with White House blessing, was also ignored. So was Senator Pat McCarran in Nevada, though the agile Pat managed to thrust himself into the Rooseveltian limelight. In California the President mentioned his "old friend" Senator McAdoo, but the situation was topsy-turvy there, for McAdoo's opponent was no tory but a leader of the "$30 every Thursday" movement named Sheridan Downey.

By the time the President had been piped aboard the *Houston,* had made a long sea cruise down through the Panama Canal to Pensacola, and had started back to Washington, some of the primary results were in. Roosevelt could feel well satisfied. Barkley won decisively in Kentucky, as did Thomas in Oklahoma. To be sure, Adams won in Colorado and McCarran was running strong in Nevada, but Roosevelt had not deeply committed himself in these races.

Moreover, the trip across the country had been one more parade of triumph for the President. In Marietta, Ohio, a little old woman symbolized much of the popular feeling when she knelt down and reverently patted the dust where he had left a footprint. The enthusiasm of the crowds bore out the comment of Republican Congressman Bruce Barton that the feeling of the masses toward Roosevelt was the controlling political influence of the time. And Roosevelt's triumph had been a wholly personal one. Farley, who had publicly supported the President after the fireside chat while secretly deploring the purge, was in Alaska. Garner had not met the President in Texas. Editorials deplored the President's meddling in local elections. Cartoonists pictured him as a donkey rider, a club wielder, a pants kicker, a big-game hunter.

Emboldened by his successes, Roosevelt on his way north turned his attention to his number-one target, the doughty and influential Senator Walter George of Georgia. The scene was so dramatic it seemed almost staged. Sitting on the platform with Roosevelt in the little country town of Barnesville was George himself, Lawrence Camp, a diffident young attorney whom the administration had induced to run against the Senator, and a host of nervous Georgia politicians. From the moment he started talking Roosevelt's heavy deliberateness of tone and manner seemed a portent. After dwelling on his many years at Warm Springs, the problems facing the South, and the need for political leadership along liberal lines, Roosevelt turned to the business at hand. He said of George:

"Let me make it clear that he is, and I hope always will be, my personal friend. He is beyond question, beyond any possible question, a gentleman and a scholar. . . ." But he and George simply did not speak the same political language. The test was in the answer to two questions: "First, has the record of the candidate shown, while differing perhaps in details, a constant active fighting attitude in favor of the broad objectives of the party and of the Government as they are constituted today; and secondly, does the candidate really, in his heart, deep down in his heart, believe in those objectives?

"I regret that in the case of my friend, Senator George, I cannot honestly answer either of these questions in the affirmative." A faint chorus of mixed cheers and boos rose from the crowd. George stirred uneasily; Camp sat motionless.

There was more in the speech, as Roosevelt dismissed another candidate, red-gallused, hard-faced, ex-Governor Eugene Talmadge, as a man of panaceas and promises, and roundly praised Camp. But the climax for the crowd came as Roosevelt turned to George and shook hands.

"Mr. President," said the Senator, "I want you to know that I accept the challenge."

"Let's always be friends," Roosevelt replied cheerily.

Next state up was South Carolina, the domain of Cotton Ed Smith. Again Roosevelt displayed his versatility. Smith's opponent, Governor Olin D. Johnston, had launched his campaign in Washington directly after a talk with the President, but now Roosevelt took a subtle approach. Without mentioning Smith by name, he ended a talk in Greenville with the remark, "I don't believe any family or man can live on fifty cents a day—" a fling at Cotton Ed, who was reputed to have said that in South Carolina a man could.

Back in Washington, the President struck the hardest blow of all against his old adversary, the urbane Millard Tydings of Maryland. At a press conference he accused Tydings—and he told reporters to put this in direct quotes—of wanting to run "with the Roosevelt prestige and the money of his conservative Republican friends both on his side." He lined up Maryland politicians behind Tydings' primary opponent, Representative David J. Lewis. He asked former Ambassador to Italy Breckinridge Long, a political leader in the state, to help out financially and personally. And he stumped intensively in Maryland for two days against Tydings during the first week of September. To give his campaign a semblance of party backing, the President got Farley to go with him. The Democratic chairman glumly watched the proceedings. "It's a bust," he told reporters.

A bust it was. During the next weeks Roosevelt's political fortunes reached the lowest point of his presidency.

Smith won decisively in South Carolina. Tydings won by a huge vote in Maryland. Maverick and other Roosevelt men lost in Texas. George came out far in front in Georgia. Talmadge was second, and Camp an ignominious third. Semi- or anti-New Dealers Alva Adams of Colorado, Pat McCarran of Nevada, Augustine Lonergan of Connecticut, all won. "It takes a long, long time to bring the past up to the present," Roosevelt remarked after Smith's victory.

Only one bright spot relieved the dark picture. Earlier in the year Hopkins and Corcoran had induced James H. Fay to enter the primary in Manhattan against the hated John O'Connor, who had used his chairmanship of the Rules Committee to thwart the President. Fay was a good choice: he had impeccable Irish antecedents, a war record, and close ties with a number of Tammany chiefs. Hopkins lined up Labor party support for Fay through La Guardia, and Roosevelt agreed to ask Patterson of the *Daily News* to back the New Deal candidate. Corcoran spent a month in New York running the campaign at the ward and precinct level. When O'Connor began to fight back hard to save his political life, Roosevelt got a reluctant Boss Flynn to help run Fay's campaign. These combined efforts defeated O'Connor by a close vote in mid-September.

By now Democrats and Republicans were locked in battle in hundreds of congressional and a score or two senatorial races. Wracked by internal splits, the Democrats had to face the somber likelihood that they would suffer a drop after the sweep of '36. The Republicans, knowing they had seen the worst and enjoying the brawls in the enemy camp, were jubilant. Some of them, indeed, were cocky to the point of insolence. Backers of a Republican candidate in Wisconsin wired Roosevelt urging him to come to Wisconsin and oppose their man. The President's opposition, they added, would guarantee his election.

Roosevelt ignored such antics, but he could not ignore the strange directions the campaigns were taking. A shift had taken place in the spirit and temper of the people. In many races the issues were not the standard old reliables like prosperity, security, reform, and peace, but vague and fearsome things such as state rights, the "rubber-stamp" Congress, presidential power, the purge itself. In other races candidates for Congress got embroiled in local issues. In South Carolina, for example, Cotton Ed raised the banner of white supremacy, and Johnston, not to be outdone, accused Smith himself of once "voting to let a big buck nigger sit next to your wife or daughter on a train." In Pennsylvania the main issue was not the New Deal but corruption; in Michigan, the sit-down strikes; in California, a state pension plan.

As party leader Roosevelt presumably had some power of campaign direction. But unlike his own presidential campaigns, where he could exploit his unmatched skill at focusing issues and at timing the attack, he lacked control over the situation. Instead of his running the campaigns, the campaigns ran away with him.

He had to spend a good deal of time simply making his position clear. In the last weeks of the campaign he found it necessary to defend Governor Frank Murphy of Michigan against charges that he had treasonably mishandled the sit-down strikes; he had to rebuke Pennsylvania Republicans for charging that he had kept hands off that state because of distaste for the Democrats there; he had to make clear that his silence about Governor Elmer Benson of Minnesota did not mean he was not in favor of Benson; he had to declare his support in California for Downey, victor over McAdoo, as a real liberal, despite Downey's "$30 every Thursday" plank, which Roosevelt opposed; he had to make clear his support of Senator F. Ryan Duffy in Wisconsin; and he had to declare for Governor Lehman and Senator Wagner of New York, candidates for re-election. Putting out campaign brush fires all over the country was no way to leave the President in a commanding position.

On election eve Roosevelt tried to pull the confused situation into focus. He reasserted that the supreme issue was the continuation of the New Deal. After a homely reference to the "dream house" he was building in Hyde Park, he said that a social gain, unlike a house, was not necessarily permanent. The great gains of Theodore Roosevelt and of Wilson, he warned, had evaporated during the subsequent administrations. The President thrust a barbed lance at the opposition. "As of today, Fascism and Communism—and old-line Tory Republicanism—are not threats to the continuation of our form of government. But I venture the challenging statement that if American democracy ceases to move forward as a living force . . . then Fascism and Communism, aided, unconsciously perhaps, by old-line Tory Republicanism, will grow in strength in our land." But political exigencies forced Roosevelt even on a national hookup to devote much of his speech to New York candidates.

The election returns dealt the Democrats a worse blow than Roosevelt had expected. Republican strength in the House almost doubled, rising from 88 to 170, and increased in the Senate by eight. The Republicans lost not a single seat. The liberal bloc in the House was halved. Wagner and Lehman both won in New York, but a brilliant and personable young district attorney, Thomas E. Dewey, came so close to upsetting Lehman that the challenger became a prospect for his party's presidential nomination in 1940. Winning over a dozen governorships, the Republicans offered new faces to the nation—Leverett Saltonstall in Massachusetts, John Bricker in Ohio, Harold Stassen in Minnesota. Taft beat Bulkley in Ohio and took over a Senate seat that he would soon convert into a national rostrum. Philip La Follette lost in Wisconsin, Murphy in Michigan, Earle in Pennsylvania.

Roosevelt tried to make the best of the situation. The New Deal had not been repudiated, he told friends. The trouble lay in party factionalism and local conditions. He pointed to corruption in Massachusetts, a race-track scandal in Rhode Island, a parkway squabble in Connecticut, Boss Frank Hague's dictatorial ways in Jersey City, strikes in the Midwest, poor Democratic candidates elsewhere. The President could point to the fact that, after all, his party still held big majorities in both Houses of Congress. But could he blink the fact that Republicans combined with anti-New Deal Democrats could control the legislature?

"Will you not encounter coalition opposition?" a reporter asked him at the first press conference after the election.

"No, I don't think so," the President answered.

"I do!" his questioner came back pertly, amid laughter.

"The trees are too close to the forest," Roosevelt went on enigmatically.

THE STRUGGLE FOR POWER

The reporter was right, and Roosevelt knew that he was right. The Republicans were making no secret of their plans to besiege the New Deal through the conservative Democrats in Congress. But the President had an eye on the forest too. The critical situation in Europe would force a political reordering at home. And he knew he would have strong cards to play against the conservatives in 1940. Meantime he showed his cheerful visage to the world. He even jested about the visage that some newspapers had given him.

"You undergraduates who see me for the first time," he told a delighted student audience at Chapel Hill in December, "have read your newspapers and heard on the air that I am, at the very least, an ogre—a consorter with Communists, a destroyer of the rich, a breaker of our ancient traditions. Some of you think of me perhaps as the inventor of the economic royalist, of the wicked utilities, of the money changers of the Temple. You have heard for six years that I was about to plunge the Nation into war; that you and your little brothers would be sent to the bloody fields of battle in Europe; that I was driving the Nation into bankruptcy; and that I breakfasted every morning on a dish of 'grilled millionaire.'" The crowd guffawed.

"Actually I am an exceedingly mild mannered person—a practitioner of peace, both domestic and foreign, a believer in the capitalistic system, and for my breakfast a devotee of scrambled eggs."

Against the advice of Garner and other of his "antediluvian friends" in Congress, as he called them, Roosevelt stood firm on his New Deal policies. Before the legislators in January 1939, he defended his program of social and economic reform. To be sure, he justified that program partly as an aid to national defense, and he stated that the country had "passed the period of internal conflict in the launching of our program of social reform." But he went on to call for the releasing of the nation's full energies "to invigorate the processes of recovery in order to preserve our reforms, and to give every man and woman who wants to work a real job at a living

Another Myth Exploded

FDR "SAYS" IT IS NOT AT ALL TRUE THAT HE "HAS GRILLED MILLIONAIRE FOR BREAKFAST;" THAT WHAT HE REALLY LIKES IS SCRAMBLED EGGS.

Dec. 6, 1938, Quincy Scott, Portland *Oregonian*

wage." And he called again for the measures Congress had denied him the year before, including reorganization.

Nor did Roosevelt indicate any compromise in a fighting party speech he gave to a Jackson Day dinner a few days later. He welcomed the return of the Republicans to a position where they could no longer excuse themselves for not having a program on the ground they had too few votes. He charged that during recent years "Republican impotence has caused powerful interests, opposed to genuine democracy, to push their way into the Democratic party, hoping to paralyze it by dividing its councils." He called on Democrats to stick together and to line up with those from other parties and with independents in a firm alliance. He prophesied that the Republican leadership, conservative at heart, would "still seek to run with the hare and hunt with the hounds, talking of balanced budgets out of one side of its mouth and in favor of opportunist raids on the Treasury out of the other." And he appealed to the memory of Andrew Jackson to keep the party a liberal party, not a Democratic Tweedledum to a Republican Tweedledee.

The President's major appointments reflected his tenacity of purpose. To the consternation of the business community Hopkins succeeded Roper as Secretary of Commerce. The priestlike Murphy of Michigan took Cummings' place as Attorney General. Felix Frankfurter, after serving six years as a recruiting sergeant for the New Deal, was appointed to Holmes's old and Cardozo's recent seat on the Supreme Court. And William O. Douglas took Brandeis' place on the high bench. So in the New Deal's sixth year there were secure liberal majorities in both cabinet and court.

But not in Congress. As the 1939 session got under way, the congressional threat to New Deal programs became more and more apparent.

The conservative coalition on the Hill would not, of course, abolish the New Deal, even if it wished to, for it could not command two-thirds majorities to override Roosevelt's vetoes. But it could stop the extension of the New Deal into new and controversial fields. To be sure, Congress passed a cut-down reorganization bill, a revised and liberalized social security measure, and several other administration measures. When it came, however, to spending programs aimed at fulfilling the President's promises of recovery, the legislators balked. Bills to finance self-liquidation projects and to lend eight hundred million dollars on housing projects passed the Senate but failed in the House amidst a general denunciation of the relief program. Relief appropriations, too, were pared sharply.

The inevitable consequence of this political stalemate was economic stalemate. With New Deal reforms secured now by a liberalized court and by determined presidential backing, investors were still immobilized largely by their fears of the government. But Congress would not tolerate a large-scale spending program, even if Roosevelt proposed it. The recovery policy was caught in dead center. Although business conditions had improved markedly since the year before, dead center still meant eight to ten million unemployed.

Some congressmen, however, were not satisfied even with stalemating the New Deal. They sought to dismantle it. And in their attempt they turned to the three classic weapons of congressional usurpation of executive power.

Perhaps the most potent of these weapons was the power to investigate. During Roosevelt's first term friendly legislators like Senator Black had used this power to arouse public opinion behind New Deal measures. The President was strong enough almost single-handed to balk hostile probes, as in the case of Tydings. But now, in his second term, the situation was reversed. At the start of the 1939 session Garner in a cabinet meeting told Roosevelt bluntly that the opposition was planning to investigate the WPA and other agencies. Something should be done about it, he said. "Jack," the President answered, "you are talking to eleven people who can't do anything about it." It was up to the congressional leaders, including Garner, he said. It was a clear indication of the extent to which Roosevelt's resources of personal influence had been drained off midway through the second term.

Even in the case of Martin Dies, the square-faced, hulking young Texan who ran the House Un-American Activities Committee, Roosevelt had to act cautiously. He detested Dies's fishing expeditions and he knew the political dangers in Dies's jabs at Ickes, Hopkins, Miss Perkins, and other New Dealers as being soft toward Communists. But the President, aside from one indignant press statement, did not risk an open counterattack against his foes. Asked by reporters to comment on the Texan's charge that Roosevelt was not co-operating with him, the President answered only with an elaborate "Ho hum." Incensed over Dies's treatment of witnesses, he protested indirectly to another committee member. When Ickes was ready to cannonade Dies with a speech entitled, "Playing with Loaded Dies," Early telephoned that the President said, "For God's sake don't do it!" Roosevelt hoped he could head Dies off by maneuvering through his leaders on Capitol Hill. But this indirection, which had worked so well during the first term, no longer seemed to turn the trick. Dies got a huge appropriation in 1939 and kept on playing ducks and drakes with the issue of Communism.

A second classic instrument of congressional attack was control over hiring administrative personnel, and here again Congress lived up to tradition. The most obvious of these controls over hiring was the old practice of senatorial courtesy, by which senators agree, in a kind of unwritten mutual defense pact, to hold up any presidential nomination when the nominee is "personally obnoxious"— i.e., a member of a hostile political faction—to one of their colleagues. In January 1939 Roosevelt deliberately flouted the rule by nominating as federal judge a Virginian who was friendly to the governor of that state but not to Senators Glass and Byrd. The President's nominee was rejected. Angry and public exchanges between Roosevelt and Glass followed, but when the dust settled, senatorial courtesy stood intact.

A third means of congressional control was the legislative power to appropriate funds annually for the bureaucracy. To the extent it dared, the coalition cut down on general funds for agency programs, but it did not dare go too far because even Republicans and anti-New Deal Democrats were sensitive to the reaction of groups benefiting from the programs. What the coalition could and did do was to cut funds for those functions behind which no congressional bloc would rally, but which in the long run might critically influence the durability and impact of the programs— namely, planning, research, statistical and economic analysis, scientific investigation, administrative management, information, staffing.

The heart of the situation was this: By 1939 coalition leaders in Congress had left their defensive posture of '37 and '38 and had moved openly to the attack. Where once they had been content to stop the New Deal from expanding, now they were trying to disrupt major federal programs or to divert them to their own purposes. Where once they had fought against presidential control over the legislative branch, now they were extending their own controls over the executive branch.

A chief executive's power to control his own establishment is always in jeopardy. At best, certain parts of the disheveled and straggling bureaucracy will escape his control if only because of its vast size. Many bureaucrats are holdovers from previous regimes and respond to ideologies and programs of the past. Such officials the President usually can remove if he knows about them; but some of them may be beyond his reach. Early in his first term Roosevelt sacked a holdover commissioner of the Federal Trade Commission mainly because the man was utterly out of sympathy with the New Deal, but the Supreme Court later ruled that his power to remove independent commissioners simply on the grounds that they differed with him over policy depended on Congress. So, too, many officials were less responsive to the change in presidential leadership than they were to the narrow professionalism and traditions of bureaucratic cliques.

Friction within government is inevitable when men are ambitious for themselves and passionately consecrated to their programs, and this was especially true of Roosevelt's jostling, bickering lieutenants. From the start fierce conflicts swept his top officialdom. The peppery, cantankerous Ickes was a ceaseless generator of friction; he jousted with Hugh Johnson, Morgenthau, Miss Perkins, Hopkins, and others, and his battle with Wallace culminated in a blazing face-to-face quarrel where charges of lying and disloyalty to the President were tossed about. Personal and administrative differences among the three TVA board members became so acute that Roosevelt had to hold long hearings in the White House and, in the end, ousted the chairman. Other rivalries that smoldered under the surface were fair game for newspaper columnists and cocktail party gossips.

Roosevelt's personality and administrative methods encouraged this turbulence. He delegated power so loosely that bureaucrats found themselves entangled in lines of authority and stepping on one another's toes. Despite his public disapproval of open brawls, Roosevelt actually tolerated them and sometimes even seemed to enjoy them. He saw some virtues in pitting bureaucrat against bureaucrat in a competitive struggle. The very nature of the New Deal programs with their improvised, experimental, and often contradictory qualities was another source of discord.

Criticism of Roosevelt's administrative methods waxed during his second term. This criticism buttressed the demands of conservatives for "less government in business, and more business in government." It was also a handy tool for congressmen bent on extending their own controls over the bureaucrats. But not all close students of the peculiar claims and needs of the American political system agreed with this criticism of Roosevelt as an administrator.

Again and again Roosevelt flouted the central rule of administration that the boss must co-ordinate the men and agencies under him —that he must make a "mesh of things." But given the situation he faced, Roosevelt had good reasons for his disdain of copybook maxims. For one thing, too much emphasis on rigid organization and channels of responsibility and control might have suffocated the freshness and vitality he loved. His technique of fuzzy delegation, as Arthur Schlesinger, Jr., has said, "often provided a testing of initiative, competence and imagination which produced far better results than playing safe by the book." Characteristically, Roosevelt himself took the burden of salving the aches and lacerations that resulted from his method of administration.

Disdaining abstract organization, Roosevelt looked at administration in terms of people. It was his sensitivity to people in all their subtle shadings and complexities that stamped him as a genius in government. He impressed them by his incredible knowledge of small details of their job; he invigorated them by his readiness to back them up when the going got rough. Yet he was no sugary dispenser of lavish praise. One of his political lieutenants never got a comment on her work, but she was conscious of "warm, constant, and continuous support and a feeling that he liked me, had confidence in my ideas and was sometimes amused at my 'goings-on' as I was myself."

One reason, then, for Roosevelt's quixotic direction was that it quickened energies and incited ideas in musty offices of government. But there were other reasons.

Again and again Roosevelt put into the same office or job men who differed from each other in temperament and viewpoint. He gave Moley and later Welles important State Department tasks that overlapped those of Hull; he divided authority in the NRA between Hugh Johnson and the general counsel, Donald Richberg; he gave his current Secretary of War, Harry Woodring, an assistant secretary who was often at odds with his chief; he gave both Ickes and Hopkins control over public works, both Ickes and Wallace control over conservation and power, both Farley and a variety of other presidential politicians control over patronage and other political functions.

Upsie Daisy!, March 28, 1935, C. K. Berryman, Washington *Star*

Roosevelt followed this seemingly weird procedure in part because it fell in naturally with his own personality. He disliked being completely committed to any one person. He enjoyed being at the center of attention and action, and the system made him the focus through which the main lines of action radiated. His facility at role-taking enabled him to deal separately with a variety of people at maximum advantage. His administrative methods tended to keep him well informed about administrative politics, too, for his bickering lieutenants were quick to bring him the various aspects of the situation.

The main reason for Roosevelt's methods, however, involved a tenacious effort to keep control of the executive branch in the face of the centrifugal forces of the American political system. By establishing in an agency one power center that counteracted another, he made each official more dependent on White House support; the President in effect became the necessary ally and partner of each. He lessened bureaucratic tendencies toward self-aggrandizement; he curbed any attempt to gang up on him. He was, in effect, adapting the old method of divide and conquer to his own purposes.

The problem, from Roosevelt's standpoint, was one of power rather than of narrow efficiency. His technique was curiously like that of Joseph Stalin, who used the overlapping delegation of function, a close student of his methods has said, to prevent "any single chain of command from making major decisions without confronting other arms of the state's bureaucracy and thus bringing the issues into the open at a high level." Roosevelt, like Stalin, was a political administrator in the sense that his first concern was power —albeit for very different ends.

How deliberate a policy was this on Roosevelt's part? While he never formalized his highly personal methods of political administration and indeed ignored all abstract formulations of administrative problems, he probably was well aware of the justification of his methods in terms of his need to keep control of his establishment. Certainly he did not embrace unorthodox managerial techniques out of ignorance of orthodox ones. His navy and gubernatorial experience had given him a close understanding of basic management problems. His recommendations to Congress for administrative reorganization were right out of the copybook, as was his request, never granted, for the right of item veto over appropriations. Many of his subordinates came to respect his methods even while they were disconcerted by them. Harold Smith, who became budget director in 1939, found the President an erratic administrator. But years later, as the size and shape of Roosevelt's job fell into better perspective, Smith told Robert Sherwood that Roose velt may have been one of history's greatest administrative geniuses. "He was a real *artist* in government," Smith concluded.

Yet a final estimate of Roosevelt's administrative role must also include the enormous amount of wasted energy, delays, and above all the attrition of Roosevelt's programs—especially the recovery program—caused by his methods. Good direction not only stimulates the ideas and energies of men; it also brings them into constructive harmony. What then can be said about Roosevelt's toleration of incessant tension and friction among his lieutenants? Certainly the main effect of this intramural sharpshooting was more destructive than constructive. Certainly Ickes' neurotic fight to wrest Forestry from Wallace during the reorganization battle was an example of wasted energies with no gain. That the New Deal often faltered in execution the President himself recognized. If, as has been said, the only genuine test of efficiency is survival, the Roosevelt recession, the continuing unemployment of 1939, and the bleeding of the President's recovery proposals in 1939 raise a serious question about the administrative adequacy of his direction.

Inevitably Roosevelt's practices produced hurt and bewilderment among his subordinates. "You are a wonderful person but you are one of the most difficult men to work with that I have ever known," Ickes blurted out on one occasion.

"Because I get too hard at times?" Roosevelt asked.

"No, you never get too hard but you won't talk frankly even with people who are loyal to you and of whose loyalty you are fully convinced. You keep your cards close up against your belly. . . ." If the President would confide in his advisers, Ickes went on, their advice would prevent him from making mistakes. Roosevelt took the criticism with good humor—but he did not change his methods.

On another occasion Democratic politicians were pressing Roosevelt to appoint a member of the Democratic National Committee as a federal judge, while the Justice Department was backing a government attorney. The pushing and hauling had reached a pitch when the President summoned representatives of both sides to the White House. They stated their cases.

"I'll tell you what I'm going to do," Roosevelt said. "I'm not going to take either man." He named his choice. "Have either of you ever heard of him?" Neither had.

"Well," the President went on. "His father was a remarkable man. Once the old man was sitting on his yacht and a big wave swept him off. Then another big wave came along and swept him back on. A remarkable man!" And that was all the explanation his visitors ever got—but Roosevelt's appointment turned out to be an excellent one.

As an artist in government Roosevelt worked with the materials at hand. The materials were not, of course, adequate. A final evaluation of Roosevelt as administrator must turn on his capacity to devise new materials out of which to fashion an administrative leadership that could stimulate men while keeping them in harness. In the end his capacity for effective administrative leadership turned on his capacity for creative political leadership.

ROOSEVELT AS A PARTY LEADER

The New Deal, wrote historian Walter Millis toward the end of 1938, "has been reduced to a movement with no program, with no effective political organization, with no vast popular party strength behind it, and with no candidate." The passage of time has not invalidated this judgment. But it has sharpened the question: Why did the most gifted campaigner of his time receive and deserve this estimate only two years after the greatest election triumph in recent American history?

The answer lay partly in the kind of political tactics Roosevelt had used ever since the time he started campaigning for president. In 1931 and 1932, he had, like any ambitious politician, tried to win over Democratic leaders and groups that embraced a great variety of attitudes and interests. Since the Democratic party was deeply divided among its sectional and ideological splinter groups, Roosevelt began the presidential campaign of 1932 with a mixed and ill-assorted group backing. Hoover's unpopularity with many elements in his own party brought various Republican and independent groups to Roosevelt's support. Inevitably the mandate of 1932 was a highly uncertain one, except that the new President must do something—anything—to cope with the Depression.

Responding to the crisis, Roosevelt assumed in his magnificent way the role of leader of all the people. Playing down his party support he mediated among a host of conflicting interest groups, political leaders, and ideological proponents. During the crisis atmosphere of 1933 his broker leadership worked. He won enormous popularity, he put through his crisis program, he restored the morale of the whole nation. The congressional elections of 1934 were less a tribute to the Democratic party than a testament of the President's wide support.

Then his ill-assorted following began to unravel at the edges. The right wing rebelled, labor erupted, Huey Long and others stepped up their harrying attacks. As a result of these political developments, the cancellation of part of the New Deal by the courts, and the need to put through the waiting reform bills, Roosevelt made a huge, sudden, and unplanned shift leftward. The shift put him in the role of leader of a great, though teeming and amorphous, coalition of center and liberal groups; it left him, in short, as party chief. From mid-1935 to about the end of 1938 Roosevelt deserted his role as broker among all groups and assumed the role of a party leader commanding his Grand Coalition of the center and left.

This role, too, the President played magnificently, most notably in the closing days of the 1936 campaign. During 1937 he spoke often of Jefferson and Jackson and of other great presidents who, he said, had served as great leaders of popular majorities. During 1938 he tried to perfect the Democratic party as an instrument of a popular majority. But in the end the effort failed—in the court fight, the defeat of effective recovery measures, and the party purge.

That failure had many causes. The American constitutional system had been devised to prevent easy capture of the government by popular majorities. The recovery of the mid-1930's not only made the whole country more confident of itself and less dependent on the leader in the White House, but it strengthened and emboldened a host of interest groups and leaders, who soon were pushing beyond the limits of New Deal policy and of Roosevelt's leadership. Too, the party system could not easily be reformed or modernized, and the anti-third-term custom led to expectations that Roosevelt was nearing the end of his political power. But the failure also stemmed from Roosevelt's limitations as a political strategist.

The trouble was that Roosevelt had assumed his role as party or majority leader not as part of a deliberate, planned political strategy but in response to a conjunction of immediate developments. As majority leader he relied on his personal popularity, on his *charisma* or warm emotional appeal. He did not try to build up a solid, organized mass base for the extended New Deal that he projected in the inaugural speech of 1937. Lacking such a mass base, he could not establish a rank-and-file majority group in Congress to push through his program. Hence the court fight ended as a congressional fight in which the President had too few reserve forces to throw into the battle.

Roosevelt as party leader, in short, never made the strategic commitment that would allow a carefully considered, thorough, and long-term attempt at party reorganization. The purge marked the bankruptcy of his party leadership. For five years the President had made a fetish of his refusal to interfere in "local" elections. When candidates—many of them stalwart New Dealers—had turned desperately to the White House for support, McIntyre or Early had flung at them the "unbreakable" rule that "the President takes no part in local elections." When the administration's good friend Key Pittman had faced a coalition of Republicans and McCarran

Democrats in 1934, all Roosevelt could say was "I wish to goodness I could speak out loud in meeting and tell Nevada that I am one thousand per cent for you!" but an "imposed silence in things like primaries is one of the many penalties of my job." When cabinet members had asked during the 1934 elections if they could make campaign speeches, Roosevelt had said, No, except in their own states.

After all this delicacy Roosevelt in 1938 completely reversed himself and threw every ounce of the administration's political weight —money, propaganda, newspaper influence, federal jobholders as well as his own name—into local campaigns in an effort to purge his foes. He mainly failed, and his failure was due in large part to his earlier policy. After five years of being ignored by the White House, local candidates and party groups were not amenable to presidential control. Why should they be? The White House had done little enough for them.

The execution of the purge in itself was typical of Roosevelt's improvising methods. Although the problem of party defections had been evident for months and the idea of a purge had been taking shape in the winter of 1938, most of the administration's efforts were marked by hurried, inadequate, and amateurish maneuvers at the last minute. In some states the White House interfered enough to antagonize the opponent within the party but not enough to insure his defeat. Roosevelt's own tactics were marked by a strange combination of rashness and irresolution, of blunt face-to-face encounters and wily, back-scene stratagems.

But Roosevelt's main failure as party leader lay not in the purge. It involved the condition of the Democratic party in state after state six years after he took over as national Democratic chief. Pennsylvania, for example, was the scene of such noisy brawling among labor, New Dealers, and old-line Democrats that Roosevelt himself compared it to Dante's Inferno. A bitter feud wracked the Democracy in Illinois. The Democrats in Wisconsin, Nebraska, and Minnesota were still reeling under their ditchings by the White House in 1934 and 1936. The party in California was split among organization Democrats, $30 every Thursday backers, and a host of other factions.

In New York the condition of the Democratic party was even more significant, for Roosevelt had detailed knowledge of politics in his home state and had no inhibitions about intervening there. He intervened so adroitly and indirectly in the New York City mayoralty election of 1933 that politicians were arguing years later as to which Democratic faction he had aided, or whether he was intent mainly on electing La Guardia. In 1936 he encouraged the formation of the Labor party in New York State to help his own re-election, and he pooh-poohed the arguments of Farley, Flynn, and other Democrats that the Labor party would some day turn against the state Democracy—as indeed it later did. By 1938 the Democratic party in New York State was weaker and more faction-ridden than it had been for many years.

It was characteristic of Roosevelt to interpret the 1938 election setbacks largely in terms of the weaknesses of local Democratic candidates and leaders. Actually the trouble lay much deeper. The President's failure to build a stronger party system at the grass roots, more directly responsive to national direction and more closely oriented around New Deal programs and issues, left a political vacuum that was rapidly filled by power groupings centered on state and local leaders holding office or contending for office. Roosevelt and his New Deal had vastly strengthened local party groups in the same way they had organized interest groups. And just as, nationally, the New Deal jolted interest groups out of their lethargy and mobilized them into political power groups that threatened to disrupt the Roosevelt coalition, so the New Deal stimulated local party groups to throw off the White House apron strings.

"If our beloved leader," wrote William Allen White to Farley early in the second term, "cannot find the least common multiple between John Lewis and Carter Glass he will have to take a maul and crack the monolith, forget that he had a party and build his policy with the pieces which fall under his hammer." The perceptive old Kansan's comment was typical of the hopes of many liberals of the day. The President had pulled so many rabbits out of his hat. Could he not produce just one more?

The purge indicated that he could not. The hat was empty. But White's suggestion posed the cardinal test of Roosevelt as party leader. How much leeway did the President have? Was it ever possible for him to build a stronger party? Or did the nature of the American party system, and especially the Democratic party, preclude the basic changes that would have been necessary to carry through the broader New Deal that the President proclaimed in his second-term inaugural?

On the face of it the forces of inertia were impressive. The American party system does not lend itself easily to change. In its major respects the national party is a holding company for complex and interlacing clusters of local groups revolving around men holding or contending for innumerable state and local offices—governors, sheriffs, state legislators, mayors, district attorneys, United States senators, county commissioners, city councilmen, and so on, all strung loosely together by party tradition, presidential leadership, and, to some extent, common ideas. As long as the American constitutional system creates electoral prizes to hold and contend for in the states and localities, the party is likely to remain undisciplined and decentralized.

Long immersed in the local undergrowth of American politics, Roosevelt was wholly familiar with the obstacles to party change. His refusal to break with some of the more unsavory local bosses like Hague and Kelly is clear evidence that he had no disposition to undertake the most obvious kind of reform. Perhaps, though, the President underestimated the possibility of party invigoration from the top.

Some New Dealers, worried by the decay of the Democratic party as a bulwark for progressive government, wanted to build up "presidential" factions pledged to the New Deal, factions that could lift the party out of the ruck of local bickering and orient it toward its national program. Attempts to build such presidential factions were abortive. They might have succeeded, however, had the President given them direction and backing. The New Deal had stimulated vigorous new elements in the party that put programs before local patronage, that were chiefly concerned with national policies of reform and recovery. By joining hands with these elements, by exploiting his own popularity and his control over the national party machinery, the President could have challenged anti-New Deal factions and tried to convert neutralists into backers of the New Deal.

Whether such an attempt would have succeeded cannot be answered because the attempt was never made. Paradoxically enough, however, the purge itself indicates that a long-run, well-organized effort might have worked in many states. For the purge did succeed under two conditions—in a Northern urban area, where there was some planning rather than total improvisation, and in those Southern states where the White House was helping a well-entrenched incumbent rather than trying to oust a well-entrenched opponent. The first was the case of O'Connor, the second the cases of Pepper and of Barkley. Indeed, the results of the purge charted a rough line between the area within the presidential reach and the area beyond it. Undoubtedly the former area would have been much bigger had Roosevelt systematically nourished New Deal strength within the party during his first term.

But he did not. The reasons that the President ignored the potentialities of the great political organization he headed were manifold. He was something of a prisoner of the great concessions he had made to gain the 1932 nomination, including the admission of Garner and other conservatives to the inner circle. His first-term successes had made his method of personal leadership look workable; overcoming crisis after crisis through his limitless resource-fulness and magnetism, Roosevelt did not bother to organize the party for the long run. As a politician eager to win, Roosevelt was concerned with his own political and electoral standing at what-ever expense to the party. It was much easier to exploit his own political skill than try to improve the rickety, sprawling party or-ganization.

The main reason, however, for Roosevelt's failure to build up the party lay in his unwillingness to commit himself to the full im-plications of party leadership, in his eternal desire to keep open alternative tactical lines of action, including a line of retreat. The personal traits that made Roosevelt a brilliant tactician—his dex-terity, his command of a variety of roles, his skill in attack and de-fense, above all his personal magnetism and *charisma*—were not the best traits for hard, long-range purposeful building of a strong popular movement behind a coherent political program. The latter would have demanded a continuing intellectual and political com-mitment to a set strategy—and this kind of commitment Roosevelt would not make.

He never forgot the great lesson of Woodrow Wilson, who got too far ahead of his followers. Perhaps, though, he never appreci-ated enough Wilson's injunction that "if the President leads the way, his party can hardly resist him." If Roosevelt had led and or-ganized the party toward well-drawn goals, if he had aroused and tied into the party the masses of farmers and workers and reliefers and white-collar workers and minority religious and racial groups, if he had met the massed power of group interests with an organ-ized movement of his own, the story of the New Deal on the do-mestic front during the second term might have been quite different.

Thus Roosevelt can be described as a great party leader only if the term is rigidly defined. On the one hand he tied the party, loosely perhaps, to a program; he brought it glorious victories; he helped point it in new ideological directions. On the other hand, he subordinated the party to his own political needs; he failed to exploit its full possibilities as a source of liberal thought and action; and he left the party, at least at its base, little stronger than when he became its leader.

Yet in an assessment of his party leadership there is a final argu-ment in Roosevelt's defense. Even while the New Deal was run-ning out domestically, new problems and new forces were coming into national and world focus. Whatever the weaknesses of his shiftiness and improvising, these same qualities gave him a flexibil-ity of maneuver to meet new conditions. That flexibility was des-perately needed as 1938 and 1939 brought crisis after crisis in world affairs.

NINETEEN

Diplomacy:
Pinpricks and Protest

During the swirling events of his second term, the President seemed to yearn even more for stability and fixity in his immediate surroundings. He still began his day around eight with breakfast in bed, a brief health checkup by his physician, Admiral Ross T. McIntyre, and a quick search through half a dozen newspapers—the New York *Times* and *Herald Tribune,* Baltimore *Sun,* Chicago *Tribune,* Washington *Post,* and Washington *Times-Herald*—with special attention to the White House stories and the editorial page. While he was still in bed or dressing, his secretaries and perhaps a cabinet member or congressman would come in for a somewhat helter-skelter and jocular parley on matters due to come up during the day. Wheeled to his office around 10:30, the President would begin a series of short appointments that stretched through the lunch hour and into the afternoon. Then came dictation time; when the mail basket was especially high the President might return to it in the evening. He got through an immense correspondence by keeping his letters brief. "Two short sentences will generally answer any known letter," he once instructed his son James.

The President's workrooms remained much the same through the years, except that his desk became increasingly cluttered by little figures, animals, lighters, flags, and the like. He seemed to look on these gadgets as old friends he hated to part with. The room that best reflected Roosevelt's personality was not his office in the executive wing of the White House but his study in the Oval Room on the second floor—a comfortable room with dark green curtains and white walls and full of chintz-covered furniture, family mementos, piles of books, stamp albums, Currier & Ives prints. With its naval paintings and ship models—the latter on stands, in bottles, or propped up where space allowed—the room had a decided navy air. Yet it was the nostalgic air of Yankee clippers and heroic encounters of the past, not one that bespoke the feverish naval race, the mammoth battleships, dirty tankers, and submarine packs of a world preparing for war.

Although he was now entering his late fifties, Roosevelt physically seemed to have changed little during his five or six years in the White House. At times his face seemed drawn and gray and then he seemed older, but such times usually followed the head colds that plagued him relentlessly in Washington. A few days of rest and sun at Warm Springs or on a cruise would erase the lines of care and fatigue, and his tanned face would look much as it had years before. The President had had no serious illness; in 1938 he suffered a fainting spell one evening at Hyde Park but he recovered almost immediately.

There was a kind of fixity in Roosevelt's immediate official circle too. In 1938 Early, McIntyre, Missy Le Hand, and Grace Tully were still in faithful attendance. James Roosevelt's service as a secretary ended in mid-1938 when he went to the Mayo Clinic to be treated for gastric ulcers. The President's military aide, Pa Watson, so won the hearts of Roosevelt and his secretaries that he stayed on as a member of the secretariat. The Reorganization Act of 1939 permitted the President to add six presidential assistants with the much-advertised "passion for anonymity," but even so he filled these places slowly.

Roosevelt's relationship with his staff preserved the dignity of his office and person while also permitting boisterous jokes and a light playfulness. He was forever deprecating Watson's fishing and hunting exploits and laying election or other bets with Early or McIntyre. Shortly after the Munich crisis, from North Carolina where he had gone to rest because of lung lesions, McIntyre wrote Missy Le Hand a note that was a take-off on the kind of letters that flooded the White House. The President rose to the occasion:

My dear Mr. McIntyre:

I am often touched, but seldom have I been so touched as by your letter to Miss Le Hand. It was one of a very small number of letters which occasionally she shows to me. Both of us were dissolved in tears.

Your one hundred per cent support in the mountains of North Carolina means more to me than carrying Vermont.

I am glad that you and your good wife are church-going people. That will keep you both from drink and from evil ways.

I hope that you and your family have not been seriously hurt by the Republican depression and that you are able to buy shoes and stockings for the children.

You are such a fine citizen that if we have to go to war with Hitler I am sure you will be the first to enlist.

Your Friend,
Franklin D. Roosevelt

Nor did foreign crisis bring any major change in the President's working habits. He still conducted business in a flurry of telephone calls, personal conferences, formal correspondence cleared with appropriate agencies, informal letters cleared with no one, chits to secretaries and cabinet officers, evening conferences. Ordinarily Roosevelt worked closely with Hull, and the two men—the one flexible, fast-moving, resourceful; the other dogged, cautious, rigid—complemented each other nicely. But as usual, Roosevelt would not confine himself within administrative channels. He often communicated directly with the icy, hardheaded Welles, with the talented Berle, with a host of ambassadors and ministers, with the Pope, with old friends at home like Cox and Baruch, with countless other friends abroad. Knowing the distant ramifications of foreign policy, searching for ideas and expedients, he discussed the world situation with Ickes and Hopkins and Wallace as well as with the State Department men.

The foreign policies that emerged from this welter were the product of no single person, although the President dominated the process. Indeed, they were more a simple response to events abroad than to a set plan or program of foreign policy making at home. Gossipy little notes from diplomats, long letters by clipper pouch, formal pronunciamentos by foreign leaders, urgent cables picked up by chattering instruments, decoded, mimeographed, and stamped "Secret and Confidential"—these brought the news of ceaselessly changing affairs abroad. Still lacking a firm strategy, Roosevelt and his policy makers struggled in the second half of his second term to divine the meaning of affairs and to fashion a role for the most powerful democracy on earth.

The tangled strands of history allow for little neatness. There was never a sharp turning point when Roosevelt's absorption with domestic matters left off and his concern for foreign affairs began. Despite the President's later talk about shifting roles from "Dr. New Deal" to "Dr. Win the War," the fitful rush of events would allow no simple shift. While Roosevelt was struggling with recession in March 1938, the Nazis overran Austria. While he was still trying to purge conservative Democrats later that year, Hitler thrust into the Sudetenland. While the President was jousting with a rebellious Congress early in 1939, Hitler swallowed the rest of Czechoslovakia and turned his eyes in new directions.

Despite the isolationist tendencies of the early New Deal, the President had never ignored the rest of the world. And now, midway through his second term, he would not allow the roar of events abroad to drown out his liberal projects at home. How to build a viable foreign policy and yet sustain the New Deal, all in a context of fast-moving events abroad and changing economic and political conditions at home—this was the central job in the latter part of his second term, and one that would challenge even Roosevelt's political dexterity and resourcefulness.

MUNICH: NO RISKS, NO COMMITMENTS

A month after seizing Austria, Hitler appealed to his people for another four years of power to consolidate the gains of the new *Gross-Deutschland.* On April 11, 1938, it was announced that a gratifying 99 per cent of the people—including Austrians—approved. Once again the Fuehrer moved fast. Ten days later he ordered his generals to draw up new plans for aggression.

Who could doubt where he would strike next? Czechoslovakia now lay like a blunt wedge driven into the heart of the new Germany. Czechoslovakia was both spawn and symbol of Versailles, a proud democracy, a buttress of the League of Nations, an ally of France and Russia, a small nation but well armed and supplied behind natural defenses, and a nation, in the Fuehrer's eyes, of Slav subhumans. As usual Hitler brought to his strategy a superb combination of military, diplomatic, and psychological power.

In Czechoslovakia the Fuehrer had an immensely useful tool for his ambitions—the minority of about three million Sudeten Germans who had long been demanding more autonomy from Prague. For several years he had been subsidizing the Nazi leader of the Sudetens, Konrad Henlein. While shouting to the world about righting the wrongs of an oppressed minority, Hitler instructed Henlein to "demand so much that we can never be satisfied." At the same time, Hitler worked to complete Prague's diplomatic isolation. He played on Polish and Rumanian fears of Moscow so that Russia would not be able to pass across those countries to come to Czechoslovakia's aid in the event of invasion. He tempted Poland and Hungary with the prospect of slices of Czech territory. As for the Western powers, Hitler divined correctly the French fear of war and he stressed to the British the oppression of the Sudetens and the folly of a great conflict over their return to the Fatherland. To protect his own flank he paid a state visit to Rome and loudly proclaimed to Mussolini, who was still anxious over the Nazi absorption of Austria, that the frontier of the Alps would be "forever inviolable."

Only two forces could stop Hitler, and he overbore both of them. One was a group of generals who feared that Germany was not strong enough to wage a major war. Alternately pleading with the military and bullying them, the Fuehrer pushed aside the veteran commanders and insisted on his plan of conquest. The other potential obstacle was united opposition from Russia and the West. But the central strategic premise on which Hitler operated—"there is no solidarity in Europe," as he put it—held true. Ironically, there was a brief moment when the two forces might have united. A small group of officers and civilian officials conspired to seize Hitler as soon as he ordered the attack on the Czechs. But their plan turned on the question whether Britain and France would come to Prague's aid.

Would they? The difference between Hitler and the Western leaders was crucial: In order to destroy Czechoslovakia the former was willing to risk a general war while Chamberlain and Daladier, to save Czechoslovakia, were not willing to risk such a war. Russia and the Western nations each feared being deserted by the other to face alone the rising German might.

The United States, of course, still carried little weight in the quivering balance of power politics. It did little more than watch and worry. Despite his preoccupation with the continuing recession and a balky Congress during the spring of 1938, Roosevelt followed European developments with care. He received a great deal of information on the complex chess game in Europe—so much, indeed, and from such varied sources that his hopes alternately rose and fell.

On the over-all course of affairs the President had fixed ideas. Looking on the Nazis and Fascists as gangsters who ultimately would have to be restrained, he had deep misgivings about Chamberlain's appeasement policies. When he heard that the prime minister was ready to recognize Mussolini's conquest of Ethiopia in return for a pact of friendship, the President said that if when a police chief made a deal with gangsters the result was no more holdups, the police chief would be a hero, but if the gangsters reneged the police chief would go to jail. Chamberlain, he felt, was taking a very long chance.

But these were private sentiments, not public action. Unwilling to throw his weight into the balance, the President was still confined to a policy of pinpricks and righteous protest. No risks, no commitments, was the motto of the White House. When he heard that a German battleship was to stop off in the West Indies, he ordered an American war vessel to be there at the same time. When Germany wanted helium from the United States for its dirigibles, the President for a time encouraged Ickes, who had control of its allotment, to stall them off. Meanwhile Hull specialized in protests. The Secretary of State repeatedly denounced international lawlessness and, when tension began to rise over Hitler's posture toward Czechoslovakia, he solemnly called attention to the Kellogg anti-war pact signed a decade before. Men of power in Europe laughed off America's moral protestations. Ciano, Italy's cynical foreign minister, noted in his diary how he listened solemnly while a visiting

American played the usual gramophone record and then turned on a record of his own.

Only one commitment was the President willing to make. Speaking in mid-August at Queen's University in Ontario, he assured the Canadians in words that Roosevelt himself had inserted in a State Department draft, that "the people of the United States will not stand idly by if domination of Canadian soil is threatened by any other Empire." But Czechoslovakia, not Canada, was next on the Nazi timetable.

By summer's end, 1938, Hitler was ready to move. Final plans were drawn up for deploying thirty-six divisions against the Czechs. To a frenzied, baying crowd of Nazis at Nürnberg he demanded "justice" for the Sudetens. Events crowded on one another during the rest of September. To Hitler's surprise and delight, Chamberlain suddenly flew to Germany. While the wind howled and rain lashed the windowpanes, the prime minister conferred with the ex-corporal in his mountain house in Berchtesgaden. Hitler shouted that he would settle affairs with the Czechs even if it meant war.

Frightened by Hitler's reckless attitude, Chamberlain returned to London to see if the cabinet would support the peaceful separation of the Sudeten Germans from Czechoslovakia. Hitler continued preparations for attack. A week later Chamberlain returned to Germany, happily bearing agreements from his country, France, and Czechoslovakia—the last obtained by putting Prague under severe pressure—for peaceful transfer of Sudeten districts. Amazed that the Czechs would submit, incensed at losing his chance of smashing them, Hitler balked. He now insisted on immediate occupation by his army. A desperate Chamberlain returned home; Hitler ordered assault regiments to their action stations; Londoners dug bomb shelters while mobilization orders went out to the fleet. As a last chance for peace Chamberlain turned to Mussolini, and the Duce, not yet ready for war, appealed to Hitler. Through the combined efforts of Mussolini and the moderates around Hitler, he was induced to join with Mussolini, Chamberlain, and Daladier in a conference where he would be granted by agreement what he wanted to take by force. Meeting in Munich on September 29, the four men arranged the partition of Czechoslovakia, and soon German troops were crossing into the Sudetenland, unopposed.

What was Roosevelt doing all this time? As the European crisis sharpened in early September he was campaigning in Maryland against Tydings and then spending some anxious days in Minnesota while Mayo Clinic surgeons operated on James's ulcers. During the critical days of September he abruptly broke off further speaking plans and hurried back to Washington. He grasped the basic elements of the situation: Hitler's determination to seize Czechoslovakia, Chamberlain's insistence on peace, the probable seizure of the Sudetenland, the likelihood of war within the next few years even if it was postponed by concessions. Could the United States play any part in the immediate crisis?

Once again, but this time in the teeth of impending disaster abroad, Roosevelt tried to throw his influence in the scale without making commitments. Again and again he and Hull called for international co-operation against lawlessness but drew the line at foreign entanglements. The President did not respond to the plea of President Eduard Beneš of Czechoslovakia that he urge Britain and France not to desert the Czechs. He would not allow Chamberlain to broadcast a direct message to the American people. He turned aside suggestions that he arbitrate. Instead he decided on an open appeal for peace to all the nations—to potential aggressor, bystander, and victim alike. But the appeal itself mentioned our spurning of "political entanglements"; it evoked polite answers from the democracies and a long diatribe from the Fuehrer filled with lies about the oppression of the Sudetens. The President then appealed to Hitler himself to agree to a conference over the crisis in some neutral spot, but with no involvement by the United States; this letter Hitler ignored, for matters were already turning his way.

September 1938 in America had been the month of a great hurricane. Breathless newscasters, working around the clock, had brought reports of winds, tidal waves, and floods in the Northeast, of the wreckage left in their wake, punctuated by the latest bulletin on the man-made storms abroad. At month's end the calm blue skies seemed to heighten the outburst of relief over Munich's outcome. "I have had a pretty strenuous two weeks," Roosevelt wrote a friend, but a cruise taken in midsummer "made it possible for me to come through except for a stupid and continuing runny nose. A few days ago I wanted to kill Hitler and amputate the nose. Today, I have really friendly feelings for the latter and no longer wish to assassinate the Fuehrer."

But the enormous sense of relief was deeply shaded by worry. Munich was probably not too great a price to pay if it insured permanent peace, Ickes said. "But will it? I doubt it very much, Hitler being the maniac that he is." Hull issued a cool statement about the pact, but Welles a day or so later publicly stated that a superb opportunity had now come to establish a new world order based on justice and law. The nation's press was divided, the more isolationist press hailing the result, other newspapers fretting over its meaning for the future. The President seemed divided too. "Good man," he had cabled Chamberlain enigmatically after Hitler agreed to the Munich meeting, but he had deep misgivings as to Chamber-

lain's appeasement policy and its implications. He told Ickes darkly
that he suspected Britain and France might offer Trinidad and
Martinique to Hitler to keep him satisfied—and if they did he would
send the fleet to take both islands.

One voice in Britain showed no mixed feelings. Said Winston
Churchill, "We have sustained a total and unmitigated defeat."

In the fall of 1938, as Hitler's truculence seemed only to increase,
the President took advantage of the lull in world affairs to reassess
his foreign policies. Again and again he called Hull and Welles in
for consultation, often while he was still in bed. Sitting in a sea of
newspapers and messages, his little cape of blue flannel slipping off
his shoulders as he waved his long cigarette holder and brandished
the latest cable, Roosevelt slowly crystallized his views. He no longer
had any doubt that appeasement was a costly gamble that would
probably fail. Nor could America escape its implications. When he
heard that the peanut vendor outside the White House had said,
"Over there, there are guns. Here there ain't no guns. Here there's
squirrels on the lawn," Roosevelt remarked that he was right, "but
he fails to mention the unfortunate fact that the fuss and pushing
and guns on the other side are coming closer to our country all the
time."

Still, the President would not tell the country about the gravity
of the situation. When Ickes urged him to do so, he said the people
simply would not believe him. Probably Roosevelt feared they
would not trust him; it was now the end of 1938, the year of the
purge and of the surge of Republican isolationist power in the
congressional elections.

Unwilling to strike boldly on the central front, the President
acted where he felt he safely could. He dispatched a bipartisan delegation to the Inter-American Congress of Lima, where Hull helped
bring about, despite Argentine opposition, a declaration of joint
action against threats to the hemisphere. Knowing of the Nazis'
vaunted strength in the air, the President laid plans for a sharply
increased air force. When a German émigré Jew shot a German
attaché in Paris and touched off a savage pogrom in Germany
against the Jews, the President publicly expressed his shock and
horror, ordered his ambassador home from Berlin to report, and
redoubled his efforts to help refugees from Germany. Keeping an
eye cocked toward the Far East, he granted a credit of twenty-five
million dollars to Chiang Kai-shek on assurances that Chinese resistance to Japan would continue.

The new year 1939 came, and with it a crucial session of Congress. Over the holidays, while his grandchildren romped through
the house and guests watched the after-supper movies, the President
dictated and redictated to Grace Tully from scribbled notes. On

January 4, 1939, he delivered some bold and urgent words to Congress:

"A war which threatened to envelop the world in flames has been averted; but it has become increasingly clear that world peace is not assured.

"All about us rage undeclared wars—military and economic. All about us are threats of new aggression—military and economic. . . .

"There comes a time in the affairs of men when they must prepare to defend, not their homes alone but the tenets of faith and humanity on which their churches, their governments and their very civilization are founded. The defense of religion, of democracy and of good faith among nations is all the same fight. To save one we must now make up our minds to save all. . . ." God-fearing democracies could not forever let pass, without effective protest, acts of aggression. "There are many methods short of war, but stronger and more effective than mere words, of bringing home to aggressor governments the aggregate sentiments of our own people."

What were these methods? Here Roosevelt pulled in his horns. Rather than call for specific changes in neutrality policy, he said, rather vaguely, "We have learned that when we deliberately try to legislate neutrality, our neutrality laws may operate unevenly and unfairly—may actually give aid to an aggressor and deny it to the victim." Quickly dropping the subject, he went on to the needs of defense.

Yet a tactic of caution and secrecy has risks of its own. During 1938 Roosevelt had smoothed the way for French and English purchase of munitions as part of a program of increasing United States arms production. Looking on this as a touchy matter, he insisted on secrecy. Unhappily, late in January 1939 one of the newest American bombers crashed in California, and in the wreckage was found the body of a French official who had been inspecting American equipment. Promptly the whole story of foreign purchase of arms came out—and in the worst possible way for the President. Isolationists stormed; the Senate Military Affairs Committee investigated. To quiet the commotion Roosevelt invited the senators in for a long talk. He insisted on secrecy, but afterward someone reported the President as saying that America's frontier "lay on the Rhine." Again the isolationists seethed with indignation. So did the President. Denouncing the report as a deliberate lie, he said that "some boob" must have said it.

Caution was not paying off. Then, in March 1939, affairs in Europe rushed to another climax.

THE STORM BREAKS

Skillfully wielding his three-pronged lance of diplomacy, threat, and subversion, Hitler on the Ides of March seized the rump state of Czechoslovakia and put Slovakia under German "protection." Hungary snatched at the bone tossed by the Fuehrer and gobbled up Ruthenia. Dictators and militarists seemed to be winning victories wherever they turned. Japan laid claim to the Spratly Islands, covering a huge area southwest of Manila. German troops occupied Memel. Smashing Loyalist resistance, Franco took Madrid at the end of the month. Ten days later Mussolini seized Albania. Earlier in March Stalin did something less dramatic but even more ominous than acts of aggression: he warned the West against "egging the Germans on" to march upon Russia.

Grimly Roosevelt read the cables. "Never in my life," he wrote a friend, "have I seen things moving in the world with more cross currents or with greater velocity." Matters changed so fast every day that he was admittedly unable to pull them into focus. Neither were others. State Department officials were divided in their views as to whether Hitler would next move west or east. Chamberlain on hearing of Hitler's move at first refused to be deflected from his course; but two weeks later he turned completely about and announced Britain's guarantee of the independence of Poland—the state that six months before had helped destroy Czechoslovakia.

The President's first step after Prague's fall was little more than the old diplomacy of protest and pinprick. He approved a statement by Welles against "acts of wanton lawlessness" and he considered imposing countervailing duties on imports from Germany. Roosevelt then indirectly sounded out Mussolini, warning him of Hitler's ambitions, on the possibility of the Duce's taking the initiative for peace—but this venture was knocked into a cocked hat by the Duce's cynical adventure in Albania a few days later. During the lull that followed the President spent hours talking about the fast-changing situation. Of certain things he was sure. The fate of Prague proved that Hitler's aim was not simply reuniting Germans. Appeasement was a failure. With Chamberlain's spine now stiffened, the chances of war had increased. And if Britain and France fell, Hitler could take over Latin-American countries by his strategy of military and economic coercion.

But what to do? Of all the somber events, Franco's triumph shook Roosevelt the hardest, for his own policies had helped shape the outcome. It was clear to him that the embargo had been a grave mistake. He asked Pittman to redouble his efforts to get the Neutrality Act revised or repealed. While the bill dragged through

the slow Senate machinery, the President decided on another, typi-
cally Rooseveltian act.

In a sudden move on a Friday night in mid-April the President
addressed identical appeals to Hitler and Mussolini. He asked them
to take their problems to the council table and in effect to "park
their guns outside." The heart of his plea had a novel twist—a direct
and unvarnished question whether they would promise not to
attack thirty-one nations, which Roosevelt named one by one. He
closed by pinning responsibility for the fate of humanity on the
heads of great governments. Explaining the message to correspondents the next day the President stressed again and again—for the
benefit of "some of our friends on the Hill"—that the message was
no departure from his policy of no entanglements, no commitments.
He was offering to serve, he said, not as a mediator but as an intermediary, as a post office or telegraph office.

In the lull between crises that was the spring of 1939 Roosevelt's
appeal came like a burst of sunlight in an April storm. Democratic
governments and peoples rejoiced; Moscow, too, expressed approval.
But the Axis leaders reacted with scorn and contempt. Visiting
Mussolini at the time, Goering dismissed the message as suggesting
an incipient brain malady; the Duce thought it might be more a
case of creeping paralysis.

But it was Hitler who delivered the main rebuttal. Appearing
before the Reichstag, after a long defense of his policies he went
over the President's plea sentence by sentence and rang every tone
on the American isolationists' register. To counter Roosevelt's appeal for the thirty-one nations, he said amid jeering applause that
he had asked each of the states listed whether it felt threatened by
Germany and each had answered no. He made much of his and
Germany's role as underdog.

"Mr. Roosevelt!" Hitler cried, "I fully understand that the vast-
ness of your nation and the immense wealth of your country allow
you to feel responsible for the history of the whole world. . . . I,
sir, am placed in a much smaller and more modest sphere. . . ."

While the harangue was essentially a string of debater's points,
Hitler spoke with such masterful irony and so cuttingly of America's
own international derelictions that he appealed to public opinion
outside Germany as well as within. He rebutted his adversary's
arguments without answering his central question about future aggression. (Perhaps he was taking a leaf from the President's own
book, for Roosevelt had made a major campaign attack out of reply-
ing to Landon at Madison Square Garden in 1936 without really
answering him.) The immediate feeling was that Hitler had had
the better of Roosevelt, and the isolationists exulted. "He asked for

it," said Nye. The President, angered by the dictators' bad manners, relapsed into silence.

Now there seemed only one weapon left—to throw into the scales the very force that Hitler had referred to: America's immense wealth. Once again Roosevelt turned to the fight to repeal or change the arms embargo provision of the Neutrality Act—the now odious provision that would force him to cut off arms to all nations, aggressor and victim alike, in the event of war.

That fight was still going badly. Since January the President had followed a strict hands-off policy on the bill, exerting no public leadership and little private influence. Hull himself feared to testify before the Senate Foreign Relations Committee. Hence much depended on the committee chairman, Pittman; but the Nevadan was not equal to the task. Concerned less with neutrality than with the price of silver for his constituents, he was no match for Borah, Johnson, La Follette, Vandenberg, and the other formidable isolationists on his committee.

Balked in the Senate, the administration now turned to the House. The President himself at last entered the lists. He told House leaders privately that repeal of the embargo would probably prevent war in Europe; but if war came, repeal would make an Axis victory less likely. He thought that the Axis had a fifty-fifty chance of winning the war and he painted a dark picture of the implications for America.

No use. The House passed a new bill but kept the essence of the embargo provision. Dismayed, Roosevelt considered ignoring the act, but he dared not go so far. With the war clouds again piling up in Europe, he called Senate leaders to the White House. Summing up for them his long fight for peace, he said: "I've fired my last shot. I think I ought to have another round in my belt." He again mentioned the strong possibility of war, the need of throwing America's material weight into the scales before it was too late. Hull was even more emphatic than the President.

The senators were sitting comfortably around the President's study in their shirt sleeves, drinks in hand. Finally Borah spoke up. All eyes turned to the lion-headed old isolationist.

"There's not going to be any war this year," he said. "All this hysteria is manufactured and artificial."

"I wish the Senator would come down to my office and read the cables," Hull said.

Borah waved him quiet. "I have sources of information in Europe that I regard as more reliable than those of the State Department."

At this Hull almost burst into tears. Roosevelt lay back on his sofa, silent. Garner after a moment went the rounds asking if there were enough votes to bring repeal up on the Senate floor. Finally he turned to the President.

"Well, Captain, we may as well face the facts. You haven't got the votes; and that's all there is to it."

That was all there was to it. Roosevelt kept his urbanity, but he insisted that the senators take responsibility. The meeting broke up. Congress adjourned early in August, the embargo requirement intact.

In all these bitter weeks, while Congress was thwarting Roosevelt's efforts abroad and pinching off the New Deal at home, there was one radiantly magnificent interlude. This was the visit of the British king and queen in June. Attending to every detail, Roosevelt set the stage for their reception with the care and gusto of a Broadway director. The royal pair played their parts brilliantly, the queen winning everyone's heart with her gracious, bonnie ways, the king looking young, strong, and earnest. Scene after scene came off perfectly: the reception by half a million Washingtonians in sweltering Washington heat; the well-schooled king even remembering to remark "Cotton Ed Smith?" when he met South Carolina's senior Senator; the state dinner in the White House climaxed with an eloquent presidential toast and with songs by Kate Smith and Marian Anderson; the inevitable wreath laying at Arlington cemetery; the drive through New York City's crowds to the World's Fair; the picnic at Hyde Park that featured hot dogs, baked beans, and strawberry shortcake; the long tête-à-tête between president and monarch ending at 1:30 in the morning when Roosevelt put his hand on the royal knee and said, "Young man, it's time for you to go to bed!"; the final good-by at the Hyde Park station, with the crowds bursting spontaneously into "Auld Lang Syne" and the President calling after the moving train, "Good luck to you! All the luck in the world!"

Yet actually it was but a brief moment of joyous pomp and pageantry in a sullen world girding for war. Indeed, war had already come—a strange war of military threat and intrigue, of calculated lies and slander, of alarums and provocations, of news blackouts and barter deals, of high-pressure diplomacy and currency raids, of propaganda barrages, mass meetings, posters, parades, radio blasts. Caught in a fog of confusion and indecision, Chamberlain and Daladier groped for a way out. They wanted to join hands with Stalin against Hitler, but they dared not pay the price Stalin demanded; nor would Poland, overly confident in her own arms. Hitler, however, marched straight to his goal. Poland was next on his list. He was willing to grant Stalin power in eastern Europe; he already planned to withdraw the grant at a later time. He fobbed off on an anxious Mussolini assurances that Britain and France would not help Poland, or if they did, would act too little and too late. By August 24, 1939, the Russians and Germans had signed their pact, Stalin had drunk a toast to Hitler, and the Fuehrer's "tremendous political overturn," as he called it, was completed. All was ready.

August 1939 in Washington was sultry and oppressive. The President received full reports of the Nazi successes, but he could not move a single pawn on the diplomatic chessboard. When he got the catastrophic news of the Russo-German pact and of Hitler's imminent attack on Poland, he sent a last despairing plea to Hitler. Poland had accepted Roosevelt's offer to conciliate, he told the Fuehrer. "All the world prays that Germany, too, will accept."

Hitler's answer came seven days later.

At ten minutes to three on the morning of September 1, 1939, the telephone rang next to the President's bed. He was awake in an instant.

"Who is it?"

"This is Bill Bullitt, Mr. President."

"Yes, Bill."

"Tony Biddle has just got through from Warsaw, Mr. President. Several German divisions are deep in Polish territory, and fighting is heavy. Tony said there were reports of bombers over the city. Then he was cut off. . . ."

"Well, Bill, it's come at last. God help us all."

After a few more words, Bullitt hung up and the President began calling Hull, Welles, and others. Soon officials were speeding to their offices through dark empty streets. For a while Welles, Hull, and Berle listened to Hitler's announcement to the Reichstag that the attack on Poland had begun and that "bombs will be met with bombs." There was little else they could do. Said Berle: "We are ending our death watch over Europe."

In the White House Roosevelt fell asleep until 6:30, when Bullitt phoned again to say that he had talked with Daladier: France would go to Poland's aid. The President, with his usual iron nerve, got a few more minutes' sleep before Ambassador Kennedy phoned from London to report that Britain would fight. Roosevelt did not try to nap again; soon Welles and his secretaries were at his bedside for instructions.

As the President set into motion long-laid plans for the emergency, his mind kept going back twenty years to the last war, when a telephone at his bedside brought news of the latest events at sea. Now the crisis hours seemed not strange to him, but more like picking up an interrupted routine. European statesmen, too, were reliving the crisis days of 1914. An anguished Chamberlain delivered an ultimatum to Hitler to withdraw his troops. In Berlin on Sunday morning, September 3, an interpreter pushed his way through a crowd of Nazi leaders in the anteroom at the Chancellery, entered Hitler's study, and slowly translated the ultimatum. When he finished, Hitler sat silent and unmoving for long seconds. Then he turned to Foreign Minister Ribbentrop, who had said that Britain would not fight. "What now?" demanded Hitler savagely. In the anteroom outside Goering gave an answer: "If we lose this war, then God help us."

That evening the President spoke to what he called "the whole of America." Until early that morning, he began, he had hoped against hope that some miracle might prevent war and end the invasion of Poland.

"You must master at the outset a simple but unalterable fact in modern foreign relations between nations. When peace has been broken anywhere, the peace of all countries everywhere is in danger.

"It is easy for you and for me to shrug our shoulders and to say that conflicts taking place thousands of miles from the continental United States, and, indeed, thousands of miles from the whole American Hemisphere, do not seriously affect the Americas—and that all the United States has to do is to ignore them and go about its own business. Passionately though we may desire detachment, we are forced to realize that every word that comes through the air, every ship that sails the sea, every battle that is fought, does affect the American future. . . .

"This nation will remain a neutral nation, but I cannot ask that every American remain neutral in thought as well. Even a neutral has a right to take account of facts. Even a neutral cannot be asked to close his mind or his conscience.

"I have said not once, but many times, that I have seen war and that I hate war. I say that again and again. . . .

"As long as it remains within my power to prevent, there will be no black-out of peace in the United States."

During the next days, as German troops and tanks plunged ever deeper into Poland, as German submarines ranged along the world's shipping lanes, the President wrestled with the problem of neutrality. He had hoped, shortly before the war, that he could order customs collectors to seize German ships as soon as war started, but the Attorney General ruled that such an act would be construed as an act of war. The President did have the satisfaction of holding up the departure of the *Bremen* from New York on various pretexts, and the huge German liner barely got home. As long as possible he delayed issuing the proclamation required under the Neutrality Act so that Britain and France could have a little extra time to get munitions. But these were trifles. The crucial job was to repeal the embargo itself, and this job the President made his main objective for the fall of 1939.

The chips were down. Polite but agonized appeals were coming in from the democratic nations at war: American material aid would be indispensable to victory. The President acted swiftly. Convening a special session, he asked Congress to repeal the embargo provisions. He denounced the Neutrality Act of 1935 as a departure from the nation's historic neutrality policy. "I regret that the Congress passed that Act. I regret equally that I signed that Act." He warned against any group assuming the exclusive label of the peace bloc. "We all belong to it."

Despite these blunt words, Roosevelt acted with great caution. In his plea for repeal he stressed peace through noninvolvement rather than what was his main goal: helping the democracies against the aggressors. He exerted every influence possible on Congress, but covertly. Cabinet members and friendly congressmen were asked to marshal votes. Patronage grievances were smoothed over. Pittman and his fellow silverites were bought off by the promise of a higher price for domestic silver. Landon and Knox were reached through newspapermen close to them and to the White House. Governors and mayors were asked to help. Prominent businessmen were lined up. Most of the job of marshaling public opinion was handled by private groups, especially by William Allen White's "Non-partisan Committee for Peace Through Revision of the Neutrality Law." The White House quietly co-operated with these groups but made no effort itself to lead a public campaign for repeal.

"I am almost literally walking on eggs," the President said to Lord Tweedsmuir, Governor General of Canada, in asking him to postpone a visit until the neutrality fight was over. ". . . I am at the moment saying nothing, seeing nothing and hearing nothing." He canceled a speech he was to give to women Democrats; he held up other business to give repeal the right of way. Reports on the Senate line-up were flashed to him daily, sometimes hourly.

On Capitol Hill, senators again roared and thundered. Isolationists rehearsed their familiar lines: ignore the "war hounds of Europe," keep out of the wily game of power politics. Tellingly they pointed to the fateful parallel to intervention in 1917: war breaks out; the President helps one side; secret commitments are made; excuses arise for taking sides. Taking their cue from the President, the advocates of repeal based their appeals on keeping America out of war, and stressed that the new bill would require belligerents to pay cash and to carry goods away in their own ships.

The lawmakers debated amid heavy pressures. A North Dakota congressman wrote the President that "you can absolutely count on my vote to lift the embargo." Eleven days later he sent a plaintive note. He had not changed his own opinions but the petitions, letters, resolutions, and telegrams from home were so strong that he probably would vote to keep the embargo. "This job of being a Representative doesn't appeal to me as strongly as it did when I first came here," he added.

Finally, at the end of October—a month after the Germans had overrun Poland—the Senate repealed the arms embargo by a vote of 63 to 30 in legislation studded with compromises and ambiguities. The House followed suit a few days later. Despite all the talk of nonpartisanship the vote was along party lines.

Even more important than neutrality legislation—at least for the long run—was a conversation the President held during October with a student of science named Alexander Sachs. Two months before, Albert Einstein had written Roosevelt about the possibility of developing a new bomb of unbelievable power, and now Sachs had come in to report on recent developments in the field of nuclear fission including, ominously enough, progress in Nazi Germany. At first Roosevelt seemed preoccupied and inattentive—it must have all seemed remote and theoretical—but in characteristic fashion once he caught on to the implications of the problem, he acted. Wheels started to turn immediately and the basis for the future Manhattan Project was laid during the next six months; because Roosevelt continued to be willing to gamble hundreds of millions of dollars against the unknown, the project went forward to the awful climax of Hiroshima.

But in the fall of 1939 all this lay far in the future. "Here in Washington the White House is very quiet," the President wrote Kennedy. "There is a general feeling of sitting quiet and waiting to see what the morrow will bring forth."

ROOSEVELT AS A POLITICAL LEADER

Back in February 1939, a friend of the President's had sent on to him a letter from a man who had long supported the administration. Written in despair and indignation, the letter spoke for the millions of Americans who could not understand Roosevelt's cautious tactics:

"Why don't you tell our idol FDR to quit beating around the bush, get on the radio and be honest with his people? Of *course* our first line of defense is the Maginot line. Of *course* we cannot afford to let France and England get licked. Of *course* we should prepare to help them—first with munitions and then if that is not enough with everything we've got.

"Why stall around? Why let these pussyfooting Senators kid the American public into the belief that we could stay out of another war? Why not talk brutal realism to the American people *before* it is too late? You and I know goddam well that if Der Fuehrer and Il Duce are convinced that we will go in—as the Gallup poll shows that the people think we will—there just won't be any war. . . .

"No bushwa about making the world safe for democracy or strict neutrality. The truth is so much more convincing: to save our own hides we must eventually halt the have-not nations in their drive to loot the have nations by force or threat of force. . . ."

All the passion in the letter left the President unmoved. "Thank him very much," he told Early. "Say delighted to get it and it came just before I left for the cruise. . . ." That was the end of it. Other persons—even heads of nations—had asked him to take the leadership against the aggressors. He had not done so.

On the contrary, the President's behavior had been almost a caricature of cautiousness. So much had he ostensibly withdrawn from the embargo repeal fight early in 1939 that Pittman was told to deny that the administration had any hand in his bill. On other matters, too, Roosevelt was utterly evasive. In January 1939 Congress was considering proposals to improve the harbor at Guam. This exchange occurred at a press conference:

REPORTER: "Can you say whether you do or do not favor the five million dollar appropriation for fortifying Guam?"

ROOSEVELT: "Is there a five million dollar appropriation for fortifying Guam?"

REPORTER: "That is my understanding of it."

ROOSEVELT: " 'Deepening the harbor.' "

REPORTER: "Guess you have got me there. . . ." [Laughter]

REPORTER: "Just so there won't be any confusion, would you make clear your stand on Guam?"

ROOSEVELT: "I don't think there is any confusion."

REPORTER: "You are for it?"

ROOSEVELT: "No, I am not." After more talk the President said he was in accord with a proposal to start dredging the harbor of Guam.

What was the matter? In the gravest international situation the nation had ever faced, where was the leadership of the man whose very name since 1933 had become the symbol of candor and courage?

When a leader fails to live up to the symbolic role he has come to occupy, his admirers cling to the image they love by imputing mistakes to the leader's advisers. Stories went the rounds in 1939 that Roosevelt's trouble really lay in Hull's timidity and in Kennedy's belief in appeasement. The stories were not true. Hull, to be sure, did seem to move slowly, but he was working against the embargo law before Roosevelt took a definite stand, and he was calling existing legislation "a wretched little bob-tailed, sawed-off" substitute for the established rules on international law while the President was using far softer words. As for Kennedy, Roosevelt knew that he had sympathized with the appeasement policies of Chamberlain and the so-called "Cliveden set" and to an extent valued him for this. But he would not let his ambassador get out of hand. When Kennedy submitted a draft of a talk he was to give in London, the President and Hull went over it line by line to adjust it to administration policy.

The President's tactics were his own. Another explanation for his caution lay in the nature of the opposition in Congress and among the people. Certainly the opposition to an internationalist or collective security program was not to be dismissed lightly. In a 1937 poll nineteen out of twenty people answered a flat "No" to the query whether the United States should enter another world war. Most of the people trusted Congress rather than the President to keep America out of war. They were powerfully drawn by the symbols of Peace and Neutrality—and they tended to equate the two. To be sure, these attitudes somewhat lacked stability and durability. But they had a terrible intensity. The late 1930's was the period when the famous aviatrix Laura Ingalls showered the White House with "peace" leaflets from her plane, when Father Coughlin and John L. Lewis were whipping up isolationist feeling, when to some fascism constituted the "wave of the future." Two decades of bitterness over World War I and its aftermath had left a hard, smarting scar tissue.

Any attempt by Roosevelt to override this feeling clearly would have been disastrous. His real mission as a political leader was to modify and guide this opinion in a direction closer to American interests as he saw them. To raise this question is again to confront the paradox of Roosevelt's leadership.

For under the impact of shattering events abroad, people's attitudes were slowly shifting. Most Americans, of course, clung to their "Keep-Out-of-War" position. But between Munich and the outbreak of war a great majority of the people swung over to the position of all help to Britain and France short of war. By September 1939 about 37 per cent of the people favored positive help to Britain, France, and Poland; less than half of these wanted to dispatch military help then or at any later time, while most favored sending food and materials. This 37 per cent interventionist element confronted a hard-core isolationist bloc that opposed any aid at all to either side. In the middle was a group of about 30 per cent that would refuse to sell to either side except on a cash-and-carry basis.

It was this vast middle group that offered the President his supreme opportunity. For this group was clinging to the symbol of nonentanglement while grasping the need of American help to nations under attack. This group, combined with the interventionists, would have given heavy backing to Roosevelt's all-aid-short-of-war policies. Was it possible that these millions of middle-of-the-roaders thought that cash and carry in 1939 meant material help to *neither* side? No; a later poll showed that 90 per cent favored cash and carry even if in practice only Britain and France got the supplies. Without question these middle attitudes were shot through with confusions and uncertainties. But this made a real leader's opportunity all the greater, for opinions that are superficial and volatile are the most subject to influence. A situation that was an opportunity for Napoleon, A. N. Whitehead has observed, would appear as an unmanageable disorder to most of us.

Roosevelt felt that events and facts themselves would educate the public. So they did—but not quickly enough. Each time in the race between aggression and American opinion victory went to the former. The early months of 1939 were the supreme test. Roosevelt's great hope was that he could demonstrate to Hitler that America would give material aid to nations the Nazis planned to attack. The President's tactic was based on a sound proposition—the best way to keep America out of war would be to keep war out of the world. But he did not lead opinion toward a position of all aid short of war. He tagged along with opinion. Sometimes, indeed—most notably when he was frightened by the reaction to the "quarantine" speech and later by the furore over America's frontier being "on the Rhine"—he lagged behind the drift of opinion favoring more commitment by the United States to joint efforts against aggression.

The President's immediate problem was not, of course, isolationist feeling in general but the mighty isolationist phalanxes in Congress. Doubtless he feared that defeat of a crucial bill on the Hill might mean a permanent setback for his hopes to aid the democracies and might so dishearten friends of America abroad as to encourage more appeasement. If such was Roosevelt's tactic with Congress, the fate of embargo repeal in the spring of 1939 suggests that he failed. Perhaps if he had taken a position against the embargo much sooner and much more openly and consistently, he could have won repeal in the spring of 1939. But the fact is that only when he knew he had the votes on the Hill did he utter the clarion call that resulted in repeal in October of that year. Once again events, not the President, had done the job of educating—and once again the time was tragically late.

No leader is a free agent. Even Hitler had to cope with grumbling and foot dragging among the military; even Stalin had to deal with backward peasants and with party rivals grasping for power. Roosevelt's plight was far more difficult. He was captain of the ship of state, but many hands reached for the tiller, and a rebellious crew manned the sails. It was only natural that this vessel should move ahead by hugging the shore, threading its way past shoal and reef, putting into harbor when the storm roared. The test of great political leadership is not whether the leader has his way; it is, first, whether the leader makes the most of existing materials he has to work with, and, second, whether he creates new materials to help him meet his goals.

At the end of 1939, as Roosevelt neared the last year of his second term, it was time to apply to him both tests of leadership. His goal had always been clear in broad outline—a prosperous people in a secure nation. By the end of 1939 this goal was still far off. Economic conditions had improved since the recession, but only back to the uncertain levels of the mid-1930's, with millions out of work. And as the President himself saw more clearly than most Americans, the nation was in grave peril.

The ship of state had not reached port; neither had it foundered. How had the captain done?

Undeniably the reefs and shoals were formidable. Any attempt to chart a clear course to port—in this case to build a liberal program for New Deal objectives—ran head on into the absence of a cohesive liberal tradition in America. Any effort to shape long-term economic programs ran up against limited understanding of economic problems. Any effort to build a consistent foreign policy that would throw the country's weight toward peace and against the aggressors encountered the fierce isolationism of most Americans. The political and governmental means to these ends were equally hard to forge. Attempts to build a stronger "presidential party" behind the New Deal fell afoul of the federal, factional make-up of the existing party system. Any effort to establish a cohesive rank-and-file group for New Deal policies in Congress splintered against the entrenched power of seniority. Even the attempt to fashion a more cohesive executive branch ran into the centrifugal tendencies of the American system and the pervasive popular fear of executive power.

But what was the factor of creative leadership in these lost battles? Could it be said that Roosevelt had tried and failed? Was it bad luck, or a rebellious crew, or a flimsy ship that had kept him from reaching port? Or was the blame his alone?

There is an important difference between the politician who is simply an able tactician, and the politician who is a creative political leader. The former accepts political conditions as given and fashions a campaign and a set of policies best suited to the existing conditions. The latter tries consciously to change the matrix of political forces amid which he operates, in order that he may better lead the people in the direction he wants to go. The former operates within slender margins; the latter, through sheer will and conviction as well as political skill, tries to widen the margins within which he operates. He seeks not merely to win votes but consciously to alter basic political forces such as public opinion, party power, interest-group pressure, the governmental system.

There were times—most notably in 1935—when Roosevelt brilliantly capitalized on every opportunity to convert New Deal aims into law. There were times—most notably in the court fight—when he tested and found the outer limits of his power. But sometimes he made no effort at all—especially in gaining lasting influence in Congress. Sometimes he tried too little and too late. And sometimes—as in the case of party consolidation and realignment and of economic program—he seemed to lack the intellectual qualities necessary to the task.

During his second term Roosevelt seemed to forget the great lesson of his inaugural speech of 1933—that courageous affirmation in itself changes the political dimensions of a situation. That speech was more than a speech—it was an act that loosened a tidal wave of support behind the new administration. The most important instrument a leader has to work with is himself—his own personality and its impact on other people. When the people's opinions are vaguely directed the way the leader is headed but lack depth and solidity, action by the leader can shift opinion in his own favor. In the parallelogram of forces in which the leader operates, such action alters the whole equation. To be sure, more than speeches was needed after 1937, for the feeling of crisis had gone and popular attitudes had hardened. But the inaugural speech of 1933 stood as an index of the leader's influence when he takes a posture of bold affirmation.

Roosevelt's failure to build a liberal coalition and a new party behind the New Deal is a further case in point. For here the materials were available for the right shaping and mixing. To be sure, most Americans during the mid-1930's as an abstract matter opposed realigning the parties along liberal and conservative lines. But when confronted in 1938 with the question of following "President Roosevelt's" proposal that old party lines be disregarded and that liberals of all parties unite to support liberal candidates for Congress, twice as many people favored as opposed the idea. The missing key was long-term and effective organization by Roosevelt of firmer support for realignment. Despite its failure, the purge showed the great potential of party realignment in the North and in the border states.

As for foreign policy, at potential turning points of public opin-

ion—most notably in 1935 and 1936, when the people's fear of war
might have been directed toward internationalist policies rather
than isolationist ones—the President had failed to give the cue the
people needed. Roosevelt did not exploit his superior information
about the foreign situation and his understanding of foreign policy
in order to guide popular attitudes.

Indeed, Roosevelt to a surprising degree was captive to the political forces around him rather than their shaper. In a democracy
such must ever be the case. But democracy assigns a place for creative political leadership too. The forces handcuffing Roosevelt
stemmed as much from his own actions and personality as from the
unyielding political environment. He could not reshape his party,
reorient foreign policy attitudes, reorganize Congress and the bureaucracy, or solve the economic problem largely because he lacked
the necessary intellectual commitment to the right union of ends
and means.

A test of Roosevelt's creative leadership, of his willingness to alter
the environment—the pressures working on him—when he had the
capacity to do so, was provided by the inner circle of his advisers.
Haphazardly brought together, embracing conservatives and liberals,
isolationists and internationalists, his brain trust helped him mediate
among opposing policies and ideas during his first term. But, despite the comings and goings of individuals, the brain trust remained an amorphous and divided group during Roosevelt's later
period of party leadership, at a time when he needed program
guidance more directly and clearly pointed toward the aims of an
expanded New Deal at home and toward firmer action abroad. Instead of compelling his advisers to serve his new needs, he allowed
them unduly to define his own purposes. Fearing commitment to
any one adviser or faction, he became overly involved in the divisions among all of them.

Roosevelt, in a sense, was captive to himself as well as to his
political environment. He was captive to his habit of mediating
among pressures rather than reshaping them, of responding eclecti-
cally to all the people around him, of balancing warring groups
and leaders against one another, of improvising with brilliance and
gusto. Impatient of theory, insatiably curious about people and their
ideas, sensitively attuned to the play of forces around him, he lacked
that burning and almost fanatic conviction that great leadership
demands.

Roosevelt was less a great creative leader than a skillful manipulator and a brilliant interpreter. Given the big, decisive event—depression at home or naked aggression abroad—he could dramatize
its significance and convey its import to the American people. But
when the crisis was less striking but no less serious, and when its

solution demanded a union of intellectual comprehension and unified and continuing strategic action, Roosevelt saw his efforts turn to dust, as in the cases of court packing, the purge, and putting his country behind efforts toward collective security. He was always a superb tactician, and sometimes a courageous leader, but he failed to achieve that combination of tactical skill and strategic planning that represents the acme of political leadership.

Finally, though, the President had to take account of another crucial factor that must finally be weighed in the scales. This was the election of 1940. All his past, all his future, would come into balance in the fateful, turbulent year that lay ahead.

LEAN DAYS FOR THE ROAD SHOW, Sept. 14, 1938, S. J. Ray, Kansas City Star

PART 5 *Through the Traps*

CHRISTMAS EVE, 1939. Bareheaded in the chill of the oncoming night, Roosevelt stood on a wooden platform next to the Washington community Christmas tree. Several thousand people craned their necks to catch a glimpse of the big, glowing face. The President's words were solemn. "In these days of strife and sadness in many other lands, let us in the nations which still live at peace forbear to give thanks only for our good fortune in our peace. Let us rather pray that we may be given strength to live for others—to live more closely to the words of the Sermon on the Mount. . . ."

In the distance loomed the brilliantly lighted White House. Bright holly wreaths festooned every window. In the gleaming East Room stood a magnificent Christmas tree trimmed in white and silver. On game racks in the kitchen hung pheasants, quail, ducks, grouse, woodcocks. Ushers and clerks staggered under the weight of tens of thousands of Christmas cards and hundreds of presents from the people to their President—fruitcakes, books, ship models, bric-a-brac, even a buck deer.

The upstairs was filled with the hustle and bustle of four generations of Roosevelts. For days they had been arriving—from eighty-five-year-old Sara, down from Hyde Park, to the newest presidential grandchild, eight months old. Around the family tree, gaily decorated under the personal supervision of the President, stacks of presents were piled waist high. By the tree on Christmas Eve, as was his cherished custom, the President read Dickens' *Christmas Carol*, holding the rapt attention of even the little children as he acted out the parts of old Scrooge and the ghosts. Then every Roosevelt, young and old, hung a red stocking over the fireplace in the President's bedroom. After the children had kissed "Grandpa" good night, the President helped stuff the stockings with presents, including toothbrush, nail file, and brightly wrapped bar of soap.

Early next morning the youngsters burst into the President's room and attacked their stockings. Roosevelt sat up in his bed, a small grandchild perched on his lap, while the room filled with

Christmas wrappings and squeals of delight. Later he helped distribute presents around the family Christmas tree, expertly carved a huge turkey at the Christmas dinner, and presided over an evening party for forty persons.

Next day snow came, and in the little interval between Christmas and New Year's the White House seemed to lie quiet and hushed under its soft white blanket. It symbolized an America at peace. Thousands of miles away French *poilus* made little sorties into devastated villages of no man's land. German tank commanders squinted through their sights. British bombardiers watched as their bombs fell lazily in long arcs below. But even the Western Front was relatively quiet—so quiet that some Americans dubbed it the "phony war." Only in Finland did war live up to its reputation. Invaded by Russia a few weeks before, the little nation was putting up a heroic resistance.

New Year's Eve came. Over a million screaming, cheering, festive men and women jammed Times Square. In the White House the President had a few friends in for a quiet evening gathering. Eleanor Roosevelt was there, gay and spirited as ever after holidays crowded with six Christmas tree ceremonies, a host of parties for children and for the poor, church services, and a hundred other duties. Shortly before midnight the radio was turned on in the President's small oval study. The group waited, eggnog glasses in hand. At the sound of midnight the President raised his glass and said with solemn emphasis: "To the United States of America."

It was 1940.

THE SPHINX

It had long been certain that 1940 would be no ordinary year in American history. For three years politicians in both parties had been jockeying and maneuvering in preparation for a crucial election year. Since fall it had seemed likely, too, that the waiting armies and bombing squadrons in Europe would swing into full action during the new year. And decisive events overseas would have fateful consequences for America.

Above all, 1940 would bring an answer to the riddle of the Sphinx: Would Roosevelt seek—and, if so, could he win—a third term? At one of the annual Gridiron dinners in Washington where costumed newsmen mocked the nation's mighty in verse and song, there had been unveiled a huge papier-mâché Sphinx. Out of the grinning mouth protruded a long cigarette holder.

The reporters had good reason to celebrate the Sphinx. For three years they had been seeking the answer by every guile and wile. For three years the President had been deftly turning aside their questions, sometimes with a quick counterthrust, sometimes with real or simulated irritation. More than once Roosevelt had told a reporter to go into the corner and don a dunce cap. But the questioning had continued. In the last press conference of 1939, Earl Godwin had tried a new approach; as the reporters trooped in he called out cheerily:

"We wish you an eventful 1940!"

"Don't be so equivocal!" the President shot back with a laugh.

"We have learned it here, Mr. President," Godwin went on.

"It is all right," said Roosevelt, still laughing. "That is very sweet of you."

What were the President's secret thoughts on the matter? Every shred of evidence, every offhand presidential remark, every list of presidential appointments was scoured for possible hints. By 1940 his intentions were a national guessing game. Most of the guessers, however, jumped to the false assumption that Roosevelt had made his decision to run or not to run, and that all his actions stemmed from this set decision.

They did not know their man. Roosevelt was not one to make a vital political decision years or even months in advance and then stick to that decision through thick and thin. His method through most of his career was to keep open alternative lines of action, to shift from one line to another as conditions demanded, to protect his route to the rear in case he wanted to make a sudden retreat, and, foxlike, to cross and snarl his trail in order to hide his real intentions. More than any situation Roosevelt ever faced, the third term demanded this kind of delicate handling.

For one thing, the President was genuinely unsure of his own desires. By 1940 both the fieldstone library at Hyde Park and his hilltop "dream house" were near completion, and they were standing invitations to return to Hyde Park life and to the memoir-writing that had enormous appeal after the grueling presidential years. More than ever by 1940 his talk was turning to the details of Dutchess County life and history. Too, the exactions and frustrations of his second term were beginning to take their toll physically. The strenuous Christmas activities left him tired rather than exhilarated. It took him weeks to subdue a case of flu during the early weeks of 1940. The weariness of his last years had already begun.

"No, no, Dan, I just can't do it," Miss Perkins remembered his saying to President Tobin of the Teamsters union early in 1940. "I have to get over this sinus. I have to have a rest. I want to go home to Hyde Park. I want to take care of my trees. I have a big planting there, Dan. I want to make the farm pay. I want to finish

Feb. 21, 1940, H. M. Talburt, © by the Washington *Daily News*

March 30, 1940, H. E. Elderman, Washington *Post*

The Sphinx

July 15, 1940, © Rube Goldberg and the New York *Sun*, Inc.

my little house on the hill. I want to write history. No, I just can't do it, Dan."

But it was not so simple as this. Roosevelt could not ignore the compelling reasons that might force him to run again. Certainly he would take the nomination himself if otherwise it would go to an anti-New Deal Democrat or to a fence straddler. Certainly he would take it if the international situation took a serious turn—if, for example, Germany should seem to be winning the war.

Faced by such a situation, some men might spend hours in mental anguish and turmoil as they strove desperately to make a decision. Not so Roosevelt. His decision was to reserve decision. Playing for time had everything to commend it. By keeping alive the possibility of running he could maintain control of the "presidential politicians" throughout the country—his personal friends in the party, high officials holding patronage jobs, programmatic New Dealers— who would jump on someone else's bandwagon only when they were sure the President was through. He could, without trying, win scores of convention delegates, including those who wanted a neutral figure to support until they saw the way the wind blew. He could husband whatever remaining influence he had with Congress. He could protect his position of strength from which to deal with foreign nations and carry weight on the international scene. Since the Republicans would meet before the Democrats, he could wait and see who would be the challenger.

None of this was remarkable; traditionally presidents considering another term had seen the uses of delay. The remarkable thing was Roosevelt's shrewdness and dexterity in keeping alive his two lines of action—of running and of refusing to run.

It was charged at the time that the President was ensuring his renomination by killing off the chances of all his prospective rivals. Quite the contrary was true. In a series of shrewd yet bold moves Roosevelt helped build up a host of presidential possibilities. His tactic was quite in keeping with his usual political and administrative leadership—to strengthen his own position by the method of divide and conquer. Now he carried the tactic to a new level: not only did he encourage the rest of the candidates to contend with one another, he enlarged the field so that there would be a host of rivals wrestling for delegate votes.

With tenacity and vigilance Roosevelt pursued this maneuver. In the spring of 1938 he privately encouraged Hopkins to try for the presidency in 1940, advised him on campaign strategy, and said that he would appoint him Secretary of Commerce in order to strengthen his position. The President did everything possible to help the Hopkins build-up until the latter's almost fatal illness in 1939. Then, during that year, he appointed former Governor Paul

V. McNutt of Indiana chief of the newly established Federal Security Agency, and he encouraged McNutt's aspirations to such an extent that the handsome, white-haired Indianan seemed to conclude that there had been a "laying on of hands." On several occasions during 1939 and early 1940 Roosevelt indicated to Hull—without absolutely committing himself—that he hoped the Secretary of State would be his successor. He told Barkley early in 1940 that "some of the folks here at the White House" were for him as the next Democratic nominee. (Barkley did not bite.) He told Governor Lehman of New York that Lehman deserved the vote of his state delegation at the convention, and the President asked Boss Flynn of the Bronx to make these arrangements. At various times he encouraged the hopes of Jackson, Wallace, and other members of the inner circle.

The President did not miss a trick. He never closed the door completely on the possibility of his own availability. Yet he told visitors time and time again that he neither desired nor intended to run. White House intimates came out with "inside dope stories" that the President would not be a candidate. Letters importuning him to be a candidate went unanswered. He pressed for Chicago as the Democratic convention site because Boss Kelly could be relied on to pack the galleries with Roosevelt supporters. In states where presidential candidates were supposed to make known their intentions before the primaries he privately arranged that he would not be asked about his candidacy. Still keeping his own intentions secret, he sent emissaries to California and other states to make peace among the factions and line them up on one pro-Roosevelt ticket. The result of these and other maneuvers was that Roosevelt kept open a line of retreat—refusal of the nomination—at the same time that he maintained a strong position in case he decided to run.

Roosevelt's basic problem, if he chose to run, was not how to get the nomination—his ability to get a decisive convention majority was never in doubt—but how to be nominated in so striking a manner that it would amount to an emphatic and irresistible call to duty. This party call would be the prelude to a call from the whole country at election time. Only a party summons in July, in short, would make possible a popular summons in November.

Standing formidably in the way of such a call was the very thing that made the call necessary—the anti-third-term tradition. Roosevelt did not doubt the potency of that tradition. No matter that the framers of the Constitution had been so hopelessly divided on re-eligibility that they had failed to establish a limit in the Constitution. No matter that the tradition had been bolstered as much by the accident of personality and circumstance as by deep popular conviction. The unwritten law was there, and Roosevelt was not one to defy it. How to get around it? All the polls showed a vast majority opposed to a third term as an abstract matter, and a clear majority opposed to a third term for Roosevelt. Yet many people, when further questioned, believed that certain circumstances— especially a crisis—would justify the President's running again.

Roosevelt's task—in the event he finally decided to run—clearly was to bring about a unanimous party draft that would neutralize the anti-third-term sentiment. Unhappily for the President, he could not openly lift a finger to bring about such a draft. To do so would be to sharpen the very fears that lay behind the no-third-term feeling, the fears that had dogged Roosevelt all through his second term—the fears of a dictatorial leader grasping for more and more power. If the President were to run again, everything depended on a spontaneous draft. Indeed, after seven years in the White House Roosevelt felt that he was entitled to such a tribute from his party.

By early 1940 there seemed little chance that Roosevelt would be given such a tribute. Three men stood in the way—Hull, Garner, and Farley.

It was a curious trio. Hull, cautious, correct, courtly, slow to act but tenacious when committed, proud of his log-cabin birth, aware at the age of sixty-eight that he had only a few years left of his long political life, stood for the old South that looked with fear on the "radicalism" of the New Deal. Garner, seventy-one years old but still tough as hickory, his tricolor face—white eyebrows, blue eyes, red complexion—hardly changing with the passing years, spoke for the new South of prairie skyscrapers, huge terminals, oil wells, the South that looked darkly on the New Deal as anti-individualistic, anticapitalistic. Farley was only fifty-one; the big tireless party chief had more friends than ever across the country, but his closest ties were with urban politicians who, little interested in policies or programs, tested every passing wind for its impact on votes, deals, tickets. Ideologically the two Southern Protestants and the Irish Catholic had little in common except varying degrees of disenchantment with the New Deal.

Politically, though, it was an ominous combination for the President. Garner, while hopeful for the presidency, was intent mainly on denying Roosevelt a third term. Hull would accept the presidential nomination if he did not have to fight for it. Farley had his eye on the White House but he could wait; running for Vice-President on a ticket headed by either Hull or Garner would give him a priceless opportunity four years later. During 1939 and early 1940 Farley kept in close touch with both men: each buttered the others up and stirred the others' resentments at Roosevelt's slights; they all united in their opposition not to the President himself, whom they professed still to love, but to the third term in principle and to the unscrupulous men who, they told one another, were leading the President astray.

Roosevelt knew that Farley was meeting with Hull and Garner. He devised a different tactic in dealing with each of his potential rivals.

Garner's candidacy the President simply dismissed. "He's just impossible," he told Farley. The once cordial relations between the two men had long turned sour. They had little contact except at cabinet meetings, where Garner, red and glowering, occasionally took issue with the President in a truculent manner. Roosevelt hinted that he would desert the Democratic cause before he would vote for the Texan for President. By early 1940 even official relations between the two men had almost ceased; Roosevelt was hoping that the Vice-President would not show up for cabinet meetings. The President was gleeful about Garner's tribulations as a presidential candidate—about Lewis's public attack on him as a "labor-baiting, poker-playing, whisky-drinking, evil old man," about Garner's sudden change of heart over an antilynching measure in the light of the Negro vote.

Farley was a different matter. Roosevelt did not want to lose the man who had so ably administered two election campaigns. But the President faced a special disadvantage. The Constitution made it politically impossible for two men from the same state to run on the same ticket. Nor would Farley be satisfied with a promise of the vice-presidency in any event. All his presidential hopes turned on Roosevelt's not being a candidate. The President sought to disarm his Postmaster General by insisting that he would not run again; but Farley's political instincts warned him to stay on the alert. Roosevelt asked Cardinal Mundelein to talk with Farley, but the cardinal failed to budge him. Farley stayed in the race.

As for Hull, Roosevelt continued to indicate that he hoped the old Tennessean would be his successor. This on the face of it seemed a dangerous maneuver, for Hull was also the person behind whom Farley and Garner would unite. But the President knew his man. Hull thought it incompatible with his position as Secretary of State to campaign for the nomination. Knowing that Roosevelt's support was all he needed, he chose to wait. Unlike Farley or Garner, he captured virtually no delegates; in the end he became utterly dependent on the President. If, on the other hand, Roosevelt ultimately decided not to run, Hull would be a suitable compromise candidate.

How much of this complex maneuvering was deliberately planned by the President, how much was sheer accident in the midst of utter confusion, no one could tell. But it was certain that by hiding his plans Roosevelt was adding to the confusion, and that he was expecting to benefit from it. The Sphinx waited.

THE HURRICANE OF EVENTS

A few weeks after the outbreak of war, when Roosevelt's standing in the polls jumped upward as it always did during international crisis, Ickes remarked to him that he was more popular than he had been for years. Roosevelt replied: "But just wait and see the nose dive that I will take about next March." As usual, his uncanny sense of timing proved right. All things considered, March 1940 was a low point even for Roosevelt's second term.

The international situation was obscure where it was not dark. Smashing through the Mannerheim Line, Soviet troops in March were forcing Finland to accept a dictated peace. Appalled by what he called the "dreadful rape of Finland," the President must have felt keenly the hopeless inadequacy of United States aid to the little nation—inadequacy stemming from Hull's caution and from Roosevelt's fear of American isolationists. Once again he had at his disposal only moral protests and pronunciamentos, and once again these went unheeded. Throughout the winter both Russia and Germany were consolidating their strength in their respective spheres of interest—but just how far was not clear.

The "phony war" maintained its leisurely pace, as both sides took advantage of the winter to build up their armies. The repeal of the embargo, enabling France and Britain to buy war materials in the United States, was proving a Pyrrhic victory. For one thing, the Allies were planning on a long war of attrition and they were slow to place orders. For another, the cash-and-carry compromise, by taking American ships off the seas, helped the German blockade of Britain almost as much as if all American ships had been torpedoed. The President tried to get around the law by allowing Americans to transfer their ships to Panamanian registry, but he had to beat a hasty retreat when Hull opposed the maneuver and William Allen White wrote that he would not have worked so hard for repeal if he had known that such a subterfuge would be resorted to.

The administration also had to use subterfuges to maintain America's neutral position. In tightening its blockade of Germany, Britain searched American ships, censored American mail, violated American "neutrality" zones. While publicly defending its neutral rights down to the last jot and tittle, the administration at first winked at British violations wherever it seemed safe to do so. But as episodes multiplied, irritation increased in America. The President had to tell his friend Winston Churchill, who had become First Lord of the Admiralty at war's outbreak, "I would not be frank

unless I told you that there has been much public criticism here."
But incidents continued, to the delight of anti-British congressmen
and orators.

March brought also the end of any peace hopes that Roosevelt
still harbored. Returning from a mission to Europe, Welles reported that he had found Rome bitter at Hitler's deals with Russia
but still banking on a German victory, Berlin intent only on a total
triumph, Paris full of corroding discouragement, and London
charged with determination, even overconfidence. There was no
sense in any further peace initiatives from America.

Balked on the diplomatic front, the President had no other way
to turn. The nation was stuck on dead center, somewhere between
neutrality and effective aid to the Allies. The mood of the country
in March 1940, Ambassador Bullitt said, was like that of England
before Munich.

On the domestic scene, too, Roosevelt's leadership was at low ebb.
To be sure, every day brought new declarations from local Democratic leaders that Roosevelt was the party's only hope, that he
must run for a third term. The President's tactic of broadening the
field in order to prevent any candidate from getting too far ahead,
seemed to be working; McNutt, for example, was bleeding so heavily from bites and scratches inflicted in the Washington jungle that
he was no longer a front runner for the nomination. And in the
early presidential primaries Roosevelt was running far ahead of any
rival. But in a more fundamental sense the President's position was
precarious.

That unmanageable creature, the American economy, was behav-
ing with its usual unpredictability. Early in March the brilliant
Treasury economist Lauchlin Currie, now one of the President's
administrative assistants, warned him that a sharp downturn was
taking place and urged a program of stimulating housing and exports and speeding up farm benefit payments. But Roosevelt had
been busy for many months doing the precise opposite of Currie's
proposals: budget slashing. As sensitive as ever to attacks on him by
the budget balancers, as unaware as ever—like most economists—of
the enormous possibilities of heavy deficit spending, Roosevelt was
cutting wherever he could without hurting essential welfare and
defense programs. He would undertake no new programs. The
man who three years before had called for bold action to help the
one-third ill-housed, ill-clothed, ill-nourished, was now turning aside
pleas that he call for stepped-up health, housing, and education
programs. The only extension of the New Deal proposed by Roosevelt during early 1940 was a paltry program for building hospitals in needy areas, a project soon forgotten. And all through the

early months of 1940 unemployment remained at a level of seven to ten million.

It was not that Roosevelt had turned against the New Deal. He was simply operating on his old political rule that he could exert leadership on only one front at a time, and he was husbanding all his strength for the crucial political problems involved in the situation abroad.

To strengthen his position in the face of that situation, the President had been engaged for some time in a tactical political shift. He was trying to line up Republican support in Congress and in the country for a bipartisan foreign policy without alienating his own party and without jettisoning the essence of the New Deal. As a grandiloquent party gesture he had Senate Republican Leader McNary and two other Republicans invited to the Jackson Day dinner. When the suspicious Republicans failed to show up, the President twitted them gently, proclaimed that *both* Hamilton and Jefferson were his heroes, and boasted that he had been less of a party man than most of his predecessors. Roosevelt's shift to bipartisanship restored his symbolic role as leader of the whole nation. But it won him few votes from Republican congressmen, who suspected that his real motive was to get their support without letting them help shape policy. It was no time for party peace. The opposition had won some local elections and was sensing victory in November. Republican presidential candidates were crisscrossing the country busily thwacking the administration's policies and failings.

It was on the left, though, that the President's position was weakest. Despite his peace efforts, the AFL and CIO were still badly split apart. Lewis was still sulking and rebellious, still upbraiding Roosevelt for his "sellout" of the CIO after its help in 1936. Some of the youth groups, too, were becoming increasingly hostile to the President; when in a speech from the White House south portico he warned American Youth Congress delegates against seeking utopias overnight, loud boos floated up in the cold winter air. And there was new and far uglier antagonism on the extreme left.

The American Communists, once friendly or at least indulgent toward the administration because of popular-front tactics dictated from Moscow, had done a flip-flop domestically as well as internationally after the Nazi-Soviet pact. Roosevelt was now at best a weak Kerensky-type pawn of the capitalists, or at worst a power-mad militarist bent on plunging his country into an imperialist war. The President did not mind the abuse, for he knew the value of Communist opposition. But he could not—and did not—ignore the Communist infiltration of sections of labor, youth groups, the press, WPA workers, and government. As usual, however, he attacked the problem indirectly rather than frontally. He put suspected government employees under supervision, and he and Eleanor Roosevelt helped the non-Communist leaders of the Workers' Alliance form a new organization of WPA workers.

The President's hold on Congress seemed weaker than ever. With their usual factionalism exacerbated by presidential nomination dogfights in both parties, the two chambers were arenas for rough-and-tumble combat. A House investigation of the National Labor Relations Board revealed a hapless administrative mess in this key New Deal agency. Republicans and conservative Democrats were readying a bill that, Roosevelt felt, while professing to assure administrative fairness, was actually a "stupid" attempt to hamstring New Deal agencies. The Hatch Act, which Roosevelt had signed the year before despite his suspicion that it was aimed at his patronage power rather than "purity in politics," was extended to cover state employees paid with federal funds. Even Hull's popular trade agreements program barely mustered enough support to gain a three-year extension. The President became so incensed at Garner's opposition to the three-year extension that he exploded one night and "Goddamned this and that" to relieve his feelings, as he told Ickes.

Such was the dismal posture of domestic affairs when Hitler once again seized the world spotlight.

At dawn on April 9 German soldiers struck across the naked Danish border. Half an hour later a dozen German destroyers suddenly emerged out of a snowstorm off the Norwegian port of Narvik, torpedoed Norwegian gunboats, and landed two thousand infantrymen. At ports along the Norwegian coast more troops were soon pouring out of barges and troopships. Danish independence was blotted out in a few hours; in two days the main ports of Norway were in the Nazi grip.

In the first fogged hours of battle it seemed that Britain and France might withstand their enemy. Indeed, the Allies themselves had been planning to occupy key areas of Norway. They were too late. The Germans had laid their plans with thoroughness and imagination; they carried them out with a brilliant mixture of power, precision, ruthlessness, treachery, deception, and surprise. The Allied countereffort was improvised, ill-planned, and inadequate. British troops landed, jousted fecklessly with the enemy, and withdrew. Amid bitter criticism Chamberlain prepared to resign; Churchill would soon take his place. Then, while the Allies were still reeling from the blow, Hitler struck again.

On May 10 a holocaust of German fire and steel began rolling across the Dutch and Belgian frontiers. Parachutists seized airfields, siren-blowing dive bombers roared through the spring air. Behind the German assault troops one hundred and twenty infantry divisions and six thousand warplanes were poised for battle. And somewhere behind this mighty force was the demonical genius, Hitler. Proclaiming the start of the battle, the Fuehrer told his troops that it would "decide the destiny of the German people for a thousand years." Ready for the attack, a half-million Allied troops moved up behind the Belgian troops.

Advancing with blinding speed, massed German tanks and dive bombers speared through Allied lines and cut around the Allied flanks in great encircling sweeps. Motorized troops and infantry poured through the gaps, converting Belgium into a vast trap for the defenders. Within five days German tanks burst through the lightly defended Ardennes hills and began their lightning dash across northern France. On May 15 Prime Minister Churchill, writing as "Former Naval Person," sent an urgent message to Roosevelt: "The scene has darkened swiftly. . . . The small countries are simply smashed up, one by one, like matchwood. . . . Mussolini will hurry in to share the loot. . . . We expect to be attacked here ourselves. . . ." The next few days brought news of disaster after disaster.

Amid this "hurricane of events," as he called it, Roosevelt showed his usual qualities amid crisis: he was serene, confident, alert, ebullient, almost nonchalant. The day after Churchill's letter he drove up to Capitol Hill and asked a cheering Congress for almost a billion dollars for increased defense. He electrified the lawmakers by setting a goal of "at least 50,000 planes a year." The President's face was grave; reporters could see the whiteness of his knuckles as he gripped the speaker's stand; but his voice was resolute as he detailed War and Navy defense needs. Moving quickly on a tide of public opinion Congress soon voted these funds and more.

Pouring through the Ardennes gap German armor curved west toward the Channel, and pinned masses of French and British troops against the sea. The retreat to Dunkerque was on. Huge crowds stood in Times Square, quiet and somber, watching the appalling news bulletins flash around the *Times* Tower. On the night of May 26 the President sat with a small group in his study. He mechanically mixed cocktails; there was no laughter or small talk. Dispatch after dispatch came in, and Roosevelt went through them quickly. "All bad, all bad," he muttered as he handed them on to Eleanor Roosevelt. Grimly he faced the microphones later in the evening. The last two weeks, he said, had shattered many illusions of American isolation. But it was no time for fear or panic. "On this Sabbath evening, in our homes in the midst of our American families, let us calmly consider what we have done and what we must do." The nation must further step up its defense, modernize its arms, enlarge its factories. The "great social gains" of the past few years must be maintained. The Fifth Column must be fought, forces of discord and division overcome. "We defend and we build a way of life, not for America alone, but for all mankind. Ours is a high duty, a noble task."

It was one thing to issue such a clarion call—it was something else to grapple with the cruel dilemma that faced the President during these weeks.

Terribly pressed, British and French leaders were naturally turning for help to the great rich democracy across the seas. In his letter of May 15 Churchill warned Roosevelt of a "Nazified Europe established with astonishing swiftness" and asked him for forty or fifty old destroyers, several hundred of the latest types of aircraft, antiaircraft equipment and ammunition, and a visit by American naval units to Irish ports. The President responded as best he dared. He was expediting the sending of as much military aid as possible, but he would have to have permission from Congress to send destroyers, and this did not seem the right moment to ask for it. The American fleet was concentrated at Hawaii, watching lest the Japanese take some advantage of the crisis.

As Allied defenses collapsed, British and French appeals became ever more frantic. Churchill warned that if England fell, new leaders might arise who could bargain off the British fleet to the Germans to gain a better peace. Ambassador Bullitt passed on a French plea for a statement by Roosevelt that the United States could not permit a French defeat, and the President had to telephone Bullitt to say that "anything of this kind is out of the question." Searching for war material and means of sending it, the President encountered a "nightmare of frustration," as Welles called it. Everything seemed short. The Navy and War Departments naturally coveted the new war equipment flowing out of factories. Legal advisers doubted that the government could sell equipment to the Allies lawfully. Secretary of War Woodring and other high officials opposed "frittering away" vital material overseas. Congress and country were wholeheartedly in favor of more defense, but divided over helping the Allies at our own expense.

The President scraped up whatever equipment he could, but it was pitifully inadequate in the face of German might. And he shied away from strong declarations and even from sending Churchill destroyers.

Roosevelt's diplomatic efforts were equally abortive. During these titanic events he sent plea after plea to Mussolini to stay out of the war. The President even offered to serve as an intermediary in approaching the Allies to satisfy Italy's "legitimate aspirations" in the Mediterranean. But as Hitler's armies advanced the Duce yearned to be in on the kill. Just before the President left Washington on June 10 to speak at the University of Virginia, a message came in from Bullitt that Italy would declare war on France that afternoon and that the French were terming it contemptuously a "stab in the back." Indignant and worried, the President set out for Charlottesville with his wife and Franklin, Jr., who was graduating from the Virginia Law School. His mind kept going over the phrase; as he said later, discretion told him not to use it and "the old red blood" said, "Use it." Blood won out. That night, after a long account of his efforts to hold Mussolini, he said in measured tones: "On this tenth day of June, 1940, the hand that held the dagger has struck it into the back of its neighbor." The President went on to declare American policy in this critical hour:

"In our American unity, we will pursue two obvious and simultaneous causes: we will extend to the opponents of force the material resources of this nation, and at the same time we will harness and speed up the use of those resources in order that we ourselves in the Americas may have equipment and training equal to the task of any emergency and every defense. . . .

"Signs and signals call for speed—full speed ahead."

Full speed was vital, for France was near collapse. In a last desperate gesture Premier Reynaud asked Roosevelt to intervene with force, or at least the threat of force. The President could only answer that the government was redoubling its efforts to send material. Roosevelt was so fearful of American opinion that he turned down Churchill's request that even this weak reply be made public to stiffen the French. Again Reynaud, who was now surrounded by ministers demanding an armistice, implored Roosevelt to lead America into the war; otherwise, he warned, France would "go under like a drowning man." At the same time Churchill warned that continued French resistance from overseas depended on the President's answer. Roosevelt hesitated. Then his answer was dispatched. He expressed his admiration for French resistance. He extended his "utmost sympathy" over developments. He was sending more and more material, but, he ended, as for military commitments—"Only the Congress can make such commitments."

Only Congress. And in the middle of this great tide of affairs a little episode reminded the President of the shoals and reefs on Capitol Hill. Chairman Walsh of the Senate Naval Affairs Committee, an Irishman and an isolationist, suddenly discovered that twenty new motor torpedo boats were to be sent to Britain. Navy Secretary Charles Edison warned the President that Walsh was in a towering rage, "threatening to force legislation prohibiting sale of anything," and the whole committee was in a lather. Reluctantly Roosevelt called off the deal.

By the time the President's last message reached Reynaud the next day, June 16, the premier was at the end of his rope. That evening he resigned his office, and Marshal Petain, who had been demanding an armistice, began to form a new cabinet. Five days later the French signed the armistice in the forest of Compiègne, where the French had accepted German capitulation twenty-two years before. Present was the exultant Fuehrer. As correspondents watched, Hitler glanced with burning contempt at the French monument celebrating the German defeat of 1918. In a "magnificent gesture of defiance," the Fuehrer snapped his hands on his hips, planted his feet wide apart, and arched his shoulders: 1918 had been avenged.

"WE WANT ROOSEVELT!"

Incredibly, during these feverish weeks, Roosevelt kept his fingers on the political situation at home. He followed closely the fights for state delegations. He jubilated over the victories scored by Roosevelt slates in California, Texas, and elsewhere. He discussed convention arrangements and platform planks with Ickes, Jackson, Douglas, Corcoran, and other third-term boosters. He watched the spirited Republican race among Dewey, Taft, Vandenberg, and a late entrant named Wendell Willkie. But he did all these things without revealing his own plans even to White House intimates. Hopkins, probably speaking for the President, asked Early to instruct all members of the administration to make no statements on the third term.

As the crisis deepened, Roosevelt's popular backing mounted sharply. Millions of Americans forgot their concern for the third-term tradition as they instinctively rallied behind their leader against the threat outside. But not all Americans, by any means—and there was one group whose opposition especially worried the President. At a time when the nation might soon be turning to its young men for succor and sacrifice, petitions against defense and aid to the Allies were showering the White House from colleges and youth groups. "Shrimps" was the best word for these young people, Roosevelt said in exasperation, but he felt concerned enough about the problem to let Eleanor Roosevelt arrange a special evening meeting early in June at the White House with the leaders of the American Youth Congress.

It was a poignant scene—the youth leaders, white and colored, grouped in the East Room, stonily polite; the President calm and genial despite sickening reports received from France during the day; Mrs. Roosevelt trying in her gracious way to establish rapport between generations; Hopkins sitting by, pale, taut, impatient at young people's failure to understand his chief's problems. At the start Roosevelt tried to create a common bond with the group. He mentioned newspaper opposition to the "radical" New Deal; he explained his Spanish Civil War policy as the result of the French and British fear of war; he said that the issue was democracy versus other forms of government. Then the questions came, fast and sharp.

What about democracy in the South, asked a conferee, where half the people don't vote? Roosevelt: "What are we going to do about it? . . . You cannot get it [solved] in a year or two." A Negro: What about segregation in the armed forces? The President turned to Hopkins, who said that even among Negroes there were two schools of thought on the matter. A Midwest YMCA leader: Why so much emphasis on national defense and so little on social defense? Roosevelt: "It is a little bit difficult in our system of government to pursue two equally important things with equal emphasis at the same time. That is darned hard." Then a long speech from the floor: "Something serious has happened" that had caused the President to forget the first line of defense—social security, education, housing, clothing, food. Billions of dollars for guns and battleships—and nothing for the people. It was not enough to blame Congress. Where was the President's leadership? "We are very—shall I say sick?—yes, but at the same time, we are a little bit angry that the President and the members of his Cabinet have not carried this fight once again to the people!"

The President looked at him. "Young man, I think you are very sincere. Have you read Carl Sandburg's *Lincoln?*"

No, the young man had not.

"I think the impression was that Lincoln was a pretty sad man," Roosevelt went on, "because he could not do all he wanted to do at one time, and I think you will find examples where Lincoln had to compromise to gain a little something. He had to compromise to make a few gains. Lincoln was one of those unfortunate people called a 'politician' but he was a politician who was practical enough to get a great many things for this country. He was a sad man because he couldn't get it all at once. And nobody can.

"Maybe you would make a much better President than I have. Maybe you will, some day. If you ever sit here, you will learn that you cannot, just by shouting from the housetops, get what you want all the time."

If sections of organized youth felt deserted and bitter, there was another group that had no mixed feelings about the President. By June 1940 hundreds of Democratic party politicos were clamoring for the President to run. He already had enough delegate votes to win the nomination easily. Then, late in June, he strengthened his position immensely by one of his quick strokes.

On the eve of the Republican convention in Philadelphia, the President appointed two eminent Republicans to his cabinet—Henry L. Stimson, seventy-three years old, a militant internationalist and a cabinet member under Taft and Hoover, as Secretary of War, and Frank Knox, Chicago newspaper publisher, Landon's running mate in 1936, and one of Uncle Ted's Rough Riders, as Secretary of the Navy. The Republicans might have ignored the matter, or they might have congratulated Roosevelt on undertaking to start his administration toward the change that the Republicans would complete in November. As Roosevelt probably anticipated, they did neither. Hysterical outcries rent the Philadelphia air, and there was even talk about reading the two renegades out of their party.

"Dirty politics!" the Republicans shouted at Roosevelt. Actually the President had been planning since the outbreak of war to make his cabinet bipartisan. He had hoped to appoint Landon as well as Knox, but this plan repeatedly fell afoul of Landon's refusal to come in unless Roosevelt publicly opposed a third term. Several other factors delayed the cabinet shuffle: Roosevelt's reluctance to oust Harry Woodring as Secretary of War; his concern that Knox's appointment might lead to difficulties with the publisher's old enemy, Boss Kelly; the arrangements that had to be made with Boss Hague of New Jersey to nominate Secretary of the Navy Edison for governor of New Jersey. When Landon in mid-May still demanded the third-term disclaimer, Roosevelt seized on a suggestion of Frankfurter's to choose Stimson. He then waited two weeks and announced the appointments just as the Republican convention was getting under way. As usual, Roosevelt's timing was perfect; the date fitted both the needs of the crisis abroad and politics at home.

The President followed with interest the turbulent Republican convention. For several ballots Dewey and Taft led the pack; then, with the help of the roaring, chanting galleries, Wendell Willkie surged ahead to an electrifying sixth-ballot victory. A utilities magnate as Republican candidate! "Nothing so extraordinary has ever happened in American politics," Ickes exclaimed. The convention seemed to arouse Roosevelt's militancy. He told his cabinet that he would break down the aura surrounding Willkie by tieing him in with the idea of the corporate state.

Now at last, with foreign and domestic events coming into focus, the President could act. On July 3 he had Hull in for lunch. The secretary of state immediately noticed a whole change of manner. To be sure, Roosevelt still deprecated the idea of running for a third term. But he talked in a "sort of impatient, incredulous tone" of the pressure on him not to let the party down. He explored Hull's weak points as a candidate. His guarded tone convinced the old Tennessean that the President would run again.

Although surprised and mystified, Hull let the matter drop. It was too late for him to act on his own even if he wished to run. Garner, too, after his drubbings by Roosevelt in presidential primaries, was now all but out of the race. There was still Farley, though, to be reckoned with. The big, bald politico could not win. But how much damage could he do to the President? By July, Farley was in a mood to do damage. He was bitter over Roosevelt's refusal to tell him of his plans, angry over Roosevelt's devious behavior on the issue of a Catholic candidate, and indignant above all over Roosevelt's failure to declare himself and let another Democrat have his chance at the presidency. In this mood Farley saw his chief at Hyde Park on a broiling day in early July. The photographers found two laughing, joking old comrades, but when they left the atmosphere quickly cooled. After desultory conversation the President shrugged his shoulders and waved toward his library and hilltop retreat.

"Jim, I don't want to run and I'm going to tell the convention so." If the President hoped that Farley would urge him to run, he was disappointed.

Having steeled himself against the President's persuasiveness, Farley said bluntly: "If you make it specific, the convention will not nominate you." Farley then launched into a brief against the third term.

"What would you do if you were in my place?" the President finally asked.

"Exactly what General Sherman did many years ago—issue a statement saying I would refuse to run if nominated and would not serve if elected."

"Jim, if nominated and elected, I could not in these times refuse to take the inaugural oath, even if I knew I would be dead within thirty days."

Farley would never forget the President's appearance at that moment—"his right hand clasping the arm of his chair as he leaned back, his left bent at the elbow to hold his cigarette, his face and eyes deadly earnest." There was a pause, and then more talk. When the political charade was over, each man had got the information he wanted. Roosevelt knew that Farley's name would go before the convention. Farley knew that Roosevelt would run—but wanted an emphatic and uncontrollable draft.

Next day Farley left for Chicago grimly determined that Roosevelt would not get that kind of draft. A week later began one of the most extraordinary conventions in history.

The Chicago Stadium, Monday morning, July 15, 1940. The corridor ringing the arena was a long congested bazaar, where bellowing hawkers peddled souvenirs, pennants, pop, hot dogs, popcorn, pictures of Roosevelt. Inside, a huge sickly gray portrait of the President looked down through the smoky haze on the gathering. The bunting around the hall was bright, the tiers of seats were gleaming red, but on the convention floor all was dull and cold. Delegates, alternates, and spectators milled about dejectedly. What's going to happen? they asked one another. What's the score? No one knew. Even the Very Important were uncertain. Ickes, watching sourly from the platform, had got no directions from the President, nor had others of the inner circle. Big Jim Farley, presiding over the convention, wanted none. Mayor Kelly mentioned the President in his welcome, but even the magic name of Roosevelt fell flat on the listless delegates and the half-filled galleries.

Soon word was spreading quickly around the floor that Hopkins was the man to see. He was in the know. Sprawling on his bed in the Blackstone Hotel, his bony frame showing through his shirt and baggy trousers, hair falling down over his pallid skull, Hopkins did indeed have a special line to the White House—a telephone in the bathroom, the only place where he was sure of privacy.

Yet even Hopkins did not really know.

Roosevelt was acting out his curious role down to the last scene. He had given no final plan or instructions to anyone—not even to Hopkins—because he was determined that the party must summon him on its own. He still wanted a genuine and emphatic draft. He would not stop Hopkins, Ickes, and the rest from working for such a draft, but neither would he help them. When they had begged him just before the convention to give them sailing orders, he had only smiled and repeated that the convention must decide. God would provide a candidate, he said. The telephone in Hopkins' bathroom was less an instrument of presidential command than a means of keeping the President informed. But that private wire, along with the sick man's residence in the White House, were the stuff and symbol of Hopkins' authority.

Only once did Roosevelt act directly to help the draft. When it was still certain, as the convention opened, that Farley was the main obstacle to a unanimous summons, the President telephoned him and gingerly—ever so gingerly—intimated that there might be no need for a ballot. "That's perfectly silly," Farley said shortly, and Roosevelt let the matter drop. In any event, the President's indirect tactics of the past year were paying off. No other strong candidate was available now. Even those party leaders who had little love for Roosevelt wanted this supreme vote-getter at the head of the ticket. And the bandwagon jumpers, waiting to see the drift of things, could sense the temper of the convention. It would be Roosevelt.

Still, the delegates were worried—worried about Willkie's popularity, worried about the third term, worried about the President's plans. Tuesday was another dull day, full of turgid oratory and restless, milling delegates. The Roosevelt men were worried too. What was Farley up to? Would Garner, Farley, and the others still work out a coalition? Byrnes, Jackson, and Ickes cooked up a scheme to take control of the convention and push the President's nomination through. Hopkins, still lacking instructions, notified the White House about the plan. Roosevelt vetoed it. He did not mind if the convention was drab, Hopkins reported back. The regular procedure must go on.

THIS CONVENTION IS BLEEDING TO DEATH, Ickes wired the President. YOUR REPUTATION AND PRESTIGE MAY BLEED WITH IT. He begged his chief to come to Chicago and supply leadership. There was no answer. Roosevelt awaited his draft. To make it seem genuine, he had devised one final twist.

Tuesday night Barkley delivered an old-fashioned, stem-winding speech. Part way through, an incidental mention of Roosevelt's name unleashed a spontaneous demonstration, but Barkley, pounding his gavel, managed to quiet the hall. Finally he came to his climax—a message Roosevelt had sent him to deliver. The President had tried "in no way whatsoever," the message began, to influence the selection or opinions of delegates. His voice rising to a roar, Barkley went on:

"Tonight, at the specific request and authorization of the President, I am making this simple fact clear to the Convention.

"The President has never had, and has not today, any desire or purpose to continue in the office of President, to be a candidate for that office, or to be nominated by the Convention for that office."

A hush spread over the hall.

"He wishes in all earnestness and sincerity to make it clear that all the delegates to this Convention are free to vote for any candidate.

"That is the message I bear to you from the President of the United States."

There was a moment of stunned silence. Delegates looked at one another uncertainly. Then, from loud-speakers around the hall, came the cry of a single, thunderous voice.

"WE WANT ROOSEVELT!"

A few delegates seized their state standards and started parading down the aisles. "EVERYBODY WANTS ROOSEVELT!" roared the loud-speakers. More delegates filed out; hundreds of spectators started pouring from the galleries onto the floor. "THE WORLD WANTS ROOSEVELT!" A long serpentine parade began weaving toward the rostrum. Down in a basement room Kelly's superintendent of sewers, a leather-lunged, potbellied little man, pressed his lips against the microphone. "ROOSEVELT!" The parade was now a wild, screaming mob. "ROOSEVELT!" Cheerleaders, bands, noisemakers added to the din, but the voice could still be heard, now a driving, drumming, ear-splitting chorus, carrying everything before it. "ROOSEVELT!" The mob surged down the aisles, waving banners, knocking down chairs, pushing people aside. "ROOSEVELT! . . . ROOSEVELT! . . . ROOSEVELT! . . ."

In an hour order was restored, but everything now was anticlimactic. Next day Roosevelt's name was put in nomination; then ailing old Senator Glass nominated Farley in a few rasping words that could hardly be heard over the scrape and shuffle and occasional boos and catcalls from the floor. Impatiently the convention waited while Garner, Tydings, and Hull were nominated, seconded, and given sad little demonstrations. The only ballot was the first: Roosevelt 946, Farley 72, Garner 61, Tydings 9, Hull 5. Then Farley, a party man to the end, moved Roosevelt's nomination by acclamation, to a roar of "ayes."

In the White House the President, surrounded by friends and aides, had listened intently to the proceedings. His draft secured, he turned immediately to the vice-presidential nomination. Until now he had not announced his choice, partly because he had hoped that Hull would accept, partly because his own draft movement was stronger the longer he held the vice-presidential prize open as bait. The night of his nomination Roosevelt began notifying Hopkins and other party leaders that his choice was Wallace. The Secretary of Agriculture was a dependable liberal, the President felt, and would appeal to the farm states, where isolationist feeling was strong. But the leaders were appalled by Roosevelt's choice. Wallace was a mystic, they complained, an inarticulate philosopher, an ex-Republican, a political innocent.

Roosevelt was adamant. "I won't deliver that acceptance speech," he said to Rosenman at breakfast Thursday morning, "until we see whom they nominate."

The real difficulty was not Wallace but the fact that a host of vice-presidential booms were under way at Chicago. Jesse Jones, Ickes, McNutt, Byrnes, and a dozen others were busily lining up delegates. Several candidates thought they had Roosevelt's support. Louis Johnson, after flying to Washington during the convention to see the President, returned to Chicago and scurried around the convention floor to report jubilantly that Roosevelt had given him the "green light." His friends were unimpressed. One of them finally said, "Oh! hell, Louis, this convention hall is full of candidates with green lights." When news spread that the President had chosen Wallace, all the other hopefuls dropped out, cursing and grumbling, except McNutt and Speaker Bankhead of Alabama. The latter, a self-styled unreconstructed Southerner, thought the White House had agreed to leave the vice-presidential nomination open if he undertook not to enter the presidential lists.

By now the convention was in a churlish temper. The delegates had gone down the line for Roosevelt; now they wanted to go ahead on their own. On a happy inspiration Eleanor Roosevelt was induced to fly from Hyde Park to talk to the delegates, but her pleasant, high-minded remarks brought only a brief calm. By Thursday evening the delegates' sore and mutinous feelings rose to a pitch. Bankhead was nominated and seconded in bitter speeches. McNutt's withdrawal announcement was almost drowned out. The galleries, packed with claques for other candidates, greeted the speeches for Wallace with jeers, hisses, and catcalls. On the platform sat Mrs. Wallace. Sadly she asked Eleanor Roosevelt: "Why are they so opposed to Henry?"

His face grim and set, Roosevelt sat by the radio in the Oval Room, playing solitaire. He listened to the convention uproar, heard the commentators describe the feeling as a revolt against presidential bossism. As the balloting neared, he put aside the cards and started writing on a pad. He asked Rosenman to "smooth it out" quickly—he might have to deliver it soon. Rosenman glanced at the paper. In a sharp and biting statement, Roosevelt had written that he could not go along with a party divided between liberalism and reaction; he would enable the party to make the choice by declining the nomination. It ended: "I so do."

The President returned to his solitaire. Outside the room Pa Watson wanted to tear the message up. "I don't give a damn who's Vice-President and neither does the country," he angrily told Rosenman. "The only thing that's important to this country is that fellow in there." When Rosenman came back into the room with the completed statement, Watson was almost in tears. Miss Le Hand, long opposed to a third term, was all smiles. As for the President, Rosenman had never seen the President look so determined.

In Chicago the balloting was under way. Back and forth the lead wavered between Wallace and Bankhead. Byrnes darted from delegation to delegation crying, "For God's sake, do you want a President or a Vice President?"

In the Oval Room Roosevelt tallied the vote. Tension mounted. The race stayed close; Bankhead led at the end, but several urban states that had passed on the roll call now threw their votes to

Wallace. The President had won his fight. By now Roosevelt was tired and bedraggled, his shirt clung to him, heavy and damp in the July heat. While word went to Chicago that he would shortly address the convention, the President was wheeled into his bedroom. Now Watson was smiling and Missy was in tears. In a few moments Roosevelt reappeared in a fresh shirt, his hair combed, as jaunty as ever.

In Chicago his voice came through strong, smooth, even, measured.

"It is very late tonight; but I have felt that you would rather that I speak to you now than wait until tomorrow.

"It is with a very full heart that I speak tonight. I must confess that I do so with mixed feelings—because I find myself, as almost everyone does sooner or later in his lifetime, in a conflict between deep personal desire for retirement on the one hand, and that quiet, invisible thing called 'conscience' on the other. . . .

"Lying awake, as I have, on many nights, I have asked myself whether I have the right, as Commander-in-Chief of the Army and Navy, to call on men and women to serve their country or to train themselves to serve and, at the same time, decline to serve my country in my personal capacity, if I am called upon to do so by the people of my country.

"In times like these—in times of great tension, of great crisis—the compass of the world narrows to a single fact. The fact which dominates our world is the fact of armed aggression, the fact of successful armed aggression, aimed at the form of Government, the kind of society that we in the United States have chosen and established for ourselves. It is a fact which no one any longer doubts—which no one is any longer able to ignore. . . .

"Like most men of my age, I had made plans for myself, plans for a private life of my own choice and for my own satisfaction, a life of that kind to begin in January, 1941. These plans, like so many other plans, had been made in a world which now seems as distant as another planet. Today all private plans, all private lives, have been in a sense repealed by an overriding public danger. . . .

"Only the people themselves can draft a President. If such a draft should be made upon me, I say to you, in the utmost simplicity, I will, with God's help, continue to serve with the best of my ability and with the fullness of my strength. . . ."

TWENTY-ONE *An Old Campaigner,*
a New Campaign

A S YOU MAY imagine," the President wrote his
Uncle Fred Delano on July 18, "the events of the past few days
have filled me more with a sense of resignation to my fate than any
feeling of exaltation." Expressing to Norris his amazement at the
conservatives' "terrific drive" to produce a situation in the convention that would force him to decline the nomination, the President
ended, "even though you and I are tired and 'want to go home,'
we are going to see this thing through together."

Roosevelt could feel well satisfied with the final results of the convention. He had soundly drubbed the conservatives, including many
of the anti-Roosevelt men who had been thwarting him ever since
the Supreme Court fight. The platform was a stout defense of the
New Deal. He had secured a running mate who was, as he said to
Norris, a "true liberal." He had gained for himself the draft he
needed. Broadly speaking, his tactics of delay and indirection had
worked. As the first ballot tally showed, no strong candidate had
been left to threaten him. The opposing forces had never got together. He had beaten "The Hater's Club," made up, he told Norris, of "strange bedfellows like Wheeler and McCarran and Tydings and Glass and John J. O'Connor and some of the wild Irishmen from Boston." His trump card—keeping open the possibility
of declining the nomination until the very end—had paid off handsomely.

On the other hand, Roosevelt had lost the thing he wanted most—
an unquestioned draft by acclamation. Farley and the others had
spoiled the stage effects for a clamorous and categorical summons by
the party. The situation had its irony. Roosevelt's nomination was
truly a draft in the sense that the impetus toward his nomination
had come not from himself but from the administration and party
leaders, and his own efforts had been indirect. But his very attempt
to forego leadership brought about a chaotic convention situation
in which leadership fell into Hopkins' hands simply because he
was believed to hold the credentials from the President. In the
eyes of many delegates Hopkins was Roosevelt's cat's-paw. The

431

forced nomination of Wallace completed the picture of a White House dictatorship over the party.

The price of victory was steep. Hundreds of delegates left Chicago for home in a bitter and rebellious frame of mind. Feeling against Wallace was so strong that he had to be dissuaded from delivering an acceptance speech at the convention. Party leadership was shaken. Farley was determined to quit the chairmanship. Other party regulars—notably Flynn—would not assume leadership unless Hopkins was sidetracked. Ickes, McNutt, and other administration leaders were hurt and angered by the President's selection of Wallace. Bankhead was telling people how Roosevelt men had sold him out at Chicago. Garner prepared to pack up and go home to Texas for good.

Republican newspapers gleefully headlined a flurry of anti-third-term Democrats who bolted the Roosevelt-Wallace ticket in the wake of the convention. Some of these had deserted their party in 1936, but they made fresh copy again four years later. The newspapers also played up the convention as a packed New Deal caucus manipulated by White House stooges, radicals, city bosses, and the "voice from the sewer." The press, of course, was heavily anti-Roosevelt. Yet the President was vulnerable. The show in Chicago had not quite come off: he had won his draft in such a way as to intensify popular suspicion of his deviousness. It was not surprising that polls showed a Republican resurgence. The parties, according to some polls, were entering the presidential battle on even terms.

The President's main trouble, though, lay in none of these, but in a big, shaggy man who, during the late July lull, was busy pumping hands and visiting rodeos in Colorado. A glittering new figure had emerged on the political scene.

THE HOARSE AND STRIDENT VOICE

Legends were sprouting profusely around Wendell Willkie by midsummer 1940, but the facts were striking enough. Born in 1892, the fourth of six children, he was descended from Germans who had left their homeland after the revolutionary disturbances earlier in that century. He grew up in Indiana amid an intellectually and politically fertile family; his father was a teacher, lawyer, and Bryanite Democrat, his mother a lawyer and a gifted public speaker. After stints at teaching, law, and the army, young Willkie spent ten years in Akron as a lawyer-businessman, then moved to New York City in 1929, where he made a meteoric rise in the utilities field. In January 1933, a few weeks before Roosevelt's first inauguration, he became head of the huge Commonwealth and Southern Corporation.

During the next seven years Willkie became the most articulate and effective business critic of the New Deal. Scorning Liberty League tactics, he shouted his denunciations from hundreds of platforms across the country and in scores of magazine articles. He sold himself as the chief victim of the New Deal, as an honest, enterprising businessman overwhelmed by big government. He had, indeed, been beaten time and again by the New Deal—beaten in his attempts to hold off the TVA, beaten in his fight against the "death-sentence" clause of the public utility holding company bill, beaten in his campaign efforts for Landon, beaten finally in the courts. It seemed a monumental piece of poetic justice that now he could take on, in direct and open combat, the author of all his misfortunes.

He was the perfect foil for Roosevelt. Like the President, Willkie was a big, attractive man, who liked to talk and to laugh; but the two antagonists were cut from sharply different cloth. Willkie's touseled hair, broad face and jaw, bulky frame, baggy, unpressed clothes gave him a countrified look that appealed to middle-class America. "A man wholly natural in manner, a man with no pose, no 'swellness,' no condescension, no clever plausibleness . . . as American as the courthouse yard in the square of an Indiana county seat . . . a good, sturdy, plain, able Hoosier," Booth Tarkington said in a description that set off the Indianan from the slick figure in the White House.

Inside this rustic form was an urbane New York cosmopolitan. Widely read and traveled, Willkie was literate enough to write book reviews for reputable journals, facile and knowledgeable enough to steal the show on "Information Please," the phenomenally popular radio program of the day, and versatile enough to win over a wide range of audiences in his vigorous, "man-to-man" talks. He was, a newspaperman noticed, "a master of timing releases, issuing denials before edition time, adding punch to a prepared speech, or making one on the spur of the moment letter-perfect enough to have been memorized, treating publishers, editors, and reporters with the skill needed to suggest to each that they were the sole beneficiaries of his gratitude and his confidence." Moreover, in seven years of crisscrossing the country in his one-man battle against the New Deal, Willkie had won the friendship of the very publishers—notably Roy Howard and Henry Luce—who had become increasingly alienated from the White House.

From the start Roosevelt saw the Republican candidate as a serious threat. Here was no solemn engineer, like Hoover, no raw novice in national politics, like Landon. Roosevelt had first met Willkie in December 1934. Their talk was friendly, but not their feelings; afterward Roosevelt told how he had outdebated his visitor and reduced him to stammered admissions, while Willkie wired his wife, an anti-New Dealer, CHARM EXAGGERATED STOP I DIDN'T TELL HIM WHAT YOU THINK OF HIM. The President felt that Willkie's utility background would hurt his opponent's chances, but the Republican selection for Vice-President of Senator McNary, a long-time supporter of public power and farm aid, was bound to take some of the sting out of any attempt to tie Willkie with the "interests."

Nor could Willkie himself easily be labeled a reactionary. He had come out publicly for many of the chief New Deal reforms. A bitter and active foe of the Klan during the 1920's, he had a deserved reputation as a friend of civil liberties. And he was an internationalist who had said, a month before the Republican convention, that "a man who thinks that the results in Europe will be of no consequence to him is a blind, foolish and silly man." Willkie was as flexible in his views as most other politicians panting for a presidential nomination. But this made him a hard man for the Democrats to label. Indeed, the Indianan himself was a Democratic bolter: he had been a delegate to the 1924 Democratic convention, he had voted for Roosevelt in 1932, and he was calling himself a Democrat as late as 1938.

All in all, Willkie and McNary were formidable opponents—the strongest ticket the Republicans could have named, Roosevelt felt. The nature of the two conventions also strengthened Willkie's hand. The Republican convention had appeared as open and unbossed as the Democratic had seemed tawdry and rigged. In fact, however, Willkie's build-up had been spurred by a great deal of money and an avalanche of propaganda; yet his sixth-ballot triumph in the convention over the Dewey and Taft "steam rollers" left him looking like a Galahad.

In mid-August Willkie made his acceptance speech in his home town in Indiana. A colossal shirt-sleeved crowd—a quarter-million strong, some said—stood in a grove in the stifling heat and heard Willkie lambaste the third-term candidate. "Only the strong can be free," he shouted in his slurred, twangy way, "and only the productive can be strong." In this speech and in the ones that followed, as his voice turned husky and then hoarse and finally became a scratchy croak, Willkie's initial strategy became clear. He would accept the major foreign and domestic policies of the New Deal. He would attack Roosevelt on three main counts: seeking dictatorial power, preventing the return of real prosperity, and failing to rearm the country fast enough in the face of foreign threat.

He was eager, Willkie proclaimed again and again, to meet "the Champ."

The Champ would not enter the ring for a while. Even before his renomination Roosevelt had decided on his campaign tactics in the event he should run again. Spurning ordinary election campaigning, he would stay close to Washington and emphasize his role as commander in chief. He would ignore the opposition. Occasionally he would travel through the eastern states on inspection trips. It would be the tactics of 1936, except that now he would be inspecting defense plants and naval depots rather than PWA projects and drought areas.

"Events move so fast in other parts of the world that it has become my duty to remain either in the White House itself or at some nearby point where I can reach Washington and even Europe and Asia by direct telephone—where, if need be, I can be back at my desk in the space of a very few hours," he had said in his acceptance speech. ". . . I shall not have the time or the inclination to engage in purely political debate."

As usual, the old campaigner had left himself an opening.

"But I shall never be loath to call the attention of the nation to deliberate or unwitting falsifications of fact, which are sometimes made by political candidates." The effect of this, of course, was that the President could enter the campaign at any moment he chose.

Roosevelt made the most of his role as commander in chief. His defense inspection trips were arranged so that he would pass through as many towns as possible. Presidential aides tried to keep state and local politicians off the President's train, but the press was given ample opportunity to picture the commander in chief watching army maneuvers and gazing fondly at aircraft carriers under construction. During a defense trip through northern New York the President met with Prime Minister Mackenzie King, and it was agreed to set up a Permanent Joint Board on Defense to consider the security of the north half of the Western Hemisphere.

Vainly the White House correspondents tried during August to get Roosevelt to answer Willkie's barbed shafts. "I don't know nothin' about politics," he said coyly.

The President's defense role was not merely a campaign tactic. By midsummer 1940 the nation was feverishly rearming, and quick decisions had to be made in the White House. Roosevelt's availability was all the more necessary because he had refused to delegate central control of defense production. When he had set up the Defense Advisory Commission at the end of May 1940, one of the members, William S. Knudsen, asked, "Who is our boss?" Roosevelt answered, laughing, "Well, I guess I am!" Administratively, it was a makeshift arrangement, but politically it enabled Roosevelt to keep his fingers on this delicate and vital phase of policy.

Diplomatic developments, too, required close attention. All over the world foreign offices were revising their estimates in the wake of France's fall. Relations with the new French government were severely strained, and the United States was caught in the middle. The Japanese military, its eyes on the Dutch and French possessions left almost undefended after Hitler's blitz, won control of the Japanese cabinet in mid-July. An even greater problem involved hemisphere defense, for it was feared that Hitler might now either force France and Holland to cede their Caribbean possessions, or he might seize them by attack or infiltration. Hull brought off a brilliant coup at the Havana Conference late in July by wangling conference approval of his program for opposing transfer of European possessions in the New World, but the situation still bristled with a host of diplomatic and military difficulties.

Despite these formidable problems, Roosevelt never forgot that he had a campaign on his hands. He arranged for Ickes to answer Willkie's speech of acceptance and watched happily the ensuing Donnybrook as Willkie became involved in answering the pugnacious Secretary's charges that the Republican nominee had been a member of Tammany Hall and had once eulogized Samuel Insull, the notorious utilities czar. The President also tried to put the creaking Democratic party machinery into shape. Farley, still galled by his treatment at Chicago, remained unwilling to continue as national chairman despite all the persuasion Roosevelt could bring to bear, and Flynn took over the job. Since the Good Neighbor League had been allowed to die, a new organization had to be set up to attract Republicans and independents; Norris and La Guardia, with the help of Corcoran and other administration aides, took on this job. Roosevelt telephoned city bosses direct to make arrangements for his campaign appearances.

It was a time of cabinet reshuffling too. To take the place of Wallace, who was already campaigning quietly, Roosevelt chose Claude R. Wickard, a "dirt farmer," as Secretary of Agriculture. Hopkins, still ailing, resigned as Secretary of Commerce in order to work directly for the President; by appointing RFC chief Jesse Jones to succeed him Roosevelt rewarded the big Texan for his cooperation at Chicago and also restored to his official family the kind of political balance the President liked, especially at election time. Frank Walker's appointment as Postmaster General maintained Catholic representation in the cabinet after Farley's departure, and Stimson's and Knox's presence gave the official family a strong bipartisan cast. During the summer two distinguished writers joined Hopkins and Rosenman to work on campaign speeches: playwright Robert Sherwood and poet Archibald MacLeish, whom Roosevelt had made Librarian of Congress the previous year.

This would be Roosevelt's ninth campaign for office, his third for the presidency. But events would not allow this to be an ordinary campaign.

LION VERSUS SEA LION

"The Battle of France is over," Churchill told a rapt House of Commons in mid-June. "I expect that the Battle of Britain is about to begin. Upon this battle depends the survival of Christian civilisation. Upon it depends our own British life, and the long continuity of our institutions and our Empire. . . . Hitler knows that he will have to break us in this island or lose the war. If we can stand up to him, all Europe may be free and the life of the world may move forward into broad, sunlit uplands. But if we fail, then the whole world, including the United States, including all that we have known and cared for, will sink into the abyss of a new Dark Age, made more sinister, and perhaps more protracted, by the lights of perverted science.

"Let us therefore brace ourselves to our duties, and so bear ourselves that, if the British Empire and its Commonwealth last for a thousand years, men will say, 'This was their finest hour.' "

Four weeks later Hitler informed his generals and admirals: "As England, in spite of the hopelessness of her military position, has so far shown herself unwilling to come to any compromise, I have decided to begin to prepare for, and if necessary to carry out, an invasion of England." Preparations must be completed by mid-August for this operation, which was given the code name "Sea Lion." The Fuehrer stressed that success depended on gaining air superiority and then controlling a sea lane across the English Channel for the invaders.

As Hitler marshaled shipping, deployed three crack armies, and mustered his awesome *Luftwaffe* for the softening up, Churchill again turned to Roosevelt for help. Destroyers, he wrote the President, were vitally necessary to repel the seaborne invasion and to protect Britain's supply routes. In the last ten days alone, the Nazis had sunk or damaged eleven British destroyers. He must have fifty or sixty of America's old, reconditioned destroyers at once. The next three months would be vital—if Britain survived this phase it ultimately would triumph.

"Mr. President," Churchill warned, "with great respect I must tell you that in the long history of the world this is a thing to do *now*."

What could Roosevelt do? He was fully aware of the dreadful urgency of the situation, but the political obstacles seemed insuperable. Senator Walsh's law provided that the President could send destroyers to Britain only if the navy certified that they were use

less for United States defense, and naval officials had recently testified as to their potential value so that Congress would not junk
them as a drain on the taxpayer. Clearly special legislation would
be necessary—and Walsh, Wheeler, Nye & Co. would be waiting
with raised hatchets. The President had toyed with the idea of allowing the destroyers to be sold to Canada on condition they be
used only in hemisphere defense, thus relieving Canadian destroyers
for service off England, but this weak subterfuge he cast aside.

It was not the President but a faction in the cabinet that broke
the stalemate. Stimson, Knox, and Ickes were pressing for action.
At a cabinet meeting August 2 Knox stated that Britain's situation
was more desperate than ever and he passed on an idea that had
been circulating for some time in private circles. This was to grant
the destroyers in exchange for military bases on British possessions
in the Americas. The idea drew wide cabinet backing. On the question whether Willkie should be consulted the cabinet was divided,
but Roosevelt decided to bring him into the picture. The President,
still assuming that legislation was necessary for the deal, calculated
that Willkie could help line up Republican support on the Hill.

From the cabinet room Roosevelt telephoned William Allen
White and asked him to talk with Willkie. White was optimistic—
had not the Republican candidate called for full aid to Britain?
But when White talked with Willkie in Colorado he found him
personally in favor of legislation to send destroyers but unwilling
to take a public stand. Willkie's difficulty lay in the Republican
isolationists who dominated his party in Congress. He did not dare
arouse this powerful group, including House Republican Leader
Joseph Martin, now the Republican national chairman.

"I know there is not two bits difference between you on the issue
pending," White telegraphed the President on August 11. "But
I can't guarantee either of you to the other, which is funny, for I
admire and respect you both."

By now Roosevelt was sorely pressed. For Willkie's rebuff came
just as the Battle of Britain broke over southeastern England. On
August 8 two hundred Stukas and Messerschmitts roared down on
British convoys. Four days later hundreds more attacked radar
stations and airfields. Then the tempo rose fast. On the 13th, 1,400
Nazi aircraft swarmed over England; two days later 1,800, the next
day 1,700. This was the Nazis' "Eagle Attack"—the knockout blow
against the Royal Air Force that was designed both to herald and to
make possible the invasion.

A cruel dilemma faced the President—the man who hated above
all to be forced into a political corner. As Americans heard radio
commentators tell of Britain's ordeal, saw pictures of London burning, of women and children huddling in subways, a wave of sym-

pathy for Britain swept the country. White's Committee to Defend America by Aiding the Allies, now boasting of six hundred chapters, built up a huge agitation on the destroyer issue. Millions signed petitions; General Pershing, old and ill, pleaded for action before it was too late; newspapers clamored that the President do something.

This same uproar, however, seemed to provoke the isolationists to new virulence. Sale of the destroyers to a nation at war, warned the Chicago *Tribune,* would be an act of war. By all the measures of opinion the isolationists were in a minority in the country, but, as usual, they were entrenched on Capitol Hill. When Ambassador Bullitt warned that if Britain fell, Hitler would turn on America, senators denounced his speech as an act "little short of treason" by a "multimillionaire, New Deal warmonger." Roosevelt knew that at best a destroyer bill would drag for weeks through Congress, at worst it would fail, with the awful effect this would have on British morale and on the chances of further American aid.

To make matters worse, Congress was already wrangling bitterly over another contentious matter, compulsory military service. Sponsored by Republican Representative James W. Wadsworth and Democratic Senator Burke of Nebraska, now a hardened anti-New Dealer, the bill was vigorously supported by Secretary Stimson, who was sorely in need of men for his newly forming army divisions. The President had taken no leadership on the bill until August 2 when, under pressure from Stimson and others, he informally came out for "a selective service training bill" in a press conference. His statement produced another explosion on the Hill. Delegations of "mothers" swarmed into congressmen's offices, religious and labor leaders protested, Senator Wheeler cried that a draft act would be Hitler's "greatest and cheapest victory," even Norris said that it would end in dictatorship.

The upshot was that by mid-August the President was committed to a draft bill now stalled in Congress, and, amid frightening reports from Britain, was thinking of sending a destroyer bill to the Hill that would pass too late if at all. In a last-minute essay at the personal influence that had once served so well, Roosevelt wrote Walsh a long, pleading letter. He tried to rebut Walsh's claims that sending the destroyers would be an act of war, that Americans thought it was too late to commit themselves as the saviors of "surrendered France and Great Britain," that Hitler would retaliate. It was not time for politics in the ordinary sense, Roosevelt said. But he could not move the Senator from Massachusetts.

What to do? Once again private citizens stepped in at the critical moment. On August 11 there had appeared in the New York *Times* a long, carefully argued letter showing how the sale of destroyers could be made under existing legislation. It was signed by Charles C. Burlingham, Dean Acheson, and two other distinguished lawyers. The idea of bypassing Congress on the matter was not new to Roosevelt, but this kind of authoritative support could help immeasurably to prepare public opinion for a presidential act. Walsh's stubborn opposition put the final capstone on Roosevelt's determination to go ahead on his own.

But now a new set of difficulties loomed. Churchill had always wanted to announce the leasing of bases to America as a spontaneous act separate from the destroyer arrangement. Tying the two matters together in one package, he argued, would make it a kind of business deal, and people would start trying to compute the money value. The embattled Prime Minister doubtless reasoned, too, that the British would consider that they had got the worst of the deal. Roosevelt took just the opposite view. Legally, he could hand over the destroyers only as part of an arrangement that would improve American defenses. Politically, he could win popular support for the measure, he felt, only if he could offer it as a good Yankee deal, so that people would say (in Roosevelt's later words), "My God, the old Dutchman and Scotchman in the White House has made a good trade."

For a moment a fatal deadlock threatened. Then Green Hackworth, State Department adviser, came up with an idea. Why not divide the bases into two lots, those in Bermuda and Newfoundland to be leased to America as an outright gift from Britain, the rest to be swapped for the destroyers? Roosevelt eagerly seized on the compromise, and Churchill reluctantly went along. On September 3, with all legal and diplomatic snags overcome, the President announced the deal.

It was barely in time. At the end of August the Battle of Britain was moving toward an agonizing climax. Day after day fagged, red-eyed pilots raced for their planes, rose to engage the invaders, and, if they lived, rose again the next day. Nazi losses were heavy, but the tide of battle was running against Britain's fighter command. In the fortnight following August 24 nearly a quarter of its thousand pilots were killed or seriously wounded. Airfields were pitted, aircraft factories gutted. Hundreds of German barges were moving down the coasts of Europe to the ports of northern France. On September 3 the German command issued operational schedules for invasion.

But the final order for Sea Lion was never to come. Infuriated by the bombing of Berlin, Hitler turned the weight of his air attack on London and gave respite to the battered fighter command. After that the *Luftwaffe* could never quite gain mastery of the air.

German naval chiefs warned the Fuehrer on September 12 that the British fleet was still in command of the Channel. The invasion date was postponed again and again. On October 12 Hitler shelved Sea Lion until spring.

Just what part the fifty overage destroyers had in the decision to postpone the invasion cannot be known; surely it was a minor factor in the Nazis' over-all estimate of the situation. Yet it was a factor at a time when the decision on Sea Lion lay in the balance. Even more important, the deal marked decisively the end of American neutrality. The United States was now in a status of "limited war." The deal came as a jolting shock to Hitler and Mussolini and forced them to consider America more seriously in their global strategy. Late in September the two dictators replied to the destroyer deal by welcoming Japan into a Tripartite Pact; this action, they hoped, would enable Japan to draw America away from Europe and would strengthen American isolationists.

The destroyer deal, too, was a decisive commitment to aiding Britain. It meant that much more military help would follow—as it did. Britain and the United States, Churchill said in Commons, would henceforth be "somewhat mixed up together" in some of their affairs for mutual advantage. "I do not view the process with any misgivings. I could not stop it if I wished; no one can stop it. Like the Mississippi, it just keeps rolling along. Let it roll. Let it roll on—full flood, inexorable, irresistible, benignant, to broader lands and better days."

For Roosevelt, the destroyer deal was a colossal political risk. He told friends that he might lose the election on the issue. Even more, if England should fall and the Nazis gain control of the British fleet, the President would be fair game for the Republicans, for in that event the fifty destroyers would be turned against their former owner. To be sure, Roosevelt had gained assurances from Churchill that the fleet would not fall in German hands—but who could guarantee the actions of a defeated nation's government seeking peace? Not only had Roosevelt dared to act—he had acted without Congress.

"Congress is going to raise hell about this," the President said to Grace Tully as he worked on the draft of the agreement, but, he added, delay might be fatal. He was right. A howl of indignation rose from Capitol Hill. The St. Louis *Post-Dispatch* published an advertisement in leading newspapers: "Mr. Roosevelt today committed an act of war. He also became America's first dictator. . . . Of all sucker real estate deals in history, this is the worst. . . ." Willkie approved the trade but denounced the bypassing of Congress, which he was soon calling "the most dictatorial and arbitrary act of any President in the history of the United States."

All this—and the election in two months. Whatever he gained from negotiating the deal—which most voters favored—he might lose from the reaction to his method of bringing it off. Roosevelt knew in advance that bypassing Congress would intensify the popular fear of presidential dictatorship that had bedeviled him for years. Yet he had gone ahead, assumed the responsibility, taken the risk. The President had performed many acts of compromise—perhaps of cowardice—in the White House, especially during his second term. But on September 3, 1940, he did much toward balancing the score. After years of foxlike retreats and evasions, he took the lion's role.

Churchill had not appealed in vain to the President's sense of the verdict of history. But Roosevelt wanted vindication on Election Day too.

THE TWO-WEEK BLITZ

By the end of September the campaign was taking on an ugly, ominous tone. As he rode through industrial areas Willkie heard workers booing and heckling, saw them spit on the sidewalk and turn their backs. He was showered with confetti in the business and financial sections, but he was pelted with fruit, stones, eggs, light bulbs in the grimy factory areas. Stories circulated about his German ancestry, about signs in his home town reading: "Nigger, don't let the sun go down on you." Roosevelt, of course, was not spared either. Besides all the shopworn slanders there were new and ingenious slurs. Leaflets asserted that the combined Roosevelt family had made millions of dollars out of the presidency. When Elliott Roosevelt received an army commission, huge buttons sprouted with the slogan, "Poppa, I wanta be a captain."

SAVE YOUR CHURCH! billboards screamed in Philadelphia. DICTATORS HATE RELIGION! VOTE STRAIGHT REPUBLICAN TICKET!

The President still did not campaign. In mid-September, to be sure, he made an admittedly political speech to the Teamsters Union convention, but he dwelt sonorously on preserving peace and extending New Deal welfare—his hearers would hardly have known that an election campaign was on. Too, he dedicated schools and issued statements on Leif Ericson and Columbus days, but all in his role of chief of state and commander in chief.

Willkie by now was in trouble. The big man, his hair more rumpled, his voice more gravelly than ever, was still drawing big crowds. His difficulty was that he could not find a winning political stance from which to strike out at his elusive foe. At the outset Willkie punched at the New Deal record on two counts: employment and defense. He had a case here: unemployment was still high;

Roosevelt had lagged behind rather than led public opinion in national defense measures; sticking to his usual administrative habits, he had not set up an integrated organization for rearmament. But the times were not propitious for an indictment on these counts. The war boom was on: as Willkie spoke in the Northwest, people were flocking back to work in aircraft factories and lumber yards; as he spoke in Pittsburgh the steel mills were humming with new orders. And Roosevelt symbolized the aroused commander in chief. Newspapers and magazines were adorned almost daily with pictures of the President next to big guns, ships, tanks.

Nor did the third-term issue seem to be paying off. Willkie made much of the undemocratic idea of the indispensable man, but here again he could not come to grips with the enemy. Democrats, taking their cue from the President, handled the question by ignoring it. Events abroad, moreover, helped maintain during September the crisis atmosphere in which the voters might find a third term acceptable. The Battle of Britain roared on; Japanese troops moved into Indochina; Italy prepared an attack on Greece.

The Republican challenger also faced divisions within his own camp. Glorifying his amateur support, leaning heavily on the thousands of Willkie Clubs that had sprung up, treating the Republican party as an allied but somewhat alien power, he had antagonized some of the professional organization men at the start. Willkie made things worse by accepting the substance of the New Deal and, on some issues, taking a more internationalist position than Roosevelt. Just a "me-too" candidate, the professionals grumbled. And they pointed to the public opinion polls as proof that such soft campaign methods were not working.

Roosevelt himself helped Willkie decide to reassess his tactics. The President had been stung by Willkie's assertions earlier in the campaign that the "third-term candidate" at the time of Munich had telephoned Hitler and Mussolini to sell Czechoslovakia down the river. To a press conference early in October the President brought a New York *Times* dispatch from Rome reporting that the Axis hoped for Roosevelt's defeat. He would not comment. "I am just quoting the press at you," he said archly.

Late in September Willkie shifted tactics. Roosevelt now was not an appeaser but a warmonger. "If his promise to keep our boys out of foreign wars is no better than his promise to balance the budget," he proclaimed in a voice that had acquired the low flat tone of a bass horn, "they're already almost on the transports." Sensing that at last he had a winning issue, Willkie went from extreme to extreme.

The President seemed all the more vulnerable to such attack because of the passage of the Selective Service Act in mid-September.

"WARMONGER!", drawn after Roosevelt sent a message to Hitler on April 18, 1939, David Low, *Europe Since Versailles*, Penguin Books, 1940, reprinted by permission of the artist, copyright © Low All Countries

BOMBPROOF SHELTER, Oct. 9, 1940, Carey Orr and D.L.B., Chicago *Tribune*

A REPORT FROM THE OLD DOMINION, Aug., 1941, Fred O. Seibel, Richmond *Times-Dispatch*

Backed by both presidential nominees, the act was a special embarrassment to the President because registration day was set for
October 16, and the first drawing of lots for October 29, just a
week before the election. Despite hints that a delay until after the
election might be the better part of discretion, Roosevelt faced his
task without flinching. He took symbolic as well as actual leadership of the "muster," as he preferred to call it, speaking movingly
to the nation on registration day and presiding magisterially at the
first drawing from the goldfish bowl.

By mid-October, Willkie's cries of warmonger were sending
tremors of fear through Democratic ranks. This was the one great,
violent, unpredictable issue. The fear of war had a hysterical tone
that seemed to spread to the whole campaign; it was solidly buttressed, moreover, by resentment at the administration among
German- and Italo-Americans. Republican orators did not allow
the latter to forget Roosevelt's stab-in-the-back remark. Flynn sent
in alarming reports on Italian sections of the Bronx, and Germans
could turn the balance in the Midwest. Worrisome stories also
reached the White House about the "Irish" isolationist vote; in
Massachusetts, Senator Walsh was campaigning for re-election on an
isolationist and almost anti-Roosevelt platform.

Newspaper opposition to the President was even stronger than
in 1936. Roosevelt's old friends Roy Howard, Henry Luce of *Time-
Life-Fortune,* and Joe Patterson of the New York *Daily News* came
out against the third term. These publishers Roosevelt long before
had written off, but he was surprised when the New York *Times*
announced for Willkie. Roosevelt dismissed the *Times* editors as
merely "self-anointed scholars" in a letter to Josephus Daniels, but
he was hurt by the switch of this newspaper that had appeal for
independent voters in the East.

Most upsetting of all were the public opinion polls. During September they had shown Roosevelt comfortably leading Willkie.
The President, however, was disturbed as well as pleased by these
figures. He feared that the final polls might show Willkie gaining
and give the impression of a horse race with his adversary likely
to pass him just before the tape. Roosevelt even speculated to Ickes
that if George Gallup, the head of the American Institute of Public
Opinion, ever wanted to sell out, this would be his best chance;
Gallup could deliberately manipulate the figures to hurt the Democrats and arrange to sell his business for a good round sum. Roosevelt was wrong about Gallup but he was right about the next poll
returns. Influenced by Willkie's cries of warmonger and by a lull
in the Battle of Britain, among other things, the October returns
showed Willkie rapidly cutting down the President's lead.

This shift was all that was needed to put the Roosevelt camp into a state of near panic. For weeks letters and telegrams had streamed into the White House urging the President to come out of his corner and fight; now the stream rose to a flood. With a single voice the party turned to its leader with a cry for help. Ickes haunted the White House pleading that the fight was lost unless the President acted. Deeply angered by Willkie's campaign Roosevelt on October 18 announced that he would answer the Republican "deliberate falsification of fact" in five election speeches. He passed out word that his lieutenants could go after Willkie with their bare hands.

"I am fighting mad," Roosevelt said to Ickes.

"I love you when you are fighting mad, Mr. President," the old gamecock replied.

No commander has ever sized up the terrain more shrewdly, rallied his demoralized battalions more tellingly, probed the enemy's weak points more unerringly, and struck more powerfully than did Roosevelt against the Republican party during the climactic two weeks before the election. Nor has any commander taken more satisfaction in the job. For it was Roosevelt's supreme good fortune that the circumstances of the election had brought together, in a sorry alliance, the reactionaries, the isolationists, the obstructionists, and the cynical laborites and left-wingers who had bruised and cut him for four years—all now under the leadership of a candidate who, the President believed, had sold out to the worst elements in his party.

Roosevelt hungered to get on the stump—yet he had to proceed cautiously. At all costs he wanted to preserve his symbolic role of commander in chief. He had said that he would not travel more than twelve hours from Washington, in case he was needed there in an emergency; and despite frantic pleas for personal appearances elsewhere, he stuck to this plan. A Secret Service ban on the presidential use of airplanes meant that the President could campaign only in parts of the Northeast. Roosevelt managed to make some automobile tours that were both defense inspections and campaign trips, but he knew that his greatest weapon was the radio, through which he could reach the whole country. Exploitation of the radio seemed all the more urgent because of Republican supremacy in the press, and it seemed all the more agreeable because Willkie was at his most graceless and ineffective at the microphone.

Roosevelt opened his campaign in Philadelphia on the night of October 23. He declared that he welcomed the chance to answer falsifications with facts. "I am an old campaigner," he proclaimed, "and I love a good fight." The huge crowd roared.

Never had the old campaigner been in better form, reporters agreed. He was in turn intimate, ironic, bitter, sly, sarcastic, indignant, solemn. He lifted his eyes in mock horror, rolled his head sidewise, shook with laughter. "He's all the Barrymores rolled in one," a reporter exclaimed.

Slowly and deliberately Roosevelt answered Willkie's charge of secret understandings.

"I give to you and to the people of this country this most solemn assurance: There is no secret treaty, no secret obligation, no secret commitment, no secret understanding in any shape or form, direct or indirect, with any other Government, or any other nation in any part of the world, to involve this nation in any war or for any other purpose."

The President struck out at a Republican charge, as he described it, that his administration had not made one man a job.

"I say that those statements are false. I say that the figures of employment, of production, of earnings, of general business activity —all prove that they are false.

"The tears, the crocodile tears, for the laboring man and laboring woman now being shed in this campaign come from those same Republican leaders who had their chance to prove their love for labor in 1932—and missed it.

"Back in 1932, those leaders were willing to let the workers starve if they could not get a job.

"Back in 1932, they were not willing to guarantee collective bargaining.

"Back in 1932, they met the demands of unemployed veterans with troops and tanks.

"Back in 1932, they raised their hands in horror at the thought of fixing a minimum wage or maximum hours for labor; they never gave one thought to such things as pensions for old age or insurance for the unemployed.

"In 1940, eight years later, what a different tune is played by them! It is a tune played against a sounding board of election day. It is a tune with overtones which whisper: 'Votes, votes, votes.'"

On the subject of economic recovery Roosevelt quoted the financial section of the New York *Times* against the editorial page. "Wouldn't it be nice," he taunted, "if the editorial writers of *The New York Times* could get acquainted with their own business experts?"

Five nights later, after driving during the day for fourteen hours through New York City streets before probably two million people, Roosevelt charged in Madison Square Garden that the Republican leaders were "playing politics with national defense." Such a charge was opportune; Italy had just invaded Greece, and several times during the day the President interrupted his street tour to telephone the State Department. He made no "stab-in-the-back" remark in the Garden—only an expression of sorrow for both the Italian and Greek peoples. Most of his speech was a slashing attack on the Republican leaders—Hoover, Taft, McNary, Vandenberg—for opposing defense measures in the past and now condemning the administration for starving the armed forces.

"Yes, it is a remarkable somersault," Roosevelt said, his voice dripping with sarcasm. "I wonder if the election could have something to do with it."

While drafting this speech Rosenman and Sherwood had hit on the rhythmic sequence of "Martin, Barton, and Fish." They handed Roosevelt a draft with this phrase to see if he would catch the rhythm. He did: his eyes twinkled as he repeated it several times, swinging his finger in cadence to show how he would put it across. The crowd in Madison Square Garden guffawed and were soon repeating the phrase with him.

Willkie was staggered by this assault on him through his weakest allies. As the campaign rose to a new peak of bitterness and intensity, he desperately doubled his bets. On October 30, the day after Roosevelt officiated at the drawing of selective service numbers, Willkie shouted that on the basis of Roosevelt's record of broken promises, his election would mean war within six months.

Roosevelt was en route to Boston the day that Willkie made this charge. By now Democratic leaders were more jittery than ever; the Gallup poll showed Willkie almost abreast of Roosevelt nationally and ahead of him in New York and other key states. Each time his train stopped for rear-platform speeches on the way to Boston messages came in from Flynn and others pleading with Roosevelt to answer Willkie's charges. The President, in fact, had already compromised on the essential issue throughout the whole campaign by stressing his love for peace and neutrality and his record on defense rather than expounding his crucial policy of aiding Britain even at the risk of war. But, as Roosevelt sat in a low-backed armchair in his private car, Hopkins handed him a telegram from Flynn insisting that he must reassure the people again about not sending Americans into foreign wars.

"But how often do they expect me to say that?" Roosevelt asked. "It's in the Democratic platform and I've repeated it a hundred times."

"Evidently," said Sherwood, "you've got to say it again—and again —and again."

The President liked the phrase. Then the speech writers ran into a snag on the sentence "Your boys are not going to be sent into foreign wars." Roosevelt in past talks had always added the words "except in case of attack"; he had, indeed, insisted on this qualification during the Chicago convention even when he was willing otherwise to compromise on the foreign policy plank. Now he wanted to drop the proviso. Rosenman asked why.

Roosevelt's face was drawn and gray. He had to bend before the fury of Willkie's attack—but he would not admit it.

"It's not necessary," he said shortly. "If we're attacked it's no longer a foreign war."

That night in Boston, after a tumultuous reception, Roosevelt catalogued the anti-New Deal voting record of "Martin, Barton and Fish" and compared it with the "soothing syrup" the Republicans spread on thick. Appealing by radio to the farming West, he wondered out loud if Martin—whom Willkie had once described as representing "all that is finest in American public life"—was slated for Secretary of Agriculture. And to the "mothers and fathers of America," he made the assurance that in years to come would be repeated mockingly by thousands of isolationist orators:

"I have said this before, but I shall say it again and again and again:

"Your boys are not going to be sent into any foreign wars."

By now Roosevelt was facing a threat from a new quarter, and he used his next campaign speech two nights later in Brooklyn to counter it. The Republicans had scored a singular coup a few nights before when John L. Lewis not only came out for Willkie but announced that he would resign as president of the CIO if Roosevelt won. The President's sole motive and goal, said the black-maned old miners' chief in his Shakespearean voice, was war. By asserting that a victory for Roosevelt would be in effect a vote of no confidence in himself, Lewis was able at last to come to grips with the slippery rival he hated—but he was doing so on the President's own ground. With the Communists also attacking the administration hysterically, Roosevelt saw his opening and struck hard.

"There is something very ominous," Roosevelt said in Brooklyn, "in this combination that has been forming within the Republican party between the extreme reactionary and the extreme radical elements of this country.

"There is no common ground upon which they can unite—we know that—unless it be their common will to power, and their impatience with the normal democratic processes to produce overnight the inconsistent dictatorial ends that they, each of them, seek." Toward the end of his speech Roosevelt quoted a Philadelphia Republican leader as having said, "The President's only supporters are paupers, those who earn less than $1200 and aren't worth *that*, and the Roosevelt family."

" 'Paupers' who are not worth their salt," Roosevelt exclaimed,

"—there speaks the true sentiment of the Republican leadership in this year of grace.

"Can the Republican leaders deny that this all too prevailing Republican sentiment is a direct, vicious, unpatriotic appeal to class hatred and class contempt?

"That, my friends, is just what I am fighting against with all my heart and soul. . . ."

While the White House moved fast to turn Lewis' district leaders against the mine leader, Roosevelt ended the campaign in Cleveland on the lofty note he loved. The Cleveland speech was perhaps the hardest he had ever had to write. Rosenman and Sherwood had not had a chance to start preparing anything until the day before, and they were exhausted. All night the two labored on the campaign train, catching cat naps on beds littered with toast crusts and gobs of cottage cheese. By midday the next day, when the draft was ready, Sherwood was shocked at Roosevelt's appearance—the dark circles under his eyes, the gray face, the sagging jowls. The President during the morning had been making rear-platform appearances, greeting people, pumping hands; he had felt compelled to say at Buffalo, "Your President says this country is not going to war." Roosevelt was dreadfully tired.

But during lunch, as the President told long, dull stories about Maine lobstermen that all present had heard many times, Sherwood saw his enormous powers of recuperation at work. Soon Roosevelt was demanding jocularly, "What have you three cutthroats been doing to my speech?" For six hours straight, except when he had to put on his leg braces and walk out to the rear platform on Pa Watson's arm, Roosevelt worked on his speech. Out of the noise and dirt of the car, out of the rhythm of the train as it chugged slowly through the falling rain, out of the chatter and scuffle of visiting politicos, out of the utter weariness of Roosevelt and his advisers, came somehow a superb campaign speech. That night forty thousand men and women cheered their hearts out as Roosevelt stood before them in a vast auditorium. He began quietly but before the end he was striking a personal and passionate note.

"During these years while our democracy advanced on many fields of battle, I have had the great privilege of being your President. No personal ambition of any man could desire more than that.

"It is a hard task. It is a task from which there is no escape day or night.

"And through it all there have been two thoughts uppermost in my mind—to preserve peace in our land; and to make the forces of democracy work for the benefit of the common people of America.

"Seven years ago I started with loyal helpers and with the trust and faith and support of millions of ordinary Americans.

"The way was difficult—the path was dark, but we have moved steadily forward to the open fields and the glowing light that shines ahead.

"The way of our lives seems clearer now, if we but follow the charts and the guides of our democratic faith.

"There is—there is a great storm raging now, a storm that makes things harder for the world. And that storm, which did not start in this land of ours, is the true reason that I would like to stick by those people of ours—yes, stick by until we reach the clear, sure footing ahead.

"And we will make it—we will make it before the next term is over.

"We will make it; and the world, we hope, will make it, too.

"When that term is over there will be another President, and many more Presidents in the years to come, and I think that, in the years to come, that word 'President' will be a word to cheer the hearts of common men and women everywhere.

"Our future belongs to us Americans.

"It is for us to design it; for us to build it. . . ."

THE FUTURE IN BALANCE

The campaign spluttered to a surly finish. Willkie, his voice still a hoarse whisper, charged once more that a third term would mean dictatorship and war. On election eve Roosevelt gave his usual "nonpartisan" talk. After urging that all vote the next day and then help restore unity, he ended with an old prayer that he remembered from Groton forty years before:

". . . Bless our land with honorable industry, sound learning, and pure manners. Save us from violence, discord, and confusion; from pride and arrogancy, and from every evil way. Defend our liberties, and fashion into one united people the multitudes brought hither out of many kindreds and tongues. . . ."

Next day fifty million Americans—millions more than ever before—streamed to the polls. Roosevelt himself was the picture of genial self-confidence when he faced reporters at the Hyde Park polling place. Patiently he posed while the photographers shot him from every angle. "Will you wave at the trees, Mr. President?" he was asked. "Go climb a tree!" Roosevelt said. "You know I never wave at trees unless they have leaves on them." But then, quickly relenting, he waved at the trees while cameras clicked.

That night the house stood dark and quiet on its height above the Hudson. On a staff above the portico the presidential flag, with its shield, eagle, and white stars, flapped quietly in the mild November air. Inside the mood was tensely gay. Much of the family was there, along with a host of friends. Little groups clustered around radios throughout the house. Roosevelt sat at the family dining-room table. In front of him were big tally sheets and a row of freshly sharpened pencils. News tickers chattered nearby.

At first the President was calm and businesslike. The early returns were mixed. Morgenthau, nervous and fussy, bustled in and out of the room. Suddenly Mike Reilly, the President's bodyguard, noticed that Roosevelt had broken into a heavy sweat. Something in the returns had upset him. It was the first time Reilly had ever seen him lose his nerve.

"Mike," Roosevelt said suddenly, "I don't want to see anybody in here."

"Including your family, Mr. President?"

"I said 'anybody,'" Roosevelt answered in a grim tone.

Reilly left the room to tell Mrs. Roosevelt and to intercept Morgenthau's next trip back to the dining room. Inside, Roosevelt sat before his charts. His coat was off; his tie hung low; his soft shirt clung around the big shoulders. The news tickers clattered feverishly. . . .

Was this the end of it all? Better by far not to have run for office again than to go down to defeat now. All his personal enemies gathered in one camp—big businessmen like Willkie, Democratic bolters like Al Smith and the rest of them, newspaper publishers like Hearst and Howard, the turncoats like John Lewis, the obstructionists on Capitol Hill, the isolationists, the Communists—would this strange coalition at last knock him down and write his epitaph in history as a power-grasping dictator rebuked by a free people?

In Hoboken and in St. Louis, in Middletown and in a South Carolina crossroads school, ballots were counted and figures phoned to the court house; numbers were tumbled onto telegraph wires, grouped with other figures, flashed to the state capitals, combined with more figures; and now the little machines were spewing them out. In the black numbers was being struck some cosmic balance—the courageous acts, the forthright utterances, the hard decisions, the great achievements, stretching from the Hundred Days to the destroyer deal, from social security to selective service. Struck in this balance, too, were the compromises and the evasions, the deals and the manipulations, the hopes unrealized, the promises unfulfilled.

The smoke curled up from the cigarette in the long holder. The Hyde Park returns were not in yet. But they would probably go against him. It was strange, in a way. He had never really left Hyde Park. He had always left part of himself in this world of tranquil estates, hard-working farmers, St. James's church, the trees and the fields and the river. He had never wholly left the world of his mother, now sitting with friends in another room. Yet this was the world he had never won over politically.

In the little black numbers marching out of the ticker, not only Roosevelt but the whole New Deal was on trial. The relentless figures were a summation of so much—of the clarion call of 1933, the sultry summer of 1935, the long trips through the country, the court fight, the purge, the pleas to the dictators, the arming of the nation. A generation of American ideas was on trial too. Eighty precincts from New Jersey reporting—what verdict would come from Newark slums and the Jersey flats on a credo that had repudiated McKinley, moved beyond Wilson, and somehow fused a dozen differing doctrines and traditions?

From all over America the atoms of judgment streamed through the ticker and took their place on the tally sheets. Still Willkie ran strong. Disappointing first returns were coming in from New York— New York, the very image of the America from which the New Deal coalition had been built. New York—the heart of his political empire, the state of Uncle Ted, of law firms like the one he had worked for on Wall Street, of Tammany bosses. New York—the state that had rebuked him in 1914, and again in 1920, then favored him by the tiny margin of 1928 and the huge avalanche of 1930.

The ash dropped from the cigarette; Mike Reilly stood stolidly outside the door. Was this the end of Jim Farley's journey to the Elks' convention; the final landing for the plane that had carried Roosevelt from Albany to the Chicago convention of 1932? Would the whole great adventure follow the Blue Eagle into defeat? New York City returns were coming in—even the city was undependable in this strange election. Here were the urban masses—the Italians, Jews, Negroes, Germans, Irish—who had benefited from the New Deal and who had sustained it. But now the New Deal was no longer new, and other, sharper issues had emerged as Hitler changed the face of politics everywhere. One report had reached Roosevelt that in New York City only the Jews were solid for him.

And so the returns poured in, filling in the little pieces that would, before the night was over, make up a vast mosaic—and an answer. The voters, in the last analysis, were not passing on a unity, on a completed sum of the New Deal. For when all its parts were added and subtracted, what remained was less a quantity than a spirit. Seven years were on trial, seven eventful years crammed with deeds; yet it was not the deeds that remained—though their monuments would long endure—so much as a distillation of the pageant of the 1930's, embodied in the spirit that was the New Deal—boldness, eclecticism, experimentation, a devotion to building the grade crossing and housing the homeless that transcended ideology and spoke the idiom of American tradition. There was in all this not so much a philosophy as a common sense. And it was the common sense of the American people that must speak tonight. . . .

Then there was a stir throughout the house. Slowly but with gathering force, the numbers on the charts started to shift their direction. Reports began to arrive of a great surge of Roosevelt strength, a surge that would go on until midnight. New York, Massachusetts, Illinois, Pennsylvania—the great urban states were falling in line behind the President. By now Roosevelt was smiling again, the door was opened, and in came family and friends with more reports of victory. Then came the usual torchlight parade from Hyde Park center, lighted by photographers' flash bulbs, and the usual homey talk by the President: "I will still be the same Franklin Roosevelt you have always known. . . ."

In the ballroom of the Hotel Commodore in New York thousands of Willkie supporters had gathered in a celebrating mood. For a time all were jubilant; then, as the sad reports poured in, the crowd slowly dwindled until only a dejected band of Willkieites remained. The candidate appeared for a short talk late in the evening. "Don't be afraid and never quit," he cried hoarsely. Not till the next day did he send Roosevelt a congratulatory wire.

The final results spelled a decisive victory for Roosevelt. The popular vote was 27,243,466 to 22,304,755; the electoral vote was 449 to 82. Besides Maine, Vermont, and six farm states, Willkie carried only Indiana and Michigan. Roosevelt won every city in the country with over 400,000 population except Cincinnati. On the other hand, Willkie had gained five million more votes than Landon had in 1936; Roosevelt's plurality was the smallest of any winning candidate since 1916. The President's margin in New York—about 225,000—was his lowest since his hairbreadth victory for governor in 1928.

But, while Roosevelt lost some support in almost every major group, he dropped off only slightly in the huge lower and lower-middle income groups. His continued substantial support among the "masses" was the key to his victory. Labor, including coal miners, stayed with the President. Lewis's efforts had fallen flat, and he duly surrendered the CIO presidency as a symbol of his total defeat by Roosevelt in the political arena. There were indications that class voting in 1940 was more solid than four years before. "I'll say it even though it doesn't sound nice," a Detroit auto unionist told reporter Samuel Lubell shortly after the election. "We've grown class conscious."

If Willkie's appeals to the workers on economic issues had proved unavailing, his raising of the war issue did cut into Roosevelt's vote.

Pro-German and Italian and anti-British elements swung sharply against the President, and these were only partly offset by the Jews, eastern seaboard Yankee internationalists, and national groups such as Poles and Norwegians who could not forget Hitler's occupation of the "old country." Roosevelt actually increased his vote in northern New England over 1936, though by a small margin.

Unquestionably Roosevelt had been lucky in at least two respects: the crisis in Europe and the first flush of returning prosperity. The former took the force out of Willkie's main foreign policy appeal; the latter took the sting out of his main domestic argument, namely the Depression. Poll after poll showed that the sharper the crisis, the more the voters clung to Roosevelt. The emergency situation seemed also wholly to counteract Willkie's third-term warnings.

Luck—but marvelous skill as well. The President's political timing had never been better, his speeches for the most part had never been more skillful, his thrusts at enemy weak points never more telling. More than this, he had exploited his one great line of communication to the people—the radio—while countering Willkie effectively in the very medium—the newspapers—that the latter could claim as peculiarly his own. Willkie was ineffective over the radio; and, while Willkie got more favorable mention in the press, Roosevelt got more *attention* in the press. The old political adage held: bad publicity is better than no publicity.

In the last analysis Roosevelt himself was the issue. His campaign poses with the guns and ships had paid off; but his captaincy of a generation paid off too. His victory was largely a personal one; the Democrats gained only six seats in the House in 1940 after the slump of 1938, and lost three in the Senate. The future had been made possible for Roosevelt, but what was foretold for his party, his program, his country, and his world, no man could tell.

EPILOGUE *The Culmination*

A MONTH AFTER Roosevelt's election Hitler threw down the gage of world battle. In a fiery speech to the Berlin armaments workers the Fuehrer pictured the global conflict as a gigantic class struggle. Britain and America, rich nations ruled by capitalists, had millions of unemployed; in Germany all had jobs, and work was the supreme value. "There are two worlds that stand opposed to each other. . . . With this world we cannot ever reconcile ourselves. . . . I can beat any other power in the world. . . ."

Three weeks later Roosevelt answered the challenge. Quoting Hitler's words, he said in a fireside chat that the Axis "not merely admits but *proclaims* that there can be no ultimate peace between their philosophy of government and our philosophy of government." Hence, he said, the United States could not encourage talk of peace until the aggressors abandoned all thought of conquering the world.

The President interpreted the election as a mandate for the United States to become a great "arsenal of democracy." In the last weeks of 1940 he slowly worked out the policies underlying Lend-Lease, under which the President would be empowered to lend or lease equipment to nations whose defense he considered necessary to the security of the United States. Britain was being stripped to the bone, Churchill had warned the President privately, and Roosevelt told reporters that he was merely trying to get rid of the "silly, foolish, old dollar sign." When Lend-Lease passed Congress, Roosevelt scored a legislative victory that was a milestone in the organizing of world resistance to Hitler.

So far, so good—even the isolationists could hardly deny that the act was a logical projection of the election mandate to step up aid

AUTHOR'S NOTE: The war years are treated synoptically for reasons explained in the preface. The concluding observations on Roosevelt's character in the third section of this Epilogue are based mainly upon the previous chapters, but these observations, I hope, may throw some light on the events pictured in broad strokes in this Epilogue.

457

to the democracies, especially at a time when Hitler was scoring a series of striking victories in the Balkans and elsewhere. But what would happen if circumstances called for something more than material help from the arsenal? Forced back on the defensive during the election, Roosevelt had made peace the supreme issue. Rearmament, aid to Britain, the destroyer deal, hemispheric unity—all these he had proclaimed as means of keeping America out of war. To be sure, in his December fireside chat he faced up to the perils involved. "If we are to be completely honest with ourselves, we must admit that there is risk in any course we may take." But then he drew quickly back on the limb. The cardinal aim was not American security, not democratic survival, not destruction of Nazism, but peace.

Circumstances soon were forcing the President's hand. With German submarine packs and battle cruisers roaming the North Atlantic in early 1941, the crucial question was insuring the safe arrival of the cargoes. Churchill sent reports of grave losses. The direct solution to the problem was outright naval escort for shipping, but Roosevelt's cautious tactics—defending Lend-Lease as a method of assuring Hitler's defeat without serious risk of war for America—now boomeranged. The more vigorously the navy tried to protect the lifelines to Britain the more likely were provocative incidents.

Once again Roosevelt was caught between divided administration counsels, between the conflicting demands of isolationists and interventionists. Once again there was a period of veering and drifting in the White House; once again Roosevelt's advisers—Stimson, Ickes, and others—lamented the President's failure to lead. And once again Roosevelt responded to the situation by improvisation and subterfuge. He publicly ordered intensified naval patrolling in the now enlarged security zones; he privately ordered a policy of seeking out German ships and planes and notifying British units of their location. On May 27, while pickets trudged dourly back and forth in front of the White House with their antiwar signs, Roosevelt announced his issuance of a proclamation of "unlimited national emergency." The next day, however, he took much of the sting out of his move by disclaiming any positive plans along new lines.

The President, said Hopkins, "would rather follow public opinion than lead it." Indeed, as Roosevelt anxiously examined public opinion polls during 1941, he once again was failing to supply the crucial factor of his own leadership in the equation of public opinion. His approach was in sharp contrast to that of his great world partner. "Nothing is more dangerous in wartime," Churchill said later in the year, "than to live in the temperamental atmosphere of a Gallup poll, always feeling one's pulse and taking one's temperature. . . . There is only one duty, only one safe course, and that is to try to be right and not to fear to do or say what you believe to be right."

ROOSEVELT AS WAR LORD

The shattering Nazi attack on Russia on June 22 came like a thunderclap amid the torpid Washington calm. Many Americans were caught between a loathing for communism as a philosophy and the practical need to work with the Russians against Nazism—but not the President. When Fulton Oursler of *Liberty* magazine sent him a proposed editorial titled "We Still Say 'To Hell with Communism,'" Roosevelt wrote back that *he* would condemn the Russian form of dictatorship equally with the German form but also would make clear that the immediate threat to America was Germany. The President spurred the sending of supplies to Russia and took steps to forestall organized opposition to such aid.

So intent was the President on immediate tactical moves rather than grand strategy that his loftiest pronouncement of the year—the Atlantic Charter, proclaimed jointly with Churchill—was almost a by-product of the Atlantic Conference of the two leaders in July. Most of the conference discussions were devoted to an intensive consideration of the host of production, logistical, co-ordinating, and intelligence matters in which the affairs of the two nations were so intertwined. The lofty pronouncements were actually scribbled on pieces of paper and issued as a press release, but their reception by a people yearning for presidential leadership and direction converted them into a historic act.

"Their countries seek no aggrandizement, territorial or other," the two leaders proclaimed. ". . . They respect the right of all people to choose the form of government under which they will live. . . . They will endeavor . . . to further the enjoyment of all states, great or small, victor or vanquished, of access . . . to the trade and to the raw materials of the world. . . . They desire to bring about the fullest collaboration between all Nations" for social security and economic welfare. "They believe that all of the Nations of the world, for realistic as well as spiritual reasons, must come to the abandonment of the use of force. . . ."

But high-sounding words were not enough by themselves. What would Roosevelt *do?* The activists around him burned with anxiety over the President's refusal to take decisive action—to provide naval escort, to order all-out naval attack in the Atlantic, even to declare war. The President still proceeded cautiously. He felt that he could act decisively only in answer to a decisive act by the enemy. Hitler, now concentrating on Russia, refused him such an act. No incidents or provocations, the Fuehrer told his admirals. The lack of an overt act deprived the President of the weapon he needed—the chance to dramatize a *situation,* to interpret an *event.* He needed such an opportunity both to arouse the people and, even more, to galvanize Congress. For legislative support was never assured; in mid-August the House of Representatives threw a scare into the administration when it extended selective service by a margin of only one vote.

Then, early in September 1941, there occurred the incident that seemed to give Roosevelt his chance—an incident implicit in presidential orders given months before. While en route to Iceland the American destroyer *Greer* learned from the British of a German submarine, trailed it for several hours, and periodically notified the British of its position; finally the submarine loosed two torpedoes against the *Greer,* both of which missed; then the *Greer* depth-charged the submarine, with unknown results. Quickly seizing on the incident, Roosevelt reported in a fireside chat that the *Greer* had been attacked, but said nothing of the preliminaries. Soon orders went out to the fleet to set up full-scale naval escorting and to "shoot on sight."

Still Hitler rejected his admirals' renewed pleas for all-out attacks on the Atlantic supply lines. Russian conquest was his goal; the United States could be dealt with later. It was in a different quarter that the decisive event occurred.

In Tokyo in mid-October 1941, the cabinet of Prince Konoye, caught between the militarists' zeal for expansion and foreign efforts to contain Japan's Asiatic ambitions, surrendered power to a new government headed by the fire-breathing general Hideki Tojo. The change tightened the Far Eastern deadlock. Tokyo was willing to settle matters with Washington only if its long-developed plans for expansion were accepted. Roosevelt and Hull wanted stabilization in the Far East but not at the expense of China or of the Good Neighbor ideals they had so often preached. Unlike Konoye, Tojo would not brook delay in further expansion. "If a hundred million people merge into one iron solidarity to go forward," the new prime minister boasted, "nothing can stop us."

The new Japanese cabinet then embarked on an elaborate double game. Conversations were to be continued with Washington, but the moment they broke down—as the militarists, at least, expected—the decision for war would be taken up at once. On November 5 operational orders were issued, with the warning: "War with Netherlands, America, England inevitable. . . ." The date for the attack was set tentatively for December 8, 1941.

Intensive negotiations then ensued between Washington and Tokyo. Roosevelt was eager to work out any acceptable stopgap arrangement in order to play for time, and the Japanese negotiators were genuinely hopeful of agreement. But fundamentally it was a case of the immovable object and the irresistible force: Japan was intent on expansion, the United States opposed further aggression in the Orient. And all the discussions took place under the harsh time limits imposed by Tojo.

Proposals and counterproposals followed, but all to no avail. By early December the President knew that the Japanese would strike soon—but he knew not where. Most reports to Washington stressed the likelihood of Japanese moves in Southeast Asia or the South Pacific. On the night of December 6, as Roosevelt, still fighting for time, dispatched a plea and a warning to Emperor Hirohito, Japanese carriers were plowing toward their positions northwest of Oahu.

That same night, commenting to Roosevelt that the Japanese would attack at their own convenience, Hopkins lamented that the United States could not strike the first blow and prevent any sort of surprise.

"No," said the President, "we can't do that. We are a democracy and a peaceful people. But we have a good record. . . ."

Early on the afternoon of the following day, Sunday, December 7, Roosevelt and Hopkins had just finished eating lunch when the telephone rang. It was Knox.

"Hello, Frank."

"Mr. President, it looks as if the Japanese have attacked Pearl Harbor."

"*No!*"

The bombs that shattered the fleet in Pearl Harbor shattered as well the stalemate in Roosevelt's war policy. In the first hours of turmoil after news of the attack there were some who could think only of the fleet's lack of readiness. Connally turned savagely on Knox with a barrage of questions. Others thought the President should issue a long review of his policy toward Japan in his war message.

But the President would have none of it. To him the only important fact was the fact of war itself. "We are in it," he kept saying to his advisers. When he appeared before a joint session next day and somberly asked Congress to declare the existence of a state of war, the two most important words in his short speech were "Hostilities exist." The crucial act had occurred for which the President could find no substitute in speech or deed. "Hostilities exist"—a few climactic hours had taught the lessons that Roosevelt had never quite been able to teach.

"I think the Boss really feels more relief than he has had for weeks," one cabinet member said to another as they left his study.

When Germany and Italy declared war on the United States four days after Pearl Harbor, world battle lines had formed.

From the President's behavior during the following weeks one might have thought that all that had gone before had been merely preparation for this hour—as perhaps it was. Roosevelt, said Sumner Welles, a close observer at the time, "demonstrated the ultimate capacity to dominate and control a supreme emergency, which is the rarest and most valuable characteristic of any statesman." It was like 1933 all over again, but projected onto an infinitely larger stage. Roosevelt was businesslike, serene, cheerful, grave, tireless, confident.

Backed now by a united people, he could exploit his superb flair for bringing warring parties together behind a common goal. Labor-management unity was a brilliant case in point. During the year before Pearl Harbor coal miners, shipbuilders, airplane-engine workers, and tens of thousands of others had gone on strike. The President had had to seize several defense plants. The central issue was "union security"—an issue so divisive that it had caused the collapse of the nation's chief mediation agency. Ten days after Pearl Harbor a "warm, confident, buoyant, serious" President summoned labor and employer delegates to the White House, told them it would be a "thrilling thing" if they could agree soon on basic problems, and proceeded to set up a board to work out a compromise on union security that was to prove one of the most creative and enduring achievements of the war administration.

All the President's command and confidence were needed during the early months of 1942, as the nation suffered staggering reversals along the vast Pacific front. Japanese forces swallowed Guam, Wake, the Philippines. Malaya, Burma, the Dutch East Indies fell. Everywhere the Axis maintained its relentless advance: in North Africa the Germans drove the British back into Egypt; they seemed to have the Russians on the point of collapse; they still exacted a heavy toll in the Atlantic. The Japanese landed in the Aleutians, reached the borders of India, threatened Australia.

Not only did Roosevelt have to maintain an air of resolution and confidence during the long, dreary days of defeat, he had to stick to the central strategic decisions—to make the main effort first against Germany while holding off Japan—in the face of the "Japan-firsters" who looked on that nation as America's only real enemy. Roosevelt worked amid a thousand pressures. He had to mediate among his own rival services, among theater commands, between war front and home front, between the desperate needs of Russians and British. As usual the more exacting problems moved relentlessly along the lines of command into his office; as usual the President tackled them cheerfully, turning quickly from crucial questions of strategy, to administrative minutiae, to galling problems of personnel; as usual he operated tirelessly among the never-ending babble of politicians, admirals, legislators, generals, diplomats, bureaucrats.

The President understood, too, that his soldiers' slow, grudging retreat was buying time for the economy to shift into high gear. Having turned from one expedient to another in the months before Pearl Harbor, he established in January 1942 a relatively centralized mobilization direction in the War Production Board. Exploitation of the nation's enormous resources was the main job of 1942 and one that called for a tenacious fight against inflation as war spending neared one hundred million dollars a day. Here again, Roosevelt seemed to have been superbly trained for the job. No longer did he face the need to decide between the agonizing alternatives—between spending and budget balancing—for which he had never been educated. That decision had been made for him. Now his job was to stave off the inflationary pressures of businessmen, labor, farmers. The notions that had run through his economic thinking for years—notions of a balanced economy, of a central harmony of interests, of mutual sacrifice for mutual gain—supplied an indispensable background for his efforts toward stabilization.

Roosevelt's utter concentration on the task at hand—winning military victory—raised difficult problems, just as his absorption with winning elections at whatever cost had created difficulties during the peace years. It was all very well for Hopkins, reflecting his chief's attitude, to apply to every policy the simple test "Will it help to win the war?" but such a test was likely to ignore broader strategic aspects of winning the war—and the relation between winning the war and defending democracy. Two examples illuminate the dilemma:

Early in 1942 Roosevelt authorized the military to uproot thousands of Japanese-Americans on the West Coast and relocate them in concentration camps in the interior. To the military this seemed a wise precaution, but in the long run it was a compromise with the ideas the nation was supposed to be fighting. Again, in September 1942, exasperated by the failure of Congress to pass a bill to stabilize the cost of living, including the prices of farm commodities, Roosevelt in effect ordered Congress to act in three weeks and warned that if the legislators failed to act he would. Congress sullenly complied. Here was an astonishing usurpation of power in a nation fighting for democratic ideas and processes.

Roosevelt would have made the same defense of his drastic actions as had another war president eighty years before. "Was it possible," Lincoln asked, "to lose the nation and yet preserve the Constitution? A limb may be amputated to save a life, but a life is never wisely given to save a limb." Yet a democratic people always faces the ultimate question, Which is life and which is limb?

ROOSEVELT AS PEACE LEADER

During 1943 the tide turned. In May, Allied forces drove the enemy out of Tunisia. Two months later they invaded Sicily; two months after that, Italy; and on September 3, 1943, Italy surrendered. Elsewhere the massive counterattack slowly gained momentum. American troops mopped up the Japanese in Guadalcanal and Buna, launched amphibious assaults in the Solomons, New Georgia, New Guinea, Tarawa. The American and British navies were winning the Battle of the Atlantic. Most decisive of all, the Russians drove the Germans back from Stalingrad early in the year after an epic siege.

By the end of 1943 victory for the Allies was no longer seriously in doubt. The question now was less whether they would win than whether they could win in such a way as to make a lasting peace more likely.

This year was also a year of the great international conferences, where questions of war strategy and postwar peace policy were taken up. Roosevelt and Churchill met at Casablanca, Washington, and Quebec; Roosevelt, Churchill, and Chiang Kai-shek met at Cairo; Roosevelt, Churchill, and Stalin met at Teheran. At this last conference the thorny problem of the second front was finally settled, and soon afterward General Dwight D. Eisenhower was made its supreme commander.

Teheran brought together three towering personalities and a "concentration of physical power and political authority unique in the whole history of mankind." Roosevelt beforehand was keenly confident of his capacity to establish a workable and mutually beneficial personal relationship with Stalin. So he did—as long as negotiations involved immediate problems of beating the Nazis. But on the longrun strategic questions involving the pattern of power in Europe after the war the President's preoccupation with military victory put him at a disadvantage to both Churchill and Stalin. Yet Roosevelt probably believed that the crowning need both for winning the war and securing the peace was the visible fact of Allied co-operation.

"I may say that I 'got along fine' with Marshal Stalin," he told the people in his Christmas Eve 1943 fireside chat, ". . . and I believe that we are going to get along very well with him and the Russian people—very well indeed." And he told Miss Perkins gleefully how he had broken the ice with Stalin by deliberately baiting Churchill about his Britishness, his cigars, and his habits.

If Roosevelt had to deal with Stalin in the posture of alliance, he had to deal with Hitler in the posture of war. It was a battle not only of armies and navies but of ideas and symbols as well. The Fuehrer, a master of propaganda, interpreted the war to his people as a struggle of the masses against the plutocratic nations of the world. The President, now the Allies' chief propagandist with a constituency of three-quarters of the world, affirmed Freedom as the supreme symbol of the cause for which the Allies fought. As Hitler sought to divest this symbol of any meaning except liberty to exploit the masses, Roosevelt sought to strengthen the idea of Freedom as a positive idea—as freedom to gain peace and security after the war. Roosevelt, in short, was compelled as a means of winning victory itself to fashion means of attaining postwar goals; one result was that during 1943 a series of "united nations" conferences began to plan postwar social and economic arrangements.

During all this time the home front was never free of storm and controversy. A "little cabinet" of Byrnes, Rosenman, Hopkins, and the President's personal chief of staff, Admiral William D. Leahy, struggled to clear bottlenecks and settle interagency feuds, but the war management reflected the familiar administrative habits of the commander in chief. Some "second-level" decisions he refused to delegate, and he continued to play officials and agencies off against one another. As in the past, the results were not altogether happy. Feeling between Hull and Welles became so sharp that the latter resigned as under secretary of state, and Wallace and Jones warred against each other so openly over international economic policy that the President removed both of them from their posts in this field. Still, the crucial goal at home—mobilization without severe inflation—was achieved.

It was in the party and legislative arena that the domestic political hostilities were sharpest. Right after Pearl Harbor Roosevelt had, quite characteristically, demanded an end to "partisan domestic politics" for the duration. He had even suggested that the two national party organizations be converted to civilian defense. But partisan politics would not die so easily. Under the inexorable calendar of American elections the regular off-year congressional contests were fought in 1942. Roosevelt carefully avoided Wilson's mistake of asking for a Democratic Congress; still, his party almost lost control of Congress. The Democratic margin in the House fell from 91 to 14, and 8 seats were lost in the Senate.

The inexorable political calendar brought also the presidential election of 1944. With the anti-third-term tradition broken, Roosevelt could eschew his devious preconvention tactics of 1940. So a

THE ONE DOLLAR QUESTION, March 14, 1944, H. M. Talburt and Don Patterson, © by the Washington *Daily News*

July 14, 1944, C. K. Berryman, Washington *Star*

week before the Democratic convention convened in mid-July 1944 Roosevelt wrote the national chairman a simple, direct letter stating that he would serve again if "the Commander in Chief of us all"— the people of the United States—should order him to do so in November.

"All that is within me cries out to go back to my home on the Hudson River," Roosevelt wrote, but "we of this generation chance to live in a day and hour when our Nation has been attacked, and when its future existence and the future existence of our chosen method of government are at stake."

When it came to the vice-presidency, though, it was the same old Roosevelt. He made half-promises to more than one aspirant, refused to tell Vice-President Wallace frankly that he could not back his nomination if it divided the convention, and yet wrote Wallace a letter stating that he was his "personal" choice. Harry Truman was surprised to find that he was the President's official choice; he would run, the Missouri Senator told Roosevelt's men, "but why the hell didn't he tell me in the first place?"

On one matter the political wheel came full circle. In June 1944 Roosevelt talked with Rosenman about the subject he had toyed with again and again in his four decades of political activity: party realignment. "We ought to have two real parties—one liberal and the other conservative," he told Rosenman. The Democratic party must get rid of its reactionary elements in the South and attract to it the Republican liberals. He asked Rosenman to take the question up with Willkie, who had just been shouldered out of the

Republican running by the G.O.P. regulars. At a secret meeting with Rosenman in New York early in July, Willkie expressed enthusiastic support for the idea of party realignment, and he agreed to work plans out jointly with the President. But on one thing Willkie was insistent. He could not meet with Roosevelt until after the election. At a time when he was still trying to keep some leverage in the Republican party he feared that co-operation with the President would be misinterpreted as a "sellout" on his part to the Democrats.

Roosevelt, however, wanted to pursue the matter before election, and it was here that his reputation for cunning and indirectness tripped him up. The more the President pressed for an early meeting the more Willkie was convinced that he was engaged in an election tactic rather than in a long-term strategic effort. A series of leaks to the press about the indirect communication between Roosevelt and Willkie served only to heighten the latter's suspicion. In any case, it was too late; for Willkie, who had always spent his energies recklessly, died of a coronary thrombosis in October. Thus was lost perhaps the supreme opportunity in a generation for party realignment.

The President now faced his fourth campaign for office—this time against the vigorous, youthful Dewey, who in 1942 had won the

Oct., 1944, Tom Little,
Nashville *Tennessean*

governorship of New York over the divided Democrats in that state. Roosevelt's tactics followed the classic pattern: long inspection trips, patient "nonpartisanship" while Dewey lambasted the "tired old men," and then a series of swift thrusts in the last few weeks of the campaign. The first of these thrusts was the most devastating—the Teamsters Union speech that answered Republican libels against "my little dog, Fala." From then on, a Democrat commented, the race was between "Roosevelt's dog and Dewey's goat."

Roosevelt's victory over Dewey by a margin of 333 electoral and about 3,600,000 popular votes was one more testament of his masterly campaigning. It was also a tribute to his supreme direction of military operations. In June, Allied armies had surged into Normandy; in midsummer American troops drove the Japanese out of Saipan and Guam; in October they landed in the Philippines. As the war fast reached its climax, issues of peace became ever more urgent.

The great tasks of peace lay ahead—but now, as the year of victory neared, Roosevelt was desperately tired. The ceaseless toil and tension of the war years were leaving their mark. Like the great actor he was, he could shake himself out of his weariness and take his old role before the people. Fighting off campaign rumors about his condition, he had handled the exacting "Fala" speech—which so easily could have flopped—with exquisite skill; he had driven gaily for hours through New York streets in a cold, driving rain. But at other times he seemed quite different. His face went slack; he slumped in his chair; his hands trembled more than ever.

Yet so swiftly did he shift from dullness to buoyancy that even while his friends were whispering to one another about their concern there would be fresh reports that the President was showing his old form.

Roosevelt was desolately lonely, too, lonely in the midst of the White House crowd. Just as he had always stayed partly in the world symbolized by Hyde Park, so he had kept around him people who had represented that world. But they were slipping away. Sara Roosevelt died in 1941, and the President remarked to Eleanor that perhaps she had departed this world at the right time, for she might not like the postwar world. Endicott Peabody died late in 1944, and Roosevelt wrote his widow that the "whole tone of things is going to be a bit different from now on, for I have leaned on the Rector in all these many years far more than most people know. . . ." McIntyre died in 1943, Missy Le Hand the following year. Eleanor Roosevelt was often away on long war tours; all four Roosevelt sons were in uniform.

On January 20, 1945, Roosevelt took the oath of office for the fourth time; to save money and energy the inaugural was held in front of the White House rather than at the Capitol. He spoke for only a few minutes. "In the days and the years that are to come, we shall work for a just and honorable peace, a durable peace, as today we work and fight for total victory in war. . . ." As the President spoke, Allied troops in Europe stood on the threshold of victory. Hitler's armies, except for a precarious hold in Hungary and northern Italy, had been forced back onto German soil. In the Pacific, American forces were preparing heavy assaults on islands barely a thousand miles from Tokyo.

"We can gain no lasting peace if we approach it with suspicion and mistrust—or with fear," the President said in his inaugural; and in this spirit he met with Churchill and Stalin two weeks later at Yalta. Roosevelt faced resolutely this supreme test of Big Three co-operation. He was tired; he was frail; Churchill noticed that his face had "a transparency, an air of purification, and often there was a far-away look in his eyes." But even at Yalta, he could be as gay, charming, and buoyant as ever. His mind moved as quickly and as acutely as ever over the great range of problems that the conference considered.

Out of the hard bargaining at Yalta issued a series of compromises. No nation had its own way. Stalin made concessions on German reparations, on voting arrangements in the projected world organization, on the question of a French zone of occupation in Germany, and on several other matters. Moreover, the date of Russia's entrance into the war against Japan was fixed. Yet Stalin also gained some large demands. While the conference did not "give" him Poland, which was already occupied by Red troops, the terms of the agreement may have facilitated ensuing Soviet control of that country. And in the Far East Stalin was granted the Kurile Islands, the southern part of Sakhalin, and extensive spheres of influence in North China.

Had Roosevelt, the man who boasted of his prowess as a "hoss-trader," finally been outbargained? Many would later cry that he had. Yet a verdict must take account of the different operating methods of the two men. Roosevelt, as always, was acting pragmatically, opportunistically, tactically. As usual, he was almost wholly concerned about the immediate job ahead—winning the war. Japan had yet to be overcome, and the military advised that the invasion and conquest of the homeland would be long and fanatically resisted. The first test of the atomic bomb was long in the future. His generals and admirals insisted—and the President agreed —that a Russian attack on Japan was essential.

Stalin, on the other hand, was thinking already of political arrangements in the postwar world. This granite-hard son of serfs, schooled in blood and violence, had always thought and acted several moves ahead of his adversaries—this was one reason he had defeated them. He had, moreover, few illusions about the postwar world; his revolutionary and Marxist background had taught him that, however friendly the Roosevelts and Churchills might be now, the inexorable laws of history would produce new tensions among nations, and Russia would have to be strong. Churchill, too, was aware of the political implications of victory; he, too, whatever his romantic Edwardian temperament, could see the storms ahead—had he not written bluntly that "the story of the human race is War"? But Churchill, unlike Stalin, did not have the continental land power to give strength to his strategy.

Roosevelt, a match for these men in the military direction of a war, was handicapped, when it came to the considerations of peace, by the belief that better days must lie ahead. Poignantly, in his inaugural address just before Yalta, he had quoted his old schoolmaster Peabody as saying that in life there would always be peaks and valleys, but that the "great fact to remember is that the trend of civilization itself is forever upward; that a line drawn through the middle of the peaks and the valleys of the centuries always has an upward trend." But Marx and Lenin seemed to have taught Stalin better than Peabody taught Roosevelt.

Such, at least, was the verdict of some of those who looked back from the years of bitterness and disillusion that followed the war. The verdict of still later years might be different. For beyond the military and political considerations of Yalta was the supreme accomplishment that Roosevelt wished to present to the world—the fact of Three Power co-operation. It was quite characteristic of him that in the existence of this accomplishment as interpreted by him to a world hungering for leadership, he should see the best chance of a lasting peace. Again and again, in his report to Congress on the Yalta Conference, his words came back to the supreme fact of the unity of the three great powers. Later generations, looking back from more tranquil years, might see this as the crowning achievement of Yalta—one that dwarfed even the most far-reaching maneuvers of the Machiavellians.

Even so, Roosevelt made one colossal—though understandable—miscalculation. His plans assumed that he, as President of the United States for another four years, would be around to keep the fact of one world alive, to symbolize it for peoples everywhere, to mediate between Stalin and Churchill. But time was fast running out.

Roosevelt's voice was strangely thick and blurred as he told Congress about Yalta. He stumbled and halted; he ad-libbed irrelevancies. At times his face and words flamed with the old eloquence, then it seemed to ebb away. Thus it was constantly in the final weeks. His body seemed to sag heavily in his chair or in the arms of his porters; his hands trembled so that the act of fixing his pince-nez or lighting his cigarette took all his powers of concentration; his gray-blue eyes clouded, his face went slack, his head hunched over. Then, suddenly, miraculously, the old gayness and vitality would return. At his last press conference in Washington the repartee raced from Canadian relations to the new peace organization to New York City politics to Yalta to night baseball; the President was as quick, humorous, and deft as ever.

At the end of March Roosevelt left for Warm Springs. The usual crowd was waiting when the train pulled into the little Georgia town. There was the usual bustle of activity at the end of the rear car. But something was different. Roosevelt's big frame, slumped in the wheel chair, seemed to joggle slightly as he was rolled along the platform. His face, once so strong and well fleshed, seemed wasted; the jaw, once so firm, quivered perceptibly. A murmur swept through the crowd.

But as usual, after a few days of rest, the gray pallor faded, some of the old vitality returned. Doctors sent reassuring reports to Eleanor Roosevelt in Washington. Sitting in his cottage, watching the fresh green countryside under the warm sun, the President was able to relax, to look over new stamps, to play with Fala, to think about the past and about the future.

It was early April, and the culmination of the war was at hand. Reports arriving daily told of victories on all battlefronts. In Europe, American and Allied troops were sweeping into the heart of Germany. In the Pacific naval forces were fighting off the heaviest Japanese air attacks of the war and clamping their grip on Okinawa. It was the culmination for Roosevelt too. He knew that war in Europe would be over in a few weeks. He knew now that Japan could not fight long against the power that would be massed against her after Germany's defeat. He knew that delegates from the united nations would meet soon in San Francisco to set up the permanent peace organization, and he knew that the United States would join it.

It was a time for rest—a time when the President could think about the long vacation that he would take in the summer and about a trip to Britain, a time when he could even toy with the idea of quitting the presidency as soon as the big jobs were done. He could think about the house at Hyde Park that was awaiting him, about the library with its mass of papers and mementos.

It was time too—though no one knew it at the moment—for a last look at the living man.

DEMOCRACY'S ARISTOCRAT

Those who knew Roosevelt best could agree fully on only one point—that he was a man infinitely complex and almost incomprehensible. "I cannot come to grips with him!" Ickes cried more than once and the words were echoed by a host of congressmen, politicos, diplomats, and bureaucrats who dealt with the canny politician in the White House. His character was not only complex, Robert Sherwood observed, it was contradictory to a bewildering degree.

The contradictions continually bemused or galled Roosevelt's lieutenants. He was almost unvaryingly kind and gracious, yet a thin streak of cruelty ran through some of his behavior. He remained unruffled and at ease under the most intense pressures; yet when pricked in certain ways he struck out at his enemies in sharp, querulous words. He found ways to evade bores and know-it-alls, yet he patiently listened to Ickes' complaints and demands hour after hour, week after week, year after year. He juggled huge figures with an almost casual air, yet he could work long minutes over a knot to save the string and over a telegram to cut it down to ten words. He liked new ideas, people, and projects, but he wanted an element of fixity in his surroundings. He shifted nimbly from one set of policies to another—from economy to spending, from central planning to trust busting, from intervention abroad to neutrality, from party action to national action.

In many little ways inconsistency ruled: in the way he thanked some subordinates for their efforts and said nothing to others, intervened in some administrative matters and ignored others, had four men doing a single job in some instances (as Flynn once complained) and one man doing four jobs in others, was unaccountably frivolous about some matters and grave about others.

And there was the most baffling quality of all—his sheer, superb courage in facing some challenges, and his caution and indirection in facing others. He acted instantly, electrically, on certain decisions, and unaccountably postponed others for months. It was not strange that he should follow Machiavelli's advice that a leader must be as brave as the lion and as shrewd as the fox, for this had long been the first lesson for politicians. But his metamorphoses from lion to fox and back to lion again mystified even his intimates.

Roosevelt's complexities stemmed in part from the demands of political life. Gladstone once remarked that he had known and studied politicians for sixty years and they still remained to him a mysterious breed. Democratic politics is a highly competitive profession, and the successful politician must know how to conceal his hand and present different faces to different groups. Too, Roosevelt took a particular delight in mystifying people by keeping something up his sleeve. But the source of his complexity lay deeper than this.

Roosevelt was a complex man mainly because he was a deeply divided man. More than almost any other political leader of his time, he experienced a lingering between two worlds.

He had been born and raised in a class and in a tradition that formed the closest American approximation to an aristocracy. At home, at Groton, at Harvard, at the right houses of Boston and New York, he had absorbed a core of beliefs and a sense of security and assurance he would never lose. His background always brought the needle of his compass, no matter how it might waver for a time, back to true north. The major premises on which this society operated might be inarticulate, or at least fuzzy, but they had meaning. These premises were: that men can live together only on the basis of certain simple, traditional ethical rules; that men are essentially good and those who are not can be improved by example and precept; that despite ups and downs the world is getting better; that the wellborn must never compromise with evil; that the gentleman must enter government to help the less fortunate, that he must enter politics to purify it. And the turn-of-the-century world seemed to validate these ideas: it was stable, secure, peaceful, expansive.

Roosevelt was projected out of this world into bizarre and unanticipated phases of the twentieth century—a decade of muckraking, a decade of Wilsonian reform at home and Wilsonian idealism abroad; a decade of postwar cynicism and reaction; then the climactic years of depression, the New Deal, abroad the rise of brutish men to power, and the coming of a new war.

Some nineteenth-century men could not effectively make the shift to the new century; insecure and frightened, they clung not only to the old moralities, as did Roosevelt, but also to the old methods, the old ways of business, the old distrust for government; they huddled within their class barriers. Roosevelt, however, made the jump with ease. He did so for several reasons: because he had not met absolute success socially at Groton or Harvard—for example, in his failure to make the best club in Cambridge—and thus was not absolutely committed to the old ways and institutions; because of the influence of Eleanor and Theodore Roosevelt; because he was drawn into the variegated political life of New York State; because he was vital and curious and ambitious.

Still other men of his generation, rejecting the past completely, found some kind of fixed mooring somewhere in this strange new world—but, again, not Roosevelt. He made no final commitment

to any part of that world—not to Wilsonian idealism, nor to business money-making, nor to radicalism, nor to internationalism.
Partly because of quick adaptability, partly because of the diverse
make-up of his intimates, partly because he had little need for
personal introspection, partly because of his tremendous self-assurance, he was able to shift back and forth among segments of this
world and to make himself at home in all of them.

Success fed on success: as Roosevelt found that he could carry
off brilliantly a variety of roles—as party leader, as man of affairs,
as bureaucrat, as Hyde Park squire, as governor, as campaigner, as
a heroic battler against polio—he played the roles more and more
to the hilt. This was one reason why he presided so joyously in the
White House, for today the great President must be a man of
many roles. Roosevelt was a superb actor in the literal sense—in
the way his face, his gestures, the tilt of his head communicated
feeling, in the perfect modulation of voice and the timing with
which he read his speeches, in his sense of the dramatic. He was
a superb actor in the far more significant sense that he was responding in each of his roles not merely to an assigned script but
to something within himself.

The result was a man of no fixed convictions about methods and
policies, flexible as a broker because he had to mediate among
conflicting worlds and experiences. To some, like Hoover, he
seemed a "chameleon on plaid" because of this enormous flexibility.
Indeed, even to some of his friends he seemed almost in a state
of anomie, lacking any guideposts at all, because he rejected so
many doctrines and dogmas. Quite naturally, because the mask
often was almost impenetratable, they could not see the inner
compass of certainty and rightness.

Caught between two worlds, Roosevelt compartmentalized his
life. The results sometimes were ludicrous, as when he tried to force
opposites to work together and could not understand why they
failed. The results were at times unfortunate, for Roosevelt's
pseudointegration of his roles weakened his capacity to supply
strong leadership and to make long-term strategic decisions or commitments when these were needed. It allowed the warring ideas
and forces in American society not only to beat against him from
outside but, because he *incorporated* as well as reflected these forces,
to divide him from within.

Yet Roosevelt's flexibility and opportunism had tremendous advantages too. In a time of whirling social change he could move fast
to head off crisis at home and abroad. In a time when experimentation was vital, he could try one method, quickly drop it, and turn
to another. In a time when Americans had to be educated in the
meaning of events, he could act as an interpreter all the more ef-

fectively because he spoke so many languages of social experience. Leading a people of sublime diversity, presiding over a nation of nations, he could say with Walt Whitman:

> Do I contradict myself?
> Very well, then, I contradict myself,
> (I am large, I contain multitudes.)

Lincoln Steffens once remarked that Theodore Roosevelt thought with his hips. Franklin Roosevelt's thinking was perhaps no more cerebral, but he thought with all five senses, perhaps with a sixth too. He had a radar set that could point in all directions, acute, sensitive, recording everything indiscriminately, and restoring the image in the responsive instrument that was Roosevelt's mind.

Was there then no hard center, no core personality, no final commitment in this man? Watching his quicksilver mind run from idea to idea, visitors could hardly believe that stone or steel lay under the bright, smooth flow of talk. But something did. The more that mask and costume are stripped away from Roosevelt, the more the turn-of-century man of Hyde Park, Groton, and Harvard stands out.

Roosevelt, for all his deviousness, was basically a moral man in the sense that he felt so intensely the need to do right that he had to *think* he did right. He believed in doing good, in showing other people how to do good, and he assumed that ultimately people would do good. By "good" he meant the Ten Commandments and the Golden Rule, as interpreted by Endicott Peabody. He meant the "simple rules of human conduct to which we always go back," as he said in 1932. He meant "old-fashioned standards of rectitude," as he said in signing the truth-in-securities bill in 1933. Significantly, Roosevelt always looked back into the past for his moralities; he did not try to fashion them anew.

These rules were not very precise, and Roosevelt did not want them to be precise. It was enough that they were there. Once when Eleanor Roosevelt raised with him the question of their children's religious upbringing, he said simply that they should go to church and learn what he had learned. "But are you sure that you believe in everything you learned?" his wife persisted. "I really never thought about it," he said with a quizzical look. "I think it is just as well not to think about things like that." But he expected others to understand his simple rules of conduct, and to understand his own allegiance to them. When Richard Whitney's financial irresponsibilities were disclosed, Roosevelt's wealthy friends wrote to compliment him on not using the unhappy incident as part of a political attack on Wall Street. The President was amazed at the letters. "I wonder what sort of man they think I am," he said.

Vague though it was, this set of moral rules embraced one idea in particular that was of cardinal importance to Roosevelt and to his country. This was the idea of man's responsibility for the well-being of his fellow man. It was simply an extension of Sara Roosevelt's notions of *noblesse oblige,* but it found enormous meaning in the new conditions of the twentieth century. For it underlay Roosevelt's most important single idea—the idea that government had a positive responsibility for the general welfare. Not that government itself must do everything, but that everything practicable must be done. Whether government does it, or private enterprise, is an operating decision dependent on many factors—but government must insure that something *is* done.

Such was the essence of Roosevelt's morality; such was the core of beliefs far below the surface.

Some politicians preach morality because it is safe to do so, because they prove thereby that they are on the right side between Good and Evil, because they reach the largest common denominator among their audience, not because they take their own preachments too seriously. Not so Roosevelt. Probably no American politician has given so many speeches that were essentially sermons rather than statements of policy. Like a preacher, he wanted and expected his sermons to serve as practical moral guides to his people. Roosevelt was so theatrical that his moral preachments were often dismissed with a smile. Actually he was deadly serious.

Only a man deadly serious and supremely confident could have spent the time Roosevelt did trying to educate and elevate not only his own people but foreign leaders who seemed to others to be beyond redemption. There was something pathetic and yet almost sublime in the way that Roosevelt sent message after message to Hitler and other dictators. Partly, of course, it was for the record; but even more it was an expression of Roosevelt's faith in the ultimate goodness and reasonableness of all men. His eternal desire to talk directly with his enemies, whether congressmen or dictators, reflected his confidence in his own persuasiveness and, even more, in the essential ethical rightness of his own position.

To Theodore Roosevelt the presidency was a "bully pulpit." To Franklin Roosevelt it was the same—"pre-eminently a place of moral leadership. . . ."

How explain, then, the "other side" of Roosevelt—his shiftiness, his compromises, his manipulations? Why did he so often act like a fox?

Roosevelt was not an absolute moralist about means because, whatever his hopes or illusions about man's possible redemption and *ultimate* goodness and reasonableness, he had few illusions about man's nature. He knew that some men were selfish, irrational,

vengeful, and mean. The practical statesman or man of affairs encounters ambitions and passions in his daily experience that put
man in a strong, harsh light. Roosevelt got his education at the
hands of tough labor leaders like Lewis, city bosses like Murphy
and Hague, agrarian demogogues like Long, and—on the level of
pure evil—Hitler and his camp followers. He learned the uses of
power.

Roosevelt overcame these men because he liked and wanted power
and, even more, because he wanted to defend the position of strength
from which he could lead *and teach* the people. To seize and hold
power, to defend that position, he got down into the dusty arena
and grappled with rival leaders on their own terms. So sure was
he of the rightness of his aims that he was willing to use Machiavellian means; and his moral certainties made him all the more effective in the struggle. To the idealists who cautioned him he responded
again and again that gaining power—winning elections—was the
first, indispensable task. He would use the tricks of the fox to
serve the purposes of the lion.

During the war years Roosevelt became interested in Kierkegaard,
and this was not surprising. The Danish theologian, with his emphasis on man's natural sinfulness, helped explain to him, Roosevelt said, why the Nazis "are human, yet they behave like demons."
From Peabody's homilies to Kierkegaard's realities, from the world
of Hyde Park to the world of Hitler, the way was long and tortuous;
the fact that Roosevelt could traverse that road so surely, with so
little impairment to his loftiest ideals, and with such courage and
good humor, was the final and true test of the man.

Holmes had been right—a second-rate intellect but a first-rate
temperament. To examine closely single aspects of Roosevelt's character—as thinker, as organizer, as manipulator, as strategist—is to
see failings and deficiencies closely interwoven with the huge capacities. But to stand back and look at the man as a whole, against
the backdrop of his people and his times, is to see the lineaments
of greatness—courage, joyousness, responsiveness, vitality, faith, and,
above all, concern for his fellow man. A democrat in manner and
conviction, he was yet a member of that small aristocracy once described by E. M. Forster—sensitive but not weak, considerate but
not fussy, plucky in his power to endure, capable of laughing and
of taking a joke. He was the true happy warrior.

WARRIOR'S HOME-COMING

Warm Springs on Thursday, April 12, was sunny and pleasant.
Roosevelt sat in his cottage looking over his stamps. He had put on
a dark blue suit and a Harvard-red tie for a painter who was doing

his portrait. Sitting in his brown leather chair near the fireplace, he seemed unusually chipper and gay. For some reason he took his draft card out of his wallet and tossed it into a basket nearby. Then he looked at some reports with intense concentration.

Suddenly the President groaned. He pressed and rubbed his temple hard—then the great head fell back inert. Carried to his bed, he lived, breathing heavily but unconscious, for about four hours. He died at 4:35 P.M.; it was fourscore years almost to the day since Lincoln's death.

The news sped to Eleanor Roosevelt in Washington, to Harry Truman, summoned suddenly to the White House from Capitol Hill, to Winston Churchill, who felt as if he had been struck a physical blow, to soldiers, sailors, and marines on far-off battle fronts. To four of these fighting men went a message from their mother: "He did his job to the end as he would want you to do." At the Capitol building a young congressman, groping for words, spoke for his generation: "He was the only person I ever knew—anywhere —who was never afraid. God, how he could take it for us all." Everywhere men and women wept, openly and without shame.

"All that is within me cries out to go back to my home on the Hudson River," Roosevelt had said nine months before, and now at last he would return. Through the dark Southern night the funeral train moved slowly back to Washington. Marines and infantrymen escorted the black, flag-draped caisson through the streets of Washington, while a huge crowd stood silent and unmoving. There was a brief, simple service in the East Room of the White House; then the body was placed again on the funeral train, and Roosevelt for the last time traveled the old, familiar route along the Pennsylvania Railroad's main line through Philadelphia and into Manhattan, then across Hell Gate bridge and up along the Hudson.

At the siding on the riverbank below the home, the coffin was moved from the train to a caisson drawn by six brown horses. There followed a lone horse, hooded, stirrups reversed and a sword hanging from the left stirrup—symbolic of a lost warrior. Marching in rigid columns of three at slow funeral cadence, the guard escorted the body up the steep winding road, through the dark woods, to the little plateau above. Behind the house, framed by the rose garden, were assembled the family and friends, old servants and retainers, and files of soldiers and sailors standing at rigid attention on the expanse of green grass.

A river breeze off the Hudson ruffled the trees above. A military band sounded the sad notes of its dirge. Muffled drums beat slowly and a bugler played the haunting notes of Taps as the coffin was slowly lowered into the grave. The warrior was home.

A NOTE ON THE STUDY OF
POLITICAL LEADERSHIP

THE LAST FEW decades have seen two important strides in the study of political leadership. In the first place, students of the subject have become more cautious in their attempt to find leadership potentials in an individual's heredity, and they have turned increasingly to environmental factors that selectively shape the nature of leadership. Secondly, they have de-emphasized the once common notion that leadership embraces a constellation of universal, innate traits and have substantially agreed that leadership involves a reciprocal relationship between personality and culture and is specific to a given situation. Both these developments have shifted emphasis from the leader as such and have directed more attention to the context in which the leader operates.[1]

This progress in the study of leadership is all the more welcome in an era when democratic peoples seek to understand the difficulties and possibilities of political leadership both in order to handle social and economic problems and to meet certain psychological needs of the people.[2] Unhappily, both the promising developments mentioned above have enormously increased the complexities involved in the study of leadership, especially in the political arena. This note seeks to describe some of those complexities and to suggest that facing up to them may nevertheless make possible better understanding of political leadership in a democratic society. The case of Franklin D. Roosevelt will be used to illustrate certain aspects of the matter.

[1] For a brief summary of the role of heredity, and especially of its interrelation with environmental factors, see Clyde Kluckhohn and Henry A. Murray, *Personality in Nature, Society, and Culture* (New York: Knopf, 1948), pp. 38-39. One of the best descriptions of the shift from the "traits" approach to the situationist approach is Alvin W. Gouldner (ed.), *Studies in Leadership* (New York: Harper, 1950), especially the Introduction; this treatment has the added merit of discussing the possibilities of generalization even in connection with the situationist approach.

[2] On this latter point, see Sebastian de Grazia, *The Political Community* (Chicago: University of Chicago Press, 1948).

I

Geneticists who have studied the matter agree that personality traits are not inherited in any simple or absolute sense. An individual's life cannot be seen as an automatic unfolding through time of the product of innate determinants of personality existing at birth. Certain potentials and certain restrictions are inherited, and the nature of these potentials and restrictions is determined by the interaction of many genes. The genetic constitution sets limits to the development of personality, but a tremendous range of possibilities exists between these limits. Different genetic structures provide varying potentialities for such vital processes as muscular responsiveness, glandular activity, reflexes, level of energy. "Biological inheritance," conclude Kluckhohn and Murray, "provides the stuff from which personality is fashioned and, as manifested in the physique at a given time-point, determines trends and sets limits within which variation is constrained." [3]

Even though genes and chromosomes are simply keys to a great variety of potentials, heredity cannot be written off. Roosevelt, for example, inherited a physique that was to enhance his personal appeal in a culture that esteems physical attractiveness. [4] He inherited certain physical potentials that would contribute to what a doctor many years later called his "extraordinarily sensitive emotional mechanism." [5] He inherited his sex—of no small importance in a society that on the whole tends to vest political power in its males. Another Roosevelt—Theodore—illustrates the influence of his (presumably) inherited asthmatic condition in the shaping of his political personality. Teased by other boys because of his weakness, he compensated for this and other humiliations by boxing, going west, leading his Rough Riders, wielding the Big Stick, shooting lions.

Aside from such obvious hereditary factors, however, the biographer's search for meaningful hereditary influences must be conducted with great prudence. Not only are the biochemical complexities involved infinitely varied and extremely difficult to measure, but at the point of birth, and indeed even in the prenatal condition, the environment begins to play on the individual a stream of converging and blending forces that will cease only with his death. These environmental forces—always interacting with the sub-

[3] *Op. cit.*, p. 39. See also Emory S. Bogardus, *Leaders and Leadership* (New York: Appleton-Century, 1934); Gardner Murphy, *Personality* (New York: Harper, 1947); L. C. Dunn and Th. Dobzhansky, *Heredity, Race, and Society* (New York: New American Library, 1946).
[4] See Murphy, *op. cit.*, p. 517.
[5] Letter, Dr. George Draper to Dr. Robert W. Lovett, Sept. 24, 1921, quoted in John Gunther, *Roosevelt in Retrospect* (New York: Harper, 1950), p. 226.

ject—liberate certain genetic potentialities, block others, and re-mold still others in a process whose main nature may not be visible even to the close observer. The tendency of some students of political leaders to see their subjects inheriting such qualities as courage, caution, chivalry, gaiety, or even an interest in particular matters like religion or transportation, must be viewed with a large dose of skepticism.[6]

On the other hand, such circumspection does not mean that a political leader's immediate forbears can be ignored. Aside from certain neural-muscular potentials that can be inherited, and along with the hereditary factors mentioned above, there is the different matter of *heritage*—those values, attitudes, and behavior patterns that are handed to a person by reason of his birth in a family that prizes and wishes to preserve them.[7] An individual may "inherit" certain traits in this sense far more significantly and durably than could possibly be the case with certain genetic potentialities.

II

The relation between emerging personality and society or culture is variously described as circular, mutual, relational, reciprocal, interactive, mutually reinforcing, but the phenomenon described is the same: the selective stimulation and restriction of the individual's potential by environmental forces that may themselves be affected by the personality, in a never-ending process of give-and-take.[8] The implication of this pattern for the student of personality is that he cannot be content with analyzing only the culture on the one hand, or only the personality on the other, as abstract entities, but he must study the interplay between the two. The implication for the student of *leadership* is that he must note the impact of the leader on the environment as well as the reverse proc-

[6] See Alfred M. Tozzer, "Biography and Biology," chapter 12 in Kluckhohn and Murray, *op. cit.* Tozzer lists trait after trait that some biographer has seen as inherited; but I think he goes too far in implying that parentage can be virtually ignored in assessing personality.

[7] I am indebted to Herman Kahn for making a point of this element in interpreting Roosevelt. An excellent example of how Roosevelt's *heritage* affected his political behavior is the dialogue between him and General Stilwell, as reported by the latter, concerning wartime relations with Chiang Kai-shek—a dialogue marked implicitly by Roosevelt's certainty of his own understanding of the Chinese because of his grandfather's financial activity in China; see Joseph W. Stilwell, *The Stilwell Papers* (New York: William Sloane Associates, 1948), pp. 251-254.

[8] On this matter, in addition to works cited above, see Hans Gerth and C. Wright Mills, *Character and Social Structure* (New York: Harcourt, Brace, 1953); Theodore M. Newcomb, *Social Psychology* (New York: Dryden Press, 1950); *The Social Sciences in Historical Study*, a report of the Committee on Historiography of the Social Science Research Council (Bulletin 64), 1954; and Muzafer Sherif and Hadley Cantril, *The Psychology of Ego-Involvement* (New York: Wiley, 1947).

ess, for by definition he is dealing with a personality of some influence—limited though it may be in some cases—on his context.[9]

Elaborate studies of leadership in primary groups have confirmed
the existence of reciprocal relations between leaders and followers
as discussed above.[10] Difficulty arises in the attempt to move from
relatively simple and limited situations to larger, more elaborate,
and more sharply politicized environments. Seligman, discussing experiments with different types of leadership in small groups, has
expressed the point well: [11]

... The democratic atmosphere of an experimental group is not the
microcosm of a democratic society. Political life occurs for the most part
in large, institutional types of organizations, in which contacts are secondary and of which rules and forms are more characteristic than they are
of face-to-face groups. Moreover, leadership in politics is associated with
emergent features of leadership to a greater extent than would be true in
an experimentally imposed one. ...

In analyzing political leadership in terms of the larger political
environment, one must of course take into account a great variety
of factors. In the United States, for example, the following are some
of the elements that must be considered: the norms and values operative in the society; the organization of political power through
parties, major socio-economic groups, and leadership both in various overtly political activities and in economic, communications,
professional, religious, and other areas; the governmental system,
with special attention to the diffusion of power between national
and state governments and among the three branches of the national government; voting behavior, including non-voting, as manifested in the various election contests that the aspiring political
leader must win; and the tensions, insecurities, expectations, passivity, and anomie or ennui among the electorate.

To say all this is, of course, to say that the analyst of any political leader must be an analyst of society; he must be historian, sociologist, social psychologist and anthropologist, as well as biographer in the usual sense. It is also to say, perhaps, that the study
of leadership in large, fluid, heterogeneous societies is no job for
mere mortals. On the other hand, putting more emphasis on the

[9] It is conceivable, of course, that some leadership might be so purely ceremonial or symbolic that the impact on the environment would be almost negli-
gible, but this would be the exceptional case.

[10] One of the best treatments on a comparative basis of several of the more important studies of interrelationships within primary groups is George C. Homans,
The Human Group (New York: Harcourt, Brace, 1950).

[11] Lester G. Seligman, "The Study of Political Leadership," *The American Political Science Review*, Vol. XLIV, No. 4, December 1950, pp. 908-909. This is a
first-rate summary of recent progress in the study of leadership, of certain implications of the new emphasis on the situationist approach, with some suggestions
for further research.

political environment, complex though that environment may be, permits a more realistic and potentially more rewarding approach because the analyst can deal with the observable, tangible, measurable elements in the matrix instead of limiting himself unduly to the subterranean, sometimes invisible, and perhaps unique elements of any one leader's temperament.[12]

The leader-in-society approach suggests three other guidelines in the study of political leadership—guidelines that may delimit the range of that study even while recognizing the many variables involved:

1. The traditional and desirable attention to the shaping of personality in childhood must be complemented by attention to developments in late adolescence and indeed through adulthood. Any act performed in adulthood, Dollard has said, will have a network of references to environmental factors and internal impulses "along the whole length of the drive sequences." The influence of parents, siblings, and school, vital though these may be, are altered by later phases of development, especially in the American context, with its changeability in time and space. Moreover, data on later personality development may be more reliable than data on childhood, because fuller and more impersonal documentation may be available in the former case.[13]

2. The environmental political factors that affect the leader's personality should not be treated as inchoate and indistinguishable forces impinging on the emerging leader but in terms of that leader's *perception* of their existence and of their relative importance. Because he is at the mercy of a conjunction of forces—in an election, perhaps, or at a convention—that he must assess long in advance, the effective political leader may be far more responsive to contextual elements, as he sizes them up, than, say, a general or industrialist may be. The study of leadership involves two tasks in this respect: it must seek to understand why the political leader assigns priorities to political influences (*i.e.*, why a Franklin Roosevelt will deal with city bosses even at the expense of antagonizing civic reformers); it must also assess independently the leader's success in setting up such priorities (*i.e.*, whether Roosevelt actually

---

[12] On this point see Bogardus, *op. cit.*, p. 11. "A new kind of autobiography is needed—one that will present the social situation, the social process, and the attitudes of all concerned." An early and pioneering study of the more general problem involved is John Dollard, *Criteria for the Life History* (New Haven: Yale University Press, 1935), in which the author emphasizes that the social situation must be carefully and continuously specified as a factor.

[13] Roosevelt might seem to be an exception to this generalization because hundreds of his early letters have been preserved, and there are extensive memoirs of his mother and of others who knew him during the early years. On the other hand, a study of these documents suggests their limitations as much as their possibilities for the explanation of personality development.

strengthened his own leadership in the long run by dealing with city bosses).[14]

3. The concept of *role-taking* is of central importance in analyzing political leadership in a fluid, variegated society. Leaders must perceive and identify with so many norms, loyalties, and interests that they can achieve adjustment only by pseudointegration—"by compartmentalizing their personalities to fit different segments of their lives," as Kluckhohn and Murray describe the process in discussing personality integration generally.[15] Just as a diverse society does not simply mold individuals in one fixed form but compels them to enact specific roles, so a heterogeneous political environment requires the leader to turn from role to role as he deals with, and even identifies with, different groups. While role-taking is traditionally viewed as a device to enable the leader to present different faces to different publics in the time-honored fashion of the politician, it also is testimony to the influence of environmental factors that compel the leader to recognize their demands and expectations. Roosevelt is an excellent case in point. However, the analyst of an important political leader must try to differentiate the roles from the central core personality, to rank order them, and—no easy task—to see whether role-taking affects that core personality. A test of the more dominant or creative leader, as described below, is the extent to which his role-taking is a means of implementing a central purpose independent of those roles, or, contrariwise, is simply a means of defining and expressing his personality.[16]

III

This last observation may also serve as an introduction to a final comment. Role-taking, carried to its ultimate degree, implies finally the absence of leadership (aside from the purely ceremonial), for the leader-actor assumes as many roles as society in all its component parts demands, and in doing so he mirrors society rather than transforms it. The creative leader, on the other hand, stands somewhat apart from society and assumes roles (as conciliator, as party chief, as representative of the whole nation, as commander-in-chief, etc.) only as a tactical means of realizing his long-term strategic ends, and in the long run seeks to broaden the environmental limits within which he operates.[17] Far from being a slave

---

[14] Cf. *The Social Sciences in Historical Study*, cited above, p. 154.
[15] *Op. cit.*, p. 523.
[16] See Newcomb, *op. cit.*, pp. 654 ff.
[17] See T. N. Whitehead, *Leadership in a Free Society* (Cambridge: Harvard University Press, 1936), in which the author argues that the executive (the leader of a bureaucracy) not only leads his human material—he organizes it. Whereas

to a role system, the great leader, as Gerth and Mills suggest, may actually smash it and set up another system in which his roles are differently structured.[18]

How great are the potentialities of creative leadership in this sense? This question cannot be answered abstractly. In the American culture one can point to certain conditions or points in time when a leader, sure of his means and of his ends, can alter the parallelogram of contextual forces amid which he operates: for example, a situation where prevailing popular attitudes are widespread but are superficial and lack depth and stability and hence are open to change brought about by systematic efforts by the leader; or a situation where groups opposed to the leader's goals are poorly organized and feebly led; or a crucial turning point confronting a society, when opposing forces are evenly balanced, and determined action by the leader may tip the scales; or a situation where the leader has the time and resources to shape a whole new alignment of power, including, for example, a reorganized and realigned party system; or a situation where possibilities exist of gaining popular acquiescence in the redefinition of a society's norms because the changed norms are identified with a widely beloved leader.[19]

All this is by no means to try to revive the discredited idea that great leaders can freely make history or refashion society.[20] On the contrary, it clearly accepts the limitations (as in part described above) on even the most creative leadership; moreover, it recognizes that the leader can bring about lasting change not by intervening sporadically and casually in the stream of events but only by altering, if he can, the channels in which the stream of events takes place. It focuses the attention of the student of leadership again on the interaction between the emerging leader and the many facets of his environment. And, in the case of the biographer, it permits him, if he wishes, to set up criteria of leadership by which his subject can be measured.

the primitive leader tried only to promote the integration of his group, the modern executive may be willing to risk endangering the integration of his followers in trying to improve their position. The essence of my estimate of Roosevelt as a political leader is that he failed to exercise creative leadership in this sense.

[18] *Op. cit.,* p. 419.

[19] The general problem is well developed in Sidney Hook, *The Hero in History* (New York: John Day, 1943), subtitled "a study in limitation and possibility." See especially his interesting distinction between the "eventful" man and the "event-making" man; I would classify Roosevelt as the former. An excellent development of the problem can be found in Elmer E. Cornwell, Jr., "Lloyd George: A Study in Political Leadership" (Ph.D. dissertation, Princeton University, 1954), in which the author examines the possibilities of creative leadership in the British context as compared with the American.

[20] For a recent warning on this score, see Allan Nevins, "Is History Made by Heroes?" *The Saturday Review,* November 5, 1955, pp. 9 ff.

ACKNOWLEDGMENTS

My debts are so heavy and so numerous that this book amounts virtually to an exercise in collective scholarship. I wish to express my deep appreciation to the following friends and colleagues for their generous help in making perceptive and painstaking critiques of the manuscript: Stephen K. Bailey, Woodrow Wilson School, Princeton University; Russell H. Bastert, C. Frederick Rudolph, and Robert C. L. Scott, all of the Department of History at Williams; John H. Blum, Department of Humanities, Massachusetts Institute of Technology; Philip K. Hastings, Department of Psychology, Williams College; William Leuchtenburg, Department of History, Columbia University; Jack Walter Peltason, Department of Political Science, University of Illinois; Lester Seligman, Department of Political Science, University of Oregon; Clinton Rossiter, Department of Government, Cornell University. I am indebted to all the foregoing both for their over-all review of the manuscript and for the special *expertise* they brought to bear in areas that they have made their particular fields of study.

La Rue Brown of Boston, a classmate of Roosevelt's at Harvard and long active in Boston law and politics, gave me valuable advice and information out of his close observation of the American political scene and of Roosevelt himself, especially in the earlier chapters and in my evaluation of the presidential personality. William B. Gates, Jr., Department of Economics, Williams College, went over the material dealing with economic problems and made some extremely useful suggestions, as did Fred Greene of the Political Science Department, Williams College, with the foreign policy chapters. John P. Roche, Department of Government, Haverford College, helped me on some of the theoretical formulations both through comments on the manuscript and through his writings on related subjects. Herbert Rosenberg went over the whole manuscript with care, paying particular attention to matters of style.

Harcourt, Brace and Company kindly secured the highly prized services of Henry Steele Commager, Eric Goldman, and C. Vann Woodward, who made many important suggestions for improving the manuscript. James Milholland of Harcourt, Brace and Company also went over the chapters and contributed comments from his close study of the historical period.

I am grateful to the entire staff of the Williams College Library for their invariably cheerful assistance on a great variety of aspects of this work, and to the staff of the Franklin D. Roosevelt Library for guiding me expertly through the great variety of material there, and especially to George Roach

488

and William J. Nichols for coping with a great number of special demands. Herman Kahn, Director of the Library and an authority on Roosevelt, has provided me with indispensable advice as to both sources and substance. I thank also the National Archives, Widener Library at Harvard, the Columbia University Library, the University of Chicago Library, and the Roper Public Opinion Collection, Williams College, for their co-operation.

To the Social Science Research Council I express appreciation for a grant to enable me to study certain theoretical aspects of political leadership, and to Williams College for financial help on travel and other expenses.

Finally, I have pitilessly enlisted my own family in the cause. My mother, Mildred Curry Baxter, and my mother-in-law, Margaret Dismorr Thompson, have made many helpful suggestions from the vantage point of having lived through more of Roosevelt's own years than have I. And my children have performed a variety of chores to the extent that their tender years allowed.

N EVER has a political leader left a more complex personal character and governmental program than did Roosevelt; but never has a leader left such ample means for the attempt to unravel the complexity. The Franklin D. Roosevelt Library at Hyde Park is a monument to his sense of responsibility to future generations, to his recognition of the needs of historians for the full record, and, no doubt, to his certainty of the high place he would hold in history once that record was carefully appraised. Above all, the Library represented his faith in the idea, as he expressed it at the dedication of the Library on June 30, 1941, that to collect and preserve its records a nation must believe in the past and in the future, and in the "capacity of its own people so to learn from the past that they can gain in judgment in creating their own future."

The Library is, of course, a collection of collections—of over 28,000 books and 40,000 other printed items; of Roosevelt's collections of autographs, colonial manuscripts and naval history manuscripts; of his collections of naval prints, paintings and books; of sound recordings of his speeches and of films of major events during his Presidency; of over 62,000 still photographs and, most important, of 3,500 cubic feet of Roosevelt's White House papers and approximately that quantity of other papers and records. It is also a place where scholars can work in this vast and diffused material with the assistance of the Library's competent and devoted staff.[1]

The White House Papers of Franklin D. Roosevelt are divided into four main series, and many smaller series; seven of the more important series that I have worked in are described below:

1. *President's Personal File.* This file contains about 9,000 folders, of which approximately two fifths are devoted to correspondence with private individuals and three fifths to special subjects or correspondence with private organizations. The material for any one correspondent may vary from a few letters to several boxes; the first few file subjects are devoted to the President himself and members of his family and are fairly extensive. Other subjects range from close associates to private citizens whose letters Roosevelt wanted for some reason to keep in his personal file. Roosevelt's answers to some of these letters are often of great value. The Library has a large subject index to these folders.

2. *"Alphabetical File."* A vast collection of letters written to Roosevelt

<hr />

[1] For a highly useful description of the nature of the collections and some of the problems and opportunities in their use, see Herman Kahn, "World War II and Its Background: Research Materials at the Franklin D. Roosevelt Library and Policies Concerning Their Use," paper delivered at the annual meeting of the American Historical Association, Chicago, December 29, 1953.

from members of the general public, some with copies of brief acknowledgments written by presidential secretaries. There is no subject arrangement of these letters. They are arranged alphabetically by name of the writer of the letter. I have not gone through this collection systematically but have sampled it for certain periods.

3. *Official File.* Another huge series of material, this group was originally planned to relate mainly to official governmental functions and there is a file subject for each major department and agency. As an example, formal departmental reports as well as informal reports to the President from his subordinates will be found in this collection. While this file is more "official" than the file listed under No. 1 above, there is no sharp or systematic distinction in the character of the material to be found in the two series.

4. *President's Secretary's File.* Roosevelt had his personal secretary put in her own separate file some of the letters and documents to which he wanted quick access. Hence this is a smaller and much more selective collection, although still one that defies descriptive generalization. It is especially valuable for the study of foreign policy. Because Miss Tully filed so much of this material, it is sometimes called the "Tully file."

5. *Press Conferences.* Transcripts of all Roosevelt's press conferences, amounting to over 1,000 separate meetings, afford a major source of week-to-week information on Roosevelt's ever-changing ideas and policies—at least to the extent to which he was willing to talk with reporters off the record. Intermixed in this collection are transcripts of occasional conferences that were held not with the press but with various groups such as businessmen, church leaders, youth leaders, and even members of Congress, and some of these are of exceptional value. In general, however, Roosevelt was so careful in the information that he gave out to the press that the transcripts rarely contain strikingly important ideas or statements.

6. *The Records of the Democratic National Committee.* The records of the Democratic National Committee in the Franklin D. Roosevelt Library are a large and important group of material. Comprising some 200 cubic feet, most of this material falls within the period 1928-1940. It consists of correspondence, campaign literature, clippings and other material created or accumulated by the Democratic National Committee in the course of conducting the campaigns of 1932, 1936 and 1940. There is a very large group of correspondence for the period 1928-1933, which is especially valuable for the study of Roosevelt's campaign for the nomination.

7. *The Papers of Harry L. Hopkins.* The great bulk of the available Hopkins papers at the Library fall in the period 1933-1940. These voluminous papers are particularly valuable for a study of Hopkins as administrator of the work relief program and the development of his ideas and his relationships with politicians and other prominent persons through the country in this period. These are the "personal" papers of Hopkins for this period. I have used them in conjunction with the official files of FERA and WPA, which are in the National Archives in Washington, D. C.

Many other groups at the Franklin D. Roosevelt Library in which I have worked are noted in the chapter bibliographies.

Aside from material at the Franklin D. Roosevelt Library, I have made particular use of the following:

1. Papers deposited in the Library of Congress, as follows: Newton D. Baker Papers, George Creel Papers, Josephus Daniels Papers, William E. Dodd, Jr., Papers, Charles Evans Hughes Papers, Harold L. Ickes Papers, Charles L. McNary Papers, George W. Norris Papers, Amos Pinchot Papers, Thomas J. Walsh Papers, William Allen White Papers. I wish to express appreciation for permission to use these papers, where such was needed, and also to thank the personnel of the Manuscripts Division, Library of Congress, for assistance in their use.

2. Interviews by the author with the following: Louis Brownlow (August 5, 1955); Benjamin Cohen (August 3, 1955); Thomas G. Corcoran (August 4, 1955); James A. Farley (April 1955); Felix Frankfurter (December 17, 1955); Ernest K. Lindley (August 4, 1955); Randolph Paul (March 1955); Eleanor Roosevelt (July 28, 1955); James H. Rowe (December 19, 1955). Interviews conducted in 1946 for earlier research which have been useful for this work are those with Paul H. Appleby, Hugo L. Black, Robert M. La Follette, Jr., Frances Perkins, and Donald R. Richberg.

3. Transcripts of interviews, Oral History Project, Columbia University, as follows: Henry Bruere, Edward J. Flynn, James W. Gerard, Arthur Krock, Langdon P. Marvin, Herbert C. Pell, William Phillips, J. David Stern, George S. Van Schaick. I am grateful for permission to use these most useful, well organized and indexed materials.

4. Minutes of the Executive Council, July 11, 1933–November 13, 1934, and of the National Emergency Council, December 19, 1933–April 28, 1936. These two councils served as somewhat enlarged cabinets, and unlike the case with the Cabinet, transcripts were made of the proceedings. Transcripts of those sessions presided over by Roosevelt provide an intimate and vivid picture of the President's month-to-month attitudes on domestic problems and personalities. These transcripts are available at the National Archives, Washington, D. C.

5. Correspondence with a number of persons participating in, or familiar with, New Deal programs or activities; these are noted in chapter bibliographies below.

6. Doctoral dissertations. I have exploited as thoroughly as I could the fund of information and ideas contained in these theses, which have been made available through that admirable institution, the Inter-Library Loan Service. Citation of such dissertations will be found in chapter bibliographies.

7. I will not try to list separately the secondary material that I have used; this too will be cited in chapter bibliographies. I do wish to pay tribute to the high caliber and enormous value of so many of the memoirs produced in the last decade or so; I have made extensive use of them. Two documentary collections that merit special mention are: Samuel I. Rosenman (ed.). *The Public Papers and Addresses of Franklin D. Roosevelt*, a well edited and superbly produced set of thirteen volumes; and Elliott Roosevelt (ed.), *F. D. R.: His Personal Letters* (4 vols., New York: Duell, Sloan and Pearce, 1947-50). The first two volumes are subtitled "Early Years" and "1905-1928," and are referred to as Vols. I and II, respectively, in chapter bibliographies; the second two volumes, covering 1928-1945, are referred to below only by page number.

CHAPTER BIBLIOGRAPHIES

The following abbreviations are used in citations in the chapter bibliographies:

FDRL   Franklin D. Roosevelt Library
LC   Library of Congress
OF   Official Files (FDRL)
OHP   Oral History Project (Columbia University)
PC   Press Conference
PLFDR   Elliott Roosevelt (ed.), *F. D. R.: His Personal Letters* (4 vols., New York: Duell, Sloan and Pearce, 1947-50)
PPAFDR   Samuel I. Rosenman (ed.), *The Public Papers and Addresses of Franklin D. Roosevelt* (13 vols., New York, 1938-50)
PPF   President's Personal Files (FDRL)
PSF   President's Secretary's File (FDRL)

Books cited in the chapter bibliographies are published in New York City unless otherwise noted. A citation like "Rossiter [chap. 11]" means that a complete citation for the Rossiter work in question will be found in the bibliography for chapter 11. When the author's name alone is used, it means that earlier in the bibliography of that same chapter will be found either a complete citation of the book in question, or a bracketed reference (as above) to the chapter bibliography containing the complete citation.

The following list is a basic list of books which are frequently cited in the chapter bibliographies; a (B) following an author's name in the bibliographies indicates that the book referred to is cited in full in this list. An author's name with a superior number (Farley[1]) is used when the basic list contains more than one book by that author; the list provides the key to the particular book.

Barkley, Alben W., *That Reminds Me* (Garden City, N. Y.: Doubleday & Company, Inc., 1954)

Beard, Charles A., *American Foreign Policy in the Making, 1932-1940* (New Haven: Yale University Press, 1946)

Burns, J. M., "Congress and the Formation of Economic Policies" (Ph.D. dissertation, Harvard University, 1947)

Cantril, Hadley (ed.), *Public Opinion 1935-1946* (Princeton: Princeton University Press, 1951)

Connally, Tom, and Alfred Steinberg, *My Name Is Tom Connally* (New York: Thomas Y. Crowell Company, 1954)

Creel, George, *Rebel at Large* (New York: G. P. Putnam's Sons, 1947)

Eccles, Marriner S., *Beckoning Frontiers* (New York: Alfred A. Knopf, 1951)

Farley, James A., *Behind the Ballots* (New York: Harcourt, Brace and Company, 1938). Farley[1].

——, *Jim Farley's Story, the Roosevelt Years* (New York: McGraw-Hill Book Company, Inc., 1948). Farley[2].

Flynn, Edward J., *You're the Boss* (New York: The Viking Press, 1947)

Flynn, John T., *Country Squire in the White House* (New York: Doubleday, Doran and Company, Inc., 1940)

Freidel, Frank, *Franklin D. Roosevelt* (2 vols., Boston: Little, Brown and Company, 1952-54)

Goldman, Eric, *Rendezvous with Destiny* (New York: Alfred A. Knopf, 1952)

Gosnell, Harold F., *Boss Platt and His New York Machine* (Chicago: University of Chicago Press, 1924). Gosnell[1].

——, *Champion Campaigner: Franklin D. Roosevelt* (New York: The Macmillan Company, 1952). Gosnell[2].

Gouldner, Alvin W. (ed.), *Studies in Leadership* (New York: Harper & Brothers, 1950)

Gunther, John, *Inside U. S. A.* (New York: Harper & Brothers, 1947). Gunther[1].

——, *Roosevelt in Retrospect* (New York: Harper & Brothers, 1950). Gunther[2].

Hoover, Herbert, *The Memoirs of Herbert Hoover.* Vol. III, *The Great Depression, 1929-1941* (New York: The Macmillan Company, 1952)

Hull, Cordell, *The Memoirs of Cordell Hull* (2 vols., New York: The Macmillan Company, 1948)

Ickes, Harold L., *The Secret Diary of Harold L. Ickes* (3 vols., New York: Simon and Schuster, 1953-54). Vol. I, *The First Thousand Days, 1933-1936* (1953): Ickes[1]. Vol. II, *The Inside Struggle, 1936-1939* (1954): Ickes[2]. Vol. III, *The Lowering Clouds, 1939-1941* (1954): Ickes[3].

Jackson, Robert H., *The Struggle for Judicial Supremacy* (New York: Alfred A. Knopf, 1941)

Langer, William L., and S. Everett Gleason, *The World Crisis and American Foreign Policy* (2 vols., New York: Harper & Brothers, 1952-53)

Lindley, Ernest K., *Franklin D. Roosevelt* (Indianapolis: The Bobbs-Merrill Company, 1931). Lindley[1].

——, *Half Way with Roosevelt* (New York: The Viking Press, 1936). Lindley[2].

——, *The Roosevelt Revolution: First Phase* (New York: The Viking Press, 1933). Lindley[3].

Michelson, Charles, *The Ghost Talks* (New York: G. P. Putnam's Sons, 1944)

Moley, Raymond, *After Seven Years* (New York: Harper & Brothers, 1939)

Morgenthau, Henry, Jr., "The Morgenthau Diaries," *Collier's*, Sept. 27—Nov. 1, 1947

Moscow, Warren, *Politics in the Empire State* (New York: Alfred A. Knopf, 1948)

Perkins, Frances, *The Roosevelt I Knew* (New York: The Viking Press, 1946)

Richberg, Donald R., *My Hero* (New York: G. P. Putnam's Sons, 1954). Richberg[1].

—, *The Rainbow* (Garden City, N. Y.: Doubleday, Doran & Co., 1936). Richberg[2].

Roosevelt, Eleanor, *This I Remember* (New York: Harper & Brothers, 1949). Roosevelt[1].

—, *This Is My Story* (New York: Harper & Brothers, 1937). Roosevelt[2].

Rosenman, Samuel I., *Working with Roosevelt* (New York: Harper & Brothers, 1952)

Sherwood, Robert E., *Roosevelt and Hopkins* (New York: Harper & Brothers, 1948)

Stiles, Lela, *The Man behind Roosevelt* (Cleveland: World Publishing Company, 1954)

Tansill, Charles C., *Back Door to War* (Chicago: Henry Regnery Company, 1952)

Timmons, Bascom N., *Garner of Texas* (New York: Harper & Brothers, 1948)

Tully, Grace G., *F. D. R., My Boss* (New York: Charles Scribner's Sons, 1949)

CHAPTER ONE

The most important material on Roosevelt's early years is in PLFDR, Vol. I (*Early Years*), which includes a score of his letters to parents and relatives in the years before he went to Groton. See also Sara Delano Roosevelt, *My Boy Franklin* (Crown Publishers, 1933), remembrances of things past from the perspective of many years; Olin Dows, *Franklin Roosevelt at Hyde Park* (American Artists Group, 1949), a colorful account; Clara and Hardy Steeholm, *The House at Hyde Park* (Viking, 1950); Noel F. Busch, *What Manner of Man?* (Harper, 1944), an interesting attempt at a psychological interpretation of Roosevelt; and John T. Flynn, which is a useful corrective to some superficial generalizations about Roosevelt's early years, but offers some questionable interpretations of its own.

The Seed and the Soil. On Roosevelt's family background, see Karl Schriftgiesser, *The Amazing Roosevelt Family* (Funk and Wagnalls, 1942), important for the Roosevelt family; and Daniel Webster Delano, *Franklin Roosevelt and the Delano Influence* (Pittsburgh: Nudi, 1946), which, while it implicitly assigns too much weight to the role of heredity, provides useful information on the other side of the family. See also Alvin Page Johnson, *Franklin D. Roosevelt's Colonial Ancestors* (Boston: Lathrop, Lee, & Shepard, 1933), an earlier account; Rita Halle Kleeman, *Gracious Lady: The Life of Sara Delano Roosevelt* (Appleton-Century, 1935), a sympathetic biography filled with noteworthy sidelights; and Hall Roosevelt, *Odyssey of an American Family* (Harper, 1939). The contrast on page 5 between industrialists and politicians as doers and talkers is from Matthew Josephson, *The Politicos* (Harcourt, Brace, 1938), p. vii. Gerald W. Johnson. writing in the New York *Herald Tribune,* is the source of the quotation on page 6 in regard to the remarkable seventh generation of Roosevelts. The quotation about the tendency of the Delanos to carry their way of life around with them, on page 7, is from the first volume of Frank Freidel's distinguished biographical series on Roosevelt, (B) p. 17. On the relation between intermarriage and the importance of heredity, page 8, see Ralph Linton, *The Cultural Background of Personality* (Appleton-Century, 1945), p. 136, although Linton refers especially to the role of intermarriage in isolated "primitive" societies. The concept of the family as the psychological broker of society is taken from Robert MacIver, *The Web of Government* (Macmillan, 1947), p. 294.

Groton: Education for What? On Groton and Peabody see Frank D. Ashburn's loving but judicious *Peabody of Groton* (Coward-McCann, 1944), and Ellery Sedgwick's reflective *The Happy Profession* (Boston: Little, Brown, 1946). George Biddle, "As I Remember Groton School," *Harper's Magazine*, Vol. 179, August 1939, pp. 292-300, and George W. Martin, "Preface to a Schoolmaster's Autobiography," in the same magazine, Vol. 188, January 1944, pp. 156-162, offer somewhat more critical views of Rector and school. PLFDR, Vol. I, includes a remarkably full set of letters from FDR during the Groton period. The Groton file (Group 14) in FDRL contains some useful data. On education for leadership in Greece see Werner Jaeger, *Paideia: the Ideals of Greek Culture* (Oxford: Basil Blackwell, 1939), Vols. I-III. I am indebted to Professor William H. Brubeck for calling my attention to literature in this field. For the history of books of advice to princes see Allan H. Gilbert, *Machiavelli's Prince and Its Forerunners* (Durham, North Carolina: Duke University Press, 1938), and for a typical "prince's book," John M. S. Allison (ed.), *Concerning the Education of a Prince* (New Haven: Yale University Press, 1941). It has been argued that while Groton contributed only a tiny fraction of her sons to the public service, the quality was high. So it was: Bronson Cutting, Joseph C. Grew, Theodore Roosevelt, Jr., Sumner Welles, Dean Acheson, and others. Two things must be noted, however: the politicians who graduated from Groton, aside from Franklin D. Roosevelt, were not very successful in electoral politics, *i.e.*, in winning elections; and men like Cutting, Welles, and Acheson had conspicuous trouble getting along with the very type of politician whom Roosevelt could either win over by charm, or defeat.

Harvard: The Gold Coast. On Roosevelt's Harvard years the Personal Letters remain of central importance, although the letters are not so frequent as in the Groton years and large gaps occur each time Sara Roosevelt takes up her Boston residence. Particularly in the Harvard years these letters raise a difficult problem: to what extent do they picture Roosevelt's activities not as they were, but as he wished his mother to see them? For example, did he ignore the intellectual side of Harvard in his letters because he thought Sara would be uninterested in it? The answer is probably not. In the first place, Roosevelt kept a diary during some of his Harvard days (now in FDRL Group 14) and this document reveals no more interest in intellectual matters than do his letters. Secondly, the other available material does not contradict—and often reinforces—the picture given in the letters. Freidel (B), Gunther[2] (B), Lindley[1] (B), *op. cit.*, are useful for the Harvard years, and Earle Looker, *This Man Roosevelt* (Brewer, Warren & Putnam, 1932) offers some interesting material. See also Harvard File, Group 14, FDRL (which throws a good deal of doubt on some published views that Roosevelt took an active part in student reform at Harvard). On the Harvard of Roosevelt's time see Samuel E. Morison, *Three Centuries of Harvard* (Cambridge: Harvard University Press, 1936), whom I have quoted on page 16 above; Samuel E. Morison (ed.), *The Development of Harvard University* (Cambridge: Harvard University Press, 1930); Henry Aaron Yeomans, *Abbott Lawrence Lowell* (Cambridge: Harvard University Press, 1948); Cleveland Amory, *The Proper Bostonians* (Dutton, 1947), a wise and witty work; Edwin E. Slosson, *Great American Universities* (Macmillan, 1910), chap. 1; "Report of the Committee on Improving Instruction in Harvard College" (Briggs report), *Harvard Graduates Magazine*, Vol. XII, June 1904, pp. 611-620. On the problem of formal education for political leadership two different approaches are Arthur J. Jones, *The Education of Youth for Leadership* (McGraw-Hill, 1938), and Karl Mannheim, *Freedom, Power, and Democratic Planning* (Oxford University Press, 1950). I am indebted to La Rue Brown of Boston, a classmate of Roosevelt's, for information and counsel on the Harvard of Roosevelt's day; and to Eleanor Roosevelt (interview, Hyde Park, N. Y., July 28, 1955) for her views on Roosevelt's early development.

CHAPTER TWO

On the reformist turmoil of the early 1900's the literature is voluminous and fascinating; only a few items can be listed here. Louis Filler, *Crusaders for American Liberalism* (Harcourt, Brace, 1939) is a richly detailed study of the muckrakers, their exposés, and their editors. The muckrakers' own writings are important if read critically; most notable, of course, is Lincoln Steffens' *Autobiography* (Harcourt, Brace, 1931), but the books of Brand Whitlock, Ray Stannard Baker, Ida Tarbell, Upton Sinclair, and their colleagues are also significant. More general works are John Chamberlain, *Farewell to Reform* (Liveright, 1932); Richard Hofstadter, *The American Political Tradition* (Knopf, 1948); Russel B. Nye, *Midwestern Progressive Politics* (Lansing: Michigan State College Press, 1951); Mark Sullivan, *Our Times* (6 vols., Scribner, 1926-35); Frederick Lewis Allen, *The Big Change* (Harper, 1952); Eric Goldman (B), to whom I am indebted for the quotation about Theodore Roosevelt on page 25.

Uncle Ted and Cousin Eleanor. Henry F. Pringle, *Theodore Roosevelt* (New York: Harcourt, Brace, revised ed., 1956) remains the best biography, at least on the period up to 1910. The volumes of *Letters of Theodore Roosevelt*, edited by Elting E. Morison (Cambridge: Harvard University Press, 1951 *et seq.*), were of more general usefulness than Roosevelt's autobiography (Macmillan, 1913), although neither has important direct reference to FDR. As for Eleanor Roosevelt, her own wonderfully frank and poignant *This Is My Story* (B) is indispensable, although discursive and sometimes trivial. The *Personal Letters*, while of course episodic, throw some light on the three-way relationship among FDR, his wife, and his mother. My source for Roosevelt's description of his political ambitions on page 25 is Grenville Clark, a fellow law clerk, writing in the Roosevelt memorial issue of the *Harvard Alumni Bulletin*, Vol. XLVII, No. 14, April 28, 1945. The material at FDRL on the 1904-1909 period is relatively sparse; there are some papers and letters from FDR's law practice (Group 14, FDRL). A well-preserved set of FDR's notes on Burgess's lectures on constitutional development (Group 14, FDRL) is of some interest, for they show that Burgess neglected—or Roosevelt failed to take notes on—some of the major *political* aspects of constitutional development, such as John Marshall's brilliant establishment of the precedent for judicial review in *Marbury* v. *Madison*. In general, however, Roosevelt's years between Harvard and the senatorship are the most difficult to document of any of his major phases. On his Saturday afternoon poker playing, see Charles C. Auchincloss to Roosevelt, August 1, 1933, PPF 707, FDRL.

The Race for the Senate. FDRL has published a most useful *Calendar of the Speeches and Other Published Statements of Franklin D. Roosevelt, 1910-1920* (1952), compiled by Robert L. Jacoby, hereafter referred to as *Calendar of Speeches.* This document not only lists speeches, statements to the press, occasional letters quoted in the press, etc., but in almost all cases provides a brief summary. Group 9, FDRL, contains newspaper clippings on the 1910 election campaign, correspondence, campaign material, some of FDR's own notes and drafts for his speeches, accounts of campaign expenses, and a number of letters to FDR and occasionally his replies. Group 21, FDRL, includes interviews by George A. Palmer, former superintendent of National Park Service at Hyde Park, of old political associates of FDR, most notably John E. Mack, Mr. and Mrs. Grant Dickinson, and Thomas F. Leonard. See also Eleanor Roosevelt[1] (B), Morgan H. Hoyt, "Roosevelt Enters Politics," *The Franklin D. Roosevelt Collector* (May 1949), a reminiscent piece by a man who accompanied FDR in some of his 1910 campaigning; *The New York Red Book*, Albany, 1911, for the official voting record; and Gosnell[2]. The most important secondary sources on the senatorial years are Freidel (B), and Alfred B. Rollins, "The Political Education of Franklin D. Roosevelt, 1909-1928" (Ph.D. dissertation, Harvard University, 1953), a phenomenally thorough and carefully researched study of these years, based not only on FDRL material but also on the papers of contemporary New York State politicians.

The College Kid and the Tammany Beast. Warren Moscow, *Politics in the Empire State* (Knopf, 1948), a journalistic but judicious treatment of parties, politicians, and voters in New York, is a helpful book for understanding the general context in which FDR operated, although it focuses on the 1930's and 1940's. For New York machine politics see Gosnell[1], M. R. Werner, *Tammany Hall* (Garden City: Doubleday, Doran, 1928), a lively and detailed historical account; Roy V. Peel, *The Political Clubs of New York City* (Putnam, 1935), an important study of the group relations within Tammany; and William L. Riordan, *Plunkitt of Tammany Hall* (Knopf, 1948). On the Sheehan fight, Lindley[1] (B), Freidel (B), and Rollins have exceptionally full treatments; see also Langdon P. Marvin, OHP, FDRL (Group 9) contains hundreds of letters to FDR from constituents, and many of FDR's replies, and several nuggets, including a copy of Boss Barnes's letter to his legislative leaders outlining strategy, and the pro-

Sheehan petition from Poughkeepsie with 265 names—"many in the same writing," Senator Roosevelt said on receiving it.

Farmer-Labor Representative. On Roosevelt's senatorship in general, the most disappointing source is his own diary, in FDRL, which he kept brilliantly for the first three days of January 1911 and then abandoned. A sympathetic and balanced account of the Howe-Roosevelt relationship, by one of Howe's assistants, can be found in Stiles (B). FDRL has (Group 9) hundreds of files of state senatorial papers; this luxuriant mass of material has been well indexed in a "Descriptive Inventory," a typed document compiled by Carl L. Spicer and Kathryn C. Fell, FDRL, 1948. FDR's correspondence files relating to bills and other legislative matters are arranged under about thirty-five subject classes of legislation; other matter is organized in "general subject files" and "name files." Some of the most useful files (all in Group 9) are Nos. 15, "Postmaster Endorsements"; 35, "Labor Bills"; 16 (patronage), 309 (Sheehan), and 323 (Stetson). See also F. Perkins (B), although Miss Perkins underestimates, I believe, the extent to which FDR moved toward socio-economic progressivism during his senatorial days.

CHAPTER THREE

Arthur S. Link, *Wilson: The Road to the White House* (Princeton: Princeton University Press, 1947), ends with an exciting and detailed account of Wilson's nomination and election campaigns. For T.R.'s role in the 1910-1912 period see George E. Mowry, *Theodore Roosevelt and the Progressive Movement* (Madison: University of Wisconsin Press, 1946), and for Taft's, Henry F. Pringle, *The Life and Times of William Howard Taft* (2 vols., Farrar & Rinehart, 1939). The story of Daniels' selection of FDR as assistant secretary is found in Josephus Daniels, *The Wilson Era* (Chapel Hill: The University of North Carolina Press, 1944). Roosevelt's role in the Wilson Conference and the Empire State Democracy is meticulously covered in Rollins [chap. 2]. Roosevelt's visit to Wilson, described on page 49 above, is not documented as fully and reliably as one might wish.

A Roosevelt on the Job. Freidel's account (B) of Roosevelt's navy years (Vol. I covers the period through the Armistice) is detailed and perceptive. The Roosevelt-Daniels relationship is reflected in their letters to each other in Carroll Kilpatrick (ed.), *Roosevelt and Daniels* (Chapel Hill: The University of North Carolina Press, 1952); the reflection is necessarily partial, but there is a discriminating introduction by the editor; see also Josephus Daniels Papers, LC. Even more useful on the two men is the sensitive, nostalgic treatment by the navy secretary's son Jonathan Daniels, *The End of Innocence* (Philadelphia: J. B. Lippincott Co., 1954). The *Letters* are rather sparse during the prewar years. FDR's own account of his wage-fixing activities in PPA (Vol. I, p. 60) is not wholly reliable. FDRL (Group 10) contains twenty-five boxes of letters and other material covering the navy period up to August 1914. The description on page 50 of bureaucracy is from C. Wright Mills's brilliant *White Collar* (Oxford University Press, 1951), p. 263.

Tammany Wins Again. Material on the 1914 race in FDRL is divided between "Personal Papers" and Correspondence—1914 senatorial race; the three boxes of the latter offer a wealth of fascinating letters and memorandums, including letters from Howe to Roosevelt while the latter was at Campobello in August 1914. Harold F. Gosnell (B, Gosnell[2]) quotes some of the documents relating to the 1914 fight, and I am indebted to him in assessing what Roosevelt learned from his defeat.

War Leader. Roosevelt's own accounts later of his war experiences must be used with great care; he liked to embroider. Material in PLFDR tends to be rather fragmentary (except during summers, when he was writing frequent letters to Eleanor at Campobello); it does include, however, Roosevelt's highly factual diary that he carefully kept on his trip to Europe. FDRL has separate boxes on Roosevelt's correspondence with Theodore Roosevelt, Woodrow Wilson, and Admiral Mahan during the navy period. There is one box on the 1918 political events. Freidel (B) provides the most exhaustive and objective study of Roosevelt's naval activities during the war. Roosevelt's image of himself as a red-tape slasher is reflected in Roosevelt to Bernard Baruch, July 21, 1937, PSF, FDRL; that at least one of his associates concurred in this picture is evident from PLFDR, Vol. II, picture facing p. 157. I am indebted to Felix Frankfurter (interview, Washington, D. C., December 19, 1955) for his views and information on Roosevelt's high capacities in his navy office. Data on Roosevelt's request for membership in the American Legion can be found in PPF 4818, FDRL.

CHAPTER FOUR

Physical changes in Roosevelt during the war years are well described in Gunther[2] (B) and vividly depicted in Stefan Lorant, *FDR: A Pictorial Biography* (Simon and Schuster, 1950); domestic aspects of these years are reported in Eleanor Roosevelt[2] (B), and in PL. His role as the young executive type is reflected in his speeches in FDRL, "Master File of Speeches," and in Donald Day, *Franklin D. Roosevelt's Own Story* (Boston: Little, Brown, 1951), an admirable collection of selections from FDR's private and public papers covering the period 1910-1945.

Challenge and Response. Accounts of the League of Nations struggle are many and varied. I have relied mainly on D. F. Fleming's authoritative *The United States and the League of Nations* (Putnam, 1932), which stresses the fight in the Senate and quotes extensively from debates; Thomas A. Bailey, *Woodrow Wilson and the Lost Peace* (Macmillan, 1944), an acute work that focuses on decisions in Paris and includes a long bibliography; and James M. Cox's garrulous, good-humored *Journey Through My Years* (Simon and Schuster, 1946), important in this connection mainly for the 1920 campaign. Roosevelt's speeches during the period are well indexed and summarized in the published *Calendar of Speeches,* and in an unpublished "Calendar of the Speeches and Other Published Statements of Franklin D. Roosevelt during the Campaign of 1920," FDRL, compiled by Robert L. Jacoby. The observer quoted on page 68 is William Bolitho.

1920—The Solemn Referendum. Chief sources for the 1920 campaign are Cox, and Lindley[1] (B), the New York *Times,* and the following in FDRL: a collection of unpublished speeches and public statements of Roosevelt during the campaign; and Group 15, which includes twenty-six boxes of correspondence and other materials containing campaign correspondence collected at the Roosevelt headquarters in New York City, papers relating to the Democratic National Convention, and an alphabetical file of general correspondence with political figures and friends, as well as five boxes of newspaper clippings, four scrapbooks, and several boxes of campaign literature. Many accounts of the meeting of Cox and Roosevelt are inaccurate; I have relied mainly on Cox, pp. 241 ff., and PL, Vol. II, pp. 496-497. Roosevelt's vice-presidential acceptance speech—perhaps his most significant during these years—is reported in full in PL, Vol. II, pp. 500-508. Marvin interview, OHP, is source for the statement that Roosevelt was cautiously optimistic on the eve of the 1920 election.

The Rising Politician. The episode described on pp. 76-77 above is based wholly on internal evidence in Sara Delano Roosevelt's letter to Roosevelt, October 14, 1917, PL, Vol. 1905-1928, pp. 274-275, although it also fits the general pattern of the family relationship at that time. Eleanor Roosevelt (interview, July 28, 1955) has commented on Roosevelt's slight feeling of alienation at Groton and Harvard despite his general adaptability. In interpreting Roosevelt's personality development my hypothesis is that biological and environmental forces represent not opposites but a continuum in which the forces are mutually interdependent and interactive. See Walter C. Langer, *Psychology and Human Living* (Appleton-Century, 1943); Ralph Linton [chap. 1]; Gardner Murphy, *Personality* (Harper, 1947); John W. Bennett and Melvin M. Tumin, *Social Life* (Knopf, 1949); Theodore M. Newcomb, *Social Psychology* (Dryden Press, 1950); Karen Horney, *The Neurotic Personality of Our Time* (W. W. Norton, 1937); Abram Kardiner and others, *The Psychological Frontiers of Society* (Columbia University Press, 1945). Alfred M. Tozzer, "Biography and Biology," *American Anthropologist,* Vol. XXXV, 1933, pp. 418-432, is a good-natured but devastating critique of attempts of biographers to specify the ancestral origin of particular qualities in their subjects.

CHAPTER FIVE

The best retrospective portrait of the 1920's is still Frederick L. Allen, *Only Yesterday* (Harper, 1931). For political aspects of the era see Karl Schriftgiesser, *This Was Normalcy* (Boston: Little, Brown, 1948); for economic, Committee on Recent Economic Changes, *Recent Economic Changes in the United States* (2 vols., McGraw-Hill, 1929); for sociological, Robert S. and Helen M. Lynd, *Middletown* (Harcourt, Brace, 1937); and for a wry look backward from the perspective of the 1930's, chap. 1 of Charles A. and Mary R. Beard, *America in Midpassage* (Macmillan, 1939). William Allen White's biography of Coolidge, *A Puritan in Babylon* (Macmillan, 1938) draws a marvelous contrast between the flint-faced president and the self-indulgent America around him. Freidel (B), Vol. II, contains a full and balanced account of Roosevelt's business activities; see also John T. Flynn (B) and Alva Johnston, "Mr. Roosevelt as a Businessman," *Saturday Evening Post,* October 31, 1936. James W. Prothro, "The Political Theory of American Business" (Ph.D. dissertation, Princeton University, 1952), is a sharp and deep-probing analysis of business attitudes in the United States.

I read this in thesis form but it has since been published as *The Dollar Decade* (Baton Rouge: Louisiana State University Press, 1954).

Ordeal. Roosevelt's political life in the 1920-28 period is hard to analyze fully because his illness limited him in activities, such as political speeches and formal messages, that ordinarily result in important documents. Gunther[2] (B) has the most illuminating description of the nature and effects of his illness and quotes previously unpublished medical diagnoses and observations. Turnley Walker, *Roosevelt and the Warm Springs Story* (A. A. Wyn, 1953) is a delightful account of that phase. Some who knew Roosevelt well believe that polio had a more lasting impact on his personality than I do; see, for example, Perkins (B), chap. 3; (for Harry Hopkins' views on the matter) Ickes[2], p. 225; Daniels to George Creel, November 12, 1947, Daniels Papers, LC. Letters in PLFDR and in FDRL show how quickly Roosevelt picked up the threads of his political life following his illness. These are organized alphabetically in Group 11, Papers of Franklin D. Roosevelt, 1920-1928. A box of miscellaneous data in Group 14, FDRL, includes first pages of Roosevelt's two abortive works, his submission for the Bok peace prize, his newspaper columns, Milton School speech, and other items. Day [chap. 4] is especially useful for the 1920's.

Dear Al and Dear Frank. A full life of Al Smith is needed. His *Up to Now* (Viking, 1929), is good reading; so is Henry F. Pringle, *Alfred E. Smith* (Macy-Masius, 1927), which is essentially a high-class campaign biography by an admirer but contains important insights. Neither of these includes Smith's significant post-1928 years, nor is there much mention of Roosevelt. FDRL has a useful file of correspondence between Smith and Roosevelt. Louis B. Wehle, *Hidden Threads of History* (Macmillan, 1953) contains several letters from Roosevelt indicating something of the latter's political plans in the 1920's. "General Correspondence," Campaign of 1920, twenty-eight boxes (Group 15), and "General Political Correspondence" (Group 11), alphabetically organized (nine boxes), comprise thirty-seven boxes of political correspondence of Roosevelt, 1920-1928; some are useful, most of the Group 15 letters are congratulations with brief replies. Correspondence with Howe, Oldfield, Van Lear Black, Hull, Jones, and other political or personal friends are of particular value. Rollins [chap. 2] is especially rewarding for the period of the 1920's, as is Freidel's broad-gaged study (B). Answers to Roosevelt's letters on party reorganization are filed separately in Group 11, but they have not been digested for 1924. "1924 Campaign Correspondence" (Group 11) in FDRL consists mostly of letters from Smith supporters with brief acknowledgments from Roosevelt or Smith, but this file with subheading "Democratic National Committee" has elaborate records on delegate sympathies, political conditions in the states, and the like.

Summons to Action. Roosevelt's weighing of political choices is described in a memorandum by Gustavus A. Rogers in his papers at FDRL, Box 4, Group 31. The drafting of Roosevelt in 1928 has been described with substantial accuracy in Eleanor Roosevelt[1] (B), a candid account of the 1928-1945 years; Edward J. Flynn (B), a temperate, knowledgeable chronicle by the head of the Democratic machine in the Bronx who joined Roosevelt's forces in 1928; Farley[1] (B), a revealing story but overfriendly to Roosevelt;

and in Lindley[1] (B). These accounts of the draft are substantiated in Howe's telegrams to Roosevelt in Howe file, FDRL, and "1928 Campaign Correspondence," Group 17, FDRL, especially Roosevelt's letter to Frederic Delano, October 8, 1928. Rollins on the 1928 draft is especially revealing. Farley's impression that Roosevelt was Smith's third choice for governor (after Lehman and one other) is not borne out in other memoirs or in documents. On the 1928 campaign the most informative material is in Rosenman (B); Perkins (B), Edward J. Flynn (B), and Lindley[1] (B) provide intriguing glimpses of the campaign, especially election night. Material in FDRL on the campaign is rather limited; the collection of typewritten copies of Roosevelt's campaign speeches in FDRL, however, covers the campaign far more fully than the excerpts that mark the beginning of Vol. I (1928-1932) of PPA. Gosnell[2] (B) and Moscow (B) offer some analysis of the 1928 election results. For the over-all picture of the 1928 presidential campaign see Roy V. Peel and Thomas C. Donnelly, *The 1928 Campaign* (Richard R. Smith, 1931). Roosevelt's feeling that he was excluded from the inner councils of Smith's presidential campaign is reflected in PLFDR, Vol. II, p. 772, memorandum of April 6, 1938.

CHAPTER SIX

Lindley[1] (B), Perkins (B), Edward J. Flynn (B), and Rosenman (B) agree on the main aspects of the Smith-Roosevelt relationship; it is unfortunate that more data is not available on the situation from Smith's point of view. PLFDR shows that the two men dealt with each other in an apparently friendly spirit during the first two or three gubernatorial years. Roosevelt wrote "for the record" in April 1938 (PLFDR, pp. 771-773) a brief memoir on Smith's expectations of guiding Roosevelt during the latter's first months in office. The Lindley quotation is from Lindley[1] (B), pp. 339-340.

The Politics of the Empire State. Moscow (B) is an informed, balanced treatment of the subject; I have relied on it heavily and borrowed from its title. Belle Zeller, *Pressure Politics in New York* (Prentice-Hall, 1937) treats in detail the complex strands of influence in the legislature. Gunther[1] has a brief but suggestive section on the state. FDRL has on permanent loan from the Office of the Governor of New York State, Albany, files on the controversy over the executive budget, containing mainly official reports and some correspondence, including a number of interesting letters between Roosevelt and his counsel. A. E. Buck, "The Budget Fight in New York," *National Municipal Review*, Vol. XVIII, No. 5, May 1929, pp. 352-354, is a succinct review that indicates Roosevelt did not monopolize virtue in the fight. PPAFDR includes a statement and a speech on the subject. One of the most fruitful sources for the gubernatorial period is Roosevelt's voluminous "Personal Correspondence, 1928-32," Group 12, organized alphabetically. Most of the invaluable correspondence with Howe is found separately in the Howe Papers, Group 36. A small fraction of the personal correspondence is available in PLFDR.

The Anatomy of Stalemate. Useful secondary material on the gubernatorial years is limited, partly because this period pales next to the succeeding one, partly because Roosevelt's own activities during the latter period shade off into the presidential contests. Lindley[1] (B) is the fullest source; while it was written midway through Roosevelt's governorship, it gains from the fact that the author was a reporter in Albany during these years and had a shrewd journalistic eye. While the book is favorable to Roosevelt, letters in FDRL and PLFDR indicate that Lindley could be critical. The four volumes of gubernatorial papers of FDR (Albany: J. B. Lyon Co., 1930-39) are the fullest source and contain messages to the legislature, speeches, etc. PPAFDR, Vol. I, offers numerous messages, reports, and speeches on the St. Lawrence; it covers to a lesser or greater extent all the main policies of the administration, with revealing introductory notes by Roosevelt. The New York State files on loan to FDRL contain filing drawers of legislative matter, departmental reports, and other documents, and occasional letters, in each of the major subject areas. A full description of Roosevelt's major projects and programs is found in Bernard Bellush, "Apprenticeship for the Presidency: Franklin D. Roosevelt as Governor of New York" (Ph.D. dissertation, Columbia University, 1950), published as *Franklin D. Roosevelt as Governor of New York* (Columbia University Press, 1955), which makes use of both the official documents and the personal correspondence.

The Power of Party. Farley was careful to send the watchful Howe copies of his form letters to party officials, so these are found in the Howe Papers. Also in these papers (Campaign Material 1930, Box 37) is the analysis of the weaknesses of the Democratic party upstate; unfortunately, the report is undated and unsigned, but internal evidence suggests Farley's authorship, probably in late 1929 or early 1930. FDRL has a volume of typewritten transcripts of virtually all Roosevelt's 1930 campaign talks. Lindley[1] (B) has an extensive account of the campaign, with particular stress on events leading to the raising of the corruption issue. Gosnell[2] (B), chap 11, presents a balanced picture, although his analysis of the election results is slight compared to Lindley's. The New York *Times* is, as usual, indispensable for the day-to-day development of the campaign. The papers of Louis McHenry Howe, 1913-1936, FDRL, are useful throughout the gubernatorial as well as earlier years.

CHAPTER SEVEN

For general developments during the 1929-1932 phase of the Depression, I have relied mainly on Broadus Mitchell, *Depression Decade* (Rinehart, 1947), a volume in the excellent series, "The Economic History of the United States"; William Starr Myers and Walter H. Newton, *The Hoover Administration* (Scribner, 1936), useful for documentary information; and Frederick L. Allen, *Since Yesterday* (Harper, 1940). Bellush [chap. 6] has a critical chapter on Roosevelt's state economic program. The observation that prosperity was the GOP's major issue of 1928 is based on Peel and Donnelly [chap. 5]. The source for the account of the Farley announcement is Farley's own memoirs of Rooseveltian politics through 1936 (Farley[1], B), and for the remark to Flynn, the Bronx leader's account, Edward J. Flynn (B). Roosevelt's exchange on economic situation is in Bellush, chap. 8, p. 3; letter to Howe in PLFDR, Vol. I, p. 92; letter to Baruch, *ibid.,* p. 244; letter from White in FDRL, Pr. Corr., 1928-32, Box 104.

The Political Uses of Corruption. On the 1931-32 nomination fight FDRL has 1,500 boxes of correspondence between Roosevelt, Howe, and Farley and Roosevelt leaders, delegates, and politicians throughout the country ("Democratic National Comm., Correspondence, 1932"), organized by states and alphabetically within states; I have gone through the material on key states. Many of the files originate in Roosevelt's 1928 correspondence on the state of the party. The Howe papers (Boxes 42-46) include important material indicating Howe's views and estimates at various times in the campaign. Farley describes his trip west in *Behind the Ballots* (B); the actual reports are in the Howe Papers, Box 42, FDRL, and make fascinating reading. Gosnell[1] (B) makes the point about the effect of the Depression on Tammany. Howells' report on his interview with Smith is in PLFDR, pp. 229-232; for an account of a somewhat similar interview see George S. Van Schaick interview, OHP.

Battle at the Grass Roots. Data on preconvention campaign costs are found in Democratic National Committee Campaign Correspondence, FDRL, noted above, mainly in Howe's correspondence with Morgenthau, Bingham, and other contributors; see also Howe papers, Box 43, Farley[1] (B), and Edward J. Flynn (B). The Democratic National Committee correspondence includes also several boxes on Massachusetts; Howe's letters to Elizabeth Marbury, from which I have quoted his retrospective comment, are especially useful. I have interviewed La Rue Brown, Boston, on the Massachusetts situation, and borrowed the term "Curley-Burley" from a New York *Times* editorial so entitled. The Villard letter is in PLFDR, p. 282; Roosevelt's letter to Murphy in Democratic National Committee correspondence, Box 409.

The Magic Two-thirds. Full and fascinating memoirs are available on the convention fight in Chicago: Farley[1], and Edward J. Flynn; Hull (B); Creel (B); Bascom N. Timmons, *Garner of Texas* (Harper, 1948); Connally and Steinberg (B); Roy V. Peel and Thomas C. Donnelly, *The 1932 Campaign* (Farrar & Rinehart, 1935), a full analysis by two scholars who attended the conventions. See also Arthur Krock interview, OHP. On the two-thirds adventure Farley covered up for Roosevelt not only at the time but in his book; I base my judgment that Roosevelt was directly involved on Edward J. Flynn, p. 90, and on PSF, Box 6, which includes two statements evidently prepared by Roosevelt: one in favor of the immediate abrogation of the two-thirds rule, and one favoring eventual abrogation. On this point see also the Democratic National Convention file, and papers recently acquired by FDRL (Group 12) which include a printed statement for issuance by Farley calling for immediate adoption of a straight majority rule; and, in PSF, Box 6, a memo dictated by Cummings June 17, 1932, on balance favoring immediate abrogation of the two-thirds tradition. Otherwise FDRL contains little on the actual convention period. The interview with Garner is from the New York *Times.* For Roosevelt's actions during the convention see Tully (B) and Rosenman (B), both of whom were with the Governor in Albany. Roosevelt described the basic tactical situation briefly in retrospect in PL., Vol. 1, p. 1090.

CHAPTER EIGHT

The struggle over Roosevelt's acceptance speech draft is vividly described in Moley (B) and Rosenman.

The Fox and the Elephant. Directly relating to the 1932 election campaign FDRL has 836 boxes of material, mainly letters received by Roosevelt during the campaign and replies, a few of the latter dictated by himself but most by assistants. I have not tried to winnow through all this immense mass of material. Howe Papers, Box 46, contains Howe's draft of his somewhat revealing story of the campaign for a newspaper syndicate and documents on the campaign organization, and Box 44 a "Synopsis of Conference of National Committeemen and National Democratic Committee," 1st session, from which Farley's remarks on club functions are taken. See also Wehle [chap. 5] on dealings with labor during the campaign. Coughlin's letter to Roosevelt re Walker is in PLFDR, p. 293. The most notable campaign speeches are in PPA, except for the Poughkeepsie speech, which is included in Moley, Appendix A, and all are in FDRL ("Master File"). The method I followed of reading the speeches themselves before reading any of the contemporary or later comments on them was revealing; I found the Commonwealth Club speech to be not nearly so strong or "progressive" a talk as some commentators later said. Moley's account of the preparation of speeches—notably the Topeka talk and the tariff references—is indispensable. Herbert Hoover's third volume of his memoirs, significantly titled *The Great Depression, 1929-1941* (B) presents many excerpts from his speeches, topically arranged. Roosevelt's letter to Olson is in PLFDR, p. 297. Election results are detailed and discussed in Gosnell[2] and in Peel and Donnelly. Roosevelt's draft of the reply to Hoover is penciled on the back of Hoover's wire; he changed the wording somewhat but not the content in dictating the final form of the wire to Moley.

The Stage is Set. Source of Sherwood comment on Roosevelt's entrance on the stage is *Roosevelt and Hopkins* (B), p. 40; according to Michelson (B), p. 50, Roosevelt expected the banking crisis to reach a climax just about Inauguration Day. Correspondence between Hoover and Roosevelt on foreign debts is in PPF 820, FDRL. Howe Papers, FDRL, include correspondence between Roosevelt and Howe on the same matter during the 1920's. Hoover gives his version of his negotiations with Roosevelt in his memoirs (B); see also Myers and Newton [chap. 7]. Moley (B) contains a detailed, though highly subjective, account of these proceedings by one who participated in many of them. A full account of the Lame Duck Congress may be found in E. P. Herring, "Second Session of the Seventy-Second Congress," *The American Political Science Review,* Vol. XXVII, No. 3, June 1933, pp. 404-422. See Myers and Newton, p. 341, for Hoover's view that if Roosevelt made the statements that Hoover wished him to, Roosevelt would be ratifying the Republican platform. Accounts or remarks on Roosevelt's cabinet making are in Moley, Farley[1, 2], Hull, Perkins, Edward J. Flynn, Tully, (all B), and Wehle [chap. 5]. The records of the Democratic National Committee, FDRL, contain several hundred letters written by backers of Cabinet aspirants, and even by aspirants themselves, but Roosevelt apparently did not pay much attention to most of these.

Roosevelt on the Eve. The text of Roosevelt's remarks on the presidency is in the New York *Times,* November 13, 1932, Sect. 8, p. 1. Broun's comment on Roosevelt is quoted by Rexford G. Tugwell, "The Preparation of a President," *Western Political Quarterly,* Vol. I, 1948; Lippmann's comment is typical of his evaluation of Roosevelt in a number of his columns in 1932; and Wilson's is from "Hudson River Progressive," *The New Republic,* Vol. 74, No. 957, April 5, 1933, pp. 219-220. Moley is important for this period, especially for a contemporary evaluation of Roosevelt as a person, pp. 10-12. On Roosevelt's hard center see also Tugwell, "Preparation of a President," cited above. Many of Roosevelt's friends remembered him from the war years as able but lacking in greatness; see, for example, William Phillips interview, OHP. Medical data on Roosevelt at this time are from Lindley[1] (B), pp. 35-38. Langdon P. Marvin, Jr., interview, OHP, recounts Roosevelt's swimming feats. The instructions to Roosevelt's staff about not mentioning his illness in correspondence is in (unsigned) letter to Mrs. Forbush, Halsted file, Group 12, FDRL. The Democratic Union folder, Group 12, FDRL, includes a wrathful letter that Roosevelt wrote to Roy Howard about attacks on Roosevelt in Howard's newspapers; this letter, however, appears never to have been sent. A description of Roosevelt's technique of handling his mail is in PPF 271, FDRL. See Moley, Lindley[1], and Tugwell on Roosevelt's advisers in 1932. Hawthorne's description of Jackson's use of men is quoted by Clinton L. Rossiter in a suggestive little article, "The Political Philosophy of F. D. Roosevelt," *The Review of Politics,* Vol. II, No. 1, p. 92. On the many strands of thought influencing the early New Dealers, see Goldman (B); Richard Hofstadter, *The American Political Tradition* (Knopf, 1948); Richard Hofstadter, *The Age of Reform* (Knopf, 1955); Henry Steele Commager, *The American Mind* (New Haven: Yale University Press, 1950); Max Lerner, *Ideas Are Weapons* (Viking, 1939). On Roosevelt's own ideas at the time see, aside from PPA, Vol. I, and PLFDR, Donald Scott Carmichael (ed.), *F. D. R. Columnist* (Chicago: Pellegrini & Cudahy, 1947), a collection of Roosevelt's columns written for the Macon (Georgia) *Daily Telegraph* in 1925 and for the Beacon (New York) *Standard* in 1928. On the failure of the right or the left to produce systematic philosophies to challenge the liberals and progressives see Louis Hartz's notable study, *The Liberal Tradition in America* (Harcourt, Brace, 1955); and for a related theme, Daniel J. Boorstin, *The Genius of American Politics* (Chicago: University of Chicago Press, 1953). Arthur S. Link, *Woodrow Wilson and the Progressive Era* (Harper, 1954) treats some of Wilson's withdrawals from pre-1913 progressive ideas. Justice Holmes's recollection of the earlier Franklin Roosevelt is from his letter to Harold J. Laski, November 23, 1932, in Mark DeWolfe Howe (ed.), *Holmes-Laski Letters* (Cambridge: Harvard University Press, 1953), Vol. II, p. 1420. My source on Holmes's comment on Roosevelt (page 157) after their meeting in 1933 is confidential.

CHAPTER NINE

Successive drafts of Roosevelt's 1933 Inaugural speech are in FDRL and include a historical note by Roosevelt; Rosenman (B), pp. 81-99, describes briefly the manner in which Roosevelt composed it. There is more than one version of the source of the "We have nothing to fear but fear" quotation; I have used Rosenman's (B). He also explains (p. 91) the discrepancy between Roosevelt's speech as delivered and the text in PPA. Description of Roosevelt's move to Washington and his first days there before Inauguration, and description of Inauguration Day, are from the New York *Times* and the Washington, D. C., newspapers.

"*A Day of Consecration.*" The Hoover remark is noted in slightly different language in both Tully (B) and Edward J. Flynn (B); both authors heard an angry Roosevelt report the incident shortly after he returned from the White House. Eleanor Roosevelt's comment on the Inaugural crowd on page 165 is from the New York *Times,* March 5, 1933.

"*Action and Action Now.*" Roosevelt's two diary excerpts are in PLFDR, pp. 333-335. He made his remarks to the press about their bank holiday stories in PC No. 2, March 10, 1933. Woodin's remark about "swift and staccato action" is quoted in Moley, p. 151. I have made wide use of Herring in describing the congressional handling of Roosevelt's "Hundred Day" bills. *Time* magazine is useful for some of the atmosphere of the period. Roosevelt's comment on the lack of constructiveness in his early measures is from PC No. 3, March 15, 1933. His comment on his farm bill is part of his editorial note in PPAFDR, p. 79 (he proposed his general farm bill on March 16, 1933, and his farm mortgage relief bill in specific detail on April 3; see also PPAFDR, p. 100).

"*A Leadership of Frankness and Vigor.*" The Minutes of the Executive Council, July 11, 1933–November 13, 1934, The National Archives, provide a vivid, month-to-month picture of the early political and administrative problems of the New Deal. Roosevelt's sheer opportunism and willingness to experiment are reflected in his actions, and in his press conferences, letters, and speeches; see PC No. 6, March 24, 1933, for his exchange with reporters on the subject of deflation. That Roosevelt was eager to reconcile spending with economy until a late date is indicated in his PPAFDR notes, especially pp. 51-52; see also PC No. 13, April 19, 1933, and PC No. 15, April 26, 1933; Roosevelt to Col. Edward M. House, May 12, 1933, PPF 222, FDRL. Roosevelt made a great point of his faithfulness to campaign and party pledges in PPAFDR, *Notes* following his messages. His views on teachers' salaries are in his letter to Daniels, March 27, 1933, PLFDR, pp. 339-340. A valuable source of information on cabinet meetings, especially Ickes' own participation (including his cat naps), is Ickes[1] (B). The Herring quotation is from his article cited above. The Roosevelt press conference quotations are from PC No. 2, March 10, 1933, and PC No. 15, April 26, 1933, respectively. The quotation from the adulatory congressman is in OF 372, FDRL, letter dated April 8, 1933.

America First. That the possibility of war with Japan came up at the second cabinet meeting is indicated in some detail in Farley[2] (B), p. 39; Ickes[1], p. 5, mentions only that relations with Japan were discussed. For the views of Roosevelt's associates on the priority of domestic over international recovery, see Hull, Ickes, Sherwood, and Moley. Baruch's letter is in PPF 88, FDRL, July 5, 1933, and Roosevelt's comment on financiers was made in PC No. 27, June 7, 1933. See also Harold G. Moulton to Frederic

A. Delano, PPF 72, FDRL, June 21, 1933, a letter Delano sent on to Roosevelt. For full but diverse accounts of the London economic conference, see Moley, Hull, and Michelson, and the Baker papers, LC; a balanced treatment appears in Allan Nevins, *The New Deal and World Affairs* (New Haven: Yale University Press, 1950). Charles A. Beard (B) presents a striking, if overdrawn, picture of Roosevelt's isolationism in 1932-33, and makes some important bibliographical observations. Roosevelt's remark on war debts is from PC No. 19, May 10, 1933. The exchange between the President and Norris is taken verbatim from an interview with Norris by Eric Goldman in his vivid and far-ranging history of recent American reformist thought and action, *Rendezvous with Destiny* (B), p. 339. My major source on the shaping of the NRA legislation is J. M. Burns, "Congress and the Formation of Economic Policies" (Ph.D. dissertation, Harvard University, 1947), which includes a study of the NRA measure based on material at FDRL and elsewhere and on interviews with some of the main participants. On Roosevelt's timing see Frederic A. Delano to Howe, PPF 72, FDRL, April 7, 1933. The White letter to Ickes is in William Allen White file, PPF 1196, FDRL; Ickes showed this letter to Roosevelt.

CHAPTER TEN

The extent to which Roosevelt took the role of bipartisan leader during 1933 and 1934 has not been fully appreciated by scholars; what has been treated in some studies as an early "conservative period" of Roosevelt that in part simply expanded on Hoover's policies can be better understood, I think, as a "middle way" incorporating main lines of action of previous administrations both Democratic and Republican, reflecting ideology and interests all across the long spectrum of Roosevelt's bipartisan support, and exploiting, of course, the atmosphere of crisis and fear. The words quoted from Roosevelt's Wisconsin speech of August 1934 came originally from a description of the New Deal by Representative (later Senator) Edward R. Burke of Nebraska; when Roosevelt saw this statement, he said, according to Moley (B), p. 290: "That's the best definition I have yet seen of the New Deal." Burke, significantly enough, later turned against the President. Friendly letters to Roosevelt from Howard, O'Neal, Du Pont, *et al.*, can be found in PPF, FDRL; see, for example, William Randolph Hearst file, PPF 62, FDRL; for Roosevelt's attitudes toward businessmen and others, see Roosevelt to Adolph J. Sabath, Nov. 7, 1933, PPF 955, FDRL; Roosevelt to Col. House, May 7, 1934, PLFDR, pp. 400-401; Minutes of the Executive Council, *passim.*

An Artist in Government. For an admirable history of presidential relations with Congress see Wilfred E. Binkley, *President and Congress* (Knopf, 1947). Roosevelt's comments on "must legislation" were voiced in PC No. 120, May 11, 1934. Garner's comment on the turmoil in the House of Representatives is reported in Ickes[1] (B), p. 162. I have used as my main source of systematic data on Roosevelt's vetoes Marvin L. Ingram, "Franklin D. Roosevelt's Exercise of the Veto Power" (Ph.D. dissertation, New York University, 1947). Lists in Roosevelt's writing of his friends and those "not with me" can be found in the "longhand file," FDRL. The comment on the delay in giving patronage to congressmen is from Herring [chap. 8]; I suspect that Herring made up this remark. Rexford G. Tugwell tells of Roosevelt's patronage deal with Senator Smith in Tugwell, "The Compromising Roosevelt," *The Western Political Quarterly*, Vol. VI, No. 2, June 1953, pp. 320-341, one of several reminiscent and discerning articles by Tugwell about his former boss; the incident is substantiated in Ickes[1], p. 164, and the Robinson incident is from the same source, pp. 19-20. The material on Herring is from his article in *The American Political Science Review* [chap. 8]; the series of which this article is one comprises a trenchant and perceptive study of congressional sessions during the New Deal years, by such authorities as Lindsay Rogers, Herring, O. R. Altman, and others. Roosevelt's shaming of an official over the telephone is from Richberg[1] (B), p. 292; on Roosevelt's tactics in dealing with the press, see Minutes of the Executive Council, December 11, 1934, and for a reaction of the press to Roosevelt's dealings with reporters, see Raymond Clapper to McIntyre, March 18, 1933, OF 4434, FDRL. Roosevelt asked the Emergency Council as well as his Cabinet to establish friendly relations with Congress.

The Broker State at Work. Miss Perkins tells of her effort to calm General Johnson in *The Roosevelt I Knew* (B), pp. 202-204, and Ickes quotes Roosevelt on Johnson rushing in with codes to sign, in his diary (B), Vol. I, p. 72. Most students of the NRA conclude that it did not markedly help recovery, and may have retarded it; I have relied mainly on Leverett S. Lyon, *et al.*, *The National Recovery Administration* (Washington, D. C.: The Brookings Institution, 1935), an authoritative and critical study; C. F. Roos, *N R A Economic Planning* (Bloomington, Ind.: The Principia Press, 1937); Mitchell [chap. 7]; 73d Congress, 1st Sess., Senate Finance Committee, *National Industrial Recovery, Hearings* on NRA extension (Washington: U.S. Govt. Print. Off., 1933), which is a mine of information and varied viewpoints. For memoirs of two NRA chiefs, see Hugh S. Johnson's lively *The Blue Eagle from Egg to Earth* (Garden City, N. Y.: Doubleday, Doran, 1935), and Richberg[2] (B). The Roosevelt-Connery exchange is in PPF 1034, FDRL. On farm politics I have made extensive use of a highly informed work, William D. Aeschbacker, "Political Activities of Agricultural Organizations, 1929-1939" (Ph.D. dissertation, University of Nebraska, July 1948). Aeschbacker lists one Farmers Union participant in agricultural policymaking; actually this participant was a congressman friendly to the Farmers Union but not actually a representative of it, according to correspondence in PPF 471, FDRL. That Roosevelt recognized the existence of farm unrest in fall 1933 is clear from Ickes[1], p. 110, and PLFDR, p. 366. The Olson letter and Roosevelt's reply are in PPF 4, FDRL. The President's close observation of economic conditions is evident especially in his press conferences, notably PC Nos. 32, 42, 51, and 88. His consideration of the use of army kitchens is noted in Minutes of the Executive Council, Sept. 5, 1933; see also Eccles (B), p. 126. The quotation about the "broadest attempt" on page 195 is from Mitchell. My main sources on early relief and public works administration are Sherwood (B), and Ickes; the Hopkins Papers, FDRL; and Records of the Works Projects Administration and of its predecessors, The National Archives.

The Politics of Broker Leadership. While I know of no systematic treatment of the problem of "broker leadership," certain works relate directly to the problem: Pendleton Herring, *The Politics of Democracy* (Rinehart, 1940), which favors the ambiguous, non-doctrinaire quality of American politics; E. E. Schattschneider, *Party Government* (Farrar and Rinehart, 1942), an argument for more responsible parties; David B. Truman, *The Governmental Process* (Knopf, 1951), which shows both the theoretical implications and the practical ramifications of the problem; Herbert Agar, *The Price of Union* (Boston: Houghton Mifflin, 1950), a luminous treatment of the general theme in American political history. For a brilliantly suggestive piece, see Max Lerner, "The Broker State," in his *Ideas for the Ice Age* (Viking, 1941), pp. 376-381. Professor Jack Peltason and I have a chapter summing up the arguments for and against "broker rule," as we call it, in *Government by the People* (Prentice-Hall, 1952), chap. 18. Peek's remark on group domination is quoted in Goldman (B), p. 351. My main sources for the Pennsylvania political situation are Ickes[1] and an exchange between Roosevelt and Pinchot, PPF 289, FDRL. On California, I have used PPF 235 and OF 300 and 1165, FDRL; Robert E. Burke, *Olson's New Deal for California* (Berkeley: University of California Press, 1953), which includes a succinct account of the 1934 election; Creel (B); George Creel Papers, LC; and Upton Sinclair, *I Candidate for Governor and How I Got Licked* (Pasadena: privately published, 1935), a detailed and, of course, vivid account by the Democratic candidate. My sources for Sinclair's Hyde Park conference are Sinclair's volume just cited, and Sinclair to author, Jan. 25, 1956. Sinclair's suspicion of some kind of Administration deal with Merriam is borne out in OF 300 (Box 16), FDRL. On Wisconsin see OF 300 (Wisconsin), FDRL; Ickes[1]; Edward N. Doan, *The La Follettes and the Wisconsin Idea* (Rinehart, 1947). On Minnesota see OF 300 (Minnesota), FDRL; Roosevelt to Farley, no date, Longhand File, FDRL; George H. Mayer, *The Political Career of Floyd B. Olson* (Minneapolis: University of Minnesota Press, 1951), a spirited and sympathetic account. On New Mexico see PPF 1201 and 3851, FDRL; Ickes[1], pp. 217, 358-359. All press conference quotations in this section are from PC No. 133, June 27, 1934.

Rupture on the Right. My source for the 1934 election returns is George Gallup, *The Political Almanac* (B. C. Forbes & Sons, 1952), a comprehensive compilation of national and state returns over recent decades. Howe's worshipful words about Roosevelt are quoted in Stiles (B), p. 290, and Ickes' comments in his diary, Vol. I, pp. 79, 127. The Stern file is PPF 1039, FDRL. Comments on Roosevelt's press conferences are based mainly on a study of the transcripts in FDRL; see also Leo C. Rosten, *The Washington Correspondents* (New York: Harcourt, Brace, 1937). Miss Perkins' picture of Roosevelt's way of speaking over the radio is from *The Roosevelt I Knew*, p. 72. Roosevelt described how he tried to visualize his audience in a letter to Helen Reynolds, October 30, 1933, PPF 234, FDRL. His curious correspondence with his critical classmate in Boston is in PPF 183, FDRL; see also PPF 23, 24, 26, 27, 28, 51, and 363, FDRL, and PC Nos. 23, 69, 78, and 141 for other material on Roosevelt's disenchantment with the right. Frederick Rudolph, "The American Liberty League, 1934-1940," *American Historical Review*, Vol. LVI, No. 1, October 1950, pp. 19-33, is a brief, illuminating review of the genesis, personalities, ideas and death of this organization. On the reaction of the right to the early New Deal see Goldman. The McIntyre memo to Roosevelt in regard to Roy Howard is in PPF 68, Oct. 6, 1934, FDRL.

CHAPTER ELEVEN

There is a vast literature on social movements: reform, protest, revolutionary, gradualist, and the like. For my particular needs I have relied mainly on Hadley Cantril, *The Psychology of Social Movements* (Wiley, 1941), a treatment of motivation in social life and of the quest for meaning in political and other contexts; Eric Hoffer, *The True Believer* (Harper, 1951), a little book on mass movements by a man who lived in, and watched carefully, the ideological breeding grounds of California; Gouldner (B), a splendidly edited study of leadership in its social setting; Crane Brinton, *The Anatomy of Revolution* (W. W. Norton, 1938).

The Little Foxes. Farley describes the "hat" interview in *Behind the Ballots* (B), pp. 240-242. Important sources on Long's career and cause are Harnett T. Kane, *Louisiana Hayride* (Morrow, 1941), which also carries the Long dynasty through 1940; Hodding Carter, "Huey Long: American Dictator," in Isabel Leighton (ed.), *The Aspirin Age* (Simon and Schuster, 1949), a trenchant, balanced piece by a Southerner; and "Louisiana: the Seamy Side of Democracy," chap. 8, in V. O. Key, Jr., *Southern Politics* (Knopf, 1949), an indispensable study. Coughlin and his movement have not had the extensive study that they deserve; I have relied mainly on a far-ranging Ph.D. dissertation by Bruce B. Mason, "American Political Protest, 1932-1936" (University of Texas, 1953), for data on Coughlin and on other leaders of protest movements during this period; and on *Fortune* magazine, February 1934, for statistics on mail and contributions. For Roosevelt's intercession with the Navy on behalf of Coughlin, see OF 306 (Coughlin), FDRL. On Townsend I have used another dissertation, the most thorough and significant study produced on the subject to date, Abraham Holtzman, "The Townsend Movement: A Study in Old Age Pressure Politics" (2 vols., Harvard University, 1952). A discerning analysis that relates the Townsend movement to underlying social and psychological behavior is Cantril, *The Psychology of Social Movements*, chap. 7. The nature of the Administration's response to Long *et al.* has been gleaned mainly from PPF 2337, FDRL, especially the Colonel House file. Minutes of the Executive Council show Roosevelt's determination and tenacity in dealing indirectly with Long, especially by withholding patronage. The Hurja political study can be found in PSF, Post Office Department Folder, FDRL; a portion of this is reproduced in PLFDR, following p. 428; and Farley describes his reaction in *Behind the Ballots*, pp. 249-252. Farley quotes Roosevelt on dealing with Coughlin in *Jim Farley's Story* (B), p. 52. PPF 3960, FDRL contains a number of letters to Roosevelt from Catholic dignitaries and laymen on Coughlin's activities. As late as September 1935 Kennedy brought Coughlin to Hyde Park for what Roosevelt described to the press as just a social visit. The concern over the Administration's political position was reflected in Ickes[1] (B), pp. 304-306, and in both of Farley's books. Hadley Cantril (B), pp. 590-598, provides evidence of a slump in Roosevelt's popularity during this period. Roosevelt to Arthur M. Schlesinger (Sr.), May 14, 1935, PPF 2501, FDRL, is an example of Roosevelt's biding his time and waiting on public opinion.

Labor: New Millions and New Leaders. An important documentary source on trade unionism during the early 1930's is *Proceedings* of the American Federation of Labor's annual convention (Washington, D. C.). For basic membership and strike data see the standard work, H. A. Millis and R. E. Montgomery, *Organized Labor* (McGraw-Hill, 1945), authoritative and pedestrian. On the rise of the C.I.O., Edward Levinson, *Labor on the March* (Harper, 1938) is rich in detail but markedly slanted in favor of the C.I.O.; Herbert Harris, *Labor's Civil War* (Knopf, 1940) gives a more balanced picture of the schism. Roosevelt's negative role in shaping the Wagner Act can be fully documented. Miss Perkins (B) says flatly that he was hardly consulted about it and that it did not appeal to him (p. 239); and this is borne out in Irving Bernstein, *The New Deal Collective Bargaining Policy* (Berkeley and Los Angeles: University of California Press, 1950), a careful and widely researched study of the passage of the Wagner Act. See also a summary of presidential conference with Senators, April 4, 1934, PSF, FDRL. On Roosevelt's views see also PC Nos. 125, 176, 299, and OF 407 (Labor). Moley (B), p. 13, describes the President as a "patron of labor"—a remark that, of course, applies to Roosevelt especially during the period Moley was close to him.

Left! Right! Left! No one is more aware than this author, especially after studying Roosevelt's ideological development, of the limitations of the terms "right" and "left." I have two excuses for using them: first, they were terms that had meaning for the political leaders of the period, including Roosevelt; and second, they are as useful as any shorthand terms can be for characterizing the ideology and program of the liberal and conservative alignments in American politics. On this score, see the useful treatment of definitions in the first-rate study, Clinton Rossiter, *Conservatism in America* (Knopf, 1955), especially p. 15. By "right" I mean ideas or policies more acceptable to, and in the short run more favorable to, businessmen, professional groups, and upper-income groups in general; and by "left" I mean the ideas or policies similarly attractive to and favoring lower income groups, industrial workers, consumers, and allied groups, and also the increased use of government for wider distribution of income and social welfare. The condition of Congress during the early weeks of 1935 is well described in a letter from Senator Key Pittman to Roosevelt, Feb. 19, 1935, PPF 745, FDRL; see also Ickes[1], pp. 302, 363-364. Data on Roosevelt's mood of early 1935 is from Ickes, *passim;* from a rather unusual letter from Roosevelt to R. J. Reager, May 22, 1935, PPF 2526, FDRL; from Lindley[2], p. 83; and from a confidential source. My chief source on the work relief bill is chap. 2 of Burns (B), a legislative history of the bill; see Paul H. Douglas, *Social Security in the United States* (Whittlesey House, 1936) for the history of the social security bill. The best evidence on Roosevelt's reaction to the Schecter decision was the historic press conference itself, printed almost in full in PPAFDR, Vol. IV, pp. 200-222; a letter from Roosevelt to Henry L. Stimson, June 10, 1935, PLFDR, pp. 484-485, shows the same reaction.

There is a thesis that Roosevelt actually was pleased that the Supreme Court voided the NRA and thus relieved him of an embarrassing burden; see Krock Interview, OHP, on this matter and also Memorandum, Richberg to McIntyre, May 1, 1935, PPF 466, FDRL; I believe, however, that the evidence preponderantly shows that Roosevelt still believed in the essence of the NRA, if more effectively administered, and that he was genuinely upset by the decision; see Levy to Roosevelt, June 24, 1935, OF 98, FDRL, and Creel (B), p. 291; it is perfectly possible, in view of Roosevelt's intellectual habits, that he had highly mixed feelings on the matter. For Roosevelt's undelivered "gold-clause" speech, see PLFDR, pp. 455-460; and for Joseph Kennedy's account of the doings of that decision day, see Tully (B), pp. 157-161. E. Pendleton Herring, "First Session of the Seventy-Fourth Congress," *The American Political Science Review*, Vol. XXIX, No. 6, Dec. 1935, pp. 985-1005, is a useful review of this crucial session. Moley, chaps. 9 and 10, offers a fascinating account of the shift in Roosevelt's position in 1935 (although I disagree with some of his interpretations). For further bibliographical notes on Roosevelt's shift leftward and on the role in this of the conservatives, see bibliography for chapter 12.

CHAPTER TWELVE

For glimpses of Roosevelt on vacation and at play during late 1935, see Ickes[1] (B), and PLFDR, *passim*. Roosevelt's comments on the 1935 legislative session are from Roosevelt to Henry Goddard Leach, August 31, 1935, PPF 324, FDRL.

Thunderbolts from the Bench. Commentary on judicial developments in the 1930's is a rich field. Aside from judicial pronouncements themselves, I have relied chiefly on the following: Charles P. Curtis, Jr., *Lions under the Throne* (Boston: Houghton Mifflin, 1947), a remarkably fresh and informed treatment of Supreme Court justices and their ideas; Jackson (B), a New Deal tract but a tract of importance; C. Herman Pritchett, *The Roosevelt Court* (Macmillan, 1948), which treats the period with vigor and competence and also cuts back across decisions of previous years; Robert K. Carr, *The Supreme Court and Judicial Review* (Farrar and Rinehart, 1942), an authoritative review of the many facets of the subject; and Wesley McCune, *The Nine Young Men* (Harper, 1947), which among its other merits treats the court as a human institution. Biography of contemporary justices is rather lean on the whole; a striking exception is Merlo J. Pusey, *Charles Evans Hughes* (2 vols., Macmillan, 1951), a lavishly factual and sympathetic picture of the Chief Justice that supplies a good deal of information about personalities behind and across the bar, and Hughes's relations with them. On the frontier element in judicial personality see Ronald F. Howell, "Conservative Influence on Constitutional Development, 1923-1937: The Judicial Theory of Justices Van Devanter, McReynolds, Sutherland, and Butler" (Ph.D. dissertation, Johns Hopkins University, 1952). Joel F. Paschal, *Mr. Justice Sutherland* (Princeton: Princeton University Press, 1951) and Samuel J. Konefsky, *Chief Justice Stone and the Supreme Court* (Macmillan, 1945) are valuable works. Cortez M. Ewing, *The Judges of the Supreme Court, 1789-1937* (Minneapolis: University of Minnesota Press, 1938) provides useful biographical information. The quotation about constitutional storks on page 230 is from Max Lerner. Jackson and Ickes agree on the impact of the *Butler* case in hardening the Administration's attitude toward the courts; Roosevelt's letters and other documents reflect a degree of acceptance by the President of the challenge. On the bonus fight, an important study of the difference between congressional and presidential politics is V. O. Key, Jr., "The Veterans and the House of Representatives: A Study of a Pressure Group and Electoral Mortality," *Journal of Politics*, Vol. V, 1943, pp. 27-40. My main source on Congress in 1936 is O. R. Altman, "Second Session of the Seventy-Fourth Congress," *The American Political Science Review*, Vol. XXX, No. 6, December 1936, a thought-provoking treatment.

Roosevelt as a Conservative. Evaluation of Roosevelt as a conservative is made triply difficult by the fluid character of Roosevelt's social and economic views, the ambiguity of the conservative tradition in the United States, and the opportunistic character of much right-wing thought in this country. To this complexity must be added the problem of definition, as noted in the bibliography for chapter 11. I am indebted especially to William Brubeck, Clinton Rossiter, C. Frederick Rudolph, and Robert C. L. Scott for advice and guidance in this area. The author, like many other Americans, heard the "Roosevelt stories," and noted that the fantastic content of the anecdotes was surpassed only by the narrator's absolute certainty that the stories were true. Roosevelt told the story about the gentleman and his top hat in PPAFDR, Vol. V, p. 385. Hofstadter's comment on the desertion of Roosevelt by his class is from Richard Hofstadter, *The American Political Tradition* (Vintage Books, 1954), p. 334. On the elements of the conservative tradition see, aside from the classical thinkers themselves such as Burke and Adams, the following contemporary writers: Rossiter [chap. 11]; Daniel Aaron, "Conservatism, Old and New," *American Quarterly Review*, Vol. VI, No. 2, Summer 1954, a short, acute piece that underlines the gap between the conservative tradition and the American right; Louis Hartz, "The Whig Tradition in America and Europe," *The American Political Science Review*, Vol. XLVI, No. 4, December 1952, which describes the "massive confusion in political thought" that lies back of our ideological development; Louis Hartz's broader treatment of the theme in *The Liberal Tradition in America* (Harcourt, Brace, 1955); Peter Viereck, *Conservatism Revisited* (Scribner, 1949), an erudite and yet "modern" treatment, with Metternich as its model; Prothro [chap. 5]; Russell Kirk, *The Conservative Mind* (Chicago: Henry Regnery Co., 1953), which touches on the degeneration of "practical conservatism" into a narrow business creed without, I think, emphasizing sufficiently the meager context and content of our conservative tradition as compared with Britain's; and Robert A. Nisbet, "Conservatism and Sociology," *The American Journal of Sociology*, Vol. LVIII, No. 2, September 1952, pp. 167-175, a notable treatment of the relation between philosophical conservatism and the sociologist's concern with group, status, and social integration. Richard W. Leopold, *Elihu Root and the Conservative Tradition* (Boston: Little, Brown, 1954), shrewdly underscores the difficulties of an American conservative operating in a culture and polity lacking conservative traditions and institutions. My comments on Roosevelt's relation to the conservative tradition stem largely from his speeches and letters and from memoirs of his associates; an especially illuminating account of his religious life is given in Perkins (B), chap. 11; and Gunther[2] (B) provides a useful miscellany of information on his personal characteristics. A copy of the intercepted Hearst instruction and a copy of the projected press release are in PSF, FDRL. On Lewis Douglas's equating of the budget and Western civilization, see Ickes[1], p. 659.

Roosevelt and the Radicals. There is a vast socialist literature, a fact attested to by the huge descriptive and critical bibliography by T. D. Seymour Bassett that comprises Vol. II of Donald D. Egbert and Stow Persons (eds.), *Socialism and American Life* (2 vols., Princeton: Princeton University Press, 1952). My chief source on socialism and the New Deal is Daniel Bell's measured yet sympathetic and even melancholy narrative "The Background and Development of Marxian Socialism in the United States," in Egbert and Persons, Vol. I. Thomas's direct answer to Smith in early 1936 was given in a radio talk later published by the Socialist party as a pamphlet, "Is the New Deal Socialism?" See also Norman Thomas, *After the New Deal, What?* (Macmillan, 1936), and Harry W. Laidler, *A Program for Modern America* (Crowell, 1936). Each step of the zigzagging Communist line was acclaimed in extensive writings by Earl Browder. The Williams College Library has an excellent collection of Socialist and Communist pamphlets. The attitude of the independent left can be found in *The Nation* and *The New Republic* during these years. For a humorous but acid picture of the President from a left-wing perspective, see Mauritz A. Hallgren, *The Gay Reformer* (Knopf, 1935). The comment of Roosevelt's friend about the Communist pat on the back is from Goldman (B), p. 352, in turn taken from an interview of Goldman with Stephen T. Early. Many instances of Roosevelt's "practicality" and of his business opponents' doctrinaire arguments can be found in FDRL; the example cited here is from PPF, FDRL, correspondence with James P. Warburg, Fred Kent, De Coursey Fales, and Joseph Day. For a sardonic, biting picture of business shibboleths on parade, see Thurman Arnold, *The Folklore of Capitalism* (New Haven: Yale University Press, 1937).

CHAPTER THIRTEEN

Most studies of the New Deal and foreign affairs stress the detail of foreign policy; a comprehensive analysis of Roosevelt as foreign policy maker and of the political considerations that dominated his actions is badly needed. Excellent studies are available on the mechanics and the politics of foreign policy making in general. For well conceived and researched accounts of the governmental institutions and political forces that Presidents must deal with in foreign policy making, see Daniel S. Cheever and H. Field Haviland, Jr., *American Foreign Policy and the Separation of Powers* (Cambridge: Harvard University Press, 1952) and Robert A. Dahl, *Congress and Foreign Policy* (Harcourt, Brace, 1950). A highly original study of rigidities and fluidities in popular and elitist attitudes on foreign policy, and one that makes considerable use of socio-psychological studies, is Gabriel A. Almond, *The American People and Foreign Policy* (Harcourt, Brace, 1950). Thomas A. Bailey, *The Man in the Street* (Macmillan, 1948) is a series of wise, witty, and wide-ranging essays on the impact of popular attitudes on foreign policy by a leading student of American diplomatic history. The quotation of Roosevelt on page 248 is from letter to Harry Emerson Fosdick, PPF 21, FDRL.

Good Neighbors and Good Fences. My analysis of Roosevelt's foreign policy is based in general on Hull (B) and on Moley (B); Nevins [chap. 8]; Beard (B), a necessary corrective to glorified treatments of Roosevelt's "world-minded" foreign policy during his first term, but one that suffers from Beard's ruggedly isolationist views and from a stubborn insistence on seeing more continuity and design in Roosevelt's foreign policies than actually existed; C. Tansill (B), which, whatever its controversial thesis, has the great virtue of being based on exceptionally wide sources, including files of the State Department; and, not least, Donald F. Whitehead, "The Making of Foreign Policy during President Roosevelt's First Term, 1933-1937" (Ph.D. dissertation, University of Chicago, 1951), which amply documents his (and my) proposition that Roosevelt followed no master plan or set strategy but rather day-to-day policies of expediency. In PSF at FDRL valuable material is available on Roosevelt's relations with Hull, David, Welles, his envoys abroad, and others; further material is widely distributed in PPF, OF, and other files. Ickes (B) and Hull supply useful data on the World Court, and Perkins (B) does so on the I.L.O. Hull is especially informative on the Good Neighbor policy; for an authoritative yet readable history of the Monroe Doctrine, see Dexter Perkins, *Hands Off* (Boston: Little, Brown, 1941).

Storm Clouds and Storm Cellars. Leonard W. Doob, *Propaganda: Its Psychology and Technique* (Holt, 1935) contains an illuminating section on the Nye Committee that is also a tribute to the capacity of a disinterested student of propaganda to see the propaganda implications of a committee with which he himself was associated. The whole story on Nye's selection as chairman of the committee is not known, but Roosevelt's passive role seems clear, and his close relations with the progressive and isolationist Republicans help explain his attitude; see also Hull, p. 398, and Connally and Steinberg (B), pp. 211-214. John C. Donovan, "Congress and the Making of Neutrality Legislation, 1935-1939" (Ph.D. dissertation, Harvard University, 1949), emphasizes the relation between the arms inquiry and isolationist feeling. Pittman's grudging cooperation with the White House and his fear of presidential discretion are shown in the Pittman file, PPF 745, FDRL. On the matter of neutrality generally, see OF 1561, FDRL. Excerpts from internal State Department communications on the approaching Ethiopian invasion, including Long's dismemberment proposals, are found in Tansill (B); on Long's earlier view of Italy and fascism, see OF 447, FDRL. Some of the more important of Roosevelt's letters on Italy are available in PLFDR (his letter to Hull, misdated August 29, 1935, in PLFDR, was actually dated August 20, 1935). Both Ickes[1], *op. cit.*, p. 450, and Sherwood (B), p. 79, agree on Roosevelt's strong sympathy with Ethiopia. As for United States relations with the League on Ethiopia, Tansill argues but does not establish that Hull and Roosevelt were actually trying to strengthen the League against Italy. My main sources for this period are Hull and Tansill, and an astute contemporary account, Allen W. Dulles and Hamilton Fish Armstrong, *Can We Be Neutral?* (Harper, 1936). Ickes and Hull both suggest that the Administration was ill-prepared for the Hoare-Laval denouement.

The Law of the Jungle. For data on Roosevelt's discouragement over the world situation in early 1936, see Ickes[1], pp. 479, 514, and PLFDR, p. 555. On the difference between Roosevelt's public position close to the isolationists and his private position close to the internationalists, especially his cautious policies on neutrality as compared with private expressions, see, for example, Moley, pp. 377-378; Minutes of the Executive Council, *passim;* PLFDR, page 547; Roosevelt to J. David Stern, Dec. 11, 1935, PPF 1039, FDRL. The following are especially useful on developments in Germany: William E. Dodd, Jr. and Martha Dodd (eds.), *Ambassador Dodd's Diary* (Harcourt, Brace, 1941); William E. Dodd Papers, LC; Frederick L. Schuman, *The Nazi Dictatorship* (Knopf, 1939); and Winston Churchill, *The Second World War,* Vol. I, *The Gathering Storm* (Boston: Houghton Mifflin, 1948). On Japan, see Joseph C. Grew, *Turbulent Era* (Boston: Houghton Mifflin, 1952).

The Politician as Foreign Policy Maker. So consistently did Roosevelt reflect a moderately isolationist view in his public pronouncements that Beard could fill page after page with quotations from Roosevelt along that line; of course, Beard's method of emphasizing public statements and paying little attention to political pressures and complexities made difficult an understanding of Roosevelt's real position. For Roosevelt's "without entanglements" statement, see PPAFDR, Vol. IV, p. 346. C. Richard Cleary, "Congress, the Executive, and Neutrality: 1935-1940" (Ph.D. dissertation, Fordham University, 1953), sees the possibility that Roosevelt was not clear about neutrality in his own mind, aside from the political difficulties of public statements; I would stress that Roosevelt's public position affected his private stand and caused some unrealism and confusion, for Cleary also finds much data showing that Roosevelt at no time strongly favored the isolationist concept of neutrality. "Roosevelt's retreat into obscure and ambiguous generalities" Cleary sees as reflecting not confusion but an attempt to cloak his basic disagreement with Congress; I think that both elements were involved. PPAFDR, Vol. IV, pp. 460-461, records both Roosevelt's and King's statements on signing the trade agreement, including the latter's reminder that it carefully safeguarded every interest. For further sources and ideas on the problem of the democratic politician dealing with the needs of political leadership, see bibliographies for chapters 18 and 19.

CHAPTER FOURTEEN

Mrs. McCormick's description of Roosevelt is from *The New York Times Magazine,* June 21, 1936, page 1. The picture of the President at work and in his various other activities is drawn from Tully, Ickes, Moley,

Perkins (all B), and other works cited. Gunther's notes on a press conference are reprinted in his *Roosevelt in Retrospect* (B), pp. 21-22; and Ickes' intimate glimpse is taken from his *Diary* (B), Vol. I, pp. 421-422. Ickes' later changed impression is evident in the subsequent volumes of his diaries; see also Frances Perkins, and Lindley[2] (B), both cited above, and Molly Dewson's unpublished autobiography, FDRL. The Roosevelt-Moley quarrel is narrated both in Moley, pp. 345-346, and in Rosenman (B), p. 105. A useful volume on the kitchen cabinet is Joseph Alsop and Robert Kintner, *Men Around the President* (Doubleday, Doran, 1939).

The Politics of the Deed. Dependable information on the impact of New Deal programs on the American people is surprisingly hard to come by. For data on recovery I have relied largely on the statistical tables in Mitchell, *Depression Decade* [chap. 7]. My unemployment figures are a rough average of his data showing estimates from eleven different sources; unemployment figures are notoriously unreliable, especially in this period, because of the difficulties of collecting data and of defining unemployment, among other reasons. Early's memorandum to the N.E.C. can be found in OF 788, FDRL, dated Feb. 24, 1936. Roosevelt's indecision on campaign tactics early in 1936 is pictured in Moley and in Ickes. For the 1936 legislative session see O. R. Altman [chap. 12], pp. 1086-1107. Max Lerner, reporting from Washington, noted Roosevelt's unaggressiveness on the corporate surplus tax, in *The Nation*, May 27, 1936, pp. 669-671; on housing legislation, see PPF 67, FDRL; on this session of Congress generally, see OF 598 and OF 1650, FDRL. Data on the organizing and financing of the Good Neighbor League can be found in PPF 1792, PSF 17, and OF 300 (Democratic National Committee), all in FDRL. I have relied largely on Moley in describing Roosevelt's attitudes and indecision in the spring of 1936. See Cantril, *Public Opinion* (B), pp. 590 ff., for public opinion polling data on popular attitudes toward Roosevelt during 1936. OF 1663, FDRL, relates especially to third parties in 1936, including rumors that the Al Smith Democratic faction might set up a third party.

"I Accept the Commission . . ." Even the main participants in the 1936 Democratic convention pay it little attention in their memoirs, but Farley[1] (B), Rosenman, and Ickes[1] provide some data. The official source is *Official Report of the Proceedings of the Democratic National Convention* (Washington, D. C., 1936). Roosevelt's exclamations to Mack, taken down by a stenographer, are found both in Tully and in PSF 16, FDRL. Both Moley and Rosenman report on the preparation of the acceptance speech. Michael F. Reilly and William J. Slocum, *Reilly of the White House* (Simon and Schuster, 1947) relates in detail the incident of Roosevelt's fall at Philadelphia. PPF 16, FDRL, provides some material on labor's participation in the 1936 campaign; for a fuller treatment see the detailed examination in William H. Riker, "The CIO in Politics, 1936-1946" (Ph.D. dissertation, Harvard University, 1948). Roosevelt's personal handling of campaign detail is shown in PPF 236 and 3565, and in OF 300 (Democratic National Committee), Special Correspondence, James A. Farley, Box 96, FDRL. OF 200-EE contains a stenographic transcript of the conferences with governors during the drought inspection trip; there are

indications that Roosevelt was specially briefed to talk with Landon about pond water. According to memoranda in PSF 17, FDRL, the La Follette brothers late in July urged on Roosevelt a drought conference toward the end both of planning a drought program and of compelling Landon to take a definite stand on drought relief; there was, however, some opposition to the idea at the White House.

"We Have Only Just Begun to Fight." Reliable information on political maneuvers, especially intraparty maneuvers, in most states is not available in any abundance. On Idaho I have used PPF 2358, FDRL (the Borah file, which includes correspondence relating to 1936); OF 300, Box 96, FDRL; and a discerning, sympathetic biography, Claudius O. Johnson, *Borah of Idaho* (Longmans, Green, 1936). On Norris, two excellent biographies treat extensively his relations with Roosevelt: Richard L. Neuberger and Stephen B. Kahn, *Integrity* (Vanguard Press, 1937), and Alfred Lief, *Democracy's Norris* (Stackpole Sons, 1939); see also PPF 880, FDRL; Democratic National Campaign Committee (1936), Box 12, FDRL; Hopkins Papers; and Roosevelt's speech endorsing Norris, PPAFDR, Vol. V, pp. 431-439. On the political situation in Wisconsin and Minnesota see memorandum Leo Crowley to McIntyre, Sept. 8, 1936, PPF 6659, FDRL; on Minnesota see Arthur Naftalin, "A History of the Farmer-Labor Party of Minnesota" (Ph.D. dissertation, University of Minnesota, 1948). On the advice to Roosevelt to break off relations with the Soviet Union see PPF 4075, FDRL. The quotation from the Beards is from their *America in Midpassage* [chap. 5], p. 326. Ickes mentions Roosevelt's comment on the New England crowds, Vol. I, p. 695; so does Richberg[1] (B), p. 205. My excerpts from the Madison Square Garden speech are taken not from PPA but from a recording of the speech at FDRL. Miss Tully reports, p. 214, that Roosevelt late in the campaign dictated this speech quickly and emphatically "because he felt strongly." The Williams College Library has a collection of 1936 campaign propaganda.

Roosevelt as a Political Tactician. Molly Dewson quotes Roosevelt on his catlike qualities in her unpublished autobiography, FDRL. His sense of the shifting qualities of American public opinion has been vindicated in Almond's study [chap. 13], among other works. On Roosevelt's sense of timing see Rosenman, p. 99, and Ickes[1], p. 602. On Roosevelt's use of polls, see OF 857; on his use of trial balloons, see Creel (B), pp. 289 ff. The story about Lewis's campaign contribution is also from Creel, pp. 297-302. The examples of political detail are from OF 200 and PPF 4128, FDRL. Roosevelt's comment on attacking the Republican leaders is from Rosenman, pp. 41, 129. My only sources for Roosevelt's expression of concern over the decreased Republican opposition in Congress are Turner Catledge, the New York *Times*, November 8, 1936, Sect. 4, p. 4, and *Newsweek*, Nov. 14, 1936, p. 13. Roosevelt commented on the election results in a letter to Josephus Daniels, Nov. 9, 1936, PPF 86, FDRL; see also Hopkins to Miss LeHand, Nov. 14, 1936, OF 1113, FDRL. The nature of Roosevelt's class support in 1936 has received considerable attention. The Gallup polls, and the failure in 1936 (but not in 1932) of the *Literary Digest* poll, which relied largely on lists of car owners and telephone users, have led to the general assumption that a relatively sharp class cleavage existed; on this see Edward G. Benson and Paul Perry, "Analysis of Democratic-Republican Strength by Population Groups," *Public Opinion Quarterly*, Vol. IV, No. 3, September 1940, pp. 464-473 Some doubt on the matter is thrown by William F. Ogburn and Lolagene C. Coombs, "The Economic Factor in the Roosevelt Elections," *The American Political Science Review*, Vol. XXXIV, 1940, p. 719. For treatments of particular areas, see Harold F. Gosnell and William G. Colman, "Political Trends in Industrial America: Pennsylvania as Example," *Public Opinion Quarterly*, Vol. IV, No. 3, September 1940, pp. 473-486; Gerhart H. Saenger, "Social Status and Political Behavior," *American Journal of Sociology*, Vol. LI, No. 2, September 1945, pp. 103-113; and, for a more long-range study, Samuel J. Eldersveld, *A Study of Urban Electoral Trends in Michigan, 1920-1940* (Ann Arbor: University of Michigan Press, 1946). The "rule of economy in politics" is from the brilliant and pioneering study of American political processes by E. E. Schattschneider [chap. 10], p. 96. Roosevelt's misgivings about European developments are found in a letter to James M. Cox, Dec. 9, 1936, PPF 53, FDRL, as well as in one to Eleanor Roosevelt, Nov. 30, 1936, PLFDR, p. 635.

CHAPTER FIFTEEN

Roosevelt told Rosenman (B), p. 144, of his inner thoughts while taking the oath of office. The second inaugural speech was one of Roosevelt's most carefully prepared addresses; the drafts in FDRL show, as Rosenman points out, extensive corrections, substitutions, and rewriting.

Bombshell. There is a voluminous literature on the court fight; almost every participant-chronicler of the New Deal devotes attention to it. Most important are Rosenman, Sherwood, Michelson, Richberg, and Connally and Steinberg (all B), and Alben W. Barkley, *That Reminds Me* (Garden City, N. Y.: Doubleday, 1954). An early work especially useful on the initial shaping of the court proposal is Joseph Alsop and Turner Catledge, *The 168 Days* (Doubleday, Doran, 1938), based largely on interviews gained by these two journalists; I have taken the comment about the banquet on the eve from them. The Ickes diaries (B) are a useful corrective to this volume, however, in showing that thinking and planning on the court problem began earlier in the first term than has been generally thought; on this point see also PPF 1820, Box 13, FDRL; PPF 2069, FDRL; Creel (B), pp. 290-292; and Cohen interview. Public opinion data are taken mainly from Cantril, *Public Opinion* (B), pp. 148-151. The polling on the court issue was conducted chiefly by the American Institute of Public Opinion (Gallup); in using these data I have taken into consideration a probability error. Ickes[2] is my chief source for Roosevelt's early shifting attitudes on ways of meeting the Supreme Court issue. A mysterious side of the court fight is why the article which George Creel wrote on the President's plan several weeks before the announcement at Roosevelt's direction, and as a trial balloon, did not attract more attention; see Creel, p. 294.

Guerilla Warfare. The fullest, most authoritative source for the court fight is E. Kimbark MacColl, "The Supreme Court and Public Opinion"

(Ph.D. dissertation, University of California, Los Angeles, 1953), although Ickes' diaries were not yet available in its writing. Another dissertation, James Johnston Anderson, "The President's Supreme Court Proposal— A Study in Presidential Leadership and Public Opinion" (Cornell University, 1940), is useful especially for historical background on the struggle between President and court. Norris's position in the fight is well covered in Lief [chap. 14]; see also Norris Papers, LC. Material on Roosevelt's views and activities is dispersed throughout a variety of PPF files, FDRL; the probable first draft of the President's court reform message is in PPF 1820, 1937, FDRL. On Republican restraint, see, aside from the biographical works cited above, McNary Papers, LC. The link that was established between the court fight and relief and labor policies is reflected in Ickes[2], p. 102; Timmons (B), p. 219; and Garner to Roosevelt, June 20, 1937, PPF 1416, FDRL. The White quotation is from Lief, p. 501, and the Borah plea to Gannett from a letter of the Senator, Borah Papers, LC, which MacColl consulted. Michelson, Farley[2] (B), Ickes, and Corcoran interview throw some light on the Administration's lobbying in Congress. I base my estimate of the impact of Roosevelt's speeches of early March on the popularity of the bill, on relative scores in the American Institute of Public Opinion polls of February through July 1937 (Cantril, pp. 149-151); that there was a causal relationship here is indicated, I think, by the high percentage of respondents who *thought* the President gained by these speeches (*ibid.*, p. 150). The fullest source on the Senate Judiciary Committee is the *Hearings* (Washington: Government Printing Office, 1937). For the activities of Hughes and other members of the court see Pusey [chap. 12]; Hughes Papers, LC; A. T. Mason, "Harlan Fiske Stone and FDR's Court Plan," *Yale Law Journal*, Vol. LXI, No. 6, June-July 1952, pp. 791 ff.; and Alsop and Catledge, *passim*. Baruch's optimism on the passage of the court bill is indicated in PPF 95, FDRL, and Corcoran's in Ickes[2]. Corcoran interview was most helpful in understanding some of the main legislative developments. I have taken Roosevelt's comment to Black from Farley[2], p. 79; using direct quotations such as these from another person's memory involves some risk, and I have done so only when other data make the statement appear reliable in substance if not in letter; in this case Ickes[2], pp. 104, 108, seems to validate the statement. Lehman's letter to Roosevelt expressing his opposition to the court plan is in PPF 93, Feb. 26, 1937, FDRL.

Breaches in the Grand Coalition. Roosevelt had not foreseen the court shift in late March and April as indicated in Michelson, Ickes, and Alsop and Catledge. On the matter of Hughes's shift see Pusey, chap. 71; an answer to Pusey by Edward S. Corwin, *The American Political Science Review*, Vol. XLVI, No. 4, December 1952, pp. 1167-1173; and a judicious treatment in Samuel Hendel, *Charles Evans Hughes and the Supreme Court* (King's Crown Press, 1951). On the tactical situation after the court decisions and Roosevelt's reaction to it, see PC No. 160, April 13, 1937, FDRL; Alsop and Catledge, pp. 154-156; and MacColl, p. 326. Roosevelt's bucolic letter to Bullitt is in PLFDR, p. 676; see also Roosevelt to E. P. Rogers, PPF 1281, April 6, 1937, FDRL. Roosevelt's militance on his return to Washington in May is reflected in PC No. 366, May 13, 1937, and in Ickes², pp. 140-141, 143. Rowe interview was helpful in under-standing why Roosevelt stuck to his guns until almost the end. The tactical aspects of Van Devanter's resignation are set forth in Jackson (B), pp. 192-193; Ickes², p. 153, and Alsop and Catledge. That Corcoran and Jackson urged Roosevelt to accept defeat or delay rather than com-promise on the bill is indicated in Ickes², p. 176, and in Alsop and Catledge; the difficulty here is that Corcoran himself was the source of Ickes' statement and probably of Alsop and Catledge's, and Corcoran was over-optimistic during most of the struggle. On Roosevelt's own tactical shift see Farley², p. 86; Ickes², *passim;* and Michelson, pp. 180-182. Roose-velt's letter to Garner is in PLFDR, pp. 692-693; see Farley², pp. 84-86, for a revealing letter at about this time from Garner to Farley. I have taken from Alsop and Catledge, p. 254, the picture of Robinson as a tormented bull. The exchange between Roosevelt and Garner is in Tim-mons, pp. 222-223.

Not with a Bang but a Whimper. The title of this section is taken, of course, from T. S. Eliot's *The Hollow Men.* Ickes says that Garner simply jettisoned the bill, but there is conflicting evidence on this. The Senate majority leader fight is described in Farley², pp. 91-94; Ickes², pp. 164, 166, 170; Timmons, pp. 223-224; and Barkley, pp. 155-156. Tully (B) and Ickes differ as to whether Corcoran or Hopkins worked on the Dieterich vote; perhaps both did. For the legislative history of the Fair Labor Standards Act see Burns (B); and for that of the Wagner housing bill, Timothy L. McDonnell, "The New Deal Makes a Public Housing Law" (Ph.D. dis-sertation, St. Louis University, 1953), a thorough and well-documented case study. Ickes, Farley², and Alsop and Catledge provide data on the Black appointment. Roosevelt's statement on the Ku Klux Klan develop-ment is from Molly Dewson's autobiography, FDRL. Max Lerner wrote a moving report on the episode, republished in *Ideas Are Weapons* [chap. 8], pp. 254-261. For critical comments by Ickes and Hopkins on the management of the court bill, see Ickes², *passim,* and Sherwood, p. 90. That the court bill never could have passed is the view of MacColl, p. v, and of Barkley, p. 153; I believe that the evidence fully supports this position. Moley (B), p. 350, quotes Roosevelt on "the one issue of the campaign." The abortive role of the Good Neighbor League in the court fight is suggested in OF 2443, FDRL. An illuminating description of the failure of the Democratic leaders in New York state to rally behind Roosevelt in 1937 is to be found in PPF 3291, FDRL.

CHAPTER SIXTEEN

Roosevelt's reaction to the court fight is noted in Eleanor Roosevelt¹ (B), p. 166; Farley² (B), p. 95; Ickes² (B), p. 179; and Corcoran interview. The letter to Green is in PPF 1769, FDRL. The stormy session with the reporters was PC No. 389, August 9, 1937. The Johnson story is in Ickes², pp. 168-169. PLFDR, p. 704, has the text of Roosevelt's letter to Bowers. Roosevelt's elation over the response of the crowds is indicated in Ickes and Farley. The Lindley-Roosevelt exchange occurred in PC No. 400, October 6, 1937. Roosevelt's concern over the reaction to his Quarantine speech poses an interesting problem. A study of press comment and a sampling of letters received by the President from members of the general public indicate a highly mixed response, but with a good deal of support for the President. Roosevelt could hardly have been thinking of this reaction when he repeatedly expressed disappointment over the adverse response to the speech; he must have been thinking of the adverse reaction in his own Administration, especially on the part of Hull, and in Congress.

Cloudburst. Roosevelt's inner responses to the recession of 1937 provide another major problem of interpretation. He went through a bewildering series of shifts in attitude, whatever his consistency in policy may have been in the fall of 1937. His encouragement of both the budget balancers and the spenders in November is a case in point. Fortunately, the Farley, Ickes and Morgenthau reports of the Cabinet discussions show a gratifying correspondence; see Farley[2], pp. 101-107; Ickes[2], pp. 223-224, 229, 240-243; and Morgenthau (B). Morgenthau's jittery statement to Roosevelt is in PSF, Box 26, FDRL. On the special session, see O. R. Altman, "Second and Third Sessions of the Seventy-Fifth Congress," *The American Political Science Review,* Vol. XXXII, No. 6, December 1938, pp. 1099-1123. There is a good deal of illuminating but somewhat fragmentary material on the economic policies and record of the New Deal; I have made particular use of Mitchell [chap. 7], from whom I have taken the words "grandly opportunistic" to describe the New Deal; C. Griffith Johnson, Jr., *The Treasury and Monetary Policy 1933-1938* (Cambridge: Harvard University Press, 1939); James D. Paris, *Monetary Policies of the United States 1932-1938* (Columbia University Press, 1938); Allan S. Everest, *Morgenthau, the New Deal, and Silver* (King's Crown Press, 1950); Arthur E. Burns and Donald S. Watson, *Government Spending and Economic Expansion* (Washington, D. C.: American Council on Public Affairs, 1940); Eccles (B); and Moley (B). See also works noted below. Ickes[2], p. 144, quotes Roosevelt's report of his statement to Garner on budget-balancing; PPAFDR, 1937, contains a half dozen comparable statements by the President on this eternal hope of his. See also Morgenthau.

Palace Struggle for a Program. Estimates of unemployment in 1937-38 are drawn from the President's special unemployment census, which found between 7.8 and 10.9 million jobless at the end of 1937, including about two million on relief. Roosevelt's exchange with Snell was reported in *Time,* January 10, 1938; his exchange with the New York banker (Fred I. Kent) is in PLFDR, pp. 758-759. A contemporary report on Roosevelt's official and kitchen cabinets, Alsop and Kintner [chap. 14], presents a revealing picture of the New Deal's programmatic divisions and unities. For economic developments in the crucial 1936-1937 period, see Kenneth D. Roose, *The Economics of Recession and Revival* (New Haven: Yale University Press, 1954); and for a somewhat different view, Sumner H. Slichter, "The Downturn of 1937," *Review of Economic Statistics,* Vol. XX, No. 3, August 1938. Roosevelt's press conferences during late 1937 and early 1938, FDRL, are an indispensable source of information on his economic thinking during the recession. Wallace's letter to Roosevelt urging leadership is in PPF 1820, March 24, 1938, FDRL.

Roosevelt as an Economist. The anecdote about Eccles' visit to the President is from pp. 327-330 of his autobiography, *Beckoning Frontiers* (B), ably edited by Sidney Hyman. There is of course a voluminous literature on Keynes; see, for example, L. R. Klein, *The Keynesian Revolution* (Macmillan, 1947); Alvin H. Hansen, *A Guide to Keynes* (McGraw-Hill, 1953); Seymour E. Harris, *John Maynard Keynes* (Scribner, 1955). R. F. Harrod, *The Life of John Maynard Keynes* (Harcourt, Brace, 1951) is a rich and moving biography by a noted British economist. Miss Perkins (B) mentions Stone's *sub rosa* comment, p. 286. The Corwin book is Edward S. Corwin, *The Twilight of the Supreme Court* (New Haven: Yale University Press, 1934). Keynes's letter to Roosevelt, Feb. 1, 1938, and the Morgenthau-drafted reply are in PPF 5235, FDRL. The relation between Keynes and Roosevelt is described in Harrod, in Harris, and in Perkins. PPF 1820 contains a letter from a number of Oxford economists, Dec. 20, 1933 (not including Keynes, a Cantabrigian, but presenting essentially Keynesian arguments). There are so many examples of Roosevelt's quick, dexterous mind in action that I cannot begin to indicate sources here. The letter from his old Hyde Park friend is Roger A. Derby to Roosevelt, July 17, 1937, PPF 758, FDRL. A clue to the thinking of lower-echelon government economists can be found in the little book by seven Harvard and Tufts economists, *An Economic Program for American Democracy* (Vanguard Press, 1938), which was the work in part of such economists and which came to the President's attention. Roosevelt's recognition of near-starvation in the latter part of his second term can be seen in PC No. 604, Dec. 8, 1939.

CHAPTER SEVENTEEN

Most of my data on popular attitudes in 1937-1938 are taken from Cantril (B), especially pp. 587, 589-590, 754-760, and from surveys published in *Fortune*. To obtain certain breakdowns, however, I have made use of the original polling data of the *Fortune* polls located in the Elmo Roper collection, Williams College, and have obtained other data from the Elmo Roper office, New York City. Information on attitudes toward Roosevelt comes mainly from periodicals during the period and from the author's observations at the time. Wesley C. Clark, *Economic Aspects of a President's Popularity* (Philadelphia: University of Pennsylvania, 1943), covering chiefly the second term, argues effectively for the author's hypothesis that a high degree of correspondence exists between presidential popularity and national income.

Squalls on Capitol Hill. The congressman making the plea was Representative Martin Dies speaking for a group of congressmen; see PPF 3458, FDRL. On Congress generally during this period, see OF 419, FDRL. There are many excellent treatments of Congress as an institution; among those based on firsthand observation of Congress are Roland Young, *This is Congress* (Knopf, 1943), especially chap. 5; T. V. Smith, *The Legislative Way of Life* (Chicago: University of Chicago Press, 1940); Ernest S. Griffith, *Congress: Its Contemporary Role* (New York University Press, 1951). H. H. Wilson, *Congress: Corruption and Compromise* (Rinehart, 1951), and

James M. Burns, *Congress on Trial* (Harper, 1949), analyze Congress in a more critical vein. Data on the 1938 Congress are from the *Congressional Directory*, 75th Congress, 3rd Session (Washington: Government Printing Office, 1937). The account of the passing of wages and hours legislation is based on Burns, *Congress on Trial*, chap. 5, and on Jerry Voorhis, *Confessions of a Congressman* (Garden City, N. Y.: Doubleday, 1947); aside from sources cited in the former, see PPF 5456, FDRL, Roosevelt to Senator Hattie Caraway, Dec. 20, 1937. The President's message to Dies is contained in OF 2730, FDRL. A detailed account of the ill-fated reorganization bill is needed; I have used Altman, "Second and Third Sessions of the Seventy-Fifth Congress, 1937-38" [chap. 16]; Lindsay Rogers, "Reorganization: Post Mortem Notes," *Political Science Quarterly*, Vol. LIII, No. 2, June 1938, pp. 161-172; Farley[2] (B), pp. 127-130; and Ickes[2] (B), *passim*.

The Broken Spell. Johnson's remark and the episode at the Press Club dinner are from *Time*, May 16, 1938, and February 14, 1938, respectively. On the question of whether any significant court or administrative reform bill could have passed, see Chapter 15 above and Roosevelt to Bowers, Jan. 15, 1937, PLFDR, pp. 651-652. Herring, *The Politics of Democracy* [chap. 10], especially p. 218, throws a good deal of light on Roosevelt's relations with Congress. Stanley High's remark is taken from his *Roosevelt—And Then?* (Harper, 1937). Analysis in this chapter of Roosevelt's relations with Congress is based largely on material scattered through many FDRL files; see especially OF 202, OF 259, OF 419, OF 1038, PPF 4142, and President's Personal Files relating by name to chairmen of congressional committees and to other legislative leaders. Data on attitudes of House Democratic Steering committee members are based on a memorandum dictated shortly afterwards by a participant (perhaps Hopkins himself) in Hopkins Papers, File 104, FDRL. It was notable that in this conference protests of rank and file House members were on the whole sharper than those of the leaders. Keller's letter is in OF 119, FDRL. Standard labor histories stress the stimulating impact of New Deal policies and recovery on unionism. Books that treat the Lewis-Roosevelt break knowledgeably are Creel (B); Cyrus Lee Sulzberger, *Sit Down with John L. Lewis* (Random, 1938); James A. Wechsler, *Labor Baron* (Morrow, 1944); Saul Alinsky, *John L. Lewis, an Unauthorized Biography* (Putnam, 1949); and Matthew Josephson, *Sidney Hillman* (Garden City, N. Y.: Doubleday, 1952). Wesley McCune, *The Farm Bloc* (Garden City, N. Y.: Doubleday, Doran, 1943) is a wise and lucid picture of the politics and personalities of the major farm groups during the New Deal. The Farm Bureau Federation membership estimate is from Orville Merton Kile, *The Farm Bureau through Three Decades* (Baltimore: Waverly Press, 1948), p. 368. Roosevelt's statement to Max Lerner is quoted in Alinsky, p. 165, and is based on statement of Lerner to Alinsky in 1948.

Too Little, Too Late. Roosevelt's private views of world developments in 1937-1938 are reflected in PLFDR; see especially pp. 716, 725, 735-736, 757, 766, 781-782. His projects for an international conference are well described in Langer and Gleason, Hull, and Tansill (all B), and in Sumner Welles, *The Time for Decision* (Harper, 1944). Some of the exchanges between Roosevelt and Welles and others on the project are in PSF, Box 23, FDRL, and drafts of the President's proposed statement are in the same file, Box 31. Keith Feiling, *The Life of Neville Chamberlain* (London: Macmillan, 1947) and Winston S. Churchill, *The Gathering Storm* [chap. 13], indicate reactions in important quarters abroad. The letter of the schoolmaster (Northrup of the Roxbury Latin School) is in PPF 2291, FDRL. Roosevelt's privately expressed sympathy for the Spanish Loyalists is indicated in the following previously cited volumes: Eleanor Roosevelt[1] (B), p. 161; Connally and Steinberg (B), p. 223; and Ickes, *passim*. The actual development of Roosevelt's attitudes on policy toward Spain is not wholly clear; for example, Welles, pp. 60-61, and Hull, pp. 491-492, disagree sharply on the President's view in January 1937 toward the Arms Embargo Act concerning Spain. On Nye and the embargo, see OF 1561, FDRL; and on the role of Catholic pressure, see Norman Thomas interview, OHRP, and Claude Bowers to author, June 14, 1955. Unhappily, neither Tansill nor Langer and Gleason throw much light on this matter or on our policy toward Spain in general. Hull, Welles, Feiling, and Ickes, and Claude G. Bowers, *My Mission to Spain* (Simon and Schuster, 1954), provide ample data on the main developments. Max Lerner, "The Case of the Spanish Embargo," in his *Ideas for the Ice Age* [chap. 10] captures the feeling of tension and anguish during the fight over lifting the embargo. Eleanor Roosevelt[1], p. 162, seems to confirm what the other sources suggest—Roosevelt's painful indecisiveness over policy toward Spain.

CHAPTER EIGHTEEN

The launching of the National Progressives of America is well described in Max Lerner, "Phil La Follette, an Interview," *The Nation*, May 14, 1938, pp. 552-555; for strategic aspects of the new party see Jay Franklin, *1940* (Viking, 1940), a vivid contemporary account. Roosevelt's reaction is indicated in PLFDR, p. 785, and in Ickes[2] (B), pp. 379, 395. On La Follette for Secretary of State, see Ickes, *ibid.*, and Sherwood (B), p. 95. Like most of Roosevelt's important political moves, the purge was not conceived overnight but was the subject of conversation a long time in advance; see Ickes[1, 2], *passim*. Roosevelt's frame of mind in the winter and spring of 1938 is reflected in two extraordinarily long and frank press conferences, one with editors and publishers of trade newspapers, April 8, 1938, and one with members of the American Society of Newspaper Editors, April 21, 1938. Both of these are included in PPAFDR.

The Donkey and the Stick. Data in FDRL on the management of the purge is widely scattered in PPF and OF files for states and individuals, and at best it is still rather fragmentary. Barkley [chap. 15], and Connally and Steinberg (B), relate their own experiences briefly. Farley[2] presents a full picture of Farley's dragging of heels during the purge. Intra–White House memoranda suggest the improvised nature of many of the purge attempts. The fullest information available in any single campaign is that on the Fay-O'Connor race; see especially PPF 2841 (Morris Ernst), PPF 245, PSF. Box 28. and Harry Hopkins to FDR, August 3, 1938, Hopkins Papers

See also Ickes[2], pp. 466, 475, and Edward J. Flynn (B), p. 150, although there is a major contradiction between these two sources on the importance of Corcoran's role. Roosevelt's election prediction is in PC 499, Nov. 11, 1938, as is the exchange with a reporter on the coalition situation.

The Struggle for Power. Roosevelt's talk at Chapel Hill is in PPAFDR, 1938 vol., pp. 613-621. He mentioned his "antediluvian" friends in a candid letter to Herbert C. Pell, FDRPL, p. 849. Floyd M. Riddick, "First Session of the Seventy-Sixth Congress," *American Political Science Review,* Vol. XXXIII, No. 6, December 1939, is a useful summary of the 1939 session. The investigating power of Congress has been well and extensively treated; two excellent recent treatments are Alan Barth, *Government by Investigation* (Viking, 1955) and Telford Taylor, *Grand Inquest* (Simon and Schuster, 1955). A full and critical treatment of the House Un-American Activities Committee, 1938-1944, is Father August R. Ogden's study, *The Dies Committee* (Washington: Catholic University of America Press, 1945). The exchange between Garner and Roosevelt at Cabinet is recorded in Ickes[2], p. 549, as is Roosevelt's cautious approach toward Dies, p. 546. On the tilt between Roosevelt and Glass over the Virginia judgeship, the President's statements are presented in PPAFDR, Vol. 1939, pp. 126-133, and the Senator's side of the case in Rixey Smith and Norman Beasley, *Carter Glass* (Longmans, Green, 1939). The nature of the congressional attack on the bureaucracy is taken from Burns, *Congress on Trial* [chap. 17], pp. 115-116. On the general problem of congressional control of the executive branch see the thoughtful little book, Louis Brownlow, *The President and the Presidency* (Chicago: Public Administration Service, 1949). One of the many virtues of Ickes' diaries is that the old curmudgeon made no attempt to hide his battles with other Cabinet members; his showdown with Wallace is described in Vol. II, pp. 38-45. Accounts of Roosevelt's methods of delegating power and the ensuing confusion are too numerous to list here, but again Ickes is a good source. The usual criticism of Roosevelt as administrator and an excellent critique of this point of view are found in a brilliant review of Ickes' first volume by Arthur Schlesinger, Jr., *The New Republic,* December 7, 1953, pp. 14-15. The comment on Roosevelt's administrative direction by a subordinate is from Molly Dewson, unpublished autobiography, FDRL. On Stalin's administrative methods see W. W. Rostow, *The Dynamics of Soviet Society* (W. W. Norton, 1952), p. 247, from which I have quoted on page 373; for Harold Smith's evaluation of Roosevelt as an administrator see Sherwood (B), pp. 72-73; see also Richberg[2] (B), pp. 286-287. Such respected students of administration as Herbert A. Simon, Donald W. Smithburg, and Victor A. Thompson, in their *Public Administration* (Knopf, 1950), p. 168, state that his way of delegating power gave his own personality a greater impact on the shaping of policy. The Roosevelt-Ickes exchange is from Ickes[2], p. 659. Rowe interview was helpful in evaluating Roosevelt as an administrator. The concept of the test of efficiency as survival is from Chester Barnard.

Roosevelt as Party Leader. The quotation from Walter Millis is taken from *The Yale Review,* October 1938. Any evaluation of Roosevelt as party leader must take into consideration the question of both what the American political party is, and what it should be. On this see E. E. Schattschneider's pioneering study [chap. 10], which combines brilliant analysis with basic postulates on party reorganization; Herring, *The Politics of Democracy* [chap. 10], a shrewd evaluation and defense of the present party arrangements; Herbert Agar, *The Price of Union* (Boston: Houghton Mifflin, 1950), a searching historical analysis; and the extensive investigations of the presidential nominating process recently being conducted under the leadership of Paul T. David at the Brookings Institution. Many examples could be cited of Roosevelt's refusal to intervene openly in Democratic primaries during the early presidential years; see Roosevelt to McIntyre, Feb. 2, 1938, PPF 4658; Roosevelt wire to Eleanor Roosevelt, July 19, 1936, PPF 3, FDRL; and Roosevelt to Frank Murphy, June 30, 1934, PPF 1662, as instances. The Pittman case is Roosevelt to Pittman, Aug. 25, 1934, PPF 745, FDRL. A good example of Roosevelt's emphasis on party after 1936 is PPAFDR, Vol. VI, pp. 113 ff., 326. The nature of Roosevelt's reaction to the 1938 election results can be seen best in Roosevelt to Pell, Nov. 12, 1938, and Roosevelt to Daniels, Nov. 14, 1938, PLFDR, Vol. II, pp. 826, 827, resp. Among those who urged party rejuvenation on Roosevelt were Emil Hurja, Box 45, Howe Papers, FDRL, and David Stern, OHP; see also OF 1535, FDRL; and Norris and Ickes Papers, LC. On the condition of the New York state and city Democracy, see PPF 149, 206, 239, FDRL; Krock and Flynn interviews, OHP; Norris Papers, LC; A. A. Berle, in *The Reporter*, Dec. 1, 1955; and Moscow (B). The White remark is from White to Farley, Dec. 28, 1937, PPF 1196, FDRL.

CHAPTER NINETEEN

Curiously, although newspapers and magazines of the period are filled with gossipy accounts about the Roosevelts and the White House, it is not easy to find a dependable description for a particular period. I have used PPF 1, FDRL, which includes a file of personal detail on the President, including letters written by his secretaries to journalists and others writing in for information; Roosevelt's own description of his working day in letter to Rep. Frank W. Fries, PPF 4142, FDRL; and Sherwood (B), p. 115. His statement on short letters is in Roosevelt to James Roosevelt, PLFDR, p. 798. One of the best descriptions of the White House environment during the second term is Joseph Alsop and Robert Kintner, *American White Paper* (Simon and Schuster, 1940), by two correspondents who had access to it. The letter to McIntyre is in PLFDR, p. 814. Langer and Gleason (B), chap. 1, have a balanced account of Roosevelt's working relationships with Hull and other officials.

Munich: No Risks, No Commitments. My main sources for the substantive account and interpretation in this chapter, aside from FDRL files and works cited in bibliographical notes for chapters 13 and 17, are: Alan Bullock, *Hitler: A Study in Tyranny* (Harper, 1953), a comprehensive biography that makes exhaustive use of German sources; Galeazzo Ciano, *Hidden Diary* (Dutton, 1953), which covers the 1937-38 period; Frederick L. Schuman, *Night over Europe* (Knopf, 1941), a brilliant and absorbing contemporary account; and Alsop and Kintner, *American White Paper*. While this last source may err in indicating a more consistent attempt at final decision making after Munich than actually occurred, in most respects it is a remarkably authentic account of White House activities and reactions during the period, based on extensive interviews and checked in the White House itself (see PPF 300, FDRL). The Ickes diary (B) is another important source. While Ickes' own bias sometimes renders misleading his accounts of his own political and administrative activities, his relative open-mindedness on foreign policy lends, I think, somewhat more authenticity to his reports of presidential and cabinet discussions in that area. Roosevelt's comment about wanting to assassinate Hitler is in Roosevelt to Frederick B. Adams, Oct. 1, 1938, PLFDR, pp. 813-814. On Roosevelt's views in the weeks after Munich see Alsop and Kintner; Hull (B); PPF 3884 (Roosevelt to an English friend on the peanut vendor's remarks, Nov. 15, 1938); and PSF, Phillips to Roosevelt, Sept. 29, 1938. The description of Roosevelt dictating his message to Congress is from Alsop and Kintner. Roosevelt's instructions to Morgenthau to keep the French plane situation confidential are in PSF 33, FDRL, handwritten note by FDR on top of a memorandum from Morgenthau. The minutes of Roosevelt's confidential session with members of the Senate Military Affairs Committee are in FDRL.

The Storm Breaks. Roosevelt's letter on the "cross currents" was to Gertrude Ely, March 25, 1939, PLFDR, p. 872. The President's indirect warning to Mussolini was via the newly appointed Italian Ambassador, whom Roosevelt asked to communicate it to the Duce; notes were taken by Sumner Welles and are to be found in PSF, Box 53, FDRL. Roosevelt's reflections on the events of March-April 1939 can be seen best in three press conferences, PC 534, March 31, 1939, PC 437, April 8, 1939, and PC 540-A, April 20, 1939. Only the last of these is not included in PPA, but it is by far the most useful, a long, probing discussion of domestic and especially foreign affairs with members of the American Society of Newspaper Editors. Roosevelt's view toward his policy toward Spain is reflected in Ickes[2], pp. 569-570, and in Bowers [chap. 17]. See also Connally and Steinberg (B), p. 226, and Morgenthau (B). Bullock, pp. 461-464, has a good account of Hitler's reply to Roosevelt; see N. H. Baynes (ed.), *The Speeches of Adolf Hitler* (London: Oxford University Press, 1942), pp. 1605-1656, for virtually the whole text. Roosevelt's reaction to Hitler's bad manners is in his letter to Francis W. Hirst, May 13, 1939, PSF 1147, FDRL. Langer and Gleason, and Alsop and Kintner have good accounts of the Neutrality bill fight of spring 1939; for an account emphasizing the nature of the various bills considered see Francis O. Wilcox, "The Neutrality Fight in Congress: 1939," *The American Political Science Review,* Vol. XXXIII, October 1939, pp. 811-825; useful though spotty notes and records of the fight are in PPF 1147 and in OF 1561 (Neutrality), FDRL. All accounts agree substantially on the proceedings of the famous White House conference where Borah spoke of his own sources of information; I have taken my language mainly from Alsop and Kintner, pp. 44-46, Connally and Steinberg, pp. 227-228, and Barkley [chap. 15], pp. 260-261. "Neutrality, Peace Legislation, and Our Foreign Policy," *Hearings* before the Committee on Foreign Relations, United States Senate, 76th Cong., 1st sess., Parts 1-22, April 5, 1939 to May 8, 1939, are a valuable source of information on attitudes toward neutrality legislation at this time. *Time* magazine, June 19, 1939, and Eleanor Roosevelt[1] present useful accounts of the royal visit from different perspectives; the meeting late at night between the King and the President is described in Daniel Roper to Roosevelt, July 5, 1939, PSF 43, FDRL. The description of the "war before the war" is taken in part from *Time* magazine, August 21, 1939. Alsop and Kintner is the chief source for the Roosevelt-Bullitt dialogue on the morning of the German attack on Poland. Charles Edison foresightedly took notes on Roosevelt's statements to the Cabinet, September 1, 1939, and these indicate Roosevelt's memories of World War I crisis times; Edison's notes are printed verbatim in PLFDR, pp. 915-917. Ickes[2], p. 700, and series of exchanges between White House and Treasury Department, PSF 42, FDRL, show that Roosevelt tried to hold up the *Bremen* from departing; see also PSF 42, FDRL, for Roosevelt's consideration of seizing German ships. OF 1561 has a rich body of materials on Roosevelt's role in getting the embargo provision repealed, including the minutes of his conference with Democratic and Republican leaders, September 20, 1939, marred unhappily by the failure of the reporter to indicate names of conferees speaking and by incomplete transcription of some of the remarks by conferees. This file also contains correspondence between Roosevelt and the changeable North Dakota Representative. Gunther[2] has a useful account of Roosevelt and the early discussions about the military exploitation of atomic energy.

Roosevelt as a Political Leader. The letter quoted here was forwarded to Roosevelt by George T. Bye, Feb. 14, 1939, PPF 2865, FDRL. PSF, Box 47, FDRL, contains exchanges between the Administration and Pittman in regard to tactics on neutrality legislation revision. The press conference involving Guam was PC 519, January 20, 1939; for another example of Rooseveltian circumspection see Langer and Gleason, p. 126. Roosevelt's attitude toward Kennedy is reflected in Ickes[2], pp. 676 and 707; Farley[2] (B), p. 198; Hull (B), pp. 763, 766. Public opinion polling data are from Cantril (B), pp. 966-970, especially items 2, 13, 14, 16, 18, 19, 20, 22-27, 30, 42-44, 49. I have rounded most figures. It is to be noted that there is a contradictory aspect to some of the findings, especially in respect to the non-extremist elements; compare items 22-23 and 24-25 in this respect. I believe, however, that this contradiction is a faithful reflection of the many-sidedness of attitudes of this element and indicate again the possibilities of attitude change induced by strong leadership. Hadley Cantril, *Gauging Public Opinion* (Princeton: Princeton University Press, 1944) has been of use in interpreting this polling material both because of his excellent interpretation of polling material and also because he uses foreign policy in the late 1930's as examples in illustrating his analyses. The Whitehead quotation is from Thomas North Whitehead, *Leadership in a Free Society* (Cambridge: Harvard University Press, 1936), p. 230. An interesting question bearing on Roosevelt's leadership is whether he saw polling results. While he rarely mentioned such results, he read newspapers that carried them, and much polling data was sent to him by friends. In the case of an important *Fortune* poll in September 1939, Robert Sherrod sent the President an advance copy of the release (see PPF 1820, 1939, folder on Neutrality, FDRL). The White House had a special file of polling returns. Evidence that the President knew before September 15, 1939 that Congress would probably repeal the embargo provision is in OF 1561, Box 2, FDRL; see also Early memo to Roosevelt, Sept. 7, 1939, PLFDR, p. 918.

My general analysis in this evaluation of Roosevelt as a political leader stems largely from the leadership studies that are described in my discussion of method; see Note on the Study of Political Leadership, above, pp. 479-485. Data on prevailing popular attitudes toward party realignment are found in Cantril (B), pp. 575-578; compare especially items 1 and 17. The statement on the importance of the leader's own personality is taken, slightly paraphrased, from Lewis A. Dexter, "Some Strategic Considerations in Innovating Leadership," in Gouldner (B), p. 592. The influence of the leader on unstructured attitudes is spelled out in Cantril, *Gauging Public Opinion,* pp. 228-229. Among other important studies of political leadership are Sidney Hook, *The Hero in History* (John Day, 1943), a fruitful study in "limitation and possibility"; and Elmer Cornwell, "Lloyd George: A Study in Political Leadership" (Ph.D. dissertation, Princeton University, 1954), a pioneering comparative study.

CHAPTER TWENTY

This description of the White House over the 1939 holidays is based on Eleanor Roosevelt[1], pp. 155-160; *Time* magazine, December 25, 1939; the New York *Times,* December 23, 1939—January 2, 1940; Ickes[3] (B), p. 100; and personal observation, December 24, 1939.

The Sphinx. Virtually all the memoirs of the time give extensive treatment to the preliminaries to the third-term campaign. All of these are worth consulting, and all, I think, give faithful accounts of factual developments and conversations without necessarily interpreting Roosevelt's motives correctly. Those motives emerge out of the total impressions and descriptions of all the memoirs involved: see Farley[2] (B), chaps. 15-25; Edward J. Flynn (B), pp. 151-157; Hull (B), chap. 62; Ickes[2, 3], *passim;* Rosenman (B), chap. 13; Michelson (B), chaps. 10-11; Perkins (B), pp. 125-128; Tully (B), pp. 236 ff.; Creel (B), pp. 311 ff.; Timmons (B), chaps. 15-16; Barkley [chap. 15], chap. 13; I have also made use of my Cohen interview, and Krock interview, OHP. There is not much on the third-term problem in the President's files, FDRL, although PSF, Box 49, contains an interesting description of Garner's probable tactics as seen from the White House. P. H. Appleby, "Roosevelt's Third-Term Decision," *The American Political Science Review,* Vol. XLVI, No. 3, September, 1952, pp. 754-765, is an indispensable analysis by an official who was on the outer fringes of the inner circle. Charles W. Stein, *The Third-Term Tradition* (Columbia University Press, 1943), amply and objectively covers the subject through 1940. My own analysis of Roosevelt's motives and methods treats the President's conscious and deliberate approach to the problem, and I have concluded that he was not sure until the convention as to whether he would accept the nomination (even though all the while keeping alternatives open). My interpretation of Roosevelt's personality, however, leads me to think that even if there had been no intensified international crisis, Roosevelt would have run again. It is inconceivable to me that a man still in his prime.

conscious of Theodore Roosevelt's difficulties after quitting the Presidency, eager to play a role on the international scene, and not very confident of the abilities of his possible successors, would give up the nomination to someone else. Roosevelt's attempts to widen the presidential field can be seen from the works cited above; on Lehman, see Roosevelt to Lehman, March 26, 1940, PPF 93, FDRL. Cantril (B) covers extensively polling of anti-third-term sentiment; see especially pp. 647-653. Contrary to general impression, the Constitution does not prohibit two men from the same state from running on the same presidential ticket, but would deny the ticket the electoral votes of the state from which both came; see the 12th Amendment. My sources on the Mundelein intercession with Farley are Farley[2], chap. 17, and Ickes[2], p. 688; FDRL files show the close relationship the President had with the Catholic hierarchy. Roosevelt's satisfaction with the confused situation in the Democratic party is reflected in Ickes[3], p. 160.

The Hurricane of Events. Langer and Gleason (B) has a remarkably detailed and vivid treatment of the Roosevelt Administration's response to the Nazi blitz in Scandinavia and on the Continent; Tansill (B) is also useful but tends to thin out during this period. The estimate on page 415 of the effect of the "cash and carry" compromise is from D. F. Fleming's excellent contemporary analysis, "Arms Embargo Debate," *Events*, November 1939, pp. 339-346. The President's early actions on the Panama registry question are not wholly clear, but that he initially favored the device is strongly indicated in Hull, p. 698, in Farley[2], p. 210, and in PPF 3684, FDRL (Watson to Roosevelt, Nov. 10, 1939); the Maritime Commission file (OF 1705, FDRL) is, however, no more than suggestive on the matter. For Roosevelt at his most disarming, see his letter to William Allen White in this connection, Nov. 13, 1939, PLFDR, pp. 953-954. Quotations from Churchill's messages to Roosevelt are taken from Churchill, *The Gathering Storm* [chap. 13] and *Their Finest Hour* (Boston: Houghton Mifflin, 1949), the first two volumes of his epic accounts of the Second World War. Currie's memo to Roosevelt on the economic situation is in PSF, Box 58, FDRL. The President's continued sensitivity on budget balancing is manifested in press conferences toward the end of 1939 and in his "budget seminar" at the beginning of 1940. The relations of the White House with the Workers Alliance and with Lasser are documented in PPF 6794, FDRL. On the administrative situation in the National Labor Relations Board see J. M. Burns, "A New House for the Labor Board," *The Journal of Politics*, Vol. III, No. 4, November 1941, pp. 486-508. Roosevelt's behavior during the crisis days of spring 1940 is indicated in Ickes and in other contemporary reports; see also an excellent account in *Time* magazine, June 10. 1940. Roosevelt agreed that it was a "hurricane of events" in letter to Edward Weeks, May 21, 1940, PPF 5553, FDRL. The description of Roosevelt receiving news of the Allied disasters on May 26 is from Rosenman, pp. 195-196. Roosevelt described his indecision over whether to use the "stab-in-the-back" phrase in letter to Edw. Bruce, June 15, 1940, FDRL. I have relied heavily on Langer and Gleason's detailed treatment of the diplomatic events of June 1940, but I would stress somewhat more than they do Roosevelt's concern about Congress and the coming national conventions and election. The description of Hitler at Compiègne is from William Shirer.

"We Want Roosevelt." Roosevelt's concern with domestic political affairs during the spring of 1940 is reflected in Ickes[3], *passim*. Hopkins' admonition against third term talk is in Hopkins to Early, June 7, 1940, Hopkins Papers, FDRL. Rowe interview was very helpful on this period. On the impact of the European crisis on Roosevelt's popularity, see Cantril, pp. 649, 756. Roosevelt agreed that the word "shrimps" was appropriate for young pacifists in letter to Roger B. Merriman, May 20, 1940, p. 1028, PLFDR; Ickes[3], p. 179, suggests the President's reaction to the isolationist sentiment. The President's evening discussion with youth leaders was transcribed and affords a striking picture of his attitudes in June of 1940, especially on domestic affairs, discounted, of course, by the special role he assumed in trying to win the confidence of the group; the transcription is included as PC No. 649-A, June 5, 1940, FDRL. For Eleanor Roosevelt's mixed but generally sympathetic attitudes toward the youth groups and their leaders, see *This I Remember* (B), chap. 12, and her column "My Day" (file in FDRL), especially Feb. 12-13, 1940. Hull, p. 858, describes his June conversation with Roosevelt on the nomination; Hull was impressed enough with the President's remarks to write down longhand notes shortly afterwards, and I have quoted from Hull. The preliminaries to the Knox and Stimson appointments were remarkably complex, stretching over many months. See Langer and Gleason, pp. 509 ff., and sources cited therein; Ickes[2, 3], *passim;* PPF 3855; Tully, p. 242 (although letter of William Bullitt in the New York *Times*, Feb. 19, 1948, p. 22, indicates that, contrary to Tully, Roosevelt had promised him the Secretaryship of the Navy, not of War); PPF 4773, FDRL; and Sherwood (B), p. 163, which is especially useful on Roosevelt's timing of the appointments. There has been some controversy as to whether Roosevelt hoped that the appointments might lead the Republicans to call off their convention; see Eliot Janeway, *The Struggle for Survival* (New Haven: Yale University Press, 1951), p. 143, and Henry Steele Commager, New York *Herald Tribune Book Review*, Feb. 3, 1952. That Roosevelt entertained any serious hopes on the matter is doubtful in view of his announcement of the appointments *just* before the convention and in view of his political realism; on the other hand, it seems entirely possible to me that he made, simply as a maneuver, the statement reported by Janeway. Farley[2], p. 244, and Ickes[3], p. 221, both report Roosevelt's campaign plans immediately upon Willkie's nomination. On the Roosevelt-Farley Hyde Park conference see Farley[2], chap. 24, and Ickes[3], p. 284: I have quoted Farley at p. 251 on Roosevelt's statement. The cardinal fact that Roosevelt did not give general directions to any representative at Chicago is amply documented in Ickes[3], pp. 193, 201, 203, 207, 235-236, 238, 240; Farley[2], p. 264; Sherwood, pp. 176-177; Eleanor Roosevelt[1], p. 218; Rosenman, p. 206; Appleby, p. 755. The convention proceedings are well described in the works cited above. Totals on the first ballot omit fractions. In describing Roosevelt's activities in the White House I have relied wholly on Rosenman's vivid description, although other sources agree that he was ready to decline the nomination had Wallace failed.

CHAPTER TWENTY-ONE

Roosevelt's letters both to Delano and to Norris are in PLFDR, pp. 1045-1047. Flynn, *You're the Boss* (B), p. 159, describes the gloom that pervaded the Democratic delegates upon convention adjournment.

The Hoarse and Strident Voice. This description of Willkie is based largely on the admirable biography, Joseph Barnes, *Willkie* (Simon and Schuster, 1952), from which I have adapted my section title. For a more critical treatment see "This Man Willkie," *The New Republic*, Vol. CIII, No. 10, Sept. 2, 1940, Pt. 2. The quotation on page 433 is from Barnes, pp. 160-1. Both Sherwood (B), p. 174, and Farley[2] (B), p. 252, indicate Roosevelt's respect for Willkie's strength as a candidate. White House planning of Roosevelt's defense trips for political advantage is reflected in data in OF 200, Box 79, FDRL. In general, material on the 1940 campaign in FDRL is rather limited and fragmentary. Roosevelt's comment as to who was "boss" is from PC 647-A, May 28, 1940, a long conference with members of his Advisory Commission, which happily was transcribed and included in the press conferences. Langer and Gleason (B) have a full treatment of diplomatic and military problems in the period after the Nazi blitz.

Lion Versus Sea Lion. All quotations from Churchill's speeches or letters in this section are from his *Their Finest Hour* [chap. 18], the second volume of his great work on World War II. Hitler's plans are taken from Bullock's *Hitler* [chap. 17]. Langer and Gleason, chap. 22, provides a full treatment of the negotiations and events leading up to the destroyer deal; see works cited therein and also Ickes[3] (B), *passim*, and Barnes, pp. 201-203, the latter on Willkie's role. Walter Johnson, *The Battle Against Isolation* (Chicago: University of Chicago Press, 1944), quotes extensively from William Allen White's correspondence on the destroyer deal. Churchill describes the Battle of Britain vividly and intimately; for a brief, dramatic account see Hanson Baldwin, "This Was Their Finest Hour," *The New York Times Magazine*, Sept. 4, 1955. Henry L. Stimson and McGeorge Bundy, *On Active Service in Peace and War* (2 vols., Harper, 1948), p. 346, describe the President's reluctance to move boldly on selective service legislation; see also PC No. 266, Aug. 2, 1940. Roosevelt's pleading letter to Walsh is in PLFDR, pp. 1056-1057 (Aug. 22, 1940). It is not certain just when Roosevelt made up his mind to go ahead on the destroyer deal without Congress, but probably he had decided before he wrote Walsh and was trying here to moderate opposition that might appear in Congress. The influence with Roosevelt of the Burlingham *et al.* letter in the *Times* is evident from the President's letter to Gilbert Montague, Sept. 19, 1940, PPF 3792. Hull (B), p. 837, relates the origin of the idea of dividing the bases into two lots. Churchill, *Their Finest Hour*, p. 330, describes the tide of battle toward the end of August 1940. Langer and Gleason as well as Tansill (B) agree that the destroyer deal marked a decisive change in American neutrality. The Nazis' hopes of strengthening isolationist opinion in the United States through the Tri-partite Pact are noted in Bullock, p. 563. That Roosevelt felt the destroyer deal would adversely affect his 'election chances is suggested in the Donovan Papers, cited in Langer and Gleason, p. 765 (footnote 61), and in Roosevelt to Walsh, Aug. 22, 1940, cited above.

The Two-Week Blitz. That the 1940 presidential election was one of the most rancorous in American history was the view of many participants and observers at the time; Barnes, pp. 206-207, 227, *Time* magazine, Oct. 14, 1940, and Harry Hopkins Papers, Confidential Political File, 1940 Campaign, FDRL, give examples of the low state of the campaign; see also OF 300, Democratic National Committee, 1940. Cantril (B), pp. 939-943, suggests the extent to which Roosevelt was following rather than leading public opinion on rearmament, although it must be kept in mind that the President's chief problem was not popular attitudes but congressional opposition. For Roosevelt's quotation of the *Times* article stating that the Axis wished Willkie to win, see PC No. 686, October 4, 1940; PPF 257, FDRL, reflects the special attention paid by the White House to all direct or indirect support for Willkie from German sources. Marquis W. Childs, *I Write from Washington* (Harper, 1942), chap. 11, provides an observer's evocative picture of Willkie campaigning. Stimson and Bundy, p. 348, suggests the political implications of Roosevelt's decision to go ahead with the draft. Watching the campaign closely, Sherwood was struck by the hysterical tone of the war issue; see his *Roosevelt and Hopkins* (B), pp. 187-188. The concern of the White House with the national-origin vote—especially the German, Italian, and Irish—is reflected in many FDRL files; see especially OF 1113; PLFDR, p. 1072; Hopkins Papers, 1940 Campaign; OF 300 (New York); and Gosnell[2], p. 187. The President's fling at the editorial writers of the *Times* is in PLFDR, pp. 1067-1068. Ickes[3], pp. 331, 344-345, tells of Flynn's and Roosevelt's worry about public opinion poll manipulation. Cantril, pp. 601-602, provides polling figures on the major party vote, and a trend can be noted in both the Roper and Gallup polls toward Willkie at the end of the campaign. Three aspects should be kept in mind in interpreting these figures: polling results are usually more dependable in depicting trends than reflecting an absolute situation; a 50-50 percentage breakdown between the two major party candidates was an especially worrisome matter for the Democrats because some of their popular strength is wasted in the South as a result of the workings of the electoral college system; and polling data interpretation calls for close attention to the dates of polls. On the near-panic in the Democratic camp in October see Democratic National Convention file, 1940, FDRL; Hopkins Papers, 1940 campaign, FDRL; PPF 2361, FDRL; PPF 2425, FDRL, among other files. The Roosevelt-Ickes exchange is in Ickes[3], p. 352. Two participants and observers, Sherwood and Rosenman (B), provide the best description of Roosevelt's two-week campaign. The special attention and planning that the White House gave to radio is clear from OF 300, Democratic National Committee, Radio Publicity Box 109, 1940, FDRL. Rosenman, p. 240, describes the origin of the "Martin-Barton-Fish" phrase; both Rosenman, p. 244, and Sherwood, p. 191, describe the drafting of the Boston speech. Hull (B), p. 862, relates with some bitterness the President's willingness to compromise on the foreign policy plank in the Democratic party platform. Krock, Krock interview, OHP, stresses that he printed the Philadelphia "pauper" remark knowing full well that the Democrats would make the most of it. Rosenman rates the Cleveland speech as Roosevelt's best up to that time, and Sherwood, pp. 195-196, and Rosenman, pp. 247-248, vividly describe its preparation. I have checked the PPAFDR version of this speech against a recording at FDRL.

The Future in the Balance. Sherwood describes the preliminaries to the drafting of Roosevelt's election eve speech and prayer, p. 197. Sources for description of Hyde Park election night activities are a detailed report in *Time* magazine, "Election Extra," November 1940; Rosenman, p. 254; Sherwood, pp. 199-200; Eleanor Roosevelt, "My Day," November 1940, FDRL; and Roosevelt to Henry Luce, Nov. 20, 1940, PPF 3338, FDRL. The last is an angry letter from the President criticizing *Time* for errors in its election night story. Roosevelt, however, did not correct the story in important respects, and his resentment probably was directed more against the invasion of his privacy than errors in the report. The *Time* description is corroborated in substance by newspaper reports and by Sherwood. Reilly describes Roosevelt's brief loss of nerve in Reilly and Slocum [chap. 14], p. 66. The early anxiety on Roosevelt's part is indicated also in Sherwood, pp. 199-200. For analysis of 1940 election results see Cantril, pp. 616-620, especially items 62, 68, 70, 72, 76, 78, 79, 80, and 82. Samuel Lubell, *The Future of American Politics* (Harper, 1951) evaluates the significance of class and ethnic voting in the 1940 election on the basis of election returns and voter interviews. Gosnell[2], pp. 185-188, has a succinct round-up of the major studies and conclusions therefrom. He cites Douglas Waples and Bernard Berelson, *Public Communications and Public Opinions* (Chicago: University of Chicago Library School, 1941, mimeographed), which measured the extent to which certain topics and persons received coverage in press and radio. A brilliant, pioneering election study, Paul F. Lazarsfeld, Bernard Berelson, and Hazel Gaudet, *The People's Choice* (Duell, Sloan and Pearce, 1944), illustrates the advantage to Roosevelt of his radio skills and illuminates many other aspects of the campaign, on the basis of elaborate studies in Erie County, Ohio. Irving Bernstein, "John L. Lewis and the Voting Behavior of the C.I.O.," *Public Opinion Quarterly*, Vol. V, No. 2, Summer 1941, pp. 233-249, is a thorough examination of this subject.

EPILOGUE

As noted in the Introduction, the first two and last sections of the Epilogue are designed chiefly to help present a rounded picture of Roosevelt's life and are not based on extensive original research at the Franklin D. Roosevelt Library or elsewhere. I have relied almost wholly on secondary sources, most of which have been listed above.

Roosevelt as War Lord. Useful works on events of 1941 aside from those previously noted are: Herbert Feis, *The Road to Pearl Harbor* (Princeton, Princeton University Press, 1950), a searching analysis by a former State Department adviser; Ray S. Cline, *Washington Command Post* (Washington: Office of the Chief of Military History, Dept. of the Army, 1951), an authoritative study; Beard (B). I do wish to mention again Langer and Gleason, *The Undeclared War* (B), on which I have relied heavily and which offers the most extensive and balanced account I know of the complex events before Pearl Harbor. Roosevelt's comments to Fulton Oursler about Russia are from PPF 212, FDRL. On Roosevelt's handling of the union status problem after Pearl Harbor see J. M. Burns, "Maintenance of Membership: A Study in Administrative Statesmanship," *The Journal of Politics,* Vol. X, No. 1, February 1948, pp. 101-116. The famous quotation from Lincoln is from J. G. Nicolay and John Hay, *Complete Works of Abraham Lincoln* (Lincoln Memorial University, 1894), Vol. X, p. 66.

Roosevelt as Peace Leader. The quotation on p. 464 is from Gunther[2] (B), p. 334. Miss Perkins (B) quotes Roosevelt's account of warming up Stalin, pp. 84-85. Roosevelt's "symbol war" with Hitler is treated in J. M. Burns, "The Roosevelt-Hitler Battle of Symbols," *The Antioch Review,* Vol. II, No. 3, September 1942, pp. 407-421. Former President Truman describes his reaction to his selection for vice-presidential candidate in 1944 in *Memoirs by Harry S. Truman* (Garden City, N. Y.: Doubleday, 1955), Vol. I, p. 193. The Roosevelt-Willkie negotiations in regard to party realignment are described fully by Rosenman (B), chap. 24, and by Barnes [chap. 21], pp. 371-379. Churchill describes Roosevelt's appearance at Yalta in *The Second World War* (6 vols., Boston: Houghton Mifflin, 1948-53), Vol. VI, p. 477. Works on the Yalta conference are too numerous to mention here, but one especially valuable volume because it excerpts from a dozen treatments of the subject is Richard F. Fenno, Jr., *The Yalta Conference* (Boston: Heath, 1955).

Democracy's Aristocrat. My analysis of Roosevelt's personality leans so heavily on the foregoing analytical narrative, and the works used and cited, that I shall not attempt a separate listing here. I will mention only the following: Eleanor Roosevelt gave me important guidelines to understanding Roosevelt in my interview with her, although I take sole responsibility for the analysis in these pages. John M. Blum's brilliant analysis of Theodore Roosevelt in *The Republican Roosevelt* (Cambridge: Harvard University Press, 1954) was extremely suggestive for my own treatment of Franklin Roosevelt, who had so much in common with his cousin. Clinton Rossiter called my attention to the Walt Whitman passage. My comments on Roosevelt's dealing with evil (in its various manifestations) lean heavily on the writings of Reinhold Neibuhr.

Warrior's Home Coming. Among the most useful accounts of Roosevelt's death are Turnley Walker, *Roosevelt and the Warm Spring Story* (A. A. Wyn, 1953), chaps. 16-17; Gunther[2]; A. M. Smith, *Thank You, Mr. President* (Harper, 1946), especially chaps. 10, 13; Reilly [chap. 14], chap. 21.

INDEX

Also by James MacGregor Burns
and available from Harcourt Brace & Company
in a Harvest paperback edition

ROOSEVELT: THE SOLDIER OF FREEDOM

My utmost for His highest

OTHER BOOKS BY OSWALD CHAMBERS

Approved Unto God

Baffled to Fight Better

Biblical Psychology

*Bringing Sons Into Glory &
Making All Things New*

Christian Disciplines

*Conformed to His Image &
The Servant As His Lord*

Daily Thoughts for Disciples

*God's Workmanship &
He Shall Glorify Me*

If You Will Ask

The Love of God

Not Knowing Where

The Place of Help

Prayer: A Holy Occupation

Shade of His Hand

*The Shadow of an Agony &
The Highest Good*

*So Send I You &
Workmen of God*

Studies in the Sermon on the Mount

Discovery House Publishers

Books, music, and videos that feed the soul with the Word of God

Box 3566 Grand Rapids, MI 49501

My utmost for His highest

The Golden Book
of
Oswald Chambers

Special Updated Edition
Edited by James Reimann

Authorized by the Oswald Chambers
Publications Associations, Ltd.

My Utmost for His Highest (Updated Edition)
© 1995, 1992 by the Oswald Chambers Publications Association, Ltd.
Original edition © 1935 by Dodd, Mead & Company, Inc. © renewed 1963
by the Oswald Chambers Publications Association, Ltd. All rights reserved

United States publication rights are held by Discovery House Publishers,
which is affiliated with RBC Ministries, Grand Rapids, Michigan 49512

Discovery House books are distributed to the trade exclusively by Barbour
Publishing, Inc., Uhrichsville, Ohio 44683

Unless otherwise indicated, Scripture quotations are from The New King
James Version. © 1979, 1980, 1982, Thomas Nelson, Inc., Publishers.

Library of Congress Cataloging-in-Publication Data

Chambers, Oswald, 1874–1917.
    My utmost for his highest : an updated edition in today's language :
the golden book of Oswald Chambers / edited by James G. Reimann.
       p. cm.
    "Authorized by the Oswald Chambers Publications Association, Ltd."
Includes index.

    ISBN: 0-929239-99-7

    1. Devotional calendars. I. Reimann, James G. II. Title.
[BV4811.C455 1995]
242'.2–dc20   95-18752
                                             CIP

Printed in the United States of America

01 02 / RRD / 15 14 13 12 11 10 9 8

Jacket Design: Diana Barnes
Photography: Matthew Barnes

This book is dedicated to the reader.

May you know God better and draw closer to Him
        as a result of applying the truths of God's Word
    expressed in this book.

Introduction

For over sixty years Oswald Chambers' *My Utmost for His Highest* has been one of the most widely read books in the Christian world. First published in England in 1927, and in the United States in 1935, these daily readings were compiled from shorthand notes of Chambers' lectures and talks by his wife, "Biddy," who was a professional stenographer.

Oswald Chambers was a powerful Bible teacher who had lectured widely in Great Britain and abroad. From 1911 to 1915 he served as principal of the Bible Training College in London. Following the outbreak of World War I he offered himself as a chaplain for the YMCA and was assigned to minister to the Australian and New Zealand troops stationed in Zeitoun, Egypt, near Cairo. It was there that he died suddenly on November 15, 1917, following surgery for a ruptured appendix. The story of his life has been chronicled in the recently published work by David McCasland, *Oswald Chambers: Abandoned to God* (Discovery House).

Because of the numerous changes in the English language over the last several decades, and the desire to reach a new generation of readers, James Reimann has updated the 1935 edition of *My Utmost for His Highest* in today's language. The enthusiastic reception given to this new edition suggests that this goal is being realized.

Among the many whose lives have been influenced by this book are contemporary Christian musicians who testify to the impact it has had on their personal walk with God. They have chosen to express their commitment to Christ by issuing a selection of recorded Christian music using the theme of "My Utmost for His Highest." The publisher is releasing this special edition of *My Utmost* to complement this musical production and introduce a new generation to the timeless truths of Scripture as taught through the enduring words of Oswald Chambers.

The Publisher

Let Us Keep to the Point

"... my earnest expectation and hope that in nothing I shall be ashamed, but with all boldness, as always, so now also Christ will be magnified in my body, whether by life or by death" (Philippians 1:20).

My Utmost for His Highest. "... my earnest expectation and hope that in nothing I shall be ashamed ...." We will all feel very much ashamed if we do not yield to Jesus the areas of our lives He has asked us to yield to Him. It's as if Paul were saying, "My determined purpose is to be my utmost for His highest— my best for His glory." To reach that level of determination is a matter of the will, not of debate or of reasoning. It is absolute and irrevocable surrender of the will at that point. An undue amount of thought and consideration for ourselves is what keeps us from making that decision, although we cover it up with the pretense that it is others we are considering. When we think seriously about what it will cost others if we obey the call of Jesus, we tell God He doesn't know what our obedience will mean. Keep to the point—He does know. Shut out every other thought and keep yourself before God in this one thing only— my utmost for His highest. I am determined to be absolutely and entirely for Him and Him alone.

My Unstoppable Determination for His Holiness. "Whether it means life or death—it makes no difference!" (see 1:21). Paul was determined that nothing would stop him from doing exactly what God wanted. But before we choose to follow God's will, a crisis must develop in our lives. This happens because we tend to be unresponsive to God's gentler nudges. He brings us to the place where He asks us to be our utmost for Him and we begin to debate. He then providentially produces a crisis where we have to decide—for or against. That moment becomes a great crossroads in our lives. If a crisis has come to you on any front, surrender your will to Jesus absolutely and irrevocably.

Will You Go Out Without Knowing?

"He went out, not knowing where he was going" (Hebrews 11:8).

Have you ever "gone out" in this way? If so, there is no logical answer possible when anyone asks you what you are doing. One of the most difficult questions to answer in Christian work is, "What do you expect to do?" You don't know what you are going to do. The only thing you know is that God knows what He is doing. Continually examine your attitude toward God to see if you are willing to "go out" in every area of your life, trusting in God entirely. It is this attitude that keeps you in constant wonder, because you don't know what God is going to do next. Each morning as you wake, there is a new opportunity to "go out," building your confidence in God. ". . . do not worry about your life . . . nor about the body . . ." (Luke 12:22). In other words, don't worry about the things that concerned you before you did "go out."

Have you been asking God what He is going to do? He will never tell you. God does not tell you what He is going to do— He reveals to you who He is. Do you believe in a miracle-working God, and will you "go out" in complete surrender to Him until you are not surprised one iota by anything He does?

Believe God is always the God you know Him to be when you are nearest to Him. Then think how unnecessary and disrespectful worry is! Let the attitude of your life be a continual willingness to "go out" in dependence upon God, and your life will have a sacred and inexpressible charm about it that is very satisfying to Jesus. You must learn to "go out" through your convictions, creeds, or experiences until you come to the point in your faith where there is nothing between yourself and God.

"*Clouds and Darkness*"

"Clouds and darkness surround Him . . ."
(Psalm 97:2).

A person who has not been born again by the Spirit of God will tell you that the teachings of Jesus are simple. But when he is baptized by the Holy Spirit, he finds that "clouds and darkness surround Him . . . ." When we come into close contact with the teachings of Jesus Christ we have our first realization of this. The only possible way to have full understanding of the teachings of Jesus is through the light of the Spirit of God shining inside us. If we have never had the experience of taking our casual, religious shoes off our casual, religious feet—getting rid of all the excessive informality with which we approach God—it is questionable whether we have ever stood in His presence. The people who are flippant and disrespectful in their approach to God are those who have never been introduced to Jesus Christ. Only after the amazing delight and liberty of realizing what Jesus Christ *does*, comes the impenetrable "darkness" of realizing who He is.

Jesus said, "The words that I speak to you are spirit, and they are life" (John 6:63). Once, the Bible was just so many words to us—"clouds and darkness"—then, suddenly, the words become spirit and life because Jesus re-speaks them to us when our circumstances make the words new. That is the way God speaks to us; not by visions and dreams, but by words. When a man gets to God, it is by the most simple way—words.

"Why Can I Not Follow You Now?"

"Peter said to Him, 'Lord, why can I not follow You now?'" (John 13:37).

There are times when you can't understand why you cannot do what you want to do. When God brings a time of waiting, and appears to be unresponsive, don't fill it with busyness, just wait. The time of waiting may come to teach you the meaning of sanctification—to be set apart from sin and made holy—or it may come after the process of sanctification has begun to teach you what service means. Never run before God gives you His direction. If you have the slightest doubt, then He is not guiding. Whenever there is doubt—wait.

At first you may see clearly what God's will is—the severance of a friendship, the breaking off of a business relationship, or something else you feel is distinctly God's will for you to do. But never act on the impulse of that feeling. If you do, you will cause difficult situations to arise which will take years to untangle. Wait for God's timing and He will do it without any heartache or disappointment. When it is a question of the providential will of God, wait for God to move.

Peter did not wait for God. He predicted in his own mind where the test would come, and it came where he did not expect it. "I will lay down my life for Your sake." Peter's statement was honest but ignorant. "Jesus answered him, ' . . . the rooster shall not crow till you have denied Me three times' " (13:38). This was said with a deeper knowledge of Peter than Peter had of himself. He could not follow Jesus because he did not know himself or his own capabilities well enough. Natural devotion may be enough to attract us to Jesus, to make us feel His irresistible charm, but it will never make us disciples. Natural devotion will deny Jesus, always falling short of what it means to truly follow Him.

The Life of Power to Follow

"And when He had spoken this, He said to him, 'Follow Me'" (John 21:19). Three years earlier Jesus had said, "Follow Me" (Matthew 4:19), and Peter followed with no hesitation. The irresistible attraction of Jesus was upon him and he did not need the Holy Spirit to help him do it. Later he came to the place where he denied Jesus, and his heart broke. Then he received the Holy Spirit and Jesus said again, "Follow Me" (John 21:19). Now no one is in front of Peter except the Lord Jesus Christ. The first "Follow Me" was nothing mysterious; it was an external following. Jesus is now asking for an internal sacrifice and yielding (see 21:18).

Between these two times Peter denied Jesus with oaths and curses (see Matthew 26:69–75). But then he came completely to the end of himself and all of his self-sufficiency. There was no part of himself he would ever rely on again. In his state of destitution, he was finally ready to receive all that the risen Lord had for him. ". . . He breathed on them, and said to them, 'Receive the Holy Spirit'" (John 20:22). No matter what changes God has performed in you, never rely on them. Build only on a Person, the Lord Jesus Christ, and on the Spirit He gives.

All our promises and resolutions end in denial because we have no power to accomplish them. When we come to the end of ourselves, not just mentally but completely, we are able to "receive the Holy Spirit." "Receive the Holy Spirit"—the idea is that of invasion. There is now only One who directs the course of your life, the Lord Jesus Christ.

Worship

"He moved from there to the mountain east of Bethel, and he pitched his tent with Bethel on the west and Ai on the east; there he built an altar to the LORD and called on the name of the LORD" (Genesis 12:8).

Worship is giving God the best that He has given you. Be careful what you do with the best you have. Whenever you get a blessing from God, give it back to Him as a love-gift. Take time to meditate before God and offer the blessing back to Him in a deliberate act of worship. If you hoard it for yourself, it will turn into spiritual dry rot, as the manna did when it was hoarded (see Exodus 16:20). God will never allow you to keep a spiritual blessing completely for yourself. It must be given back to Him so that He can make it a blessing to others.

Bethel is the symbol of fellowship with God; Ai is the symbol of the world. Abram "pitched his tent" between the two. The lasting value of our public service for God is measured by the depth of the intimacy of our private times of fellowship and oneness with Him. Rushing in and out of worship is wrong every time—there is always plenty of time to worship God. Days set apart for quiet can be a trap, detracting from the need to have daily quiet time with God. That is why we must "pitch our tents" where we will always have quiet times with Him, however noisy our times with the world may be. There are not three levels of spiritual life—worship, waiting, and work. Yet some of us seem to jump like spiritual frogs from worship to waiting, and from waiting to work. God's idea is that the three should go together as one. They were always together in the life of our Lord and in perfect harmony. It is a discipline that must be developed; it will not happen overnight.

Intimate with Jesus

> "Jesus said to him, 'Have I been with you so long, and yet you have not known Me, Philip?' "
> (John 14:9).

These words were not spoken as a rebuke, nor even with surprise; Jesus was encouraging Philip to draw closer. Yet the last person we get intimate with is Jesus. Before Pentecost the disciples knew Jesus as the One who gave them power to conquer demons and to bring about a revival (see Luke 10:18–20). It was a wonderful intimacy, but there was a much closer intimacy to come: ". . . I have called you friends . . ." (John 15:15). True friendship is rare on earth. It means identifying with someone in thought, heart, and spirit. The whole experience of life is designed to enable us to enter into this closest relationship with Jesus Christ. We receive His blessings and know His Word, but do we really know Him?

Jesus said, "It is to your advantage that I go away . . ." (John 16:7). He left that relationship to lead them even closer. It is a joy to Jesus when a disciple takes time to walk more intimately with Him. The bearing of fruit is always shown in Scripture to be the visible result of an intimate relationship with Jesus Christ (see John 15:1–4).

Once we get intimate with Jesus we are never lonely and we never lack for understanding or compassion. We can continually pour out our hearts to Him without being perceived as overly emotional or pitiful. The Christian who is truly intimate with Jesus will never draw attention to himself but will only show the evidence of a life where Jesus is completely in control. This is the outcome of allowing Jesus to satisfy every area of life to its depth. The picture resulting from such a life is that of the strong, calm balance that our Lord gives to those who are intimate with Him.

Is My Sacrifice Living?

"Abraham built an altar . . . ,
and he bound Isaac his son
and laid him on the altar . . ."
(Genesis 22:9).

This event is a picture of the mistake we make in thinking that the ultimate God wants of us is the sacrifice of death. What God wants is the sacrifice *through* death which enables us to do what Jesus did, that is, sacrifice our lives. Not—"Lord, I am ready to go with You . . . to death" (Luke 22:33). But—"I am willing to be identified with Your death so that I may sacrifice my life to God."

We seem to think that God wants us to give up things! God purified Abraham from this error, and the same process is at work in our lives. God never tells us to give up things just for the sake of giving them up, but He tells us to give them up for the sake of the only thing worth having, namely, life with Himself. It is a matter of loosening the bands that hold back our lives. Those bands are loosened immediately by identification with the death of Jesus. Then we enter into a relationship with God whereby we may sacrifice our lives to Him.

It is of no value to God to give Him your life for death. He wants you to be a "living sacrifice"—to let Him have all your strengths that have been saved and sanctified through Jesus (Romans 12:1). This is what is acceptable to God.

$P_{rayerful}$ Inner-searching

"Your whole spirit . . . ." The great, mysterious work of the Holy Spirit is in the deep recesses of our being which we cannot reach. Read Psalm 139. The psalmist implies—"O Lord, You are the God of the early mornings, the God of the late nights, the God of the mountain peaks, and the God of the sea. But, my God, my soul has horizons further away than those of early mornings, deeper darkness than the nights of earth, higher peaks than any mountain peaks, greater depths than any sea in nature. You who are the God of all these, be my God. I cannot reach to the heights or to the depths; there are motives I cannot discover, dreams I cannot realize. My God, search me."

Do we believe that God can fortify and protect our thought processes far beyond where we can go? ". . . the blood of Jesus Christ His Son cleanses us from all sin" (1 John 1:7). If this verse means cleansing only on our conscious level, may God have mercy on us. The man who has been dulled by sin will say that he is not even conscious of it. But the cleansing from sin we experience will reach to the heights and depths of our spirit if we will "walk in the light as He is in the light" (1:7). The same Spirit that fed the life of Jesus Christ will feed the life of our spirit. It is only when we are protected by God with the miraculous sacredness of the Holy Spirit that our spirit, soul, and body can be preserved in pure uprightness until the coming of Jesus—no longer condemned in God's sight.

We should more frequently allow our minds to meditate on these great, massive truths of God.

The $Opened$ $Sight$

This verse is the greatest example of the true essence of the message of a disciple of Jesus Christ in all of the New Testament.

God's first sovereign work of grace is summed up in the words, ". . . that they may receive forgiveness of sins . . . ." When a person fails in his personal Christian life, it is usually because he has never *received* anything. The only sign that a person is saved is that he has received something from Jesus Christ. Our job as workers for God is to open people's eyes so that they may turn themselves from darkness to light. But that is not salvation; it is conversion—only the effort of an awakened human being. I do not think it is too broad a statement to say that the majority of so-called Christians are like this. Their eyes are open, but they have received nothing. Conversion is not regeneration. This is a neglected fact in our preaching today. When a person is born again, he knows that it is because he has received something as a gift from Almighty God and not because of his own decision. People may make vows and promises, and may be determined to follow through, but none of this is salvation. Salvation means that we are brought to the place where we are able to receive something from God on the authority of Jesus Christ, namely, forgiveness of sins.

This is followed by God's second mighty work of grace: ". . . an inheritance among those who are sanctified . . . ." In sanctification, the one who has been born again deliberately gives up his right to himself to Jesus Christ, and identifies himself entirely with God's ministry to others.

What My Obedience to God Costs Other People

"As they led Him away, they laid hold of a certain man, Simon . . . , and on him they laid the cross that he might bear it after Jesus" (Luke 23:26).

If we obey God, it is going to cost other people more than it costs us, and that is where the pain begins. If we are in love with our Lord, obedience does not cost us anything—it is a delight. But to those who do not love Him, our obedience does cost a great deal. If we obey God, it will mean that other people's plans are upset. They will ridicule us as if to say, "You call this Christianity?" We could prevent the suffering, but not if we are obedient to God. We must let the cost be paid.

When our obedience begins to cost others, our human pride entrenches itself and we say, "I will never accept anything from anyone." But we must, or disobey God. We have no right to think that the type of relationships we have with others should be any different from those the Lord Himself had (see Luke 8:1–3).

A lack of progress in our spiritual life results when we try to bear all the costs ourselves. And actually, we cannot. Because we are so involved in the universal purposes of God, others are immediately affected by our obedience to Him. Will we remain faithful in our obedience to God and be willing to suffer the humiliation of refusing to be independent? Or will we do just the opposite and say, "I will not cause other people to suffer"? We can disobey God if we choose, and it will bring immediate relief to the situation, but it will grieve our Lord. If, however, we obey God, He will care for those who have suffered the consequences of our obedience. We must simply obey and leave all the consequences with Him.

Beware of the inclination to dictate to God what consequences you would allow as a condition of your obedience to Him.

Have You Ever Been Alone with God?

"When they were alone, He explained all things to His disciples" (Mark 4:34).

Our Solitude with Him. Jesus doesn't take us aside and explain things to us all the time; He explains things to us as we are able to understand them. The lives of others are examples for us, but God requires us to examine our own souls. It is slow work—so slow that it takes God all of time and eternity to make a man or woman conform to His purpose. We can only be used by God after we allow Him to show us the deep, hidden areas of our own character. It is astounding how ignorant we are about ourselves! We don't even recognize the envy, laziness, or pride within us when we see it. But Jesus will reveal to us everything we have held within ourselves before His grace began to work. How many of us have learned to look inwardly with courage?

We have to get rid of the idea that we understand ourselves. That is always the last bit of pride to go. The only One who understands us is God. The greatest curse in our spiritual life is pride. If we have ever had a glimpse of what we are like in the sight of God, we will never say, "Oh, I'm so unworthy." We will understand that this goes without saying. But as long as there is any doubt that we are unworthy, God will continue to close us in until He gets us alone. Whenever there is any element of pride or conceit remaining, Jesus can't teach us anything. He will allow us to experience heartbreak or the disappointment we feel when our intellectual pride is wounded. He will reveal numerous misplaced affections or desires—things over which we never thought He would have to get us alone. Many things are shown to us, often without effect. But when God gets us alone over them, they will be clear.

Have You Ever Been Alone with God?

"When He was alone . . . the twelve asked Him about the parable" (Mark 4:10).

His Solitude with Us. When God gets us alone through suffering, heartbreak, temptation, disappointment, sickness, or by thwarted desires, a broken friendship, or a new friendship—when He gets us absolutely alone, and we are totally speechless, unable to ask even one question, then He begins to teach us. Notice Jesus Christ's training of the Twelve. It was the disciples, not the crowd outside, who were confused. His disciples constantly asked Him questions, and He constantly explained things to them, but they didn't understand until after they received the Holy Spirit (see John 14:26).

As you journey with God, the only thing He intends to be clear is the way He deals with your soul. The sorrows and difficulties in the lives of others will be absolutely confusing to you. We think we understand another person's struggle until God reveals the same shortcomings in our lives. There are vast areas of stubbornness and ignorance the Holy Spirit has to reveal in each of us, but it can only be done when Jesus gets us alone. Are we alone with Him now? Or are we more concerned with our own ideas, friendships, and cares for our bodies? Jesus cannot teach us anything until we quiet all our intellectual questions and get alone with Him.

Called by God

"I heard the voice of the Lord,
saying: 'Whom shall I send,
and who will go for Us?'
Then I said, 'Here am I!
Send me'"
(Isaiah 6:8).

God did not direct His call to Isaiah—Isaiah overheard God saying, "... who will go for Us?" The call of God is not just for a select few but for everyone. Whether I hear God's call or not depends on the condition of my ears, and exactly what I hear depends upon my spiritual attitude. "Many are called, but few are chosen" (Matthew 22:14). That is, few prove that they are the chosen ones. The chosen ones are those who have come into a relationship with God through Jesus Christ and have had their spiritual condition changed and their ears opened. Then they hear "the voice of the Lord" continually asking, "... who will go for Us?" However, God doesn't single out someone and say, "Now, *you* go." He did not force His will on Isaiah. Isaiah was in the presence of God, and he overheard the call. His response, performed in complete freedom, could only be to say, "Here am I! Send me."

Remove the thought from your mind of expecting God to come to force you or to plead with you. When our Lord called His disciples, He did it without irresistible pressure from the outside. The quiet, yet passionate, insistence of His "Follow Me" was spoken to men whose every sense was receptive (Matthew 4:19). If we will allow the Holy Spirit to bring us face to face with God, we too will hear what Isaiah heard—"the voice of the Lord." In perfect freedom we too will say, "Here am I! Send me."

Do You Walk in White? "We were buried with Him . . . that just as Christ was raised from the dead . . . even so we also should walk in newness of life" (Romans 6:4).

No one experiences complete sanctification without going through a "white funeral"—the burial of the old life. If there has never been this crucial moment of change through death, sanctification will never be more than an elusive dream. There must be a "white funeral," a death with only one resurrection— a resurrection into the life of Jesus Christ. Nothing can defeat a life like this. It has oneness with God for only one purpose—to be a witness for Him.

Have you really come to your last days? You have often come to them in your mind, but have you really experienced them? You cannot die or go to your funeral in a mood of excitement. Death means you stop being. You must agree with God and stop being the intensely striving kind of Christian you have been. We avoid the cemetery and continually refuse our own death. It will not happen by striving, but by yielding to death. It is dying—being "baptized into His death" (Romans 6:3).

Have you had your "white funeral," or are you piously deceiving your own soul? Has there been a point in your life which you now mark as your last day? Is there a place in your life to which you go back in memory with humility and overwhelming gratitude, so that you can honestly proclaim, "Yes, it was then, at my 'white funeral,' that I made an agreement with God."

"This is the will of God, your sanctification . . ." (1 Thessalonians 4:3). Once you truly realize this is God's will, you will enter into the process of sanctification as a natural response. Are you willing to experience that "white funeral" now? Will you agree with Him that this is your last day on earth? The moment of agreement depends on you.

The Voice of the Nature of God

"I heard the voice of the Lord, saying: 'Whom shall I send, and who will go for Us?'"
(Isaiah 6:8).

When we talk about the call of God, we often forget the most important thing, namely, the nature of Him who calls. There are many things calling each of us today. Some of these calls will be answered, and others will not even be heard. The call is the expression of the nature of the One who calls, and we can only recognize the call if that same nature is in us. The call of God is the expression of God's nature, not ours. God providentially weaves the threads of His call through our lives, and only we can distinguish them. It is the threading of God's voice directly to us over a certain concern, and it is useless to seek another person's opinion of it. Our dealings over the call of God should be kept exclusively between ourselves and Him.

The call of God is not a reflection of my nature; my personal desires and temperament are of no consideration. As long as I dwell on my own qualities and traits and think about what I am suited for, I will never hear the call of God. But when God brings me into the right relationship with Himself, I will be in the same condition Isaiah was. Isaiah was so attuned to God, because of the great crisis he had just endured, that the call of God penetrated his soul. The majority of us cannot hear anything but ourselves. And we cannot hear anything God says. But to be brought to the place where we can hear the call of God is to be profoundly changed.

The Call of the Natural Life

"When it pleased God . . . to reveal His Son in me . . ."
(Galatians 1:15–16).

The call of God is not a call to serve Him in any particular way. My contact with the nature of God will shape my understanding of His call and will help me realize what I truly desire to do for Him. The call of God is an expression of His nature; the service which results in my life is suited to me and is an expression of my nature. The call of the natural life was stated by the apostle Paul—"When it pleased God . . . to reveal His Son in me, that I might *preach* Him [that is, *purely and solemnly express* Him] among the Gentiles . . . ."

Service is the overflow which pours from a life filled with love and devotion. But strictly speaking, there is no *call* to that. Service is what I bring to the relationship and is the reflection of my identification with the nature of God. Service becomes a natural part of my life. God brings me into the proper relationship with Himself so that I can understand His call, and then I serve Him on my own out of a motivation of absolute love. Service to God is the deliberate love-gift of a nature that has heard the call of God. Service is an expression of my nature, and God's call is an expression of His nature. Therefore, when I receive His nature and hear His call, His divine voice resounds throughout His nature and mine and the two become one in service. The Son of God reveals Himself in me, and out of devotion to Him service becomes my everyday way of life.

"It Is the Lord!"

"Thomas answered and said to Him, 'My Lord and my God!' " (John 20:28).

"Jesus said to her, 'Give Me a drink' " (John 4:7). How many of us are expecting Jesus Christ to quench our thirst when we should be satisfying Him! We should be pouring out our lives, investing our total beings, not drawing on Him to satisfy us. "You shall be witnesses to Me . . ." (Acts 1:8). That means lives of pure, uncompromising, and unrestrained devotion to the Lord Jesus, which will be satisfying to Him wherever He may send us.

Beware of anything that competes with your loyalty to Jesus Christ. The greatest competitor of true devotion to Jesus is the service we do for Him. It is easier to serve than to pour out our lives completely for Him. The goal of the call of God is His satisfaction, not simply that we should do something *for* Him. We are not sent to do battle for God, but to be used by God in His battles. Are we more devoted to service than we are to Jesus Christ Himself?

Vision and Darkness

"When the sun was going down, a deep sleep fell upon Abram, and behold, horror and great darkness fell upon him" (Genesis 15:12).

Whenever God gives a vision to a Christian, it is as if He puts him in "the shadow of His hand" (Isaiah 49:2). The saint's duty is to be still and listen. There is a "darkness" that comes from too much light—that is the time to listen. The story of Abram and Hagar in Genesis 16 is an excellent example of listening to so-called good advice during a time of darkness, rather than waiting for God to send the light. When God gives you a vision and darkness follows, wait. God will bring the vision He has given you to reality in your life if you will wait on His timing. Never try to help God fulfill His word. Abram went through thirteen years of silence, but in those years all of his self-sufficiency was destroyed. He grew past the point of relying on his own common sense. Those years of silence were a time of discipline, not a period of God's displeasure. There is never any need to pretend that your life is filled with joy and confidence; just wait upon God and be grounded in Him (see Isaiah 50:10–11).

Do I trust at all in the flesh? Or have I learned to go beyond all confidence in myself and other people of God? Do I trust in books and prayers or other joys in my life? Or have I placed my confidence in God *Himself*, not in His blessings? "I am Almighty God . . ." —El-Shaddai, the All-Powerful God (Genesis 17:1). The reason we are all being disciplined is that we will know God is real. As soon as God becomes real to us, people pale by comparison, becoming shadows of reality. Nothing that other saints do or say can ever upset the one who is built on God.

Are You Fresh for Everything?

Sometimes we are fresh and eager to attend a prayer meeting, but do we feel that same freshness for such mundane tasks as polishing shoes?

Being born again by the Spirit is an unmistakable work of God, as mysterious as the wind, and as surprising as God Himself. We don't know where it begins—it is hidden away in the depths of our soul. Being born again from above is an enduring, perpetual, and eternal beginning. It provides a freshness all the time in thinking, talking, and living—a continual surprise of the life of God. Staleness is an indication that something in our lives is out of step with God. We say to ourselves, "I have to do this thing or it will never get done." That is the first sign of staleness. Do we feel fresh this very moment or are we stale, frantically searching our minds for something to do? Freshness is not the result of obedience; it comes from the Holy Spirit. Obedience keeps us "in the light as He is in the light . . ." (1 John 1:7).

Jealously guard your relationship with God. Jesus prayed "that they may be one just as We are one"—with nothing in between (John 17:22). Keep your whole life continually open to Jesus Christ. Don't pretend to be open with Him. Are you drawing your life from any source other than God Himself? If you are depending on something else as your source of freshness and strength, you will not realize when His power is gone.

Being born of the Spirit means much more than we usually think. It gives us new vision and keeps us absolutely fresh for everything through the never-ending supply of the life of God.

Recall What God Remembers

"Thus says the LORD: 'I remember . . . the kindness of your youth . . .'" (Jeremiah 2:2).

Am I as spontaneously kind to God as I used to be, or am I only expecting God to be kind to me? Does everything in my life fill His heart with gladness, or do I constantly complain because things don't seem to be going my way? A person who has forgotten what God treasures will not be filled with joy. It is wonderful to remember that Jesus Christ has needs which we can meet—"Give Me a drink" (John 4:7). How much kindness have I shown Him in the past week? Has my life been a good reflection on His reputation?

God is saying to His people, "You are not in love with Me now, but I remember a time when you were." He says, "I remember . . . the love of your betrothal . . ." (Jeremiah 2:2). Am I as filled to overflowing with love for Jesus Christ as I was in the beginning, when I went out of my way to prove my devotion to Him? Does He ever find me pondering the time when I cared only for Him? Is that where I am now, or have I chosen man's wisdom over true love for Him? Am I so in love with Him that I take no thought for where He might lead me? Or am I watching to see how much respect I get as I measure how much service I should give Him?

As I recall what God remembers about me, I may also begin to realize that He is not what He used to be to me. When this happens, I should allow the shame and humiliation it creates in my life, because it will bring godly sorrow, and "godly sorrow produces repentance . . ." (2 Corinthians 7:10).

Am I Looking to God?

Do we expect God to come to us with His blessings and save us? He says, *"Look to Me, and be saved . . . ."* The greatest difficulty spiritually is to concentrate on God, and His blessings are what make it so difficult. Troubles almost always make us look to God, but His blessings tend to divert our attention elsewhere. The basic lesson of the Sermon on the Mount is to narrow all your interests until your mind, heart, and body are focused on Jesus Christ. "Look to Me . . . ."

Many of us have a mental picture of what a Christian should be, and looking at this image in other Christians' lives becomes a hindrance to our focusing on God. This is not salvation—it is not simple enough. He says, in effect, "Look to Me and you *are* saved," not "You will be saved someday." We will find what we are looking for if we will concentrate on Him. We get distracted from God and irritable with Him while He continues to say to us, "Look to Me, and be saved . . . ." Our difficulties, our trials, and our worries about tomorrow all vanish when we look to God.

Wake yourself up and look to God. Build your hope on Him. No matter how many things seem to be pressing in on you, be determined to push them aside and look to Him. "Look to Me . . . ." Salvation *is* yours the moment you look.

Transformed by Beholding

"We all, with unveiled face, beholding as in a mirror the glory of the Lord, are being transformed into the same image . . ."
(2 Corinthians 3:18).

The greatest characteristic a Christian can exhibit is this completely unveiled openness before God, which allows that person's life to become a mirror for others. When the Spirit fills us, we are transformed, and by beholding God we become mirrors. You can always tell when someone has been beholding the glory of the Lord, because your inner spirit senses that he mirrors the Lord's own character. Beware of anything that would spot or tarnish that mirror in you. It is almost always something good that will stain it—something good, but not what is best.

The most important rule for us is to concentrate on keeping our lives open to God. Let everything else including work, clothes, and food be set aside. The busyness of things obscures our concentration on God. We must maintain a position of beholding Him, keeping our lives completely spiritual through and through. Let other things come and go as they will; let other people criticize us as they will; but never allow anything to obscure the life that "is hidden with Christ in God" (Colossians 3:3). Never let a hurried lifestyle disturb the relationship of abiding in Him. This is an easy thing to allow, but we must guard against it. The most difficult lesson of the Christian life is learning how to continue "beholding as in a mirror the glory of the Lord . . . ."

God's Overpowering Purpose

The vision Paul had on the road to Damascus was not a passing emotional experience, but a vision that had very clear and emphatic directions for him. And Paul stated, "I was not disobedient to the heavenly vision" (Acts 26:19). Our Lord said to Paul, in effect, "Your whole life is to be overpowered or subdued by Me; you are to have no end, no aim, and no purpose but Mine." And the Lord also says to us, "You did not choose Me, but *I chose you* and appointed you that you should go . . ." (John 15:16).

When we are born again, if we are spiritual at all, we have visions of what Jesus wants us to be. It is important that I learn not to be "disobedient to the heavenly vision"—not to doubt that it can be attained. It is not enough to give mental assent to the fact that God has redeemed the world, nor even to know that the Holy Spirit can make all that Jesus did a reality in my life. I must have the foundation of a personal relationship with Him. Paul was not given a message or a doctrine to proclaim. He was brought into a vivid, personal, overpowering relationship with Jesus Christ. Acts 26:16 is tremendously compelling ". . . to make you a minister and a witness . . . ." There would be nothing there without a personal relationship. Paul was devoted to a Person, not to a cause. He was absolutely Jesus Christ's. He saw nothing else and he lived for nothing else. "For I determined not to know anything among you except Jesus Christ and Him crucified" (1 Corinthians 2:2).

Leave Room for God

As servants of God, we must learn to make room for Him—to give God "elbow room." We plan and figure and predict that this or that will happen, but we forget to make room for God to come in as He chooses. Would we be surprised if God came into our meeting or into our preaching in a way we had never expected Him to come? Do not look for God to come in a particular way, but *do look for Him.* The way to make room for Him is to expect Him to come, but not in a certain way. No matter how well we may know God, the great lesson to learn is that He may break in at any minute. We tend to overlook this element of surprise, yet God never works in any other way. Suddenly—God meets our life—". . . when it pleased God . . . ."

Keep your life so constantly in touch with God that His surprising power can break through at any point. Live in a constant state of expectancy, and leave room for God to come in as He decides.

Look Again and Consecrate

"If God so clothes the grass of the field . . . , will He not much more clothe you . . . ?"
(Matthew 6:30).

A simple statement of Jesus is always a puzzle to us because we will not be simple. How can we maintain the simplicity of Jesus so that we may understand Him? By receiving His Spirit, recognizing and relying on Him, and obeying Him as He brings us the truth of His Word, life will become amazingly simple. Jesus asks us to consider that "if God so clothes the grass of the field . . ." how "much more" will He clothe you, if you keep your relationship right with Him? Every time we lose ground in our fellowship with God, it is because we have disrespectfully thought that we knew better than Jesus Christ. We have allowed "the cares of this world" to enter in (Matthew 13:22), while forgetting the "much more" of our heavenly Father.

"Look at the birds of the air . . ." (6:26). Their function is to obey the instincts God placed within them, and God watches over them. Jesus said that if you have the right relationship with Him and will obey His Spirit within you, then God will care for your "feathers" too.

"Consider the lilies of the field . . ." (6:28). They grow where they are planted. Many of us refuse to grow where God plants us. Therefore, we don't take root anywhere. Jesus said if we would obey the life of God within us, He would look after all other things. Did Jesus Christ lie to us? Are we experiencing the "much more" He promised? If we are not, it is because we are not obeying the life God has given us and have cluttered our minds with confusing thoughts and worries. How much time have we wasted asking God senseless questions while we should be absolutely free to concentrate on our service to Him? Consecration is the act of continually separating myself from everything except that which God has appointed me to do. It is not a one-time experience but an ongoing process. Am I continually separating myself and looking to God every day of my life?

A warning which needs to be repeated is that "the cares of this world and the deceitfulness of riches," and the lust for other things, will choke out the life of God in us (Matthew 13:22). We are never free from the recurring waves of this invasion. If the frontline of attack is not about clothes and food, it may be about money or the lack of money; or friends or lack of friends; or the line may be drawn over difficult circumstances. It is one steady invasion, and these things will come in like a flood, unless we allow the Spirit of God to raise up the banner against it.

"I say to you, do not worry about your life . . . ." Our Lord says to be careful only about one thing—our relationship to Him. But our common sense shouts loudly and says, "That is absurd, I *must* consider how I am going to live, and I *must* consider what I am going to eat and drink." Jesus says you must not. Beware of allowing yourself to think that He says this while not understanding your circumstances. Jesus Christ knows our circumstances better than we do, and He says we must not think about these things to the point where they become the primary concern of our life. Whenever there are competing concerns in your life, be sure you always put your relationship to God first.

"Sufficient for the day is its own trouble" (6:34). How much trouble has begun to threaten you today? What kind of mean little demons have been looking into your life and saying, "What are your plans for next month—or next summer?" Jesus tells us not to worry about any of these things. Look again and think. Keep your mind on the "much more" of your heavenly Father (6:30).

How Could Someone So Persecute Jesus!

"Saul, Saul, why are you persecuting Me?" (Acts 26:14).

Are you determined to have your own way in living for God? We will never be free from this trap until we are brought into the experience of the baptism of "the Holy Spirit and fire" (Matthew 3:11). Stubbornness and self-will will always stab Jesus Christ. It may hurt no one else, but it wounds His Spirit. Whenever we are obstinate and self-willed and set on our own ambitions, we are hurting Jesus. Every time we stand on our own rights and insist that this is what we intend to do, we are persecuting Him. Whenever we rely on self-respect, we systematically disturb and grieve His Spirit. And when we finally understand that it is Jesus we have been persecuting all this time, it is the most crushing revelation ever.

Is the Word of God tremendously penetrating and sharp in me as I hand it on to you, or does my life betray the things I profess to teach? I may teach sanctification and yet exhibit the spirit of Satan, the very spirit that persecutes Jesus Christ. The Spirit of Jesus is conscious of only one thing—a perfect oneness with the Father. And He tells us, "Take My yoke upon you and learn from Me, for I am gentle and lowly in heart, and you will find rest for your souls" (Matthew 11:29). All I do should be based on a perfect oneness with Him, not on a self-willed determination to be godly. This will mean that others may use me, go around me, or completely ignore me, but if I will submit to it for His sake, I will prevent Jesus Christ from being persecuted.

How Could Someone Be So Ignorant!

"Who are You, Lord?"
(Acts 26:15).

"The LORD spoke thus to me with a strong hand . . ." (Isaiah 8:11). There is no escape when our Lord speaks. He always comes using His authority and taking hold of our understanding. Has the voice of God come to you directly? If it has, you cannot mistake the intimate insistence with which it has spoken to you. God speaks in the language you know best—not through your ears, but through your circumstances.

God has to destroy our determined confidence in our own convictions. We say, "I know that this is what I should do"—and suddenly the voice of God speaks in a way that overwhelms us by revealing the depths of our ignorance. We show our ignorance of Him in the very way we decide to serve Him. We serve Jesus in a spirit that is not His, and hurt Him by our defense of Him. We push His claims in the spirit of the devil; our words sound all right, but the spirit is that of an enemy. "He . . . rebuked them, and said, 'You do not know what manner of spirit you are of' " (Luke 9:55). The spirit of our Lord in His followers is described in 1 Corinthians 13.

Have I been persecuting Jesus by an eager determination to serve Him in my own way? If I feel I have done my duty, yet have hurt Him in the process, I can be sure that this was not my duty. My way will not be to foster a meek and quiet spirit, only the spirit of self-satisfaction. We presume that whatever is unpleasant is our duty! Is that anything like the spirit of our Lord—"I *delight* to do Your will, O my God . . ." (Psalm 40:8).

The Dilemma of Obedience

"Samuel was afraid to tell
Eli the vision"
(1 Samuel 3:15).

God never speaks to us in dramatic ways, but in ways that are easy to misunderstand. Then we say, "I wonder if that is God's voice?" Isaiah said that the Lord spoke to him "with a strong hand," that is, by the pressure of his circumstances (Isaiah 8:11). Without the sovereign hand of God Himself, nothing touches our lives. Do we discern His hand at work, or do we see things as mere occurrences?

Get into the habit of saying, "Speak, LORD," and life will become a romance (1 Samuel 3:9). Every time circumstances press in on you, say, "Speak, LORD," and make time to listen. Chastening is more than a means of discipline—it is meant to bring me to the point of saying, "Speak, LORD." Think back to a time when God spoke to you. Do you remember what He said? Was it Luke 11:13, or was it 1 Thessalonians 5:23? As we listen, our ears become more sensitive, and like Jesus, we will hear God all the time.

Should I tell my "Eli" what God has shown to me? This is where the dilemma of obedience hits us. We disobey God by becoming amateur providences and thinking, "I must shield 'Eli,'" who represents the best people we know. God did not tell Samuel to tell Eli—he had to decide that for himself. God's message to you may hurt your "Eli," but trying to prevent suffering in another's life will prove to be an obstruction between your soul and God. It is at your own risk that you prevent someone's right hand being cut off or right eye being plucked out (see Matthew 5:29–30).

Never ask another person's advice about anything God makes you decide before Him. If you ask advice, you will almost always side with Satan. ". . . I did not immediately confer with flesh and blood . . ." (Galatians 1:16).

Do You See Your Calling?

Our calling is not primarily to be holy men and women, but to be proclaimers of the gospel of God. The one all-important thing is that the gospel of God should be recognized as *the* abiding reality. Reality is not human goodness, or holiness, or heaven, or hell—it is redemption. The need to perceive this is the most vital need of the Christian worker today. As workers, we have to get used to the revelation that redemption is the only reality. Personal holiness is an effect of redemption, not the cause of it. If we place our faith in human goodness we will go under when testing comes.

Paul did not say that he separated himself, but "when it pleased God, who separated me . . ." (Galatians 1:15). Paul was not overly interested in his own character. And as long as our eyes are focused on our own personal holiness, we will never even get close to the full reality of redemption. Christian workers fail because they place their desire for their own holiness above their desire to know God. "Don't ask me to be confronted with the strong reality of redemption on behalf of the filth of human life surrounding me today; what I want is anything God can do for me to make me more desirable in my own eyes." To talk that way is a sign that the reality of the gospel of God has not begun to touch me. There is no reckless abandon to God in that. God cannot deliver me while my interest is merely in my own character. Paul was not conscious of himself. He was recklessly abandoned, totally surrendered, and separated by God for one purpose—to proclaim the gospel of God (see Romans 9:3).

The Call of God

"Christ did not send me to baptize, but to preach the gospel . . ."
(1 Corinthians 1:17).

Paul states here that the call of God is to preach the gospel. But remember what Paul means by "the gospel," namely, the reality of redemption in our Lord Jesus Christ. We are inclined to make sanctification the goal of our preaching. Paul refers to personal experiences only by way of illustration, never as the end of the matter. We are not commissioned to preach salvation or sanctification—we are commissioned to lift up Jesus Christ (see John 12:32). It is an injustice to say that Jesus Christ labored in redemption to make me a saint. Jesus Christ labored in redemption to redeem the whole world and to place it perfectly whole and restored before the throne of God. The fact that we can experience redemption illustrates the power of its reality, but that experience is a byproduct and not the goal of redemption. If God were human, how sick and tired He would be of the constant requests we make for our salvation and for our sanctification. We burden His energies from morning till night asking for things for ourselves or for something from which *we* want to be delivered! When we finally touch the underlying foundation of the reality of the gospel of God, we will never bother Him anymore with little personal complaints.

The one passion of Paul's life was to proclaim the gospel of God. He welcomed heartbreak, disillusionment, and tribulation for only one reason—these things kept him unmovable in his devotion to the gospel of God.

The Compelling Force of the Call

"Woe is me if I do not preach the gospel!" (1 Corinthians 9:16).

Beware of refusing to hear the call of God. Everyone who is saved is called to testify to the fact of his salvation. That, however, is not the same as the call to preach, but is merely an illustration which can be used in preaching. In this verse, Paul was referring to the stinging pains produced in him by the compelling force of the call to preach the gospel. Never try to apply what Paul said regarding the call to preach to those souls who are being called to God for salvation. There is nothing easier than getting saved, because it is solely God's sovereign work— "Look to Me, and be saved . . ." (Isaiah 45:22). Our Lord never requires the same conditions for discipleship that he requires for salvation. We are condemned to salvation through the Cross of Christ. But discipleship has an option with it—"*If* anyone . . ." (Luke 14:26).

Paul's words have to do with our being made servants of Jesus Christ, and our permission is never asked as to what we will do or where we will go. God makes us as broken bread and poured-out wine to please Himself. To be "separated to the gospel" means being able to hear the call of God (Romans 1:1). Once someone begins to hear that call, a suffering worthy of the name of Christ is produced. Suddenly, every ambition, every desire of life, and every outlook is completely blotted out and extinguished. Only one thing remains—". . . *separated to the gospel* . . . ." Woe be to the soul who tries to head in any other direction once that call has come to him. The Bible Training College exists so that each of you may know whether or not God has a man or woman here who truly cares about proclaiming His gospel and to see if God grips you for this purpose. Beware of competing calls once the call of God grips you.

Becoming the "Filth of the World"

"We have been made as the filth of the world . . ."
(1 Corinthians 4:13).

These words are not an exaggeration. The only reason they may not be true of us who call ourselves ministers of the gospel is not that Paul forgot or misunderstood the exact truth of them, but that we are too cautious and concerned about our own desires to allow ourselves to become the refuse or "filth of the world." "Fill up in my flesh what is lacking in the afflictions of Christ . . ." (Colossians 1:24) is not the result of the holiness of sanctification, but the evidence of consecration—being "separated *to* the gospel of God . . ." (Romans 1:1).

"Beloved, do not think it strange concerning the fiery trial which is to try you . . ." (1 Peter 4:12). If we do think the things we encounter are strange, it is because we are fearful and cowardly. We pay such close attention to our own interests and desires that we stay out of the mire and say, "I won't submit; I won't bow or bend." And you don't have to—you can be saved by the "skin of your teeth" if you like. You can refuse to let God count you as one who is "separated to the gospel . . . ." Or you can say, "I don't care if I am treated like 'the filth of the world' as long as the gospel is proclaimed." A true servant of Jesus Christ is one who is willing to experience martyrdom for the reality of the gospel of God. When a moral person is confronted with contempt, immorality, disloyalty, or dishonesty, he is so repulsed by the offense that he turns away and in despair closes his heart to the offender. But the miracle of the redemptive reality of God is that the worst and the vilest offender can never exhaust the depths of His love. Paul did not say that God separated him to show what a wonderful man He could make of him, but *"to reveal His Son in me . . ."* (Galatians 1:16).

The Compelling Majesty of His Power

"The love of Christ compels us . . ."
(2 Corinthians 5:14).

Paul said that he was overpowered, subdued, and held as in a vise by "the love of Christ." Very few of us really know what it means to be held in the grip of the love of God. We tend so often to be controlled simply by our own experience. The one thing that gripped and held Paul, to the exclusion of everything else, was the love of God. "The love of Christ compels us . . . ." When you hear that coming from the life of a man or woman it is unmistakable. You will know that the Spirit of God is completely unhindered in that person's life.

When we are born again by the Spirit of God, our testimony is based solely on what God has done for us, and rightly so. But that will change and be removed forever once you "receive power when the Holy Spirit has come upon you . . ." (Acts 1:8). Only then will you begin to realize what Jesus meant when He went on to say, ". . . you shall be *witnesses to Me* . . . ." Not witnesses to what Jesus can do—that is basic and understood—but "witnesses to Me . . . ." We will accept everything that happens as if it were happening to Him, whether we receive praise or blame, persecution or reward. No one is able to take this stand for Jesus Christ who is not totally compelled by the majesty of His power. It is the only thing that matters, and yet it is strange that it's the last thing we as Christian workers realize. Paul said that he was gripped by the love of God and that is why he acted as he did. People could perceive him as mad or sane—he did not care. There was only one thing he lived for—to persuade people of the coming judgment of God and to tell them of "the love of Christ." This total surrender to "the love of Christ" is the only thing that will bear fruit in your life. And it will always leave the mark of God's holiness and His power, never drawing attention to your personal holiness.

Are You Ready To Be Poured Out As an Offering?

"If I am being poured out as a drink offering on the sacrifice and service of your faith, I am glad and rejoice with you all" (Philippians 2:17).

Are you willing to sacrifice yourself for the work of another believer—to pour out your life sacrificially for the ministry and faith of others? Or do you say, "I am not willing to be poured out right now, and I don't want God to tell me how to serve Him. I want to choose the place of my own sacrifice. And I want to have certain people watching me and saying, 'Well done.'"

It is one thing to follow God's way of service if you are regarded as a hero, but quite another thing if the road marked out for you by God requires becoming a "doormat" under other people's feet. God's purpose may be to teach you to say, "I know how to be abased . . ." (Philippians 4:12). Are you ready to be sacrificed like that? Are you ready to be less than a mere drop in the bucket—to be so totally insignificant that no one remembers you even if they think of those you served? Are you willing to give and be poured out until you are used up and exhausted—not seeking to be ministered to, but to minister? Some saints cannot do menial work while maintaining a saintly attitude, because they feel such service is beneath their dignity.

Are You Ready To Be Poured Out As an Offering?

"I am already being poured out as a drink offering . . ."
(2 Timothy 4:6).

Are you ready to be poured out as an offering? It is an act of your will, not your emotions. *Tell* God you are ready to be offered as a sacrifice for Him. Then accept the consequences as they come, without any complaints, in spite of what God may send your way. God sends you through a crisis in private, where no other person can help you. From the outside your life may appear to be the same, but the difference is taking place in your will. Once you have experienced the crisis in your will, you will take no thought of the cost when it begins to affect you externally. If you don't deal with God on the level of your will first, the result will be only to arouse sympathy for yourself.

"Bind the sacrifice with cords to the horns of the altar" (Psalm 118:27). You must be willing to be placed on the altar and go through the fire; willing to experience what the altar represents—burning, purification, and separation for only one purpose—the elimination of every desire and affection not grounded in or directed toward God. But *you* don't eliminate it, God does. You "bind the sacrifice . . . to the horns of the altar" and see to it that you don't wallow in self-pity once the fire begins. After you have gone through the fire, there will be nothing that will be able to trouble or depress you. When another crisis arises, you will realize that things cannot touch you as they used to do. What fire lies ahead in your life?

Tell God you are ready to be poured out as an offering, and God will prove Himself to be all you ever dreamed He would be.

Spiritual Dejection

> "We were hoping that it was He who was going to redeem Israel. Indeed, besides all this, today is the third day since these things happened"
> (Luke 24:21).

Every fact that the disciples stated was right, but the conclusions they drew from those facts were wrong. Anything that has even a hint of dejection spiritually is always wrong. If I am depressed or burdened, I am to blame, not God or anyone else. Dejection stems from one of two sources—I have either satisfied a lust or I have not had it satisfied. In either case, dejection is the result. *Lust* means "I must have it at once." Spiritual lust causes me to demand an answer from God, instead of seeking God Himself who gives the answer. What have I been hoping or trusting God would do? Is today "the third day" and He has still not done what I expected? Am I therefore justified in being dejected and in blaming God? Whenever we insist that God should give us an answer to prayer we are off track. The purpose of prayer is that we get ahold of God, not of the answer. It is impossible to be well physically and to be dejected, because dejection is a sign of sickness. This is also true spiritually. Dejection spiritually is wrong, and we are always to blame for it.

We look for visions from heaven and for earth-shaking events to see God's power. Even the fact that we are dejected is proof that we do this. Yet we never realize that all the time God is at work in our everyday events and in the people around us. If we will only obey, and do the task that He has placed closest to us, we will see Him. One of the most amazing revelations of God comes to us when we learn that it is in the everyday things of life that we realize the magnificent deity of Jesus Christ.

The Cost of Sanctification

> "May the God of peace
> Himself sanctify you
> completely . . ."
> (1 Thessalonians 5:23).

When we pray, asking God to sanctify us, are we prepared to measure up to what that really means? We take the word *sanctification* much too lightly. Are we prepared to pay the cost of sanctification? The cost will be a deep restriction of all our earthly concerns, and an extensive cultivation of all our godly concerns. Sanctification means to be intensely focused on God's point of view. It means to secure and to keep all the strength of our body, soul, and spirit for God's purpose alone. Are we really prepared for God to perform in us everything for which He separated us? And after He has done His work, are we then prepared to separate ourselves to God just as Jesus did? "For their sakes I sanctify Myself . . ." (John 17:19). The reason some of us have not entered into the experience of sanctification is that we have not realized the meaning of sanctification from God's perspective. Sanctification means being made one with Jesus so that the nature that controlled Him will control us. Are we really prepared for what that will cost? It will cost absolutely everything in us which is not of God.

Are we prepared to be caught up into the full meaning of Paul's prayer in this verse? Are we prepared to say, "Lord, make me, a sinner saved by grace, as holy as You can"? Jesus prayed that we might be one with Him, just as He is one with the Father (see John 17:21–23). The resounding evidence of the Holy Spirit in a person's life is the unmistakable family likeness to Jesus Christ, and the freedom from everything which is not like Him. Are we prepared to set ourselves apart for the Holy Spirit's work in us?

Are You Exhausted Spiritually?

"The everlasting God . . .
neither faints nor is weary"
(Isaiah 40:28).

Exhaustion means that our vital energies are completely worn out and spent. Spiritual exhaustion is never the result of sin, but of service. Whether or not you experience exhaustion will depend on where you get your supplies. Jesus said to Peter, "Feed My sheep," but He gave him nothing with which to feed them (John 21:17). The process of being made broken bread and poured-out wine means that *you* have to be the nourishment for other people's souls until they learn to feed on God. They must drain you completely —to the very last drop. But be careful to replenish your supply, or you will quickly be utterly exhausted. Until others learn to draw on the life of the Lord Jesus directly, they will have to draw on His life through you. You must literally be their source of supply, until they learn to take their nourishment from God. We owe it to God to be our best for His lambs and sheep, as well as for Him.

Have you delivered yourself over to exhaustion because of the way you have been serving God? If so, then renew and rekindle your desires and affections. Examine your reasons for service. Is your source based on your own understanding or is it grounded on the redemption of Jesus Christ? Continually look back to the foundation of your love and affection and remember where your Source of power lies. You have no right to complain, "O Lord, I am so exhausted." He saved and sanctified you to exhaust you. Be exhausted for God, but remember that He is your supply. "All my springs are in you" (Psalm 87:7).

Is Your Ability To See God Blinded?

"Lift up your eyes on high, and see who has created these things . . ." (Isaiah 40:26).

The people of God in Isaiah's time had blinded their minds' ability to see God by looking on the face of idols. But Isaiah made them look up at the heavens; that is, he made them begin to use their power to think and to visualize correctly. If we are children of God, we have a tremendous treasure in nature and will realize that it is holy and sacred. We will see God reaching out to us in every wind that blows, every sunrise and sunset, every cloud in the sky, every flower that blooms, and every leaf that fades, if we will only begin to use our blinded thinking to visualize it.

The real test of spiritual focus is being able to bring your mind and thoughts under control. Is your mind focused on the face of an idol? Is the idol yourself? Is it your work? Is it your idea of what a servant should be, or maybe your experience of salvation and sanctification? If so, then your ability to see God is blinded. You will be powerless when faced with difficulties and will be forced to endure in darkness. If your power to see has been blinded, don't look back on your own experiences, but look to God. It is God you need. Go beyond yourself and away from the faces of your idols and away from everything else that has been blinding your thinking. Wake up and accept the ridicule that Isaiah gave to his people, and deliberately turn your thoughts and your eyes to God.

One of the reasons for our sense of futility in prayer is that we have lost our power to visualize. We can no longer even imagine putting ourselves deliberately before God. It is actually more important to be broken bread and poured-out wine in the area of intercession than in our personal contact with others. The power of visualization is what God gives a saint so that he can go beyond himself and be firmly placed into relationships he never before experienced.

Is Your Mind Stayed on God?

"You will keep him in perfect peace, whose mind is stayed on You, because he trusts in You"
(Isaiah 26:3).

Is your mind stayed on God or is it starved? Starvation of the mind, caused by neglect, is one of the chief sources of exhaustion and weakness in a servant's life. If you have never used your mind to place yourself before God, begin to do it now. There is no reason to wait for God to come to you. You must turn your thoughts and your eyes away from the face of idols and look to Him and be saved (see Isaiah 45:22).

Your mind is the greatest gift God has given you and it ought to be devoted entirely to Him. You should seek to be "bringing every thought into captivity to the obedience of Christ . . ." (2 Corinthians 10:5). This will be one of the greatest assets of your faith when a time of trial comes, because then your faith and the Spirit of God will work together. When you have thoughts and ideas that are worthy of credit to God, learn to compare and associate them with all that happens in nature—the rising and the setting of the sun, the shining of the moon and the stars, and the changing of the seasons. You will begin to see that your thoughts are from God as well, and your mind will no longer be at the mercy of your impulsive thinking, but will always be used in service to God.

"We have sinned with our fathers . . . [and] . . . did not remember . . ." (Psalm 106:6–7). Then prod your memory and wake up immediately. Don't say to yourself, "But God is not talking to me right now." He ought to be. Remember whose you are and whom you serve. Encourage yourself to remember, and your affection for God will increase tenfold. Your mind will no longer be starved, but will be quick and enthusiastic, and your hope will be inexpressibly bright.

Are You Listening to God?

"They said to Moses, 'You speak with us, and we will hear; but let not God speak with us, lest we die'" (Exodus 20:19).

We don't consciously and deliberately disobey God—we simply don't listen to Him. God has given His commands to us, but we pay no attention to them—not because of willful disobedience, but because we do not truly love and respect Him. "If you love Me, keep My commandments" (John 14:15). Once we realize we have constantly been showing disrespect to God, we will be filled with shame and humiliation for ignoring Him.

"You speak with us, . . . but let not God speak with us . . . ." We show how little love we have for God by preferring to listen to His servants rather than to Him. We like to listen to personal testimonies, but we don't want God Himself to speak to us. Why are we so terrified for God to speak to us? It is because we know that when God speaks we must either do what He asks or tell Him we will not obey. But if it is simply one of God's servants speaking to us, we feel obedience is optional, not imperative. We respond by saying, "Well, that's only your own idea, even though I don't deny that what you said is probably God's truth."

Am I constantly humiliating God by ignoring Him, while He lovingly continues to treat me as His child? Once I finally do hear Him, the humiliation I have heaped on Him returns to me. My response then becomes, "Lord, why was I so insensitive and obstinate?" This is always the result once we hear God. But our real delight in finally hearing Him is tempered with the shame we feel for having taken so long to do so.

The Devotion of Hearing

"Samuel answered, 'Speak, for
Your servant hears'"
(1 Samuel 3:10).

Just because I have listened carefully and intently to one thing from God does not mean that I will listen to everything He says. I show God my lack of love and respect for Him by the insensitivity of my heart and mind toward what He says. If I love my friend, I will instinctively understand what he wants. And Jesus said, "You are My friends . . ." (John 15:14). Have I disobeyed some command of my Lord's this week? If I had realized that it was a command of Jesus, I would not have deliberately disobeyed it. But most of us show incredible disrespect to God because we don't even hear Him. He might as well never have spoken to us.

The goal of my spiritual life is such close identification with Jesus Christ that I will always hear God and know that God always hears me (see John 11:41). If I am united with Jesus Christ, I hear God all the time through the devotion of hearing. A flower, a tree, or a servant of God may convey God's message to me. What hinders me from hearing is my attention to other things. It is not that I don't want to hear God, but I am not devoted in the right areas of my life. I am devoted to things and even to service and my own convictions. God may say whatever He wants, but I just don't hear Him. The attitude of a child of God should always be, "Speak, for Your servant hears." If I have not developed and nurtured this devotion of hearing, I can only hear God's voice at certain times. At other times I become deaf to Him because my attention is to other things—things which I think I must do. This is not living the life of a child of God. Have you heard God's voice today?

The Discipline of Hearing

"Whatever I tell you in the dark, speak in the light, and what you hear in the ear, preach on the housetops"
(Matthew 10:27).

Sometimes God puts us through the experience and discipline of darkness to teach us to hear and obey Him. Song birds are taught to sing in the dark, and God puts us into "the shadow of His hand" until we learn to hear Him (Isaiah 49:2). "Whatever I tell you in the dark. . ."—pay attention when God puts you into darkness, and keep your mouth closed while you are there. Are you in the dark right now in your circumstances, or in your life with God? If so, then remain quiet. If you open your mouth in the dark, you will speak while in the wrong mood—darkness is the time to listen. Don't talk to other people about it; don't read books to find out the reason for the darkness; just listen and obey. If you talk to other people, you cannot hear what God is saying. When you are in the dark, listen, and God will give you a very precious message for someone else once you are back in the light.

After every time of darkness, we should experience a mixture of delight and humiliation. If there is only delight, I question whether we have really heard God at all. We should experience delight for having heard God speak, but mostly humiliation for having taken so long to hear Him! Then we will exclaim, "How slow I have been to listen and understand what God has been telling me!" And yet God has been saying it for days and even weeks. But once you hear Him, He gives you the gift of humiliation, which brings a softness of heart—a gift that will always cause you to listen to God *now*.

"Am I My Brother's Keeper?"

"None of us lives to himself . . ." (Romans 14:7).

Has it ever dawned on you that you are responsible spiritually to God for other people? For instance, if I allow any turning away from God in my private life, everyone around me suffers. We "sit *together* in the heavenly places . . ." (Ephesians 2:6). "If one member suffers, all the members suffer with it . . ." (1 Corinthians 12:26). If you allow physical selfishness, mental carelessness, moral insensitivity, or spiritual weakness, everyone in contact with you will suffer. But you ask, "Who is sufficient to be able to live up to such a lofty standard?" "Our sufficiency is from God . . ." and God alone (2 Corinthians 3:5).

"You shall be witnesses to Me . . ." (Acts 1:8). How many of us are willing to spend every bit of our nervous, mental, moral, and spiritual energy for Jesus Christ? That is what God means when He uses the word *witness*. But it takes time, so be patient with yourself. Why has God left us on the earth? Is it simply to be saved and sanctified? No, it is to be at work in service to Him. Am I willing to be broken bread and poured-out wine for Him? Am I willing to be of no value to this age or this life except for one purpose and one alone—to be used to disciple men and women to the Lord Jesus Christ. My life of service to God is the way I say "thank you" to Him for His inexpressibly wonderful salvation. Remember, it is quite possible for God to set any of us aside if we refuse to be of service to Him—". . . lest, when I have preached to others, I myself should become disqualified" (1 Corinthians 9:27).

The Inspiration of Spiritual Initiative

"Arise from the dead . . ."
(Ephesians 5:14).

Not all initiative, the willingness to take the first step, is inspired by God. Someone may say to you, "Get up and get going! Take your reluctance by the throat and throw it overboard—just do what needs to be done!" That is what we mean by ordinary human initiative. But when the Spirit of God comes to us and says, in effect, "Get up and get going," suddenly we find that the initiative is inspired.

We all have many dreams and aspirations when we are young, but sooner or later we realize we have no power to accomplish them. We cannot do the things we long to do, so our tendency is to think of our dreams and aspirations as dead. But God comes and says to us, "Arise from the dead . . . ." When God sends His inspiration, it comes to us with such miraculous power that we are able to "arise from the dead" and do the impossible. The remarkable thing about spiritual initiative is that the life and power comes after we "get up and get going." God does not give us overcoming life—He gives us life *as we overcome*. When the inspiration of God comes, and He says, "Arise from the dead . . . ," we have to get ourselves up; God will not lift us up. Our Lord said to the man with the withered hand, "Stretch out your hand" (Matthew 12:13). As soon as the man did so, his hand was healed. But he had to take the initiative. If we will take the initiative to overcome, we will find that we have the inspiration of God, because He immediately gives us the power of life.

Taking the Initiative Against Depression

"Arise and eat"
(1 Kings 19:5).

The angel in this passage did not give Elijah a vision, or explain the Scriptures to him, or do anything remarkable. He simply told Elijah to do a very ordinary thing, that is, to get up and eat. If we were never depressed, we would not be alive—only material things don't suffer depression. If human beings were not capable of depression, we would have no capacity for happiness and exaltation. There are things in life that are designed to depress us; for example, things that are associated with death. Whenever you examine yourself, always take into account your capacity for depression.

When the Spirit of God comes to us, He does not give us glorious visions, but He tells us to do the most ordinary things imaginable. Depression tends to turn us away from the everyday things of God's creation. But whenever God steps in, His inspiration is to do the most natural, simple things—things we would never have imagined God was in, but as we do them we find Him there. The inspiration that comes to us in this way is an initiative against depression. But we must take the first step and do it in the inspiration of God. If, however, we do something simply to overcome our depression, we will only deepen it. But when the Spirit of God leads us instinctively to do something, the moment we do it the depression is gone. As soon as we arise and obey, we enter a higher plane of life.

Taking the Initiative Against Despair

"Rise, let us be going"
(Matthew 26:46).

In the Garden of Gethsemane, the disciples went to sleep when they should have stayed awake, and once they realized what they had done it produced despair. The sense of having done something irreversible tends to make us despair. We say, "Well, it's all over and ruined now; what's the point in trying anymore." If we think this kind of despair is an exception, we are mistaken. It is a very ordinary human experience. Whenever we realize we have not taken advantage of a magnificent opportunity, we are apt to sink into despair. But Jesus comes and lovingly says to us, in essence, "Sleep on now. That opportunity is lost forever and you can't change that. But get up, and let's go on to the next thing." In other words, let the past sleep, but let it sleep in the sweet embrace of Christ, and let us go on into the invincible future with Him.

There will be experiences like this in each of our lives. We will have times of despair caused by real events in our lives, and we will be unable to lift ourselves out of them. The disciples, in this instance, had done a downright unthinkable thing—they had gone to sleep instead of watching with Jesus. But our Lord came to them taking the spiritual initiative against their despair and said, in effect, "Get up, and do the next thing." If we are inspired by God, what is the next thing? It is to trust Him absolutely and to pray on the basis of His redemption.

Never let the sense of past failure defeat your next step.

Taking the Initiative
Against Drudgery

When it comes to taking the initiative against drudgery, we have to take the first step as though there were no God. There is no point in waiting for God to help us—He will not. But once we arise, immediately we find He is there. Whenever God gives us His inspiration, suddenly taking the initiative becomes a moral issue—a matter of obedience. Then we must act to be obedient and not continue to lie down doing nothing. If we will arise and shine, drudgery will be divinely transformed.

Drudgery is one of the finest tests to determine the genuineness of our character. Drudgery is work that is far removed from anything we think of as ideal work. It is the utterly hard, menial, tiresome, and dirty work. And when we experience it, our spirituality is instantly tested and we will know whether or not we are spiritually genuine. Read John 13. In this chapter, we see the Incarnate God performing the greatest example of drudgery—washing fishermen's feet. He then says to them, "If I then, your Lord and Teacher, have washed your feet, you also ought to wash one another's feet" (John 13:14). The inspiration of God is required if drudgery is to shine with the light of God upon it. In some cases the way a person does a task makes that work sanctified and holy forever. It may be a very common everyday task, but after we have seen it done, it becomes different. When the Lord does something through us, He always transforms it. Our Lord takes our human flesh and transforms it, and now every believer's body has become "the temple of the Holy Spirit" (1 Corinthians 6:19).

Taking the Initiative Against Daydreaming

"Arise, let us go from here" (John 14:31).

Daydreaming about something in order to do it properly is right, but daydreaming about it when we should be doing it is wrong. In this passage, after having said these wonderful things to His disciples, we might have expected our Lord to tell them to go away and meditate over them all. But Jesus never allowed idle daydreaming. When our purpose is to seek God and to discover His will for us, daydreaming is right and acceptable. But when our inclination is to spend time daydreaming over what we have already been told to do, it is unacceptable and God's blessing is never on it. God will take the initiative against this kind of daydreaming by prodding us to action. His instructions to us will be along the lines of this: "Don't sit or stand there, just go!"

If we are quietly waiting before God after He has said to us, "Come aside by yourselves . . ." then that is meditation before Him to seek His will (Mark 6:31). Beware, however, of giving in to mere daydreaming once God has spoken. Allow Him to be the source of all your dreams, joys, and delights, and be careful to go and obey what He has said. If you are in love with someone, you don't sit and daydream about that person all the time—you go and do something for him. That is what Jesus Christ expects us to do. Daydreaming after God has spoken is an indication that we do not trust Him.

Do You Really Love Him?

If what we call love doesn't take us beyond ourselves, it is not really love. If we have the idea that love is characterized as cautious, wise, sensible, shrewd, and never taken to extremes, we have missed the true meaning. This may describe affection and it may bring us a warm feeling, but it is not a true and accurate description of love.

Have you ever been driven to do something for God not because you felt that it was useful or your duty to do so, or that there was anything in it for you, but simply because you love Him? Have you ever realized that you can give things to God that are of value to Him? Or are you just sitting around daydreaming about the greatness of His redemption, while neglecting all the things you could be doing for Him? I'm not referring to works which could be regarded as divine and miraculous, but ordinary, simple human things—things which would be evidence to God that you are totally surrendered to Him. Have you ever created what Mary of Bethany created in the heart of the Lord Jesus? "She has done a good work for Me."

There are times when it seems as if God watches to see if we will give Him even small gifts of surrender, just to show how genuine our love is for Him. To be surrendered to God is of more value than our personal holiness. Concern over our personal holiness causes us to focus our eyes on ourselves, and we become overly concerned about the way we walk and talk and look, out of fear of offending God. ". . . but perfect love casts out fear . . ." once we are surrendered to God (1 John 4:18). We should quit asking ourselves, "Am I of any use?" and accept the truth that we really are not of much use to Him. The issue is never of being of use, but of being of value to God Himself. Once we are totally surrendered to God, He will work through us all the time.

The Discipline of Spiritual Perseverance

"Be still, and know that I am God . . ."
(Psalm 46:10).

Perseverance is more than endurance. It is endurance combined with absolute assurance and certainty that what we are looking for is going to happen. Perseverance means more than just hanging on, which may be only exposing our fear of letting go and falling. Perseverance is our supreme effort of refusing to believe that our hero is going to be conquered. Our greatest fear is not that we will be damned, but that somehow Jesus Christ will be defeated. Also, our fear is that the very things our Lord stood for—love, justice, forgiveness, and kindness among men—will not win out in the end and will represent an unattainable goal for us. Then there is the call to spiritual perseverance. A call not to hang on and do nothing, but to work deliberately, knowing with certainty that God will never be defeated.

If our hopes seem to be experiencing disappointment right now, it simply means that they are being purified. Every hope or dream of the human mind will be fulfilled if it is noble and of God. But one of the greatest stresses in life is the stress of waiting for God. He brings fulfillment, "because you have kept My command to persevere . . ." (Revelation 3:10).

Continue to persevere spiritually.

The Determination to Serve

"The Son of Man did not come to be served, but to serve . . ."
(Matthew 20:28).

Jesus also said, "Yet I am among you as the One who serves" (Luke 22:27). Paul's idea of service was the same as our Lord's—". . . ourselves your bondservants for Jesus' sake" (2 Corinthians 4:5). We somehow have the idea that a person called to the ministry is called to be different and above other people. But according to Jesus Christ, he is called to be a "doormat" for others—called to be their spiritual leader, but never their superior. Paul said, "I know how to be abased . . ." (Philippians 4:12). Paul's idea of service was to pour his life out to the last drop for others. And whether he received praise or blame made no difference. As long as there was one human being who did not know Jesus, Paul felt a debt of service to that person until he did come to know Him. But the chief motivation behind Paul's service was not love for others but love for his Lord. If our devotion is to the cause of humanity, we will be quickly defeated and broken-hearted, since we will often be confronted with a great deal of ingratitude from other people. But if we are motivated by our love for God, no amount of ingratitude will be able to hinder us from serving one another.

Paul's understanding of how Christ had dealt with him is the secret behind his determination to serve others. "I was formerly a blasphemer, a persecutor, and an insolent man . . ." (1 Timothy 1:13). In other words, no matter how badly others may have treated Paul, they could never have treated him with the same degree of spite and hatred with which he had treated Jesus Christ. Once we realize that Jesus has served us even to the depths of our meagerness, our selfishness, and our sin, nothing we encounter from others will be able to exhaust our determination to serve others for His sake.

The Delight of Sacrifice

Once "the love of God has been poured out in our hearts by the Holy Spirit," we deliberately begin to identify ourselves with Jesus Christ's interests and purposes in others' lives (Romans 5:5). And Jesus has an interest in every individual person. We have no right in Christian service to be guided by our own interests and desires. In fact, this is one of the greatest tests of our relationship with Jesus Christ. The delight of sacrifice is that I lay down my life for my Friend, Jesus (see John 15:13). I don't throw my life away, but I willingly and deliberately lay it down for Him and His interests in other people. And I do this for no cause or purpose of my own. Paul spent his life for only one purpose—that he might win people to Jesus Christ. Paul always attracted people to his Lord, but never to himself. He said, "I have become all things to all men, that I might by all means save some" (1 Corinthians 9:22).

When someone thinks that to develop a holy life he must always be alone with God, he is no longer of any use to others. This is like putting himself on a pedestal and isolating himself from the rest of society. Paul was a holy person, but wherever he went Jesus Christ was always allowed to help Himself to his life. Many of us are interested only in our own goals, and Jesus cannot help Himself to our lives. But if we are totally surrendered to Him, we have no goals of our own to serve. Paul said that he knew how to be a "doormat" without resenting it, because the motivation of his life was devotion to Jesus. We tend to be devoted, not to Jesus Christ, but to the things which allow us more spiritual freedom than total surrender to Him would allow. Freedom was not Paul's motive at all. In fact, he stated, "I could wish that I myself were accursed from Christ for my brethren . . ." (Romans 9:3). Had Paul lost his ability to reason? Not at all! For someone who is in love, this is not an overstatement. And Paul was in love with Jesus Christ.

The Destitution of Service

"... though the more abundantly I love you, the less I am loved"
(2 Corinthians 12:15).

Natural human love expects something in return. But Paul is saying, "It doesn't really matter to me whether you love me or not. I am willing to be completely destitute anyway; willing to be poverty-stricken, not just for your sakes, but also that I may be able to get you to God." "For you know the grace of our Lord Jesus Christ, that though He was rich, yet for your sakes He became poor . . ." (2 Corinthians 8:9). And Paul's idea of service was the same as our Lord's. He did not care how high the cost was to himself—he would gladly pay it. It was a joyful thing to Paul.

The institutional church's idea of a servant of God is not at all like Jesus Christ's idea. His idea is that we serve Him by being the servants of others. Jesus Christ actually "out-socialized" the socialists. He said that in His kingdom the greatest one would be the servant of all (see Matthew 23:11). The real test of a saint is not one's willingness to preach the gospel, but one's willingness to do something like washing the disciples' feet—that is, being willing to do those things that seem unimportant in human estimation but count as everything to God. It was Paul's delight to spend his life for God's interests in other people, and he did not care what it cost. But before we will serve, we stop to ponder our personal and financial concerns— "What if God wants me to go over there? And what about my salary? What is the climate like there? Who will take care of me? A person must consider all these things." All that is an indication that we have reservations about serving God. But the apostle Paul had no conditions or reservations. Paul focused his life on Jesus Christ's idea of a New Testament saint; that is, not one who merely proclaims the gospel, but one who becomes broken bread and poured-out wine in the hands of Jesus Christ for the sake of others.

Our Misgivings About Jesus

"The woman said to Him, 'Sir, You have nothing to draw [water] with, and the well is deep' " (John 4:11).

Have you ever said to yourself, "I am impressed with the wonderful truths of God's Word, but He can't really expect me to live up to that and work all those details into my life!" When it comes to confronting Jesus Christ on the basis of His qualities and abilities, our attitudes reflect religious superiority. We think His ideals are lofty and they impress us, but we believe He is not in touch with reality—that what He says cannot actually be done. Each of us thinks this about Jesus in one area of our life or another. These doubts or misgivings about Jesus begin as we consider questions that divert our focus away from God. While we talk of our dealings with Him, others ask us, "Where are you going to get enough money to live? How will you live and who will take care of you?" Or our misgivings begin within ourselves when we tell Jesus that our circumstances are just a little too difficult for Him. We say, "It's easy to say, 'Trust in the Lord,' but a person has to live; and besides, Jesus has nothing with which to draw water—no means to be able to give us these things." And beware of exhibiting religious deceit by saying, "Oh, I have no misgivings about Jesus, only misgivings about myself." If we are honest, we will admit that we never have misgivings or doubts about ourselves, because we know exactly what we are capable or incapable of doing. But we do have misgivings about Jesus. And our pride is hurt even at the thought that He can do what we can't.

My misgivings arise from the fact that I search within to find how He will do what He says. My doubts spring from the depths of my own inferiority. If I detect these misgivings in myself, I should bring them into the light and confess them openly—"Lord, I have had misgivings about You. I have not believed in Your abilities, but only my own. And I have not believed in Your almighty power apart from my finite understanding of it."

The Impoverished Ministry of Jesus

"Where then do You get that living water?"
(John 4:11).

"The well is deep"—and even a great deal deeper than the Samaritan woman knew! (4:11). Think of the depths of human nature and human life; think of the depth of the "wells" in you. Have you been limiting, or impoverishing, the ministry of Jesus to the point that He is unable to work in your life? Suppose that you have a deep "well" of hurt and trouble inside your heart, and Jesus comes and says to you, "Let not your heart be troubled . . ." (John 14:1). Would your response be to shrug your shoulders and say, "But, Lord, the well is too deep, and even You can't draw up quietness and comfort out of it." Actually, that is correct. Jesus doesn't bring anything up from the wells of human nature—He brings them down from above. We limit the Holy One of Israel by remembering only what we have allowed Him to do for us in the past, and also by saying, "Of course, I cannot expect God to do this particular thing." The thing that approaches the very limits of His power is the very thing we as disciples of Jesus ought to believe He will do. We impoverish and weaken His ministry in us the moment we forget He is almighty. The impoverishment is in us, not in Him. We will come to Jesus for Him to be our comforter or our sympathizer, but we refrain from approaching Him as our Almighty God.

The reason some of us are such poor examples of Christianity is that we have failed to recognize that Christ is almighty. We have Christian attributes and experiences, but there is no abandonment or surrender to Jesus Christ. When we get into difficult circumstances, we impoverish His ministry by saying, "Of course, He can't do anything about this." We struggle to reach the bottom of our own well, trying to get water for ourselves. Beware of sitting back, and saying, "It can't be done." You will know it can be done if you will look to Jesus. The well of your incompleteness runs deep, but make the effort to look away from yourself and to look toward Him.

"Do You Now Believe?"

" 'By this we believe . . . .'
Jesus answered them, 'Do
you now believe?' "
(John 16:30–31).

Now we believe. . . ." But Jesus asks, "Do you . . . ? Indeed the hour is coming . . . that you . . . will leave Me alone" (16:31–32). Many Christian workers have left Jesus Christ alone and yet tried to serve Him out of a sense of duty, or because they sense a need as a result of their own discernment. The reason for this is actually the absence of the resurrection life of Jesus. Our soul has gotten out of intimate contact with God by leaning on our own religious understanding (see Proverbs 3:5–6). This is not deliberate sin and there is no punishment attached to it. But once a person realizes how he has hindered his understanding of Jesus Christ, and caused uncertainties, sorrows, and difficulties for himself, it is with shame and remorse that he has to return.

We need to rely on the resurrection life of Jesus on a much deeper level than we do now. We should get in the habit of continually seeking His counsel on everything, instead of making our own commonsense decisions and then asking Him to bless them. He cannot bless them; it is not in His realm to do so, and those decisions are severed from reality. If we do something simply out of a sense of duty, we are trying to live up to a standard that competes with Jesus Christ. We become a prideful, arrogant person, thinking we know what to do in every situation. We have put our sense of duty on the throne of our life, instead of enthroning the resurrection life of Jesus. We are not told to "walk in the light" of our conscience or in the light of a sense of duty, but to "walk in the light *as He is in the light . . .*" (1 John 1:7). When we do something out of a sense of duty, it is easy to explain the reasons for our actions to others. But when we do something out of obedience to the Lord, there can be no other explanation—just obedience. That is why a saint can be so easily ridiculed and misunderstood.

What Do You Want the Lord To Do for You?

" 'What do you want Me to do for you?' He said, 'Lord, that I may receive my sight' " (Luke 18:41).

Is there something in your life that not only disturbs you, but makes you a disturbance to others? If so, it is always something you cannot handle yourself. "Then those who went before warned him that he should be quiet; but he cried out all the more . . ." (18:39). Be persistent with your disturbance until you get face to face with the Lord Himself. Don't deify common sense. To sit calmly by, instead of creating a disturbance, serves only to deify our common sense. When Jesus asks what we want Him to do for us about the incredible problem that is confronting us, remember that He doesn't work in common-sense ways, but only in supernatural ways.

Look at how we limit the Lord by only remembering what we have allowed Him to do for us in the past. We say, "I always failed there, and I always will." Consequently, we don't ask for what we want. Instead, we think, "It is ridiculous to ask God to do this." If it is an impossibility, it is the very thing for which we have to ask. If it is not an impossible thing, it is not a real disturbance. And God will do what is absolutely impossible.

This man received his sight. But the most impossible thing for you is to be so closely identified with the Lord that there is literally nothing of your old life remaining. God will do it if you will ask Him. But you have to come to the point of believing Him to be almighty. We find faith by not only believing what Jesus says, but, even more, by trusting Jesus Himself. If we only look at what He says, we will never believe. Once we see Jesus, the impossible things He does in our lives become as natural as breathing. The agony we suffer is only the result of the deliberate shallowness of our own heart. We *won't* believe; we *won't* let go by severing the line that secures the boat to the shore—we prefer to worry.

The Piercing Question   "Do you love Me?"
(John 21:17).

Peter's response to this piercing question is considerably different from the bold defiance he exhibited only a few days before when he declared, "Even if I have to die with You, I will not deny You!" (Matthew 26:35; also see verses 33–34). Our natural individuality, or our natural self, boldly speaks out and declares its feelings. But the true love within our inner spiritual self can be discovered only by experiencing the hurt of this question of Jesus Christ. Peter loved Jesus in the way any natural man loves a good person. Yet that is nothing but emotional love. It may reach deeply into our natural self, but it never penetrates to the spirit of a person. True love never simply declares itself. Jesus said, "Whoever *confesses* Me before men [that is, confesses his love by everything he does, not merely by his words], him the Son of Man also will confess before the angels of God" (Luke 12:8).

Unless we are experiencing the hurt of facing every deception about ourselves, we have hindered the work of the Word of God in our lives. The Word of God inflicts hurt on us more than sin ever could, because sin dulls our senses. But this question of the Lord intensifies our sensitivities to the point that this hurt produced by Jesus is the most exquisite pain conceivable. It hurts not only on the natural level, but also on the deeper spiritual level. "For the Word of God is living and powerful . . . , piercing even to the division of soul and spirit . . ."—to the point that no deception can remain (Hebrews 4:12). When the Lord asks us this question, it is impossible to think and respond properly, because when the Lord speaks directly to us, the pain is too intense. It causes such a tremendous hurt that any part of our life which may be out of line with His will can feel the pain. There is never any mistaking the pain of the Lord's Word by His children, but the moment that pain is felt is the very moment at which God reveals His truth to us.

Have You Felt the Pain Inflicted by the Lord?

"He said to him the third time, '. . . do you love Me?' "
(John 21:17).

Have you ever felt the pain, inflicted by the Lord, at the very center of your being, deep down in the most sensitive area of your life? The devil never inflicts pain there, and neither can sin nor human emotions. Nothing can cut through to that part of our being but the Word of God. "Peter was grieved because He said to him the third time, 'Do you love Me?' " Yet he was awakened to the fact that at the center of his personal life he was devoted to Jesus. And then he began to see what Jesus' patient questioning meant. There was not the slightest bit of doubt left in Peter's mind; he could never be deceived again. And there was no need for an impassioned response; no need for immediate action or an emotional display. It was a revelation to him to realize how much he did love the Lord, and with amazement he simply said, "Lord, You know all things . . . ." Peter began to see how very much he did love Jesus, and there was no need to say, "Look at this or that as proof of my love." Peter was beginning to discover within himself just how much he really did love the Lord. He discovered that his eyes were so fixed on Jesus Christ that he saw no one else in heaven above or on the earth below. But he did not know it until the probing, hurting questions of the Lord were asked. The Lord's questions always reveal the true me to myself.

Oh, the wonder of the patient directness and skill of Jesus Christ with Peter! Our Lord never asks questions until the perfect time. Rarely, but probably once in each of our lives, He will back us into a corner where He will hurt us with His piercing questions. Then we will realize that we do love Him far more deeply than our words can ever say.

This is love in the making. The love of God is not created—it is His nature. When we receive the life of Christ through the Holy Spirit, He unites us with God so that His love is demonstrated in us. The goal of the indwelling Holy Spirit is not just to unite us with God, but to do it in such a way that we will be one with the Father in exactly the same way Jesus was. And what kind of oneness did Jesus Christ have with the Father? He had such a oneness with the Father that He was obedient when His Father sent Him down here to be poured out for us. And He says to us, "As the Father has sent Me, I also send you" (John 20:21).

Peter now realizes that he does love Him, due to the revelation that came with the Lord's piercing question. The Lord's next point is—"Pour yourself out. Don't testify about how much you love Me and don't talk about the wonderful revelation you have had, just 'Feed My sheep.'" Jesus has some extraordinarily peculiar sheep: some that are unkempt and dirty, some that are awkward or pushy, and some that have gone astray! But it is impossible to exhaust God's love, and it is impossible to exhaust my love if it flows from the Spirit of God within me. The love of God pays no attention to my prejudices caused by my natural individuality. If I love my Lord, I have no business being guided by natural emotions—I have to feed His sheep. We will not be delivered or released from His commission to us. Beware of counterfeiting the love of God by following your own natural human emotions, sympathies, or understandings. That will only serve to revile and abuse the true love of God.

Is This True of Me?

It is easier to serve or work for God without a vision and without a call, because then you are not bothered by what He requires. Common sense, covered with a layer of Christian emotion, becomes your guide. You may be more prosperous and successful from the world's perspective, and will have more leisure time, if you never acknowledge the call of God. But once you receive a commission from Jesus Christ, the memory of what God asks of you will always be there to prod you on to do His will. You will no longer be able to work for Him on the basis of common sense.

What do I count in my life as "dear to myself"? If I have not been seized by Jesus Christ and have not surrendered myself to Him, I will consider the time I decide to give God and my own ideas of service as dear. I will also consider my own life as "dear to myself." But Paul said he considered his life dear so that he might fulfill the ministry he had received, and he refused to use his energy on anything else. This verse shows an almost noble annoyance by Paul at being asked to consider himself. He was absolutely indifferent to any consideration other than that of fulfilling the ministry he had received. Our ordinary and reasonable service to God may actually compete against our total surrender to Him. Our reasonable work is based on the following argument which we say to ourselves, "Remember how useful you are here, and think how much value you would be in that particular type of work." That attitude chooses our own judgment, instead of Jesus Christ, to be our guide as to where we should go and where we could be used the most. Never consider whether or not you are of use— but always consider that "you are not your own" (1 Corinthians 6:19). You are His.

Is He Really My Lord?

Joy comes from seeing the complete fulfillment of the specific purpose for which I was created and born again, not from successfully doing something of my own choosing. The joy our Lord experienced came from doing what the Father sent Him to do. And He says to us, "As the Father has sent Me, I also send you" (John 20:21). Have you received a ministry from the Lord? If so, you must be faithful to it—to consider your life valuable only for the purpose of fulfilling that ministry. Knowing that you have done what Jesus sent you to do, think how satisfying it will be to hear Him say to you, "Well done, good and faithful servant" (Matthew 25:21). We each have to find a niche in life, and spiritually we find it when we receive a ministry from the Lord. To do this we must have close fellowship with Jesus and must know Him as more than our personal Savior. And we must be willing to experience the full impact of Acts 9:16—"I will show him how many things he must suffer for My name's sake."

"Do you love Me?" Then, "Feed My sheep" (John 21:17). He is not offering us a choice of how we can serve Him; He is asking for absolute loyalty to His commission, a faithfulness to what we discern when we are in the closest possible fellowship with God. If you have received a ministry from the Lord Jesus, you will know that the need is not the same as the call—the need is the opportunity to exercise the call. The call is to be faithful to the ministry you received when you were in true fellowship with Him. This does not imply that there is a whole series of differing ministries marked out for you. It does mean that you must be sensitive to what God has called you to do, and this may sometimes require ignoring demands for service in other areas.

Taking the Next Step

". . . in much patience, in tribulations, in needs, in distresses" (2 Corinthians 6:4).

When you have no vision from God, no enthusiasm left in your life, and no one watching and encouraging you, it requires the grace of Almighty God to take the next step in your devotion to Him, in the reading and studying of His Word, in your family life, or in your duty to Him. It takes much more of the grace of God, and a much greater awareness of drawing upon Him, to take that next step, than it does to preach the gospel.

Every Christian must experience the essence of the incarnation by bringing the next step down into flesh-and-blood reality and by working it out with his hands. We lose interest and give up when we have no vision, no encouragement, and no improvement, but only experience our everyday life with its trivial tasks. The thing that really testifies for God and for the people of God in the long run is steady perseverance, even when the work cannot be seen by others. And the only way to live an undefeated life is to live looking to God. Ask God to keep the eyes of your spirit open to the risen Christ, and it will be impossible for drudgery to discourage you. Never allow yourself to think that some tasks are beneath your dignity or too insignificant for you to do, and remind yourself of the example of Christ in John 13:1–17.

The Source of Abundant Joy

"In all these things we are more than conquerors through Him who loved us" (Romans 8:37).

Paul was speaking here of the things that might seem likely to separate a saint from the love of God. But the remarkable thing is that *nothing* can come between the love of God and a saint. The things Paul mentioned in this passage can and do disrupt the close fellowship of our soul with God and separate our natural life from Him. But none of them is able to come between the love of God and the soul of a saint on the spiritual level. The underlying foundation of the Christian faith is the undeserved, limitless miracle of the love of God that was exhibited on the Cross of Calvary; a love that is not earned and can never be. Paul said this is the reason that "in all these things we are more than conquerors." We are super-victors with a joy that comes from experiencing the very things which look as if they are going to overwhelm us.

Huge waves that would frighten an ordinary swimmer produce a tremendous thrill for the surfer who has ridden them. Let's apply that to our own circumstances. The things we try to avoid and fight against—tribulation, suffering, and persecution—are the very things that produce abundant joy in us. "We are more than conquerors through Him" "*in* all these things"; not in spite of them, but in the midst of them. A saint doesn't know the joy of the Lord in spite of tribulation, but *because* of it. Paul said, "I am exceedingly joyful in all our tribulation" (2 Corinthians 7:4).

The undiminished radiance, which is the result of abundant joy, is not built on anything passing, but on the love of God that nothing can change. And the experiences of life, whether they are everyday events or terrifying ones, are powerless to "separate us from the love of God which is in Christ Jesus our Lord" (Romans 8:39).

To become one with Jesus Christ, a person must be willing not only to give up sin, but also to surrender his whole way of looking at things. Being born again by the Spirit of God means that we must first be willing to let go before we can grasp something else. The first thing we must surrender is all of our pretense or deceit. What our Lord wants us to present to Him is not our goodness, honesty, or our efforts to do better, but real solid sin. Actually, that is all He can take from us. And what He gives us in exchange for our sin is real solid righteousness. But we must surrender all pretense that we are anything, and give up all our claims of even being worthy of God's consideration.

Once we have done that, the Spirit of God will show us what we need to surrender next. Along each step of this process, we will have to give up our claims to our rights to ourselves. Are we willing to surrender our grasp on all that we possess, our desires, and everything else in our lives? Are we ready to be identified with the death of Jesus Christ?

We will suffer a sharp painful disillusionment before we fully surrender. When people really see themselves as the Lord sees them, it is not the terribly offensive sins of the flesh that shock them, but the awful nature of the pride of their own hearts opposing Jesus Christ. When they see themselves in the light of the Lord, the shame, horror, and desperate conviction hit home for them.

If you are faced with the question of whether or not to surrender, make a determination to go on through the crisis, surrendering all that you have and all that you are to Him. And God will then equip you to do all that He requires of you.

Turning Back or
Walking with Jesus?

"Do you also want to go
away?"
(John 6:67).

What a penetrating question! Our Lord's words often hit home
for us when He speaks in the simplest way. In spite of the fact
that we know who Jesus is, He asks, "Do you also want to go
away?" We must continually maintain an adventurous attitude
toward Him, despite any potential personal risk.

"From that time many of His disciples went back and
walked with Him no more" (6:66). They turned back from
walking with Jesus; not into sin, but away from Him. Many
people today are pouring their lives out and working for Jesus
Christ, but are not really walking with Him. One thing God
constantly requires of us is a oneness with Jesus Christ. After
being set apart through sanctification, we should discipline our
lives spiritually to maintain this intimate oneness. When God
gives you a clear determination of His will for you, all your
striving to maintain that relationship by some particular
method is completely unnecessary. All that is required is to live
a natural life of absolute dependence on Jesus Christ. Never try
to live your life with God in any other way than His way. And
His way means absolute devotion to Him. Showing no concern
for the uncertainties that lie ahead is the secret of walking with
Jesus.

Peter saw in Jesus only someone who could minister salvation to him and to the world. But our Lord wants us to be fellow laborers with Him.

In verse 70 Jesus lovingly reminded Peter that he was chosen to go with Him. And each of us must answer this question
for ourselves and no one else: "Do you also want to go away?"

March 9

Being an Example of His Message

"Preach the word!"
(2 Timothy 4:2).

We are not saved only to be instruments for God, but to be His sons and daughters. He does not turn us into spiritual agents but into spiritual messengers, and the message must be a part of us. The Son of God was His own message—"The words that I speak to you are spirit, and they are life" (John 6:63). As His disciples, our lives must be a holy example of the reality of our message. Even the natural heart of the unsaved will serve if called upon to do so, but it takes a heart broken by conviction of sin, baptized by the Holy Spirit, and crushed into submission to God's purpose to make a person's life a holy example of God's message.

There is a difference between giving a testimony and preaching. A preacher is someone who has received the call of God and is determined to use all his energy to proclaim God's truth. God takes us beyond our own aspirations and ideas for our lives, and molds and shapes us for His purpose, just as He worked in the disciples' lives after Pentecost. The purpose of Pentecost was not to teach the disciples something, but to make them the incarnation of what they preached so that they would literally become God's message in the flesh. ". . . you shall be witnesses to Me . . ." (Acts 1:8).

Allow God to have complete liberty in your life when you speak. Before God's message can liberate other people, His liberation must first be real in you. Gather your material carefully, and then allow God to "set your words on fire" for His glory.

March 10

Obedience to the
"Heavenly Vision"

"I was not disobedient to the
heavenly vision"
(Acts 26:19).

If we lose "the heavenly vision" God has given us, we alone are responsible—not God. We lose the vision because of our own lack of spiritual growth. If we do not apply our beliefs about God to the issues of everyday life, the vision God has given us will never be fulfilled. The only way to be obedient to "the heavenly vision" is to give our utmost for His highest—our best for His glory. This can be accomplished only when we make a determination to continually remember God's vision. But the acid test is obedience to the vision in the details of our everyday life—sixty seconds out of every minute, and sixty minutes out of every hour, not just during times of personal prayer or public meetings.

"Though it tarries, wait for it . . ." (Habakkuk 2:3). We cannot bring the vision to fulfillment through our own efforts, but must live under its inspiration until it fulfills itself. We try to be so practical that we forget the vision. At the very beginning we saw the vision but did not wait for it. We rushed off to do our practical work, and once the vision was fulfilled we could no longer even see it. Waiting for a vision that "tarries" is the true test of our faithfulness to God. It is at the risk of our own soul's welfare that we get caught up in practical busy-work, only to miss the fulfillment of the vision.

Watch for the storms of God. The only way God plants His saints is through the whirlwind of His storms. Will you be proven to be an empty pod with no seed inside? That will depend on whether or not you are actually living in the light of the vision you have seen. Let God send you out through His storm, and don't go until He does. If you select your own spot to be planted, you will prove yourself to be an unproductive, empty pod. However, if you allow God to plant you, you will "bear much fruit" (John 15:8).

It is essential that we live and "walk in the light" of God's vision for us (1 John 1:7).

Total Surrender

"Peter began to say to Him,
'See, we have left all and
followed You' "
(Mark 10:28).

Our Lord replies to this statement of Peter by saying that this surrender is "for My sake and the gospel's" (10:29). It was not for the purpose of what the disciples themselves would get out of it. Beware of surrender that is motivated by personal benefits that may result. For example, "I'm going to give myself to God because I want to be delivered from sin, because I want to be made holy." Being delivered from sin and being made holy are the result of being right with God, but surrender resulting from this kind of thinking is certainly not the true nature of Christianity. Our motive for surrender should not be for any personal gain at all. We have become so self-centered that we go to God only for something from Him, and not for God Himself. It is like saying, "No, Lord, I don't want you; I want myself. But I do want You to clean me and fill me with Your Holy Spirit. I want to be on display in Your showcase so I can say, 'This is what God has done for me.' " Gaining heaven, being delivered from sin, and being made useful to God are things that should never even be a consideration in real surrender. Genuine total surrender is a personal sovereign preference for Jesus Christ Himself.

Where does Jesus Christ figure in when we have a concern about our natural relationships? Most of us will desert Him with this excuse—"Yes, Lord, I heard you call me, but my family needs me and I have my own interests. I just can't go any further" (see Luke 9:57–62). "Then," Jesus says, "you 'cannot be My disciple' " (see Luke 14:26–33).

True surrender will always go beyond natural devotion. If we will only give up, God will surrender Himself to embrace all those around us and will meet their needs, which were created by our surrender. Beware of stopping anywhere short of total surrender to God. Most of us have only a vision of what this really means, but have never truly experienced it.

God's Total Surrender to Us

"For God so loved the world that He gave . . ."
(John 3:16).

Salvation does not mean merely deliverance from sin or the experience of personal holiness. The salvation which comes from God means being completely delivered from myself, and being placed into perfect union with Him. When I think of my salvation experience, I think of being delivered from sin and gaining personal holiness. But salvation is so much more! It means that the Spirit of God has brought me into intimate contact with the true Person of God Himself. And as I am caught up into total surrender to God, I become thrilled with something infinitely greater than myself.

To say that we are called to preach holiness or sanctification is to miss the main point. We are called to proclaim Jesus Christ (see 1 Corinthians 2:2). The fact that He saves from sin and makes us holy is actually part of the effect of His wonderful and total surrender to us.

If we are truly surrendered, we will never be aware of our own efforts to remain surrendered. Our entire life will be consumed with the One to whom we surrender. Beware of talking about surrender if you know nothing about it. In fact, you will never know anything about it until you understand that John 3:16 means that God completely and absolutely gave Himself to us. In our surrender, we must give ourselves to God in the same way He gave Himself for us—totally, unconditionally, and without reservation. The consequences and circumstances resulting from our surrender will never even enter our mind, because our life will be totally consumed with Him.

Yielding

The first thing I must be willing to admit when I begin to examine what controls and dominates me is that I am the one responsible for having yielded myself to whatever it may be. If I am a slave to myself, I am to blame because somewhere in the past I yielded to myself. Likewise, if I obey God I do so because at some point in my life I yielded myself to Him.

If a child gives in to selfishness, he will find it to be the most enslaving tyranny on earth. There is no power within the human soul itself that is capable of breaking the bondage of the nature created by yielding. For example, yield for one second to anything in the nature of lust, and although you may hate yourself for having yielded, you become enslaved to that thing. (Remember what lust is—"I must have it now," whether it is the lust of the flesh or the lust of the mind.) No release or escape from it will ever come from any human power, but only through the power of redemption. You must yield yourself in utter humiliation to the only One who can break the dominating power in your life, namely, the Lord Jesus Christ. ". . . He has anointed Me . . . to proclaim liberty to the captives . . ." (Luke 4:18 and Isaiah 61:1).

When you yield to something, you will soon realize the tremendous control it has over you. Even though you say, "Oh, I can give up that habit whenever I like," you will know you can't. You will find that the habit absolutely dominates you because you willingly yielded to it. It is easy to sing, "He will break every fetter," while at the same time living a life of obvious slavery to yourself. But yielding to Jesus will break every kind of slavery in any person's life.

The Discipline of Dismay

"As they followed they were afraid" (Mark 10:32).

At the beginning of our life with Jesus Christ, we were sure we knew all there was to know about following Him. It was a delight to forsake everything else and to throw ourselves before Him in a fearless statement of love. But now we are not quite so sure. Jesus is far ahead of us and is beginning to seem different and unfamiliar—"Jesus was going before them; and they were amazed" (10:32).

There is an aspect of Jesus that chills even a disciple's heart to its depth and makes his entire spiritual life gasp for air. This unusual Person with His face set "like a flint" (Isaiah 50:7) is walking with great determination ahead of me, and He strikes terror right through me. He no longer seems to be my Counselor and Friend and has a point of view about which I know nothing. All I can do is stand and stare at Him in amazement. At first I was confident that I understood Him, but now I am not so sure. I begin to realize that there is a distance between Jesus and me and I can no longer be intimate with Him. I have no idea where He is going, and the goal has become strangely distant.

Jesus Christ had to understand fully every sin and sorrow that human beings could experience, and that is what makes Him seem unfamiliar. When we see this aspect of Him, we realize we really don't know Him. We don't recognize even one characteristic of His life, and we don't know how to begin to follow Him. He is far ahead of us, a Leader who seems totally unfamiliar, and we have no friendship with Him.

The discipline of dismay is an essential lesson which a disciple must learn. The danger is that we tend to look back on our times of obedience and on our past sacrifices to God in an effort to keep our enthusiasm for Him strong (see Isaiah 1:10–11). But when the darkness of dismay comes, endure until it is over, because out of it will come the ability to follow Jesus truly, which brings inexpressibly wonderful joy.

The Master Will Judge

"We must all appear before the judgment seat of Christ . . ."
(2 Corinthians 5:10).

Paul says that we must all, preachers and other people alike, "appear before the judgment seat of Christ." But if you will learn here and now to live under the scrutiny of Christ's pure light, your final judgment will bring you only delight in seeing the work God has done in you. Live constantly reminding yourself of the judgment seat of Christ, and walk in the knowledge of the holiness He has given you. Tolerating a wrong attitude toward another person causes you to follow the spirit of the devil, no matter how saintly you are. One carnal judgment of another person only serves the purposes of hell in you. Bring it immediately into the light and confess, "Oh, Lord, I have been guilty there." If you don't, your heart will become hardened through and through. One of the penalties of sin is our acceptance of it. It is not only God who punishes for sin, but sin establishes itself in the sinner and takes its toll. No struggling or praying will enable you to stop doing certain things, and the penalty of sin is that you gradually get used to it, until you finally come to the place where you no longer even realize that it is sin. No power, except the power that comes from being filled with the Holy Spirit, can change or prevent the inherent consequences of sin.

"If we walk in the light *as He is in the light . . .*" (1 John 1:7). For many of us, walking in the light means walking according to the standard we have set up for another person. The deadliest attitude of the Pharisees that we exhibit today is not hypocrisy but that which comes from unconsciously living a lie.

March 16

"We make it our aim . . . to be well pleasing to Him" (2 Corinthians 5:9).

"We make it our aim . . . ." It requires a conscious decision and effort to keep our primary goal constantly in front of us. It means holding ourselves to the highest priority year in and year out; not making our first priority to win souls, or to establish churches, or to have revivals, but seeking only "to be well pleasing to Him." It is not a lack of spiritual experience that leads to failure, but a lack of working to keep our eyes focused and on the right goal. At least once a week examine yourself before God to see if your life is measuring up to the standard He has for you. Paul was like a musician who gives no thought to audience approval, if he can only catch a look of approval from his Conductor.

Any goal we have that diverts us even to the slightest degree from the central goal of being "approved to God" (2 Timothy 2:15) may result in our rejection from further service for Him. When you discern where the goal leads, you will understand why it is so necessary to keep "looking unto Jesus" (Hebrews 12:2). Paul spoke of the importance of controlling his own body so that it would not take him in the wrong direction. He said, "I discipline my body and bring it into subjection, lest . . . I myself should become disqualified" (1 Corinthians 9:27).

I must learn to relate everything to the primary goal, maintaining it without interruption. My worth to God publicly is measured by what I really am in my private life. Is my primary goal in life to please Him and to be acceptable to Him, or is it something less, no matter how lofty it may sound?

Will I Bring Myself Up to This Level?

"... perfecting holiness in the fear of God" (2 Corinthians 7:1).

"Therefore, having these promises . . . ." I claim God's promises for my life and look to their fulfillment, and rightly so, but that shows only the human perspective on them. God's perspective is that through His promises I will come to recognize His claim of ownership on me. For example, do I realize that my "body is the temple of the Holy Spirit," or am I condoning some habit in my body which clearly could not withstand the light of God on it? (1 Corinthians 6:19). God formed His Son in me through sanctification, setting me apart from sin and making me holy in His sight (see Galatians 4:19). But I must begin to transform my natural life into spiritual life by obedience to Him. God instructs us even in the smallest details of life. And when He brings you conviction of sin, do not "confer with flesh and blood," but cleanse yourself from it at once (Galatians 1:16). Keep yourself cleansed in your daily walk.

I must cleanse myself from all filthiness in my flesh and my spirit until both are in harmony with the nature of God. Is the mind of my spirit in perfect agreement with the life of the Son of God in me, or am I mentally rebellious and defiant? Am I allowing the mind of Christ to be formed in me? (see Philippians 2:5). Christ never spoke of His right to Himself, but always maintained an inner vigilance to submit His spirit continually to His Father. I also have the responsibility to keep my spirit in agreement with His Spirit. And when I do, Jesus gradually lifts me up to the level where He lived—a level of perfect submission to His Father's will—where I pay no attention to anything else. Am I perfecting this kind of holiness in the fear of God? Is God having His way with me, and are people beginning to see God in my life more and more?

Be serious in your commitment to God and gladly leave everything else alone. Literally put God first in your life.

Abraham's Life of Faith   "He went out, not knowing
                                      where he was going"
                                     (Hebrews 11:8).

In the Old Testament, a person's relationship with God was
seen by the degree of separation in that person's life. This separation is exhibited in the life of Abraham by his separation
from his country and his family. When we think of separation
today, we do not mean to be literally separated from those family members who do not have a personal relationship with God,
but to be separated mentally and morally from their viewpoints. This is what Jesus Christ was referring to in Luke 14:26.

Living a life of faith means never knowing where you are
being led. But it does mean loving and knowing the One who is
leading. It is literally a life of *faith*, not of understanding and
reason—a life of knowing Him who calls us to go. Faith is rooted in the knowledge of a Person, and one of the biggest traps
we fall into is the belief that if we have faith, God will surely
lead us to success in the world.

The final stage in the life of faith is the attainment of character, and we encounter many changes in the process. We feel
the presence of God around us when we pray, yet we are only
momentarily changed. We tend to keep going back to our everyday ways and the glory vanishes. A life of faith is not a life of
one glorious mountaintop experience after another, like soaring
on eagles' wings, but is a life of day-in and day-out consistency;
a life of walking without fainting (see Isaiah 40:31). It is not
even a question of the holiness of sanctification, but of something which comes much farther down the road. It is a faith that
has been tried and proved and has withstood the test. Abraham
is not a type or an example of the holiness of sanctification, but
a type of the life of faith—a faith, tested and true, built on the
true God. "*Abraham believed God . . .*" (Romans 4:3).

"Shall I hide from Abraham
what I am doing . . . ?"
(Genesis 18:17).

The Delights of His Friendship. Genesis 18 brings out the delight of true friendship with God, as compared with simply feeling His presence occasionally in prayer. This friendship means being so intimately in touch with God that you never even need to ask Him to show you His will. It is evidence of a level of intimacy which confirms that you are nearing the final stage of your discipline in the life of faith. When you have a right-standing relationship with God, you have a life of freedom, liberty, and delight; you *are* God's will. And all of your commonsense decisions are actually His will for you, unless you sense a feeling of restraint brought on by a check in your spirit. You are free to make decisions in the light of a perfect and delightful friendship with God, knowing that if your decisions are wrong He will lovingly produce that sense of restraint. Once he does, you must stop immediately.

The Difficulties of His Friendship. Why did Abraham stop praying when he did? He stopped because he still was lacking the level of intimacy in his relationship with God, which would enable him boldly to continue on with the Lord in prayer until his desire was granted. Whenever we stop short of our true desire in prayer and say, "Well, I don't know, maybe this is not God's will," then we still have another level to go. It shows that we are not as intimately acquainted with God as Jesus was, and as Jesus would have us to be—". . . that they may be one just as We are one . . ." (John 17:22). Think of the last thing you prayed about— were you devoted to your desire or to God? Was your determination to get some gift of the Spirit for yourself or to get to God? "For your Father knows the things you have need of before you ask Him" (Matthew 6:8). The reason for asking is so you may get to know God better. "Delight yourself also in the LORD, and He shall give you the desires of your heart" (Psalm 37:4). We should keep praying to get a perfect understanding of God Himself.

Identified or Simply Interested?

> "I have been crucified with Christ . . ."
> (Galatians 2:20).

The inescapable spiritual need each of us has is the need to sign the death certificate of our sin nature. I must take my emotional opinions and intellectual beliefs and be willing to turn them into a moral verdict against the nature of sin; that is, against any claim I have to my right to myself. Paul said, "I have been crucified with Christ . . . ." He did not say, "I have made a determination to imitate Jesus Christ," or, "I will really make an effort to follow Him"—but—"I have been *identified* with Him in His death." Once I reach this moral decision and act on it, all that Christ accomplished *for* me on the Cross is accomplished *in* me. My unrestrained commitment of myself to God gives the Holy Spirit the opportunity to grant to me the holiness of Jesus Christ.

"... it is no longer I who live . . . ." My individuality remains, but my primary motivation for living and the nature that rules me are radically changed. I have the same human body, but the old satanic right to myself has been destroyed.

"... and the life which I now live in the flesh," not the life which I long to live or even pray that I live, but the life I now live in my mortal flesh—the life which others can see, "I live by faith in the Son of God . . . ." This faith was not Paul's own faith in Jesus Christ, but the faith in the Son God had given to him (see Ephesians 2:8). It is no longer a faith in faith, but a faith that transcends all imaginable limits—a faith that comes only from the Son of God.

The Burning Heart

"Did not our heart burn within us . . . ?" (Luke 24:32).

We need to learn this secret of the burning heart. Suddenly Jesus appears to us, fires are set ablaze, and we are given wonderful visions; but then we must learn to maintain the secret of the burning heart—a heart that can go through anything. It is the simple, dreary day, with its commonplace duties and people, that smothers the burning heart—unless we have learned the secret of abiding in Jesus.

Much of the distress we experience as Christians comes not as the result of sin, but because we are ignorant of the laws of our own nature. For instance, the only test we should use to determine whether or not to allow a particular emotion to run its course in our lives is to examine what the final outcome of that emotion will be. Think it through to its logical conclusion, and if the outcome is something that God would condemn, put a stop to it immediately. But if it is an emotion that has been kindled by the Spirit of God and you don't allow it to have its way in your life, it will cause a reaction on a lower level than God intended. That is the way unrealistic and overly emotional people are made. And the higher the emotion, the deeper the level of corruption, if it is not exercised on its intended level. If the Spirit of God has stirred you, make as many of your decisions as possible irrevocable, and let the consequences be what they will. We cannot stay forever on the "mount of transfiguration," basking in the light of our mountaintop experience (see Mark 9:1–9). But we must obey the light we received there; we must put it into action. When God gives us a vision, we must transact business with Him at that point, no matter what the cost.

> We cannot kindle when we will
>> The fire which in the heart resides,
> The spirit bloweth and is still,
>> In mystery our soul abides;
> But tasks in hours of insight willed
> Can be through hours of gloom fulfilled.

Am I Carnally Minded? "Where there are envy, strife, and divisions among you, are you not carnal . . . ?" (1 Corinthians 3:3).

The natural man, or unbeliever, knows nothing about carnality. The desires of the flesh warring against the Spirit, and the Spirit warring against the flesh, which began at rebirth, are what produce carnality and the awareness of it. But Paul said, "Walk in the Spirit, and you shall not fulfill the lust of the flesh" (Galatians 5:16). In other words, carnality will disappear.

Are you quarrelsome and easily upset over small things? Do you think that no one who is a Christian is ever like that? Paul said they are, and he connected these attitudes with carnality. Is there a truth in the Bible that instantly awakens a spirit of malice or resentment in you? If so, that is proof that you are still carnal. If the process of sanctification is continuing in your life, there will be no trace of that kind of spirit remaining.

If the Spirit of God detects anything in you that is wrong, He doesn't ask you to make it right; He only asks you to accept the light of truth, and then He will make it right. A child of the light will confess sin instantly and stand completely open before God. But a child of the darkness will say, "Oh, I can explain that." When the light shines and the Spirit brings conviction of sin, be a child of the light. Confess your wrongdoing, and God will deal with it. If, however, you try to vindicate yourself, you prove yourself to be a child of the darkness.

What is the proof that carnality has gone? Never deceive yourself; when carnality is gone you will know it—it is the most real thing you can imagine. And God will see to it that you have a number of opportunities to prove to yourself the miracle of His grace. The proof is in a very practical test. You will find yourself saying, "If this had happened before, I would have had the spirit of resentment!" And you will never cease to be the most amazed person on earth at what God has done for you on the inside.

If you become a necessity to someone else's life, you are out of God's will. As a servant, your primary responsibility is to be a "friend of the bridegroom" (3:29). When you see a person who is close to grasping the claims of Jesus Christ, you know that your influence has been used in the right direction. And when you begin to see that person in the middle of a difficult and painful struggle, don't try to prevent it, but pray that his difficulty will grow even ten times stronger, until no power on earth or in hell could hold him away from Jesus Christ. Over and over again, we try to be amateur providences in someone's life. We are indeed amateurs, coming in and actually preventing God's will and saying, "This person should not have to experience this difficulty." Instead of being friends of the Bridegroom, our sympathy gets in the way. One day that person will say to us, "You are a thief; you stole my desire to follow Jesus, and because of you I lost sight of Him."

Beware of rejoicing with someone over the wrong thing, but always look to rejoice over the right thing. ". . . the friend of the bridegroom . . . rejoices greatly because of the bridegroom's voice. Therefore this joy of mine is fulfilled. He must increase, but I must decrease" (3:29–30). This was spoken with joy, not with sadness—at last they were to see the Bridegroom! And John said this was his joy. It represents a stepping aside, an absolute removal of the servant, never to be thought of again.

Listen intently with your entire being until you hear the Bridegroom's voice in the life of another person. And never give any thought to what devastation, difficulties, or sickness it will bring. Just rejoice with godly excitement that His voice has been heard. You may often have to watch Jesus Christ wreck a life before He saves it (see Matthew 10:34).

Goodness and purity should never be traits that draw attention to themselves, but should simply be magnets that draw people to Jesus Christ. If my holiness is not drawing others to Him, it is not the right kind of holiness; it is only an influence which awakens undue emotions and evil desires in people and diverts them from heading in the right direction. A person who is a beautiful saint can be a hindrance in leading people to the Lord by presenting only what Christ has done for him, instead of presenting Jesus Christ Himself. Others will be left with this thought—"What a fine person that man is!" That is not being a true "friend of the bridegroom"—*I* am increasing all the time; *He* is not.

To maintain this friendship and faithfulness to the Bridegroom, we have to be more careful to have the moral and vital relationship to Him above everything else, including obe-dience. Sometimes there is nothing to obey and our only task is to maintain a vital connection with Jesus Christ, seeing that nothing interferes with it. Only occasionally is it a matter of obedience. At those times when a crisis arises, we have to find out what God's will is. Yet most of our life is not spent in trying to be consciously obedient, but in maintaining this relation-ship—being the "friend of the bridegroom." Christian work can actually be a means of diverting a person's focus away from Jesus Christ. Instead of being friends "of the bridegroom," we may become amateur providences of God to someone else, working against Him while we use His weapons.

Spiritual Vision Through Personal Purity

"Blessed are the pure in heart, for they shall see God" (Matthew 5:8).

Purity is not innocence—it is much more than that. Purity is the result of continued spiritual harmony with God. We have to grow in purity. Our life with God may be right and our inner purity unblemished, yet occasionally our outer life may become spotted and stained. God intentionally does not protect us from this possibility, because this is the way we recognize the necessity of maintaining our spiritual vision through personal purity. If the outer level of our spiritual life with God is impaired to the slightest degree, we must put everything else aside until we make it right. Remember that spiritual vision depends on our character—it is *"the pure in heart"* who *"see God."*

God makes us pure by an act of His sovereign grace, but we still have something that we must carefully watch. It is through our bodily life coming in contact with other people and other points of view that we tend to become tarnished. Not only must our "inner sanctuary" be kept right with God, but also the "outer courts" must be brought into perfect harmony with the purity God gives us through His grace. Our spiritual vision and understanding is immediately blurred when our "outer court" is stained. If we want to maintain personal intimacy with the Lord Jesus Christ, it will mean refusing to do or even think certain things. And some things that are acceptable for others will become unacceptable for us.

A practical help in keeping your personal purity unblemished in your relations with other people is to begin to see them as God does. Say to yourself, "That man or that woman is *perfect in Christ Jesus!* That friend or that relative is *perfect in Christ Jesus!*"

Spiritual Vision Through Personal Character

"Come up here, and I will show you things which must take place . . ." (Revelation 4:1).

A higher state of mind and spiritual vision can only be achieved through the higher practice of personal character. If you live up to the highest and best that you know in the outer level of your life, God will continually say to you, "Friend, come up even higher." There is also a continuing rule in temptation which calls you to go higher; but when you do, you only encounter other temptations and character traits. Both God and Satan use the strategy of elevation, but Satan uses it in temptation, and the effect is quite different. When the devil elevates you to a certain place, he causes you to fasten your idea of what holiness is far beyond what flesh and blood could ever bear or achieve. Your life becomes a spiritual acrobatic performance high atop a steeple. You cling to it, trying to maintain your balance and daring not to move. But when God elevates you by His grace into heavenly places, you find a vast plateau where you can move about with ease.

Compare this week in your spiritual life with the same week last year to see how God has called you to a higher level. We have all been brought to see from a higher viewpoint. Never allow God to show you a truth which you do not instantly begin to live up to, applying it to your life. Always work through it, staying in its light.

Your growth in grace is not measured by the fact that you haven't turned back, but that you have an insight and understanding into where you are spiritually. Have you heard God say, "Come up higher," not audibly on the outer level, but to the innermost part of your character?

"Shall I hide from Abraham what I am doing . . . ?" (Genesis 18:17). God has to hide from us what He does, until, due to the growth of our personal character, we get to the level where He is then able to reveal it.

Isn't There Some Misunderstanding?

" 'Let us go to Judea again.'
The disciples said to Him,
'. . . are You going there
again?' "
(John 11:7-8).

Just because I don't understand what Jesus Christ says, I have no right to determine that He must be mistaken in what He says. That is a dangerous view, and it is never right to think that my obedience to God's directive will bring dishonor to Jesus. The only thing that will bring dishonor is not obeying Him. To put my view of His honor ahead of what He is plainly guiding me to do is never right, even though it may come from a real desire to prevent Him from being put to an open shame. I know when the instructions have come from God because of their quiet persistence. But when I begin to weigh the pros and cons, and doubt and debate enter into my mind, I am bringing in an element that is not of God. This will only result in my concluding that His instructions to me were not right. Many of us are faithful to our ideas about Jesus Christ, but how many of us are faithful to Jesus Himself? Faithfulness to Jesus means that I must step out even when and where I can't see anything (see Matthew 14:29). But faithfulness to my own ideas means that I first clear the way mentally. Faith, however, is not intellectual understanding; faith is a deliberate commitment to the Person of Jesus Christ, even when I can't see the way ahead.

Are you debating whether you should take a step of faith in Jesus, or whether you should wait until you can clearly see how to do what He has asked? Simply obey Him with unrestrained joy. When He tells you something and you begin to debate, it is because you have a misunderstanding of what honors Him and what doesn't. Are you faithful to Jesus, or faithful to your ideas about Him? Are you faithful to what He says, or are you trying to compromise His words with thoughts that never came from Him? "Whatever He says to you, do it" (John 2:5).

Our Lord's Surprise Visits

"You also be ready . . ." (Luke 12:40).

A Christian worker's greatest need is a readiness to face Jesus Christ at any and every turn. This is not easy, no matter what our experience has been. This battle is not against sin, difficulties, or circumstances, but against being so absorbed in our service to Jesus Christ that we are not ready to face Jesus Himself at every turn. The greatest need is not facing our beliefs or doctrines, or even facing the question of whether or not we are of any use to Him, but the need is to face *Him.*

Jesus rarely comes where we expect Him; He appears where we least expect Him, and always in the most illogical situations. The only way a servant can remain true to God is to be ready for the Lord's surprise visits. This readiness will not be brought about by service, but through intense spiritual reality, expecting Jesus Christ at every turn. This sense of expectation will give our life the attitude of childlike wonder He wants it to have. If we are going to be ready for Jesus Christ, we have to stop being religious. In other words, we must stop using religion as if it were some kind of a lofty lifestyle—we must be spiritually real.

If you are avoiding the call of the religious thinking of today's world, and instead are "looking unto Jesus" (Hebrews 12:2), setting your heart on what He wants, and thinking His thoughts, you will be considered impractical and a daydreamer. But when He suddenly appears in the work of the heat of the day, you will be the only one who is ready. You should trust no one, and even ignore the finest saint on earth if he blocks your sight of Jesus Christ.

"He . . . wondered that there was no intercessor . . ."
(Isaiah 59:16).

The reason many of us stop praying and become hard toward God is that we only have an emotional interest in prayer. It sounds good to say that we pray, and we read books on prayer which tell us that prayer is beneficial—that our minds are quieted and our souls are uplifted when we pray. But Isaiah implied in this verse that God is amazed at such thoughts about prayer.

Worship and intercession must go together; one is impossible without the other. Intercession means raising ourselves up to the point of getting the mind of Christ regarding the person for whom we are praying (see Philippians 2:5). Instead of worshiping God, we recite speeches to God about how prayer is supposed to work. Are we worshiping God or disputing Him when we say, "But God, I just don't see how you are going to do this"? This is a sure sign that we are not worshiping. When we lose sight of God, we become hard and dogmatic. We throw our petitions at His throne and dictate to Him what we want Him to do. We don't worship God, nor do we seek to conform our minds to the mind of Christ. And if we are hard toward God, we will become hard toward other people.

Are we worshiping God in a way that will raise us up to where we can take hold of Him, having such intimate contact with Him that we know His mind about the ones for whom we pray? Are we living in a holy relationship with God, or have we become hard and dogmatic?

Do you find yourself thinking that there is no one interceding properly? Then be that person yourself. Be a person who worships God and lives in a holy relationship with Him. Get involved in the real work of intercession, remembering that it truly is work—work that demands all your energy, but work which has no hidden pitfalls. Preaching the gospel has its share of pitfalls, but intercessory prayer has none whatsoever.

Heedfulness or Hypocrisy in Ourselves?

"If anyone sees his brother sinning a sin which does not lead to death, he will ask, and He will give him life for those who commit sin not leading to death" (1 John 5:16).

If we are not heedful and pay no attention to the way the Spirit of God works in us, we will become spiritual hypocrites. We see where other people are failing, and then we take our discernment and turn it into comments of ridicule and criticism, instead of turning it into intercession on their behalf. God reveals this truth about others to us not through the sharpness of our minds but through the direct penetration of His Spirit. If we are not attentive, we will be completely unaware of the source of the discernment God has given us, becoming critical of others and forgetting that God says, ". . . he will ask, and He will give him life for those who commit sin not leading to death." Be careful that you don't become a hypocrite by spending all your time trying to get others right with God before you worship Him yourself.

One of the most subtle and illusive burdens God ever places on us as saints is this burden of discernment concerning others. He gives us discernment so that we may accept the responsibility for those souls before Him and form the mind of Christ about them (see Philippians 2:5). We should intercede in accordance with what God says He will give us, namely, "life for those who commit sin not leading to death." It is not that we are able to bring God into contact with our minds, but that we awaken ourselves to the point where God is able to convey His mind to us regarding the people for whom we intercede.

Can Jesus Christ see the agony of His soul in us? He can't unless we are so closely identified with Him that we have His view concerning the people for whom we pray. May we learn to intercede so wholeheartedly that Jesus Christ will be completely and overwhelmingly satisfied with us as intercessors.

Helpful or Heartless Toward Others?

"It is Christ . . . who also makes intercession for us. . . . the Spirit . . . makes intercession for the saints . . ." (Romans 8:34, 27).

Do we need any more arguments than these to become intercessors—that Christ "always lives to make intercession" (Hebrews 7:25), and that the Holy Spirit "makes intercession for the saints"? Are we living in such a relationship with others that we do the work of intercession as a result of being the children of God who are taught by His Spirit? We should take a look at our current circumstances. Do crises which affect us or others in our home, business, country, or elsewhere, seem to be crushing in on us? Are we being pushed out of the presence of God and left with no time for worship? If so, we must put a stop to such distractions and get into such a living relationship with God that our relationship with others is maintained through the work of intercession, where God works His miracles.

Beware of getting ahead of God by your very desire to do His will. We run ahead of Him in a thousand and one activities, becoming so burdened with people and problems that we don't worship God, and we fail to intercede. If a burden and its resulting pressure come upon us while we are not in an attitude of worship, it will only produce a hardness toward God and despair in our own souls. God continually introduces us to people in whom we have no interest, and unless we are worshiping God the natural tendency is to be heartless toward them. We give them a quick verse of Scripture, like jabbing them with a spear, or leave them with a hurried, uncaring word of counsel before we go. A heartless Christian must be a terrible grief to our Lord.

Are our lives in the proper place so that we may participate in the intercession of our Lord and the Holy Spirit?

April 1

The Glory That's Unsurpassed

"... the Lord Jesus ... has sent me that you may receive your sight ..." (Acts 9:17).

When Paul received his sight, he also received spiritual insight into the Person of Jesus Christ. His entire life and preaching from that point on were totally consumed with nothing but Jesus Christ—"For I determined not to know anything among you except Jesus Christ and Him crucified" (1 Corinthians 2:2). Paul never again allowed anything to attract and hold the attention of his mind and soul except the face of Jesus Christ.

We must learn to maintain a strong degree of character in our lives, even to the level that has been revealed in our vision of Jesus Christ.

The lasting characteristic of a spiritual man is the ability to understand correctly the meaning of the Lord Jesus Christ in his life, and the ability to explain the purposes of God to others. The overruling passion of his life is Jesus Christ. Whenever you see this quality in a person, you get the feeling that he is truly a man after God's own heart (see Acts 13:22).

Never allow anything to divert you from your insight into Jesus Christ. It is the true test of whether you are spiritual or not. To be unspiritual means that other things have a growing fascination for you.

> Since mine eyes have looked on Jesus,
>   I've lost sight of all beside,
> So enchained my spirit's vision,
>   Gazing on the Crucified.

"If You Had Known!"

"If you had known . . . in this your day, the things that make for your peace! But now they are hidden from your eyes"
(Luke 19:42).

Jesus entered Jerusalem triumphantly and the city was stirred to its very foundations, but a strange god was there—the pride of the Pharisees. It was a god that seemed religious and upright, but Jesus compared it to "whitewashed tombs which indeed appear beautiful outwardly, but inside are full of dead men's bones and all uncleanness" (Matthew 23:27).

What is it that blinds you to the peace of God "in this your day"? Do you have a strange god—not a disgusting monster but perhaps an unholy nature that controls your life? More than once God has brought me face to face with a strange god in my life, and I knew that I should have given it up, but I didn't do it. I got through the crisis "by the skin of my teeth," only to find myself still under the control of that strange god. I am blind to the very things that make for my own peace. It is a shocking thing that we can be in the exact place where the Spirit of God should be having His completely unhindered way with us, and yet we only make matters worse, increasing our blame in God's eyes.

"If you had known . . . ." God's words here cut directly to the heart, with the tears of Jesus behind them. These words imply responsibility for our own faults. God holds us accountable for what we refuse to see or are unable to see because of our sin. And "now they are hidden from your eyes" because you have never completely yielded your nature to Him. Oh, the deep, unending sadness for what might have been! God never again opens the doors that have been closed. He opens other doors, but He reminds us that there are doors which we have shut—doors which had no need to be shut. Never be afraid when God brings back your past. Let your memory have its way with you. It is a minister of God bringing its rebuke and sorrow to you. God will turn what might have been into a wonderful lesson of growth for the future.

The Way to Permanent Faith

"Indeed the hour is coming . . . that you will be scattered . . ."
(John 16:32).

Jesus was not rebuking the disciples in this passage. Their faith was real, but it was disordered and unfocused, and was not at work in the important realities of life. The disciples were scattered to their own concerns and they had interests apart from Jesus Christ. After we have the perfect relationship with God, through the sanctifying work of the Holy Spirit, our faith must be exercised in the realities of everyday life. We will be scattered, not into service but into the emptiness of our lives where we will see ruin and barrenness, to know what internal death to God's blessings means. Are we prepared for this? It is certainly not of our own choosing, but God engineers our circumstances to take us there. Until we have been through that experience, our faith is sustained only by feelings and by blessings. But once we get there, no matter where God may place us or what inner emptiness we experience, we can praise God that all is well. That is what is meant by faith being exercised in the realities of life.

". . . you . . . will leave Me alone." Have we been scattered and have we left Jesus alone by not seeing His providential care for us? Do we not see God at work in our circumstances? Dark times are allowed and come to us through the sovereignty of God. Are we prepared to let God do what He wants with us? Are we prepared to be separated from the outward, evident blessings of God? Until Jesus Christ is truly our Lord, we each have goals of our own which we serve. Our faith is real, but it is not yet permanent. And God is never in a hurry. If we are willing to wait, we will see God pointing out that we have been interested only in His blessings, instead of in God Himself. The sense of God's blessings is fundamental.

". . . be of good cheer, I have overcome the world" (16:33). Unyielding spiritual fortitude is what we need.

His Agony and Our Access

"Jesus came with them to a place called Gethsemane, and said to the disciples . . . . 'Stay here and watch with Me'" (Matthew 26:36, 38).

We can never fully comprehend Christ's agony in the Garden of Gethsemane, but at least we don't have to misunderstand it. It is the agony of God and man in one Person, coming face to face with sin. We cannot learn about Gethsemane through personal experience. Gethsemane and Calvary represent something totally unique—they are the gateway into life for us.

It was not death on the cross that Jesus agonized over in Gethsemane. In fact, He stated very emphatically that He came with the purpose of dying. His concern here was that He might not get through this struggle as the Son of Man. He was confident of getting through it as the Son of God—Satan could not touch Him there. But Satan's assault was that our Lord would come through for us on His own solely as the Son of Man. If Jesus had done that, He could not have been our Savior (see Hebrews 9:11–15). Read the record of His agony in Gethsemane in light of His earlier wilderness temptation— ". . . the devil . . . departed from Him until an opportune time" (Luke 4:13). In Gethsemane, Satan came back and was overthrown again. Satan's final assault against our Lord as the *Son of Man* was in Gethsemane.

The agony in Gethsemane was the agony of the Son of God in fulfilling His destiny as the Savior of the world. The veil is pulled back here to reveal all that it cost Him to make it possible for us to become sons of God. His agony was the basis for the simplicity of our salvation. The Cross of Christ was a triumph for the *Son of Man*. It was not only a sign that our Lord had triumphed, but that He had triumphed to save the human race. Because of what the Son of Man went through, every human being has been provided with a way of access into the very presence of God.

The Collision of God and Sin

"... who Himself bore our sins in His own body on the tree ..."
(1 Peter 2:24).

The Cross of Christ is the revealed truth of God's judgment on sin. Never associate the idea of martyrdom with the Cross of Christ. It was the supreme triumph, and it shook the very foundations of hell. There is nothing in time or eternity more absolutely certain and irrefutable than what Jesus Christ accomplished on the Cross—He made it possible for the entire human race to be brought back into a right-standing relationship with God. He made redemption the foundation of human life; that is, He made a way for every person to have fellowship with God.

The Cross was not something that *happened to* Jesus—He came to die; the Cross was His purpose in coming. He is "the Lamb slain from the foundation of the world" (Revelation 13:8). The incarnation of Christ would have no meaning without the Cross. Beware of separating *"God was manifested in the flesh ..."* from *"... He made Him ... to be sin for us ..."* (1 Timothy 3:16; 2 Corinthians 5:21). The purpose of the incarnation was redemption. God came in the flesh to take sin away, not to accomplish something for Himself. The Cross is the central event in time and eternity, and the answer to all the problems of both.

The Cross is not the cross of a man, but the Cross of God, and it can never be fully comprehended through human experience. The Cross is God exhibiting His nature. It is the gate through which any and every individual can enter into oneness with God. But it is not a gate we pass right through; it is one where we abide in the life that is found there.

The heart of salvation is the Cross of Christ. The reason salvation is so easy to obtain is that it cost God so much. The Cross was the place where God and sinful man merged with a tremendous collision and where the way to life was opened. But all the cost and pain of the collision was absorbed by the heart of God.

April 6

Why We Lack Understanding

"He commanded them that they should tell no one the things they had seen, till the Son of Man had risen from the dead" (Mark 9:9).

As the disciples were commanded, you should also say nothing until the Son of Man has risen in you—until the life of the risen Christ so dominates you that you truly understand what He taught while here on earth. When you grow and develop the right condition inwardly, the words Jesus spoke become so clear that you are amazed you did not grasp them before. In fact, you were not able to understand them before because you had not yet developed the proper spiritual condition to deal with them.

Our Lord doesn't hide these things from us, but we are not prepared to receive them until we are in the right condition in our spiritual life. Jesus said, "I still have many things to say to you, but you cannot bear them now" (John 16:12). We must have a oneness with His risen life before we are prepared to bear any particular truth from Him. Do we really know anything about the indwelling of the risen life of Jesus? The evidence that we do is that His Word is becoming understandable to us. God cannot reveal anything to us if we don't have His Spirit. And our own unyielding and headstrong opinions will effectively prevent God from revealing anything to us. But our insensible thinking will end immediately once His resurrection life has its way with us.

". . . tell no one . . . ." But so many people do tell what they saw on the Mount of Transfiguration—their mountaintop experience. They have seen a vision and they testify to it, but there is no connection between what they say and how they live. Their lives don't add up because the Son of Man has not yet risen in them. How long will it be before His resurrection life is formed and evident in you and in me?

His Resurrection Destiny

"Ought not the Christ to have
suffered these things and to
enter into His glory?"
(Luke 24:26).

Our Lord's Cross is the gateway into His life. His resurrection means that He has the power to convey His life to me. When I was born again, I received the very life of the risen Lord from Jesus Himself.

Christ's resurrection destiny—His foreordained purpose—was to bring "many sons to glory" (Hebrews 2:10). The fulfilling of His destiny gives Him the right to make us sons and daughters of God. We never have exactly the same relationship to God that the Son of God has, but we are brought by the Son into the relation of sonship. When our Lord rose from the dead, He rose to an absolutely new life—a life He had never lived before He was God Incarnate. He rose to a life that had never been before. And what His resurrection means for us is that we are raised to His risen life, not to our old life. One day we will have a body like His glorious body, but we can know here and now the power and effectiveness of His resurrection and can "walk in newness of life" (Romans 6:4). Paul's determined purpose was to "know Him and the power of His resurrection" (Philippians 3:10).

Jesus prayed, ". . . as You have given Him authority over all flesh that He should give eternal life to as many as You have given Him" (John 17:2).The term *Holy Spirit* is actually another name for the experience of eternal life working in human beings here and now. The Holy Spirit is the deity of God who continues to apply the power of the atonement by the Cross of Christ to our lives. Thank God for the glorious and majestic truth that His Spirit can work the very nature of Jesus into us, if we will only obey Him.

Have You Seen Jesus?

"After that, He appeared in another form to two of them . . ."
(Mark 16:12).

Being saved and seeing Jesus are not the same thing. Many people who have never seen Jesus have received and share in God's grace. But once you have seen Him, you can never be the same. Other things will not have the appeal they did before.

You should always recognize the difference between what you see Jesus to be and what He has done for you. If you see only what He has done for you, your God is not big enough. But if you have had a vision, seeing Jesus as He really is, experiences can come and go, yet you will endure "as seeing Him who is invisible" (Hebrews 11:27). The man who was blind from birth did not know who Jesus was until Christ appeared and revealed Himself to him (see John 9). Jesus appears to those for whom He has done something, but we cannot order or predict when He will come. He may appear suddenly, at any turn. Then you can exclaim, "Now I see Him!" (see John 9:25).

Jesus must appear to you and to your friend individually; no one can see Jesus with your eyes. And division takes place when one has seen Him and the other has not. You cannot bring your friend to the point of seeing; God must do it. Have you seen Jesus? If so, you will want others to see Him too. "And they went and told it to the rest, but they did not believe them either" (Mark 16:13). When you see Him, you must tell, even if they don't believe.

> O could I tell, you surely would believe it!
> O could I only say what I have seen!
> How should I tell or how can you receive it,
> How, till He bringeth you where I have been?

"... our old man was crucified
with Him, that the body
of sin might be done away
with, that we should no
longer be slaves of sin"
(Romans 6:6).

Co-Crucifixion. Have you made the following decision about sin—that it must be completely killed in you? It takes a long time to come to the point of making this complete and effective decision about sin. It is, however, the greatest moment in your life once you decide that sin must die in you—not simply be restrained, suppressed, or counteracted, but crucified—just as Jesus Christ died for the sin of the world. No one can bring anyone else to this decision. We may be mentally and spiritually convinced, but what we need to do is actually make the decision that Paul urged us to do in this passage.

Pull yourself up, take some time alone with God, and make this important decision, saying, "Lord, identify me with Your death until I know that sin is dead in me." Make the moral decision that sin in you must be put to death.

This was not some divine future expectation on the part of Paul, but was a very radical and definite experience in his life. Are you prepared to let the Spirit of God search you until you know what the level and nature of sin is in your life—to see the very things that struggle against God's Spirit in you? If so, will you then agree with God's verdict on the nature of sin—that it should be identified with the death of Jesus? You cannot "reckon yourselves to be dead indeed to sin" (6:11) unless you have radically dealt with the issue of your will before God.

Have you entered into the glorious privilege of being crucified with Christ, until all that remains in your flesh and blood is His life? "I have been crucified with Christ; it is no longer I who live, but Christ lives in me . . ." (Galatians 2:20).

*Complete and
Effective Divinity*

"If we have been united
together in the likeness of
His death, certainly we
also shall be in the likeness
of His resurrection . . ."
(Romans 6:5).

Co-Resurrection. The proof that I have experienced crucifixion
with Jesus is that I have a definite likeness to Him. The Spirit of
Jesus entering me rearranges my personal life before God. The
resurrection of Jesus has given Him the authority to give the life
of God to me, and the experiences of my life must now be built
on the foundation of His life. I can have the resurrection life of
Jesus here and now, and it will exhibit itself through holiness.

The idea all through the apostle Paul's writings is that after
the decision to be identified with Jesus in His death has been
made, the resurrection life of Jesus penetrates every bit of my
human nature. It takes the omnipotence of God—His complete
and effective divinity—to live the life of the Son of God in
human flesh. The Holy Spirit cannot be accepted as a guest in
merely one room of the house—He invades all of it. And once I
decide that my "old man" (that is, my heredity of sin) should be
identified with the death of Jesus, the Holy Spirit invades me.
He takes charge of everything. My part is to walk in the light
and to obey all that He reveals to me. Once I have made that
important decision about sin, it is easy to "reckon" that I am
actually "dead indeed to sin," because I find the life of Jesus in
me all the time (Romans 6:11). Just as there is only one kind of
humanity, there is only one kind of holiness—the holiness of
Jesus. And it is His holiness that has been given to me. God
puts the holiness of His Son into me, and I belong to a new
spiritual order.

Complete and Effective Dominion

"Death no longer has dominion over Him. . . . the life that He lives, He lives to God. Likewise you also, reckon yourselves to be dead indeed to sin, but alive to God . . ." (Romans 6:9–11).

Co-Eternal Life. Eternal life is the life which Jesus Christ exhibited on the human level. And it is this same life, not simply a copy of it, which is made evident in our mortal flesh when we are born again. Eternal life is not a gift from God; eternal life is the gift *of God*. The energy and the power which was so very evident in Jesus will be exhibited in us by an act of the absolute sovereign grace of God, once we have made that complete and effective decision about sin.

"You shall receive power when the Holy Spirit has come upon you . . ." (Acts 1:8)—not power as a gift from the Holy Spirit; the power is the Holy Spirit, not something that He gives us. The life that was in Jesus becomes ours because of His Cross, once we make the decision to be identified with Him. If it is difficult to get right with God, it is because we refuse to make this moral decision about sin. But once we do decide, the full life of God comes in immediately. Jesus came to give us an endless supply of life—". . . that you may be filled with all the fullness of God" (Ephesians 3:19). Eternal life has nothing to do with time. It is the life which Jesus lived when He was down here, and the only Source of life is the Lord Jesus Christ.

Even the weakest saint can experience the power of the deity of the Son of God, when he is willing to "let go." But any effort to "hang on" to the least bit of our own power will only diminish the life of Jesus in us. We have to keep letting go, and slowly, but surely, the great full life of God will invade us, penetrating every part. Then Jesus will have complete and effective dominion in us, and people will take notice that we have been with Him.

What To Do When Your Burden Is Overwhelming

"Cast your burden on the LORD . . ."
(Psalm 55:22).

We must recognize the difference between burdens that are right for us to bear and burdens that are wrong. We should never bear the burdens of sin or doubt, but there are some burdens placed on us by God which He does not intend to lift off. God wants us to roll them back on Him—to literally "cast your burden," which He has given you, "on the LORD . . . ." If we set out to serve God and do His work but get out of touch with Him, the sense of responsibility we feel will be overwhelming and defeating. But if we will only roll back on God the burdens He has placed on us, He will take away that immense feeling of responsibility, replacing it with an awareness and understanding of Himself and His presence.

Many servants set out to serve God with great courage and with the right motives. But with no intimate fellowship with Jesus Christ, they are soon defeated. They do not know what to do with their burden, and it produces weariness in their lives. Others will see this and say, "What a sad end to something that had such a great beginning!"

"Cast your burden on the LORD . . . ." You have been bearing it all, but you need to deliberately place one end on God's shoulder. ". . . the government will be upon His shoulder" (Isaiah 9:6). Commit to God whatever burden He has placed on you. Don't just cast it aside, but put it over onto Him and place yourself there with it. You will see that your burden is then lightened by the sense of companionship. But you should never try to separate yourself from your burden.

"Take My yoke upon you and learn from Me . . ."
(Matthew 11:29).

"Whom the LORD loves He chastens . . ." (Hebrews 12:6). How petty our complaining is! Our Lord begins to bring us to the point where we can have fellowship with Him, only to hear us moan and groan, saying, "Oh Lord, just let me be like other people!" Jesus is asking us to get beside Him and take one end of the yoke, so that we can pull together. That's why Jesus says to us, "My yoke is easy and My burden is light" (Matthew 11:30). Are you closely identified with the Lord Jesus like that? If so, you will thank God when you feel the pressure of His hand upon you.

". . . to those who have no might He increases strength" (Isaiah 40:29). God comes and takes us out of our emotionalism, and then our complaining turns into a hymn of praise. The only way to know the strength of God is to take the yoke of Jesus upon us and to learn from Him.

". . . the joy of the LORD is your strength" (Nehemiah 8:10). Where do the saints get their joy? If we did not know some Christians well, we might think from just observing them that they have no burdens at all to bear. But we must lift the veil from our eyes. The fact that the peace, light, and joy of God is in them is proof that a burden is there as well. The burden that God places on us squeezes the grapes in our lives and produces the wine, but most of us see only the wine and not the burden. No power on earth or in hell can conquer the Spirit of God living within the human spirit; it creates an inner invincibility.

If your life is producing only a whine, instead of the wine, then ruthlessly kick it out. It is definitely a crime for a Christian to be weak in God's strength.

The Failure To Pay Close Attention

"The high places were not removed from Israel. Nevertheless the heart of Asa was loyal all his days" (2 Chronicles 15:17).

Asa was not completely obedient in the outward, visible areas of his life. He was obedient in what he considered the most important areas, but he was not entirely right. Beware of ever thinking, "Oh, that thing in my life doesn't matter much." The fact that it doesn't matter much to you may mean that it matters a great deal to God. Nothing should be considered a trivial matter by a child of God. How much longer are we going to prevent God from teaching us even one thing? But He keeps trying to teach us and He never loses patience. You say, "I know I am right with God"—yet the "high places" still remain in your life. There is still an area of disobedience. Do you protest that your heart is right with God, and yet there is something in your life He causes you to doubt? Whenever God causes a doubt about something, stop it immediately, no matter what it may be. Nothing in our lives is a mere insignificant detail to God.

Are there some things regarding your physical or intellectual life to which you have been paying no attention at all? If so, you may think you are all correct in the important areas, but you are careless—you are failing to concentrate or to focus properly. You no more need a day off from spiritual concentration on matters in your life than your heart needs a day off from beating. As you cannot take a day off morally and remain moral, neither can you take a day off spiritually and remain spiritual. God wants you to be entirely His, and it requires paying close attention to keep yourself fit. It also takes a tremendous amount of time. Yet some of us expect to rise above all of our problems, going from one mountaintop experience to another, with only a few minutes' effort.

Can You Come Down From the Mountain?

"While you have the light,
    believe in the light . . ."
(John 12:36).

We all have moments when we feel better than ever before, and we say, "I feel fit for anything; if only I could always be like this!" We are not meant to be. Those moments are moments of insight which we have to live up to even when we do not feel like it. Many of us are no good for the everyday world when we are not on the mountaintop. Yet we must bring our everyday life up to the standard revealed to us on the mountaintop when we were there.

Never allow a feeling that was awakened in you on the mountaintop to evaporate. Don't place yourself on the shelf by thinking, "How great to be in such a wonderful state of mind!" Act immediately—do something, even if your only reason to act is that you would rather not. If, during a prayer meeting, God shows you something to do, don't say, "I'll do it"—just *do it!* Pick yourself up by the back of the neck and shake off your fleshly laziness. Laziness can always be seen in our cravings for a mountaintop experience; all we talk about is our planning for our time on the mountain. We must learn to live in the ordinary "gray" day according to what we saw on the mountain.

Don't give up because you have been blocked and confused once—go after it again. Burn your bridges behind you, and stand committed to God by an act of your own will. Never change your decisions, but be sure to make your decisions in the light of what you saw and learned on the mountain.

All or Nothing?

"When Simon Peter heard that it was the Lord, he put on his outer garment . . . and plunged into the sea" (John 21:7).

Have you ever had a crisis in your life in which you deliberately, earnestly, and recklessly abandoned everything? It is a crisis of the will. You may come to that point many times externally, but it will amount to nothing. The true deep crisis of abandonment, or total surrender, is reached internally, not externally. The giving up of only external things may actually be an indication of your being in total bondage.

Have you deliberately committed your will to Jesus Christ? It is a transaction of the will, not of emotion; any positive emotion that results is simply a superficial blessing arising out of the transaction. If you focus your attention on the emotion, you will never make the transaction. Do not ask God what the transaction is to be, but make the determination to surrender your will regarding whatever you see, whether it is in the shallow or the deep, profound places internally.

If you have heard Jesus Christ's voice on the waves of the sea, you can let your convictions and your consistency take care of themselves by concentrating on maintaining your intimate relationship to Him.

Readiness

"God called to him . . . .
And he said, 'Here I am'"
(Exodus 3:4).

When God speaks, many of us are like people in a fog, and we give no answer. Moses' reply to God revealed that he knew where he was and that he was ready. Readiness means having a right relationship to God and having the knowledge of where we are. We are so busy telling God where we would like to go. Yet the man or woman who is ready for God and His work is the one who receives the prize when the summons comes. We wait with the idea that some great opportunity or something sensational will be coming our way, and when it does come we are quick to cry out, "Here I am." Whenever we sense that Jesus Christ is rising up to take authority over some great task, we are there, but we are not ready for some obscure duty.

Readiness for God means that we are prepared to do the smallest thing or the largest thing—it makes no difference. It means we have no choice in what we want to do, but that whatever God's plans may be, we are there and ready. Whenever any duty presents itself, we hear God's voice as our Lord heard His Father's voice, and we are ready for it with the total readiness of our love for Him. Jesus Christ expects to do with us just as His Father did with Him. He can put us wherever He wants, in pleasant duties or in menial ones, because our union with Him is the same as His union with the Father. ". . . that they may be one just as We are one . . ." (John 17:22).

Be ready for the sudden surprise visits of God. A ready person never needs to *get* ready—he *is* ready. Think of the time we waste trying to get ready once God has called! The burning bush is a symbol of everything that surrounds the person who is ready, and it is on fire with the presence of God Himself.

*Beware of the Least
Likely Temptation*

"Joab had defected to
Adonijah, though he had
not defected to Absalom"
(1 Kings 2:28).

Joab withstood the greatest test of his life, remaining absolutely loyal to David by not turning to follow after the fascinating and ambitious Absalom. Yet toward the end of his life he turned to follow after the weak and cowardly Adonijah. Always remain alert to the fact that where one person has turned back is exactly where anyone may be tempted to turn back (see 1 Corinthians 10:11–13). You may have just victoriously gone through a great crisis, but now be alert about the things that may appear to be the least likely to tempt you. Beware of thinking that the areas of your life where you have experienced victory in the past are now the least likely to cause you to stumble and fall.

We are apt to say, "It is not at all likely that having been through the greatest crisis of my life I would now turn back to the things of the world." Do not try to predict where the temptation will come; it is the least likely thing that is the real danger. It is in the aftermath of a great spiritual event that the least likely things begin to have an effect. They may not be forceful and dominant, but they are there. And if you are not careful to be forewarned, they will trip you. You have remained true to God under great and intense trials—now beware of the undercurrent. Do not be abnormally examining your inner self, looking forward with dread, but stay alert; keep your memory sharp before God. Unguarded strength is actually a double weakness, because that is where the least likely temptations will be effective in sapping strength. The Bible characters stumbled over their strong points, never their weak ones.

". . . kept by the power of God . . ."—that is the only safety. (1 Peter 1:5).

Can a Saint Falsely Accuse God?

"All the promises of God in Him are Yes, and in Him Amen . . ."
(2 Corinthians 1:20).

Jesus' parable of the talents recorded in Matthew 25:14–30 was a warning that it is possible for us to misjudge our capacities. This parable has nothing to do with natural gifts and abilities, but relates to the gift of the Holy Spirit as He was first given at Pentecost. We must never measure our spiritual capacity on the basis of our education or our intellect; our capacity in spiritual things is measured on the basis of the promises of God. If we get less than God wants us to have, we will falsely accuse Him as the servant falsely accused his master when he said, "You expect more of me than you gave me the power to do. You demand too much of me, and I cannot stand true to you here where you have placed me." When it is a question of God's Almighty Spirit, never say, "I can't." Never allow the limitation of your own natural ability to enter into the matter. If we have received the Holy Spirit, God expects the work of the Holy Spirit to be exhibited in us.

The servant justified himself, while condemning his lord on every point, as if to say, "Your demand on me is way out of proportion to what you gave to me." Have we been falsely accusing God by daring to worry after He has said, "But seek first the kingdom of God and His righteousness, and all these things shall be added to you"? (Matthew 6:33). Worrying means exactly what this servant implied—"I know your intent is to leave me unprotected and vulnerable." A person who is lazy in the natural realm is always critical, saying, "I haven't had a decent chance," and someone who is lazy in the spiritual realm is critical of God. Lazy people always strike out at others in an independent way.

Never forget that our capacity and capability in spiritual matters is measured by, and based on, the promises of God. Is God able to fulfill His promises? Our answer depends on whether or not we have received the Holy Spirit.

Don't Hurt the Lord

"Have I been with you so long, and yet you have not known Me, Philip?" (John 14:9).

Our Lord must be repeatedly astounded at us—astounded at how "un-simple" we are. It is our own opinions that make us dense and slow to understand, but when we are simple we are never dense; we have discernment all the time. Philip expected the future revelation of a tremendous mystery, but not in Jesus, the Person he thought he already knew. The mystery of God is not in what is going to be—it is now, though we look for it to be revealed in the future in some overwhelming, momentous event. We have no reluctance to obey Jesus, but it is highly probable that we are hurting Him by what we ask—"Lord, show us the Father . . ." (14:8). His response immediately comes back to us as He says, "Can't you see Him? He is always right here or He is nowhere to be found." We look for God to exhibit Himself *to* His children, but God only exhibits Himself *in* His children. And while others see the evidence, the child of God does not. We want to be fully aware of what God is doing in us, but we cannot have complete awareness and expect to remain reasonable or balanced in our expectations of Him. If all we are asking God to give us is experiences, and the awareness of those experiences is blocking our way, we hurt the Lord. The very questions we ask hurt Jesus, because they are not the questions of a child.

"Let not your heart be troubled . . ." (14:1, 27). Am I then hurting Jesus by allowing my heart to be troubled? . If I believe in Jesus and His attributes, am I living up to my belief? Am I allowing anything to disturb my heart, or am I allowing any questions to come in which are unsound or unbalanced? I have to get to the point of the absolute and unquestionable relationship that takes everything exactly as it comes from Him. God never guides us at some time in the future, but always here and now. Realize that the Lord is here *now*, and the freedom you receive is immediate.

April 21

The Light That Never Fails

"We all, with unveiled face, beholding . . . the glory of the Lord . . ."
(2 Corinthians 3:18).

A servant of God must stand so very much alone that he never realizes he is alone. In the early stages of the Christian life, disappointments will come—people who used to be lights will flicker out, and those who used to stand with us will turn away. We have to get so used to it that we will not even realize we are standing alone. Paul said, ". . . no one stood with me, but all forsook me . . . . But the Lord stood with me and strengthened me . . ." (2 Timothy 4:16–17). We must build our faith not on fading lights but on the Light that never fails. When "important" individuals go away we are sad, until we see that they are meant to go, so that only one thing is left for us to do—to look into the face of God for ourselves.

Allow nothing to keep you from looking with strong determination into the face of God regarding yourself and your doctrine. And every time you preach make sure you look God in the face about the message first, then the glory will remain through all of it. A Christian servant is one who perpetually looks into the face of God and then goes forth to talk to others. The ministry of Christ is characterized by an abiding glory of which the servant is totally unaware—". . . Moses did not know that the skin of his face shone while he talked with Him" (Exodus 34:29).

We are never called on to display our doubts openly or to express the hidden joys and delights of our life with God. The secret of the servant's life is that he stays in tune with God all the time.

Do You Worship the Work?

"We are God's fellow workers . . ."
(1 Corinthians 3:9).

Beware of any work for God that causes or allows you to avoid concentrating on Him. A great number of Christian workers worship their work. The only concern of Christian workers should be their concentration on God. This will mean that all the other boundaries of life, whether they are mental, moral, or spiritual limits, are completely free with the freedom God gives His child; that is, a worshiping child, not a wayward one. A worker who lacks this serious controlling emphasis of concentration on God is apt to become overly burdened by his work. He is a slave to his own limits, having no freedom of his body, mind, or spirit. Consequently, he becomes burned out and defeated. There is no freedom and no delight in life at all. His nerves, mind, and heart are so overwhelmed that God's blessing cannot rest on him.

But the opposite case is equally true—once our concentration is on God, all the limits of our life are free and under the control and mastery of God alone. There is no longer any responsibility on you for the work. The only responsibility you have is to stay in living constant touch with God, and to see that you allow nothing to hinder your cooperation with Him. The freedom that comes after sanctification is the freedom of a child, and the things that used to hold your life down are gone. But be careful to remember that you have been freed for only one thing—to be absolutely devoted to your co-Worker.

We have no right to decide where we should be placed, or to have preconceived ideas as to what God is preparing us to do. God engineers everything; and wherever He places us, our one supreme goal should be to pour out our lives in wholehearted devotion to Him in that particular work. "Whatever your hand finds to do, do it with your might . . ." (Ecclesiastes 9:10).

The Warning Against Desiring Spiritual Success

"Do not rejoice in this, that the spirits are subject to you . . ."
(Luke 10:20).

Worldliness is not the trap that most endangers us as Christian workers; nor is it sin. The trap we fall into is extravagantly desiring spiritual success; that is, success measured by, and patterned after, the form set by this religious age in which we now live. Never seek after anything other than the approval of God, and always be willing to go "outside the camp, bearing His reproach" (Hebrews 13:13). In Luke 10:20, Jesus told the disciples not to rejoice in successful service, and yet this seems to be the one thing in which most of us do rejoice. We have a commercialized view—we count how many souls have been saved and sanctified, we thank God, and then we think everything is all right. Yet our work only begins where God's grace has laid the foundation. Our work is not to save souls, but to disciple them. Salvation and sanctification are the work of God's sovereign grace, and our work as His disciples is to disciple others' lives until they are totally yielded to God. One life totally devoted to God is of more value to Him than one hundred lives which have been simply awakened by His Spirit. As workers for God, we must reproduce our own kind spiritually, and those lives will be God's testimony to us as His workers. God brings us up to a standard of life through His grace, and we are responsible for reproducing that same standard in others.

Unless the worker lives a life that "is hidden with Christ in God" (Colossians 3:3), he is apt to become an irritating dictator to others, instead of an active, living disciple. Many of us are dictators, dictating our desires to individuals and to groups. But Jesus never dictates to us in that way. Whenever our Lord talked about discipleship, He always prefaced His words with an "if," never with the forceful or dogmatic statement—"You must." Discipleship carries with it an option.

Many of us suffer from the unbalanced tendency to "be ready" only "out of season." The season does not refer to time; it refers to us. This verse says, "Preach the Word! Be ready in season and out of season." In other words, we should "be ready" whether we feel like it or not. If we do only what we feel inclined to do, some of us would never do anything. There are some people who are totally unemployable in the spiritual realm. They are spiritually feeble and weak, and they refuse to do anything unless they are supernaturally inspired. The proof that our relationship is right with God is that we do our best whether we feel inspired or not.

One of the worst traps a Christian worker can fall into is to become obsessed with his own exceptional moments of inspiration. When the Spirit of God gives you a time of inspiration and insight, you tend to say, "Now that I've experienced this moment, I will always be like this for God." No, you will not, and God will make sure of that. Those times are entirely the gift of God. You cannot give them to yourself when you choose. If you say you will only be at your best for God, as during those exceptional times, you actually become an intolerable burden on Him. You will never do anything unless God keeps you consciously aware of His inspiration to you at all times. If you make a god out of your best moments, you will find that God will fade out of your life, never to return until you are obedient in the work He has placed closest to you, and until you have learned not to be obsessed with those exceptional moments He has given you.

The Supreme Climb

"Take now your son . . . and offer him . . . as a burnt offering on one of the mountains of which I shall tell you"

(Genesis 22:2).

A person's character determines how he interprets God's will (see Psalm 18:25–26). Abraham interpreted God's command to mean that he had to kill his son, and he could only leave this traditional belief behind through the pain of a tremendous ordeal. God could purify his faith in no other way. If we obey what God says according to our sincere belief, God will break us from those traditional beliefs that misrepresent Him. There are many such beliefs which must be removed—for example, that God removes a child because his mother loves him too much. That is the devil's lie and a travesty on the true nature of God! If the devil can hinder us from taking the supreme climb and getting rid of our wrong traditional beliefs about God, he will do so. But if we will stay true to God, God will take us through an ordeal that will serve to bring us into a better knowledge of Himself.

The great lesson to be learned from Abraham's faith in God is that he was prepared to do anything for God. He was there to obey God, no matter what contrary belief of his might be violated by his obedience. Abraham was not devoted to his own convictions or else he would have slain Isaac and said that the voice of the angel was actually the voice of the devil. That is the attitude of a fanatic. If you will remain true to God, God will lead you directly through every barrier and right into the inner chamber of the knowledge of Himself. But you must always be willing to come to the point of giving up your own convictions and traditional beliefs. Don't ask God to test you. Never declare as Peter did that you are willing to do anything, even "to go . . . both to prison and to death" (Luke 22:33). Abraham did not make any such statement—he simply remained true to God, and God purified his faith.

What Do You Want?

"Do you seek great things for yourself?"
(Jeremiah 45:5).

Are you seeking great things for yourself, instead of seeking to be a great person? God wants you to be in a much closer relationship with Himself than simply receiving His gifts—He wants you to get to know Him. Even some large thing we want is only incidental; it comes and it goes. But God never gives us anything incidental. There is nothing easier than getting into the right relationship with God, unless it is not God you seek, but only what He can give you.

If you have only come as far as asking God for things, you have never come to the point of understanding the least bit of what surrender really means. You have become a Christian based on your own terms. You protest, saying, "I asked God for the Holy Spirit, but He didn't give me the rest and the peace I expected." And instantly God puts His finger on the reason— you are not seeking the Lord at all; you are seeking something for yourself. Jesus said, "Ask, and it will be given to you . . ." (Matthew 7:7). Ask God for what you want and do not be concerned about asking for the wrong thing, because as you draw ever closer to Him, you will cease asking for things altogether. "Your Father knows the things you have need of before you ask Him" (Matthew 6:8). Then why should you ask? So that you may get to know Him.

Are you seeking great things for yourself? Have you said, "Oh, Lord, completely fill me with your Holy Spirit"? If God does not, it is because you are not totally surrendered to Him; there is something you still refuse to do. Are you prepared to ask yourself what it is you want from God and why you want it? God always ignores your present level of completeness in favor of your ultimate future completeness. He is not concerned about making you blessed and happy right now, but He's continually working out His ultimate perfection for you— ". . . that they may be one just as We are one . . ." (John 17:22).

W_{hat} Y_{ou} W_{ill} G_{et}

"I will give your life to you
as a prize in all places,
wherever you go"
(Jeremiah 45:5).

This is the firm and immovable secret of the Lord to those who trust Him—"I will give your life to you . . . ." What more does a man want than his life? It is the essential thing. ". . . your life . . . as a prize . . ." means that wherever you may go, even if it is into hell, you will come out with your life and nothing can harm it. So many of us are caught up in exhibiting things for others to see, not showing off property and possessions, but our blessings. All these things that we so proudly show have to go. But there is something greater that can never go—the life that "is hidden with Christ in God" (Colossians 3:3).

Are you prepared to let God take you into total oneness with Himself, paying no more attention to what you call the great things of life? Are you prepared to surrender totally and let go? The true test of abandonment or surrender is in refusing to say, "Well, what about this?" Beware of your own ideas and speculations. The moment you allow yourself to think, "What about this?" you show that you have not surrendered and that you do not really trust God. But once you do surrender, you will no longer think about what God is going to do. Abandonment means to refuse yourself the luxury of asking any questions. If you totally abandon yourself to God, He immediately says to you, "I will give your life to you as a prize . . . ." The reason people are tired of life is that God has not given them anything— they have not been given their life "as a prize." The way to get out of that condition is to abandon yourself to God. And once you do get to the point of total surrender to Him, you will be the most surprised and delighted person on earth. God will have you absolutely, without any limitations, and He will have given you your life. If you are not there, it is either because of disobedience in your life or your refusal to be simple enough.

Gracious Uncertainty

" . . . it has not yet been revealed what we shall be . . ."
(1 John 3:2).

Our natural inclination is to be so precise—trying always to forecast accurately what will happen next—that we look upon uncertainty as a bad thing. We think that we must reach some predetermined goal, but that is not the nature of the spiritual life. The nature of the spiritual life is that we are certain in our uncertainty. Consequently, we do not put down roots. Our common sense says, "Well, what if I were in that circumstance?" We cannot presume to see ourselves in any circumstance in which we have never been.

Certainty is the mark of the commonsense life—gracious uncertainty is the mark of the spiritual life. To be certain of God means that we are uncertain in all our ways, not knowing what tomorrow may bring. This is generally expressed with a sigh of sadness, but it should be an expression of breathless expectation. We are uncertain of the next step, but we are certain of God. As soon as we abandon ourselves to God and do the task He has placed closest to us, He begins to fill our lives with surprises. When we become simply a promoter or a defender of a particular belief, something within us dies. That is not believing God—it is only believing our belief about Him. Jesus said, " . . . unless you . . . become as little children . . ." (Matthew 18:3). The spiritual life is the life of a child. We are not uncertain of God, just uncertain of what He is going to do next. If our certainty is only in our beliefs, we develop a sense of self-righteousness, become overly critical, and are limited by the view that our beliefs are complete and settled. But when we have the right relationship with God, life is full of spontaneous, joyful uncertainty and expectancy. Jesus said, " . . . believe also in Me" (John 14:1), not, "Believe certain things about Me." Leave everything to Him and it will be gloriously and graciously uncertain how He will come in—but you can be certain that He will come. Remain faithful to Him.

*S*pontaneous *L*ove

"Love suffers long and is
kind . . ."
(1 Corinthians 13:4).

Love is not premeditated—it is spontaneous; that is, it bursts forth in extraordinary ways. There is nothing of precise certainty in Paul's description of love. We cannot predetermine our thoughts and actions by saying, "Now I will never think any evil thoughts, and I will believe everything that Jesus would have me to believe." No, the characteristic of love is spontaneity. We don't deliberately set the statements of Jesus before us as our standard, but when His Spirit is having His way with us, we live according to His standard without even realizing it. And when we look back, we are amazed at how unconcerned we have been over our emotions, which is the very evidence that real spontaneous love was there. The nature of everything involved in the life of God in us is only discerned when we have been through it and it is in our past.

The fountains from which love flows are in God, not in us. It is absurd to think that the love of God is naturally in our hearts, as a result of our own nature. His love is there only because it "has been poured out in our hearts by the Holy Spirit . . ." (Romans 5:5).

If we try to prove to God how much we love Him, it is a sure sign that we really don't love Him. The evidence of our love for Him is the absolute spontaneity of our love, which flows naturally from His nature within us. And when we look back, we will not be able to determine why we did certain things, but we can know that we did them according to the spontaneous nature of His love in us. The life of God exhibits itself in this spontaneous way because the fountains of His love are in the Holy Spirit.

Faith—Not Emotion

"We walk by faith, not by sight" (2 Corinthians 5:7).

For a while, we are fully aware of God's concern for us. But then, when God begins to use us in His work, we begin to take on a pitiful look and talk only of our trials and difficulties. And all the while God is trying to make us do our work as hidden people who are not in the spotlight. None of us would be hidden spiritually if we could help it. Can we do our work when it seems that God has sealed up heaven? Some of us always want to be brightly illuminated saints with golden halos and with the continual glow of inspiration, and to have other saints of God dealing with us all the time. A self-assured saint is of no value to God. He is abnormal, unfit for daily life, and completely unlike God. We are here, not as immature angels, but as men and women, to do the work of this world. And we are to do it with an infinitely greater power to withstand the struggle because we have been born from above.

If we continually try to bring back those exceptional moments of inspiration, it is a sign that it is not God we want. We are becoming obsessed with the moments when God did come and speak with us, and we are insisting that He do it again. But what God wants us to do is to "walk by faith." How many of us have set ourselves aside as if to say, "I cannot do anything else until God appears to me"? He will never do it. We will have to get up on our own, without any inspiration and without any sudden touch from God. Then comes our surprise and we find ourselves exclaiming, "Why, He was there all the time, and I never knew it!" Never live for those exceptional moments—they are surprises. God will give us His touches of inspiration only when He sees that we are not in danger of being led away by them. We must never consider our moments of inspiration as the standard way of life—our work is our standard.

The Patience To Wait for the Vision

"Though it tarries, wait for it . . ." (Habakkuk 2:3).

Patience is not the same as indifference; patience conveys the idea of someone who is tremendously strong and able to withstand all assaults. Having the vision of God is the source of patience because it gives us God's true and proper inspiration. Moses endured, not because of his devotion to his principles of what was right, nor because of his sense of duty to God, but because he had a vision of God. ". . . he endured as seeing Him who is invisible" (Hebrews 11:27). A person who has the vision of God is not devoted to a cause or to any particular issue—he is devoted to God Himself. You always know when the vision is of God because of the inspiration that comes with it. Things come to you with greatness and add vitality to your life because everything is energized by God. He may give you a time spiritually, with no word from Himself at all, just as His Son experienced during His time of temptation in the wilderness. When God does that, simply endure, and the power to endure will be there because you see God.

"Though it tarries, wait for it . . . ." The proof that we have the vision is that we are reaching out for more than we have already grasped. It is a bad thing to be satisfied spiritually. The psalmist said, "What shall I render to the Lord . . . ? I will take up the cup of salvation . . ." (Psalm 116:12–13). We are apt to look for satisfaction within ourselves and say, "Now I've got it! Now I am completely sanctified. Now I can endure." Instantly we are on the road to ruin. Our reach must exceed our grasp. Paul said, "Not that I have already attained, or am already perfected; but I press on . . ." (Philippians 3:12). If we have only what we have experienced, we have nothing. But if we have the inspiration of the vision of God, we have more than we can experience. Beware of the danger of spiritual relaxation.

Vital Intercession

". . . praying always with all prayer and supplication in the Spirit . . ."
(Ephesians 6:18).

As we continue on in our intercession for others, we may find that our obedience to God in interceding is going to cost those for whom we intercede more than we ever thought. The danger in this is that we begin to intercede in sympathy with those whom God was gradually lifting up to a totally different level in direct answer to our prayers. Whenever we step back from our close identification with God's interest and concern for others and step into having emotional sympathy with them, the vital connection with God is gone. We have then put our sympathy and concern for them in the way, and this is a deliberate rebuke to God.

It is impossible for us to have living and vital intercession unless we are perfectly and completely sure of God. And the greatest destroyer of that confident relationship to God, so necessary for intercession, is our own personal sympathy and preconceived bias. Identification with God is the key to intercession, and whenever we stop being identified with Him it is because of our sympathy with others, not because of sin. It is not likely that sin will interfere with our intercessory relationship with God, but sympathy will. It is sympathy with ourselves or with others that makes us say, "I will not allow that thing to happen." And instantly we are out of that vital connection with God.

Vital intercession leaves you with neither the time nor the inclination to pray for your own "sad and pitiful self." You do not have to struggle to keep thoughts of yourself out, because they are not even there to be kept out of your thinking. You are completely and entirely identified with God's interests and concerns in other lives. God gives us discernment in the lives of others to call us to intercession for them, never so that we may find fault with them.

Vicarious Intercession

". . . having boldness to enter
the Holiest by the blood
of Jesus . . ."
(Hebrews 10:19).

Beware of thinking that intercession means bringing our own
personal sympathies and concerns into the presence of God,
and then demanding that He do whatever we ask. Our ability to
approach God is due entirely to the vicarious, or substitutionary, identification of our Lord with sin. We have "boldness to
enter the Holiest *by the blood of Jesus.*"

Spiritual stubbornness is the most effective hindrance to
intercession, because it is based on a sympathetic "understanding" of things we see in ourselves and others that we think
needs no atonement. We have the idea that there are certain
good and virtuous things in each of us that do not need to be
based on the atonement by the Cross of Christ. Just the slug-
gishness and lack of interest produced by this kind of thinking
makes us unable to intercede. We do not identify ourselves
with God's interests and concerns for others, and we get irritated with Him. Yet we are always ready with our own ideas,
and our intercession becomes only the glorification of our
own natural sympathies. We have to realize that the identification of Jesus with sin means a radical change of all of our sympathies and interests. Vicarious intercession means that we
deliberately substitute God's interests in others for our natural
sympathy with them.

Am I stubborn or substituted? Am I spoiled or complete
in my relationship to God? Am I irritable or spiritual? Am I
determined to have my own way or determined to be identified with Him?

Judgment and the Love of God

"The time has come for judgment to begin at the house of God . . ."

(1 Peter 4:17).

The Christian servant must never forget that salvation is God's idea, not man's; therefore, it has an unfathomable depth. Salvation is the great thought of God, not an experience. Experience is simply the door through which salvation comes into the conscious level of our life so that we are aware of what has taken place on a much deeper level. Never preach the experience—preach the great thought of God behind the experience. When we preach, we are not simply proclaiming how people can be saved from hell and be made moral and pure; we are conveying good news about God.

In the teachings of Jesus Christ the element of judgment is always brought out—it is the sign of the love of God. Never sympathize with someone who finds it difficult to get to God; God is not to blame. It is not for us to figure out the reason for the difficulty, but only to present the truth of God so that the Spirit of God will reveal what is wrong. The greatest test of the quality of our preaching is whether or not it brings everyone to judgment. When the truth is preached, the Spirit of God brings each person face to face with God Himself.

If Jesus ever commanded us to do something that He was unable to equip us to accomplish, He would be a liar. And if we make our own inability a stumbling block or an excuse not to be obedient, it means that we are telling God that there is something which He has not yet taken into account. Every element of our own self-reliance must be put to death by the power of God. The moment we recognize our complete weakness and our dependence upon Him will be the very moment that the Spirit of God will exhibit His power.

Liberty and the Standards of Jesus

"Stand fast therefore in the liberty by which Christ has made us free . . ." (Galatians 5:1).

A spiritually-minded person will never come to you with the demand—"Believe this and that"; a spiritually-minded person will demand that you align your life with the standards of Jesus. We are not asked to believe the Bible, but to believe the One whom the Bible reveals (see John 5:39–40). We are called to present liberty for the conscience of others, not to bring them liberty for their thoughts and opinions. And if we ourselves are free with the liberty of Christ, others will be brought into that same liberty—the liberty that comes from realizing the absolute control and authority of Jesus Christ.

Always measure your life solely by the standards of Jesus. Submit yourself to His yoke, and His alone; and always be careful never to place a yoke on others that is not of Jesus Christ. It takes God a long time to get us to stop thinking that unless everyone sees things exactly as we do, they must be wrong. That is never God's view. There is only one true liberty—the liberty of Jesus at work in our conscience enabling us to do what is right.

Don't get impatient with others. Remember how God dealt with you—with patience and with gentleness. But never water down the truth of God. Let it have its way and never apologize for it. Jesus said, "Go . . . and make _disciples_ . . ." (Matthew 28:19), not, "Make converts to your own thoughts and opinions."

Building for Eternity

> "Which of you, intending to build a tower, does not sit down first and count the cost, whether he has enough to finish it . . ."
> (Luke 14:28).

Our Lord was not referring here to a cost which we have to count, but to a cost which He has already counted. The cost was those thirty years in Nazareth, those three years of popularity, scandal, and hatred, the unfathomable agony He experienced in Gethsemane, and the assault upon Him at Calvary—the central point upon which all of time and eternity turn. Jesus Christ has counted the cost. In the final analysis, people are not going to laugh at Him and say, "This man began to build and was not able to finish" (14:30).

The conditions of discipleship given to us by our Lord in verses 26, 27, and 33 mean that the men and women He is going to use in His mighty building enterprises are those in whom He has done everything. "If anyone comes to Me and does not hate his father and mother, wife and children, brothers and sisters, yes, and his own life also, *he cannot be My disciple*" (14:26). This verse teaches us that the only men and women our Lord will use in His building enterprises are those who love Him personally, passionately, and with great devotion—those who have a love for Him that goes far beyond any of the closest relationships on earth. The conditions are strict, but they are glorious.

All that we build is going to be inspected by God. When God inspects us with His searching and refining fire, will He detect that we have built enterprises of our own on the foundation of Jesus? (see 1 Corinthians 3:10–15). We are living in a time of tremendous enterprises, a time when we are trying to work for God, and that is where the trap is. Profoundly speaking, we can never work for God. Jesus, as the Master Builder, takes us over so that He may direct and control us completely for His enterprises and His building plans; and no one has any right to demand where he will be put to work.

The Faith to Persevere

"Because you have kept My command to persevere . . ." (Revelation 3:10).

Perseverance means more than endurance—more than simply holding on until the end. A saint's life is in the hands of God like a bow and arrow in the hands of an archer. God is aiming at something the saint cannot see, but our Lord continues to stretch and strain, and every once in a while the saint says, "I can't take any more." Yet God pays no attention; He goes on stretching until His purpose is in sight, and then He lets the arrow fly. Entrust yourself to God's hands. Is there something in your life for which you need perseverance right now? Maintain your intimate relationship with Jesus Christ through the perseverance of faith. Proclaim as Job did, "Though He slay me, yet will I trust Him" (Job 13:15).

Faith is not some weak and pitiful emotion, but is strong and vigorous confidence built on the fact that God is holy love. And even though you cannot see Him right now and cannot understand what He is doing, you know *Him.* Disaster occurs in your life when you lack the mental composure that comes from establishing yourself on the eternal truth that God is holy love. Faith is the supreme effort of your life—throwing yourself with abandon and total confidence upon God.

God ventured His all in Jesus Christ to save us, and now He wants us to venture our all with total abandoned confidence in Him. There are areas in our lives where that faith has not worked in us as yet—places still untouched by the life of God. There were none of those places in Jesus Christ's life, and there are to be none in ours. Jesus prayed, "This is eternal life, that they may know You . . ." (John 17:3). The real meaning of eternal life is a life that can face anything it has to face without wavering. If we will take this view, life will become one great romance—a glorious opportunity of seeing wonderful things all the time. God is disciplining us to get us into this central place of power.

Reaching Beyond Our Grasp

"Where there is no revelation [or prophetic vision], the people cast off restraint . . ." (Proverbs 29:18).

There is a difference between holding on to a principle and having a vision. A principle does not come from moral inspiration, but a vision does. People who are totally consumed with idealistic principles rarely *do* anything. A person's own idea of God and His attributes may actually be used to justify and rationalize his deliberate neglect of his duty. Jonah tried to excuse his disobedience by saying to God, ". . . I know that You are a gracious and merciful God, slow to anger and abundant in lovingkindness, One who relents from doing harm" (Jonah 4:2). I too may have the right idea of God and His attributes, but that may be the very reason why I do not do my duty. But wherever there is vision, there is also a life of honesty and integrity, because the vision gives me the moral incentive.

Our own idealistic principles may actually lull us into ruin. Examine yourself spiritually to see if you have vision, or only principles.

> Ah, but a man's reach should exceed his grasp,
> Or what's a heaven for?

"Where there is no revelation [or prophetic vision] . . . ." Once we lose sight of God, we begin to be reckless. We cast off certain restraints from activities we know are wrong. We set prayer aside as well and cease having God's vision in the little things of life. We simply begin to act on our own initiative. If we are eating only out of our own hand, and doing things solely on our own initiative without expecting God to come in, we are on a downward path. We have lost the vision. Is our attitude today an attitude that flows from our vision of God? Are we expecting God to do greater things than He has ever done before? Is there a freshness and a vitality in our spiritual outlook?

Take the Initiative

Add means that we have to do something. We are in danger of forgetting that we cannot do what God does, and that God will not do what we can do. We cannot save nor sanctify our-selves—God does that. But God will not give us good habits or character, and He will not force us to walk correctly before Him. We have to do all that ourselves. We must "work *out*" our "own salvation" which God has worked in us (Philippians 2:12). *Add* means that we must get into the habit of doing things, and in the initial stages that is difficult. To take the initiative is to make a beginning—to instruct yourself in the way you must go.

Beware of the tendency to ask the way when you know it perfectly well. Take the initiative—stop hesitating—take the first step. Be determined to act immediately in faith on what God says to you when He speaks, and never reconsider or change your initial decisions. If you hesitate when God tells you to do something, you are being careless, spurning the grace in which you stand. Take the initiative yourself, make a decision of your will right now, and make it impossible to go back. Burn your bridges behind you, saying, "I *will* write that letter," or "I *will* pay that debt"; and then do it! Make it irrevocable.

We have to get into the habit of carefully listening to God about everything, forming the habit of finding out what He says and heeding it. If, when a crisis comes, we instinctively turn to God, we will know that the habit has been formed in us. We have to take the initiative where we *are*, not where we have not yet been.

"Love One Another"

Love is an indefinite thing to most of us; we don't know what we mean when we talk about love. Love is the loftiest preference of one person for another, and spiritually Jesus demands that this sovereign preference be for Himself (see Luke 14:26). Initially, when "the love of God has been poured out in our hearts by the Holy Spirit" (Romans 5:5), it is easy to put Jesus first. But then we must practice the things mentioned in 2 Peter 1 to see them worked out in our lives.

The first thing God does is forcibly remove any insincerity, pride, and vanity from my life. And the Holy Spirit reveals to me that God loved me not because I was lovable, but because it was His nature to do so. Now He commands me to show the same love to others by saying, ". . . love one another as I have loved you" (John 15:12). He is saying, "I will bring a number of people around you whom you cannot respect, but you must exhibit My love to them, just as I have exhibited it to you." This kind of love is not a patronizing love for the unlovable—it is His love, and it will not be evidenced in us overnight. Some of us may have tried to force it, but we were soon tired and frustrated.

"The Lord . . . is longsuffering toward us, not willing that any should perish . . ." (2 Peter 3:9). I should look within and remember how wonderfully He has dealt with me. The knowledge that God has loved me beyond all limits will compel me to go into the world to love others in the same way. I may get irritated because I have to live with an unusually difficult person. But just think how disagreeable I have been with God! Am I prepared to be identified so closely with the Lord Jesus that His life and His sweetness will be continually poured out through Me? Neither natural love nor God's divine love will remain and grow in me unless it is nurtured. Love is spontaneous, but it has to be maintained through discipline.

The Habit of Having No Habits

"If these things are yours and abound, you will be neither barren nor unfruitful . . ."
(2 Peter 1:8).

When we first begin to form a habit, we are fully aware of it. There are times when we are aware of becoming virtuous and godly, but this awareness should only be a stage we quickly pass through as we grow spiritually. If we stop at this stage, we will develop a sense of spiritual pride. The right thing to do with godly habits is to immerse them in the life of the Lord until they become such a spontaneous expression of our lives that we are no longer aware of them. Our spiritual life continually causes us to focus our attention inwardly for the determined purpose of self-examination, because each of us has some qualities we have not yet added to our lives.

Your god may be your little Christian habit—the habit of prayer or Bible reading at certain times of your day. Watch how your Father will upset your schedule if you begin to worship your habit instead of what the habit symbolizes. We say, "I can't do that right now; this is my time alone with God." No, this is your time alone with your habit. There is a quality that is still lacking in you. Identify your shortcoming and then look for opportunities to work into your life that missing quality.

Love means that there are no visible habits—that your habits are so immersed in the Lord that you practice them without realizing it. If you are consciously aware of your own holiness, you place limitations on yourself from doing certain things—things God is not restricting you from at all. This means there is a missing quality that needs to be added to your life. The only supernatural life is the life the Lord Jesus lived, and He was at home with God anywhere. Is there someplace where you are not at home with God? Then allow God to work through whatever that particular circumstance may be until you increase in Him, adding His qualities. Your life will then become the simple life of a child.

The Habit of Keeping a Clear Conscience

" . . . strive to have a conscience without offense toward God and men" (Acts 24:16).

God's commands to us are actually given to the life of His Son in us. Consequently, to our human nature in which God's Son has been formed (see Galatians 4:19), His commands are difficult. But they become divinely easy once we obey.

Conscience is that ability within me that attaches itself to the highest standard I know, and then continually reminds me of what that standard demands that I do. It is the eye of the soul which looks out either toward God or toward what we regard as the highest standard. This explains why conscience is different in different people. If I am in the habit of continually holding God's standard in front of me, my conscience will always direct me to God's perfect law and indicate what I should do. The question is, will I obey? I have to make an effort to keep my conscience so sensitive that I can live without any offense toward anyone. I should be living in such perfect harmony with God's Son that the spirit of my mind is being renewed through every circumstance of life, and that I may be able to quickly "prove what is that good and acceptable and perfect will of God" (Romans 12:2; also see Ephesians 4:23).

God always instructs us down to the last detail. Is my ear sensitive enough to hear even the softest whisper of the Spirit, so that I know what I should do? "Do not grieve the Holy Spirit of God . . ." (Ephesians 4:30). He does not speak with a voice like thunder—His voice is so gentle that it is easy for us to ignore. And the only thing that keeps our conscience sensitive to Him is the habit of being open to God on the inside. When you begin to debate, stop immediately. Don't ask, "Why can't I do this?" You are on the wrong track. There is no debating possible once your conscience speaks. Whatever it is—drop it, and see that you keep your inner vision clear.

The Habit of Enjoying Adversity

" . . . that the life of Jesus also may be manifested in our body"
(2 Corinthians 4:10).

We have to develop godly habits to express what God's grace has done in us. It is not just a question of being saved from hell, but of being saved so that "the life of Jesus also may be manifested in our body." And it is adversity that makes us exhibit His life in our mortal flesh. Is my life exhibiting the essence of the sweetness of the Son of God, or just the basic irritation of "myself" that I would have apart from Him? The only thing that will enable me to enjoy adversity is the acute sense of eagerness of allowing the life of the Son of God to evidence itself in me. No matter how difficult something may be, I must say, "Lord, I am delighted to obey You in this." Instantly, the Son of God will move to the forefront of my life, and will manifest in my body that which glorifies Him.

You must not debate. The moment you obey the light of God, His Son shines through you in that very adversity; but if you debate with God, you grieve His Spirit (see Ephesians 4:30). You must keep yourself in the proper condition to allow the life of the Son of God to be manifested in you, and you cannot keep yourself fit if you give way to self-pity. Our circumstances are the means God uses to exhibit just how wonderfully perfect and extraordinarily pure His Son is. Discovering a new way of manifesting the Son of God should make our heart beat with renewed excitement. It is one thing to choose adversity, and quite another to enter into adversity through the orchestrating of our circumstances by God's sovereignty. And if God puts you into adversity, He is adequately sufficient to "supply all your need" (Philippians 4:19).

Keep your soul properly conditioned to manifest the life of the Son of God. Never live on your memories of past experiences, but let the Word of God always be living and active in you.

The Habit of Rising to the Occasion

". . . that you may know what is the hope of His calling . . ."
(Ephesians 1:18).

Remember that you have been saved so that the life of Jesus may be manifested in your body (see 2 Corinthians 4:10). Direct the total energy of your powers so that you may achieve everything your election as a child of God provides; rise every time to whatever occasion may come your way.

You did not do anything to achieve your salvation, but you must do something to exhibit it. You must "work out your own salvation" which God has worked in you already (Philippians 2:12). Are your speech, your thinking, and your emotions evidence that you are working it "out"? If you are still the same miserable, grouchy person, set on having your own way, then it is a lie to say that God has saved and sanctified you.

God is the Master Designer, and He allows adversities into your life to see if you can jump over them properly—"By my God I can leap over a wall" (Psalm 18:29). God will never shield you from the requirements of being His son or daughter. First Peter 4:12 says, "Beloved, do not think it strange concerning the fiery trial which is to try you, as though some strange thing happened to you . . . ." Rise to the occasion—do what the trial demands of you. It does not matter how much it hurts as long as it gives God the opportunity to manifest the life of Jesus in your body.

May God not find complaints in us anymore, but spiritual vitality—a readiness to face anything He brings our way. The only proper goal of life is that we manifest the Son of God; and when this occurs, all of our dictating of our demands to God disappears. Our Lord never dictated demands to His Father, and neither are we to make demands on God. We are here to submit to His will so that He may work through us what He wants. Once we realize this, He will make us broken bread and poured-out wine with which to feed and nourish others.

The Habit of Recognizing God's Provision

"... you may be partakers of the divine nature ..." (2 Peter 1:4).

We are made "partakers of the divine nature," receiving and sharing God's own nature through His promises. Then we have to work that divine nature into our human nature by developing godly habits. The first habit to develop is the habit of recognizing God's provision for us. We say, however, "Oh, I can't afford it." One of the worst lies is wrapped up in that statement. We talk as if our heavenly Father has cut us off without a penny! We think it is a sign of true humility to say at the end of the day, "Well, I just barely got by today, but it was a severe struggle." And yet all of Almighty God is ours in the Lord Jesus! And He will reach to the last grain of sand and the remotest star to bless us if we will only obey Him. Does it really matter that our circumstances are difficult? Why shouldn't they be! If we give way to self-pity and indulge in the luxury of misery, we remove God's riches from our lives and hinder others from entering into His provision. No sin is worse than the sin of self-pity, because it removes God from the throne of our lives, replacing Him with our own self-interests. It causes us to open our mouths only to complain, and we simply become spiritual sponges—always absorbing, never giving, and never being satisfied. And there is nothing lovely or generous about our lives.

Before God becomes satisfied with us, He will take everything of our so-called wealth, until we learn that He is our Source; as the psalmist said, "All my springs are in You" (Psalm 87:7). If the majesty, grace, and power of God are not being exhibited in us, God holds us responsible. "God is able to make all grace abound toward you, that you ... may have an abundance ..." (2 Corinthians 9:8)—then learn to lavish the grace of God on others, generously giving of yourself. Be marked and identified with God's nature, and His blessing will flow through you all the time.

*His Ascension
and Our Access*

"It came to pass, while He blessed them, that He was parted from them and carried up into heaven"
(Luke 24:51).

We have no experiences in our lives that correspond to the events in our Lord's life after the transfiguration. From that moment forward His life was altogether substitutionary. Up to the time of the transfiguration, He had exhibited the normal, perfect life of a man. But from the transfiguration forward—Gethsemane, the Cross, the resurrection—everything is unfamiliar to us. His Cross is the door by which every member of the human race can enter into the life of God; by His resurrection He has the right to give eternal life to anyone, and by His ascension our Lord entered heaven, keeping the door open for humanity.

The transfiguration was completed on the Mount of Ascension. If Jesus had gone to heaven directly from the Mount of Transfiguration, He would have gone alone. He would have been nothing more to us than a glorious Figure. But He turned His back on the glory, and came down from the mountain to identify Himself with fallen humanity.

The ascension is the complete fulfillment of the transfiguration. Our Lord returned to His original glory, but not simply as the Son of God—He returned to His father as the *Son of Man* as well. There is now freedom of access for anyone straight to the very throne of God because of the ascension of the Son of Man. As the Son of Man, Jesus Christ deliberately limited His omnipotence, omnipresence, and omniscience. But now they are His in absolute, full power. As the Son of Man, Jesus Christ now has all the power at the throne of God. From His ascension forward He is the King of kings and Lord of lords.

Living Simply— Yet Focused

"Look at the birds of the air
. . . . Consider the lilies
of the field . . ."
(Matthew 6:26, 28).

Consider the lilies of the field, how they grow: they neither toil nor spin"—they simply *are*! Think of the sea, the air, the sun, the stars, and the moon—all of these simply *are* as well—yet what a ministry and service they render on our behalf! So often we impair God's designed influence, which He desires to exhibit through us, because of our own conscious efforts to be consistent and useful. Jesus said there is only one way to develop and grow spiritually, and that is through focusing and concentrating on God. In essence, Jesus was saying, "Do not worry about being of use to others; simply believe on Me." In other words, pay attention to the Source, and out of you "will flow rivers of living water" (John 7:38). We cannot discover the source of our natural life through common sense and reasoning, and Jesus is teaching here that growth in our spiritual life comes not from focusing directly on it, but from concentrating on our Father in heaven. Our heavenly Father knows our circumstances, and if we will stay focused on Him, instead of our circumstances, we will grow spiritually—just as "the lilies of the field."

The people who influence us the most are not those who detain us with their continual talk, but those who live their lives like the stars in the sky and "the lilies of the field"—simply and unaffectedly. Those are the lives that mold and shape us.

If you want to be of use to God, maintain the proper relationship with Jesus Christ by staying focused on Him, and He will make use of you every minute you live—yet you will be unaware, on the conscious level of your life, that you are being used of Him.

God does not keep His child immune from trouble; He promises, "I will be with him in trouble . . ." (Psalm 91:15). It doesn't matter how real or intense the adversities may be; nothing can ever separate him from his relationship to God. "In all these things we are more than conquerors . . ." (Romans 8:37). Paul was not referring here to imaginary things, but to things that are dangerously real. And he said we are "super-victors" in the midst of them, not because of our own ingenuity, nor because of our courage, but because none of them affects our essential relationship with God in Jesus Christ. I feel sorry for the Christian who doesn't have something in the circumstances of his life that he wishes were not there.

"Shall tribulation . . . ?" Tribulation is never a grand, highly welcomed event; but whatever it may be—whether exhausting, irritating, or simply causing some weakness—it is not able to "separate us from the love of Christ." Never allow tribulations or the "cares of this world" to separate you from remembering that God loves you (Matthew 13:22).

"Shall . . . distress . . . ?" Can God's love continue to hold fast, even when everyone and everything around us seems to be saying that His love is a lie, and that there is no such thing as justice?

"Shall . . . famine . . . ?" Can we not only believe in the love of God but also be "more than conquerors," even while we are being starved?

Either Jesus Christ is a deceiver, having deceived even Paul, or else some extraordinary thing happens to someone who holds on to the love of God when the odds are totally against him. Logic is silenced in the face of each of these things which come against him. Only one thing can account for it—the *love of God in Christ Jesus*. "Out of the wreck I rise" every time.

Taking Possession of Our Own Soul

"By your patience possess your souls"
(Luke 21:19).

When a person is born again, there is a period of time when he does not have the same vitality in his thinking or reasoning that he previously had. We must learn to express this new life within us, which comes by forming the mind of Christ (see Philippians 2:5). Luke 21:19 means that we take possession of our souls through patience. But many of us prefer to stay at the entrance to the Christian life, instead of going on to create and build our soul in accordance with the new life God has placed within us. We fail because we are ignorant of the way God has made us, and we blame things on the devil that are actually the result of our own undisciplined natures. Just think what we could be when we are awakened to the truth!

There are certain things in life that we need not pray about—moods, for instance. We will never get rid of moodiness by praying, but we will by kicking it out of our lives. Moods nearly always are rooted in some physical circumstance, not in our true inner self. It is a continual struggle not to listen to the moods which arise as a result of our physical condition, but we must never submit to them for a second. We have to pick ourselves up by the back of the neck and shake ourselves; then we will find that we can do what we believed we were unable to do. The problem that most of us are cursed with is simply that we *won't*. The Christian life is one of spiritual courage and determination lived out in our flesh.

Having God's "Unreasonable" Faith

"Seek first the kingdom of God and His righteousness, and all these things shall be added to you" (Matthew 6:33).

When we look at these words of Jesus, we immediately find them to be the most revolutionary that human ears have ever heard. ". . . seek first the kingdom of God . . . ." Even the most spiritually-minded of us argue the exact opposite, saying, "But I *must* live; I *must* make a certain amount of money; I *must* be clothed; I *must* be fed." The great concern of our lives is not the kingdom of God but how we are going to take care of ourselves to live. Jesus reversed the order by telling us to get the right relationship with God first, maintaining it as the primary concern of our lives, and never to place our concern on taking care of the other things of life.

". . . do not worry about your life . . ." (6:25). Our Lord pointed out that from His standpoint it is absolutely unreasonable for us to be anxious, worrying about how we will live. Jesus did not say that the person who takes no thought for anything in his life is blessed—no, that person is a fool. But Jesus *did* teach that His disciple must make his relationship with God the dominating focus of his life, and to be cautiously carefree about everything else in comparison to that. In essence, Jesus was saying, "Don't make food and drink the controlling factor of your life, but be focused absolutely on God." Some people are careless about what they eat and drink, and they suffer for it; they are careless about what they wear, having no business looking the way they do; they are careless with their earthly matters, and God holds them responsible. Jesus is saying that the greatest concern of life is to place our relationship with God first, and everything else second.

It is one of the most difficult, yet critical, disciplines of the Christian life to allow the Holy Spirit to bring us into absolute harmony with the teaching of Jesus in these verses.

The Explanation for Our Difficulties

"... that they all may be one, as You, Father, are in Me, and I in You, that they also may be one in Us ..."
(John 17:21).

If you are going through a time of isolation, seemingly all alone, read John 17. It will explain exactly why you are where you are—because Jesus has prayed that you "may be one" with the Father as He is. Are you helping God to answer that prayer, or do you have some other goal for your life? Since you became a disciple, you cannot be as independent as you used to be.

God reveals in John 17 that His purpose is not just to answer our prayers, but that through prayer we might come to discern His mind. Yet there is one prayer which God must answer, and that is the prayer of Jesus—"... that they may be one just as We are one ..." (17:22). Are we as close to Jesus Christ as that?

God is not concerned about our plans; He doesn't ask, "Do you want to go through this loss of a loved one, this difficulty, or this defeat?" No, He allows these things for His own purpose. The things we are going through are either making us sweeter, better, and nobler men and women, or they are making us more critical and fault-finding, and more insistent on our own way. The things that happen either make us evil, or they make us more saintly, depending entirely on our relationship with God and its level of intimacy. If we will pray, regarding our own lives, "Your will be done" (Matthew 26:42), then we will be encouraged and comforted by John 17, knowing that our Father is working according to His own wisdom, accomplishing what is best. When we understand God's purpose, we will not become small-minded and cynical. Jesus prayed nothing less for us than absolute oneness with Himself, just as He was one with the Father. Some of us are far from this oneness; yet God will not leave us alone until we *are* one with Him—because Jesus prayed, "... that they *all* may be one ...."

Our Careful Unbelief

"... do not worry about your life, what you will eat or what you will drink, nor about your body, what you will put on" (Matthew 6:25).

Jesus summed up commonsense carefulness in the life of a disciple as *unbelief*. If we have received the Spirit of God, He will squeeze right through our lives, as if to ask, "Now where do I come into this relationship, this vacation you have planned, or these new books you want to read?" And He always presses the point until we learn to make Him our first consideration. Whenever we put other things first, there is confusion.

"... do not worry about your life ...." Don't take the pressure of your provision upon yourself. It is not only wrong to worry, it is unbelief; worrying means we do not believe that God can look after the practical details of our lives, and it is never anything but those details that worry us. Have you ever noticed what Jesus said would choke the Word He puts in us? Is it the devil? No—"the cares of this world" (Matthew 13:22). It is always our little worries. We say, "I will not trust when I cannot see"—and that is where unbelief begins. The only cure for unbelief is obedience to the Spirit.

The greatest word of Jesus to His disciples is *abandon*.

"When I saw Him, I fell at His feet as dead" (Revelation 1:17).

It may be that, like the apostle John, you know Jesus Christ intimately. Yet when He suddenly appears to you with totally unfamiliar character-istics, the only thing you can do is fall "at His feet as dead." There are times when God cannot reveal Himself in any other way than in His majesty, and it is the awesomeness of the vision which brings you to the delight of despair. You experience this joy in hopelessness, realizing that if you are ever to be raised up it must be by the hand of God.

"He laid His right hand on me . . ." (1:17). In the midst of the awesomeness, a touch comes, and you know it is the right hand of Jesus Christ. You know it is not the hand of restraint, correction, nor chastisement, but the right hand of the Everlasting Father. Whenever His hand is laid upon you, it gives inexpressible peace and comfort, and the sense that "underneath are the everlasting arms" (Deuteronomy 33:27), full of support, provision, comfort, and strength. And once His touch comes, nothing at all can throw you into fear again. In the midst of all His ascended glory, the Lord Jesus comes to speak to an insignificant disciple, saying, "Do not be afraid" (Revelation 1:17). His tenderness is inexpressibly sweet. Do I know Him like that?

Take a look at some of the things that cause despair. There is despair which has no delight, no limits whatsoever, and no hope of anything brighter. But the delight of despair comes when "I know that in me (that is, in my flesh) nothing good dwells . . ." (Romans 7:18). I delight in knowing that there is something in me which must fall prostrate before God when He reveals Himself to me, and also in knowing that if I am ever to be raised up it must be by the hand of God. God can do nothing for me until I recognize the limits of what is humanly possible, allowing Him to do the impossible.

The Good or the Best?

"If you take the left, then I
will go to the right; or, if
you go to the right, then I
will go to the left"
(Genesis 13:9).

As soon as you begin to live the life of faith in God, fascinating and physically gratifying possibilities will open up before you. These things are yours by right, but if you are living the life of faith you will exercise your right to waive your rights, and let God make your choice for you. God sometimes allows you to get into a place of testing where your own welfare would be the appropriate thing to consider, if you were not living the life of faith. But if you are, you will joyfully waive your right and allow God to make your choice for you. This is the discipline God uses to transform the natural into the spiritual through obedience to His voice.

Whenever our *right* becomes the guiding factor of our lives, it dulls our spiritual insight. The greatest enemy of the life of faith in God is not sin, but good choices which are not quite good enough. The good is always the enemy of the best. In this passage, it would seem that the wisest thing in the world for Abram to do would be to choose. It was his right, and the people around him would consider him to be a fool for not choosing.

Many of us do not continue to grow spiritually because we prefer to choose on the basis of our rights, instead of relying on God to make the choice for us. We have to learn to walk according to the standard which has its eyes focused on God. And God says to us, as He did to Abram, ". . . walk before Me . . ." (Genesis 17:1).

May 25

Our thinking about prayer, whether right or wrong, is based on our own mental conception of it. The correct concept is to think of prayer as the breath in our lungs and the blood from our hearts. Our blood flows and our breathing continues "without ceasing"; we are not even conscious of it, but it never stops. And we are not always conscious of Jesus keeping us in perfect oneness with God, but if we are obeying Him, He always is. Prayer is not an exercise, it is the life of the saint. Beware of anything that stops the offering up of prayer. "Pray without ceasing . . ."—maintain the childlike habit of offering up prayer in your heart to God all the time.

Jesus never mentioned unanswered prayer. He had the unlimited certainty of knowing that prayer is always answered. Do we have through the Spirit of God that inexpressible certainty that Jesus had about prayer, or do we think of the times when it seemed that God did not answer our prayer? Jesus said, ". . . everyone who asks receives . . ." (Matthew 7:8). Yet we say, "But . . . , but . . . ." God answers prayer in the best way—not just sometimes, but every time. However, the evidence of the answer in the area we want it may not always immediately follow. Do we expect God to answer prayer?

The danger we have is that we want to water down what Jesus said to make it mean something that aligns with our common sense. But if it were only common sense, what He said would not even be worthwhile. The things Jesus taught about prayer are supernatural truths He reveals to us.

$The \ Life \ To \ Know \ Him$ " . . . tarry in the city of Jerusalem until you are endued with power from on high" (Luke 24:49).

The disciples had to tarry, staying in Jerusalem until the day of Pentecost, not only for their own preparation but because they had to wait until the Lord was actually glorified. And as soon as He was glorified, what happened? "Therefore being exalted to the right hand of God, and having received from the Father the promise of the Holy Spirit, He poured out this which you now see and hear" (Acts 2:33). The statement in John 7:39—". . . for the Holy Spirit was not yet given, because Jesus was not yet glorified"—does not pertain to us. The Holy Spirit *has been* given; the Lord *is* glorified—our waiting is not dependent on the providence of God, but on our own spiritual fitness.

The Holy Spirit's influence and power were at work before Pentecost, but *He* was not here. Once our Lord was glorified in His ascension, the Holy Spirit came into the world, and He has been here ever since. We have to receive the revealed truth that He is here. The attitude of receiving and welcoming the Holy Spirit into our lives is to be the continual attitude of a believer. When we receive the Holy Spirit, we receive reviving life from our ascended Lord.

It is not the baptism of the Holy Spirit that changes people, but the power of the ascended Christ coming into their lives through the Holy Spirit. We all too often separate things that the New Testament never separates. The baptism of the Holy Spirit is not an experience apart from Jesus Christ—it is the evidence of the ascended Christ.

The baptism of the Holy Spirit does not make you think of time or eternity—it is one amazing glorious *now.* "This is eternal life, that they may know You . . ." (John 17:3). Begin to know Him now, and never finish.

"In that day you will ask Me nothing"
(John 16:23).

When is "that day"? It is when the ascended Lord makes you one with the Father. "In that day" you will be one with the Father just as Jesus is, and He said, "In that day you will ask Me nothing." Until the resurrection life of Jesus is fully exhibited in you, you have questions about many things. Then after a while you find that all your questions are gone—you don't seem to have any left to ask. You have come to the point of total reliance on the resurrection life of Jesus, which brings you into complete oneness with the purpose of God. Are you living that life now? If not, why aren't you?

"In that day" there may be any number of things still hidden to your understanding, but they will not come between your heart and God. "In that day you will ask Me nothing"—you will not need to ask, because you will be certain that God will reveal things in accordance with His will. The faith and peace of John 14:1 has become the real attitude of your heart, and there are no more questions to be asked. If anything is a mystery to you and is coming between you and God, never look for the explanation in your mind, but look for it in your spirit, your true inner nature—that is where the problem is. Once your inner spiritual nature is willing to submit to the life of Jesus, your understanding will be perfectly clear, and you will come to the place where there is no distance between the Father and you, His child, because the Lord has made you one. "In that day you will ask Me nothing."

Untroubled Relationship

In that day you will ask in My name . . . ," that is, in My nature. Not—"You will use My name as some magic word," but—"You will be so intimate with Me that you will be one with Me." "That day" is not a day in the next life, but a day meant for here and now. ". . . for the Father Himself loves you . . ."—the Father's love is evidence that our union with Jesus is complete and absolute. Our Lord does not mean that our lives will be free from external difficulties and uncertainties, but that just as He knew the Father's heart and mind, we too can be lifted by Him into heavenly places through the baptism of the Holy Spirit, so that He can reveal the teachings of God to us.

". . . whatever you ask the Father in My name . . ." (16:23). "That day" is a day of peace and an untroubled relationship between God and His saint. Just as Jesus stood unblemished and pure in the presence of His Father, we too by the mighty power and effectiveness of the baptism of the Holy Spirit can be lifted into that relationship—". . . that they may be one just as We are one . . ." (John 17:22).

". . . He will give you" (John 16:23). Jesus said that because of His name God will recognize and respond to our prayers. What a great challenge and invitation—to pray in His name! Through the resurrection and ascension power of Jesus, and through the Holy Spirit He has sent, we can be lifted into such a relationship. Once in that wonderful position, having been placed there by Jesus Christ, we can pray to God in Jesus' name—in His nature. This is a gift granted to us through the Holy Spirit, and Jesus said, ". . . whatever you ask the Father in My name He will give you." The sovereign character of Jesus Christ is tested and proved by His own statements.

"Yes—But . . . !"

Suppose God tells you to do something that is an enormous test of your common sense, totally going against it. What will you do? Will you hold back? If you get into the habit of doing something physically, you will do it every time you are tested until you break the habit through sheer determination. And the same is true spiritually. Again and again you will come right up to what Jesus wants, but every time you will turn back at the true point of testing, until you are determined to abandon yourself to God in total surrender. Yet we tend to say, "Yes, but—suppose I do obey God in this matter, what about . . . ?" Or we say, "Yes, I will obey God if what He asks of me doesn't go against my common sense, but don't ask me to take a step in the dark."

Jesus Christ demands the same unrestrained, adventurous spirit in those who have placed their trust in Him that the natural man exhibits. If a person is ever going to do anything worthwhile, there will be times when he must risk everything by his leap in the dark. In the spiritual realm, Jesus Christ demands that you risk everything you hold on to or believe through common sense, and leap by faith into what He says. Once you obey, you will immediately find that what He says is as solidly consistent as common sense.

By the test of common sense, Jesus Christ's statements may seem mad, but when you test them by the trial of faith, your findings will fill your spirit with the awesome fact that they are the very words of God. Trust completely in God, and when He brings you to a new opportunity of adventure, offering it to you, see that you take it. We act like pagans in a crisis—only one out of an entire crowd is daring enough to invest his faith in the character of God.

P_{ut} G_{od} F_{irst}

"Jesus did not commit Himself
to them . . . for He knew
what was in man"
(John 2:24–25).

Put Trust in God First. Our Lord never put His trust in any person. Yet He was never suspicious, never bitter, and never lost hope for anyone, because He put His trust in God first. He trusted absolutely in what God's grace could do for others. If I put my trust in human beings first, the end result will be my despair and hopelessness toward everyone. I will become bitter because I have insisted that people be what no person can ever be—absolutely perfect and right. Never trust anything in yourself or in anyone else, except the grace of God.

Put God's Will First. "Behold, I have come to do Your will, O God" (Hebrews 10:9).

A person's obedience is to what he sees to be a need—our Lord's obedience was to the will of His Father. The rallying cry today is, "We must get to work! The heathen are dying without God. We must go and tell them about Him." But we must first make sure that God's "needs" and His will in us personally are being met. Jesus said, ". . . tarry . . . until you are endued with power from on high" (Luke 24:49). The purpose of our Christian training is to get us into the right relationship to the "needs" of God and His will. Once God's "needs" in us have been met, He will open the way for us to accomplish His will, meeting His "needs" elsewhere.

Put God's Son First. "Whoever receives one little child like this in My name receives Me" (Matthew 18:5).

God came as a baby, giving and entrusting Himself to me. He expects my personal life to be a "Bethlehem." Am I allowing my natural life to be slowly transformed by the indwelling life of the Son of God? God's ultimate purpose is that His Son might be exhibited in me.

"He said to me, 'Son of man, can these bones live?' " (Ezekiel 37:3).

Can a sinner be turned into a saint? Can a twisted life be made right? There is only one appropriate answer—"O Lord God, You know" (37:3). Never forge ahead with your religious common sense and say, "Oh, yes, with just a little more Bible reading, devotional time, and prayer, I see how it can be done."

It is much easier to *do* something than to trust in God; we see the activity and mistake panic for inspiration. That is why we see so few fellow workers *with* God, yet so many people working *for* God. We would much rather work for God than believe in Him. Do I really believe that God will do in me what I cannot do? The degree of hopelessness I have for others comes from never realizing that God has done anything for me. Is my own personal experience such a wonderful realization of God's power and might that I can never have a sense of hopelessness for anyone else I see? Has any spiritual work been accomplished in me at all? The degree of panic activity in my life is equal to the degree of my lack of personal spiritual experience.

"Behold, O My people, I will open your graves . . ." (37:12). When God wants to show you what human nature is like separated from Himself, He shows it to you in yourself. If the Spirit of God has ever given you a vision of what you are apart from the grace of God (and He will only do this when His Spirit is at work in you), then you know that in reality there is no criminal half as bad as you yourself could be without His grace. My "grave" has been opened by God and "I know that in me (that is, in my flesh) nothing good dwells" (Romans 7:18). God's Spirit continually reveals to His children what human nature is like apart from His grace.

Are You Obsessed by Something?

"Who is the man that fears the LORD?" (Psalm 25:12).

Are you obsessed by something? You will probably say, "No, by nothing," but all of us are obsessed by something—usually by ourselves, or, if we are Christians, by our own experience of the Christian life. But the psalmist says that we are to be obsessed by God. The abiding awareness of the Christian life is to be God Himself, not just thoughts about Him. The total being of our life inside and out is to be absolutely obsessed by the presence of God. A child's awareness is so absorbed in his mother that although he is not consciously thinking of her, when a problem arises, the abiding relationship is that with the mother. In that same way, we are to "live and move and have our being" in God (Acts 17:28), looking at everything in relation to Him, because our abiding awareness of Him continually pushes itself to the forefront of our lives.

If we are obsessed by God, nothing else can get into our lives—not concerns, nor tribulation, nor worries. And now we understand why our Lord so emphasized the sin of worrying. How can we dare to be so absolutely unbelieving when God totally surrounds us? To be obsessed by God is to have an effective barricade against all the assaults of the enemy.

"He himself shall dwell in prosperity . . ." (Psalm 25:13). God will cause us to "dwell in prosperity," keeping us at ease, even in the midst of tribulation, misunderstanding, and slander, if our "life is hidden with Christ in God" (Colossians 3:3). We rob ourselves of the miraculous, revealed truth of this abiding companionship with God. "God is our refuge . . ." (Psalm 46:1). Nothing can break through His shelter of protection.

"The Secret of the LORD"

"The secret of the LORD is
with those who fear
Him . . ."
(Psalm 25:14).

What is the sign of a friend? Is it that he tells you his secret sorrows? No, it is that he tells you his secret joys. Many people will confide their secret sorrows to you, but the final mark of intimacy is when they share their secret joys with you. Have we ever let God tell us any of His joys? Or are we continually telling God our secrets, leaving Him no time to talk to us? At the beginning of our Christian life we are full of requests to God. But then we find that God wants to get us into an intimate relationship with Himself—to get us in touch with His purposes. Are we so intimately united to Jesus Christ's idea of prayer—"Your will be done" (Matthew 6:10)—that we catch the secrets of God? What makes God so dear to us is not so much His big blessings to us, but the tiny things, because they show His amazing intimacy with us—He knows every detail of each of our individual lives.

"Him shall He teach in the way He chooses" (Psalm 25:12). At first, we want the awareness of being guided by God. But then as we grow spiritually, we live so fully aware of God that we do not even need to ask what His will is, because the thought of choosing another way will never occur to us. If we are saved and sanctified, God guides us by our everyday choices. And if we are about to choose what He does not want, He will give us a sense of doubt or restraint, which we must heed. Whenever there is doubt, stop at once. Never try to reason it out, saying, "I wonder why I shouldn't do this?" God instructs us in what we choose; that is, He actually guides our common sense. And when we yield to His teachings and guidance, we no longer hinder His Spirit by continually asking, "Now, Lord, what is Your will?"

The Never-forsaking God

"He Himself has said, 'I will never leave you nor forsake you'" (Hebrews 13:5).

What line of thinking do my thoughts take? Do I turn to what God says or to my own fears? Am I simply repeating what God says, or am I learning to truly hear Him and then to respond after I have heard what He says? "For He Himself has said, 'I will never leave you nor forsake you.' So we may boldly say: 'The LORD is my helper; I will not fear. What can man do to me?'" (13:5–6).

"I will never leave you . . ."—not for any reason; not my sin, selfishness, stubbornness, nor waywardness. Have I really let God say to me that He will never leave me? If I have not truly heard this assurance of God, then let me listen again.

"I will never . . . forsake you." Sometimes it is not the difficulty of life but the drudgery of it that makes me think God will forsake me. When there is no major difficulty to overcome, no vision from God, nothing wonderful or beautiful—just the everyday activities of life—do I hear God's assurance even in these?

We have the idea that God is going to do some exceptional thing—that He is preparing and equipping us for some extraordinary work in the future. But as we grow in His grace we find that God is glorifying Himself here and now, at this very moment. If we have God's assurance behind us, the most amazing strength becomes ours, and we learn to sing, glorifying Him even in the ordinary days and ways of life.

God's Assurance

"He Himself has said . . . .
So we may boldly say . . ."
(Hebrews 13:5–6).

My assurance is to be built upon God's assurance to me. God says, "I will never leave you," so that then I "may boldly say, 'The LORD is my helper; I will not fear'" (13:5–6). In other words, I will not be obsessed with apprehension. This does not mean that I will not be tempted to fear, but I will remember God's words of assurance. I will be full of courage, like a child who strives to reach the standard his father has set for him. The faith of many people begins to falter when apprehensions enter their thinking, and they forget the meaning of God's assurance—they forget to take a deep spiritual breath. The only way to remove the fear from our lives is to listen to God's assurance to us.

What are you fearing? Whatever it may be, you are not a coward about it—you are determined to face it, yet you still have a feeling of fear. When it seems that there is nothing and no one to help you, say to yourself, "But 'The LORD is my helper' this very moment, even in my present circumstance." Are you learning to listen to God before you speak, or are you saying things and then trying to make God's Word fit what you have said? Take hold of the Father's assurance, and then say with strong courage, "I will not fear." It does not matter what evil or wrong may be in our way, because "He Himself has said, 'I will never leave you . . . .'"

Human frailty is another thing that gets between God's words of assurance and our own words and thoughts. When we realize how feeble we are in facing difficulties, the difficulties become like giants, we become like grasshoppers, and God seems to be nonexistent. But remember God's assurance to us—"I will never . . . forsake you." Have we learned to sing after hearing God's keynote? Are we continually filled with enough courage to say, "The LORD is my helper," or are we yielding to fear?

"Work Out" What God "Works in" You

"... work out your own salvation ... for it is God who works in you ..." (Philippians 2:12–13).

Your will agrees with God, but in your flesh there is a nature that renders you powerless to do what you know you ought to do. When the Lord initially comes in contact with our conscience, the first thing our conscience does is awaken our will, and our will always agrees with God. Yet you say, "But I don't know if my will is in agreement with God." Look to Jesus and you will find that your will and your conscience are in agreement with Him every time. What causes you to say "I will not obey" is something less deep and penetrating than your will. It is perversity or stubbornness, and they are never in agreement with God. The most profound thing in a person is his will, not sin.

The will is the essential element in God's creation of human beings—sin is a perverse nature which entered into people. In someone who has been born again, the source of the will is Almighty God. "... for it is God who works in you both to will and to do for His good pleasure." With focused attention and great care, you have to "work out" what God "works in" you—not *work* to accomplish or earn "your own salvation," but *work it out* so you will exhibit the evidence of a life based with determined, unshakable faith on the complete and perfect redemption of the Lord. As you do this, you do not bring an opposing will up against God's will—God's will *is* your will. Your natural choices will be in accordance with God's will, and living this life will be as natural as breathing. Stubbornness is an unintelligent barrier, refusing enlightenment and blocking its flow. The only thing to do with this barrier of stubbornness is to blow it up with "dynamite," and the "dynamite" is obedience to the Holy Spirit.

Do I believe that Almighty God is the Source of my will? God not only expects me to do His will, but He is in me to do it.

June 6

The Greatest Source of Power

Am I fulfilling this ministry of intercession deep within the hidden recesses of my life? There is no trap nor any danger at all of being deceived or of showing pride in true intercession. It is a hidden ministry that brings forth fruit through which the Father is glorified. Am I allowing my spiritual life to waste away, or am I focused, bringing everything to one central point—the atonement of my Lord? Is Jesus Christ more and more dominating every interest of my life? If the central point, or the most powerful influence, of my life is the atonement of the Lord, then every aspect of my life will bear fruit for Him.

However, I must take the time to realize what this central point of power is. Am I willing to give one minute out of every hour to concentrate on it? "If you abide in Me . . ."—that is, if you continue to act, and think, and work from that central point—"you will ask what you desire, and it shall be done for you" (John 15:7). Am I abiding? Am I taking the time to abide? What is the greatest source of power in my life? Is it my work, service, and sacrifice for others, or is it my striving to work for God? It should be none of these—what ought to exert the greatest power in my life is the atonement of the Lord. It is not on what we spend the greatest amount of time that molds us the most, but whatever exerts the most power over us. We must make a determination to limit and concentrate our desires and interests on the atonement by the Cross of Christ.

"Whatever you ask in My name, that I will do . . . ." The disciple who abides in Jesus *is* the will of God, and what appears to be his free choices are actually God's foreordained decrees. Is this mysterious? Does it appear to contradict sound logic or seem totally absurd? Yes, but what a glorious truth it is to a saint of God.

What's Next To Do?

"If you know these things, blessed are you if you do them" (John 13:17).

Be determined to know more than others. If you yourself do not cut the lines that tie you to the dock, God will have to use a storm to sever them and to send you out to sea. Put everything in your life afloat upon God, going out to sea on the great swelling tide of His purpose, and your eyes will be opened. If you believe in Jesus, you are not to spend all your time in the calm waters just inside the harbor, full of joy, but always tied to the dock. You have to get out past the harbor into the great depths of God, and begin to know things for yourself—begin to have spiritual discernment.

When you know that you should do something and you do it, immediately you know more. Examine where you have become sluggish, where you began losing interest spiritually, and you will find that it goes back to a point where you did not do something you knew you should do. You did not do it because there seemed to be no immediate call to do it. But now you have no insight or discernment, and at a time of crisis you are spiritually distracted instead of spiritually self-controlled. It is a dangerous thing to refuse to continue learning and knowing more.

The counterfeit of obedience is a state of mind in which you create your own opportunities to sacrifice yourself, and your zeal and enthusiasm are mistaken for discernment. It is easier to sacrifice yourself than to fulfill your spiritual destiny, which is stated in Romans 12:1–2. It is much better to fulfill the purpose of God in your life by discerning His will than it is to perform great acts of self-sacrifice. "Behold, to obey is better than sacrifice . . ." (1 Samuel 15:22). Beware of paying attention or going back to what you once were, when God wants you to be something that you have never been. "If anyone wills to do His will, he shall know . . ." (John 7:17).

Then What's Next To Do?

Ask if you have not received. There is nothing more difficult than asking. We will have yearnings and desires for certain things, and even suffer as a result of their going unfulfilled, but not until we are at the limit of desperation will we *ask*. It is the sense of not being spiritually real that causes us to ask. Have you ever asked out of the depths of your total insufficiency and poverty? "If any of you lacks wisdom, let him ask of God . . ." (James 1:5), but be sure that you do lack wisdom before you ask. You cannot bring yourself to the point of spiritual reality anytime you choose. The best thing to do, once you realize you are not spiritually real, is to ask God for the Holy Spirit, basing your request on the promise of Jesus Christ (see Luke 11:13). The Holy Spirit is the one who makes everything that Jesus did for you real in your life.

"Everyone who asks receives . . . ." This does not mean that you will not *get* if you do not ask, but it means that until you come to the point of asking, you will not *receive* from God (see Matthew 5:45). To be able to receive means that you have to come into the relationship of a child of God, and then you comprehend and appreciate mentally, morally, and with spiritual understanding, that these things come from God.

"If any of you lacks wisdom . . . ." If you realize that you are lacking, it is because you have come in contact with spiritual reality—do not put the blinders of reason on again. The word *ask* actually means "beg." Some people are poor enough to be interested in their poverty, and some of us are poor enough spiritually to show our interest. Yet we will never receive if we ask with a certain result in mind, because we are asking out of our lust, not out of our poverty. A pauper does not ask out of any reason other than the completely hopeless and painful condition of his poverty. He is not ashamed to beg—blessed are the *paupers* in spirit (see Matthew 5:3).

And After That What's Next To Do?

Seek if you have not found. "You ask and do not receive, because you ask amiss . . ." (James 4:3). If you ask for things from life instead of from God, "you ask amiss"; that is, you ask out of your desire for self-fulfillment. The more you fulfill yourself the less you will seek God. ". . . seek, and you will find . . . ." Get to work—narrow your focus and interests to this one thing. Have you ever sought God with your whole heart, or have you simply given Him a feeble cry after some emotionally painful experience? ". . . seek, [focus,] and you will find . . . ."

"Ho! Everyone who thirsts, come to the waters. . ." (Isaiah 55:1). Are you thirsty, or complacent and indifferent—so satisfied with your own experience that you want nothing more of God? Experience is a doorway, not a final goal. Beware of building your faith on experience, or your life will not ring true and will only sound the note of a critical spirit. Remember that you can never give another person what you have found, but you can cause him to have a desire for it.

". . . knock, and it will be opened to you" (Luke 11:9). "Draw near to God . . ." (James 4:8). Knock—the door is closed, and your heartbeat races as you knock. "Cleanse your hands . . ." (4:8). Knock a bit louder—you begin to find that you are dirty. ". . . purify your hearts . . ." (4:8). It is becoming even more personal—you are desperate and serious now—you will do anything. "Lament . . ." (4:9). Have you ever lamented, expressing your sorrow before God for the condition of your inner life? There is no thread of self-pity left, only the heart-rending difficulty and amazement which comes from seeing what kind of person you really are. "Humble yourselves . . ." (4:10). It is a humbling experience to knock at God's door—you have to knock with the crucified thief. ". . . to him who knocks it will be opened" (Luke 11:10).

Where sin and sorrow stops, and the song of the saint starts.
Do I really want to get there? I can right now. The questions
that truly matter in life are remarkably few, and they are all
answered by these words—"Come to Me." Our Lord's words
are not, "Do this, or don't do that," but—"Come to me." If I
will simply come to Jesus, my real life will be brought into harmony with my real desires. I will actually cease from sin, and
will find the song of the Lord beginning in my life.

Have you ever come to Jesus? Look at the stubbornness of
your heart. You would rather do anything than this one simple
childlike thing—"Come to Me." If you really want to experience
ceasing from sin, you must come to Jesus.

Jesus Christ makes Himself the test to determine your genuineness. Look how He used the word *come.* At the most unexpected moments in your life there is this whisper of the Lord—
"Come to Me," and you are immediately drawn to Him.
Personal contact with Jesus changes everything. Be "foolish"
enough to come and commit yourself to what He says. The
attitude necessary for you to come to Him is one where your
will has made the determination to let go of everything and
deliberately commit it all to Him.

". . . and I will give you rest"—that is, "I will sustain you,
causing you to stand firm." He is not saying, "I will put you to
bed, hold your hand, and sing you to sleep." But, in essence, He
is saying, "I will get you out of bed—out of your listlessness
and exhaustion, and out of your condition of being half dead
while you are still alive. I will penetrate you with the spirit of
life, and you will be sustained by the perfection of vital activity." Yet we become so weak and pitiful and talk about "suffering" the will of the Lord! Where is the majestic vitality and the
power of the Son of God in that?

Getting There

"They said to Him, 'Rabbi . . .
where are You staying?'
He said to them, 'Come
and see' "
(John 1:38–39).

Where our self-interest sleeps and the real interest is awakened.
"They . . . remained with Him that day . . . ." That is about all
some of us ever do. We stay with Him a short time, only to
wake up to our own realities of life. Our self-interest rises up
and our abiding with Him is past. Yet there is no circumstance
of life in which we cannot abide in Jesus.

"You are Simon . . . . You shall be called Cephas" (1:42).
God writes our new name only on those places in our lives
where He has erased our pride, self-sufficiency, and self-interest. Some of us have our new name written only in certain
spots, like spiritual measles. And in those areas of our lives we
look all right. When we are in our best spiritual mood, you
would think we were the highest quality saints. But don't dare
look at us when we are not in that mood. A true disciple is one
who has his new name written all over him—self-interest,
pride, and self-sufficiency have been completely erased.

Pride is the sin of making "self" our god. And some of us
today do this, not like the Pharisee, but like the tax collector (see
Luke 18:9–14). For you to say, "Oh, I'm no saint," is acceptable
by human standards of pride, but it is unconscious blasphemy
against God. You defy God to make you a saint, as if to say, "I
am too weak and hopeless and outside the reach of the atonement by the Cross of Christ." Why aren't you a saint? It is either
that you do not want to be a saint, or that you do not believe
that God can make you into one. You say it would be all right if
God saved you and took you straight to heaven. That is exactly
what He will do! And not only do we make our home with
Him, but Jesus said of His Father and Himself, ". . . We will come
to him and make Our home with him" (John 14:23). Put no
conditions on your life—let Jesus be everything to you, and He
will take you home with Him not only for a day, but for eternity.

Where our individual desire dies and sanctified surrender lives.
One of the greatest hindrances in coming to Jesus is the excuse
of our own individual temperament. We make our temperament and our natural desires barriers to coming to Jesus. Yet
the first thing we realize when we do come to Jesus is that He
pays no attention whatsoever to our natural desires. We have
the idea that we can dedicate our gifts to God. However, you
cannot dedicate what is not yours. There is actually only one
thing you can dedicate to God, and that is your right to yourself
(see Romans 12:1). If you will give God your right to yourself,
He will make a holy experiment out of you—and His experiments always succeed. The one true mark of a saint of God is
the inner creativity that flows from being totally surrendered to
Jesus Christ. In the life of a saint there is this amazing Well,
which is a continual Source of original life. The Spirit of God is
a Well of water springing up perpetually fresh. A saint realizes
that it is God who engineers his circumstances; consequently
there are no complaints, only unrestrained surrender to Jesus.
Never try to make your experience a principle for others, but
allow God to be as creative and original with others as He is
with you.

If you abandon everything to Jesus, and come when He
says, "Come," then He will continue to say, "Come," through
you. You will go out into the world reproducing the echo of
Christ's "Come." That is the result in every soul who has abandoned all and come to Jesus.

Have I come to Him? Will I come *now*?

G_{et} $Moving!$

In the matter of determination. The Spirit of Jesus is put into me by way of the atonement by the Cross of Christ. I then have to build my thinking patiently to bring it into perfect harmony with my Lord. God will not make me think like Jesus—I have to do it myself. I have to bring "every thought into captivity to the obedience of Christ" (2 Corinthians 10:5). "Abide in Me"— in intellectual matters, in money matters, in every one of the matters that make human life what it is. Our lives are not made up of only one neatly confined area.

Am I preventing God from doing things in my circumstances by saying that it will only serve to hinder my fellowship with Him? How irrelevant and disrespectful that is! It does not matter what my circumstances are. I can be as much assured of abiding in Jesus in any one of them as I am in any prayer meeting. It is unnecessary to change and arrange my circumstances myself. Our Lord's inner abiding was pure and unblemished. He was at home with God wherever His body was. He never chose His own circumstances, but was meek, submitting to His Father's plans and directions for Him. Just think of how amazingly relaxed our Lord's life was! But we tend to keep God at a fever pitch in our lives. We have none of the serenity of the life which is "hidden with Christ in God" (Colossians 3:3).

Think of the things that take you out of the position of abiding in Christ. You say, "Yes, Lord, just a minute—I still have this to do. Yes, I will abide as soon as this is finished, or as soon as this week is over. It will be all right, Lord. I will abide then." *Get moving*—begin to abide *now*. In the initial stages it will be a continual effort to abide, but as you continue, it will become so much a part of your life that you will abide in Him without any conscious effort. Make the determination to abide in Jesus wherever you are now or wherever you may be placed in the future.

Get Moving!

"Also . . . add to your
faith . . ."
(2 Peter 1:5).

In the matter of drudgery. Peter said in this passage that we have become "partakers of the divine nature" and that we should now be "giving all diligence," concentrating on forming godly habits (1:4–5). We are to "add" to our lives all that character means. No one is born either naturally or supernaturally with character; it must be developed. Nor are we born with habits—we have to form godly habits on the basis of the new life God has placed within us. We are not meant to be seen as God's perfect, bright-shining examples, but to be seen as the everyday essence of ordinary life exhibiting the miracle of His grace. Drudgery is the test of genuine character. The greatest hindrance in our spiritual life is that we will only look for big things to do. Yet, "Jesus . . . took a towel and . . . began to wash the disciples' feet . . ." (John 13:3–5).

We all have those times when there are no flashes of light and no apparent thrill to life, where we experience nothing but the daily routine with its common everyday tasks. The routine of life is actually God's way of saving us between our times of great inspiration which come from Him. Don't always expect God to give you His thrilling moments, but learn to live in those common times of the drudgery of life by the power of God.

It is difficult for us to do the "adding" that Peter mentioned here. We say we do not expect God to take us to heaven on flowery beds of ease, and yet we act as if we do! I must realize that my obedience even in the smallest detail of life has all of the omnipotent power of the grace of God behind it. If I will do my duty, not for duty's sake but because I believe God is engineering my circumstances, then at the very point of my obedience all of the magnificent grace of God is mine through the glorious atonement by the Cross of Christ.

"Will You Lay Down Your Life?"

"Greater love has no one than this, than to lay down one's life for his friends. . . . I have called you friends . . ." (John 15:13, 15).

Jesus does not ask me to die for Him, but to lay down my life for Him. Peter said to the Lord, "I will lay down my life for Your sake," and he meant it (John 13:37). He had a magnificent sense of the heroic. For us to be incapable of making this same statement Peter made would be a bad thing—our sense of duty is only fully realized through our sense of heroism. Has the Lord ever asked you, "Will you lay down your life for My sake?" (John 13:38). It is much easier to die than to lay down your life day in and day out with the sense of the high calling of God. We are not made for the bright-shining moments of life, but we have to walk in the light of them in our everyday ways. There was only one bright-shining moment in the life of Jesus, and that was on the Mount of Transfiguration. It was there that He emptied Himself of His glory for the second time, and then came down into the demon-possessed valley (see Mark 9:1–29). For thirty-three years Jesus laid down His life to do the will of His Father. "By this we know love, because He laid down His life for us. And we also ought to lay down our lives for the brethren" (1 John 3:16). Yet it is contrary to our human nature to do so.

If I am a friend of Jesus, I must deliberately and carefully lay down my life for Him. It is a difficult thing to do, and thank God that it is. Salvation is easy for us, because it cost God so much. But the exhibiting of salvation in my life is difficult. God saves a person, fills him with the Holy Spirit, and then says, in effect, "Now you work it out in your life, and be faithful to Me, even though the nature of everything around you is to cause you to be unfaithful." And Jesus says to us, ". . . I have called you friends. . . ." Remain faithful to your Friend, and remember that His honor is at stake in your bodily life.

June 16

*Beware of
Criticizing Others*

"Judge not, that you be not judged"
(Matthew 7:1).

Jesus' instructions with regard to judging others is very simply put; He says, *"Don't."* The average Christian is the most piercingly critical individual known. Criticism is one of the ordinary activities of people, but in the spiritual realm nothing is accomplished by it. The effect of criticism is the dividing up of the strengths of the one being criticized. The Holy Spirit is the only one in the proper position to criticize, and He alone is able to show what is wrong without hurting and wounding. It is impossible to enter into fellowship with God when you are in a critical mood. Criticism serves to make you harsh, vindictive, and cruel, and leaves you with the soothing and flattering idea that you are somehow superior to others. Jesus says that as His disciple you should cultivate a temperament that is never critical. This will not happen quickly but must be developed over a span of time. You must constantly beware of anything that causes you to think of yourself as a superior person.

There is no escaping the penetrating search of my life by Jesus. If I see the little speck in your eye, it means that I have a plank of timber in my own (see 7:3–5). Every wrong thing that I see in you, God finds in me. Every time I judge, I condemn myself (see Romans 2:17–24). Stop having a measuring stick for other people. There is always at least one more fact, which we know nothing about, in every person's situation. The first thing God does is to give us a thorough spiritual cleaning. After that, there is no possibility of pride remaining in us. I have never met a person I could despair of, or lose all hope for, after discerning what lies in me apart from the grace of God.

June 17

*K*eep Recognizing Jesus

"... Peter ... walked on the water to go to Jesus. But when he saw that the wind was boisterous, he was afraid ..."
(Matthew 14:29-30).

The wind really was boisterous and the waves really were high, but Peter didn't see them at first. He didn't consider them at all; he simply recognized his Lord, stepped out in recognition of Him, and "walked on the water." Then he began to take those things around him into account, and instantly, down he went. Why couldn't our Lord have enabled him to walk at the bottom of the waves, as well as on top of them? He could have, yet neither could be done without Peter's continuing recognition of the Lord Jesus.

We step right out with recognition of God in some things, then self-consideration enters our lives and down we go. If you are truly recognizing your Lord, you have no business being concerned about how and where He engineers your circumstances. The things surrounding you *are* real, but when you look at them you are immediately overwhelmed, and even unable to recognize Jesus. Then comes His rebuke, "... why did you doubt?" (14:31). Let your actual circumstances be what they may, but keep recognizing Jesus, maintaining complete reliance upon Him.

If you debate for even one second when God has spoken, it is all over for you. Never start to say, "Well, I wonder if He really did speak to me?" Be reckless immediately—totally unrestrained and willing to risk everything—by casting your all upon Him. You do not know when His voice will come to you, but whenever the realization of God comes, even in the faintest way imaginable, be determined to recklessly abandon yourself, surrendering everything to Him. It is only through abandonment of yourself and your circumstances that you will recognize Him. You will only recognize His voice more clearly through recklessness—being willing to risk your all.

The Service of Passionate Devotion

"...do you love Me?...
Tend My sheep"
(John 21:16).

Jesus did not say to make converts to your way of thinking, but He said to look after His sheep, to see that they get nourished in the knowledge of Him. We consider what we do in the way of Christian work as service, yet Jesus Christ calls service to be what we *are* to Him, not what we *do* for Him. Discipleship is based solely on devotion to Jesus Christ, not on following after a particular belief or doctrine. "If anyone comes to Me and does not hate . . . , he cannot be My disciple" (Luke 14:26). In this verse, there is no argument and no pressure from Jesus to follow Him; He is simply saying, in effect, "If you want to be My disciple, you must be devoted solely to Me." A person touched by the Spirit of God suddenly says, "Now I see who Jesus is!"—that is the source of devotion.

Today we have substituted doctrinal belief for personal belief, and that is why so many people are devoted to causes and so few are devoted to Jesus Christ. People do not really want to be devoted to Jesus, but only to the cause He started. Jesus Christ is deeply offensive to the educated minds of today, to those who only want Him to be their Friend, and who are unwilling to accept Him in any other way. Our Lord's primary obedience was to the will of His Father, not to the needs of people—the saving of people was the natural outcome of His obedience to the Father. If I am devoted solely to the cause of humanity, I will soon be exhausted and come to the point where my love will waver and stumble. But if I love Jesus Christ personally and passionately, I can serve humanity, even though people may treat me like a "doormat." The secret of a disciple's life is devotion to Jesus Christ, and the characteristic of that life is its seeming insignificance and its meekness. Yet it is like a grain of wheat that "falls into the ground and dies"—it will spring up and change the entire landscape (John 12:24).

Have You Come to "When" Yet?

"The LORD restored Job's losses when he prayed for his friends" (Job 42:10).

A pitiful, sickly, and self-centered kind of prayer and a determined effort and selfish desire to be right with God are never found in the New Testament. The fact that I am trying to be right with God is actually a sign that I am rebelling against the atonement by the Cross of Christ. I pray, "Lord, I will purify my heart if You will answer my prayer—I will walk rightly before You if You will help me." But I *cannot* make myself right with God; I *cannot* make my life perfect. I can only be right with God if I accept the atonement of the Lord Jesus Christ as an absolute gift. Am I humble enough to accept it? I have to surrender all my rights and demands, and cease from every self-effort. I must leave myself completely alone in His hands, and then I can begin to pour my life out in the priestly work of intercession. There is a great deal of prayer that comes from actual disbelief in the atonement. Jesus is not just beginning to save us—He has already saved us completely. It is an accomplished fact, and it is an insult to Him for us to ask Him to do what He has already done.

If you are not now receiving the "hundredfold" which Jesus promised (see Matthew 19:29), and not getting insight into God's Word, then start praying for your friends—enter into the ministry of the inner life. "The LORD restored Job's losses *when he prayed for his friends.*" As a saved soul, the real business of your life is intercessory prayer. Whatever circumstances God may place you in, always pray immediately that His atonement may be recognized and as fully understood in the lives of others as it has been in yours. Pray for your friends *now,* and pray for those with whom you come in contact *now.*

The Ministry of the Inner Life

"You are . . . a royal priesthood . . ."
(1 Peter 2:9).

By what right have we become "a royal priesthood"? It is by the right of the atonement by the Cross of Christ that this has been accomplished. Are we prepared to purposely disregard ourselves and to launch out into the priestly work of prayer? The continual inner-searching we do in an effort to see if we are what we ought to be generates a self-centered, sickly type of Christianity, not the vigorous and simple life of a child of God. Until we get into this right and proper relationship with God, it is simply a case of our "hanging on by the skin of our teeth," although we say, "What a wonderful victory I have!" Yet there is nothing at all in that which indicates the miracle of redemption. Launch out in reckless, unrestrained belief that the redemption is complete. Then don't worry anymore about yourself, but begin to do as Jesus Christ has said, in essence, "Pray for the friend who comes to you at midnight, pray for the saints of God, and pray for all men." Pray with the realization that you are perfect only in Christ Jesus, not on the basis of this argument: "Oh, Lord, I have done my best; please hear me now."

How long is it going to take God to free us from the unhealthy habit of thinking only about ourselves? We must get to the point of being sick to death of ourselves, until there is no longer any surprise at anything God might tell us about ourselves. We cannot reach and understand the depths of our own meagerness. There is only one place where we are right with God, and that is in Christ Jesus. Once we are there, we have to pour out our lives for all we are worth in this ministry of the inner life.

The Unchanging Law of Judgment

> "With what judgment you judge, you will be judged, and with the measure you use, it will be measured back to you" (Matthew 7:2).

This statement is not some haphazard theory, but it is an eternal law of God. Whatever judgment you give will be the very way you are judged. There is a difference between retaliation and retribution. Jesus said that the basis of life is retribution—"with the measure you use, it will be measured back to you." If you have been shrewd in finding out the shortcomings of others, remember that will be exactly how you will be measured. The way you pay is the way life will pay you back. This eternal law works from God's throne down to us (see Psalm 18:25–26).

Romans 2:1 applies it in even a more definite way by saying that the one who criticizes another is guilty of the very same thing. God looks not only at the act itself, but also at the possibility of committing it, which He sees by looking at our hearts. To begin with, we do not believe the statements of the Bible. For instance, do we really believe the statement that says we criticize in others the very things we are guilty of ourselves? The reason we see hypocrisy, deceit, and a lack of genuineness in others is that they are all in our own hearts. The greatest characteristic of a saint is humility, as evidenced by being able to say honestly and humbly, "Yes, all those, as well as other evils, would have been exhibited in me if it were not for the grace of God. Therefore, I have no right to judge."

Jesus said, "Judge not, that you be not judged" (Matthew 7:1). He went on to say, in effect, "If you do judge, you will be judged in exactly the same way." Who of us would dare to stand before God and say, "My God, judge me as I have judged others"? We have judged others as sinners—if God should judge us in the same way, we would be condemned to hell. Yet God judges us on the basis of the miraculous atonement by the Cross of Christ.

"Acquainted With Grief"

"He is . . . a Man of sorrows and acquainted with grief" (Isaiah 53:3).

We are not "acquainted with grief" in the same way our Lord was acquainted with it. We endure it and live through it, but we do not become intimate with it. At the beginning of our lives we do not bring ourselves to the point of dealing with the reality of sin. We look at life through the eyes of reason and say that if a person will control his instincts, and educate himself, he can produce a life that will slowly evolve into the life of God. But as we continue on through life, we find the presence of something which we have not yet taken into account, namely, sin—and it upsets all of our thinking and our plans. Sin has made the foundation of our thinking unpredictable, uncontrollable, and irrational.

We have to recognize that sin is a fact of life, not just a shortcoming. Sin is blatant mutiny against God, and either sin or God must die in my life. The New Testament brings us right down to this one issue—if sin rules in me, God's life in me will be killed; if God rules in me, sin in me will be killed. There is nothing more fundamental than that. The culmination of sin was the crucifixion of Jesus Christ, and what was true in the history of God on earth will also be true in your history and in mine—that is, sin will kill the life of God in us. We must mentally bring ourselves to terms with this fact of sin. It is the only explanation why Jesus Christ came to earth, and it is the explanation of the grief and sorrow of life.

Reconciling Yourself to the Fact of Sin

"This is your hour, and the power of darkness" (Luke 22:53).

Not being reconciled to the fact of sin—not recognizing it and refusing to deal with it—produces all the disasters in life. You may talk about the lofty virtues of human nature, but there is something in human nature that will mockingly laugh in the face of every principle you have. If you refuse to agree with the fact that there is wickedness and selfishness, something down-right hateful and wrong, in human beings, when it attacks your life, instead of reconciling yourself to it, you will compromise with it and say that it is of no use to battle against it. Have you taken this "hour, and the power of darkness" into account, or do you have a view of yourself which includes no recognition of sin whatsoever? In your human relationships and friend-ships, have you reconciled yourself to the fact of sin? If not, just around the next corner you will find yourself trapped and you will compromise with it. But if you will reconcile yourself to the fact of sin, you will realize the danger immediately and say, "Yes, I see what this sin would mean." The recognition of sin does not destroy the basis of friendship—it simply establishes a mutual respect for the fact that the basis of sinful life is disas-trous. Always beware of any assessment of life which does not recognize the fact that there is sin.

Jesus Christ never trusted human nature, yet He was never cynical nor suspicious, because He had absolute trust in what He could do for human nature. The pure man or woman is the one who is shielded from harm, not the innocent person. The so-called innocent man or woman is never safe. Men and women have no business trying to be innocent; God demands that they be pure and virtuous. Innocence is the characteristic of a child. Any person is deserving of blame if he is unwilling to reconcile himself to the fact of sin.

Receiving Yourself
in the Fires of Sorrow

"... what shall I say? 'Father, save Me from this hour'? But for this purpose I came to this hour. 'Father, glorify Your name'"
(John 12:27–28).

As a saint of God, my attitude toward sorrow and difficulty should not be to ask that they be prevented, but to ask that God protect me so that I may remain what He created me to be, in spite of all my fires of sorrow. Our Lord received Himself, accepting His position and realizing His purpose, in the midst of the fire of sorrow. He was saved not _from_ the hour, but _out_ of the hour.

We say that there ought to be no sorrow, but there is sorrow, and we have to accept and receive ourselves in its fires. If we try to evade sorrow, refusing to deal with it, we are foolish. Sorrow is one of the biggest facts in life, and there is no use in saying it should not be. Sin, sorrow, and suffering _are,_ and it is not for us to say that God has made a mistake in allowing them.

Sorrow removes a great deal of a person's shallowness, but it does not always make that person better. Suffering either gives me to myself or it destroys me. You cannot find or receive yourself through success, because you lose your head over pride. And you cannot receive yourself through the monotony of your daily life, because you give in to complaining. The only way to find yourself is in the fires of sorrow. Why it should be this way is immaterial. The fact is that it is true in the Scriptures and in human experience. You can always recognize who has been through the fires of sorrow and received himself, and you know that you can go to him in your moment of trouble and find that he has plenty of time for you. But if a person has not been through the fires of sorrow, he is apt to be contemptuous, having no respect or time for you, only turning you away. If you will receive yourself in the fires of sorrow, God will make you nourishment for other people.

Drawing on the
Grace of God—Now

"We . . . plead with you not
to receive the grace of
God in vain"
(2 Corinthians 6:1).

The grace you had yesterday will not be sufficient for today. Grace is the overflowing favor of God, and you can always count on it being available to draw upon as needed. ". . . in much patience, in tribulations, in needs, in distresses"—that is where our patience is tested (6:4). Are you failing to rely on the grace of God there? Are you saying to yourself, "Oh well, I won't count this time"? It is not a question of praying and asking God to help you—it is taking the grace of God *now*. We tend to make prayer the preparation for our service, yet it is never that in the Bible. Prayer is the practice of drawing on the grace of God. Don't say, "I will endure this until I can get away and pray." Pray *now*—draw on the grace of God in your moment of need. Prayer is the most normal and useful thing; it is not simply a reflex action of your devotion to God. We are very slow to learn to draw on God's grace through prayer.

". . . in stripes, in imprisonments, in tumults, in labors . . ." (6:5)—in all these things, display in your life a drawing on the grace of God, which will show evidence to yourself and to others that you are a miracle of His. Draw on His grace now, not later. The primary word in the spiritual vocabulary is *now*. Let circumstances take you where they will, but keep drawing on the grace of God in whatever condition you may find yourself. One of the greatest proofs that you are drawing on the grace of God is that you can be totally humiliated before others without displaying even the slightest trace of anything but His grace.

". . . having nothing . . . ." Never hold anything in reserve. Pour yourself out, giving the best that you have, and always be poor. Never be diplomatic and careful with the treasure God gives you. ". . . and yet possessing all things"—this is poverty triumphant (6:10).

The Overshadowing of God's Personal Deliverance

" '. . . I am with you to deliver you,' says the LORD" (Jeremiah 1:8).

God promised Jeremiah that He would deliver him personally—
". . . your life shall be as a prize to you . . ." (Jeremiah 39:18).
That is all God promises His children. Wherever God sends us,
He will guard our lives. Our personal property and possessions
are to be a matter of indifference to us, and our hold on these
things should be very loose. If this is not the case, we will have
panic, heartache, and distress. Having the proper outlook is evidence of the deeply rooted belief in the overshadowing of God's
personal deliverance.

The Sermon on the Mount indicates that when we are on
a mission for Jesus Christ, there is no time to stand up for ourselves. Jesus says, in effect, "Don't worry about whether or not
you are being treated justly." Looking for justice is actually a
sign that we have been diverted from our devotion to Him.
Never look for justice in this world, but never cease to give it. If
we look for justice, we will only begin to complain and to
indulge ourselves in the discontent of self-pity, as if to say,
"Why should I be treated like this?" If we are devoted to Jesus
Christ, we have nothing to do with what we encounter, whether
it is just or unjust. In essence, Jesus says, "Continue steadily on
with what I have told you to do, and I will guard your life. If
you try to guard it yourself, you remove yourself from My
deliverance." Even the most devout among us become atheistic
in this regard—we do not believe Him. We put our common
sense on the throne and then attach God's name to it. We *do*
lean to our own understanding, instead of trusting God with all
our hearts (see Proverbs 3:5–6).

Held by the Grip of God

Never choose to be a worker for God, but once God has placed His call on you, woe be to you if you "turn aside to the right hand or to the left" (Deuteronomy 5:32). We are not here to work for God because we have chosen to do so, but because God has "laid hold of" us. And once He has done so, we never have this thought, "Well, I'm really not suited for this." What you are to preach is also determined by God, not by your own natural leanings or desires. Keep your soul steadfastly related to God, and remember that you are called not simply to convey your testimony but also to preach the gospel. Every Christian must testify to the truth of God, but when it comes to the call to preach, there must be the agonizing grip of God's hand on you—your life is in the grip of God for that very purpose. How many of us are held like that?

Never water down the Word of God, but preach it in its undiluted sternness. There must be unflinching faithfulness to the Word of God, but when you come to personal dealings with others, remember who you are—you are not some special being created in heaven, but a sinner saved by grace.

"Brethren, I do not count myself to have apprehended; but one thing I do . . . I press toward the goal for the prize of the upward call of God in Christ Jesus" (Philippians 3:13–14).

The Strictest Discipline

"If your right hand causes you to sin, cut it off and cast it from you, for it is more profitable for you that one of your members perish, than for your whole body to be cast into hell" (Matthew 5:30).

Jesus did not say that everyone must cut off his right hand, but that "if your right hand causes you to sin" in your walk with Him, then it is better to "cut it off." There are many things that are perfectly legitimate, but if you are going to concentrate on God you cannot do them. Your right hand is one of the best things you have, but Jesus says that if it hinders you in following His precepts, then "cut it off." The principle taught here is the strictest discipline or lesson that ever hit humankind.

When God changes you through regeneration, giving you new life through spiritual rebirth, your life initially has the characteristic of being maimed. There are a hundred and one things that you dare not do—things that would be sin for you, and would be recognized as sin by those who really know you. But the unspiritual people around you will say, "What's so wrong with doing that? How absurd you are!" There has never yet been a saint who has not lived a maimed life initially. Yet it is better to enter into life maimed but lovely in God's sight than to appear lovely to man's eyes but lame to God's. At first, Jesus Christ through His Spirit has to restrain you from doing a great many things that may be perfectly right for everyone else but not right for you. Yet, see that you don't use your restrictions to criticize someone else.

The Christian life is a maimed life initially, but in verse 48 Jesus gave us the picture of a perfectly well-rounded life—"You shall be *perfect,* just as your Father in heaven is perfect."

D_o I_t N_{ow}!

"Agree with your adversary
quickly . . ."
(Matthew 5:25).

In this verse, Jesus Christ laid down a very important principle by saying, "Do what you know you must do—*now*. Do it quickly. If you don't, an inevitable process will begin to work 'till you have paid the last penny' (5:26) in pain, agony, and distress." God's laws are unchangeable and there is no escape from them. The teachings of Jesus always penetrate right to the heart of our being.

Wanting to make sure that my adversary gives me all my rights is a natural thing. But Jesus says that it is a matter of inescapable and eternal importance to me that I pay my adversary what I owe him. From our Lord's standpoint it doesn't matter whether I am cheated or not, but what does matter is that I don't cheat someone else. Am I insisting on having my own rights, or am I paying what I owe from Jesus Christ's standpoint?

Do it quickly—bring yourself to judgment now. In moral and spiritual matters, you must act immediately. If you don't, the inevitable, relentless process will begin to work. God is determined to have His child as pure, clean, and white as driven snow, and as long as there is disobedience in any point of His teaching, He will allow His Spirit to use whatever process it may take to bring us to obedience. The fact that we insist on proving that we are right is almost always a clear indication that we have some point of disobedience. No wonder the Spirit of God so strongly urges us to stay steadfastly in the light! (see John 3:19–21).

"Agree with your adversary quickly . . . ." Have you suddenly reached a certain place in your relationship with someone, only to find that you have anger in your heart? Confess it quickly—make it right before God. Be reconciled to that person—*do it now!*

$\mathcal{T}$he Inevitable Penalty

There is no heaven that has a little corner of hell in it. God is determined to make you pure, holy, and right, and He will not allow you to escape from the scrutiny of the Holy Spirit for even one moment. He urged you to come to judgment immediately when He convicted you, but you did not obey. Then the inevitable process began to work, bringing its inevitable penalty. Now you have been "thrown into prison, [and] . . . you will by no means get out of there till you have paid the last penny" (5:25–26). Yet you ask, "Is this a God of mercy and love?" When seen from God's perspective, it is a glorious ministry of love. God is going to bring you out pure, spotless, and undefiled, but He wants you to recognize the nature you were exhibiting—the nature of demanding your right to yourself. The moment you are willing for God to change your nature, His recreating forces will begin to work. And the moment you realize that God's purpose is to get you into the right relationship with Himself and then with others, He will reach to the very limits of the universe to help you take the right road. Decide to do it right now, saying, "Yes, Lord, I *will* write that letter," or, "I *will* be reconciled to that person now."

These sermons of Jesus Christ are meant for your will and your conscience, not for your head. If you dispute these verses from the Sermon on the Mount with your head, you will dull the appeal to your heart.

If you find yourself asking, "I wonder why I'm not growing spiritually with God?"—then ask yourself if you are paying your debts from God's standpoint. Do *now* what you will have to do someday. Every moral question or call comes with an "ought" behind it—the knowledge of knowing what we ought to do.

The Conditions of Discipleship

"If anyone comes to Me and does not hate his father and mother, wife and children, brothers and sisters, yes, and his own life also . . . . And whoever does not bear his cross and come after Me . . . . So likewise, whoever of you does not forsake all that he has cannot be My disciple" (Luke 14:26–27, 33).

If the closest relationships of a disciple's life conflict with the claims of Jesus Christ, then our Lord requires instant obedience to Himself. Discipleship means personal, passionate devotion to a Person—our Lord Jesus Christ. There is a vast difference between devotion to a person and devotion to principles or to a cause. Our Lord never proclaimed a cause—He proclaimed personal devotion to Himself. To be a disciple is to be a devoted bondservant motivated by love for the Lord Jesus. Many of us who call ourselves Christians are not truly devoted to Jesus Christ. No one on earth has this passionate love for the Lord Jesus unless the Holy Spirit has given it to him. We may admire, respect, and revere Him, but we cannot love Him on our own. The only One who truly loves the Lord Jesus is the Holy Spirit, and it is He who has "poured out in our hearts" the very "love of God" (Romans 5:5). Whenever the Holy Spirit sees an opportunity to glorify Jesus through you, He will take your entire being and set you ablaze with glowing devotion to Jesus Christ.

The Christian life is a life characterized by true and spontaneous creativity. Consequently, a disciple is subject to the same charge that was leveled against Jesus Christ, namely, the charge of inconsistency. But Jesus Christ was always consistent in His relationship to God, and a Christian must be consistent in his relationship to the life of the Son of God in him, not consistent to strict, unyielding doctrines. People pour themselves into their own doctrines, and God has to blast them out of their preconceived ideas before they can become devoted to Jesus Christ.

The Concentration of Personal Sin

"Woe is me, for I am undone! Because I am a man of unclean lips . . ." (Isaiah 6:5).

When I come into the very presence of God, I do not realize that I am a sinner in an indefinite sense, but I suddenly realize and the focus of my attention is directed toward the concentration of sin in a particular area of my life. A person will easily say, "Oh yes, I know I am a sinner," but when he comes into the presence of God he cannot get away with such a broad and indefinite statement. Our conviction is focused on our specific sin, and we realize, as Isaiah did, what we really are. This is always the sign that a person is in the presence of God. There is never any vague sense of sin, but a focusing on the concentration of sin in some specific, personal area of life. God begins by convicting us of the very thing to which His Spirit has directed our mind's attention. If we will surrender, submitting to His conviction of that particular sin, He will lead us down to where He can reveal the vast underlying nature of sin. That is the way God always deals with us when we are consciously aware of His presence.

This experience of our attention being directed to our concentration of personal sin is true in everyone's life, from the greatest of saints to the worst of sinners. When a person first begins climbing the ladder of experience, he might say, "I don't know where I've gone wrong," but the Spirit of God will point out some definite and specific thing to him. The effect of Isaiah's vision of the holiness of the Lord was the directing of his attention to the fact that he was "a man of unclean lips." "He touched my mouth with it, and said: 'Behold, this has touched your lips; your iniquity is taken away, and your sin purged'" (6:7). The cleansing fire had to be applied where the sin had been concentrated.

Fretting means getting ourselves "out of joint" mentally or spiritually. It is one thing to say, "Do not fret," but something very different to have such a nature that you find yourself unable to fret. It's easy to say, "Rest in the Lord, and wait patiently for Him" (37:7) until our own little world is turned upside down and we are forced to live in confusion and agony like so many other people. Is it possible to "rest in the Lord" then? If this "Do not" doesn't work there, then it will not work anywhere. This "Do not" must work during our days of difficulty and uncertainty, as well as our peaceful days, or it will never work. And if it will not work in your particular case, it will not work for anyone else. Resting in the Lord is not dependent on your external circumstances at all, but on your relationship with God Himself.

Worrying always results in sin. We tend to think that a little anxiety and worry are simply an indication of how wise we really are, yet it is actually a much better indication of just how wicked we are. Fretting rises from our determination to have our own way. Our Lord never worried and was never anxious, because His purpose was never to accomplish His own plans but to fulfill God's plans. Fretting is wickedness for a child of God.

Have you been propping up that foolish soul of yours with the idea that your circumstances are too much for God to handle? Set all your opinions and speculations aside and "abide under the shadow of the Almighty" (Psalm 91:1). Deliberately tell God that you will not fret about whatever concerns you. All our fretting and worrying is caused by planning without God.

Don't Plan Without God   "Commit your way to the
                                    LORD, trust also in Him,
                                    and He shall bring it to
                                    pass"
                                    (Psalm 37:5).

Don't plan without God. God seems to have a delightful way of upsetting the plans we have made, when we have not taken Him into account. We get ourselves into circumstances that were not chosen by God, and suddenly we realize that we have been making our plans without Him—that we have not even considered Him to be a vital, living factor in the planning of our lives. And yet the only thing that will keep us from even the possibility of worrying is to bring God in as the greatest factor in all of our planning.

In spiritual issues it is customary for us to put God first, but we tend to think that it is inappropriate and unnecessary to put Him first in the practical, everyday issues of our lives. If we have the idea that we have to put on our "spiritual face" before we can come near to God, then we will never come near to Him. We must come as we are.

Don't plan with a concern for evil in mind. Does God really mean for us to plan without taking the evil around us into account? "Love . . . thinks no evil" (1 Corinthians 13:4–5). Love is not ignorant of the existence of evil, but it does not take it into account as a factor in planning. When we were apart from God, we did take evil into account, doing all of our planning with it in mind, and we tried to reason out all of our work from its standpoint.

Don't plan with a rainy day in mind. You cannot hoard things for a rainy day if you are truly trusting Christ. Jesus said, "Let not your heart be troubled . . ." (John 14:1). God will not keep your heart from being troubled. It is a command—"*Let not . . . .*" To do it, continually pick yourself up, even if you fall a hundred and one times a day, until you get into the habit of putting God first and planning with Him in mind.

Visions Becoming Reality

"The parched ground shall
become a pool . . ."
(Isaiah 35:7).

We always have a vision of something before it actually becomes
real to us. When we realize that the vision is real, but is not yet
real in us, Satan comes to us with his temptations, and we are
inclined to say that there is no point in even trying to continue.
Instead of the vision becoming real to us, we have entered into a
valley of humiliation.

> Life is not as idle ore,
>> But iron dug from central gloom,
>> And battered by the shocks of doom
> To shape and use.

God gives us a vision, and then He takes us down to the
valley to batter us into the shape of that vision. It is in the valley
that so many of us give up and faint. Every God-given vision
will become real if we will only have patience. Just think of the
enormous amount of free time God has! He is never in a hurry.
Yet we are always in such a frantic hurry. While still in the light
of the glory of the vision, we go right out to do things, but the
vision is not yet real in us. God has to take us into the valley and
put us through fires and floods to batter us into shape, until we
get to the point where He can trust us with the reality of the
vision. Ever since God gave us the vision, He has been at work.
He is getting us into the shape of the goal He has for us, and yet
over and over again we try to escape from the Sculptor's hand in
an effort to batter ourselves into the shape of our own goal.

The vision that God gives is not some unattainable castle in
the sky, but a vision of what God wants you to be down here.
Allow the Potter to put you on His wheel and whirl you around
as He desires. Then as surely as God is God, and you are you,
you will turn out as an exact likeness of the vision. But don't
lose heart in the process. If you have ever had a vision from
God, you may try as you will to be satisfied on a lower level, but
God will never allow it.

All Efforts of Worth and
Excellence Are Difficult

"Enter by the narrow gate . . . .
Because narrow is the gate
and difficult is the way
which leads to life . . ."
(Matthew 7:13-14).

If we are going to live as disciples of Jesus, we have to remember that all efforts of worth and excellence are difficult. The Christian life is gloriously difficult, but its difficulty does not make us faint and cave in—it stirs us up to overcome. Do we appreciate the miraculous salvation of Jesus Christ enough to be our utmost for His highest—our best for His glory?

God saves people by His sovereign grace through the atonement of Jesus, and "it is God who works in you both to will and to do for His good pleasure" (Philippians 2:13). But we have to "work out" that salvation in our everyday, practical living (Philippians 2:12). If we will only start on the basis of His redemption to do what He commands, then we will find that we can do it. If we fail, it is because we have not yet put into practice what God has placed within us. But a crisis will reveal whether or not we have been putting it into practice. If we will obey the Spirit of God and practice in our physical life what God has placed within us by His Spirit, then when a crisis does come we will find that our own nature, as well as the grace of God, will stand by us.

Thank God that He does give us difficult things to do! His salvation is a joyous thing, but it is also something that requires bravery, courage, and holiness. It tests us for all we are worth. Jesus is "bringing many sons to glory" (Hebrews 2:10), and God will not shield us from the requirements of sonship. God's grace produces men and women with a strong family likeness to Jesus Christ, not pampered, spoiled weaklings. It takes a tremendous amount of discipline to live the worthy and excellent life of a disciple of Jesus in the realities of life. And it is always necessary for us to make an effort to live a life of worth and excellence.

*W*ill To Be Faithful

". . . choose for yourselves this day whom you will serve . . ." (Joshua 24:15).

A person's will is embodied in the actions of the whole person. I cannot *give up* my will—I must exercise it, putting it into action. I must *will* to obey, and I must *will* to receive God's Spirit. When God gives me a vision of truth, there is never a question of what He will do, but only of what I will do. The Lord has been placing in front of each of us some big proposals and plans. The best thing to do is to remember what you did before when you were touched by God. Recall the moment when you were saved, or first recognized Jesus, or realized some truth. It was easy then to yield your allegiance to God. Immediately recall those moments each time the Spirit of God brings some new proposal before you.

". . . choose for yourselves this day whom you will serve. . . ." Your choice must be a deliberate determination—it is not something into which you will automatically drift. And everything else in your life will be held in temporary suspension until you make a decision. The proposal is between you and God—do not "confer with flesh and blood" about it (Galatians 1:16). With every new proposal, the people around us seem to become more and more isolated, and that is where the tension develops. God allows the opinion of His other saints to matter to you, and yet you become less and less certain that others really understand the step you are taking. You have no business trying to find out where God is leading—the only thing God will explain to you is Himself.

Openly declare to Him, "I will be faithful." But remember that as soon as you choose to be faithful to Jesus Christ, "You are witnesses against yourselves . . ." (Joshua 24:22). Don't consult with other Christians, but simply and freely declare before Him, "I will serve You." *Will* to be faithful—and give other people credit for being faithful too.

Will You Examine Yourself?

> "Joshua said to the people, 'You cannot serve the LORD . . . '"
> (Joshua 24:19).

Do you have even the slightest reliance on anything or anyone other than God? Is there a remnant of reliance left on any natural quality within you, or on any particular set of circumstances? Are you relying on yourself in any manner whatsoever regarding this new proposal or plan which God has placed before you? Will you examine yourself by asking these probing questions? It really is true to say, "I cannot live a holy life," but you can decide to let Jesus Christ make you holy. "You cannot serve the LORD . . ."—but you can place yourself in the proper position where God's almighty power will flow through you. Is your relationship with God sufficient for you to expect Him to exhibit His wonderful life in you?

"The people said to Joshua, 'No, but we will serve the LORD!'" (24:21). This is not an impulsive action, but a deliberate commitment. We tend to say, "But God could never have called *me* to this. I'm too unworthy. It can't mean *me*." It does mean you, and the more weak and feeble you are, the better. The person who is still relying and trusting in anything within himself is the last person to even come close to saying, "I will serve the Lord."

We say, "Oh, if only I really could believe!" The question is, "*Will* I believe?" No wonder Jesus Christ placed such emphasis on the sin of unbelief. "He did not do many mighty works there because of their unbelief" (Matthew 13:58). If we really believed that God meant what He said, just imagine what we would be like! Do I really dare to let God be to me all that He says He will be?

The Spiritually Lazy Saint

"Let us consider one another in order to stir up love and good works, not forsaking the assembling of ourselves together . . ." (Hebrews 10:24-25).

We are all capable of being spiritually lazy saints. We want to stay off the rough roads of life, and our primary objective is to secure a peaceful retreat from the world. The ideas put forth in these verses from Hebrews 10 are those of stirring up one another and of keeping ourselves together. Both of these require initiative—our willingness to take the first step toward Christ-realization, not the initiative toward self-realization. To live a distant, withdrawn, and secluded life is diametrically opposed to spirituality as Jesus Christ taught it.

The true test of our spirituality occurs when we come up against injustice, degradation, ingratitude, and turmoil, all of which have the tendency to make us spiritually lazy. While being tested, we want to use prayer and Bible reading for the purpose of finding a quiet retreat. We use God only for the sake of getting peace and joy. We seek only our enjoyment of Jesus Christ, not a true realization of Him. This is the first step in the wrong direction. All these things we are seeking are simply effects, and yet we try to make them causes.

"Yes, I think it is right," Peter said, ". . . to stir you up by reminding you . . ." (2 Peter 1:13). It is a most disturbing thing to be hit squarely in the stomach by someone being used of God to stir us up—someone who is full of spiritual activity. Simple active work and spiritual activity are not the same thing. Active work can actually be the counterfeit of spiritual activity. The real danger in spiritual laziness is that we do not want to be stirred up—all we want to hear about is a spiritual retirement from the world. Yet Jesus Christ never encourages the idea of retirement—He says, "Go and tell My brethren . . ." (Matthew 28:10).

The Spiritually Vigorous Saint

"... that I may know Him ..."
(Philippians 3:10).

A saint is not to take the initiative toward self-realization, but toward knowing Jesus Christ. A spiritually vigorous saint never believes that his circumstances simply happen at random, nor does he ever think of his life as being divided into the secular and the sacred. He sees every situation in which he finds himself as the means of obtaining a greater knowledge of Jesus Christ, and he has an attitude of unrestrained abandon and total surrender about him. The Holy Spirit is determined that we will have the realization of Jesus Christ in every area of our lives, and He will bring us back to the same point over and over again until we do. Self-realization only leads to the glorification of good works, whereas a saint of God glorifies Jesus Christ through his good works. Whatever we may be doing—even eating, drinking, or washing disciples' feet—we have to take the initiative of realizing and recognizing Jesus Christ in it. Every phase of our life has its counterpart in the life of Jesus. Our Lord realized His relationship to the Father even in the most menial task. "Jesus, knowing ... that He had come from God and was going to God, ... took a towel ... and began to wash the disciples' feet ..." (John 13:3–5).

The aim of a spiritually vigorous saint is "that I may know Him ..." Do I know Him where I am today? If not, I am failing Him. I am not here for self-realization, but to know Jesus Christ. In Christian work our initiative and motivation are too often simply the result of realizing that there is work to be done and that we must do it. Yet that is never the attitude of a spiritually vigorous saint. His aim is to achieve the realization of Jesus Christ in every set of circumstances.

The Spiritually Self-Seeking Church

"... till we all come ... to the measure of the stature of the fullness of Christ ..." (Ephesians 4:13).

Reconciliation means the restoring of the relationship between the entire human race and God, putting it back to what God designed it to be. This is what Jesus Christ did in redemption. The church ceases to be spiritual when it becomes self-seeking, only interested in the development of its own organization. The reconciliation of the human race according to His plan means realizing Him not only in our lives individually, but also in our lives collectively. Jesus Christ sent apostles and teachers for this very purpose—that the corporate Person of Christ and His church, made up of many members, might be brought into being and made known. We are not here to develop a spiritual life of our own, or to enjoy a quiet spiritual retreat. We are here to have the full realization of Jesus Christ, for the purpose of building His body.

Am I building up the body of Christ, or am I only concerned about my own personal development? The essential thing is my personal relationship with Jesus Christ—"... that I may know Him ..." (Philippians 3:10). To fulfill God's perfect design for me requires my total surrender—complete abandonment of myself to Him. Whenever I only want things for myself, the relationship is distorted. And I will suffer great humiliation once I come to acknowledge and understand that I have not really been concerned about realizing Jesus Christ Himself, but only concerned with knowing what He has done for me.

> My goal is God Himself, not joy nor peace,
> Nor even blessing, but Himself, my God.

Am I measuring my life by this standard or by something less?

The Price of the Vision

Our soul's personal history with God is often an account of the death of our heroes. Over and over again God has to remove our friends to put Himself in their place, and that is when we falter, fail, and become discouraged. Let me think about this personally—when the person died who represented for me all that God was, did I give up on everything in life? Did I become ill or disheartened? Or did I do as Isaiah did and see the Lord?

My vision of God is dependent upon the condition of my character. My character determines whether or not truth can even be revealed to me. Before I can say, "I saw the Lord," there must be something in my character that conforms to the likeness of God. Until I am born again and really begin to see the kingdom of God, I only see from the perspective of my own biases. What I need is God's surgical procedure—His use of external circumstances to bring about internal purification.

Your priorities must be God first, God second, and God third, until your life is continually face to face with God and no one else is taken into account whatsoever. Your prayer will then be, "In all the world there is no one but You, dear God; there is no one but You."

Keep paying the price. Let God see that you are willing to live up to the vision.

Suffering Afflictions and Going the Second Mile

> "I tell you not to resist an evil person. But whoever slaps you on your right cheek, turn the other to him also" (Matthew 5:39).

This verse reveals the humiliation of being a Christian. In the natural realm, if a person does not hit back, it is because he is a coward. But in the spiritual realm, it is the very evidence of the Son of God in him if he does not hit back. When you are insulted, you must not only not resent it, but you must make it an opportunity to exhibit the Son of God in your life. And you cannot imitate the nature of Jesus—it is either in you or it is not. A personal insult becomes an opportunity for a saint to reveal the incredible sweetness of the Lord Jesus.

The teaching of the Sermon on the Mount is not, "Do your duty," but is, in effect, "Do what is not your duty." It is not your duty to go the second mile, or to turn the other cheek, but Jesus said that if we are His disciples, we will always do these things. We will not say, "Oh well, I just can't do any more, and I've been so misrepresented and misunderstood." Every time I insist on having my own rights, I hurt the Son of God, while in fact I can prevent Jesus from being hurt if I will take the blow myself. That is the real meaning of filling "up in my flesh what is lacking in the afflictions of Christ . . ." (Colossians 1:24). A disciple realizes that it is his Lord's honor that is at stake in his life, not his own honor.

Never look for righteousness in the other person, but never cease to be righteous yourself. We are always looking for justice, yet the essence of the teaching of the Sermon on the Mount is—Never look for justice, but never cease to give it.

My Life's Spiritual Honor and Duty

"I am a debtor both to Greeks and to barbarians . . ."
(Romans 1:14).

Paul was overwhelmed with the sense of his indebtedness to Jesus Christ, and he spent his life to express it. The greatest inspiration in Paul's life was his view of Jesus Christ as his spiritual creditor. Do I feel that same sense of indebtedness to Christ regarding every unsaved soul? As a saint, my life's spiritual honor and duty is to fulfill my debt to Christ in relation to these lost souls. Every tiny bit of my life that has value I owe to the redemption of Jesus Christ. Am I doing anything to enable Him to bring His redemption into evident reality in the lives of others? I will only be able to do this as the Spirit of God works into me this sense of indebtedness.

I am not a superior person among other people—I am a bondservant of the Lord Jesus. Paul said, ". . . you are not your own . . . you were bought at a price . . ." (1 Corinthians 6:19–20). Paul sold himself to Jesus Christ and he said, in effect, "I am a debtor to everyone on the face of the earth because of the gospel of Jesus; I am free only that I may be an absolute bondservant of His." That is the characteristic of a Christian's life once this level of spiritual honor and duty becomes real. Quit praying about yourself and spend your life for the sake of others as the bondservant of Jesus. That is the true meaning of being broken bread and poured-out wine in real life.

The Concept of Divine Control

"... how much more will your Father who is in heaven give good things to those who ask Him!" (Matthew 7:11).

Jesus is laying down the rules of conduct in this passage for those people who have His Spirit. He urges us to keep our minds filled with the concept of God's control over everything, which means that a disciple must maintain an attitude of perfect trust and an eagerness to ask and to seek.

Fill your mind with the thought that God is there. And once your mind is truly filled with that thought, when you experience difficulties it will be as easy as breathing for you to remember, "My heavenly Father knows all about this!" This will be no effort at all, but will be a natural thing for you when difficulties and uncertainties arise. Before you formed this concept of divine control so powerfully in your mind, you used to go from person to person seeking help, but now you go to God about it. Jesus is laying down the rules of conduct for those people who have His Spirit, and it works on the following principle: God is my Father, He loves me, and I will never think of anything that He will forget, so why should I worry?

Jesus said there are times when God cannot lift the darkness from you, but you should trust Him. At times God will appear like an unkind friend, but He is not; He will appear like an unnatural father, but He is not; He will appear like an unjust judge, but He is not. Keep the thought that the mind of God is behind all things strong and growing. Not even the smallest detail of life happens unless God's will is behind it. Therefore, you can rest in perfect confidence in Him. Prayer is not only asking, but is an attitude of the mind which produces the atmosphere in which asking is perfectly natural. "Ask, and it will be given to you ..." (7:7).

The Miracle of Belief

"My speech and my preaching were not with persuasive words of human wisdom . . ."
(1 Corinthians 2:4).

Paul was a scholar and an orator of the highest degree; he was not speaking here out of a deep sense of humility, but was saying that when he preached the gospel, he would veil the power of God if he impressed people with the excellency of his speech. Belief in Jesus is a miracle produced only by the effectiveness of redemption, not by impressive speech, nor by wooing and persuading, but only by the sheer unaided power of God. The creative power of redemption comes through the preaching of the gospel, but never because of the personality of the preacher.

Real and effective fasting by a preacher is not fasting from food, but fasting from eloquence, from impressive diction, and from everything else that might hinder the gospel of God being presented. The preacher is there as the representative of God—". . . as though God were pleading through us . . ." (2 Corinthians 5:20). He is there to present the gospel of God. If it is only because of my preaching that people desire to be better, they will never get close to Jesus Christ. Anything that flatters me in my preaching of the gospel will result in making me a traitor to Jesus, and I prevent the creative power of His redemption from doing its work.

"And I, if I am lifted up . . . , will draw all peoples to Myself" (John 12:32).

Through the miracle of redemption, Saul of Tarsus was instantly changed from a strong-willed and forceful Pharisee into a humble and devoted bondservant of the Lord Jesus.

There is nothing miraculous or mysterious about the things we can explain. We control what we are able to explain, consequently it is only natural to seek an explanation for everything. It is not natural to obey, yet it is not necessarily sinful to disobey. There can be no real disobedience, nor any moral virtue in obedience, unless a person recognizes the higher authority of the one giving the orders. If this recognition does not exist, even the one giving the orders may view the other person's disobedience as freedom. If one rules another by saying, "You must do this," and, "You will do that," he breaks the human spirit, making it unfit for God. A person is simply a slave for obeying, unless behind his obedience is the recognition of a holy God.

Many people begin coming to God once they stop being religious, because there is only one master of the human heart—Jesus Christ, not religion. But "Woe is me" if after seeing *Him* I still *will not* obey (Isaiah 6:5, also see verse 1). Jesus will never insist that I obey, but if I don't, I have already begun to sign the death certificate of the Son of God in my soul. When I stand face to face with Jesus Christ and say, "I will not obey," He will never insist. But when I do this, I am backing away from the recreating power of His redemption. It makes no difference to God's grace what an abomination I am, if I will only come to the light. But "Woe is me" if I refuse the light (see John 3:19–21).

The Submission of the Believer

Our Lord never insists on having authority over us. He never says, "You *will* submit to me." No, He leaves us perfectly free to choose—so free, in fact, that we can spit in His face or we can put Him to death, as others have done; and yet He will never say a word. But once His life has been created in me through His redemption, I instantly recognize His right to absolute authority over me. It is a complete and effective domination, in which I acknowledge that "You are worthy, O Lord . . ." (Revelation 4:11). It is simply the unworthiness within me that refuses to bow down or to submit to one who is worthy. When I meet someone who is more holy than myself, and I don't recognize his worthiness, nor obey his instructions for me, it is a sign of my own unworthiness being revealed. God teaches us by using these people who are a little better than we are; not better intellectually, but more holy. And He continues to do so until we willingly submit. Then the whole attitude of our life is one of obedience to Him.

If our Lord insisted on our obedience, He would simply become a taskmaster and cease to have any real authority. He never insists on obedience, but when we truly see Him we will instantly obey Him. Then He is easily Lord of our life, and we live in adoration of Him from morning till night. The level of my growth in grace is revealed by the way I look at obedience. We should have a much higher view of the word *obedience*, rescuing it from the mire of the world. Obedience is only possible between people who are equals in their relationship to each other; like the relationship between father and son, not that between master and servant. Jesus showed this relationship by saying, "I and My Father are one" (John 10:30). ". . . though He was a Son, yet He learned obedience by the things which He suffered" (Hebrews 5:8). The Son was obedient as our Redeemer, *because He was the Son,* not in order to become God's Son.

Dependent on God's Presence

"Those who wait on the LORD . . . shall walk and not faint"
(Isaiah 40:31).

There is no thrill for us in walking, yet it is the test for all of our steady and enduring qualities. To "walk and not faint" is the highest stretch possible as a measure of strength. The word *walk* is used in the Bible to express the character of a person—". . . John . . . looking at Jesus *as He walked* . . . said, 'Behold the Lamb of God!' " (John 1:35–36). There is nothing abstract or obscure in the Bible; everything is vivid and real. God does not say, "Be spiritual," but He says, "Walk before Me . . ." (Genesis 17:1).

When we are in an unhealthy condition either physically or emotionally, we always look for thrills in life. In our physical life this leads to our efforts to counterfeit the work of the Holy Spirit; in our emotional life it leads to obsessions and to the destruction of our morality; and in our spiritual life, if we insist on pursuing only thrills, on mounting up "with wings like eagles" (40:31), it will result in the destruction of our spirituality.

Having the reality of God's presence is not dependent on our being in a particular circumstance or place, but is only dependent on our determination to keep the Lord before us continually. Our problems arise when we refuse to place our trust in the reality of His presence. The experience the psalmist speaks of—"We will not fear, even though . . ." (Psalm 46:2)— will be ours once we are grounded on the truth of the reality of God's presence, not just a simple awareness of it, but an understanding of the reality of it. Then we will exclaim, "He has been here all the time!" At critical moments in our lives it is necessary to ask God for guidance, but it should be unnecessary to be constantly saying, "Oh, Lord, direct me in this, and in that." Of course He will, and in fact, He is doing it already! If our everyday decisions are not according to His will, He will press through them, bringing restraint to our spirit. Then we must be quiet and wait for the direction of His presence.

The Doorway to the Kingdom

"Blessed are the poor in spirit . . ."
(Matthew 5:3).

Beware of thinking of our Lord as only a teacher. If Jesus Christ is only a teacher, then all He can do is frustrate me by setting a standard before me I cannot attain. What is the point of presenting me with such a lofty ideal if I cannot possibly come close to reaching it? I would be happier if I never knew it. What good is there in telling me to be what I can never be—to be "pure in heart" (5:8), to do more than my duty, or to be completely devoted to God? I must know Jesus Christ as my Savior before His teaching has any meaning for me other than that of a lofty ideal which only leads to despair. But when I am born again by the Spirit of God, I know that Jesus Christ did not come only to *teach*—He came to *make me what He teaches I should be*. The redemption means that Jesus Christ can place within anyone the same nature that ruled His own life, and all the standards God gives us are based on that nature.

The teaching of the Sermon on the Mount produces a sense of despair in the natural man—exactly what Jesus means for it to do. As long as we have some self-righteous idea that we can carry out our Lord's teaching, God will allow us to continue until we expose our own ignorance by stumbling over some obstacle in our way. Only then are we willing to come to Him as paupers and receive from Him. "Blessed are the poor in spirit . . . ." This is the first principle in the kingdom of God. The underlying foundation of Jesus Christ's kingdom is poverty, not possessions; not making decisions for Jesus, but having such a sense of absolute futility that we finally admit, "Lord, I cannot even begin to do it." Then Jesus says, "Blessed are you . . ." (5:11). This is the doorway to the kingdom, and yet it takes us so long to believe that we are actually poor! The knowledge of our own poverty is what brings us to the proper place where Jesus Christ accomplishes His work.

The Death Side. In sanctification God has to deal with us on the death side as well as on the life side. Sanctification requires our coming to the place of death, but many of us spend so much time there that we become morbid. There is always a tremendous battle before sanctification is realized—something within us pushing with resentment against the demands of Christ. When the Holy Spirit begins to show us what sanctification means, the struggle starts immediately. Jesus said, "If anyone comes to Me and does not hate . . . his own life . . . he cannot be My disciple" (Luke 14:26).

In the process of sanctification, the Spirit of God will strip me down until there is nothing left but myself, and that is the place of death. Am I willing to be myself and nothing more? Am I willing to have no friends, no father, no brother, and no self-interest—simply to be ready for death? That is the condition required for sanctification. No wonder Jesus said, "I did not come to bring peace but a sword" (Matthew 10:34). This is where the battle comes, and where so many of us falter. We refuse to be identified with the death of Jesus Christ on this point. We say, "But this is so strict. Surely He does not require that of me." Our Lord _is_ strict, and He _does_ require that of us.

Am I willing to reduce myself down to simply "me"? Am I determined enough to strip myself of all that my friends think of me, and all that I think of myself? Am I willing and determined to hand over my simple naked self to God? Once I am, He will immediately sanctify me completely, and my life will be free from being determined and persistent toward anything except God (see 1 Thessalonians 5:23–24).

When I pray, "Lord, show me what sanctification means for me," He will show me. It means being made one with Jesus. Sanctification is not something Jesus puts in me—it is _Himself_ in me (see 1 Corinthians 1:30).

$\mathcal{S}$anctification

"But of Him you are in Christ
Jesus, who became for
us . . . sanctification . . ."
(1 Corinthians 1:30).

The Life Side. The mystery of sanctification is that the perfect
qualities of Jesus Christ are imparted as a gift to me, not gradually, but instantly once I enter by faith into the realization that
He "became for [me] . . . sanctification . . . ." Sanctification
means nothing less than the holiness of Jesus becoming mine
and being exhibited in my life.

The most wonderful secret of living a holy life does not lie
in imitating Jesus, but in letting the perfect qualities of Jesus
exhibit themselves in my human flesh. Sanctification is "Christ
in you . . ." (Colossians 1:27). It is *His* wonderful life that is
imparted to me in sanctification—imparted by faith as a sovereign gift of God's grace. Am I willing for God to make sanctification as real in me as it is in His Word?

Sanctification means the impartation of the holy qualities
of Jesus Christ to me. It is the gift of His patience, love, holiness, faith, purity, and godliness that is exhibited in and
through every sanctified soul. Sanctification is not drawing
from Jesus the power to be holy—it is drawing from Jesus the
very holiness that was exhibited in Him, and that He now
exhibits in me. Sanctification is an impartation, not an imitation. Imitation is something altogether different. The perfection
of everything is in Jesus Christ, and the mystery of sanctification is that all the perfect qualities of Jesus are at my disposal.
Consequently, I slowly but surely begin to live a life of inexpressible order, soundness, and holiness—". . . kept by the
power of God . . ." (1 Peter 1:5).

$H$is Nature and Our Motives

> ". . . unless your righteousness exceeds the righteousness of the scribes and Pharisees, you will by no means enter the kingdom of heaven" (Matthew 5:20).

The characteristic of a disciple is not that he does good things, but that he is good in his motives, having been made good by the supernatural grace of God. The only thing that exceeds right-*doing* is right-*being*. Jesus Christ came to place within anyone who would let Him a new heredity that would have a righteousness exceeding that of the scribes and Pharisees. Jesus is saying, "If you are My disciple, you must be right not only in your actions, but also in your motives, your aspirations, and in the deep recesses of the thoughts of your mind." Your motives must be so pure that God Almighty can see nothing to rebuke. Who can stand in the eternal light of God and have nothing for Him to rebuke? Only the Son of God, and Jesus Christ claims that through His redemption He can place within anyone His own nature and make that person as pure and as simple as a child. The purity that God demands is impossible unless I can be remade within, and that is exactly what Jesus has undertaken to do through His redemption.

No one can make himself pure by obeying laws. Jesus Christ does not give us rules and regulations—He gives us His teachings which are truths that can only be interpreted by His nature which He places within us. The great wonder of Jesus Christ's salvation is that He changes our heredity. He does not change human nature—He changes its source, and thereby its motives as well.

A_m I Blessed Like This?

"Blessed are . . ."
(Matthew 5:3-11).

When we first read the statements of Jesus, they seem wonderfully simple and unstartling, and they sink unnoticed into our subconscious minds. For instance, the Beatitudes initially seem to be merely soothing and beautiful precepts for overly spiritual and seemingly useless people, but of very little practical use in the rigid, fast-paced workdays of the world in which *we* live. We soon find, however, that the Beatitudes contain the "dynamite" of the Holy Spirit. And they "explode" when the circumstances of our lives cause them to do so. When the Holy Spirit brings to our remembrance one of the Beatitudes, we say, "What a startling statement that is!" Then we must decide whether or not we will accept the tremendous spiritual upheaval that will be produced in our circumstances if we obey His words. That is the way the Spirit of God works. We do not need to be born again to apply the Sermon on the Mount literally. The literal interpretation of the Sermon on the Mount is as easy as child's play. But the interpretation by the Spirit of God as He applies our Lord's statements to our circumstances is the strict and difficult work of a saint.

The teachings of Jesus are all out of proportion when compared to our natural way of looking at things, and they come to us initially with astonishing discomfort. We gradually have to conform our walk and conversation to the precepts of Jesus Christ as the Holy Spirit applies them to our circumstances. The Sermon on the Mount is not a set of rules and regulations—it is a picture of the life we will live when the Holy Spirit is having His unhindered way with us.

The Way to Purity

"Those things which proceed out of the mouth come from the heart . . . . For out of the heart proceed evil thoughts, murders, adulteries, fornications, thefts, false witness, blasphemies. These are the things which defile a man . . ."
(Matthew 15:18–20).

Initially we trust in our ignorance, calling it innocence, and next we trust our innocence, calling it purity. Then when we hear these strong statements from our Lord, we shrink back, saying, "But I never felt any of those awful things in my heart." We resent what He reveals. Either Jesus Christ is the supreme authority on the human heart, or He is not worth paying any attention to. Am I prepared to trust the penetration of His Word into my heart, or would I prefer to trust my own "innocent ignorance"? If I will take an honest look at myself, becoming fully aware of my so-called innocence and putting it to the test, I am very likely to have a rude awakening that what Jesus Christ said is true, and I will be appalled at the possibilities of the evil and the wrong within me. But as long as I remain under the false security of my own "innocence," I am living in a fool's paradise. If I have never been an openly rude and abusive person, the only reason is my own cowardice coupled with the sense of protection I receive from living a civilized life. But when I am open and completely exposed before God, I find that Jesus Christ is right in His diagnosis of me.

The only thing that truly provides protection is the redemption of Jesus Christ. If I will simply hand myself over to Him, I will never have to experience the terrible possibilities that lie within my heart. Purity is something far too deep for me to arrive at naturally. But when the Holy Spirit comes into me, He brings into the center of my personal life the very Spirit that was exhibited in the life of Jesus Christ, namely, the *Holy* Spirit, which is absolute unblemished purity.

The Way to Knowledge

"If anyone wills to do His will, he shall know concerning the doctrine . . ." (John 7:17).

The golden rule to follow to obtain spiritual understanding is not one of intellectual pursuit, but one of obedience. If a person wants scientific knowledge, then intellectual curiosity must be his guide. But if he desires knowledge and insight into the teachings of Jesus Christ, he can only obtain it through obedience. If spiritual things seem dark and hidden to me, then I can be sure that there is a point of disobedience somewhere in my life. Intellectual darkness is the result of ignorance, but spiritual darkness is the result of something that I do not intend to obey.

No one ever receives a word from God without instantly being put to the test regarding it. We disobey and then wonder why we are not growing spiritually. Jesus said, "If you bring your gift to the altar, and there remember that your brother has something against you, leave your gift there before the altar, and go your way. First be reconciled to your brother, and then come and offer your gift" (Matthew 5:23–24). He is saying, in essence, "Don't say another word to me; first be obedient by making things right." The teachings of Jesus hit us where we live. We cannot stand as impostors before Him for even one second. He instructs us down to the very last detail. The Spirit of God uncovers our spirit of self-vindication and makes us sensitive to things that we have never even thought of before.

When Jesus drives something home to you through His Word, don't try to evade it. If you do, you will become a religious impostor. Examine the things you tend simply to shrug your shoulders about, and where you have refused to be obedient, and you will know why you are not growing spiritually. As Jesus said, "*First . . . go . . . .*" Even at the risk of being thought of as fanatical, you must obey what God tells you.

God's Purpose or Mine?   "He made His disciples get into the boat and go before Him to the other side . . ." (Mark 6:45).

We tend to think that if Jesus Christ compels us to do something and we are obedient to Him, He will lead us to great success. We should never have the thought that our dreams of success are God's purpose for us. In fact, His purpose may be exactly the opposite. We have the idea that God is leading us toward a particular end or a desired goal, but He is not. The question of whether or not we arrive at a particular goal is of little importance, and reaching it becomes merely an episode along the way. What we see as only the process of reaching a particular end, God sees as the goal itself.

What is my vision of God's purpose for me? Whatever it may be, His purpose is for me to depend on Him and on His power *now.* If I can stay calm, faithful, and unconfused while in the middle of the turmoil of life, the goal of the purpose of God is being accomplished in me. God is not working toward a particular finish—His purpose is the process itself. What He desires for me is that I see "Him walking on the sea" with no shore, no success, nor goal in sight, but simply having the absolute certainty that everything is all right because I see "Him walking on the sea" (6:49). It is the process, not the outcome, that is glorifying to God.

God's training is for now, not later. His purpose is for this very minute, not for sometime in the future. We have nothing to do with what will follow our obedience, and we are wrong to concern ourselves with it. What people call preparation, God sees as the goal itself.

God's purpose is to enable me to see that He can walk on the storms of my life right now. If we have a further goal in mind, we are not paying enough attention to the present time. However, if we realize that moment-by-moment obedience is the goal, then each moment as it comes is precious.

Do You See Jesus in Your Clouds?

"Behold, He is coming with clouds . . ."
(Revelation 1:7).

In the Bible clouds are always associated with God. Clouds are the sorrows, sufferings, or providential circumstances, within or without our personal lives, which actually seem to contradict the sovereignty of God. Yet it is through these very clouds that the Spirit of God is teaching us how to walk by faith. If there were never any clouds in our lives, we would have no faith. "The clouds are the dust of His feet" (Nahum 1:3). They are a sign that God is there. What a revelation it is to know that sorrow, bereavement, and suffering are actually the clouds that come along with God! God cannot come near us without clouds—He does not come in clear-shining brightness.

It is not true to say that God wants to teach us something in our trials. Through every cloud He brings our way, He wants us to *unlearn* something. His purpose in using the cloud is to simplify our beliefs until our relationship with Him is exactly like that of a child—a relationship simply between God and our own souls, and where other people are but shadows. Until other people become shadows to us, clouds and darkness will be ours every once in a while. Is our relationship with God becoming more simple than it has ever been?

There is a connection between the strange providential circumstances allowed by God and what we know of Him, and we have to learn to interpret the mysteries of life in the light of our knowledge of God. Until we can come face to face with the deepest, darkest fact of life without damaging our view of God's character, we do not yet know Him.

". . . they were fearful as they entered the cloud" (Luke 9:34). Is there anyone except Jesus in your cloud? If so, it will only get darker until you get to the place where there is "no one anymore, but only Jesus . . ." (Mark 9:8; also see verses 2–7).

The Teaching of Disillusionment

"Jesus did not commit Himself to them . . . , for He knew what was in man"
(John 2:24-25).

Disillusionment means having no more misconceptions, false impressions, and false judgments in life; it means being free from these deceptions. However, though no longer deceived, our experience of disillusionment may actually leave us cynical and overly critical in our judgment of others. But the disillusionment that comes from God brings us to the point where we see people as they really are, yet without any cynicism or any stinging and bitter criticism. Many of the things in life that inflict the greatest injury, grief, or pain, stem from the fact that we suffer from illusions. We are not true to one another as *facts*, seeing each other as we really are; we are only true to our misconceived *ideas* of one another. According to our thinking, everything is either delightful and good, or it is evil, malicious, and cowardly.

Refusing to be disillusioned is the cause of much of the suffering of human life. And this is how that suffering happens—if we love someone, but do not love God, we demand total perfection and righteousness from that person, and when we do not get it we become cruel and vindictive; yet we are demanding of a human being something which he or she cannot possibly give. There is only one Being who can completely satisfy to the absolute depth of the hurting human heart, and that is the Lord Jesus Christ. Our Lord is so obviously uncompromising with regard to every human relationship because He knows that every relationship that is not based on faithfulness to Himself will end in disaster. Our Lord trusted no one, and never placed His faith in people, yet He was never suspicious or bitter. Our Lord's confidence in God, and in what God's grace could do for anyone, was so perfect that He never despaired, never giving up hope for any person. If our trust is placed in human beings, we will end up despairing of everyone.

July 30

Becoming Entirely His

"Let patience have its perfect work, that you may be perfect and complete, lacking nothing"
(James 1:4).

Many of us appear to be all right in general, but there are still some areas in which we are careless and lazy; it is not a matter of sin, but the remnants of our carnal life that tend to make us careless. Carelessness is an insult to the Holy Spirit. We should have no carelessness about us either in the way we worship God, or even in the way we eat and drink.

Not only must our relationship to God be right, but the outward expression of that relationship must also be right. Ultimately, God will allow nothing to escape; every detail of our lives is under His scrutiny. God will bring us back in countless ways to the same point over and over again. And He never tires of bringing us back to that one point until we learn the lesson, because His purpose is to produce the finished product. It may be a problem arising from our impulsive nature, but again and again, with the most persistent patience, God has brought us back to that one particular point. Or the problem may be our idle and wandering thinking, or our independent nature and self-interest. Through this process, God is trying to impress upon us the one thing that is not entirely right in our lives.

We have been having a wonderful time in our studies over the revealed truth of God's redemption, and our hearts are perfect toward Him. And His wonderful work in us makes us know that overall we are right with Him. "Let patience have its perfect work . . . ." The Holy Spirit speaking through James said, "Now let your patience become a finished product." Beware of becoming careless over the small details of life and saying, "Oh, that will have to do for now." Whatever it may be, God will point it out with persistence until we become entirely His.

Learning About
His Ways

"When Jesus finished commanding His twelve disciples . . . He departed from there to teach and to preach in their cities" (Matthew 11:1).

He comes where He commands us to leave. If you stayed home when God told you to go because you were so concerned about your own people there, then you actually robbed them of the teaching of Jesus Christ Himself. When you obeyed and left all the consequences to God, the Lord went into your city to teach, but as long as you were disobedient, you blocked His way. Watch where you begin to debate with Him and put what you call your duty into competition with His commands. If you say, "I know that He told me to go, but my duty is here," it simply means that you do not believe that Jesus means what He says.

He teaches where He instructs us not to teach.

"Master . . . let us make three tabernacles . . ." (Luke 9:33).

Are we playing the part of an amateur providence, trying to play God's role in the lives of others? Are we so noisy in our instruction of other people that God cannot get near them? We must learn to keep our mouths shut and our spirits alert. God wants to instruct us regarding His Son, and He wants to turn our times of prayer into mounts of transfiguration. When we become certain that God is going to work in a particular way, He will never work in that way again.

He works where He sends us to wait.

". . . tarry . . . until . . ." (Luke 24:49).

"Wait on the LORD" and He will work (Psalm 37:34). But don't wait sulking spiritually and feeling sorry for yourself, just because you can't see one inch in front of you! Are we detached enough from our own spiritual fits of emotion to "wait patiently for Him"? (37:7). Waiting is not sitting with folded hands doing nothing, but it is learning to do what we are told.

These are some of the facets of His ways that we rarely recognize.

The Teaching of Adversity

"In the world you will have tribulation, but be of good cheer, I have overcome the world" (John 16:33).

The typical view of the Christian life is that it means being delivered from all adversity. But it actually means being delivered in adversity, which is something very different. "He who dwells in the secret place of the Most High shall abide under the shadow of the Almighty. No evil shall befall you, nor shall any plague come near your dwelling . . ." (Psalm 91:1, 10)—the place where you are at one with God.

If you are a child of God, you will certainly encounter adversities, but Jesus says you should not be surprised when they come. "In the world you will have tribulation; but be of good cheer, I have overcome the world." He is saying, "There is nothing for you to fear." The same people who refused to talk about their adversities before they were saved often complain and worry after being born again because they have the wrong idea of what it means to live the life of a saint.

God does not give us overcoming life—He gives us life as we overcome. The strain of life is what builds our strength. If there is no strain, there will be no strength. Are you asking God to give you life, liberty, and joy? He cannot, unless you are willing to accept the strain. And once you face the strain, you will immediately get the strength. Overcome your own timidity and take the first step. Then God will give you nourishment—"To him who overcomes I will give to eat from the tree of life . . ." (Revelation 2:7). If you completely give of yourself physically, you become exhausted. But when you give of yourself spiritually, you get more strength. God never gives us strength for tomorrow, or for the next hour, but only for the strain of the moment. Our temptation is to face adversities from the standpoint of our own common sense. But a saint can "be of good cheer" even when seemingly defeated by adversities, because victory is absurdly impossible to everyone, except God.

The Compelling Purpose of God

"He . . . said to them,
'Behold, we are going up to
Jerusalem . . .'"
(Luke 18:31).

Jerusalem, in the life of our Lord, represents the place where He reached the culmination of His Father's will. Jesus said, "I do not seek My own will but the will of the Father who sent Me" (John 5:30). Seeking to do "the will of the Father" was the one dominating concern throughout our Lord's life. And whatever He encountered along the way, whether joy or sorrow, success or failure, He was never deterred from that purpose. ". . . He steadfastly set His face to go to Jerusalem . . ." (Luke 9:51).

The greatest thing for us to remember is that we go up to Jerusalem to fulfill God's purpose, not our own. In the natural life our ambitions are our own, but in the Christian life we have no goals of our own. We talk so much today about our decisions for Christ, our determination to be Christians, and our decisions for this and that, but in the New Testament the only aspect that is brought out is the compelling purpose of God. "You did not choose Me, but I chose you . . ." (John 15:16).

We are not taken into a conscious agreement with God's purpose—we are taken into God's purpose with no awareness of it at all. We have no idea what God's goal may be; as we continue, His purpose becomes even more and more vague. God's aim appears to have missed the mark, because we are too nearsighted to see the target at which He is aiming. At the beginning of the Christian life, we have our own ideas as to what God's purpose is. We say, "God means for me to go over there," and, "God has called me to do this special work." We do what we think is right, and yet the compelling purpose of God remains upon us. The work we do is of no account when compared with the compelling purpose of God. It is simply the scaffolding surrounding His work and His plan. "He took the twelve aside . . ." (Luke 18:31). God takes us aside all the time. We have not yet understood all there is to know of the compelling purpose of God.

The Brave Friendship of God

"He took the twelve aside . . ."
(Luke 18:31).

Oh, the bravery of God in trusting us! Do you say, "But He has been unwise to choose me, because there is nothing good in me and I have no value"? That is exactly why He chose you. As long as you think that you are of value to Him He cannot choose you, because you have purposes of your own to serve. But if you will allow Him to take you to the end of your own self-sufficiency, then He can choose you to go with Him "to Jerusalem" (18:31). And that will mean the fulfillment of purposes which He does not discuss with you.

We tend to say that because a person has natural ability, he will make a good Christian. It is not a matter of our equipment, but a matter of our poverty; not of what we bring with us, but of what God puts into us; not a matter of natural virtues, of strength of character, of knowledge, or of experience—all of that is of no avail in this concern. The only thing of value is being taken into the compelling purpose of God and being made His friends (see 1 Corinthians 1:26–31). God's friendship is with people who know their poverty. He can accomplish nothing with the person who thinks that he is of use to God. As Christians we are not here for our own purpose at all—we are here for the purpose of God, and the two are not the same. We do not know what God's compelling purpose is, but whatever happens, we must maintain our relationship with Him. We must never allow anything to damage our relationship with God, but if something does damage it, we must take the time to make it right again. The most important aspect of Christianity is not the work we do, but the relationship we maintain and the surrounding influence and qualities produced by that relationship. That is all God asks us to give our attention to, and it is the one thing that is continually under attack.

The Bewildering Call of God

" '. . . and all things that are written by the prophets concerning the Son of Man will be accomplished.' . . . But they understood none of these things . . .' " (Luke 18:31, 34).

God called Jesus Christ to what seemed absolute disaster. And Jesus Christ called His disciples to see Him put to death, leading every one of them to the place where their hearts were broken. His life was an absolute failure from every standpoint except God's. But what seemed to be failure from man's standpoint was a triumph from God's standpoint, because God's purpose is never the same as man's purpose.

This bewildering call of God comes into our lives as well. The call of God can never be understood absolutely or explained externally; it is a call that can only be perceived and understood internally by our true inner-nature. The call of God is like the call of the sea—no one hears it except the person who has the nature of the sea in him. What God calls us to cannot be definitely stated, because His call is simply to be His friend to accomplish His own purposes. Our real test is in truly believing that God knows what He desires. The things that happen do not happen by chance—they happen entirely by the decree of God. God is sovereignly working out His own purposes.

If we are in fellowship and oneness with God and recognize that He is taking us into His purposes, then we will no longer strive to find out what His purposes are. As we grow in the Christian life, it becomes simpler to us, because we are less inclined to say, "I wonder why God allowed this or that?" And we begin to see that the compelling purpose of God lies behind everything in life, and that God is divinely shaping us into oneness with that purpose. A Christian is someone who trusts in the knowledge and the wisdom of God, not in his own abilities. If we have a purpose of our own, it destroys the simplicity and the calm, relaxed pace which should be characteristic of the children of God.

"In that day you will ask in
My name . . ."
(John 16:26).

We too often think of the Cross of Christ as something we have to get through, yet we get *through* for the purpose of getting *into* it. The Cross represents only one thing for us—complete, entire, absolute identification with the Lord Jesus Christ—and there is nothing in which this identification is more real to us than in prayer.

"Your Father knows the things you have need of before you ask Him" (Matthew 6:8). Then why should we ask? The point of prayer is not to get answers from God, but to have perfect and complete oneness with Him. If we pray only because we want answers, we will become irritated and angry with God. We receive an answer every time we pray, but it does not always come in the way we expect, and our spiritual irritation shows our refusal to identify ourselves truly with our Lord in prayer. We are not here to prove that God answers prayer, but to be living trophies of God's grace.

". . . I do not say to you that I shall pray the Father for you; for the Father Himself loves you . . ." (John 16:26–27). Have you reached such a level of intimacy with God that the only thing that can account for your prayer life is that it has become one with the prayer life of Jesus Christ? Has our Lord exchanged your life with His vital life? If so, then "in that day" you will be so closely identified with Jesus that there will be no distinction.

When prayer seems to be unanswered, beware of trying to place the blame on someone else. That is always a trap of Satan. When you seem to have no answer, there is always a reason—God uses these times to give you deep personal instruction, and it is not for anyone else but you.

Prayer in the
Father's House

". . . they found Him in the temple . . . . And He said to them, '. . . Did you not know that I must be about My Father's business?' " (Luke 2:46, 49).

Our Lord's childhood was not immaturity waiting to grow into manhood—His childhood is an eternal fact. Am I a holy, innocent child of God as a result of my identification with my Lord and Savior? Do I look at my life as being in my Father's house? Is the Son of God living in His Father's house within me?

The only abiding reality is God Himself, and His order comes to me moment by moment. Am I continually in touch with the reality of God, or do I pray only when things have gone wrong—when there is some disturbance in my life? I must learn to identify myself closely with my Lord in ways of holy fellowship and oneness that some of us have not yet even begun to learn. ". . . I must be about My Father's business"— and I must learn to live every moment of my life in my Father's house.

Think about your own circumstances. Are you so closely identified with the Lord's life that you are simply a child of God, continually talking to Him and realizing that everything comes from His hands? Is the eternal Child in you living in His Father's house? Is the grace of His ministering life being worked out through you in your home, your business, and in your circle of friends? Have you been wondering why you are going through certain circumstances? In fact, it is not that *you* have to go through them. It is because of your relationship with the Son of God who comes, through the providential will of His Father, into your life. You must allow *Him* to have His way with you, staying in perfect oneness with Him.

The life of your Lord is to become your vital, simple life, and the way He worked and lived among people while here on earth must be the way He works and lives in you.

Prayer in the Father's Honor

". . . that Holy One who is to be born will be called the Son of God" (Luke 1:35).

If the Son of God has been born into my human flesh, then am I allowing His holy innocence, simplicity, and oneness with the Father the opportunity to exhibit itself in me? What was true of the Virgin Mary in the history of the Son of God's birth on earth is true of every saint. God's Son is born into me through the direct act of God; then I as His child must exercise the right of a child—the right of always being face to face with my Father through prayer. Do I find myself continually saying in amazement to the commonsense part of my life, "Why did you want me to turn here or to go over there? 'Did you not know that I must be about My Father's business?' " (Luke 2:49). Whatever our circumstances may be, that holy, innocent, and eternal Child must be in contact with His Father.

Am I simple enough to identify myself with my Lord in this way? Is He having His wonderful way with me? Is God's will being fulfilled in that His Son has been formed in me (see Galatians 4:19), or have I carefully pushed Him to one side? Oh, the noisy outcry of today! Why does everyone seem to be crying out so loudly? People today are crying out for the Son of God to be put to death. There is no room here for God's Son right now—no room for quiet, holy fellowship and oneness with the Father.

Is the Son of God praying in me, bringing honor to the Father, or am I dictating my demands to Him? Is He ministering in me as He did in the time of His manhood here on earth? Is God's Son in me going through His passion, suffering so that His own purposes might be fulfilled? The more a person knows of the inner life of God's most mature saints, the more he sees what God's purpose really is: to ". . . fill up in my flesh what is lacking in the afflictions of Christ . . ." (Colossians 1:24). And when we think of what it takes to "fill up," there is always something yet to be done.

*Prayer in the
Father's Hearing*

"Jesus lifted up His eyes and
said, 'Father, I thank You
that You have heard Me'"
(John 11:41).

When the Son of God prays, He is mindful and consciously aware of only His Father. God always hears the prayers of His Son, and if the Son of God has been formed in me (see Galatians 4:19) the Father will always hear my prayers. But I must see to it that the Son of God is exhibited in my human flesh. ". . . your body is the temple of the Holy Spirit . . ." (1 Corinthians 6:19), that is, your body is the Bethlehem of God's Son. Is the Son of God being given His opportunity to work in me? Is the direct simplicity of His life being worked out in me exactly as it was worked out in His life while here on earth? When I come into contact with the everyday occurrences of life as an ordinary human being, is the prayer of God's eternal Son to His Father being prayed in me? Jesus says, "In that day you will ask in My name . . ." (John 16:26). What day does He mean? He is referring to the day when the Holy Spirit has come to me and made me one with my Lord.

Is the Lord Jesus Christ being abundantly satisfied by your life, or are you exhibiting a walk of spiritual pride before Him? Never let your common sense become so prominent and forceful that it pushes the Son of God to one side. Common sense is a gift that God gave to our human nature—but common sense is not the gift of His Son. Supernatural sense is the gift of His Son, and we should never put our common sense on the throne. The Son always recognizes and identifies with the Father, but common sense has never yet done so and never will. Our ordinary abilities will never worship God unless they are transformed by the indwelling Son of God. We must make sure that our human flesh is kept in perfect submission to Him, allowing Him to work through it moment by moment. Are we living at such a level of human dependence upon Jesus Christ that His life is being exhibited moment by moment in us?

The Holy Suffering of the Saint

> "Let those who suffer according to the will of God commit their souls to Him in doing good . . ."
> (1 Peter 4:19).

Choosing to suffer means that there must be something wrong with you, but choosing God's will—even if it means you will suffer—is something very different. No normal, healthy saint ever chooses suffering; he simply chooses God's will, just as Jesus did, whether it means suffering or not. And no saint should ever dare to interfere with the lesson of suffering being taught in another saint's life.

The saint who satisfies the heart of Jesus will make other saints strong and mature for God. But the people used to strengthen us are never those who sympathize with us; in fact, we are hindered by those who give us their sympathy, because sympathy only serves to weaken us. No one better understands a saint than the saint who is as close and as intimate with Jesus as possible. If we accept the sympathy of another saint, our spontaneous feeling is, "God is dealing too harshly with me and making my life too difficult." That is why Jesus said that self-pity was of the devil (see Matthew 16:21–23). We must be merciful to God's reputation. It is easy for us to tarnish God's character because He never argues back; He never tries to defend or vindicate Himself. Beware of thinking that Jesus needed sympathy during His life on earth. He refused the sympathy of people because in His great wisdom He knew that no one on earth understood His purpose (see 16:23). He accepted only the sympathy of His Father and the angels (see Luke 15:10).

Look at God's incredible waste of His saints, according to the world's judgment. God seems to plant His saints in the most useless places. And then we say, "God intends for me to be here because I am so useful to Him." Yet Jesus never measured His life by how or where He was of the greatest use. God places His saints where they will bring the most glory to Him, and we are totally incapable of judging where that may be.

This Experience Must Come

"Elijah went up by a whirlwind into heaven. And Elisha . . . saw him no more"
(2 Kings 2:11–12).

It is not wrong for you to depend on your "Elijah" for as long as God gives him to you. But remember that the time will come when he must leave and will no longer be your guide and your leader, because God does not intend for him to stay. Even the thought of that causes you to say, "I cannot continue without my 'Elijah.'" Yet God says you must continue.

Alone at Your "Jordan" (2:14). The Jordan River represents the type of separation where you have no fellowship with anyone else, and where no one else can take your responsibility from you. You now have to put to the test what you learned when you were with your "Elijah." You have been to the Jordan over and over again with Elijah, but now you are facing it alone. There is no use in saying that you cannot go—the experience is here, and you must go. If you truly want to know whether or not God is the God your faith believes Him to be, then go through your "Jordan" alone.

Alone at Your "Jericho" (2:15). Jericho represents the place where you have seen your "Elijah" do great things. Yet when you come alone to your "Jericho," you have a strong reluctance to take the initiative and trust in God, wanting, instead, for someone else to take it for you. But if you remain true to what you learned while with your "Elijah," you will receive a sign, as Elisha did, that God is with you.

Alone at Your "Bethel" (2:23). At your "Bethel" you will find yourself at your wits' end but at the beginning of God's wisdom. When you come to your wits' end and feel inclined to panic—don't! Stand true to God and He will bring out His truth in a way that will make your life an expression of worship. Put into practice what you learned while with your "Elijah"—use his mantle and pray (see 2:13–14). Make a determination to trust in God, and do not even look for Elijah anymore.

August 11

The Theology of
Resting in God

"Why are you fearful, O you
of little faith?"
(Matthew 8:26).

When we are afraid, the least we can do is pray to God. But our Lord has a right to expect that those who name His name have an underlying confidence in Him. God expects His children to be so confident in Him that in any crisis they are the ones who are reliable. Yet our trust is only in God up to a certain point, then we turn back to the elementary panic-stricken prayers of those people who do not even know God. We come to our wits' end, showing that we don't have even the slightest amount of confidence in Him or in His sovereign control of the world. To us He seems to be asleep, and we can see nothing but giant, breaking waves on the sea ahead of us.

". . . O you of little faith!" What a stinging pain must have shot through the disciples as they surely thought to themselves, "We missed the mark again!" And what a sharp pain will go through us when we suddenly realize that we could have produced complete and utter joy in the heart of Jesus by remaining absolutely confident in Him, in spite of what we were facing.

There are times when there is no storm or crisis in our lives, and we do all that is humanly possible. But it is when a crisis arises that we instantly reveal upon whom we rely. If we have been learning to worship God and to place our trust in Him, the crisis will reveal that we can go to the point of breaking, yet without breaking our confidence in Him.

We have been talking quite a lot about sanctification, but what will be the result in our lives? It will be expressed in our lives as a peaceful resting in God, which means a total oneness with Him. And this oneness will make us not only blameless in His sight, but also a profound joy to Him.

"Do Not Quench the Spirit"

"Do not quench the Spirit"
(1 Thessalonians 5:19).

The voice of the Spirit of God is as gentle as a summer breeze—so gentle that unless you are living in complete fellowship and oneness with God, you will never hear it. The sense of warning and restraint that the Spirit gives comes to us in the most amazingly gentle ways. And if you are not sensitive enough to detect His voice, you will quench it, and your spiritual life will be impaired. This sense of restraint will always come as a "still small voice" (1 Kings 19:12), so faint that no one except a saint of God will notice it.

Beware if in sharing your personal testimony you continually have to look back, saying, "Once, a number of years ago, I was saved." If you have put your "hand to the plow" and are walking in the light, there is no "looking back"—the past is instilled into the present wonder of fellowship and oneness with God (Luke 9:62; also see 1 John 1:6–7). If you get out of the light, you become a sentimental Christian, and live only on your memories, and your testimony will have a hard metallic ring to it. Beware of trying to cover up your present refusal to "walk in the light" by recalling your past experiences when you did "walk in the light" (1 John 1:7). Whenever the Spirit gives you that sense of restraint, call a halt and make things right, or else you will go on quenching and grieving Him without even knowing it.

Suppose God brings you to a crisis and you almost endure it, but not completely. He will engineer the crisis again, but this time some of the intensity will be lost. You will have less discernment and more humiliation at having disobeyed. If you continue to grieve His Spirit, there will come a time when that crisis cannot be repeated, because you have totally quenched Him. But if you will go on through the crisis, your life will become a hymn of praise to God. Never become attached to anything that continues to hurt God. For you to be free of it, God must be allowed to hurt whatever it may be.

The Discipline of the Lord

"My son, do not despise the chastening of the LORD, nor be discouraged when you are rebuked by Him" (Hebrews 12:5).

It is very easy to grieve the Spirit of God; we do it by despising the discipline of the Lord, or by becoming discouraged when He rebukes us. If our experience of being set apart from sin and being made holy through the process of sanctification is still very shallow, we tend to mistake the reality of God for something else. And when the Spirit of God gives us a sense of warning or restraint, we are apt to say mistakenly, "Oh, that must be from the devil."

"Do not quench the Spirit" (1 Thessalonians 5:19), and do not despise Him when He says to you, in effect, "Don't be blind on this point anymore—you are not as far along spiritually as you thought you were. Until now I have not been able to reveal this to you, but I'm revealing it to you right now." When the Lord disciplines you like that, let Him have His way with you. Allow Him to put you into a right-standing relationship before God.

". . . nor be discouraged when you are rebuked by Him." We begin to pout, become irritated with God, and then say, "Oh well, I can't help it. I prayed and things didn't turn out right anyway. So I'm simply going to give up on everything." Just think what would happen if we acted like this in any other area of our lives!

Am I fully prepared to allow God to grip me by His power and do a work in me that is truly worthy of Himself? Sanctification is not my idea of what I want God to do for me—sanctification is God's idea of what He wants to do for me. But He has to get me into the state of mind and spirit where I will allow Him to sanctify me completely, whatever the cost (see 1 Thessalonians 5:23–24).

The Evidence of the New Birth

"You must be born again" (John 3:7).

The answer to Nicodemus' question, "How can a man be born when he is old?" is: Only when he is willing to die to everything in his life, including his rights, his virtues, and his religion, and becomes willing to receive into himself a new life that he has never before experienced (3:4). This new life exhibits itself in our conscious repentance and through our unconscious holiness.

"But as many as received Him . . ." (John 1:12). Is my knowledge of Jesus the result of my own internal spiritual perception, or is it only what I have learned through listening to others? Is there something in my life that unites me with the Lord Jesus as my personal Savior? My spiritual history must have as its underlying foundation a personal knowledge of Jesus Christ. To be born again means that I see Jesus.

". . . unless one is born again, he cannot see the kingdom of God" (John 3:3). Am I seeking only for the evidence of God's kingdom, or am I actually recognizing His absolute sovereign control? The new birth gives me a new power of vision by which I begin to discern God's control. His sovereignty was there all the time, but with God being true to His nature, I could not see it until I received His very nature myself.

"Whoever has been born of God does not sin . . ." (1 John 3:9). Am I seeking to stop sinning or have I actually stopped? To be born of God means that I have His supernatural power to stop sinning. The Bible never asks, "Should a Christian sin?" The Bible emphatically states that *a Christian must not sin.* The work of the new birth is being effective in us when we do not commit sin. It is not merely that we have the power not to sin, but that we have actually stopped sinning. Yet 1 John 3:9 does not mean that we *cannot* sin—it simply means that if we will obey the life of God in us, that we *do not have to sin.*

$Does\ He\ Know\ Me\ .\ .\ .\ ?$ "He calls his own . . . by name . . ."
(John 10:3).

When I have sadly misunderstood Him? (see John 20:11–18).
It is possible to know all about doctrine and still not know
Jesus. A person's soul is in grave danger when the knowledge of
doctrine surpasses Jesus, avoiding intimate touch with Him.
Why was Mary weeping? Doctrine meant no more to her than
the grass under her feet. In fact, any Pharisee could have made
a fool of Mary doctrinally, but one thing they could never
ridicule was the fact that Jesus had cast seven demons out of
her (see Luke 8:2); yet His blessings were nothing to her in
comparison with knowing Jesus Himself. ". . . she turned
around and saw Jesus standing there, and did not know that it
was Jesus. . . . Jesus said to her, 'Mary!' " (John 20:14, 16). Once
He called Mary by her name, she immediately knew that she
had a personal history with the One who spoke. "She turned
and said to Him, 'Rabboni!' " (20:16).

When I have stubbornly doubted? (see John 20:24–29).
Have I been doubting something about Jesus—maybe an experience to which others testify, but which I have not yet experienced? The other disciples said to Thomas, "We have seen the
Lord" (20:25). But Thomas doubted, saying, "Unless I see . . . I
will not believe" (20:25). Thomas needed the personal touch of
Jesus. When His touches will come we never know, but when
they do come they are indescribably precious. "Thomas . . . said
to Him, 'My Lord and my God!' " (20:28).

When I have selfishly denied Him? (see John 21:15–17).
Peter denied Jesus Christ with oaths and curses (see Matthew
26:69–75), and yet after His resurrection Jesus appeared to
Peter alone. Jesus restored Peter in private, and then He
restored him publicly before the others. And Peter said to Him,
"Lord . . . You know that I love You" (John 21:17).

Do I have a personal history with Jesus Christ? The one
true sign of discipleship is intimate oneness with Him—a
knowledge of Jesus that nothing can shake.

Are You Discouraged or Devoted?

"... Jesus ... said to him, 'You still lack one thing. Sell all that you have ... and come, follow Me.' But when he heard this, he became very sorrowful, for he was very rich" (Luke 18:22–23).

Have you ever heard the Master say something very difficult to you? If you haven't, I question whether you have ever heard Him say anything at all. Jesus says a tremendous amount to us that we listen to, but do not actually hear. And once we do hear Him, His words are harsh and unyielding.

Jesus did not show the least concern that this rich young ruler should do what He told him, nor did Jesus make any attempt to keep this man with Him. He simply said to him, "Sell all that you have ... and come, follow Me." Our Lord never pleaded with him; He never tried to lure him—He simply spoke the strictest words that human ears have ever heard, and then left him alone.

Have I ever heard Jesus say something difficult and unyielding to me? Has He said something personally to me to which I have deliberately listened—not something I can explain for the sake of others, but something I have heard Him say directly to me? This man understood what Jesus said. He heard it clearly, realizing the full impact of its meaning, and it broke his heart. He did not go away as a defiant person, but as one who was sorrowful and discouraged. He had come to Jesus on fire with zeal and determination, but the words of Jesus simply froze him. Instead of producing enthusiastic devotion to Jesus, they produced heartbreaking discouragement. And Jesus did not go after him, but let him go. Our Lord knows perfectly well that once His word is truly heard, it will bear fruit sooner or later. What is so terrible is that some of us prevent His words from bearing fruit in our present life. I wonder what we will say when we finally make up our minds to be devoted to Him on that particular point? One thing is certain—He will never throw our past failures back in our faces.

Have You Ever Been Speechless with Sorrow?

"When he heard this, he became very sorrowful, for he was very rich" (Luke 18:23).

The rich young ruler went away from Jesus speechless with sorrow, having nothing to say in response to Jesus' words. He had no doubt about what Jesus had said or what it meant, and it produced in him a sorrow with no words with which to respond. Have you ever been there? Has God's Word ever come to you, pointing out an area of your life, requiring you to yield it to Him? Maybe He has pointed out certain personal qualities, desires, and interests, or possibly relationships of your heart and mind. If so, then you have often been speechless with sorrow. The Lord will not go after you, and He will not plead with you. But every time He meets you at the place where He has pointed, He will simply repeat His words, saying, "If you really mean what you say, these are the conditions."

"Sell all that you have . . ." (18:22). In other words, rid yourself before God of everything that might be considered a possession until you are a mere conscious human being standing before Him, and then give God that. That is where the battle is truly fought—in the realm of your will before God. Are you more devoted to your idea of what Jesus wants than to Jesus Himself? If so, you are likely to hear one of His harsh and unyielding statements that will produce sorrow in you. What Jesus says *is* difficult—it is only easy when it is heard by those who have His nature in them. Beware of allowing anything to soften the hard words of Jesus Christ.

I can be so rich in my own poverty, or in the awareness of the fact that I am nobody, that I will never be a disciple of Jesus. Or I can be so rich in the awareness that I am somebody that I will never be a disciple. Am I willing to be destitute and poor even in my sense of awareness of my destitution and poverty? If not, that is why I become discouraged. Discouragement is disillusioned self-love, and self-love may be love for my devotion to Jesus—not love for Jesus Himself.

God intends for us to live a well-rounded life in Christ Jesus,
but there are times when that life is attacked from the outside.
Then we tend to fall back into self-examination, a habit that we
thought was gone. Self-awareness is the first thing that will
upset the completeness of our life in God, and self-awareness
continually produces a sense of struggling and turmoil in our
lives. Self-awareness is not sin, and it can be produced by nervous emotions or by suddenly being dropped into a totally new
set of circumstances. Yet it is never God's will that we should be
anything less than absolutely complete in Him. Anything that
disturbs our rest in Him must be rectified at once, and it is not
rectified by being ignored but only by coming to Jesus Christ. If
we will come to Him, asking Him to produce Christ-awareness
in us, He will always do it, until we fully learn to abide in Him.

Never allow anything that divides or destroys the oneness
of your life with Christ to remain in your life without facing it.
Beware of allowing the influence of your friends or your circumstances to divide your life. This only serves to sap your
strength and slow your spiritual growth. Beware of anything
that can split your oneness with Him, causing you to see yourself as separate from Him. Nothing is as important as staying
right spiritually. And the only solution is a very simple one—
"Come to Me . . . ." The intellectual, moral, and spiritual depth
of our reality as a person is tested and measured by these
words. Yet in every detail of our lives where we are found not to
be real, we would rather dispute the findings than come to
Jesus.

*C*hrist-*A*wareness

". . . and I will give you rest"
(Matthew 11:28).

Whenever anything begins to disintegrate your life with Jesus Christ, turn to Him at once, asking Him to re-establish your rest. Never allow anything to remain in your life that is causing the unrest. Think of every detail of your life that is causing the disintegration as something to fight against, not as something you should allow to remain. Ask the Lord to put awareness of Himself in you, and your self-awareness will disappear. Then He will be your all in all. Beware of allowing your self-aware-ness to continue, because slowly but surely it will awaken self-pity, and self-pity is satanic. Don't allow yourself to say, "Well, they have just misunderstood me, and this is something over which they should be apologizing to me; I'm sure I must have this cleared up with them already." Learn to leave others alone regarding this. Simply ask the Lord to give you Christ-aware-ness, and He will steady you until your completeness in Him is absolute.

A complete life is the life of a child. When I am fully con-scious of my awareness of Christ, there is something wrong. It is the sick person who really knows what health is. A child of God is not aware of the will of God because he is the will of God. When we have deviated even slightly from the will of God, we begin to ask, "Lord, what is your will?" A child of God never prays to be made aware of the fact that God answers prayer, because he is so restfully certain that God always answers prayer.

If we try to overcome our self-awareness through any of our own commonsense methods, we will only serve to strengthen our self-awareness tremendously. Jesus says, "Come to Me . . . and I will give you rest," that is, Christ-awareness will take the place of self-awareness. Wherever Jesus comes He establishes rest—the rest of the completion of activity in our lives that is never aware of itself.

A u g u s t 2 0

The Ministry of the Unnoticed

"Blessed are the poor in spirit . . ."
(Matthew 5:3).

The New Testament notices things that do not seem worthy of notice by our standards. "Blessed are the poor in spirit . . . ." This literally means, "Blessed are the paupers." Paupers are remarkably commonplace! The preaching of today tends to point out a person's strength of will or the beauty of his character—things that are easily noticed. The statement we so often hear, "Make a decision for Jesus Christ," places the emphasis on something our Lord never trusted. He never asks us to decide for Him, but to yield to Him—something very different. At the foundation of Jesus Christ's kingdom is the genuine loveliness of those who are commonplace. I am truly blessed in my poverty. If I have no strength of will and a nature without worth or excellence, then Jesus says to me, "Blessed are you, because it is through your poverty that you can enter My kingdom." I cannot enter His kingdom by virtue of my goodness—I can only enter it as an absolute pauper.

The true character of the loveliness that speaks for God is always unnoticed by the one possessing that quality. Conscious influence is prideful and unchristian. If I wonder if I am being of any use to God, I instantly lose the beauty and the freshness of the touch of the Lord. "He who believes in Me . . . out of his heart will flow rivers of living water" (John 7:38). And if I examine the outflow, I lose the touch of the Lord.

Who are the people who have influenced us most? Certainly not the ones who thought they did, but those who did not have even the slightest idea that they were influencing us. In the Christian life, godly influence is never conscious of itself. If we are conscious of our influence, it ceases to have the genuine loveliness which is characteristic of the touch of Jesus. We always know when Jesus is at work because He produces in the commonplace something that is inspiring.

"I Indeed . . . But He"

Have I ever come to the point in my life where I can say, "I indeed . . . but He . . ."? Until that moment comes, I will never know what the baptism of the Holy Spirit means. *I indeed* am at the end, and I cannot do anything more—*but* He begins right there—He does the things that no one else can ever do. Am I prepared for His coming? Jesus cannot come and do His work in me as long as there is anything blocking the way, whether it is something good or bad. When He comes to me, am I prepared for Him to drag every wrong thing I have ever done into the light? That is exactly where He comes. Wherever I know I am unclean is where He will put His feet and stand, and wherever I think I am clean is where He will remove His feet and walk away.

Repentance does not cause a sense of sin—it causes a sense of inexpressible unworthiness. When I repent, I realize that I am absolutely helpless, and I know that through and through I am not worthy even to carry His sandals. Have I repented like that, or do I have a lingering thought of possibly trying to defend my actions? The reason God cannot come into my life is that I am not at the point of complete repentance.

"He will baptize you with the Holy Spirit and fire." John is not speaking here of the baptism of the Holy Spirit as an experience, but as a work performed by Jesus Christ. "*He* will baptize you . . . ." The only experience that those who are baptized with the Holy Spirit are ever conscious of is the experience of sensing their absolute unworthiness.

"*I indeed*" was this in the past, "*but He*" came and something miraculous happened. Get to the end of yourself where you can do nothing, but where He does everything.

Prayer—Battle in
"The Secret Place"

"When you pray, go into your room, and when you have shut your door, pray to your Father who is in the secret place, and your Father who sees in secret will reward you openly" (Matthew 6:6).

Jesus did not say, "Dream about your Father who is in the secret place," but He said, "... *pray* to your Father who is in the secret place...." Prayer is an effort of the will. After we have entered our secret place and shut the door, the most difficult thing to do is to pray. We cannot seem to get our minds into good working order, and the first thing we have to fight is wandering thoughts. The great battle in private prayer is overcoming this problem of our idle and wandering thinking. We have to learn to discipline our minds and concentrate on willful, deliberate prayer.

We must have a specially selected place for prayer, but once we get there this plague of wandering thoughts begins, as we begin to think to ourselves, "This needs to be done, and I have to do that today." Jesus says to "shut your door." Having a secret stillness before God means deliberately shutting the door on our emotions and remembering Him. God is in secret, and He sees us from "the secret place"—He does not see us as other people do, or as we see ourselves. When we truly live in "the secret place," it becomes impossible for us to doubt God. We become more sure of Him than of anyone or anything else. Enter into "the secret place," and you will find that God was right in the middle of your everyday circumstances all the time. Get into the habit of dealing with God about everything. Unless you learn to open the door of your life completely and let God in from your first waking moment of each new day, you will be working on the wrong level throughout the day. But if you will swing the door of your life fully open and "pray to your Father who is in the secret place," every public thing in your life will be marked with the lasting imprint of the presence of God.

August 23

The Spiritual Search

"What man is there among you who, if his son asks for bread, will give him a stone?"
(Matthew 7:9).

The illustration of prayer that our Lord used here is one of a good child who is asking for something good. We talk about prayer as if God hears us regardless of what our relationship is to Him (see Matthew 5:45). Never say that it is not God's will to give you what you ask. Don't faint and give up, but find out the reason you have not received; increase the intensity of your search and examine the evidence. Is your relationship right with your spouse, your children, and your fellow students? Are you a "good child" in those relationships? Do you have to say to the Lord, "I have been irritable and cross, but I still want spiritual blessings"? You cannot receive and will have to do without them until you have the attitude of a "good child."

We mistake defiance for devotion, arguing with God instead of surrendering. We refuse to look at the evidence that clearly indicates where we are wrong. Have I been asking God to give me money for something I want, while refusing to pay someone what I owe him? Have I been asking God for liberty while I am withholding it from someone who belongs to me? Have I refused to forgive someone, and have I been unkind to that person? Have I been living as God's child among my relatives and friends? (see Matthew 7:12).

I am a child of God only by being born again, and as His child I am good only as I "walk in the light" (1 John 1:7). For most of us, prayer simply becomes some trivial religious expression, a matter of mystical and emotional fellowship with God. We are all good at producing spiritual fog that blinds our sight. But if we will search out and examine the evidence, we will see very clearly what is wrong—a friendship, an unpaid debt, or an improper attitude. There is no use praying unless we are living as children of God. Then Jesus says, regarding His children, "Everyone who asks receives . . ." (Matthew 7:8).

Sacrifice and Friendship

We will never know the joy of self-sacrifice until we surrender in every detail of our lives. Yet self-surrender is the most difficult thing for us to do. We make it conditional by saying, "I'll surrender if . . . !" Or we approach it by saying, "I suppose I have to devote my life to God." We will never find the joy of self-sacrifice in either of these ways.

But as soon as we do totally surrender, abandoning ourselves to Jesus, the Holy Spirit gives us a taste of His joy. The ultimate goal of self-sacrifice is to lay down our lives for our Friend (see 15:13–14). When the Holy Spirit comes into our lives, our greatest desire is to lay down our lives for Jesus. Yet the thought of self-sacrifice never even crosses our minds, because sacrifice is the Holy Spirit's ultimate expression of love.

Our Lord is our example of a life of self-sacrifice, and He perfectly exemplified Psalm 40:8, "I delight to do Your will, O my God . . . ." He endured tremendous personal sacrifice, yet with overflowing joy. Have I ever yielded myself in absolute submission to Jesus Christ? If He is not the One to whom I am looking for direction and guidance, then there is no benefit in my sacrifice. But when my sacrifice is made with my eyes focused on Him, slowly but surely His molding influence becomes evident in my life (see Hebrews 12:1–2).

Beware of letting your natural desires hinder your walk in love before God. One of the cruelest ways to kill natural love is through the rejection that results from having built the love on natural desires. But the one true desire of a saint is the Lord Jesus. Love for God is not something sentimental or emotional—for a saint to love as God loves is the most practical thing imaginable.

"I have called you friends. . . ." Our friendship with Jesus is based on the new life He created in us, which has no resemblance or attraction to our old life but only to the life of God. It is a life that is completely humble, pure, and devoted to God.

Are You Ever Troubled? "Peace I leave with you, My peace I give to you . . ." (John 14:27).

Where are times in our lives when our peace is based simply on our own ignorance. But when we are awakened to the realities of life, true inner peace is impossible unless it is received from Jesus. When our Lord speaks peace, He creates peace, because the words that He speaks are always "spirit, and they are life" (John 6:63). Have I ever received what Jesus speaks? ". . . My peace I give to you . . ."—a peace that comes from looking into His face and fully understanding and receiving His quiet contentment.

Are you severely troubled right now? Are you afraid and confused by the waves and the turbulence God sovereignly allows to enter your life? Have you left no stone of your faith unturned, yet still not found any well of peace, joy, or comfort? Does your life seem completely barren to you? Then look up and receive the quiet contentment of the Lord Jesus. Reflecting His peace is proof that you are right with God, because you are exhibiting the freedom to turn your mind to Him. If you are not right with God, you can never turn your mind anywhere but on yourself. Allowing anything to hide the face of Jesus Christ from you either causes you to become troubled or gives you a false sense of security.

With regard to the problem that is pressing in on you right now, are you "looking unto Jesus" (Hebrews 12:2) and receiving peace from Him? If so, He will be a gracious blessing of peace exhibited in and through you. But if you only try to worry your way out of the problem, you destroy His effectiveness in you, and you deserve whatever you get. We become troubled because we have not been taking Him into account. When a person confers with Jesus Christ, the confusion stops, because there is no confusion in Him. Lay everything out before Him, and when you are faced with difficulty, bereavement, and sorrow, listen to Him say, "Let not your heart be troubled . . ." (John 14:27).

Living Your Theology

"Walk while you have the light, lest darkness overtake you . . ."
(John 12:35).

Beware of not acting upon what you see in your moments on the mountaintop with God. If you do not obey the light, it will turn into darkness. "If therefore the light that is in you is darkness, how great is that darkness!" (Matthew 6:23). The moment you forsake the matter of sanctification or neglect anything else on which God has given you His light, your spiritual life begins to disintegrate within you. Continually bring the truth out into your real life, working it out into every area, or else even the light that you possess will itself prove to be a curse.

The most difficult person to deal with is the one who has the prideful self-satisfaction of a past experience, but is not working that experience out in his everyday life. If you *say* you are sanctified, *show it.* The experience must be so genuine that it shows in your life. Beware of any belief that makes you self-indulgent or self-gratifying; that belief came from the pit of hell itself, regardless of how beautiful it may sound.

Your theology must work itself out, exhibiting itself in your most common everyday relationships. Our Lord said, ". . . unless your righteousness *exceeds* the righteousness of the scribes and Pharisees, you will by no means enter the kingdom of heaven" (Matthew 5:20). In other words, you must be more moral than the most moral person you know. You may know all about the doctrine of sanctification, but are you working it out in the everyday issues of your life? Every detail of your life, whether physical, moral, or spiritual, is to be judged and measured by the standard of the atonement by the Cross of Christ.

The Purpose of Prayer

"... one of His disciples said
to Him, 'Lord, teach us to
pray ...'"
(Luke 11:1).

Prayer is not a normal part of the life of the natural man. We hear it said that a person's life will suffer if he doesn't pray, but I question that. What will suffer is the life of the Son of God in him, which is nourished not by food, but by prayer. When a person is born again from above, the life of the Son of God is born in him, and he can either starve or nourish that life. Prayer is the way that the life of God in us is nourished. Our common ideas regarding prayer are not found in the New Testament. We look upon prayer simply as a means of getting things for ourselves, but the biblical purpose of prayer is that we may get to know God Himself.

"Ask, and you will receive ..." (John 16:24). We complain before God, and sometimes we are apologetic or indifferent to Him, but we actually *ask* Him for very few things. Yet a child exhibits a magnificent boldness to ask! Our Lord said, "... unless you ... become as little children ..." (Matthew 18:3). Ask and God will do. Give Jesus Christ the opportunity and the room to work. The problem is that no one will ever do this until he is at his wits' end. When a person is at his wits' end, it no longer seems to be a cowardly thing to pray; in fact, it is the only way he can get in touch with the truth and the reality of God Himself. Be yourself before God and present Him with your problems—the very things that have brought you to your wits' end. But as long as you think you are self-sufficient, you do not need to ask God for anything.

To say that "prayer changes things" is not as close to the truth as saying, "Prayer changes *me* and then I change things." God has established things so that prayer, on the basis of redemption, changes the way a person looks at things. Prayer is not a matter of changing things externally, but one of working miracles in a person's inner nature.

The Unsurpassed Intimacy of Tested Faith

"Jesus said to her, 'Did I not say to you that if you would believe you would see the glory of God?' " (John 11:40).

Every time you venture out in your life of faith, you will find something in your circumstances that, from a commonsense standpoint, will flatly contradict your faith. But common sense is not faith, and faith is not common sense. In fact, they are as different as the natural life and the spiritual. Can you trust Jesus Christ where your common sense cannot trust Him? Can you venture out with courage on the words of Jesus Christ, while the realities of your commonsense life continue to shout, "It's all a lie"? When you are on the mountaintop, it's easy to say, "Oh yes, I believe God can do it," but you have to come down from the mountain to the demon-possessed valley and face the realities that scoff at your Mount-of-Transfiguration belief (see Luke 9:28–42). Every time my theology becomes clear to my own mind, I encounter something that contradicts it. As soon as I say, "I believe 'God shall supply all [my] need,'" the testing of my faith begins (Philippians 4:19). When my strength runs dry and my vision is blinded, will I endure this trial of my faith victoriously or will I turn back in defeat?

Faith must be tested, because it can only become your intimate possession through conflict. What is challenging your faith right now? The test will either prove your faith right, or it will kill it. Jesus said, "Blessed is he who is not offended because of Me" (Matthew 11:6). The ultimate thing is confidence in Jesus. "We have become partakers of Christ if we hold the beginning of our confidence steadfast to the end . . ." (Hebrews 3:14). Believe steadfastly on Him and everything that challenges you will strengthen your faith. There is continual testing in the life of faith up to the point of our physical death, which is the last great test. Faith is absolute trust in God—trust that could never imagine that He would forsake us (see Hebrews 13:5–6).

Usefulness or Relationship? "Do not rejoice in this, that the spirits are subject to you, but rather rejoice because your names are written in heaven" (Luke 10:20).

Jesus Christ is saying here, "Don't rejoice in your successful service *for* Me, but rejoice because of your right relationship *with* Me." The trap you may fall into in Christian work is to rejoice in successful service—rejoicing in the fact that God has used you. Yet you will never be able to measure fully what God will do through you if you do not have a right-standing relationship with Jesus Christ. If you keep your relationship right with Him, then regardless of your circumstances or whoever you encounter each day, He will continue to pour "rivers of living water" through you (John 7:38). And it is actually by His mercy that He does not let you know it. Once you have the right relationship with God through salvation and sanctification, remember that whatever your circumstances may be, you have been placed in them by God. And God uses the reaction of your life to your circumstances to fulfill His purpose, as long as you continue to "walk in the light as He is in the light" (1 John 1:7).

Our tendency today is to put the emphasis on service. Beware of the people who make their request for help on the basis of someone's usefulness. If you make usefulness the test, then Jesus Christ was the greatest failure who ever lived. For the saint, direction and guidance come from God Himself, not some measure of that saint's usefulness. It is the work that God does through us that counts, not what we do for Him. All that our Lord gives His attention to in a person's life is that person's relationship with God—something of great value to His Father. Jesus is "bringing many *sons* to glory . . ." (Hebrews 2:10).

"My Joy . . . Your Joy"

"These things I have spoken to you, that My joy may remain in you, and that your joy may be full" (John 15:11).

What was the joy that Jesus had? Joy should not be confused with happiness. In fact, it is an insult to Jesus Christ to use the word *happiness* in connection with Him. The joy of Jesus was His absolute self-surrender and self-sacrifice to His Father—the joy of doing that which the Father sent Him to do—". . . who for the joy that was set before Him endured the cross . . ." (Hebrews 12:2). "I delight to do Your will, O my God . . ." (Psalm 40:8). Jesus prayed that our joy might continue fulfilling itself until it becomes the same joy as His. Have I allowed Jesus Christ to introduce His joy to me?

Living a full and overflowing life does not rest in bodily health, in circumstances, nor even in seeing God's work succeed, but in the perfect understanding of God, and in the same fellowship and oneness with Him that Jesus Himself enjoyed. But the first thing that will hinder this joy is the subtle irritability caused by giving too much thought to our circumstances. Jesus said, ". . . the cares of this world, . . . choke the word, and it becomes unfruitful" (Mark 4:19). And before we even realize what has happened, we are caught up in our cares. All that God has done for us is merely the threshold—He wants us to come to the place where we will be His witnesses and proclaim who Jesus is.

Have the right relationship with God, finding your joy there, and out of you "will flow rivers of living water" (John 7:38). Be a fountain through which Jesus can pour His "living water." Stop being hypocritical and proud, aware only of yourself, and live "your life . . . hidden with Christ in God" (Colossians 3:3). A person who has the right relationship with God lives a life as natural as breathing wherever he goes. The lives that have been the greatest blessing to you are the lives of those people who themselves were unaware of having been a blessing.

August 31

Destined To Be Holy

"... it is written, 'Be holy, for I am holy'"
(1 Peter 1:16).

We must continually remind ourselves of the purpose of life. We are not destined to happiness, nor to health, but to holiness. Today we have far too many desires and interests, and our lives are being consumed and wasted by them. Many of them may be right, noble, and good, and may later be fulfilled, but in the meantime God must cause their importance to us to decrease. The only thing that truly matters is whether a person will accept the God who will make him holy. At all costs, a person must have the right relationship with God.

Do I believe I need to be holy? Do I believe that God can come into me and make me holy? If through your preaching you convince me that I am unholy, I then resent your preaching. The preaching of the gospel awakens an intense resentment because it is designed to reveal my unholiness, but it also awakens an intense yearning and desire within me. God has only one intended destiny for mankind—holiness. His only goal is to produce saints. God is not some eternal blessing-machine for people to use, and He did not come to save us out of pity—He came to save us because He created us to be holy. Atonement through the Cross of Christ means that God can put me back into perfect oneness with Himself through the death of Jesus Christ, without a trace of anything coming between us any longer.

Never tolerate, because of sympathy for yourself or for others, any practice that is not in keeping with a holy God. Holiness means absolute purity of your walk before God, the words coming from your mouth, and every thought in your mind—placing every detail of your life under the scrutiny of God Himself. Holiness is not simply what God gives me, but what God has given me that is being exhibited in my life.

A Life of Pure and Holy Sacrifice

"He who believes in Me . . . out of his heart will flow . . ."
(John 7:38).

Jesus did not say, "He who believes in Me will realize all the blessings of the fullness of God," but, in essence, "He who believes in Me will have everything he receives escape out of him." Our Lord's teaching was always *anti*-self-realization. His purpose is not the development of a person—His purpose is to make a person exactly like Himself, and the Son of God is characterized by self-expenditure. If we believe in Jesus, it is not what we gain but what He pours through us that really counts. God's purpose is not simply to make us beautiful, plump grapes, but to make us grapes so that He may squeeze the sweetness out of us. Our spiritual life cannot be measured by success as the world measures it, but only by what God pours through us—and we cannot measure that at all.

When Mary of Bethany "broke the flask . . . of very costly oil . . . and poured it on [Jesus'] head," it was an act for which no one else saw any special occasion; in fact, ". . . there were some who . . . said, 'Why was this fragrant oil wasted?' " (Mark 14:3–4). But Jesus commended Mary for her extravagant act of devotion, and said, ". . . wherever this gospel is preached . . . what this woman has done will also be told as a memorial to her" (Mark 14:9). Our Lord is filled with overflowing joy whenever He sees any of us doing what Mary did—not being bound by a particular set of rules, but being totally surrendered to Him. God poured out the life of His Son "that the world through Him might be saved" (John 3:17). Are we prepared to pour out our lives for Him?

"He who believes in Me . . . out of his heart will flow rivers of living water"—and hundreds of other lives will be continually refreshed. Now is the time for us to break "the flask" of our lives, to stop seeking our own satisfaction, and to pour out our lives before Him. Our Lord is asking who of us will do it for Him?

Pouring Out the Water of Satisfaction

"He would not drink it, but poured it out to the LORD"
(2 Samuel 23:16).

What has been like "water from the well of Bethlehem" to you recently—love, friendship, or maybe some spiritual blessing (23:16)? Have you taken whatever it may be, even at the risk of damaging your own soul, simply to satisfy yourself? If you have, then you cannot pour it out "to the LORD." You can never set apart for God something that you desire for yourself to achieve your own satisfaction. If you try to satisfy yourself with a blessing from God, it will corrupt you. You must sacrifice it, pouring it out to God—something that your common sense says is an absurd waste.

How can I pour out "to the LORD" natural love and spiritual blessings? There is only one way—I must make a determination in my mind to do so. There are certain things other people do that could never be received by someone who does not know God, because it is humanly impossible to repay them. As soon as I realize that something is too wonderful for me, that I am not worthy to receive it, and that it is not meant for a human being at all, I must pour it out "to the LORD." Then these very things that have come to me will be poured out as "rivers of living water" all around me (John 7:38). And until I pour these things out to God, they actually endanger those I love, as well as myself, because they will be turned into lust. Yes, we can be lustful in things that are not sordid and vile. Even love must be transformed by being poured out "to the LORD."

If you have become bitter and sour, it is because when God gave you a blessing you hoarded it. Yet if you had poured it out to Him, you would have been the sweetest person on earth. If you are always keeping blessings to yourself and never learning to pour out anything "to the LORD," other people will never have their vision of God expanded through you.

$H_{is}!$

"They were Yours, You gave them to Me . . ."
(John 17:6).

A missionary is someone in whom the Holy Spirit has brought about this realization: "You are not your own" (1 Corinthians 6:19). To say, "I am not my own," is to have reached a high point in my spiritual stature. The true nature of that life in actual everyday confusion is evidenced by the deliberate giving up of myself to another Person through a sovereign decision, and that Person is Jesus Christ. The Holy Spirit interprets and explains the nature of Jesus to me to make me one with my Lord, not that I might simply become a trophy for His showcase. Our Lord never sent any of His disciples out on the basis of what He had done for them. It was not until after the resurrection, when the disciples had perceived through the power of the Holy Spirit who Jesus really was, that He said, "Go" (Matthew 28:19; also see Luke 24:49 and Acts 1:8).

"If anyone comes to Me and does not hate his father and mother, wife and children, brothers and sisters, yes, and his own life also, he cannot be My disciple" (Luke 14:26). He was not saying that this person cannot be good and upright, but that he cannot be someone over whom Jesus can write the word *Mine*. Any one of the relationships our Lord mentions in this verse can compete with our relationship with Him. I may prefer to belong to my mother, or to my wife, or to myself, but if that is the case, then, Jesus said, "[You] cannot be My disciple." This does not mean that I will not be saved, but it does mean that I cannot be entirely *His*.

Our Lord makes His disciple His very own possession, becoming responsible for him. ". . . you shall be witnesses to Me . . ." (Acts 1:8). The desire that comes into a disciple is not one of *doing* anything for Jesus, but of *being* a perfect delight to Him. The missionary's secret is truly being able to say, "I am His, and He is accomplishing His work and His purposes through me."

Be entirely His!

September 4

Watching With Jesus

"Watch with Me." Jesus was saying, in effect, "Watch with no private point of view at all, but watch solely and entirely with Me." In the early stages of our Christian life, we do not watch *with* Jesus, we watch *for* Him. We do not watch with Him through the revealed truth of the Bible even in the circumstances of our own lives. Our Lord is trying to introduce us to identification with Himself through a particular "Gethsemane" experience of our own. But we refuse to go, saying, "No, Lord, I can't see the meaning of this, and besides, it's very painful." And how can we possibly watch with Someone who is so incomprehensible? How are we going to understand Jesus sufficiently to watch with Him in His Gethsemane, when we don't even know why He is suffering? We don't know how to watch with Him— we are only used to the idea of Jesus watching with us.

The disciples loved Jesus Christ to the limit of their natural capacity, but they did not fully understand His purpose. In the Garden of Gethsemane they slept as a result of their own sorrow, and at the end of three years of the closest and most intimate relationship of their lives they "all . . . forsook Him and fled" (26:56).

"They were all filled with the Holy Spirit . . ." (Acts 2:4). "They" refers to the same people, but something wonderful has happened between these two events—our Lord's death, resurrection, and ascension—and the disciples have now been invaded and "filled with the Holy Spirit." Our Lord had said, "You shall receive power when the Holy Spirit has come upon you . . ." (Acts 1:8). This meant that they learned to watch *with* Him the rest of their lives.

The Far-reaching Rivers of Life

"He who believes in Me . . .
out of his heart will flow
rivers of living water"
(John 7:38).

A river reaches places which its source never knows. And Jesus said that, if we have received His fullness, "rivers of living water" will flow out of us, reaching in blessing even "to the end of the earth" (Acts 1:8) regardless of how small the visible effects of our lives may appear to be. We have nothing to do with the outflow—"This is the work of God, that you *believe* . . ." (John 6:29). God rarely allows a person to see how great a blessing he is to others.

A river is victoriously persistent, overcoming all barriers. For a while it goes steadily on its course, but then comes to an obstacle. And for a while it is blocked, yet it soon makes a pathway around the obstacle. Or a river will drop out of sight for miles, only later to emerge again even broader and greater than ever. Do you see God using the lives of others, but an obstacle has come into your life and you do not seem to be of any use to God? Then keep paying attention to the Source, and God will either take you around the obstacle or remove it. The river of the Spirit of God overcomes all obstacles. Never focus your eyes on the obstacle or the difficulty. The obstacle will be a matter of total indifference to the river that will flow steadily through you if you will simply remember to stay focused on the Source. Never allow anything to come between you and Jesus Christ— not emotion nor experience—nothing must keep you from the one great sovereign Source.

Think of the healing and far-reaching rivers developing and nourishing themselves in our souls! God has been opening up wonderful truths to our minds, and every point He has opened up is another indication of the wider power of the river that He will flow through us. If you believe in Jesus, you will find that God has developed and nourished in you mighty, rushing rivers of blessing for others.

Fountains of Blessings

"The water that I shall give him will become in him a fountain of water springing up into everlasting life" (John 4:14).

The picture our Lord described here is not that of a simple stream of water, but an overflowing fountain. Continue to "be filled" (Ephesians 5:18) and the sweetness of your vital relationship to Jesus will flow as generously out of you as it has been given to you. If you find that His life is not springing up as it should, you are to blame—something is obstructing the flow. Was Jesus saying to stay focused on the Source so that you may be blessed personally? No, you are to focus on the Source so that out of you "will flow rivers of living water"—irrepressible life (John 7:38).

We are to be fountains through which Jesus can flow as "rivers of living water" in blessing to everyone. Yet some of us are like the Dead Sea, always receiving but never giving, because our relationship is not right with the Lord Jesus. As surely as we receive blessings from Him, He will pour out blessings through us. But whenever the blessings are not being poured out in the same measure they are received, there is a defect in our relationship with Him. Is there anything between you and Jesus Christ? Is there anything hindering your faith in Him? If not, then Jesus says that out of you "will flow rivers of living water." It is not a blessing that you pass on, or an experience that you share with others, but a river that continually flows through you. Stay at the Source, closely guarding your faith in Jesus Christ and your relationship to Him, and there will be a steady flow into the lives of others with no dryness or deadness whatsoever.

Is it excessive to say that rivers will flow out of one individual believer? Do you look at yourself and say, "But I don't see the rivers"? Through the history of God's work you will usually find that He has started with the obscure, the unknown, the ignored, but those who have been steadfastly true to Jesus Christ.

Do It $Yourself$

". . . casting down arguments and every high thing that exalts itself against the knowledge of God . . ." (2 Corinthians 10:5).

Determinedly Demolish Some Things. Deliver-ance from sin is not the same as deliverance from human nature. There are things in human nature, such as prejudices, that the saint can only destroy through sheer neglect. But there are other things that have to be destroyed through violence, that is, through God's divine strength imparted by His Spirit. There are some things over which we are not to fight, but only to "stand still, and see the salvation of the Lord . . ." (Exodus 14:13). But every theory or thought that raises itself up as a fortified barrier "against the knowledge of God" is to be determinedly demolished by drawing on God's power, not through human effort or by compromise (see 2 Corinthians 10:4).

It is only when God has transformed our nature and we have entered into the experience of sanctification that the fight begins. The warfare is not against sin; we can never fight against sin—Jesus Christ conquered that in His redemption of us. The conflict is waged over turning our natural life into a spiritual life. This is never done easily, nor does God intend that it be so. It is accomplished only through a series of moral choices. God does not make us holy in the sense that He makes our character holy. He makes us holy in the sense that He has made us innocent before Him. And then we have to turn that innocence into holy character through the moral choices we make. These choices are continually opposed and hostile to the things of our natural life which have become so deeply entrenched—the very things that raise themselves up as forti-fied barriers "against the knowledge of God." We can either turn back, making ourselves of no value to the kingdom of God, or we can determinedly demolish these things, allowing Jesus to bring another son to glory (see Hebrews 2:10).

Do It Yourself

Determinedly Discipline Other Things. This is another difficult aspect of the strenuous nature of sainthood. Paul said, according to the Moffatt translation of this verse, ". . . I take every project prisoner to make it obey Christ . . . ." So much Christian work today has never been disciplined, but has simply come into being by impulse! In our Lord's life every project was disciplined to the will of His Father. There was never the slightest tendency to follow the impulse of His own will as distinct from His Father's will—"the Son can do nothing of Himself . . ." (John 5:19). Then compare this with what we do—we take "every thought" or project that comes to us by impulse and jump into action immediately, instead of imprisoning and disciplining ourselves to obey Christ.

Practical work for Christians is greatly overemphasized today, and the saints who are "bringing every thought [and project] into captivity" are criticized and told that they are not determined, and that they lack zeal for God or zeal for the souls of others. But true determination and zeal are found in obeying God, not in the inclination to serve Him that arises from our own undisciplined human nature. It is inconceivable, but true nevertheless, that saints are not "bringing every thought [and project] into captivity," but are simply doing work for God that has been instigated by their own human nature, and has not been made spiritual through determined discipline.

We have a tendency to forget that a person is not only committed to Jesus Christ for salvation, but is also committed, responsible, and accountable to Jesus Christ's view of God, the world, and of sin and the devil. This means that each person must recognize the responsibility to "be transformed by the renewing of [his] mind. . . ." (Romans 12:2).

"When you were under the fig tree, I saw you" (John 1:48).

Worshiping in Everyday Occasions. We presume that we would be ready for battle if confronted with a great crisis, but it is not the crisis that builds something within us—it simply reveals what we are made of already. Do you find yourself saying, "If God calls me to battle, of course I will rise to the occasion"? Yet you won't rise to the occasion unless you have done so on God's training ground. If you are not doing the task that is closest to you now, which God has engineered into your life, when the crisis comes, instead of being fit for battle, you will be revealed as being unfit. Crises always reveal a person's true character.

A private relationship of worshiping God is the greatest essential element of spiritual fitness. The time will come, as Nathanael experienced in this passage, that a private "fig-tree" life will no longer be possible. Everything will be out in the open, and you will find yourself to be of no value there if you have not been worshiping in everyday occasions in your own home. If your worship is right in your private relationship with God, then when He sets you free, you will be ready. It is in the unseen life, which only God saw, that you have become perfectly fit. And when the strain of the crisis comes, you can be relied upon by God.

Are you saying, "But I can't be expected to live a sanctified life in my present circumstances; I have no time for prayer or Bible study right now; besides, my opportunity for battle hasn't come yet, but when it does, of course I will be ready"? No, you will not. If you have not been worshiping in everyday occasions, when you get involved in God's work, you will not only be useless yourself but also a hindrance to those around you.

God's training ground, where the missionary weapons are found, is the hidden, personal, worshiping life of the saint.

Missionary Weapons

"If I then, your Lord and Teacher, have washed your feet, you also ought to wash one another's feet" (John 13:14).

Ministering in Everyday Opportunities. Ministering in everyday opportunities that surround us does not mean that we select our own surroundings—it means being God's very special choice to be available for use in any of the seemingly random surroundings which He has engineered for us. The very character we exhibit in our present surroundings is an indication of what we will be like in other surroundings.

The things Jesus did were the most menial of everyday tasks, and this is an indication that it takes all of God's power in me to accomplish even the most common tasks in His way. Can I use a towel as He did? Towels, dishes, sandals, and all the other ordinary things in our lives reveal what we are made of more quickly than anything else. It takes God Almighty Incarnate in us to do the most menial duty as it ought to be done.

Jesus said, "I have given you an example, that you should do as I have done to you" (13:15). Notice the kind of people that God brings around you, and you will be humiliated once you realize that this is actually His way of revealing to you the kind of person you have been to Him. Now He says we should exhibit to those around us exactly what He has exhibited to us.

Do you find yourself responding by saying, "Oh, I will do all that once I'm out on the mission field"? Talking in this way is like trying to produce the weapons of war while in the trenches of the battlefield—you will be killed while trying to do it.

We have to go the "second mile" with God (see Matthew 5:41). Yet some of us become worn out in the first ten steps. Then we say, "Well, I'll just wait until I get closer to the next big crisis in my life." But if we do not steadily minister in everyday opportunities, we will do nothing when the crisis comes.

Going Through Spiritual Confusion

> "Jesus answered and said, 'You do not know what you ask' " (Matthew 20:22).

There are times in your spiritual life when there is confusion, and the way out of it is not simply to say that you should not be confused. It is not a matter of right and wrong, but a matter of God taking you through a way that you temporarily do not understand. And it is only by going through the spiritual confusion that you will come to the understanding of what God wants for you.

The Shrouding of His Friendship (see Luke 11:5–8). Jesus gave the illustration here of a man who appears not to care for his friend. He was saying, in effect, that is how the heavenly Father will appear to you at times. You will think that He is an unkind friend, but remember—He is not. The time will come when everything will be explained. There seems to be a cloud on the friendship of the heart, and often even love itself has to wait in pain and tears for the blessing of fuller fellowship and oneness. When God appears to be completely shrouded, will you hang on with confidence in Him?

The Shadow on His Fatherhood (see Luke 11:11–13). Jesus said that there are times when your Father will appear as if He were an unnatural father—as if He were callous and indifferent—but remember, He is not. "Everyone who asks receives . . ." (Luke 11:10). If all you see is a shadow on the face of the Father right now, hang on to the fact that He will ultimately give you clear understanding and will fully justify Himself in everything that He has allowed into your life.

The Strangeness of His Faithfulness (see Luke 18:1–8). "When the Son of Man comes, will He really find faith on the earth?" (Luke 18:8). Will He find the kind of faith that counts on Him in spite of the confusion? Stand firm in faith, believing that what Jesus said is true, although in the meantime you do not understand what God is doing. He has bigger issues at stake than the particular things you are asking of Him right now.

*After Surrender—
Then What?*

"I have finished the work
      which You have given Me
   to do"
(John 17:4).

True surrender is not simply surrender of our external life but surrender of our will—and once that is done, surrender is complete. The greatest crisis we ever face is the surrender of our will. Yet God never forces a person's will into surrender, and He never begs. He patiently waits until that person willingly yields to Him. And once that battle has been fought, it never needs to be fought again.

Surrender for Deliverance. "Come to Me . . . and I will give you rest" (Matthew 11:28). It is only after we have begun to experience what salvation really means that we surrender our will to Jesus for rest. Whatever is causing us a sense of uncertainty is actually a call to our will—"Come to Me." And it is a voluntary coming.

Surrender for Devotion. "If anyone desires to come after Me, let him deny himself . . ." (Matthew 16:24). The surrender here is of my self to Jesus, with His rest at the heart of my being. He says, "If you want to be My disciple, you must give up your right to yourself to Me." And once this is done, the remainder of your life will exhibit nothing but the evidence of this surrender, and you never need to be concerned again with what the future may hold for you. Whatever your circumstances may be, Jesus is totally sufficient (see 2 Corinthians 12:9 and Philippians 4:19).

Surrender for Death. ". . . another will gird you . . ." (John 21:18; also see verse 19). Have you learned what it means to be girded for death? Beware of some surrender that you make to God in an ecstatic moment in your life, because you are apt to take it back again. True surrender is a matter of being "united together [with Jesus] in the likeness of His death" (Romans 6:5) until nothing ever appeals to you that did not appeal to Him.

And after you surrender—then what? Your entire life should be characterized by an eagerness to maintain unbroken fellowship and oneness with God.

Arguments or Obedience? " . . . the simplicity that is in Christ"
(2 Corinthians 11:3).

Simplicity is the secret to seeing things clearly. A saint does not *think* clearly until a long time passes, but a saint ought to *see* clearly without any difficulty. You cannot think through spiritual confusion to make things clear; to make things clear, you must obey. In intellectual matters you can think things out, but in spiritual matters you will only think yourself into further wandering thoughts and more confusion. If there is something in your life upon which God has put His pressure, then obey Him in that matter. Bring all your "arguments and . . . every thought into captivity to the obedience of Christ" regarding the matter, and everything will become as clear as daylight to you (2 Corinthians 10:5). Your reasoning capacity will come later, but reasoning is not how we see. We see like children, and when we try to be wise we see nothing (see Matthew 11:25).

Even the very smallest thing that we allow in our lives that is not under the control of the Holy Spirit is completely sufficient to account for spiritual confusion, and spending all of our time thinking about it will still never make it clear. Spiritual confusion can only be conquered through obedience. As soon as we obey, we have discernment. This is humiliating, because when we are confused we know that the reason lies in the state of our mind. But when our natural power of sight is devoted and submitted in obedience to the Holy Spirit, it becomes the very power by which we perceive God's will, and our entire life is kept in simplicity.

What To Renounce

"We have renounced the hidden things of shame . . ."
(2 Corinthians 4:2).

Have you "renounced the hidden things of shame" in your life—the things that your sense of honor or pride will not allow to come into the light? You can easily hide them. Is there a thought in your heart about anyone that you would not like to be brought into the light? Then renounce it as soon as it comes to mind—renounce everything in its entirety until there is no hidden dishonesty or craftiness about you at all. Envy, jealousy, and strife don't necessarily arise from your old nature of sin, but from the flesh which was used for these kinds of things in the past (see Romans 6:19 and 1 Peter 4:1–3). You must maintain continual watchfulness so that nothing arises in your life that would cause you shame.

". . . not walking in craftiness. . ." (2 Corinthians 4:2). This means not resorting to something simply to make your own point. This is a terrible trap. You know that God will allow you to work in only one way—the way of truth. Then be careful never to catch people through the other way—the way of deceit. If you act deceitfully, God's blight and ruin will be upon you. What may be craftiness for you, may not be for others—God has called you to a higher standard. Never dull your sense of being your utmost for His highest—your best for His glory. For you, doing certain things would mean craftiness coming into your life for a purpose other than what is the highest and best, and it would dull the motivation that God has given you. Many people have turned back because they are afraid to look at things from God's perspective. The greatest spiritual crisis comes when a person has to move a little farther on in his faith than the beliefs he has already accepted.

Praying to God in Secret

"When you pray, go into your room, and when you have shut your door, pray to your Father who is in the secret place . . ."
(Matthew 6:6).

The primary thought in the area of religion is—keep your eyes on God, not on people. Your motivation should not be the desire to be known as a praying person. Find an inner room in which to pray where no one even knows you are praying, shut the door, and talk to God in secret. Have no motivation other than to know your Father in heaven. It is impossible to carry on your life as a disciple without definite times of secret prayer.

"When you pray, do not use vain repetitions . . ." (6:7). God does not hear us because we pray earnestly—He hears us solely on the basis of redemption. God is never impressed by our earnestness. Prayer is not simply getting things from God—that is only the most elementary kind of prayer. Prayer is coming into perfect fellowship and oneness with God. If the Son of God has been formed in us through regeneration (see Galatians 4:19), then He will continue to press on beyond our common sense and will change our attitude about the things for which we pray.

"Everyone who *asks* receives . . ." (Matthew 7:8). We pray religious nonsense without even involving our will, and then we say that God did not answer—but in reality we have never *asked* for anything. Jesus said, ". . . you will ask what you desire . . ." (John 15:7). Asking means that our will must be involved. Whenever Jesus talked about prayer, He spoke with wonderful childlike simplicity. Then we respond with our critical attitude, saying, "Yes, but even Jesus said that we must *ask*." But remember that we have to ask things of God that are in keeping with the God whom Jesus Christ revealed.

September 16

Is There Good in Temptation?

"No temptation has overtaken you except such as is common to man . . ."
(1 Corinthians 10:13).

The word *temptation* has come to mean something bad to us today, but we tend to use the word in the wrong way. Temptation itself is not sin; it is something we are bound to face simply by virtue of being human. Not to be tempted would mean that we were already so shameful that we would be beneath contempt. Yet many of us suffer from temptations we should never have to suffer, simply because we have refused to allow God to lift us to a higher level where we would face temptations of another kind.

A person's inner nature, what he possesses in the inner, spiritual part of his being, determines what he is tempted by on the outside. The temptation fits the true nature of the person being tempted and reveals the possibilities of his nature. Every person actually determines or sets the level of his own temptation, because temptation will come to him in accordance with the level of his controlling, inner nature.

Temptation comes to me, suggesting a possible shortcut to the realization of my highest goal—it does not direct me toward what I understand to be evil, but toward what I understand to be good. Temptation is something that confuses me for a while, and I don't know whether something is right or wrong. When I yield to it, I have made lust a god, and the temptation itself becomes the proof that it was only my own fear that prevented me from falling into the sin earlier.

Temptation is not something we can escape; in fact, it is essential to the well-rounded life of a person. Beware of thinking that you are tempted as no one else—what you go through is the common inheritance of the human race, not something that no one has ever before endured. God does not save us from temptations—He sustains us in the midst of them (see Hebrews 2:18 and 4:15–16).

His Temptation and Ours

"We do not have a High Priest who cannot sympathize with our weaknesses, but was in all points tempted as we are, yet without sin"
(Hebrews 4:15).

Until we are born again, the only kind of temptation we understand is the kind mentioned in James 1:14, "Each one is tempted when he is drawn away by his own desires and enticed." But through regeneration we are lifted into another realm where there are other temptations to face, namely, the kind of temptations our Lord faced. The temptations of Jesus had no appeal to us as unbelievers because they were not at home in our human nature. Our Lord's temptations and ours are in different realms until we are born again and become His brothers. The temptations of Jesus are not those of a mere man, but the temptations of God as Man. Through regeneration, the Son of God is formed in us (see Galatians 4:19), and in our physical life He has the same setting that He had on earth. Satan does not tempt us just to make us do wrong things—he tempts us to make us lose what God has put into us through regeneration, namely, the possibility of being of value to God. He does not come to us on the premise of tempting us to sin, but on the premise of shifting our point of view, and only the Spirit of God can detect this as a temptation of the devil.

Temptation means a test of the possessions held within the inner, spiritual part of our being by a power outside us and foreign to us. This makes the temptation of our Lord explainable. After Jesus' baptism, having accepted His mission of being the One "who takes away the sin of the world" (John 1:29) He "was led up by the Spirit into the wilderness" (Matthew 4:1) and into the testing devices of the devil. Yet He did not become weary or exhausted. He went through the temptation "without sin," and He retained all the possessions of His spiritual nature completely intact.

Are You Going on With Jesus?

"You are those who have continued with Me in My trials" (Luke 22:28).

It is true that Jesus Christ is with us through our temptations, but are we going on with Him through His temptations? Many of us turn back from going on with Jesus from the very moment we have an experience of what He can do. Watch when God changes your circumstances to see whether you are going on with Jesus, or siding with the world, the flesh, and the devil. We wear His name, but are we going on with Him? "From that time many of His disciples went back and walked with Him no more" (John 6:66).

The temptations of Jesus continued throughout His earthly life, and they will continue throughout the life of the Son of God in us. Are we going on with Jesus in the life we are living right now?

We have the idea that we ought to shield ourselves from some of the things God brings around us. May it never be! It is God who engineers our circumstances, and whatever they may be we must see that we face them while continually abiding with Him in His temptations. They are *His* temptations, not temptations to us, but temptations to the life of the Son of God in us. Jesus Christ's honor is at stake in our bodily lives. Are we remaining faithful to the Son of God in everything that attacks His life in us?

Are you going on with Jesus? The way goes through Gethsemane, through the city gate, and on "outside the camp" (Hebrews 13:13). The way is lonely and goes on until there is no longer even a trace of a footprint to follow—but only the voice saying, "Follow Me" (Matthew 4:19).

The Divine Commandment of Life

> ". . . be perfect, just as your Father in heaven is perfect" (Matthew 5:48).

Our Lord's exhortation to us in verses 38–48 is to be generous in our behavior toward everyone. Beware of living according to your natural affections in your spiritual life. Everyone has natural affections—some people we like and others we don't like. Yet we must never let those likes and dislikes rule our Christian life. "If we walk in the light as He is in the light, we have fellowship with one another" (1 John 1:7), even those toward whom we have no affection.

The example our Lord gave us here is not that of a good person, or even of a good Christian, but of God Himself. ". . . be perfect, just as your Father in heaven is perfect." In other words, simply show to the other person what God has shown to you. And God will give you plenty of real life opportunities to prove whether or not you are "perfect, just as your Father in heaven is perfect." Being a disciple means deliberately identifying yourself with God's interests in other people. Jesus says, "A new commandment I give to you, that you love one another; as I have loved you, that you also love one another. By this all will know that you are My disciples, if you have love for one another" (John 13:34–35).

The true expression of Christian character is not in good-doing, but in God-likeness. If the Spirit of God has transformed you within, you will exhibit divine characteristics in your life, not just good human characteristics. God's life in us expresses itself as *God's* life, not as human life trying to be godly. The secret of a Christian's life is that the supernatural becomes natural in him as a result of the grace of God, and the experience of this becomes evident in the practical, everyday details of life, not in times of intimate fellowship with God. And when we come in contact with things that create confusion and a flurry of activity, we find to our own amazement that we have the power to stay wonderfully poised even in the center of it all.

The Missionary's Predestined Purpose

> "Now the LORD says, who formed Me from the womb to be His Servant . . ." (Isaiah 49:5).

The first thing that happens after we recognize our election by God in Christ Jesus is the destruction of our preconceived ideas, our narrow-minded thinking, and all of our other allegiances— we are turned solely into servants of God's own purpose. The entire human race was created to glorify God and to enjoy Him forever. Sin has diverted the human race onto another course, but it has not altered God's purpose to the slightest degree. And when we are born again we are brought into the realization of God's great purpose for the human race, namely, that He created us for Himself. This realization of our election by God is the most joyful on earth, and we must learn to rely on this tremendous creative purpose of God. The first thing God will do is force the interests of the whole world through the channel of our hearts. The love of God, and even His very nature, is introduced into us. And we see the nature of Almighty God purely focused in John 3:16—*"For God so loved the world . . . ."*

We must continually keep our soul open to the fact of God's creative purpose, and never confuse or cloud it with our own intentions. If we do, God will have to force our intentions aside no matter how much it may hurt. A missionary is created for the purpose of being God's servant, one in whom God is glorified. Once we realize that it is through the salvation of Jesus Christ that we are made perfectly fit for the purpose of God, we will understand why Jesus Christ is so strict and relentless in His demands. He demands absolute righteousness from His servants, because He has put into them the very nature of God.

Beware lest you forget God's purpose for your life.

The Missionary's Master and Teacher

To have a master and teacher is not the same thing as being mastered and taught. Having a master and teacher means that there is someone who knows me better than I know myself, who is closer than a friend, and who understands the remotest depths of my heart and is able to satisfy them fully. It means having someone who has made me secure in the knowledge that he has met and solved all the doubts, uncertainties, and problems in my mind. To have a master and teacher is this and nothing less—". . . for One is your Teacher, the Christ . . ." (Matthew 23:8).

Our Lord never takes measures to make me do what He wants. Sometimes I wish God would master and control me to make me do what He wants, but He will not. And at other times I wish He would leave me alone, and He does not.

"You call Me Teacher and Lord . . ."—but *is* He? *Teacher, Master,* and *Lord* have little place in our vocabulary. We prefer the words *Savior, Sanctifier,* and *Healer.* The only word that truly describes the experience of being mastered is *love,* and we know little about love as God reveals it in His Word. The way we use the word *obey* is proof of this. In the Bible, obedience is based on a relationship between equals; for example, that of a son with his father. Our Lord was not simply God's servant— He was His Son. ". . . *though He was a Son,* yet He learned obedience. . ." (Hebrews 5:8). If we are consciously aware that we are being mastered, that idea itself is proof that we have no master. If that is our attitude toward Jesus, we are far away from having the relationship He wants with us. He wants us in a relationship where He is so easily our Master and Teacher that we have no conscious awareness of it—a relationship where all we know is that we are His to obey.

The Missionary's Goal

"He . . . said to them,
'Behold, we are going up to
Jerusalem . . .'"
(Luke 18:31).

In our natural life our ambitions change as we grow, but in the Christian life the goal is given at the very beginning, and the beginning and the end are exactly the same, namely, our Lord Himself. We start with Christ and we end with Him—". . . till we all come . . . to the measure of the stature of the fullness of Christ . . ." (Ephesians 4:13), not simply to our own idea of what the Christian life should be. The goal of the missionary is to do God's will, not to be useful or to win the lost. A missionary *is* useful and he *does* win the lost, but that is not his goal. His goal is to do the will of his Lord.

In our Lord's life, Jerusalem was the place where He reached the culmination of His Father's will upon the cross, and unless we go there with Jesus we will have no friendship or fellowship with Him. Nothing ever diverted our Lord on His way to Jerusalem. He never hurried through certain villages where He was persecuted, or lingered in others where He was blessed. Neither gratitude nor ingratitude turned our Lord even the slightest degree away from His purpose to go "up to Jerusalem."

"A disciple is not above his teacher, nor a servant above his master" (Matthew 10:24). In other words, the same things that happened to our Lord will happen to us on our way to our "Jerusalem." There will be works of God exhibited through us, people will get blessed, and one or two will show gratitude while the rest will show total ingratitude, but nothing must divert us from going "up to [our] Jerusalem."

". . . there they crucified Him . . ." (Luke 23:33). That is what happened when our Lord reached Jerusalem, and that event is the doorway to our salvation. The saints, however, do not end in crucifixion; by the Lord's grace they end in glory. In the meantime our watchword should be summed up by each of us saying, "I too go 'up to Jerusalem.'"

The "Go" of Preparation

"If you bring your gift to the altar, and there remember that your brother has something against you, leave your gift there before the altar, and go your way. First be reconciled to your brother, and then come and offer your gift" (Matthew 5:23–24).

It is easy for us to imagine that we will suddenly come to a point in our lives where we are fully prepared, but preparation is not suddenly accomplished. In fact, it is a process that must be steadily maintained. It is dangerous to become settled and complacent in our present level of experience. The Christian life requires preparation *and* more preparation.

The sense of sacrifice in the Christian life is readily appealing to a new Christian. From a human standpoint, the one thing that attracts us to Jesus Christ is our sense of the heroic, and a close examination of us by our Lord's words suddenly puts this tide of enthusiasm to the test. ". . . *go* your way. First be reconciled to your brother. . . ." The "go" of preparation is to allow the Word of God to examine you closely. Your sense of heroic sacrifice is not good enough. The thing the Holy Spirit will detect in you is your nature that can never work in His service. And no one but God can detect that nature in you. Do you have anything to hide from God? If you do, then let God search you with His light. If there is sin in your life, don't just *admit* it—*confess* it. Are you willing to obey your Lord and Master, whatever the humiliation to your right to yourself may be?

Never disregard a conviction that the Holy Spirit brings to you. If it is important enough for the Spirit of God to bring it to your mind, it is the very thing He is detecting in you. You were looking for some big thing to give up, while God is telling you of some tiny thing that must go. But behind that tiny thing lies the stronghold of obstinacy, and you say, "I will not give up my right to myself"—the very thing that God intends you to give up if you are to be a disciple of Jesus Christ.

The "Go" of Relationship

Our Lord's teaching can be summed up in this: the relationship that He demands for us is an impossible one unless He has done a super-natural work in us. Jesus Christ demands that His disciple does not allow even the slightest trace of resentment in his heart when faced with tyranny and injustice. No amount of enthusiasm will ever stand up to the strain that Jesus Christ will put upon His servant. Only one thing will bear the strain, and that is a personal relationship with Jesus Christ Himself—a relationship that has been examined, purified, and tested until only one purpose remains and I can truly say, "I am here for God to send me where He will." Everything else may become blurred, but this relationship with Jesus Christ must never be.

The Sermon on the Mount is not some unattainable goal; it is a statement of what will happen in me when Jesus Christ has changed my nature by putting His own nature in me. Jesus Christ is the only One who can fulfill the Sermon on the Mount.

If we are to be disciples of Jesus, we must be made disciples supernaturally. And as long as we consciously maintain the determined purpose to be His disciples, we can be sure that we are not disciples. Jesus says, "You did not choose Me, but *I chose you* . . ." (John 15:16). That is the way the grace of God begins. It is a constraint we can never escape; we can disobey it, but we can never start it or produce it ourselves. We are drawn to God by a work of His supernatural grace, and we can never trace back to find where the work began. Our Lord's making of a disciple is supernatural. He does not build on any natural capacity of ours at all. God does not ask us to do the things that are naturally easy for us—He only asks us to do the things that we are perfectly fit to do through His grace, and that is where the cross we must bear will always come.

The "Go" of Reconciliation   "If you ... remember that
                                  your brother has something
                                  against you ..."
                                 (Matthew 5:23).

This verse says, "If you bring your gift to the altar, and there remember that your brother has something against you ...." It is not saying, "If you search and find something because of your unbalanced sensitivity," but, "If you ... remember ...." In other words, if something is brought to your conscious mind by the Spirit of God—"First be reconciled to your brother, and then come and offer your gift" (5:24). Never object to the intense sensitivity of the Spirit of God in you when He is instructing you down to the smallest detail.

"First be reconciled to your brother ...." Our Lord's directive is simple—"First be reconciled ...." He says, in effect, "Go back the way you came—the way indicated to you by the conviction given to you at the altar; have an attitude in your mind and soul toward the person who has something against you that makes reconciliation as natural as breathing." Jesus does not mention the other person—He says for *you* to go. It is not a matter of your rights. The true mark of the saint is that he can waive his own rights and obey the Lord Jesus.

"... and then come and offer your gift." The process of reconciliation is clearly marked. First we have the heroic spirit of self-sacrifice, then the sudden restraint by the sensitivity of the Holy Spirit, and then we are stopped at the point of our conviction. This is followed by obedience to the Word of God, which builds an attitude or state of mind that places no blame on the one with whom you have been in the wrong. And finally there is the glad, simple, unhindered offering of your gift to God.

". . . someone said to Him,
'Lord, I will follow You
wherever You go'"
(Luke 9:57).

Our Lord's attitude toward this man was one of severe discouragement, "for He knew what was in man" (John 2:25). We would have said, "I can't imagine why He lost the opportunity of winning that man! Imagine being so cold to him and turning him away so discouraged!" Never apologize for your Lord. The words of the Lord hurt and offend until there is nothing left to be hurt or offended. Jesus Christ had no tenderness whatsoever toward anything that was ultimately going to ruin a person in his service to God. Our Lord's answers were not based on some whim or impulsive thought, but on the knowledge of "what was in man." If the Spirit of God brings to your mind a word of the Lord that hurts you, you can be sure that there is something in you that He wants to hurt to the point of its death.

Luke 9:58. These words destroy the argument of serving Jesus Christ because it is a pleasant thing to do. And the strictness of the rejection that He demands of me allows for nothing to remain in my life but my Lord, myself, and a sense of desperate hope. He says that I must let everyone else come or go, and that I must be guided solely by my relationship to Him. And He says, ". . . the Son of Man has nowhere to lay His head."

Luke 9:59. This man did not want to disappoint Jesus, nor did he want to show a lack of respect for his father. We put our sense of loyalty to our relatives ahead of our loyalty to Jesus Christ, forcing Him to take last place. When your loyalties conflict, always obey Jesus Christ whatever the cost.

Luke 9:61. The person who says, "Lord, I will follow You, but . . .," is the person who is intensely ready to go, but never goes. This man had reservations about going. The exacting call of Jesus has no room for good-byes; good-byes, as we often use them, are pagan, not Christian, because they divert us from the call. Once the call of God comes to you, start going and never stop.

The "Go" of Unconditional Identification

"Jesus . . . said to him, 'One thing you lack: Go your way, sell whatever you have and give to the poor . . . and come, take up the cross, and follow Me'" (Mark 10:21).

The rich young ruler had the controlling passion to be perfect. When he saw Jesus Christ, he wanted to be like Him. Our Lord never places anyone's personal holiness above everything else when He calls a disciple. Jesus' primary consideration is my absolute annihilation of my right to myself and my identification with Him, which means having a relationship with Him in which there are no other relationships. Luke 14:26 has nothing to do with salvation or sanctification, but deals solely with unconditional identification with Jesus Christ. Very few of us truly know what is meant by the absolute "go" of unconditional identification with, and abandonment and surrender to, Jesus.

"Then Jesus, looking at him, loved him . . ." (Mark 10:21). This look of Jesus will require breaking your heart away forever from allegiance to any other person or thing. Has Jesus ever looked in this way at you? This look of Jesus transforms, penetrates, and captivates. Where you are soft and pliable with God is where the Lord has looked at you. If you are hard and vindictive, insistent on having your own way, and always certain that the other person is more likely to be in the wrong than you are, then there are whole areas of your nature that have never been transformed by His gaze.

"One thing you lack . . . ." From Jesus Christ's perspective, oneness with Him, with nothing between, is the only good thing.

". . . sell whatever you have . . . ." I must humble myself until I am merely a living person. I must essentially renounce possessions of all kinds, not for salvation (for only one thing saves a person and that is absolute reliance in faith upon Jesus Christ), but to follow Jesus. ". . . come. . . and follow Me." And the road is the way He went.

The Awareness of the Call

We are inclined to forget the deeply spiritual and supernatural touch of God. If you are able to tell exactly where you were when you received the call of God and can explain all about it, I question whether you have truly been called. The call of God does not come like that; it is much more supernatural. The realization of the call in a person's life may come like a clap of thunder or it may dawn gradually. But however quickly or slowly this awareness comes, it is always accompanied with an undercurrent of the supernatural—something that is inexpressible and produces a "glow." At any moment the sudden awareness of this incalculable, supernatural, surprising call that has taken hold of your life may break through—"I chose you ..." (John 15:16). The call of God has nothing to do with salvation and sanctification. You are not called to preach the gospel because you are sanctified; the call to preach the gospel is infinitely different. Paul describes it as a compulsion that was placed upon him.

If you have ignored, and thereby removed, the great supernatural call of God in your life, take a review of your circumstances. See where you have put your own ideas of service or your particular abilities ahead of the call of God. Paul said, "... woe is me if I do not preach the gospel!" He had become aware of the call of God, and his compulsion to "preach the gospel" was so strong that nothing else was any longer even a competitor for his strength.

If a man or woman is called of God, it doesn't matter how difficult the circumstances may be. God orchestrates every force at work for His purpose in the end. If you will agree with God's purpose, He will bring not only your conscious level but also all the deeper levels of your life, which you yourself cannot reach, into perfect harmony.

The Assigning of the Call

"I now rejoice in my sufferings for you, and fill up in my flesh what is lacking in the afflictions of Christ, for the sake of His body, which is the church . . ." (Colossians 1:24).

We take our own spiritual consecration and try to make it into a call of God, but when we get right with Him He brushes all this aside. Then He gives us a tremendous, riveting pain to fasten our attention on something that we never even dreamed could be His call for us. And for one radiant, flashing moment we see His purpose, and we say, "Here am I! Send me" (Isaiah 6:8).

This call has nothing to do with personal sanctification, but with being made broken bread and poured-out wine. Yet God can never make us into wine if we object to the fingers He chooses to use to crush us. We say, "If God would only use His own fingers, and make me broken bread and poured-out wine in a special way, then I wouldn't object!" But when He uses someone we dislike, or some set of circumstances to which we said we would never submit, to crush us, then we object. Yet we must never try to choose the place of our own martyrdom. If we are ever going to be made into wine, we will have to be crushed—you cannot drink grapes. Grapes become wine only when they have been squeezed.

I wonder what finger and thumb God has been using to squeeze you? Have you been as hard as a marble and escaped? If you are not ripe yet, and if God *had* squeezed you anyway, the wine produced would have been remarkably bitter. To be a holy person means that the elements of our natural life experience the very presence of God as they are providentially broken in His service. We have to be placed into God and brought into agreement with Him before we can be broken bread in His hands. Stay right with God and let Him do as He likes, and you will find that He is producing the kind of bread and wine that will benefit His other children.

September 30

The Place of Exaltation

". . . Jesus took . . . them up
on a high mountain apart
by themselves . . ."
(Mark 9:2).

We have all experienced times of exaltation on the mountain,
when we have seen things from God's perspective and have
wanted to stay there. But God will never allow us to stay there.
The true test of our spiritual life is in exhibiting the power to
descend from the mountain. If we only have the power to go
up, something is wrong. It is a wonderful thing to be on the
mountain with God, but a person only gets there so that he
may later go down and lift up the demon-possessed people in
the valley (see 9:14–18). We are not made for the mountains,
for sunrises, or for the other beautiful attractions in life—those
are simply intended to be moments of inspiration. We are
made for the valley and the ordinary things of life, and that is
where we have to prove our stamina and strength. Yet our spiritual selfishness always wants repeated moments on the mountain. We feel that we could talk and live like perfect angels, if we
could only stay on the mountaintop. Those times of exaltation
are exceptional and they have their meaning in our life with
God, but we must beware to prevent our spiritual selfishness
from wanting to make them the only time.

We are inclined to think that everything that happens is to
be turned into useful teaching. In actual fact, it is to be turned
into something even better than teaching, namely, character.
The mountaintop is not meant to *teach* us anything, it is meant
to *make* us something. There is a terrible trap in always asking,
"What's the use of this experience?" We can never measure spiritual matters in that way. The moments on the mountaintop
are rare moments, and they are meant for something in God's
purpose.

The Place of Humiliation

> "If You can do anything, have compassion on us and help us"
> (Mark 9:22).

After every time of exaltation, we are brought down with a sudden rush into things as they really are, where it is neither beautiful, poetic, nor thrilling. The height of the mountaintop is measured by the dismal drudgery of the valley, but it is in the valley that we have to live for the glory of God. We see His glory on the mountain, but we never *live* for His glory there. It is in the place of humiliation that we find our true worth to God—that is where our faithfulness is revealed. Most of us can do things if we are always at some heroic level of intensity, simply because of the natural selfishness of our own hearts. But God wants us to be at the drab everyday level, where we live in the valley according to our personal relationship with Him. Peter thought it would be a wonderful thing for them to remain on the mountain, but Jesus Christ took the disciples down from the mountain and into the valley, where the true meaning of the vision was explained (see 9:5–6, 14–23).

"If you can do anything . . . ." It takes the valley of humiliation to remove the skepticism from us. Look back at your own experience and you will find that until you learned who Jesus really was, you were a skillful skeptic about His power. When you were on the mountaintop you could believe anything, but what about when you were faced with the facts of the valley? You may be able to give a testimony regarding your sanctification, but what about the thing that is a humiliation to you right now? The last time you were on the mountain with God, you saw that all the power in heaven and on earth belonged to Jesus—will you be skeptical now, simply because you are in the valley of humiliation?

October 2

The Place of Ministry

"He said to them, 'This kind [of unclean spirit] can come out by nothing but prayer and fasting.'" (Mark 9:29).

His disciples asked Him privately, 'Why could we not cast it out?'" (9:28). The answer lies in a personal relationship with Jesus Christ. "This kind can come out by nothing but" concentrating on Him, and then doubling and redoubling that concentration on Him. We can remain powerless forever, as the disciples were in this situation, by trying to do God's work without concentrating on His power, and by following instead the ideas that we draw from our own nature. We actually slander and dishonor God by our very eagerness to serve Him without knowing Him.

When you are brought face to face with a difficult situation and nothing happens externally, you can still know that freedom and release will be given because of your continued concentration on Jesus Christ. Your duty in service and ministry is to see that there is nothing between Jesus and yourself. Is there anything between you and Jesus even now? If there is, you must get through it, not by ignoring it as an irritation, or by going up and over it, but by facing it and getting through it into the presence of Jesus Christ. Then that very problem itself, and all that you have been through in connection with it, will glorify Jesus Christ in a way that you will never know until you see Him face to face.

We must be able to "mount up with wings like eagles" (Isaiah 40:31), but we must also know how to come down. The power of the saint lies in the coming down and in the living that is done in the valley. Paul said, "I can do all things through Christ who strengthens me" (Philippians 4:13) and what he was referring to were mostly humiliating things. And yet it is in our power to refuse to be humiliated and to say, "No, thank you, I much prefer to be on the mountaintop with God." Can I face things as they actually are in the light of the reality of Jesus Christ, or do things as they really are destroy my faith in Him, and put me into a panic?

The Vision and the Reality

Thank God for being able to see all that you have not yet been. You have had the vision, but you are not yet to the reality of it by any means. It is when we are in the valley, where we prove whether we will be the choice ones, that most of us turn back. We are not quite prepared for the bumps and bruises that must come if we are going to be turned into the shape of the vision. We have seen what we are not, and what God wants us to be, but are we willing to be battered into the shape of the vision to be used by God? The beatings will always come in the most common, everyday ways and through common, everyday people.

There are times when we do know what God's purpose is; whether we will let the vision be turned into actual character depends on us, not on God. If we prefer to relax on the mountaintop and live in the memory of the vision, then we will be of no real use in the ordinary things of which human life is made. We have to learn to live in reliance upon what we saw in the vision, not simply live in ecstatic delight and conscious reflection upon God. This means living the realities of our lives in the light of the vision until the truth of the vision is actually realized in us. Every bit of our training is in that direction. Learn to thank God for making His demands known.

Our little "I am" always sulks and pouts when God says *do*. Let your little "I am" be shriveled up in God's wrath and indignation—"I AM WHO I AM ... has sent me to you" (Exodus 3:14). He must dominate. Isn't it piercing to realize that God not only knows where we live, but also knows the gutters into which we crawl! He will hunt us down as fast as a flash of lightning. No human being knows human beings as God does.

The Nature of Degeneration

The Bible does not say that God punished the human race for one man's sin, but that the nature of sin, namely, my claim to my right to myself, entered into the human race through one man. But it also says that another Man took upon Himself the sin of the human race and put it away—an infinitely more profound revelation (see Hebrews 9:26). The nature of sin is not immorality and wrongdoing, but the nature of self-realization which leads us to say, "I am my own god." This nature may exhibit itself in proper morality or in improper immorality, but it always has a common basis—my claim to my right to myself. When our Lord faced either people with all the forces of evil in them, or people who were clean-living, moral, and upright, He paid no attention to the moral degradation of one, nor any attention to the moral attainment of the other. He looked at something we do not see, namely, the nature of man (see John 2:25).

Sin is something I am born with and cannot touch—only God touches sin through redemption. It is through the Cross of Christ that God redeemed the entire human race from the possibility of damnation through the heredity of sin. God nowhere holds a person responsible for having the heredity of sin, and does not condemn anyone because of it. Condemnation comes when I realize that Jesus Christ came to deliver me from this heredity of sin, and yet I refuse to let Him do so. From that moment I begin to get the seal of damnation. "This is the condemnation [and the critical moment], that the light has come into the world, and men loved darkness rather than light . . . " (John 3:19).

If Jesus Christ is going to regenerate me, what is the problem He faces? It is simply this—I have a heredity in which I had no say or decision; I am not holy, nor am I likely to be; and if all Jesus Christ can do is tell me that I must be holy, His teaching only causes me to despair. But if Jesus Christ is truly a regenerator, someone who can put His own heredity of holiness into me, then I can begin to see what He means when He says that I have to be holy. Redemption means that Jesus Christ can put into anyone the hereditary nature that was in Himself, and all the standards He gives us are based on that nature—*His teaching is meant to be applied to the life which He puts within us.* The proper action on my part is simply to agree with God's verdict on sin as judged on the Cross of Christ.

The New Testament teaching about regeneration is that when a person is hit by his own sense of need, God will put the Holy Spirit into his spirit, and his personal spirit will be energized by the Spirit of the Son of God—". . . until Christ is formed in you" (Galatians 4:19). The moral miracle of redemption is that God can put a new nature into me through which I can live a totally new life. When I finally reach the edge of my need and know my own limitations, then Jesus says, "Blessed are you . . ." (Matthew 5:11). But I must get to that point. God cannot put into me, the responsible moral person that I am, the nature that was in Jesus Christ unless I am aware of my need for it.

Just as the nature of sin entered into the human race through one man, the Holy Spirit entered into the human race through another Man (see Romans 5:12–19). And redemption means that I can be delivered from the heredity of sin, and that through Jesus Christ I can receive a pure and spotless heredity, namely, the Holy Spirit.

The Nature of Reconciliation

> "He made Him who knew no sin to be sin for us, that we might become the righteousness of God in Him" (2 Corinthians 5:21).

Sin is a fundamental relationship—it is not wrong *doing*, but wrong *being*—it is deliberate and determined independence from God. The Christian faith bases everything on the extreme, self-confident nature of sin. Other faiths deal with *sins*—the Bible alone deals with *sin*. The first thing Jesus Christ confronted in people was the heredity of sin, and it is because we have ignored this in our presentation of the gospel that the message of the gospel has lost its sting and its explosive power.

The revealed truth of the Bible is not that Jesus Christ took on Himself our fleshly sins, but that He took on Himself the heredity of sin that no man can even touch. God made His own Son "to be sin" that He might make the sinner into a saint. It is revealed throughout the Bible that our Lord took on Himself the sin of the world through *identification with us,* not through *sympathy for us.* He deliberately took on His own shoulders, and endured in His own body, the complete, cumulative sin of the human race. "He made Him who knew no sin *to be sin for us . . .*" and by so doing He placed salvation for the entire human race solely on the basis of redemption. Jesus Christ reconciled the human race, putting it back to where God designed it to be. And now anyone can experience that reconciliation, being brought into oneness with God, on the basis of what our Lord has done on the cross.

A man cannot redeem himself—redemption is the work of God, and is absolutely finished and complete. And its application to individual people is a matter of their own individual action or response to it. A distinction must always be made between the revealed truth of redemption and the actual conscious experience of salvation in a person's life.

Isn't it humiliating to be told that we must come to Jesus! Think of the things about which we will not come to Jesus Christ. If you want to know how real you are, test yourself by these words—"Come to Me . . . ." In every dimension in which you are not real, you will argue or evade the issue altogether rather than come; you will go through sorrow rather than come; and you will do anything rather than come the last lap of the race of seemingly unspeakable foolishness and say, "Just as I am, I come." As long as you have even the least bit of spiritual disrespect, it will always reveal itself in the fact that you are expecting God to tell you to do something very big, and yet all He is telling you to do is to "Come . . . ."

"Come to Me . . . ." When you hear those words, you will know that something must happen in you before you can come. The Holy Spirit will show you what you have to do, and it will involve anything that will uproot whatever is preventing you from getting through to Jesus. And you will never get any further until you are willing to do that very thing. The Holy Spirit will search out that one immovable stronghold within you, but He cannot budge it unless you are willing to let Him do so.

How often have you come to God with your requests and gone away thinking, "I've really received what I wanted this time!" And yet you go away with nothing, while all the time God has stood with His hands outstretched not only to take you but also for you to take Him. Just think of the invincible, unconquerable, and untiring patience of Jesus, who lovingly says, "Come to Me . . . ."

Building on the Atonement

I cannot save and sanctify myself; I cannot make atonement for sin; I cannot redeem the world; I cannot right what is wrong, purify what is impure, or make holy what is unholy. That is all the sovereign work of God. Do I have faith in what Jesus Christ has done? He has made the perfect atonement for sin. Am I in the habit of constantly realizing it? The greatest need we have is not to *do* things, but to *believe* things. The redemption of Christ is not an experience, it is the great act of God which He has performed through Christ, and I have to build my faith on it. If I construct my faith on my own experience, I produce the most unscriptural kind of life—an isolated life, with my eyes focused solely on my own holiness. Beware of that human holiness that is not based on the atonement of the Lord. It has no value for anything except a life of isolation—it is useless to God and a nuisance to man. Measure every kind of experience you have by our Lord Himself. We cannot do anything pleasing to God unless we deliberately build on the foundation of the atonement by the Cross of Christ.

The atonement of Jesus must be exhibited in practical, unassuming ways in my life. Every time I obey, the absolute deity of God is on my side, so that the grace of God and my natural obedience are in perfect agreement. Obedience means that I have completely placed my trust in the atonement, and my obedience is immediately met by the delight of the supernatural grace of God.

Beware of the human holiness that denies the reality of the natural life—it is a fraud. Continually bring yourself to the trial or test of the atonement and ask, "Where is the discernment of the atonement in this, and in that?"

How Will I Know?

"Jesus answered and said, 'I thank You, Father . . . that You have hidden these things from the wise and prudent and have revealed them to babes'"
(Matthew 11:25).

We do not grow into a spiritual relationship step by step—we either have a relationship or we do not. God does not continue to cleanse us more and more from sin—"But if we walk in the light," we *are* cleansed "from all sin" (1 John 1:7). It is a matter of obedience, and once we obey, the relationship is instantly perfected. But if we turn away from obedience for even one second, darkness and death are immediately at work again.

All of God's revealed truths are sealed until they are opened to us through obedience. You will never open them through philosophy or thinking. But once you obey, a flash of light comes immediately. Let God's truth work into you by immersing yourself in it, not by worrying into it. The only way you can get to know the truth of God is to stop trying to find out and by being born again. If you obey God in the first thing He shows you, then He instantly opens up the next truth to you. You could read volumes on the work of the Holy Spirit, when five minutes of total, uncompromising obedience would make things as clear as sunlight. Don't say, "I suppose I will understand these things someday!" You can understand them now. And it is not study that brings understanding to you, but obedience. Even the smallest bit of obedience opens heaven, and the deepest truths of God immediately become yours. Yet God will never reveal more truth about Himself to you, until you have obeyed what you know already. Beware of becoming one of the "wise and prudent." "If anyone wills to do His will, he shall know . . ." (John 7:17).

God's Silence—
Then What?

"When He heard that he was sick, He stayed two more days in the place where He was" (John 11:6).

Has God trusted you with His silence—a silence that has great meaning? God's silences are actually His answers. Just think of those days of absolute silence in the home at Bethany! Is there anything comparable to those days in your life? Can God trust you like that, or are you still asking Him for a visible answer? God will give you the very blessings you ask if you refuse to go any further without them, but His silence is the sign that He is bringing you into an even more wonderful understanding of Himself. Are you mourning before God because you have not had an audible response? When you cannot hear God, you will find that He has trusted you in the most intimate way possible—with absolute silence, not a silence of despair, but one of pleasure, because He saw that you could withstand an even bigger revelation. If God has given you a silence, then praise Him—He is bringing you into the mainstream of His purposes. The actual evidence of the answer in time is simply a matter of God's sovereignty. Time is nothing to God. For a while you may have said, "I asked God to give me bread, but He gave me a stone instead" (see Matthew 7:9). He did not give you a stone, and today you find that He gave you the "bread of life" (John 6:35).

A wonderful thing about God's silence is that His stillness is contagious—it gets into you, causing you to become perfectly confident so that you can honestly say, "I know that God has heard me." His silence is the very proof that He has. As long as you have the idea that God will always bless you in answer to prayer, He will do it, but He will never give you the grace of His silence. If Jesus Christ is bringing you into the understanding that prayer is for the glorifying of His Father, then He will give you the first sign of His intimacy—silence.

The true test of a person's spiritual life and character is not what he does in the extraordinary moments of life, but what he does during the ordinary times when there is nothing tremendous or exciting happening. A person's worth is revealed in his attitude toward the ordinary things of life when he is not under the spotlight (see John 1:35–37 and 3:30). It is painful work to get in step with God and to keep pace with Him—it means getting your second wind spiritually. In learning to walk with God, there is always the difficulty of getting into His stride, but once we have done so, the only characteristic that exhibits itself is the very life of God Himself. The individual person is merged into a personal oneness with God, and God's stride and His power alone are exhibited.

It is difficult to get into stride with God, because as soon as we start walking with Him we find that His pace has surpassed us before we have even taken three steps. He has different ways of doing things, and we have to be trained and disciplined in His ways. It was said of Jesus—"He will not fail nor be discouraged . . ." (Isaiah 42:4) because He never worked from His own individual standpoint, but always worked from the standpoint of His Father. And we must learn to do the same. Spiritual truth is learned through the atmosphere that surrounds us, not through intellectual reasoning. It is God's Spirit that changes the atmosphere of our way of looking at things, and then things begin to be possible which before were impossible. Getting into God's stride means nothing less than oneness with Him. It takes a long time to get there, but keep at it. Don't give up because the pain is intense right now—get on with it, and before long you will find that you have a new vision and a new purpose.

Individual Discouragement and Personal Growth

Moses saw the oppression of his people and felt certain that he was the one to deliver them, and in the righteous indignation of his own spirit he started to right their wrongs. After he launched his first strike for God and for what was right, God allowed Moses to be driven into empty discouragement, sending him into the desert to feed sheep for forty years. At the end of that time, God appeared to Moses and said to him, " '. . . bring My people . . . out of Egypt.' But Moses said to God, 'Who am I that I should go . . . ?' " (Exodus 3:10–11). In the beginning Moses had realized that he was the one to deliver the people, but he had to be trained and disciplined by God first. He was right in his individual perspective, but he was not the person for the work until he had learned true fellowship and oneness with God.

We may have the vision of God and a very clear understanding of what God wants, and yet when we start to do it, there comes to us something equivalent to Moses' forty years in the wilderness. It's as if God had ignored the entire thing, and when we are thoroughly discouraged, God comes back and revives His call to us. And then we begin to tremble and say, "Who am I that I should go . . . ?" We must learn that God's great stride is summed up in these words—"I AM WHO I AM . . . has sent me to you" (Exodus 3:14). We must also learn that our individual effort for God shows nothing but disrespect for Him—our individuality is to be rendered radiant through a personal relationship with God, so that He may be "well pleased" (Matthew 3:17). We are focused on the right individual perspective of things; we have the vision and can say, "I know this is what God wants me to do." But we have not yet learned to get into God's stride. If you are going through a time of discouragement, there is a time of great personal growth ahead.

*The Key to the
Missionary's Work*

> "Jesus came and spoke to them, saying, 'All authority has been given to Me in heaven and on earth. Go therefore and make disciples of all the nations . . .'"
> (Matthew 28:18–19).

The key to the missionary's work is the authority of Jesus Christ, not the needs of the lost. We are inclined to look on our Lord as one who assists us in our endeavors for God. Yet our Lord places Himself as the absolute sovereign and supreme Lord over His disciples. He does not say that the lost will never be saved if we don't go—He simply says, "Go therefore and make disciples of all the nations . . . ." He says, "Go on the basis of the revealed truth of My sovereignty, teaching and preaching out of your living experience of Me."

"Then the eleven disciples went . . . to the mountain which Jesus had appointed for them" (28:16). If I want to know the universal sovereignty of Christ, I must know Him myself. I must take time to worship the One whose name I bear. Jesus says, "Come to Me . . ."—that is the place to meet Jesus—"all you who labor and are heavy laden . . ." (Matthew 11:28)—and how many missionaries are! We completely dismiss these wonderful words of the universal Sovereign of the world, but they are the words of Jesus to His disciples meant for here and now.

"Go therefore . . . ." To "go" simply means to live. Acts 1:8 is the description of *how* to go. Jesus did not say in this verse, "Go into Jerusalem, Judea, and Samaria," but, ". . . you shall *be witnesses* to Me in [all these places]." He takes upon Himself the work of sending us.

"If you abide in Me, and My words abide in you . . ." (John 15:7) —that is the way to keep *going*. Where we are placed is then a matter of indifference to us, because God sovereignly engineers our *goings*.

"None of these things move me; nor do I count my life dear to myself, so that I may finish my race with joy, and the ministry which I received from the Lord Jesus . . ." (Acts 20:24). That is how to keep going until we are gone from this life.

The Key to the Missionary's Message

"He Himself is the propitiation for our sins, and not for ours only but also for the whole world"
(1 John 2:2).

The key to the missionary's message is the propitiation of Christ Jesus—His sacrifice for us that completely satisfied the wrath of God. Look at any other aspect of Christ's work, whether it is healing, saving, or sanctifying, and you will see that there is nothing limitless about those. But—"The Lamb of God who takes away the sin of the world!"—that is limitless (John 1:29). The missionary's message is the limitless importance of Jesus Christ as the propitiation for our sins, and a missionary is someone who is immersed in the truth of that revelation.

The real key to the missionary's message is the "remissionary" aspect of Christ's life, not His kindness, His goodness, or even His revealing of the fatherhood of God to us. ". . . repentance and *remission* of sins should be preached . . . to all nations . . ." (Luke 24:47). The greatest message of limitless importance is that "He Himself is the propitiation for our sins . . . ." The missionary's message is not nationalistic, favoring nations or individuals; it is "for the whole world." When the Holy Spirit comes into me, He does not consider my partialities or preferences; He simply brings me into oneness with the Lord Jesus.

A missionary is someone who is bound by marriage to the stated mission and purpose of his Lord and Master. He is not to proclaim his own point of view, but is only to proclaim "the Lamb of God." It is easier to belong to a faction that simply tells what Jesus Christ has done for me, and easier to become a devotee of divine healing, or of a special type of sanctification, or of the baptism of the Holy Spirit. But Paul did not say, "Woe is me if I do not preach what Christ has done for me," but, ". . . woe is me if I do not preach the gospel!" (1 Corinthians 9:16). And this is the gospel—"the Lamb of God who takes away the sin of the world!"

The Key to the Master's Orders

"Pray the Lord of the harvest
to send out laborers into
His harvest"
(Matthew 9:38).

The key to the missionary's difficult task is in the hand of God, and that key is prayer, not work—that is, not work as the word is commonly used today, which often results in the shifting of our focus away from God. The key to the missionary's difficult task is also not the key of common sense, nor is it the key of medicine, civilization, education, or even evangelization. The key is in following the Master's orders—the key is prayer. "Pray the Lord of the harvest . . . ." In the natural realm, prayer is not practical but absurd. We have to realize that prayer is foolish from the commonsense point of view.

From Jesus Christ's perspective, there are no nations, but only *the world*. How many of us pray without regard to the persons, but with regard to only one Person—Jesus Christ? He owns the harvest that is produced through distress and through conviction of sin. This is the harvest for which we have to pray that laborers be sent out to reap. We stay busy at work, while people all around us are ripe and ready to be harvested; we do not reap even one of them, but simply waste our Lord's time in over-energized activities and programs. Suppose a crisis were to come into your father's or your brother's life—are you there as a laborer to reap the harvest for Jesus Christ? Is your response, "Oh, but I have a special work to do!" No Christian has a special work to do. A Christian is called to be Jesus Christ's own, "a servant [who] is not greater than his master" (John 13:16), and someone who does not dictate to Jesus Christ what he intends to do. Our Lord calls us to no special work—He calls us to Himself. "Pray the Lord of the harvest," and He will engineer your circumstances to send you out as His laborer.

The Key of the Greater Work

". . . I say to you, he who believes in Me, . . . greater works than these he will do, because I go to My Father" (John 14:12).

Prayer does not equip us for greater works—prayer *is* the greater work. Yet we think of prayer as some commonsense exercise of our higher powers that simply prepares us for God's work. In the teachings of Jesus Christ, prayer is the working of the miracle of redemption in me, which produces the miracle of redemption in others, through the power of God. The way fruit remains firm is through prayer, but remember that it is prayer based on the agony of Christ in redemption, not on my own agony. We must go to God as His child, because only a child gets his prayers answered; a "wise" man does not (see Matthew 11:25).

Prayer is *the* battle, and it makes no difference where you are. However God may engineer your circumstances, your duty is to pray. Never allow yourself this thought, "I am of no use where I am," because you certainly cannot be used where you have not yet been placed. Wherever God has placed you and whatever your circumstances, you should pray, continually offering up prayers to Him. And He promises, "Whatever you ask in My name, that I will do . . ." (14:13). Yet we refuse to pray unless it thrills or excites us, which is the most intense form of spiritual selfishness. We must learn to work according to God's direction, and He says to *pray.* "Pray the Lord of the harvest to send out laborers into His harvest" (Matthew 9:38).

There is nothing thrilling about a laboring person's work, but it is the laboring person who makes the ideas of the genius possible. And it is the laboring saint who makes the ideas of his Master possible. When you labor at prayer, from God's perspective there are always results. What an astonishment it will be to see, once the veil is finally lifted, all the souls that have been reaped by you, simply because you have been in the habit of taking your orders from Jesus Christ.

The Key to the Missionary's Devotion

"... they went forth for His name's sake ..." (3 John 7).

Our Lord told us how our love for Him is to exhibit itself when He asked, "Do you love Me?" (John 21:17). And then He said, "Feed My sheep." In effect, He said, "Identify *yourself* with *My* interests in other people," not, "Identify *Me* with *your* interests in other people." First Corinthians 13:4–8 shows us the characteristics of this love—it is actually the love *of God* expressing itself. The true test of my love for Jesus is a very practical one, and all the rest is sentimental talk.

Faithfulness to Jesus Christ is the supernatural work of redemption that has been performed in me by the Holy Spirit—"the love of God has been poured out in our hearts by the Holy Spirit ..." (Romans 5:5). And it is that love in me that effectively works through me and comes in contact with everyone I meet. I remain faithful to His name, even though the commonsense view of my life may seemingly deny that, and may appear to be declaring that He has no more power than the morning mist.

The key to the missionary's devotion is that he is attached to nothing and to no one except our Lord Himself. It does not mean simply being detached from the external things surrounding us. Our Lord was amazingly in touch with the ordinary things of life, but He had an inner detachment except toward God. External detachment is often an actual indication of a secret, growing, inner attachment to the things we stay away from externally.

The duty of a faithful missionary is to concentrate on keeping his soul completely and continually open to the nature of the Lord Jesus Christ. The men and women our Lord sends out on His endeavors are ordinary human people, but people who are controlled by their devotion to Him, which has been brought about through the work of the Holy Spirit.

The Unheeded Secret

The great enemy of the Lord Jesus Christ today is the idea of practical work that has no basis in the New Testament but comes from the systems of the world. This work insists upon endless energy and activities, but no private life with God. The emphasis is put on the wrong thing. Jesus said, "The kingdom of God does not come with observation . . . . For indeed, the kingdom of God is within you" (Luke 17:20–21). It is a hidden, obscure thing. An active Christian worker too often lives to be seen by others, while it is the innermost, personal area that reveals the power of a person's life.

We must get rid of the plague of the spirit of this religious age in which we live. In our Lord's life there was none of the pressure and the rushing of tremendous activity that we regard so highly today, and a disciple is to be like His Master. The central point of the kingdom of Jesus Christ is a personal relationship with Him, not public usefulness to others.

It is not the practical activities that are the strength of this Bible Training College—its entire strength lies in the fact that here you are immersed in the truths of God to soak in them before Him. You have no idea of where or how God is going to engineer your future circumstances, and no knowledge of what stress and strain is going to be placed on you either at home or abroad. And if you waste your time in over-activity, instead of being immersed in the great fundamental truths of God's redemption, then you will snap when the stress and strain do come. But if this time of soaking before God is being spent in getting rooted and grounded in Him, which may appear to be impractical, then you will remain true to Him whatever happens.

Is God's Will My Will?

Sanctification is not a question of whether God is willing to sanctify me—is it *my* will? Am I willing to let God do in me everything that has been made possible through the atonement of the Cross of Christ? Am I willing to let Jesus become sanctification to me, and to let His life be exhibited in my human flesh? (see 1 Corinthians 1:30). Beware of saying, "Oh, I am longing to be sanctified." No, you are not. Recognize your need, but stop longing and make it a matter of action. Receive Jesus Christ to become sanctification for you by absolute, unquestioning faith, and the great miracle of the atonement of Jesus will become real in you.

All that Jesus made possible becomes mine through the free and loving gift of God on the basis of what Christ accomplished on the cross. And my attitude as a saved and sanctified soul is that of profound, humble holiness (there is no such thing as proud holiness). It is a holiness based on agonizing repentance, a sense of inexpressible shame and degradation, and also on the amazing realization that the love of God demonstrated itself to me while I cared nothing about Him (see Romans 5:8). He completed everything for my salvation and sanctification. No wonder Paul said that nothing "shall be able to separate us from the love of God which is in Christ Jesus our Lord" (Romans 8:39).

Sanctification makes me one with Jesus Christ, and in Him one with God, and it is accomplished only through the magnificent atonement of Christ. Never confuse the effect with the cause. The effect in me is obedience, service, and prayer, and is the outcome of inexpressible thanks and adoration for the miraculous sanctification that has been brought about in me because of the atonement through the Cross of Christ.

Impulsiveness or Discipleship?

"But you, beloved, building yourselves up on your most holy faith . . ." (Jude 20).

There was nothing of the nature of impulsive or thoughtless action about our Lord, but only a calm strength that never got into a panic. Most of us develop our Christianity along the lines of our own nature, not along the lines of God's nature. Impulsiveness is a trait of the natural life, and our Lord always ignores it, because it hinders the development of the life of a disciple. Watch how the Spirit of God gives a sense of restraint to impulsiveness, suddenly bringing us a feeling of self-conscious foolishness, which makes us instantly want to vindicate ourselves. Impulsiveness is all right in a child, but is disastrous in a man or woman—an impulsive adult is always a spoiled person. Impulsiveness needs to be trained into intuition through discipline.

Discipleship is built entirely on the supernatural grace of God. Walking on water is easy to someone with impulsive boldness, but walking on dry land as a disciple of Jesus Christ is something altogether different. Peter walked on the water to go to Jesus, but he "followed Him at a distance" on dry land (Mark 14:54). We do not need the grace of God to withstand crises—human nature and pride are sufficient for us to face the stress and strain magnificently. But it does require the supernatural grace of God to live twenty-four hours of every day as a saint, going through drudgery, and living an ordinary, unnoticed, and ignored existence as a disciple of Jesus. It is ingrained in us that we have to do exceptional things for God—but we do not. We have to be exceptional in the ordinary things of life, and holy on the ordinary streets, among ordinary people—and this is not learned in five minutes.

We are in danger of getting into a bargaining spirit with God when we come to Him—we want the witness of the Spirit before we have done what God tells us to do.

Why doesn't God reveal Himself to you? He cannot. It is not that He will not, but He cannot, because you are in the way as long as you won't abandon yourself to Him in total surrender. Yet once you do, immediately God witnesses to Himself—He cannot witness to you, but He instantly witnesses to His own nature in you. If you received the witness of the Spirit before the reality and truth that comes from obedience, it would simply result in sentimental emotion. But when you act on the basis of redemption, and stop the disrespectfulness of debating with God, He immediately gives His witness. As soon as you abandon your own reasoning and arguing, God witnesses to what He has done, and you are amazed at your total disrespect in having kept Him waiting. If you are debating as to whether or not God can deliver from sin, then either let Him do it or tell Him that He cannot. Do not quote this or that person to Him. Simply obey Matthew 11:28, "Come to Me, all you who labor and are heavy laden . . . ." *Come,* if you are weary, and *ask,* if you know you are evil (see Luke 11:9–13).

The Spirit of God witnesses to the redemption of our Lord, and to nothing else. He cannot witness to our reason. We are inclined to mistake the simplicity that comes from our natural commonsense decisions for the witness of the Spirit, but the Spirit witnesses only to His own nature, and to the work of redemption, never to our reason. If we are trying to make Him witness to our reason, it is no wonder that we are in darkness and uncertainty. Throw it all overboard, trust in Him, and He will give you the witness of the Spirit.

Nothing of the Old Life! "If anyone is in Christ, he is a new creation, old things have passed away, behold, all things have become new" (2 Corinthians 5:17).

Our Lord never tolerates our prejudices—He is directly opposed to them and puts them to death. We tend to think that God has some special interest in our particular prejudices, and are very sure that He will never deal with us as He has to deal with others. We even say to ourselves, "God has to deal with other people in a very strict way, but of course He knows that my prejudices are all right." But we must learn that God accepts nothing of the old life! Instead of being on the side of our prejudices, He is deliberately removing them from us. It is part of our moral education to see our prejudices put to death by His providence, and to watch how He does it. God pays no respect to anything we bring to Him. There is only one thing God wants of us, and that is our unconditional surrender.

When we are born again, the Holy Spirit begins to work His new creation in us, and there will come a time when there is nothing remaining of the old life. Our old gloomy outlook disappears, as does our old attitude toward things, and "all things are of God" (5:18). How are we going to get a life that has no lust, no self-interest, and is not sensitive to the ridicule of others? How will we have the type of love that "is kind . . . is not provoked, [and] thinks no evil"? (1 Corinthians 13:4–5). The only way is by allowing nothing of the old life to remain, and by having only simple, perfect trust in God—such a trust that we no longer want God's blessings, but only want God Himself. Have we come to the point where God can withdraw His blessings from us without our trust in Him being affected? Once we truly see God at work, we will never be concerned again about the things that happen, because we are actually trusting in our Father in heaven, whom the world cannot see.

"Thanks be to God who
always leads us in triumph
in Christ . . ."
(2 Corinthians 2:14).

The proper perspective of a servant of God must not simply be as near to the highest as he can get, but it must be *the* highest. Be careful that you vigorously maintain God's perspective, and remember that it must be done every day, little by little. Don't think on a finite level. No outside power can touch the proper perspective.

The proper perspective to maintain is that we are here for only one purpose—to be captives marching in the procession of Christ's triumphs. We are not on display in God's showcase—we are here to exhibit only one thing—the "captivity [of our lives] to the obedience of Christ" (2 Corinthians 10:5). How small all the other perspectives are! For example, the ones that say, "I am standing all alone, battling for Jesus," or, "I have to maintain the cause of Christ and hold down this fort for Him." But Paul said, in essence, "I am in the procession of a conqueror, and it doesn't matter what the difficulties are, for I am always led in triumph." Is this idea being worked out practically in us? Paul's secret joy was that God took him as a blatant rebel against Jesus Christ, and made him a captive—and that became his purpose. It was Paul's joy to be a captive of the Lord, and he had no other interest in heaven or on earth. It is a shameful thing for a Christian to talk about getting the victory. We should belong so completely to the Victor that it is always His victory, and "we are more than conquerors through Him . . ." (Romans 8:37).

"We are to God the fragrance of Christ . . ."(2 Corinthians 2:15). We are encompassed with the sweet aroma of Jesus, and wherever we go we are a wonderful refreshment to God.

Submitting to God's Purpose "I have become all things to all men, that I might by all means save some" (1 Corinthians 9:22).

A Christian worker has to learn how to be God's man or woman of great worth and excellence in the midst of a multitude of meager and worthless things. Never protest by saying, "If only I were somewhere else!" All of God's people are ordinary people who have been made extraordinary by the purpose He has given them. Unless we have the right purpose intellectually in our minds and lovingly in our hearts, we will very quickly be diverted from being useful to God. We are not workers for God by choice. Many people deliberately choose to be workers, but they have no purpose of God's almighty grace or His mighty Word in them. Paul's whole heart, mind, and soul were consumed with the great purpose of what Jesus Christ came to do, and he never lost sight of that one thing. We must continually confront ourselves with one central fact—". . . Jesus Christ and Him crucified" (1 Corinthians 2:2).

"I chose you . . ." (John 15:16). Keep these words as a wonderful reminder in your theology. It is not that you have gotten God, but that He has gotten you. God is at work bending, breaking, molding, and doing exactly as He chooses. And why is He doing it? He is doing it for only one purpose—that He may be able to say, "This is My man, and this is My woman." We have to be in God's hand so that He can place others on the Rock, Jesus Christ, just as He has placed us.

Never choose to be a worker, but once God has placed His call upon you, woe be to you if you "turn aside . . . to the right or the left . . ." (Deuteronomy 28:14). He will do with you what He never did before His call came to you, and He will do with you what He is not doing with other people. Let Him have His way.

What is a Missionary?

"Jesus said to them again, '. . . As the Father has sent Me, I also send you' " (John 20:21).

A missionary is someone sent by Jesus Christ just as He was sent by God. The great controlling factor is not the needs of people, but the command of Jesus. The source of our inspiration in our service for God is behind us, not ahead of us. The tendency today is to put the inspiration out in front—to sweep everything together in front of us and make it conform to our definition of success. But in the New Testament the inspiration is put behind us, and is the Lord Jesus Himself. The goal is to be true to Him—to carry out *His* plans.

Personal attachment to the Lord Jesus and to His perspective is the one thing that must not be overlooked. In missionary work the great danger is that God's call will be replaced by the needs of the people, to the point that human sympathy for those needs will absolutely overwhelm the meaning of being sent by Jesus. The needs are so enormous, and the conditions so difficult, that every power of the mind falters and fails. We tend to forget that the one great reason underneath all missionary work is not primarily the elevation of the people, their education, nor their needs, but is first and foremost the command of Jesus Christ—"Go therefore and make disciples of all the nations . . ." (Matthew 28:19).

When looking back on the lives of men and women of God, the tendency is to say, "What wonderfully keen and intelligent wisdom they had, and how perfectly they understood all that God wanted!" But the keen and intelligent mind behind them was the mind of God, not human wisdom at all. We give credit to human wisdom when we should give credit to the divine guidance of God being exhibited through childlike people who were "foolish" enough to trust God's wisdom and His supernatural equipment.

The Method of Missions   "Go therefore and make disciples of all the nations . . ."
(Matthew 28:19).

Jesus Christ did not say, "Go and save souls" (the salvation of souls is the supernatural work of God), but He said, "Go . . . make disciples of all the nations . . . ." Yet you cannot make disciples unless you are a disciple yourself. When the disciples returned from their first mission, they were filled with joy because even the demons were subject to them. But Jesus said, in effect, "Don't rejoice in successful service—the great secret of joy is that you have the right relationship with Me" (see Luke 10:17–20). The missionary's great essential is remaining true to the call of God, and realizing that his one and only purpose is to disciple men and women to Jesus. Remember that there is a passion for souls that does not come from God, but from our desire to make converts to our point of view.

The challenge to the missionary does not come from the fact that people are difficult to bring to salvation, that backsliders are difficult to reclaim, or that there is a barrier of callous indifference. No, the challenge comes from the perspective of the missionary's own personal relationship with Jesus Christ—"Do you believe that I am able to do this?" (Matthew 9:28). Our Lord unwaveringly asks us that question, and it confronts us in every individual situation we encounter. The one great challenge to us is—do I know my risen Lord? Do I know the power of His indwelling Spirit? Am I wise enough in God's sight, but foolish enough according to the wisdom of the world, to trust in what Jesus Christ has said? Or am I abandoning the great supernatural position of limitless confidence in Christ Jesus, which is really God's only call for a missionary? If I follow any other method, I depart altogether from the methods prescribed by our Lord—"All authority has been given to Me . . . . *Go therefore . . .*" (Matthew 28:18–19).

Justification by Faith

"If when we were enemies we were reconciled to God through the death of His Son, much more, having been reconciled, we shall be saved by His life" (Romans 5:10).

I am not saved by believing—I simply realize I am saved by believing. And it is not repentance that saves me—repentance is only the sign that I realize what God has done through Christ Jesus. The danger here is putting the emphasis on the effect, instead of on the cause. Is it my obedience, consecration, and dedication that make me right with God? It is never that! I am made right with God because, prior to all of that, Christ died. When I turn to God and by belief accept what God reveals, the miraculous atonement by the Cross of Christ instantly places me into a right relationship with God. And as a result of the supernatural miracle of God's grace I stand justified, not because I am sorry for my sin, or because I have repented, but because of what Jesus has done. The Spirit of God brings justification with a shattering, radiant light, and I know that I am saved, even though I don't know how it was accomplished.

The salvation that comes from God is not based on human logic, but on the sacrificial death of Jesus. We can be born again solely because of the atonement of our Lord. Sinful men and women can be changed into new creations, not through their repentance or their belief, but through the wonderful work of God in Christ Jesus which preceded all of our experience (see 2 Corinthians 5:17–19). The unconquerable safety of justification and sanctification is God Himself. We do not have to accomplish these things ourselves—they have been accomplished through the atonement of the Cross of Christ. The supernatural becomes natural to us through the miracle of God, and there is the realization of what Jesus Christ has already done—*"It is finished!"* (John 19:30).

"He made Him who knew no sin to be sin for us, that we might become the righteousness of God in Him" (2 Corinthians 5:21).

The modern view of the death of Jesus is that He died for our sins out of sympathy for us. Yet the New Testament view is that He took our sin on Himself not because of sympathy, but because of His identification with us. He was *made . . . to be sin . . . .*" Our sins are removed because of the death of Jesus, and the only explanation for His death is His obedience to His Father, not His sympathy for us. We are acceptable to God not because we have obeyed, nor because we have promised to give up things, but because of the death of Christ, and for no other reason. We say that Jesus Christ came to reveal the fatherhood and the lovingkindness of God, but the New Testament says that He came to take "away the sin of the world!" (John 1:29). And the revealing of the fatherhood of God is only to those to whom Jesus has been introduced as Savior. In speaking to the world, Jesus Christ never referred to Himself as One who revealed the Father, but He spoke instead of being a stumbling block (see John 15:22–24). John 14:9, where Jesus said, "He who has seen Me has seen the Father," was spoken to His disciples.

That Christ died for me, and therefore I am completely free from penalty, is never taught in the New Testament. What is taught in the New Testament is that "He died for all" (2 Corinthians 5:15)—not, "He died my death"—and that through identification with His death I can be freed from sin, and have His very righteousness imparted as a gift to me. The substitution which is taught in the New Testament is twofold—"For He made Him who knew no sin to be sin for us, *that we might become the righteousness of God in Him.*" The teaching is not Christ *for* me unless I am determined to have Christ formed *in* me (see Galatians 4:19).

F_{aith}

"Without faith it is impossible
to please Him . . ."
(Hebrews 11:6).

Faith in active opposition to common sense is mistaken enthusiasm and narrow-mindedness, and common sense in opposition to faith demonstrates a mistaken reliance on reason as the basis for truth. The life of faith brings the two of these into the proper relationship. Common sense and faith are as different from each each other as the natural life is from the spiritual, and as impulsiveness is from inspiration. Nothing that Jesus Christ ever said is common sense, but is revelation sense, and is complete, whereas common sense falls short. Yet faith must be tested and tried before it becomes real in your life. "We know that all things work together for good . . ." (Romans 8:28) so that no matter what happens, the transforming power of God's providence transforms perfect faith into reality. Faith always works in a personal way, because the purpose of God is to see that perfect faith is made real in His children.

For every detail of common sense in life, there is a truth God has revealed by which we can prove in our practical experience what we believe God to be. Faith is a tremendously active principle that always puts Jesus Christ first. The life of faith says, "Lord, You have said it, it appears to be irrational, but I'm going to step out boldly, trusting in Your Word" (for example, see Matthew 6:33). Turning intellectual faith into our personal possession is *always* a fight, not just sometimes. God brings us into particular circumstances to educate our faith, because the nature of faith is to make the object of our faith very real to us. Until we know Jesus, God is merely a concept, and we can't have faith in Him. But once we hear Jesus say, "He who has seen Me has seen the Father" (John 14:9) we immediately have something that is real, and our faith is limitless. Faith is the entire person in the right relationship with God through the power of the Spirit of Jesus Christ.

The Trial of Faith

"If you have faith as a mustard seed . . . nothing will be impossible for you" (Matthew 17:20).

We have the idea that God rewards us for our faith, and it may be so in the initial stages. But we do not earn anything through faith— faith brings us into the right relationship with God and gives Him His opportunity to work. Yet God frequently has to knock the bottom out of your experience as His saint to get you in direct contact with Himself. God wants you to understand that it is a life of *faith*, not a life of emotional enjoyment of His blessings. The beginning of your life of faith was very narrow and intense, centered around a small amount of experience that had as much emotion as faith in it, and it was full of light and sweetness. Then God withdrew His conscious blessings to teach you to "walk by faith" (2 Corinthians 5:7). And you are worth much more to Him now than you were in your days of conscious delight with your thrilling testimony.

Faith by its very nature must be tested and tried. And the real trial of faith is not that we find it difficult to trust God, but that God's character must be proven as trustworthy in our own minds. Faith being worked out into reality must experience times of unbroken isolation. Never confuse the trial of faith with the ordinary discipline of life, because a great deal of what we call the trial of faith is the inevitable result of being alive. Faith, as the Bible teaches it, is faith in God coming against everything that contradicts Him—a faith that says, "I will remain true to God's character whatever He may do." The highest and the greatest expression of faith in the whole Bible is— "Though He slay me, yet will I trust Him" (Job 13:15).

"You Are Not Your Own"

"Do you not know that . . . you are not your own?" (1 Corinthians 6:19).

There is no such thing as a private life, or a place to hide in this world, for a man or woman who is intimately aware of and shares in the sufferings of Jesus Christ. God divides the private life of His saints and makes it a highway for the world on one hand and for Himself on the other. No human being can stand that unless he is identified with Jesus Christ. We are not sanctified for ourselves. We are called into intimacy with the gospel, and things happen that appear to have nothing to do with us. But God is getting us into fellowship with Himself. Let Him have His way. If you refuse, you will be of no value to God in His redemptive work in the world, but will be a hindrance and a stumbling block.

The first thing God does is get us grounded on strong reality and truth. He does this until our cares for ourselves individually have been brought into submission to His way for the purpose of His redemption. Why shouldn't we experience heartbreak? Through those doorways God is opening up ways of fellowship with His Son. Most of us collapse at the first grip of pain. We sit down at the door of God's purpose and enter a slow death through self-pity. And all the so-called Christian sympathy of others helps us to our deathbed. But God will not. He comes with the grip of the pierced hand of His Son, as if to say, "Enter into fellowship with Me; arise and shine." If God can accomplish His purposes in this world through a broken heart, then why not thank Him for breaking yours?

Obedience or Independence?

Our Lord never insists on our obedience. He stresses very definitely what we *ought* to do, but He never *forces* us to do it. We have to obey Him out of a oneness of spirit with Him. That is why whenever our Lord talked about discipleship, He prefaced it with an "If," meaning, "You do not need to do this unless you desire to do so." "*If* anyone desires to come after Me, let him deny himself . . ." (Luke 9:23). In other words, "To be My disciple, let him give up his right to himself to Me." Our Lord is not talking about our eternal position, but about our being of value to Him in this life here and now. That is why He sounds so stern (see Luke 14:26). Never try to make sense from these words by separating them from the One who spoke them.

The Lord does not give me rules, but He makes His standard very clear. If my relationship to Him is that of love, I will do what He says without hesitation. If I hesitate, it is because I love someone I have placed in competition with Him, namely, myself. Jesus Christ will not force me to obey Him, but I must. And as soon as I obey Him, I fulfill my spiritual destiny. My personal life may be crowded with small, petty happenings, altogether insignificant. But if I obey Jesus Christ in the seemingly random circumstances of life, they become pinholes through which I see the face of God. Then, when I stand face to face with God, I will discover that through my obedience thousands were blessed. When God's redemption brings a human soul to the point of obedience, it always produces. If I obey Jesus Christ, the redemption of God will flow through me to the lives of others, because behind the deed of obedience is the reality of Almighty God.

A Bondservant of Jesus

"I have been crucified with Christ, it is no longer I who live, but Christ lives in me . . ."
(Galatians 2:20).

These words mean the breaking and collapse of my independence brought about by my own hands, and the surrendering of my life to the supremacy of the Lord Jesus. No one can do this for me, I must do it myself. God may bring me up to this point three hundred and sixty-five times a year, but He cannot push me through it. It means breaking the hard outer layer of my individual independence from God, and the liberating of myself and my nature into oneness with Him; not following my own ideas, but choosing absolute loyalty to Jesus. Once I am at that point, there is no possibility of misunderstanding. Very few of us know anything about loyalty to Christ or understand what He meant when He said, ". . . for My sake" (Matthew 5:11). That is what makes a strong saint.

Has that breaking of my independence come? All the rest is religious fraud. The one point to decide is—will I give up? Will I surrender to Jesus Christ, placing no conditions whatsoever as to how the brokenness will come? I must be broken from my own understanding of myself. When I reach that point, immediately the reality of the supernatural identification with Jesus Christ takes place. And the witness of the Spirit of God is unmistakable—"I have been crucified with Christ . . . ."

The passion of Christianity comes from deliberately signing away my own rights and becoming a bondservant of Jesus Christ. Until I do that, I will not begin to be a saint.

One student a year who hears God's call would be sufficient for God to have called the Bible Training College into existence. This college has no value as an organization, not even academically. Its sole value for existence is for God to help Himself to lives. Will we allow Him to help Himself to us, or are we more concerned with our own ideas of what we are going to be?

The Authority of Truth   "Draw near to God and He
will draw near to you"
(James 4:8).

It is essential that you give people the opportunity to act on the truth of God. The responsibility must be left with the individual—you cannot act for him. It must be his own deliberate act, but the evangelical message should always lead him to action. Refusing to act leaves a person paralyzed, exactly where he was previously. But once he acts, he is never the same. It is the apparent folly of the truth that stands in the way of hundreds who have been convicted by the Spirit of God. Once I press myself into action, I immediately begin to live. Anything less is merely existing. The moments I truly live are the moments when I act with my entire will.

When a truth of God is brought home to your soul, never allow it to pass without acting on it internally in your will, not necessarily externally in your physical life. Record it with ink and with blood—work it into your life. The weakest saint who transacts business with Jesus Christ is liberated the second he acts and God's almighty power is available on his behalf. We come up to the truth of God, confess we are wrong, but go back again. Then we approach it again and turn back, until we finally learn we have no business going back. When we are confronted with such a word of truth from our redeeming Lord, we must move directly to transact business with Him. "Come to Me . . ." (Matthew 11:28). His word *come* means "to act." Yet the last thing we want to do is come. But everyone who does come knows that, at that very moment, the supernatural power of the life of God invades him. The dominating power of the world, the flesh, and the devil is now paralyzed; not by your act, but because your act has joined you to God and tapped you in to His redemptive power.

Partakers of His Sufferings

"... but rejoice to the extent that you partake of Christ's sufferings ..." (1 Peter 4:13).

If you are going to be used by God, He will take you through a number of experiences that are not meant for you personally at all. They are designed to make you useful in His hands, and to enable you to understand what takes place in the lives of others. Because of this process, you will never be surprised by what comes your way. You say, "Oh, I can't deal with that person." Why can't you? God gave you sufficient opportunities to learn from Him about that problem; but you turned away, not heeding the lesson, because it seemed foolish to spend your time that way.

The sufferings of Christ were not those of ordinary people. He suffered "according to the will of God" (1 Peter 4:19), having a different point of view of suffering from ours. It is only through our relationship with Jesus Christ that we can understand what God is after in His dealings with us. When it comes to suffering, it is part of our Christian culture to want to know God's purpose beforehand. In the history of the Christian church, the tendency has been to avoid being identified with the sufferings of Jesus Christ. People have sought to carry out God's orders through a shortcut of their own. God's way is always the way of suffering—the way of the "long road home."

Are we partakers of Christ's sufferings? Are we prepared for God to stamp out our personal ambitions? Are we prepared for God to destroy our individual decisions by supernaturally transforming them? It will mean not knowing why God is taking us that way, because knowing would make us spiritually proud. We never realize at the time what God is putting us through—we go through it more or less without understanding. Then suddenly we come to a place of enlightenment, and realize—"God has strengthened me and I didn't even know it!"

Martha believed in the power available to Jesus Christ; she believed that if He had been there He could have healed her brother; she also believed that Jesus had a special intimacy with God, and that whatever He asked of God, God would do. But— she needed a closer personal intimacy with Jesus. Martha's theology had its fulfillment in the future. But Jesus continued to attract and draw her in until her belief became an intimate possession. It then slowly emerged into a personal inheritance— "Yes, Lord, I believe that You are the Christ . . ." (11:27).

Is the Lord dealing with you in the same way? Is Jesus teaching you to have a personal intimacy with Himself? Allow Him to drive His question home to you—"Do you believe this?" Are you facing an area of doubt in your life? Have you come, like Martha, to a crossroads of overwhelming circumstances where your theology is about to become a very personal belief? This happens only when a personal problem brings the awareness of our personal need.

To believe is to commit. In the area of intellectual learning I commit myself mentally, and reject anything not related to that belief. In the realm of personal belief I commit myself morally to my convictions and refuse to compromise. But in intimate personal belief I commit myself spiritually to Jesus Christ and make a determination to be dominated by Him alone.

Then, when I stand face to face with Jesus Christ and He says to me, "Do you believe this?" I find that faith is as natural as breathing. And I am staggered when I think how foolish I have been in not trusting Him earlier.

The Undetected Sacredness of Circumstances

"We know that all things work together for good to those who love God . . ." (Romans 8:28).

The circumstances of a saint's life are ordained of God. In the life of a saint there is no such thing as chance. God by His providence brings you into circumstances that you can't understand at all, but the Spirit of God understands. God brings you to places, among people, and into certain conditions to accomplish a definite purpose through the intercession of the Spirit in you. Never put yourself in front of your circumstances and say, "I'm going to be my own providence here; I will watch this closely, or protect myself from that." All your circumstances are in the hand of God, and therefore you don't ever have to think they are unnatural or unique. Your part in intercessory prayer is not to agonize over how to intercede, but to use the everyday circumstances and people God puts around you by His providence to bring them before His throne, and to allow the Spirit in you the opportunity to intercede for them. In this way God is going to touch the whole world with His saints.

Am I making the Holy Spirit's work difficult by being vague and unsure, or by trying to do His work for Him? I must do the human side of intercession—utilizing the circumstances in which I find myself and the people who surround me. I must keep my conscious life as a sacred place for the Holy Spirit. Then as I lift different ones to God through prayer, the Holy Spirit intercedes for them.

Your intercessions can never be mine, and my intercessions can never be yours, ". . . but the Spirit Himself makes intercession" in each of our lives (Romans 8:26). And without that intercession, the lives of others would be left in poverty and in ruin.

November 7

The Unrivaled Power of Prayer

"We do not know what we should pray for as we ought, but the Spirit Himself makes intercession for us with groanings which cannot be uttered" (Romans 8:26).

We realize that we are energized by the Holy Spirit for prayer; and we know what it is to pray in accordance with the Spirit; but we don't often realize that the Holy Spirit Himself prays prayers in us which we cannot utter ourselves. When we are born again of God and are indwelt by the Spirit of God, He expresses for us the unutterable.

"He," the Holy Spirit in you, "makes intercession for the saints according to the will of God" (8:27). And God searches your heart, not to know what your conscious prayers are, but to find out what the prayer of the Holy Spirit is.

The Spirit of God uses the nature of the believer as a temple in which to offer His prayers of intercession. ". . . your body is the temple of the Holy Spirit . . ." (1 Corinthians 6:19). When Jesus Christ cleansed the temple, ". . . He would not allow anyone to carry wares through the temple" (Mark 11:16). The Spirit of God will not allow you to use your body for your own convenience. Jesus ruthlessly cast out everyone who bought and sold in the temple, and said, "My house shall be called a house of prayer . . . . But you have made it a 'den of thieves' " (Mark 11:17).

Have we come to realize that our "body is the temple of the Holy Spirit"? If so, we must be careful to keep it undefiled for Him. We have to remember that our conscious life, even though only a small part of our total person, is to be regarded by us as a "temple of the Holy Spirit." He will be responsible for the unconscious part which we don't know, but we must pay careful attention to and guard the conscious part for which we are responsible.

Sacred Service

> "I now rejoice in my sufferings for you, and fill up in my flesh what is lacking in the afflictions of Christ . . ."
> (Colossians 1:24).

The Christian worker has to be a sacred "go-between." He must be so closely identified with his Lord and the reality of His redemption that Christ can continually bring His creating life through him. I am not referring to the strength of one individual's personality being superimposed on another, but the real presence of Christ coming through every aspect of the worker's life. When we preach the historical facts of the life and death of our Lord as they are conveyed in the New Testament, our words are made sacred. God uses these words, on the basis of His redemption, to create something in those who listen which otherwise could never have been created. If we simply preach the effects of redemption in the human life instead of the revealed, divine truth regarding Jesus Himself, the result is not new birth in those who listen. The result is a refined religious lifestyle, and the Spirit of God cannot witness to it because such preaching is in a realm other than His. We must make sure that we are living in such harmony with God that as we proclaim His truth He can create in others those things which He alone can do.

When we say, "What a wonderful personality, what a fascinating person, and what wonderful insight!" then what opportunity does the gospel of God have through all of that? It cannot get through, because the attraction is to the messenger and not the message. If a person attracts through his personality, that becomes his appeal. If, however, he is identified with the Lord Himself, then the appeal becomes what Jesus Christ can do. The danger is to glory in men, yet Jesus says we are to lift up only *Him* (see John 12:32).

After sanctification, it is difficult to state what your purpose in life is, because God has moved you into His purpose through the Holy Spirit. He is using you now for His purposes throughout the world as He used His Son for the purpose of our salvation. If you seek great things for yourself, thinking, "God has called me for this and for that," you barricade God from using you. As long as you maintain your own personal interests and ambitions, you cannot be completely aligned or identified with God's interests. This can only be accomplished by giving up all of your personal plans once and for all, and by allowing God to take you directly into His purpose for the world. Your understanding of your ways must also be surrendered, because they are now the ways of the Lord.

I must learn that the purpose of my life belongs to God, not me. God is using me from His great personal perspective, and all He asks of me is that I trust Him. I should never say, "Lord, this causes me such heartache." To talk that way makes me a stumbling block. When I stop telling God what I want, He can freely work His will in me without any hindrance. He can crush me, exalt me, or do anything else He chooses. He simply asks me to have absolute faith in Him and His goodness. Self-pity is of the devil, and if I wallow in it I cannot be used by God for His purpose in the world. Doing this creates for me my own cozy "world within the world," and God will not be allowed to move me from it because of my fear of being "frost-bitten."

God's command is, "Take now," not later. It is incredible how we debate! We know something is right, but we try to find excuses for not doing it immediately. If we are to climb to the height God reveals, it can never be done later—it must be done now. And the sacrifice must be worked through our will before we actually perform it.

"So Abraham rose early in the morning . . . and went to the place of which God had told him" (22:3). Oh, the wonderful simplicity of Abraham! When God spoke, he did not "confer with flesh and blood" (Galatians 1:16). Beware when you want to "confer with flesh and blood" or even your own thoughts, insights, or understandings—anything that is not based on your personal relationship with God. These are all things that compete with and hinder obedience to God.

Abraham did not choose what the sacrifice would be. Always guard against self-chosen service for God. Self-sacrifice may be a disease that impairs your service. If God has made your cup sweet, drink it with grace; or even if He has made it bitter, drink it in communion with Him. If the providential will of God means a hard and difficult time for you, go through it. But never decide the place of your own martyrdom, as if to say, "I will only go to there, but no farther." God chose the test for Abraham, and Abraham neither delayed nor protested, but steadily obeyed. If you are not living in touch with God, it is easy to blame Him or pass judgment on Him. You must go through the trial before you have any right to pronounce a verdict, because by going through the trial you learn to know God better. God is working in us to reach His highest goals until His purpose and our purpose become one.

The Changed Life

"If anyone is in Christ, he is a new creation, old things have passed away, behold, all things have become new" (2 Corinthians 5:17).

What understanding do you have of the salvation of your soul? The work of salvation means that in your real life things are dramatically changed. You no longer look at things in the same way. Your desires are new and the old things have lost their power to attract you. One of the tests for determining if the work of salvation in your life is genuine is—has God changed the things that really matter to you? If you still yearn for the old things, it is absurd to talk about being born from above—you are deceiving yourself. If you are born again, the Spirit of God makes the change very evident in your real life and thought. And when a crisis comes, you are the most amazed person on earth at the wonderful difference there is in you. There is no possibility of imagining that *you* did it. It is this complete and amazing change that is the very evidence that you are saved.

What difference has my salvation and sanctification made? For instance, can I stand in the light of 1 Corinthians 13, or do I squirm and evade the issue? True salvation, worked out in me by the Holy Spirit, frees me completely. And as long as I "walk in the light as He is in the light" (1 John 1:7), God sees nothing to rebuke because His life is working itself into every detailed part of my being, not on the conscious level, but even deeper than my consciousness.

Faith or Experience?

"... the Son of God, who loved me and gave Himself for me" (Galatians 2:20).

We should battle through our moods, feelings, and emotions into absolute devotion to the Lord Jesus. We must break out of our own little world of experience into abandoned devotion to Him. Think who the New Testament says Jesus Christ is, and then think of the despicable meagerness of the miserable faith we exhibit by saying, "I haven't had this experience or that experience"! Think what faith in Jesus Christ claims and provides—He can present us faultless before the throne of God, inexpressibly pure, absolutely righteous, and profoundly justified. Stand in absolute adoring faith "in Christ Jesus, who became for us wisdom from God—and righteousness and sanctification and redemption ..." (1 Corinthians 1:30). How dare we talk of making a sacrifice for the Son of God! We are saved from hell and total destruction, and then we talk about making sacrifices!

We must continually focus and firmly place our faith in Jesus Christ—not a "prayer meeting" Jesus Christ, or a "book" Jesus Christ, but the New Testament Jesus Christ, who is God Incarnate, and who ought to strike us dead at His feet. Our faith must be in the One from whom our salvation springs. Jesus Christ wants our absolute, unrestrained devotion to Himself. We can never *experience* Jesus Christ, or selfishly bind Him in the confines of our own hearts. Our faith must be built on strong determined confidence in Him.

It is because of our trusting in experience that we see the steadfast impatience of the Holy Spirit against unbelief. All of our fears are sinful, and we create our own fears by refusing to nourish ourselves in our faith. How can anyone who is identified with Jesus Christ suffer from doubt or fear! Our lives should be an absolute hymn of praise resulting from perfect, irrepressible, triumphant belief.

Discovering Divine Design

"As for me, being on the way,
the Lord led me . . ."
(Genesis 24:27).

We should be so one with God that we don't need to ask continually for guidance. Sanctification means that we are made the children of God. A child's life is normally obedient, until he chooses disobedience. But as soon as he chooses to disobey, an inherent inner conflict is produced. On the spiritual level, inner conflict is the warning of the Spirit of God. When He warns us in this way, we must stop at once and be renewed in the spirit of our mind to discern God's will (see Romans 12:2). If we are born again by the Spirit of God, our devotion to Him is hindered, or even stopped, by continually asking Him to guide us here and there. ". . . the Lord led me . . ." and on looking back we see the presence of an amazing design. If we are born of God we will see His guiding hand and give Him the credit.

We can all see God in exceptional things, but it requires the growth of spiritual discipline to see God in every detail. Never believe that the so-called random events of life are anything less than God's appointed order. Be ready to discover His divine designs anywhere and everywhere.

Beware of being obsessed with consistency to your own convictions instead of being devoted to God. If you are a saint and say, "I will never do this or that," in all probability this will be exactly what God will require of you. There was never a more inconsistent being on this earth than our Lord, but He was never inconsistent with His Father. The important consistency in a saint is not to a principle but to the divine life. It is the divine life that continually makes more and more discoveries about the divine mind. It is easier to be an excessive fanatic than it is to be consistently faithful, because God causes an amazing humbling of our religious conceit when we are faithful to Him.

"What Is That to You?"

"Peter . . . said to Jesus, 'But Lord, what about this man?' Jesus said to him, '. . . what is that to you? You follow Me' " (John 21:21-22).

One of the hardest lessons to learn comes from our stubborn refusal to refrain from interfering in other people's lives. It takes a long time to realize the danger of being an amateur providence, that is, interfering with God's plan for others. You see someone suffering and say, "He will not suffer, and I will make sure that he doesn't." You put your hand right in front of God's permissive will to stop it, and then God says, "What is that to you?" Is there stagnation in your spiritual life? Don't allow it to continue, but get into God's presence and find out the reason for it. You will possibly find it is because you have been interfering in the life of another—proposing things you had no right to propose, or advising when you had no right to advise. When you do have to give advice to another person, God will advise through you with the direct understanding of His Spirit. Your part is to maintain the right relationship with God so that His discernment can come through you continually for the purpose of blessing someone else.

Most of us live only within the level of consciousness—consciously serving and consciously devoted to God. This shows immaturity and the fact that we're not yet living the real Christian life. Maturity is produced in the life of a child of God on the unconscious level, until we become so totally surrendered to God that we are not even aware of being used by Him. When we are consciously aware of being used as broken bread and poured-out wine, we have yet another level to reach—a level where all awareness of ourselves and of what God is doing through us is completely eliminated. A saint is never consciously a saint—a saint is consciously dependent on God.

Still Human!

". . . whatever you do, do all to the glory of God" (1 Corinthians 10:31).

In the Scriptures, the great miracle of the incarnation slips into the ordinary life of a child; the great miracle of the transfiguration fades into the demon-possessed valley below; the glory of the resurrection descends into a breakfast on the seashore. This is not an anticlimax, but a great revelation of God.

We have a tendency to look for wonder in our experience, and we mistake heroic actions for real heroes. It's one thing to go through a crisis grandly, yet quite another to go through every day glorifying God when there is no witness, no limelight, and no one paying even the remotest attention to us. If we are not looking for halos, we at least want something that will make people say, "What a wonderful man of prayer he is!" or, "What a great woman of devotion she is!" If you are properly devoted to the Lord Jesus, you have reached the lofty height where no one would ever notice you personally. All that is noticed is the power of God coming through you all the time.

We want to be able to say, "Oh, I have had a wonderful call from God!" But to do even the most humbling tasks to the glory of God takes the Almighty God Incarnate working in us. To be utterly unnoticeable requires God's Spirit in us making us absolutely humanly His. The true test of a saint's life is not successfulness but faithfulness on the human level of life. We tend to set up success in Christian work as our purpose, but our purpose should be to display the glory of God in human life, to live a life "hidden with Christ in God" in our everyday human conditions (Colossians 3:3). Our human relationships are the very conditions in which the ideal life of God should be exhibited.

The Eternal Goal

"By Myself I have sworn, says the LORD, because you have done this thing . . . I will bless you . . ."
(Genesis 22:16–17).

Abraham, at this point, has reached the place where he is in touch with the very nature of God. He now understands the reality of God.

> My goal is God Himself . . .
>
> At any cost, dear Lord, by any road.

"At any cost . . . by any road" means submitting to God's way of bringing us to the goal.

There is no possibility of questioning God when He speaks, if He speaks to His own nature in me. Prompt obedience is the only result. When Jesus says, "Come," I simply come; when He says, "Let go," I let go; when He says, "Trust God in this matter," I trust. This work of obedience is the evidence that the nature of God is in me.

God's revelation of Himself to me is influenced by my character, not by God's character.

> 'Tis because I am ordinary,
>
> Thy ways so often look ordinary to me.

It is through the discipline of obedience that I get to the place where Abraham was and I see who God is. God will never be real to me until I come face to face with Him in Jesus Christ. Then I will know and can boldly proclaim, "In all the world, my God, there is none but Thee, there is none but Thee."

The promises of God are of no value to us until, through obedience, we come to understand the nature of God. We may read some things in the Bible every day for a year and they may mean nothing to us. Then, because we have been obedient to God in some small detail, we suddenly see what God means and His nature is instantly opened up to us. "All the promises of God in Him are Yes, and in Him Amen . . ." (2 Corinthians 1:20). Our "Yes" must be born of obedience; when by obedience we ratify a promise of God by saying, "Amen," or, "So be it." That promise becomes ours.

Winning into Freedom

"If the Son makes you free,
you shall be free indeed"
(John 8:36).

If there is even a trace of individual self-satisfaction left in us, it always says, "I can't surrender," or "I can't be free." But the spiritual part of our being never says "I can't"; it simply soaks up everything around it. Our spirit hungers for more and more. It is the way we are built. We are designed with a great capacity for God, but sin, our own individuality, and wrong thinking keep us from getting to Him. God delivers us from sin—we have to deliver ourselves from our individuality. This means offering our natural life to God and sacrificing it to Him, so He may transform it into spiritual life through our obedience.

God pays no attention to our natural individuality in the development of our spiritual life. His plan runs right through our natural life. We must see to it that we aid and assist God, and not stand against Him by saying, "I can't do that." God will not discipline us; we must discipline ourselves. God will not bring our "arguments . . . and every thought into captivity to the obedience of Christ" (2 Corinthians 10:5)—we have to do it. Don't say, "Oh, Lord, I suffer from wandering thoughts." *Don't* suffer from wandering thoughts. Stop listening to the tyranny of your individual natural life and win freedom into the spiritual life.

"If the Son makes you free . . . ." Do not substitute *Savior* for *Son* in this passage. The *Savior* has set us free from sin, but this is the freedom that comes from being set free from myself by the *Son*. It is what Paul meant in Galatians 2:20 when he said, "I have been crucified with Christ . . . ." His individuality had been broken and his spirit had been united with his Lord; not just merged into Him, but made one with Him. ". . . you shall be free indeed"—free to the very core of your being; free from the inside to the outside. We tend to rely on our own energy, instead of being energized by the power that comes from identification with Jesus.

"When He Has Come"

"When He has come, He will convict the world of sin . . ."
(John 16:8).

Very few of us know anything about conviction of sin. We know the experience of being disturbed because we have done wrong things. But conviction of sin by the Holy Spirit blots out every relationship on earth and makes us aware of only one— "Against You, You only, have I sinned . . ." (Psalm 51:4). When a person is convicted of sin in this way, he knows with every bit of his conscience that God would not dare to forgive him. If God did forgive him, then this person would have a stronger sense of justice than God. God does forgive, but it cost the breaking of His heart with grief in the death of Christ to enable Him to do so. The great miracle of the grace of God is that He forgives sin, and it is the death of Jesus Christ alone that enables the divine nature to forgive and to remain true to itself in doing so. It is shallow nonsense to say that God forgives us because He is love. Once we have been convicted of sin, we will never say this again. The love of God means Calvary—nothing less! The love of God is spelled out on the Cross and nowhere else. The only basis for which God can forgive me is the Cross of Christ. It is there that His conscience is satisfied.

Forgiveness doesn't merely mean that I am saved from hell and have been made ready for heaven (no one would accept forgiveness on that level). Forgiveness means that I am forgiven into a newly created relationship which identifies me with God in Christ. The miracle of redemption is that God turns me, the unholy one, into the standard of Himself, the Holy One. He does this by putting into me a new nature, the nature of Jesus Christ.

The Forgiveness of God

"In Him we have . . . the forgiveness of sins . . ." (Ephesians 1:7).

Beware of the pleasant view of the fatherhood of God: God is so kind and loving that of course He will forgive us. That thought, based solely on emotion, cannot be found anywhere in the New Testament. The only basis on which God can forgive us is the tremendous tragedy of the Cross of Christ. To base our forgiveness on any other ground is unconscious blasphemy. The only ground on which God can forgive our sin and reinstate us to His favor is through the Cross of Christ. There is no other way! Forgiveness, which is so easy for us to accept, cost the agony at Calvary. We should never take the forgiveness of sin, the gift of the Holy Spirit, and our sanctification in simple faith, and then forget the enormous cost to God that made all of this ours.

Forgiveness is the divine miracle of grace. The cost to God was the Cross of Christ. To forgive sin, while remaining a holy God, this price had to be paid. Never accept a view of the fatherhood of God if it blots out the atonement. The revealed truth of God is that without the atonement He cannot forgive—He would contradict His nature if He did. The only way we can be forgiven is by being brought back to God through the atonement of the Cross. God's forgiveness is possible only in the supernatural realm.

Compared with the miracle of the forgiveness of sin, the experience of sanctification is small. Sanctification is simply the wonderful expression or evidence of the forgiveness of sins in a human life. But the thing that awakens the deepest fountain of gratitude in a human being is that God has forgiven his sin. Paul never got away from this. Once you realize all that it cost God to forgive you, you will be held as in a vise, constrained by the love of God.

"It is Finished!"

"I have finished the work
which You have given Me
to do"
(John 17:4).

The death of Jesus Christ is the fulfillment in history of the very mind and intent of God. There is no place for seeing Jesus Christ as a martyr. His death was not something that happened to Him—something that might have been prevented. His death was the very reason He came.

Never build your case for forgiveness on the idea that God is our Father and He will forgive us because He loves us. That contradicts the revealed truth of God in Jesus Christ. It makes the Cross unnecessary, and the redemption "much ado about nothing." God forgives sin only because of the death of Christ. God could forgive people in no other way than by the death of His Son, and Jesus is exalted as Savior because of His death. "We see Jesus . . . *for the suffering of death* crowned with glory and honor . . ." (Hebrews 2:9). The greatest note of triumph ever sounded in the ears of a startled universe was that sounded on the Cross of Christ—"It is finished!" (John 19:30). That is the final word in the redemption of humankind.

Anything that lessens or completely obliterates the holiness of God, through a false view of His love, contradicts the truth of God as revealed by Jesus Christ. Never allow yourself to believe that Jesus Christ stands with us, and against God, out of pity and compassion, or that He became a curse for us out of sympathy for us. Jesus Christ became a curse for us by divine decree. Our part in realizing the tremendous meaning of His curse is the conviction of sin. Conviction is given to us as a gift of shame and repentance; it is the great mercy of God. Jesus Christ hates the sin in people, and Calvary is the measure of His hatred.

Shallow and Profound

"Whether you eat or drink, or whatever you do, do all to the glory of God"
(1 Corinthians 10:31).

Beware of allowing yourself to think that the shallow aspects of life are not ordained by God; they are ordained by Him equally as much as the profound. We sometimes refuse to be shallow, not out of our deep devotion to God but because we wish to impress other people with the fact that we are not shallow. This is a sure sign of spiritual pride. We must be careful, for this is how contempt for others is produced in our lives. And it causes us to be a walking rebuke to other people because they are more shallow than we are. Beware of posing as a profound person—God became a baby.

To be shallow is not a sign of being sinful, nor is shallowness an indication that there is no depth to your life at all—the ocean has a shore. Even the shallow things of life, such as eating and drinking, walking and talking, are ordained by God. These are all things our Lord did. He did them as the Son of God, and He said, "A disciple is not above his teacher . . ." (Matthew 10:24).

We are safeguarded by the shallow things of life. We have to live the surface, commonsense life in a commonsense way. Then when God gives us the deeper things, they are obviously separated from the shallow concerns. Never show the depth of your life to anyone but God. We are so nauseatingly serious, so desperately interested in our own character and reputation, we refuse to behave like Christians in the shallow concerns of life.

Make a determination to take no one seriously except God. You may find that the first person you must be the most critical with, as being the greatest fraud you have ever known, is yourself.

The Distraction of Contempt

"Have mercy on us, O LORD, have mercy on us! For we are exceedingly filled with contempt"
(Psalm 123:3).

What we must beware of is not damage to our belief in God but damage to our Christian disposition or state of mind. "Take heed to your spirit, that you do not deal treacherously" (Malachi 2:16). Our state of mind is powerful in its effects. It can be the enemy that penetrates right into our soul and distracts our mind from God. There are certain attitudes we should never dare to indulge. If we do, we will find they have distracted us from faith in God. Until we get back into a quiet mood before Him, our faith is of no value, and our confidence in the flesh and in human ingenuity is what rules our lives.

Beware of "the cares of this world . . ." (Mark 4:19). They are the very things that produce the wrong attitudes in our soul. It is incredible what enormous power there is in simple things to distract our attention away from God. Refuse to be swamped by "the cares of this world."

Another thing that distracts us is our passion for vindication. St. Augustine prayed, "O Lord, deliver me from this lust of always vindicating myself." Such a need for constant vindication destroys our soul's faith in God. Don't say, "I must explain myself," or, "I must get people to understand." Our Lord never explained anything—He left the misunderstandings or misconceptions of others to correct themselves.

When we discern that other people are not growing spiritually and allow that discernment to turn to criticism, we block our fellowship with God. God never gives us discernment so that we may criticize, but that we may intercede.

Direction of Focus

"Behold, as the eyes of servants look to the hand of their masters . . . , so our eyes look to the LORD our God . . ."
(Psalm 123:2).

This verse is a description of total reliance on God. Just as the eyes of a servant are riveted on his master, our eyes should be directed to and focused on God. This is how knowledge of His countenance is gained and how God reveals Himself to us (see Isaiah 53:1). Our spiritual strength begins to be drained when we stop lifting our eyes to Him. Our stamina is sapped, not so much through external troubles surrounding us but through problems in our thinking. We wrongfully think, "I suppose I've been stretching myself a little too much, standing too tall and trying to look like God instead of being an ordinary humble person." We have to realize that no effort can be too high.

For example, you came to a crisis in your life, took a stand for God, and even had the witness of the Spirit as a confirmation that what you did was right. But now, maybe weeks or years have gone by, and you are slowly coming to the conclusion—"Well, maybe what I did showed too much pride or was superficial. Was I taking a stand a bit too high for me?" Your "rational" friends come and say, "Don't be silly. We knew when you first talked about this spiritual awakening that it was a passing impulse, that you couldn't hold up under the strain. And anyway, God doesn't expect you to endure." You respond by saying, "Well, I suppose I was expecting too much." That sounds humble to say, but it means that your reliance on God is gone, and you are now relying on worldly opinion. The danger comes when, no longer relying on God, you neglect to focus your eyes on Him. Only when God brings you to a sudden stop will you realize that you have been the loser. Whenever there is a spiritual drain in your life, correct it immediately. Realize that something has been coming between you and God, and change or remove it at once.

The Secret of Spiritual Consistency

"God forbid that I should boast except in the cross of our Lord Jesus Christ . . ." (Galatians 6:14).

When a person is newly born again, he seems inconsistent due to his unrelated emotions and the state of the external things or circumstances in his life. The apostle Paul had a strong and steady underlying consistency in his life. Consequently, he could let his external life change without internal distress because he was rooted and grounded in God. Most of us are not consistent spiritually because we are more concerned about being consistent externally. In the external expression of things, Paul lived in the basement, while his critics lived on the upper level. And these two levels do not begin to touch each other. But Paul's consistency was down deep in the fundamentals. The great basis of his consistency was the agony of God in the redemption of the world, namely, the Cross of Christ.

State your beliefs to yourself again. Get back to the foundation of the Cross of Christ, doing away with any belief not based on it. In secular history the Cross is an infinitesimally small thing, but from the biblical perspective it is of more importance than all the empires of the world. If we get away from dwelling on the tragedy of God on the Cross in our preaching, our preaching produces nothing. It will not transmit the energy of God to man; it may be interesting, but it will have no power. However, when we preach the Cross, the energy of God is released. ". . . it pleased God through the foolishness of the message preached to save those who believe. . . . we preach Christ crucified . . ." (1 Corinthians 1:21, 23).

November 25

The Focal Point of Spiritual Power

"... except in the cross of our Lord Jesus Christ ..." (Galatians 6:14).

If you want to know the power of God (that is, the resurrection life of Jesus) in your human flesh, you must dwell on the tragedy of God. Break away from your personal concern over your own spiritual condition, and with a completely open spirit consider the tragedy of God. Instantly the power of God will be in you. "Look to Me ..." (Isaiah 45:22). Pay attention to the external Source and the internal power will be there. We lose power because we don't focus on the right thing. The effect of the Cross is salvation, sanctification, healing, etc., but we are not to preach any of these. We are to preach "Jesus Christ and Him crucified" (1 Corinthians 2:2). The proclaiming of Jesus will do its own work. Concentrate on God's focal point in your preaching, and even if your listeners seem to pay it no attention, they will never be the same again. If I share my own words, they are of no more importance than your words are to me. But if we share the truth of God with one another, we will encounter it again and again. We have to focus on the great point of spiritual power—the Cross. If we stay in contact with that center of power, its energy is released in our lives. In holiness movements and spiritual experience meetings, the focus tends to be put not on the Cross of Christ but on the effects of the Cross.

The feebleness of the church is being criticized today, and the criticism is justified. One reason for the feebleness is that there has not been this focus on the true center of spiritual power. We have not dwelt enough on the tragedy of Calvary or on the meaning of redemption.

The Consecration of Spiritual Power

". . . by whom the world has been crucified to me, and I to the world" (Galatians 6:14).

If I dwell on the Cross of Christ, I do not simply become inwardly devout and solely interested in my own holiness—I become strongly focused on Jesus Christ's interests. Our Lord was not a recluse nor a fanatical holy man practicing self-denial. He did not physically cut Himself off from society, but He was inwardly disconnected all the time. He was not aloof, but He lived in another world. In fact, He was so much in the common everyday world that the religious people of His day accused Him of being a glutton and a drunkard. Yet our Lord never allowed anything to interfere with His consecration of spiritual power.

It is not genuine consecration to think that we can refuse to be used of God now in order to store up our spiritual power for later use. That is a hopeless mistake. The Spirit of God has set a great many people free from their sin, yet they are experiencing no fullness in their lives—no true sense of freedom. The kind of religious life we see around the world today is entirely different from the vigorous holiness of the life of Jesus Christ. "I do not pray that You should take them out of the world, but that You should keep them from the evil one" (John 17:15). We are to be in the world but not of it—to be separated internally, not externally (see John 17:16).

We must never allow anything to interfere with the consecration of our spiritual power. Consecration (being dedicated to God's service) is our part; sanctification (being set apart from sin and being made holy) is God's part. We must make a deliberate determination to be interested only in what God is interested in. The way to make that determination, when faced with a perplexing problem, is to ask yourself, "Is this the kind of thing in which Jesus Christ is interested, or is it something in which the spirit that is diametrically opposed to Jesus is interested?"

The Riches
of the Destitute

"... being justified freely by
His grace ..."
(Romans 3:24).

The gospel of the grace of God awakens an intense longing in human souls and an equally intense resentment, because the truth that it reveals is not palatable or easy to swallow. There is a certain pride in people that causes them to give and give, but to come and accept a gift is another thing. I will give my life to martyrdom; I will dedicate my life to service—I will do anything. But do not humiliate me to the level of the most hell-deserving sinner and tell me that all I have to do is accept the gift of salvation through Jesus Christ.

We have to realize that we cannot earn or win anything from God through our own efforts. We must either receive it as a gift or do without it. The greatest spiritual blessing we receive is when we come to the knowledge that we are destitute. Until we get there, our Lord is powerless. He can do nothing for us as long as we think we are sufficient in and of ourselves. We must enter into His kingdom through the door of destitution. As long as we are "rich," particularly in the area of pride or independence, God can do nothing for us. It is only when we get hungry spiritually that we receive the Holy Spirit. The gift of the essential nature of God is placed and made effective in us by the Holy Spirit. He imparts to us the quickening life of Jesus, making us truly alive. He takes that which was "beyond" us and places it "within" us. And immediately, once "the beyond" has come "within," it rises up to "the above," and we are lifted into the kingdom where Jesus lives and reigns (see John 3:5).

The holiness movements of today have none of the rugged reality of the New Testament about them. There is nothing about them that needs the death of Jesus Christ. All that is required is a pious atmosphere, prayer, and devotion. This type of experience is not supernatural nor miraculous. It did not cost the sufferings of God, nor is it stained with "the blood of the Lamb" (Revelation 12:11). It is not marked or sealed by the Holy Spirit as being genuine, and it has no visual sign that causes people to exclaim with awe and wonder, "That is the work of God Almighty!" Yet the New Testament is about the work of God and nothing else.

The New Testament example of the Christian experience is that of a personal, passionate devotion to the Person of Jesus Christ. Every other kind of so-called Christian experience is detached from the Person of Jesus. There is no regeneration—no being born again into the kingdom in which Christ lives and reigns supreme. There is only the idea that He is our pattern. In the New Testament Jesus Christ is the Savior long before He is the pattern. Today He is being portrayed as the figurehead of a religion—a mere example. He is that, but He is infinitely more. He is salvation itself; He is the gospel of God!

Jesus said, ". . . when He, the Spirit of truth, has come, . . . He will glorify Me . . ." (John 16:13–14). When I commit myself to the revealed truth of the New Testament, I receive from God the gift of the Holy Spirit, who then begins interpreting to me what Jesus did. The Spirit of God does in me internally all that Jesus Christ did for me externally.

"By the Grace of God I Am What I Am"

> "By the grace of God I am what I am, and His grace toward me was not in vain . . ."
>
> (1 Corinthians 15:10).

The way we continually talk about our own inabilities is an insult to our Creator. To complain over our incompetence is to accuse God falsely of having overlooked us. Get into the habit of examining from God's perspective those things that sound so humble to men. You will be amazed at how unbelievably inappropriate and disrespectful they are to Him. We say things such as, "Oh, I shouldn't claim to be sanctified; I'm not a saint." But to say that before God means, "No, Lord, it is impossible for You to save and sanctify me; there are opportunities I have not had and so many imperfections in my brain and body; no, Lord, it isn't possible." That may sound wonderfully humble to others, but before God it is an attitude of defiance.

Conversely, the things that sound humble before God may sound exactly the opposite to people. To say, "Thank God, I know I am saved and sanctified," is in God's eyes the purest expression of humility. It means you have so completely surrendered yourself to God that you know He is true. Never worry about whether what you say sounds humble before others or not. But always be humble before God, and allow Him to be your all in all.

There is only one relationship that really matters, and that is your personal relationship to your personal Redeemer and Lord. If you maintain that at all costs, letting everything else go, God will fulfill His purpose through your life. One individual life may be of priceless value to God's purposes, and yours may be that life.

The Law and the Gospel

"Whoever shall keep the whole law, and yet stumble in one point, he is guilty of all" (James 2:10).

The moral law does not consider our weaknesses as human beings; in fact, it does not take into account our heredity or infirmities. It simply demands that we be absolutely moral. The moral law never changes, either for the highest of society or for the weakest in the world. It is enduring and eternally the same. The moral law, ordained by God, does not make itself weak to the weak by excusing our shortcomings. It remains absolute for all time and eternity. If we are not aware of this, it is because we are less than alive. Once we do realize it, our life immediately becomes a fatal tragedy. "I was alive once without the law, but when the commandment came, sin revived and I died" (Romans 7:9). The moment we realize this, the Spirit of God convicts us of sin. Until a person gets there and sees that there is no hope, the Cross of Christ remains absurd to him. Conviction of sin always brings a fearful, confining sense of the law. It makes a person hopeless—". . . sold under sin" (Romans 7:14). I, a guilty sinner, can never work to get right with God— it is impossible. There is only one way by which I can get right with God, and that is through the death of Jesus Christ. I must get rid of the underlying idea that I can ever be right with God because of my obedience. Who of us could ever obey God to absolute perfection!

We only begin to realize the power of the moral law once we see that it comes with a condition and a promise. But God never coerces us. Sometimes we wish He would make us be obedient, and at other times we wish He would leave us alone. Whenever God's will is in complete control, He removes all pressure. And when we deliberately choose to obey Him, He will reach to the remotest star and to the ends of the earth to assist us with all of His almighty power.

*C*hristian *P*erfection

"Not that I have already
attained, or am already
perfect . . ."
(Philippians 3:12).

It is a trap to presume that God wants to make us perfect specimens of what He can do—God's purpose is to make us one
with Himself. The emphasis of holiness movements tends to be
that God is producing specimens of holiness to put in His
museum. If you accept this concept of personal holiness, your
life's determined purpose will not be for God, but for what you
call the evidence of God in your life. How can we say, "It could
never be God's will for me to be sick"? If it was God's will to
bruise His own Son (Isaiah 53:10), why shouldn't He bruise
you? What shines forth and reveals God in your life is not your
relative consistency to an idea of what a saint should be, but
your genuine, living relationship with Jesus Christ, and your
unrestrained devotion to Him whether you are well or sick.

Christian perfection is not, and never can be, human perfection. Christian perfection is the perfection of a relationship
with God that shows itself to be true even amid the seemingly
unimportant aspects of human life. When you obey the call of
Jesus Christ, the first thing that hits you is the pointlessness of
the things you have to do. The next thought that strikes you is
that other people seem to be living perfectly consistent lives.
Such lives may leave you with the idea that God is unnecessary—that through your own human effort and devotion you
can attain God's standard for your life. In a fallen world this
can never be done. I am called to live in such a perfect relationship with God that my life produces a yearning for God in the
lives of others, not admiration for myself. Thoughts about
myself hinder my usefulness to God. God's purpose is not to
perfect me to make me a trophy in His showcase; He is getting
me to the place where He can use me. Let Him do what He
wants.

"Not by Might nor by Power"

"My speech and my preaching were not with persuasive words of human wisdom, but in demonstration of the Spirit and of power . . ."
(1 Corinthians 2:4).

If in preaching the gospel you substitute your knowledge of the way of salvation for confidence in the power of the gospel, you hinder people from getting to reality. Take care to see while you proclaim your knowledge of the way of salvation, that you yourself are rooted and grounded by faith in God. Never rely on the clearness of your presentation, but as you give your explanation make sure that you are relying on the Holy Spirit. Rely on the certainty of God's redemptive power, and He will create His own life in people.

Once you are rooted in reality, nothing can shake you. If your faith is in experiences, anything that happens is likely to upset that faith. But nothing can ever change God or the reality of redemption. Base your faith on that, and you are as eternally secure as God Himself. Once you have a personal relationship with Jesus Christ, you will never be moved again. That is the meaning of sanctification. God disapproves of our human efforts to cling to the concept that sanctification is merely an experience, while forgetting that even our sanctification must also be sanctified (see John 17:19). I must deliberately give my sanctified life to God for His service, so that He can use me as His hands and His feet.

Life without war is impossible in the natural or the supernatural realm. It is a fact that there is a continuing struggle in the physical, mental, moral, and spiritual areas of life.

Health is the balance between the physical parts of my body and all the things and forces surrounding me. To maintain good health I must have sufficient internal strength to fight off the things that are external. Everything outside my physical life is designed to cause my death. The very elements that sustain me while I am alive work to decay and disintegrate my body once it is dead. If I have enough inner strength to fight, I help to produce the balance needed for health. The same is true of the mental life. If I want to maintain a strong and active mental life, I have to fight. This struggle produces the mental balance called thought.

Morally it is the same. Anything that does not strengthen me morally is the enemy of virtue within me. Whether I overcome, thereby producing virtue, depends on the level of moral excellence in my life. But we must fight to be moral. Morality does not happen by accident; moral virtue is acquired.

And spiritually it is also the same. Jesus said, "In the world you will have tribulation . . ." (John 16:33). This means that anything which is not spiritual leads to my downfall. Jesus went on to say, ". . . but be of good cheer, I have overcome the world." I must learn to fight against and overcome the things that come against me, and in that way produce the balance of holiness. Then it becomes a delight to meet opposition.

Holiness is the balance between my nature and the law of God as expressed in Jesus Christ.

"The Temple of the Holy Spirit"

" . . . only in regard to the throne will I be greater than you" (Genesis 41:40).

I am accountable to God for the way I control my body under His authority. Paul said he did not "set aside the grace of God"—make it ineffective (Galatians 2:21). The grace of God is absolute and limitless, and the work of salvation through Jesus is complete and finished forever. I am not being saved—I am saved. Salvation is as eternal as God's throne, but I must put to work or use what God has placed within me. To "work out [my] own salvation" (Philippians 2:12) means that I am responsible for using what He has given me. It also means that I must exhibit in my own body the life of the Lord Jesus, not mysteriously or secretly, but openly and boldly. "I discipline my body and bring it into subjection . . ." (1 Corinthians 9:27). Every Christian can have his body under absolute control for God. God has given us the responsibility to rule over all "the temple of the Holy Spirit," including our thoughts and desires (1 Corinthians 6:19). We are responsible for these, and we must never give way to improper ones. But most of us are much more severe in our judgment of others than we are in judging ourselves. We make excuses for things in ourselves, while we condemn things in the lives of others simply because we are not naturally inclined to do them.

Paul said, "I beseech you . . . that you present your bodies a living sacrifice . . ." (Romans 12:1). What I must decide is whether or not I will agree with my Lord and Master that my body will indeed be His temple. Once I agree, all the rules, regulations, and requirements of the law concerning the body are summed up for me in this revealed truth—my body is "the temple of the Holy Spirit."

December 5

"My Rainbow in the Cloud"

"I set My rainbow in the cloud, and it shall be for the sign of the covenant between Me and the earth" (Genesis 9:13).

It is the will of God that human beings should get into a right-standing relationship with Him, and His covenants are designed for this purpose. Why doesn't God save me? He has accomplished and provided for my salvation, but I have not yet entered into a relationship with Him. Why doesn't God do everything we ask? He has done it. The point is—will I step into that covenant relationship? All the great blessings of God are finished and complete, but they are not mine until I enter into a relationship with Him on the basis of His covenant.

Waiting for God to act is fleshly unbelief. It means that I have no faith in Him. I wait for Him to do something in me so I may trust in that. But God won't do it, because that is not the basis of the God-and-man relationship. Man must go beyond the physical body and feelings in his covenant with God, just as God goes beyond Himself in reaching out with His covenant to man. It is a question of faith in God—a very rare thing. We only have faith in our feelings. I don't believe God until He puts something tangible in my hand, so that I know I have it. Then I say, "Now I believe." There is no faith exhibited in that. God says, "Look to Me, and be saved . . ." (Isaiah 45:22).

When I have really transacted business with God on the basis of His covenant, letting everything else go, there is no sense of personal achievement—no human ingredient in it at all. Instead, there is a complete overwhelming sense of being brought into union with God, and my life is transformed and radiates peace and joy.

Repentance

"Godly sorrow produces
repentance leading to
salvation . . ."
(2 Corinthians 7:10).

Conviction of sin is best described in the words:

> My sins, my sins, my Savior,
> How sad on Thee they fall.

Conviction of sin is one of the most uncommon things that ever happens to a person. It is the beginning of an understanding of God. Jesus Christ said that when the Holy Spirit came He would convict people of sin (see John 16:8). And when the Holy Spirit stirs a person's conscience and brings him into the presence of God, it is not that person's relationship with others that bothers him but his relationship with God—"Against You, You only, have I sinned, and done this evil in your sight . . ." (Psalm 51:4). The wonders of conviction of sin, forgiveness, and holiness are so interwoven that it is only the forgiven person who is truly holy. He proves he is forgiven by being the opposite of what he was previously, by the grace of God. Repentance always brings a person to the point of saying, "I have sinned." The surest sign that God is at work in his life is when he says that and means it. Anything less is simply sorrow for having made foolish mistakes—a reflex action caused by self-disgust.

The entrance into the kingdom of God is through the sharp, sudden pains of repentance colliding with man's respectable "goodness." Then the Holy Spirit, who produces these struggles, begins the formation of the Son of God in the person's life (see Galatians 4:19). This new life will reveal itself in conscious repentance followed by unconscious holiness, never the other way around. The foundation of Christianity is repentance. Strictly speaking, a person cannot repent when he chooses—repentance is a gift of God. The old Puritans used to pray for "the gift of tears." If you ever cease to understand the value of repentance, you allow yourself to remain in sin. Examine yourself to see if you have forgotten how to be truly repentant.

The Impartial Power of God

"By one offering He has perfected forever those who are being sanctified"
(Hebrews 10:14).

We trample the blood of the Son of God underfoot if we think we are forgiven because we are sorry for our sins. The only reason for the forgiveness of our sins by God, and the infinite depth of His promise to forget them, is the death of Jesus Christ. Our repentance is merely the result of our personal realization of the atonement by the Cross of Christ, which He has provided for us. ". . . Christ Jesus . . . became for us wisdom from God—and righteousness and sanctification and redemption . . ." (1 Corinthians 1:30). Once we realize that Christ has become all this for us, the limitless joy of God begins in us. And wherever the joy of God is not present, the death sentence is still in effect.

No matter who or what we are, God restores us to right standing with Himself only by means of the death of Jesus Christ. God does this, not because Jesus pleads with Him to do so but because He died. It cannot be earned, just accepted. All the pleading for salvation which deliberately ignores the Cross of Christ is useless. It is knocking at a door other than the one which Jesus has already opened. We protest by saying, "But I don't want to come that way. It is too humiliating to be received as a sinner." God's response, through Peter, is, ". . . there is no other name . . . by which we must be saved" (Acts 4:12). What at first appears to be heartlessness on God's part is actually the true expression of His heart. There is unlimited entrance His way. "In Him we have redemption through His blood . . ." (Ephesians 1:7). To identify with the death of Jesus Christ means that we must die to everything that was never a part of Him.

God is just in saving bad people only as He makes them good. Our Lord does not pretend we are all right when we are all wrong. The atonement by the Cross of Christ is the propitiation God uses to make unholy people holy.

"Those who are Christ's have crucified the flesh with its passions and desires"
(Galatians 5:24).

The natural life itself is not sinful. But we must abandon sin, having nothing to do with it in any way whatsoever. Sin belongs to hell and to the devil. I, as a child of God, belong to heaven and to God. It is not a question of giving up sin, but of giving up my right to myself, my natural independence, and my self-will. This is where the battle has to be fought. The things that are right, noble, and good from the natural standpoint are the very things that keep us from being God's best. Once we come to understand that natural moral excellence opposes or counteracts surrender to God, we bring our soul into the center of its greatest battle. Very few of us would debate over what is filthy, evil, and wrong, but we do debate over what is good. It is the good that opposes the best. The higher up the scale of moral excellence a person goes, the more intense the opposition to Jesus Christ. "Those who are Christ's have crucified the flesh . . . ." The cost to your natural life is not just one or two things, but everything. Jesus said, "If anyone desires to come after Me, let him deny himself . . ." (Matthew 16:24). That is, he must deny his right to himself, and he must realize who Jesus Christ is before he will bring himself to do it. Beware of refusing to go to the funeral of your own independence.

The natural life is not spiritual, and it can be made spiritual only through sacrifice. If we do not purposely sacrifice the natural, the supernatural can never become natural to us. There is no high or easy road. Each of us has the means to accomplish it entirely in his own hands. It is not a question of praying, but of sacrificing, and thereby performing His will.

The Offering of the Natural

"It is written that Abraham had two sons: the one by a bondwoman, the other by a freewoman"
(Galatians 4:22).

Paul was not dealing with sin in this chapter of Galatians, but with the relation of the natural to the spiritual. The natural can be turned into the spiritual only through sacrifice. Without this a person will lead a divided life. Why did God demand that the natural must be sacrificed? God did not demand it. It is not God's perfect will, but His permissive will. God's perfect will was for the natural to be changed into the spiritual through obedience. Sin is what made it necessary for the natural to be sacrificed.

Abraham had to offer up Ishmael before he offered up Isaac (see Genesis 21:8–14). Some of us are trying to offer up spiritual sacrifices to God before we have sacrificed the natural. The only way we can offer a spiritual sacrifice to God is to "present [our] bodies a living sacrifice . . ." (Romans 12:1). Sanctification means more than being freed from sin. It means the deliberate commitment of myself to the God of my salvation, and being willing to pay whatever it may cost.

If we do not sacrifice the natural to the spiritual, the natural life will resist and defy the life of the Son of God in us and will produce continual turmoil. This is always the result of an undisciplined spiritual nature. We go wrong because we stubbornly refuse to discipline ourselves physically, morally, or mentally. We excuse ourselves by saying, "Well, I wasn't taught to be disciplined when I was a child." Then discipline yourself now! If you don't, you will ruin your entire personal life for God.

God is not actively involved with our natural life as long as we continue to pamper and gratify it. But once we are willing to put it out in the desert and are determined to keep it under control, God will be with it. He will then provide wells and oases and fulfill all His promises for the natural (see Genesis 21:15–19).

Individuality

Individuality is the hard outer layer surrounding the inner spiritual life. Individuality shoves others aside, separating and isolating people. We see it as the primary characteristic of a child, and rightly so. When we confuse individuality with the spiritual life, we remain isolated. This shell of individuality is God's created natural covering designed to protect the spiritual life. But our individuality must be yielded to God so that our spiritual life may be brought forth into fellowship with Him. Individuality counterfeits spirituality, just as lust counterfeits love. God designed human nature for Himself, but individuality corrupts that human nature for its own purposes.

The characteristics of individuality are independence and self-will. We hinder our spiritual growth more than any other way by continually asserting our individuality. If you say, "I can't believe," it is because your individuality is blocking the way; individuality can never believe. But our spirit cannot help believing. Watch yourself closely when the Spirit of God is at work in you. He pushes you to the limits of your individuality where a choice must be made. The choice is either to say, "I will not surrender," or to surrender, breaking the hard shell of individuality, which allows the spiritual life to emerge. The Holy Spirit narrows it down every time to one thing (see Matthew 5:23–24). It is your individuality that refuses to "be reconciled to your brother" (5:24). God wants to bring you into union with Himself, but unless you are willing to give up your right to yourself, He cannot. ". . . let him deny himself . . ."—deny his independent right to himself. Then the real life—the spiritual life—is allowed the opportunity to grow.

Personality

Personality is the unique, limitless part of our life that makes us distinct from everyone else. It is too vast for us even to comprehend. An island in the sea may be just the top of a large mountain, and our personality is like that island. We don't know the great depths of our being, therefore we cannot measure ourselves. We start out thinking we can, but soon realize that there is really only one Being who fully understands us, and that is our Creator.

Personality is the characteristic mark of the inner, spiritual man, just as individuality is the characteristic of the outer, natural man. Our Lord can never be described in terms of individuality and independence, but only in terms of His total Person—"I and My Father are one" (John 10:30). Personality merges, and you only reach your true identity once you are merged with another person. When love or the Spirit of God come upon a person, he is transformed. He will then no longer insist on maintaining his individuality. Our Lord never referred to a person's individuality or his isolated position, but spoke in terms of the total person—". . . that they may be one just as We are one . . . ." Once your rights to yourself are surrendered to God, your true personal nature begins responding to God immediately. Jesus Christ brings freedom to your total person, and even your individuality is transformed. The transformation is brought about by love—personal devotion to Jesus. Love is the overflowing result of one person in true fellowship with another.

" . . . men always ought to
pray and not lose heart"
(Luke 18:1).

You cannot truly intercede through prayer if you do not
believe in the reality of redemption. Instead, you will simply be
turning intercession into useless sympathy for others, which
will serve only to increase the contentment they have for
remaining out of touch with God. True intercession involves
bringing the person, or the circumstance that seems to be
crashing in on you, before God, until you are changed by His
attitude toward that person or circumstance. Intercession
means to "fill up . . . [with] what is lacking in the afflictions of
Christ" (Colossians 1:24), and this is precisely why there are so
few intercessors. People describe intercession by saying, "It is
putting yourself in someone else's place." That is not true!
Intercession is putting yourself in God's place; it is having His
mind and His perspective.

As an intercessor, be careful not to seek too much information from God regarding the situation you are praying
about, because you may be overwhelmed. If you know too
much, more than God has ordained for you to know, you can't
pray; the circumstances of the people become so overpowering
that you are no longer able to get to the underlying truth.

Our work is to be in such close contact with God that we
may have His mind about everything, but we shirk that responsibility by substituting doing for interceding. And yet intercession is the only thing that has no drawbacks, because it keeps
our relationship completely open with God.

What we must avoid in intercession is praying for someone to be simply "patched up." We must pray that person completely through into contact with the very life of God. Think of
the number of people God has brought across our path, only to
see us drop them! When we pray on the basis of redemption,
God creates something He can create in no other way than
through intercessory prayer.

The $Great$ $Life$

"Peace I leave with you, My peace I give to you, not as the world gives do I give to you. Let not your heart be troubled . . ."
(John 14:27).

Whenever we experience something difficult in our personal life, we are tempted to blame God. But we are the ones in the wrong, not God. Blaming God is evidence that we are refusing to let go of some disobedience somewhere in our lives. But as soon as we let go, everything becomes as clear as daylight to us. As long as we try to serve two masters, ourselves and God, there will be difficulties combined with doubt and confusion. Our attitude must be one of complete reliance on God. Once we get to that point, there is nothing easier than living the life of a saint. We encounter difficulties when we try to usurp the authority of the Holy Spirit for our own purposes.

God's mark of approval, whenever you obey Him, is peace. He sends an immeasurable, deep peace; not a natural peace, "as the world gives," but the peace of Jesus. Whenever peace does not come, wait until it does, or seek to find out why it is not coming. If you are acting on your own impulse, or out of a sense of the heroic, to be seen by others, the peace of Jesus will not exhibit itself. This shows no unity with God or confidence in Him. The spirit of simplicity, clarity, and unity is born through the Holy Spirit, not through your decisions. God counters our self-willed decisions with an appeal for simplicity and unity.

My questions arise whenever I cease to obey. When I do obey God, problems come, not between me and God, but as a means to keep my mind examining with amazement the revealed truth of God. But any problem that comes between God and myself is the result of disobedience. Any problem that comes while I obey God (and there will be many), increases my overjoyed delight, because I know that my Father knows and cares, and I can watch and anticipate how He will unravel my problems.

"Approved to God"

"Be diligent to present yourself approved to God, a worker who does not need to be ashamed, rightly dividing the word of truth" (2 Timothy 2:15).

If you cannot express yourself well on each of your beliefs, work and study until you can. If you don't, other people may miss out on the blessings that come from knowing the truth. Strive to re-express a truth of God to yourself clearly and understandably, and God will use that same explanation when you share it with someone else. But you must be willing to go through God's winepress where the grapes are crushed. You must struggle, experiment, and rehearse your words to express God's truth clearly. Then the time will come when that very expression will become God's wine of strength to someone else. But if you are not diligent and say, "I'm not going to study and struggle to express this truth in my own words; I'll just borrow my words from someone else," then the words will be of no value to you or to others. Try to state to yourself what you believe to be the absolute truth of God, and you will be allowing God the opportunity to pass it on through you to someone else.

Always make it a practice to stir your own mind thoroughly to think through what you have easily believed. Your position is not really yours until you make it yours through suffering and study. The author or speaker from whom you learn the most is not the one who teaches you something you didn't know before, but the one who helps you take a truth with which you have quietly struggled, give it expression, and speak it clearly and boldly.

$W_{restling}$ B_{efore} G_{od} "Take up the whole armor of
                                        God . . . praying always . . ."
                                      (Ephesians 6:13,18).

You must learn to wrestle *against* the things that hinder your communication with God, and wrestle in prayer *for* other people; but to wrestle *with* God in prayer is unscriptural. If you ever do wrestle with God, you will be crippled for the rest of your life. If you grab hold of God and wrestle with Him, as Jacob did, simply because He is working in a way that doesn't meet with your approval, you force Him to put you out of joint (see Genesis 32:24–25). Don't become a cripple by wrestling with the ways of God, but be someone who wrestles before God with the things of this world, because "we are more than conquerors through Him . . ." (Romans 8:37). Wrestling before God makes an impact in His kingdom. If you ask me to pray for you, and I am not complete in Christ, my prayer accomplishes nothing. But if I am complete in Christ, my prayer brings victory all the time. Prayer is effective only when there is completeness—"take up the whole armor of God . . . ."

Always make a distinction between God's perfect will and His permissive will, which He uses to accomplish His divine purpose for our lives. God's perfect will is unchangeable. It is with His permissive will, or the various things that He allows into our lives, that we must wrestle before Him. It is our reaction to these things allowed by His permissive will that enables us to come to the point of seeing His perfect will for us. "We know that all things work together for good to those who love God . . ." (Romans 8:28)—to those who remain true to God's perfect will—His calling in Christ Jesus. God's permissive will is the testing He uses to reveal His true sons and daughters. We should not be spineless and automatically say, "Yes, it is the Lord's will." We don't have to fight or wrestle *with God,* but we must wrestle before God *with things.* Beware of lazily giving up. Instead, put up a glorious fight and you will find yourself empowered with His strength.

Redemption—Creating the Need it Satisfies

"The natural man does not receive the things of the Spirit of God, for they are foolishness to him . . ."
(1 Corinthians 2:14).

The gospel of God creates the sense of need for the gospel. Is the gospel hidden to those who are servants already? No, Paul said, "But even if our gospel is veiled, it is veiled to those who are perishing, whose minds the god of this age has blinded, who do not believe . . ." (2 Corinthians 4:3–4). The majority of people think of themselves as being completely moral, and have no sense of need for the gospel. It is God who creates this sense of need in a human being, but that person remains totally unaware of his need until God makes Himself evident. Jesus said, "Ask, and it will be given to you . . ." (Matthew 7:7). But God cannot give until a man asks. It is not that He wants to withhold something from us, but that is the plan He has established for the way of redemption. Through our asking, God puts His process in motion, creating something in us that was nonexistent until we asked. The inner reality of redemption is that it creates all the time. And as redemption creates the life of God in us, it also creates the things which belong to that life. The only thing that can possibly satisfy the need is what created the need. This is the meaning of redemption—it creates and it satisfies.

Jesus said, "And I, if I am lifted up from the earth, will draw all peoples to Myself" (John 12:32). When we preach our own experiences, people may be interested, but it awakens no real sense of need. But once Jesus Christ is "lifted up," the Spirit of God creates an awareness of the need for Him. The creative power of the redemption of God works in the souls of men only through the preaching of the gospel. It is never the sharing of personal experiences that saves people, but the truth of redemption. "The words that I speak to you are spirit, and they are life" (John 6:63).

Test of Faithfulness

"We know that all things work together for good to those who love God . . ." (Romans 8:28).

It is only a faithful person who truly believes that God sovereignly controls his circumstances. We take our circumstances for granted, saying God is in control, but not really believing it. We act as if the things that happen were completely controlled by people. To be faithful in every circumstance means that we have only one loyalty, or object of our faith—the Lord Jesus Christ. God may cause our circumstances to suddenly fall apart, which may bring the realization of our unfaithfulness to Him for not recognizing that He had ordained the situation. We never saw what He was trying to accomplish, and that exact event will never be repeated in our life. This is where the test of our faithfulness comes. If we will just learn to worship God even during the difficult circumstances, He will change them for the better very quickly if He so chooses.

Being faithful to Jesus Christ is the most difficult thing we try to do today. We will be faithful to our work, to serving others, or to anything else; just don't ask us to be faithful to Jesus Christ. Many Christians become very impatient when we talk about faithfulness to Jesus. Our Lord is dethroned more deliberately by Christian workers than by the world. We treat God as if He were a machine designed only to bless us, and we think of Jesus as just another one of the workers.

The goal of faithfulness is not that we will do work for God, but that He will be free to do His work through us. God calls us to His service and places tremendous responsibilities on us. He expects no complaining on our part and offers no explanation on His part. God wants to use us as He used His own Son.

The Focus of Our Message "I did not come to bring peace but a sword" (Matthew 10:34).

Never be sympathetic with a person whose situation causes you to conclude that God is dealing harshly with him. God can be more tender than we can conceive, and every once in a while He gives us the opportunity to deal firmly with someone so that He may be viewed as the tender One. If a person cannot go to God, it is because he has something secret which he does not intend to give up—he may admit his sin, but would no more give up that thing than he could fly under his own power. It is impossible to deal sympathetically with people like that. We must reach down deep in their lives to the root of the problem, which will cause hostility and resentment toward the message. People want the blessing of God, but they can't stand something that pierces right through to the heart of the matter.

If you are sensitive to God's way, your message as His servant will be merciless and insistent, cutting to the very root. Otherwise, there will be no healing. We must drive the message home so forcefully that a person cannot possibly hide, but must apply its truth. Deal with people where they are, until they begin to realize their true need. Then hold high the standard of Jesus for their lives. Their response may be, "We can never be that." Then drive it home with, "Jesus Christ says you must." "But how can we be?" "You can't, unless you have a new Spirit" (see Luke 11:13).

There must be a sense of need created before your message is of any use. Thousands of people in this world profess to be happy without God. But if we could be truly happy and moral without Jesus, then why did He come? He came because that kind of happiness and peace is only superficial. Jesus Christ came to "bring . . . a sword" through every kind of peace that is not based on a personal relationship with Himself.

The Right Kind of Help

"And I, if I am lifted up . . .
will draw all peoples to
Myself"
(John 12:32).

Very few of us have any understanding of the reason why Jesus Christ died. If sympathy is all that human beings need, then the Cross of Christ is an absurdity and there is absolutely no need for it. What the world needs is not "a little bit of love," but major surgery.

When you find yourself face to face with a person who is spiritually lost, remind yourself of Jesus Christ on the cross. If that person can get to God in any other way, then the Cross of Christ is unnecessary. If you think you are helping lost people with your sympathy and understanding, you are a traitor to Jesus Christ. You must have a right-standing relationship with Him yourself, and pour your life out in helping others in His way—not in a human way that ignores God. The theme of the world's religion today is to serve in a pleasant, non-confrontational manner.

But our only priority must be to present Jesus Christ crucified—to lift Him up all the time (see 1 Corinthians 2:2). Every belief that is not firmly rooted in the Cross of Christ will lead people astray. If the worker himself believes in Jesus Christ and is trusting in the reality of redemption, his words will be compelling to others. What is extremely important is for the worker's simple relationship with Jesus Christ to be strong and growing. His usefulness to God depends on that, and that alone.

The calling of a New Testament worker is to expose sin and to reveal Jesus Christ as Savior. Consequently, he cannot always be charming and friendly, but must be willing to be stern to accomplish major surgery. We are sent by God to lift up Jesus Christ, not to give wonderfully beautiful speeches. We must be willing to examine others as deeply as God has examined us. We must also be sharply intent on sensing those Scripture passages that will drive the truth home, and then not be afraid to apply them.

December 20

Experience or God's Revealed Truth?

"We have received . . . the Spirit who is from God, that we might know the things that have been freely given to us by God" (1 Corinthians 2:12).

My experience is not what makes redemption real—redemption is reality. Redemption has no real meaning for me until it is worked out through my conscious life. When I am born again, the Spirit of God takes me beyond myself and my experiences, and identifies me with Jesus Christ. If I am left only with my personal experiences, I am left with something not produced by redemption. But experiences produced by redemption prove themselves by leading me beyond myself, to the point of no longer paying any attention to experiences as the basis of reality. Instead, I see that only the reality itself produced the experiences. My experiences are not worth anything unless they keep me at the Source of truth—Jesus Christ.

If you try to hold back the Holy Spirit within you, with the desire of producing more inner spiritual experiences, you will find that He will break the hold and take you again to the historic Christ. Never support an experience which does not have God as its Source and faith in God as its result. If you do, your experience is anti-Christian, no matter what visions or insights you may have had. Is Jesus Christ Lord of your experiences, or do you place your experiences above Him? Is any experience dearer to you than your Lord? You must allow Him to be Lord over you, and pay no attention to any experience over which He is not Lord. Then there will come a time when God will make you impatient with your own experience, and you can truthfully say, "I do not care what I experience—I am sure of Him!"

Be relentless and hard on yourself if you are in the habit of talking about the experiences you have had. Faith based on experience is not faith; faith based on God's revealed truth is the only faith there is.

The Drawing of the Father "No one can come to Me unless the Father who sent Me draws him . . ."
(John 6:44).

When God begins to draw me to Himself, the problem of my will comes in immediately. Will I react positively to the truth that God has revealed? Will I come to Him? To discuss or deliberate over spiritual matters when God calls is inappropriate and disrespectful to Him. When God speaks, never discuss it with anyone as if to decide what your response may be (see Galatians 1:15–16). Belief is not the result of an intellectual act, but the result of an act of my will whereby I deliberately commit myself. But will I commit, placing myself completely and absolutely on God, and be willing to act solely on what He says? If I will, I will find that I am grounded on reality as certain as God's throne.

In preaching the gospel, always focus on the matter of the will. Belief must come from the *will* to believe. There must be a surrender of the will, not a surrender to a persuasive or powerful argument. I must deliberately step out, placing my faith in God and in His truth. And I must place no confidence in my own works, but only in God. Trusting in my own mental understanding becomes a hindrance to complete trust in God. I must be willing to ignore and leave my feelings behind. I must *will* to believe. But this can never be accomplished without my forceful, determined effort to separate myself from my old ways of looking at things. I must surrender myself completely to God.

Everyone has been created with the ability to reach out beyond his own grasp. But it is God who draws me, and my relationship to Him in the first place is an inner, personal one, not an intellectual one. I come into the relationship through the miracle of God and through my own will to believe. Then I begin to get an intelligent appreciation and understanding of the wonder of the transformation in my life.

Sharing in the Atonement

"God forbid that I should boast except in the cross of our Lord Jesus Christ . . ." (Galatians 6:14).

The gospel of Jesus Christ always forces a decision of our will. Have I accepted God's verdict on sin as judged on the Cross of Christ? Do I have even the slightest interest in the death of Jesus? Do I want to be identified with His death—to be completely dead to all interest in sin, worldliness, and self? Do I long to be so closely identified with Jesus that I am of no value for anything except Him and His purposes? The great privilege of discipleship is that I can commit myself under the banner of His Cross, and that means death to sin. You must get alone with Jesus and either decide to tell Him that you do not want sin to die out in you, or that at any cost you want to be identified with His death. When you act in confident faith in what our Lord did on the cross, a supernatural identification with His death takes place immediately. And you will come to know through a higher knowledge that your old life was "crucified with Him" (Romans 6:6). The proof that your old life is dead, having been "crucified with Christ" (Galatians 2:20), is the amazing ease with which the life of God in you now enables you to obey the voice of Jesus Christ.

Every once in a while our Lord gives us a glimpse of what we would be like if it were not for Him. This is a confirmation of what He said—". . . without Me you can do nothing" (John 15:5). That is why the underlying foundation of Christianity is personal, passionate devotion to the Lord Jesus. We mistake the joy of our first introduction into God's kingdom as His purpose for getting us there. Yet God's purpose in getting us into His kingdom is that we may realize all that identification with Jesus Christ means.

The Hidden Life

The Spirit of God testifies to and confirms the simple, but almighty, security of the life that "is hidden with Christ in God." Paul continually brought this out in his New Testament letters. We talk as if living a sanctified life were the most uncertain and insecure thing we could do. Yet it is the most secure thing possible, because it has Almighty God in and behind it. The most dangerous and unsure thing is to try to live without God. For one who is born again, it is easier to live in a right-standing relationship with God than it is to go wrong, provided we heed God's warnings and "walk in the light" (1 John 1:7).

When we think of being delivered from sin, being "filled with the Spirit" (Ephesians 5:18), and "walk[ing] in the light," we picture the peak of a great mountain. We see it as very high and wonderful, but we say, "Oh, I could never live up there!" However, when we do get there through God's grace, we find it is not a mountain peak at all, but a plateau with plenty of room to live and to grow. "You enlarged my path under me, so my feet did not slip" (Psalm 18:36).

When you really see Jesus, I defy you to doubt Him. If you see Him when He says, "Let not your heart be troubled . . ." (John 14:27), I defy you to worry. It is virtually impossible to doubt when He is there. Every time you are in personal contact with Jesus, His words are real to you. "My peace I give to you . . ." (John 14:27)—a peace which brings an unconstrained confidence and covers you completely, from the top of your head to the soles of your feet. ". . . your life is hidden with Christ in God," and the peace of Jesus Christ that cannot be disturbed has been imparted to you.

*His Birth and
Our New Birth*

" 'Behold, the virgin shall be
with child, and bear a Son,
and they shall call His
name Immanuel,' which is
translated, 'God with us' "
(Matthew 1:23).

His Birth in History. ". . . that Holy One who is to be born will be called the Son of God (Luke 1:35). Jesus Christ was born *into* this world, not *from* it. He did not emerge out of history; He came into history from the outside. Jesus Christ is not the best human being the human race can boast of—He is a Being for whom the human race can take no credit at all. He is not man becoming God, but God Incarnate—God coming into human flesh from outside it. His life is the highest and the holiest entering through the most humble of doors. Our Lord's birth was an advent—the appearance of God in human form.

His Birth in Me. "My little children, for whom I labor in birth again until Christ is formed in you . . ." (Galatians 4:19). Just as our Lord came into human history from outside it, He must also come into me from outside. Have I allowed my personal human life to become a "Bethlehem" for the Son of God? I cannot enter the realm of the kingdom of God unless I am born again from above by a birth totally unlike physical birth. "You must be born again" (John 3:7). This is not a command, but a fact based on the authority of God. The evidence of the new birth is that I yield myself so completely to God that "Christ is formed" in me. And once "Christ is formed" in me, His nature immediately begins to work through me.

God Evident in the Flesh. This is what is made so profoundly possible for you and for me through the redemption of man by Jesus Christ.

December 25

"Walk in the Light"

"If we walk in the light as He is in the light . . . the blood of Jesus Christ His Son cleanses us from all sin" (1 John 1:7).

To mistake freedom from sin only on the conscious level of our lives for complete deliverance from sin by the atonement through the Cross of Christ is a great error. No one fully knows what sin is until he is born again. Sin is what Jesus Christ faced at Calvary. The evidence that I have been delivered from sin is that I know the real nature of sin in me. For a person to really know what sin is requires the full work and deep touch of the atonement of Jesus Christ, that is, the imparting of His absolute perfection.

The Holy Spirit applies or administers the work of the atonement to us in the deep unconscious realm as well as in the conscious realm. And it is not until we truly perceive the unrivaled power of the Spirit in us that we understand the meaning of 1 John 1:7, which says, ". . . the blood of Jesus Christ His Son cleanses us from all sin." This verse does not refer only to conscious sin, but also to the tremendously profound understanding of sin which only the Holy Spirit in me can accomplish.

I must "walk in the light as He is in the light . . ." —not in the light of my own conscience, but in God's light. If I will walk there, with nothing held back or hidden, then this amazing truth is revealed to me: ". . . the blood of Jesus Christ His Son cleanses [me] from all sin" so that God Almighty can see nothing to rebuke in me. On the conscious level it produces a keen, sorrowful knowledge of what sin really is. The love of God working in me causes me to hate, with the Holy Spirit's hatred for sin, anything that is not in keeping with God's holiness. To "walk in the light" means that everything that is of the darkness actually drives me closer to the center of the light.

Where the Battle is Won or Lost

" 'If you will return, O Israel,'
says the LORD . . ."
(Jeremiah 4:1).

Our battles are first won or lost in the secret places of our will in God's presence, never in full view of the world. The Spirit of God seizes me and I am compelled to get alone with God and fight the battle before Him. Until I do this, I will lose every time. The battle may take one minute or one year, but that will depend on me, not God. However long it takes, I must wrestle with it alone before God, and I must resolve to go through the hell of renunciation or rejection before Him. Nothing has any power over someone who has fought the battle before God and won there.

I should never say, "I will wait until I get into difficult circumstances and then I'll put God to the test." Trying to do that will not work. I must first get the issue settled between God and myself in the secret places of my soul, where no one else can interfere. Then I can go ahead, knowing with certainty that the battle is won. Lose it there, and calamity, disaster, and defeat before the world are as sure as the laws of God. The reason the battle is lost is that I fight it first in the external world. Get alone with God, do battle before Him, and settle the matter once and for all.

In dealing with other people, our stance should always be to drive them toward making a decision of their will. That is how surrendering to God begins. Not often, but every once in a while, God brings us to a major turning point—a great crossroads in our life. From that point we either go toward a more and more slow, lazy, and useless Christian life, or we become more and more on fire, giving our utmost for His highest—our best for His glory.

December 27

Continuous Conversion

". . . unless you are converted
and become as little children, you will by no means
enter the kingdom of heaven"
(Matthew 18:3).

These words of our Lord refer to our initial conversion, but we should continue to turn to God as children, being continuously converted every day of our lives. If we trust in our own abilities, instead of God's, we produce consequences for which God will hold us responsible. When God through His sovereignty brings us into new situations, we should immediately make sure that our natural life submits to the spiritual, obeying the orders of the Spirit of God. Just because we have responded properly in the past is no guarantee that we will do so again. The response of the natural to the spiritual should be continuous conversion, but this is where we so often refuse to be obedient. No matter what our situation is, the Spirit of God remains unchanged and His salvation unaltered. But we must "put on the new man . . ." (Ephesians 4:24). God holds us accountable every time we refuse to convert ourselves, and He sees our refusal as willful disobedience. Our natural life must not rule—God must rule in us.

To refuse to be continuously converted puts a stumbling block in the growth of our spiritual life. There are areas of self-will in our lives where our pride pours contempt on the throne of God and says, "I won't submit." We deify our independence and self-will and call them by the wrong name. What God sees as stubborn weakness, we call strength. There are whole areas of our lives that have not yet been brought into submission, and this can only be done by this continuous conversion. Slowly but surely we can claim the whole territory for the Spirit of God.

Deserter or Disciple?

"From that time many of His disciples went back and walked with Him no more" (John 6:66).

When God, by His Spirit through His Word, gives you a clear vision of His will, you must "walk in the light" of that vision (1 John 1:7). Even though your mind and soul may be thrilled by it, if you don't "walk in the light" of it you will sink to a level of bondage never envisioned by our Lord. Mentally disobeying the "heavenly vision" (Acts 26:19) will make you a slave to ideas and views that are completely foreign to Jesus Christ. Don't look at someone else and say, "Well, if he can have those views and prosper, why can't I?" You have to "walk in the light" of the vision that has been given to *you*. Don't compare yourself with others or judge them—that is between God and them. When you find that one of your favorite and strongly held views clashes with the "heavenly vision," do not begin to debate it. If you do, a sense of property and personal right will emerge in you— things on which Jesus placed no value. He was against these things as being the root of everything foreign to Himself—". . . for one's life does not consist in the abundance of the things he possesses" (Luke 12:15). If we don't see and understand this, it is because we are ignoring the underlying principles of our Lord's teaching.

Our tendency is to lie back and bask in the memory of the wonderful experience we had when God revealed His will to us. But if a New Testament standard is revealed to us by the light of God, and we don't try to measure up, or even feel inclined to do so, then we begin to backslide. It means your conscience does not respond to the truth. You can never be the same after the unveiling of a truth. That moment marks you as one who either continues on with even more devotion as a disciple of Jesus Christ, or as one who turns to go back as a deserter.

"And Every Virtue We Possess"

"... All my springs are in you" (Psalm 87:7).

Our Lord never "patches up" our natural virtues, that is, our natural traits, qualities, or characteristics. He completely remakes a person on the inside—"... put on the new man ..." (Ephesians 4:24). In other words, see that your natural human life is putting on all that is in keeping with the new life. The life God places within us develops its own new virtues, not the virtues of the seed of Adam, but of Jesus Christ. Once God has begun the process of sanctification in your life, watch and see how God causes your confidence in your own natural virtues and power to wither away. He will continue until you learn to draw your life from the reservoir of the resurrection life of Jesus. Thank God if you are going through this drying-up experience!

The sign that God is at work in us is that He is destroying our confidence in the natural virtues, because they are not promises of what we are going to be, but only a wasted reminder of what God created man to be. We want to cling to our natural virtues, while all the time God is trying to get us in contact with the life of Jesus Christ—a life that can never be described in terms of natural virtues. It is the saddest thing to see people who are trying to serve God depending on that which the grace of God never gave them. They are depending solely on what they have by virtue of heredity. God does not take our natural virtues and transform them, because our natural virtues could never even come close to what Jesus Christ wants. No natural love, no natural patience, no natural purity can ever come up to His demands. But as we bring every part of our natural bodily life into harmony with the new life God has placed within us, He will exhibit in us the virtues that were characteristic of the Lord Jesus.

> And every virtue we possess
> Is His alone.

Yesterday

"You shall not go out with
haste, . . . for the LORD
will go before you, and the
God of Israel will be your
rear guard"
(Isaiah 52:12).

Security from Yesterday. ". . . God requires an account of
what is past" (Ecclesiastes 3:15). At the end of the year we
turn with eagerness to all that God has for the future, and yet
anxiety is apt to arise when we remember our yesterdays. Our
present enjoyment of God's grace tends to be lessened by the
memory of yesterday's sins and blunders. But God is the God
of our yesterdays, and He allows the memory of them to turn
the past into a ministry of spiritual growth for our future.
God reminds us of the past to protect us from a very shallow
security in the present.

Security for Tomorrow. ". . . the LORD will go before you
. . . ." This is a gracious revelation—that God will send His
forces out where we have failed to do so. He will keep watch so
that we will not be tripped up again by the same failures, as
would undoubtedly happen if He were not our "rear guard."
And God's hand reaches back to the past, settling all the claims
against our conscience.

Security for Today. "You shall not go out with haste . . . ."
As we go forth into the coming year, let it not be in the haste
of impetuous, forgetful delight, nor with the quickness of
impulsive thoughtlessness. But let us go out with the patient
power of knowing that the God of Israel will go before us. Our
yesterdays hold broken and irreversible things for us. It is true
that we have lost opportunities that will never return, but God
can transform this destructive anxiety into a constructive
thoughtfulness for the future. Let the past rest, but let it rest in
the sweet embrace of Christ.

Leave the broken, irreversible past in His hands, and step
out into the invincible future with Him.

Subject Index

A

abandon(ment) 1/31, 2/27, 4/17, 4/28, 4/29, 5/8, 5/23, 5/30, 6/13, 6/18, 7/11, 7/12, 8/25, 9/28, 10/22, 11/13

abiding in God/Jesus 1/23, 3/22, 6/7, 6/12, 6/14, 8/19, 9/19, 10/14

Abraham (Abram) 1/6, 1/8, 1/19, 3/19, 3/20, 4/26, 5/25, 11/11, 11/17, 12/10

Absalom 4/19

access to God 4/5, 5/17

Adam 12/30

Adonijah 4/19

adversity 5/14, 5/15, 5/19, 8/2

affliction 7/14, 8/8, 11/9, 12/13

Ai 1/6

alone with God 1/12, 1/13

anger 6/30, 8/6

apprehension 6/5

armor of God 12/16

Asa 4/15

ascension of Jesus 9/5

ascension power 5/29

assurance 6/4, 6/5, 8/29, 10/28

atonement 4/8, 5/4, 6/7, 6/12, 6/14, 6/15, 6/20, 6/21, 6/22, 7/7, 8/27, 9/1, 10/9, 10/20, 10/28, 11/20, 12/8, 12/23, 12/26

attributes of God 5/9

authority of God/Holy Spirit/Jesus 1/10, 4/8, 4/11, 4/18, 5/6, 7/19, 10/14, 10/27, 12/5, 12/14, 12/25

B

backsliding 12/29

Bartimaeus 2/29

beatitudes (also see Sermon on the Mount) 7/25

belief/believing 4/26, 4/29, 5/6, 5/18, 6/1, 6/19, 6/21, 7/17, 7/18, 8/27, 8/29, 9/6, 9/15, 10/28, 11/6, 11/13, 12/11, 12/15, 12/20, 12/22

bereavement 7/29, 8/26

Bethany 10/11

Bethel 1/6, 8/11

Bethlehem 5/31, 8/9, 9/3, 12/25

blasphemy 6/12, 11/20

blessings of God 1/22, 4/28, 9/6, 9/7, 10/23, 10/31, 11/28, 12/19

bondservant 7/2, 7/15, 7/18, 11/3

born again 1/3, 1/20, 1/24, 2/4, 3/5, 3/8, 4/8, 4/12, 5/20, 6/6, 7/13, 7/21, 8/15, 8/24, 8/28, 9/18, 9/21, 10/10, 10/23, 11/8, 11/12, 11/14, 11/25, 11/29, 12/21, 12/24, 12/25, 12/26

bread, broken 2/2, 2/9, 2/10, 2/15, 2/25, 5/15, 7/15, 9/30, 11/15

brokenness 11/3

burdens 3/31, 4/13, 4/14

C

call of God/Jesus 1/1, 1/14, 1/16, 1/17, 1/31, 2/1, 2/2, 3/4, 3/5, 3/13, 5/15, 6/16, 6/28, 8/5, 9/13, 9/27, 9/30, 10/4, 10/13, 10/25, 10/26, 10/27, 11/3, 12/2, 12/16, 12/20

call to preach/ministry 2/2, 2/23, 3/10, 6/28, 9/29

Calvary 3/7, 4/5, 5/7, 11/19, 11/20, 11/21, 12/26

carelessness 7/31

carnality 3/23

character, attainment of 3/19, 9/8, 10/1, 10/4

Subject Index

Subject Index

Subject Index

Subject Index

To locate verses that appear at the top of each day's devotional, see the dates set in bold type. All other dates correspond with verses used within the devotional.

Scripture Index

The Oswald Chambers Library

Spiritual guidance from the author
of *My Utmost for His Highest*.
Powerful insights on topics of interest
to every believer.

MY UTMOST FOR HIS HIGHEST

Updated Edition—hardcover
Prayer Edition (Original)—hardcover
Large Print Edition (Original)—softcover

APPROVED UNTO GOD with FACING REALITY
—The Spiritual Life of the Christian Worker

These talks encourage us to become competent servants of
Jesus Christ, spiritually fit and mentally fit, for the great task
entrusted to us. Do not read this book unless you mean business,
but if you do you will find wisdom and understanding on every
page.
Softcover. 128 pages.

BAFFLED TO FIGHT BETTER
—Job and the Problem of Suffering

This brief commentary provides unique insight into the book
of Job. It shows how human pain and suffering can drive us to
God and bring new understanding of His majesty, goodness,
and plan for our lives.
Softcover. 144 pages.

BIBLICAL PSYCHOLOGY
—Christ-centered Solutions for Daily Problems

A resource for every Christian worker, this volume presents a Scripture-based understanding of one's own psychological experiences, enabling one to present the truth of God effectively to people perplexed by moral problems of their own inner life of feeling, thought, and will.

Softcover. 256 pages.

BRINGING SONS INTO GLORY &
MAKING ALL THINGS NEW

This two-in-one volume focuses on the life of Jesus and its relationship to the life of His disciples today. Compelling and thorough, this unabridged collection challenges those who have not made a total commitment to Christ and comforts those who aim to please Him in every aspect of daily living.

Softcover. 224 pages.

CHRISTIAN DISCIPLINES
—Build Strong Christian Character through these disciplines: Divine Guidance, Suffering, Peril, Prayer, Loneliness, and Patience

In this new edition of a classic work, Chambers concentrates on six disciplines that build strong Christian character: divine guidance, and the childlike expectation we should have when we come to God for leading; suffering, an opportunity for God's glory to be revealed; peril and how our dependency on God makes us more available to do His work; prayer, an avenue to Christlikeness; loneliness, or solitude, an opportunity for intimate communion with God; and patience, an anchoring in God that holds us through the troubles and circumstances of the world.

Softcover. 224 pages.

CONFORMED TO HIS IMAGE &
THE SERVANT AS HIS LORD
—Lessons on Living Like Jesus

Oswald Chambers' invitation to let go of the "old you" and become a new creature in Christ. And not only an invitation— a practical guide that will move you out of spiritual failure, frustration, and listlessness into the Christian life as you have imagined it could be.

Softcover. 224 pages.

DAILY THOUGHTS FOR DISCIPLES

Designed to be read like *My Utmost for His Highest*, this devotional book presents 365 daily readings collected from a variety of Chambers' writings for those who take their faith seriously. Each devotion provides a brief, concentrated thought based on a single Scripture verse. Profound insight from a master of devotional writing.

Hardcover. 384 pages.

GOD'S WORKMANSHIP &
HE SHALL GLORIFY ME
—The Holy Spirit and the Life of the Believer

A two-in-one volume that provides many practical insights on the Spirit's work in the minds and hearts of believers and shows how the Holy Spirit in us brings greater unity to the body of Christ. It includes a thorough discussion of the doctrine of the Holy Spirit and explains what He can mean to our everyday lives.

Softcover. 224 pages.

IF YOU WILL ASK
—Reflections on the Power of Prayer

In this small but powerful book on prayer, Chambers reveals the key problem with the way many of us pray today—the focus of our prayers is on ourselves instead of on God. He explains that the purpose of prayer is not to get healed, get a job, or get whatever we want; the purpose is to get "the life of God in us."

Softcover. 96 pages.

THE LOVE OF GOD
—An Intimate Look at the Father-Heart of God

For those who are spiritually weary, *The Love of God* is filled with the cool refreshment of God's love. It is a book for people who want to deepen and strengthen their relationship with the heavenly Father.

Softcover. 128 pages.

NOT KNOWING WHERE
—A Spiritual Journey Through the Book of Genesis

Here Chambers presents studies of the great pioneers of the faith: Noah, Abraham, and Joseph. In them we see faith's response to God's call, to clashing circumstances, to the subtle temptations of the Adversary, and to the terrific costs and benefits of friendship and fellowship with God.

Softcover. 208 pages.

THE PLACE OF HELP
—God's Provision for Our Daily Needs

This devotional study upholds Jesus Christ as the only unshakable source of help. Chambers provides a vital, unique perspective on the complexities and challenges of our Christian experience. Each of the forty-eight devotionals looks from a different perspective at the believer's life and his relationship to our great and wonderful God.

Softcover. 256 pages.

PRAYER: A HOLY OCCUPATION

A comprehensive collection of Chambers' writings on prayer, *Prayer: A Holy Occupation* describes prayer as work, an act of obedience and of the will. Chambers' chief objectives in prayer were to know Jesus, to learn His will, and to get himself aligned with that will.

Hardcover. 192 pages.

SHADE OF HIS HAND
—Ecclesiastes and the Purpose of Life

Chambers' study of Ecclesiastes brings his extraordinary discernment to a most perplexing biblical book. Throughout *Shade of His Hand*, his mission is to relieve the despair and pessimism of modern times by pointing us to God, who is the only source of hope and light. Those who practice God's presence can confidently rest in the shade of His hand.

Softcover. 176 pages.

THE HIGHEST GOOD &
THE SHADOW OF AN AGONY
—Seeing Life from God's Perspective

The Highest Good and *The Shadow of an Agony* examine the psalms, the gospels, and Paul's letters to answer questions relating to Christian character and conduct, to explain human pain and suffering, and to help us see life from God's perspective.

Softcover. 240 pages.

SO SEND I YOU &
WORKMEN OF GOD
—Recognizing and Answering God's Call to Service

So Send I You examines the Christian's call to missionary service. This portion of the book explores the nature of God's call to every person and how to hear His call in one's life. *Workmen of God* offers a challenging approach to spiritual discernment and diagnosis. This material shows how godly Christians can work for the cure of souls with passion and power.

Softcover. 240 pages.

About Oswald Chambers

OSWALD CHAMBERS: ABANDONED TO GOD

The life story of the author of *My Utmost for His Highest*, this volume unveils Chambers' active, devout, Christ-centered life from which flowed this century's best-loved devotional book and many other inspirational classics. Includes photos.

Hardcover. 336 pages.

"Oswald Chambers was a man for all time. His mind was the mind of Christ and so his words are compelling because they reflect the thoughts of our Savior. I am not the first to say that no book outside the Bible has influenced me as much as *My Utmost for His Highest*. In David McCasland's book we have, at last, the story of this remarkable man's life and how, having honored God, God is now honoring him with the only fame that really matters."

—Cal Thomas, Syndicated Columnist

Order from your favorite bookstore or from:

Discovery House Publishers
Box 3566
Grand Rapids, MI 49501
Call toll-free: 1-800-653-8333

Journal

Journal

Journal

Journal

Journal

Journal

Note to the Reader